FUNDAMENTALS OF FEDERAL INCOME TAXATION

Fundamentals of Federal Income Taxation

is based on

Federal Taxation of
Income, Estates and Gifts

by

BORIS I. BITTKER

With the collaboration of

Michael Asimow
Louis A. Del Cotto
Meade Emory
James S. Eustice
Alan L. Feld
Thomas J. Gallagher, Jr.
Norman H. Lane
Michael B. Lang
John W. Lee
Lawrence Lokken

FUNDAMENTALS OF FEDERAL INCOME TAXATION

BORIS I. BITTKER

Sterling Professor of Law, Yale University

Edited by

RICHARD L. DOERNBERG NORTON L. STEUBEN

MARTIN J. MCMAHON, JR. MARY MOERS WENIG

FOR STUDENT USE

WARREN, GORHAM & LAMONT

Boston • New York

WARREN, GORHAM & LAMONT, INC.

210 South Street

Boston, Massachusetts 02111

ISBN 0-88262-963-8

Library of Congress Catalog Card No. 83-60097

PRINTED IN THE UNITED STATES OF AMERICA

Preface

This abridgement of *Federal Taxation of Income, Estates and Gifts* is designed to provide students of law, accounting, and business with orientation and background for a basic course on the federal personal income tax. Although the content and emphasis of such courses vary widely from instructor to instructor, I hope that most of the material included in this volume will be useful to most students. Instructors may wish to assign or recommend some of the material, such as the chapters covering the Internal Revenue Service, tax procedures, and litigation, as background reading even if the area is not explicitly dealt with in class.

Pedagogical considerations have determined not only the scope of this work, but also the extent to which it incorporates such recent legislation as the Economic Recovery Tax Act of 1981 and the Tax Equity and Fiscal Responsibility Act of 1982, as well as the level of detail in the citations. Although the result is not a brief essay, it is selective rather than comprehensive; and it is not intended for use as a reference work. Unlike practitioners, students do not need to revise their thinking every time a Tax Court judge hems or haws or the Commissioner lifts an eyebrow.

I am greatly indebted to Richard L. Doernberg, Martin J. McMahon, Jr., Norton L. Steuben, and Mary Moers Wenig for their skill in pruning the original four-volume work down to manageable length, a process that entailed scores of difficult (and, I would like to think, painful) decisions. James Isaacs and Marci Kelly performed nobly as research assistants in preparing the manuscript for the printer. I also acknowledge with thanks the secretarial assistance, under the pressure of a tight schedule, of Cathy Briganti, Elizabeth Doyle, and Pam Standish. I would also thank Anne S. Bittker for extirpating many stylistic infelicities and typographical errors, but she pursued these delinquencies with such enthusiasm that the chase was its own reward.

BORIS I. BITTKER

March 1983

Summary of Contents

[*A detailed Table of Contents begins at page ix.*]

Table of Contents

Chapter 1
FEDERAL INCOME TAXATION—CONSTITUTIONALITY AND BASIC STRUCTURAL AND DEFINITIONAL CONCEPTS

Chapter 2
INCOME—THE EFFECT OF OFFSETTING LIABILITIES

Chapter 3

GIFTS, BEQUESTS, PRIZES, AND SCHOLARSHIPS

Chapter 4

LIFE INSURANCE, ANNUITY, AND ENDOWMENT CONTRACTS AND EMPLOYEE DEATH BENEFITS

Chapter 5

COMPENSATION FOR PERSONAL INJURIES AND SICKNESS

Chapter 6

INTEREST ON FEDERAL, STATE, AND LOCAL OBLIGATIONS

Chapter 7

EMPLOYEE FRINGE BENEFITS AND OTHER EXCLUSIONS FROM GROSS INCOME

Chapter 8

EXPENSES INCURRED IN BUSINESS AND PROFIT-ORIENTED ACTIVITIES

Chapter 9

SPECIALLY TREATED BUSINESS AND PROFIT-ORIENTED EXPENSES

Chapter 10
COST RECOVERY, DEPRECIATION AND AMORTIZATION

Chapter 11
DEPLETION

Chapter 12
LOSSES AND OTHER BUSINESS DEDUCTIONS

Chapter 13
BUSINESS CREDITS

Chapter 14
PERSONAL EXEMPTIONS AND ITEMIZED DEDUCTIONS

Chapter 15
INTEREST PAID OR ACCRUED ON INDEBTEDNESS

Chapter 16
TAXES

Chapter 17
BAD DEBTS

Chapter 18
CASUALTY LOSSES

Chapter 19
CHARITABLE CONTRIBUTIONS

Chapter 20
MEDICAL AND DENTAL EXPENSES

Chapter 21
PERSONAL CREDITS

Chapter 22
REALIZATION OF GAINS AND LOSSES—TAXABLE EVENTS

Chapter 23
SALES OF PROPERTY—BASIS AND AMOUNT REALIZED

Chapter 24

NONRECOGNITION TRANSACTIONS

Chapter 25

TAXATION OF CAPITAL GAINS AND LOSSES—BASIC STRUCTURE AND DEFINITIONS

Chapter 26

CAPITAL GAINS AND LOSSES—"SALE OR EXCHANGE" AND HOLDING PERIOD REQUIREMENTS

Chapter 27

QUASI-CAPITAL ASSETS, UNSTATED INTEREST, AND OTHER SPECIALLY TREATED ITEMS

Chapter 28
RECAPTURE OF DEPRECIATION AND OTHER TAX ALLOWANCES

Chapter 29
DEFERRED COMPENSATION–CONTRACTS AND OTHER NONQUALIFIED ARRANGEMENTS

Chapter 30
ASSIGNMENTS OF INCOME

Chapter 31

EFFECT OF COMMUNITY-PROPERTY SYSTEM

Chapter 32

ALIMONY AND OTHER MARITAL SUPPORT PAYMENTS

Chapter 33

REALLOCATION OF INCOME AND DEDUCTIONS AND DISALLOWANCE OF DEDUCTIONS

Chapter 34

GRANTOR TRUSTS

Chapter 35

CASH AND ACCRUAL ACCOUNTING

Chapter 36

INSTALLMENT AND OTHER DEFERRED PAYMENT SALES, LONG-TERM CONTRACTS, AND OTHER SPECIAL PROBLEMS

Chapter 37

INDIRECT METHODS OF COMPUTING INCOME

Chapter 38

THE INTERNAL REVENUE SERVICE

Chapter 42
INTEREST, CIVIL PENALTIES, AND TAX CRIMES

Chapter 43
TAX LITIGATION

CHAPTER 1

Federal Income Taxation—Constitutionality and Basic Structural and Definitional Concepts

¶1.1 CONSTITUTIONAL STATUS OF THE FEDERAL INCOME TAX

1. Introductory. The Constitution vests Congress with the power

> To lay and collect Taxes, Duties, Imposts and Excises, to pay the Debts and provide for the common Defence and general Welfare of the

> United States; but all Duties, Imposts and Excises shall be uniform throughout the United States; . . .

and

> To make all Laws which shall be necessary and proper for carrying into Execution the foregoing Powers. . . . [1]

Like all other federal powers, the right of Congress to levy and collect taxes is subject to a wide range of constitutional limits, including the due process clause, the right to trial by jury in criminal cases, and the prohibition of unreasonable searches and seizures. In addition, the taxing power is singled out by the Constitution for a special restriction—the "direct tax" clause—that led the Supreme Court to hold the 1894 income tax law unconstitutional,[2] an event providing the impetus for the Sixteenth Amendment, as explained below.

2. The Direct Tax Clause of the Constitution. The power to tax conferred on Congress by Article I, Section 8, is subject to the procedural requirement that all revenue bills must originate in the House of Representatives [3] and to the substantive requirement of Article I, Section 9 that "direct" taxes must be apportioned among the states, expressed in the following language: "No Capitation, or other direct, Tax shall be laid, unless in Proportion to the Census or Enumeration herein before directed to be taken." [4] The apportionment requirement is repeated and amplified by Article I, Section 2:

> Representatives and direct Taxes shall be apportioned among the several States which may be included within this Union, according to their respective Numbers, which shall be determined by adding to the whole Number of free Persons, including those bound to Service for a Term of Years, and excluding Indians not taxed, three fifths of all other Persons.[5]

Congress could readily apportion a poll tax among the states in proportion to population, save for difficulties caused by the constitutional requirement that untaxed Indians be excluded from the count and, until the Civil War, that three-fifths of the number of slaves be included. But apportionment of most other, if not all other, types of taxes would require a different rate for

---

[1] U.S. Const., Art. I, §8, Cls. 1, 18. For a recent discussion of the terms "duties," "taxes," etc., see Michelin Tire Corp. v. Wages, 423 US 276, 287-301 (1976).

[2] Pollock v. Farmers' Loan & Trust Co., 158 US 601 (1895). This was the "second" (and final) *Pollock* case; for the first installment, see infra note 7.

[3] U.S. Const., Art. I, §7, Cl. 1; see Flint v. Stone Tracy Co., 220 US 107 (1911) (revenue bill originating in House may be amended by the Senate).

[4] U.S. Const., Art. I, §9, Cl. 4.

[5] U.S. Const. Art I, §2, Cl.3.

every state in order to insure that the aggregate amount paid by each state was proportional to its population rather than to the value of the taxable items within its borders. The operation of the apportionment system can be illustrated by a federal tax on land, imposed in 1861 as "a direct tax of twenty millions of dollars" which was apportioned among the states, territories, and District of Columbia by statute (e.g., "To the State of Maine, four hundred and twenty thousand eight hundred and twenty-six dollars").[6] The President was then authorized to assign the states, territories, and District of Columbia to collection districts, to apportion "to each county and State district its proper quota of direct tax," and to establish the amount payable by the taxpayers in each district.

The scope of the apportionment rule is as murky as its purpose. The constitutional term "capitation tax" meant a per capita or poll tax, and there was general agreement that a periodic tax on the ownership of real estate—the kind of tax that produces the bulk of municipal revenue today—was also a "direct tax" as that term was used in the Constitution. Beyond this there was no consensus.

So far as the federal income tax is concerned, the Supreme Court's most important pronouncements on this subject were *Springer v. US* and *Pollock v. Farmers' Loan & Trust Co.,* decided in 1980 and 1895 respectively.[7] In *Springer,* the Court unanimously upheld the validity of the Civil War income tax, which embraced "the annual gains, profits, and income of every person . . . whether derived from any kind of property, rents, interests, dividends, or salaries, or from any profession, trade, employment, or vocation . . . or from any other source whatever." [8] Citing the *Hylton* case and other cases holding that taxes on the receipts of insurance companies, state bank notes, and inheritances were all indirect taxes, the Court ruled that the federal income tax was also indirect, saying, "Our conclusions are, that direct taxes, within the meaning of the Constitution, are only capitation taxes, as expressed in that instrument, and taxes on real estate; and that the tax of which the plaintiff in error complains is within the category of an excise or duty." [9]

In the *Pollock* case, however, the Court held by a vote of six to two (one Justice not sitting) that the 1894 federal income tax was unconstitutional insofar as it taxed income from real estate:

> [I]t is admitted that a tax on real estate is a direct tax. Unless, therefore, a tax upon rents or income issuing out of lands is intrinsically so different from a tax on the land itself that it belongs to a wholly

[6] 12 Stat. 292 (1861). Other examples of direct taxes are cited in Springer v. US, 102 US 586, 598-599 (1880).

[7] Springer v. US, supra note 6; Pollock v. Farmers' Loan & Trust Co., supra note 2, and 157 US 429 (1895).

[8] 13 Stat. 469, 479 (1865).

[9] Springer v. US, supra note 6, at 602.

> different class of taxes, such taxes must be regarded as falling within the same category as a tax on real estate *eo nomine*. . . . An annual tax upon the annual value or annual user of real estate appears to us the same in substance as an annual tax on the real estate, which would be paid out of the rent or income. . . . If, by calling a tax indirect when it is essentially direct, the rule of protection could be frittered away, one of the great landmarks defining the boundary between the Nation and the States of which it is composed, would have disappeared, and with it one of the bulwarks of private rights and private property.[10]

The *Springer* case was distinguished by the Court because none of the income of the taxpayer there in question was derived from real estate—a factual distinction that probably would have seemed immaterial to the *Springer* Court.

In addition to holding that the inclusion of rents in the income tax base was unconstitutional, the Court in the *Pollock* case decided, all eight Justices agreeing, that the inclusion of municipal bond interest in the tax base constituted "a tax on the power of the States and their instrumentalities to borrow money" and that, so viewed, it was an unconstitutional violation of the federal system of government. This determination was not of fundamental importance because an income tax exemption for interest from state and municipal bonds was entirely feasible; indeed, all later income tax statutes have explicitly exempted such income.[11] It might even have been politically possible to reenact a federal income tax with an exemption for income derived from real property.

But two other questions were left unanswered because the Court was equally divided; and while these questions remained in doubt, reenactment of an income tax law was not likely. The first question was whether a tax on income from personal property was an improper direct tax. This was a fundamental issue because if investment income had to be excluded from the tax base, a federal income tax would fall almost entirely on earned income—wages, salaries, professional fees, etc.—and business profits; and a tax with so restricted a base was not calculated to whet the political appetite. Second, the

---

[10] Id. at 580, 581, 583.

The author, formerly the incumbent of a Yale professorship established in honor of Charles F. Southmayd, cannot resist noting that Southmayd was credited by Joseph H. Choate, who argued the *Pollock* case, with working out the theory that a tax on rent was necessarily a tax on the property from which the rent was derived, thus providing "the keystone of the whole argument, and indeed, of the decision [*Pollock*] which overthrew the Act of Congress." Choate, Memorial of Charles F. Southmayd, in Arguments and Addresses of Joseph Hodges Choate 139, 148 (Hicks, Ed., West 1926). See, however, 26 Cong. Rec. 6826-6827 (1894), which shows that this argument was made during the debate *preceding* enactment of the 1894 tax, when an amendment to exempt rents from real estate on the ground that their inclusion would be unconstitutional was rejected.

[11] Infra ¶6.2.

Court failed to decide whether the granting of a minimum exemption of $4,000 to individuals violated the uniformity clause of Article I, Section 8, Clause 1, of the Constitution: "[A]ll Duties, Imposts and Excises shall be uniform throughout the United States."

One week after the first *Pollock* decision, counsel for the appellants applied for a rehearing on the undecided questions, and the Attorney General in response suggested that the whole case be reargued. In a second opinion, the previous holding as to income from real estate was reaffirmed by a vote of five to four.[12] The same five Justices agreed that a tax on income from personal property (e.g., dividends and interest) was an invalid direct tax; and they also held that the invalid provisions were not separable from the rest of the tax, so that the statute was invalid in toto.

The Court did not find it necessary in the second *Pollock* opinion to pass on the other question that was left undecided by the first opinion: Did the $4,000 exemption violate the uniformity clause of Article I? A few years later, however, the Supreme Court held in *Knowlton v. Moore* that a federal inheritance tax was constitutional despite certain exemptions.[13] The term "uniform throughout the United States," it held, required geographical uniformity, so that persons and property would be taxed in the same manner without regard to geographical location, rather than "intrinsic" uniformity (i.e., without exemptions).

The *Pollock* case is often described as a "judicial veto" preventing Congress from taxing income until the Sixteenth Amendment was adopted in 1913. In point of fact, however, the decision intimated that a tax on salaries, wages, and business profits would not be a "direct tax" and hence would not have to be apportioned,[14] thus leaving Congress free to tax income from these sources if it was willing to exempt unearned income. While unearned income is only a small fraction of total *national* income, it becomes an increasingly important component of *individual* income as income rises; and this meant that taxing earned income but not income from investments was not politically acceptable. Congress also was free after *Pollock* to enact an *apportioned* income tax, though such a contraption would have required different rate schedules for each state. For these reasons, foes of the income tax hailed the *Pollock* case for sounding its death knell, while its friends turned their major attention to the arduous task of amending the Constitution to permit all types of income to be taxed without apportionment.

In the meantime, Congress enacted a corporate income tax, which was promptly attacked as a direct tax that, not being apportioned among the states in proportion to their population, was unconstitutional. In *Flint v. Stone Tracy Co.,* however, the Supreme Court adhered to its suggestion in the *Pollock* case

---

[12] Pollock v. Farmers' Loan & Trust Co., supra note 2.

[13] Knowlton v. Moore, 178 US 41 (1900).

[14] Pollock v. Farmers' Loan & Trust Co., supra note 2, at 635.

that a tax on the conduct of business would qualify as an excise or indirect tax, not subject to the apportionment rule, and it upheld the 1909 tax as an excise tax on the privilege of doing business in a corporate capacity:

> Within the category of indirect taxation . . . is embraced a tax upon business done in a corporate capacity, which is the subject-matter of the tax imposed in the act under consideration. The *Pollock Case* construed the tax there levied as direct, because it was imposed upon property simply because of its ownership. In the present case the tax is not payable unless there be a carrying on or doing of business in the designated capacity, and this is made the occasion for the tax, measured by the standard prescribed. The difference between the acts is not merely nominal, but rests upon substantial differences between the mere ownership of property and the actual doing of business in a certain way.[15]

3. The Sixteenth Amendment. While this litigation concerning the constitutionality of the 1909 corporate income tax was on its way to the Supreme Court, a proposed amendment to the Constitution was being ratified in one state after another. This process continued until February of 1913, when the Secretary of State certified that the Sixteenth Amendment had been duly ratified. Henceforth, any discussion of the direct tax clause of Article I would have to take account of the new amendment: "The Congress shall have power to lay and collect taxes on incomes, from whatever source derived, without apportionment among the several States, and without regard to any census or enumeration."

Ratification of the Sixteenth Amendment was followed by enactment of the Revenue Act of 1913, which imposed an income tax on both individuals and corporations. Despite the constitutional change, more litigation over the validity of income taxation ensued. It was argued (a) that the Sixteenth Amendment applied only to a tax reaching every species of income ("from whatever source derived") and all potential taxpayers, with no exceptions; (b) that the Revenue Act of 1913, having exempted some taxpayers and types of income, could not claim the protection of the Sixteenth Amendment; and hence (c) that the 1913 tax was a direct tax, invalid under the *Pollock* case for want of apportionment. The Supreme Court rejected this theory in *Brushaber v. Union Pacific R.R.,* decided in 1916:

> It is clear on the face of [the Sixteenth Amendment] that it does not purport to confer power to levy income taxes in a generic sense—an authority already possessed and never questioned—or to limit and distinguish between one kind of income taxes and another, but that the whole purpose of the Amendment was to relieve all income taxes when imposed

---

[15] Flint v. Stone Tracy Co., supra note 3, at 150.

> from apportionment from a consideration of the source whence the income was derived. Indeed in the light of the history which we have given and of the decision in the *Pollock Case* and the ground upon which the ruling in that case was based, there is no escape from the conclusion that the Amendment was drawn for the purpose of doing away for the future with the principle upon which the *Pollock Case* was decided, that is, of determining whether a tax on income was direct not by a consideration of the burden placed on the taxed income upon which it directly operated, but by taking into view the burden which resulted on the property from which the income was derived, since in express terms the Amendment provides that income taxes, from whatever source the income may be derived, shall not be subject to the regulation of apportionment.[16]

As construed by the Supreme Court in the *Brushaber* case, the power of Congress to tax income derives from Article I, Section 8, Clause 1, of the original Constitution rather than from the Sixteenth Amendment, which simply eliminated the requirement that an income tax, to the extent that it is a direct tax, must be apportioned among the states.[17] A corollary of this conclusion is that any direct tax that is not imposed on "income" remains subject to the rule of apportionment. Since the Sixteenth Amendment does not purport to define the term "direct tax," the scope of that constitutional phrase remains as debatable as it was before 1913; but the practical significance of the issue was greatly reduced once income taxes, even if direct, were relieved from the requirement of apportionment.

¶ 1.2 THE FEDERAL INCOME TAX AND STATE LAW

1. Introductory. The Internal Revenue Code is a national law, but it taxes transactions whose legal effects are almost always prescribed by state rather than federal law. Without this body of state law to prescribe the rights and liabilities arising from the daily activities of millions of taxpayers, the federal tax collector would be a fish out of water. For example, so simple a matter as the deduction of a worthless debt under IRC §166(a)(1) on the

---

[16] Brushaber v. Union Pacific R.R., 240 US 1, 17-18 (1916). See also Stanton v. Baltic Mining Co., 240 US 103, 112-113 (1916) (hinting that *Pollock* was based on the "mistaken theory" that the constitutional validity of an income tax should be determined by reference to the origin or source of the income taxed).

[17] The "no new power to tax" aspect of the *Brushaber* opinion creates difficulty in at least one peripheral area, viz., whether, if Congress lacked the power to tax state and municipal bond interest before the Sixteenth Amendment (as *Pollock* held), its ratification remedied this gap by permitting Congress to tax income "from whatever source derived."

ground that the taxpayer's claim against the debtor is barred by the statute of limitations depends on the length of the state's limitations period, the effect of a seal or recordation, the effect on the statute of limitations of an oral acknowledgment of the debt, and other factors that are governed by state law and vary from one state to another.[18] Before the federal tax effect of a transaction can be determined, a host of threshold determinations of this type is almost always required. The answers to these preliminary questions are often so clear as to be taken for granted. This does not mean that the Code is independent of state law but only that its reliance on state law is so pervasive that it rarely rises to the conscious level.

The notion that state law plays a secondary role, however, is widespread. For the most part, this misapprehension is traceable to cases like *Lucas v. Earl*, in which the Supreme Court held that a married man performing personal services was taxable on his earnings in their entirety, even though one-half had been assigned by him to his wife under a contract that was valid under state law.[19] Because the contract transferred to the taxpayer's wife the right to collect and retain one-half of his salary as a matter of state law, but failed to relieve him of the obligation to pay federal income taxes on that amount, the decision may seem at first blush to reject state law in favor of an overriding federal legal structure—an impression that is strengthened by the Supreme Court's statement that "this case is not to be decided by attenuated subtleties." In point of fact, however, in deciding that the revenue act in question taxed "salaries to those who earned them," not to their assignees, the Court in no sense rejected any state law. Indeed, state, rather than federal, law supplied the very foundation of the decision by establishing that the amount divided between the taxpayer and his wife under the agreement was compensation for his services (rather than, for example, a gift or a loan), that it was "earned" by him rather than by his wife or someone else, and that in the absence of the agreement he would have been entitled to collect and retain the entire amount paid by the employer.

In *Lucas v. Earl*, and in many other cases like it, the courts were compelled to decide the issues before them without much aid from the statutory language of the Internal Revenue Code. Although it is usually prolix rather than concise, the Code provided no explicit guide for the Court in *Lucas v. Earl*; the controlling provisions were Sections 211(a) and 213(a) of the Revenue Act of 1918, imposing a tax on "the net income of every individual" and defining income in the broad terms that are now found, with minor variations, in IRC

---

[18] Infra ¶17.3.

[19] Lucas v. Earl, 281 US 111 (1930), discussed infra ¶30.2. The taxable years before the Court were 1920-1921, long before the enactment of the optional joint return that now provides essentially the same tax effect that was claimed by the couple in *Lucas v. Earl*.

§61(a). Given the husband-wife agreement to divide their earnings equally, the Court had to decide whether the wife's share of the husband's salary was income "of" the husband, who had performed the personal services, or "of" the wife, who was entitled to receive it under the marital agreement. As suggested above, state law was important, indeed indispensable, to the result reached by the Court; but this was not because state law shed any light on the meaning of the naked term "of" as used in the Revenue Act of 1918.

Elsewhere in the Internal Revenue Code, however, terms taken from state law (for example, "trust," "marriage," "corporation," "contract," "debenture," "lease," and "real property") occur in profusion.[20] Since terms like these can have one meaning in New York and another in Hawaii, how should they be interpreted when used in a national law taxing transactions whose substantive legal results are almost always prescribed by state law?

In *Burnet v. Harmel,* a leading case discussing this issue, the Supreme Court said:

> The exertion of [Congress' power to tax income] is not subject to state control. It is the will of Congress which controls, and the expression of its will in legislation, in the absence of language evidencing a different purpose, is to be interpreted so as to give a uniform application to a nationwide scheme of taxation. . . . State law may control only when the federal taxing act, by express language or necessary implication, makes its own operation dependent upon state law. . . . The state law creates legal interests, but the federal statute determines when and how they shall be taxed.[21]

If a transaction or event has identical legal consequences in substantially all states but is given a peculiar label by the law of a particular locality, it is easy for the courts to conclude that local usage is not controlling and that the federal tax liability generated by the transaction should be uniform across the nation. But if there are substantive differences in the legal rights attached by local law to the activity, it is far less clear whether Congress intended to adopt—or to disregard—the local usage. The *Harmel* case establishes a presumption in favor of "uniform application." This seems plausible, but there are, unfortunately, at least two types of uniformity.

The competing possibilities can be illustrated by the problem created by the personal earnings of minor children, which in some states they are entitled

---

[20] The Code also uses terms of its own invention that are akin to, but not identical with, state-law terms. Thus, "earnings and profits" as used in IRC §316(a) is not a state-law term, though it bears a resemblance to the state-law concept of "earned surplus"; and there is a similar relationship between the "complete liquidation" of a corporation (IRC §331) and its "dissolution" under state law.

[21] Burnet v. Harmel, 287 US 103, 110 (1932).

to retain for themselves but in other states must pay over to their parents. Before the enactment of the statutory predecessor of IRC §73 in 1944,[22] the Internal Revenue Code did not state explicitly whether the child or the parent was required to report this type of income, and the controlling provision was IRC §1, imposing a tax on the income "of" every individual. If this vague term were interpreted to require children to report their wages and other earnings whether they were entitled to retain them under local law or not, national uniformity would be achieved in the sense that the income of minors would be taxed everywhere to the person performing the services. On the other hand, if the earnings were taxed to whichever person was entitled by local law to receive and spend them, another type of national uniformity would be achieved; the governing factor—nationwide—would be legal control over the funds in question. The *Harmel* presumption in favor of "uniform application" does not resolve this conflict between two types of uniformity.

The *Harmel* formulation is also ambiguous in stating that "state law may control only when the federal taxing act, by express language or necessary implication, makes its own operation dependent upon state law." In an ultimate sense, of course, state law *never* controls; even when the Code expressly adopts state law for some purpose, this is done by Congress, which may revoke its acceptance of the state rules whenever it chooses.

Moreover, the reference in *Harmel* to state law that is adopted by "express language or necessary implication" seems, at first blush, to suggest that most legal terms used by the Code have an independent national meaning, and that only a few are used in their local sense. Precisely the opposite is true. The Internal Revenue Code attaches tax significance to state-created legal rights, and most legal terms are used as abbreviated references to these substantive rights. This is why Randolph Paul wrote, over forty years ago, that "much of our federal tax law is not federal tax law at all, but non-tax state law."[23]

Paul's observation is illustrated by the Supreme Court's 1965 decision in *CIR v. Clay Brown,* holding that the term "sale" in IRC §1222(3), referring to "the sale or exchange of a capital asset," is used in its customary sense rather than in a special tax sense:

> The transaction was a sale under local law. . . . "Capital gain" and "capital asset" are creatures of the tax law and the Court has been inclined to give these terms a narrow, rather than a broad, construction. . . . A "sale," however, is a common event in the non-tax world; and since it is used in the Code without limiting definition and without legislative history indicating a contrary result, its common and ordinary meaning

---

[22] See infra ¶30.4.

[23] Paul, The Effect on Federal Taxation of Local Rules of Property, in Paul, Selected Studies in Federal Taxation 1, 5 (Callaghan, 2d ser. 1938).

should at least be persuasive of its meaning as used in the Internal Revenue Code.[24]

Though not in direct conflict, *Harmel* and *Clay Brown* manifest divergent approaches to the meaning of common legal terms, although both opinions interpret the same word ("sale") as used in the same provision of the Internal Revenue Code: *Harmel* suggests that a uniform national "tax" definition should be adopted unless "express language or necessary implication" assigns a dominant role to the state definition, while *Clay Brown* implies that the term's nontax meaning, which necessarily comes from state law, should ordinarily control. Against this background, it is useful to examine the two possible extremes and then the middle ground, viz., (a) provisions of the Internal Revenue Code explicitly imposing a uniform national definition on a familiar state-law term; (b) provisions of the Code that explicitly subordinate national uniformity to state law; and (c) the broad intermediate area, illustrated by both *Harmel* and *Clay Brown,* in which the Code uses legal terms without explicitly indicating whether they are to retain their customary local sense or be given a uniform national interpretation.

2. Federal Definitions Superseding State Law. The Internal Revenue Code contains a few provisions that supersede the usual local meaning of familiar legal terms by substituting a uniform federal definition. An example is IRC §704(e), which attaches certain tax consequences to partnership interests created by "gift" and then goes on to provide that "for purposes of this section, an interest purchased by one member of a family [as defined] from another shall be considered to be created by gift from the seller. . . ." Another example is IRC §6013(d)(2), providing that a person "legally separated from his spouse under a decree . . . of separate maintenance shall not be considered as married," which prevents a couple from filing a joint return under IRC §6013(a),[25] even though they are "married" under the law of the marital domicile for local-law purposes.

These federal definitions do not purport to alter the substantive legal rights created by state law: A "purchase" under state law remains a purchase for local purposes, despite its treatment as a gift by IRC §704(e)(3); a couple separated under a legal decree remain married for local purposes if the law of their marital domicile so provides, even though they are not allowed to file a

---

[24] CIR v. Brown, 380 US 563, 569-571 (1965); see also Crane v. CIR, 331 US 1, 6 (1947) ("the words of statutes—including revenue acts—should be interpreted where possible in their ordinary, everyday senses"). These references to common usage do not explicitly defer to the meaning of the particular term under the governing state law; but when the term is a legal one, state law is the usual source of its meaning.

[25] See infra ¶39.3.

joint federal tax return. Thus, the federal definition does not "violate," or even "disregard," state law; instead, it treats some of the substantive legal rights created by state law as irrelevant to a particular issue of federal tax liability.

3. Explicit Federal Adoption of State Law. At the other end of the spectrum from these relatively scarce federal definitions that supersede the local meaning of a legal term are Code provisions—also rather uncommon—explicitly providing that a state usage or determination is controlling. Thus, if a married couple is not divorced, legally separated, or subject to a written separation agreement, payments by one spouse to support the other are deductible by the payor and taxable to the recipient only if there is "a decree entered after March 1, 1954, requiring the husband to make the payments for [the wife's] support or maintenance." [26] A more unusual example of explicit federal deference to state law is to be found in IRC §162(c)(2), providing that a bribe, kickback, or other payment may not be deducted as a business expense if it violates a state criminal or occupational licensing law, "but only if such State law is generally enforced." [27]

While this list of Code provisions explicitly bowing to state common law, statutes, or agency determinations could be extended, even the most complete catalogue would be a thin pamphlet. In the overwhelming majority of cases, when the Internal Revenue Code uses a familiar legal term, it neither explicitly adopts its local meaning nor explicitly supersedes it with a uniform national definition. The effect of this practice is discussed in the next paragraph.

4. State Meaning Neither Supplanted Nor Endorsed. Often the Code uses a legal term without either adopting its state-law meaning or explicitly supplanting the local meaning with a uniform federal definition. Since statutory construction is an art rather than a science, generalizations about the meaning of such terms when used in the Internal Revenue Code are perilous and must always be accompanied by an acknowledgment that exceptions are bound to occur. With this caveat, and in the absence of an actual word count by a lexicographer, I venture to assert that when the Code uses familiar legal terms, it rarely infuses them with a national meaning but, instead, ordinarily defers to state law by employing the terms as abbreviated ways of designating events and relationships that create taxable income, deductions, and other tax consequences. Indeed, the only alternative to these shorthand expressions

---

[26] IRC §71(a)(3), discussed infra ¶32.1.

[27] This provision is another example of the ambiguity inherent in the concept of "uniform national application" of the revenue laws. It treats alike all taxpayers who violate state laws that are generally enforced by the particular state where the activity occurs, but this uniformity is achieved at the cost of treating differently taxpayers who engage in identical illegal activities in states that are lax in enforcing their laws. See infra ¶8.3.

would be detailed descriptions in the Code of the underlying facts triggering federal tax consequences, a practice that might increase the clarity of the Code but would require an even wordier statute than Congress has seen fit to enact. Thus, a Code provision referring to "contracts" conveys in a single word a meaning that would, in the alternative, require paragraphs of black-letter law describing the concepts of offer, acceptance, consideration, capacity to contract, etc. Moreover, the use of such terms ordinarily points to the state law applicable to a particular set of facts, rather than to a more generalized national standard.

Common legal terms may be employed by Congress, not only to incorporate by reference a complex set of facts but also as a way of attaching tax consequences to the facts, only if they have a particular legal effect under state law. In these instances, the term refers to the legal result, as well as implying the existence of the underlying facts. For example, the references in IRC §642(c)(2) to "mental disability" to change a will or trust refer to a want of legal power under the applicable state law, by reason of mental deficiency, to perform the specified acts. Thus, a person would be embraced by the statutory phrase if an attempt by him to change a will or trust would be ineffective in his own state, even if his emotional or cognitive disorientation would be characterized as mere eccentricity in a more tolerant state.

The principal exception to this common use of legal terms as abbreviated references to the taxpayer's state-prescribed legal rights, liabilities, or status occurs when the applicable state law attaches an unconventional meaning to the term. If used as an idiosyncratic label for a transaction, event, or status that seems to be outside the intended reach of the tax provision in question, the local term may be rejected in favor of a more conventional, nationally uniform definition. Conversely, the taxpayer's rights, liabilities, or status will be subjected to a tax provision if within its intended scope, even if they are denoted by an unconventional local label that differs from the term used by the Code. What is important in these circumstances is not that the state in question attaches different legal consequences to an activity or set of facts than do other states, but that its label clashes with the term employed by the Code, either because the Code's term is used locally to denote legal results that the Code provision was not intended to comprehend or because a different label is used locally for results within the Code's intended scope.

Since the labels employed by a particular state's common or statutory law are not controlling, it should occasion no surprise that the federal courts are not bound by the labels that taxpayers chose to bestow on a contract or transaction. A transaction may be treated as a mortgage for federal tax purposes, for example, even though the documents consistently describe it as a sale of the property coupled with a leaseback by the buyer to the seller.[28] When

[28] Infra ¶22.6.

a label used by the parties does not accurately denote the transaction's legal consequences under state law, a different characterization in applying the Internal Revenue Code may actually conform to, rather than depart from, the characterization that would be adopted for local purposes by the state courts.

Finally, a few legal terms used in the Code have been the subject of extensive interpretation in federal tax litigation, in which nationally applicable principles have been developed with minimal reliance on state law. This is most likely to occur with broad, amorphous terms whose local meanings evolved in contexts far removed from the federal tax issues created by their use in the Code. For example, the Supreme Court has held that the term "gift" as used in IRC §102(a) (excluding "the value of property acquired by gift" from the donee's gross income) is not used "in the common-law sense." [29] This conclusion is quite understandable. Federal income tax problems involving the meaning of "gift" arise most frequently in transactions that have a compensatory flavor, leading the IRS to assert that the transfer was not a tax-free "gift" but a receipt of taxable compensation. For private-law purposes, however, the principal situation invoking the term "gift" is a transfer of property that the purported donor (or, more frequently, his executor) seeks to recover. In deciding whether the transferee is entitled to retain the property under state law, it is not necessary to distinguish between "gifts" and payments of compensation, since in either case the transfer is legally effective. By contrast, in applying IRC §102(a), this distinction is all-important. It is, therefore, not surprising that the federal tax cases interpreting the term "gift" as used in IRC §102(a) give little attention to local law.

5. The Effect of State Adjudications. As pointed out earlier, virtually every federal income tax question entails threshold issues of state law, since the taxpayer's rights, liabilities, and status under local law are the infrastructure on which federal tax liability rests. For example, whenever the federal tax consequences of a contract must be determined, whether by the IRS at the audit level or by the federal courts in a litigated case, there must be either an implicit assumption or an explicit determination that the parties to the agreement had legal capacity to contract, that the statute of frauds was either inapplicable or satisfied, that enforcement of the obligations is not barred by the statute of limitations or laches, and that the contract in all other respects is valid and subsisting. In the overwhelming bulk of tax matters, private-law issues like these are conceded rather than contested, but sometimes a legal issue arising under state law must be decided in the course of a federal tax case. When this occurs, the federal court performs substantially the same function as when it decides a similar state issue in a diversity-of-citizenship case, and

---

[29] CIR v. Duberstein, 363 US 278, 285 (1960), discussed infra ¶3.2.

hence it "may be said to be, in effect, sitting as a state court." [30] In this capacity, and in the absence of an authoritative decision by the highest state court, the federal court must give "proper regard"—but not conclusive force—to decisions of the state's trial and intermediate appellate courts when determining, as best it can, how the local issue would be decided by the highest state court.[31] In unusual circumstances a state-law issue may be certified by the federal court to a state court for an authoritative ruling.[32]

What if the local issue that is being disputed in the federal tax proceeding has already been decided by a state court in litigation by which the taxpayer is bound? Assume, for example, that the taxpayer seeks to deduct a debt as worthless under IRC §166(a)(1), offering as evidence of worthlessness a state court judgment, in a suit brought by him against the debtor, holding that collection is barred by the statute of limitations. If the government asserts that the debt is not yet worthless because the state court applied the wrong statute of limitations,[33] much can be said for treating the issue as foreclosed by the state judgment since it is binding on the taxpayer, whether it correctly interprets state law or not.[34] If the debtor happens to be the taxpayer's child, however, the taxpayer may not have prosecuted the case as vigorously as possible and may even have preferred to lose than to win. In such a nonadversary situation, the local judgment may be tantamount to a consent decree, entered without much attention to the issues by a busy judge who is eager to clear a heavy docket.

The tension between the state judgment's conclusive determination of the taxpayer's private-law rights under local law and federal fear of perfunctory decisions, collusion, and even fraud in nonadversary local proceedings has generated a series of dramatic cases in the Supreme Court. In *CIR v. Bosch's Estate,* the most recent, the Court apparently disregarded both of these factors by announcing that the federal court must follow the same procedure in

---

[30] CIR v. Bosch's Est., 387 US 456, 465 (1967); see also 382 F.2d 295 (2d Cir. 1967) (decision on remand). But the "state court" analogy does not hold for the Supreme Court, which will ordinarily not reexamine a federal appellate court's determination of local law. 387 US at 462 (Point II).

[31] CIR v. Bosch's Est., supra note 30; Linder v. CIR, 68 TC 292, 298-299 (1977) (Tax Court effort to determine whether New Jersey Supreme Court would follow an earlier, outmoded decision); Newman v. CIR, 68 TC 494 (1977) (effect of retroactive state court rulings).

[32] See Imel v. US, 523 F.2d 853 (10th Cir. 1975); US v. Baldwin, 586 F.2d 324 (4th Cir. 1978).

[33] Since the Commissioner cannot be a party to the private lawsuit, the judgment is not res judicata as to the government, nor does the principle of collateral estoppel apply.

[34] See Rev. Rul. 73-142, 1973-1 CB 405 (state decree holding that decedent did not have power to appoint successor trustees binding in applying federal estate tax because, whether correct or not, it effectively terminated decedent's power).

ascertaining state law when the taxpayer's rights have already been determined by a state court as it would in the absence of such a specific determination. The result, evidently, is that a decision of the highest state court is controlling even if the lawsuit was of a nonadversary nature, whereas decisions of the state trial and intermediate appellate courts are to receive "proper regard" but are not conclusive even if rendered in an adversary lawsuit.[35]

¶1.3 PERVASIVE JUDICIAL DOCTRINES

1. Introductory. During the nineteenth century, the practice of construing taxing statutes strictly against the government was said to be "founded so firmly upon principles of equity and natural justice as not to admit reasonable doubt." [36] As explained by Mr. Justice Story in 1842:

> In every case . . . of doubt, [taxing] statutes are construed most strongly against the government, and in favor of the subjects or citizens, because burdens are not to be imposed, nor presumed to be imposed, beyond what the statutes expressly and clearly import. Revenue statutes are in no just sense either remedial laws or laws founded upon any permanent public policy, and therefore are not to be liberally construed.[37]

This approach, which bracketed taxing statutes with laws imposing criminal penalties or forfeitures, was not without challenge even in its heyday, and by now has been largely abandoned.[38]

Contemporary courts apply tax laws with greater tolerance—some would say enthusiasm; and if strict construction is still a watchword, it is more likely to be used against the taxpayer in cases deciding the scope of statutory exceptions, deductions, and similar allowances than against the government.[39]

---

[35] CIR v. Bosch's Est., supra note 30. Although the Court cited the legislative history of the tax provision in dispute (the marital deduction authorized by IRC §2056 of the estate tax law) to support its conclusion about the effect of state law, the opinion seemingly stakes out a much wider area of application.

[36] Cahoon v. Coe, 57 NH 556, 570 (1876).

[37] US v. Wigglesworth, 28 F.Cas. 595, 597 (C.C.D. Mass. 1842).

[38] But see Ivan Allen Co. v. US, 422 US 617, 627 (1975) (penalty taxes to be strictly construed against government); Fullman, Inc. v. US, 434 US 528, 533 n.8 (1978) (strict construction principle not applicable to penalties that can be easily avoided by following statutory guidelines).

[39] See, e.g., Corn Prods. Ref. Co. v. CIR, 350 US 46 (1955) (strict construction of term "capital assets" in order to reduce "preferential treatment" for capital gains); Interstate Transit Lines v. CIR, 319 US 590, 593 (1943) (income tax deductions are a "matter of legislative grace and . . . the burden of clearly showing the right to the

Often, however, what one taxpayer loses from the strict construction of a statutory provision, another taxpayer gains. If the term "capital asset" is narrowly defined to deny the benefit of the lower tax rate for capital gains to a taxpayer who sells his property at a profit, for example, the same narrow construction will inure to the benefit of other taxpayers incurring losses on the sale of similar property, since they will not be subjected to the special limitations on the deductibility of capital losses.[40]

Quite aside from the possibility that a court's effort to help out the Treasury in a close case may give the government a Pyrrhic victory, it is far from clear why the Internal Revenue Code should be construed strictly against *either* the taxpayer *or* the government.[41] A more salutary attitude was advocated by Mr. Justice Holmes, responding to the once-popular adage that statutes in derogation of the common law should be strictly construed:

> The Legislature has the power to decide what the policy of the law shall be, and if it has intimated its will, however indirectly, that will should be recognized and obeyed. The major premise of the conclusion expressed in a statute, the change of policy that induces the enactment, may not be set out in terms, but it is not an adequate discharge of duty for courts to say: We see what you are driving at, but you have not said it, and therefore we shall go on as before.[42]

In applying the Internal Revenue Code to particular transactions, the courts frequently distinguish between "tax avoidance" and "tax evasion" and between "form" and "substance," assert that transactions are to be taken at face value for tax purposes only if they are imbued with a "business purpose or reflect economic reality," and integrate all steps in a prearranged plan rather than give effect to each step as though it were an isolated transaction. These presuppositions or criteria are so pervasive that they resemble a preamble to the Code, describing the framework within which all statutory provisions are to function. But these judicial presuppositions, like the canons of statutory construction, are more successful in establishing attitudes and moods than in supplying crisp answers to specific questions.

---

claimed deduction is on the taxpayer"); Stiles v. CIR, 69 TC 558, 563 (1978) (as exceptions to the general rule, relief provisions are to be strictly construed).

[40] Infra ¶25.12.

[41] Of course, the taxpayer has the burden of proof in litigated cases as respects factual issues, as explained infra ¶43.4; the discussion in the text is concerned with the resolution of legal questions.

[42] Johnson v. US, 163 F. 30, 32 (1st Cir. 1908) (Mr. Justice Holmes on circuit). For a similar comment by Mr. Justice Stone in a tax case, see White v. US, 305 US 281, 292 (1938) (duty of courts, in tax cases as in other litigation, is to decide "what [the] construction fairly should be").

2. Tax Avoidance vs. Tax Evasion. Although the terms are occasionally used interchangeably, "tax avoidance" and "tax evasion" are usually differentiated—the former phrase denoting lawful modes of minimizing or avoiding tax liability; the latter, fraudulent behavior. The line between lawful conduct (which, of course, may or may not achieve its tax reduction objective) and fraudulent or criminal misconduct is discussed elsewhere in this work;[43] for present purposes, the term "tax evasion" can be reserved for conduct that entails deception, concealment, destruction of records, and the like, while "tax avoidance" refers to behavior that the taxpayer hopes will serve to reduce his tax liability but that he is prepared to disclose fully to the IRS.

Used in this sense, "tax avoidance" embraces a virtually unlimited spectrum of personal, financial, and business transactions. Taxpayers often organize corporations, establish trusts, make gifts, sell property, and borrow money—to mention only a few obvious areas—in ways or at times selected to reduce their tax liabilities. In many cases, the tax savings is so clearly granted by the statute that even the most severe moralist would direct any criticism at Congress rather than at the taxpayer. When the Internal Revenue Code requires the taxpayer to pick one of several options to be chosen (e.g., cash or accrual accounting, straight-line or accelerated depreciation, etc.), for example, it would be quixotic to gladden the heart of the Commissioner of Internal Revenue by electing the most costly. Citizens who want to make a voluntary contribution to the Treasury can do so by sending in their checks at any time; there is no reason to use the tax return as a vehicle for such generosity.

In any event, the issue for consideration here is not whether taxpayers who seek to minimize their taxes by transactions of the types just described should be condemned as tightfisted, but whether the courts—staffed not by moral philosophers but by jurists—will uphold their legal claims. It is clear that the courts do not regard themselves as invested with a roving commission to extirpate tax avoidance. There are three classic statements justifying judicial disregard of the taxpayer's motive if, though close to the dividing line, he stays on the nontaxable side—all quoted so frequently that experienced tax lawyers know them by heart. One is a 1930 observation by Mr. Justice Holmes:

> The only purpose of the [taxpayer] was to escape taxation. . . . The fact that it desired to evade the law, as it is called, is immaterial, because the very meaning of a line in the law is that you may intentionally go as close to it as you can if you do not pass it.[44]

The second statement is by Judge Learned Hand:

---

[43] Infra ¶42.4.

[44] Superior Oil Co. v. Mississippi, 280 US 390, 395-396 (1930).

> [A] transaction, otherwise within an exception of the tax law, does not lose its immunity, because it is actuated by a desire to avoid, or, if one choose, to evade, taxation. Any one may so arrange his affairs that his taxes shall be as low as possible; he is not bound to choose that pattern which will best pay the Treasury; there is not even a patriotic duty to increase one's taxes.[45]

The third is also by Judge Learned Hand:

> Over and over again courts have said that there is nothing sinister in so arranging one's affairs as to keep taxes as low as possible. Everybody does so, rich or poor; and all do right, for nobody owes any public duty to pay more than the law demands: taxes are enforced exactions, not voluntary contributions. To demand more in the name of morals is mere cant.[46]

The statement that tax avoidance is practiced by rich and poor alike must be taken as exaggeration since wage earners have few opportunities to "arrange [their] affairs" so as to reduce their taxes; and it is not clear why Judge Hand felt impelled to *commend* persons engaged in tax avoidance for "do[ing] right," rather than merely to uphold their privilege to do so. These reservations aside, his central message—"the doctrine that a man's motive to avoid taxation will not establish his liability if the transaction does not do so without it" [47]—is widely accepted.

It would be a mistake, however, to conclude that the flavor of a stew is never impaired by a lavish infusion of tax avoidance. After asserting that the taxpayer's purpose was a neutral circumstance, both Holmes and Hand in the first two opinions quoted above went on to resolve the tax question in favor of the government, and it is hard to escape the conclusion that the aroma of tax avoidance contributed to the outcome.[48] Even if the taxpayer's purpose was wholly irrelevant in these cases, however, there are other circumstances in which it cannot be disregarded.

First, the Code contains many statutory provisions that explicitly make

---

[45] Helvering v. Gregory, 69 F.2d 809, 810 (2d Cir. 1934), aff'd sub nom. Gregory v. Helvering, 293 US 465 (1935), discussed infra, text at notes 60 and 61.

[46] CIR v. Newman, 159 F.2d 848, 850-851 (2d Cir.) (dissenting opinion), cert. denied, 331 US 859 (1947).

[47] Chisholm v. CIR, 79 F.2d 14, 15 (2d Cir. 1935), cert. denied, 296 US 641 (1936).

[48] In Superior Oil Co. v. Mississippi, supra note 44, at 394, the Court said that a crucial document (relied on by the taxpayer to establish that a transaction was in interstate commerce and immune to a state sales tax) "seems to have had no other use than . . . to try to convert a domestic transaction into one of interstate commerce"; in Helvering v. Gregory, supra note 45, the taxpayer created a transitory corporation that was promptly, and pursuant to plan, liquidated.

tax avoidance an operative factor in determining tax liability. Thus, IRC §532 imposes a special tax on "every corporation . . . formed or availed of for the purpose of avoiding the income tax with respect to its shareholders"; and IRC §357(b)(1), involving assumptions of debt in certain transfers to controlled corporations, requires a determination of whether "the principal purpose of the taxpayer . . . was a purpose to avoid Federal income tax." Difficulties in administering statutory distinctions between transactions that are, and those that are not, dominated by tax-avoidance objectives have more than once led Congress to impose a disability on all transactions in the suspect category, whether guilty or not.[49]

Second, in deciding whether to accept at face value the form in which a transaction was cast by the taxpayer or to probe for its substance or net effect, revenue agents and courts sometimes respond to the aroma of tax avoidance like hounds to the scent of foxes. They are likely to suspect that the form adopted by the taxpayer is a self-serving declaration—"motive is a persuasive interpreter of equivocal conduct" [50]—if the Internal Revenue Code seems to be more influential in shaping a transaction than its nontax results.

Finally, when construing ambiguous statutory language, the courts often reject interpretations that would sanctify legal formalities and thereby foster tax avoidance. Since the statute as construed will affect all taxpayers, however, the state of mind of the litigant who happens to come before the court (however significant it may be in determining whether the forms he has used correspond to the substance of his transaction) is less important in such cases than the objectives of taxpayers as a group. If the court concludes that they are likely to engage in the particular transaction primarily to reduce taxes rather than to achieve nontax business or personal objectives, the statutory provision will often be construed strictly in favor of the government, and this meaning will be visited upon all taxpayers, even those who are wholly innocent of any tax-avoidance purpose.

3. Form vs. Substance. When today's federal income tax was still in its swaddling clothes, the Supreme Court treated the superiority of substance over form as a well-settled principle in tax matters, saying (in 1921):

> We recognize the importance of regarding matters of substance and disregarding forms in applying the provisions of the Sixteenth Amendment and income tax laws enacted thereunder. In a number of cases . . . we have under varying conditions followed the rule.[51]

---

[49] E.g., IRC §267(a)(1), denying any deduction for losses on sales between related taxpayers, whether at a fair market price or not (infra ¶33.1), and IRC §166(d)(1), providing that nonbusiness bad debts create capital rather than ordinary losses (infra ¶17.6).

[50] Texas & N.O.R.R. v. Brotherhood of Ry. Clerks, 281 US 548, 559 (1930).

[51] US v. Phellis, 257 US 156, 168 (1921).

More recently, the substance-over-form principle has been called "the cornerstone of sound taxation." [52]

There are times, however, when form—and form alone—determines the tax consequences of a transaction. For example, a taxpayer with several blocks of stock of the same company, purchased over a period of time at different prices, can sell either high-cost or low-cost shares merely by delivering one certificate rather than another or even, when a particular lot of shares cannot be traced to a separate certificate, by designating which shares he intends to sell.[53] Whichever form is employed to separate the shares sold from those retained, it will have no nontax ramifications. There are also a few statutory provisions that, the courts have held, deliberately elevate form above substance. An example is IRC §71(b), providing that a payment under a decree of divorce or separate maintenance is not taxable to the recipient if the decree fixes the amount "as a sum which is payable for the support of minor children of the husband," a condition that requires "specific earmarking" and cannot be satisfied by evidence that in substance, though not in form, the payment was made for the support of the children.[54]

Despite these examples of the occasional preeminence of form, in deciding federal tax cases the courts are ordinarily willing if not eager to take account of the substance behind the veil of form.[55] Unfortunately, however, it is almost impossible to distill useful generalizations from the welter of substance-over-form cases. First, the facts of particular cases are usually complicated, and it is rarely clear which facts are crucial to the decision and which are irrelevant; this uncertainty about the precedential value of the decision is often compounded by the failure of courts to say whether their conclusions rest on findings of fact that might have gone the other way if a witness had been more credible or additional evidence had been offered on a particular point.

Another barrier to generalizing from the decided cases is uncertainty whether the courts, in particular cases, are interpreting the statutory provision on which the taxpayer relies or enunciating a principle to be applied throughout the Internal Revenue Code. In his famous opinion in the *Gregory* case, for example, Judge Learned Hand said of certain transactions:

> [T]heir only defect was that they were not what [the statutory predecessor of IRC §368(a)(1)] means by a "reorganization," because the transactions were no part of the conduct of the business of either or both companies; so viewed they were a sham. . . . [56]

---

[52] Weinert's Est. v. CIR, 294 F.2d 750, 755 (5th Cir. 1961).

[53] Infra ¶23.7.

[54] See CIR v. Lester, 366 US 299 (1960), discussed infra ¶32.2.

[55] Tax cases, of course, are not unique in searching for substance; a common analogue is the piercing of the corporate veil in private lawsuits. See Ballantine, Ballantine on Corporations §122 (Callaghan, rev. ed. 1946).

[56] Helvering v. Gregory, supra note 45, at 811.

Despite this reference to the meaning of a particular statutory provision, Judge Hand's language is regularly quoted as having much broader significance. A related source of difficulty is the common judicial practice of citing the substance-over-form doctrine in combination with other broad concepts (e.g., the business purpose and step transaction doctrines and the requirement of an accurate accounting method), thus obscuring the independent force of each of these grounds of decision.

Finally, for the reasons just canvassed, when a case holding that the form chosen by a particular taxpayer does not accurately reflect the substance of his transaction is compared with a decision supporting another taxpayer's version of a similar transaction, it is difficult, if not impossible, to ascertain whether the decisions are in conflict. Occasionally the Supreme Court grants certiorari because of a conflict among the circuit courts in cases of this type; but if each case rests on the "genuineness" of the particular taxpayer's transaction, the nature of the "conflict" is unclear.

The substance-over-form doctrine is invoked by the government with greatest success when the transaction under examination entails self-dealing, since in these circumstances the form used often has minimal, if any, nontax consequences and is often chosen solely because it is expected to reduce taxes. For example, a purported credit sale of property by parents to their children may, on analysis, be akin to a gift of the property because neither the parents nor the children take seriously the purported obligation to pay the agreed price.

Transactions at arm's length between the taxpayer and outsiders are far less vulnerable to substance-over-form attacks by the government than self-dealing transactions. For nontax reasons, the parties usually fully express their understanding in the documents, so that the chosen form ordinarily embodies the substance of their transaction. This fusion of form and substance is fostered if, as often occurs, they have divergent tax interests. Thus, when a business pays an employee for services, the desire to deduct the payment as a business expense usually leads the employer to resist suggestions by the recipient that the payment be disguised as a tax-free gift rather than reported as taxable wages.[57]

This frequent opposition of interests does not mean that the characterization adopted by the parties to an arm's-length bargain is invariably conclusive. The employer, to continue with the example just used, may be a tax-exempt organization or a persistently unsuccessful enterprise with more deductions than it can use; if so, it may be willing to cooperate with the employee either as a costless gesture of benevolence or in return for a concession by him. A similar bargain may be struck when two parties expect to be taxed at very

[57] See IRC §274(b)(1), discussed infra ¶9.4.

different rates; if they can devise a legal form that will assign the tax advantages to the party who can best "use" them, the tax savings thus achieved can be divided between them. Thus, the amount to be paid under an alimony agreement is often affected by the fact that the husband's right to deduct the payment will reduce his taxes more than receiving the same amount will increase the wife's taxes;[58] railroads and airlines with a long history of business losses often lease equipment rather than buy it, thereby enabling the lessor to derive a tax advantage from depreciation deductions or investment credits that would be useless to the lessee; and many tax shelters similarly serve to shift tax allowances to investors who can deduct them from top-bracket income.

If the transaction as consummated is clothed in a form that fairly reflects its substance, it will ordinarily pass muster despite the conscious pursuit of tax benefits; in this respect, it resembles an individual taxpayer's isolated decision to pursue a tax-minimizing route rather than a taxable one. On the other hand, if the form of the transaction does not coincide with its substance, the fact that it was negotiated at arm's length by unrelated taxpayers will not protect it against attack by the government, since the assumption of opposing tax interests is inapplicable. The government can, for example, successfully invoke the substance-over-form doctrine in order to treat a purported lease of business equipment with an option in the "lessee" to purchase the property as a sale on credit if the option price is nominal in amount or the term of the lease is coextensive with the anticipated useful life of the property.

The presence of a third party with whom the taxpayer has bargained at arm's length will also fail to protect a tax-avoidance plan if the formalities employed by the taxpayer have no significant impact on the other contracting party and are tolerated or accepted by him as an accommodation rather than viewed as an integral part of the basic transaction. This phenomenon is characteristic of cases in which the taxpayer engages in preliminary mumbo jumbo to prepare assets for an impending sale or effects the transfer through a conduit rather than directly. An acerbic comment by Chief Judge John R. Brown of the Court of Appeals for the Fifth Circuit can stand as a summary of this attitude. Refusing to allow the taxpayers in a complex transaction to hide behind a facade entailing the use of an intermediary named, by an appropriate fortuity, W. R. Deal, he said: "The Deal deal was not the real deal. That ends it."[59]

Although the substance-over-form doctrine is ordinarily a one-way street, taxpayers are sometimes permitted to repudiate the form of a transaction entered into in ignorance, especially if the taxpayer was deceived by another

---

[58] See infra ¶32.1.

[59] Blueberry Land Co. v. CIR, 361 F.2d 93, 102 (5th Cir. 1966). See also Waterman S.S. Corp. v. CIR, 430 F.2d 1185 (5th Cir. 1970) ("another attempt to ward off tax blows with paper armor").

party or other mitigating circumstances make it possible to characterize the form as a trap for the unwary. The courts, however, have not gone so far as to require "informed consent" before holding a taxpayer to his own red tape, and these cases of lenience, though important, remain exceptional.

4. Business Purpose. As applied to tax matters, the business purpose doctrine originated with the *Gregory* case, involving the sole shareholder of a corporation that owned certain marketable securities which she wanted to obtain in her personal capacity for sale to a third party.[60] A straightforward distribution of the securities to her in anticipation of the sale would have been taxable as a dividend. To avoid this result, the securities were transferred to a newly created second corporation, whose stock was issued to the taxpayer; she then dissolved the new corporation, receiving the securities as a liquidating distribution. Under the statutory predecessor of IRC §368(a)(1), taken literally, this transaction was a tax-free corporate reorganization, and the trial court held that "a statute so meticulously drafted must be interpreted as a literal expression of the taxing policy" and that the second corporation was entitled to recognition, despite its transitory life as a vehicle to transfer the securities from the first corporation to its sole shareholder.[60.1] The Court of Appeals for the Second Circuit reversed, holding that the transaction did not qualify as a "reorganization" when the purpose of the statutory definition of that term was taken into account and the Supreme Court affirmed, observing:

> Putting aside . . . the question of motive in respect of taxation altogether, and fixing the character of the proceeding by what actually occurred, what do we find? Simply an operation having no business or corporate purpose—a mere device which put on the form of a corporate reorganization as a disguise for concealing its real character, and the sole object and accomplishment of which was the consummation of a preconceived plan, not to reorganize a business or any part of a business, but to transfer a parcel of corporate shares to the petitioner.[60.2]

Though its career was launched by a decision concerned only with whether the steps employed by the taxpayer to achieve her objective was a "reorganization" within the meaning of the statutory predecessor of IRC §368(a)(1), the business purpose standard rapidly proliferated as an implied requirement of other statutory provisions. In 1949 Judge Learned Hand summarized its jurisdiction as follows:

---

[60] Gregory v. Helvering, supra note 45, at 811.

[60.1] Gregory v. CIR, 27 BTA 223, 225 (1932)

[60.2] Gregory v. Helvering, supra note 45, at 469.

The doctrine of *Gregory v. Helvering* . . . means that in construing words of a tax statute which describes commercial or industrial transactions we are to understand them to refer to transactions entered upon for commercial or industrial purposes and not to include transactions entered upon for no other motive but to escape taxation.[61]

5. Step Transactions. The step transaction doctrine, requiring the interrelated steps of an integrated transaction to be taken as a whole rather than treated separately, began as an interpretation of a detailed statutory provision,[62] as did the business purpose doctrine; but it has also been a successful cultural imperialist, on which the sun never sets. Its control is especially pronounced in the corporate-shareholder area.

While it is usually comparatively simple to foresee the results that flow from the step transaction doctrine if it applies, it is more difficult to predict whether it will be adopted as the proper method of analyzing a set of facts. At one extreme, if the parties have agreed to take a series of steps, no one of which will be legally effective unless all are consummated, application of the step transaction doctrine is ordinarily assured. In the absence of such an all-or-nothing plan, however, predictions are more perilous. Sometimes a series of steps, though independent, may occur simultaneously or in rapid succession; the taxpayer may simply seize upon the fact that he is engaged in negotiations or has a lawyer at hand to achieve several independent objectives, each of which would be pursued on its own even if the others had to be abandoned. Recognizing this possibility, the Tax Court has said: "The test [for applying the step transaction doctrine] is, were the steps taken so interdependent that the legal relations created by one transaction would have been fruitless without a completion of the series?"[63]

Despite intimations to the contrary in the early cases, the step transaction

---

[61] CIR v. Transport Trading & Terminal Corp., 176 F.2d 570, 572 (2d Cir. 1949), cert. denied, 338 US 955 (1950).

[62] It is dangerous to be dogmatic in pinpointing the source of a protean doctrine, particularly since in its earlier days it was sometimes regarded as an aspect of the pervasive injunction to look at substance rather than form; but the earliest explicit statement of the step transaction doctrine seems to be Warner Co. v. CIR, 26 BTA 1225, 1228 (1932) (Acq.) (Section 204(a)(7) of the Revenue Act of 1926, relating to corporate reorganizations, "permits, if it does not require, an examination of the several steps taken which culminated in the taxpayer's acquisition of the . . . assets"). See also Carter Publications, Inc. v. CIR, 28 BTA 160, 164 (1933) (Acq.) ("the whole series of acts, corporate and otherwise, constituted only a single transaction").

[63] Manhattan Bldg. Co. v. CIR, 27 TC 1032, 1042 (1957) (Acq.), citing American Bantam Car Co. v. CIR, 11 TC 397 (1948), aff'd per curiam, 177 F.2d 513 (3d Cir. 1949), cert. denied, 339 US 920 (1950).

doctrine does not require a prior agreement committing the parties to the entire series of steps once the first is taken; there is ample authority for linking several prearranged or contemplated steps, even in the absence of a contractual obligation or financial compulsion to follow through.[64] Moreover, while simultaneity is often the best evidence of interdependence, the step transaction doctrine has been applied to events separated by as much as five years and, on other facts, held inapplicable to events occurring within a period of thirty minutes.[65]

Although step transaction cases often, perhaps even usually, are concerned with whether a particular step with significant legal or business consequences should be treated as part of a larger single transaction, there are also many cases in which particular steps in an integrated transaction are disregarded as transitory events or empty formalities. The classic formulation of this variation of the step transaction doctrine, in *Minnesota Tea Co. v. Helvering,* is: "A given result at the end of a straight path is not made a different result because reached by following a devious path." [66] The unnecessary step in this case was a distribution of cash by a bankrupt corporation to its shareholders, who were required to pay the funds over to the company's creditors. In holding that this was only a "devious path" by which corporate funds were routed to the creditors (rather than a true distribution to the shareholders), the Court said:

> The preliminary distribution to the stockholders was a meaningless and unnecessary incident in the transmission of the fund to the creditors . . . so transparently artificial that further discussion would be a needless waste of time. The relation of the stockholders to the matter was that of a mere conduit.[67]

When the step transaction doctrine is thus employed to eliminate transitory or unnecessary steps, it overlaps and becomes almost indistinguishable from the business purpose doctrine (under which the unnecessary step is disregarded because lacking in business purpose) and the substance-over-form principle (nullifying the unnecessary step as a formality that merely obscures the substance of the transaction). The *Gregory* case, for example, is often cited in support of the business purpose and substance-over-form doctrines, but it

---

[64] See King Enterprises, Inc. v. US, 418 F.2d 511 (Ct. Cl. 1969).

[65] Douglas v. CIR, 37 BTA 1122 (1938) (Acq.) (five-year delay in consummating a corporate reorganization resulting from nonassignability of contracts and disputed claims); Henricksen v. Braicks, 137 F.2d 632 (9th Cir. 1943) (liquidation treated as independent of transfer of assets to new corporation thirty minutes later).

[66] Minnesota Tea Co. v. Helvering, 302 US 609, 613 (1938).

[67] Id. at 613-614.

could be equally validly viewed as a step transaction case; indeed, it is cited in the *Minnesota Tea* case in support of the "devious path" formula.[68] A typical amalgamation of all three ideas is the following statement in an IRS revenue ruling:

> The two steps of the transaction described above were part of a prearranged integrated plan and may not be considered independently of each other for Federal income tax purposes. The receipt by A of the additional stock of X in exchange for the sole proprietorship assets is transitory and without substance for tax purpose since it is apparent that the assets of the sole proprietorship were transferred to X for the purpose of enabling Y to acquire such assets without the recognition of gain to A.[69]

6. Disavowal of Form by Taxpayers. When taxpayers invoke the substance-over-form, business purpose, or step transaction doctrine in order to escape the normal tax consequences of a transaction to which they are parties, the judicial reaction gravitates between two extremes.

At one end of the spectrum, taxpayers are often told that the government can cut through their red tape if it wishes, but that it is equally free to leave them entangled in the form they selected.[70] This judicial refusal to permit taxpayers to repudiate their own handiwork is occasionally supported by the traditional elements of estoppel. The form, as characterized by the taxpayer on the tax return, may be accepted at face value by the IRS; and if the taxpayer later attempts to discard the form and portray events in a more realistic light, it may be administratively difficult or even impossible to correct all related prior returns of the taxpayer and other parties to the same transaction, because memories have faded or the statute of limitations has run.[71] But, even when no irretrievable waves have been set in motion, taxpayers have sometimes been denied the right to invoke the substance-over-form doctrine:

> It would be quite intolerable to pyramid the existing complexities of tax law by a rule that the tax shall be that resulting from the form of

---

[68] Id. at 614.

[69] Rev. Rul. 70-140, 1970-1 CB 73.

[70] See Burnet v. Commonwealth Improvement Co., 287 US 415 (1932) (having elected to do business in corporate form, taxpayer must accept tax disadvantages of doing so); see also Higgins v. Smith, 308 US 473 (1940) (government can pierce corporate veil in similar situation if it chooses).

[71] See Unvert v. CIR, 72 TC 807 (1979) (review of cases on quasi-estoppel). For mitigation of the statute of limitations in the case of inconsistency by either the taxpayer or the IRS, see infra ¶41.9.

transaction taxpayers have chosen or from any other form they might have chosen, whichever is less.[72]

This attitude may be buttressed by a belief that a taxpayer's repudiation of a form deliberately chosen by him is unappealing conduct even when prejudice to the government's interest cannot be proved.

At the opposite extreme from the foregoing line of authority, many cases hold that the substance-over-form doctrine is a two-way street, open to the taxpayer as well as to the government. In a graphic expression of this attitude, the Court of Appeals for the Ninth Circuit said, "One should not be garotted by the tax collector for calling one's agreement by the wrong name." [73] In a similar vein, the Supreme Court has permitted taxpayers to disavow a tax-oriented contract on showing that its form conflicted with economic reality, despite the government's willingness to accept the contract as written.[74] The case involved an effort to shift liability for social security taxes on the wages of musicians from bandleaders to ballroom operators by vesting the latter with rights under a standard union contract that were not intended to be enforced. Despite this barefaced denial of the employment realities, the IRS was willing to accept the agreement, perhaps because the ballroom operators were more responsible taxpayers than the bandleaders; but the Supreme Court allowed the operators to repudiate the fictitious employer-employee relationship.

Between these two extremes can be found cases allowing taxpayers to escape from the forms selected by them but imposing a more stringent burden of proof than is ordinarily applicable in ordinary tax cases. Describing this middle ground, the Tax Court has observed that "the so-called 'two-way street' seems to run downhill for the Commissioner and uphill for the taxpayer." [74.1] For example, when the sales price of a going business is allocated by the parties among its components (e.g., inventory, depreciable assets, and a covenant not to compete), some courts permit a unilateral repudiation of the agreed allocation by the buyer or seller only on "strong proof" of its failure to reflect economic reality; and in the Court of Appeals for the Third Circuit, the taxpayer can disavow the allocation only on showing that it was induced by mistake, fraud, or the like.[75]

---

[72] Television Indus., Inc. v. CIR, 284 F.2d 322, 325 (2d Cir. 1960).

[73] Pacific Rock & Gravel Co. v. US, 297 F.2d 122, 125 (9th Cir. 1961). Despite this auspicious comment, the taxpayer lost; since the court attributed its action to a murky agreement, perhaps it was a case of suicide rather than garrotting.

[74] Bartels v. Birmingham, 332 US 126 (1947) (three Justices dissenting).

[74.1] Rogers v. CIR, ¶70,192 P-H Memo TC (1970), aff'd, 445 F.2d 1020 (2d Cir. 1971).

[75] See, e.g., Ullman v. CIR, 264 F.2d 305 (2d Cir. 1959) ("strong proof"); CIR v. Danielson, 378 F.2d 771 (3d Cir. 1967) (evidence sufficient to vary the terms of a written contract under common law, such as mistake or fraud); infra ¶26.7.

¶1.4 THE MEANING OF "INCOME"—INTRODUCTORY

Nowhere in the Internal Revenue Code is there a definition of the term "income." Section 61(a), the Code's basic definitional provision, undertakes only the more limited task of defining "gross income," which it describes as "all income from whatever source derived, including (but not limited to) the following items [compensation from services, interest, dividends, etc.]." [76] Thus, IRC §61(a) puts all items that constitute "income" (and no others) into "gross income," but it does not purport to answer the threshold question whether a particular item is, or is not, "income."

When recommending enactment of IRC §61(a) in 1954, the House Ways and Means Committee pointed out that the statutory phrase "all income from whatever source derived" was taken from the Sixteenth Amendment and said that "the word 'income' is used [by IRC §61(a)] in its constitutional sense." [77] The Senate Finance Committee's report makes a similar reference to the Sixteenth Amendment, and both reports state that the concept of income employed by the 1939 Code was carried forward without change into the 1954 Code.[78] Like the 1954 Code, however, the 1939 Code defined "gross income" but not "income" itself; and the same is true of its statutory predecessors.

There is no hope, however, of finding an authoritative definition of "income" in the legislative and public debates that preceded and accompanied ratification of the Sixteenth Amendment. The Sixteenth Amendment did not confer the power to tax income on Congress; that power had existed from the founding of the Republic. The Sixteenth Amendment served the more limited (though critical) function of permitting Congress to tax individuals on certain types of income (primarily rents, interest, and dividends) without apportioning the tax among the states in proportion to population.[79] Given this limited mission, the Sixteenth Amendment did not elicit an outpouring of popular or professional views about the meaning of the term "income."

It was obvious enough to everyone that ratification of the Sixteenth Amendment would result in an individual income tax on such major sources as interest, rents, dividends, business profits, wages, salaries, and other compensation for personal services. But if an inquisitive legislator, journalist, or man in the street had wondered about the peripheral items that the Internal Revenue Service and courts had to deal with in later years—stock dividends, cancellation of indebtedness, unlawful receipts, windfalls, compensation for personal injuries or loss of life, etc.—few answers would have been found in

---

[76] See also IRC §6501(e)(1)(A) (special definition of "gross income" for purposes of extended statute of limitations), discussed infra ¶41.4.

[77] H. Rep. No. 1337, 83d Cong., 2d Sess. A18 (1954).

[78] S. Rep. No. 1622, 83d Cong., 2d Sess. 168-169 (1954).

[79] See supra ¶1.1.

the few places where help might have been sought. Dictionary definitions of the term "income" were too terse to be helpful; accounting principles were relatively undeveloped in the early years of this century; and there was no consensus among economists, who in any event concentrated then, as now, on macroeconomic issues to the exclusion of details. Nor was much to be learned from the administrative and judicial history of the prior income tax laws. As for the congressional debate on the Revenue Act of 1913, it proceeded in important part on the mistaken theory that the power to tax income was derived from the Sixteenth Amendment and that the scope of the term "income" was a constitutional issue that could not be influenced by congressional action.[80]

The newly minted Revenue Act of 1913, with its undefined concept of "income," soon came before the courts for interpretation. The most important of the early cases, *Eisner v. Macomber,* concerned the power of Congress to tax a shareholder on the value of a dividend of common stock paid to her by a corporation whose share capital consisted solely of one class of common stock. The Court held that the tax was unconstitutional:

> [The stock dividend] does not alter the preexisting proportionate interest of any stockholder or increase the intrinsic value of his holding or of the aggregate holdings of the other stockholders as they stood before. The new certificates simply increase the number of the shares, with consequent dilution of the value of each share. . . .
>
> The essential and controlling fact is that the stockholder has received nothing out of the company's assets for his separate use and benefit; on the contrary, every dollar of his original investment, together with whatever accretions and accumulations have resulted from employment of his money and that of the other stockholders in the business of the company, still remains the property of the company, and subject to business risks which may result in wiping out the entire investment. Having regard to the very truth of the matter, to substance and not to form, he has received nothing that answers the definition of income within the meaning of the Sixteenth Amendment.[81]

In reaching this conclusion, the Supreme Court reaffirmed a definition of income that it had previously enunciated in construing the 1909 corporation income tax but elevated the definition from the status of statutory construction to constitutional dogma:

> [W]e find little to add to the succinct definition . . .—"Income may be defined as the gain derived from capital, from labor, or from both

---

[80] Id.

[81] Eisner v. Macomber, 252 US 189, 211 (1920).

combined," provided it be understood to include profit gained through a sale or conversion of capital assets. . . .

Brief as it is, it indicates the characteristic and distinguishing attribute of income essential for a correct solution of the present controversy. The Government, although basing its argument upon the definition as quoted, placed chief emphasis upon the word "gain," which was extended to include a variety of meanings; while the significance of the next three words was either overlooked or misconceived. *"Derived-from-capital"*; the *"gain-derived-from capital,"* etc. Here we have the essential matter: *not* a gain *accruing* to capital, not a *growth* or *increment* of value *in* the investment; but a gain, a profit, something of exchangeable value *proceeding from* the property, *severed from* the capital however invested or employed, and *coming in,* being *"derived,"*— that is, *received* or *drawn by* the recipient (the taxpayer) for his *separate* use, benefit and disposal; *that* is income derived from property. Nothing else answers the description.

The same fundamental conception is clearly set forth in the Sixteenth Amendment—"incomes, *from* whatever *source derived*"— the essential thought being expressed with a conciseness and lucidity entirely in harmony with the form and style of the Constitution.[82]

Aside from its direct impact on the taxability of stock dividends, a minor issue when viewed in proper perspective, the most important implications of *Eisner v. Macomber*'s definition of income are:

1. That Congress cannot tax as income the increase in net worth enjoyed by a taxpayer as a result of appreciation in the value of assets between the beginning and end of the taxable year, because this gain has not yet been "severed" from the taxpayer's capital.[83]
2. That corporate earnings cannot be taxed pro rata to the shareholders unless distributed to them, because undistributed corporate income, though increasing the value of the shareholder's stock, has not been "received . . . for his separate use."
3. That windfalls, payments for personal injuries, gifts, bequests, and similar amounts cannot be taxed as income, because they are not "derived from capital, from labor, or from both combined." [84]

These three corollaries of *Eisner v. Macomber* have not been directly challenged by Congress; they are, rather, part of the basic framework of the federal income tax. But as pointed out subsequently in this work, Congress has nibbled around the edges of each one, and judicial decisions subsequent to *Eisner v. Macomber* have undermined it as a foundation for all three.

---

[82] Id. at 207-208.
[83] See infra ¶1.5.
[84] See infra ¶¶3.1 (gifts), 5.1 (personal injuries and sickness).

The decision itself was not unanimous. Mr. Justice Holmes responded briefly, but decisively, to the lengthy majority opinion:

> I think the word "incomes" in the Sixteenth Amendment should be read in "a sense most obvious to the common understanding at the time of its adoption." . . . For it was for public adoption that it was proposed. . . . The known purpose of this Amendment was to get rid of nice questions as to what might be direct taxes, and I cannot doubt that most people not lawyers would suppose when they voted for it that they put a question like the present to rest.[85]

Mr. Justice Brandeis also dissented, invoking the conception of income held by the general public and the business community:

> In terse, comprehensive language befitting the Constitution, [the people of the United States] empowered Congress "to lay and collect taxes on incomes from whatever source derived." They intended to include thereby everything which by reasonable understanding can fairly be regarded as income. That stock dividends representing profits are so regarded, not only by the plain people, but by investors and financiers, and by most of the courts of the country, is shown, beyond peradventure, by their acts and by their utterances.[86]

In the long run, the relaxed if not populist conception of income espoused by Holmes and Brandeis prevailed, as did their views in so many other constitutional areas, over the awesome finality of the majority's definition. In *United States v. Kirby Lumber Co.,* the Supreme Court held that income was realized by a corporation on purchasing some of its own bonds for less than the price at which they had been issued.[87] Arguing that the transaction improved its balance sheet but did not produce any gain that was "severed" from its capital, the taxpayer relied on the definition in *Eisner v. Macomber*; and the court below, in harmony with the conclusion of other courts, agreed with this claim. But a unanimous Court, speaking through Mr. Justice Holmes, denigrated the weight of *Eisner v. Macomber*'s definition:

> We see nothing to be gained by the discussion of judicial definitions. The [taxpayer] has realized within the year an accession to income, if we take words in their plain popular meaning, as they should be taken here.[88]

The next step in reducing the authority of *Eisner v. Macomber* was taken

---

[85] Eisner v. Macomber, supra note 81, at 219-220.

[86] Id. at 237.

[87] US v. Kirby Lumber Co., 284 US 1 (1931), discussed infra ¶2.4.

[88] Id. at 3. Holmes' reference to the "plain popular meaning" of the term income is reminiscent of his dissent in Eisner v. Macomber, supra note 81.

in 1940, when the Court held in *Helvering v. Bruun* that a landlord realized gain on the forfeiture of a leasehold for nonpayment of rent, the tenant having erected a building that added about $50,000 to the value of the property.[89] The taxpayer argued that this increase in value was not "severed" from his investment or received "for his separate use, benefit, and disposal." The Court, however, held that the event generated taxable income:

> Here, as a result of a business transaction, the respondent received back his land with a new building on it, which added an ascertainable amount to its value. It is not necessary to recognition of taxable gain that he should be able to sever the improvement begetting the gain from his original capital. If that were necessary, no income could arise from the exchange of property; whereas such gain has always been recognized as realized taxable gain.[90]

Although the *Bruun* opinion did not reject the famous definition promulgated by *Eisner v. Macomber,* it watered down the requirement of a realization by suggesting that any definite event—here the forfeiture of a leasehold—could be properly employed as the occasion for taking account of the taxpayer's gain.

There were other steps in the erosion of *Eisner v. Macomber*'s definition, but the coup de grace was delivered by the Supreme Court in 1955, when it decided in *CIR v. Glenshaw Glass Co.* that punitive damages awarded to two taxpayers in private antitrust actions were taxable.[91] Rather than attempt even a verbal reconciliation of these windfalls with the concept of "gain derived from capital, from labor, or from both combined," the Court consigned the *Eisner v. Macomber* definition to an insignificant role:

> The Court was there [in *Eisner v. Macomber*] endeavoring to determine whether the distribution of a corporate stock dividend constituted a realized gain to the shareholder, or changed "only the form, not the essence," of his capital investment. . . . It was held that the taxpayer had "received nothing out of the company's assets for his separate use and benefit." . . . The distribution, therefore, was held not a taxable event. In that context—distinguishing gain from capital—the definition served a useful purpose. But it was not meant to provide a touchstone to all future gross income questions. . . .
>
> Here we have instances of undeniable accessions to wealth, clearly realized, and over which the taxpayers have complete dominion. The mere fact that the payments were extracted from the wrongdoers as punishment for unlawful conduct cannot detract from their character as

---

[89] Helvering v. Bruun, 309 US 461 (1940).

[90] Id. at 468-469. For IRC §§109 and 1019, the statutory aftermath of the *Bruun* case, see infra ¶7.10.

[91] CIR v. Glenshaw Glass Co., 348 US 426 (1955).

taxable income to the recipients. . . . [W]e find no . . . evidence of intent to exempt these payments.[92]

When the *Eisner v. Macomber* definition lost its claim to exclusivity, "income" as a constitutional concept was relegated to a minor role, which can be summarized as follows:

1. If Congress explicitly directs that a particular item is to be included in the tax base, there is no need to decide whether it constitutes "income" unless a tax on the item is a "direct" tax. In this rare situation, the tax can be sustained only if it (a) is apportioned among the states according to population or (b) is relieved of that requirement by the Sixteenth Amendment because the item constitutes "income" in the constitutional sense.
2. If an item is not explicitly mentioned by the Code and gets into the tax base because it constitutes "gross income" within the meaning of IRC §61(a), that determination simultaneously establishes that it is "income" in the constitutional sense. Any doubt about its status under the direct tax clause, therefore, is dispelled by the Sixteenth Amendment, which uses the term "income" in at least as broad a sense as IRC §61(a).

While *Glenshaw Glass* completed the process, begun by the *Kirby Lumber* case, of limiting the *Eisner v. Macomber* definition, it did little to resolve the continuing problems of statutory interpretation inherent in IRC §61(a)'s use of the term "income." To be sure, the Court announced that the statutory phrase "gains or profits and income derived from any source whatever" (used by Section 22(a) of the 1939 Code, the predecessor of IRC §61(a)) "was used by Congress to exert in this field 'the full measure of its taxing power' " by including "all gains except those specifically exempted." [93] But this generalization is clearly too broad; it is obvious that Congress did not intend to tax a number of major items (e.g., home-produced goods and the rental value of owner-occupied residences), even though they constitute "gains" and are not specifically exempted. Two other important exclusions from income that are taken for granted, though not explicitly mandated by the Code, are social security benefits and gain from shrewd purchases at a bargain price.[94] Moreover, if the term "gains" includes unrealized appreciation in the taxpayer's net worth, it is quite clear that Congress has chosen not to tax this kind of income even though it is not specifically exempted;[95] and the Court in *Glenshaw Glass*

---

[92] Id. at 430-431.

[93] Id. at 429-430.

[94] See Hunley v. CIR, ¶66,066 P-H Memo TC (1966) (bargain purchases); infra ¶3.2 (social security).

[95] See infra ¶1.5.

described the punitive damages received by the taxpayers as "clearly realized," though without indicating whether it regarded realization as indispensable.

Another source of uncertainty in the *Glenshaw Glass* opinion is its use of the ambiguous term "gain." Does it embrace, for example, the receipt by an employee of a bonus that was erroneously computed and will have to be repaid on demand, the collection of a debt that was written off in an earlier year as uncollectible, compensation for injury to the taxpayer's reputation caused by slander, or funds obtained by false pretenses with no intent to repay? As will be seen,[96] these questions have all been presented to the IRS or the courts for adjudication, and *Glenshaw Glass* provides little help in resolving them. But to expect more would be to misapprehend *Glenshaw Glass,* whose principal lesson is: "Put not your faith in definitions."

¶1.5 REALIZATION

Under the definition of income most widely accepted by economists, an increase in the taxpayer's net worth during the relevant accounting period constitutes income and a decline in net worth is an offset against income.[97] The economist's reason for taking increases and decreases in the value of the taxpayer's assets into account periodically is that unrealized appreciation and depreciation alter the taxpayer's economic well-being and can be voluntarily realized by a sale, so that a decision to *retain* the assets is the functional equivalent (save for brokerage commissions and other transaction costs) of selling them and promptly reinvesting the proceeds in the same assets.

Taxing unrealized appreciation would require annual valuations of everyone's assets and that assessing closely held enterprises, real estate, intangibles like patents and franchises, and other property that is not regularly traded in a public market would be a cumbersome, abrasive, and unpredictable administrative task. Moreover, taxing unrealized appreciation would compel many taxpayers to sell or mortgage their assets in order to pay the tax; and the resulting involuntary and distress sales would be especially resented in the case of assets that are highly prized as a source of occupational opportunities or emotional satisfaction, such as farms, family businesses, heirlooms, and personal residences.

---

[96] For erroneously computed amounts, see infra ¶2.3; for collection of previously charged-off debts, see infra ¶1.10, for compensation for slander, see infra ¶1.9; for unlawful receipts, see infra ¶2.5.

[97] See Simons, Personal Income Taxation 50, 61-62, 206 (University of Chicago Press, 1938):

> Personal income may be defined as the algebraic sum of (1) the market value of rights exercised in consumption and (2) the change in the value of the store of property rights between the beginning and end of the period in question.

Another powerful deterrent to legislation putting taxpayers on an inventory method of computing income is a deep-seated distrust of "paper profits." The economic theorist may be entirely correct in asserting that a taxpayer who thinks that his unrealized appreciation is illusory should sell out while he can and that the failure to do so is tantamount to an expression of faith in the property's current market price, but this analysis is almost certainly not consciously accepted by the man in the street.

Whatever may be said for or against taxing unrealized appreciation, the federal income tax from the outset has refrained from taxing gains until they have been "realized" in some way. The Code does not explicitly require a realization of income,[98] but, despite occasional judicial statements that all gains are embraced by IRC §61(a) unless specifically excluded by statute,[99] realization is so basic to the taxing structure of existing law that the general principle is simply not challenged. Like other fundamental concepts, however, it is a bit vague around the edges, giving rise to some troublesome peripheral issues.

If, for example, an art collector trades an oil painting that cost $1,000, but is worth $10,000, for a $10,000 racehorse, the collector's gain is "realized" for tax purposes, even though he would be hard pressed to say whether the horse's head represented the gain and its tail the original investment, or vice versa—and despite the inconvenience of "severing" one from the other. Of course, the swap terminated the collector's investment in the painting, and it can be said that he "realized" the gain even if it is reinvested along with his original principal in a newly acquired indivisible asset, since he is no longer affected by fluctuations in the value of the work of art.

Another situation in which gain can be taxed even though it has been realized only in a loose sense is typified by *Helvering v. Bruun,* involving a landlord whose tenant defaulted in the payment of rent under a long-term lease after erecting a building on the leased premises. On regaining possession of the property, the landlord was held to realize income equal to the value of the building, even though he could not "sever the improvement begetting the gain from his original capital." [100] If an increase in the value of the property attributable to the building erected by the tenant can be taxed to the landlord as income, it is hard to see why he cannot also be taxed—if Congress so desires—on an increase in value resulting from trees and shrubs planted by the tenant, an adjacent highway built by the state, or an improvement in the national economy.

---

[98] Perhaps the inclusion of "gains derived from dealings in property" in gross income by virtue of IRC §61(a)(3) implies that gain is not taxable before there is a "dealing," but this is hardly a specific exclusion of unrealized appreciation.

[99] See discussion of the *Glenshaw Glass Co.* case, supra ¶1.4.

[100] Helvering v. Bruun, 309 US 461, 469 (1940), discussed supra ¶1.4.

A few months after deciding the *Bruun* case, the Supreme Court denigrated the concept of realization still further, describing it as a rule "founded on administrative convenience"—quite a demotion from the constitutional status it enjoyed under *Eisner v. Macomber.*[101] This slighting reference to "the rule that income is not taxable until realized" appears in *Helvering v. Horst,* which was concerned with whether the income from certain negotiable interest coupons was taxable to their original owner or to his son, to whom he gave the coupons and who cashed them at maturity shortly after the gift. The rationale adopted for taxing the donor was that Congress could have taxed the donor on the interest as it accrued during his ownership of the coupons and that, having refrained as a matter of administrative convenience from taxing him at this early stage, Congress implicitly indicated that he should be taxed if he gave the coupons away before they matured. Thus, without overruling or even explicitly mentioning *Eisner v. Macomber,* the Court came close to sanctioning a tax on increases in the taxpayer's net worth.

Though badly eroded as a constitutional principle, if not wholly undermined, realization as a rule of administrative convenience (or legislative generosity) remains largely intact. As will be seen at many points hereafter,[102] however, any action that significantly alters the taxpayer's relationship to an asset may constitute a "realization" of gain even though the event does not "sever" the gain from the taxpayer's original capital.

¶1.6 IMPUTED INCOME

1. Introductory. Under existing law, two major sources of untaxed income are the goods and services produced by the taxpayer for personal consumption and the taxpayer's use of his own residence and other durable goods. These items are not exempted from tax by specific statutory provisions, but congressional silence on the subject is clearly tantamount to an affirmative grant of immunity. The first of these categories of so-called imputed income is exemplified by a house painter whose home needs repainting at an estimated cost of $600 for the labor. If he is paid $10 per hour for overtime work and his marginal tax rate is 20 percent, he can earn enough in seventy-five hours of overtime to hire someone to paint his house—$750 (75 × $10), less income tax of $150, leaves $600. But if he does the job himself, he will not be taxed on the value of his labor; and if he can complete the work in sixty hours, he can either read a couple of good books during the remaining fifteen hours or work for pay and earn $150, or $120 net after taxes.

---

[101] Helvering v. Horst, 311 US 112 (1940), discussed infra ¶30.3.

[102] E.g., infra ¶22.2.

The second category of imputed income can be illustrated by comparing individuals *A* and *B*, each with $50,000 to invest. *A* buys securities with an 8 percent yield, using the annual income of $4,000 to rent a home. *B* buys a similar home for $40,000, invests the remaining $10,000 in securities and uses the annual income of $800 for repairs and real property taxes on the home. *A* and *B* are in substantially identical economic positions (assuming that depreciation on *B*'s home is offset by increases in its market value), but *A* must report $4,000 of gross income each year, while *B*'s gross income is only $800, which is partly counterbalanced by a deduction for the local property taxes.

2. Self-Help. The house painter illustration is, of course, just one example of imputed income generated by the taxpayer's own services; a comprehensive list of comparable activity would be as diverse as life itself—lawyers who write their own wills, parents who tutor their own children, housekeepers who perform domestic services, tinkerers who repair their own appliances, homeowners who mow their own lawns and raise their own vegetables, entertainers who perform for their families instead of taking them to the movies, and infants who suck their own thumbs.[103] The list would also include taxpayers who help relatives, friends, and nonprofit organizations with unpaid services, instead of working for pay and donating the compensation to these beneficiaries.

In a few situations the exclusion of imputed income is temporary rather than permanent; if a do-it-yourself project increases the value of the family residence, for example, the taxpayer may ultimately sell it at a profit that is attributable in part to his labor. In most cases, however, the taxpayer's labor does not increase the value of any property, so that its value is permanently excluded from income. Ranked by the number of persons involved and the economic significance of the work, domestic services performed in the home by housewives almost certainly dwarf any other type of imputed income.

Despite the importance of imputed income from services performed by taxpayers for themselves and their families, Congress has never sought to tax this source of economic gain. Most tax theorists have acquiesced, though sometimes grumblingly, in this decision. For one thing, an attempt to reach all sources of imputed income would require the taxpayer to keep a record of the time spent on a wide range of activities in the home, and a serious effort by the IRS to verify the time sheets or the values placed by the taxpayer on the services would be intolerably abrasive. Moreover, in theory, there is no reason to distinguish homeowners who mow their own lawns or work an extra hour in order to hire someone to do the job for them from their neighbors who lie in hammocks sipping lemonade while their grass grows tall because an hour

---

[103] For the thumb-sucking example, I am indebted to McIntyre & Oldman, Taxation of the Family in a Comprehensive and Simplified Income Tax, 90 Harv. L. Rev. 1572, 1611 (1977).

of leisure is worth as much to them as a neatly trimmed lawn is to the first group of homeowners. Rigorous consistency in the treatment of imputed income, therefore, would require taxing not just the value of unpaid services rendered by the taxpayer to himself but the value of leisure as well. If this were done, the tax would resemble a tax on the earnings the taxpayer could realize by bestirring himself; and while such a tax on vagrancy might be momentarily seductive to the theorist, it is not likely to command much support on Capitol Hill or among voters.

Although there has never been any serious effort to alter the exemption of imputed income, its economic significance is slightly reduced by several provisions of current law. First, taxpayers get a tax credit for the cost of hiring someone to look after their children while at work, subject to restrictions described in a later chapter.[104] Another statutory provision is the earned income credit granted by IRC §43, which reduces the tax disparity between taxpayers who live on investment income and are therefore able to devote as much time as they want to keeping house and similar pursuits, and taxpayers who must work for a living and have less time to satisfy their own needs.[105] The relationship of the child care and earned income credits to the exemption of imputed income becomes even more evident when we note that the rationale for both credits would be weakened if imputed income and leisure were taxable, since staying at home would then no longer create a tax advantage as compared with paid employment outside the home.[106]

In practice, the exemption of imputed income generates some troublesome peripheral issues, primarily for farmers, restaurateurs, and other taxpayers who produce goods for the public but also consume some of their own output. If a farmer who raises $10,000 worth of crops at an aggregate cost of $6,000 uses 10 percent of his output for home consumption, the proper way to separate his taxable business income from his exempt imputed income is to report the $9,000 received for the products sold to customers and deduct $5,400 of expenses (i.e., the portion of his expenses attributable to the crops sold to others), so that taxable income is $3,600. If instead he includes in gross income both the cash received from others ($9,000) and the value of the home-consumed produce ($1,000) and deducts all his agricultural expenses, the resulting income of $4,000 will include $400 of "profit" generated by raising produce for personal consumption.

Imputed income can also arise when a salesman working on a commission

[104] IRC §44A, discussed infra ¶21.1.

[105] For IRC §43, see infra ¶21.3.

[106] If imputed income were taxable, however, an earned income allowance might be supported on a secondary ground, viz., to offset the special costs incurred by taxpayers who work outside the home (e.g., for lunches, transportation, more formal clothing, etc.); see infra ¶8.2.

basis makes a sale to himself. When the issue was first litigated, the Tax Court held that an insurance broker did not realize income when a company he represented allowed him to purchase a policy on his own life for the regular premium less the customary commission. But the decision was reversed by the Court of Appeals for the Fifth Circuit, and the Tax Court bowed to its judgment in a later case.[107]

Purchasing a policy for less than its regular price is a perquisite of the insurance salesman's business status and may even be one of the attractions of representing the company whose policies he sells. Courtesy discounts, however, allowed by employers on merchandise purchased by employees are not ordinarily taxable;[107.1] and self-employed businessmen are not taxed when they buy merchandise for personal consumption at a wholesale price, even if they get this advantage only because they do business with the supplier.

Imputed income arises not only from services performed by taxpayers for themselves but also from working without pay for relatives, friends, or nonprofit organizations. An exception to this immunity is the occasional entertainer or lecturer who is about to receive a fee for a performance and who arranges, at the last minute, for payment to an organization whose work he or she wishes to support; in these circumstances, the fee ordinarily is includable in gross income. With a little foresight and attention to the paper work, however, the benefactor can usually avoid being taxed on the income from benefit nights or similar events.[108] On analysis, there is no significant economic difference between addressing envelopes for a political party, lending one's name and prestige to its appeals for funds, and singing at a benefit performance for which tickets are sold. In each case the organization gets valuable services without charge, and in each case the volunteers could provide assistance of equal value by working at their regular occupations and endorsing their paychecks to the organization. But the direct services enjoy the immunity accorded to imputed income; the alternative of working for pay and turning over the proceeds to the organization, though functionally equivalent, is a taxable event.

The recent popularity of communes among young people raises a long-latent aspect of the immunity of imputed income, viz., the taxability of reciprocal back scratching. If a lawyer writes a will for a plumber in exchange for repair of a leaky faucet in his home, both should report income from the transaction even though no money changes hands.[109] But if a group of parents organize a car pool or cooperative nursery school and take turns in providing the necessary services, even the most relentless Commissioner of Internal

[107] CIR v. Minzer, 279 F.2d 338 (5th Cir. 1960), rev'g Minzer v. CIR, 31 TC 1130 (1959); Bailey v. CIR, 41 TC 663 (1964).

[107.1] Benjamin v. Hoey, 139 F.2d 945 (2d Cir. 1944).

[108] See infra ¶30.2.

[109] See Treas. Regs. §1.61-2(d) (services for services).

Revenue would hesitate to assert that taxable income was generated by their activities. This prudence might be rationalized on the theory that the participants derive tax-free imputed income from their own services, the benefits provided by the other parents being tax-free gifts to the recipient. This theory collides with reality, however, if the parents do not help each other in the spirit of "disinterested generosity" that is the hallmark of a tax-free gift but, rather, on a quid pro quo basis (in the same way that the lawyer and plumber agree to exchange services in the earlier example).[110]

So long as nonmarket transactions of this type are restricted to the arena of personal life and remain of minor economic significance, the IRS is unlikely to mount an effort to treat them as exchanges of services rather than as tax-free imputed income. If the Treasury were confronted by hundreds of utopian communities in which money was obsolete, however, its reaction might shift from benign neglect to a vigorous effort to uncover taxable income; and the courts would then be forced to say whether the commune was held together by love—so that the services rendered to each member by the others were tax-free gifts—or by a practical (and taxable) agreement that "those who don't work, don't eat."

3. Owner-Occupied Residences. As pointed out earlier, taxpayers who own their own homes enjoy the economic benefit of occupancy without being taxed on the rental value of the property; in effect, their investments are treated as nonproductive. Thus, just as two house painters can paint their own homes without reporting any income but will gain the privilege of paying an income tax if each paints the other's house, so neighbors who realize no income from occupying their own homes will become taxable if each lives rent-free in the other's home. At one time it was thought that including imputed rent in taxable income would be unconstitutional, but today there is little if any justification for this doubt.

To eliminate the existing immunity of this type of imputed income, which has been a consistent feature of the federal income tax since 1913, the homeowner could be treated as a landlord, required to include the fair rental value of the property in gross income and permitted to deduct local taxes, mortgage interest, repairs, depreciation, and other expenses. (If the result was a negative amount, consistency would suggest allowing the hypothetical landlord to deduct his loss, just as he could deduct the identical amount if he rented the premises to an outsider at the hypothetical rent.) This reform has long been supported by economists; but some have reservations about the administrative feasibility of computing net rental values, and others are concerned about the impact of a change in the tax rules on taxpayers who bought residences expecting the current law to continue indefinitely. In any event,

---

[110] CIR v. Duberstein, 363 US 278 (1960), discussed infra ¶3.2. See also Rev. Rul. 79-24, 1979-1 CB 565 (income realized by members of services-for-services barter club).

proposals by tax theorists for change have had few responsive echoes on Capitol Hill.

Imputed income is also generated by automobiles, household furnishings, clothing, pleasure boats, and other consumer durable goods, and by the practice of keeping a minimum balance in non-interest-bearing checking accounts in order to enjoy "free" banking services.

¶1.7 "GAIN"—TAX-FREE RECOVERY OF CAPITAL

On selling property for more than its cost, a taxpayer's gain is not the entire sales price but the difference between the sales price and his cost; and if the asset is sold for less than cost, the taxpayer realizes a loss rather than a gain. This elementary principle is now embodied in IRC §1001(a), but it was accepted by the Treasury and the courts even before it was explicitly prescribed by Congress. Some of the early cases concerned with the meaning of "income" implied (or were understood to imply) that the taxpayer has a *constitutional* right to deduct the cost of property from the sales price in computing taxable gain. The reasoning of these cases was that (a) a tax on the sales price of property (i.e., unreduced by cost) would be a direct tax and (b) since the sales price is not "income," a tax thereon is not relieved by the Sixteenth Amendment from the constitutional rule that direct taxes must be apportioned among the states according to their population.

The Supreme Court came close to grappling with this issue in *Stanton v. Baltic Mining Co.,* where it seemed to hold that an allowance for the cost of property sold was a matter of legislative grace rather than constitutional right.[111] In a murky opinion, the Court upheld the tax as an excise that did not need the support of the Sixteenth Amendment. It is not clear, however, whether the decision was intended to be confined to mining corporations (which encounter particular difficulty in allocating the cost of mineral deposits to the output of a particular year) or to embrace all taxpayers engaged in business operations.

The courts have not been called upon to choose between these competing interpretations of *Baltic Mining* because Congress has affirmatively sanctioned a tax-free recovery of the taxpayer's capital in the overwhelming bulk of important situations in which the issue arises. On selling property, for example, the taxpayer can offset its cost (or other basis) either under IRC §1001(a) or, if inventory property is involved, as part of the cost of goods sold.[112] Business expenses and such other costs as depreciation, interest, and

---

[111] Stanton v. Baltic Mining Co., 240 US 103 (1916).

[112] For IRC §1001(a), see infra ¶22.1; for inventory property, see infra ¶35.4. See also Sullenger v. CIR, 11 TC 1076 (1948). (Nonacq.), holding that a merchant's cost of goods sold included payments for merchandise in excess of the legal prices set by

taxes are also deductible, except in unusual circumstances.[113]

Moreover, the tax-free recovery of capital is so basic a presupposition of the federal income tax law that it has been permitted by administrative practice or judicial decision in a variety of situations, even when there is no explicit statutory authorization for such an offset.[114] For example, the courts have recognized that a taxpayer whose business goodwill is tortiously destroyed by a competitor is taxable on damages paid by the wrongdoer only if, and to the extent that, the recovery exceeds the cost or other basis of the lost goodwill.[115] Similarly, taxpayers receiving damages for injury to property or for easements have been allowed to exclude these amounts from income because they were less than the basis of the property and there was no practical way to allocate an appropriate fraction of the basis to the portion of the property that was affected.[116]

Although tax-free recovery of the taxpayer's capital is ordinarily a prerequisite to "income" or "gain," taxpayers sometimes realize income although their receipts are less than their business outlays. One instance is

---

the Office of Price Administration during World War II and stating that this result was required by the Constitution. Since the court seemed to conclude that the deduction was in any event authorized by Congress and sanctioned by administrative practice, the constitutional reference might be regarded as dictum, though it obviously was important, and possibly even essential, to the result. In 1976 the IRS withdrew its 1952 acquiescence in *Sullenger* and substituted a nonacquiescence, probably because the case might have to be attacked when disallowing so-called questionable payments to foreign officials for business favors. 1976-1 CB 1; see infra ¶8.3. For cases rejecting the *Sullenger* constitutional theory, see CIR v. Weisman, 197 F.2d 221 (1st Cir. 1952) (unlawful portion of wages paid to employees not deductible because not a "reasonable" allowance); Pedone v. US, 151 F.Supp. 288 (Ct. Cl.), cert. denied, 355 US 829 (1957).

[113] Infra ¶8.1.

[114] Clark v. CIR, 40 BTA 333 (1939) (reimbursement for error by tax adviser) Rev. Rul. 57-47, 1957-1 CB 23 (acquiescence in *Clark* case except as to interest or amount deducted under IRC §212(3) with tax benefit); Cox v. Kraemer, 88 F.Supp. 835 (D.Conn. 1948) (legislative reimbursement of legal expenses for successful defense of charge of official misconduct). In *Cox* the taxpayer was allowed to exclude the grant, although the legal expenses for which he was reimbursed were deducted when incurred; this aspect of the decision is of doubtful validity, unless based on the court's alternative theory that the payment was a tax-free gift.

[115] See Raytheon Prod. Corp. v. CIR, 144 F.2d 110 (1st Cir.), cert. denied, 323 US 779 (1944), stating that an offset of basis against the recovery would have been permitted if the taxpayer had proved that the goodwill had been purchased or had otherwise acquired a basis. The court did not cite IRC §1001(a) as authority for offsetting basis, perhaps because the statutory phrase ("the sale or other disposition of property") requires a little stretching to embrace a recovery of damages for tortious destruction.

[116] Inaja Land Co. v. CIR, 9 TC 727 (1947) (Acq.) (payment for diverting polluted waters into taxpayer's fishing area and for an easement to continue the practice);

familiar to every reader of this volume, viz., the computation of income from professional practice without allowing the cost of professional training to be deducted as a business expense when paid or incurred, to be amortized during the years of active practice, or to be deducted as a loss on retirement or death.[117]

Finally, some tax allowances provide for a tax-free recovery of capital in a formal sense but must be taken at a time when they may be useless. For example, an investment in purchased goodwill cannot be deducted until it becomes wholly worthless; since this event often follows a long series of loss years, there may be no income to be offset by the deduction.[118] But these situations are limited in number, and they qualify rather than undermine the basic premise that taxpayers are entitled to a tax-free recovery of capital in computing income.

¶1.8 WINDFALL RECEIPTS—GAIN WITHOUT PAIN

1. Punitive Damages. In *CIR v. Glenshaw Glass Co.,* decided in 1955, the Supreme Court held that exemplary damages for fraud and the punitive two-thirds portion of a treble-damage antitrust recovery, received by a business corporation in settlement of a lawsuit against a competitor, were includable in the successful litigant's gross income.[119] In a companion case, the Court came to the same conclusion regarding a corporation's recovery of "insider profits" from a director who traded in its securities in violation of the Securities Exchange Act of 1934.[120] In both cases, the taxpayers argued that the receipts did not constitute "income" within the meaning of the definition enunciated in *Eisner v. Macomber*—"income may be defined as the gain derived from capital, from labor, or from both combined" [121]—because neither the taxpayer's capital nor the taxpayer's labor had generated the recovery. But the Court held that the definition in *Eisner v. Macomber* "was not meant to provide a touchstone to all future gross income questions" and that

---

Strother v. CIR, 55 F.2d 626 (4th Cir.), aff'd on other issues, 287 US 314 (1932) (damages for removing unknown amount of coal from taxpayer's mine).

[117] See infra ¶9.6.

[118] See infra ¶10.6.

[119] CIR v. Glenshaw Glass Co., 348 US 426 (1955), discussed supra ¶1.4. The taxpayer conceded that one-third of the recovery was taxable, and the government conceded that the taxpayer's legal fees in obtaining the recovery were deductible.

See Park & Tilford Distillers Corp. v. US, 107 F.Supp. 941, 942 (Ct. Cl.), cert. denied, 345 US 917 (1952): "If Congress were to select one kind of receipt of money which, above all others, would be a fair mark for taxation, it might well be 'windfalls.' "

[120] General Am. Investors Co. v. CIR, 348 US 434 (1955).

[121] Eisner v. Macomber, 252 US 189, 207 (1920), discussed supra ¶1.4.

Congress intended "to tax all gains except those specifically exempted." It continued:

> Here we have instances of undeniable accessions to wealth, clearly realized, and over which the taxpayers have complete dominion. The mere fact that the payments were extracted from the wrongdoers as punishment for unlawful conduct cannot detract from their character as taxable income to the recipients. Respondents concede, as they must, that the recoveries are taxable to the extent that they compensate for damages actually incurred. It would be an anomaly that could not be justified in the absence of clear congressional intent to say that a recovery for actual damages is taxable but not the additional amount extracted as punishment for the same conduct which caused the injury. And we find no such evidence of intent to exempt these payments.[122]

Sometimes punitive damages, taxable under the *Glenshaw Glass* case, are claimed along with compensatory damages that are exempt from tax (e.g., because they reimburse the taxpayer for an impairment of damaged capital). If the claim results in a lump-sum judgment or settlement, it must be allocated between the taxable and tax-free components by reference to the parties' own characterization, the relative amounts demanded in the complaint, or some other suitable yardstick.

2. Found Property, Free Samples, Etc. The regulations provide that treasure trove (i.e., property found by the taxpayer) constitutes gross income to the extent of its value for the taxable year in which it is reduced to "undisputed possession." [122.1] In a case involving a taxpayer who found about $4,500 in old currency in a piano seven years after purchasing it at an auction for $15, the court held that the currency was taxable in the year of discovery rather than when the piano was purchased.[123] But a later year might have been appropriate if the taxpayer had advertised for the true owner and refrained from exerting dominion over the property until the search was abandoned, at least if state law imposed such an obligation on the finder. If the piano itself had proved to be more valuable than anticipated at the time of acquisition, however, the taxpayer's bargain purchase would not have generated income until the property was sold, at which time the gain would be the difference between its cost and the amount realized on the sale.

Free samples are as American as apple pie and almost as prevalent as junk mail, but the taxability of the recipient is a murky issue that has generated

[122] General Am. Investors Co. v. CIR, supra note 120, at 430-431.

[122.1] Treas. Regs. §1.61-14(a).

[123] Cesarini v. US, 296 F.Supp. 3 (N.D. Ohio 1969), aff'd per curiam, 428 F.2d 812 (6th Cir. 1970).

surprisingly little litigation. A rigorous application of the *Glenshaw Glass* theory would lead to taxing the recipient, even if the taxpayer took the unusual step of returning the unsolicited merchandise if under state law there was no legal obligation to do so. Despite the breadth of the language used in *Glenshaw Glass,* it is hard to believe that it was meant to impose so extreme a rule of taxability or to tax the more ambiguous taxpayer who retains the free samples as a kind of involuntary warehouseman. Moreover, in many cases the samples are worth so little as to invoke the maxim *de minimis non curat lex*; sometimes, indeed, they may be worth just what the recipient paid for them.

On the other hand, a taxpayer who sells the merchandise should clearly be taxed. Should the tax, however, be imposed at the time of receipt or sale? As a test of taxability, the unequivocal act of selling the merchandise is more easily applied than the taxpayer's intent at the time of receipt, since the latter is not likely to be publicly disclosed.[124] In some circumstances, however, the mere retention of property may be unequivocal evidence of an exercise of dominion and a receipt of benefit.[125]

3. Unclaimed Deposits and Uncashed Checks. When acting as trustees, brokers, or agents, taxpayers often receive money or other property that the true owners abandon or fail to claim for so long that their rights are barred by the statute of limitations. This situation often arises when the taxpayer is a debtor (for example, a bank or public utility holding deposits or refunds for customers who cannot be located). If not claimed by the state under an escheat statute, assets of this type were taxed to the custodian even before *Glenshaw Glass*;[126] but the validity of these early cases might have been challenged on

---

[124] Rev. Rul. 70-498, 1970-2 CB 6 (book reviewer taxable on unsolicited books when books given to charity and charitable deduction claimed), superseding Rev. Rul. 70-330, 1970-1 CB 14 (book reviewer taxable on unsolicited books if he accepts them); see Haverly v. US, 513 F.2d 224 (7th Cir.), cert. denied, 423 US 912 (1975) (sample textbooks sent by publishers to principal of public school and donated by him to school library; held, "intent to exercise complete dominion over unsolicited samples is demonstrated by donating those samples to a charitable institution and taking a tax deduction therefor," and value constitutes gross income).

[125] See Hornung v. CIR, 47 TC 428 (1967) (Acq.) (professional football player taxed (1) on value of automobile received from sports magazine as most valuable player in championship game because it did not qualify as tax-free gift under IRC §102 or as award for noteworthy service under IRC §74 (infra ¶3.5) and (2) on rental value of two other automobiles made available by manufacturer; use of cars was an accession to wealth under *Glenshaw Glass* and was not a tax-free gift since manufacturer had a commercial motive.

[126] See, e.g., Fidelity-Philadelphia Trust Co. v. CIR, 23 TC 527 (1954) (bank deposits); Lehman v. CIR, ¶42,540 P-H Memo BTA (1942) (dividends held for unknown transferees of customers; held, taxable to firm on expiration of statute of limitations); Boston Consol. Gas Co. v. CIR, 128 F.2d 473 (1st Cir. 1942) (unclaimed deposits held by utility and transferred to surplus); Chicago, Rock Island & Pac. Ry.

the ground that accessions to wealth resulting from the lethargy, amnesia, or disappearance of the taxpayer's customers are not gains "derived from capital, from labor, or from both combined," as required by *Eisner v. Macomber.*

Any doubt about the propriety of taxing unclaimed property to the custodian is dispelled by *Glenshaw Glass,* but the proper taxable year is less obvious. When the property itself is not segregated and the taxpayer's only mode of acknowledging liability to the true owner is a reserve account or other book entry, the concept of "dominion" is not easily applied. Cash received from a customer, for example, may have been deposited in the taxpayer's regular bank account when received, so that in a sense dominion has been exercised from the outset. But since the taxpayer simultaneously admits the offsetting liability, the transaction might be analogized to a borrowing of funds, which does not generate tax liability unless, and until, the debt is discharged by less than full payment.[127]

Once the offsetting liability is eliminated by the statute of limitations, however, taxing the custodian is reasonable even if refunds might be made thereafter as a matter of good business judgment; and earlier taxability is appropriate if the taxpayer's own behavior (for example, a book entry eliminating the liability) evinces a judgment that the chance of repayment is minimal or if repayment was unlikely from the outset (for example, an overcharge paid by an unknown customer). Moreover, if unclaimed assets are a recurrent phenomenon in the taxpayer's business, an accounting method that does not systematically credit these amounts to income may not clearly reflect income as required by IRC §446(b). Finally, if checks issued by an accrual-basis taxpayer to pay wages, interest, refunds, and other deductible expenses are not presented to the taxpayer's bank for payment or are returned because the addressee cannot be found, the taxpayer is required to include these amounts in income to correct for the previous deductions, even if the liability remains outstanding.

¶1.9 REIMBURSEMENT FOR WRONGFUL DEATH OR INJURY

In a series of early rulings and cases, the Internal Revenue Service and the courts held that damages for wrongful death, defamation, alienation of affections, breach of contract to marry, and similar invasions of "personal" or "family" rights were not includable in the recipient's gross income.[128] The

v. CIR, 47 F.2d 990 (7th Cir.), cert. denied, 284 US 618 (1931) (excess fares collected by railroad from unknown passengers).

[127] See infra ¶2.4.

[128] I.T. 2420, VII-2 CB 123 (1928) (compensation for death of taxpayer's husband in sinking of *Lusitania*), declared obsolete by Rev. Rul. 69-43, 1969-1 CB 310, after being reaffirmed by Rev. Rul. 54-19, 1954-1 CB 179 (recovery under state wrongful-

exclusion of these receipts was based partly on the theory that they were not "derived from capital, from labor, or from both combined" and hence did not constitute "income" under *Eisner v. Macomber,*[129] and partly on the absence of a statutory provision specifically requiring their inclusion in gross income.[130] These theories, however, were undermined by the Supreme Court's 1955 decision in *CIR v. Glenshaw Glass Co.,* holding that the *Eisner v. Macomber* definition was not exhaustive, that windfall receipts were taxable without regard to whether they were derived from capital or labor, and that Congress intended to tax all "accessions to wealth" unless specifically exempted.[131]

These early exclusions also rested on a more fundamental ground, viz., that "compensatory" recoveries for personal wrongs do not create any gain or income:

> If an individual is possessed of a personal right that is not assignable and not susceptible of any appraisal in relation to market values, and thereafter receives either damages or payment in compromise for an invasion of that right, it can not be held that he thereby derives any gain or profit. It is clear, therefore, that the Government cannot tax him on any portion of the sum received.[132]

It has long been established, however, that "compensatory" receipts must be included in gross income to the extent that they exceed the cost or other basis of property transferred, relinquished, or lost by the taxpayer in the event giving rise to the recovery.[133] Recoveries for defamation of the taxpayer's business reputation, for example, are taxable even though the payment is purely compensatory, intended to restore the *status quo ante* without enriching the taxpayer.[134]

---

death statute); Sol. Op. 132, I-1 CB 92 (1922) (superseded but reiterated in part by Rev. Rul. 74-77, 1974-1 CB 33) (alienation of affections; slander and libel of "personal character," not affecting "business reputation or property rights"; payment received by parent for surrendering custody of a minor child); McDonald v. CIR, 9 BTA 1340 (1928) (Acq.) (damages for breach of contract to marry); I.T. 2422, VII-2 CB 186 (1928) (declared obsolete by Rev. Rul. 67-466, 1967-2 CB 427); Hawkins v. CIR, 6 BTA 1023 (1927) (libel and slander).

[129] Eisner v. Macomber, 252 US 189 (1920), discussed supra ¶1.4.

[130] US v. Supplee-Biddle Hardware Co., 265 US 189 (1924).

[131] CIR v. Glenshaw Glass Co., supra note 119.

[132] Sol. Op. 132, supra note 128, at 93; see also Hawkins v. CIR, supra note 128.

[133] See Raytheon Prod. Corp. v. CIR, 144 F.2d 110 (1st Cir.), cert. denied, 323 US 779 (1944) (recovery for destruction of goodwill).

[134] See Agar v. CIR, ¶60,021 P-H Memo TC (1960) (settlement of libel claim taxable in absence of evidence that anything was paid for damage to taxpayer's personal, rather than business, reputation), aff'd per curiam on other grounds, 290 F.2d 283 (2d Cir. 1961).

Taxing a recovery for "personal" injury or deprivation may be a harsh response to the taxpayer's misfortune, but it is not significantly different from taxing wages and salaries without allowing an offsetting deduction for the exhaustion of the taxpayer's physical prowess and mental agility during his working life.[135] Since defamation or alienation of affections does not entail the loss of something for which the taxpayer paid cold cash, this analogy would imply that compensation for such a wrong is an accession to the taxpayer's wealth that must be included in gross income unless Congress chooses to grant an explicit exemption.

The Supreme Court referred in *Glenshaw Glass* to "the long history of departmental rulings holding personal injury recoveries nontaxable" [136], and this comment suggests the possibility that they were subsequently sanctified by congressional acquiescence, whether their origin was legitimate or not. It is not fanciful to suggest that the basic theory of these cases and rulings has been approved by silence. Indeed, it is probable that most of the lawyers in Congress know that wrongful-death recoveries are regularly excluded from gross income by the decedent's executor and heirs. The theory that long-standing administrative rulings can acquire the force of law if the statute is repeatedly reenacted without change is often criticized [137] and rarely applied, but the rulings cited in *Glenshaw Glass* may qualify for this unusual legislative blessing.

In any event, the IRS seems content to let sleeping dogs lie; despite the breadth of the Supreme Court's language in *Glenshaw Glass,* the IRS subsequently issued several additional "personal right" rulings.[138]

So far, we have looked only at recoveries for tortious invasions of the taxpayer's rights. If, before any misconduct occurs, the taxpayer is paid for a release of claims that might otherwise arise in the future, the courts have refused to sanction an exclusion, holding instead that the payment is taxable.[139] The cases involved payments by motion-picture companies wishing to

---

[135] See Bourne v. CIR, 23 BTA 1288, 1292 (1931), aff'd, 62 F.2d 648 (4th Cir.), cert. denied, 290 US 650 (1933) (no deduction allowable for human depreciation).

[136] CIR v. Glenshaw Glass Co., supra note 119 at 432 n.8.

[137] For discussion of the reenactment doctrine, see infra ¶38.4.

[138] Rev. Rul. 55-132, 1955-1 CB 213 (damages received by prisoners of war); Rev. Rul. 56-518, 1956-2 CB 25, as clarified by Rev. Rul. 57-505, 1957-2 CB 50 (West Germany's payments to victims of Nazi persecution); Rev. Rul. 58-370, 1958-2 CB 14, and Rev. Rul. 69-212, 1969-1 CB 34 (similar payments by Austria); but see Stanford v. CIR, 297 F.2d 298 (9th Cir. 1961) (private pension paid by German company not covered by Rev. Rul. 56-518). See also Revenue Act of 1962, P.L. No. 87-834, §27(a), 76 Stat. 960, 1067 (exempting from income tax awards by Attorney General to persons of Japanese ancestry evacuated from their homes during World War II).

[139] Ehrlich v. Higgins, 52 F.Supp. 805 (S.D.N.Y. 1943); Starrels v. CIR, 304 F.2d 574 (9th Cir. 1962), and cases there cited; see also US v. Garber, 607 F.2d 92 (5th Cir.

use the name or biography of a real person without interference by him or his family. The issue has not always been faced head on, however, either because the recipient has been unable to segregate the amount paid for a release of future claims from undeniably taxable amounts paid for advice, documents, or similar assistance or because, when the payment is made to heirs, it is not clear that they have any legally protected rights to release.

¶1.10 THE RECOVERY OF DEDUCTED ITEMS—TAX BENEFIT PRINCIPLES

1. Introductory. Taxpayers who recover or collect items that were deducted in an earlier year are ordinarily taxed on the amount received unless the prior deduction was of no "tax benefit" because it did not reduce the taxpayer's tax liability. Because each year's income tax return must be based on the facts as known during that year, the deduction in good faith of amounts that are recovered in later years is a familiar phenomenon. Creditors, for example, often deduct seemingly worthless claims but subsequently collect part or all of the debt when the debtor's financial state unexpectedly improves.

In the early days of the federal income tax, it was not clear that taxpayers were taxable on recovering these previously deducted amounts. If the deduction was erroneous when taken, the IRS could assess a deficiency for the year in which the error occurred (assuming that the year was not closed by the statute of limitations);[140] but if the deduction was justified on the facts as then known, it could not be retroactively disallowed, even if the statute of limitations had not run. As for the year of recovery, it was once thought anomalous to require income to be reported when taxpayers merely collected amounts that were owing to them or received refunds of amounts that had been paid by mistake, especially since *Eisner v. Macomber* defined the term "income" as used in the Sixteenth Amendment and the tax law as "gain derived from capital, from labor, or from both combined." [141] As late as 1929, for example, the Board of Tax Appeals seemed uncertain about the validity of a Treasury regulation providing that income was realized on collecting a debt previously charged off as worthless.[142] Within a few months, however, the Board of Tax

---

1979) (professional blood donor convicted of willful failure to report income from sale of blood).

[140] Ordinarily a deficiency may not be assessed more than three years from the due date of the return. See IRC §6501(a), discussed infra ¶41.2.

[141] Eisner v. Macomber, 252 US 189 (1920), discussed supra ¶1.4.

[142] Treas. Regs. 62, Art. 151, issued pursuant to the Revenue Act of 1921, carrying forward a principle enunciated by Treas. Regs. 33, Art. 125, under the Revenue Act of 1913.

Appeals accepted the so-called tax benefit rule enunciated by this regulation;[143] by 1931 it was described as a principle that "seems to be taken for granted, as indeed it must be,"[144] and it has been a basic part of the federal income tax structure ever since.

Although the taxability of recoveries of previously deducted amounts rests primarily on judge-made rather than statutory law, the courts have not devoted much attention to its rationale, and, when they have felt impelled to explain the principle, their theories have not been wholly consistent. These theories have included: the prior deduction of a bad debt converts the capital represented by the debt into income on the debt's subsequent collection, treating the recovery of a bad debt as income is required to accurately reflect income, and deducting a bad debt implies a consent by the taxpayer to be taxed on a future recovery of the debt.

While divergent, these theories share the view that the recoveries do not constitute economic gain in the ordinary sense and that their inclusion in income is an anomaly requiring explanation. The premise, evidently, is that a creditor's collection of a just debt does not increase his net worth, even if he previously concluded that the debtor would never pay. Thus, the taxpayer is treated as realizing income only because he deducted amounts that, it now appears, exceeded his actual loss or cost. The tax benefit rule does not, however, insure that the tax on the recovery will be equal to the tax savings generated by the prior deduction. Since marginal tax rates vary from year to year, particularly in the case of individuals, the increased tax in the year of recovery will almost always either exceed or be less than the tax reduction enjoyed in the earlier year.[145]

Once the courts concluded that recovered amounts are taxable because they are linked to a prior tax deduction, the door was opened to taxpayer claims that recoveries should be taxed only if the deduction actually reduced the taxpayer's tax liability for the earlier year. As a limitation on the basic principle of taxing recoveries of previously deducted items, this aspect of the tax benefit principle has had a checkered career in the courts for more than a decade, and the IRS also wavered between accepting and rejecting it. In 1942, however, Congress gave it formal endorsement by enacting the statutory predecessor of IRC §111, which excludes from gross income the recovery of certain previously deducted items if the deduction "did not result in a reduction of

[143] Excelsior Printing Co. v. CIR, 16 BTA 886 (1929).

[144] Putnam Nat'l Bank v. CIR, 50 F.2d 158 (5th Cir. 1931).

[145] In Perry v. US, 160 F.Supp. 270 (Ct. Cl. 1958), the Court of Claims adopted an "exact tax benefit" rule, under which the recovery was taxed at the rate that was applicable to the deduction; but it later overruled this decision and accepted the prevailing judicial view that the recovery is to be taxed at whatever rate is in effect for the year of receipt. Alice Phelan Sullivan Corp. v. US, 381 F.2d 399 (Ct. Cl. 1967).

the taxpayer's tax" in prior years. Although IRC §111 accords this treatment explicitly only to the recovery of previously deducted bad debts, taxes (whether deducted or taken as a credit), and "delinquency amounts" (primarily interest on past-due taxes), the tax benefit principle is applied by the regulations to a much wider assortment of items.[146]

As employed since the enactment of IRC §111, the tax benefit rule is "both a rule of inclusion and exclusion: recovery of an item previously deducted must be *included* in income; that portion of the recovery not resulting in a prior tax benefit is *excluded.*" [147] Section 111 is addressed solely to the exclusionary aspect of the tax benefit rule, as a shield for the taxpayer; but by necessary implication it ratifies the judge-made inclusionary component of the rule as a sword for the government, without which there would be no raw material on which IRC §111 could operate. In the discussion that follows, the threshold issue of inclusion will be examined first;[148] and then the exclusionary aspect of the tax benefit rule, which serves to qualify its inclusionary requirement, will be discussed.[149]

2. Inclusion of Recovered Items. As pointed out above, the inclusionary component of the tax benefit rule comes into play on the recovery [150] of an item that would not be includable in income except for the fact that it was previously deducted or credited in computing the taxpayer's federal income tax liability for a prior year.[151] This principle embraces a wide range of receipts, including collections of debts that were previously deducted as worthless, refunds of previously deducted state and local taxes,[152] and reimbursements of previously deducted losses (e.g., payments by a tort-feasor). In the same vein, if a business expense is paid by a check that is never cashed by the payee, the amount must be taken back into income, though the date when such an adjustment becomes mandatory is not clear.[153]

---

[146] Treas. Regs. §1.111-1(a) (second sentence); infra, text at note 158.

[147] Putoma Corp. v. CIR, 66 TC 652, 664 n.10 (1976), aff'd, 601 F.2d 734 (5th Cir. 1979).

[148] Infra, text at note 150.

[149] Infra, text at note 158.

[150] For problems in determining whether there has been a "recovery" to which the inclusionary aspect of the tax benefit rule applies, see Weyher v. CIR, 66 TC 825 (1976) (on sale of mortgaged property, seller recovered prepaid interest); Tennessee Carolina Transp., Inc. v. CIR, 582 F.2d 378 (6th Cir. 1978) (expensed supplies were "recovered" by corporation when distributed to shareholders in a corporate liquidation; extended dissent in Tax Court by seven judges).

[151] For the recovery of items that could have been, but were not, deducted in earlier years, see infra note 156.

[152] IRC §§111(b)(2), 111(b)(3).

[153] See Roxy Custom Clothes Corp. v. US, 171 F.Supp. 851 (Ct. Cl. 1959) (income when accounts payable was credited to eliminate liability); Lime Cola Co. v. CIR, 22

If a debt incurred by the taxpayer gave rise to a tax deduction when incurred (e.g., an accrual basis taxpayer's liability for wages or business supplies) but is discharged for less than its face amount, the *Kirby Lumber Co.* principle overlaps the tax benefit doctrine in certain respects, creating problems that are discussed elsewhere in this work.[154]

The inclusionary component of the tax benefit rule applies to the foregoing items (and some others) because they involve the partial or complete recovery of amounts that were previously deducted or credited. In the absence of a prior tax allowance, however, the tax benefit rule does not require the inclusion in income of recoveries that do not increase the taxpayer's net worth. Thus, it does not embrace the refund of an amount paid for personal services or a nondeductible tax (for example, the federal income tax or a local real property tax paid by a taxpayer who did not itemize his personal deductions) or the recovery of long-lost property (for example, forgotten bank accounts or misplaced jewelry). These events do not generate income even if the taxpayer never expected to see the items again and views the recovery as a windfall.

The status of a recovered amount that was *improperly* deducted is problematical. If the error was apparent on the face of the return, so that the IRS should have known that the deduction was erroneous, it has been held that the government's sole remedy is to assess a deficiency for the deduction year; if the statute of limitations has run, the IRS cannot seize upon a subsequent recovery and compel it to be included in income.[155]

An amount received in respect of an item that could have been—but was not—deducted in an earlier year is not includable in gross income when received.[156] A contrary rule would open the door, whenever a debt or other item is collected after a long delay, to an assertion by the IRS that it could have been deducted in an earlier year and that the current receipt is a taxable recovery unless the hypothetical deduction would have produced no tax benefit.

When the inclusionary branch of the tax benefit rule is applicable, it is necessary to determine whether the taxable recovery constitutes ordinary in-

---

TC 593, 601 (1954) (income when amount was credited to surplus); G.M. Standifer Constr. Corp. v. CIR, 30 BTA 184 (1934), appeal dism'd, 78 F.2d 285 (9th Cir. 1935) (income in year of settlement).

[154] US v. Kirby Lumber Co., 284 US 1 (1931), discussed infra ¶2.4.

[155] Canelo v. CIR, 53 TC 217, 226-227 (1969) (Acq.) aff'd per curiam, 447 F.2d 484 (9th Cir. 1971); Mayfair Minerals, Inc. v. CIR, 56 TC 82, 89-91 (1971), aff'd per curiam, 456 F.2d 622 (5th Cir. 1972); Unvert v. CIR, 72 TC 807 (1979), aff'd, 48 AFTR2d 5860 (9th Cir. 1981). The court of appeals in *Unvert* held that the recovery of an amount previously deducted was includable in income regardless of the propriety of the deduction, whether or not the taxpayer was estopped.

[156] Boehm v. CIR, 146 F.2d 553 (2d Cir.), aff'd on other issues, 326 US 287 (1945), rehearing denied, 326 US 811 (1946).

come or capital gain. In making this determination, as explained elsewhere in this work,[157] the courts often impress the character of the original transaction on the recovery rather than view it as an isolated transaction.

3. Exclusion of Items Deducted Without Tax Benefit. The exclusionary aspect of the tax benefit rule, embodied in IRC §111, qualifies the rule's inclusionary principle by excluding the recovery from income if, and to the extent that, the earlier deduction or credit was of no tax benefit. This result is achieved by a "recovery exclusion," defined by IRC §111(b)(4) as the amount by which the earlier deduction or credit failed to reduce the taxpayer's taxes less any exclusion already allowed. Although IRC §111(a) explicitly sanctions a recovery exclusion for only three categories of recoveries—bad debts, prior taxes, and "delinquency amounts" (interest or other amounts paid or accrued for delays or failures in filing tax returns, paying taxes, etc.)—the regulations extend the same treatment to "all other losses, expenditures, and accruals made the basis of deductions," with the exception of deductions for depreciation, depletion, amortization, or bond premiums.[158]

In determining whether a recovered item produced a tax benefit when it was deducted, the regulations assume that the deduction was used only if, and to the extent that, the taxpayer's income exceeded his other deductions.[159] This method of computing the tax benefit attributable to the recovered items is favorable to the taxpayer, since it assumes that the recovered items were the last to be deducted. Moreover, if the statute of limitations has run, this presumption is buttressed by the subsidiary presumption that all other deductions taken were valid. On the other hand, the taxpayer cannot introduce deductions, however valid, that were not claimed on the return to establish that deducting the recovered item produced no tax benefit.

The regulations provide that recoveries of deductions for depreciation, depletion, amortization, and amortizable bond premiums are not subject to the "rule of exclusion." [160] Thus, the sole statutory remedy for a taxpayer incurring deductions for depreciation, amortization, and depletion in a loss year is the net operating loss carryover authorized by IRC §172, which permits excess business deductions to be used in profitable years within a specified carryover period.[161]

The taxpayer must look to the net operating loss carryover rather than to IRC §111 for a remedy in another important category of cases, which can

---

[157] Infra ¶25.12.

[158] Treas. Regs. §1.111-1(a).

[159] Treas. Regs. §1.111-1(b)(3), Example. See also IRC §111(d), which provides that in computing the recovery exclusion, an increase in an unexpired carryover shall be treated as a reduction in tax.

[160] Treas. Regs. §1.111-1(a).

[161] For IRC §172, see infra ¶12.9.

be illustrated by a business venture with expenditures for wages, supplies, and other deductible items that exceed income in one year, followed by substantial receipts in a later year. The receipts flow from and in a sense serve to recoup the expenditures, but it has been held that they cannot be excluded under IRC §111 even if the prior deductions were of no tax benefit.[162] In reaching this conclusion, the court relied on the annual accounting rationale of *Burnet v. Sanford & Brooks Co.,* holding that taxable income is realized when payment is received under a long-term contract, even if the taxpayer incurred a loss over the life of the project.[163] On the other hand, refunds and abatements of amounts paid or accrued for wages or supplies qualify for exclusion if they were deducted without tax benefit, since these receipts are "recoveries" within the meaning of IRC §111(a).

Because IRC §111 is concerned with recoveries of items that were previously deducted or credited, a receipt must be closely associated with the prior allowance to qualify for exclusion. Thus, if in 1980 a taxpayer accepted property worth $3,000 in settlement of a $5,000 claim and deducted the remaining $2,000 as a bad debt, the transaction is closed; and if the property is sold in 1983 for $5,000, the taxpayer's gain of $2,000 is not a "recovery" of the bad debt and, hence, cannot be excluded under IRC §111 even if the 1980 deduction produced no tax benefit.[164] On the other hand, if the taxpayer collects an additional $1,000 from the debtor in 1984 (for example, because the 1980 settlement was induced by fraud), this receipt would qualify as a partial recovery of the 1980 deduction.

In addition to requiring that a previously deducted item be recovered, IRC §111 presupposes that the recovery is received by the taxpayer who took the deduction. This principle ordinarily bars relief under IRC §111 when otherwise qualified items are recovered by the original taxpayer's successor in interest (by liquidation, merger, etc.), but this barrier is lifted by IRC §381(c)(12) for certain corporate liquidations and other reorganizations.[165] Moreover, since a partnership is treated for most income tax purposes as a conduit, each partner takes into account his distributive share of the firm's recoveries.[166]

4. Tax Detriment and Reverse Tax Benefit. The tax benefit doctrine is not the only judicial and legislative departure from the annual accounting

---

[162] US v. Rexach, 482 F.2d 10 (1st Cir.), cert. denied, 414 US 1039 (1973), on remand, 411 F.Supp. 1288 (D.P.R. 1975).

[163] Burnet v. Sanford & Brooks Co., 282 US 359 (1931), discussed infra ¶35.1.

[164] Rev. Rul. 66-320, 1966-2 CB 37, relying on Allen v. Trust Co. of Ga., 180 F.2d 527 (5th Cir.), cert. denied, 340 US 814 (1950).

[165] IRC §381(c)(12); but see Ridge Realization Corp. v. CIR, 45 TC 508, 523-526 (1966) (Nonacq.) (successor entitled to use IRC §111).

[166] Treas. Regs. §1.702-1(a)(8).

principle seeking to harmonize a transaction's tax consequences when it is finally closed with its tax treatment in an earlier year.

Among these analogues to the tax benefit rule, the most important is probably IRC §1341, applicable when a taxpayer must refund an amount in excess of $3,000 that was included in income in an earlier year because he apparently had an unrestricted right to receive and retain it. In the year of repayment, the taxpayer is permitted by IRC §1341 to pay the lesser of (a) a tax computed in the usual fashion after deducting the refunded amount and (b) a tax computed in the usual fashion on his other income (before deducting the refunded amount) minus the tax detriment suffered in the year when the refunded amount was received and included in income.[167] This approach guarantees that the tax saved by deducting the refunded amount will be at least as great as the tax paid when the item was received.

If, however, the taxpayer takes the deduction in the usual way in the year of repayment (the first of the alternatives just described), the deduction allowable under IRC §1341 is limited by what might be termed a "reverse tax benefit" rule, which serves to protect the government against a deduction that is excessive when compared with the amount included in income in the earlier year. For example, if, because of percentage depletion,[168] only 72 percent of the receipt subject to repayment was included in income, then only 72 percent of the repayment is deductible.[169]

¶1.11 INDIRECT RECEIPTS: PAYMENT OF TAXPAYER'S EXPENSES, BARGAIN PURCHASES, ETC.

1. Introductory. In *Old Colony Trust Co. v. CIR,* decided in 1929, the Supreme Court held that a corporate officer was required to include in gross income amounts paid by his employer to defray his state and federal income taxes.[170] In *United States v. Boston & Maine R.R.,* a companion case decided at the same time, the Court held that the taxpayer realized income when its federal income taxes were paid by the lessee of all its properties, as required under a ninety-nine-year lease.[171]

Acknowledging that they would be taxable on amounts otherwise owing to them that were paid at their direction to creditors, the taxpayers in these cases argued that (1) since the amounts to be reimbursed each year depended on the applicable tax laws, there was no clearly defined "amount otherwise owing," (2) payment of their income taxes should not be regarded as "income,"

---

[167] For IRC §1341, see infra ¶2.3.

[168] For percentage depletion, see infra ¶11.3.

[169] US v. Skelly Oil Co., 394 US 678, 685-686 (1969) (divided court).

[170] Old Colony Trust Co. v. CIR, 279 US 716 (1929).

[171] US v. Boston & Maine R.R., 279 US 732, 733 (1929).

since they were not received by them but were paid directly to the government, and (3) the rejection by Congress of a 1917 proposal to prohibit agreements to pay another person's income tax impliedly sanctioned the exclusion of such payments from the obligee's gross income.[172] They also raised the specter of complex computations if the government's theory was accepted, since each taxpayer was entitled to be reimbursed for the disputed taxes, if owing, thus producing a never-ending but continually narrowing circle.

The Court rejected the taxpayer's claim in the *Old Colony* case in short order:

> The payment of the tax by the employers was in consideration of the services rendered by the employee and was a gain derived by the employee from his labor. The form of the payment is expressly declared [by the statute] to make no difference. . . . It is therefore immaterial that the taxes were directly paid over to the Government. The discharge by a third person of an obligation to him is equivalent to receipt by the person taxed.[173]

The Court reached the same result in the *Boston & Maine* case, saying that the lessee's payment of the lessor's taxes under the lease "is merely a short cut whereby that which the lessee specifically agreed to pay as part of the rental [is paid] by discharging the obligation of the lessor to pay the tax to the Government."[174]

In retrospect, the outcome in these cases seems a foregone conclusion; but if the taxpayers had managed to persuade the Court to exclude the reimbursed amounts from their income, it is a virtual certainty that Congress would have amended the statute to insure their taxability. The most common illustration of the *Old Colony* principle is the taxability of employees on their gross compensation, including amounts withheld by the employer to pay the employee's social security taxes, even though participation is compulsory and does not entitle employees to name their own beneficiaries.[175] Another common example is the payment by a closely held corporation of its principal shareholder's personal expenses, an event that is treated as a constructive distribution to him of the amounts paid on his behalf.[176]

---

[172] S. Rep. No. 1039, 64th Cong., 2d Sess. (1917), reprinted in 1939-1 (Part 2) CB 47.

[173] Old Colony Trust Co. v. CIR, supra note 170, at 729.

[174] US v. Boston & Maine R.R., supra note 171, at 734.

[175] See Rev. Rul. 74-75, supra note 170; see also Escofil v. CIR, 464 F.2d 358 (3d Cir. 1972) (social security taxes withheld from employee's wages not deductible, which necessarily implies that they are includable in gross income).

[176] See, e.g., Sachs v. CIR, 277 F.2d 879 (8th Cir.), cert. denied, 364 US 833 (1960) (corporate payment of fine imposed on dominant shareholder for filing fraudulent corporate tax returns).

In practice, the *Old Colony* principle requires the drawing of troublesome lines to distinguish items that are properly attributable to the taxpayer, even though paid to someone else, from items that are not attributable to the taxpayer, especially in the following situations:

1. *Gifts and renunciations.* If a married couple directs a corporation in which they own stock to pay their next quarterly dividend to their children, *Old Colony* clearly attributes the dividend to the shareholders, just as though they had received the dividend check and endorsed it over to their children. But if they make a no-strings-attached gift of the stock to the children, the dividends declared thereafter are paid to the children, not because of parental instructions, within the meaning of *Old Colony,* but because the children are now the owners of the stock; and hence the dividends are taxed to the children rather than to the parents. This distinction between an effective gift of the income-producing "tree" and an ineffective gift of the "fruit," which is often difficult to draw, is discussed in detail elsewhere in this work.[177]

A similarly troubled area is the renunciation of income to be produced by the taxpayer's personal services, as in the case of an entertainer who agrees to perform for the benefit of a charity, where it is necessary to determine whether he contributed the receipts from his services to the charity (so as to be taxable under *Old Colony*) or contributed his services to the charity, so that it became the source of the profits.[178]

2. *Payments benefitting payor.* *Old Colony* does not apply to payments satisfying obligations of the payor (e.g., an employer's payment of its own share of federal social security taxes),[179] even though the employee derives a benefit as a by-product of the primary obligor's payments. Thus, it has been held that a shareholder bringing a derivative action against his corporation is not taxable when the corporation pays his legal fees pursuant to a state law imposing primary obligation for these fees on the corporation.[180]

When, however, damages resulting from the taxpayer's tortious behavior are paid by his insurance company, as in the case of an automobile accident caused by his negligence, he is not required to include the payment in income, even though his liability to the victim is thereby discharged. Although somewhat anomalous, this exemption is sanctioned by practice and may perhaps be explained on the ground that, as between the taxpayer and the insurer, the latter is primarily liable, so that payment discharged its *own* obligation.

---

[177] See infra ¶30.3.

[178] See infra ¶30.2.

[179] For amounts withheld from wages and contributed to federal or state retirement plans, see Cohen v. CIR, 63 TC 267 (1974), aff'd per curiam, 543 F.2d 725 (9th Cir. 1976) (federal employee taxed on contributions); Sibla v. CIR, 68 TC 422 (1977), aff'd on other issues, 611 F.2d 1260 (9th Cir. 1981) (state system; same result), and cases there cited.

[180] Ingalls v. Patterson, 158 F.Supp. 627 (D.Ala. 1958).

2. Pyramiding Effect of Tax Reimbursement Agreements ("Tax on a Tax"). In the *Old Colony* and *Boston & Maine* cases, the taxpayers argued vehemently that the government was seeking to pyramid their tax liabilities:

> It is next argued against the payment of this tax that if these payments by the employer constitute income to the employee, the employer will be called upon to pay the tax imposed upon this additional income, and that the payment of the additional tax will create further income which will in turn be subject to tax, with the result that there would be a tax upon a tax. This it is urged is the result of the Government's theory, when carried to its logical conclusion, and results in an absurdity which Congress could not have contemplated.[181]

The central drafting problem raised by a tax reimbursement agreement, which determines whether it will have a pyramiding effect, can be illustrated by two polar cases.

First, assume that an employer agrees to pay an employee a bonus of $1,000 in 1982 and to reimburse him in 1983 for the amount of federal income tax payable on the 1982 bonus. The reimbursement will be part of the employee's 1983 income under *Old Colony,* but the 1983 tax on the reimbursement must be borne by him since the employer did not guarantee that he would receive $1,000 net of all taxes. Since only the tax for 1982 is reimbursed, such a one-round agreement does not generate a "tax on a tax."

At the opposite extreme is a full-reimbursement agreement, under which the employee is guaranteed a bonus of $1,000 net after income taxes. Such an arrangement can take either of two forms. One is a lagged full-reimbursement agreement, under which the employer promises to reimburse the employee in 1983 for the 1982 tax on his 1982 bonus, in 1984 for the 1983 tax paid under *Old Colony* on the reimbursement received in 1983, in 1985 for any tax that may be imposed on the reimbursement received in 1984, and so on until the government ceases to impose a tax, either for reasons of administrative policy or because the amount would be less than one cent. Since even the highest marginal income tax rate is less than 100 percent, the amounts to be reimbursed will gradually diminish and eventually drop below one cent; but with large amounts and high tax rates this may not occur for many years. Assuming an original payment of $100,000 and a constant tax rate of 70 percent, it would take thirty-three years for the reimbursement to drop below $1 and fifteen more for it to become less than one-half of one cent.

The operation of a lagged full-reimbursement agreement is illustrated by Table 1-1 (see page 1-60), which assumes that the original payment is $1,000, that the IRS imposes a tax on every round of reimbursement, and that all

---

[181] Old Colony Trust Co. v. CIR, supra note 170, at 730-731.

payments are subject to a tax of 20 percent. The calculation would be more complicated if the tax rate varied from year to year.

Instead of "lagging" the reimbursements, the parties can accomplish the same objective (a bonus, after taxes, of $1,000) by a single-sum full-reimbursement agreement, under which the employer agrees to pay the employee, in the year the services are performed, an amount that will, after taxes, yield a net amount of $1,000.

The amount to be paid under a single-sum full-reimbursement agreement can be determined either by trial and error or, if the recipient is subject to a constant rate of tax, by the following algebraic formula:

$$\text{Gross amount} = \frac{a}{1 - r}$$

where a = net amount and r = tax rate.

The computation, based on the hypothesized facts, is set out in Table 1-2 (see page 1-61).

Table 1-1

Lagged Full Reimbursement of Payee's Income Taxes

Year	*Received by Payee*	*Tax (20%) on Amount Received*
1	$1,000.00	$200.00
2	200.00	40.00
3	40.00	8.00
4	8.00	1.60
5	1.60	.32
6	.32	.06
7	.06	.01
8	.01	-0-
Totals	$1,249.99	$249.99

A more complicated formula is required if the amount of the payment is subject to more than a single tax rate.

A single-sum full-reimbursement agreement produces the same result (save for the rounding of fractions) for all parties, including the Treasury, as a lagged full-reimbursement agreement (Table 1-1, where the one-cent difference results from rounding of fractions), assuming that the applicable tax rate does not change from year to year.

Table 1-2

Computation of Single-Sum Full Reimbursement of Payee's Income Taxes

Inserting the amounts hypothesized in the text:

$$\text{Gross amount} = \frac{\$1,000}{1 - 0.2}$$

$$= \frac{\$1,000}{0.8}$$

$$= \$1,250.$$

Proof: $1,250 less tax of 20% ($250) equals $1,000.

Though a catchy slogan, the phrase "tax on a tax" is less than accurate. No matter how many rounds of reimbursement occur, the amount paid each time is part of the compensation bargain, which in the event of pyramiding would be taxed to the employee as such. If taxing these payments entails a "tax on a tax," so does the tax on the *original* salary payment, since the amount included in income is the gross amount received, including the part that must be used to pay the tax.

In 1952, after a long period of uncertainty in the treatment of tax reimbursements, the Treasury announced that all federal income taxes reimbursed by a tax reimbursement agreement would be taxed, regardless of the number of rounds involved. Under this policy, however, the IRS accepts the construction placed on the contract by the parties; when the reimbursements stop, so do the tax assessments.[182]

Since the income tax on the payee under a tax reimbursement agreement depends not on the amount of salary, rent, or other item paid to him but on his *taxable* income, the parties must either include in the contract a method of computing the amount of tax to be reimbursed or resolve troublesome interpretative questions after the fact. Moreover, the method to be used will

---

[182] Mim. 6779, 1952-1 CB 8 (agreements between lessors and lessees); IR Mim. 51, 1952-2 CB 65 (all types of agreements). These rulings were listed as obsolete by Rev. Rul. 71-498, 1971-2 CB 434, but the principles announced therein are still followed; see T.D. 7483, 1977-1 CB 310 (Temp. Regs. §34.3402-1(d), Example (4)) (state lottery prize that includes payment of withheld taxes).

affect, sometimes drastically, the cost to the payor of entering into such an agreement.

At one extreme, for example, the agreement may provide that the amount to be reimbursed is the tax actually payable by the recipient on his taxable income for the applicable year, less the amount of tax that would have been payable if the salary, rent, or other payment (or, in each subsequent year, the reimbursement received in that year) had not been received. The obligor under a tax reimbursement agreement of this type is affected by such extraneous and unpredictable factors as the payee's marital status, personal exemptions and deductions, and participation in tax shelters.

At the opposite extreme, the amount to be paid can be computed on the assumption that the taxable receipt was the only gross income received by a hypothetical taxpayer with specified characteristics (e.g., either unmarried without dependents or itemized deductions, etc., or a corporation with no other receipts or deductions). By gearing the amount to such a hypothetical taxpayer, the agreement relieves the payor of involvement with the payee's personal characteristics; but the amount due will be either more or less than the tax actually allocable to the underlying payment.

3. Bargain Purchases. When a taxpayer purchases property for less than it is worth, he is ordinarily not taxed on the fruits of his astute negotiations when the purchase takes place;[183] but since the property's basis in his hands is its cost, he will realize gain on selling the property at its fair market value. The tax results, however, are quite different for a "bargain purchase" in the sense in which this term is used by tax practitioners, viz., to denote a purchase of property for less than fair market value when the difference reflects an extraneous objective, such as the seller's desire to confer an economic advantage on the buyer. In *CIR v. Smith,* involving the sale of stock by an employer to an employee for less than fair market value pursuant to a stock option granted to him as additional compensation, the Supreme Court held that the taxpayer realized gain equal to the "spread" between the value of the stock and the lower amount paid by him on exercising the option.[184]

In effect, the bargain purchase was treated in *CIR v. Smith* as a shortcut method by which the employer transferred the amount of the spread to the employee as compensation.[185] In the *Smith* case the purpose of the transaction was to compensate the taxpayer for his services; but in other situations the sale of property for less than its fair market value may be a way of paying rent,

---

[183] See Hunley v. CIR, ¶66,066 P-H Memo TC (1966) (bargain purchase not taxed despite broad reference to "accessions to wealth" in *Glenshaw Glass* case).

[184] CIR v. Smith, 324 US 177, 181, rehearing denied, 324 US 695 (1945). For computation of the seller's gain or loss on a bargain sale, see infra ¶23.6.

[185] For the extensive subsequent statutory and administrative developments in the stock option area, see infra ¶29.4.

distributing a dividend to shareholders, making an intra-family gift, or accomplishing some other objective. *Old Colony* holds that indirect receipts have the same tax effect as amounts received directly, but the transaction's characterization depends on all the surrounding facts and circumstances. In some instances this analysis may produce both income and an offsetting deduction or capital gain rather than ordinary income.

SELECTED BIBLIOGRAPHY

Bittker, Galvin, Musgrave & Pechman, A "Comprehensive Tax Base" as a Goal of Income Tax Reform, 80 Harv. L. Rev. 925 (1967) and 81 Harv. L. Rev. 44, 63, and 1016 (1968).

Bittker & Kanner, The Tax Benefit Rule, 26 U.C.L.A. L. Rev. 265 (1978).

Blum, How the Courts, Congress and the IRS Try to Limit Legal Tax Avoidance, 10 J. Tax. 300 (1959).

Cahn, Local Law in Federal Taxation, 52 Yale L.J. 799 (1943).

Chirelstein, Learned Hand's Contribution to the Law of Tax Avoidance, 77 Yale L.J. 440, 456 (1968).

Congressional Budget Office, The Tax Treatment of Homeownership: Issues and Options (1981).

Goode, Imputed Rent of Owner-Occupied Dwellings Under the Income Tax, 15 J. Fin. 504 (1960).

Griswold, An Argument Against the Doctrine That Deductions Should Be Narrowly Construed as a Matter of Legislative Grace, 56 Harv. L. Rev. 1142 (1943).

Gunn, Tax Avoidance, 76 Mich. L. Rev. 733 (1978).

Haskell & Kauffman, Taxation of Imputed Income, 17 Nat'l Tax J. 232 (1964).

Isenbergh, Musings on Form and Substance in Taxation, 49 U. of Chi. L. Rev. 859, 863–884 (1982).

Lowndes, Current Conceptions of Taxable Income, 25 Ohio St. L.J. 151, 173 (1964).

Murray, Step Transactions, 24 U. Miami L. Rev. 60 (1969).

Newman, Transferability, Utility, and Taxation, 30 U. Kan. L. Rev. 27 (1981).

Rosen, Substance Over Form—A Taxpayer's Weapon, 1970 So. Calif. Tax Inst. ¶689.

Rottschaefer, The Concept of Income in Federal Taxation, 13 Minn. L. Rev. 637 (1929).

Surrey, The Supreme Court and the Federal Income Tax: Some Implications of the Recent Decisions, 35 Ill. L. Rev. 779, 782 (1941).

Surrey & Warren, The Income Tax Project of the American Law Institute: Gross Income, Deductions, Accounting, Gains and Losses, Cancellation of Indebtedness, 66 Harv. L. Rev. 761 (1953).

Winston, Industrial Development Bonds After TEFRA, 61 Taxes 20 (1983).

Wolfman, *Bosch*, Its Implications and Aftermath: The Effect of State Court Adjudications on Federal Tax Litigation, 3 U. Miami Inst. on Est. Plan. ¶69.205.4 (1969).

Wueller, Concepts of Taxable Income, 53 Polit. Sci. Q. 83, 557 (1938) and 54 Polit. Sci. Q. 555 (1939).

CHAPTER 2

Income—The Effect of Offsetting Liabilities

¶2.1 THE EFFECT OF OFFSETTING LIABILITIES AND OBLIGATIONS: IN GENERAL

If a taxpayer receives money or other property burdened with an obligation to return or repay it, he is not ordinarily enriched by the transaction and therefore does not realize any "income" within the meaning of IRC §61(a). This is obvious enough if the taxpayer is a trustee or bailee, who is entrusted with property but holds it for the benefit of the true owner.[1] It is equally fundamental that borrowed funds are not income to the debtor, since the increase in his assets is offset by an increase of an equal amount in his liabilities.[2] If, however, the offsetting liability barring a tax on the trustee or debtor when the property or funds are received is terminated in some way (e.g., by the statute of limitations or abandonment by the beneficial owner), the

[1] See infra ¶2.2.

[2] See Matarese v. CIR, ¶75,184 P-H Memo TC (1975). For the status of funds that are ostensibly borrowed, but with no intent to repay, see cases cited infra ¶2.5.

resulting increase in the recipient's wealth must be reported as income at that time.[3]

The obligation of a trustee, bailee, or borrower to return or repay is usually consensual, unconditional, and honored; and these characteristics justify the conclusion that the taxpayer has not realized any income or gain in transactions of this type. But if property or money is received subject to a contingent or disputed offsetting obligation, a different tax result may be warranted because the taxpayer's liability does not fully counterbalance the economic advantage of receiving or holding the property. The major categories of transactions producing income even though the taxpayer does not get a clear title to the property or is burdened with a legal obligation are:

1. *Claim of right.* Property may be received under a "claim of right," where the offsetting obligation to return the property is either unknown to the taxpayer or disputed by him. In general, the taxpayer is required to report the property when received, despite the cloud on his title, but is allowed a deduction when, as, and if he returns the property.[4]

2. Unlawful conduct. Property may be obtained by unlawful conduct, where the taxpayer does not intend to honor his obligation to return the property. In general, the taxpayer is not permitted to use the offsetting obligation as a defense against reporting illegal receipts; but if he disgorges them, a deduction is permitted.[5]

3. Conditional obligations. Funds may be received subject to an obligation that may or may not mature, such as a manufacturer's money-back guaranty, or obligation to repair or replace property for a specified period of time.[6] In general, the sale is treated as complete for tax purposes when made and the sales price must be taken into income at that time; the obligation to make refunds, repairs, or other adjustments is treated as too contingent to justify a tax deduction unless and until the triggering event actually occurs.

4. Attenuated obligations. Obligations like the liability of a bank or a utility company to refund deposits to customers who move away or cannot be found may lose their potency because of the passage of time or other factors. In general, the taxpayer must report unclaimed deposits and similar amounts as income when the likelihood of repayment becomes very slim, even though an obligation to refund the funds on demand continues to exist in theory, especially if the amounts are transferred from a reserve account to surplus on the taxpayer's books.[7]

---

[3] See infra ¶2.4.

[4] See infra ¶2.3.

[5] See infra ¶2.5.

[6] See infra ¶35.3.

[7] See supra ¶1.8.

¶2.2 NOMINAL VS. BENEFICIAL OWNERSHIP—AMOUNTS RECEIVED BY TRUSTEES, NOMINEES, AGENTS, AND OTHER CONDUITS

In circumstances so diverse as to defy useful generalizations, funds are received by persons who are acting for the benefit of others. In many of these situations, it is so obvious that the initial recipient is not required to include the funds in gross income that one scarcely sees the issue. In other situations, however, the proper result is a bit more obscure. If the office messenger is given $10 a month by each employee who wants a daily cup of coffee, can just the receipts and expenses be reflected on the messenger's tax return, or can they be disregarded unless there is an excess or shortage for the taxable year?

In some situations the tax liability of the recipient of funds will be the same whether the amount received is disregarded or reflected on the tax return since, if included, it is offset by a deduction of an equal amount. But the resulting "wash" is not necessarily identical with disregarding the transaction entirely. For example, if an employee defrays the expenses of a business trip with personal funds, under a reimbursement arrangement with the employer, the employee's tax liability will be the same whether the transaction is treated as a loan to the employer that is subsequently repaid [8] or as a deductible business expense coupled with the later receipt of income; but the latter treatment increases the taxpayer's gross income and hence affects such procedural matters as the obligation to file a tax return and the statute of limitations on an assessment.[9] Moreover, if the outlay and receipt occur in different years, the cash-basis employee's actual tax liability may depend on which treatment is proper.[10]

This amorphous area of the law is complicated by frequent use of the term "conduit" to epitomize the statutory status of organizations whose income is taxed, in whole or in part, to the beneficiaries or real parties in interest rather than to the recipient and, conversely, by its use as a pejorative label for an intermediary employed to disguise or effect a plan of tax avoidance. The principal situations in which recipients of funds or property are viewed as conduits, nominees, agents, or constructive trustees are summarized below.

---

[8] See Flower v. CIR, 61 TC 140, 156 (1973), aff'd by unpublished opinion (5th Cir., Dec. 12, 1974) (expenditures under reimbursement agreement treated as loans); see generally infra ¶9.5 (obligation to substantiate certain expenses).

[9] See infra ¶¶39.1 (gross income bench mark for filing returns), 41.4 (extended statute of limitations when more than 25 percent is omitted from gross income).

[10] See Burnett v. CIR, 356 F.2d 755 (5th Cir. 1966) (advances by attorney to clients, subject to repayment on successful completion of litigation, not deductible when made); Rev. Rul. 78-388, 1978-2 CB 110 (moving expenses not deductible by accrual-basis business entitled to reimbursement by public agency).

1. Nominees to receive and expend funds for principals. In a series of cases, it has been held that organizations created by members of an industry to receive and expend funds for the common benefit of the contributing members (e.g., to advertise a franchised product) are not taxable entities if the funds are received pursuant to an agreement explicitly requiring their use in programs controlled by the contributing members.[11] If, however, the recipient organization has substantial discretion over the use to which the funds are put and is not required to refund unexpended balances to the contributing members on a termination of the advertising program, the IRS will seek to tax the organization.[12]

If otherwise applicable, the trust fund theory embraces funds received for an illegal purpose, as in the case of a bagman for a corrupt public official.[13] The courts are realistic enough, however, to recognize that some thieves are not to be trusted, and assertions by self-styled intermediaries that they paid the illicit funds over to third parties are sometimes received with skepticism and rejected if not proved up to the hilt.[14]

2. *"Cost companies."* A formal device for the sharing of expenses is a "cost company," created by members of the same industry to conduct mining or other operations under an agreement to share expenses and output. Since they actively conduct business operations, these captive companies differ from purely passive corporations used to hold title to property, which are ordinarily but not always treated as conduits. In 1977, the IRS withdrew an earlier ruling holding that cost companies were mere conduits, and ruled instead that they constitute separate taxable entities, required to compute their own income, deductions, credits, and tax liabilities.[15]

3. *Employees hired out by employer.* Employees obligated to turn over their outside earnings to their employer are ordinarily viewed as mere agents, so that the fees or wages are taxable to the employer rather than to the employee.[16]

---

[11] Ford Dealers Advertising Fund, Inc. v. CIR, 55 TC 761 (1971) (Nonacq.), aff'd per curiam, 456 F.2d 255 (5th Cir. 1972); see also Florists' Transworld Delivery Ass'n v. CIR, 67 TC 333 (1976) (Nonacq.) (same as to organization of retail florists operating as a clearinghouse between florists taking orders and receiving payment for members located in other cities who filled and delivered the orders).

[12] See Rev. Rul. 74-138, 1974-2 CB 14; Rev. Rul. 74-319, 1974-2 CB 15.

[13] See, e.g., Pierson v. CIR, ¶76,281 P-H Memo TC (1976).

[14] See Pendola v. CIR, 50 TC 509, 519 (1968) (corrupt IRS employee who recruited co-workers in large-scale fraudulent activities taxed on amounts received from tax preparer on failure to prove how much was paid over to others, even though it appeared that he paid "whatever was needed to get the job done").

[15] Rev. Rul. 77-1, 1977-1 CB 161 (ruling to be applied only prospectively, with additional time allowed to existing cost companies to restructure their arrangements to conform to new rules).

[16] See Rev. Rul. 65-282, 1965-2 CB 21 (employees of legal aid society not taxed

4. *Gift or sale of property subject to income charge.* When property is acquired by gift or purchase under an arrangement requiring the transferee to pay the income to the transferor or some other person for a period of time or until a specified sum has been paid, it is necessary to determine whether the transferee is only a conduit through which the income passes to the owner or is himself the beneficial owner of the income. The determination usually turns on whether the transferor retains an income interest,[17] or the income is diverted to the transferor as part of the unpaid purchase price or to meet some other obligation.[18]

5. *Statutory conduits.* Under rules beyond the scope of this work, the Code treats partnerships, estates and trusts, Subchapter S corporations, real estate investment trusts, and mutual funds as conduits, either in whole or in part.

6. *Tax-avoidance transactions.* In many tax-avoidance transactions, intermediaries are used as camouflage; and when unmasked, they are described—and sometimes castigated—as nominees, agents, dummies, conduits, and the like.

¶2.3 AMOUNTS RECEIVED UNDER "CLAIM OF RIGHT"

1. Introductory. Taxpayers frequently receive funds in circumstances permitting them to use the funds as their own but are subsequently required to repay part or all of the amount received—for example, because the amount was paid by mistake or erroneously computed, or because a controversy regarding the payment is decided against the taxpayer. Amounts of this type are ordinarily includable in gross income when received under the claim of right doctrine, enunciated by the Supreme Court in *North American Oil Consolidated v. Burnet.*[19] In holding for the government, the Supreme Court ruled that the crucial fact was that the taxpayer had received funds under a "claim of right"—a phrase taken from the law of adverse possession of real property—even though the validity of its claim was disputed. In a logical extension of *North American Oil Consolidated,* the Court of Appeals for the Second

---

on court-awarded fees for representing indigent defendants); see generally infra ¶30.2; but see CIR v. Laughton, 113 F.2d 103 (9th Cir. 1940) (employee was taxed on income received by his wholly owned corporation).

[17] See Malloy v. CIR, 5 TC 1112 (1945) (receipt of partnership interest subject to obligation to pay widow of transferor a fixed sum out of profits).

[18] See Hibler v. CIR, 46 TC 66 (1966) (business acquired for cash plus percentage of income until $70,000 was received; held, payments were part of purchase price and not excludable by transferee).

[19] North American Oil Consol. v. Burnet, 286 US 417 (1932).

Circuit held, only a year later, that the claim of right doctrine encompasses (1) disputed amounts that the taxpayer obtained by posting a bond for repayment, since this neither imposed any restrictions on use of the funds nor added to the taxpayer's existing contingent liability to repay, as well as (2) disputed amounts that *could* be obtained by posting a bond, since the taxpayer cannot "alter at will the accrual of income by failing to exercise an option to receive it." [20]

2. Scope of Claim of Right Doctrine. An exhaustive catalog of the circumstances triggering application of the claim of right doctrine can hardly be compiled, since almost any business or profit-oriented transaction, and even some personal activities, can result in the receipt of funds that the taxpayer may have to repay in a later year but can use freely in the interim.[21] The principal areas of uncertainty or dispute in applying the claim of right doctrine are:

1. Disclaimers. Since the tax liability on receiving a disputed amount can exceed the tax reduction that will occur if the amount is actually repaid in a later year,[22] a taxpayer may seek to avoid application of the claim of right doctrine by rejecting a payment when it is proferred, depositing it into a special account, or otherwise acknowledging that its status is subject to controversy. A prompt repayment should establish that the amount was not received under a claim of right, unless the taxpayer's action is merely a ploy for tax avoidance purposes or the repayment is rejected by the original payor as unfounded.[23] Recent cases in this area have required cash-basis taxpayers to make actual repayment in the year of receipt, not merely to disclaim the right to retain the amount;[24] but if acknowledgment of an obligation to repay is *contemporaneous*

---

[20] CIR v. Brooklyn Union Gas Co., 62 F.2d 505, 507 (2d Cir. 1933).

[21] See, e.g., Healy v. CIR, 345 US 278 (salaries paid by insolvent corporation repaid by recipients); Griffin v. Smith, 101 F.2d 348 (7th Cir. 1938) (excessive salaries repaid in settlement of shareholders' suit); Phillips v. CIR, 262 F.2d 668 (9th Cir. 1959) (stock claimed by taxpayer but later held to belong to another person); Van Wagoner v. US, 368 F.2d 95 (5th Cir. 1966) (commissions on prepaid insurance premiums); Walet v. CIR, 31 TC 461 (1958) (short-swing profits repaid under Section 16(b) of Securities Exchange Act), aff'd without discussion of this point, 272 F.2d 694 (5th Cir. 1959).

[22] But see IRC §1341, discussed infra, text at notes 36-47.

[23] See Crellin's Est. v. CIR, 203 F.2d 812 (9th Cir.), cert. denied, 346 US 873 (1953) (refund of dividends, paid under mistaken belief that retained earnings would be subject to personal holding company tax, disregarded); Miller v. CIR, ¶63,341 P-H Memo TC (1963), aff'd by order, 15 AFTR2d 321 (9th Cir.) (not officially reported), cert. denied, 382 US 888 (1965) (wages taxed to discharged employee, although out of religious conviction she attempted to refund them by deposit to employer's credit in bank account and bank, on employer's instructions, held amount in trust for taxpayer).

[24] See, e.g., Quinn v. CIR, 524 F.2d 617, 624 (7th Cir. 1975) (cash-basis taxpayer

with receipt of the payment, this may establish that the payment is a loan, rather than an amount received under a claim of right.[25]

2. *Special accounts, escrows, etc.* Taxpayers who are not prepared to refund a disputed amount may seek to avoid the claim of right doctrine by depositing it into an escrow or custodial account. In general, actions that can be rescinded by the taxpayer, such as depositing the amount in a special bank account under the taxpayer's sole control, are ineffective.[26] But formal escrows, joint accounts in the names of both the taxpayer and the other claimant, and special accounts subject to withdrawal limitations are effective if established prior to receipt and probably even thereafter but in the same year.[27]

3. *Conduits, trustees, etc.* Amounts paid to trustees, agents, and other intermediaries are not received under a claim of right and hence are not taxed to them, even if they are entrusted with discretionary powers exercisable on behalf of the real parties in interest.[28] But this exemption from the claim of right doctrine does not encompass recipients who are not mere conduits or agents and who, properly or improperly, exercise control over the funds for their own benefit.[29]

4. *Prepaid income.* In an early decision holding that an accrual-basis automobile club was taxable on prepaid membership fees, despite its obligation to provide services on demand to the members, the IRS relied on *North American Oil Consolidated,* and the Supreme Court seemed to endorse this rationale.[30] In later cases reaching the same result, however, the Supreme

---

must make repayment, not merely promise to do so; promissory note as evidence of obligation not sufficient).

[25] Gilbert v. CIR, 552 F.2d 478 (2d Cir. 1977) (despite conviction for embezzlement, taxpayer did not realize taxable income on making unauthorized withdrawals of corporate funds, where he did not intend to retain amounts, used them for corporate purposes, accounted for them to corporate directors, and signed secured promissory notes for full amount taken).

[26] CIR v. Alamitos Land Co., 112 F.2d 648 (9th Cir.), cert. denied, 311 US 679 (1940) (bank account under taxpayer's control).

[27] See Mutual Tel. Co. v. US, 204 F.2d 160 (9th Cir. 1953) (utility company's receipts under disputed rate increase not taxable where deposited into account subject to withdrawal only with utility commission's consent); Preston v. CIR, 35 BTA 312 (1937) (joint account with other claimant).

[28] See, e.g., Lashells' Est. v. CIR, 208 F.2d 430 (6th Cir. 1953) (commissions or commercial bribes not taxable to go-between).

[29] See, e.g., Angelus Funeral Home v. CIR, 47 TC 391 (1967), aff'd, 407 F.2d 210 (9th Cir.), cert. denied, 396 US 824 (1969) (prepayments for funeral expenses under one form of contract not taxable because received by taxpayer as custodian or trustee, although tied to use of taxpayer's facilities; amounts received under another contract taxable for want of restraints on taxpayer's use of funds); Latimer v. CIR, 55 TC 515 (1970) (fire insurance proceeds received by lessor under lease requiring use of funds to replace damaged building, but actually applied to other purposes).

[30] Automobile Club of Mich. v. CIR, 353 US 180 (1957).

Court refrained from relying on *North American Oil Consolidated,* stressing instead the IRS' authority to require taxpayers to use an accounting method that clearly reflects income, as well as Congress' repeal of certain statutory provisions that explicitly authorized the deferral of prepaid income.[31] In this important area, therefore, the claim of right doctrine has receded into the shadows.

5. *Illegal receipts.* The tax status of illegal receipts is another area in which the claim of right doctrine once played a leading role, only to disappear as a significant factor when the Supreme Court reexamined the subject, as explained later in this chapter.[32]

3. Deduction of Repaid Amounts. In *North American Oil Consolidated,* the Supreme Court required the taxpayer to report an amount it received in 1917 as income for that year, although its right to retain the amount was not finally settled until 1922.[33] Since the taxpayer ultimately prevailed in its claim to the disputed amount, the Court did not have to pass on the effect of a repayment; but it observed that a deduction in 1922 would have been allowable if a taxpayer had been required to refund the 1917 receipts. No statutory authority was cited for this dictum, but the relevant provisions of current law in the case of corporate taxpayers are IRC §162, relating to business expenses, and IRC §165, relating to losses.[34]

If the taxpayer is an individual rather than a corporation, however, the status of a repayment is more complicated. Repayments can be deducted if they qualify under IRC §165(c)(1), relating to losses incurred in the taxpayer's trade or business, IRC §165(c)(2), relating to losses that are incurred in transactions entered into for profit but are not connected with a trade or business, or IRC §212, relating to expenses incurred for the production of income. If, however, the disputed amount was generated by a hobby or similar activity, the taxpayer's right to a deduction on repayment is open to question. While the IRS might argue that the repayment cannot be deducted because the loss does not fit into one of these provisions, it is obviously unfair to disregard the taxpayer's contingent obligation to repay when computing the taxpayer's taxable gain, as required by the claim of right doctrine, and then to disallow a deduction if the contingency is resolved against the taxpayer. For this reason, the Treasury evidently concedes the propriety of a deduction in

---

[31] American Auto. Ass'n v. US, 367 US 687 (1961); see generally infra ¶35.3.

[32] See infra ¶2.5.

[33] Supra note 19.

[34] For IRC §§162 and 165, see generally infra ¶¶8.1 and 12.1, respectively. For the possibility that IRC §1341 supplies an independent statutory foundation for deducting repayments, see infra, text at note 36.

this situation,[35] perhaps on the theory that a deduction in the event of repayment is an appropriate corollary of the claim of right doctrine itself.

4. Effect of Repayment on Tax Liability—IRC §1341. In *United States v. Lewis,* holding that an employee who repaid in 1946 part of an erroneously computed bonus received in 1944 could not reopen his 1944 return in order to recalculate his tax liability, the Supreme Court refused to depart from the claim of right doctrine "merely because it results in an advantage or disadvantage to a taxpayer." [36] For the taxpayer in *Lewis,* a refund for the earlier year was preferable, either because his marginal tax rate was higher in that year than in the year of repayment, because a refund is paid with interest, or both; but for other taxpayers, as the Court noted, a deduction in the year of repayment could be more valuable than a refund, even with interest. In a later case, the Supreme Court observed that "these discrepancies were accepted as an unavoidable consequence of the annual accounting system." [37]

Under IRC §1341, enacted in 1954 in response to the *Lewis* case, however, qualified taxpayers get the better of these alternatives. The tax liability for the year of repayment is the lesser of (1) a tax computed in the normal fashion after deducting the repayment, and (2) a hypothetical tax for the repayment year, computed without the deduction, less the decrease in tax that would have resulted for the earlier year if the repaid amount had been excluded from that year's gross income. These alternative computations—under which "the taxpayer always wins and the Government always loses" [38] are made for the year of repayment, without reopening the return for the earlier year; and since the remedial mechanism does not entail a refund for the earlier year, the taxpayer is not credited with interest. In determining the decrease in the prior year's tax that would have resulted from excluding the repaid amount, the arithmetic effects of the hypothetical exclusion on such matters as deductions for charitable contributions and medical expenses (resulting from the percentage limitations on these deductions) are taken into account; but if the statute of limitations has run on corrections for that year, income and deductions that were erroneously omitted are not corrected.[39]

Section 1341 comes into play if (1) an item was included in gross income for a prior taxable year because it then appeared that the taxpayer had an

---

[35] See Treas. Regs. §1.1341-1(h), Example (deduction allowed under IRC §1341 for repayment following sale of personal residence at a gain; moreover, no indication that amount repaid was less than the gain); but see National Life & Accident Ins. Co. v. US, 244 F.Supp. 135 (M.D. Tenn. 1965) (no deduction for interest refunded on early redemption of U.S. bonds, in absence of explicit statutory provision).

[36] US v. Lewis, 340 US 590, 592 (1951).

[37] US v. Skelly Oil Co., 349 US 678, 681 (1969).

[38] ID. at 692 (Mr. Justice Stewart, dissenting).

[39] See Treas. Regs. §1.1341-1(d)(4)(ii).

unrestricted right to such item; (2) a deduction is allowable for the current taxable year because it was established after the prior year that the taxpayer did not have an unrestricted right to the item or a portion thereof; and (3) the deduction exceeds $3,000.

The first of these conditions deserves close attention. Section 1341 was enacted primarily to deal with the repayment of amounts received under a "claim of right." [40] But the operative language of IRC §1341(a)(1) refers to items included in gross income "because it appeared that the taxpayer had an unrestricted right to such item," and this phrase is broader and, possibly, also narrower than the claim of right doctrine. It is broader in that it encompasses amounts included in gross income by an accrual-basis taxpayer, such as billed but uncollected fees. On the other hand, by confining relief to amounts to which the taxpayer apparently had "an unrestricted right," IRC §1341(a)(1) seems to deny relief to amounts that are in dispute when received, even if they must be included in income because received under a *claim* of right.

Without resolving this problem, the regulations provide that items are covered by IRC §1341(a)(1) if "it appeared from all the facts available in the year of inclusion that the taxpayer had an unrestricted right to such item." [41] In applying this standard, an important 1968 ruling looks to the facts that were available *to the taxpayer* and goes on to distinguish between three types of "appearances": (1) a "semblance" of an unrestricted right; (2) an unchallengeable right, which is more than an apparent right; and (3) no right at all, which is less than an apparent right.[42] If the taxpayer's right to the item was unchallengeable in the year of inclusion (type 2 in the foregoing sumary) but was undermined by facts arising subsequently, IRC §1341 does not apply, because it was not established until a later year that the taxpayer did not have an unrestricted right to the item *in the year of inclusion.* [43] As examples, the ruling cites the repayment of prepaid interest when a debt is paid in advance and the payment of liquidated damages under a contract; in these cases, the taxpayer is entitled to a deduction, but not to IRC §1341 relief. At the other end of the spectrum are amounts to which the taxpayer had no right at all (type 3), such as embezzled funds, which are also outside the scope of IRC §1341, although here too the taxpayer is entitled to a deduction for amounts repaid.[44]

This leaves type 1 items—the gold mean, as it were—to which the

---

[40] Treas. Regs. §§1.1341.1(a)(1), 1.1341.1(a)(2) ("claim of right" defined for purposes of IRC §1341 by reference to its statutory language); but see IRC §7806(b) (no interpretative inferences to be drawn from descriptive matter, etc.).

[41] Treas. Regs. §1.1341.1(a)(2).

[42] Rev. Rul. 68-153, 1968-1 CB 371.

[43] See, e.g., Rev. Rul. 58-226, 1958-1 CB 318 (refund of prepaid interest); Rev. Rul. 67-48, 1967-1 CB 50 (liquidated damages for breach of employment contract).

[44] See, e.g., McKinney v. US, 574 F.2d 1240 (5th Cir. 1978), cert. denied, 439 US 1072 (1979) (repayment of embezzled funds).

taxpayer has a right that "appears" unrestricted in the year of inclusion, but that turns out to be fatally defective. Typical items meeting this standard are commissions received or accrued by a salesman for the performance of services, subject to a condition requiring a refund or credit in a later year if the customer fails to pay the salesman's employer for the goods.[45]

Even if the taxpayer includes in gross income and later repays an item meeting the standards of IRC §1341(a)(1), IRC §1341 does not apply unless IRC §1341(a)(2) is also satisfied—a deduction must be "allowable" for the current taxable year because it was "established" after the close of the inclusion year that the taxpayer did not have an unrestricted right to all or part of the item. Notwithstanding an occasional loose reference to amounts that are "deductible under the provisions of section 1341," [46] it is clear that the taxpayer must look elsewhere—primarily to IRC §§162 and 165—to establish that a deduction is "allowable"; IRC §1341 is concerned exclusively with the *computation* of tax liability.[47]

¶2.4 INCOME FROM DISCHARGE OF DEBT FOR LESS THAN FACE AMOUNT

1. Introductory. Borrowed funds are excluded from gross income even though they increase the taxpayer's assets and can be used as he sees fit, because the obligation to repay increases his liabilities by the same amount, so that the receipt of a loan produces no gain.[48] Sometimes, however, the taxpayer is able to discharge the debt for less than the amount received. Although this means that the taxpayer has received and excluded from income more than he pays out, the federal income tax was almost twenty years old before the courts unequivocally accepted the government's theory that the discharge of a debt for less than its face amount could generate income. An obstacle to government success in this early period was that an improvement in the debtor's financial status resulting from settling a debt for less than its full amount did not seem to entail a gain derived by the taxpayer-debtor from either capital or labor, as required by *Eisner v. Macomber.* [49] Moreover, if the creditor accepts less than the amount due because the debtor is in financial

---

[45] See, e.g., Rev. Rul. 72-78, 1972-1 CB 45 (IRC §1341 applies to salesman's advance commissions, refunded because of customer's failure to pay in the following year); see also Rev. Rul. 68-153, supra note 42 (refund by utility company to customers on retroactive reduction of rates by state utility commission).

[46] See Blanton v. CIR, 46 TC 527, 529 (1966).

[47] See US v. Skelly Oil Co., supra note 37, at 683 ("it is necessary to refer to other portions of the Code to discover how much of a deduction is allowable").

[48] Supra ¶2.1.

[49] Eisner v. Macomber, 252 US 189 (1920), discussed supra ¶1.4; see, e.g., Meyer Jewelry Co. v. CIR, 3 BTA 1319 (1926).

distress, taxing the debtor may have seemed anomalous, even heartless. This reluctance to kick someone when he is down may have carried over to a very different situation, viz., gain realized by a corporate debtor on open-market purchases of its own bonds at less than their face amount, where the decline in value is attributable to an increase in the interest rate on obligations of equivalent risk, rather than to doubts about collectibility.

The government's early efforts to tax gain from below-face debt cancellations encountered still another obstacle in 1926, when the Supreme Court decided *Bowers v. Kerbaugh-Empire Co.* [50] In this case, its first pronouncement on the subject, the Court held that no income was realized by a corporation that borrowed German marks before World War I, converted the borrowed funds into dollars, advanced the dollars to a subsidiary (which lost the funds in unsuccessful business activities), and then repaid the loans after the war with devalued marks costing about $685,000 less in dollars than the borrowed marks were worth when received. Observing that "the whole transaction was a loss," the Court said: "The loss was less than it would have been if [the] marks had not declined in value; but the mere diminution of loss is not gain, profit, or income." [51]

Despite this inauspicious beginning, the government persisted in trying to establish that the discharge of debt for less than its face amount could generate income. In *United States v. Kirby Lumber Co.,* decided by the Supreme Court in 1931, the Court upheld the government's contention, dismissing the constitutional doubts that had clouded the area, without even citing Eisner v. Macomber:

> Here [i.e., in *Kirby Lumber*] there was no shrinkage of assets [as in *Kerbaugh-Empire*] and the taxpayer made a clear gain. As a result of its dealings it made available $137,521.30 [of] assets previously offset by the obligation of bonds now extinct. We see nothing to be gained by the discussion of judicial definitions. The defendant in error has realized within the year an accession to income, if we take words in their plain popular meaning, as they should be taken here.[52]

Kirby Lumber's result was entirely justifiable, but its cryptic rationale set afloat several erroneous ideas, leading to a confusing patchwork of rules and exceptions that dominates the area to this day.

First, the Court carried forward the *Kerbaugh-Empire* theory that the

[50] Bowers v. Kerbaugh-Empire Co., 271 US 170 (1926).

[51] Id. at 175.

[52] US v. Kirby Lumber Co., 284 US 1, 3 (1931). Although the opinion refers to "extinct" bonds, it was held later that it is immaterial whether the bonds are retired or held for reissue. See Montana, Wyo. & S.R.R. v. CIR, 31 BTA 62 (1934), aff'd per curiam, 77 F.2d 1007 (3d Cir.), cert. denied, 296 US 604 (1935).

taxability of a debt discharge depends on analyzing "the transaction as a whole"—not merely whether the taxpayer borrowed more than it paid back. Such an analysis is usually impossible, however, since borrowed funds are ordinarily absorbed into the business so completely that tracing the travels of interchangeable dollars lacks even the surface plausibility that it could claim in *Kerbaugh-Empire.*[53] Even where funds can be traced to a particular project, as in *Kerbaugh-Empire,* the attribution is artificial. In most cases, the borrowed funds free up funds that can be used to finance other projects, which may or may not be profitable. It is unclear, therefore, how an examination of "the transaction as a whole" can be limited to the fate of projects directly financed by the borrowed funds.

More important, the debtor's business activities will have the tax results prescribed by the Internal Revenue Code, whether they are financed with borrowed funds or not and, if borrowed funds are used, whether the taxpayer pays the debt in full or not. This means that the debtor's business expenses, losses, depreciation, and other financial drains will be recognized as they occur, to the extent permitted by law. If borrowed funds are invested, the full amount borrowed will be deductible (unless used to defray nondeductible items); and if the taxpayer later settles the debt for less than its face amount, an exclusion of the difference from income because the funds were lost would be tantamount to a double deduction for a single loss. Thus, if a taxpayer borrows $1,000, loses this amount in a business venture, and settles the debt for $100, his tax return will reflect $1,000 of deductions, although his out-of-pocket loss is only $100. If the $900 difference between the amount borrowed and the amount repaid is excluded from income under *Kerbaugh-Empire* because of the business loss, that event will be doing double duty—first by creating $1,000 of deductions, and then by shielding $900 against the *Kirby Lumber* principle.

The second theme in the *Kirby Lumber* opinion focuses not on the long-term results of the borrowing transaction, but on the immediate impact of the repayment. According to the Court, the taxpayer "realized within the year an accession to income."[54] This conclusion, however, merely reflects the fact that the bonds were listed on the liability side of the balance sheet at their face amount, while the cash used to purchase the bonds was, of course, shown at full value. If the company's assets and liabilities to creditors had been valued at their respective aggregate fair market values, the company's net worth would have been the same after the repurchase as it was before.

Finally, the reference in the *Kirby Lumber* opinion to dealings that "made

---

[53] For cases in which the taxpayer was unable to trace borrowed funds into business losses, see Capitol Coal Corp. v. CIR, 26 TC 1183 (1956), aff'd, 250 F.2d 361 (2d Cir. 1957); Church's English Shoes, Ltd. v. CIR, 229 F.2d 957 (2d Cir. 1956).

[54] Supra note 52.

available $137,521.30 [of] assets previously offset by the [repurchased bonds]" has been a continual source of confusion. If this comment means that repurchase of the bonds for less than their face amount reduced the taxpayer's liabilities by more than its assets and, hence, increased its net worth, this phenomenon would occur whether the taxpayer invested the borrowed funds successfully or not. If the reference to "available assets" means that the taxpayer borrowed more than it paid back, that is similarly unaffected by interim gains or losses attributable to the borrowed funds.

Since borrowed funds are obviously worth their face amount and assets acquired on credit in an arm's length transaction are also worth what the buyer agrees to pay, a taxpayer who ultimately pays back less than he received enjoys a financial benefit whether the funds were invested successfully, lost in a business venture, spent for food and clothing, or given to a charity. Thus, the tax treatment of below-face debt discharges would have been much simplified if it had been based at the outset on the fact that borrowed funds are excluded from gross income because of the assumption that they will be repaid in full and on the simple corollary that a tax adjustment is required when this assumption proves erroneous, regardless of the use to which the taxpayer put the borrowed funds. Unfortunately, *Kerbaugh-Empire* linked the tax treatment of the debt discharge to the fate of the borrowed funds, and *Kirby Lumber* carried forward this idea by distinguishing rather than repudiating *Kerbaugh-Empire,* seeming thereby to sanction an open-ended inquiry into the debtor's financial history in order to determine whether the discharge of the debt generated a "clear gain."

Despite this tangled net of judicial rules, Congress has chosen to remain largely quiescent. In 1954, the Code was amended to provide explicitly that "income from discharge of indebtedness" is includable in gross income;[55] but this statutory change leaves to the courts the task of determining when the discharge of a debt produces, and when it does not produce, income. The same is true of IRC §§108 and 1017, which give business taxpayers a last clear chance to avoid realizing income on the discharge of a debt by electing to reduce the basis of their depreciable assets.[56] This election comes into play only if the taxpayer realizes income under the judicially prescribed rules. When applicable, it does not permanently exclude the taxpayer's gain from gross income, but rather postpones its realization by increasing the gain (or decreasing the loss) realized when the property is disposed of and by reducing the taxpayer's depreciation deductions in the interim.

Finally, application of the *Kirby Lumber* principle is complicated by the fact that debts are often described as having been discharged for less than their face amount, when in fact they have been paid in full. For example, an

---

[55] IRC §61(a)(12).

[56] See infra, text at note 79.

employee who borrows $50 from his employer may authorize the deduction of that amount from his next paycheck; when the deduction is made, the debt is for all practical purposes *paid,* even though no cash changes hands. The employee realizes $50 of income on the "cancellation" of his debt, but it is not "cancellation of indebtedness" income taxed to him by virtue of the *Kirby Lumber* case. It is, rather, compensation for his services, and it would have been taxable as such even if *Kirby Lumber* had been decided against the IRS. There are many other examples of this phenomenon—a debt that, superficially viewed, was cancelled without payment but that, on analysis, is found to have been paid in full. Unfortunately, in prescribing the proper tax treatment for these spurious cancellation-of-indebtedness cases, the courts have sometimes confused them with the genuine article.[57]

2. Nature of the Debt. As a general rule, income from the discharge of indebtedness should depend not on the type of debt incurred, but merely on the spread between the amount received by the debtor and the amount paid by him to satisfy his obligation. The courts, however, have engrafted a number of exceptions on *Kirby Lumber* that depend on apparently irrelevant considerations, such as whether the debtor was personally liable on the debt and whether the debt was incurred for cash or other consideration.

1. *Nature and amount of the consideration.* The bonds in *Kirby Lumber* were issued in exchange for the taxpayer's preferred stock with dividends in arrears, but the case has often been thought to have involved bonds issued for cash, perhaps because the Court said that the taxpayer, on issuing the bonds, "received their par value."[58] Despite this misconception, the *Kirby Lumber* principle has been regularly applied to bonds issued or assumed by the taxpayer to acquire business assets,[59] but obligations arising in other noncash transactions, such as bonds distributed as dividends, have sometimes been held outside the reach of that case.[60]

The computation of income resulting from the discharge of a debt becomes more complicated if the taxpayer gets more or less than its face

---

[57] The term "spurious" is not intended to imply doubt about the legal effectiveness of the discharge; what is spurious is the implication that the debt was discharged for less than its face amount. See infra, text at note 5 74-79.

[58] US v. Kirby Lumber Co., supra note 52, at 2.

[59] See, e.g., Helvering v. American Chicle Co., 291 US 426 (1934) (purchase for less than face of a predecessor company's bonds, which had been assumed by the taxpayer on purchasing predecessor's assets).

[60] See CIR v. Rail Joint Co., 61 F.2d 751 (2d Cir. 1932); see also Bradford v. CIR, 233 F.2d 935 (6th Cir. 1956) (note issued to bank to obtain reduction of debt owed by taxpayer's husband; taxpayer is described as issuing her note "without receiving any consideration in return," although it might have been treated as an indirect way of getting cash to reduce husband's debt).

amount on issuance. When bonds are issued at a premium or discount, for example, the premium received by the obligor is an indirect way of reducing the nominal interest rate, while discount is an indirect way of increasing the nominal interest. In general, therefore, the issuing taxpayer must report the premium as additional income (or may deduct the discount) in installments over the life of the bond.[61] On discharging such an obligation, the taxpayer's gain under the *Kirby Lumber* principle is the excess of the issue price, plus any previously deducted discount or minus any premium previously reported as income, over the amount paid on repurchase.[62]

2. *Nonrecourse debts.* If the taxpayer borrows on a nonrecourse basis, pledging real estate or other property as security for the debt, several cases hold or suggest that the taxable amount cannot exceed the value of the released collateral when the debt is discharged.[63] This restriction can be defended if the taxpayer acquires property subject to an existing debt in excess of its value and pays the latter amount (or more) to discharge the debt, since in this situation the taxpayer receives (and excludes from income) only the value of the property and hence realizes no gain on repaying that amount. But if the property when received was worth more than the existing debt, acquisition of the property subject to the liability is functionally equivalent to buying it with a nonrecourse purchase-money mortgage or purchasing it for cash and then pledging it for a nonrecourse loan; and if the debt is later settled for less than its face amount, there is no sound reason for excluding the spread from income.

3. *Disputed liabilities.* The Treasury regulations under IRC §108 define "indebtedness" as "an obligation, absolute and not contingent, to pay on demand or within a given time, in cash or another medium, a fixed amount."[64] This definition has in effect been adopted by the courts in applying the *Kirby Lumber* principle. Because the debt must be "absolute and not contingent," settlement of a claim does not generate income under IRC §61(a)(12) if the debtor disputes liability for the amount claimed by the alleged creditor,[65] since the amount payable is, in a realistic sense, whatever the parties agree upon in their settlement negotiations. For this reason, discharge of the debt does not increase the taxpayer's net worth, as required by the *Kirby Lumber* principle. If, for example, business equipment is bought for $1,000 on credit and the buyer refuses to pay because of an alleged misrepresentation or breach of warranty, a settlement of the debt for $750 is not a taxable event but

---

[61] For bond premium and discount, see Treas. Regs. §§1.161-12(c)(2) and 1.163-4, discussed infra ¶15.3.

[62] For an illustrative computation, see Treas. Regs. §1.61-12(c)(5); see also CIR v. National Alfalfa Dehydrating & Milling Co., 417 US 134 (1974).

[63] See, e.g., Collins v. CIR, ¶63,285 P-H Memo TC (1963) (income limited to the value of collateral released on complete cancellation of the debt).

[64] Treas. Regs. §1.108(b)-1(c) (issued under IRC §108(b), repealed in 1976).

[65] See N. Sobel, Inc. v. CIR, 40 BTA 1263 (1939) (Nonacq.). The no-income result presupposes a bona fide dispute but not necessarily a valid defense.

a retroactive reduction of the purchase price to $750; and the amount actually paid, rather than the original price of $1,000, will be the taxpayer's basis in computing depreciation on the property and gain or loss when it is ultimately disposed of.[66]

When applicable, the judicially created "retroactive reduction of purchase price" exception to *Kirby Lumber* [67] has the same effect as an election under IRC §108—no income when the debt is discharged, but lower depreciation deductions if the property is depreciable and more gain (or less loss) when it is eventually disposed of. But the judicial exception is evidently available to individual taxpayers who cannot make an election under IRC §108 because the property acquired on credit is a personal residence or other nonbusiness property.

3. Effect of Method by Which Debt Is Discharged. There are a number of ways, other than a payment of cash, to eliminate, scale down, or modify debts; and these alternatives introduce tax complications.

1. Modification of original obligation and substitution of new obligation. Debtors often induce creditors to extend the time of payment, reduce the interest rate, release collateral, or eliminate restrictions imposed by a loan agreement, without reducing the principal amount due. Changes of this type do not generate income under the *Kirby Lumber* principle, even if the fair market value of the new obligations is less than the face amount of the old debt and the latter is discharged in exchange for the new obligations.[68]

If, however, there is a reduction in the amount due, the resulting increase in the taxpayer's net worth brings the *Kirby Lumber* principle into play, whether there is an exchange of obligations or simply an agreement by the creditor to accept a scaled-down amount. The most appropriate treatment of a reduction in the debt's face amount would be to bifurcate the transaction by treating the difference between the face amount of the old debt and the fair market value of the new debt as cancellation-of-indebtedness income, to be taxed immediately, with any difference between the fair market value and the face amount of the new debt being viewed as premium or discount to be amortized over the life of the new obligation.

2. *Exchange of stock for debt.* The cases and a longstanding ruling adopt the theory that the substitution of common stock for debt "does not effect a cancellation, reduction, or discharge of indebtedness but rather amounts to a

---

[66] CIR v. Sherman, 135 F.2d 68 (6th Cir. 1943).

[67] For statutory codification of this principle by the Bankruptcy Tax Act of 1980, see IRC §108(e)(5).

[68] See Rev. Rul. 58-546, 1958-2 CB 143 (on bond-for-bond exchange, which changed interest rates and maturities but not face amount, obligor realized gain only to extent of cancellation of liability for accrued interest previously deducted with tax benefit).

transformation from a fixed indebtedness to a capital stock liability."[69] Though not entirely persuasive, the theory is firmly entrenched in both the case law and administrative practice, and it is in any event of limited importance since the exchange would ordinarily constitute a tax-free recapitalization of the debtor.[70] The theory was indirectly codified by the Bankruptcy Tax Act of 1980,[71] since amended IRC §108(e)(8) refers to "the stock-for-debt exception" in determining a debtor's income from the discharge of indebtedness; but the same provision goes on to provide that this exception shall not apply (1) to the issuance of nominal or token shares or (2) in the case of an unsecured creditor, if the ratio of the value of the stock received to the debt cancelled or exchanged for stock is less than 50 percent of the ratio applicable to all unsecured creditors participating in the workout of the debt.

3. *Use of property to discharge debt.* The debtor may use property rather than cash to effect a settlement of his debt. If the property is worth less than the face amount of the debt, a transfer to the creditor in discharge of the debt raises a *Kirby Lumber* problem; and if the debtor's basis for the property exceeds, or is less than, its fair market value, the transaction simultaneously raises an issue of gain or loss on the disposition of appreciated or depreciated property. The courts have not unbundled transactions of this type, however, but have instead ordinarily treated them as sales of the property for the face amount of the cancelled debt.[72]

4. *Three-party transactions.* If a creditor sells a claim against a debtor to a third party for less than its face amount, the debtor does not realize income under the *Kirby Lumber* case, since the debt is not discharged but simply transferred to a new creditor. If, however, the debt is acquired by a person related to the debtor from a person who is not related to the debtor, the acquisition is imputed to the debtor, to the extent provided by regulations to be issued by the IRS.[73] The tainted relationships triggering this imputation are specified by IRC §108(e)(4).

---

[69] Rev. Rul. 59-222, 1959-1 CB 80; Motor Mart Trust v. CIR, 4 TC 931 (1945) (Acq.), aff'd, 156 F.2d 122 (1st Cir. 1946), and cases there cited.

[70] See, e.g., Hummel-Ross Fibre Corp. v. CIR, 40 BTA 821 (1939) (Acq.).

[71] Infra, text following note 78.

[72] See Unique Art Mfg. Co., 8 TC 1341 (1947) (Acq.); but see Bialock v. CIR, 35 TC 649, 661 (Acq.) (1961) (transfer of property to discharge debt with face amount in excess of property's value generated debt-discharge income). While it is unclear whether the IRS has ever pushed for bifurcation in an appropriate case, the regulations appear to recognize that where a debt is cancelled in exchange for property, only a portion of the resulting gain may be pure debt-discharge income. See Treas. Regs. §1.1017-1(b)(5).

[73] See also Bradford v. CIR, 233 F.2d 935 (6th Cir. 1956), where an intermediary was used and the parties acknowledged that he acted as an agent for the debtor, not as a principal; Forrester v. CIR, 4 TC 907 (1945) (Acq.)(husband and wife treated as separate).

4. "Spurious" Cancellations of Indebtedness—Gifts, Etc. Debts are often cancelled not to effect a financial adjustment of the debtor-creditor relationship, but as an indirect way of achieving a quite different objective. An example is the employee who borrows $50 from his employer, with the understanding that the debt will be deducted from his next paycheck. When this occurs, the debt is "cancelled" in form, but it is in fact paid in full even though no cash changes hands. The employee must report the $50 as income, not because the debt has been cancelled for less than its face amount within the meaning of the *Kirby Lumber* case but because he has been paid in full for his services.

This distinction between genuine cancellations of indebtedness for less than the face amount and spurious cancellations [74] can be illustrated by analyzing the tax treatment of the creditor. If the creditor accepts less than the amount due in a *Kirby Lumber* situation (a genuine cancellation for less than face), he is ordinarily entitled to deduct the difference between the amount due and the amount received as a loss or worthless debt. By contrast, the creditor who agrees to a spurious cancellation (e.g., the employer who cancels the employee's debt by docking his pay) is not entitled to a bad-debt deduction, since no loss has been suffered.

Spurious cancellations of indebtedness are frequently employed as an indirect way to make gifts to relatives, friends, and nonprofit organizations. If a proud grandparent loans money to a favorite grandchild for college tuition and is overcome by emotion on graduation day, tears up the promissory notes, and announces that the debt is forgiven, the transaction is clearly outside the proper ambit of *Kirby Lumber.* Since the transaction is a gift, the grandchild does not report any debt-discharge income.

The Supreme Court held in *Helvering v. American Dental Co.* that the cancellation of a debt in a wholly commercial context can qualify as a tax-free gift to the debtor,[75] but it later observed in *CIR v. Jacobson* that such an "extraordinary transaction" is "hardly likely," [76] and this has proved, for practical purposes, to be a requiem for the *American Dental* case. To qualify as a gift, the transaction must stem from "detached and disinterested generosity . . . affection, respect, admiration, charity or like impulses." [77] If (but only if) the debt cancellation is attributable to motives of this type, the tax exemption accorded to gifts by IRC §102 prevails over the *Kirby Lumber* principle.

5. Effect of Debtor's Insolvency. If a debtor is in extremis (financially speaking) when his debt is cancelled for less than its face amount, he may be entitled to partial or complete relief from the *Kirby Lumber* principle by virtue

---

[74] For use of the term "spurious" in this context, see supra note 57.

[75] Helvering v. American Dental Co., 318 US 322 (1943).

[76] CIR v. Jacobson, 336 US 28 (1949).

[77] CIR v. Duberstein, 363 US 278, 285 (1960), discussed infra ¶3.2.

of a complex network of administrative, judicial, and statutory rules. Although not internally self-consistent, these rules have all been influenced by a dominant theme—that a debtor does not realize income when his debts are discharged in bankruptcy—which originated in a 1923 IRS ruling.[78] This "fresh start" approach was codified and expanded by IRC §108(a)(1), enacted as part of the Bankruptcy Tax Act of 1980. Subject to certain elections and limitations, this provision excludes from the bankrupt's gross income any amount that would otherwise be includable by reason of the discharge of the taxpayer's indebtedness if (a) the discharge occurs in "a title 11 case," defined by IRC §108(d)(2) to mean a case under Title 11 USC (relating to bankruptcy), if the taxpayer is under the jurisdiction of the court and the discharge is granted either by the court or pursuant to a plan approved by the court; (b) the discharge occurs when the taxpayer is insolvent; or (c) regardless of the financial vitality of the debtor, the debt is "qualified business indebtedness."

Under IRC §108(b), the amount excluded from gross income under IRC §108(a)(1)(A), relating to discharges of debt in bankruptcy, are applied to reduce the taxpayer's "tax attributes" in the following order: (1) net operating losses for the taxable year of the discharge and net operating loss carryovers to that year; (2) carryovers to or from the year of the discharge allowed under IRC §§38 (investment tax credit), 40 (work-incentive programs), 44B (new jobs credit), and 44E (alcohol used as fuel); (3) net capital losses and capital loss carryovers; (4) basis reductions under IRC §1017; and (5) foreign tax credit carryovers.[79] These tax attributes are reduced by one dollar for each dollar excluded from gross income, except for credits, which are reduced by 50 cents per dollar of excluded gross income. Excluded debt discharge income that cannot be absorbed by the taxpayer's tax attributes is disregarded.

If an insolvent debtor's obligations are discharged by agreement with creditors without a bankruptcy proceeding, the income from the discharge is excluded from gross income and the debtor's tax attributes are reduced as though the debt had been discharged in bankruptcy. But this procedure applies only to the extent of the debtor's insolvency, defined by IRC §108(d)(3) as the excess of the taxpayer's liabilities over the fair market value of the taxpayer's assets, determined immediately before the discharge. Any debt discharge income in excess of the amount by which the taxpayer is insolvent is treated as realized by a solvent taxpayer.

---

[78] I.T. 1564, II-1 CB 59 (1923). This ruling was carried into the regulations in 1935 and was declared obsolete in 1969. See Treas. Regs. 86, §22(a)-14 (1935); Rev. Rul. 69-43, 1969-1 CB 310.

[79] The amount of the discharge can be applied first to reduce basis in depreciable property upon this taxpayer's election. See IRC §108(b)(5).

6. Solvent Debtors—Election to Apply Debt-Discharge Income Against Basis of Property. The 1980 legislation does not alter the preexisting rules determining whether a cancellation of a solvent taxpayer's debt is includable in gross income, but a pre-1980 election to exclude such amounts is now allowed by IRC §§108(c) and 1017 only to the extent of the taxpayer's basis in depreciable property (including, if the taxpayer so elects, realty held for sale to customers). This election is open to all corporate taxpayers, but individuals may make it only if the indebtedness was incurred or assumed in connection with property used in a trade or business. The election serves to postpone realization of the gain rather than to exclude it permanently. This is because the reduced basis will result in lower depreciation deductions for depreciable property and more taxable gain (or a smaller deductible loss) on a subsequent disposition of the property. If the debt-discharge income exceeds the aggregate pre-discharge adjusted basis of the taxpayer's depreciable property (and, if the taxpayer elects, of the real property held for sale to customers), the excess must be reported as income in the year of the discharge, under IRC §108(c)(2).

¶2.5 INCOME FROM UNLAWFUL ACTIVITIES

If property is obtained by unlawful conduct and the taxpayer intends to disregard his legal obligation to make restitution, he is ordinarily not allowed to use the offsetting liability as a shield against tax liability; he resembles the parricide who asked for mercy because he was an orphan. Instead, the unlawful receipts must be included in gross income, and the wrongdoer may take a deduction only if and when he reimburses the victim for the loss. This result was reached only after a series of confusing and conflicting Supreme Court decisions. The story begins with the Revenue Act of 1913, which taxed income from a variety of sources, including "any lawful business carried on for gain or profit." [80] Three years later Congress eliminated the qualifying word "lawful" from the statute, without announcing any reason for the change.[81] With the advent of Prohibition, the Treasury relied on this unexplained change in the law when prosecuting bootleggers for failing to report their income from the unlawful sale of liquor, arguing that it manifested a legislative intent to tax the profits of illegal as well as lawful activities.

In *United States v. Sullivan* the Supreme Court agreed that the profits of an unlawful business were taxable, saying: "We see no reason . . . why the fact that a business is unlawful should exempt it from paying the taxes that if lawful it would have to pay." [82] In an opinion by Mr. Justice Holmes, the Court went

---

[80] Revenue Act of 1913, P.L. No. 16, §IIB, 38 Stat. 114, 167.

[81] Revenue Act of 1916, P.L. No. 271, §2(a), 39 Stat. 756, 757.

[82] US v. Sullivan, 274 US 259, 263 (1927).

on to dispose of the defendant's claim that the Fifth Amendment exempted him from filing a return:

> Most of the items [called for by the return] warranted no complaint. It would be an extreme if not an extravagant application of the Fifth Amendment to say that it authorized a man to refuse to state the amount of his income because it had been made in crime.[83]

Although the *Sullivan* case was decided by the Supreme Court in 1927, the scope of the privilege against self-incrimination, so far as tax returns are concerned, remains unclear to this day.[84] When income from unlawful activities is reported, the taxpayer often supplies his name, address, and net income (usually in round figures, with such laconic labels as "miscellaneous income" or "income from various sources"), leaving the rest of the return blank. Returns like these invite intensive scrutiny by the IRS, but taxpayers are rarely prosecuted for failing to supply more information, either because the Fifth Amendment is thought to protect them against making further disclosure or because juries are thought unlikely to convict for mere silence. Instead, revenue agents endeavor to verify the accuracy of the reported amounts by reconstructing the taxpayer's financial history from purchases, investments, loans, and so on.[85]

The *Sullivan* case did not discuss the taxability of illegal receipts when the wrongdoer can be compelled by the victim to disgorge the fruits of the crime. The Supreme Court did not address this question until 1946, when it held in *CIR v. Wilcox* that embezzled funds are not includable in the embezzler's gross income because, like borrowed funds, they are received subject to a duty of repayment.[86] The Court left open the possibility that the embezzler would become taxable if and when his obligation to repay was terminated by the statute of limitations or by an act of forgiveness on the part of the victim.

Six years after deciding *Wilcox,* the Supreme Court had to decide whether the defendant in *Rutkin v. United States* was taxable on $250,000 extorted by threats of violence from an ex-partner in a "high seas venture" (i.e., bootlegging).[87] In theory, extortion resembles embezzlement in imposing an obligation on the wrongdoer to reimburse his victim on demand, but in practice, an extortioner is less likely to be asked for repayment; if the victim's fear of exposure or violence keeps him from complaining to the police when he is first approached, he will probably remain silent thereafter. For this reason, the

[83] Id. at 263-264.

[84] See infra ¶40.2.

[85] See infra ¶¶40.2 (self-incrimination), 42.4 (prosecution for failure to supply information), 37.1 (indirect methods of computing income).

[86] CIR v. Wilcox, 327 US 404 (1946).

[87] Rutkin v. US, 343 US 130, rehearing denied, 343 US 952 (1952).

Supreme Court held in the *Rutkin* case that extorted funds are taxable. This decision evoked a vigorous dissent by four of the nine Justices, who could see no valid distinction between embezzled and extorted funds. The dissenters were not prepared, however, to extend the "borrower" analogy to criminal activity that was sufficiently sustained and regular to constitute a "business." Thus, they distinguished the profits generated by gambling and bootlegging from the "sporadic loot of an embezzler, an extortioner or a robber," on the theory that the commission of these felonies does not comprise a "business." [88]

The distinction drawn by the majority in *Rutkin* between embezzled funds (held nontaxable in the *Wilcox* case) and extorted funds (held taxable in the *Rutkin* case) lasted for less than ten years. In *James v. United States,* the Supreme Court overruled *Wilcox,* holding that income from illegal activity is taxable despite the recipient's legal obligation to make restitution.[89] The offsetting liability should be disregarded, according to Mr. Chief Justice Warren, because the taxpayer himself does not intend to honor this obligation and because "as a practical matter" he has enough control over the funds to derive economic value from them. The majority in *James* went on to suggest that if the taxpayer actually made restitution to his victim, he would be entitled to a deduction in the year of repayment.[90]

The *James* case evidently embraces all illegal receipts, even if the culprit promises restitution, though a chink in this generalization should probably be left for malefactors whose victims agree before the end of the taxable year to treat the improper taking as a loan.[91] The theft-loan dichotomy is also encountered if the taxpayer purports to borrow funds for legitimate business transactions but is actually engaged in swindling the investors. If the investment facade is given credence, the receipts are nontaxable borrowed funds, but if the intent to cheat is dominant, they are the taxable fruits of larceny or embezzlement.[92]

A final problem in the taxability of income from unlawful activity is the

---

[88] Id. at 140-141.

[89] James v. US, 366 US 213 (1961).

[90] Id. at 220-222. See also Rev. Rul. 65-254, 1965-2 CB 50 (repayment of embezzled funds is a loss, deductible under IRC §§165(a) and 165(c)(2), relating to transactions entered into for profit).

[91] But see Buff v. CIR, 496 F.2d 847 (2d Cir. 1974) (bookkeeper taxed on embezzled funds despite promise within same year to make restitution, embodied in confession of judgment; judgment "not worth the paper it was written on"); Quinn v. CIR, 524 F.2d 617 (7th Cir. 1975) (embezzler taxed despite his action in giving promissory note to victimized bank in same year).

[92] See In re Diversified Brokers Co., 487 F.2d 355 (8th Cir. 1973) (receipts in "Ponzi" pyramiding scheme treated as loans to corporate borrower rather than as embezzled funds); Moore v. US, 412 F.2d 974 (5th Cir. 1969) (Billy Sol Estes operations treated as swindle resulting in taxable income, not as investments).

plight of the victim. The issue is whether the victim or the government will have the superior claim. In general, if the victim can trace and identify his property, as in the case of a stolen work of art, he can get it back, even if the thief has nothing left with which to pay his taxes. Even if the property cannot be traced (e.g., cash), the victim will ordinarily be familiar with the facts sooner than the government, and this prior knowledge will usually enable him to establish an enforceable claim against any assets that can be discovered in the criminal's possession before the government's tax lien takes hold. But situations can also be imagined in which the victim's right to reimbursement will be subordinated to the government's right to collect taxes on the unlawful income, because the government acts first. This possibility, though probably unusual as a practical matter, is offensive; but a corrective could be provided by Congress without going so far as to confer a blanket tax exemption on unlawful receipts, for example, by giving the victim's claim a high priority in distributing the malefactor's wealth among all claimants, including the government itself.[93]

SELECTED BIBLIOGRAPHY

Bittker, Taxing Income From Unlawful Activities, 25 Case W. Res. L. Rev. 130 (1974).

Bittker & Thompson, Income From the Discharge of Indebtedness, 66 Calif. L. Rev. 1159 (1979).

Emanuel, The Scope of Section 1341, 53 Taxes 644 (1975).

Lister, The Use and Abuse of Pragmatism: The Judicial Doctrine of Claim of Right, 21 Tax L. Rev. 263 (1966).

Popkin, The Taxation of Borrowing, 56 Ind. L.J. 43 (1980).

Rabinovitz, Effect of Prior Year's Transactions on Federal Income Tax Consequences of Current Receipts or Payments, 28 Tax L. Rev. 85 (1972).

Wootton, The Claim of Right Doctrine and Section 1341, 34 Tax Lawyer 297 (1981).

---

[93] See infra ¶39.5 (federal tax liens).

CHAPTER 3

Gifts, Bequests, Prizes, and Scholarships

¶3.1 GIFTS AND BEQUESTS—INTRODUCTORY

The value of property acquired by gift, bequest, devise, or inheritance has been excluded from the recipient's gross income, with only minor changes of statutory language, since 1913.[1] Like many other durable features of the federal income tax, however, this exclusion (now embodied in IRC §102) entered the law without a formal congressional explanation, and this deficiency has not been remedied in the decades since its enactment. Taxing gifts and bequests as income may have seemed objectionable to Congress because gratuitous receipts do not increase the aggregate stock of goods and services available for consumption but simply transfer wealth from one person to another. Moreover, if gifts were taxed to the recipient, it would be necessary

[1] From 1913 to 1926 the statute referred to property acquired by "gift, bequest, devise or descent"; in 1926 "descent" was replaced by "inheritance" because the latter "more appropriately [refers to] both real and personal property." S. Rep. No. 52, 69th Cong., 1st Sess. (1926), reprinted in 1939-1 (Part 2) CB 332, 347.

to draw a line between taxable gifts and tax-free family support.[2] It is also possible that the early legislators may have refrained from treating gifts and bequests as taxable income lest amounts received irregularly or only once in a lifetime be taxed at a capriciously high rate.

Many tax theorists have criticized this legislative decision on the ground that a taxpayer's economic well-being is improved as much by a gift or bequest as by the fruits of his own labor or capital; but most tax reformers have avoided a direct assault on IRC §102, preferring to push for peripheral changes in existing law (e.g., taxing unrealized appreciation when property is transferred by gift or at death) and for a separate system of taxing gratuitous receipts. As a result, few provisions of existing law resemble their 1913 antecedents as much as IRC §102.

While excluding from gross income the value of property acquired by gift, bequest, devise, or inheritance, IRC §102 does not exempt the income produced by the property after the transfer.[3] Were it not for this limitation, set out in IRC §102(b)(1), the income from a family fortune would be immunized from tax for all time, once the property passed from the person who created the fortune to his donees or heirs. The application of IRC §102(b)(1) is simple enough in the case of ordinary gifts of money or investment property; the recipient is not taxed at the time of the transfer, but must report the income generated thereafter. But the statutory provision is more complex and operates somewhat erratically if the donor or testator creates divided interests in the transferred property (e.g., income to *A* for life, remainder to *B*), since the full benefit of the exclusion ordinarily goes to the remainderman, with the result that the life tenant must report all of the income, even though he or she may be the primary target of the donor's generous impulse.[4]

If the subject of the gift or bequest is not money but securities, real estate, or other property, the new owner must ascertain his or her "basis" for the property in order to compute gain or loss on a subsequent sale, depreciation, and other tax allowances. In the case of lifetime transfers, the donee does not get a new basis for the property but, in general, takes over the donor's basis.[5] The status of inherited property in the hands of the decedent's estate and heirs, however, is quite different. Property received by will or intestate succession, along with nonprobate property included in the decedent's gross estate for federal estate tax purposes (e.g., gifts subject to a reserved power of control), acquires a new basis equal to the value of the property on the date

---

[2] For the distinction between taxable gifts and tax-free support under the federal gift tax, see Rev. Rul. 68-379, 1968-2 CB 414.

[3] IRC §102(b)(1).

[4] Infra ¶3.4.

[5] IRC §1015, discussed infra ¶23.3.

of death.[6] The new basis is often called a "stepped-up" basis because the date-of-death value in a period of inflation and economic growth is usually higher than the decedent's own basis, but a "stepped-down" basis is also possible. In either event, the decedent's unrealized gain or loss (i.e., the difference between his basis and the value of the property at his death) is disregarded for income tax purposes. These rules are subject to important qualifications, which are discussed in detail in a later chapter.[7]

¶3.2 EXCLUSION OF GIFTS FROM GROSS INCOME

1. Introductory. Neither Congress nor the Treasury has ever promulgated an authoritative definition of the term "gift" as used in IRC §102(a), preferring instead to leave the task of interpreting the naked statutory language to the courts. In *CIR v. Duberstein,* decided in 1960, the Supreme Court declined to announce a comprehensive, all-purpose definition; and it summarized the decisional law as follows:

> We are of [the] opinion that the governing principles are necessarily general . . . and that the problem is one which, under the present statutory framework, does not lend itself to any more definitive statement that would produce a talisman for the solution of concrete cases. . . .
>
> The course of decision here makes it plain that the statute does not use the term "gift" in the common-law sense, but in a more colloquial sense. . . . A gift in the statutory sense, . . . proceeds from a "detached and disinterested generosity," . . . "out of affection, respect, admiration, charity or like impulses." . . . And in this regard, the most critical consideration, as the Court was agreed in the leading case here, is the transferor's "intention." . . . "What controls is the intention with which payment, however voluntary, has been made." [8]

---

[6] IRC §1014, discussed infra ¶23.4.

[7] Infra ¶¶23.3, 23.4.

[8] CIR v. Duberstein, 363 US 278, 283-286 (1960) (citations omitted). The earlier cases cited by the Supreme Court in its summary of the governing principles are Old Colony Trust Co. v. CIR, 279 US 716 (1929) (corporation's payment of income taxes on officer's salary was additional taxable compensation, not tax-free gift); Bogardus v. CIR, 302 US 34 (1937) (on selling stock, shareholders authorized distribution of about $600,000 as "a gift or honorarium" to sixty-four employees and other associates of their company in appreciation of their loyalty; held (four Justices dissenting), payments, stemming from "spontaneous generosity," were tax-free gifts); Robertson v. US, 343 US 711 (1952) (composer taxed on $25,000 award for best symphonic work by native-born composer; payment was "for services rendered" even though donor derived no economic benefit therefrom); and CIR v. LoBue, 351 US 243 (1956) (employee realized income on exercising stock option granted in recognition of his contribution to em-

The Court went on to comment on a series of principles or presumptions offered by the government in support of its proposed test:

> We think, to the extent they are correct, that these propositions are not principles of law but rather maxims of experience . . . Some of them simply represent truisms . . . Others are overstatements of possible evidentiary inferences relevant to a factual determination on the totality of circumstances in the case . . . But these inferences cannot be stated in absolute terms. . . . The taxing statute does not make nondeductibility by the transferor a condition on the "gift" exclusion;[9] nor does it draw any distinction, in terms, between transfers by corporations and individuals, as to the availability of the "gift" exclusion to the transferee. The conclusion whether a transfer amounts to a "gift" is one that must be reached on considerations of all the factors.[10]

The Court's concern with "all the factors" resulted in its placing great weight on the conclusions of the trial court and narrowing the range of appellate review:

> The nontechnical nature of the statutory standard, the close relationship of it to the data of practical human experience, and the multiplicity of relevant factual elements, with their various combinations, creating the necessity of ascribing the proper force to each, confirm us in our conclusion that primary weight in this area must be given to the conclusions of the trier of fact.[11]

Finally, the Court applied these principles to the facts of the two cases under review. In *Duberstein* itself, the Tax Court held that a Cadillac automobile received by the taxpayer from a businessman to whom he had occasionally given the names of potential customers was not a tax-free gift under IRC §102(a), even though the taxpayer insisted that the transferor "owed him [nothing]" and the latter said that the car was "a present." The Tax Court's judgment had been reversed by the court of appeals, but it was reinstated by the Supreme Court:

---

ployer's success—"none of the earmarks of a gift" were present, and "company was not giving something away for nothing").

[9] In 1960, when *Duberstein* was decided, the Code did not connect the transferor's right to deduct the payment with the transferee's right to exclude it from gross income as a gift. In 1962, however, IRC §274(b) was enacted, limiting the transferor's deduction for certain "business gifts" to $25 for any single donee during a taxable year. The treatment of the transferor under IRC §274(b) follows from the treatment of the transferee, however, not vice versa; see infra ¶9.4.

[10] CIR v. Duberstein, supra note 8, at 287-288.

[11] Id. at 289-291.

> [I]t cannot be said that the conclusion of the Tax Court was "clearly erroneous." It seems to us plain that as trier of the facts it was warranted in concluding that despite the characterization of the transfer of the Cadillac by the parties and the absence of any obligation, even of a moral nature, to make it, it was at bottom a recompense for Duberstein's past services, or an inducement for him to be of further service in the future.[12]

The Court had more difficulty with a companion case *(Stanton v. United States),* decided at the same time, which involved the employee of a church's real estate subsidiary who received a "gratuity" of $20,000 on resigning to enter business for himself. The trial court held that the transfer was a "gift," but the court of appeals reversed, noting that there was "no evidence that personal affection enter[ed] into the payment." The appellate court also noted that the resolution authorizing the payment required the employee to release any claim against the employer for pension and retirement benefits, even though there was undisputed testimony that this proviso reflected an abundance of caution because the employee had no such rights.[13] A majority of the Supreme Court voted to remand the case to the trial court for further findings, because the simple conclusion that the transfer was a "gift" made it impossible to determine whether the trial court had applied the proper legal standards to the facts. On remand, the district court made detailed findings of fact, again concluding that the payment was a gift, and its judgment was affirmed on appeal on the ground that the findings were not clearly erroneous.[14]

As the foregoing extracts from the *Duberstein* case suggest, the common-law meaning of the term "gift" has not played a significant role in judicial interpretations of IRC §102(a). In point of fact, the common-law elements of an effective gift (donative intent, delivery, and acceptance),[15] though ordinarily present in transfers that satisfy IRC §102(a), are rarely at issue in the disputed cases.

In addition to holding that IRC §102(a) does not use the term "gift" in its common-law sense, the courts have held that the statutory term does not necessarily have the same meaning as it has for federal estate and gift tax

---

[12] Id. at 291-292.

[13] Stanton v. US, 268 F.2d 727 (2d Cir. 1959), vacated and remanded, 363 US 278 (1960).

[14] Stanton v. US, 186 F. Supp. 393 (E.D.N.Y. 1960), aff'd per curiam, 287 F.2d 876, 877 (2d Cir. 1961). Compare Ruestow v. CIR, ¶78,147 P-H Memo TC (1978) (severance pay taxable where payment was in part motivated by employer's desire to retain employee's goodwill and to create impression that it was a good firm to work for).

[15] See 7 Powell, The Law of Real Property ¶971A (Rohan, rev. ed. 1976); Edson v. Lucas, 40 F.2d 398 (8th Cir. 1930).

purposes. This inspired Judge Jerome N. Frank to suggest that the terms "gift," "gaft," and "geft" might be used to denote the separate income, gift, and estate tax usages.[16]

Turning now from the general principles governing interpretation of the term "gift" as used in IRC §102(a) to the litigated cases, we find that the overwhelming bulk of disputes is concentrated in a few areas.

2. Tips. For many years the Treasury regulations have provided that tips (including a professor's honoraria and a clergyman's marriage fees) must be included in gross income, and the courts have sustained this rule.[17] Most disputes in this area involve the validity of estimates by the Internal Revenue Service of the amounts received by persons failing to keep accurate records of their receipts.[18]

Recipients of tips almost always regard them as a normal if not indispensable component of their compensation, but the emphasis in the *Duberstein* case on the intention of the *transferor* suggests that a tip *could* qualify as a tax-free gift on proof that the patron was motivated by "detached and disinterested generosity" or similar impulses rather than by a desire to pay for services or avoid an embarrassing insult.[19] In practice, however, taxpayers in industries where tips are customary have rarely endeavored to divide their receipts between taxable tips and tax-free gifts, probably in tacit acknowledgment that pure generosity is seldom encountered in this setting and, even when it occurs, is difficult to prove.[20]

If the link between the parties is not the rendition of services by one to the other in a context normally calling for tips, there is a stronger case for excluding the payment under IRC §102(a). If the payments are not made to elicit or reward special treatment or to avoid embarrassment, a test that focuses on the attitude of the payor tends to weight the scales in favor of tax-free gifts; on the other hand, if the recipient views the receipts as supplemental compensation, though from a sporadic source, this tends to undermine

---

[16] See Farid-Es-Sultaneh v. CIR, 160 F.2d 812 (2d Cir. 1947) (concerned with "gift" as used by IRC §1015, but presumably same approach would apply to IRC §102); CIR v. Beck's Est., 129 F.2d 243 (2d Cir. 1942) ("gift," "gaft," and "geft").

[17] Treas. Regs. §1.61-2(a)(1); Roberts v. CIR, 176 F.2d 221 (9th Cir. 1949).

[18] See infra ¶37.1 (indirect methods of computing income).

[19] See US v. McCormick, 67 F.2d 867 (2d Cir. 1933), cert. denied, 291 US 662 (1934) (tax evasion conviction of city clerk for failing to report "contributions" by bridegrooms wanting to obtain marriage certificates promptly and without embarrassment; some payments "were practically extorted"); see also Roberts v. CIR, supra note 17 (history of tipping; "there is an element of compulsion in tipping").

[20] But see Johnson v. CIR, ¶72,180 P-H Memo TC (1972) (transfer from elderly person to nurse was gift, excludable under IRC §102); see also Johnson v. CIR, 48 TC 636 (1967) (Acq.) (transfers by an old but alert rancher to employees were gifts).

their characterization as gifts.[21] The same tension is characteristic of birthday and Christmas "gifts" received by entertainers and other public personalities from their fans.[22] In some situations it may be possible to classify the patrons by motive, treating some as generous donors of tax-free gifts and the others as customers paying for services.[23]

3. Payments to Retired Employees. The judicial response has been divided with respect to "in appreciation" payments to employees at or after retirement—payments that would not have been made except for the employee's faithful services, but that are often also motivated by personal affection and esteem. In the leading case of *Bogardus v. CIR,* involving bonuses paid by the acquiring corporation in a reorganization to sixty-four former and current employees of the acquired corporation in gratitude for their aid in building up the business, a majority of the Supreme Court held that the payments were excludable from gross income because they were neither intended to compensate for past or future services nor paid under legal or other compulsion, but stemmed instead from "spontaneous generosity." [24]

Since *Duberstein,* the courts have focused on the employer's intent; but there have been few "in appreciation" cases, perhaps because IRC §274(b) ordinarily limits the payor's deduction to a maximum of $25 if a business gift is excludable from the recipient's income.[25] Since this restriction is usually of no concern to tax-exempt organizations, however, "in appreciation" cases continue to arise in this sector.[26]

---

[21] See Olk v. US, 536 F.2d 876 (9th Cir.), cert. denied, 429 US 920 (1976) ("tokes" given by successful gamblers to casino dealers, who are forbidden to show favoritism, nevertheless are taxable because "contributed by those with whom the taxpayers have some personal or functional contact in the course of performance of . . . services").

[22] See Webber v. CIR, 219 F.2d 834 (10th Cir. 1955) (radio minister taxed on amounts received in response to solicitation; although amounts were larger on his birthday and wedding anniversary, there was "no evidence tending to show that the contributions were referred to [by the contributors] as gifts; or that any of the contributors knew the petitioners personally or had any personal relationship with them which would form the basis for personal gifts as distinguished from contributions to the perpetuation of the programs which the contributors enjoyed and desired to support financially").

[23] Kralstein v. CIR, 38 TC 810 (1962) (Acq.) (20 percent of amount received at testimonial dinner determined to be tax-free gifts).

[24] Bogardus v. CIR, supra note 8.

[25] See Brimm v. CIR, ¶68,231 P-H Memo TC (1968) (payment by school on ceasing operations "in appreciation and recognition of [professor's] past services and achievements"; held, excludable); for taxable payments, see Rev. Rul. 76-516, 1976-2 CB 24 (payments to retired volunteer firemen or widows). For IRC §274(b) (deduction for business gifts limited to $25 per donee), see infra ¶9.4.

[26] See, e.g., Sweeney's Est. v. CIR, ¶79,387 P-H Memo TC (1979) (retired physician-founder taxable on amounts received from camp for diabetic children, although

4. Employee Death Benefits. Upon the death of an employee, employers sometimes pay death benefits to the decedent's surviving spouse and children; and, as in the case of "in appreciation" transfers, these payments may reflect personal affection but simultaneously serve to acknowledge the employee's services. Before *CIR v. Duberstein,* death benefits were usually excluded from gross income as gifts under IRC §102(a).[27] In *Hellstrom's Estate v. CIR,* a leading pre-*Duberstein* case, for example, the court concluded that the corporate employer's "principal motive" in paying benefits to a deceased employee's widow was a "desire to do an act of kindness" for her:

> [T]he payment was made to petitioner and not to her husband's estate; . . . there was no obligation on the part of the corporation to pay any additional compensation to petitioner's husband; it derived no benefit from the payment; petitioner performed no services for the corporation and . . . those of her husband had been fully compensated for.[28]

After *Duberstein* the Tax Court, concluding that the Supreme Court had adopted a more restrictive construction of the term "gift," made "an abrupt swerve"[29] toward taxability, while the federal district courts, believing that *Hellstrom* was consistent with *Duberstein,* continued to apply it.[30] Of particular importance to closely held corporations, however, is the possibility that, when charity begins at home by payments to persons owning a controlling block of stock, the transaction may be treated as a constructive dividend.[31]

Since death benefits paid to a deceased employee's beneficiaries or estate are excludable from the recipient's gross income under IRC §101(b) up to $5,000,[32] the protection accorded to "gifts" by IRC §102(a) is needed only for amounts in excess of $5,000. But if the recipient successfully relies on IRC

---

directors asserted that payments were authorized not to compensate past services, but "to show good will, esteem or kindness."); Rev. Rul. 55-422, 1955-1 CB 14 (payments by congregations to retiring clergymen excluded from income if not made pursuant to agreement; if the recipient does not undertake to perform future services; if there was a close personal relationship; if the amount paid reflected the congregation's financial position and recipient's needs; and if the recipient had been adequately compensated in the past); but see Perkins v. CIR, 34 TC 117 (1960) (payments to retired minister by a conference of churches to which several congregations contributed; requirements of Rev. Rul. 55-442 not met).

[27] See I.T. 3329, 1939-2 CB 153, modified by I.T. 4027, 1950-2 CB 9.

[28] Hellstrom's Est. v. CIR, 24 TC 916, 920 (1955).

[29] Carter's Est. v. CIR, 453 F.2d 61, 65 (2d Cir. 1971); see also Jensen v. US, 511 F.2d 265 (5th Cir. 1975), commenting that the five factors listed in *Hellstrom* and reiterated in Poyner v. CIR, 301 F.2d 287 (4th Cir. 1962), are neither the only relevant factors in determining whether a transfer is a gift nor of equal relevance in all cases.

[30] See Carter's Est. v. CIR, supra note 29, at 66-67, citing cases.

[31] Poyner v. CIR, supra note 29.

[32] For IRC §101(b), see infra ¶4.6.

§102(a) to exclude the excess over $5,000, the employer is denied a deduction by IRC §274(b), disallowing deductions for business gifts in excess of $25 annually per payee.[33] Since the employer will often derive a larger tax benefit from a deduction than the tax cost to the recipient of including the same amount in gross income, the employer may well fix the amount to be paid on the assumption that it will be deductible and then buttress its claim for a deduction by explicitly characterizing the payment as additional compensation.[34]

5. Employer, Governmental, and Institutional Charity. An employer's charitable aid to its employees, like "in appreciation" gifts and death benefits, may manifest a combination of motives. While expressing concern for its employees' welfare, the employer may expect improved productivity and morale. For their part, the employees may view benefits as a pure manifestation of affection, as merely part of their compensatory package, or as a mixture of the two. Against this background, the IRS has promulgated a "no income if you can eat it or drink it" doctrine.[35] In addition to acknowledging that the employer can act as Santa Claus, the IRS has ruled that amounts contributed by an employer for the rehabilitation of employees suffering personal injuries or property damage as the result of a tornado do not constitute taxable income to the employees if the payments are measured by need rather than by services rendered or length of service.[36]

If, instead of receiving benefits from their employer in an aura of good feeling, the employees are assisted through difficult days by strike benefits paid by their union, the tax status of the payments depends on the relative weight of imponderables similar to those determining whether payments by the employer are taxable. On the one hand, unions pay benefits to their members (and sometimes to nonmembers) to insure solidarity and reduce defections from the cause—objectives that point toward taxability;[37] on the other hand, the motivation may be compassion, which is a hallmark of a tax-free gift.[38]

A broad range of governmental disbursements made "in the interest of the general welfare" has been excluded from gross income, including social

[33] Infra ¶9.4.

[34] Compare Carter's Est. v. CIR, supra note 29 (exclusion of death benefits from gross income), with Bank of Palm Beach & Trust Co. v. US, 476 F.2d 1343 (Ct. Cl. 1973) (deduction by *Carter* employer allowed for pre-IRC §274(b) year).

[35] Rev. Rul. 59-58, 1959-1 CB 17 (value of turkey, ham, or other item of merchandise of nominal value distributed by employer to employees at holiday times is not taxable).

[36] Rev. Rul. 131, 1953-2 CB 112.

[37] Colwell v. CIR, 64 TC 584, 587 (1975) (union's payments to nonmember honoring picket line, in amount based on wages, held includable in gross income).

[38] See US v. Kaiser, 363 US 299 (1960).

security benefits, disaster relief, and payments to families with low income or to persons who are elderly or disabled.[39] In a series of pre-1978 rulings, the IRS exempted federal and state unemployment benefits from tax, but held that private benefits paid under private plans are taxable to the extent they exceed the recipient's contributions.[40] Congress later reduced this disparity by enacting IRC §85, which now provides for a phaseout of the tax exemption accorded to federal and state unemployment benefits for taxpayers with adjusted gross income in excess of $12,000 or, if a joint return is filed, $18,000.

6. Intra-Family Transfers. Most tax advisers would probably say that a child's weekly allowance is a tax-free gift within the meaning of IRC §102(a);[41] but if a payment can qualify as a "gift" only if there is no "anticipated benefit," no return in the form of services rendered, and no "moral duty" to make the payment—the indicia endorsed by *Duberstein*— conscientious parents may have some difficulty in characterizing their payments as gifts within the meaning of IRC §102(a). Threats to reduce or stop an allowance if children neglect their domestic chores are common, and the payments often stem not from spontaneous generosity but from social if not moral compulsion—"Billy's parents give him *five* dollars a week, and he doesn't even have to wash the dishes!" In holding that tips to waiters are not tax-free gifts, the courts referred to the scowls and insults vented on patrons who leave nothing. A repetition of these transitory stigmata can be avoided by eating in a different restaurant; but parents who withdraw their child's allowance have no easy refuge from allegations of niggardly behavior. If, however, a revenue agent attempted to use the *Duberstein* criteria to deny an exclusion for children's allowances, it is almost certain that the courts would somehow or other bring them within the shelter of IRC §102(a).

There are other intra-family transfers that are regularly treated as tax-free even though the *Duberstein* criteria might be thought to deny "gift" status. For

---

[39] See Rev. Rul. 76-144, 1976-1 CB 17 (federal payments to needy victims of major disasters; payments are "from a general welfare fund in the interest of the general welfare"); Rev. Rul. 70-217, 1970-1 CB 12 (social security benefits); Rev. Rul. 73-87, 1973-1 CB 39 (federally funded anti-poverty program); Rev. Rul. 57-102, 1957-1 CB 26 (payment by state to blind person); Rev. Rul. 78-170, 1978-1 CB 24 (state-financed credits against winter energy bills of elderly low-income individuals).

[40] Compare Rev. Rul. 76-63, 1976-1 CB 14 (federal unemployment compensation exempt), with Rev. Rul. 71-70, 1971-1 CB 28 (union's payment of unemployment benefits to unemployed members taxable) and Rev. Rul. 59-9, 1959-1 CB 232 (unemployment benefits funded by recipients held gross income to extent of excess over recipient's contribution).

[41] If the child works in a parent's business, however, the compensation can qualify for deduction by the parent and is taxable to the child. See infra ¶¶30.2 (salaries to children), 30.4 (earnings of minor children).

example, a promise to pay a student's college tuition and living expenses on condition that the recipient maintains a specified scholastic average may be stimulated by affection, but it also exacts a quid pro quo and imposes a moral—in some situations a legal—duty to make the payment if the condition is satisfied.[42] Amounts paid by breadwinners to support their spouses and minor children are routinely excluded from the beneficiary's gross income even though they satisfy a legal obligation. Intra-family transfers of this type can be properly viewed as excludable by a higher authority than the language of IRC §102(a), viz., a basic presupposition—so obvious that it does not require explicit mention in the Code—that Congress never intended to tax them.[43]

The IRS has ruled that a wife is not required to include in income property received at the time of divorce in exchange for her surrender of dower rights.[44] It is likely that a wife who gave up her dower rights in exchange for stock pursuant to an antenuptial agreement would be accorded a comparable exclusion for the stock, since it was accepted by her in exchange for the dower rights she would otherwise have acquired on marriage.[45]

7. Payments for Companionship, Etc. Transfers of cash and property by a taxpayer to a companion or sexual partner have been classified in a few litigated cases as tax-free gifts or taxable compensation, depending on whether the recipient appears to be a beneficiary of generosity or a purveyor of services.[46] The increased frequency and social acceptability of informal alliances make it likely that financial arrangements between consenting adults will

---

[42] Cf. Robertson v. US, supra note 8, holding that a prize was taxable to the recipient even though the donor derived no economic benefit from the recipient's prizewinning entry; see also Smith v. CIR, ¶55,183 P-H Memo TC (1955), aff'd, 249 F.2d 218 (5th Cir. 1957) (holding enforceable parent's promise to transfer farmland to son for abandoning plans to play professional baseball, completing school, and endeavoring to develop the land).

[43] The Supreme Court asserted in CIR v. Glenshaw Glass Co., 348 US 426, 430 (1955), that Congress intended "to tax all gains except those specifically exempted [by statute]," but this statement is clearly too sweeping. See discussion at supra ¶1.8.

[44] Rev. Rul. 67-221, 1967-2 CB 63.

[45] See Farid-Es-Sultaneh v. CIR, supra note 16.

[46] See Pascarelli v. CIR, 55 TC 1082 (1971), aff'd without published opinion, 485 F.2d 681 (3d Cir. 1973) (male friend gave taxpayer large sums of money and a house, which they occupied for over twenty years, and she assisted him in business "with the same spirit of cooperation that would motivate a wife to strive to help her husband advance in his business"; held, tax-free gifts rather than income); Blevins v. CIR, ¶55,211 P-H Memo TC (1955), aff'd per curiam, 238 F.2d 621 (6th Cir. 1956) (payments of cash by taxpayer's male friend taxable, not gifts in contemplation of marriage; he was already married and not considering divorce). The exclusion of gifts from gross income presumably embraces recoveries in cases like Marvin v. Marvin, 18 Cal. 3d 660 (1976) (agreements between nonmarital partners enforced unless they rest on "unlawful meretricious considerations").

ordinarily be regarded as a sharing of resources, comparable to marital support, and that only blatant commercial traffic will be characterized as compensatory.

¶3.3 EXCLUSION OF INHERITED PROPERTY FROM GROSS INCOME

1. Bequest or Compensation for Services? The exclusion from gross income accorded since 1913 by IRC §102(a) to "gifts" also encompasses property acquired by "bequest, devise, or inheritance." This long-standing statutory parallelism between transfers during life and transfers at death is mirrored by the litigated cases; as is true of gifts, the principal source of dispute in the case of property acquired from a decedent is the shadowy borderline between the exercise of benevolence and the discharge of a moral or legal obligation.

As early as 1923, in its first pronouncement on the subject, the Supreme Court held in *United States v. Merriam* that testamentary bequests to the decedent's executors in lieu of commissions constituted tax-free bequests:

> The distinction to be drawn is between compensation fixed by will for services to be rendered by the executor and a legacy to one upon the implied condition that he shall clothe himself with the character of executor. In the former case he must perform the service to earn the compensation. In the latter case he need do no more than in good faith comply with the condition in order to receive the bequest.[47]

Although never overruled, the *Merriam* case has not inspired much judicial enthusiasm,[48] and it rests on an unpersuasive interpretation of the decedent's will. It is difficult to imagine why a decedent would want a specified person to "clothe himself with the character of executor" except to perform the customary fiduciary services, nor is it likely that such a person would be entitled to receive or retain the legacy if he promptly resigned, for he would not yet have cloaked himself "with the character of executor." In any event, it is clear that the executor is taxable on a purported bequest in lieu of statutory compensation if he is *required* to perform the services, and this condition would seem to be the normal expectation of testators leaving such bequests.

---

[47] US v. Merriam, 263 US 179, 187 (1923).

[48] See Bank of New York v. Helvering, 132 F.2d 773 (2d Cir. 1943) (legacy tax-free to the extent that it exceeded the statutory commissions; discontent with *Merriam* rationale expressed, but "if it is to be overruled, the Supreme Court, not we, must overrule it"); Wolder v. CIR, 493 F.2d 608 (2d Cir.), cert. denied, 419 US 828 (1974) (***Duberstein*** embodied "an entirely different viewpoint from *Merriam*" in interpreting the term "gift" in IRC §102(a)).

There is an even larger category of litigated cases that entails a comprehensive examination of facts that are often hard to reconstruct, where the issue is whether a legacy is a tax-free transfer under IRC §102(a) or belated compensation for services rendered by the legatee to the decedent during his life. If the decedent did not *agree* to leave anything by will to the beneficiary, a legacy ordinarily qualifies as a tax-free bequest; but if the bequest discharges a promise to reward the beneficiary, an exclusion under IRC §102(a) is inconsistent with the rationale of *Duberstein.*[49] The more vague and informal the understanding, the more it resembles a garden-variety bequest by a lonely testator who rewards a distant relative or friend providing solace in the form of personal attention in preference to close relatives who contented themselves with verbal professions of affection. If, however, the disputed amount was paid to satisfy a judgment or settle a claim against the estate by a taxpayer alleging that the decedent breached an agreement to leave him a legacy as compensation for services, the payment is invariably held to be taxable.[50]

2. Settlement of Will Contests. In *Lyeth v. Hoey,* the Supreme Court held that an amount received in settlement of a will contest was "acquired by . . . inheritance" within the meaning of IRC §102(a).[51] The Court held that the scope of this phrase was not determined by local characterizations, so that it was irrelevant that the taxpayer's rights were viewed as "contractual" rather than "testamentary" by local law; and that "bequest, devise, [and] inheritance" as used by Congress were "comprehensive terms embracing all acquisitions in the devolution of a decedent's estate." In effect, the Court held that, in applying IRC §102(a), property acquired in settlement of a claim should be treated as it would have been if the taxpayer's claim had been honored rather than disputed. A corollary of this "relation back" theory is that if the original claim would have generated taxable income had it been paid in due course (e.g., compensation for services), the amount paid to settle the claim is equally taxable.[52]

In *Lyeth v. Hoey* the taxpayer's status as an heir of the decedent was

---

[49] See Wolder v. CIR, 493 F.2d 608 (2d Cir.) cert. denied, 419 US 828 (1974) (bequest to decedent's attorney pursuant to formal agreement by which he agreed to render legal services without charge; held, taxable); Rev. Rul. 67-375, 1967-2 CB 60 (bequest pursuant to written agreement to care for decedent held taxable; "bequest" as used in IRC §102(a) "generally implies bounty, gift, or gratuity").

[50] See Cotnam v. CIR, 263 F.2d 119 (5th Cir. 1959) (judgment against intestate decedent's administrator based on oral contract to leave taxpayer one-fifth of his estate if she would serve as "attendant or friend"); Braddock v. US, 434 F.2d 631 (9th Cir. 1970) (oral agreement to leave entire estate in return for taxpayer's agreement to cook, clean, and help with decedent's farm work).

[51] Lyeth v. Hoey, 305 US 188 (1938).

[52] See Parker v. US, 573 F.2d 42 (Ct. Cl. 1978) (settlement of will contest allocated between claim for inheritance, which was excludable, and claim for income from inherited property, which was taxable).

conceded, but the same principle has been applied to a person whose right to take as an intestate successor was itself in doubt.[53] This approach makes it unnecessary to determine in the federal tax case whether the taxpayer was in fact an heir or legatee under a prior will, but the settlement among the concerned parties is ordinarily a sufficient guaranty that the claim was not wholly spurious.[54]

¶3.4 GIFTS AND BEQUESTS OF INCOME, REMAINDERS, AND OTHER DIVIDED INTERESTS

The exclusion of IRC §102(a) does not embrace the income from property acquired by gift, bequest, devise, or inheritance. This restriction, embodied in IRC §102(b)(1), prevents the permanent immunization of the investment income generated by family fortunes. The application of IRC §102(b)(1) in the case of most gifts and bequests of income-producing property is quite straightforward: The recipient is not taxed on receiving the property itself but must report the dividends, interest, rents, or other investment income generated by the property thereafter.

The distinction between donated property and the income from donated property is more complicated if the donor transfers the right to receive the income to one donee and a remainder interest in the property to a different donee. In *Irwin v. Gavit,* a landmark decision under pre-1942 law, a life tenant argued that the "property" that he acquired by inheritance was the right to collect the income and that his periodic receipts were therefore excludable from gross income.[55] Rejecting this interpretation of pre-1942 law, the Supreme Court said:

> The language quoted [the statutory predecessors of IRC §§102(a) and 102(b)(1), providing that gross income included "the income from, but not the value of, property acquired by gift, bequest, devise or descent]

---

[53] US v. Gavin, 159 F.2d 613 (9th Cir. 1947) (payment to person claiming as decedent's illegitimate child held tax-free, though claimant agreed to refrain from asserting her paternity and consented to probate decree finding against relationship).

[54] But see White v. Thomas, 116 F.2d 147 (5th Cir. 1940), cert. denied, 313 US 581 (1941), where a payment of $125,000 in settlement of a claim against executors and testamentary trustees was based on the decedent's alleged inter vivos gift to the claimant of a ranch that was then devised to the trustee by the decedent's will. The court implied that the taxpayer's claim was fraudulent ("a business venture in litigation") but also advanced a less tenable ground for denying an exclusion under IRC §102(a), viz., that the claim was settled for cash rather than for "a part of the very thing [the ranch] claimed."

[55] Irwin v. Gavit, 268 US 161 (1925). The issue in this case was complicated by the fact that trusts and estates were not taxed as separate entities during the tax years before the Court (1913-1915), with the result that their income was taxed to no one if the beneficiaries were exempted.

> assumes the gift of a corpus and contrasts it with the income arising from it, but was not intended to exempt income properly so-called simply because of a severance between it and the principal fund.[56]

Although *Irwin v. Gavit* reached its conclusion by interpreting what is now IRC §102(b)(1), in 1942, for the sake of clarity, Congress gave explicit statutory sanction to this interpretation by enacting what is now IRC §102(b)(2).

Under *Irwin v. Gavit* and IRC §102(b)(2), when the ownership of income-producing property is divided between a life tenant and remainderman, the entire benefit of the statutory exclusion inures to the benefit of the remainderman, and the life tenant is taxed in full on his receipts.[57] Congress might, in the alternative, have divided the exclusion between the life tenant and the remainderman. For example, if the transferred property has an adjusted basis and fair market value of $100,000 and the life tenant, *A,* is a thirty-year-old male, his life estate is worth about $87,000 and *B*'s remainder about $13,000.[58] These interests could be exempted from tax, with the excess over them taxed as income, by (a) allowing *A* to deduct an appropriate portion of $87,000 each year from the income actually received and (b) requiring *B* to report the difference between $13,000 and the adjusted basis of the transferred property as income, either when his remainder vests or in aliquot portions in the preceding years. Under this alternative approach, the aggregate amount taxed would be the same as under *Irwin v. Gavit,* but the tax burden would be divided between *A* and *B* instead of being imposed solely on *A.* By codifying *Irwin v. Gavit,* however, Congress assigned the entire benefit of the exclusion to *B,* even though the life tenant is usually the primary object of the donor's or testator's bounty.

Because the amounts received by the taxpayer in *Irwin v. Gavit* were explicitly payable from trust income, the Court was not required to pass on the status of amounts payable without regard to the amount of income generated by the transferred property. In 1942 Congress enacted the second sentence of IRC §102(b), which denies the exclusion to periodic payments if and to the extent that they are paid, credited, or distributed from income. Lump-sum payments, however, are distinguished from amounts that are to be paid "at intervals" and are excludable from gross income." [59]

The final sentence of IRC §102(b), enacted in 1954, serves to indicate that

---

[56] Irwin v. Gavit, supra note 55, at 167.

[57] This treatment of the life tenant is made more explicit by IRC §273, denying life tenants the right to amortize the value of the life estate, and by IRC §1001(e), denying them any basis on a sale of the interest except in conjunction with a sale by the remainderman. See infra ¶23.7.

[58] For allocation between life tenants and remaindermen in the case of decedents dying after December 31, 1970, see Treas. Regs. §20.2031-10(f), Tables A(1) (male), A(2) (female).

[59] Lindau v. CIR, 21 TC 911 (1954) (Acq.).

Subchapter J (relating to trusts and estates) takes precedence over IRC §102, so that amounts included in the gross income of a beneficiary of a trust or estate under IRC §652, §662 or §667 cannot be excluded under IRC §102.[60]

¶3.5 PRIZES AND AWARDS

1. Introductory. Under IRC §74, prizes and awards are includable in gross income unless the amount (a) is received in recognition of religious, charitable, or similar meritorious achievement, provided the recipient is selected without action on his part and is not required to render substantial future services, or (b) constitutes a tax-exempt scholarship or fellowship grant under IRC §117.[61] Enacted in 1954 to eliminate "the confusion resulting from certain court decisions," [62] IRC §74 was the first statutory provision to deal explicitly with this subject. Before 1954 the only basis for exclusion was the statutory predecessor of IRC §102, relating to gifts,[63] which the Supreme Court in *Robertson v. United States* held was not applicable to a taxpayer winning a cash award for the best symphonic work submitted in a contest established by an individual philanthropist to encourage young composers.[64]

Because IRC §74(a) provides that prizes and awards are includable in gross income unless exempted by IRC §74(b) or §117, it impliedly prevents prizes from being treated as tax-free gifts under IRC §102, even if the payment otherwise satisfies the latter provision's requirements and would have been an excludable gift under pre-1954 law. But IRC §102 may apply in some borderline situations notwithstanding the donor's use of the term "prize or award." [65]

---

[60] See Treas. Regs. §1.102-1(d).

[61] For IRC §117, see infra ¶3.6; see also Rev. Rul. 66-241, 1966-2 CB 40 (when an award constitutes a scholarship, IRC §117 applies rather than §74).

[62] S. Rep. No. 1622, 83d Cong., 2d Sess. 13, 178-179 (1954).

[63] See Rev. Rul. 54-110, 1954-1 CB 28 (Pulitzer prize in recognition of past achievement or present abilities is a nontaxable gift; it does not discharge a contractual obligation or constitute payment for services rendered).

[64] Robertson v. US, 343 US 711 (1952).

[65] See, e.g., IRC §274(b)(1)(C), which implies that an "award" by an employer to an employee for safety achievement could qualify as a tax-free gift under IRC §102. In Simmons v. US, 308 F.2d 160 (4th Cir. 1962), the court concluded that the prize under examination was not within the exclusion of IRC §74(b); but before holding that it was taxable under IRC §74(a), the court went on to consider (and to reject) the taxpayer's argument that it could be considered a tax-free gift under IRC §102.

2. Awards for Meritorious Achievement. The general rule of IRC §74(a) is subject to the exception of IRC §74(b), excluding prizes and awards from gross income if granted "primarily in recognition of religious, charitable, scientific, educational, artistic, literary, or civic achievement." The regulations interpret this exception as satisfied primarily by awards for past achievement, as in the case of the Nobel and Pulitzer prizes.[66] The meritorious achievement standard of IRC §74(b) disqualifies many types of receipt. Attempts to stretch the terms "artistic" and "civic" to encompass athletic achievement have failed; the term "civic" has been held to imply "positive action, exemplary, unselfish, and broadly advantageous to the community."[67]

An award for educational, civic, or other meritorious achievement is not disqualified under IRC §74(b) by the fact that the prizewinner's accomplishments occurred in the course of employment, provided the grantor is not the employer.[68] The statute itself does not explicitly disqualify payments by the employer, but the regulations do; and this interpretation is supported by the legislative history of IRC §74.[69] A related point is that the award must be made "primarily" in recognition of the taxpayer's achievement.[70]

In addition to meritorious achievement, the taxpayer must display the virtue of humility, or at least patience, since a prize is exempt under IRC §74(b) only if the recipient "was selected without any action on his part to enter the contest or proceeding." If the entrant is not *too* pushy, however, the award can qualify under an IRS ruling permitting candidates who are selected in a preliminary screening without action on their part to appear for a personal interview or fill out a biographical form before the final selection occurs.[71]

---

[66] Treas. Regs. §1.74-1(b); S. Rep. No. 1622, supra note 62, which also refers to "past" achievement and to the Nobel and Pulitzer prizes.

[67] Simmons v. US, supra note 65 (fisherman taxed on $25,000 prize for catching banded fish in Third Annual American Beer Fishing Derby; IRC §74(b) requires "genuinely meritorious achievement"); Wills v. CIR, 411 F.2d 537 (9th Cir. 1969) (automobile awarded to "most popular Dodger" of 1962 baseball season).

[68] See Rev. Rul. 61-92, 1961-1 CB 11 (Rockefeller Public Service Award to outstanding federal employees).

[69] Treas. Regs. §1.74-1(a); S. Rep. No. 1622, supra note 62, at 179 (IRC §74(b) not intended to exempt prizes from employer to employee in "recognition of some achievement in connection with his employment, such as having the largest sales record or best production record during a certain period"); but see supra note 65 for the possibility that some employer-employee awards may qualify as tax-free gifts under IRC §102.

[70] Rogallo v. US, 475 F.2d 1 (4th Cir. 1973) (award to inventor on condition that rights in discovery be assigned to grantor not excludable).

[71] Rev. Rul. 57-67, 1957-1 CB 33 (award to students for academic and citizenship achievement held exempt; students selected by their high school faculties and judged on regional basis after filling out forms and appearing for personal interviews); but see Rev. Rul. 72-163, 1972-1 CB 26 (writer invited to apply for grant; held, submission of resumé and summary of project is excessive "action on his part").

Finally, prizes cannot be excluded from income if they are conditioned on the recipient's rendition of substantial future services.[72] This restriction, however, does not preclude a personal appearance to accept an award.[73]

When a taxable prize is paid in goods or services rather than money, the regulations provide that it is to be valued at its fair market value.[74] The amount taxable to the winner should not be less than he could realize on a sale,[75] even if the grantor purchased it for less than that amount because it was entitled to a dealer or quantity discount. If the taxpayer must either use the prize personally or forfeit it (e.g., travel accommodations), the inability to convert it into cash does not negate a fair market value; but a substantial discount from the retail price or fair market value of identical transferable property may be warranted, provided the prize does not take the place of goods or services that the taxpayer would have purchased in any event.[76] Moreover, if push comes to shove, a taxpayer who finds the prize unappealing—a lifetime supply of Fig Newtons or a set of plastic dwarfs for the front lawn—and is unwilling to run the valuation gauntlet can decline to accept the award and thereby avoid the risk of a tax assessment exceeding his personal estimate of the prize's worth.[77]

In order to moderate the impact of tax progression on recipients, who almost always use the cash receipts and disbursements method of reporting income, large cash awards (e.g., in lotteries) are sometimes payable in installments. Under the usual principles of cash-basis tax accounting, a stretch-out of payments is ordinarily effective, unless the obligor's promise to pay is buttressed by an escrow or a similar security arrangement or is evidenced by negotiable promissory notes.[78]

---

[72] Rev. Rul. 68-20, 1968-1 CB 55 (winner of beauty contest required to participate in pageant, pose for photographs and engage in personal appearances; the ruling might have questioned whether demonstration of "talent, charm, and grooming" constitutes "artistic" or "civic" achievement); see also Mueller v. CIR, 338 F.2d 1015 (1st Cir. 1964) (awards to scientists expected to work in tax-exempt grantor institute's laboratory; held, taxable).

[73] Rev. Rul. 58-89, 1958-1 CB 40.

[74] Treas. Regs. §1.74-1(a)(2).

[75] McCoy v. CIR, 38 TC 841, 844 (1962) (Acq.) (taxpayer disposed of car received as a prize for $3,600 after driving it from place of award to his home; the court attributed $300 of depreciation to this use of the car, concluding that its value was $3,900 when received despite the fact that the grantor had paid $4,500 for it).

[76] See Turner v. CIR, ¶54,142 P-H Memo TC (1954) (steamship tickets with retail value of $2,200 used by taxpayer; held, under pre-1954 law, $1,400 taxable).

[77] Rev. Rul. 57-374, 1957-2 CB 69 (no tax when prizewinner refused to accept an all-expense-paid trip).

[78] See Rev. Rul. 62-74, 1962-1 CB 68 (winner taxed on discounted value of right to receive prize in installments, where full amount was deposited in escrow account by sponsor); Rev. Rul. 67-203, 1967-1 CB 105 (minor who won Irish Sweepstakes must

¶3.6 SCHOLARSHIPS AND FELLOWSHIPS

1. Introductory. Section 117 excludes scholarships and fellowships (including the value of contributed services and accommodations) from gross income, subject to certain conditions; if the recipient is not a candidate for a degree, for example, the exclusion is limited to $300 for each month of the grant up to a lifetime maximum of thirty-six months. Amounts received and expended for travel, research, clerical help, or equipment are also excluded from income if the expenses are incident to the scholarship or fellowship.[79] Scholarships and fellowships that do not qualify for exclusion under IRC §117 are taxable by virtue of IRC §74(a).[80]

The regulations state flatly that the taxability of scholarships and fellowships is governed solely by IRC §117, so that a grant exceeding the dollar limit of IRC §117(b) cannot qualify for full exemption under the "meritorious achievement" rule of IRC §74(b), presumably on the theory that grantees of fellowships are expected to pursue their studies and that this constitutes disqualifying "substantial future services" within the meaning of IRC §74(b).[81]

Prior to the enactment of IRC §117 no statutory provision explicitly governed the tax treatment of scholarships and fellowships, and they could be excluded from income only if they constituted "property acquired by gift" within the meaning of the statutory predecessor of IRC §102.[82] In 1954 Congress enacted IRC §§74 and 117, thereby ousting IRC §102 (relating to gifts) from jurisdiction over scholarships and fellowships, except for grants by individuals who are stimulated by family or philanthropic motives.[83]

The 1954 legislative committee reports observe that pre-1954 law failed to provide a "clear-cut method of distinguishing between taxable and nontaxable grants [so that] the tax status of these grants presently must be decided on a case-by-case method"; but the reports supply little justification for the new statutory rules (which, in application, have proved no more clear than the

---

report present value of winnings deposited with Irish court, to be held until he comes of age); for cash basis accounting, see infra ¶35.2.

[79] For the right of professors and other scholars to deduct unreimbursed research expenses as business expenses, see infra ¶¶8.3, 9.12.

[80] For IRC §74, see supra ¶3.5.

[81] Treas. Regs. §1.117-1(a).

[82] See I.T. 4056, 1951-2 CB 8 (grant for an individual's education, no services being rendered in consideration therefor, is a tax-free gift), declared obsolete by Rev. Rul. 69-43, 1969-1 CB 310.

[83] See Treas. Regs. §§1.117-3(a) and 1.117-3(c) ("scholarship" and "fellowship grant" defined to exclude amounts paid *by an individual* to aid a relative, friend, or other individual in pursuing his studies or research "where the grantor is motivated by family or philanthropic considerations").

pre-1954 rules), nor do they explain why any scholarships and fellowships should be excluded from income.

When scholarship and fellowship awards to candidates for degrees are restricted to applicants demonstrating financial need, the exclusion provided by IRC §117 is often irrelevant since there would be no tax liability in any event. Moreover, so long as charitable benefactions to nonstudents are excluded from income under IRC §102, there is little reason not to extend the same tax treatment to recipients of similar institutional generosity who are required to stay in school to qualify for the grant. But some grants, especially to persons who are not candidates for degrees, are not based on financial need, so that the tax exemption of current law is a benefit that falls on rich and poor alike, with a value that varies with the recipient's marginal rate of tax. If IRC §117 grows out of a legislative intent to foster study and research, it is not a very rational way of achieving this objective.

2. The Meaning of "Scholarship" and "Fellowship Grant." When it enacted IRC §117, Congress did not supply a statutory definition of the terms "scholarship" and "fellowship grant." In the regulations, "scholarship" is defined as an amount paid or allowed to (or for the benefit of) a student, whether an undergraduate or graduate, to aid him in the pursuit of his studies; a "fellowship grant" is a similar amount to aid an individual in the pursuit of study or research.[84] Both terms include not only cash but also the value of services and accommodations (e.g., room, board, and laundry service), tuition and other fees furnished or remitted to the grantee, and family allowances.[85]

Problems arise with respect to grants by business, nonprofit, and governmental organizations to students engaged in vocational, graduate, and professional training if they (a) are required or expected to accept or resume employment with the grantor or (b) render personal services (e.g., as hospital interns or apprentice teachers) that advance their educational objectives and simultaneously relieve the grantor of the expense of hiring others to perform the same tasks.[86] Rather than leave these issues wholly to the courts, the Treasury staked out a position in the regulations, viz., (1) that amounts representing "compensation for past, present, or future employment services or . . . payment for services which are subject to the direction or supervision of the grantor"

[84] Treas. Regs. §§1.117-3(a), 1.117-3(c).

[85] See Rev. Rul. 77-263, 1977-2 CB 47 (athletic scholarship held excludable under IRC §117 where limited to value of tuition and fees, room and board, and books and supplies necessary for studies, less value of any other scholarship received and any wages earned during school year).

[86] Employment is mentioned in IRC §117(b)(1), but this provision does little to resolve the problem raised in the text.

cannot qualify as scholarships or fellowships even though paid to enable the grantee to pursue his studies or research, and (2) that a parallel disqualification applies if the grantee's studies or research are "primarily for the benefit of the grantor." [87]

In line with the first of these interpretations, the Tax Court has held that compensation for services does not become a scholarship or fellowship simply because the recipient's objective is professional training.[88] The second disqualifying condition set out in the regulations (study or research for the grantor's benefit) is mitigated by two minor concessions: (a) It does not apply if the "primary purpose" of the studies or research is to further the training of the recipient in his individual capacity, provided the amount paid does not represent compensation or payment for his services;[89] and (b) incidental benefits to the grantor are not fatal, nor is a requirement that the grantee submit progress reports to the grantor.

Although the two disqualifying conditions described above would clearly have been justifiable under pre-1954 law, when an exclusion was warranted only if the scholarship or fellowship was a "gift" reflecting the grantor's generosity, taxpayers have argued that they are inconsistent with the 1954 legislation. This attack on the validity of the regulations was rejected by the Supreme Court in 1969, when it held in *Bingler v. Johnson* that a grant by a business corporation to enable an employee to work on a doctoral dissertation, on condition that he return to the company's employ at the end of a leave of absence, was not a "scholarship" within the meaning of IRC §117(a).[90] Acknowledging that the legislative history was not clear, the Court concluded that the regulations constituted a reasonable contemporaneous interpretation of the legislative statutory language:

> Here, the definitions supplied by the Regulation clearly are prima facie proper, comporting as they do with the ordinary understanding of "scholarships" and "fellowships" as relatively disinterested, "no-strings" educational grants, with no requirement of any substantial *quid pro quo* from the recipients. . . . The thrust of the provision [of the regulations] dealing with compensation is that bargained-for payments, given only as a *quo* in return for the *quid* of services rendered—whether past, present, or future—should not be excludable from income as "scholarship" funds.[91]

In the years since *Bingler v. Johnson* was decided, few grants by employers

---

[87] Treas. Regs. §1.117-4(c).

[88] Proskey v. CIR, 51 TC 918, 924-925 (1969).

[89] See Rev. Rul. 75-280, 1975-2 CB 47.

[90] Bingler v. Johnson, 394 US 741 (1969).

[91] Id. at 749, 757-758.

to current or prospective employees have been able to avoid the stigma of being a "quo" for past, present, or future services, except by meeting the test of IRC §117(b)(1) (payments for services required of all candidates for the same degree), discussed below.[92] In many situations the disqualification results from the performance of services that, while advancing the taxpayer's educational objective, also relieve the grantor of the expense of hiring others to perform the same tasks. In other situations, the grantee's studies or research do not enable the grantor to reduce its staff or avoid hiring other persons, but—like the grant in *Bingler v. Johnson*—serve to upgrade the skills or increase the supply of qualified persons who are required or expected to work for the grantor. The quid pro quo test of *Bingler v. Johnson* can apply to trainees in any occupation, but the most persistent losers have been hospital interns and residents, nurses, and teachers.[93] A limited offset to the dismal record racked up by these groups in the litigated cases was provided by Congress in 1976 and 1978, however, in the form of an exclusion from gross income when student loans are cancelled for the benefit of physicians, nurses, and teachers who work in specified geographical areas, such as rural communities and low-income urban areas with a shortage of trained personnel.[94]

Although IRC §117 was enacted on the theory that it would provide clear-cut criteria for determining the excludability of educational grants, the cases and revenue rulings have employed a case-by-case approach, examining all the circumstances under which the grant was made.[95] Where research or teaching assistantships are involved, the key factors include the extent of faculty supervision, freedom of the grantee to pursue individual goals, consid-

---

[92] Congress, however, looks after its federal flock. Section 117(c), enacted in 1980, exalts federal employment above more common pursuits by providing that amounts received under a federal program that would qualify for exclusion but for the fact that future federal employment is required are excludable despite this condition, to the extent used for qualified tuition and related expenses (as defined).

[93] See Adams v. CIR, 71 TC 477 (1978) (hospital intern taxed; divided court); Burstein v. US, 43 AFTR2d 1132 (Ct. Cl. Trial Judge 1979) (not officially reported) (hospital residents allowed to exclude grants received from hospital that separated salaries from grants—a rare exception to a "near unanimous group" of over fifty cases denying exclusion to hospital residents), and cases there cited; Logan v. US, 518 F.2d 143 (6th Cir. 1975) (teaching assistant); Rev. Rul. 70-220, 1970-1 CB 26 (nurses and sanitarians).

[94] See Rev. Rul. 73-256, 1973-1 CB 56, as modified by Rev. Rul. 74-540, 1974-2 CB 38 (cancellation of student loan when debtor works for specified period in rural or other deprived area, etc., constitutes taxable quid pro quo, not a tax-free scholarship). To encourage doctors and others to practice in areas with a shortage of trained personnel, Section 2117 of the Tax Reform Act of 1976 and Section 162 of the Revenue Act of 1978 exempt certain cancellations before January 1, 1983 from inclusion in gross income.

[95] See, e.g., Zolany v. CIR, 49 TC 389, 395 (1968) ("each case must turn upon its own particular facts and circumstances"); Rev. Rul. 72-263, 1972-1 CB 40.

eration of financial need in making grants, existence of equivalent research or teaching requirements for all similarly situated students, the university's treatment of the grant, the receipt of degree-related academic credit, and the extent to which the student's activities are tied to the needs of the university. When studies are subsidized by a business employer, however, the grants are almost always income to the employee, save in extraordinary circumstances where the possible benefits to the employer are nominal or if IRC §127, relating to employer-financed educational assistance programs for their employees, is applicable.[96]

When funds are provided by one entity to another (e.g., a grant by a federal agency to a tax-exempt hospital), the tax recipient's claim to an exclusion is likely to be disallowed if he fails the quid pro quo test of *Bingler v. Johnson* with regard to either the immediate payor or the original source of the funds.[97]

Business corporations often establish and finance private foundations to grant scholarships to the children of their employees. The IRS' policy is to apply the exclusion of IRC §117 to these programs, provided the grants are "controlled and limited by substantial nonemployment factors to such an extent that the preferential treatment derived from employment does not continue to be of any significance beyond an initial qualifier." [98] Under the IRS

---

[96] See, e.g., Ehrhart v. CIR, 470 F.2d 940 (1st Cir. 1973) (living allowances paid for employees while attending university taxable despite absence of obligation to return; company's primary objective was that graduates would remain as employees and "hearts can be won as well as coerced"); for a rare case excluding an employer's subventions, see Broniwitz v. CIR, ¶68,221 P-H Memo TC (1968) (full-time student directed own course of study, was under no obligation to work for employer after graduation, and was paid amounts commensurate with ability for required work for employer during the summer). With respect to grantor benefits other than employment of the grantee, see Rev. Rul. 73-564, 1973-2 CB 28 (right to patents and inventions arising out of research grant); Rev. Rul. 74-95, 1974-1 CB 39 (rights to publication); Rev. Rul. 72-263, 1972-1 CB 40 (right to patents and royalty-free use of copyrighted materials).

For IRC §127 (employer-financed educational assistance programs for employees), see infra ¶7.4.

[97] See Johnson v. CIR, ¶78,090 P-H Memo TC (1978) (board of education held to be grantor where it selected recipient of grant and provided her with employee benefits; irrelevant that board was reimbursed by federal agency and institution); Rev. Rul. 64-213, 1964-2 CB 40 (students working as newspaper interns were paid by university from funds contributed by the newspapers; held, newspapers were grantor); Rev. Rul. 73-564, supra note 96 (foundation made funds available to college to pay designated professor while on leave, indirectly controlled his research, and had preferential right to patents and inventions; held, foundation is grantor).

[98] Rev. Proc. 76-47, 1976-2 CB 670, amplified by Rev. Proc. 77-32, 1977-2 CB 541. For plans under which educational institutions remit tuition charges for faculty children, see Treas. Regs. §1.117-3(a) (last sentence).

rules, the taint arising from the fact that the parent's employment is a threshold qualifying factor is dispelled if the program satisfies specified conditions (including use of an independent selection committee and such objective criteria as the candidate's academic performance and financial need), including a percentage test designed to disqualify grants that are a relatively automatic consequence of the parent's status as an employee.

3. Candidates for Degrees. In the case of candidates for degrees, there is no dollar limit on the exclusion of scholarships and fellowships, but IRC §117(b)(1) disqualifies "that portion of any amount received which represents payment for teaching, research, or other services in the nature of part-time employment required as a condition to receiving the scholarship or the fellowship grant," unless similar services are required of all candidates for the same degree. Under the regulations approved by *Bingler v. Johnson,* however, the Treasury does not need the limited disqualification imposed by IRC §117(b)(1) on payments for part-time employment, since they are not "scholarships" or "fellowship grants" under the threshold rules defining those terms.[99] On the other hand, the taxpayer cannot draw any benefit from IRC §117(b)(1)'s exemption of payments for services required of all degree candidates, because, not being "scholarships or fellowship grants" under *Bingler v. Johnson,* the payments are removed from IRC §117(b)(1)'s jurisdiction.

4. Noncandidates for Degrees. If the recipient of a "scholarship" or "fellowship grant" is not a candidate for a degree at an educational organization,[100] there are two additional barriers to an exclusion.

First, by virtue of IRC §117(b)(2)(A), the exclusion applies only if the grantor is a nonprofit organization described in IRC §501(c)(3) (relating to religious, charitable, educational, and similar organizations); a foreign government; an international organization; the United States (or an instrumentality or agency thereof); a state, territory, or possession of the United States or political subdivision thereof; or the District of Columbia. Presumably the primary legislative purpose of this provision was to disqualify grants by ordinary business corporations (the most notable group omitted from the list) to past, present, or prospective employees.[101]

---

[99] See Logan v. US, supra note 93.

[100] The term "educational organization" is defined by IRC §170(b)(1)(A)(ii) (institution normally having a regular faculty, curriculum, and regularly organized body of students in attendance); for the term "candidate for a degree," see Treas. Regs. §1.117-3(e).

[101] See Williamsen v. CIR, 32 TC 154 (1959) (taxpayer bears burden of proving that private corporation making grant was agent of United States and not independent contractor); Rev. Rul. 61-66, 1961-1 CB 19 (where tax-exempt university was conduit

The second restriction on grants to persons who are not candidates for degrees is the dollar limit of IRC §117(b)(2)(B), under which (1) the exclusion for any one taxable year cannot exceed $300 times the number of months for which grants were received, and (2) no exclusion is allowed after the taxpayer has been permitted to exclude amounts for an aggregate of thirty-six months (whether or not consecutive) when he was not a candidate for a degree. All funds paid to the grantee are included in computing the $300 limit unless specifically designated to cover expenses for travel, research, clerical help, or equipment.[102]

SELECTED BIBLIOGRAPHY

Del Cotto, The Trust Annuity as Income: The Constitutional Problem of Taxing Gifts and Bequests as Income, 23 Tax L. Rev. 231 (1968).

Dodge, Beyond Estate and Gift Tax Reform: Including Gifts and Bequests in Income, 91 Harv. L. Rev. 1177 (1978).

Kemp, Federal Tax Aspects of Will Contests, 23 U. Miami L. Rev. 72 (1968).

Klein, An Enigma in the Federal Income Tax: The Meaning of the Word "Gift," 48 Minn. L. Rev. 215 (1963).

McNulty, Tax Policy and Tuition Credit Legislation: Federal Income Tax Allowances for Personal Costs of Higher Education, 61 Calif. L. Rev. 1 (1973).

Stuart, Tax Status of Scholarship and Fellowship Grants: Frustration of Legislative Purpose and Approaches to Obtain the Exclusion Granted by Congress, 25 Emory L.J. 357 (1976).

Tucker, Federal Income Taxation of Scholarships and Fellowships: A Practical Analysis, 8 Ind. L. Rev. 749 (1975).

Wolfman, Federal Tax Policy and the Support of Science, 114 U. Pa. L. Rev. 171 (1965).

---

for grant from one individual to another, individual is grantor; no exclusion under IRC §117).

[102] See Rev. Rul. 71-344, 1971-2 CB 94 (amount specifically designated for expenses held excludable).

CHAPTER 4

Life Insurance, Annuity, and Endowment Contracts and Employee Death Benefits

¶4.1 LIFE INSURANCE, ANNUITY, AND ENDOWMENT CONTRACTS: IN GENERAL

Several of the Internal Revenue Code's most important exclusions from gross income are authorized by a complex set of provisions relating to amounts received under life insurance, annuity, and endowment contracts. This network of rules (labyrinth is a more appropriate metaphor) is discussed in detail hereafter, but can be summarized as follows:

1. Death Benefits. Amounts paid under a life insurance contract by reason of the death of the insured are ordinarily excluded from the beneficiary's gross income by IRC §101(a).[1] Section 101(a) embraces both lump-sum

[1] See infra ¶4.2.

and installment payments, but the latter are ordinarily apportioned between the amount that would have been paid at the date of death, which is exempt, and the post-death earnings on the face amount, which are usually taxed.

2. Annuities. Each annuity payment is divided by IRC §72(b) into two components: A portion is excluded from gross income as a return of capital (viz., the cost of the contract), and the balance must be included in gross income under IRC §72(a) since it represents gain or yield on the taxpayer's investment in the contract.[2] This division between taxable income and tax-free recoveries of capital applies to "any amount received as an annuity" (a phrase that connotes periodic payments at regular intervals of the aggregate amount stated in the contract) and can ordinarily be computed by reference to mortality and compound interest tables. The statutory scheme also covers amounts payable for a fixed period of years.

3. Other Payments. Other amounts paid under life insurance annuity, and endowment contracts are, in general, treated by IRC §72(e) either as tax-free refunds of the taxpayer's premiums or as profits on his investment in the contract.[3]

In application, the foregoing basic rules are complicated by many factors, including the following:

1. *Combination of components.* Many contracts combine two or more of the components mentioned above. Life insurance policies, for example, often provide for installment payments for the duration of the beneficiary's life. In these instances, two or all three of the above rules may apply to the same contract. Conversely, two ostensibly separate contracts are sometimes written by the insurer only in combination and are viewed as a unit in determining the characterization and proper treatment of a particular payment.

2. *Noncommercial contracts.* Both IRC §72 and §101 are primarily concerned with contracts written by regulated insurance companies. But many other contracts, such as agreements by employers to pay death benefits and annuities to employees, must be fitted into the statutory framework and are treated as life insurance and annuity contracts if they sufficiently resemble commercial policies.[4] On the other hand, some private and noncommercial transactions are excluded from IRC §§72 and 101.[5]

3. *Overlapping statutory provisions.* Finally, IRC §§72 and 101 are primarily concerned with individuals who purchase life insurance, annuity, or

[2] See infra ¶4.3.
[3] See infra ¶4.4.
[4] See infra ¶¶4.2, 4.6.
[5] See infra ¶4.3.

endowment contracts to provide for their own well-being or the support of their dependents. The statutory provisions are not confined to this standard situation, but departures from it (for example, a contract assigned in a commercial setting for the benefit of the insured's creditors) may trigger the application of other statutory provisions, thus altering the tax results that would be reached by IRC §§72 and 101 if they had sole jurisdiction over the transaction.[6]

¶4.2 LIFE INSURANCE PROCEEDS PAID AT DEATH

1. Introductory. By virtue of IRC §101(a)(1), amounts received under a life insurance contract, if paid by reason of the death of the insured, are ordinarily excluded from the beneficiary's gross income. This exclusion, in force since 1913, is now based on a legislative policy judgment rather than on a perception of constitutional compulsion.[7]

The exclusion of life insurance proceeds has much in common with the statutory exclusion of bequests.[8] If the decedent had saved the premiums instead of purchasing life insurance, the savings plus the accumulated yield could have been transferred to the survivors as a tax-free bequest. The analogy between life insurance proceeds and bequests is weakened, of course, by the possibility of mortality gains and losses, which are unique to life insurance. Moreover, the proceeds of life insurance have nothing in common with a bequest when paid to an employer to reimburse the business loss suffered on the death of an officer or employee.

The exclusion of life insurance benefits from gross income applies only to payments by reason of the insured's death.[9] Post-death interest or earnings are

---

[6] See infra ¶4.3 (special rules).

[7] In US v. Supplee-Biddle Hardware Co., 265 US 189 (1924), the Court held that the exclusion granted by the Revenue Act of 1918 embraced corporate beneficiaries of life insurance as well as individuals, saying that life insurance proceeds "are not usually classed as income" and reserving judgment whether "Congress could call the proceeds of such indemnity, income, and validly tax it as such." Since 1926, however, certain transferees of life insurance policies have been taxed on the proceeds to the extent that they get more than they paid for the policy (infra, text at note 29); and this treatment was upheld as constitutional in James F. Waters, Inc. v. CIR, 160 F.2d 596 (9th Cir.), cert. denied, 332 US 767 (1947).

The long-standing exclusionary rule of IRC §101(f) was qualified in 1982 by the enactment of IRC §101(f), denying the exclusion to certain amounts received under so-called flexible premium life insurance contracts, in order to tax the investment yield on such contracts, as distinguished from their insurance components.

[8] See supra ¶3.1.

[9] See infra ¶4.4. But see Rev. Rul. 79-87, 1979-1 CB 73 (exclusion covers amounts

ordinarily taxable, the exclusion being limited to the date-of-death value of the future payments.[10] Finally, the exclusion is ordinarily denied to purchasers of a policy and other transferees for value, who are taxed if they receive more than they paid for the policy.[11]

2. Amounts Paid by Reason of Insured's Death. The proceeds of life insurance paid by reason of the death of the insured are excluded from gross income by IRC §101(a), whether payment is direct or in trust and regardless of the person or entity to whom it is paid.[12] The exclusion applies to installment payments as well as to lump-sum settlements, except that the interest component of amounts paid after the insured's death is ordinarily subject to tax.[13]

The regulations interpret the statutory phrase "amounts received . . . under a life insurance contract" to embrace death benefit payments "having the characteristics of life insurance proceeds," even though paid under workmen's compensation contracts, endowment contracts, or accident and health insurance policies.[14] But the contract must exhibit the risk-shifting and risk-distribution characteristics of insurance.[15] Contracts having the requisite insurance characteristics can qualify, however, even if not written by regulated insurance companies.[16] These contracts are distinguished from payments by a self-insuring employer financing payments from its regular resources.[17] But it is not easy to stake out a boundary between these two situations, and this presages difficulties in deciding when death benefits paid under an employee benefit plan to a deceased employee's family qualify as life insurance under

---

paid under variable life insurance policy, where benefits may increase or decrease depending on investment results, but not below a specified minimum).

[10] See infra, text at note 24.

[11] See infra, text at note 29.

[12] Treas. Regs. §1.101-1(a)(1).

[13] See infra, text at note 24.

[14] Treas Regs. §1.101-1(a)(1). See Atlantic Oil Co. v. Patterson, 331 F.2d 516 (5th Cir. 1964) (IRC §101(a) exclusion denied to trucking company that insured lives of its drivers for its own benefit; for want of insurable interest, policy treated as wagering contract).

[15] Kess v. US, 451 F.2d 1229 (6th Cir. 1971) (exclusion denied to single-premium life insurance policy and annuity contract issued without evidence of insurability because the company's commitments offset each other).

[16] Ross v. Odom, 401 F.2d 464 (5th Cir. 1968) (actuarially sound and determinable obligation); Moyer's Est. v. CIR, 32 TC 515, 535 (1959) (benefits excludable under IRC §101(a); fund was a mutual insurance company for federal tax purposes). See also Epmeier v. US, 199 F.2d 508 (7th Cir. 1952), construing the statutory phrase "accident or health insurance" to include a self-insured employer's plan for employees, which led to the enactment of IRC §105, discussed infra ¶5.2.

[17] See Davis v. US, 323 F.Supp. 858 (S.D. W. Va. 1971), holding that a West Virginia state retirement system did not meet the criteria of Ross v. Odom, supra note 16; Essenfeld v. CIR, 311 F.2d 208 (2d Cir. 1962) (employer-employee retirement contract not a "life insurance contract").

IRC §101(a) and when they fall outside its jurisdiction.[18]

In addition to being paid "under a life insurance contract," the proceeds must be "paid by reason of the death of the insured" to qualify for exclusion under IRC §101(a). Designed primarily to separate death benefits from such lifetime payments as dividends and cash surrender values, this requirement rarely creates any interpretative difficulties.[19] For example, if a policy of life insurance is pledged as security for a debt, the creditor, even if irrevocably designated as the beneficiary, gets the proceeds not "by reason of the death of the insured," but because there is an unpaid balance on the debt.[20] The Internal Revenue Service has ruled that this principle applies to so-called creditors' life insurance, purchased by dealers engaged in retail installment sales in amounts equal to the unpaid balance of the customer's debt.[21] Since the insurance described in the ruling was limited in amount to the customer's unpaid balance, there could be no surplus. If a surplus is possible, it presumably would be (a) uncollectible for want of an insurable interest, (b) held for the benefit of the customer's estate, or (c) taxed to the creditor as the fruits of a gambling contract, rather than excluded as true life insurance.

On the other hand, if the taxpayer owns an insurance policy on someone else's life and can receive and use the proceeds for his own purposes, he is entitled to the exclusion even if the policy facilitates payment of an obligation or achievement of a desired objective, such as acquisition of the insured's business interest under a buy-sell agreement or payment of a death benefit to the insured's family.[22] When the proceeds of a policy are used to settle a dispute about ownership of the contract, however, it is often difficult to determine whether the recipient has been paid by reason of the insured's death, as required by IRC §101(a), or because of an extraneous claim for damages, lost profits, unpaid wages, or the like; and the issues may be further complicated by a question of insurable interest under state law.[23]

---

[18] For the relationship between the exclusion of life insurance proceeds under IRC §101(a) and the exclusion of employee death benefits up to $5,000 by IRC §101(b), see infra ¶4.6.

[19] See Rev. Rul. 55-63, 1955-1 CB 227 (employer purchased life insurance on employees' lives, naming itself as beneficiary, pursuant to program guaranteeing payment of death benefits to employee's estate or beneficiaries; held, employer was only a conduit and recipients were entitled to exclusion).

[20] See Treas. Regs. §1.101-1(b)(4) (IRC §101 inapplicable to amounts received by pledgee of a policy).

[21] Rev. Rul. 70-254, 1970-1 CB 31.

[22] See Mushro v. CIR, 50 TC 43 (1968) (Nonacq.) (surviving partners held to have received insurance proceeds on life of deceased partner although his widow was nominal beneficiary because proceeds were applied to their obligation to purchase decedent's partnership interest under buy-sell agreement).

[23] See e.g., Salmonson v. US, 11 AFTR2d 1568 (E.D. Wash. 1963) (not officially reported) (deceased employee's widow received taxable employment benefits, not excludable proceeds of key-man insurance).

3. Effect of Settlement Options. The general rule of IRC §101(a) provides for the exclusion of life insurance death benefits whether paid "in a single sum or otherwise"; but when payments are made over a period of time after the insured's death, the exclusion embraces only the principal and not the interest or other increments added by the insurer to compensate the beneficiary for the delay. The simplest situation of this type is an agreement under which the insurer holds the proceeds intact after the insured's death, pays interest to the beneficiary, and pays over the principal at a designated date or on the beneficiary's request or death. Under IRC §101(c), the interest is includable in the recipient's gross income;[24] but the principal, when received, qualifies for exclusion under IRC §101(a).

There was until 1954 no explicit statutory provision covering settlement options paying a combination of income and capital for the beneficiary's life or a term certain. In 1954, Congress enacted IRC §101(d), requiring the interest component of installment payments to be separated from the principal and included in gross income. Thus, the exclusion granted by IRC §101(a) embraces only the amount payable at death (or the value at that time of the future payments if the policy does not provide for a lump-sum settlement), which is prorated over the installments as they are received. The 1954 rule is mitigated by IRC §101(d)(1)(B) if the beneficiary is the insured's surviving spouse, to the extent of $1,000 of interest per year.[25] This special exemption applies only to installment payments described by IRC §101(d) and not to interest-only payments under IRC §101(c).[26]

Thus, if the insurance policy provides for installment payments for a specified period of years, the amount held by the insurer [27] is prorated equally over the installments and the excess is includable in the beneficiary's gross income. The result is that the amount payable at death (or, if the policy does not provide for a lump-sum settlement, the value at death of the future payments) is excluded over the life of the annuity, but everything above that

---

[24] Section 101(c) applies whether the interim payments are labeled interest or an annuity, provided they do not reduce the capital sum to be paid at a later date. Under Treas. Regs. §1.101-3(a), a settlement is to be treated as an interest-only agreement unless the periodic payments result in a "substantial diminution" of the principal.

[25] Qualification as a "surviving spouse" is determined under IRC §101(d)(3) as of the date of death and is not forfeited by remarriage. See Rev. Rul. 72-164, 1972 CB 28. Payments under two or more policies on the same decedent must be aggregated in applying the $1,000 annual limit. Treas. Regs. §1.101-4(a)(1)(ii).

[26] This discrimination against an interest-only option is not explained by the legislative history. In order to prevent interest-only settlements from posing as installment options by the obvious device of paying out a nominal amount of capital along with the interest, Treas. Regs. §1.101-3(a) specifies that IRC §101(d) applies only if the payments produce a "substantial diminution" of the principal amount.

[27] The term "amount held by an insurer" is defined by IRC §101(d)(2) and Treas. Regs. §1.101-4(b).

amount is includable in gross income. These principles are illustrated by Example 4-1, which assumes that (a) a beneficiary (other than the decedent's surviving spouse) elects to receive the amount payable at death ($150,000) in ten annual installments of $16,500 each, based on a certain guaranteed interest rate, plus such excess earnings as may be realized and declared by the insurer, and (b) as a result of excess earnings, the installment for a particular year is $17,500. The amount includable in income for that year is $2,500, determined as shown in Example 4-1.

Example 4-1
Payments for Ten Years Certain

1. Amount received	$17,500
2. Less: Prorated amount excludable under IRC §101(a) ($150,000/10)	15,000
3. Amount includable in gross income	$ 2,500

If the payments are not guaranteed for a specified term of years but are to continue so long as the beneficiary lives (with no refund in the event of early death), the amount held by the insurer must be prorated over the beneficiary's life expectancy, determined by the mortality tables used by the insurer in fixing the benefits to be paid. Amounts in excess of this prorated annual amount are includable in the beneficiary's gross income. Thus, the amount excluded from gross income over the beneficiary's life will equal the amount that would have been payable at death if, but only if, the beneficiary's life corresponds exactly to his or her life expectancy.

Annuities payable for the beneficiary's life often contain a refund feature, such as a guarantee that payments will be made for at least a specified number of years or until the payments aggregate the amount that would have been paid in a lump sum on the insured's death. Although IRC §101(d) makes no explicit mention of refunds, the regulations require such commitments to be valued separately and deducted from the "amount held by the insurer" before it is prorated over the annuity payments.[28] As a result, the value of a refund is not excluded from the first beneficiary's gross income. If the first beneficiary dies early, however, and payments are made to his or her estate or to a secondary beneficiary pursuant to the refund feature, they are excluded from the recipient's gross income.

---

[28] Treas. Regs. §1.101-4(e).

4. Transferees for Value. With some exceptions, transferees for value of life insurance contracts may not exclude the benefits from gross income but are, instead, taxed by IRC §101(a)(2) on the proceeds, less amounts paid by them to acquire the policy and for later premiums and other payments. If a policy is purchased as an investment in a commercial setting, taxing the purchaser's gain seems more appropriate than an exclusion. If this was its objective, however, IRC §101(a)(2) is both too broad and too narrow. It denies the exclusion if an existing policy is sold by the insured to a member of his family, even if the transaction is an estate-planning device rather than a business arrangement.[29] On the other hand, IRC §101(a)(2) does not deny the exclusion to the proceeds of a policy serving the exclusively commercial function, provided it is *taken out by* (rather than *transferred to*) the beneficiary.

The regulations interpret the phrase "transfer for a valuable consideration, by assignment or otherwise," as used in IRC §101(a)(2), to embrace "any absolute transfer for value of a right to receive all or a part of the proceeds of a life insurance policy," but not the assignment of a policy as collateral security.[30] In a few cases, the apparent breadth of the "transfer for value" concept has been mitigated by exempting transfers for value that did not effect a significant change in the beneficial ownership of a policy. More commonly, however, the transfer-for-value disqualification is strictly interpreted against the taxpayer, resulting in a denial of the exclusion in situations involving a technical transfer for value, even if there was no risk of speculation on the death of the insured.[31]

To limit or overrule these severe interpretations, Congress intervened to exempt two categories of transactions from the transfer-for-value rule.

1. *Carryover basis.* Section 101(a)(2)(A) exempts transfers if the transferee's basis for determining gain or loss is determined in whole or in part by reference to the transferor's basis, as in the case of a transfer by gift or in a tax-free corporate reorganization. The regulations, however, deny the exemption if there was an earlier transfer for value.[32]

2. *Transfers to insured and certain others.* The second category of exempt transfers for value, described by IRC §101(a)(2)(B), consists of transfers to the insured, a partner of the insured, a partnership of which the insured is

[29] See Hacker v. CIR, 36 BTA 659 (1937) (no implied exemption from transfer-for-value rule for transfer to a member of the insured's family having "a special claim upon his bounty").

[30] Treas. Regs. §1.101-1(b)(4).

[31] See James F. Waters, Inc. v. CIR, supra note 7 (transfer of policy to corporation controlled by insured).

[32] Treas. Regs. §1.101-1(b)(3); Treas. Regs. 1.101-1(b)(5), illustrated by Example (6); see also James F. Waters, Inc. v. CIR, supra note 7 (after a transfer for value, gratuitous transferee stands in shoes of donor).

a member, or a corporation of which the insured is a shareholder or officer. These exceptions to the transfer-for-value rule, which protect policies transferred for "legitimate business reasons rather than for speculation purposes," [33] are of particular importance in drafting buy-sell contracts for the transfer of closely held enterprises on the death of a key person. Despite its broad objective, IRC §101(a)(2)(B) does not accord transfers among shareholders of a closely held corporation the immunity that is granted to transfers among partners, nor does it exempt transfers by the insured's corporation to one of his co-shareholders, although a comparable transfer by a partnership to one of the insured's co-partners is permitted. Moreover, IRC §101(a)(2)(B) does not immunize transfers to the spouse or children of the insured or of his partners.

5. Life Insurance as Alimony. When payments under a life insurance contract are includable in the gross income of a spouse under IRC §71 (relating to alimony) or §682 (relating to the income of an estate or trust in case of divorce, etc.), their tax status is determined not by the normal tax rules of IRC §101, but by the statutory provisions relating to alimony and similar payments.[34]

¶4.3 ANNUITY PAYMENTS

1. Introductory. The tax treatment of amounts received under an annuity contract is prescribed by IRC §72. Because this provision is addressed to complicated financial arrangements that over the years have evoked a series of different statutory rules, a description of the basic transaction and a brief review of the legislative history are essential to an understanding of current law.

The tax problem can be illustrated by assuming that a fifty-six-year-old male taxpayer paid $5,000 to an insurance company, either in a lump sum or in installments, for an annuity contract under which he was to be paid $1,000 a year, starting at age sixty-five and continuing for the rest of his life, with no refund if he should die prematurely (i.e., either before reaching sixty-five, or thereafter but before receiving as much as the $5,000 paid in).[35] If the taxpayer

[33] S. Rep. No. 1622, 83d Cong., 2d Sess. 14 (1954). Although the exemptions of IRC §101(a)(2)(B) are limited to persons having a business relationship with the insured, it does not explicitly require the transfer to serve the enterprise's business purposes.

[34] IRC §101(e); for the tax treatment of alimony, see infra ¶32.2.

[35] An annuity contract without a cash value or refund feature is unusual and is

lives exactly as long as the average person reflected by the mortality tables used by the company in fixing the amount to be paid (fourteen years), he will receive a total of $14,000 under the contract. From his point of view, this result can be analogized to a deposit of $5,000 in a savings bank, followed by annual withdrawals, starting at age sixty-five and continuing until his death, of the interest plus enough of the principal to make up $1,000. If the annuitant's life is longer or shorter than the average, however, he will benefit from a "mortality gain" or suffer a "mortality loss."

Before 1934, annuitants were allowed to recover the cost of an annuity contract ($5,000 in the example above) tax-free from the earliest receipts; but everything received thereafter was includable in gross income.[36] In 1934, however, the cost recovery approach was replaced by a statutory plan under which each annual payment was taxable to the extent of 3 percent of the cost of the contract (a percentage based on the investment assumptions of insurance companies at that time); the balance of the annual payment was excluded from gross income as a return of the annuitant's premium; and the payments became taxable in full as soon as the aggregate excluded amount equaled the annuitant's cost.

For long-lived annuitants, the 1934 change accelerated the annuitant's receipt of gross income and slowed down the recovery of his investment, but it did not alter the aggregate amounts included and excluded over the long haul. For short-lived annuitants, however, the 1934 legislation differed from prior law by requiring income to be reported even though the annuitant died before recovering his investment tax-free.

This feature of the 1934 law led to an attack on its constitutionality in *Egtvedt v. United States,*[37] involving a forty-five-year-old taxpayer (with a life expectancy of twenty years) who could not have recovered his investment tax-free unless he lived to ninety-eight—an unlikely event, despite the assurance in *Poor Richard's Almanac* that "pensioners never die; annuitants live forever." The court rejected the taxpayer's claim that the 1934 provision was an unconstitutional direct tax on his property rather than a tax on income, partly on the ground that he failed to prove "what part of the payments [received by him] during the taxable years actually represent[ed] earnings on the amounts paid by him as consideration for the policies and what part was simply a return of capital."[38] Moving to a more fundamental level, the court denied that the taxpayer had any constitutional right to a tax-free recovery of his capital:

prohibited by some states; the example is deliberately simplified to illustrate the basic principles.

[36] See Klein v. CIR, 6 BTA 617 (1927) (Acq.).

[37] Egtvedt v. US, 112 Ct. Cl. 80 (1948).

[38] Egtvedt v. US, supra note 37, at 93.

> [W]e think an investment of funds in an annuity is a transaction which is materially different from an ordinary business transaction entered into for profit where the concept of gain or loss might be applicable. To some extent one who has invested his money in an annuity may be said to have "spent it," that is, to have parted with it in order to obtain contractual rights which are not inherent, in the same degree at least, in the mere ownership of property.[39]

Finally, without going so far as to say that Congress could tax annuity payments without making *any* allowance for a tax-free recovery of the taxpayer's cost, the court in *Egtvedt* held out little hope for a successful attack on any statutory scheme taxing "a fair approximation"[40] of the income component of the average annuity.

Although constitutional, the 1934 rule continued to elicit criticism, for reasons summarized by the Senate Finance Committee in 1954:

> This present rule is objectionable because it is erratic. Where the amount paid for the annuity represents a large proportion of its value at the time payments begin, the present rule does not return to the annuitant on a tax-free basis the amount he paid for the annuity during his lifetime. On the other hand, where the amount the annuitant paid for the annuity represents a small proportion of its value at the time payments begin, the exclusion is used up rapidly. In such cases the annuitant finds that after being retired for a few years and becoming accustomed to living on a certain amount of income after tax, he suddenly has to make a sizable downward adjustment in his living standard because, when his exclusion is used up, the annuity income becomes fully taxable.[41]

To avoid these features of the 1934 rule, Congress enacted, as part of the 1954 Code, the current method of separating the income component of annuity payments from the return-of-capital component, which spreads the tax-free portion of the annuity income evenly over the annuitant's lifetime.

2. "Amounts Received as an Annuity"—The Exclusion Ratio of IRC §72. Section 72 of current law distinguishes between "amounts received as an annuity" under an annuity, endowment, or life insurance contract and other amounts received under such contracts.[42] The distinction is not elucidated by the statute, but the regulations provide that payments qualify as "amounts received as an annuity" only if (a) they are received on or after the "annuity

---

[39] Id. at 94-95. For nondeductibility of the loss if the annuitant fails to recover his investment, see infra ¶4.5.

[40] Egtvedt v. US, supra note 37, at 95-96.

[41] S. Rep. No. 1622, supra note 33, at 11.

[42] Section 72's jurisdiction is not limited to contracts issued by regulated insurance companies but includes some noncommercial contracts as well. See infra ¶4.5.

starting date,"[43] (b) they are payable in periodic installments at regular intervals, and (c) the aggregate amount payable can be determined either directly from the contract (e.g., $10,000, payable in quarterly installments of $1,000 each) or indirectly by the use of mortality tables or compound interest computations (e.g., $1,000 annually for the life of John Jones, or $500 quarterly until $10,000 plus interest of 6 percent on the declining balance is exhausted).[44]

Payments meeting these standards are subject to the "exclusion ratio" of IRC §72(b), under which a uniform fraction of the "amount received as an annuity" is excluded from gross income (as a tax-free recovery of the annuitant's investment in the contract), while the balance of the payment is includable in gross income unless it qualifies for exclusion under some other provision of law.[45] All other payments, which the Code lumps together under the catchall phrase "amounts not received as an annuity," are, in general, either treated as a recovery of the cost of the policy or, if in excess of that amount, included in gross income.[46]

The exclusion ratio is the "investment in the contract" (the premiums or other consideration paid, adjusted for any tax-free recoveries before the annuity starting date and for any refund feature) divided by the "expected return" (the aggregate amount to be received, computed under actuarial tables prescribed by the Treasury, if the payments depend on the life expectancy of one or more individuals).[47] To determine the amount to be excluded, the annuity payments received during the taxable year are multiplied by the exclusion ratio; the remainder is includable in gross income under IRC §72(a). Once determined, the exclusion ratio ordinarily continues unchanged throughout the life of the contract, so that a long-lived annuitant may be able to exclude from gross income more than his investment in the contract.[48]

Important concepts employed in computing the exclusion ratio of IRC §72(b) are:

1. *Investment in the contract.* The taxpayer's "investment in the contract" is the aggregate amount of the premiums or other consideration paid, less premium refunds, dividends, and any excludable amounts received under

---

[43] For this term, see IRC §72(c)(4).

[44] See Treas. Regs. §1.72-2(b)(2), which contains certain minor exceptions to the principles set out in the text, as well as a more important exception for variable annuities. For the latter, see infra, text at note 55.

[45] E.g., as an accident or health benefit excludable under IRC §104 or §105; see infra, text at note 65.

[46] See infra, text at note 55; for amounts paid by reason of the death of the insured, see supra ¶4.2. See also Price v. US, 459 F.Supp. 362 (D.Md. 1978) (excess contributions taxed when returned, but exclusion ratio remains stable).

[47] See IRC §72(c), defining the terms "investment in the contract" and "expected return." These statutory definitions are expanded by Treas. Regs. §§1.72-5 and 1.72-6.

[48] Treas. Regs. §1.72-4(a)(4).

the contract before the annuity starting date.[49] To avoid periodic changes in the exclusion ratio, dividends and other nonannuity amounts received on or after the annuity starting date are included in gross income under IRC §72(e)(1)(A) rather than applied to reduce the taxpayer's investment in the contract.

2. *Employer contributions.* In computing the premiums or other consideration paid for the contract, amounts contributed by an employer are treated as paid by the employee only (a) if they were includable in his gross income [50] or (b) if, had they been paid directly to him, they would have been excluded from his gross income.[51] This means that annuities under qualified pension and profit-sharing plans are, in general, treated as purchased by the employee only to the extent of his after-tax contributions, if any. If the employee has made no contributions, all amounts received by him are includable in gross income.

3. *Adjustment for refund feature.* To protect against loss of the annuitant's investment if he dies prematurely, annuity contracts often contain a refund feature, such as an agreement to make payments for ten years even if the annuitant dies during this period, or to continue payments after the annuitant's death until the aggregate amount paid by the insurer equals the premiums received by it. Under IRC §72(c)(2), the value of these guaranteed payments must be subtracted from the cost of the contract in computing the exclusion ratio.

4. *Transferees.* For donees and other transferees whose basis in the annuity contract is determined by reference to its basis in the hands of the transferor, the latter's premiums and other payments are included in determining the transferee's investment in the contract. Purchasers and other transferees for value, however, may take into account only the amount paid by them for the contract and for premiums thereafter.[52]

5. *Employee contributions recoverable in three years.* To avoid complex computations for small exclusions, IRC §72(d) provides a cost recovery principle for annuities if (a) part of the consideration for the contract was contributed by an employer and (b) the consideration contributed by the employee will be recovered during the three-year period beginning with receipt of the first annuity payment.[53] When IRC §72(d) applies, the employee (or, if he died

---

[49] Treas. Regs. §1.72-6(a).

[50] IRC §72(f)(1). See, e.g., IRC §§83 and 403(c), discussed infra ¶29.3; see also US v. Drescher, 179 F.2d 863 (2d Cir.), cert. denied, 340 US 821 (1950) (employee taxed on annuity contract purchased by employer).

[51] IRC §72(f)(2).

[52] IRC §72(g)(1); Treas. Regs. §1.72-10; see also IRC §72(g)(2) (reduction of consideration by amounts received tax-free by the transferee).

[53] The starting date for the three-year period under IRC §72(d) is the date on which an amount is *received* as an annuity, not the "annuity starting date," which is

before any payments began, his beneficiary) excludes from gross income all amounts received as an annuity until his contributions have been recovered.[54]

3. Variable Annuities. If the amount to be paid under an annuity contract varies in response to the insurer's investment experience, cost-of-living indices, or other fluctuating criteria, the "expected return" cannot be predicted with accuracy; and this in turn makes it impossible to compute an exclusion ratio in the usual manner. The regulations cope with this problem by (a) treating the amount received by the beneficiary as an annuity payment only to the extent that it does not exceed the taxpayer's investment in the contract (less the value of any refund feature) divided by the number of anticipated periodic payments; (b) applying an exclusion ratio of 100 percent to this amount, thus excluding it from gross income in its entirety; and (c) requiring any additional amounts received to be included in gross income.[55]

Since the amount excluded in any taxable year cannot exceed the larger of (a) the amount actually received or (b) the ratable portion of the taxpayer's investment, the taxpayer would not recover his investment tax-free received less than the excludable amount in any year and lived no longer than his life expectancy. To correct for this deficiency, the regulations permit the taxpayer to elect to recompute the excludable annuity portion of payments received after a shortfall,[56] thus restoring the possibility of recovering his investment tax-free if investment experience under the contract improves.

Variable annuity contracts giving the policyholder control over the insurer's investment decisions are not viewed by the IRS as genuine annuity contracts subject to IRC §72, but as custodial accounts generating income that is includable in the policyholder's gross income as realized.[57]

4. Effect of Original Annuitant's Death. If the beneficiary of a single-life annuity contract without a refund feature dies while receiving annuity payments, the issuer's obligation to make payments ceases and there is nothing to be inherited by the annuitant's estate or legatees. If, however, the contract provides for a joint-and-survivor annuity or includes a refund feature, the

---

defined by IRC §72(c)(4) as the first day of the first period for which an annuity payment is received.

[54] Treas. Regs. §1.72-13(a)(5) provides that contributions with respect to a self-employed individual that are deductible under IRC §404(a) (so-called H.R. 10 or Jenkins-Keogh plans).

[55] Treas. Regs. §§1.72-2(b)(3), 1.72-4(d)(3).

[56] Treas. Regs. §1.72-4(d)(3)(ii).

[57] See Rev. Rul. 77-85, 1977-1 CB 12; see also Investment Annuity, Inc. v. Blumenthal, 442 F.Supp. 681 (D.D.C. 1977) (Rev. Rul. 77-85 invalid), rev'd, 609 F.2d 1 (D.C. Cir. 1979) (district court lacked jurisdiction).

payments will continue for the agreed period and their value at the annuitant's death usually must be included in the decedent's gross estate for federal estate tax purposes.[58] The decedent's beneficiaries do not get a date-of-death basis for their rights under the annuity contract in these situations; instead, they inherit the decedent's exclusion ratio and basis for the contract.[59]

Section 691(d), however, provides that amounts received as an annuity during the survivor's life-expectancy period in excess of the amount determined by the exclusion ratio shall be considered as income in respect of a decedent under IRC §691(a). This does not change the status of these amounts directly, but it permits the survivor to take a deduction for an allocable portion of the death taxes resulting from inclusion of the contract in the first annuitant's estate.[60]

5. Noncommercial and Private Annuities. Although IRC §72 applies to all contracts that "are considered to be life insurance, endowment, and annuity contracts in accordance with the customary practice of life insurance companies," it is immaterial that the issuer is not an insurance company,[61] and it encompasses some contracts issued by persons who are not subject to state insurance regulations and who do not pool the mortality risks of a large number of lives.[62]

If the policy is not purchased for cash, however, but with appreciated property, it is necessary to take account of the purchaser's gain on the transfer. Under Revenue Ruling 69-74, the transferor's gain, computed by subtracting the adjusted basis of the transferred property from the present value of the annuity, is taxed ratably over the annuitant's life expectancy.[63] This result is accomplished by using the property's adjusted basis rather than its value in determining the exclusion ratio, so that the annuitant's tax-free recovery is limited to the property's adjusted basis. If the transferred property was a capital asset, the taxable portion of each annuity payment is divided between

---

[58] See IRC §2039, relating to inclusion of annuities in the gross estate for federal estate tax purposes; IRC §2033, relating to inclusion in gross estate of property in which the decedent had an ownership interest.

[59] See IRC §1014(b)(9)(A).

[60] See Treas. Regs. §1.691(d)-1, illustrating the deduction and limiting it to the period of the survivor's life expectancy.

[61] Treas. Regs. §1.72-2(a)(1).

[62] See Heard v. CIR, 40 TC 7 (1963), aff'd, 326 F.2d 962 (8th Cir.), cert. denied, 377 US 978 (1964) (IRC §72 applies to annuities under Federal Civil Service Retirement Act; extensive discussion); Treas. Regs. §1.72-2(a)(3)(iii); Rev. Rul. 72-438; 1972-2 CB 38 (policyholder's investment in noncommercial contract determined by reference to cost of comparable contract issued by insurance companies).

[63] Rev. Rul. 69-74, 1969-1 CB 43; see also Bell's Est. v. CIR, 60 TC 469 (1973) (excess of annuity contract's fair market value over taxpayer's adjusted basis realized in year of exchange).

ordinary income and capital gain until the capital gain has been recognized in full; thereafter, the taxable portions of the annuity payments are taxed as ordinary income in their entirety.

6. Special Rules. The general rules prescribed by IRC §72 are qualified in a variety of circumstances, the most important of which are the following:

1. *Interest.* Periodic payments that represent only an investment yield on the premiums are treated as interest rather than as payments under IRC §72.

2. *Alimony.* Section 72 does not apply to payments includable in a spouse's gross income by reason of IRC §71 (relating to alimony and separate maintenance payments) or §682 (relating to income of an estate or trust in case of divorce, etc.).[64]

3. *Accident and health benefits.* Section 72 does not apply to amounts received as accident or health benefits, which are governed by IRC §§104 and 105.[65] If an employer-established plan provides both for payments taxable under IRC §72 and payments excluded from gross income under IRC §104 or §105, employee contributions allocable to the accident and health benefits are excluded in determining the employee's investment in the contract.[66]

4. *Employee death benefits.* If by reason of an employee's death, the employee's beneficiary receives payments to which IRC §72 applies, the aggregate amount of premiums or other consideration paid or deemed paid or contributed by the employee includes amounts excludable from the beneficiary's gross income under IRC §101(b), whether or not paid as an annuity.[67]

¶4.4 OTHER RECEIPTS UNDER LIFE INSURANCE, ANNUITY, AND ENDOWMENT CONTRACTS

1. Introductory. Section 72(e) prescribes the tax treatment of amounts received under life insurance, annuity, and endowment contracts that are not subject to either IRC §101(a) (life insurance proceeds "paid by reason of the death of the insured") or §72(b) ("amounts received as an annuity").[68] These

---

[64] IRC §72(k); for IRC §§71 and 682, see infra ¶¶32.1 and 32.4, respectively.

[65] See infra ¶¶5.1, 5.2.

[66] Treas. Regs. §1.72-15(c).

[67] Treas. Regs. §1.72-8(b); see Treas. Regs. §1.101-2(a)(2) (third sentence); IRC §101(b)(2)(D) (amount excluded determined by reference to date-of-death value). For IRC §101(b), see infra ¶4.6.

[68] For IRC §§101(a) and 72(b), see supra ¶¶4.2 and 4.3, respectively.

receipts—the residue, as it were, after the more specialized rules of IRC §§101(a) and 72(b) have exerted jurisdiction over their respective territories—are collectively designated by the statutory label "amounts not received as an annuity." As a general rule, receipts subject to IRC §72(e) are included in gross income only to the extent that, when added to amounts previously excluded from gross income, they exceed the aggregate premiums or other consideration paid for the contract.

This cost recovery approach is subject to two exceptions.

First, under IRC §72(e), as amended in 1982, amounts received under annuity contracts (and, to the extent prescribed by regulations to be issued, under endowment and life insurance contracts) *before* the annuity starting date are treated as taxable withdrawals of income earned on the investment to the extent of such income, the remainder being treated as returns of capital. In addition, IRC §72(q) imposes a penalty tax on certain receipts allocable to investments made less than ten years before the payment.

Second, amounts received under an annuity contract *after* the annuity starting date, which are included in gross income whether or not the taxpayer's investment has been recovered.[69] The reason for this qualification is that the exclusion ratio, which provides a method of recovering the investment over the life of an annuity contract, is computed as of the annuity starting date; and if subsequent nonannuity receipts were treated as tax-free recoveries of the annuitant's cost, it would be necessary to recompute the exclusion ratio every time that such a nonannuity payment was received.

By virtue of IRC §72(h), enacted in 1954, a taxpayer who elects to receive a lump sum in a series of annuity payments is not required to include the lump sum in gross income if an option to receive the annuity is exercised within sixty days after the lump sum first becomes payable. The regulations seem to interpret this provision to include agreements to take an annuity in lieu of the lump sum even though the option elected is not contained in the original contract.[70]

2. Sales and Other Dispositions of Policies. If a policyholder sells or otherwise disposes of contractual rights under a life insurance, endowment, or annuity policy (other than by electing a settlement option), the transaction is subject to the general rules of IRC §1001, relating to gain or loss on a disposition of property.[71] If the contract is a capital asset in the owner's hands, any

---

[69] IRC §72(e)(1)(A). This exception is itself subject, in turn, to the qualification set out in IRC §72(e)(2) (payments in full discharge of the contract or on its surrender, redemption, or maturity are subject to the general rule of IRC §72(e)(1)(B)).

[70] See Treas. Regs. §1.72-12 (exercises option or "irrevocably agrees" to take an option).

[71] For IRC §1001, see infra ¶22.2. There is no explicit comprehensive exemption for settlement options, but it is usually assumed that the election of a particular option does not constitute a sale or other disposition of the policyholder's other rights under

excess of the amount received over the premiums or other consideration paid for the contract will constitute capital gain, unless the transaction does not constitute a "sale or exchange" of the contract,[72] is a device to convert ordinary income into capital gain,[73] or otherwise falls outside the intended range of the capital gain and loss provisions.[74]

Section 1035, enacted in 1954, exempts certain exchanges of life insurance, endowment, and annuity contracts from the basic principle that gain or loss is recognized on a sale or other disposition of property. This nonrecognition treatment applies to the exchange of (1) a life insurance contract for a life insurance, endowment, or annuity contract; (2) an endowment contract for an annuity contract or for an endowment contract whose payments begin no later than payments under the surrendered contract; or (3) an annuity contract for another annuity contract.[75]

If an exchange qualifies under IRC §1035 except for the fact that the transferor receives cash or other property in addition to a policy that can be received tax-free, the transferor's gain is recognized to the extent of the disqualified property ("boot") received; but any loss on the exchange is not recognized. The transferor's basis for the contract received is the same as the basis of the transferred contract, with an adjustment for gain (if any) recognized on the exchange.[76]

¶4.5 DEDUCTIBILITY OF PREMIUMS AND LOSSES

1. Deductibility of Premiums. Since no statutory provision explicitly authorizes a deduction for premiums, a deduction is permissible only if the expense can be fitted into a broader class of deductible expenditures (e.g., business expenses). But even if the premiums seem at first blush to be covered by such a provision, the road bristles with obstacles, and premiums are seldom deductible. The principal barriers are the following:

---

the contract, by analogy to Rev. Rul. 72-265, 1972-1 CB 222 (conversion of debenture in accordance with its terms into stock of issuer does not result in realization of income).

[72] See Hawkins v. CIR, ¶44,349 P-H Memo TC (1944), rev'd on another issue, 152 F.2d 221 (5th Cir. 1945) (surrender of insurance policies to issuer for cash value not a sale or exchange; held, gain taxable as ordinary income); see generally infra ¶26.1.

[73] See CIR v. Phillips, 275 F.2d 33, 36 n.3 (4th Cir. 1960) (paid-up endowment policy sold by taxpayer to his law partners twelve days before maturity; held, ordinary income); see also infra ¶26.1.

[74] See Gallun v. CIR, 327 F.2d 809 (7th Cir. 1964) (assignment-of-income theory).

[75] See S. Rep. No. 1622, supra note 33, at 110-111; Treas. Regs. §1.1035-1 (both contracts must relate to same insured); Rev. Rul. 72-358, 1972-2 CB 473 (contracts may be issued by different companies).

[76] See IRC §1031(d), discussed infra ¶24.2.

1. *Nondeductibility of personal expenditures.* In the ordinary case, the premiums constitute "personal, living and family expenses," which, by virtue of IRC §262, cannot be deducted except pursuant to express statutory authority.[77] Except for contributions to qualified pension plans and similar arrangements with an insurance component, this restriction bars a deduction for virtually all premiums paid for policies serving personal objectives. Premiums paid as alimony or as charitable contributions, however, are deductible if the contract belongs to the ex-spouse or charitable donee.[78]

2. *Business expenses.* Business expenses are usually deductible under IRC §162, and IRC §212 allows individuals to deduct similar expenses incurred in connection with income-producing property.[79] Thus, if an employer augments an employee's salary by paying premiums on the employee's life insurance, annuity, or endowment policy, the premiums are deductible if the total amount paid does not exceed reasonable compensation.[80] It should be remembered, however, that business expenses can be deducted only if "ordinary and necessary"—a phrase that has been applied several times, not entirely convincingly, to disallow deductions for life insurance premiums when the insured was not closely connected with the taxpayer, even though the latter would suffer financially from the death of the insured.[81]

3. *Capital outlay.* Premiums paid for the savings component of life insurance, annuity, and endowment contracts are nondeductible if paid by the owner of the policy, because they constitute an investment or capital outlay. This barrier to a deduction applies even if the policy is purchased for business reasons.[82]

The premiums are taken into account, however, in determining the tax status of payments to the insured.[83] Since this cost recovery principle is also applied in computing gain on annuity and endowment policies purchased for personal reasons, the "capital outlay" rationale for disallowing a deduction

---

[77] For IRC §262, see infra ¶14.3; see also Treas. Regs. §1.262-1(b)(1) (premiums paid by insured for life insurance are not deductible).

[78] See infra ¶¶32.2 (insurance premiums as alimony), 19.1 (charitable contributions).

[79] For IRC §§162 and 212, see infra ¶¶8.1 and 8.5, respectively.

[80] For discussion, see Champion Trophy Mfg. Co. v. CIR, ¶72,250 P-H Memo TC (1972).

[81] Goedel v. CIR, 39 BTA 1 (1939) (premiums paid by stock dealer on life of President of United States, whose death might disrupt the stock market); Rev. Rul. 55-714, 1955-2 CB 51 (manager denied deduction for insurance on lives of entertainers whom he represented for percentage of their gross income); infra ¶8.3 (re "ordinary and necessary" test).

[82] For discussion of the "capital outlay" restriction on business expenditures, see infra ¶8.4; see also Chism Ice Cream Co. v. CIR, ¶62,006 P-H Memo TC (1962) (premiums on retirement income policy; held, nondeductible capital investment), aff'd on other issues sub nom. Chism's Est. v. CIR, 322 F.2d 956 (9th Cir. 1963).

[83] See supra ¶¶4.2, 4.3.

when the premiums are paid is more accurate than the "personal, living, and family expenses" theory of IRC §262.

4. *Expenses allocable to exempt income.* Section 265(1) bars a deduction for amounts allocable to income that is "wholly exempt" from income taxation. It has been held that IRC §265(1) applies to premiums paid for life insurance, presumably on the theory that the proceeds are ordinarily "wholly exempt."[84] Section 265(1) is not construed, however, to bar a deduction for premiums paid by an employer to compensate an employee for services on the theory that the premiums are "allocable" to the compensation (which is taxable to the employee) rather than to the exempt proceeds received by the employee's beneficiaries.[85]

5. *Premiums paid by beneficiary of business life insurance.* Section 264(a)(1) disallows any deduction for life insurance premiums paid on policies covering the life of any officer, employee, or person financially interested in the taxpayer's trade or business if the taxpayer is directly or indirectly a beneficiary under the policy. This specialized provision applies whether the proceeds are exempt from income taxation or not, but is confined to premiums paid in a business context.[86] To trigger the disallowance of deductions under IRC §264(a)(1), the taxpayer must be "directly or indirectly a beneficiary under [the] policy." Not surprisingly, this phrase has been broadly construed to encompass policies pledged as collateral for the taxpayer's debts,[87] policies in which the taxpayer's interest is limited to a specified fractional or dollar amount,[88] and policies on the lives of employees if the employer is entitled to the cash surrender value on termination of employment.[89]

Although premiums paid by debtors on insurance policies pledged to secure their obligations are disallowed by IRC §264(a)(1) even if the loan is incurred for business purposes, creditors who pay premiums to keep pledged policies in force are not subject to the same constraint, since the insured is not

[84] Jones v. CIR, 231 F.2d 655 (3d Cir. 1956); see also Treas. Regs. §1.264-1(a) (last sentence).

[85] See Treas. Regs. §1.264-1(b) (second sentence), assuming deductibility of the premiums when paid as compensation.

[86] Because of the historic link (discussed infra ¶8.5) between IRC §162, relating to business expenses, and IRC §212, relating to expenses incurred by individuals in connection with income-producing property, it has been held that IRC §264(a)(1) applies to both classes of expenses. See Meyer v. US, 175 F.2d 45 (2d Cir. 1949).

[87] See Rev. Rul. 68-5, 1968-1 CB 99 (policies on the life of officer of taxpayer corporation, pledged to secure Small Business Administration loan).

[88] Desks, Inc. v. CIR, 18 TC 674 (1952) (Acq.) (taxpayer entitled to proceeds in excess of debt owed by predecessor); Rev. Rul. 66-203, 1966-2 CB 104 (premiums disallowed in whole, although taxpayer's interest limited to policy's cash surrender value and declined by ten percentage points each year).

[89] Rev. Rul. 70-148, 1970-1 CB 60.

financially interested *in the creditor's business.*[90] But if the creditor has a contractual or implied right to be reimbursed for the premiums (whether by the debtor or from the proceeds of the policy), the IRS evidently regards the payments as nondeductible capital outlays unless the right to reimbursement is worthless.[91]

2. Losses. If a life insurance policy expires during the life of the insured, the owner of the policy cannot deduct the cost of the policy as a loss.[92] The "mortality loss" attributable to the insured's longevity is denied recognition for tax purposes because the premiums provided full value in the form of protection against premature death while the policy was in force. This rationale can be illustrated by reference to a vacationer who purchased life insurance from an airport vending machine before embarking on a flight. If he announced that he suffered a loss because he arrived safely at his destination, his comment would be regarded as gallows humor rather than sober economic analysis. Since his family was protected during the flight, he received his money's worth; and the protection was part of the nondeductible cost of the vacation.

The premiums paid by a business enterprise to protect itself against loss from a key employee's death on a business trip are nondeductible by virtue of IRC §265(1). If the employee arrives safely, the cost of protection in the interim is a genuine business expense, but a deduction for the "loss" is not allowed under current law.

The no-loss principle has also been employed to deny a deduction when a policyholder surrenders or sells a life insurance policy for its cash value and receives less than the premiums paid for the policy.[93] In effect, the policy is treated as having a basis equal to the premiums paid less the cost of the interim protection, the cash surrender value being viewed as a suitable measure of this difference.[94] If, however, the taxpayer receives less than the policy's cash surrender value (e.g., because of the insurer's insolvency), the difference should be deductible under IRC §165(c)(2), since the savings component of life insur-

---

[90] Rev. Rul. 75-46, 1975-1 CB 55; see also Rev. Rul. 70-254, 1970-1 CB 31 (premiums on credit life insurance deductible by creditor).

[91] Rev. Rul. 75-46, supra note 90; see also First Nat'l Bank & Trust Co. of Tulsa v. Jones, 143 F.2d 652, 653 (10th Cir. 1944) ("advancements made for insurance premiums, without reasonable hope or expectancy of repayment," deductible as ordinary and necessary business expenses if justified as "proper business precaution").

[92] Rev. Rul. 56-634, 1956-2 CB 291, 292 ("the purchased protection was provided during the years for which the premium was paid so that no loss results").

[93] London Shoe Co. v. CIR, 80 F.2d 230 (2d Cir. 1935), cert. denied, 298 US 663 (1936) (surrender to insurer).

[94] On proper proof, a different measure might be accepted by the courts. See Brawerman, Income Tax Problems of Non-Business Life Insurance, 1952 So. Calif. Tax Inst. 267, 282-283.

ance (reflected by its cash surrender value) is comparable to an investment in securities or other assets.[95]

Annuitants who outlive their life expectancies are not taxed on their mortality gains,[96] but short-lived annuitants have not been successful in establishing that a mortality loss should give rise to a deduction for tax purposes. Their claims have been rejected because the annuity contract was not purchased in a transaction entered into for profit, because the taxpayer suffered no loss since he got what he bargained for (i.e., a guaranteed income for life), or for both reasons.[97]

¶4.6 EMPLOYEE DEATH BENEFITS

1. Introductory. Under IRC §101(b)(1), the beneficiaries of the estate of a deceased employee may exclude from gross income certain death benefits paid by an employer by reason of the employee's death, up to an aggregate amount of $5,000. Except for the $5,000 limitation, the exclusion granted by IRC §101(b)(1) is extremely broad: It is available whether the benefits are paid in a single sum or in installments,[98] outright or in trust, to the deceased employee's beneficiaries or to his estate, directly by the employer or indirectly on his behalf, by one employer or several, and whether the employee was on active duty or retired at the time of death.

The status of an "employee" is determined by the usual common-law rules,[99] which do not embrace independent contractors; and IRC §101(b)(3) explicitly excludes self-employed persons, even if they qualify as "employees" under IRC §401(c)(1) (relating to retirement plans for self-employed taxpayers).

Since the exclusion may not exceed $5,000 per employee, it is necessary to allocate the exclusion if benefits aggregating more than $5,000 are paid to two or more beneficiaries of the same deceased employee. The regulations

---

[95] See Cohen v. CIR, 44 BTA 709 (1941) (Acq.) (loss attributable to insurer's financial difficulties incurred in transaction entered into for profit, one judge dissenting). For IRC §165(c)(2), see infra ¶12.2.

[96] See supra ¶4.3.

[97] White v. US, 19 AFTR2d 658 (N.D. Tex. 1966) (not officially reported) (jury verdict); Industrial Trust Co. v. Broderick, 94 F.2d 927 (1st Cir.), cert. denied, 304 US 572 (1938); Rev. Rul. 72-193, 1972-1 CB 58; Evans v. Rothensies, 114 F.2d 958, 961-962 (3d Cir. 1940).

[98] If, however, the benefit is held by the employer under an agreement to pay interest, the exclusion of IRC §101(b)(1) covers only the capital amount, not the interest payments. See IRC §101(c); Treas. Regs. §1.101-3; supra ¶4.2.

[99] Rev. Rul. 54-547, 1954-2 CB 57; see also infra ¶39.6.

provide for an allocation in the same proportion that each beneficiary's share bears to the total amount paid or payable.[100]

2. Nonforfeitable Rights in Employee During Life. Under IRC §101(b)(2)(B), the $5,000 exclusion does not embrace amounts that the employee had a nonforfeitable right to receive while living.[101] As interpreted by the regulations, this provision disqualifies not only accrued salary, unpaid leave, bonuses, and other items of compensation that would have been paid in due course to the employee, but also amounts that he would have been able to collect only on retirement or termination of his employment.[102] This disqualification of amounts to which the employee had a nonforfeitable right is not applicable to lump-sum distributions by certain qualified pension, profit-sharing, stock bonus, and annuity plans.[103]

3. Annuity Payments. Death benefits do not qualify for the $5,000 exclusion if received by the employee's survivor under a joint-and-survivor annuity contract after the employee himself has received an annuity payment or would have received such a payment had he lived. This limitation, imposed by IRC §101(b)(2)(C), is similar to the disqualification of benefits to which the employee had a nonforfeitable right during his life, since the employee would have received the entire amount payable under the joint-and-survivor annuity contract if he had outlived the secondary beneficiary.

Other annuity contracts are subject to IRC §101(b)(2)(D), which in effect permits the exclusion granted by IRC §101(b)(1) to be treated as the cost of the contract in applying IRC §72, the general statutory provision governing the taxability of annuity payments.[104] The result of this treatment is that part of each annuity payment can be excluded from gross income by the beneficiary (up to an aggregate of $5,000), but the interest component is subject to tax.

4. Employee Death Benefits as Tax-Free Proceeds of Life Insurance. If benefits paid by an employer to the employee's beneficiaries or estate can qualify as the proceeds of "life insurance" within the meaning of IRC

---

[100] Treas. Regs. §1.101-2(c); for examples, see Rev. Rul. 72-555, 1972-2 CB 44; Treas. Regs. §1.101-2(c)(2), Example; Treas. Regs. §1.101-2(e)(2), Examples (1)(ii), (2).

[101] For the meaning of "nonforfeitable," see Pollnow v. CIR, 35 TC 715 (1961) (Acq.) (forfeiture of rights on conviction of crime or willful disloyalty to employer); Rev. Rul. 71-361, 1971-2 CB 90 (rights forfeited if employee quits before retirement, was discharged for cause, or engaged after retirement in competition with employer).

[102] See Treas. Regs. §1.101-2(d)(1)(i).

[103] Treas. Regs. §1.101-2(d).

[104] Treas. Regs. §§1.101-2(a)(2) (third sentence); 1.101-2(e). Note that the nonforfeitable disqualification of IRC §101(b)(2)(B) is also applicable to annuity payments.

§101(a), they can be excluded from gross income regardless of the dollar amount.[105] Since the unlimited exclusion of insurance proceeds embraces all "death benefit payments having the characteristics of life insurance payable by reason of death" [106] regardless of the payor's business, there is a troublesome area of overlap between IRC §101(a) and §101(b). The scope of the crucial phrase "payments having the characteristics of life insurance" is examined elsewhere in this work.[107]

5. Employee Death Benefits as Tax-Free Gifts. When paid voluntarily by the employer, employee death benefits can sometimes qualify as "gifts" within the meaning of IRC §102(a), in which event they are excluded from the recipient's gross income regardless of the dollar amount.[108] The government argues, however, that the 1954 extension of IRC §101(b)(1) to noncontractual payments is evidence that Congress endorsed the IRS theory that payments to the widows of employees are "generally" not tax-free gifts.[109]

In practice, the existence of IRC §101(b)(1) provides a safe harbor for the first $5,000 of employee death benefits; but it does not seem to reduce the taxpayer's ability to prove that amounts in excess of $5,000 are excludable gifts under IRC §102. If the employee succeeds in this endeavor, however, the employer's deduction for the gift is limited to $25 per donee per year by IRC §274(b), a restriction that encourages employers to describe death benefits in excess of $5,000 as belated compensation rather than as acts of disinterested generosity.[110]

6. Employee Death Benefits as Income in Respect of Decedents. Section 101(b) applies if benefits qualify as "income in respect of a decedent" under IRC §691, in the nature of deferred compensation or the continuation of the decedent's salary. Payments of this type retain their compensatory character in the hands of the recipient. Thus, the payments qualify for the $5,000 exclusion of IRC §101(b)(2)(A); but any excess is includable in gross income, subject to the usual remote possibility of being excluded as gifts from the employer to the employee's survivor.[111]

---

[105] See supra ¶4.2.

[106] Treas. Regs. §1.101-1(a)(1).

[107] Supra ¶4.2.

[108] For discussion of this possibility, see supra ¶3.2.

[109] Rev. Rul. 62-102, 1962-2 CB 37; see also Fanning v. Conly, 357 F.2d 37 (2d Cir. 1966) (benefits above first $5,000 qualified as tax-free gifts).

[110] For discussion of IRC §274(b), see infra ¶9.4.

[111] Rev. Rul. 68-124, 1968-1 CB 44 (bonuses held to be income in respect of a decedent, subject to $5,000 death benefit exclusion); Nilssen's Est. v. US, 322 F.Supp. 260 (D.Minn. 1971) (payments to employee's surviving spouse under retirement contract subject to IRC §691, despite inclusion of value of contract for federal estate tax purposes).

SELECTED BIBLIOGRAPHY

Banoff & Hartz, It's No Sin to SCIN! A Reply to Professor Blum on Self-Cancelling Installment Notes—The New SCIN Game? 60 Taxes 187 (1982).

Blum, Self-Cancelling Installment Notes—The New SCIN Game? 60 Taxes 183 (1982).

Ginsberg, Future Payment Sales After the 1980 Revision Act, 39 NYU Inst. on Fed. Tax. Ch. 43 (1981).

Goldstein, Tax Aspects of Corporate Business Use of Life Insurance, 18 Tax L. Rev. 133 (1963).

Treanor, Code Section 101: The Thin Line Between Life Insurance and Employee Death Benefits, 37 J. Tax. 176 (1972).

CHAPTER 5

Compensation for Personal Injuries and Sickness

¶5.1 COMPENSATION FOR PERSONAL INJURIES AND SICKNESS

1. Introductory. Compensation for personal injuries and sickness is excluded from gross income by IRC §104(a), subject to qualifications examined below. The imposition of an income tax on compensation received by persons who have been blinded or crippled by accident would no doubt be regarded as heartless, unless their recoveries from tort-feasors were correspondingly increased. The exclusion, however, also embraces less emotionally charged receipts, such as compensation for the loss of wages during temporary absences from work, if paid under a workmen's compensation act or taxpayer-financed health and accident insurance policy or if recovered in a tort suit; and this immunity is inconsistent with the usual practice of taxing substitutes for amounts that would be includable in gross income if received in the normal course of events.[1]

The exclusionary principle underlying IRC §104(a) is subject to two major qualifications. Receipts attributable to deductions allowed in prior years under IRC §213 (relating to medical expenses in excess of 5 percent of the taxpayer's adjusted gross income) are not excludable; since the medical expenses have already reduced the taxpayer's income, an exclusion of the reimbursement would constitute a double benefit. Amounts received for medical

[1] See Raytheon Prod. Corp. v. CIR, 144 F.2d 110 (1st Cir.), cert. denied, 323 US 779 (1944).

expenses that were not deducted (e.g., because not yet paid or below the deductible floor), however, are excludable under IRC §104, if otherwise qualified, along with advance payments for future medical expenses.[2] The second major limitation on the exclusion of IRC §104(a) concerns the proceeds of accident or health insurance financed by the taxpayer's employer, which are subjected by IRC §105 to stricter rules than benefits under taxpayer-financed insurance.[3]

2. Workmen's Compensation. Compensation for personal injuries and sickness is excludable from gross income under IRC §104(a)(1) if received under a workmen's compensation act.[4] Recognizing that this phrase is hazy around the edges, the regulations reach out to encompass any "statute in the nature of a workmen's compensation act which provides compensation to employees for personal injuries or sickness incurred in the course of employment," a liberalization applied by the IRS to many compensation plans for public employees.[5] The regulations also extend the exclusion to payments to the survivors of employees killed in the line of duty.[6] Disabled employees whose benefits under a workmen's compensation act continue even if they are able to find other employment do not lose the exclusion.[7]

Adhering to the original concept of workmen's compensation, the regulations provide that IRC §104(a)(1) does not apply to retirement benefits to the extent determined by reference to the employee's age, length of service, or prior contributions, even though retirement is occasioned by occupational injury or sickness.[8] If an employee compensation plan combines disability and retirement elements (as is true of many public plans for public employees), the benefits qualify for exclusion under IRC §104(a)(1) only to the extent attributable to personal injury or sickness incurred in the course of employment, without reference to the employee's age, length of service, or prior contributions.[9]

---

[2] For IRC §213, see infra ¶20.1; see also Rev. Rul. 75-230, 1975-1 CB 93 (in absence of express allocation by parties, settlement of personal injury suit allocated first to previously deducted medical expenses); Rev. Rul. 75-232, 1975-1 CB 94 (payment for future medical expenses excludable but will reduce amount deductible under IRC §213).

[3] Infra ¶5.2.

[4] The exclusion does not apply to amounts attributable to medical expenses allowed as deductions under IRC §213. See supra note 2.

[5] Treas. Regs. §1.104-1(b).

[6] Id.; see also Robinson v. CIR, 42 TC 403 (1964) (Acq.) (death not in line of duty; exclusion denied).

[7] Rev. Rul. 72-44, 1972-1 CB 32 (Question 4).

[8] Treas. Regs. §1.104-1(b); see Waller v. US, 180 F.2d 194 (D.C. Cir. 1950).

[9] Treas. Regs. §1.104-1(b); Rev. Rul. 72-44, supra note 7 (service-disabled firemen received one-half regular salary if employed for less than twenty years but full salary

The regulations also provide that compensation for nonoccupational injuries or sickness is not excludable under IRC §104(a)(1).[10] Despite this static view of the term "workmen's compensation act," the IRS has not endeavored to confine the concept of an injury "arising out of and in the course of employment" to its scope as of 1918, when the statutory predecessor of IRC §104(a)(1) was enacted. Thus, workmen's compensation payments for injuries resulting from horseplay in the plant or accidents while driving to work are excludable under IRC §104, even if they would not have been regarded as employment-related in 1918; and it seems likely that the tax exclusion will continue to expand with the concept of service-connected injuries.[11]

3. Military Disability Pensions. Pensions, annuities, and similar allowances for personal injuries or sickness resulting from active service in the armed forces of any country or the United States Public Health Service, Coast and Geodetic Survey, or Foreign Service are excludable under IRC §104(a)(4), subject to severe restrictions imposed by the Tax Reform Act of 1976. Under the 1976 legislation, the IRC §104(a)(4) exclusion is limited to combat-related injuries (defined to include personal injury or sickness from armed conflict, extra hazardous service, simulated war exercises, or instrumentalities of war) and to amounts that the taxpayer could receive by applying to the Veterans Administration for disability compensation. Two grandfather clauses, however, preserve IRC §104(a)(4)'s broader pre-1976 benefits for taxpayers who, on or before September 24, 1975, (a) were entitled to receive excludable amounts or (b) were members of or subject to a binding written commitment to join one of the affected federal services.

The principal litigation under IRC §104(a)(4) has concerned members of the armed forces who were retired for length of service when they might have been retired for disability. If the retirement board made no determination of disability, an exclusion is not warranted even if the taxpayer can prove that disability existed and could have been found by the appropriate military

---

if employed for twenty years or more; held, latter group can exclude only amount determined without regard to length of service, viz., one-half regular salary).

[10] Treas. Regs. §1.104-1(b); McDonald v. CIR, 33 TC 540 (1959) (insufficient evidence of service connection); Golden v. CIR, ¶71,162 P-H Memo TC (1971) (despite "valiant effort" by retired municipal judge to show that hypertension was service-connected, IRC §104(a)(1) not applicable); Rev. Rul. 72-191, 1972-1 CB 45 (nonoccupational benefits cannot be excluded under IRC §104(a)(1)), amplified by Rev. Rul. 75-499, 1975-2 CB 43 (benefits may qualify as excludable proceeds of health and accident insurance or unemployment compensation).

[11] For an illustration of the expansive contemporary view of workmen's compensation coverage, see Beauchesne v. David London & Co., 375 A.2d 920 (R.I. 1977) (employee got drunk at office Christmas party and fell out of window; held, compensable).

board.[12] If, however, the board erroneously failed to find that the taxpayer was disabled, the IRS has ruled that a later correction of its action qualifies the payments for exclusion, retroactively to the date when the finding of disability should have been made.[13] These principles remain applicable to the residual situations in which the exclusion of IRC §104(a)(4) is still available after the 1976 changes.

Proof that the Internal Revenue Code keeps abreast of international events may be found in IRC §104(a)(5), enacted in 1976, which permits government employees injured in a terrorist attack while abroad in the performance of official duties to exclude from gross income disability income attributable to the injuries.[14]

In limited circumstances, disability payments to servicemen and other government employees that are outside the ambit of IRC §104(a)(4) may qualify for exclusion under IRC §105(d),[15] relating to employer-financed accident and health plans, and benefits to them are also affected by special provisions in the statutes regulating their retirement and other benefits.[16]

4. Damages. Since 1918, IRC §104(a)(2) and its statutory predecessors have excluded from gross income damages received, whether by suit or agreement, on account of personal injuries or sickness.[17] The rationale for the exclusion, which is interpreted by the regulations to embrace claims based on "tort or tort type rights," [18] is presumably that the recovery does not generate a gain or profit but only makes the taxpayer whole by compensating for a loss.[19] But the exclusion clearly embraces compensation for lost wages if

---

[12] Pangburn v. CIR, 13 TC 169 (1949); but see Prince v. US, 119 F.Supp. 421 (Ct. Cl. 1954) (retirement based on length of service treated as based on disability).

[13] Rev. Rul. 74-582, 1974-2 CB 34 (retroactive change effective where original retirement for length of service was erroneous; but if taxpayer elected to retire for length of service, subsequent change is effective only prospectively); Strickland v. CIR, 540 F.2d 1196 (4th Cir. 1976) (exclusion allowed despite administrative delay in granting disability status); Rev. Rul. 78-161, 1978-1 CB 31 (retroactive determination of service-connected disability by V.A. accepted, following *Strickland;* earlier contrary ruling revoked).

[14] See S. Rep. No. 94-938, reprinted in 1976-3 CB (Vol. 3) 49 at 704; see also Hostage Relief Act of 1980, 94 Stat. 1967, §201 (compensation from United States excluded from income of American hostage in Iran).

[15] Treas. Regs. §1.104-1(e).

[16] See Treas. Regs. §1.104-1(e), listing relevant nontax statutes.

[17] Like other items excludable under IRC §104(a), damage recoveries are includable in gross income to the extent attributable to medical expenses previously deducted under IRC §213. See supra note 4.

[18] Treas. Regs. §1.104-1(c). For receipts under no-fault insurance policies, see Rev. Rul. 73-155, infra note 29; see also US v. Garber, 589 F.2d 843 (5th Cir. 1979) (amounts received by commercial blood donor not damages for personal injuries).

[19] For a series of early IRS rulings excluding from gross income recoveries for

occasioned by personal injury or sickness, despite the usual principle that recoveries are taxable if they compensate for amounts that would have been taxable if received in due course.[20] The IRS has ruled that punitive awards also qualify for the exclusion if attributable to personal injuries or sickness.[21] On the other hand, income accruing on an award of damages (e.g., interest earned on damages held by a court for the benefit of a minor) is not excludable under IRC §104(a)(2).

The exclusion from the recipient's gross income of recoveries for personal injuries and wrongful death is deeply entrenched in private tort law, and juries are often instructed that the plaintiff will not be taxed on the award.[22] Thus, a repeal of IRC §104(a)(2) would create shock waves throughout the personal injury area and would no doubt lead to larger verdicts and higher insurance premiums.

The phrase "personal injuries or sickness" as used in IRC §104(a)(2) embraces emotional distress, libel, slander, and other nonphysical wrongs, but not damage to the taxpayer's business reputation.[23] When this distinction requires apportioning a lump-sum settlement between its excludable and taxable components, the taxpayer has the burden of establishing a reasonable basis for the division.[24] The exclusion has been denied, however, to payments for agreeing to a future invasion of the taxpayer's privacy (e.g., depicting the taxpayer's family in a motion picture).[25] It seems equally clear that a person

---

wrongful death, alienation of affections, breach of promise to marry, and libel and slander because they do not produce a gain, see supra ¶1.9.

[20] See supra note 1.

[21] Rev. Rul. 75-45, 1975-1 CB 47 (damages "whether compensatory or punitive" are excludable); Rev. Rul. 58-418, 1958-2 CB 18 (punitive component of settlement of libel action taxable as income).

[22] See Norfolk & Western Ry. v. Liepelt, 444 US 490 (1980) (tax-free status of award under Federal Employers' Liability Act and effect of taxes on employee's future earnings admissible); McWeeney v. New York, N.H. & H.R.R., 282 F.2d 34, 39 (2d Cir.), cert. denied, 364 US 870 (1960) (instruction proper but not mandatory); but see Domeracki v. Humble Oil & Ref. Co., 443 F.2d 1245, 1248-1251 (3d Cir.), cert. denied, 404 US 883 (1971) (upon request, instruction re tax exclusion must be given).

[23] Seay v. CIR, 58 TC 32 (1972) (Acq.) ($45,000 of $105,000 received by ex-employee in settlement of claims for breach of contract and wrongful discharge, designated as "compensation for . . . personal embarrassment, mental and physical strain and injury to health and personal reputation in the community," held excludable); Wolfson v. CIR, ¶78,445 P-H Memo TC (1978), aff'd, 48 AFTR2d 5351 (6th Cir. 1981) (damages found to be for injury to professional reputation; court raises but leaves open possibility that such damages constitute nontaxable return of capital, because issue not argued by taxpayer).

[24] See Seay v. CIR, supra note 23; Wallace v. CIR, ¶76,219 P-H Memo TC (1976) (failure to allocate recovery between injury to personal reputation and injury to business reputation).

[25] See Roosevelt v. CIR, 43 TC 77 (1964) (extended discussion of issue and

engaged in a hazardous calling, such as a motion-picture stunt actor, cannot use IRC §104(a)(2) to shield amounts received for a release of the right to sue for injuries that might be sustained in the future.

5. Taxpayer-Financed Accident or Health Insurance. Payments for personal injuries or sickness received through accident or health insurance are excludable from gross income under IRC §104(a)(3), unless attributable to amounts previously deducted as medical expenses under IRC §213. This exclusion does not embrace amounts received by an employee, however, if paid by the employer or attributable to employer contributions that were not includable in the employee's gross income.[26] Payments under employer-financed arrangements are not necessarily taxable, but their status is governed by IRC §105.[27] If contributions are made by both the employer and the employee, the benefits must be apportioned between employer-financed amounts subject to IRC §105, and employee-financed amounts governed by IRC §104(a)(3).[28]

The primary function of IRC §104(a)(3) is to exempt from taxation amounts received under ordinary accident and health insurance policies purchased by the taxpayer. It also embraces amounts received by a sole proprietor as compensation for income lost as a result of disability or sickness and similar payments received by a corporation as compensation for a key employee's absence from work because of disability.[29] Moreover, the exclusion is not

---

relevant cases); see also Treas. Regs. §1.104-1(c) (exclusion embraces "damages" based on "tort or tort type rights").

[26] In the case of self-employed persons, certain contributions deductible under IRC §404 (relating to qualified pension, profit-sharing, or annuity plans) are treated by the last sentence of IRC §104(a) as made by the employer, so that distributions under the plan to the self-employed person cannot be treated as the proceeds of accident or health insurance and excluded under IRC §104(a)(3); moreover, by virtue of IRC §105(g), these amounts are not covered by IRC §105. As a result, jurisdiction over these amounts is vested in IRC §72(m) rather than in IRC §§104 and 105; see Treas. Regs. §§1.104-1(d) (last sentence), 1.105-1(a). See also Chosiad v. CIR, ¶80,408 P-H Memo TC (1980) (when contributory plan provides both retirement and accident or health benefits, latter are presumed attributable to employer contributions in absence of contrary showing).

[27] Infra ¶5.2.

[28] Treas. Regs. §§1.104-1(d), 1.105-1(c); Rev. Rul. 63-181, 1963-2 CB 74 (allocation of receipts under employer-employee contributory group insurance policy in proportion to percentages of premiums paid).

[29] Rev. Rul. 58-90, 1958-1 CB 88 (sole proprietor); Rev. Rul. 55-264, 1955-1 CB 11 (exclusion not applicable to reimbursement for business overhead expenses during prolonged disability due to injury or sickness). Rev. Rul. 73-155, 1973-1 CB 50, provides that disability benefits received by an injured auto passenger from the owner's insurer under a no-fault provision are excludable under IRC §104(a)(3). It is not clear why the IRS cited IRC §104(a)(3) (insurance) rather than IRC §104(a)(2) (damages) as authority for this ruling.

limited to commercial insurance companies, but also encompasses payments from funds and other plans that spread the risk of loss by indemnifying participants, such as a company-wide fund maintained by employee contributions.[30]

¶5.2 EMPLOYER-FINANCED ACCIDENT AND HEALTH PLANS

1. Introductory. Before 1954, the status of wage continuation payments received by a sick employee depended on whether they constituted "amounts received through accident or health insurance for personal injuries or sickness" within the meaning of the statutory predecessor of IRC §104(a)(3). When the Court of Appeals for the Seventh Circuit held in *Epmeier v. United States* that a self-insured company's own wage continuation plan for employees constituted "accident or health insurance," [31] the IRS announced that it would not follow *Epmeier* "in the absence of further clarification from the Congress," [32] fearing that the decision would encourage closely held corporations to allow their executives and shareholder-employees to go to Florida on "sick leave" every winter and to treat their salaries as excludable insurance receipts.

Congress responded to *Epmeier* by transferring jurisdiction over employer-financed accident and health insurance benefits from the statutory predecessor of IRC §104(a)(3) to a new provision, IRC §105. This shift was effected by making IRC §104(a)(3) inapplicable to insurance payments received by an employee if paid by the employer or attributable to employer contributions not includable in the employee's gross income.[33] Under IRC §105(a), payments under employer-financed plans must be included in the employee's gross income unless they meet the special tests of IRC §105(b), §105(c), or §105(d). The 1954 rules regarding employer-financed insurance were buttressed by the contemporaneous enactment of (1) IRC §105(e), defining the term "accident or health insurance" to include various "plans" and "funds," and (2) IRC §106, providing that employees are not taxable on contributions by their employers to accident or health plans compensating them for personal injuries or sickness.

As enacted in 1954, IRC §105 granted an exclusion to amounts received

---

[30] See Haynes v. US, 353 US 81 (1957); Treas. Regs. §1.104-1(d).

[31] Epmeier v. US, 199 F.2d 508 (7th Cir. 1952). Although the taxpayer was itself a life insurance company, the *Epmeier* plan did not involve conventional insurance, and the Supreme Court later reached the same result as to a plan created by a utility company for its employees. Haynes v. US, supra note 30.

[32] IR-047 (March 26, 1953), 1953 P-H Fed. Taxes ¶76,437.

[33] For allocation of benefits if the plan is financed jointly by employees and their employer, see supra note 31.

by employees under employer-financed accident and health plans if the payment (1) reimbursed the employee for medical expenses, (2) compensated for permanent bodily injury, or (3) qualified as "sick pay." The exclusion of sick pay proved to be a prolific source of litigation and criticism, and it was severely pruned in 1976 by amendments to IRC §105(d), which confine its benefits to taxpayers who are permanently and totally disabled, under the age of sixty-five, and meet other tests. Moreover, the sick pay exclusion is phased out if the taxpayer's adjusted gross income exceeds $15,000.

2. Accident and Health Insurance. The operative provisions of IRC §105 apply to "amounts received by an employee through accident or health insurance for personal injuries or sickness," [34] and IRC §105(e)(1) states that "an accident or health plan for employees" shall be treated as "insurance." [35] This explicit reference to "plans," which need not be insured or funded, carries forward the theory that an indemnification arrangement can constitute "insurance" even though not backed by a formal policy issued by a commercial insurance company.[36] When enacting IRC §105(e) in 1954, Congress deliberately refrained from requiring employer-financed plans to meet the elaborate standards that must be satisfied by qualified pension and profit-sharing plans; this tolerance came to an end in 1978, when IRC §105(h) was enacted to impose special rules on discriminatory self-insured medical reimbursement plans.

The 1954 use by Congress of the vague term "plan," unaccompanied at that time by any restrictions on discrimination in favor of the controlling shareholders of closely held corporations or highly compensated employees, opened the door to abuse. This risk was increased by liberal regulations, which provided that a plan may cover "one or more employees," that different plans may be established for "different employees or classes of employees," that the plan need not be in writing, that a "program, policy, or custom having the effect of a plan" will suffice, and that an employee's rights need not be enforceable, provided notice or knowledge of the plan was reasonably available to the employee when the injury or sickness was sustained.[37] Despite this flabby concept of a "plan," the courts held that a plan "signifies something more than

[34] By virtue of IRC §105(g), the term "employee" does not embrace self-employed individuals, so their accident and health insurance benefits are not covered by IRC §105. See supra note 26.

[35] Section 105(e)(2) spreads the same umbrella over sickness and disability funds for public employees.

[36] Supra note 31.

[37] Treas. Regs. §1.105-5(a). But see Chism's Est. v. CIR, 322 F.2d 956 (9th Cir. 1963) (plan not reduced to writing, employees not formally notified, and employee rights subject to change without their consent; held, Tax Court could properly conclude that no plan existed).

merely one or more ad hoc benefit payments." [38] In addition to surmounting the "ad hoc" hurdle, an accident or health plan must be for the benefit of "employees" to qualify under IRC §105. This criterion does not preclude a plan that benefits shareholder-employees, but they must be included by virtue of their status as employees, rather than as shareholders.[39]

Most of the litigated disputes regarding the existence of a "plan" involved wage continuation payments to shareholder-employees rather than reimbursement of their medical expenses or compensation for permanent bodily injury. For the controlling shareholders of closely held enterprises, it was tempting to describe Florida vacations as periods of convalescence from illness.[40] This possibility of abuse was drastically reduced in 1976, when Congress restricted the sick pay exclusion to employees afflicted with permanent and total disability and provided for a phaseout of even this limited exclusion if the employee's adjusted gross income exceeds $15,000. These restrictions do not apply to the exclusion of reimbursed medical expenses and payments for permanent bodily injury under IRC §§105(b) and 105(c); but these items are more easily verified than sick pay.

3. Reimbursed Medical Expenses. Accident and health insurance payments made directly or indirectly to an employee specifically to reimburse expenses incurred for "medical care" [41] of the taxpayer or the taxpayer's spouse or dependents are excludable from the employee's gross income under IRC §105(b), unless attributable to deductions allowed under IRC §213 (relating to the deduction of medical expenses) in prior taxable years. The exclusion is allowed if the sick or injured person is a "dependent" of the taxpayer as

---

[38] Kaufman's Est. v. CIR, 35 TC 663, 666 (1961), aff'd per curiam, 300 F.2d 128 (6th Cir. 1962); see also Lang v. CIR, 41 TC 352, 356-357 (1963) ("plan" as used in IRC §105 "presupposes a predetermined course of action under prescribed circumstances," not merely the "favorable exercise of discretion by the employer when sickness arises").

[39] American Foundry v. CIR, 536 F.2d 289 (9th Cir. 1976) ("rational" basis for benefits, other than ownership of business, if required); Leidy's Est. v. CIR, ¶75,340 P-H Memo TC (1975), aff'd per curiam, 549 F.2d 798 (4th Cir. 1976) (payments to controlling shareholder and mother treated as constructive dividends to him); Levine v. CIR, 50 TC 422 (1968) (payments to taxpayer for more than five years; on basis of employer's financial circumstances, court concluded that payments to ordinary employees would have been restricted to shorter period and that taxpayer's payments continued only because he was controlling shareholder).

[40] See Kaufman's Est. v. CIR, supra note 38 (part-time consulting services by corporate officer; held, compensation, not sick pay).

[41] "Indirect" payments include amounts paid to a physician or hospital or to the employee's spouse or dependents. See Treas. Regs. §1.105-2. For the definition of "medical care" under IRC §213(e), see infra ¶20.1.

defined by IRC §152,[42] whether or not the additional requirements for a "dependency exemption" are met.

4. Payments for Permanent Bodily Injury. Section 105(c) excludes payments for permanent bodily injury (as defined), incurred by the taxpayer or the taxpayer's spouse or dependents, provided the amount is computed by reference to the nature of the injury and without regard to the length of the employee's absence from work.[43] If computed without regard to the taxpayer's absence from work, however, payments for permanent bodily injury can be excluded whether paid in a lump sum or installments.[44] Section 105(c) covers payments for the permanent loss or loss of use of a member or function of the body, or for permanent disfigurement. The regulations provide that the term "disfigurement" is subject to "a reasonable interpretation in the light of all the particular facts and circumstances" and that disfigurement "shall be considered permanent when it may reasonably be expected to continue for the life of the individual." [45]

5. Pre-1977 Sick Pay. From 1954 to 1976, IRC §105(d) permitted employees to exclude wages or payments in lieu of wages, up to a weekly rate of $100, for periods of absence from work on account of personal injuries or sickness. This exclusion was drastically curtailed for taxable years beginning after December 31, 1976. In application, the earlier rules created difficulties that will no doubt continue to be litigated for pre-1977 taxable years for some time to come, including whether there was a plan in existence and, if so, whether the payments were made pursuant to it; whether the employee was "absent from work" on account of injuries or sickness; and whether the statutorily imposed waiting periods and dollar and percentage limits were complied with.[46]

6. Post-1976 Sick Pay—Permanent and Total Disability. Under IRC §105(d) as amended in 1976, wage continuation payments are excluded from gross income only if the taxpayer (1) has not attained age sixty-five before the

---

[42] For the scope of the term "dependent," see infra ¶14.2.

[43] See Rev. Rul. 74-603, 1974-2 CB 35.

[44] Treas. Regs. §1.105-3 (penultimate sentence).

[45] Id.; see Rev. Rul. 63-181, 1963-2 CB 74 (lump-sum payment for permanent and total disability due to acute cancerous condition constitutes payment for permanent loss of use of member or function of the body).

[46] Treas. Regs. §§1.105-4(a)(3)(ii), 1.105-4(b) (effect of holiday or vacation in computing period of disability); Treas. Regs. §§1.105-4(a)(3), 1.105-6 (employees retired before January 1, 1975); Rev. Proc. 76-12, 1976-1 CB 552 (exclusion terminates when employer's mandatory or customary retirement age is reached). Treas. Regs. §1.105-4(e), 1.105-4(f) (waiting period, dollar, and percentage limitations).

close of the taxable year,[47] (2) retired on disability when permanently and totally disabled, and (3) is absent from work on account of permanent and total disability. The second and third of these requirements, which are set out separately in IRC §105(d)(1), overlap in part but are independently significant in that the employee must be permanently disabled at retirement but must continue to be absent from work because of the disability. Thus, if there is an unexpected remission, the employee would not satisfy the third requirement. Permanent and total disability is defined by IRC §105(d)(4) as inability to engage in any substantial gainful activity by reason of a medically determinable physical or mental impairment that has lasted or can be expected to last for a continuous period of twelve months or more or to result in death.

The exclusion is limited to a weekly rate of $100, and is phased out, dollar for dollar, if the taxpayer's adjusted gross income (including the disability income itself) exceeds $15,000. In the case of married couples, each spouse is entitled to the $100 weekly exclusion if disabled; but a joint return must be filed if they live together, and the $15,000 phaseout applies to their joint AGI.

7. Discriminatory Medical Expense Reimbursement Plans. Before 1980 it was possible for employer-financed plans to qualify for tax benefits under IRC §105 even if they discriminated in favor of shareholder-employees and highly compensated employees and excluded rank-and-file workers.[48] Section 105(g), enacted in 1978, limits the blanket exclusion of benefits paid under an employer's self-insured medical reimbursement plan, without altering the tax results of payments under plans covered by policies of accident or health insurance. The heart of the 1978 legislation is IRC §105(h)(1), providing that if a self-insured medical reimbursement plan is discriminatory as to eligibility and/or benefits (as defined), the normal exclusion from gross income allowed by IRC §105(b) does not apply to any "excess reimbursement" paid to a "highly compensated individual." This operative rule is backed up by a set of definitions.

1. *Nondiscriminatory plans.* To qualify as nondiscriminatory, a plan must satisfy both an eligibility and a benefits test.

The *eligibility* test is satisfied only if the plan benefits either (a) at least 70 percent of all employees or 80 percent of eligible employees if at least 70 percent are eligible or (b) such employees as qualify under a classification established by the employer and found by the IRS not to discriminate in favor of highly compensated participants. These alternative eligibility standards,

---

[47] Recipients of payments to which both IRC §105(d) and the annuity rules of IRC §72 would otherwise apply are subject solely to IRC §105(d) until attaining age sixty-five or until an irrevocable election is made to rely on IRC §72. See IRC §105(d)(6).

[48] For the limited restrictions imposed on plans by the regulations and case law, see supra, text at notes 36-40.

which resemble those applicable to qualified employee pension and profit-sharing plans, are relaxed by IRC §105(h)(3)(B), permitting the exclusion of employees with less than three years of service, employees under the age of 25, part-time and seasonal employees, employees covered by certain collective bargaining agreements, and certain nonresident aliens.

The *benefits* test requires all benefits provided for highly compensated individuals to be provided for all other participants.

2. *Excess reimbursement.* The term "excess reimbursement," which determines the taxable amount in the case of a highly compensated individual's benefits under a discriminatory plan, is given a twofold meaning by IRC §105(h)(7). First, the entire amount constitutes excess reimbursement under IRC §105(h)(7)(A) if the benefit is available to a highly compensated individual but not to a "broad cross-section" of employees. Second, in the case of benefits that are not disqualified by IRC §105(h)(7)(A), a payment to a highly compensated individual constitutes "excess reimbursement" in an amount determined by multiplying the individual's reimbursements for the plan year by a fraction, of which the numerator is the total amount reimbursed to highly compensated individuals and the denominator is the total amount reimbursed to all employees under the plan.

3. *Highly compensated individuals.* The highly compensated group consists of the employer's five highest paid officers; shareholders owning (directly, indirectly, or constructively) more than 10 percent of the employer's stock; and the highest paid 25 percent of all employees, other than nonparticipating employees excluded by IRC §105(h)(3)(B).

4. *The bottom line.* The statutory distinction between discriminatory and nondiscriminatory plans may acquire more teeth with the passage of time. In the interim, however, highly compensated individuals who itemize their personal deductions will often find that IRC §105(h) is a paper tiger, since the inclusion of excess reimbursement in gross income will be offset by a medical expense deduction under IRC §213, except for the nondeductible amount prescribed by the percentage limit of IRC §213(a)(1) (5 percent of adjusted gross income).[49]

8. Exclusion of Employer Contributions From Employee's Gross Income. Section 106 provides that an employer's contributions to an accident or health plan to compensate employees for personal injuries or sickness are not includable in the employee's gross income. Were it not for this exclusion, an employer's payment of premiums to an insurer or contributions to a disability fund would ordinarily constitute additional compensation to the employee, unless the amounts attributable to individuals could not be ascertained or the employee's rights were too tenuous to constitute "income." If IRC

[49] For IRC §213(a)(1), see generally infra ¶20.1.

§106 applies, amounts received by the employee when disability occurs are subject to IRC §105(a) rather than to §104(a)(3).

Since IRC §106 applies only to contributions to "accident or health plans," amounts attributable to other benefits are not excludable under IRC §106, but might qualify for exclusion on some other ground (such as IRC §79, relating to group term life insurance).[50]

9. Employer-Financed Accident and Health Benefits Paid Without Regard to a "Plan." Section 105 has no jurisdiction over accident and health benefits paid by an employer to an employee in the absence of "insurance" or a "plan." The status of such sporadic benefits can only be determined by an analysis of the circumstances leading to the payment itself. Among the possibilities are the following:

1. Additional compensation, taxable to the employee as such.[51]
2. A gift, excludable under IRC §102 if motivated by affection or similar impulses rather than by a profit-making purpose.[52]
3. Damages, excludable under IRC §104(a)(2).[53]
4. A constructive dividend, if paid to a shareholder-employee or a shareholder's relative.[54]
5. An employee death benefit, excludable to the extent provided by IRC §101(b).[55]

SELECTED BIBLIOGRAPHY

Bittker, Tax Reform and Disability Pensions—The Equal Treatment of Equals, 55 Taxes 363 (1977).

Colvin, Coping With the Anti-Discrimination Requirement of Medical Reimbursement Plans, 50 J. Tax. 104 (1979).

James & Lowe, Reassessing Medical Reimbursement Plans After Changes in the Law and Regulations, 54 J. Tax. 80 (1981).

James & Lowe, Consequences of Maintaining Discriminatory Self-Insured Medical Reimbursement Plans, 54 J. Tax. 89 (1981).

Note, Income Taxes and the Computation of Lost Future Earnings in Wrongful Death and Personal Injury Cases, 29 Md. L. Rev. 177 (1969).

---

[50] See Treas. Regs. §1.106-1; for IRC §79, see infra ¶7.2.

[51] See Charlie Sturgill Motor Co. v. CIR, ¶73,281 P-H Memo TC (1973) (Issue 4; employer's payment of medical expenses treated as additional compensation).

[52] For IRC §102, see supra ¶3.2.

[53] For IRC §104(a)(2), see supra ¶5.1.

[54] See Leidy's Est. v. CIR, supra note 39.

[55] For IRC §101(b), see supra ¶4.6.

CHAPTER 6

Interest on Federal, State, and Local Obligations

¶6.1 FEDERAL OBLIGATIONS

From 1913 to 1917, interest on federal obligations was excluded from the recipient's gross income. In 1917, this blanket exemption was replaced by a more selective approach, providing for an exemption only to the extent granted by the law authorizing particular obligations to be issued. Thereafter, no wholly exempt federal obligations were issued; but in some instances a partial tax exemption was granted, under which the interest was exempt from the federal "normal" income tax but not from the "surtax." When the distinction between the normal tax and surtax was eliminated in 1954, Congress enacted a credit to honor its commitment to investors in partially tax-exempt federal obligations; but this provision was repealed in 1976 as unnecessary since no such bonds remained outstanding.

Thus, interest on federal obligations now enjoys no special tax immunity. There are, however, some differences between federal and private obligations as respects the year when interest must be reported.[1]

---

[1] See IRC §1232A(a)(2)(B) (U.S. savings bonds not subject to constant interest method of reporting original issue discount); see generally infra ¶27.4.

¶6.2 STATE AND LOCAL OBLIGATIONS—IN GENERAL

1. Introductory. Since 1913, interest on the obligations of states and their political subdivisions has been excluded from the obligee's gross income. When this provision, now IRC §103(a)(1), was first enacted, it was widely thought that taxing the recipients of such income would impose an unconstitutional burden on the borrowing power of state and local governments. With the waning of the doctrine of intergovernmental tax immunity, the exclusion has been preserved by Congress as a kind ofnd of revenue sharing, which enables states and cities to borrow funds at an interest cost usually estimated to be about 70 percent of the rate paid on taxable obligations of similar quality.

The benefit derived by bondholders from the tax exemption accorded to interest on state and local obligations depends on the investor's marginal tax rate and the differential between the interest rate on exempt obligations and the rate on taxable obligations of equal quality. For example, if all state and local bonds were purchased by individual taxpayers who would otherwise be subject to a 50 percent tax rate on the interest, at a time when comparable private obligations carried an interest rate of 10 percent, the exempt issuers would have to pay only 5 percent (or a shade more) to float their securities, since a 5 percent exempt yield is the equivalent of a 10 percent taxable yield to an investor subject to a 50 percent marginal tax rate. On these assumptions, the entire benefit of the tax exemption would pass through to the cities and states, which would be able to borrow at 5 percent, while taxable borrowers would have to pay 10 percent to sell bonds of equal risk. The investors, on the other hand, would derive no benefit from the tax exemption, since their economic position would be the same whether they buy tax-free bonds and keep the 5 percent yield or buy taxable bonds with a 10 percent yield, pay their taxes, and keep 5 percent. Though they would claim the exemption, they would be mere conduits through which the benefit would pass to the governmental borrowers.

Turning to real life, however, we find that the interest rate on tax-exempt bonds (in 1982) is not 5 percent, but twice that, or more. In the view of most economists, this relationship reflects the fact that in recent years cities and states have had a virtually insatiable appetite for funds, leading them to flood the market with tax-exempt obligations. But this process is inherently self-destructive; if the supply of bonds is so great that they are not all purchased by top-bracket taxpayers, the borrowers must appeal to taxpayers in ever lower tax brackets, and this requires higher rates of interest than 5 percent. For taxpayers subject to a 30 percent marginal tax rate, for example, industrial bonds paying 10 percent produce a net return after taxes of 7 percent; and these taxpayers will not buy tax-exempt bonds unless they too offer a 7 percent return. To bring these teachers, pharmacists, and other plebian investors into the tax-exempt bond market, the interest rate must be boosted from 5 percent—enough to attract the top-bracket investors—to 7 percent.

Once this happens, however, the top-bracket taxpayers, who would have been content with 5 percent, get a windfall, since all tax exempt bonds, not merely the ones offered to teachers and pharmacists, will be paying 7 percent. In effect, the tax benefit will trickle up. The teachers and pharmacists will get no benefit from this trickle-up phenomenon, since for them there is no difference between 10 percent taxable and 7 percent exempt. But taxpayers subject to higher marginal tax rates will derive a benefit; and the amount of the benefit will rise with income. But even the top-bracket taxpayers will not get the full benefit of the exclusion; it will be shared by them with cities and states, who will be able to borrow at 7 percent when comparable industrial bonds must pay 10 percent.

2. Qualified Obligations. Although IRC §103 is often described as an exclusion for state and municipal bond interest, it is broader in scope, encompassing interest paid on "obligations," whether evidenced by bonds or not, including ordinary commercial debts incurred by state and local governments for services and supplies; and it extends to states, territories, U.S. possessions, and their political subdivisions, as well as the District of Columbia. Certain "industrial development bonds" and "arbitrage bonds," however, are disqualified by recent legislation, as explained below.[2] Moreover, the exclusion is offset to some extent by IRC §265, forbidding the taxpayer to deduct interest on debts incurred or continued to purchase or carry exempt obligations, as well as expenses otherwise qualifying for deduction under IRC §212 if allocable to exempt interest.[3]

The principal questions arising under IRC §103(a)(1) are:

1. *Is the obligor a "political subdivision" of a state, territory, or possession?* In *CIR v. Shamberg's Estate,* a landmark decision, the issue was whether the Port of New York Authority, created by a compact between New York and New Jersey, was a "political subdivision" within the meaning of IRC §103(a)(1).[4] The Court of Appeals for the Second Circuit held that it was, citing several opinions of the Attorney General ruling that the exclusion was not limited to a "true governmental subdivision such as a county, township, etc.," but extended as well to "any subdivision of the state created for a public purpose although authorized to exercise a portion

---

[2] See infra ¶6.3.

[3] See infra ¶6.4.

[4] CIR v. Shamberg's Est., 144 F.2d 998 (2d Cir. 1944), cert. denied, 323 US 792 (1945).

of the sovereign power of the state only to a limited degree." The court also pointed to the long-standing reference in the Treasury regulations to obligations issued "by or on behalf of" the state, observing that the words "on behalf of" must have been intended to refer to bonds "issued by a state agency to carry out a public purpose where the [state] is not named as obligor." [5]

2. *Does the payment constitute "interest" on an "obligation"?* Interest paid by a state or political subdivision qualifies for exclusion even though the obligation is not evidenced by bonds or promissory notes in conventional form.[6] It has been held, however, that IRC §103(a)(1) does not apply to interest on obligations arising from involuntary transactions between the state and the taxpayer (e.g., condemnation awards), on the ground that the congressional intent was to avoid burdening the state's "borrowing power" and that this function is not impaired by a tax on interest if the taxpayer must accept whatever interest rate the state chooses to prescribe by statute.[7] The same rationale applies to interest on other obligations that do not arise in a "borrowing" transaction, such as a state lottery or bank.[8]

Obligations can qualify for the exclusion, however, even if they are not secured by the issuer's general credit or taxing power; thus, interest can be tax-exempt even if payable out of special funds or revenues derived from specific property.[9] Moreover, if property acquired for public purposes is subject to a preexisting indebtedness, interest on the deferred payments is exempt

---

[5] CIR v. Shamberg's Est., supra note 4, at 1005-1006. See Treas. Regs. §1.103-1(b) ("by or on behalf of"); Rev. Rul. 63-20, 1963-1 CB 24 (conditions that must be met to establish that obligations of nonprofit corporations are issued "on behalf of" a state or political subdivision within meaning of Treas. Regs. §1.103-1(b)); Philadelphia Nat'l Bank v. US, 666 F.2d 834 (3d Cir. 1981) (obligations issued by Temple University not qualified, despite some state-related and state-supported features).

[6] Rev. Rul. 60-179, 1960-1 CB 37 (interest on debt evidenced by written agreement of purchase and sale can be excluded); see also Marsh Monument Co. v. US, 301 F.Supp. 1316 (E.D. Mich. 1969) (commercial contract with implicit interest; held, qualified for exclusion).

[7] See Drew v. US, 551 F.2d 85 (5th Cir. 1977) (interest under deferred-payment agreement for sale of land under threat of condemnation; held, not excludable), and cases there cited; Newman v. CIR, 68 TC 433 (1977) (interest included in state retirement annuity under pension plan for civil service employees not excludable).

[8] See Newman v. CIR, supra note 7; Fox v. US, 397 F.2d 119 (8th Cir. 1968) (interest on certificates of deposit issued by a state bank not exempt); Rev. Rul. 78-140, 1978-1 CB 27 (lottery prize paid in annual installments; portion designated as "interest" not excludable).

[9] Treas. Regs. §1.103-1(b) (special assessments); see also Independent Gravel Co. v. CIR, 56 TC 698 (1971) (special tax bills issued as payment for street and sewer improvements, assessed against adjacent landowners), and cases there cited.

under IRC §103(a) whether the public body assumes the debt or takes subject to it,[10] since the acquisition is tantamount to a purchase of property with borrowed funds, to be paid solely out of the revenues produced by the acquired property.

3. Bond Discount and Premium. If a state or municipal obligation is issued at a discount, the difference between the issue price and amount paid at maturity ("original issue discount") is "interest" qualifying for exclusion under IRC §103(a)(1). The IRS ruled in 1973 that original-issue discount accrues ratably over the term of the obligation and is apportioned on a calendar-day basis among successive holders of the debt in proportion to the length of each one's ownership.[11] If securities issued at a discount are redeemed before maturity, the earned discount received upon redemption is excluded from gross income by IRC §103(a)(1), but the unearned discount is treated as gain on the sale of a capital asset.[12]

If exempt bonds are issued or purchased for more than par, the premium cannot be amortized by a deduction against income, as is permitted by IRC §171(a) in the case of taxable securities,[13] since the premium is paid for the exempt interest and in effect reduces the amount thereof. Under IRC §1016(a)(5), however, a ratable portion of the premium must be applied each year to reduce the taxpayer's basis for the security to reflect the fact that the premium is recovered in annual installments as the interest accrues or is received.

4. Exempt-Interest Distributions by Mutual Funds. To enable small investors to invest in diversified portfolios of exempt securities, IRC §852 permits regulated investment companies to pass tax-exempt bond interest through to their shareholders. To qualify, the fund must invest at least 50 percent of the value of its assets in tax-exempt securities and distribute at least 90 percent of both its investment company taxable income and its net income from exempt securities. Correlative amendments to IRC §265, relating to interest paid on debt to purchase or carry tax-exempt securities,[14] put the shareholders in substantially the same position that they would have occupied had they purchased the exempt securities directly.

---

[10] Kings County Dev. Co. v. CIR, 93 F.2d 33 (9th Cir. 1937), cert. denied, 304 US 559 (1938) (prearranged assumption of debt).

[11] Rev. Rul. 73-112, 1973-1 CB 47. For the treatment of original issue discount on governmental bonds issued after July 1, 1982, see IRC §1232A, discussed infra ¶27.4.

[12] Rev. Rul. 80-143, 1980-1 CB 19.

[13] For the application of IRC §171 to taxable bonds, see infra ¶12.12.

[14] For IRC §265, see infra ¶6.4.

¶6.3 SPECIAL CLASSES OF STATE AND LOCAL OBLIGATIONS

1. Industrial Development Bonds. Once it was decided that bond interest was excluded from gross income by IRC §103(a)(1) even though payment depended on the revenues to be received by an obligor having no power to levy taxes or assessments (as in *Shamberg's Estate,* involving bonds issued by the Port of New York Authority),[15] it was only a short step to an exclusion for interest on so-called industrial development bonds. These are obligations issued by a state-owned corporation or political subdivision to finance the construction of a factory or other business facility, which is then leased to a private enterprise, whose rental payments are used by the issuer-landlord to pay the interest and eventually retire the bonds. When industrial development bonds are issued to construct a facility for a single occupant, the interest savings attributable to tax exemption may be passed on by the public agency to the private enterprise in the form of reduced rents.

The IRS initially adopted a benign attitude toward the increasing volume of industrial development bonds issued after World War II, but the Treasury became restive as the device came to be used as a financing arrangement for ordinary business facilities, with the municipality or other political subdivision acting merely as a complaisant conduit for a modest fee. In 1968 Congress was galvanized into action by a Treasury announcement that it was about to revoke a series of favorable IRS rulings and would issue proposed regulations under IRC §103 providing that industrial development bonds were obligations of the private corporation occupying the facilities rather than of the state or political subdivision ostensibly issuing them. Congress responded promptly to this dramatic announcement by enacting the statutory predecessor of IRC §103(b). Because it provides that an "industrial development bond" (IDB) is not to be treated as an obligation under IRC §103(a)(1) except in the case of certain exempt activities and small issues, the crux of IRC §103(b) is its definition of this basic term. The main features of the complex definition are:

1. *The "trade or business" and "security interest" tests.* An IDB is defined by IRC §103(b)(2) as any obligation (1) that is part of an issue whose proceeds are to be used in a trade or business carried on by a nonexempt person (the "trade or business" test) and (2) whose principal or interest is either (a) secured by an interest in trade or business property (or payments in respect thereof) or (b) to be derived from payments in respect of property or borrowed money used or to be used in a trade or business (the "security interest" test). The classic case of an IDB, satisfying both of these tests, is a bond to finance the construction of a factory to be leased for its estimated useful life to a private

[15] CIR v. Shamberg's Est., supra note 4.

business corporation, with principal and interest payable solely from the rents to be paid by the lessee.

The "trade or business" test is satisfied if all or a major portion (defined by the regulations as more than 25 percent) [16] of the proceeds is lent or is used to acquire, construct, or reconstruct facilities to be leased or sold to a nonexempt person for use in its business.

The security-interest test looks to the terms of the indenture or underlying arrangement (including any separate agreements between the parties and "all the facts and circumstances surrounding the issuance of the bonds") to determine whether payment of principal or interest in whole or in major part either (a) is secured by business or property or payments in respect thereof or (b) is to be derived from payments in respect of business property or borrowed money used or to be used in a business.

2. *Exempt activities.* Even though otherwise constituting an IDB, an obligation is not disqualified if substantially all of the proceeds of the issue of which it is a part are used to provide facilities which ordinarily benefit the general public, such as (a) residential real property for family units; (b) sports facilities; (c) convention or trade show facilities; (d) airports, docks, wharves, mass commuting facilities, parking facilities, or storage or training facilities directly related to the foregoing; (e) sewage, solid-waste, or local electric-energy or gas facilities; (f) air or water pollution control facilities; (g) water facilities, if available to the general public; or (h) qualified mass commuting vehicles leased to a governmental mass transit system.

3. *Industrial parks.* An exception similar to those for "exempt activities" is granted by IRC §103(b)(5), under which an IDB qualifies for tax exemption if substantially all of the proceeds of the issue of which it is a part are to be used for the acquisition or development of land for an industrial park.

4. *Small issues.* Finally, an IDB qualifies for tax exemption under IRC §103(b)(6) if it is part of an issue with an aggregate authorized face amount of $1 million or less, substantially all of the proceeds of which are to be used (a) for the acquisition, construction, reconstruction, or improvement of land or depreciable property, or (b) to redeem a qualified prior small issue. The $1 million limit can be raised to $10 million if the issuer so elects, under regulations issued by the Treasury.

This exemption for so-called small issues is scheduled to terminate at the end of 1986, and obligations issued between 1983 and the expiration date cannot qualify if the funds are to be used for such purposes as tennis clubs, massage parlors, and racetracks or if more than 25 percent of the proceeds are to be used for certain other purposes, including automobile service facilities, restaurants, and taverns.

5. *Disqualification of bonds held by "substantial user" of facilities.* The

[16] Treas. Regs. §1.103-7(b)(3)(iii).

exemptions summarized above do not apply to bonds held by a substantial user of the facilities or by a related person as defined by IRC §103(b)(6)(C).[17]

2. Arbitrage Bonds. Arbitrage bonds enabled state and local governments, equipped only with the tax exemption granted by IRC §103(a)(1) to their obligations, to go into business for themselves. For example, by issuing $1 million of bonds at the favorable interest rate fostered by IRC §103(a)(1) (e.g., 4 percent) and investing the proceeds in federal obligations bearing the higher rate required by their taxable status (e.g., 5 percent), a community could profit from the margin between the amount received on the federal obligations ($50,000 per year) and the debt service ($40,000 per year) on its own obligations. Congress responded to this problem by enacting IRC §103(c) as part of the Tax Reform Act of 1969. Briefly summarized, IRC §103(c) denies the exclusion to interest on any "arbitrage bond"—defined as an obligation all or a major portion of the proceeds of which is reasonably expected to be used, directly or indirectly, (1) to acquire taxable securities or obligations that may be expected to produce a materially higher yield over the term of the governmental issue than is payable on the latter issue, or (2) to replace funds used directly or indirectly for such acquisitions. The breadth of the statutory definition is narrowed by IRC §103(c)(4), under which obligations do not become arbitrage bonds solely because (1) the proceeds are invested for a temporary period until needed for the nonarbitrage purpose for which the obligations were issued or (2) a portion of the proceeds is invested as part of a reasonably required reserve or replacement fund, provided the amount does not exceed 15 percent of the proceeds (or more if the issuer proves that a higher amount is necessary).

3. Scholarship Funding Bonds. In 1976 Congress enacted IRC §103(a)(2), conferring tax exemption on "qualified scholarship funding bonds" as defined by IRC §103(e). The reason this exemption was not already implicit in the basic exemption of state and local obligations was that the issuers of the bonds might not have been considered political subdivisions and, even if the issuer qualified, the bonds might have been considered arbitrage bonds. The Joint Committee on Taxation explained the scope of IRC §103(a)(2) as follows:

> This provision adds to the list of exempt obligations described in section 103(a) those obligations of not-for-profit corporations organized by, or requested to act by, a State or a political subdivision of a State (or of a possession of the United States), solely to acquire student loan notes incurred under the Higher Education Act of 1965. The entire income of these corporations (after payment of expenses and provision for

[17] See Treas. Regs. §1.103-11 (defining "substantial user").

debt service requirements) must accrue to the State or political subdivision, or be required to be used to purchase additional student loan notes.[18]

4. Obligations of Public Housing Agencies. Under Section 11(b) of the United States Housing Act of 1937, as amended in 1974, interest on the obligations of "public housing agencies" authorized to engage or assist in the development or operation of low-income housing qualifies for tax exemption.[19] Unlike IRC §103(a), this provision (which is not part of the Internal Revenue Code) does not require the obligations to be issued "by" or "on behalf of" a political body as those terms have been interpreted by the regulations and IRS rulings.

5. Bonds to Finance Mortgages on Owner-Occupied Residences. Section 103A, enacted in 1980, provides that "mortgage subsidy bonds"—obligations whose proceeds are to be used directly or indirectly for mortgages on owner-occupied residences—do not qualify for the tax exemption granted by IRC §103 unless they constitute "qualified mortgage bonds" or "qualified veterans' mortgage bonds." The former term is defined in great detail, by reference to the mortgagor's prior home-owning history, the economic characteristics of the area, and the purchase price of the residence, in order to channel the tax subsidy to families in special need of assistance.

The 1980 legislation also tightens up IRC §103(b)(4)(A). Residential rental projects now qualify for relief from the industrial development bond rules only if a specified percentage of the units is to be occupied by low- or moderate-income individuals.

¶6.4 NONDEDUCTIBILITY OF INTEREST AND INVESTMENT EXPENSES ATTRIBUTABLE TO TAX-EXEMPT INTEREST

1. Introductory. Section 265 disallows certain otherwise allowable deductions arising from the taxpayer's ownership of tax-exempt securities. The most important of these restrictions is IRC §265(2), providing that interest on indebtedness "incurred or continued to purchase or carry [tax-exempt] obligations" may not be deducted. Less important, because the amounts are usually nominal, is the disallowance by IRC §265(1) of deductions otherwise allowable under IRC §212 (relating to expenses incurred for the production of in-

[18] Joint Comm. on Taxation, 94th Cong., 2d Sess., General Explanation of the Tax Reform Act of 1976, reprinted in 1976-3 CB (Vol. 2) 621.

[19] 42 USC §1437i(b).

come).[20] Sections 265(1) and 265(2) can apply whether or not the taxpayer is *currently* receiving interest from tax-exempt securities or had a tax-avoidance motive in purchasing them.

2. Disallowance of Interest Deduction. Although IRC §163(a) permits taxpayers to deduct "all interest paid or accrued during the taxable year on indebtedness," [21] IRC §265(2) disallows the deduction if the indebtedness is "incurred or continued to purchase or carry obligations the interest on which is wholly exempt" from the federal income tax. The function of this restriction can be illustrated by assuming that a taxpayer receiving $10,000 of taxable dividends annually from stock worth $100,000 borrows $200,000 at 5 percent to purchase $200,000 of tax-exempt bonds yielding 4 percent, pledging both classes of securities as collateral for the loan. Although the investment of the borrowed funds in tax-exempt securities generates a loss of $2,000 per year (one percent of $200,000) when taken in isolation, Example 6-1 demonstrates that it would produce a net economic gain of $3,000 annually if the taxpayer's marginal tax rate were 50 percent and IRC §265(2) did not exist.

Example 6-1

Use of Borrowed Funds to Purchase Tax-Exempt Securities In Absence of IRC §265(c)

	Before Purchasing Exempt Securities	*After Purchasing Exempt Securities*
1. Dividends received	$10,000	$10,000
2. Exempt interest received ...	-0-	8,000
3. Gross economic income	$10,000	$18,000
4. Less: Interest paid	-0-	10,000
5. Net economic income	$10,000	$ 8,000
6. Less: Nontaxable portion of line 5	-0-	8,000
7. Taxable income	$10,000	-0-
8. Tax on line 7 (50%)	5,000	-0-
9. Net "take-home" (line 5 less line 8)	$ 5,000	$ 8,000

In applying IRC §265(2), the central interpretative issue is whether the

[20] For IRC §212, see infra ¶8.5.

[21] For IRC §163, see infra ¶15.1.

taxpayer's indebtedness was "incurred or continued to purchase or carry" tax-exempt obligations. This nexus between the taxpayer's debts and the exempt securities is readily established, or rebutted, at the extremes. If, for example, a taxpayer with no resources borrows funds and purchases tax-exempt securities, pledging them to secure the loan, an inference that the debt was "incurred . . . to purchase" the exempt securities within the meaning of IRC §265(2) is clearly warranted and virtually irrebuttable. Such an inference would not be justified, however, if a taxpayer withdrew funds from a savings account to purchase tax-exempt securities at a time when he was paying interest on a long-standing mortgage on his personal residence.

Unfortunately, there are innumerable situations along the spectrum between these two extremes. Generalizations are of limited utility in disposing of these intermediate cases, but a succinct summary by the Tax Court of the applicable principles can hardly be improved on:

> It is now well settled that the statutory disallowance is not activated merely by the simultaneous existence of an indebtedness and the holding of tax-exempt obligations. . . . Thus, a taxpayer is not automatically required to liquidate such obligations to obtain needed funds rather than retain such obligations and obtain those funds by way of independent borrowing. . . . On the other hand, it is equally clear that a taxpayer cannot insulate himself from the prohibition of Section 265(2) by merely juggling the use of his available assets so as to create a surface sanitation of the indebtedness from the acquisition or holding of the tax-exempt obligations. . . . The touchstone for decision is the *purpose* of the taxpayer in incurring or continuing the indebtedness . . . and the burden of proof is on the [taxpayer]. . . . "The finding of the taxpayer's purpose does not depend solely upon looking into his mind and learning what he was thinking; although his intentions are relevant, purpose may be inferred from his conduct and from the circumstances that confronted him." To these elements may be added the further element of timing, which "can be just as important to the taxpayer as it is to the athlete or comedian." . . . Expressed in another way, the deduction will be barred if there is "a sufficiently direct relationship" between the incurring or continuing of the indebtedness and the acquisition or holding of the tax-exempt obligations.[22]

In 1972 the IRS issued Revenue Procedure 72-18, containing a set of guidelines for taxpayers and revenue agents regarding the application of IRC §265(2).[23] Starting with a pledge of allegiance to the "purpose" test, Revenue

---

[22] Indian Trail Trading Post, Inc. v. CIR, 60 TC 497, 500 (1973), aff'd per curiam, 503 F.2d 102 (6th Cir. 1974) (citations omitted).

[23] Rev. Proc. 72-18, 1972-1 CB 740.

Procedure 72-18 states that the requisite purpose may be established by either direct or circumstantial evidence. Direct evidence of a purpose to *purchase* exempt obligations exists, under Revenue Procedure 72-18, if the proceeds of indebtedness are used for and are directly traceable to the purchase of exempt obligations; direct evidence of a purpose to *carry* exempt securities exists if exempt securities are used as collateral for a debt. In particular cases, however, the surrounding circumstances might rebut the ultimate conclusion of a tainted purpose. Revenue Procedure 72-18 itself acknowledges this possibility by exempting funds borrowed for a business purpose that are temporarily invested in tax-exempt securities. Having identified the two instances summarized above of "direct evidence" of the tainted purpose, Revenue Procedure 72-18 goes on to provide that, in their absence, a tainted purpose will not ordinarily be inferred if a taxpayer's investment in exempt obligations is "insubstantial."

In the absence of direct evidence (and if the taxpayer is not protected by the de minimis test), Revenue Procedure 72-18 provides for resorting to circumstantial evidence to ascertain the taxpayer's purpose. In general, debt incurred for personal purposes (e.g., to purchase a residence or goods and services for consumption) is not viewed as having a sufficiently direct relationship to the ownership of exempt securities to be reached by IRC §265(2). Debt incurred or continued by an individual for reasons connected with the active conduct of a trade or business is also generally free of the tainted purpose under Revenue Procedure 72-18.[24] On the other hand, if an individual taxpayer's outstanding debt is not directly connected with personal expenditures or the active conduct of a trade or business, the tainted purpose will be inferred from the fact that he owns exempt obligations.[25]

3. Interest Paid by Banks. Under administrative rulings that have won legislative approval, the IRS holds that a bank's obligation to its depositors is not "indebtedness" within the meaning of IRC §265(2), so that only other types of debt are taken into account in determining whether a bank has incurred or continued indebtedness to purchase or carry tax-exempt securities.[26] Under the IRS guidelines, IRC §265(2) is ordinarily not applicable to

---

[24] Id. §4.03.

[25] See id. §4.04, which provides that "portfolio investments" include real estate if not connected with the active conduct of a trade or business and sets out additional factors to be considered in determining whether an inference of the tainted purpose should be drawn or has been rebutted. Revenue Procedure 72-18 was modified by Rev. Proc. 74-8, 1974-1 CB 419 to clarify the status of a substantial interest in a business corporation.

[26] See Rev. Proc. 70-20, §2.02, 1970-2 CB 499, amplified by Rev. Proc. 78-34, 1978-2 CB 535; Investors Diversified Servs., Inc. v. US, 575 F.2d 843 (Ct. Cl. 1978) (bank deposit exception).

a bank's short-term obligations, such as certificates of deposit, federal funds transactions, day-to-day borrowing from Federal Reserve banks, or repurchase agreements relating to taxable securities, unless there is a direct connection between the borrowing and the tax-exempt securities. This tolerance does not extend to capital notes, however, unless issued to increase the bank's capital to a level consistent with generally accepted banking practice pursuant to federal or state regulatory requirements or to finance buildings or other physical facilities.[27]

4. Disallowance of Investment Expenses. Section 265(1) disallows amounts otherwise deductible under IRC §212 (relating to expenses for the production of income) if allocable to exempt interest, whether or not any exempt interest is actually received or accrued.[28] Items disallowed by IRC §265(1) include payments for investment advice, safe-deposit and custodial facilities, clerical assistance, fiduciary services, and legal advice.[29] If the taxpayer's portfolio includes both exempt and taxable securities, IRC §212 expenses must be allocated between the two classes, ordinarily in proportion to the amount of income derived from each.

SELECTED BIBLIOGRAPHY

Bedell, The Interest Deduction: Its Current Status, 32 NYU Inst. on Fed. Tax. 1117, 1138–1151 (1974).

Bittker, Equity, Efficiency, and Income Tax Theory: Do Misallocations Drive Out Inequities? 16 San Diego L. Rev. 735 (1979).

Craven, Disallowance of Interest Deduction to Owner of Tax-Exempt Bonds, 24 Tax Lawyer 287 (1971).

Gabinet, The Municipal Bond Interest Exemption: Comments on a Running Battle, 24 Case W. Res. L. Rev. 64 (1972).

Ritter, Federal Income Tax Treatment of Municipal Obligations: Industrial Development Bonds, 25 Tax Lawyer 511 (1972).

---

[27] Rev. Proc. 70-20, §3.10, supra note 26.

[28] For IRC §212, see generally infra ¶8.5. In addition to disallowing deductions under IRC §212 if allocable to exempt interest, IRC §265(1) disallows all otherwise allowable deductions if allocable to exempt income other than interest. For this aspect of IRC §265(1), see infra ¶9.12.

[29] See Whittemore v. US, 383 F.2d 824 (8th Cir. 1967) (parenthetical reference in IRC §265(1) to "expenses for the production of income" seems to refer only to IRC §212(1), but IRC §212(2) expenses are also subject to disallowance; fiduciary commissions and attorney's fees relating to trust assets, consisting of taxable and exempt securities, disallowed in part); Jamison v. CIR, 8 TC 173 (1947) (Acq.) (investor's office expenses); Weil's Est. v. CIR, ¶54,202 P-H Memo TC (1954) (legal and other fees relating to appointment of committee for incompetent).

CHAPTER 7

Employee Fringe Benefits and Other Exclusions From Gross Income

¶7.1 NONSTATUTORY EXCLUSION OF FRINGE BENEFITS

The tax status under current law of fringe benefits furnished to employees and other persons performing personal services is veiled in uncertainty, except as clarified by explicit statutory provisions covering a few items. On the one hand, the Supreme Court held in *CIR v. Glenshaw Glass Co.* that Congress intended "to tax all gains except those specifically exempted" and the regulations provide that if services are paid for other than in money the fair market value of the property or services taken in payment must be included in income.[1] On the other hand, the Internal Revenue Service's administrative approach has been that the value of employee fringe benefits are not generally "considered income to the employees even if the employer's sole reason for providing them is to confer a benefit upon the employees." [2] This relaxed view, however, has never been embodied in either an official statement of the applicable rules or a catalog of excludable items. There are, in fact, only a few isolated rulings and litigated cases exempting fringe benefits from taxation, and they can be matched in number by cases holding that a few other benefits are taxable.[3]

In 1975, the Treasury issued a "discussion draft" of proposed regulations governing the tax status of fringe benefits.[4] The draft sanctioned the exclusion of employee fringe benefits from income if the facilities, goods, or services are (a) owned or controlled by the employer for business reasons unrelated to use or consumption by the employees, (b) available to employees on terms involving no substantial additional cost to the employer, and (c) available to employees generally or to groups of employees classified by reference to the nature of their work, seniority, or similar factors and not primarily limited to highly compensated employees. Benefits not meeting these conditions could still be excluded under a de minimis rule (embracing any amount "so small as to make accounting for it unreasonable or administratively impractical") or if all the facts and circumstances indicated that the benefit did not constitute compensation. Caught in a heated cross fire between critics who thought that the proposed regulations were too lenient and those who thought they were too severe, however, the Treasury Department withdrew its draft in 1976.[5] Thereafter, Congress enacted Public Law 95-427, forbidding the Treasury to issue any regulations on fringe benefits before 1980, a date that was later extended to 1984; and a Task Force of the House Committee on Ways and Means proposed legislation—as yet unenacted—to govern this area.[6]

---

[1] CIR v. Glenshaw Glass Co., 348 US 426, 430 (1955), discussed supra ¶1.4; Treas. Regs. §1.61-2(d)(2).

[2] Brief for US at 39, Rudolph v. US, 370 US 269 (1962); see generally infra ¶9.2.

[3] For exempted benefits, see Rev. Rul. 131, 1953-2 CB 112 (disaster relief to employees, based on need); Rev. Rul. 59-58, 1959-1 CB 17 (value of turkey, ham, or other merchandise of nominal value distributed on holidays to employees to promote good relations not taxable; rule not applicable to cash, gift certificates, or other items with readily convertible cash value). For taxable benefits, see Dole v. CIR, 43 TC 697 (Acq.), aff'd per curiam, 351 F.2d 308 (1st Cir. 1965) (employee use of company-owned residence and automobile); Rev. Rul. 73-13, 1973-1 CB 42 (estate planning, tax advice, etc.); Rev. Rul. 57-130, 1957-1 CB 108 (executive's health resort expenses).

[4] 40 Fed. Reg. 41,118 (1975).

[5] Withdrawal notice, 41 Fed. Reg. 56,334 (1976).

[6] See H. Rep. No. 95-1232, reprinted in 1978-2 CB 365; for the Task Force's Draft

Any renewed effort to bring coherence to this area will have to come to grips with the following factors, which individually create difficulties and cannot be fully reconciled with each other:

1. *The personal-business borderline.* Some fringe benefits serve the supplier's business purposes at the same time that they confer economic advantages on the recipient. A manufacturer of consumer products, for example, may request or require its employees to use its products and report on their quality, novelty, or other features; business firms often hold employee conventions and meetings at resort hotels; newspapers pay the restaurant bills of their food critics; airlines and hotels invite travel agents to use their facilities at a discount or without charge; publishers furnish free books to professors; and employees expected to respond to the employer's calls after business hours are sometimes supplied with telephones, automobiles, or other facilities. It is far from clear that Congress, if it had focused on the question, would have intended the naked term "income" as used in the Internal Revenue Code to encompass items like these, which can often be characterized as conditions of employment.

2. *Constructive receipt.* Employees who arrange to have part of their agreed salary diverted by the employer to personal goods and services are taxed on the diverted amounts, even if the items might qualify as fringe benefits if provided to employees at the employer's instigation.[7] In theory, the same principle should apply to employees who gravitate toward an employer known to provide in-kind benefits, since a diversion occurs here too; but it is obviously difficult to detect.

3. *Impact of IRC § 83.* Section 83(a) provides that if property is transferred in connection with the performance of services, the person rendering the services must include in income the excess of value of the property over the amount (if any) paid for it. The broad language of IRC §83 seems to encompass not only the purchase of merchandise at an employee's discount, but other transfers of property in connection with services.[8]

4. *Exclusion of gifts.* Some fringe benefits, though granted only to employees, manifest a spirit of generosity, affection, or respect and hence have a fighting chance to be excluded from gross income as "gifts" under IRC §102(a).[9]

5. *De minimis items.* Fringe benefits of minor value may fit within the statutory concept of "income" and fail to qualify as tax-free gifts because

---

Proposal on Fringe Benefits and an explanatory accompanying letter of transmittal, see [1979] 5 P-H Fed. Taxes ¶59,605.

[7] For the treatment of employer payments benefiting the employee and the related doctrine of constructive receipt, see supra ¶1.11; infra ¶35.2.

[8] For IRC §83, see infra ¶29.3.

[9] For IRC §102(a), see supra ¶3.2.

employees expect them as a matter of course;[10] but the voluntary reporting of de minimis items is bound to be sporadic. As for enforcement efforts, they may be unduly expensive, not merely in a cost-effective sense but also because the public regards the pursuit of minor items as ludicrous, Scrooge-like, or oppressive. The question then arises whether scrupulous taxpayers can disregard these items only if the IRS has formally exempted them or can, instead, assume that common sense is the order of the day until they are officially told otherwise.

6. *Valuation.* Fringe benefits entail a restriction of choice, so that in many situations the employee is not a willing buyer from a willing seller; and this may mean that the benefit is not worth as much as a salary increase equal to the benefit's fair market value.[11] The valuation of fringe benefits is also complicated if employees are given access to, but do not make equal use of, the facility, like a subsidized cafeteria, golf course, or vacation lodge.

7. *Costless items.* In the 1975 Treasury discussion draft on fringe benefits, the use by employees of facilities entailing no additional expense to the employer (e.g., empty seats on a company plane) counted heavily in favor of tax exemption.[12] Critics of the draft correctly pointed out that the value of the facility to the employee is not diminished by this fact; that some marginal costs (e.g., for insurance, clerical expense, etc.) are usually incurred when employees use empty facilities; and that some allegedly unused facilities might, at least in theory, be sold to the public at a discount. A tax that discourages the use of empty facilities without raising an appreciable amount of revenue resembles the puritan prohibition on bearbaiting, which was forbidden not because it gave pain to the bear but because it gave pleasure to the spectators.

¶7.2 GROUP TERM LIFE INSURANCE

Section 79 requires employees to include in gross income an amount equal to the cost of group term life insurance on the employee's life under a policy carried directly or indirectly by the employer, except for the cost of $50,000 of such insurance. In effect, IRC §79 permits the employee to exclude the cost of the first $50,000 of coverage under the policy. The value of this tax-free fringe benefit is enhanced by the fact that any contributions by the employee toward the purchase of the policy are credited against its excess coverage.

---

[10] See Rev. Rul. 59-58, supra note 3.

[11] The 1975 Treasury discussion draft on fringe benefits, supra note 7, proposed to value includable benefits at the amount that the employee would have had to pay in arm's-length transactions for similar facilities. For the valuation of prizes and awards, see supra ¶3.5 (discounting retail values to reflect lack of taxpayer's choice).

[12] Supra note 7.

Thus, if a $75,000 policy costs $1,500 per year, of which the employee pays $200, the employer's payment of the remaining $1,300 is tax-free to the extent of $1,000 (the cost of $50,000 of coverage) and taxable only to the extent of $300—$500, the cost of the excess $25,000 of insurance, less the employee's $200 contribution, which is wholly allocated to this portion of the policy. Because the exclusion granted by IRC §79 is confined to insurance on the life of "an employee," it does not embrace insurance on partners, self-employed persons, or members of an employee's family.[13]

The principal features of the exclusion granted by IRC §79 are:

1. *Group insurance.* Only *group* insurance qualifies for the exclusion. As interpreted by the regulations, the statutory standard requires (a) that life insurance be provided under a "plan" of group insurance making term life insurance available to a group, which must include all employees or a class or classes determined on the basis of factors precluding individual selection; and (b) that the amount of coverage be determined by a formula based on such objective factors as salary, years of service, and position.[14]

2. *Term life insurance.* Section 79 applies only to "term life insurance." [15] If a policy provides both term and permanent insurance, it qualifies under IRC §79 only if the portion of the premium allocable to the qualified group term coverage is specified and the policy provides that the remainder of the premium is not to be paid by the employer.[16]

3. *Unlimited coverage.* The $50,000 limit and the concomitant restriction on the premiums that can be excluded from gross income by the employee are eliminated by IRC §79(b) for three classes of group term life insurance policies: (a) insurance on the lives of retired or disabled ex-employees; (b) policies whose proceeds are payable to the employer or a qualified charitable organization; and (c) policies provided under a contract described by IRC §72(m)(3), relating to qualified employee pension and profit-sharing plans.

---

[13] See Treas. Regs. §1.79-1(b)(2) (incorporating by reference the employer-employee relationship rules of IRC §3401(c), relating to withholding of taxes from wages, and excluding independent contractors and self-employed persons); Treas. Regs. §1.79-3(f)(2) (cost of insurance on life of employee's spouse or other relatives not exempted by IRC §79); but see Treas. Regs. §1.61-2(d)(2)(ii)(*b*) ("incidental" cost of insurance, not exceeding $2,000 of coverage, on life of employee's spouse or child can be disregarded).

[14] Treas. Regs. §§1.79-1(b)(1)(i), 1.79-1(b)(1)(iii). If fewer than ten full-time employees are covered at some time during the calendar year, stricter standards must be met. See Treas. Regs. §§1.79-1(b)(1)(iii)(*d*); Rev. Rul. 75-528, 1975-2 CB 35 (disqualification of plan including fewer than ten full-time employees if medical evidence other than questionnaire is used).

[15] Treas. Regs. §§1.79-1(b)(1)(i), 1.79-1(b)(1)(ii).

[16] Treas. Regs. §1.79-1(b)(1)(ii). For the distinction between "term" and "permanent" life insurance, see Rev. Rul. 71-360, 1971-2 CB 87; Rev. Rul. 75-91, 1975-1 CB 39; see also Rev. Proc. 79-29, 1979-1 CB 571 (procedure for separating excludable cost of qualifying term coverage from taxable cost of permanent benefits).

4. *Key employees.* Section 79(d), enacted in 1982, disallows the $50,000 exclusion in the case of key employees (as defined by IRC §416, relating to so-called top-heavy plans), if the plan of group insurance violates a set of nondiscrimination rules, which are designed to insure a reasonably broad coverage of employees and benefits that do not favor key employees.

¶7.3 GROUP LEGAL SERVICES

As an incentive to the establishment of prepaid legal services plans, IRC §120 provides that amounts contributed by employers to qualified group legal services plans for employees or their spouses or dependents are excludable from the employee's gross income and that amounts paid to the employee under such a plan as reimbursement for legal services are also excludable. To qualify under IRC §120, a group legal services plan must meet the following conditions:

1. *Coverage.* The arrangement must be a "separate written plan of an employer for the exclusive benefit of his employees or their spouses or dependents" [17] to provide personal, as opposed to business, legal services through prepayment (or other advance arrangements) by the employer of legal fees.

2. *Discrimination and eligibility.* The contributions or benefits and the classification of employees qualifying under the plan must not discriminate in favor of officers, shareholders, self-employed persons, or highly compensated employees.

3. *Insiders.* Not more than 25 percent of the amounts contributed during a taxable year may be provided for employees who are shareholders or owners (or their spouses or dependents) and own more than 5 percent of the employer's stock, capital, or interest in profits at any time during the year.

4. *Recipients of contributions.* Contributions under the plan must be paid to organizations specified by IRC §120(c)(5).[18]

¶7.4 EDUCATIONAL ASSISTANCE PROGRAMS

Under IRC §127, employees can exclude from gross income expenses paid or incurred by their employers for educational assistance, if the benefits are

---

[17] "Dependent" is used by IRC §120 as defined by IRC §152; as explained infra ¶14.1, the term can include many persons for whom the taxpayer is not entitled to claim a dependency exemption.

[18] The organizations specified in IRC §120(c)(5) include insurance companies or organizations providing personal legal services for prepayment or a premium, organizations described in IRC §501(c)(2), "providers of legal services" under the plan, and combinations of the foregoing.

furnished under an "educational assistance program." To qualify, the program must be "a separate written plan of an employer for the exclusive benefit of his employes to provide such employees with educational assistance," and it must satisfy four requirements set out in IRC §127(b)(1): (1) The program must benefit employees qualifying under a classification found by the IRS not to be discriminatory in favor of officers, owners or highly compensated employees, or their dependents;[19] (2) not more than 5 percent of the employer's expenses for the taxable year may be provided to the class of shareholders or owners (or to their spouses or dependents), consisting of individuals who own (directly or constructively) more than 5 percent of the stock or of the capital or profits interest in the employer; (3) eligible employees must not be granted, explicitly or in practice, a choice between educational assistance and taxable remuneration; and (4) eligible employees must receive reasonable notification of the program's terms.

Since the cost of job related education can ordinarily be excluded from the employee's gross income if defrayed by the employer or be deducted as a business expense under IRC §162 if defrayed by the employee,[20] the principal function of IRC §127 is to exclude two classes of educational benefits from the employee's gross income: (a) education (whether job-related or not) that either satisfies the minimum educational requirements for qualification in the individual's occupation or qualifies him for a new occupation and (b) education pursued for cultural or recreational reasons.[21]

Section 127(c)(6) preserves existing law by providing explicitly that the enactment of IRC §127 does not affect the application of IRC §117, §162, or §212 to amounts that are not covered by IRC §127.

¶7.5 MEALS AND LODGING FURNISHED TO EMPLOYEES FOR CONVENIENCE OF THE EMPLOYER

1. Introductory. Section 119 excludes from gross income the value of meals and lodging furnished to employees for the convenience of the employer on the employer's business premises, subject to certain conditions discussed below. Enacted in 1954, IRC §119 was designed to end the confusion that had

[19] In judging whether the plan is discriminatory, unionized employees can be excluded if educational assistance benefits were subject to good-faith collective bargaining, subject to scrutiny by the Secretary of Labor.

[20] See infra ¶9.6.

[21] For the nondeductibility of educational expenses of this type, and the employee's correlative obligation to report employer-defrayed expenses as income, see infra ¶9.6.

arisen under a "convenience of the employer" doctrine developed by the IRS and the courts without the aid of any explicit statutory foundation. During this pre-statutory period, the IRS and courts gravitated between two polar theories, viz., that meals and lodging furnished by an employer did not constitute "income" to the employee if they were not "considered" by the employer to be compensation for services, and the more objective theory that they were excludable only if furnished as a matter of business necessity to enable the employees to perform their duties properly.[22] In *CIR v. Kowalski,* decided in 1977, the Supreme Court held that IRC §119(1) codified the "business necessity" rationale for the convenience-of-the-employer doctrine; (2) is limited to meals and lodging furnished in kind, excluding cash; and (3) preempts the field, leaving no room for the exclusion of so-called noncompensatory cash allowances under either IRC §119 or §61.[23]

2. Convenience of the Employer. Neither meals nor lodging can be excluded from the employee's gross income under IRC §119 unless they are furnished "for the convenience of the employer." Since virtually all benefits, including wages and salaries, serve the employer's "convenience" in the sense that they help to get the employer's work done, the statutory phrase must be used by IRC §119 in a narrower sense. In a pre-1954 case, cited with evident approval by the Supreme Court in *Kowalski,* the Tax Court said that meals and lodging are furnished for the employer's convenience when they resemble conditions of employment:

> [T]he subsistence and quarters [in a particular case] were not supplied by the employer and received by the employee "for his personal convenience, comfort or pleasure, but solely because he could not otherwise perform the services required of him." In other words, though there was an element of gain to the employee, in that he received subsistence and quarters which otherwise he would have had to supply for himself, he had nothing he could take, appropriate, use and expend according to his own dictates, but rather, the ends of the employer's business dominated and controlled, just as in the furnishing of a place to work and in the supplying of the tools and machinery with which to work. The fact that certain personal wants and needs of the employee were satisfied was plainly secondary and incidental to the employment.[24]

In the case of lodging, IRC §119(a)(2) sanctions an exclusion only if

---

[22] See CIR v. Kowalski, 434 US 77 (1977).
[23] Id.
[24] Van Rosen v. CIR, 17 TC 834, 838 (1951).

employee "is required to accept such lodging . . . as a condition of his employment." Although separately stated, this requirement seems to add nothing to the "employer's convenience" standard; both are satisfied by a showing that the employee must occupy the housing furnished by the employer in order to perform the duties of his employment properly. As interpreted by the cases and rulings, IRC §119(a)(2) applies if the lodging is furnished at a site lacking alternative housing (e.g., a remote construction site) [25] or if the employee must be available for duty at all times (e.g., caretakers, hotel managers, etc).[26]

The regulations interpret IRC §119(a)(1) as encompassing meals "furnished for a substantial noncompensatory business reason of the employer." [27] After stating that this amorphous standard is to be applied to "all the surrounding facts and circumstances," the regulations put some flesh on the skeleton by stating that "substantial noncompensatory business reasons" include (1) having the employee available for emergency calls during the meal period, (2) a business need restricting the employee to a short meal period (e.g., thirty or forty-five minutes) when quick meals elsewhere are not feasible,[28] and (3) the absence of sufficient eating facilities in the vicinity of the employer's premises.[29]

3. Business Premises. To qualify for the exclusion of IRC §119, meals and lodging must be furnished on the employer's "business premises." This requirement, which was not included in the pre-1954 nonstatutory convenience-of-the-employer doctrine, is construed by the regulations to mean "the

---

[25] See Olkjer v. CIR, 32 TC 464, 468 (1959) (Acq.) (construction site in Greenland where no other housing was available; "facilities so furnished were not only for the employer's convenience but were indispensable if any work was to be accomplished").

[26] Treas. Regs. §1.119-1(d), Example (5) (state institution; employee required to be available for duty at all times); Coyner v. Bingler, 344 F.2d 736, 737-738 (3d Cir. 1965) (caretaker of building whose duties "made it a practical necessity for him and his wife to live there"). Cases denying an exclusion include McDonald v. CIR, 66 TC 223 (1976) (multinational corporation furnished western-style housing to executive stationed in Japan; no proof that proper performance of duties required such facilities).

[27] Treas. Regs. §1.119-1(a)(2)(i) (first sentence).

[28] It is heartening to know that *some* places have not been invaded by fast-food outlets.

[29] Treas. Regs. §1.119-1(a)(2)(ii)*(c);* Rev. Rul. 71-411, 1971-2 CB 103 (exclusion allowed for employees subject to phone calls while eating at desks or in company dining area); Treas. Reg. §1.119-1(a)(2)(ii)(e) (exclusion allowed for meal furnished immediately after working hours if duties required employee to miss excludable meal); Treas. Reg. §1.119-1(d), Example (9) (if noncompensatory reason applies to substantially all employees, all can exclude); Treas. Reg. §1.119-1(a)(2)(ii)(d) (food service employees can exclude one meal, either before or after working hours, for every meal period worked); Treas. Reg. §1.119-1(a)(2)(i) (last sentence) (if lodging is furnished for employer convenience, all meals furnished without charge on premises are excluded).

place of employment of the employee."[30] The courts have construed this term to include (1) living quarters that constitute an integral part of the business property or (2) premises on which the company carries on some of its business activities, as well as the employer's residence in the case of domestic servants even though no business is conducted there.[31] Section 119(c), enacted in 1981, provides that a "camp" located in a foreign country shall be considered part of the employer's business premises. "Camp" is defined as lodging (1) provided by or on behalf of the employer for the employer's convenience because the job site is in a remote area where satisfactory housing is not available on the open market, (2) located as near as practicable to the job site, and (3) furnished in a common area or enclave not available to the public and normally accommodating ten or more employees.

4. Employee Status. Section 119 refers to meals and lodging furnished by or on behalf of employers to *employees* (or their spouses or dependents). Although the exclusion can be claimed by shareholder-employees of closely held corporations, it is necessary to determine in these cases whether the taxpayer receives the benefits *as an employee* or because he or she is a shareholder.[32] Partners are not ordinarily employees of their firms, but it has been held that a partner receiving payments for services without regard to the firm's income can qualify as an employee under IRC §119.[33]

5. Compensatory Character of Benefits. The regulations state that meals furnished for a substantial noncompensatory business reason qualify for the exclusion "even though such meals are also furnished for a compensatory reason" and that lodging can satisfy the standards of IRC §119(b)(1) even though "furnished as compensation" under the terms of an employment con-

---

[30] Treas. Regs. §1.119-1(c)(1).

[31] Dole v. CIR, 43 TC 697, 707 (1965) (Acq.), aff'd per curiam, 351 F.2d 308 (1st Cir. 1965); Benninghoff v. CIR, 71 TC 216 (1978) (policeman employed by Canal Zone government cannot treat entire Zone as employer's business premises); see also Treas. Regs. §1.119-1(c)(1) (premises leased for business purposes qualify); CIR v. Anderson, 371 F.2d 59 (6th Cir. 1966), cert. denied, 387 US 906 (1967) (residence constructed by motel corporation two blocks away; not qualified for exclusion although occupied by manager on 24-hour call; employee did not perform significant part of duties in residence); compare Lindeman v. CIR, 60 TC 609 (1973) (Acq.) (hotel manager occupying separate residence on hotel property; held, "business premises" because manager, subject to 24-hour call, could view hotel from, and made part-time business use of, residence); Bob Jones Univ. v. US, 670 F.2d 167 (Ct.Cl. 1982) (dormitory counselors on 24-hour call entitled to exclude value of lodging furnished by university; contra for faculty and staff).

[32] See Wilhelm v. US, 257 F.Supp. 16 (D. Wyo. 1966) (Subchapter S corporation); Atlanta Biltmore Hotel Corp. v. CIR, 349 F.2d 677 (5th Cir. 1965) (exclusion denied; major shareholder had no significant managerial duties).

[33] Armstrong v. Phinney, 394 F.2d 661 (5th Cir. 1968).

tract or statute.[34] Indeed, by accepting the business necessity rationale for IRC §119 [35] and thereby downgrading the compensatory nature of the benefits, the regulations permit meals and lodging to be excluded from the employee's gross income even if they are the employee's *sole* reward for the services rendered.[36]

6. Miscellaneous Matters

1. *Cash allowances and charges.* In *CIR v. Kowalski,* the Supreme Court held that IRC §119(a)(1) applies only to meals furnished in kind and that cash allowances to reimburse employees for the cost of meals must be included in their gross income.[37] It is not clear, however, whether *Kowalski* would tax employees on the value of meals that they are authorized to charge to the employer's account or would instead treat this as an "in kind" arrangement.

In 1978, Congress added IRC §§119(b)(2) and 119(b)(3), both concerned with charges for meals. Section 119(b)(2) provides that in determining whether meals are furnished for the convenience of the employer, neither the fact that a charge is made nor the fact that the employee may accept or decline the meals shall be taken into account. In the absence of this provision, these circumstances could be viewed as inconsistent with the convenience-of-the-employer requirement, since the charge, coupled with the employee's option to make independent arrangements for meals, suggests that the services could be properly performed even if meals were not furnished by the employer. If the employee must pay for meals whether he accepts them or not, IRC §119(b)(3) comes into play. If, despite the charge, the meals are furnished for the convenience of the employer, the amount paid by the employee is excluded from his gross income, whether it comes from the employee's own funds or is deducted from his stated compensation.

2. *Meals and lodging for employee's family.* In 1978, Congress amended IRC §119 by explicitly exempting meals and lodging furnished to the employee's spouse and dependents, as well as those furnished to the employee.[38]

---

[34] Treas. Regs. §§1.119-1(a)(2)(i) (meals), 1.119-1(b) (lodging); Treas. Regs. §1.119-1(d), Example (5) (meals and lodging furnished to civil service employee on 24-hour call; excludable although regarded as compensation under applicable state statute).

[35] See CIR v. Kowalski, supra note 22.

[36] See Coyner v. Bingler, supra note 26 (caretaker whose sole compensation for extra duties was housing); Rev. Rul. 68-354 (meals and housing excludable, though they were sole compensation for extra duties by employees volunteering to be on 24-hour call).

[37] CIR v. Kowalski, supra note 22; see also Treas. Regs. §1.119-1(c)(2) (same).

[38] For the scope of the term "dependent" (which is not limited to persons for which the taxpayer is entitled to a dependency exemption), see IRC §152(a), discussed infra ¶14.2.

3. *Value of taxable meals and lodging.* When employer-furnished meals and lodging are taxable, their fair market value is ordinarily the amount to be included in gross income, even if the taxpayer would have preferred more or less expensive facilities in lieu of those supplied by the employer.[39]

¶7.6 HOMES AND RENTAL ALLOWANCES FURNISHED TO MINISTERS

Ministers are permitted by IRC §107 to exclude from gross income the rental value of a home provided to them as part of their compensation, as well as rental allowances to the extent used to rent or provide a home. The exclusion of allowances dates from 1954, but the rental value of housing furnished by the employer in kind has been excludable by statute since 1921, presumably because parsonages can sometimes be analogized to premises supplied for the convenience of the minister's congregation.[40] In appropriate cases, a minister can exclude both types of benefits (e.g., the rental value of a house and a cash allowance earmarked for utility services).[41] Section 107 does not, however, authorize ministers to deduct rental expenses defrayed from their own resources or to exclude portions of a salary that are not designated by the employer as a rental allowance.[42]

Although IRC §107 refers only to "a minister of the gospel," it embraces clergymen of all faiths;[43] but the cases and rulings confine the benefits of IRC §107 to persons who are "duly ordained, commissioned, or licensed."[44] If, however, a self-styled minister has any followers, their acknowledgment of his or her leadership should constitute a sufficient commission or license if this

---

[39] See McDonald v. CIR, supra note 26 (corporate executive taxed on expensive Japanese housing, not on lesser amount spent by typical executives of similar rank for housing in United States); Heyward v. CIR, 36 TC 739 (1961), aff'd per curiam, 201 F.2d 307 (4th Cir. 1962) (isolation of company-supplied housing affects its fair rental value); but see supra ¶3.5 (re valuation of taxable prizes and awards).

[40] Revenue Act of 1921, P.L. No. 98, §213(b)(11), 42 Stat. 239, which displaced O.D. 862, 4 CB 85 (1921) (rental value of parsonage includable in gross income); for the 1954 change, see S. Rep. No. 1622, 83d Cong., 2d Sess. 186 (1954); see also Williamson v. CIR, 224 F.2d 377 (8th Cir. 1955) (rental allowance held excludable under pre-1954 "convenience of employer" doctrine).

[41] Rev. Rul. 59-350, 1959-2 CB 45.

[42] Treas. Regs. §1.107-1(b); see Eden v. CIR, 41 TC 605 (1964) (no official designation; exclusion denied).

[43] Salkov v. CIR, 46 TC 190, 194 (1966) (Acq.) (no legislative intent to exclude non-Christian faiths or persons who are equivalent to "ministers").

[44] See Kirk v. CIR, 425 F.2d 492 (D.C. Cir.), cert. denied, 400 US 853 (1970); Salkov v. CIR, supra note 43, at 196 ("reasonably clear" that "self-appointed ministers" do not qualify); Rev. Rul. 59-270, 1959-2 CB 44 ("ministers" of music and education who were not ordained, commissioned, or licensed as ministers of the gospel held not qualified).

is their only official mode of vesting the individual with sacerdotal powers.[45] If the taxpayer in question belongs to a religious group with an ordination procedure and is not qualified to perform sacerdotal functions for want of an official license, however, the benefits of IRC §107 are properly denied.[46] Being authorized to perform some sacredotal functions, but not all, qualifies one as a minister.[47]

In addition to being a minister, the taxpayer must receive the home or rental allowance "as part of his compensation," which is construed by the regulations to mean "as remuneration for services which are ordinarily the duties of a minister of the gospel." [48] In practice, the distinction between a religious body's "religious" and "secular" activities is difficult to draw,[49] and it runs the risk of offending religious sensibilities, since some denominations regard the "social gospel" as central to their calling.

Rental allowances qualify for the exclusion under IRC §107 only to the extent used "to rent or provide a home," but the term "home" encompasses a dwelling place, furnishings, and such appurtenances as a garage.[50]

A minister's business expenses are nondeductible under IRC §265(1) if allocable to income exempt from tax under IRC §107.[51]

¶7.7 HOUSING AND SUBSISTENCE FURNISHED TO MILITARY PERSONNEL

Members of the uniformed services are subject to the basic rules of the Internal Revenue Code, but a few provisions prescribe special time limits and allowances to take account of the hazards, travel obligations, and other fea-

---

[45] See Salkov v. CIR, supra note 43, implying that a congregation's selection of its leader constitutes a commission or license.

[46] See Kirk v. CIR, supra note 44.

[47] Salkov v. CIR, supra note 43 (Jewish cantor commissioned by recognized national body and installed by local congregation with power to perform certain religious functions; qualified under IRC §107 even though he cannot perform all functions of ordained rabbi).

[48] Treas. Regs. §1.107-1(a).

[49] See Colbert v. CIR, 61 TC 449 (1974) (ordained minister serving with Christian Anti-Communism Crusade to combat communism by lectures, broadcasts, publications, evangelistic services, and other means; held, not qualified); Boyer v. CIR, 69 TC 521 (1977) (Acq.) (minister teaching data processing in state college not qualified, despite purported assignment by church).

[50] Treas. Regs. §§1.107-1(b), 1.107-1(c) (purchase of home as well as direct housing expenses); see also Rev. Rul. 59-350, supra note 41 (cost of utilities qualifies for exclusion).

[51] Deason v. CIR, 41 TC 465 (1964) (Acq.) (minister's salary of $1,300 was exempt under IRC §107 to extent of $1,239; held, automobile expenses nondeductible to extent allocable to exempt portion); but see Rev. Rul. 62-212, 1962-2 CB 41 (IRC §265(1) does not prevent deduction of interest and taxes on residence by minister receiving allowance exempt under IRC §107).

tures of military life. Because these provisions turn on the individual's status in a particular branch of the uniformed services, however, the Code and regulations do not contain a complete compendium of the relevant rules. Thus, it is often necessary to consult legislation and regulations peculiar to the armed forces and other uniformed services to determine the applicability of these provisions to a specific person.[52] The principal aspects of these allowances are:

1. *Scope of provisions.* Some tax allowances are available to members of the "armed forces," a term that means the U.S. Army, Navy, Air Force, Marine Corps, and Coast Guard; others are available to members of the "uniformed services," a term that includes not only the armed forces but also the Environmental Science Services Administration and the Public Health Service.

2. *Quarters and subsistence allowances.* The basic compensation of uniformed personnel is subject to tax, but the regulations provide that the value of their quarters and subsistence is excluded from income, along with cash allowances for subsistence, uniforms, and commutation of quarters.[53]

3. *Moving and storage expenses.* For members of the armed forces on active duty, IRC §217(g) liberalizes the rules relating to the treatment of reimbursed moving expenses. If the move is pursuant to military orders incident to a permanent change of station, the value of moving and storage services provided in kind and cash reimbursements and allowances (to the extent of the expenses paid or incurred) are excludable from gross income. Unreimbursed expenses can be deducted to the extent permitted by IRC §217, but without regard to the minimum distance and time limits of IRC §217(c).[54]

4. *Combat pay.* Pursuant to IRC §112, compensation, other than retirement pay or pensions, for any month during which a member of the armed forces served in a combat zone or was hospitalized because of wounds, disease, or injury incurred in a combat zone is excluded from gross income in its entirety for personnel below the grade of commissioned officer and up to $500

---

[52] See, e.g., Scott v. US, 33 AFTR2d 858 (D.S.C. 1973) (not officially reported) (examining military statutes at length to ascertain status of retired officer teaching in Junior ROTC program).

[53] Treas. Regs. §1.61-2(b); see Rev. Rul. 60-65, 1960-1 CB 21 (Treas. Regs. §1.61-2 applies to National Guard); Scott v. US, supra note 52 (contra as to retired officer in JROTC); Rev. Rul. 70-281, 1970-1 CB 16 (family separation allowances excluded); Rev. Rul. 61-5, 1961-1 CB 8 (cost-of-living allowance to defray excess cost of quarters excluded); Treas. Regs. §1.61-2(b) (exclusion does not include per diem in lieu of subsistence or mileage); see also Rev. Rul. 76-2, 1976-1 CB 82 (temporary lodging allowance includable in gross income but deductible as provided by IRC §217, discussed infra ¶9.9).

[54] For IRC §217, see generally infra ¶9.9.

per month for commissioned officers.[55] Section 112(d), enacted in 1972, permits members of the armed forces and civilian employees in a "missing status" during the Vietnam War to exclude from gross income their compensation for active service.

5. *Mustering-out pay.* Under IRC §113, mustering-out payments for service in the armed forces are excluded from gross income.

6. *Reductions in retirement pay to provide family annuities.* To put members of the uniformed services on a par with participants in qualified civilian pension plans, IRC §122 excludes from gross income reductions in retired or retainer pay to purchase annuities for surviving spouses and children. The annuity is treated as having a zero cost, since the money withheld to compensate for the extended annuity was excluded from gross income.

7. *Abatement of taxes on death.* Under IRC §692, members of the armed forces who die while serving in a combat zone or because of wounds, disease, or injury incurred in combat are exempted from income taxes for the year of death and any prior taxable years ending on or after the first day of combat service. In addition, taxes for prior years that are unpaid at the date of death are not to be assessed, if assessed are to be abated, and if collected are to be credited or refunded.

¶7.8 COMMUTER TRANSPORTATION

To encourage conservation in the use of energy, IRC §124 excludes from gross income the value of "qualified transportation" furnished by employers between an employee's residence and place of employment. To qualify under IRC §124, the transportation must be provided under a separate written plan that does not discriminate in favor of officers, shareholders, or highly compensated employees; the plan must provide that the transportation is supplied in addition to any other compensation otherwise payable to the employee; and the vehicle must have a seating capacity of at least eight adults in addition to the driver, and its reasonably expected use must constitute a prescribed fraction of its full capacity. The exclusion does not encompass the value of transportation furnished to self-employed individuals.

¶7.9 EMPLOYEE-CHOSEN BENEFITS ("CAFETERIA PLANS")

Under IRC §125, employees are not required to include otherwise nontaxable fringe benefits in gross income merely because they are permitted by an

---

[55] Based on personal experience, the author suggests caution in the deliberate use of IRC §112 as a tax shelter.

employer's "cafeteria plan" to choose between taxable and nontaxable benefits. Section 125 thus supersedes the pervasive but nonstatutory principle that taxpayers who choose nontaxable benefits in lieu of cash must be viewed as though they had taken the cash and used it to purchase the benefits actually chosen.[56]

The statutory term "cafeteria plan" means a written plan under which all participants are employees who can choose among two or more benefits, consisting of nontaxable benefits or cash, property, or other taxable benefits. Except for the exclusion of certain plans providing for deferred compensation,[57] IRC §125 does not specify the types of nontaxable benefits that can be offered by a cafeteria plan. Section 125(f) defines "nontaxable benefit" as any benefit that, but for the taxpayer's right to choose, is not includable in gross income.

So far as rank-and-file employees are concerned, a cafeteria plan does not have to be generally available or nondiscriminatory. Highly compensated participants, however, cannot exclude cafeteria plan benefits from gross income under IRC §125(a) if the plan discriminates in favor of (a) highly compensated individuals as to eligibility to participate or (b) highly compensated participants as to contributions and benefits. In applying these nondiscrimination standards, IRC §125(g)(1) confers automatic immunity on plans maintained under a collective bargaining agreement.

¶7.10 LESSEE IMPROVEMENTS ON LESSOR'S PROPERTY

Section 109 excludes from the gross income of lessors of real property any income (other than rent) realized on the termination of a lease, representing the value of buildings or other improvements constructed by the lessee. Under a related provision, IRC §1019, the lessor's basis for the building is neither increased nor decreased by the excluded income. Taken in combination, these provisions have the effect of postponing recognition of the lessor's windfall profit until the property is sold or otherwise disposed of.

Section 109 does not apply to "rent," a qualification interpreted by the regulations to deny the exclusion to the value of buildings or improvements representing in whole or in part "a liquidation in kind of lease rentals."[58] The principal interpretative problem under IRC §109 is the distinction between

---

[56] See infra ¶35.2; infra ¶29.2 (deferred compensation where employer would have been willing to pay cash).

[57] IRC §125(d)(2); for cash-or-deferred plans, see IRC §402(a)(8). In 1980, Congress concluded that the blanket exclusion of deferred compensation from the benefits that can be offered by cafeteria plans was too restrictive, and it amended IRC §125(d)(2) to permit employee elections to have the employer pay contributions to a qualified profit-sharing or stock bonus plan with a cash-or-deferred option.

[58] Treas. Regs. §1.109-1(a). For the tenant's right to depreciate the cost of leasehold improvements, see infra ¶10.5.

taxable rent and excludable windfalls. The resolution of the problem turns on the intention of the parties to the lease.[59] If the improvements constructed have an estimated useful life exceeding the term of the lease, rent might be indicated; but not conclusively.[60]

¶7.11 REIMBURSEMENT OF LIVING EXPENSES AND OTHER NONDEDUCTIBLE AMOUNTS

Section 123 provides that an individual whose principal residence is damaged or destroyed by fire or other casualty can exclude from gross income amounts received under an insurance contract to reimburse the resulting additional living expenses, to the extent that they exceed the expenses that would have been incurred for the taxpayer and other members of the taxpayer's household during the period that the residence cannot be used or occupied. The exclusion is also allowed if access to the residence is denied by government action attributable to a casualty or threat thereof.

In computing the amount qualifying for exclusion, the taxpayer must take into account both increases and decreases in expenses incurred after the casualty in maintaining the normal standard of living of the taxpayer's household, such as rent, transportation, food, utilities, and miscellaneous services; but amounts that are unaffected by the casualty (e.g., mortgage payments) are disregarded.[61]

Section 123 permits qualifying amounts to be excluded from gross income, but it does not speak to the treatment of amounts that exceed the taxpayer's increased living expenses, are received from sources other than an insurance company, or compensate for the loss of use of property other than a principal residence (e.g., a vacation home or automobile). Stepping boldly into this breach, the regulations state flatly that any insurance recovery for increased living expenses in excess of the limit prescribed by IRC §123 is includable in gross income,[62] and this construction of an ambiguous statute is supported by several pre-1969 cases holding that amounts of this type are includable in gross income.[63]

---

[59] See Treas. Regs. §1.61-8(c) (whether tenant's improvements constitute rent to lessor depends on intention of parties, disclosed either by terms of lease or by surrounding circumstances).

[60] M.E. Blatt Co. v. US, 305 US 267, 277 (1938) (intention to constitute rent must be "plainly disclosed"); see Porter v. US, 11 AFTR2d 1426 (not officially reported) (W.D. Tenn. 1963) ("intention" submitted to jury).

[61] For the allocation of lump-sum payments covering increased living expenses, property damage, and loss of rental income, see Treas. Regs. §1.123-1(a)(4)(ii).

[62] Treas. Regs. §1.123-1(a)(5).

[63] Millsap v. CIR, 387 F.2d 420 (8th Cir. 1968); Arnold v. US, 289 F.Supp. 206 (E.D.N.Y. 1968); McCabe v. CIR, 54 TC 1745 (1970); but see Taylor v. US, 28 AFTR2d 6108 (N.D. Ala. 1964) (not officially reported) (contra).

These cases and the regulations under IRC §123 seem to imply that all amounts reimbursing the taxpayer for nondeductible living expenses are taxable unless excluded from gross income by a specific statutory provision, such as IRC §123 or §102, (relating to gifts). In a series of rulings, however, the IRS has held that amounts received to reimburse living expenses incurred in a nonemployment context on behalf of other persons or organizations are not taxable, even if unreimbursed expenses of the same type cannot be deducted.[64] Moreover, it is assumed—so universally that the issue has evidently not been litigated—that payments under an automobile liability policy to persons injured by the taxpayer's negligence are not includable in the taxpayer's gross income. To be sure, these amounts are paid to the victim rather than to the taxpayer. But unless the taxpayer is judgment-proof, they inure to his or her economic benefit; and amounts paid directly to injured persons by drivers who are uninsured or whose liability exceeds the policy limits cannot be deducted unless the accident occurs while driving for business purposes.

¶7.12 ALIMONY, SEPARATE MAINTENANCE, AND SUPPORT PAYMENTS

Alimony, separate maintenance, and support payments by one spouse, or former spouse, to the other are ordinarily deductible by the payor and taxable to the recipient. When the payments do not meet certain statutory conditions, however, they cannot be deducted by the payor; and as a corollary, they are excluded from the recipient's gross income.[65]

¶7.13 GOVERNMENT SUBSIDIES

Government subsidies are ordinarily includable in gross income unless they qualify for exclusion under a particular statutory provision, such as IRC §102 (gifts), which has been construed to embrace federal disaster aid and similar assistance, or IRC §1032 (contributions to a corporation's capital).[66] In addition to these broad exclusions, which do not explicitly refer to govern-

---

[64] See Rev. Rul. 80-99, 1980-1 CB 10 (reimbursement of speaker's travel expenses by political organizations), and rulings there cited; Rev. Rul. 55-555, 1955-2 CB 20 (car pool expenses); Rev. Rul. 63-77, 1963-1 CB 177 (interviews with prospective employers).

[65] Infra ¶32.1.

[66] See supra ¶3.2 (institutional charity); for the long-standing administrative exclusion of social security benefits, see supra ¶3.2; for agricultural support payments, see IRC §77.

ment subsidies, IRC §126(a) lists a number of federal and state subsidies that are excluded from gross income if and to the extent that the payment (1) is made primarily for the purpose of conserving soil and water resources, protecting or restoring the environment, improving forests, or providing a habitat for wildlife, as determined by the Secretary of Agriculture; and (2) does not substantially increase the annual income derived from the property, as determined by the IRS. A similar exclusion is allowed by IRC §621 for subsidies for the exploration, development, or mining of strategic minerals.

No deduction or credit is allowable for expenditures financed by these excludable subsidies, and they cannot be included in the basis of the benefited property.[67]

On the sale or other disposition of property acquired, improved, or otherwise modified by expenditures financed with these excluded amounts, IRC §1255 provides for the recapture on a sliding scale of amounts excluded under IRC §126, subject to rules similar to those applicable to the recapture of excess depreciation under IRC §1245.[68]

SELECTED BIBLIOGRAPHY

Bartlett, "Tax Treatment of Replacements of Leased Property and of Leasehold Improvements Made by a Lessee," 30 Tax Lawyer 105 (1976).

Bassey, Cafeteria Medical Reimbursement Plans: Terms Causing Problems As Deadlines Near, 51 J. Tax. 334 (1979).

Bruttomesso, Group-Term Life Insurance Plans, 46 J. Tax. 182 (1977).

Caplin, Educational Assistance Programs: A New Fringe Benefit for 1979-1983, 57 Taxes 75 (1979).

Kragen & Speer, IRC Section 119: Is Convenience of the Employer a Valid Concept? 29 Hastings L.J. 921 (1978).

Litwin, Designing a Qualified Group Legal Services Plan, 56 Taxes 123 (1978).

Newman, Transferability, Utility, and Taxation, 30 U. Kan. L. Rev. 27 (1981).

Popkin, The Taxation of Employee Fringe Benefits, 22 Boston Coll. L. Rev. 439 (1981).

Taft, Tax Benefits for the Clergy: The Unconstitutionality of Section 107, 62 Geo. L.J. 1261 (1974).

Wasserman, Principles in Taxation of Nonstatutory Fringe Benefits, 32 Tax Lawyer 137 (1978).

---

[67] IRC §§126(d), 126(e). IRC §126(c) allows the taxpayer to elect out of IRC §126 for any excludable amount or part thereof.

[68] For IRC §1245, see infra ¶28.2.

CHAPTER 8

Expenses Incurred in Business and Profit-Oriented Activities

¶8.1 INTRODUCTORY

1. Statutory Framework. In determining the taxable income of taxpayers engaged in business or profit-oriented activities, the Internal Revenue Code focuses on net profits rather than on gross receipts or gross income. The central importance of net profits is illustrated by Example 8-1, involving a merchant with sales of $1 million, cost of goods sold of $800,000, and selling and other business expenses of $150,000. On these assumptions, business profits are $50,000, as shown by Example 8-1.

Example 8-1

Computation of Gross Receipts, Gross Income, and Business Profits

1. Gross receipts (sales)	$1,000,000
2. Less: Cost of goods sold	800,000
3. Equals: Gross income	$ 200,000
4. Less: Business expenses	150,000
5. Equals: Business profits	$ 50,000

From business profits (a nonstatutory term that is similar to adjusted gross income if the taxpayer engages in no other relevant transactions for the taxable year), it is necessary to deduct either the so-called itemized deductions (charitable contributions, medical expenses, interest, etc.) or the zero bracket amount and the taxpayer's personal and dependency exemptions to reach taxable income, the statutory base on which the income tax is actually computed.[1]

In the case of wage earners and salaried employees, the Code similarly focuses on net profits rather than on gross receipts or gross income, but the spread is usually much smaller than for merchants and manufacturers. Thus, gross receipts and gross income are often identical if the taxpayer does not sell any goods, and gross income is often reduced by only a few minor items (e.g., union dues, safe-deposit box rentals, etc.) in arriving at net profits. In the same vein, when determining the taxable income of a taxpayer who sells securities, a personal residence, or other appreciated assets, the profit realized, rather than the sales proceeds, is taxed.

Whatever the nature of the taxpayer's economic activities, Congress has chosen to allow virtually all expenses incurred in business or profit-oriented transactions to be deducted. This basic principle stands in sharp contrast to the legislative treatment of the taxpayer's personal activities, which give rise to only a few circumscribed deductions. Unlike the cost *of living,* then, the cost *of earning a living* is ordinarily fully deductible.

Tax allowances for the cost of earning income are not required by the Constitution but instead embody a fundamental legislative decision to impose a *net income* tax rather than a sales tax, value added tax or gross income tax. Business-related payments are not automatically deductible, however; like personal expenditures, they can be deducted only if and to the extent authorized by the Internal Revenue Code. The difference between the two categories is that the Code provisions sanctioning the deduction of business and profit-oriented expenses are expressed in very broad terms, while the itemized personal deductions cover only a few of the manifold items comprising the cost of living and are subject to tight limits.

The broad—but not unqualified—principle of taxing net income rather than gross receipts or gross income is effected by the following statutory provisions:

1. *Business expenses.* IRC §162 allows taxpayers to deduct "all the ordinary and necessary expenses paid or incurred during the taxable year in carrying on any trade or business."

---

[1] For the terms "adjusted gross income" and "zero bracket amount," see IRC §62 and infra ¶14.5, respectively.

2. *Depreciation and Accelerated Cost Recovery System.* IRC §167 and §168 authorize annual depreciation and cost recovery deductions for buildings, equipment, and other assets that wear out or become obsolete while used in the taxpayer's business or profit-oriented activities. Because assets of this type contribute to income throughout their useful lives, they cannot be deducted under IRC §162 when purchased, but the annual depreciation and cost recovery deductions reflect the gradual erosion of the taxpayer's investment in the income-generating enterprise.

3. *Losses.* IRC §165 permits losses sustained during the taxable year to be deducted if incurred in the taxpayer's business or in a transaction entered into for profit.

4. *Expenses of producing income.* IRC §212 authorizes the deduction of all ordinary and necessary expenses paid or incurred by individuals, trusts, and estates during the taxable year for (a) the production or collection of income or (b) the management, conservation or maintenance of property held for the production of income. Section 212 is primarily concerned with expenses attributable to marketable securities and other passive investments, such as the cost of investment advice and custodial services. When expenses of this type are incurred by corporations, it is generally assumed that they qualify as business expenses under IRC §162.

5. *Hobbies.* IRC §183 authorizes the deduction of expenses incurred in hobbies ("activities not engaged in for profit"), defined as activities not meeting the standards of IRC §162 or IRC §§212(1) and 212(2); but the deductions, roughly speaking, cannot exceed the gross income generated by the activity. Thus, a hobby can generate a taxable gain or a break-even result for the taxpayer, but not a deductible loss.

6. *Cost of goods sold.* Under IRC §471, which authorizes the Treasury to prescribe regulations relating to inventories, the taxpayer is permitted to deduct the cost of goods sold from gross receipts in computing gross income.[2]

7. *Specialized provisions.* In addition to the foregoing provisions, there are a number of more specialized deductions, limited to particular business activities or industries.

Viewed as a whole, this network of provisions enables taxpayers to deduct virtually all business and profit-oriented expenditures at some time during the life of the enterprise—when the cost is paid or incurred, during the asset's useful life, when it is sold, or when the business venture is terminated. The few exceptions to this basic principle of deductibility, which are discussed below,

---

[2] See also Treas. Regs. §1.61-3(a): "In a manufacturing, merchandising, or mining business, 'gross income' means the total sales, less the cost of goods sold, plus any [incidental or investment] income."

were mandated by Congress primarily to curb exaggerated claims and other forms of tax abuse.

2. Business and Profit-Oriented Expenses. Although the deduction authorized by IRC §162(a) for all ordinary and necessary expenses incurred "in carrying on any trade or business" is the Code's most fundamental tax deduction, the term "trade or business" is not defined by either the Code or the regulations; and there is no authoritative judicial definition of the term. A much-quoted definition—to the effect that "carrying on any trade or business" as used in IRC §162(a) "involves holding one's self out to others as engaged in the selling of goods or services" [3]—seems to imply, erroneously, that taxpayers working throughout their lives for a single employer are not engaged in a trade or business because they do not hold themselves out to serve all comers. Nevertheless, it is well established that an employee's calling is a trade or business, even if the services are not offered to the public.[4]

Before IRC §212 was enacted in 1942, the courts had to determine whether the activities of individual investors in managing their own marketable securities constituted a trade or business, so that expenditures for investment advice, clerical assistance, safe-deposit rentals, and similar services were deductible under the statutory predecessor of IRC §162. In *Higgins v. CIR,* decided in 1941, the Supreme Court held that the management of one's own securities, even on a large enough scale to require an office and staff, was not a trade or business within the meaning of IRC §162.[5] With the enactment of IRC §212, it is no longer necessary to distinguish between "business" and "profit-oriented (or "investor") expenses in deciding whether a deduction is permissible. If the taxpayer is an individual, both types of expenses are deductible; except in special circumstances,[6] it is not necessary to decide whether the deduction rests on IRC §162 or §212.

Neither IRC §162 nor §212 applies, however, unless the activity giving rise to the expense is conducted for profit rather than pleasure. Activities not engaged in for profit, usually described as hobbies, may produce income as a by-product (e.g., profit on selling one's personal residence or collection of family memorabilia); but these incidental profits, even if large in amount, do not qualify the activity as a business under IRC §162 or as an income-producing activity under IRC §212. Section 183 distinguishes between activities that

---

[3] Deputy v. DuPont, 308 US 488, 499 (1940) (Mr. Justice Frankfurter, concurring).

[4] See Noland v. CIR, 269 F.2d 108, 111 (4th Cir.), cert. denied, 361 US 885 (1959) ("every person who works for compensation is engaged in the business of earning his pay," so that expenses essential to continuance of employment are deductible under statutory predecessor of IRC §162(a)).

[5] Higgins v. CIR, 312 US 212 (1941).

[6] See infra ¶8.5.

are, and those that are not, engaged in for profit; and the regulations specify nine factors that are relevant in making this determination.[7] Because the function of these regulations is to exclude activities engaged in for profit from IRC §183's rules, they are discussed below in conjunction with IRC §183 itself; but it should be noted here that they are useful guideposts to IRC §§162 and 212 as well, since an exclusion from IRC §183 virtually insures that the activity is either a trade or business within the meaning of IRC §162 or a profit-oriented activity within the meaning of IRC §212.

3. Relation to Itemized Deductions. It is not unusual for expenses qualifying for deduction under IRC §162 or §212 to qualify also as so-called itemized deductions under specific provisions, such as IRC §§163 (interest) and 164 (taxes), that do not require the item to arise in a business or profit-oriented activity. In general, these twice-blessed deductions are viewed as business expenses if this classification is more favorable to the taxpayer than treating them as itemized deductions. Thus, mortgage interest and local real property taxes paid in respect of an individual taxpayer's place of business can be deducted under IRC §62(1) in computing adjusted gross income, so that taxpayers get the benefit of these deductions in addition to the zero bracket amount allowed by IRC §63(d).[8]

Moreover, IRC §§162 and 212 ordinarily take precedence over the more specific itemized deductions when the latter are subject to special restrictions. Thus, IRC §164, allowing certain taxes to be deducted whether incurred in a business or profit-related activity or not, does not encompass any federal taxes; but if a federal tax qualifies as an expense under IRC §162 or §212, it is deductible even though not listed in IRC §164(a). On the other hand, Congress has sometimes assigned second-fiddle status to IRC §162; thus IRC §162(b) provides that charitable contributions in excess of the percentage limitations imposed by IRC §170, relating to the deduction of charitable contributions, may not be deducted under IRC §162. In no event, however, does the fact that an expenditure is deductible under more than one statutory provision permit it to be deducted twice.[9]

4. Expenses Paid on Behalf of Another Person. It is well established that expenses can be deducted under IRC §162 or §212 only if they are incurred in *the taxpayer's own* business or profit-oriented activities.[10] This sound principle is sometimes said to prohibit a taxpayer from deducting "the expenses of another taxpayer's business" or "expenses incurred for the benefit of another person." When properly employed, however, the expense-of-another notion is

---

[7] Infra ¶9.10.

[8] For the zero bracket amount, see infra ¶14.4.

[9] Treas. Regs. §1.161-1.

[10] See Treas. Regs. §1.162-1(a).

less a rule of law than a tool of analysis, which directs attention to the reason why the item was paid by the taxpayer claiming the deduction. In *Deputy v. DuPont,* the leading expense-of-another case, the Supreme Court held that a principal shareholder of the DuPont Company could not deduct under IRC §162 expenses incurred to assist the corporation in a plan to compensate executives in a manner the corporation could not have employed directly.[11] The Court held that the taxpayer's expenses "proximately result[ed] not from the taxpayer's business but from the business of the DuPont Company," and it prohibited any "blending" of the corporation's business with the business of its stockholders. After enunciating its anti-blending principle, the Court went on to hold that the expenses incurred by the taxpayer were not "ordinary"—a barrier to deductions under IRC §162. In the absence of evidence "that stockholders or investors, in . . . enhancing and conserving their estates, ordinarily or frequently lend such assistance to employee stock purchase plans of their corporations," the taxpayer's expenses could not be deducted.

On analysis, therefore, *Deputy v. DuPont* does not prohibit the deduction of the expenses of another person. In effect, the taxpayer was required to stand on his own two feet. Evidence that the transactions enhanced the company's business operations was not enough to establish that they advanced any business conducted by the taxpayer or that, if they did, they were "ordinary" expenses of the taxpayer's own business rather than extraordinary ones.[12]

The factual basis of *Deputy v. DuPont* was recognized, and appropriately distinguished, by the Tax Court in *Gould v. CIR,* which rejected the expense-of-another shibboleth.[13] The taxpayer in *Gould* was the president and sole shareholder of a failing corporation ("GPH") and was simultaneously an employee and minority shareholder of a successful corporation ("IMC") in the same industry. Under pressure from the directors of IMC, who feared damage to their company's reputation if GPH went into bankruptcy, he paid about $30,000 to settle GPH's obligations, for which he had no personal liability. The Tax Court allowed him to deduct the payment under IRC §162(a) because the taxpayer's "employment with IMC constituted a business, and he is entitled to deduct expenditures that have the requisite relationship to such employment."[14]

The expense-of-another problem arises with some frequency when executives deduct travel and entertainment expenses incurred in promoting their employer's business. In *Schmidlapp v. CIR,* involving a bank officer whose

---

[11] Deputy v. DuPont, supra note 3.

[12] See infra ¶8.3.

[13] Gould v. CIR, 64 TC 132 (1975).

[14] Id. at 134-136; see also Conley v. CIR, ¶77,406 P-H Memo TC (1977) (payment of wholly owned corporation's debts to protect taxpayer's business reputation; deduction allowed).

employer "expected that as part of [the taxpayer's] duties he would entertain at his own expense visitors whose favor the bank desired," Judge Learned Hand held that the officer could deduct the expenses "so far as they really were to drum up business for the bank." [15] Since this evidentiary burden was satisfied, Judge Hand did not regard the expense-of-another principle as a barrier to a deduction. Although some later cases have suggested that the employer's failure to reimburse the employee for such expenses is evidence that they serve personal rather than business purposes,[16] *Schmidlapp* properly recognizes that employers sometimes prefer to pay a "gross" salary and shift the burden of these expenses to the employee, an arrangement that may be more economical than allowing employees to charge entertainment expenses to the employer.

The basic IRS ruling in this area offers the following temperate summary of the applicable legal principles:

> Reimbursement for such expenses to the corporation officer or a resolution requiring the assumption of such expenses by him would tend to indicate that they are a necessary expense of his office. Although the presence of such evidence does not conclusively determine that the expenses are deductible, neither does the absence of such evidence of itself necessarily result in the disallowance of deductions, provided it can be established otherwise that the expenses are a necessary expense of the office.[17]

The ruling properly treats an employer's resolution requiring employees to defray their own traveling and entertainment expenses as neither indispensable nor conclusive. Commission salesmen, for example, do not need to be advised that travel and entertainment can serve their financial interests by promoting the employer's goods and services. Conversely, a formal declaration by the employer may be camouflage—a shabby attempt to furnish a fringe benefit to the employee at the expense of the Treasury—rather than a genuine statement of business policy.

The expense-of-another rationale has been used in a few cases to disallow the deduction of entertainment expenses by an employee who was entitled to be reimbursed by the employer but failed to press the claim.[18] The result may

---

[15] Schmidlapp v. CIR, 96 F.2d 680, 681-682 (2d Cir. 1938).

[16] Noland v. CIR, supra note 4, at 113. The court in *Noland* may have meant only that an adverse inference arises if an employer whose practice is to reimburse all appropriate entertainment expenses explicitly declines to reimburse the payment in dispute.

[17] Rev. Rul. 57-502, 1957-2 CB 118.

[18] E.g., Heidt v. CIR, 274 F.2d 25 (7th Cir. 1959); see also Rev. Rul. 78-141, 1978-1 CB 58 (attorney reimbursing client for expenses caused by erroneous advice cannot deduct payment as business expense under IRC §162 or loss under IRC §165 if he refrains from filing claim under malpractice insurance policy because of fear

be justified by the circumstances of the particular cases, but an employee's mere failure to enforce a right of reimbursement is neutral; what is material is the *reason* for the failure. If the employee is careless or lazy in failing to request reimbursement, the payment is not a business expense, though it might be viewed as creating a debt that will become deductible if and when the right to be reimbursed expires. Conversely, a salesman may be right in thinking that his success depends on results, that the expenditure helps to produce the results expected by the employer, and that it is better to absorb the expense—as an offset to his salary—than to insist on enforcing a reimbursement arrangement.

A right to be reimbursed is a more solid barrier to a deduction if there is no business reason why the taxpayer should not press the claim when it matures. Taxpayers often incur expenses on behalf of customers, clients, or other persons under reimbursement arrangements. In this context, the taxpayer's expenditure is better viewed as a loan or advance to the party on whose behalf the payment is made than as a deductible expense of the taxpayer's business. If the taxpayer's right to be reimbursed becomes worthless, the loss will be reflected by a bad debt deduction.

5. Charitable Contributions as Business Expenses. Section 162(b) disallows deductions under IRC §162(a) for contributions or gifts that would qualify as deductible charitable contributions were it not for the percentage limitations or time-of-payment requirements imposed by IRC §170 on the deductibility of charitable contributions. This limitation applies only to payments that are "in fact contributions or gifts to organizations described in Section 170." [19] Thus, payments to a hospital in consideration for its agreement to provide services and facilities to the taxpayer's employees are deductible without regard to the limitations of IRC §162(b), since the payments are not in fact contributions or gifts. However, the merely incidental benefit to the taxpayer's business resulting from a payment to a charity does not remove the payment from the gift or contribution category.

6. Business and Profit-Oriented Expenses as Capital Losses. Occasionally an amount that would usually be deductible under IRC §§162 or 212 against ordinary income is so closely linked to a current or prior transaction involving a capital asset that the expense must be treated as a capital loss rather than as a deduction in computing ordinary income. Conversely, a loss on the sale of a capital asset sometimes results in a deduction from ordinary income, rather than a capital loss, because the transaction was an integral part

---

of premium increase or cancellation of policy); Hills v. CIR, 691 F.2d 997 (11th Cir. 1982) (contra for casualty loss on taxpayer's personal residence; extensive analysis).

[19] Treas. Regs. §1.162-15(a)(2).

of the taxpayer's business operations, rather than the type of investment activity which the capital gain and loss provisions were designed to encompass.[20]

7. Estimating and Substantiating Deductible Amounts. In addition to establishing that an expenditure was paid or incurred for business or profit-oriented purposes within the meaning of IRC §162 or §212, the taxpayer must prove the *amount* spent for qualified purposes. If the actual amount of an expenditure cannot be established by such documentary evidence as an invoice, paid bill, or canceled check, oral testimony by the taxpayer or other persons may suffice; but self-serving declarations are subject to close scrutiny.

In establishing the right to deductions, taxpayers are enormously aided by the *Cohan* rule, promulgated in 1930 by the Court of Appeals for the Second Circuit in *Cohan v. CIR.*[21] The Board of Tax Appeals found that George M. Cohan, in conducting his business as a Broadway producer, "was required to and did spend large sums of money in traveling and entertaining"; but it upheld the disallowance by the IRS of any deductions because "the amounts claimed are bare estimates unsupported by any vouchers or book-keeping entries of any kind" and it could not determine what amounts were expended for personal expenses. In an opinion by Judge Learned Hand, however, the appellate court reversed, holding that the Board should have made the best estimate possible in the circumstances:

> Absolute certainty in such matters is usually impossible and is not necessary; the Board should make as close an approximation as it can, bearing heavily if it chooses upon the taxpayer whose inexactitude is of his own making. But to allow nothing at all appears to us inconsistent with saying that something was spent. True, we do not know how many trips Cohan made, nor how large his entertainments were; yet there was obviously some basis for computation, if necessary by drawing upon the Board's personal estimates of the minimum of such expenses. The amount may be trivial and unsatisfactory, but there was basis for some allowance, and it was wrong to refuse any, even though it were the traveling expenses of a single trip. It is not fatal that the result will inevitably be speculative; many important decisions must be such.[22]

Despite an outdated premise that record-keeping is not a customary part of everyday life, *Cohan* has been expanded to cover virtually the entire corpus of the tax law. Although rendered inapplicable to travel and entertainment expenses by IRC §274, it remains a major factor in the allowance of virtually

[20] See infra ¶25.1.

[21] Cohan v. CIR, 11 BTA 743 (1928), rev'd, 39 F.2d 540 (2d Cir. 1930).

[22] Id. at 543-544.

all other deductions under IRC §162. It should be noted, however, that taxpayers relying on *Cohan* must make a threshold showing that they spent more for deductible items than was allowed by the IRS; if the IRS has already applied *Cohan* in allowing the claimed deduction in part, it may be very difficult to establish that a more generous estimate is required. Moreover, *Cohan* does not require a partial allowance for an item that is either wholly deductible or wholly nondeductible, no matter how difficult it is to categorize the item.

¶8.2 THE BUSINESS-PERSONAL BORDERLINE

1. Introductory. Most expenses can be readily classified as purely personal or purely business; but many others serve personal purposes while simultaneously advancing the taxpayer's business or profit-oriented pursuits. Common examples are uniforms, meals and lodging during business travel, and medical care required by occupational injuries. In deciding whether expenses along the business-personal borderline can be deducted under IRC §162 or §212 as ordinary and necessary expenses of carrying on the taxpayer's business or profit-oriented activities or are disallowed by IRC §262, prohibiting any deduction for "personal, living, or family expenses" unless otherwise expressly allowed, the IRS, courts, and Congress have vacillated between four main approaches:

1. *Inherently personal.* One possibility is the denial of any deduction for "inherently personal" expenses, even though they also serve business purposes or needs. At a minimum, this concept prohibits deductions for expenses that are incurred whether the taxpayer works or not.[23] Thus, the Tax Court has rejected the claim that a taxpayer's living expenses were a cost of selling labor, analogous to a merchant's cost of goods sold.[24] The "inherently personal" concept has also been used to disallow deductions claimed by a young couple for the care of their infant child while they both were at work [25] although the expenses would not have been incurred but for their employment. In the same vein, expenses are often viewed as inherently personal and, therefore, nondeductible, even though they exceed the level that the taxpayer would have incurred in the absence of pressure from employers or customers, such as the

[23] See Sparkman v. CIR, 112 F.2d 774 (9th Cir. 1940) (dentures to correct radio actor's speech defect nondeductible); Fred W. Amend Co. v. CIR, 454 F.2d 399 (7th Cir. 1971) (businessman's use of Christian Science practitioner as consultant; held, inherently personal); Rev. Rul. 78-128, 1978-1 CB 39 (health spa expenses of law-enforcement officer required to keep in top physical condition nondeductible).

[24] Reading v. CIR, 70 TC 730, 733-734 (1978).

[25] Smith v. CIR, 40 BTA 1038 (1939), aff'd per curiam, 113 F.2d 114 (2d Cir. 1940); for the subsequent enactment of a legislative remedy, see infra ¶21.1.

excess cost of clothing when stylish dress is expected in the taxpayer's occupation.

2. *Excess cost.* A second possibility is to allow a deduction only if, and to the extent that, the expense was increased by the exigencies of the taxpayer's business or profit-oriented activities. This approach was adopted in 1920 by the Treasury in dealing with the cost of meals and lodging incurred by taxpayers on business trips, but was abandoned when Congress enacted the statutory predecessor of IRC §162(a)(2), permitting these expenses to be deducted in full. The excess cost theory was endorsed by the Supreme Court in *Fausner v. CIR,* involving a commercial airline pilot's expenses of getting to and from his place of employment with his flight equipment and overnight bag.[26] Holding that the expenses were personal because they would have been incurred even if the taxpayer had no occupational baggage, the Court indicated that a deduction would have been in order for any *additional* expenses incurred to transport job-required tools and materials.

3. *Allocation.* Third, expenses can be allocated between their business and personal components, with only the amount assigned to the business function being deductible. This approach is often applied to expenditures for dual-purpose facilities, such as a physician's automobile, when business and personal uses can be separated by reference to the amount of time, space, etc., devoted to each.

4. *Primary purpose.* Finally, a deduction is sometimes allowed for the full amount of the expense if it was incurred primarily for business or profit-oriented activities, and the personal benefit was a mere by-product. This approach is characteristic of cases and rulings permitting taxpayers to deduct educational expenses and the cost of business entertainment, where personal benefits are usually inevitable despite the primacy of the taxpayer's business goal.

Neither the bare language nor the legislative history of IRC §162, §212, or §262 supplies a firm basis for choosing among these conflicting principles, and there is no possible way to reconcile all of the cases and rulings. There is, unfortunately, no theoretically satisfactory boundary between business expenses that provide incidental personal benefits and personal expenditures that incidentally serve business purposes. No matter how generously the Code defines business expenses in an effort to insure that all business-related expenses can be deducted, there will always be some nondeductible items beyond the line that contribute in some way to the production of income. On the other hand, no matter how severely the term "business expense" is defined, many items will continue to qualify for deduction although they confer "personal" benefits on the taxpayer. Even the most puritanical definition of busi-

[26] Fausner v. CIR, 413 US 838 (1973), discussed infra ¶9.1.

ness expense, for example, is not likely to prevent self-employed taxpayers from deducting the cost of air-conditioning their offices, upholstering their swivel chairs, or adding gadgets to their telephones, even if they derive personal pleasure from these amenities.

The most common categories of borderline expenses have produced their own bodies of law which are summarized below. In a few areas, Congress has not been satisfied with the tax results reached by the general rules of IRC §162 or §212 and has intervened with special legislation.

1. *Food and shelter.* With the exception of meals and lodging while the taxpayer is away from home on a business or profit-oriented trip, which are deductible under special rules discussed below,[27] food and shelter are quintessential nondeductible personal expenses.[28] Yet it would be too dogmatic to assert that they can never qualify for deduction under IRC §162 or §212. There are evidently no rulings or litigated cases involving professional food tasters or restaurant critics, for example, but they would have a reasonably solid case for deducting at least the excess cost of their meals, if not the entire amount.

2. *Clothing and personal grooming.* The basic IRS ruling on expenditures to acquire and maintain uniforms provides that they constitute business expenses if they are (1) specifically required as a condition of employment and (2) not suitable for ordinary wear.[29] The latter requirement is evidently satisfied by a showing that the uniform is distinctive. The disallowance of deductions for clothing suited to ordinary usage is presumably intended to forestall claims by bankers, lawyers, sales clerks in fashionable stores, and others who dress expensively to satisfy the actual or imagined wishes of their employers or customers.[30] When its twin conditions are satisfied, the ruling permits the taxpayer to deduct the entire cost of procuring and maintaining the uniform, even if it does not exceed the cost of ordinary clothing. By confining its scope to "uniforms," the ruling impliedly disqualifies overalls and other heavy-duty

[27] Infra ¶9.1.

[28] See Moscini v. CIR, ¶77,245 P-H Memo TC (1977) (policeman cannot deduct excess cost of restaurant meals over home-prepared meals, even though departmental regulations prohibited carrying bag lunch or eating in patrol car); but see Green v. CIR, 74 TC 1229 (1980) (taxpayer in business of selling blood plasma allowed to deduct excess cost of high-protein diet).

[29] Rev. Rul. 70-474, 1970-2 CB 35 (re police officers, firemen, letter carriers, nurses, bus drivers and railroad employees).

[30] Pevsner v. CIR, 628 F.2d 467 (5th Cir. 1980), rev'g ¶79,311 P-H Memo TC (1979) (manager of boutique not allowed to deduct cost of fashionable clothes and accessories); but see Yeomans v. CIR, 30 TC 757 (1958) (Nonacq.) (high-fashion clothing required by fashion coordinator's job deductible, but amounts claimed severely limited because allocation between business and personal use not clearly established by taxpayer).

clothing worn by blue-collar workers, even if specially chosen to withstand the conditions of employment.[31] Despite the ruling's insistence on *employer* compulsion, the courts have held that self-employed taxpayers may deduct the cost of uniforms required by the nature of their occupations.[32]

Although TV entertainers, circus clowns, and similar performers can no doubt deduct the cost of cosmetics, hairstyling, etc., ordinary mortals must treat grooming expenses as nondeductible costs of living, even if mandated by employers accustomed to obedience, like the United States Army.[33]

3. *Medical expenses.* Medical expenses, even if occasioned by occupational injuries or required to perform business services properly, are rarely deductible under IRC §162; but they may be deducted as itemized personal deductions under IRC §213, subject to its percentage limitations.[34]

4. *Care of taxpayer's dependents during working hours.* In *Smith v. CIR,* the Tax Court held that a two-job married couple could not deduct, as a business expense under IRC §162, the cost of nursemaids employed to care for their young child during working hours.[35] Although Congress subsequently enacted a deduction for expenses of this type, which was later converted into the credit now allowed by IRC §44A, the principle of the *Smith* case remains in force except where superseded by this legislation.[36]

5. *Commuting expenses.* The cost of getting to and from work is incurred only by taxpayers who work and not by those who live on investment income or are supported by others, but it has long been established that commuting expenses are not deductible business expenses.[37] The rationale for this rule is that taxpayers living away from their business locations do so for personal convenience rather than for business reasons.[38] In actuality, there is sometimes no housing to be had at any price within walking distance of the taxpayer's place of employment; and even more often, none is available at a price commensurate with the taxpayer's wages. But despite the weakness of its rationale, the nondeductibility of commuting expenses remains a cardinal principle in the application of IRC §§162 and 212.

---

[31] See Rev. Rul. 57-143, 1957-1 CB 89 (painter's work clothing, required by his union, not a "uniform"); Donnelly v. CIR, 262 F.2d 411 (2d Cir. 1959) (heavy-duty work clothing not deductible); but see Bushey v. CIR, ¶71,149 P-H Memo TC (1971) (specially designed work clothing, special work shoes, and safety glasses all required in taxpayer's employment; held, deductible).

[32] Harsaghy v. CIR, 2 TC 484 (Acq.) (1943) (private-duty nurse); Motrud v. CIR, 44 TC 208, 216 (1965) (independent contractor operating wholesale dairy route).

[33] Drake v. CIR, 52 TC 842, 844 (1969) (Acq.) (soldier's haircuts).

[34] See infra ¶20.2.

[35] Smith v. CIR, supra note 25.

[36] See infra ¶21.1.

[37] Treas. Regs. §§1.162-2(e), 1.212-1(f), 1.262-1(b)(5).

[38] For IRC §217, permitting the cost of moving to a new principal place of business to be deducted, see infra ¶9.9.

6. *Entertainment expenses.* Of all dual-purpose items, entertainment expenses are the most susceptible to exaggeration and fraud. For this reason, their deductibility is governed not only by the usual standards of IRC §162 or §212 but also by a network of special rules under IRC §274.[39]

7. *Business use of personal residences.* Another area particularly subject to abuse is the alleged business and profit-oriented use of the taxpayer's personal residence. By virtue of IRC §280A, enacted in 1976 and discussed below,[40] severe restrictions are imposed on deductions for depreciation and maintenance of home offices, vacation homes held for part-time rental purposes, and similar properties.

8. *Education.* Education to fulfill the taxpayer's cultural aspirations is a nondeductible cost of living, but many educational courses serve both personal and business objectives, and some training has a purely vocational function. To qualify for a deduction under IRC §162 or §212, however, educational expenses not only must avoid being classified as "living expenses" under IRC §262 but must also qualify as current expenses rather than long-term capital expenditures. Further discussion of this subject, therefore, follows an examination of the capital expenditure issue.[41]

9. *Litigation expenses.* Litigation costs can be deducted under IRC §162 or §212 only if they can avoid being classified either as personal expenses (e.g., the cost of getting a divorce) or as capital expenditures (e.g., the cost of clearing title to property).

10. *Expenses to protect taxpayer's reputation.* In a tangled group of cases the courts have distinguished payments, legal fees, and other expenditures to protect the taxpayer's personal reputation, which are nondeductible living expenses, from outlays to protect the taxpayer's business reputation, which are deductible under IRC §162 or §212 unless classified as capital expenditures. In some cases, the courts look to the nature of the events giving rise to the payments in deciding whether they are deductible under IRC §162 or §212. Thus, an accountant who pleaded nolo contendere in a criminal tax evasion case was denied a deduction for the cost of his unsuccessful defense in a later professional disciplinary proceeding because the tax offense was caused by personal misconduct rather than by his business activities.[42] On the other hand, if the claim affecting the taxpayer's reputation originates in the taxpayer's business activities, the expenses are ordinarily deductible, even

---

[39] Infra ¶9.3.

[40] Infra ¶9.11.

[41] Infra ¶8.4.

[42] Bell v. CIR, 320 F.2d 953 (8th Cir. 1963); see also Lewis v. CIR, 253 F.2d 821 (2d Cir. 1958) (fees to defend incompetency proceeding nondeductible, despite possible adverse effect on taxpayer's status as author); but see Draper v. CIR, 26 TC 201 (1956) (Acq.) (legal expenses to prosecute libel suit against person alleging performer was Communist; held, deductible), disapproved by the *Lewis* case.

though the claim adversely affects the taxpayer's personal reputation as well as his or her business standing.[43]

Even if the payments have an exclusively business origin and objective, the taxpayer must prove that they are current expenses rather than capital expenditures, since outlays of the latter type must be capitalized and are taken into account when the resulting goodwill is abandoned or sold. Deductions under IRC §162 are not warranted, however, if payment of some other enterprise's debts is not proximately related to the taxpayer's own business reputation.[44]

11. *Expenses of public officials.* While in office, a public official may deduct unreimbursed current expenses, including the cost of contesting a recall election.[45] Expenses of political campaigns, however, are neither deductible nor amortizable, whether the candidate is seeking election to an initial term or is an incumbent and whether he or she is elected or defeated.

12. *Correlation between exclusions and deductions.* In general, taxpayers whose employers or customers furnish them with dual-purpose items (e.g., work clothing or travel expenses) are entitled to exclude these items from gross income if the expenses could have been deducted under IRC §162 or §212 had they been incurred and paid by the taxpayer.[46] Conversely, the receipts should be included in gross income if direct payments would not have been deductible. There are, however, some exceptions to this principle of parity. For example, meals and lodging furnished in kind for the employer's convenience are excluded from the employee's gross income by virtue of IRC §119, but cannot be deducted if procured and paid for by the employee, even if they serve the identical function of facilitating performance of the taxpayer's duties.[47] The result is an anomalous distinction that depends more on the form of the transaction than its substance.

---

[43] Pepper v. CIR, 36 TC 886 (1961) (Acq.) (lawyer's payments to clients who invested funds on his recommendation in another client's business, on discovering that latter was engaged in fraud); but see Friedman v. Delaney, 171 F.2d 269 (1st Cir. 1948), cert. denied, 336 US 936 (1949) (contra).

[44] See Cloud v. CIR, ¶76,027 P-H Memo TC (1976) (lawyer's payment of incorporated motel's expenses; no showing of relationship to professional reputation); see also *Welch v. Helvering,* discussed infra ¶8.3.

[45] See IRC §7701(a)(26) ("trade or business" includes performance of functions of public office); Rev. Rul. 71-470, 1971-2 CB 121 (recall election); Rev. Rul. 73-356, 1973-2 CB 31 (amounts expended by congressman for newsletters, etc. to constituents).

[46] Even when the inclusion-deduction alternative constitutes the norm, however, the regulations allow employees to exclude the item if they properly account to the employer. See Treas. Regs. §1.162-17; Rev. Rul. 76-71, 1976-1 CB 308 (employer reimbursement of tuition paid for business educational expense); Rev. Rul. 76-65, 1976-1 CB 46 (tuition fees paid directly by employer not compensatory because they would have been deductible if paid by employees).

[47] For IRC §119, see supra ¶7.5.

¶8.3 "ORDINARY AND NECESSARY" AND SIMILAR QUALIFICATIONS ON DEDUCTIBILITY OF BUSINESS AND PROFIT-ORIENTED EXPENSES

1. Introductory. To quality for deduction under IRC §162 or §212, an expense must be both "ordinary" and "necessary." This qualification has been included in the tax law since the Revenue Act of 1913, but its scope has never been authoritatively delineated and remains uncertain to this day.

2. Scope of "Ordinary and Necessary." In *Welch v. Helvering,* the most widely quoted opinion dealing with the term "ordinary," Mr. Justice Cardozo described the test as not whether the payments are "habitual or normal in the sense that the taxpayer will have to make them often," but rather whether the payment is normal, common, and accepted under the circumstances by the business community. That this does not offer much in the way of precision, as Cardozo himself acknowledged:

> Here, indeed, as so often in other branches of the law, the decisive distinctions are those of degree and not of kind. One struggles in vain for any verbal formula that will supply a ready touchstone. The standard set up by the statute is not a rule of law; it is rather a way of life. Life in all its fullness must supply the answer to the riddle.[48]

Another much-cited definition of "ordinary" appears in *Deputy v. Du-Pont,* decided by the Supreme Court a few years after *Welch v. Helvering:*

> Ordinary has the connotation of normal, usual, or customary. To be sure, an expense may be ordinary though it happen but once in the taxpayer's lifetime. . . . Yet the transaction which gives rise to it must be of common or frequent occurrence in the type of business involved. . . . Hence, the fact that a particular expense would be an ordinary or common one in the course of one business and so deductible under [IRC §162] does not necessarily make it such in connection with another business. . . . One of the extremely relevant circumstances is the nature and scope of the particular business out of which the expense in question accrued. The fact that an obligation to pay has arisen is not sufficient. It is the kind of transaction out of which the obligation arose and its normalcy in the particular business which are crucial and controlling.[49]

As for the statutory term "necessary," *Welch v. Helvering* suggests that

---

[48] Welch v. Helvering, 290 US 111, 115 (1933).
[49] Deputy v. DuPont, 308 US 488, 495-496 (1940).

it requires no more than that the expenses be "appropriate and helpful" [50] in developing the taxpayer's business; they need not be indispensable or unavoidable. Moreover, the courts have tended to accept the taxpayer's own judgment of the business value of expenditures, rather than to decide this commercial issue de novo.

Although Mr. Justice Cardozo acknowledged in *Welch v. Helvering* that it would be "a futile task" to attempt to harmonize all the cases applying these generalities to what he called "life in all its fullness" a few major functions assigned by the courts to the "ordinary and necessary" standard can be identified:

1. *Capital expenditures.* In *CIR v. Tellier,* the Supreme Court said:

> The principal function of the term "ordinary" in §162(a) is to clarify the distinction, often difficult, between those expenses that are currently deductible and those that are in the nature of capital expenditures, which, if deductible at all, must be amortized over the useful life of the asset.[51]

Viewed as a prohibition against deductions for capital expenditures, however, the phrase "ordinary and necessary" is a handkerchief thrown over something that is already covered by a blanket. This is because IRC §263(a), denying any deduction for amounts paid for the acquisition, improvement, or betterment of property, explicitly embodies the basic principle that a capital expenditure may not be deducted from current income and takes precedence over IRC §162.

2. *Personal expenses.* The "ordinary and necessary" standard is occasionally invoked to disallow deductions for personal expenses. An example is *Henry v. CIR,* in which the Tax Court held that a tax lawyer-accountant could not deduct the cost of maintaining a yacht, despite his claim that its red, white, and blue pennant bearing the magic numerals "1040" stimulated inquiries and brought him clients.[52] Operating a yacht for this purpose was, in the court's opinion, not normal under the circumstances and, therefore, not "ordinary." Furthermore, because the expenditure "may well have been made to further ends which are primarily personal," the court declined to defer to the taxpayer's judgment as to whether the expense was "necessary" in the sense of "appropriate and helpful," requiring instead that the taxpayer prove that the expense was "necessary" in the more common sense of the word, a burden he could not meet. The same result could have been reached without ascribing

---

[50] Welch v. Helvering, supra note 48, at 113.

[51] CIR v. Tellier, 383 US 687, 689-690 (1966).

[52] Henry v. CIR, 36 TC 879, 884 (1961); see also Brown v. CIR, 446 F.2d 926 (8th Cir. 1971) (expense of photographic safari not a "necessary" expense of corporate executive's occupation, although films used to advertise employer's product).

a special meaning to the term "necessary," however, in reliance on IRC §262, prohibiting the deduction of "personal, living, or family expenses." Though harmless, the use of "ordinary and necessary" as a barrier to the deduction of personal expenses adds nothing of substance of the government's primary safeguards.

3. *Reasonableness of amount.* It has been held that "the element of reasonableness is inherent in the phrase 'ordinary and necessary' in both IRC §162 and §212."[53] In practice, however, the concept of reasonableness adds little if anything to the statutory requirement that expenses must be "ordinary and necessary." If the amount of an otherwise deductible expense is determined by an impersonal market or fixed in arm's-length bargaining between the taxpayer and an independent supplier, there is no reason to pare it down for tax purposes. Indeed, the best evidence that an amount is "reasonable" is that it was paid by the taxpayer to an independent party for the goods or services in question.

On the other hand, payments between related parties, such as members of the same family, may serve personal as well as business or profit motives, and may not be, in fact, what they purport to be. If the amount is excessive, the payment is pro tanto not an "expense" of carrying on a business or of conserving and maintaining income-producing property, but a gift, dividend, loan, or other nondeductible item.

4. *Ordinary vs. extraordinary.* Courts sometimes contrast "ordinary" expenses with "extraordinary" ones on the theory that IRC §§162 and 212 do not permit unusual, idiosyncratic, or unique expenditures to be deducted, even if they are helpful or appropriate in carrying on the taxpayer's business or profit-oriented activities. This distinction is sanctioned by *Welch v. Helvering,* where the Supreme Court suggested that allowing extraordinary expenses to be deducted would "open the door to many bizarre analogies"; but the Court was there primarily worried about attempts to deduct personal expenses and capital expenditures, and it conceded that the term "ordinary" does not require payments to be "habitual or normal in the sense that the same taxpayer will have to make them often."[54]

In a few subsequent cases, however, taxpayers have been denied the right to deduct payments that served business purposes and were not capital expenditures, on the ground that the payment was unusual or extraordinary. In *Goedel v. CIR,* for example, a stock dealer was denied a deduction for premi-

---

[53] CIR v. Lincoln Elec. Co., 176 F.2d 815, 817 (6th Cir. 1949) (one judge dissenting), cert. denied, 338 US 949 (1950); see also Bingham's Trust v. CIR, 325 US 365, 370 (1945) (same as to "ordinary and necessary" as used in IRC §212); Treas. Regs. §1.212-1(d) (to be deductible under IRC §212, expenses "must be reasonable in amount"), §1.162-2(a) (same for traveling expenses).

[54] Welch v. Helvering, supra note 48, at 114.

ums paid for insurance on the life of the President of the United States, whose death it was feared would disrupt the stock market.[55] Other cases in this category have disallowed deductions for services performed by a minister who advised the taxpayer and his employees about business problems, using prayer rather than business skill; for hush money paid by an attorney to silence an accuser whose derogatory charges adversely affected his professional reputation; and for kickbacks paid to a customer's purchasing agent.[56]

In some of these cases, there was at least a latent suspicion that the expenditure either served personal rather than business objectives or contravened public policy. To the extent that they rest solely on the theory that unusual or extraordinary payments are not deductible even if helpful and appropriate in carrying on the taxpayer's business, however, they are anomalous. There is no sound reason to deny a deduction merely because the taxpayer is unusually imaginative or innovative.

3. Frustration of Public Policy. In an important series of cases involving taxable years before 1970, the courts disallowed deductions—usually for unlawful payments and bribes—whose allowance, it was thought or assumed, would frustrate public policy by encouraging unlawful conduct. The principal rationale was that it is neither "ordinary" nor "necessary" to violate the law. Recognizing, however, that fines and unlawful payments are sometimes unavoidable or necessary for the enterprise to continue in business (e.g., fines for traffic infractions by companies operating fleets of taxis and trucks despite sedulous efforts to discipline careless drivers) but feeling that it was distasteful to allow bribes and some other payments to be deducted, the courts gravitated between the impulse to measure net income accurately regardless of moral considerations and a more demanding "frustration of public policy" doctrine. In 1924, for example, the Board of Tax Appeals disallowed a deduction for the cost of defending a perjury action, growing out of testimony given by the taxpayer in an investigation of payoffs to officers of construction unions, with the comment:

> We do not believe that it is in the interest of sound public policy that the commission of illegal acts should be so far protected or recognized that their cost is regarded as a legitimate and proper deduction in the

---

[55] Goedel v. CIR, 39 BTA 1, 12 (1939); see also Rev. Rul. 55-714, 1955-2 CB 51 (manager of entertainer entitled to percentage of latter's gross income cannot deduct premiums paid for insurance on entertainer's life in absence of evidence that practice is customary in the industry).

[56] Trebilcock v. CIR, 64 TC 852 (1975) (Acq.), aff'd by order, 557 F.2d 1226 (6th Cir. 1977) (spiritual advice); Bonney v. CIR, 247 F.2d 237 (2d Cir.), cert. denied, 355 US 906 (1957) (hush money); United Draperies, Inc. v. CIR, 340 F.2d 936 (7th Cir. 1964), cert. denied, 382 US 813 (1965) (kickbacks).

computation of net income under the revenue laws of the United States.[57]

In later cases, however, this seemingly simple line proved difficult to apply. In a series of important cases, the Supreme Court held that fines paid by a trucking company for violations of state maximum-weight laws were nondeductible even if the offenses were inadvertent; that illegal gambling enterprises could deduct wages and rental payments even though both types of expenditures violated state law; that opticians could deduct payments to eye doctors who recommended them to their patients because the payments did not violate any "sharply defined national or state policies," although the contracts were unenforceable under local law as a matter of public policy; and that the deduction of legal fees paid in unsuccessfully defending a prosecution for fraud in the sale of securities did not frustrate public policy.[58]

These decisions and others by the lower federal courts not only were difficult to reconcile, but they left many related issues unsettled, such as the status of payments that violated trade practices, administrative rules, or civil statutes but were not punishable by fine or imprisonment; the effect of an absence of criminal intent, if it resulted in a reduced level of punishment; and the deductibility of payments to settle private lawsuits involving conduct in violation of law, including the punitive portion of treble-damage actions.

Rather than leave the many uncertainties in the frustration-of-public-policy doctrine to be decided by the courts on a case-by-case basis, Congress preempted the field in 1969 by amending IRC §162 to disallow deductions for specific categories of payments, stating that the new provisions are "intended to be all-inclusive" and that "public policy, in other circumstances, generally is not sufficiently clearly defined to justify the disallowance of deductions."[59] As amended in 1971, the 1969 rules are embodied in IRC §§162(c) (illegal bribes, kickbacks, and other payments), 162(f) (fines and penalties), and 162(g) (treble damages under the antitrust laws). These rules were augmented in 1982 by the enactment of IRC §280E, which singles out taxpayers

---

[57] Backer v. CIR, 1 BTA 214, 217 (1924). The deduction of legal fees incurred in defending against charges of criminal misconduct in the taxpayer's business was later sanctioned by the Supreme Court in CIR v. Tellier, supra note 51.

The *Backer* approach to the expenses of unlawful enterprises was codified in 1982 by the enactment of IRC §280E, disallowing any deduction or credit for amounts paid or incurred in carrying on a business of trafficking in drugs ("controlled substances") if the business is prohibited by federal or state law.

[58] Tank Truck Rentals, Inc. v. CIR, 356 US 30, 33 (1958) (violations of state maximum-weight laws); Hoover Motor Express Co. v. US, 356 US 38 (1958) (same, inadvertent violations); CIR v. Sullivan, 356 US 27 (1958) (gambling enterprise); Lilly v. CIR, 343 US 90 (1952) (payments to eye doctors); CIR v. Tellier, supra note 51 (legal fees in defending prosecution for fraud in sale of securities).

[59] S. Rep. No. 91-552, reprinted in 1969-3 CB 423, 597.

engaged in the trade or business of illegal trafficking in controlled drugs, and denies all deductions otherwise allowable under IRC §162 or any other section.

The legislative intent to preempt the frustration-of-public-policy doctrine, as restated by the regulations, seems to apply to both IRC §162 and §212.[60] As is often true of preempting attempts, however, the statutory rules may have left some crevices to be filled by the otherwise outmoded frustration doctrine. The IRS has ruled, for example, that IRC §165, relating to losses, does not sanction a deduction for a taxpayer's loss from the seizure and forfeiture of his slot machines when his possession became unlawful for nonpayment of the federal tax on coin-operated gaming devices, and the Tax Court similarly disallowed deductions to a taxpayer whose vehicles were confiscated because they were used to transport marijuana.[61]

4. Fines and Penalties. Section 162(f) prohibits any deduction under IRC §162(a) for "any fine or similar penalty paid to a government for the violation of any law." This provision codifies the Supreme Court's decision in *Tank Truck Rentals, Inc.* and *Hoover Motor Express,* disallowing any deduction whether the violation was deliberate or inadvertent.[62] The ambiguous term "similar penalty" encompasses "payments of sanctions which are imposed under civil statutes but which in general terms serve the same purpose as a fine exacted under a criminal statute" [63] and certain additions to tax or late filing charges imposed in respect to the late filing of a tax return.[64]

---

[60] Treas. Regs. §§1.162-1(a), 1.212-1(p); see also Rev. Rul. 74-323, 1974-2 CB 40 (advertising expenses deductible although in violation of Civil Rights Act of 1964, since public-policy doctrine was preempted by IRC §§162(c), 162(f), and 162(g)—none of which applies to these expenses).

[61] Rev. Rul. 77-126, 1977-1 CB 47 (public-policy doctrine not codified and limited as respects IRC §165); Holt v. CIR, 69 TC 75 (1977) (loss disallowed under IRC §165 without reaching government's contention that IRC §162(f) precluded deduction, where taxpayer used vehicle to transport marijuana); see also Mazzei v. CIR, 61 TC 497 (1974), denying a theft loss on public-policy grounds to a taxpayer who was defrauded by his confederates in a scheme to manufacture counterfeit currency; although the case involved a pre-1970 year, the IRS would presumably contend for the same result in later years, since the deduction was claimed under IRC §165 rather than IRC §162; but see Rev. Rul. 80-211, 1980-2 CB 57 (punitive damages imposed on business for breach of contract and fraud in ordinary conduct of business deductible because not explicitly precluded by statutory limits of IRC §162).

[62] Supra note 58.

[63] S. Rep. No. 92-437 (1971), reprinted in 1972-1 CB 559, 600; see also Rev. Rul. 78-196, 1978-1 CB 45 ("liquidity deficiency penalty" imposed by federal banking agency on savings and loan association for failure to maintain prescribed level of liquid assets held nondeductible); S & B Restaurant, Inc. v. CIR, 73 TC 1226 (1980) (payments by taxpayer discharging sewage waste, under agreement with state agency until central sewer became available; held, not "fine or similar penalty").

[64] Treas. Regs. §1.162-21; see also Treas. Regs. §1.212-1(p); Tucker v. CIR, 69 TC

5. Bribes, Kickbacks, and Similar Payments. Section 162(c), enacted in 1958 and amended in 1969 and 1971, disallows deductions under IRC §162(a) for three categories of payments:

1. *Illegal payments to government officials or employees.* Section 162(c)(1) disallows deductions for amounts paid directly or indirectly to any governmental official or employee if the payment is an illegal bribe or kickback. If the recipient is an official or employee of a foreign government (including, under the regulations, revolutionary groups that have not been accorded diplomatic recognition), the payment cannot be deducted if it is unlawful under the Foreign Corrupt Practices Act of 1977, even if it is condoned by the foreign recipient's government and hence does not violate local law. This exportation of our legal standards can be viewed as a laudable effort to protect innocent foreigners from corruption by rich American entrepreneurs or, alternatively, as an imperialistic imposition of our political standards on countries with a different conception of the way government officials are to be compensated. The burden of proving that a payment is an illegal bribe or kickback or that it is unlawful under the Foreign Corrupt Practices Act is placed by IRC §162(c)(1) on the IRS, which must prove this issue by clear and convincing evidence.[65] Proof of the amount, nature, purpose, and ultimate beneficiaries of such payments is obviously difficult, not only because of the difficulties encountered by both taxpayers and the IRS in getting nonresident aliens to testify here, but also because perjury is standard operating procedure when thieves try to save their own skins.

2. *Other illegal payments.* Section 162(c)(2) similarly disallows direct or indirect payments to any person if the payment constitutes an illegal bribe, illegal kickback, or other illegal payment under any U.S. law subjecting the payor to a criminal penalty or to the loss of a license or privilege to engage in a trade or business. If the payment is illegal under state law, however, it is disallowed only if the state law is "generally enforced." Kickbacks include payments for the referral of a client, patient, or customers, and the burden of proving illegality is on the IRS.

The Tax Court has distinguished between (a) unlawful discounts or rebates to which the taxpayer's customers become entitled when the transaction is negotiated and agreed upon and (b) unlawful payments not made pursuant to the agreement between the buyer and seller. Allowances of the first type are

---

675 (1978) (school teacher must include in gross income amounts withheld from salary for participation in illegal strike; IRC §162(f) prohibits deduction of penalty); Conley v. CIR, supra note 14 (penalties for failure to pay withholding taxes nondeductible); Rev. Rul. 78-196, supra note 63 (same as to interest-like deficiency penalty imposed by federal loan agency).

[65] Treas. Regs. §1.162-18(a)(5).

customarily treated as allowable reductions of gross income, unaffected by IRC §162(c); payments of the second type, on the other hand, have been disallowed.[66]

3. *Kickbacks, rebates, and bribes under Medicare and Medicaid.* Section 162(c)(3), added in 1971, denies any deduction for kickbacks, rebates, or bribes by physicians and other providers of goods or services in connection with Medicare and Medicaid, including payments for the referral of clients, patients, or customers. Unlike IRC §§162(c)(1) and 162(c)(2), IRC §162(c)(3) does not require the payment to be unlawful. No reason was given by Congress for singling out payments under these social welfare programs for special treatment while disregarding similar payments under other programs, but the context was a series of highly publicized investigations into Medicare and Medicaid abuses.

6. Treble-Damage Payments Under Federal Antitrust Laws. Section 162(g) disallows deductions under IRC §162(a) for two-thirds of any damages paid under the Clayton Antitrust Act, whether the action is settled or goes to judgment, if the taxpayer is convicted or pleads guilty or nolo contendere to an indictment or information charging a violation or the antitrust laws. If the only proceeding against the taxpayer is a private antitrust action or a civil suit by the government, IRC §162(g) does not apply, presumably on the theory that the government's failure to institute a criminal prosecution betokens a milder degree of misconduct. Only two-thirds of the payment is disallowed, on the theory that the balance constitutes the restitution of gains previously included in the taxpayer's gross income.

7. Lobbying Expenses and Other Political Activities. In 1918, relying on the "ordinary and necessary" requirement of the statutory predecessor of IRC §162, the Treasury promulgated regulations disallowing any deduction for expenditures for lobbying, the promotion or defeat of legislation, and political contributions. With minor changes in language, this restriction has been carried forward to the present day, except as modified since 1962 by IRC §162(e). Alluding to the "insidious influences" of money on politics, the Supreme Court held in *Textile Mills Securities Corp. v. CIR* that the regulation

[66] See Pittsburgh Milk Co. v. CIR, 26 TC 707 (1956) (Acq.) (milk sold for net prices below legal minimum with books showing sales at legal minimum and reduction charged to advertising); Coed Records, Inc. v. CIR, 47 TC 422 (1967) (record company not allowed to deduct illegal payments to disc jockeys and other radio station employees for preferential treatment); cf. United Draperies, Inc. v. CIR, supra note 56 (illegal kickbacks to employees of customers).

was a reasonable interpretation of the statutory phrase "ordinary and necessary" and that the taxpayer could not deduct the cost of lobbying for legislation authorizing the return to German business interests of properties seized by the United States during World War I under the Trading with the Enemy Act.[67] In *Cammarano v. United States,* the Supreme Court held that the regulation applied to expenses incurred by beer and liquor dealers in publicity campaigns urging voters to defeat state initiative measures that would have made it impossible for them to continue in business, rejecting the taxpayer's claim that the restriction violated the First Amendment.[68]

Section 162(e) permits the deduction of certain expenses related to proposed or existing legislation "of direct interest" to the taxpayer but preserves the restrictive rule of prior law in other respects. These restrictions are buttressed by IRC §276, which prohibits the deduction of amounts spent for political advertising or for admission to political dinners and similar events. Thus, the status under IRC §§162 and 212 of expenditures for political purposes now depends on three sets of rules:

1. *Appearances and statements regarding legislation.* Section 162(e)(1) authorizes the deduction of all ordinary and necessary expenses paid or incurred in direct connection with (1) appearances before and statements to individual members and committees of Congress and state and local legislative bodies with respect to legislation or proposed legislation of direct interest to the taxpayer and (2) the communication of information between taxpayers and organizations to which they belong if similarly related to legislation of direct interest to the taxpayer. The regulations provide that (a) legislation or proposed legislation is of direct interest to the taxpayer if it will, or may reasonably be expected to, affect his trade or business either positively or negatively, but not merely because it may affect business in general; (b) a taxpayer does not have a direct interest in appropriations bills or in such matters as nominations, appointments, or the operation of the legislative body (but professional lobbyists presumably have a direct interest in any other actual or proposed legislation of direct interest to their clients); and (c) legislation or proposed legislation is of direct interest to an expert who specializes in the field of the legislation and appears to provide testimony as either an invited expert witness or on his own "if it is customary for individuals in his type of employment to publicly express their views in respect of matters in their field of competence" (e.g., a university professor teaching in the money and banking field who testifies on his own behalf regarding proposed banking legislation).[69]

---

[67] Textile Mills Sec. Corp. v. CIR, 314 US 326, 337 (1941).

[68] Cammarano v. US, 358 US 498 (1959).

[69] See Treas. Regs. §1.162-20(c)(2)(ii); Jordan v. CIR, 60 TC 770 (1973)

2. *Other political expenditures.* Lobbying and political expenditures not within the IRC §162(e)(1) categories are generally not deductible.[70] In particular, IRC §162(e)(2) disallows as business expenses any expenditures for participation or intervention in a political campaign[71] or in connection with an attempt to influence the general public with respect to legislative matters, elections, or referendums. This rule prohibits deductions incurred in "grass roots" campaigns to develop a point of view among the public generally, even if it relates to a matter of direct interest to the taxpayer's business. Difficulties sometimes arise in distinguishing nondeductible attempts to influence the public from deductible advertising expenses that are designed to keep the taxpayer's name before the public but also disseminate general economic, financial, and social views.[72]

3. *Advertising in political publications, admission to political events, etc.* Section 276(a) disallows three types of political expenditures: (1) advertising in a political party's convention program or in any other publication if the proceeds are intended to, or do, directly or indirectly inure to or for the use of a political party or candidate; (2) admission to a dinner or program whose proceeds are intended to, or do, directly or indirectly inure to or for the use of a political party or candidate; and (3) admission to an inaugural ball, gala, parade, or concert or to any similar event identified with a political party or a political candidate. This provision attempts to disallow deductions for political contributions disguised as advertising expenses.

In applying IRC §276(a), IRC §276(b)(1) defines "political party" in the same manner as IRC §271, relating to bad debts owed by political organizations.[73] The term "political candidate" includes not only persons already selected or nominated by a political party but also anyone generally believed to be currently, or who in the reasonably foreseeable future will be, seeking nomination or election to any public office.[74]

(Acq.) (employment benefits for Georgia Highway Department employees of direct interest to one such employee); Rev. Rul. 68-414, 1968-2 CB 74 (professional lobbyist).

[70] See Treas. Regs. §1.162-20(c)(1).

[71] Individuals may receive a credit for a limited portion of political campaign contributions under IRC §41.

[72] Compare Cammarano v. US, supra note 68 (contributions to campaign to defeat a prohibition referendum held nondeductible) and Revere Racing Ass'n v. Scanlon, 232 F.2d 816 (1st Cir. 1956) (advertising to influence voters to continue pari-mutuel betting held nondeductible) with Treas. Regs. §1.162-20(a)(2) (advertising encouraging contributions to the Red Cross and purchase of United States Savings Bonds deductible).

[73] See Treas. Regs. §1.276-1(f)(1); Treas. Regs. §1.271-1(b)(1), discussed infra ¶17.9.

[74] Treas. Regs. §1.276-1(f)(2).

¶8.4 CAPITAL EXPENDITURES

1. Introductory. The deductibility of expenses under IRC §§162 and 212 is limited by IRC §263(a)(1), which disallows deductions for "any amount paid out for new buildings or for permanent improvements or betterments made to increase the value of any property or estate," or for amounts "expended in restoring property or in making good the exhaustion thereof for which an allowance is or has been made."[75] As interpreted by the regulations, IRC §263 prohibits any deduction for "the cost of acquisition, construction, or erection of buildings, machinery and equipment, furniture and fixtures, and similar property having a useful life substantially beyond the taxable year," or for "amounts paid or incurred (1) to add to the value, or substantially prolong the useful life, of property owned by the taxpayer, such as plant or equipment, or (2) to adapt property to a new or different use."[76]

As explained by the Supreme Court in *CIR v. Idaho Power Co.:*

> The purpose of §263 is to reflect the basic principle that a capital expenditure may not be deducted from current income. It serves to prevent a taxpayer from utilizing currently a deduction properly attributable, through amortization, to later tax years when the capital asset becomes income producing.[77]

In furtherance of this objective, capital expenditures constitute (or are added to) the basis of the acquired or improved property. They are then either (a) depreciated or amortized over the property's useful life in the taxpayer's business or income-producing activity or (b) if the property is not subject to exhaustion through use (e.g., land), held in abeyance until the property is sold or otherwise disposed of, at which time the cost is deducted from the amount realized in computing gain or loss on the disposition. Thus, the basic difference between business expenses and capital expenditures is that expenses are deducted when paid or incurred, while capital expenditures are written off over a longer period of time.

The distinction between "expenses" (as the term is used by IRC §§162 and 212) and nondeductible capital expenditures is also inherent in the concept of an "expense," viewed as a cost allocable to the current year's

---

[75] The allowances for exhaustion referred to by IRC §263(2) include cost recovery, depreciation, amortization, and depletion. See Treas. Regs. §§1.263(a)-1(a)(1) and 1.263(a)-1(a)(2).

[76] Treas. Regs. §§1.263(a)-2(a), 1.263(a)-1(b).

[77] CIR v. Idaho Power Co., 418 US 1, 16 (1974) (taxpayer is prohibited by IRC §263 from depreciating equipment used to construct its own capital facilities); see also infra text following note 89. The term "capital asset" is used by the Court in *Idaho Power* as a synonym for "capital expenditure," not in its technical sense as defined by IRC §1221.

operations. The same basic principle is also embodied in IRC §§446(a) and 446(b), requiring use of an accounting method that "clearly reflects income"—a standard requiring that "expenditures for such items as plant and equipment, which have a useful life extending substantially beyond the taxable year, shall be charged to a capital account and not to an expense account." [78]

In the overwhelming bulk of cases, nondeductible capital expenditures are readily identifiable. There are, however, many other situations in which the usual criteria of a capital expenditure are either over-inclusive or under-inclusive. The criteria, if applied rigorously, would classify numerous purchases of minor items as capital expenditures—an accountant's fountain pen, a carpenter's screwdriver, or a lawyer's copy of the Internal Revenue Code.

A rule of reason is essential; if every cost contributing to the profits of future periods were disallowed, it would be necessary to divide almost every salary and contribution between its immediate impact on the customer and its contribution to long-lived goodwill. Recognizing this, the Supreme Court has said that "the presence of an ensuing benefit that may have some future aspect is not controlling; many expenses concededly deductible have prospective effect beyond the taxable year." [79] In this spirit, the regulations explicitly permit farmers to deduct the cost of "ordinary tools of short life or small cost, such as hand tools, including shovels, rakes, etc."; and professional taxpayers are allowed to deduct the cost of "books, furniture, and professional instruments and equipment, the useful life of which is short." [80]

2. Expenditures to Acquire, Clear Title to, and Dispose of Property. Among the capital expenditures listed in the regulations are the cost of acquiring property, the cost of defending or perfecting title thereto, and commissions paid in purchasing securities.[81] Numerous cases have also required the capitalization of legal and accounting fees incurred in connection with the acquisition of property.

Costs incurred in defending or perfecting title to property are easily viewed as capital expenditures, since the elimination of a disputed claim or cloud on the taxpayer's title increases its value. But expenses in connection with the acquisition of property sometimes seem, at least at first blush, to

---

[78] Treas. Regs. §1.446-1(a)(4)(ii). See also Treas. Regs. §§1.461-1(a)(1), 1.461-1(a)(2) (re assets with a useful life "which extends substantially beyond the close of the taxable year").

[79] CIR v. Lincoln Sav. & Loan Ass'n, 403 US 345, 354 (1971).

[80] Treas. Regs. §§1.162-12 (farmers), 1.162-6 (professional expenses); see also Treas. Regs. §1.162-3 (incidental materials and supplies can be deducted when purchased if inventories and records of consumption are not kept, provided taxable income is clearly reflected).

[81] Treas. Regs. §§1.263(a)-2(a), 1.263(a)-2(c), 1.263(a)-2(e).

qualify either as business expenses under IRC §162 or as expenses of managing, conserving, or maintaining property under IRC §212; and if they do not increase the value of the property, they do not seem to be disallowed as capital expenditures by IRC §263. In *Woodward v. CIR,* however, the Supreme Court held that the expenses incurred by shareholders in litigation pursuant to a state statute requiring shareholders voting in favor of the perpetual extension of a corporate charter to purchase all dissenting stock at "its real value," had to be capitalized, rejecting the taxpayer's argument that the expenses were not incurred in acquiring or defending or perfecting title, but solely to determine the stock's value.[82] A companion case, *United States v. Hilton Hotels Corp.,* involved fees paid by the taxpayer in an appraisal proceeding brought by shareholders of a controlled subsidiary who dissented to its merger into the taxpayer.[83] The taxpayer relied heavily on the fact that title to the dissenting shares vested in the subsidiary as soon as the dissenters registered their opposition to the merger, giving them the status thereafter of creditors; but the Court held that this was a distinction without a difference and disallowed a deduction for the fees.

This "origin-of-the-claim" principle has also been applied to litigation expenses incurred in enforcing a corporate buy-sell agreement;[84] but when the dispute involved both the ownership of property and the taxpayer's right to receive accumulated income therefrom, the taxpayer was required to capitalize only the amount allocable to the former aspect of the litigation.[85]

In cases involving the disposition of property, it has long been established that selling commissions cannot be deducted (except by dealers) but must be offset against the amount realized in computing the taxpayer's gain or loss on a sale of property.[86] Since *Woodward,* the same principle has been applied to other expenses incurred in the sale of property, such as legal and accounting fees.[87]

The effect of capitalizing an acquisition expenditure is to hold it in abey-

---

[82] Woodward v. CIR, 397 US 572, 576 (1970).

[83] US v. Hilton Hotels Corp., 397 US 580 (1970).

[84] Ransburg v. US, 440 F.2d 1140 (10th Cir. 1971).

[85] Boagni v. CIR, 59 TC 708 (1973) (Acq.) (expenses to establish ownership of royalty interest capitalized; expenses to establish taxpayer's share of accumulated royalties deductible).

[86] Treas. Regs. §1.263(a)-2(e).

[87] See Third Nat'l Bank in Nashville v. US, 427 F.2d 343 (6th Cir. 1970) (expenses incurred by minority shareholders in appraisal proceeding following dissent to merger); Munn v. CIR, 455 F.2d 1028 (Ct. Cl. 1972) (proceeding to collect proceeds of sale; expenses capitalized even though sale was at a loss); Madden v. CIR, 514 F.2d 1149 (9th Cir. 1975), cert. denied, 424 US 912 (1976) (expenses of opposing condemnation in unsuccessful effort to get public agency to take an easement rather than title); Baier's Est. v. CIR, 533 F.2d 117 (3d Cir. 1976) (dispute over terms of disposition of capital asset).

ance for tax purposes until the property is disposed of, and this affects both the year when the expenditure is reflected on the tax return and whether it will reduce ordinary income or capital gain. By contrast, disposition expenses are usually paid or incurred when the gain or loss on the disposition is recognized and the only issue is whether the expenses can be deducted from ordinary income or must be used as an offset in computing the taxpayer's capital gain or loss. If the expenditures are paid or incurred *after* the disposition is completed, *Arrowsmith v. CIR* requires the taxpayer to treat them as capital losses rather than deduct them from ordinary income.[88]

3. Self-Constructed Assets. If a taxpayer uses its own equipment, facilities, and staff to construct or improve an asset whose useful life extends substantially beyond the taxable year, it is well-established that direct construction costs, such as tools, materials, and labor, may not be currently deducted but must instead be charged to capital account. In *CIR v. Idaho Power Co.,* the Supreme Court held that the same principle applies to depreciation on the company's construction equipment.[89] The Court rejected the taxpayer's theory that IRC §263, denying deductions for amounts "paid out" for new buildings or permanent improvements or betterments, was inapplicable because depreciation is not "paid out," noting that the *cost* of the construction equipment *was* paid out when it was acquired.

The effect of *Idaho Power Co.* is not to disallow permanently the construction equipment depreciation, but to require it to be spread over the useful life of the improvements or, if attributable to land or other nondepreciable property, to be held in abeyance until the underlying property is disposed of, at which time the disallowed depreciation (being part of the property's basis) will reduce the gain or increase the loss realized by the taxpayer on the disposition. This puts taxpayers who construct their own factories or equipment in the same position as those who have the work done by an independent contractor, because an element of the contractor's cost will be depreciation on construction equipment.

On the authority of *Idaho Power Co.,* and IRC §446(b), requiring use of an accounting method that clearly reflects income, taxpayers have been required to capitalize a variety of indirect construction-related expenses, including vacation pay, payroll taxes, health and welfare benefits, general overhead costs, and, in some instances, executive salaries.[90] Overhead costs are probably

---

[88] See Arrowsmith v. US, 344 US 6 (1952), discussed infra ¶25.13.

[89] CIR v. Idaho Power Co., supra note 77 at 13-14.

[90] Louisville & Nashville R.R. v. CIR, 66 TC 962 (1976) (vacation and holiday pay, payroll taxes, health and welfare benefits, and cost of transporting construction materials on taxpayer's own tracks required to be capitalized); Adolph Coors Co. v. CIR, 519 F.2d 1280 (10th Cir. 1975), cert. denied, 423 US 1087 (1976) (method of accounting whereby only direct construction costs are capitalized and overhead is

subject to capitalization only if they bear a direct and close relationship to the taxpayer's construction activity, as judged by generally accepted accounting practices; and there may be room for a de minimis exception if the taxpayer's internal construction and replacement activity is not substantial.

Capitalized construction-related depreciation, though not deducted, must be charged against the basis of the construction equipment under IRC §1016(a)(1) lest the same amount be used to reduce the taxpayer's gain (or increase the loss) both on disposition of the new property and on disposition of the construction equipment.

4. Expenditures to Investigate, Start, Enter, or Expand a Business. The principle that the cost of acquiring a long-lived asset is a capital expenditure rather than a current business expense applies not only to obvious items like marketable securities, land, buildings, and tangible equipment but also to intangibles acquired on purchasing an existing business as a going concern, such as commercial goodwill, industrial knowhow, franchises, staff experience, and favorable contracts with employees and suppliers.[91] Expenditures in investigating a potential acquisition, as well as commissions, legal fees, and other expenses incurred in consummating the transaction, are also capital expenditures, includable in the cost basis of the acquired assets, rather than deductible expenses under IRC §162 or §212.

Even if the investigation does not result in a consummated transaction, the courts and the IRS have denied deductions for the expenses incurred. The leading case is *Frank v. CIR,* which held that travel and legal expenses in searching for a newspaper or radio station to purchase and operate were not deductible under (a) IRC §162, because the taxpayers were not engaged in any trade or business, (b) IRC §212, because they had no interest in an income-producing asset, or (c) IRC §165(c)(2), relating to losses on transactions entered into for profit, because they decided not to enter into any transaction after the preliminary investigation.[92]

Since taxpayers who purchase a business as a going concern must capitalize the purchase price, including amounts allocable to its goodwill and industrial know-how, it is not surprising that the IRS contends that taxpayers

---

charged to cost of goods sold does not clearly reflect income); Chevy Chase Motor Co. v. CIR, ¶77,227 P-H Memo TC (1977) (salary of president-shareholder of real estate development firm capitalized to extent of time devoted to supervising construction).

[91] See Treas. Regs. §1.263(a)-2(h).

[92] Frank v. CIR, 20 TC 511 (1953). See also Rev. Rul. 57-418, 1957-2 CB 143 (expenditures in search of a business or investment are deductible "only where the activities are more than investigatory and the taxpayer has actually entered into a transaction for profit and the project is later abandoned"); Seed v. CIR, 52 TC 880 (1969) (Acq.) (deductible loss under IRC §165(c)(2) for legal expenses, etc., on abandonment of business venture following denial of application for charter).

creating an enterprise from scratch must capitalize expenditures incurred in training the staff during the start-up or pre-operating period. In *Richmond Television Corp. v. United States,* the Court of Appeals for the Fourth Circuit summarized this principle as follows:

> [E]ven though a taxpayer has made a firm decision to enter into business and over a considerable period of time spent money in preparation for entering that business, he still has not "engaged in carrying on any trade or business" within the intendment of Section 162(a) until such time as the business has begun to function as a going concern and performed those activities for which it was organized.[93]

The distinction between pre-operating and operating expenses was readily applied in *Richmond Television Corp.,* which involved expenditures before the taxpayer was legally licensed to engage in its projected broadcasting business. As applied to the generality of businesses, however, the line of demarcation between a business that is getting ready to operate and one that is already operating is usually indistinct, particularly when the issue is whether a going concern is preparing to enter into a new line of business or is merely expanding its existing operations. The difficulty of identifying new lines of business can be illustrated by a line of cases in which the IRS unsuccessfully sought to disallow deductions to banks for expenditures associated with entry into the consumer credit card field (e.g., Master Card). The start-up costs, which include computer programming, credit evaluations, and promotional activities, were allowed by the courts as business expenses under IRC §162 on the theory that banks have always engaged in the business of making loans to their customers and that "the credit card system enables a bank to carry on an old business in a new way" rather than to enter a "new business." [94]

Difficulties in this area stem not from any weakness in the theory that pre-operating expenditures to create intangibles should be capitalized, but from the impossibility of systematically administering this principle in practice

---

[93] Richmond Television Corp. v. US, 345 F.2d 901, 907 (4th Cir.), rev'd and remanded on another issue, 382 US 68 (1965); for decision on remand, see 354 F.2d 410 (4th Cir. 1965).

[94] Colorado Springs Nat'l Bank v. US, 505 F.2d 1185, 1190 (10th Cir. 1974); Iowa-Des Moines Nat'l Bank v. CIR, 592 F.2d 433 (8th Cir. 1979); in both cases, however, a one-time membership fee paid by the bank to join a Master Card association was held to be a capital expenditure. See also Briarcliff Candy Corp. v. CIR, 475 F.2d 775 (2d Cir. 1973) (expenditures by candy manufacturer to create a franchise division to expand sales in retail outlets held deductible). For a rare case in which an existing enterprise was held to have expanded into a new line of business, see Mid-State Prods. Co. v. CIR, 21 TC 696, 713-714 (1954) (Acq.) (company engaged in buying shell eggs and selling frozen eggs required to capitalize expenditures to enter business of producing and selling dried eggs).

and, previously, the absence of a method of amortizing pre-operating costs over the taxable years in which the new venture was conducted. These difficulties were substantially ameliorated, however, by the enactment in 1980 of IRC §195, allowing taxpayers to elect to amortize over not less than sixty months start-up expenditures for the creation or acquisition of a new business, if incurred after July 29, 1980.[95]

5. Advertising Expenses. Efforts by taxpayers in the early years of income taxation to capitalize the cost of large-scale advertising campaigns and to amortize the capitalized amount over a period of years were successfully opposed by the IRS on the ground that allocating advertising expenditures between current expenses and capital outlays was not feasible.[96] In a leading early case, for example, the Board of Tax Appeals rejected the taxpayer's claim that the cost of free samples, distributed in its early years to promote and expand a regional business into a national enterprise, constituted part of its invested capital in determining its liability under a tax on excess wartime profits.[97]

Although the courts did not entirely foreclose the propriety of capitalizing some advertising expenditures, they were never satisfied in the litigated cases with the taxpayer's allocation between current and long-term benefits; and in time this hardened into a rule of law that capitalization is proper only if the taxpayer can establish "with reasonable certainty the benefits resulting in later years from the expenditure." [98] If the IRS disallowed current deductions for advertising, the taxpayer would have to bear—and would probably fail to carry—the burden of establishing the currently deductible component of the expenditure; but the IRS has eschewed this tactic,[99] and its long acquiescence in the current deduction of advertising costs may have been implicitly ratified by congressional silence.

The result, as a practical matter, is that advertising expenses are deductible (assuming a sufficient nexus between the expenditure and the taxpayer's

---

[95] For IRC §195, see infra ¶12.13.

[96] See E.H. Sheldon & Co. v. CIR, 214 F.2d 655 (6th Cir. 1954), and cases there cited. *Sheldon* allowed the taxpayer to deduct costs incurred in publishing a trade catalogue having a useful life in excess of one year; as to this issue, neither the Tax Court nor the IRS currently follows *Sheldon.* See Best Lock Corp. v. CIR, 31 TC 1217 (1959); Rev. Rul. 68-360, 1968-2 CB 197. As to other forms of advertising not resulting in tangible assets like catalogues, however, the rationale of *Sheldon* still prevails.

[97] Northwestern Yeast Co. v. CIR, 5 BTA 232 (1926) (Acq.).

[98] E.H. Sheldon & Co. v. CIR, supra note 96, at 659; see also Durovic v. CIR, 542 F.2d 1328 (7th Cir. 1976) (cost of free samples must be capitalized; amortization denied in absence of proof of limited useful life).

[99] Treas. Regs. §1.162-20(a)(2) (expenditures for institutional and goodwill advertising to keep taxpayer's name before the public are deductible if related to "the patronage the taxpayer might reasonably expect in the future").

business), even if long-term benefits are the taxpayer's primary objective. Occasional judicial comments to the effect that advertising costs constitute nondeductible capital expenditures generally involve expenditures for physical assets with an extended life, such as catalogues and billboards.[100] Thus, advertising expenditures to construct goodwill are deductible business expenses, unlike expenditures to purchase goodwill.

6. Expenses of Finding Employment. The pre-operating/operating distinction applied to businesses has a counterpart in the tax treatment of expenditures incurred in seeking or finding employment. The most frequently cited case in this area is *McDonald v. CIR,* in which the Supreme Court held that a state judge appointed to fill a term could not deduct his campaign expenses in seeking election to a regular term, since they "were not expenses incurred in being a judge but in trying to be a judge for the next ten years." [101] The relevance of the case to ordinary employees, however, is complicated by the difficulty of envisioning "judgeship" as a continuing occupation of reelection is necessary to continue in office. In any event, the IRS ruled in 1975 that employment-seeking expenses are deductible regardless of success if the search is for employment in the taxpayer's existing trade or business, relying on the familiar principle that an employee is engaged in the business of providing services to various employers, not merely in the business of working for his or her current employer.[102]

If, however, the employee is seeking employment for the first time, the 1975 ruling disallows any deduction even if employment is actually secured; and the same principle applies if the taxpayer seeks employment in a new trade or business.[103] The basis for this conclusion is not explicitly stated, but it presumably rests on the theory that the expenses are not incurred "in carrying on" the taxpayer's trade or business, as required by IRC §162(a).

Under the 1975 ruling, currently unemployed taxpayers are viewed as still

---

[100] See Best Lock Corp. v. CIR, supra note 96 (cost of catalogues with useful life of more than one year must be capitalized); Alabama Coca-Cola Bottling Co. v. CIR, ¶69,123 P-H Memo TC (1969) (same as to cost of signs, clocks, and scoreboard with useful lives of more than one year).

[101] McDonald v. CIR, 323 US 57, 60 (1944).

[102] See Rev. Rul. 75-120, 1975-1 CB 55; see also McKinley v. CIR, ¶78,428 P-H Memo TC (1978) (electrician allowed to deduct cost of traveling to different union halls to seek employment); Rev. Rul. 78-93, 1978-1 CB 38 (career counseling expense allowed attorney and part-time law professor who secured full-time teaching position).

[103] The IRS, however, does not appear to apply this distinction where a prospective employer reimburses an applicant's expenses in connection with an interview conducted at the employer's invitation. See Rev. Rul. 63-77, 1963-1 CB 177 (reimbursements not includable in gross income; no discussion or mention of applicant's previous employment status).

engaged in the business of providing the type of services performed for the prior employer, unless "there is a substantial lack of continuity between the time of [the employee's] past employment and the seeking of new employment." Although not confined to students, this "hiatus" theory has been most frequently applied against taxpayers leaving their employment for an extended period of graduate study or other training.[104]

7. Expenditures to Create or Preserve Taxpayer's Business Reputation. The deductibility under IRC §162 of expenditures relating to the taxpayer's business reputation depends on whether they are incurred to *create* a reputation or to *preserve* an existing reputation; the former category must be capitalized, while the latter can be deducted. This distinction can be traced back to *Welch v. Helvering,* in which the Supreme Court held that the taxpayer could not deduct amounts paid by him to reimburse the customers of a family business, with which he had been connected, for their losses when the company went into bankruptcy and received a discharge from its debts.[105] His purpose in paying off the debts, for which he was not legally liable, was to reestablish his own standing, credit, and relations with the customers of the prior business on going into business for his own account.

Viewing *Welch v. Helvering* as involving "a capital outlay to acquire good will for a new business," [106] the courts have subsequently allowed taxpayers to deduct similar payments on showing that they served to preserve and protect the goodwill or reputation of an *existing* business. In *Dunn & McCarthy, Inc. v. CIR,* for example, a corporation was permitted to deduct amounts paid to employees who had lent funds to its former president, who had lost the money gambling at the racetrack and died insolvent. The court did not think the payments were "extraordinary"—"It was the kind of outlay which we believe many corporations would make, and have made, under similar circumstances." [107]

---

[104] See Sherman v. CIR, ¶77,301 P-H Memo TC (1977) (business manager held to be carrying on trade or business while attending graduate school for two years, although he was denied leave of absence by former employer and took job with another employer on completing studies); Canter v. US, 354 F.2d 352 (Ct. Cl. 1965) (nurse who discontinued nursing activities for more than four years while obtaining degrees in nursing was not carrying on a trade or business); Corbett v. CIR, 55 TC 884 (1971) (same as to teacher who discontinued teaching and commenced full-time study leading to a Ph.D.).

[105] Welch v. Helvering, supra note 48.

[106] Dunn & McCarthy, Inc. v. CIR, 139 F.2d 242, 244 (2d Cir. 1943).

[107] Id. at 244; see also Pepper v. CIR, supra note 43 (lawyer allowed to deduct payments to reimburse clients for losses suffered through another client's dishonesty); Rev. Rul. 56-359, 1956-2 CB 115 (insurance broker reimbursed customer for losses when insurance company represented by him failed; held, deductible expenses of protecting business by preserving confidence of customers); but see Carl Reimers Co. v.

8. Repairs vs. Improvements and Replacements. The regulations under IRC §162 provides that (a) the cost of incidental repairs that neither materially increase the value of the property nor appreciably prolong its life, but simply keep it in an ordinarily efficient operating condition, may be deducted as business expenses, provided the basis of the property is not increased by the amount expended, but that (b) repairs in the nature of replacements, to the extent that they arrest deterioration and appreciably prolong the property's life, must be capitalized and depreciated.[108] The regulations under IRC §263 similarly distinguish between "incidental repairs" and capital expenditures that add to the value or substantially prolong the useful life of property or adapt it to a new or different use.[109] In a much-quoted decision, the Board of Tax Appeals distinguished between repairs and replacements as follows:

> To repair is to restore to a sound state or to mend, while a replacement connotes a substitution. A repair is an expenditure for the purpose of keeping the property in an ordinarily efficient operating condition. It does not add to the value of the property, nor does it appreciably prolong its life. It merely keeps the property in an operating condition over its probable useful life for the uses for which it was acquired. Expenditures for that purpose are distinguishable from those for replacements, alterations, improvements, or additions which prolong the life of the property, increase its value, or make it adaptable to a different use.[110]

In a later case, the Tax Court observed that it "is none too easy" to apply this distinction.[111] Seldom has a court applied so mild a label to a chimera.

The impact of the criteria that are most frequently cited to distinguish repairs from replacements can be summarized as follows:

1. *Material increase in property's value.* The principle that expenditures materially adding to the asset's value are capital expenditures is closely related to the principle that expenditures creating or enhancing an asset with a useful life of more than one year must be capitalized.[112] In *Hotel Kingkade v. CIR,*

CIR, 211 F.2d 66 (2d Cir. 1954) (payment of bankrupt predecessor's debts to qualify for admission to a business association; held, capital expenditure to get into a new field).

[108] Treas. Regs. §1.162-4; see also Jones v. US, 279 F. Supp. 772 (D.Del. 1968) (applying repair-capital expenditure distinction to deny deduction under IRC §212).

[109] Treas. Regs. §1.263(a)-1(b).

[110] Illinois Merchants Trust Co. v. CIR, 4 BTA 103, 106 (1926) (Acq.) (cost of shoring up walls and repairing foundation of building threatened by lowering of water level; held, deductible).

[111] Midland Empire Packing Co. v. CIR, 14 TC 635, 640 (1950) (Acq.) (cost of oilproofing a leaking basement to prevent contamination of the taxpayer's meat products held deductible).

[112] Treas. Regs. §§1.263(a)-2(a), 1.263(a)-1(b).

for example, the Court of Appeals for the Tenth Circuit held that payments for carpets, refrigerators, repairs, and similar rehabilitation expenditures to replace a hotel's worn-out and discarded equipment were capital outlays. Rejecting the taxpayer's contention that the expenditures merely kept the hotel in a reasonably efficient operating condition, the court said: "Some were for repairs of a permanent nature which materially added to the value of the property and appreciably prolonged its life as an operating hotel; and others were for replacements of furnishings and equipment having a useful life in excess of one year." [113]

Recognizing that "any properly performed repair adds value as compared with the situation existing immediately prior to the repair," however, the Tax Court has stated that "the proper test is whether the expenditure materially enhances the value, use, life expectancy, strength, or capacity [of the property] as compared with the status of the assets prior to the condition necessitating the expenditure." [114] Applying this standard, the courts have frequently allowed major expenditures to be deducted when necessitated by casualties, distinguishing these unexpected outlays from the cost of replacing or rehabilitating assets that were exhausted or became obsolete in normal use.[115]

2. *Material increase in property's life.* Expenditures materially prolonging the property's life, especially as part of a general rehabilitation program, are ordinarily classified as capital expenditures, including minor items that, in isolation, would qualify as repairs.[116] On the other hand, the fact that materials and supplies used to effect repairs have a long life does not preclude their classification as current expenses; otherwise, every nail, shingle, and pane of glass would have to be capitalized.[117]

3. *Repairs in the nature of replacements.* The regulations classify "repairs in the nature of replacements" as capital expenditures if they arrest

[113] Hotel Kingkade v. CIR, 180 F.2d 310, 312 (10th Cir. 1950); see also Treas. Reg. §1.263(a)-1(a)(2) (amounts spent to make good exhaustion for which depreciation allowances were allowed must be capitalized).

[114] Oberman Mfg. Co. v. CIR, 47 TC 471, 483 (1967) (Acq.) (insertion of expansion joint in roof to prevent leaks deductible).

[115] See Midland Empire Packing Co. v. CIR, supra note 111; American Bemberg Corp. v. CIR, 10 TC 361 (1948) (Nonacq.), aff'd per curiam, 177 F.2d 200 (6th Cir. 1949) (drilling and grouting of building foundations, required by subsoil cave-ins); compare Phillips & Easton Supply Co. v. CIR, 20 TC 455, 459 (1953) (new floor installed to replace a worn-out floor, not because of accelerated deterioration due to sudden external condition; held, capital expenditure).

[116] See Stoelzing v. CIR, 266 F.2d 374 (3d Cir. 1959) (reconversion of neglected building to commercial use by concentrating in one year repairs that prior owner should have made as a matter of good housekeeping over a period of time).

[117] See US v. Wehrli, 400 F.2d 686 (10th Cir. 1968) ("replacement of a broken windowpane, a damaged lock, or a door, or even a periodic repainting of the entire structure, may well be treated as a deductible repair expenditure even though the benefits endure quite beyond the current year").

deterioration and appreciably prolong the life of the property, contrasting these items with "incidental repairs." [118] The distinction between incidental repairs and replacements is one of degree. The replacement of small parts of a machine or building as they wear out is easily characterized as a deductible expense, but major replacement items usually must be capitalized. Structural alterations, however, also often qualify as repairs,[119] particularly if they "are of relatively minor proportions of the physical structure and of any of its major parts, . . . where the building as a whole may not be considered to have gained appreciably in expectancy of useful life over its expectancy when built." [120]

4. *Adaptation to new or different use.* Alterations adapting a building or machine to a new or different use are capital expenditures, in the nature of improvements or betterments.[121]

9. Expenditures to Raise Equity Capital. The cost of raising equity capital, such as fees and commissions paid by a corporation to underwriters for selling its stock and the related legal, accounting, and printing expenses, cannot be deducted as a business expense. This rule has been explained as based on the premise that the expenditures "should be charged against the proceeds of the stock and not recouped out of operating earnings" because "the benefits of acquiring the capital will inure [to] the corporation over a long period of years." [122]

In *Emerson Electric Manufacturing Co. v. CIR,* [123] the Board of Tax Appeals analogized the cost of raising equity capital to the cost of floating a bond issue, the expenses of which are written off over the life of the indebtedness. But while the cost of raising borrowed funds can be amortized over the life of the loan and organizational expenses can be either amortized over the period prescribed by IRC §248 or deducted as a loss when the corporation dissolves, these analogies have been rejected for the cost of raising equity capital on the theory that "money paid out to acquire capital does not result

---

[118] Treas. Regs. §1.162-4.

[119] Compare Phillips & Easton Supply Co. v. CIR, supra note 115 (floor; not deductible), and Alexander Sprunt & Son v. CIR, 24 BTA 599 (1931) (Acq.), rev'd on other grounds, 64 F.2d 424 (4th Cir. 1933) (wall; not deductible), with Farmers Creamery Co. v. CIR, 14 TC 879 (1950) (Acq.) (replacement of less than one-half of deteriorated building's walls, ceilings, and floors; deductible); and Midland Empire Packing Co. v. CIR, supra note 111.

[120] Buckland v. US, 66 F.Supp. 681, 683 (D.Conn. 1946) (expenditures amounting to 35 percent of value of building to correct leaky walls and roof; deductible, where no major unit was wholly replaced).

[121] See Coors Porcelain Co. v. CIR, 52 TC 682, 696-697 (1969), aff'd on other issues, 429 F.2d 1 (10th Cir. 1970) (conversion of machine from oscillating to rotary action); West Virginia Steel Corp. v. CIR, 34 TC 851, 859-860 (1960) (rewiring of factory and adjacent storage area to rearrange equipment for more efficient operations).

[122] Emerson Elec. Mfg. Co. v. CIR, 3 BTA 932, 935 (1926).

[123] Id.

in the acquisition of any asset other than the capital itself," so that there is nothing to be amortized or deducted as worthless.[124] Yet, a corporation that does not recover the out-of-pocket expenses incurred to raise its equity capital sustains a loss, just as clearly as though the unrecovered expenses had been incurred to float a bond issue or to acquire its charter.

10. Deduction and Rapid Amortization of Certain Capital Expenditures. There are numerous capital outlays that Congress has authorized taxpayers to deduct currently or to amortize over an arbitrary period of years, even if the asset has a useful life of indefinite duration. The most important of these specialized statutory deductions are discussed in Chapter 26.

¶8.5 NONBUSINESS PROFIT-ORIENTED ACTIVITIES OF INDIVIDUALS

1. Introductory. Sections 212(1) and 212(2) allow individuals to deduct all ordinary and necessary expenses paid or incurred during the taxable year for the production or collection of income or for the management, conservation, or maintenance of property held for the production of income. With minor exceptions, therefore, it does not matter whether or not a taxpayer's profit-oriented activities constitute a trade or business within the meaning of IRC §162; in either case, the individual's tax liability is based on net rather than gross income.

Until 1942, the only statutory foundation for the deduction of profit-oriented expenses was the predecessor of IRC §162, relating to expenses incurred in carrying on a trade or business, and the IRS ruled that expenses were not deductible unless the taxpayer's profit-making activities could qualify as a trade or business. This view was endorsed by *Higgins v. CIR,* decided in 1942, which held that the management of one's own securities, even on a scale large enough to require an office or staff, was not a trade or business within the meaning of IRC §162 and upheld the disallowance of a deduction for the expenses incurred in connection with the management of the securities.[125] The practical results of *Higgins* were anomalous. Under the statutory predecessor of IRC §165(c)(2), the taxpayer in *Higgins* could deduct *losses* on the sale of his securities but not *amounts* paid for investment advice, safe-deposit rental,

---

[124] Van Keuren v. CIR, 28 BTA 480, 487 (1933); see also Treas. Regs. §1.248-1(b)(3)(i) (expenses of issuing stock not amortizable under IRC §248); Rev. Rul. 72-348, 1972-2 CB 97 (conversion of bonds into stock does not generate deduction for previously unamortized bond discount); but see Rev. Rul. 73-463, 1973-2 CB 34 (mutual fund can deduct cost of issuing stock after its initial 90-day offering period).

[125] Higgins v. CIR, supra note 5 (clerical assistance, office space).

and bookkeeping services related to the same securities. Moreover, his real estate activities constituted a trade or business, so that the expenses of those activities were deductible. Since only the net income from renting real estate was taxable, it was not surprising that Congress decided to tax only the net income from investing or speculating in stocks or bonds and other profit-seeking activities by enacting, in 1942, the statutory predecessors of IRC §§212(1) and 212(2).

Three years later, the Supreme Court was called upon to render its first interpretation of IRC §212. In *Bingham's Trust v. CIR* the Court held that legal fees incurred by the trustees of a testamentary trust in connection with the payment of certain legacies were deductible.[126] In deciding that the expenses were incurred by the trust in *managing* property held for the production of income, even though they did not directly produce any income, the Court stressed the parallelism between IRC §§162 and 212. In general, therefore, the term "ordinary and necessary" as used in both provisions is interpreted in the same manner; and the same is true of such issues as whether an expense is reasonable in amount, personal in character, or a nondeductible capital outlay.[127] A similar parallelism characterizes the rulings and cases on the deductibility of expenses for travel, entertainment, education, hobbies, home offices, and vacation homes.[128]

Some statutory provisions, however, explicitly distinguish between IRC §162 on the one hand, and IRC §§212(1) and 212(2), on the other, although it is not always clear whether the legislative distinction was deliberate or inadvertent. If a reference to business expenses seems to overlook IRC §212 items by mistake, the IRS may seek to put them back on a plane of equality by administrative action.[129] When there is an operational difference, however it is necessary to determine whether the taxpayer's profit-oriented activities constitute a trade or business. The principal areas generating distinctions or interpretative problems include the following:

---

[126] Bingham's Trust v. CIR, supra note 53.

[127] See Treas. Regs. §§1.212-1(d) and 1.212-1(f) (personal items); Treas. Regs. §1.212-1(n) (capital outlays).

[128] For travel, see Lowrey v. CIR, § 65,206 P-H Memo TC (1965) (expenses of travel to look after out-of-state investment property allowed under IRC §212(2)); Kanelos v. CIR, §43,429 P-H Memo TC (1943) (same re cost of traveling to Dublin to collect proceeds of lottery ticket in Irish Sweepstakes); Dicker v. CIR, ¶63,082 P-H Memo TC (196) (expenses of profitable trip to Las Vegas disallowed, presumably on the assumption that taxpayer was lucky rather than truly profit-oriented).

To put IRC §162 and IRC §212 deductions for travel and entertainment on a plane of equality so far as substantiation is concerned, IRC §2174(a)(2)(B) provides that IRC §212 activities shall be treated for this purpose as a trade or business.

[129] See, e.g., infra ¶9.1 (meals and lodging while away from home); supra ¶8.3 (frustration of public policy).

1. Section 212 refers only to "individuals." Because trusts and estates are taxed in the same manner as individuals, they also benefit from the provision; and individual partners can deduct their respective shares of a partnership's IRC §212 expenses.[130] Although corporations are not covered by IRC §212, the paucity of litigation concerning corporate investment expenses suggests that corporations regularly deduct under IRC §162 expenses of the type that individuals are authorized to deduct under IRC §212 and that the IRS does not disallow these expenses even if the corporate activities do not constitute a trade or business.[131]

2. Trade and business expenses are deductible from gross income in computing the adjusted gross income of individuals, with exceptions in the case of employees; but IRC §212 expenses can be deducted from gross income only if attributable to property held for the production of rents or royalties; otherwise they are allowable only if itemized by the taxpayer under IRC §63(b).[132]

3. Trade and business expenses enter into the computation of net operating losses under IRC §172 regardless of amount; but IRC §212 expenses are taken into account in computing net operating losses only to the extent of the taxpayer's related income.

4. Section 280A, restricting deductions for home offices, contains exceptions for certain trade or business uses but not for use of the property in activities covered by IRC §212.

5. Expenses allocable to tax-exempt interest cannot be deducted under IRC §212, but they can be deducted under IRC §162 if they qualify as business expenses.[133]

2. Standards for Deduction. Echoing the Supreme Court's language in *Bingham's Trust v. CIR,* the regulations provide that, to be deducted under IRC §212(1) or §212(2), expenses "must be reasonable in amount and must bear a reasonable and proximate relation to the production or collection of taxable income or to the management, conservation, or maintenance of property held for the production of income." [134]

1. *Proximate relationship to profit-oriented activity.* In using the phrase "reasonable and proximate relation" in *Bingham's Trust,* the Supreme Court

---

[130] For trusts and estates, see IRC §641(b); Bingham's Trust v. CIR, supra note 53. For the pass-through of IRC §212 items to partners, see Treas. Regs. §§1.702-1(a)(8), 1.703-1(a)(2)(vi).

[131] See Treas. Regs. §1.861-8(e)(4) (re expenses of "stewardship" functions undertaken for a corporation's "own benefit as an investor" in subsidiaries and other related corporations); Howell v. CIR, 57 TC 546, 553 (1972) (Acq.) ("nothing unique or improper about a corporation engaging in exclusively investment activity").

[132] See IRC §§62(1) and 62(2).

[133] IRC §265(1).

[134] Treas. Regs. §1.212-1(d).

rejected the IRS' claim that expenses can be deducted under IRC §§212(1) and 212(2) only if they produce income directly; but too relaxed a construction of the phrase is not warranted. In *Lykes v. CIR,* for example, the Supreme Court held that legal expenses incurred in contesting a gift tax deficiency of about $150,000 did not become deductible under IRC §212 merely because the taxpayer would have to use income-producing property to pay the deficiency if he lost the case.[135] (The particular issue before the Court in *Lykes* would now be decided differently under IRC §212(3), which was enacted in 1954; but the general principle enunciated in *Lykes* is still controlling.) A contrary rule, as the Court pointed out, would permit taxpayers to deduct the cost of defending an action for damages caused by the taxpayer's negligence in driving an automobile for pleasure. Under *Lykes,* the deductibility of expenses under IRC §212 turns on their "immediate purposes" rather than on "the more remote contributions they might make to the conservation of a taxpayer's income-producing assets by reducing his general liabilities."

2. *Origin-of-the-claim test.* In *United States v. Gilmore* the Supreme Court held that IRC §212(2) did not authorize a taxpayer to deduct legal expenses incurred in a divorce proceeding.[136] The expenses were disallowed even though attributable to the taxpayer's successful resistance to his wife's claim that certain assets, primarily controlling stock interests in three automobile agencies franchised by General Motors, constituted community property—a claim that if upheld might have resulted in the loss of his salaried posts with the companies and in cancellation of their franchises. In a companion case, *United States v. Patrick,* the Court held that legal expenses incurred by a husband in arranging a property settlement incident to a divorcc could not be deducted, even though "the fees were incurred not to resist a liability, but to arrange how it could be met without depriving the taxpayer of income-producing property, the loss of which would have destroyed his capacity to earn income."[137]

In both *Gilmore* and *Patrick,* the Supreme Court mentioned but did not pass on the government's alternative argument that the expenses in dispute were nondeductible capital outlays. In a sequel to the *Gilmore* litigation, however, the taxpayer was allowed to add the disallowed expenses to the basis of the stock in computing gain on a later sale; and the IRS evidently accepts this otherwise debatable practice.[138]

3. *Production or collection of income.* Because expenses can be deducted under IRC §§212(1) or 212(2) if paid or incurred either (a) for the production or collection of income or (b) for the management, conservation, or maintenance of property held for the production of income, it is not necessary in

---

[135] Lykes v. CIR, 343 US 118 (1952); see also Treas. Regs. §1.212-1(m).

[136] US v. Gilmore, 372 US 39, 45 (1963).

[137] US v. Patrick, 372 US 53, 56 (1963).

[138] Gilmore v. US, 245 F.Supp. 383 (N.D. Cal. 1965).

particular cases to assign expenses to one of these functions rather than the other; and many expenses serve both functions simultaneously. In illustrating the scope of IRC §212, for example, the regulations refer to such investment expenses as custodial and advisory fees, clerical help, and office rent,[139] which ordinarily serve both to produce income and to manage income-producing property. Furthermore, the regulations acknowledge that expenses can be incurred to produce income and that property can be held for the production of income even though no income is being *currently* received.[140] Moreover, expenses can be deducted if related to income received in prior years or to investment property held merely to minimize a loss. Although the cases and rulings have not explicitly developed a concept of "reasonable investment judgment" to epitomize the requirements of IRC §§212(1) and 212(2), such a parallel to the reasonable business judgment concept used in applying IRC §162 is implicit in the law of this area.

The reference in IRC §212(1) to the "production or collection of income" is not restricted to investment income. Taxpayers have been allowed, for example, to deduct expenses incurred in collecting alimony, lottery prizes, damages for copyright infringement, and claims for wrongful discharge from employment.[141]

The principal bone of contention under IRC §212(1) is the distinction—developed primarily under IRC §162 but equally applicable to IRC §§212(1) and 212(2)—between currently deductible capital expenses and nondeductible outlays, such as expenditures to create or acquire a new investment or to qualify for entry into a new occupation.[142] In some circumstances, these expenditures are disqualified both as capital outlays and as personal expenses. To illustrate these restrictions, the regulations provide that IRC §212 does not sanction the deduction of commuting expenses, expenses in seeking employment, campaign expenses of candidates for political office, or bar examination fees and similar expenses incurred to secure the right to practice a profession.[143]

4. *Management of property held for production of income.* To be deductible under IRC §212(2), expenses must be paid or incurred for the management, conservation, or maintenance of property held for the production of

[139] Treas. Regs. §1.212-1(g).

[140] Treas. Regs. §1.212-1(b).

[141] See, e.g., Treas. Regs. §1.262-1(b)(7); Hesse v. CIR, 60 TC 685 (1973) (Acq.), aff'd by unpublished opinion (3d Cir., March 10, 1975), cert. denied, 423 US 834 (1975) (legal fees for obtaining alimony); Howard v. CIR, ¶75,170 P-H Memo TC (1975) (allocation between deductible portion attributable to alimony and nondeductible portion attributable to property settlement and child support payments).

[142] For the distinction between expenses and capital outlays, see generally supra ¶8.4.

[143] Treas. Regs. §1.212-1(f).

income. This statutory standard embodies two independent requirements: (1) The property must be held for the production of income; and (2) the expense must entail management, conservation, or maintenance of the property.

The first requirement excludes property held for recreation, pleasure, or other personal uses, such as the taxpayer's residence. But property can be converted from nonqualifying to qualifying uses (or vice versa),[144] and an allocation of expenses is appropriate in the case of such dual-use property as an automobile used by an investor to visit rental properties as well as for personal transportation.

The second requirement—that the expenses be incurred for the management, conservation, or maintenance of property—also echoes the case law under IRC §162 by implicitly precluding the deduction of capital outlays, such as expenses incurred in improving property and in defending, perfecting, or quieting title.[145] Any expenditure to defend or perfect title to income-producing property necessarily helps to assure that the income flow will continue; but the greater swallows up the lesser—if incurred to defend or protect title, the expenditure cannot be deducted as a conservation expense, unless the proceeding also involves the recovery of interest, rents, damages, or other amounts includable in income, in which event an appropriate portion of the expenses can be deducted under IRC §212(1) because incurred for the collection of income.[146]

3. Common Categories of "Nonbusiness" Expenses. Although it is impossible to describe the outer limits of IRC §212(1) and 212(2) except in vague terms, most cases and rulings involve expenses incurred in the three contexts discussed below.

1. *Investments in securities.* Investment expenses of the type involved in *Higgins v. CIR* (custodial and clerical expenses, rent, etc.) are clearly deductible.[147] Although fees paid to investment advisers are deductible, taxpayers who supervise their own investments may encounter skepticism if they deduct

[144] For the conversion of personal residences to business or investment status, see Treas. Regs. §1.212-1(h).

[145] Treas. Regs. §1.212-1(k).

[146] See Treas. Regs. §1.212-1(k); Helvering v. Stormfeltz, 142 F.2d 982 (8th Cir. 1944) (unliquidated claim not held for production of income; expenses not for maintenance, etc., of any specific property since taxpayer sued for money, but portion allocable to recovery of interest deductible); but see Cruttenden v. CIR, 70 TC 191 (1978), aff'd, 644 F.2d 1368 (9th Cir. 1981) (expense of recovering stock loaned to enable borrower to obtain bank loan; held, deductible because no dispute over title).

[147] See Treas. Regs. §1.212-1(g) (advisory and custodial fees, clerical help, office rent, and similar expenses); Rev. Rul. 75-548, 1975-2 CB 331 (bank service charge paid by participants in automatic investment service); Rev. Rul. 62-21, 1962-1 CB 37 (premium for indemnity bond required to replace lost stock certificates).

large travel expenses in attending to relatively modest assets, since personal pleasure may overshadow the profit-oriented activity.[148] Expenses incurred by shareholders in proxy fights are deductible under IRC §212 if "proximately" related either to the production or collection of income or to the management, conservation, or maintenance of property held for the production of income.[149] This standard should be readily satisfied if the dispute concerns corporate business or financial policies, even if the company's dividend practices are not directly involved.

Controlling shareholders of closely held corporations must be prepared to show that unusual expenses are attributable to managing, conserving, or maintaining their investment, rather than expenditures in the nature of capital contributions to increase the value of their stock.[150]

2. *Real estate.* Because taxpayers holding real estate for rental are ordinarily viewed as engaged in a trade or business even if their activities are modest in scale, they can usually deduct their expenses under IRC §162. For rental property below the "business" threshold, however, IRC §§212(1) and 212(2) sanction deductions for management expenses, repairs, travel to visit the properties, and clerical assistance (1) provided they are not capital outlays and (2) subject to allocation or other restrictions in the case of property devoted to both personal and rental purposes.[151] Similar expenses incurred in holding property for capital appreciation or future development are also deductible;[152] but, unlike expenses in connection with rental property, these expenses are not deductible from gross income in computing adjusted gross income.

---

[148] See Kinney v. CIR, 66 TC 122, 127 (1976) (shareholder's travel to visit corporate plants; no evidence of "rationally planned, systematic investigation"; taxpayer did not negate disguised personal motive for the travel or establish that cost was reasonable relative to size of investment); Walters v. CIR, ¶69,005 P-H Memo TC (1969) (transportation to watch stock ticker at broker's office held nondeductible because activity served as entertainment; insufficient showing of relationship to taxpayer's investment activities); but see Henderson v. CIR, ¶68,022 P-H Memo TC (1968) (transportation to bank, broker's office, and safe-deposit box and to meet with manager of custodial account; held, deductible).

[149] See Rev. Rul. 64-236, 1964-2 CB 64, following Graham v. CIR, 326 F.2d 878 (4th Cir. 1964), rather than the more relaxed business judgment standard of Surasky v. US, 325 F.2d 191 (5th Cir. 1963).

[150] See, e.g., Hewett v. CIR, 47 TC 483 (1967) (shareholder payment to salesman for selling corporate stock; nondeductible); Kaplan v. CIR, 21 TC 134 (1953) (Acq.) (travel and entertainment paid for by shareholder).

[151] See, e.g., Coors v. CIR, 60 TC 368 (1973) (Acq.) (amount paid agency to manage and rent condominium unit); Hilton v. CIR, ¶71,102 P-H Memo TC (1971) (travel and lodging to collect rent).

[152] See, e.g., Harris v. CIR, ¶78,332 P-H Memo TC (1978) (expenses to keep unimproved land free of trash and debris); Markward v. CIR, ¶78,312 P-H Memo TC (1978) (repairs and maintenance on farm bought as investment).

Brokerage commissions paid to purchase or sell property cannot be deducted, however, but must instead be added to the cost of the acquired property or offset against the selling price of the property disposed of, as the case may be.

3. *Trust and estates.* Reasonable administration expenses of trusts and estates, including fiduciary fees and legal expenses incurred in performing the duties of administration, are deductible in the years to which they are properly allocable, provided the amounts are not allocable to tax-exempt income or deducted in computing the net estate for federal estate tax purposes.[153] In the case of grantor trusts, however, the expenses pass through for deduction by the grantor.[154]

The regulations similarly authorize the deduction of reasonable amounts paid or incurred for the services of guardians for minors and other ordinary and necessary expenses in connection with the production or collection of the minor's income or the management, conservation or maintenance of the minor's property held for the production of income.[155]

Professional fiduciaries can deduct the expenses of earning their fees under IRC §162, and nonprofessional fiduciaries can treat them as expenses of producing income under IRC §212(1).[156] But the IRS has successfully resisted efforts by nonprofessional fiduciaries to deduct legal fees and settlement payments in defending suits alleging mismanagement or negligence in performing their fiduciary duties.[157]

The regulations provide that: "Expenses paid or incurred in protecting or asserting one's rights to property of a decedent as heir or legatee, or as beneficiary under a testamentary trust, are not deductible." [158] Taxpayers seeking to establish their rights under inter vivos trusts are subject to the same restriction.[159] The rationale for disallowance of the expenses is that they are incurred to establish or defend the claimant's rights, rather than to produce income or conserve existing property; the disputed claim is not itself viewed as property held for the production of income.[160] In a few cases, however, trust

[153] IRC §642(g); Treas. Regs. §1.212-1(i).

[154] Rev. Rul. 58-53, 1958-1 CB 152.

[155] Treas. Regs. §1.212-1(j).

[156] See Rev. Rul. 72-316, 1972-1 CB 96 (nonprofessional trustee can deduct premiums for indemnification insurance under IRC §212); Rev. Rul. 55-447, 1955-2 CB 533 (inexperienced nonprofessional executor allowed to deduct payments to coexecutors for special assistance).

[157] See Fayen v. CIR, 34 TC 630 (1960).

[158] Treas. Regs. §1.212-1(k).

[159] See, e.g., Lucas v. CIR, 388 F.2d 472 (1st Cir. 1967); but see Matthews v. US, 425 F.2d 738 (Ct. Cl. 1970) (primary purpose test applied to allow deduction of legal fees incurred to revoke grantor trust).

[160] See, e.g., Perret v. CIR, 55 TC 712 (1971) (expenses of disinherited son to

beneficiaries have fared better than the regulations seem to permit.[161]

4. Expenses in Connection With the Determination, Collection, or Refund of Taxes. Section 212(3) permits individuals, trusts, and estates to deduct all the ordinary and necessary expenses paid or incurred during the taxable year in connection with the determination, collection, or refund of any tax, whether federal, state, local, or foreign.[162] Since the expenses need not be related to business or profit-oriented activities and can be deducted whether the tax itself is deductible or not, IRC §212(3) is properly viewed as a "personal" deduction, rather than a profit-oriented deduction like IRC §§212(1) and 212(2). Corporations can deduct their tax-related expenses under IRC §162.

Before the enactment of IRC §212(3) in 1954, expenses incurred in determining or contesting taxes could be deducted by individuals under IRC §162 if related to a trade or business (e.g., legal fees in determining liability for a manufacturer's excise tax) or if IRC §212(1) or §212(2) applied. Section 212(2) applied if the tax related to income-producing property (e.g., real property taxes on the taxpayer's rental property); and IRC §212(1) applied to refund actions, regardless of the nature of the tax, to the extent that the expense was allocable to the recovery of interest.

Congress enacted IRC §212(3) without explaining why expenses related to taxes attributable to wholly personal activities, such as gifts and purchases of consumer goods, *should* be deductible. Perhaps the implicit rationale was that taxes are involuntary levies and that the deductibility of tax-related expenses would encourage resistance to arbitrary determinations by the taxing bureaucracy and thus contribute to a social sense of fairness in the taxing process.

The regulations state that taxpayers can deduct not only the expenses of tax counsel and of preparing returns, but also expenses paid or incurred in proceedings to determine or contest the extent of tax liability. Since it covers expenses "in connection with" the determination, collection, or refund of taxes, IRC §212(3) permits taxpayers to deduct such associated expenses as appraisal fees to determine the amount of a charitable contribution and legal fees incurred in civil or criminal proceedings for tax evasion.[163]

---

acquire share of estate); Bliss v. US, 373 F.2d 936 (Ct. Cl. 1967) (attempt to upset will); Kelce v. CIR, ¶78,506, P-H Memo TC (1978) (expenses of establishing dower rights); Delp v. CIR, 30 TC 1230 (1958) (payments for promise not to contest will).

[161] See Tyler v. CIR, 6 TC 135 (1946) (Acq.) (fees paid to establish share of annual income of estate); Geary v. CIR, 9 TC 8 (1947) (Acq.) (fees paid by life beneficiary challenging trustee's charges to income); Hendrick v. CIR, 35 TC 1223 (1961) (Acq.) (remainderman's expenses for surveillance of trustee's administration).

[162] Treas. Regs. §1.212-1(l).

[163] Rev. Rul. 67-461, 1967-2 CB 125 (charitable contribution); Rev. Rul. 58-180, 1958-1 CB 153 (casualty loss); Rev. Rul. 68-662, 1968-2 CB 69 (expenses incurred by

But all good things have limits. A graduate of New York University's LL.M. program in taxation was informed in 1979 by the Tax Court that he could not deduct the cost of a year's tuition, meals, and lodging as an expense of preparing his federal income tax returns.[164] The opinion does not state whether his failure to learn the controlling principles was caused by inattention in class or faulty instruction; in any event, the additional lesson cost him nothing, since he appeared pro se.

The principal areas of dispute in the application of IRC §212(3) are:

1. *Divorce planning.* After an unsuccessful effort to confine IRC §212(3) to expenses related to taxes resulting from past or settled facts, as distinguished from advice about the molding of events so as to minimize future tax liabilities, the IRS ruled that the cost of advice relating to the federal income, gift, and estate tax consequences incident to a divorce proceeding could be deducted under IRC §212(3), provided the fees attributable to the tax advice were properly substantiated and separated from amounts attributable to nontax matters.[165]

2. *Estate planning.* In *Merians v. CIR,* decided by the Tax Court in 1973, the IRS conceded in argument that legal fees for estate planning are deductible to the extent allocable to tax advice (estimated by the court at 20 percent of the total bill), even though the plan entailed the molding of future events and did not grow out of any current compulsion.[166]

Some estate planning expenses may be deductible apart from IRC §212(3), such as the expense of creating a revocable trust to facilitate management of the taxpayer's income-producing property; but most such expenses, if not deductible under *Merians,* are either personal expenses incurred in transferring assets to objects of the taxpayer's bounty or capital expenditures.

3. *Capital expenditures.* The IRS has argued on several occasions that expenses for tax advice should be disallowed if they are related to a capital expenditure. Although rejected in an important Court of Claims case,[167] this theory cannot be written off as yet, especially in the light of *CIR v. Idaho Power Co.,* in which the Supreme Court indicated that when a provision authorizing a deduction conflicts with IRC §263, prohibiting deductions for capital expenditures, the latter takes precedence. Section 211 seems to subordinate IRC §212 to IRC §263 in the same way that IRC §161 subordinates IRC §167, the provision involved in the *Idaho Power Co.* case.

---

corporate office in unsuccessful defense of criminal case charging evasion of personal and corporate taxes; held, deductible because disposition affects issue of tax liability).

[164] Wassenaar v. CIR, 72 TC 1195 (1979) ("It strains our credulity to conclude that the petitioner's total expenses of $2,781 incurred while attending NYU . . . bear any reasonable relationship to the preparation of his tax return").

[165] Rev. Rul. 72-545, 1972-2 CB 179.

[166] Merians v. CIR, 60 TC 187 (1973) (Acq.).

[167] Sharples v. US, 533 F.2d 550 (Ct. Cl. 1976).

4. *Sham and fraudulent transactions.* Payments for tax advice that turns out to be erroneous are deductible under IRC §212(3). But if the taxpayer knowingly pays for assistance in effecting a sham transaction or committing fraud, it is virtually inconceivable that the expense is within the intended scope of IRC §212(3), even though if the statutory language is taken literally, the payment can be described as occurring "in connection with the determination" of a tax.[168]

5. *Taxes of another person.* Although IRC §212(3) does not explicitly provide that expenses, to be deductible, relate to the tax liability of the person paying or incurring them, this requirement is implicit; otherwise a deduction would be allowable for gifts effected by paying the bills of a relative's tax counsel.[169] On the other hand, persons who succeed to someone else's tax liability, such as a shareholder of a liquidating corporation or a donee whose donor failed to pay the gift tax, have been allowed to deduct expenses incurred in resisting their own secondary or transferee liability.[170]

SELECTED BIBLIOGRAPHY

Allington, Deductibility of Estate Planning Fees, 60 A.B.A.J. 482 (1974).

Chu & Magraw, The Deductibility of Questionable Foreign Payments, 87 Yale L.J. 1091 (1978).

Cook, Repairs Expense Versus Capital Expenditures, 13 Tax L. Rev. 231 (1958).

Galvin, Investigation and Start-Up Costs: Tax Consequences and Considerations for New Businesses, 56 Taxes 413 (1978).

Halperin, Business Deductions for Personal Living Expenses: A Uniform Approach to an Unsolved Problem, 122 U. Pa. L. Rev. 859 (1974).

Klein, Income Taxation and Commuting Expenses: Tax Policy and the Need for Nonsimplistic Analysis of "Simple" Problems, 54 Cornell L. Rev. 871 (1969).

Krebs, Grassroots Lobbying Defined: The Scope of IRC Section 162(e)(2)(B), 56 Taxes 516 (1978).

---

[168] Compare Dooley v. CIR, 332 F.2d 463 (7th Cir. 1964) (deduction denied for advice re sham transaction), with Ippolito v. CIR, ¶65,167 P-H Memo TC (1965), aff'd as to other issues, 364 F.2d 744 (2d Cir. 1966) (deduction allowed for advice re similar scheme).

[169] See Davis v. US, 370 US 65, 74 (1962) (fees of attorney for tax advice to taxpayer's spouse in separation and divorce proceeding not deductible); Biggs v. CIR, ¶68,240 P-H Memo TC (1968), aff'd on other issues, 440 F.2d 1 (6th Cir. 1971) (advice re wife's separate tax return not deductible); Moyer v. CIR, ¶76,069 P-H Memo TC (1976), aff'd by unpublished opinion (3d Cir., Oct. 17, 1977) (fees of tax counsel allocable equally to corporation and taxpayer-officer but paid in full by latter; held, only one-half deductible).

[170] Sharples v. US, supra note 167 (transferee liability); Bonnyman v. US, 156 F.Supp. 625 (E.D. Tenn.), aff'd per curiam, 261 F.2d 835 (6th Cir. 1958) (donee's liability for unpaid gift tax).

BUSINESS EXPENSES

Lee, Command Performance: The Tax Treatment of Employer Mandated Expenses, 7 U. Rich. L. Rev. 1, 39 et seq. (1972).

Lee & Murphy, Capital Expenditures: A Result in Search of a Rationale, 15 U. Rich. L. Rev. 473 (1981).

Malloy & Bratton, Unreimbursed Expenses—A Problem Area, 55 Taxes 257 (1977).

Special Subcommittee of the Committee on Practice and Procedure, New York State Bar Association Tax Section, Report on the Internal Revenue Service "Slush Fund" Investigation, 32 Tax L. Rev. 161 (1977).

Taggart, Fines, Penalties, Bribes, and Damage Payments and Recoveries, 25 Tax L. Rev. 611 (1970).

CHAPTER 9

Specially Treated Business and Profit-Oriented Expenses

¶9.1 TRAVEL AND TRANSPORTATION

1. Introductory. In 1921, the general rule of IRC §162(a), relating to trade or business expenses, was augmented by the statutory predecessor of IRC §162(a)(2), explicitly allowing taxpayers to deduct traveling expenses while "away from home in the pursuit of a trade or business," including amounts expended for meals and lodging.[1] Since the business traveler's automobile expenses and plane fares would be deductible under the general rule of IRC §162(a), the primary function of the special rule of IRC §162(a)(2) is to allow the entire cost of meals and lodging incurred in business trips to be deducted. Before 1921, these expenses were deductible only if, and to the extent that, they exceeded "any expenditures ordinarily required for such purposes when at home." [2] Difficulties in administering this excess cost principle led to the enactment of the statutory predecessor of IRC §162(a)(2). For most taxpayers, of course, the cost of lodging when on a business trip is a dead loss because the cost of maintaining the taxpayer's personal residence in the interim is not diminished, and meals on the road usually cost more than they would at home; but IRC §162(a)(2) applies even if the travel does not entail an increase in the taxpayer's living expenses. In 1962, Congress qualified the statutory language of IRC §162(a) to disallow amounts expended for meals and lodging "which are lavish or extravagant under the circumstances," and it imposed severe substantiation requirements under IRC §274(d) to cope with exaggerated and unfounded claims. In addition, foreign travel is subject to special limitations under IRC §274(c) and (h).

Although there is no explicit authorization in IRC §212 for the deduction of expenses for meals and lodging incurred on trips related to an investor's income-producing property, other statutory provisions assume that IRC §§162 and 212 are parallel in this respect.[3] Given the antiquity—as the age of tax provisions is measured—of IRC §162(a)(2), it is little short of astonishing to find that we still do not know with assurance whether the term "home," as used in the statutory phrase "away from home," refers to the taxpayer's permanent place of abode or to his business headquarters. The IRS has long espoused the view that "home" as used in IRC §162(a)(2) ordinarily means the place where the taxpayer is employed or conducts his business, often called the taxpayer's "tax home." Several cases, however, have held that "home" was used by Congress in its normal and customary meaning of residence or place of abode.[4]

---

[1] In addition to the cost of transportation, meals, and lodging, travel expenses include such incidentals as sample rooms, telephone and telegraph charges, public stenographers, laundry and cleaning bills, and parking fees. See Treas. Regs. §1.162-2(a); Rev. Rul. 63-145, 1963-2 CB 86; Rev. Rul. 74-433, 1974-2 CB 92 (fees and tips for waiters and baggagemen, parking fees, and tolls).

For the possibility that travel expenses incurred for business purposes are capital expenditures rather than currently deductible expenses, see Rev. Rul. 68-194, 1968-1 CB 87 (author's travel expenses in producing manuscript must be capitalized).

[2] T.D. 3101, 3 CB 191 (1920).

[3] See IRC §§274(c), 274(d), 274(h); see also Harris v. CIR, ¶78,332 P-H Memo TC (1978) (allowing meals to be deducted as travel expenses under IRC §212).

[4] Wallace v. CIR, 144 F.2d 407 (9th Cir. 1944).

In 1946, the Supreme Court had an opportunity to resolve this debate when it decided *CIR v. Flowers,* involving a lawyer whose permanent residence was in Jackson, Mississippi, but who was employed as vice-president and general counsel of a railroad with its business headquarters in Mobile, Alabama, and who deducted the cost of getting from Jackson to Mobile and his meals and lodging while there. Declining to take the bait, the Court construed IRC §162(a)(2) to impose three conditions on the deductibility of traveling expenses:

1. The expense must be a reasonable and necessary traveling expense, as that term is generally understood. This includes such items as transportation fares and food and lodging expenses incurred while traveling.
2. The expense must be incurred "while away from home."
3. The expense must be incurred in pursuit of business. This means that there must be a direct connection between the expenditure and the carrying on of the trade or business of the taxpayer or of his employer, and that the expenditure must be necessary or appropriate to the development and pursuit of the business or trade.[5]

After observing that "whether particular expenditures fulfill these three conditions . . . is purely a question of fact in most instances," the Court held that the facts of the *Flowers* case demonstrated that the taxpayer's expenses were not incurred in pursuit of the railroad's business but, rather, arose from his personal desire to maintain a residence remote from his place of employment:

> Travel expenses in pursuit of business within the meaning of [the statutory predecessor of IRC §162(a)(2)] could arise only when the railroad's business forced the taxpayer to travel and to live temporarily at some place other than Mobile, thereby advancing the interests of the railroad. Business trips are to be identified in relation to business demands and the traveler's business headquarters. The exigencies of business rather than the personal conveniences and necessities of the traveler must be the motivating factors.[6]

The business exigency principle set out in *Flowers* would have barred any deduction for the taxpayer's meals and lodging in Jackson, whether it was viewed as his home or not, since he was there as a matter of personal preference rather than for business reasons. If he traveled on business to a third city, however, the business exigency principle would be satisfied; and the second

---

[5] CIR v. Flowers, 326 US 465, 470 (1946).

[6] Id. at 473-474.

condition ("away from home") would also be satisfied, whether "home" refers to the taxpayer's residence or business headquarters.

The taxpayer's inability in *Flowers* to satisfy the business exigency test made it unnecessary for the Court to decide whether his "home" was Jackson, where he and his family lived, or Mobile, where his business office was located; and this unresolved aspect of the statutory phrase "away from home" has continued to trouble taxpayers, the IRS, and the lower courts in later cases. This lingering conceptual confusion seldom affects the result in actual practice, however, because "the Commissioner's definition of 'home' as 'business headquarters' will produce the same result as the third *Flowers* condition in the overwhelming bulk of cases arising under §162(a)(2)."[7]

The crucial business exigency test, however, is difficult to apply in many situations. The principal areas creating difficulties are examined below.

2. "Away From Home"—The "Sleep or Rest" Rule. In *United States v. Correll,* involving a traveling salesman who left home early in the morning on daily trips of 150-175 miles, ate breakfast and lunch en route, and returned home in time for dinner, the Supreme Court upheld the assertion by the IRS that the phrase "away from home" requires the taxpayer to be "away from home" overnight or, at least, for a period requiring either sleep or rest.[8] While acknowledging that this "sleep or rest" rule is somewhat arbitrary, the Court found that it at least avoids the inequity of permitting a deduction for one taxpayer and denying a deduction for another merely because the former traveled a further distance away from his home during the day before returning. As a matter of statutory construction, the Court suggested that the term "meals and lodging" as a unit implied that the cost of meals are deductible only where the travel also entails lodging expenses.

Following *Correll,* in a ruling concerned with railroad employees but of wider import, the IRS made the sleep-or-rest principle more concrete:

---

[7] Rosenspan v. US, 438 F.2d 905, 911 (2d Cir. 1971), cert. denied, 404 US 864 (1971); but see Daly v. CIR, 631 F.2d 351 (4th Cir. 1980) (taxpayer resided in Virginia and traveled regularly to call on customers in sales territory, consisting of Delaware, New Jersey, and eastern Pennsylvania; held, tax home was Virginia, where he prepared sales reports and other business papers, even though 44 percent of trips were to Philadelphia or surrounding 28-mile area).

In CIR v. Stidger, 386 US 287 (1967), the Supreme Court held that a Marine Corps officer was not "away from home" while at his permanent duty station, even though his family was required to reside elsewhere. This did not constitute a ruling that "home" as used in IRC §162(a)(2) means "business headquarters" for the generality of taxpayers, since the Court relied heavily on the special circumstances of members of the armed forces, reflected by a statutory system of allowances for their living expenses.

[8] US v. Correll, 389 US 299 (1967).

> [A]bsence [from home] need not be for an entire 24-hour day or throughout the hours from dusk until dawn, but it must be of such duration or nature that the taxpayers cannot reasonably be expected to complete the round trip without being released from duty, or otherwise stopping (with their employer's tacit or expressed concurrence) the performance of their regular duties, for sufficient time to obtain substantial sleep or rest.
>
> However, the Service does not consider the brief interval during which employees may stop, or be released from duty, for sufficient time to eat, but not to obtain substantial sleep or rest, as being an adequate rest period to satisfy the requirement for deducting the cost of meals on business trips completed within one day.[9]

3. Commuting and Transportation Expenses. The entrenched principle that commuting expenses are not deductible is based on the theory that these expenses are incurred not for business reasons but because the taxpayer prefers to live at a distance from his place of employment or business. The Tax Court has applied this uncompromising rule to deny a deduction for the commuting expenses of employees working at a nuclear test site in a remote area of the Nevada desert, located sixty-five miles from the nearest habitable community.[10] Although the classic commuter travels to and from the same office every day, the disallowance rule also applies to taxpayers like nurses, office "temporaries," and river pilots, who go to a different jobsite every day in response to instructions from an employer or central registry.[11]

In a few situations, however, transportation expenses can be deducted under the general rule of IRC §162(a) despite the anti-commuting principle:

1. *Tools and bulky equipment.* In *Fausner v. CIR,* the Supreme Court held that an airline pilot could not deduct the cost of commuting by private automobile, despite the fact that he had to take two flight and overnight bags

---

[9] Rev. Rul. 75-170, 1975-1 CB 60; see also Rev. Rul. 75-168, 1975-1 CB 58 (truck driver on round trips of several hundred miles may deduct cost of meals and lodging during layover of about eight hours during which employer tacitly agreed to release him from duties to obtain necessary sleep or rest).

[10] Coombs v. CIR, 67 TC 426, 473-477 (1976), affirmed as to daily trips between the taxpayer's residence and the work site, but reversed as to the cost of lodging and extra meals when overtime work required overnight stays at the site, 608 F.2d 1269 (9th Cir. 1979); see also Ireland v. US, 621 F.2d 731 (5th Cir. 1980) (commuting expenses defrayed by employer constituted income to taxpayer even though taxpayer moved to reduce intra-company friction between taxpayer and another executive officer); Hall v. CIR, ¶80,485 P-H Memo TC (1980) (damages paid to settle claim for negligent driving while commuting; held, non-deductible).

[11] Steinhort v. CIR, 335 F.2d 496 (5th Cir. 1964) (river pilots); Marot v. CIR, 36 TC 238 (1961) (nurse on twenty-four hour call).

with him, because he would have traveled by private automobile in any event.[12] The Court stated that an allocation would be permissible, however, if a taxpayer incurred *additional* expenses to transport job-required tools and materials to and from work. To illustrate this possibility, an IRS ruling describes a taxpayer who ceased to commute by public transportation and began to use an automobile and trailer when transportation of bulky equipment became essential.[13] In practice, taxpayers claiming deductions for automobile expenses to transport tools face a formidable problem of proving that they would not have used their automobiles in any event.

2. *Transportation expenses between business sites.* In addition to commuting between their personal residences and business headquarters, many taxpayers must leave their headquarters during the day to see customers, patients, clients, and suppliers elsewhere in the same city. Although they are not "away from home" for a period requiring sleep or rest and hence cannot deduct the cost of *meals* while on these daily trips, their automobile expenses, taxi fares, and other *transportation* expenses are ordinary and necessary expenses paid or incurred in carrying on their trade or business within the meaning of the general rule of IRC §162(a).

4. Temporary vs. Indefinite Employment. In applying IRC §162(a)(2), the IRS has distinguished for many years between "temporary" employment and employment of "indefinite" or "indeterminate" duration, permitting employees employed temporarily at a distance from their places of abode to deduct the cost of meals and lodging at temporary jobsites on the theory that they are "away from home" while there.[14] By contrast, taxpayers who accept employment of indefinite or indeterminate duration at a distant location cannot deduct the cost of living at the site even if it is inconvenient to move their personal residences to the new location. The purpose of the "temporary employment" rule is to mitigate the hardship incurred by taxpayers who must bear extra living expenses while at jobsites to which it would not be reasonable to move their families because of the short duration of the employment at the location.[15] Employment is generally treated as temporary by the IRS if its anticipated and actual duration at a location is less than one year, but an actual

---

[12] Fausner v. CIR, 413 US 838 (1973).

[13] Rev. Rul. 75-380, 1975-2 CB 59. The ruling limits the deductions to the cost of renting the trailer, excluding a deduction for the excess of the automobile expenses over the prior cost of traveling by public transportation. See, however, Kallander v. US, 526 F.2d 1131 (Ct. Cl. 1975), which assumes that the excess of automobile expenses over public transportation expenses can be deducted by a taxpayer who proves that he would have used public facilities except for the weight of his business equipment.

[14] See Peurifoy v. CIR, 358 US 59 (1958) (suggesting that "temporary" principle does not satisfy *Flowers* criteria, but applying it because it was accepted by IRS).

[15] Tucker v. CIR, 55 TC 783, 786 (1971).

or anticipated stay of one year or more strongly indicates an indefinite or permanent stay.[16]

5. Homeless Taxpayers. An itinerant taxpayer with no permanent place of abode cannot deduct the cost of meals and lodging while on the road.[17] For courts interpreting the term "home" as used in IRC §162(a)(2) as the taxpayer's place of abode, the rationale for disallowing the cost of meals and lodging incurred by itinerant taxpayers is that they have no home to be away from; courts equating "home" with business headquarters ("tax home") reach the same result, either by holding that an itinerant's home is wherever he is working at the moment or by giving the term "home" its conventional meaning for this limited class of taxpayers.[18] Taxpayers who travel continuously often keep personal belongings in a relative's home or maintain other permanent links with a particular locality. Whether the links create a place of abode for the taxpayer is a question of fact that can be resolved only by a detailed inquuiry into the taxpayer's personal habits.[19]

6. Taxpayers With Two Employers or Places of Business. Taxpayers with two employers or two places of business can deduct the cost of getting from one site to the other during the same day, on the theory that it is an ordinary and necessary expense of carrying out the taxpayer's combined trade or business of working at both locations.[20] Similarly, away-from-home travel expenses incurred by a taxpayer who is required to travel between two jobs which are widely separated are deductible. The leading case is *Sherman v. CIR,* where the taxpayer had a proprietorship in New York City and was employed in Worcester, Massachusetts.[21] On finding that Worcester was his tax home, the Tax Court allowed a deduction for the expenses of traveling to and from New York City, including meals and lodging while there.

---

[16] Rev. Rul. 74-291, 1974-1 CB 42.

[17] Rosenspan v. US, supra note 7, and cases there cited.

[18] Id. at 908 (taxpayer had no home in conventional sense); James v. US, 308 F.2d 204 (9th Cir. 1962) (implying that "home" of taxpayer without fixed and permanent place of abode is located wherever taxpayer happens to be).

[19] For typical cases, see Cummins v. CIR, ¶76,286 P-H Memo TC (1976) (family residence ceased being tax home as of date of taxpayer's divorce); Michael v. CIR, ¶78,463 P-H Memo TC (1978) (parents' home not taxpayer's home despite sincere contrary belief, since she was only there two weeks every year); but see Rambo v. CIR, 69 TC 920 (1978) (cabin in Montana was tax home in light of taxpayer's ties to area and actual presence there for four to six weeks during each year at issue); see also Rev. Rul. 73-529, 1973-2 CB 37 (tests to be applied to itinerant taxpayer who has no regular or principal place of business).

[20] Rev. Rul. 55-109, 1955-1 CB 261.

[21] Sherman v. CIR, 16 TC 332, 337 (1951) (Acq.).

The extent to which a taxpayer with two employers can deduct overnight meal and lodging expenses depends on where his "tax home" is. The IRS considers the taxpayer's principal place of business to be his tax home; if he maintains homes at both spots, he can deduct meal and lodging expenses at the minor post if properly attributable to the taxpayer's presence there in actual performance of his business duties.[22] This is so even if the taxpayer maintains his family at the minor post of duty.[23] The principal post is generally ascertained on an objective basis, considering the time spent at each location, the proportion of income and business generated by each, and other relevant factors.

While the taxpayer's "tax home" must be identified in order to determine the deductibility of meals and lodging, the principal/minor distinction is not applied to transportation expenses, since they are deductible if incurred for business reasons whether the taxpayer is "away from home" or not.

7. Federal and State Legislators. The last sentence of IRC §162(a)(2) provides that a congressman's district "shall be considered his home" for travel-expense purposes, but that no more than $3,000 may be deducted for away-from-home living expenses per taxable year.

In *Montgomery v. CIR,* the Court of Appeals for the Sixth Circuit held that a state legislator had two places of business, one at the state capital and the other in his home district, and upheld the Tax Court's finding of fact that his principal post was at the state capital, which barred a deduction for his living expenses while there.[24] The Economic Recovery Tax Act of 1981 added IRC §162(h), providing an elective special rule governing the away-from-home expenses of state legislators.

8. Two-Job Married Couples. When husband and wife are employed or conduct businesses in two widely separated locations, they cannot deduct living expenses incurred at either site.[25] The husband's living expenses at his duty post are not attributable to business exigencies; and his living expenses when he is at his wife's duty post are also personal rather than business expenses. The same is true, mutatis mutandis, for the wife. The cost of getting from one site to the other is also not deductible since it is animated by personal rather than business reasons.

---

[22] Rev. Rul. 63-82, 1963-1 CB 33.

[23] Rev. Rul. 55-604, 1955-2 CB 49 (deduction limited to portion of meals and lodging properly attributable to taxpayer's presence at post while in actual performance of duties).

[24] Montgomery v. CIR, 532 F.2d 1088 (6th Cir. 1976).

[25] See Foote v. CIR, 67 TC 1 (1976), and cases there cited.

¶9.2 COMBINED BUSINESS-PLEASURE TRAVEL

In practice, IRC §162(a)(2) has been plagued by the fact that travel frequently entails both business and personal components; taxpayers tend to exaggerate the business reasons for trips that combine business with pleasure, while revenue agents naturally listen skeptically to the taxpayer's explanation. In an effort to separate fact from fiction, the IRS, Congress, and the courts have addressed themselves to the following troublesome aspects of this area:

1. *Primary Purpose.* Traveling expenses to and from a destination at which the taxpayer engages in both business and personal activities are deductible if the trip is "related primarily" to the taxpayer's trade or business, but not if it is "primarily personal in nature." [26] In the latter case, expenses at the destination are deductible to the extent properly allocable to the business activities conducted there; conversely, expenses at the destination cannot be deducted if properly allocable to personal activities, even if the trip was undertaken primarily for business reasons. Whether a trip is primarily related to taxpayer's business or is primarily personal in nature depends on all the facts and circumstances, especially the relative amount of time devoted to each category of activities.[27]

2. *Foreign Travel.* In addition to satisfying the basic tests for deductibility imposed by IRC §162(a) or §212, travel outside the United States must run the gauntlet of IRC §274(c), disallowing any deduction for expenses not allocable to business or profit-oriented activities, including an appropriate fraction of the taxpayer's expenses in getting to and from the business destination. For example, if a taxpayer travels primarily for business purposes from New York City to London, flies to Paris for nonbusiness activities, and returns to New York City via London, the expenses of the London-Paris-London leg of the trip are nondeductible, even without regard to IRC §274(c); but if IRC §274(c) applies, part of the cost of getting from New York City to London and back is also disallowed.[28]

Section 274(c) does not apply if the travel outside the United States does not exceed seven consecutive days, or if the time attributable to nonbusiness activities constitutes less than 25 percent of the total time; and the regulations

---

[26] Treas. Regs. §1.162-2(b)(1).

[27] Treas. Regs. §1.162-2(b)(2). See Buddy Schoellkopf Prods., Inc. v. CIR, 65 TC 640, 662 (1975) (Acq.) (president's Alaskan Arctic hunt primarily personal, not to test cold-weather gear); Stroope v. CIR, ¶75,348 P-H Memo TC (1975) (real estate salesman's Hawaiian trip predominantly for vacation rather than investigation of real estate opportunities); Ballantine v. CIR, 46 TC 272 (1966) (Acq.) (newspaper publisher's South American trip for personal satisfaction despite claim that it furnished newspaper with writing based on first-hand experience).

[28] See Treas. Regs. §1.274-4(g), Example (7).

also exempt travel expenses if (1) the taxpayer incurring the expenses did not have "substantial control over the arranging of the business trip" or (2) obtaining a personal vacation or holiday was not a major consideration in the decision to make the trip.[29] Moreover, IRC §274(c) applies only to expenses incurred by the traveler and does not affect the deductibility of travel paid or incurred by the traveler's employer or client.[30]

3. *Conventions.* For conventions and other meetings, the test of deductibility prescribed by the regulations is "whether there is a sufficient relationship between the taxpayer's trade or business and his attendance at the convention or other meeting so that he is benefitting or advancing the interests of his trade or business by such attendance." [31] Expenses of attending conventions for nonbusiness purposes cannot be deducted under IRC §162(a). If a trip made primarily to attend a business meeting includes some personal activities, the expense attributable to the latter do not qualify for deduction; but the taxpayer's transportation expenses in getting to and from the business location are deductible in full.

In 1976, Congress concluded that the basic rules of IRC §162(a) and the special rules applied to foreign travel by IRC §274(c) were insufficient to cope with the problem of conventions ostensibly held for business or educational purposes, but conducted outside the United States primarily because of the recreational and sightseeing opportunities. Congress responded by enacting IRC §274(h), which, as revised in 1980, denies any deduction for the cost of attending a convention or seminar held outside the "North American area"—defined as the United States, its possessions, the Trust Territory of the Pacific, Canada and Mexico—unless, taking into account certain statutory factors, it is as reasonable for the meeting to be held outside the North American area as within it. Any meeting on a cruise ship automatically fails the reasonableness test. Otherwise, business expenses and travel for a trip that is primarily for a business purpose and meets the reasonableness test are deductible provided they are not lavish or extravagant.

4. *Expenses of Spouses.* If a taxpayer is accompanied by his or her spouse on a business trip, the latter's travel expenses are deductible only if his or her presence serves a bona fide business purpose, a standard that is not satisfied

---

[29] Treas. Regs. §§1.274-4(f)(5), 1.274-4(g).

[30] Treas. Regs. §1.274-4(a).

[31] Treas. Regs. §1.162-2(d); Rev. Rul. 63-266, 1963-2 CB 88 (agenda of convention need not deal specifically with duties and responsibilities of taxpayer's own position; regulations are satisfied if agenda is sufficiently related to taxpayer's position to show that attendance was for business purposes); Rev. Rul. 59-316, 1959-2 CB 57 (business purpose not established merely by showing that taxpayer was appointed or elected delegate); Reed v. CIR, 35 TC 199 (1969) (general practitioner's attendance at meeting in Yugoslavia of International Law Association not sufficiently related to his legal practice).

by the performance of incidental services.[32] The Tax Court is usually skeptical of claims that the presence of the taxpayer's spouse served a business purpose; but taxpayers seem to fare better in the federal "district" and appellate courts, especially if the taxpayer's employer encourages married couples to travel together on business trips and reimburses their combined expenses.[33]

¶9.3 ENTERTAINMENT, AMUSEMENT, AND RECREATION

1. Introductory. The deductibility of entertainment expenses has long been a disaster area, producing results that do not satisfy taxpayers, practitioners, the IRS, Congress, or the general public. The roots of the problem are that a bright line cannot be drawn between business and pleasure, that administrators and judges are fallible human beings, and that any mechanical rule is bound to put numerous items on the wrong side of the line. Among the complicating factors in the proper classification of entertainment expenses are the following: (a) by joining in the merriment themselves, taxpayers who defray the bills derive personal benefits from the activity unless they are ascetics; (b) business guests are sometimes personal friends whom the taxpayer would have entertained in any event; (c) the type and level of entertainment are usually within the taxpayer's control, making it difficult to determine whether the expenditures are animated by business needs or personal preference; and (d) the taxpayer is sometimes subsequently the beneficiary of reciprocal entertainment, supplied (and deducted) by his guests in an informal but effective mutual back-scratching arrangement.

Taxpayers have long deducted their own share of restaurant, nightclub, and theater expenses, as well as the amount attributable to business guests, despite decisions holding this to be a nondeductible personal expense unless it exceeds the amount the taxpayer would normally spend on himself.[34] But in a 1963 ruling the IRS said that it did not intend to depart from its practice of applying this rule "largely to abuse cases where taxpayers claim deductions for substantial amounts of personal living expenses." [35] No reference was made in the ruling to the cost of theater tickets and other entertainment expenses. The difficulty of deciding whether customers are friends or friends are custom-

---

[32] Treas. Regs. §1.162-2(c); Rev. Rul. 56-168, 1956-1 CB 93 (spouse's presence not "necessary" despite performance of typing and similar services).

[33] See Rieley v. CIR, ¶64,066 P-H Memo TC (1964); US v. Disney, 413 F.2d 783 (9th Cir. 1969) (employer "virtually insisted" on presence of executives' wives to enhance company's reputation for producing family entertainment), and cases there cited.

[34] Sutter v. CIR, 21 TC 170, 173 (1953) (Acq.).

[35] Rev. Rul. 63-144, 1963-2 CB 129, 135; see also LaForge v. CIR, 434 F.2d 370 (2d Cir. 1970) (taxpayer's meals not deductible except to extent of excess over normal amount; but implying that full amount is deductible if taxpayer can show that IRS applies *Sutter* rule only to cases of abuse and that his case does not fall in that category).

ers has been noted by the Tax Court, which aptly observed that business associates frequently become friends and the mere fact that a guest is a business contact does not justify deducting the cost of entertainment having a primarily personal purpose.[36] In a similar vein, the IRS has ruled that the cost of lunches is not a deductible ordinary and necessary business expense when a group of business people regularly have lunch together for personal reasons and each pays the entire bill in rotation.[37]

The fact that some taxpayers could exploit the amorphous rules governing travel and entertainment expenses led President Kennedy in 1961 to propose the complete disallowance of deductions for entertainment. This blanket proposal was rejected by Congress, but it enacted major changes in the tax treatment of expenditures for entertainment, amusement, and recreation, as well as limits on the deductibility of business-related travel expenses and business gifts. To be deductible, expenditures for entertainment, amusement, or recreation must constitute "ordinary and necessary expenses" incurred in carrying on the taxpayer's business or profit-oriented activities, as required by IRC §§162 and 212; but they must also satisfy the more severe business-relationship standards of IRC §274(a) and be substantiated in the manner required by IRC §274(d), as summarized below.

2. Entertainment Activities. Section 274(a)(1)(A) disallows deductions for an item with respect to an activity "which is of a type generally considered to constitute entertainment, amusement, or recreation," unless the taxpayer establishes that it was (a) "directly related to" the "active conduct" of the taxpayer's trade or business or (b) "associated with" the active conduct of the business and directly preceded or followed "a substantial and bona fide business discussion."[38] For this purpose, activities subject to IRC §212, relating to expenses incurred for the production of income and other profit-oriented activities, are treated as a trade or business by virtue of IRC §274(a)(2)(B).

As examples of "entertainment," the regulations list activities at night clubs, cocktail lounges, theaters, country clubs, golf and athletic clubs, sporting events, hunting, fishing, vacation and similar trips, as well as food and beverages and lodging or transportation provided to a business customer or the customer's family.[39] But the meaning of "entertainment" is interpreted in light of the taxpayer's trade or business. For example, a theater critic's attendance at a performance in a professional capacity is not entertainment and a fashion show sponsored by a dress manufacturer for buyers is not entertainment; but

---

[36] Challenge Mfg. Co. v. CIR, 37 TC 650, 659-660 (1962) (Acq.).

[37] Rev. Rul. 63-144, supra note 35, at 133.

[38] Treas. Regs. §1.274-2(c). For the details of IRC §274(a), see Rev. Rul. 63-144, 1963-2 CB 129 (answers to ninety-three questions relating to entertainment, travel, and business gifts).

[39] Treas. Regs. §1.274-2(b)(1).

a fashion show sponsored by an appliance distributor for spouses of appliance retailers is entertainment. Similarly, food, lodging, and transportation in the form of "supper money" for employees working overtime, hotel lodging for employees traveling away from home, and the provision of an automobile used primarily for the active conduct of the employee's business do not constitute entertainment. To prevent taxpayers from attempting to avoid IRC §274(a) by reclassifying entertainment expenses, the regulations provide, with some exceptions, that dual-status activities that may be either, on the one hand, entertainment or, on the other hand, the expense of advertising, public relations, travel or business gifts, will be treated as entertainent.[40]

As examples of entertainment that is "directly related" to the active conduct of the taxpayer's business, the regulations cite the entertainment of business representatives and civic leaders at the opening of a hotel, the maintenance of a hospitality suite at a business convention where the taxpayer's products are displayed, and the award of vacation trips as prizes to the taxpayer's dealers.[41] By contrast, entertainment at theaters, nightclubs, and sporting events is said by the regulations not to be "directly related," unless the taxpayer clearly proves the contrary; and the same principles apply to entertainment at country clubs and cocktail lounges if the group includes persons other than business associates.[42]

If not "directly related" to the "active conduct" of the taxpayer's business, expenses are deductible only if the entertainment directly preceded or followed a substantial business discussion and was "associated with" the active conduct of the taxpayer's business.[43] To illustrate these requirements, the regulations cite only two instances—entertainment at a business convention if a business program is the principal activity of the meeting; and entertainment on the day of a substantial business discussion or, if the persons entertained are from out of town, on the preceding or following evening.[44] Entertainment is "associated with the active conduct of the taxpayer's trade or business if the taxpayer establishes that he had a clear business purpose in making the expenditure, such as to obtain new business or to encourage the continuation of

---

[40] Treas. Regs. §1.274-2(b)(1)(iii).

[41] Treas. Regs. §§1.274-2(c)(4), 1.274-2(c)(5); see Hippodrome Oldsmobile, Inc. v. US, 474 F.2d 959 (6th Cir. 1973) (entertainment on pleasure boat not "directly related" to active conduct of business, where taxpayer refrained from initiating discussions in belief that "soft sell" was best approach).

[42] Treas. Regs. §1.274-2(c)(7).

[43] See Treas. Regs. §1.274-2(d).

[44] Treas. Regs. §1.274-2(d)(3). See Leon v. CIR, ¶78,367 P-H Memo TC (1978) (home dinner parties neither directly related to nor associated with the active conduct of business); Walliser v. CIR, 72 TC 433 (1979) (same as to bank officer's payment of expenses on vacation tours with customers, despite qualification of expenses under IRC §162).

an existing business relationship."[45] If entertainment of business guests meets either the "directly related" or the "associated" test, expenses allocable to spouses (including the taxpayer's) are treated as "associated" with the active conduct of the taxpayer's business.[46]

3. Entertainment Facilities. As enacted in 1962, IRC §274(a) imposed on the deduction of expenses relating to entertainment *facilities* similar, but more stringent, rules than were imposed on entertainment *activities,* but, in 1978, Congress decided that even greater limitations should be imposed. The 1962 rules allowed expenses for entertainment facilities to be deducted if (1) they were ordinary and necessary, (2) the facility was used primarily for the furtherance of the taxpayer's business, and (3) the expense in question was "directly related" to the active conduct of the taxpayer's business. As enacted in 1978, however, IRC §274(a)(1)(B) disallows any deductions for facilities used in connection with an activity constituting entertainment, amusement, or recreation. An entertainment facility is any personal or real property owned, rented, or used by a taxpayer during the taxable year for, or in connection with, any activity of a type "generally considered" to constitute entertainment, amusement, or recreation. Examples of entertainment facilities include yachts, hunting lodges, fishing camps, swimming pools, tennis courts, bowling alleys, automobiles, airplanes, apartments, hotel suites, and vacation homes.[47] Section 274(a)(2)(A) provides that dues and fees paid to social, athletic, and sporting clubs constitute items with respect to facilities; but the regulations exempt clubs operated solely to provide lunches in circumstances conducive to business discussions, and an IRS ruling provides that dues paid to professional associations and civic organizations are also generally outside the jurisdiction of IRC §274(a)(1)(B).[48]

After disallowing all deductions for entertainment facilities, however, the 1978 legislation lifts this draconic general rule for clubs, provided the taxpayer establishes under IRC §274(a)(2)(C) that the facility was used primarily for the furtherance of the taxpayer's business and that the item was related directly to the active conduct of the business—the same conditions that were formerly applicable to all types of facilities. The blanket disallowance imposed by IRC §274(a)(1)(B) is also inapplicable to deductions that are otherwise allowable even if unconnected with the taxpayer's business or profit-oriented transaction. The owner of a hunting lodge, for example, can deduct mortgage interest, real

---

[45] Treas. Regs. §1.274-2(d)(4).

[46] Treas. Regs. §1.274-2(e)(2), 1.274-2(e)(3).

[47] Treas. Regs. §§1.274-2(e)(2), 1.274-2(e)(3).

[48] Treas. Regs. §1.274-2(e)(3) (luncheon clubs); Rev. Rul. 63-144, 1963-2 CB 129, 138-139 (professional organizations, etc.).

estate taxes, and casualty losses even though it is not used primarily for business purposes. Section 274(a)(1)(B) is also inapplicable in a variety of other circumstances that Congress did not view as fraught with abuse, such as business meals or entertainment in a club with respect to which the taxpayer is not allowed a deduction for dues or fees, if the "quiet business meal" or "associated with business" test is satisfied for entertainment activities, and otherwise allowable meal and lodging expenses incurred while away from home overnight.

Finally, expenses of individuals and Subchapter S corporations for apartments, hotel suites, vacation homes, and other dwelling units—even if they satisfy all of the requirements of IRC §274—are subject to the special disallowance rules imposed by IRC §280A, discussed below.[49]

4. Exempted Expenses. Section 274(e) exempts a variety of expenses for entertainment, amusement, and recreation from the business-relationship and disallowance rules of IRC §274(a). The exempted items cannot be deducted, however, unless they are ordinary and necessary expenses of carrying on the taxpayer's business or profit-oriented activities within the meaning of IRC §162 or §212, and they may be subject to the substantiation rules of IRC §274(d).[50] Most of the excepted items represent compensation, fringe benefits, or conditions of employment for employees of the taxpayer incurring the expenses, rather than entertainment involving the taxpayer. Of particular note is the "quiet business meal" exclusion, under which expenses for food and beverages furnished in circumstances conducive to a business discussion (such as a life insurance agent's meeting with a client at lunch during a normal business day) are excepted. The regulations, however, deny this exemption to events entailing "major distractions not conducive to business discussions."[51]

¶9.4 BUSINESS GIFTS

Section 274(b) disallows a deduction under IRC §162 or §212 in excess of $25 per donee per year for "business gifts."[52] The term "gift" for this

---

[49] Infra ¶9.11.

[50] The regulations exempt some expenses from the substantiation requirements as well as from the business-relationship tests. See Treas. Regs. §1.274-5(c)(7).

[51] Treas. Regs. §1.274-2(f)(2)(i)(*b*).

[52] Although the statutory language could be interpreted to disallow *any* deduction if the $25 limit is exceeded, it has been sensibly interpreted to disallow only the excess over $25. Feinstein v. CIR, ¶75,193 P-H Memo TC (1975). For a question-and-answer explanation of IRC §274(b), see Rev. Rul. 63-144, supra note 35.

purpose means an item that (a) is excludable from the recipient's income under IRC §102 (such as a Christmas turkey), but (b) is not excludable under any other statutory provision, such as a scholarship (IRC §117), a prize (IRC §74(b)), or the first $5,000 of an employee's death benefit (IRC §101(b)). The $25 annual limit of IRC §274(b), which is based on the cost of the donated item to the donor,[53] is computed on an aggregate basis for each donee. Gifts are taken into account whether made to the donee directly or indirectly, such as a gift to a spouse or other family member of an individual having business connections with the taxpayer.[54] Similarly, gifts to a corporation or other business entity for eventual personal use by an identifiable employee, shareholder, or owner are treated as made to the ultimate individual beneficiary.[55]

Because business gifts and entertainment are often difficult to distinguish, the regulations require that expenditures that may be considered either gifts or entertainment are to be considered entertainment, a principle that brings the strict rules of IRC §274(a) into play. But an expenditure for packaged food or beverages transferred to the donee for consumption at a later time constitutes a gift, as do tickets to theaters and other places of entertainment, if the taxpayer does not accompany the recipient to the event, unless the taxpayer elects to treat the item as entertainment.[56]

Section 274(b)(1) exempts from the $25 limit and the substantiation requirements: (1) items costing the taxpayer not more than $4 each, on which the taxpayer's name is imprinted and which are distributed generally (e.g., desk calendars and recalcitrant ballpoint pens); (2) signs, display racks, and other promotional items to be used on the recipient's business premises; and (3) items of tangible personal property awarded to employees for length of service, productivity or safety achievements. The third category of gifts qualifies for the exclusion only if they either (a) cost the taxpayer not more than $400 each, or (b) are "qualified plan awards," defined to mean items awarded under a permanent written plan that does not discriminate in favor of officers, shareholders, or highly compensated employees and that cost not more than $1,600, provided the average cost of all items awarded under all of the taxpayer's plans during the taxable year does not exceed $400. The exemption of these items from the $25 limit of IRC §274(b) does not automatically establish that they are deductible, but ordinarily they qualify as business expenses under IRC §162.

---

[53] Treas. Regs. §1.274-3(c).
[54] Treas. Regs. §1.274-3(d)(1).
[55] Treas. Regs. §1.274-3(d)(2).
[56] Treas. Regs. §1.274-2(b)(1)(iii)(*b*).

¶9.5 SUBSTANTIATION

In order to deduct expenses for travel, entertainment, amusement, recreation, or business gifts, the taxpayer must meet the stiff substantiation requirements of IRC §274(d). These rules, which are elaborately amplified by the regulations, supersede the *Cohan* doctrine, holding that if taxpayer incurs deductible expenses but cannot prove the exact amount, the trial court must make "as close an approximation as it can" rather than disallow the deduction entirely.[57] The regulations provide that "no deduction shall be allowed a taxpayer for [items subject to IRC §274(d)] on the basis of . . . approximations or unsupported testimony of the taxpayer." [58] The taxpayer is required to substantiate, by adequate records or sufficient evidence corroborating his own statement, four aspects of the deducted item: (1) its amount; (2) the time and place of the travel, entertainment, or use of the facility or the date and description of the gift; (3) the business purpose of the item; and (4) the business relationship between the taxpayer and the person entertained, using the facility, or receiving the gift.[59] Since IRC §274(d) is concerned only with substantiation, it comes into force only if the taxpayer establishes that the item is otherwise deductible under the substantive rules laid down by IRC §§162, 212, 274(a), etc.

1. *Adequate records.* To substantiate an item by adequate records, the taxpayer must maintain (1) an account book, diary, statement of expense, or similar record in which each element of the expenditure is recorded "at or near the time of the expenditure" and (2) documentary evidence (i.e., receipts, paid bills, etc.) for away-from-home lodging expenditures and any other expenditures of $25 or more. An adequate record must include a written statement of business purpose, unless it is evident from the surrounding facts and circumstances, such as a salesman's travel to call on customers on an established sales route. Documentary evidence should establish the amount, date, place and character of the expenditure. A hotel receipt with the date of lodging and separate amounts for charges such as lodging, meals, and telephone calls may be sufficient; but a cancelled check with a bill from the payee might only establish the cost element. On substantial compliance with the adequate-records requirement, the taxpayer may be permitted to establish a particular element of an expenditure with other "adequate evidence" instead of being required to produce full substantiation.

2. *Taxpayer's corroborated statement.* In lieu of adequate records, taxpayers may rely on their own written or oral statements, if corroborated by

---

[57] Cohan v. CIR, 39 F.2d 540 (2d Cir. 1930), discussed supra ¶8.1.

[58] Treas. Regs. §1.274-5(a).

[59] See Treas. Regs. §1.274-5(b).

other evidence "sufficient to establish each element." [60] Direct corroborative evidence is required as to all elements of the expenditure except its business purpose and the business relationship between the taxpayer and the persons entertained; these elements can be proved by circumstantial evidence.

3. *Exceptional circumstances.* The foregoing requirements are relaxed by the regulations if the taxpayer is unable to meet them "by reason of the inherent nature of the situation in which an expenditure was made" or because the records were lost through circumstances beyond the taxpayer's control. In the first situation, the regulations require the taxpayer to present other evidence of each element "which possesses the highest degree of probative value possible under the circumstances," while in the latter situation the deductions can be substantiated by a "reasonable reconstruction" of the expenditures.[61]

4. *Separate or aggregated expenditures.* In applying the substantiation rules, each separate payment (e.g., for breakfast, lunch, and dinner) constitutes a separate "expenditure," but concurrent or repetitious payments during a single event (e.g., several rounds of drinks in a cocktail lounge) are treated as a single expenditure.

5. *Exempted expenditures.* The substantiation rules of IRC §274(d) do not apply to items that are deductible without regard to their connection with a business or income-producing activity, such as interest, certain taxes, and casualty losses.[62] Pursuant to authority granted by IRC §274(d) (last sentence), the regulations also exempt from the substantiation requirements several of the items exempted by IRC §274(e) from the substantive business-relationship rules of IRC §274(a).[63]

6. *Employee expenses.* An employee incurring expenses solely for his employer's benefit that are charged to the employer or for which the employee receives advances, reimbursements, or similar payments is partly relieved of the IRC §274(d) substantiation burden if an adequate accounting to the employer is required and made.[64] The term "adequate accounting" means the submission to the employer of an account book or similar record with supporting documentary evidence, which together conform to the "adequate records" requirement discussed above.[65] If the employee satisfies the adequate-accounting standard and the payments received from the employer equal his deductible expenses on his employer's behalf, both expenses and reimbursements can be omitted from the employee's tax return; if the payments received exceed the deductible expenses, however, the excess must be included in gross in-

---

[60] Treas. Regs. §1.274-5(c)(3).

[61] Treas. Regs. §§1.274-5(c)(4) and 1.274-5(c)(5).

[62] Treas. Regs. §1.274-6.

[63] Treas. Regs. §1.274-5(c)(7).

[64] Treas. Regs. §1.274-5(e). These expenses may also be exempted from the business-relationship rules of IRC §274(a); see IRC §274(e)(4)(A).

[65] Treas. Regs. §1.274-5(e)(4); see also Treas. Regs. §§1.274-5(c)(3), 1.274-5(c)(4).

come.[66] A proper accounting by an employee shifts the obligation to comply with the requirements of IRC §274(d) to the employer.[67] In the absence of an accounting, however, or if the reimbursement exceeds the expense, the employee must satisfy the substantiation requirements.[68]

The regulations authorize the IRS to treat subsistence reimbursement arrangements, per diem allowances, and mileage allowances, "if in accordance with reasonable business practice," as equivalent to substantiation by adequate records for purposes of the basic substantiation requirements of IRC §274(d) and as satisfying the adequate-accounting requirement in the case of employees accounting to employers.[69] Pursuant to this authority, the IRS prescribes per diem and automobile mileage allowances from time to time.[70]

¶9.6 EDUCATIONAL EXPENSES

1. Introductory. Educational expenses can generally be assigned to one of the following three categories:

1. *Personal expenses,* such as tuition paid by a practicing attorney to satisfy a cultural interest in the history of art by pursuing a course of study after the day's work. Expenses of this type are nondeductible, both because they are "personal" or "living" expenses within the meaning of IRC §262 and because they do not serve business or profit-oriented objectives as required by IRC §§162 and 212.

2. *Business expenses,* such as costs incurred by a practicing attorney or accountant in attending a tax institute to keep in touch with current developments, which are deductible under IRC §162 because they are ordinary and necessary expenses of carrying on the taxpayer's trade or business.[71]

3. *Capital expenditures,* such as the cost of vocational or professional education undertaken in order to qualify for entry into a new occupation. Like other capital outlays, expenditures of this type cannot be deducted; but one would expect—if approaching the issue de novo—that the expenditure would either (a) be depreciable over the taxpayer's life expectancy or anticipated

---

[66] Treas. Regs. §1.274-5(e)(2).

[67] Treas. Regs. §1.274-2(f)(2)(iv).

[68] Treas. Regs. §1.274-5(e)(2)(iii).

[69] Treas. Regs. §1.274-5(f).

[70] See, for example, Rev. Proc. 80-32, 1980-2 CB 767 (20 cents for first 15,000 miles of business use each year and 11 cents per mile thereafter (and for all miles of a fully depreciated car), in lieu of all operating and fixed costs, including depreciation, maintenance, repairs, gasoline, oil, insurance, and registration fees, plus parking fees and tolls; basis of vehicle must be reduced by straight-line depreciation).

[71] Treas. Regs. §1.162-5(c)(1); Coughlin v. CIR, 203 F.2d 307 (2d Cir. 1953).

years of remunerative service or (b) be held in abeyance and deducted as a loss on retirement, death, or irreversible failure to find employment in the chosen field. But the IRS and the courts do not sanction either of these methods of recognizing that educational expenditures to enter an occupation constitute, over the long haul, an expense of earning a living in the taxpayer's chosen field.

In addition to these "pure" cases, many educational expenditures serve both personal and business objectives, thus falling into two or all three of the foregoing categories. For example, an accountant who attends law school solely to improve skills in current job could be viewed as incurring a business expense, but as simultaneously making a capital expenditure facilitating entry into a new occupation should that be desired at a later time. When a single course of study simultaneously serves both personal and business objectives, the expenditure is usually assigned entirely to its disadvantageous component because the taxpayer cannot carry the burden of proving the portion qualifying as a business expense.[72]

Briefly summarized, the regulations permit a taxpayer to deduct expenses (1) to maintain or improve skills required by the taxpayer's employment or other trade or business or (2) to meet requirements imposed by the employer or applicable law or regulations as a condition of retaining the taxpayer's established employment relationship, status, or rate of compensation;[73] but the taxpayer must *also* show that the expenses *do not* (3) meet the minimum educational requirements of the taxpayer's employment or other trade or business or (4) constitute part of a program of study qualifying the taxpayer for a new trade or business.[74] Thus, the taxpayer must *pass one* of the two positive tests (the "skill maintenance" and "employer mandate" tests) and *avoid both* of the two negative tests (the "entry level" and "upward bound" tests).

It should be noted that the regulations deal only with expenditures by individuals for their own benefit. An employer's right to deduct the cost of training employees or applicants for employment depends on whether, under the basic principles of IRC §162, the cost is a current business expense or a capital expenditure. The regulations are also limited to the effect of IRC §162; hence, they do not speak to the possibility of deducting educational expenses under other statutory provisions, such as IRC §§212(1) and 212(2) (expenses to produce income or conserve income-producing property), §212(3) (expenses of determining tax liability), and §213 (medical expenses), such as the cost of attending lectures on the management of income-producing property or on computing one's tax liability. Finally, the regulations do not

---

[72] See Treas. Regs. §1.162-5(b)(1).

[73] See infra, text following note 75.

[74] See infra, text at note 83.

define the term "education," leaving the status of payments for advice, counseling, and other functions to be decided under more general principles if the activity can be distinguished from "education."

2. Maintaining Skills or Meeting Employer Requirements. Provided that an educational expenditure does not violate either the "entry level" or the "upward bound" standard, it can be deducted under IRC §162 if it satisfies either the "skill maintenance" or "employer mandate" standard of the regulations,[75] unless the course of study constitutes the minimum educational requirement for entry into the taxpayer's occupation or qualifies the taxpayer for entry into a new occupation.

1. *The skill-maintenance standard.* The skill-maintenance standard is satisfied by education that "maintains or improves skills required by the individual in his employment or other trade or business." [76] The term "required" means "appropriate, helpful, or needed." [77] The cost of *maintaining* the taxpayer's skills may be likened to the cost of keeping business equipment in an ordinarily efficient operating condition, which is the hallmark of a deductible repair; education *improving* the taxpayer's skills, by contrast, can be deducted even though it resembles a nondeductible expenditure increasing the value or prolonging the life of depreciable property.

The skill-maintenance standard is ultimately factual and is difficult to apply. It is most easily satisfied by refresher courses and other brief programs focusing on current developments in the taxpayer's chosen field,[78] but the status of broader education is more problematical. The Tax Court has allowed classroom teachers and a minister to deduct expenses for college courses in broad subject areas,[79] but more typically the cases hold that generalized programs of study, even if they increase the taxpayer's "general level of competence," are only tenuously related to the skills required by the taxpayer's occupation rather than of direct proximate benefit.[80]

---

[75] Treas. Regs. §1.162-5(a)(1).

[76] Treas. Regs. §§1.162-5(a)(1), 1.162-5(c)(1).

[77] See Rev. Rul. 60-97, 1960-1 CB 69, 70, declared obsolete by Rev. Rul. 72-619, 1972-2 CB 650; principle presumably still valid.

[78] Treas. Regs. §1.162-5(c)(1); see also Coughlin v. CIR, supra note 71 (cost of attending NYU Institute on Federal Taxation); Beatty v. CIR, ¶80,196 P-H Memo TC (1980) (aeronautical engineer could deduct MBA program costs since duties required interpersonal and management skills).

[79] Glasgow v. CIR, ¶72,077 P-H Memo TC (1972), aff'd per curiam, 486 F.2d 1045 (10th Cir. 1973) (minister); Ford v. CIR, 487 F.2d 1025 (9th Cir. 1973) (social studies teacher could deduct cost of studying linguistics and anthropology at a foreign university).

[80] See, e.g., Mullen v. CIR, ¶70,211 P-H Memo TC (1970) (manager of engineering department; insufficient showing of relationship of courses in history and philosophy to occupational skills); Carroll v. CIR, 418 F.2d 91 (7th Cir. 1969) (policeman pursuing

2. *The employer-mandate standard.* In lieu of satisfying the skill-maintenance standard, the taxpayer may rely on the employer-mandate standard by establishing that the expenditures were for education meeting the employer's express requirements or the requirements of applicable law or regulations, imposed as a condition to retention of an established employment relationship, status, or rate of compensation.[81] If the skill-maintenance and employer-mandate standards overlap, the employer-mandate rules apply. To avoid abuse, however, the regulations specify that the employer-mandate standard is satisfied only by educational requirements that are imposed for a bona fide business purpose of the employer. Moreover, the employer-mandate standard applies only to "the minimum education" necessary to retain the taxpayer's established employment relationship, status, or rate of compensation. The cost of education beyond this minimum, even if required by the employer, can be deducted only if it meets the skill-maintenance standard.[82]

The inclusion of applicable laws and regulations as a source of compulsion in the employer-mandate standard is particularly pertinent to public school teachers, who are frequently required by state statutes or regulations to take additional courses to preserve their accreditation; but it also embraces such self-employed persons as lawyers and doctors, if required by local law to get educational booster shots from time to time in order to continue in practice.

3. Entry-Level and Upward-Bound Education. Even if the taxpayer meets the skill-maintenance or employer-mandate standard, expenditures for education are not deductible under IRC §162 if they violate either the entry-level or the upward-bound standard.

1. *Entry-level education.* Any deduction under IRC §162 for education required to meet the minimum educational requirements for qualification in the taxpayer's employment or other trade or business is disallowed. This encompasses not only education required to enter an occupation but also education required of temporary employees or provisional appointees to preserve their status. On the other hand, taxpayers meeting the minimum educational requirements in force at the time of entry are treated as continuing to

---

college studies as philosophy major; although college education improved job skills of all students, this relationship is insufficient).

[81] Treas. Regs. §§1.162-5(a)(2), 1.162-5(c)(2). The employer-mandate standard originated in Hill v. CIR, 181 F.2d 906 (4th Cir. 1950) (teacher required by regulations to pursue college courses or pass examination for renewal of teaching certificate; held, tuition deductible).

[82] Treas. Regs. §1.162-5(c)(2); see also Kandell v. CIR, ¶71,287 P-H Memo T-C (1971) (financial studies required by employer to qualify for promotion to account executive but not to retain job as clerk; held, not deductible).

meet these requirements despite a subsequent increase in educational standards.[83]

The distinction in the regulations between temporary employees, who cannot deduct the cost of education required to obtain full status, and qualified employees, who must pursue additional studies to retain their established status, is not easily drawn. The regulations illustrate the distinction in typical situations encountered by public school teachers.[84]

2. *Upward-bound education.* The second category of nondeductible expenses comprises education that "is part of a program of study being pursued by [the taxpayer] which will lead to qualifying him in a new trade or business." [85] Because upward-bound education is tantamount to entry-level education for the new occupation, the expenses are disallowed even if they satisfy the skill-maintenance or employer-mandate standard.

The central interpretive problem in applying the upward-bound test is distinguishing education helping the taxpayer to qualify for "a new trade or business" from education that merely trains the taxpayer for "new duties [involving] the same general type of work as is involved in the individual's present employment," since only the former category is disqualified by the regulations. As examples of "changes in duties which do not constitute new trades or businesses," the regulations refer to shifts by classroom teachers from one subject to another, as well as changes in assignment from classroom teacher to guidance counselor or principal.[86] The regulations illustrate the distinction between new occupations and new duties by ruling that law is a new occupation from the perspective of an engineer or accountant, but that psychiatry and psychoanalysis are in the same boat.[87] Applying the distinction to other occupations, the Tax Court has ruled that the following occupations are separate trades or businesses: licensed public accountant and certified public accountant, intern pharmacist and registered pharmacist, counselor to children with learning disabilities and social worker, member of the New York bar and member of the California bar, "tax expert" (employed as a revenue agent) and "tax attorney," and college teacher of mathematics and college teacher of law.[88]

---

[83] Treas. Regs. §1.162-5(b)(2)(i); Treas. Regs. §1.162-5(b)(2)(iii), Example (1), Situation 4.

[84] See Treas. Regs. §1.162-5(b)(2)(ii), (iii), Example (1); see also Toner v. CIR, 623 F.2d 315 (3rd Cir. 1980), cert. denied, 450 US 916 (1981) (unlicensed parochial-school teacher could deduct cost of getting bachelor's degree, since it did not qualify her for new occupation).

[85] Treas. Regs. §§1.162(b)(3)(i), 1.162(b)(3)(ii), Example (2) (engineer, accountant, etc., required by employer to obtain bachelor of laws degree cannot deduct expenses); Bodley v. CIR, 56 TC 1357, 1360 (1971) (law course).

[86] Treas. Regs. §1.162-5(b)(3)(i).

[87] Treas. Regs. §1.162-5(b)(3)(ii), Examples (1), (2), (4).

[88] Glenn v. CIR, 62 TC 270, 275 (1974) (licensed public accountant cannot deduct cost of review course to qualify for CPA status); Antzoulatos v. CIR, ¶75,327 P-H

4. Educational Travel. When taxpayers claim that expenditures for travel are deductible because the travel itself is "a form of education," the regulations (1) require evidence that the expenditures "are attributable to a period of travel that is directly related to the duties of the individual in his employment or other trade or business," (2) provide that this condition is satisfied only if "the major portion of the activities during such period is of a nature which directly maintains or improves skills required by the individual in [his] employment or other trade or business," and (3) state that employer approval of the travel does not itself establish the required relationship between the travel "and the duties of the individual in the particular position."[89]

The boundary between travel for business and travel for pleasure is especially murky in the case of teachers, who as a class are both especially likely to derive occupational benefits from travel and especially likely to travel for personal pleasure. Some teachers and other taxpayers can demonstrate a special kinship between foreign travel and the needs of their own occupation—teachers of languages, anthropology, and art are prime examples.[90] Beyond this, virtually all teachers—and many other taxpayers—can assert that observing the techniques of foreign colleagues will shed light on their own occupational practices. For this reason the results in litigated cases depend heavily on the trial court's assessment of the taxpayer's credibility and the validity of the asserted relationship between the sights seen on the trip and the taxpayer's daily work.[91] Even when the necessary link between the travel and the needs of the taxpayer's occupation has been established, it may be necessary to allocate the expenses actually incurred among the business component of the travel, personal side trips, expenses of the taxpayer's spouse, and other nonbusiness items.

Memo TC (1975) (intern and registered pharmacist); Burnstein v. CIR, 66 TC 492 (1976) (teacher of disabled children and social worker); Weiler v. CIR, 54 TC 398 (1970) (revenue agent and attorney; court rejects concept of "federal income tax expert" as unitary occupation); Sharon v. CIR, 591 F.2d 1273 (9th Cir. 1978), cert. denied, 442 US 941 (1979) (bar review course taken by New York lawyer to prepare for California bar examination); Bouchard v. CIR, ¶77,273 P-H Memo TC (1977) (college teacher of mathematics and college teacher of law; expenses disallowed, since law degree qualified taxpayer to practice law as well as teach it).

[89] Treas. Regs. §1.162-5(d).

[90] See Marlin v. CIR, 54 TC 560 (1970) (Acq.) (trip to France by married couple, both teachers; husband, who taught Latin, denied deduction despite visits to Roman ruins; wife, who taught history and collected slides and other teaching aids on trip, allowed to deduct her share of expenses); Adelson v. US, 342 F.2d 332 (9th Cir. 1965) (travel expenses incurred by teacher of English and journalism denied; trip resembled ordinary tourist's sightseeing trip).

[91] See Steinmann v. CIR, ¶71,295 P-H Memo TC (1971) (professor of management can deduct expenses of observing foreign business techniques); Postman v. CIR, ¶74,145 P-H Memo TC (1974) (architect's foreign travel not deductible, despite claimed "new understanding and appreciation of various styles of architecture").

A taxpayer who travels away from home "primarily to obtain education" may deduct not only the transportation expenses under IRC §162(a)(2), but also the cost of meals and lodging (except to the extent allocable to sightseeing, recreation, or other personal activities), provided the educational expenses are themselves deductible.[92] On the other hand, if the travel is primarily personal, the transportation expenses are not deductible, and meals and lodging qualify for deduction only for the period spent in deductible educational pursuits. In determining whether a trip is primarily to obtain education of a deductible character, "all the facts and circumstances" are taken into account; an important factor is the relative amount of time devoted to educational pursuits as against personal activities.[93]

5. Interruption of Employment or Business Activities by Education. If the taxpayer's studies are pursued on a full-time basis for an extended period, rather than after working hours, the IRS sometimes argues that the taxpayer has abandoned his or her business and that the expenses are incurred to enter a business at an indefinite future time rather than to carry on an existing business. Moreover, part-time employment during an extended period of studies (e.g., as a college research or teaching assistant) may be viewed as a method of financing the studies rather than as an occupation to which the education is subsidiary.[94]

In Revenue Ruling 68-591, the IRS ruled that a suspension of business activities for a period of a year or less, if followed by a resumption of the same employment, trade or business, is a "temporary" interruption rather than an abandonment of the taxpayer's business status.[95] This implied that a longer interruption, at least if the taxpayer is not on leave of absence, is evidence that the taxpayer is no longer carrying on a trade or business. The cases, however, make it clear that the distinction between temporary and indefinite suspensions is based on all of the facts, not merely the elapsed time between periods of gainful activity.[96]

---

[92] Treas. Regs. §1.162-5(e).

[93] Id.; see Rev. Rul. 74-292, 1974-1 CB 43 (doctor who combined vacation abroad with brief professional association; travel expenses disallowed in their entirety).

[94] See Jungreis v. CIR, 55 TC 581 (1970), in which Judge Tannenwald, concurring, concluded (at 593) that "petitioner herein worked because he studied. He did not study because he worked."

[95] Rev. Rul. 68-591, 1968-2 CB 73; see also Rev. Rul. 77-32, 1977-1 CB 38.

[96] See Sherman v. CIR, ¶77,301 P-H Memo TC (1977) (taxpayer was carrying on business during two-year program at business school), and cases there cited; see also Wyatt v. CIR, 56 TC 517, 520 (1971) (fact that taxpayer was member in good standing of profession by virtue of valid certificate or license does not by itself establish that she was "carrying on" a business).

¶9.7 COMPENSATION FOR PERSONAL SERVICES

1. Introductory. Section 162(a)(1) specifies that the deduction for ordinary and necessary business expenses includes "a reasonable allowance for salaries or other compensation for personal services actually rendered." Although the provision was originally added to permit deductions under the now defunct World War I excess profits tax for amounts accrued but not paid, for purposes of current tax the provision has come to be interpreted as *disallowing unreasonable amounts* even though paid. This power to disallow the deduction of payments actually made is almost never exercised, however, unless the employer and employee are related parties or unrelated persons engaging simultaneously in another transaction, such as a sale of property with a concomitant employment contract, where a purported payment for services may be in whole or in part a disguised gift, loan, dividend, or payment for property.

Since only genuine business expenses are deductible under IRC §162(a), however, payments disguised as wages or salaries could be disallowed by the IRS even if the statutory reference to a "reasonable allowance" had not been enacted. There is no such specific limitation, for example, on the deduction of payments for materials, supplies, interest, or rent, nor does IRC §212 explicitly restrict compensation payments to a reasonable amount; but the concept of an ordinary and necessary "expense," buttressed by the substance-over-form doctrine, forbids the deduction of payments inflated to disguise a nondeductible transfer. Indeed, the regulations refer to payments "in the form of compensation," "ostensible" salaries, and payments that "are a distribution of earnings,"[97] confirming a primary if not exclusive concern with amounts that are in fact not payments for services.

If there is no extraneous relationship between the employer and the employee, the amount fixed by them as payment for the services is almost always ipso facto reasonable, since they meet the willing-buyer, willing-seller criterion used in determining the fair market value of goods and services.

2. Criteria of Reasonableness. No single factor is determinative of the reasonableness of compensation; the situation must be considered as a whole. Although attempts to elaborate on the facts and circumstances relevant to the ultimate factual determination inevitably bog down in platitudes, the following factors are generally relevant:

1. *Services performed.* Significant services contributing importantly to the taxpayer's financial success buttress a larger compensation deduction, especially if the employee has special qualifications, training, or experience. Conversely, if the employee performs insignificant or part-time services or if

---

[97] Treas. Regs. §§1.162-7(b)(1), 1.162-8, 1.162-9.

the services require no special training or experience, the compensation should be correspondingly smaller.

2. *Comparison with other employees.* The reasonableness of compensation is frequently supported by reference to amounts paid by similar taxpayers to similar employees, and the regulations encourage comparisons with the compensation "paid for like services by like enterprises under like circumstances." [98] Salaries paid to other employees of the taxpayer or to the same employee in a prior year are sometimes relevant, providing the taxpayer's entire salary scale is not out of line.[99]

3. *Employer's earnings.* The employer's prosperity justifies a higher level of compensation, but salaries tending to reduce dividends are suspect, especially if the dividends would go to the employees whose compensation is being challenged.[100]

4. *Ownership.* Employees who own stock or are related to controlling shareholders are the primary targets for disallowance, particularly if the amount of compensation is roughly pro rata to stock ownership, since proportionality inevitably suggests that part of the compensation may be a disguised dividend.[101] Stock ownership becomes less significant if control is divided between unrelated persons who can be expected to bargain with each other at arm's length,[102] and it is, of course, possible for vigorous negotiations to take place between members of the same family over their relative financial rewards. Salaries paid to persons who are neither owners nor related to the owners of the business are rarely challenged by the IRS.

5. *Economic conditions.* The effect of improved general economic conditions on the appropriate level of compensation is ambiguous: On the one hand, higher costs of living can justify increased compensation, but improvements in the economy may account for a company's success more than the talents of its executives.[103]

---

[98] Treas. Regs. §1.162-7(b)(3).

[99] See, e.g., Robert Louis Stevenson Apartments v. CIR, 337 F.2d 681 (8th Cir. 1964) (same amount paid same employee in prior years; evidence of reasonable compensation); Standard Asbestos Mfg. & Insulating Co. v. CIR, 276 F.2d 289 (8th Cir. 1960), cert. denied, 364 US 826 (1960) (increase in challenged salaries when less-well-paid officers did not get commensurate increase; evidence of unreasonable compensation).

[100] See, e.g., Charles McCandless Tile Serv. v. US, 422 F.2d 1336 (Ct. Cl. 1970) (denying deduction because part of amount paid was disguised dividend, although compensation was otherwise reasonable).

[101] See Charles McCandless Tile Serv. v. US, supra note 100 (compensation in proportion to shareholdings); see also CIR v. R.J. Reynolds Tobacco Co., 260 F.2d 9 (4th Cir. 1958) (public company, but compensation based on stock ownership).

[102] See Ziegler Steel Serv. Corp. v. CIR, ¶62,057 P-H Memo TC (1962) (nothing to suggest that employee could dominate corporation through ownership of 50 percent of stock where balance was owned by unrelated persons).

[103] See, e.g., Petro-Chem Marketing Co. v. US, 602 F.2d 959 (Ct. Cl. 1979) (part of compensation unreasonable since large profits partly due to chaotic conditions in petrochemical industry).

6. *Employer's dividend policy.* Although the reasonableness of shareholder-employee salaries can be separated in theory from the company's dividend policy, a low distribution level is sometimes cited as evidence of excessive compensation.[104] But the IRS ruled in 1979 that, although a closely held corporation's failure to pay more than an insubstantial portion of its earnings in dividends "is a very significant factor to be taken into account in determining the deductibility of compensation paid by the corporation to its shareholder-employees," deductions would not be denied on this ground alone if an examination of all facts and circumstances, including the corporation's dividend history, indicated that the compensation was reasonable compensation for services rendered.[105]

7. *Contingent compensation.* Evaluating the reasonableness of compensation paid under a long-term contract geared to sales, profits, or other variable amounts is especially difficult, since the amount paid may skyrocket as a result of circumstances unrelated to the employee's contributions. The regulations provide that if contingent compensation is paid pursuant to a bona fide bargain between the employer and employee, made before the services are rendered and reasonable at that time, a deduction will be allowed even though the amount paid turns out to be unreasonable.[106] A number of cases, nevertheless, hold that agreements valid when made at arm's length with an employee may become unreasonable if the employee subsequently acquires control of the employing corporation.[107]

3. Status of Unreasonable Compensation. The regulations provide that absent evidence justifying other treatment, amounts paid ostensibly as compensation, but which the taxpayer was not allowed to deduct, will nevertheless be included in the gross income of the recipient. The precise treatment, however, depends on the circumstances of each case; a payment, for example, may be treated as a dividend if it bears a close relationship to stockholdings in a corporate employer, or as part of the sales price of property if the payment is in fact a disguised purchase of property by the payor.[108] Moreover, payments reclassified as "dividends" may be taxable to someone other than the recipient.

---

[104] E.g., Charles McCandless Tile Serv. v. US, supra note 100 (payment deemed reasonable but held in part a disguised dividend); Treas. Regs. §1.162-7(b)(1) ("ostensible salary paid by a corporation may be a distribution of a dividend on stock"); but see Edwin's, Inc. v. US, 501 F.2d 675, 677 n.5 (7th Cir. 1974) ("absence of dividends might be a red flag," but it does not require disallowance of compensation "demonstrated to be reasonable under all of the circumstances").

[105] Rev. Rul. 79-8, 1979-1 CB 92.

[106] Treas. Regs. §1.162-7(b)(2).

[107] E.g., City Chevrolet Co. v. CIR, ¶54,261 P-H Memo TC (1954), aff'd per curiam, 228 F.2d 894 (4th Cir. 1956), cert. denied, 351 US 939 (1956).

[108] Treas. Regs. §1.162-8.

For example, if an ostensible salary paid to a controlling shareholder's child is viewed as a dividend, the parent-shareholder is taxed on assignment-of-income principles, and the child is the recipient of a tax-free gift.

¶9.8 RENTAL PAYMENTS

Section 162(a)(3) provides that business expenses include "rentals or other payments required to be made as a condition to the continued use or possession, for purposes of the trade or business, or property to which the taxpayer has not taken or is not taking title or in which he has no equity." [109] The affirmative message of the provision—that rents, royalties, and similar payments are deductible if incurred to use property for business purposes—is scarcely necessary: their deductible status is self-evident. The negative message—that taxpayers cannot deduct capital outlays to purchase property—is also self-evident today, though in 1916, when the "no equity" restriction was enacted, Congress evidently thought that an explicit warning was required to prevent taxpayers from deducting mortgage payments on business property.

In application, IRC §162(a)(3) is troublesome primarily in lease-option and sale-leaseback arrangements, where the taxpayer's relationship to business property is ambiguous. If the taxpayer leases property for its fair market value, subject to an option to purchase at its estimated future value or for an amount to be determined by appraisal when the option is exercised, the rental payments while the option remains inchoate are deductible if the property is used for business purposes. On the other hand, if the interim rental payments exceed the property's fair rental value and are applicable against the purchase price, the lessee's economic status may be virtually indistinguishable from that of a purchaser who finances acquisition of the property with a mortgage. In this event, the rental payments cannot be deducted but are instead recharacterized as interest and amortization on the hypothetical mortgage; the taxpayer can then deduct the interest component of the periodic payments and can depreciate the property over its estimated useful life. The same tax results follow if a sale-leaseback is recharacterized as a mortgage.

The characterization problem just described arises most frequently in transactions involving real estate and business equipment; but the same legal issues are posed by royalty agreements involving trademarks, other intangible assets, and mineral property, where the licensee has an option to purchase and can apply the interim payments against the option price.[110]

---

[109] There is no explicit counterpart in IRC §212, but similar principles are applied by the courts. See Daniel v. CIR, ¶78,277 P-H Memo TC (1978) (option to purchase; IRC §§162(a)(3) and 212 equivalent).

[110] Goldfields of America, Ltd. v. CIR, 44 BTA 200 (1941) (minimum royalties

Although IRC §162(a)(3) does not explicitly deal with payments to acquire a leasehold for business purposes, the regulations provide that the cost is deductible in equal portions over the life of the lease;[111] and IRC §178 provides rules for determining whether renewal periods will be included in the amortization period.

¶9.9 MOVING EXPENSES

1. Introductory. Section 217 permits a deduction for certain moving expenses incurred by both employees and self-employed taxpayers as a result of commencing work at a new location. Prior to the enactment of IRC §82 (requiring reimbursement for moving expenses to be included in income) and §217, the cost of moving the taxpayer's residence from one permanent place of business to another was a nondeductible personal expense, but amounts paid by employers to reimburse the moving expenses of an existing employee (as distinguished from a new employee) were viewed as incurred "primarily for the benefit of the employer" and hence were not includable in the employee's gross income.

Amounts deductible under IRC §217 are invested with a quasi-business character by IRC §62(8), which permits them to be deducted in computing adjusted gross income whether the taxpayer itemizes "personal" deductions or not.

The salient features of IRC §217 are:

1. *Work commencement.* Under IRC §217(a), the moving expenses must be incurred "in connection with the commencement of work by the taxpayer as an employee or as a self-employed individual at a new principal place of work." Although the work-commencement requirement is not satisfied unless the taxpayer actually commences work at the new location, it is not essential that the taxpayer be transferred by an employer from the old duty post to the new place of work. Thus, IRC §217 encompasses employees beginning work for a new employer, self-employed taxpayers changing locations, and persons beginning work for the first time.

The regulations provide that "the move must bear a reasonable proximity both in time and place to [the commencement of work] at the new principal

---

paid before production and applied to purchase price under option to buy not deductible); J. Strickland & Co. v. US, 352 F.2d 1016 (6th Cir. 1965), cert. denied, 384 US 950 (1966) ("inordinately large" minimum royalty payments and large advertising and promotional campaign by "licensee," coupled with option to purchase vested in its controlling shareholders, indicated purported license of trademarks was purchase and sale).

[111] Treas. Regs. §1.162-11(a).

place of work." [112] In general, the time requirement is satisfied by moving expenses incurred within one year of the commencement of work; whether expenses incurred thereafter qualify depends on the facts and circumstances of each case. The move is generally not reasonably "proximate in place" to the commencement of work at the new location if the new duty post is closer to the old residence than to the new one.

2. *Minimum distance.* Presumably on the theory that short residential moves are animated more by personal preferences than by business pressure, IRC §217(c)(1) requires the new principal place of work to be (a) at least thirty-five miles farther from the taxpayer's former residence than was the former principal place of work or (b) if the taxpayer had no former principal place of work, at least thirty-five miles from the taxpayer's former residence.

3. *Duration of employment.* To prevent taxpayers from using temporary jobs as a pretext for deducting the expenses of moving for personal reasons from one residence to another, IRC §217(c)(2) imposes a duration-of-employment condition which is met if the taxpayer is a full-time employee (not necessarily for the same employer) in the general location of the new principal place of work during at least thirty-nine weeks of the twelve-month period immediately following arrival there. A self-employed taxpayer must perform services as a self-employed person or as an employee on a full-time basis during at least seventy-eight weeks of the twenty-four-month period starting with arrival, of which thirty-nine weeks must occur during the first twelve-month period. These duration requirements are waived by IRC §217(d)(1) if the taxpayer is unable to satisfy the conditions by reason of death, disability, or certain other involuntary circumstances.

2. Qualifying Expenses and Dollar Limits. Taxpayers meeting the requirements of IRC §217 may deduct five categories of "moving expenses," listed in IRC §217(b), subject to certain dollar limits, provided the amounts are "reasonable." [113] The five categories, each of which is elaborated by the regulations,[114] are (a) the cost of moving household goods and personal effects of the taxpayer and his family from the former residence to the new one, including expenses for packing and in-transit storage;[115] (b) the cost of one trip (including meals and lodging) between the two residences for the taxpayer and each family member; (c) the cost of traveling (including meals and lodging) between the old residence and the location of the new principal place of

[112] Treas. Regs. §1.217-2(a)(3).

[113] For the term "reasonable expenses," see Treas. Regs. §1.217-2(b)(2)(i) (cost of moving by shortest and most direct route, excluding detours for scenic pleasure; meals and lodging must not be lavish or extravagant; etc.).

[114] Treas. Regs. §1.217-2(b).

[115] See Rev. Rul. 66-305, 1966-2 CB 102 (cost of moving household pets qualifies); Aksomitas v. CIR, 50 TC 679, 686 (1968) (contra as to forty-five foot yacht).

business, after obtaining employment, for the principal purpose of finding a new residence; (d) the cost of meals and lodging while at temporary quarters in the general location of the new principal place of work during any period of thirty consecutive days after obtaining employment; and (e) "qualified residence sale, purchase, or lease expenses"—an elaborately defined miscellany, including commissions, attorney's fees, and similar expenses incurred in selling the old residence or purchasing the new one and comparable expenses attributable to terminating or entering into residential leases.

The first two categories of moving expenses can be deducted regardless of amount, provided they are reasonable. By contrast, the deduction for categories (c) and (d) may not exceed $1,500, and the deduction for category (e) expenses may not exceed $3,000 less the amount allowable as a deduction for categories (c) and (d).[116]

3. Moving Expenses and Travel Away From Home. Taxpayers cannot deduct both moving expenses under IRC §217 and the cost of meals and lodging at the new duty post under IRS §162(a)(2). Moving expenses are deductible under IRC §217 only if the taxpayer will be employed at the new principal place of work on a permanent or indefinite basis, while IRC §162(a)(2) permits living expenses at a duty post to be deducted only if the taxpayer's employment there is "temporary."[117]

4. Reimbursed Moving Expenses. To eliminate the distinctions prevailing under prior law between taxpayers whose moving expenses were defrayed by their employers and those who paid their own expenses, IRC §82 was enacted in 1969 to require amounts received, directly or indirectly, as payments or reimbursements for the expenses of moving from one residence to another to be included in gross income if attributable to the taxpayer's employment. Taken in combination, therefore, IRC §§82 and 217 force all taxpayers to comply with the conditions prescribed by IRC §217 in order to deduct their moving expenses.

¶9.10 HOBBIES AND OTHER ACTIVITIES NOT ENGAGED IN FOR PROFIT

1. Introductory. Although it has been clear from the inception of the federal income tax that costs incurred by a taxpayer in carrying on a hobby or other recreational activity are not deductible, it has never been easy to administer the distinction between business and profit-oriented activities on

---

[116] IRC §217(b)(3); these dollar amounts are halved for a married person filing a separate return. For the treatment of two-job married couples, see IRC §217(b)(3)(B).

[117] See Goldman v. CIR, 497 F.2d 382 (6th Cir. 1974), cert. denied, 419 US 1021 (1974); Treas. Regs. §1.217-2(a)(1) (fourth sentence).

the one hand and not-for-profit activities on the other. In the early cases, taxpayers managed to establish that their country estates, racing stables, and other costly pursuits were conducted for profit rather than for pleasure in a surprisingly large number of cases.[118] Discontented with the outcome of these hobby/business cases, Congress enacted a provision in 1943, which became Section 270 of the 1954 Code, under which an individual, but not a corporation, whose losses from a trade or business exceeded the enterprise's gross income by $50,000 or more for each of five consecutive years, could not deduct the excess losses. The threshold question of whether the activity was a hobby or a business was left to the courts, to be decided on a case-by-case basis with reference to all of the facts and circumstances. If the activity was found to be conducted for pleasure rather than for profit, the losses were entirely disallowed; but if the taxpayer succeeded in establishing that it was a business, IRC §270 disallowed losses in excess of $50,000 per year, subject to qualification for special circumstances.

In 1969 Congress concluded that IRC §270 had not worked well and replaced it with IRC §183. Section 183 applies only to individual taxpayers, trusts, estates and Subchapter S corporations.[119] If an activity is not engaged in for profit, deductions attributable to the activity are allowable only to the extent permitted by IRC §183. A separate "not engaged in for profit" determination must be made for each "activity" conducted by the taxpayer. A pro-taxpayer presumption provides, in general, that an activity producing gross income in excess of its deductions for two or more taxable years during a period of five consecutive years (seven in the case of horse breeding, etc.) is engaged in for profit unless the IRS establishes the contrary.

2. Activity "Not Engaged In for Profit." Section 183(c) defines an "activity not engaged in for profit" as any activity other than one for which deductions are allowable under IRC §162, relating to expenses in carrying on the taxpayer's trade or business, or IRC §212(1) or §212(2), relating to expenses for the production or collection of income or for the management,

---

[118] See, e.g., Ellsworth v. CIR, ¶62,032 P-H Memo TC (1962) (uninterrupted losses aggregating almost $700,000 over thirteen years in operating "Folly Farm" held to be business rather than hobby).

[119] For the application of IRC §183 to partnerships, see Rev. Rul. 77-320, 1977-2 CB 78 (IRC §183 applied at partnership level and reflected in partners' distributive shares), limited by Rev. Rul. 78-22, 1978-1 CB 72.

As for corporations (other than Subchapter S corporations), Treas. Regs. §1.183-1(a) provides that no inference is to be drawn from IRC §183 or the regulations thereunder as to whether a corporation's activities are engaged in for profit. Since the factors set forth in the regulations for determining whether an activity is carried on for profit are a distillation of prior case law, however, they seem equally applicable to corporations. See Smith v. CIR, ¶79,324 P-H Memo TC (1979) (corporate-owned Lipizzan horses held for profit, despite twenty-year period of losses; analysis of facts similar to approach under IRC §183 in cases involving individual taxpayers).

conservation, or maintenance of property held for the production of income. Although this definition incorporates the standards applied by IRC §§162, 212(1), and 212(2) to determine whether expenses attributable to a particular activity are deductible, the regulations under IRC §183 lay down an independent set of interpretative principles to determine whether an activity is or is not engaged in for profit. Because the IRC §183 regulations are a distillation of the prior case law, however, the chance of conflict with the standards employed by IRC §§162 and 212 is minimal.

The regulations under IRC §183 require the determination of whether an activity is engaged in for profit to be made by reference to "objective standards" rather than the taxpayer's "subjective intent." But while the object of the activity must be to make a profit, the taxpayer need not necessarily have a "reasonable expectation" of making a profit.[120] In determining whether an activity is engaged in for profit, "all facts and circumstances with respect to the activity are to be taken into account." [121] The regulations then set out and illustrate nine "relevant factors" that "should normally be taken into account," along with a warning that no one factor, nor even a majority of them, is controlling and that factors not explicitly specified may be relevant.[122] The nine listed factors are:

1. The manner in which the taxpayer carries on the activity (e.g., accurate books and records, abandonment of unprofitable methods, and similarity of operating procedures to comparable profitable enterprises).[123]
2. The expertise of the taxpayer or his advisers (e.g., preparatory study of business, economic, and scientific practices, or consultations with experts regarding these matters).[124]
3. The amount of time and effort devoted by the taxpayer to the activity (e.g., extensive attention or withdrawal from other activities to devote full time to the activity).[125]

---

[120] Treas. Regs. §1.183-2(a).

[121] Treas. Regs. §1.183-2(b); see also Rev. Rul. 79-300, 1979-2 CB 112 (IRC §183 not applicable to investment in federally subsidized housing project, despite expectation of losses for twenty years, because of legislative intent to encourage investment by allowing losses to be deducted).

[122] Treas. Regs. §1.183-2(b).

[123] See Lyon v. CIR, ¶77,239 P-H Memo TC (1977) (failure to maintain records and unbusinesslike approach; activity not engaged in for profit); Allen v. CIR, 72 TC 28 (1979) (Acq.) (taxpayers operated ski lodge in business-like manner, experimenting with different modes of operating it in hope of making profit).

[124] See also Benz v. CIR, 63 TC 375 (1974) (taxpayer was "a relative novice"; breeding activity held a hobby).

[125] See Hawkins v. CIR, ¶79,101 P-H Memo TC (1979) (publication of isolated book of poetry not activity engaged in for profit).

4. An expectation that assets used in the activity may appreciate in value, unless current operations and sales of the property (e.g., farmland) at a profit are separate activities.
5. The taxpayer's experience in converting other unprofitable activities into profitable enterprises.
6. The taxpayer's history of income or losses in the activity (e.g., whether losses were incurred in a start-up period, which is a common experience, or have continued without adequate explanation thereafter; unforeseen losses from drought, fire, or depressed market conditions; etc.).
7. The amount of occasional profits, if any, that are earned, in relation to the losses and as compared to the amount invested by the taxpayer and the value of the assets used in the activity.
8. The taxpayer's financial status (poor taxpayers are not oblivious to large losses; wealthy ones may be willing to accept losses, especially if they generate offsetting tax, personal, or recreational benefits).
9. Elements of personal pleasure or recreation in conducting the activity. While the derivation of pleasure from the activity does not negate a profit-making objective, recreational elements are an adverse factor; conversely, the fact that an activity "lacks any appeal other than profit" may denote a profit motivation.

While this catalogue of the amorphous Big Nine Factors may be the best that can be done to illuminate the intractable issue of whether an activity is or is not "engaged in for profit," it is obvious that some of the indicia (e.g., accurate books and records, preliminary investigations, and consultations with experts) may be no more than camouflage, of doubtful evidentiary value once their observance becomes self-conscious.

3. Scope of Term "Activity." Although the term "activity" is not defined by IRC §183, its scope can be of crucial importance. The taxpayer, for example, may wish to amalgamate two or more undertakings or enterprises into a single "activity" if the resulting consolidated financial statement shows a profit, because one of them, if viewed in isolation, might be treated as an activity not engaged in for profit.

The regulations provide that the most significant facts and circumstances in determining whether the taxpayer is engaged in a single activity or several activities are "the degree of organizational and economic interrelationship of various undertakings, the business purpose which is (or might be) served by carrying on the various undertakings separately or together in a trade or in a business setting, and the similarity of various undertakings." [126] As an exam-

[126] Treas. Regs. §1.183-1(d)(1).

ple, the regulations state that farming and holding land with the intent to profit from appreciation will be viewed as a single activity only if the income derived from farming exceeds the deductions attributable to farming which would have been incurred as a result of merely holding the land as an investment (such as interest on the mortgage, real property taxes, and depreciation on improvements).[127]

4. Allowable Deductions. Deductions attributable to each activity are marshalled into three tiers by IRC §183(b) and the regulations thereunder,[128] which are then treated as follows:

1. Tier 1 consists of deductions that are allowable without regard to whether the activity is engaged in for profit, such as IRC §§163 (interest), 164 (certain taxes), and 165(c)(3) (casualty losses). These items can be deducted in full, subject to any limitations to which they are otherwise subject (e.g., disallowance of the first $100 of a casualty loss).

2. Tier 2 consists of deductions that would be allowable if the activity in question had been conducted for profit but that do not result in adjustments to the basis of property, such as business expenses under IRC §162(a) and profit-oriented expenses under IRC §212(a) or §212(2). These items can be deducted only to the extent that the activity produced gross income in excess of its tier 1 deductions.

3. Tier 3 consists of deductions that would be allowable if the activity had been conducted for profit but that (unlike tier 2 deductions) result in basis adjustments, such as accelerated cost recovery, amortization, the first $100 of a casualty loss, and partially worthless bad debts. These deductions are allowable only to the extent that the activity's gross income exceeds the sum of its tier 1 and tier 2 deductions. If any tier 3 deductions are allowed, the property's basis must be correspondingly adjusted.[129]

These principles are illustrated by Example 10-1, which assumes that a taxpayer who races cars as a hobby receives a prize of $5,000 in a competition and incurs the following expenses, all with respect to a single car: (1) uninsured collision damage of $1,800 (before taking account of the $100 nondeductible floor on nonbusiness casualty losses, but after giving effect to the 10 percent of adjusted gross income floor); (2) gasoline, oil, and repairs of $1,300; and (3) depreciation of $2,500.

---

[127] Id.; see also Rev. Rul. 78-22, 1978-1 CB 72 (horse racing conducted as sole proprietor and as member of partnership constituted two separate activities); Engdahl v. CIR, 72 TC 659 (1979) (Acq.) (property purchased to breed and raise horses; land and horse-related activities combined into single activity).

[128] Section 183(b) establishes only two categories of deductions, but the regulations split the second category into two subspecies. Treas. Regs. §1.183-1(b)(1).

[129] See Treas. Regs. §§1.183-1(b)(2), 1.183-1(b)(3) (allocation of adjustments between assets).

Example 10-1

Deductions as Limited by IRC §183

1. Tier 1 deduction—casualty loss ($1,800 less nondeductible $100)		$1,700
2. Tier 2 deductions		
a. Gross income from activity	$5,000	
b. Less: Tier 1 deductions	1,700	
c. Balance	$3,300	
d. Deductions not affecting basis	$1,300	
e. Lesser of line 2c and line 2d		1,300
3. Tier 3 deductions		
a. Gross income from activity	$5,000	
b. Less: Tier 1 and 2 deductions	3,000	
c. Balance	$2,000	
d. Depreciation and first $100 of casualty loss	$2,600	
e. Lesser of line 3e and line 3d		2,000
4. Total deductions		$5,000

As shown in Example 10-1, the taxpayer is entitled to deductions of $5,000 (line 4), and the car is subject to a basis adjustment of $2,000 (line 3e).

It is sometimes necessary to determine whether the taxpayer's operations constitute one "activity" or more than one in applying the three-tier system to the taxpayer's deductions. For example, assume that a taxpayer engages in enterprise *A,* which produces $1,000 of gross income and $1,000 of tier 2 deductions, and enterprise *B,* which produces no gross income and $1,000 of tier 1 deductions. If the enterprises qualify as separate "activities" under IRC §183(b), the taxpayer must report $1,000 of gross income and can deduct the tier 2 deductions of $1,000 in respect of enterprise *A* and the tier 1 deductions of $1,000 in respect of enterprise *B.* If the enterprises constitute a single activity, however, the tier 1 deductions are offset against the gross income of $1,000, resulting in disallowance of the tier 2 deductions.

5. Presumption of For-Profit Operation. Section 183(d) provides that if the gross income from an activity exceeds the deductions attributable to it for any two or more taxable years during the five-year period ending with the current taxable year, a rebuttable presumption arises that the activity was engaged in for profit during the taxable year. The five-year period is extended to seven years if the activity consists in major part of the breeding, training, showing, or racing of horses.

This comparison between the activity's gross income and its deductions is made by treating the activity, provisionally, as engaged in for profit; if, on this assumption, the gross income exceeds the deductions (excluding the IRC §1202 net capital gain deduction and the net operating loss deduction under IRC §172), for the requisite two years, the activity is presumed to be conducted for profit during the second profit year and all subsequent years during the same five- or seven-year period. A taxpayer's failure to qualify for the rebuttable presumption, however, does not justify an inference that the activity is *not* conducted for profit.

Section 183(e) permits taxpayers to postpone a determination of whether the presumption applies until the close of the fourth taxable year (or the sixth year, in the case of horse breeding, etc.) following the first taxable year in which the taxpayer engaged in the activity. If there are two profitable years in the applicable five- or seven-year period, the presumption applies to all five or seven years, including years preceding the profit years. If the presumption does not come into force or is rebutted, however, the time for assessing deficiencies is extended by IRC §183(e)(4).

¶9.11 RESIDENTIAL PROPERTY USED FOR BUSINESS AND PROFIT-ORIENTED PURPOSES—HOME OFFICES, VACATION HOMES, ETC.

1. Introductory. Section 280A severely limits individuals (including trusts, estates, and members of partnerships) and Subchapter S corporations in deducting expenses attributable to the business or profit-oriented use of a dwelling unit, whether owned or leased by the taxpayer, if the property is also used by the taxpayer as a residence during the taxable year. Although aimed primarily at deductions claimed for offices located in the taxpayer's residence and for vacation homes that are offered for rent when not occupied by the taxpayer, IRC §280A also applies to dwelling units used for business entertainment or other profit-oriented purposes, assuming the requisite amount of personal residential use in the same taxable year. Section 280A(b), however, exempts from the general disallowance rule all deductions that are allowable without regard to business or income producing activities, such as taxes, interest, and casualty losses.

Because use of the property "by the taxpayer . . . as a residence" is defined by IRC §§280A(d)(1) and 280A(d)(2) to mean any use of a dwelling unit "for personal purposes" by the taxpayer, members of the taxpayer's family, or certain other persons, IRC §280A can apply even if the taxpayer never sets foot on the premises and even if none of the tainted persons actually sleep there. Use of the property as a residence is defined by IRC §280A(d) to mean use of the unit for personal purposes for more than fourteen days or more than 10 percent of the days for which it is rented at a fair rental, whichever is greater—taking into account personal use not only by the taxpayer but also by other persons with an interest in the property, by their families (as defined by IRC §267(c)(4)), by persons using the property under a reciprocal arrangement entitling the taxpayer to use another dwelling unit, or by any other person except an employee subject to IRC §119 (relating to lodging furnished for the convenience of the employer), unless a fair rental is charged. Thus, a vacation home is subject to the jurisdiction of IRC §280A if the owners allow their child's college roommate to occupy it without charge for two months, even though it is rented to outsiders under an arm's-length lease for the other ten months of the taxable year. Furthermore, rental of a dwelling unit to a family member (as defined in IRC §267(c)(4)) is considered personal use, even if the rental is for fair rental value, unless the relative rents the dwelling unit for use as his principal residence.[130]

2. Exempted Uses. Section 280A(c) exempts four categories of uses from the blanket disallowance of IRC §280A(a)—certain home offices, storage of inventory, rental, and day care services—but these exempted uses generate deductions only if they are sanctioned by a substantive provision authorizing deductions, such as IRC §162 (business expenses), §165 (losses), §168 (cost recovery), or §212 (nonbusiness expenses of profit-oriented activities). The cost of adding a new room to the taxpayer's residence, for example, is a nondeductible capital expenditure even if the space is used exclusively for an exempted business use. Moreover, deductions allocable to exempted uses are subject to a gross-income limit described below.

1. *Certain home offices.* Section 280A(c)(1) exempts deductions allocable to portions of a dwelling unit used exclusively and regularly (a) as the principal place of business for any trade or business of the taxpayer; (b) as a place of business to meet or deal with patients, clients, or customers in the normal course of the taxpayer's business; or (c) in the case of a separate structure that is not attached to the dwelling unit, in connection with the taxpayer's trade or business. These standards are clearly intended to disqualify residential space used by investors to study stock market quotations and keep records, by business executives to read or prepare business reports, by teachers to prepare for class and grade examinations, and by most self-employed taxpayers whose principal office is located elsewhere.[131]

---

[130] IRC §280A(d)(3).

[131] See Weightman v. CIR, ¶81,301 P-H Memo TC (1981) (IRC §280A(c) satisfied by college professor's showing that part of bedroom was used exclusively as home office, despite absence of partition or other physical demarcation; but home office was not principal place of business despite claim that home research activities were more important than teaching; also, no showing that home office was used for employer's convenience); Baie v. CIR, 74 TC 105 (1980) (no deduction for room in house used

The "principal place of business" exception accommodates primarily self-employed taxpayers working out of their homes and employees whose employers do not provide them with office space; but it also embraces taxpayers with two or more businesses, one of which is conducted from an office in the taxpayer's home.[132]

The exception for home offices in which the taxpayer meets patients, clients, and customers covers mostly physicians, other professionals, and salesmen who meet with clients in a secondary office at home. In theory, there is no justification for distinguishing these taxpayers from others (e.g., musicians and professors) with a bona fide secondary place of business at home; but the IRS can obviously separate genuine from fictitious claims with greater confidence if the taxpayer must establish that the office is used to meet third persons.

Finally, the separate-structure exception is especially suited to artists and self-employed artisans with a secondary studio at home; but it also embraces other taxpayers using a separate structure exclusively and regularly in connection with a trade or business. Here again, enforcement is facilitated by the statutory standard; but this administrative objective is reached at the expense of urban taxpayers, who are not likely to have a studio in the backyard unless they are successful enough to own a country estate.

If the taxpayer is an employee, the statutory standards are buttressed by a requirement that the exclusive use of the business area must be for the convenience of the employer; thus, expenses allocable to a separate structure used by an employee after working hours and on weekends as a matter of personal convenience do not qualify, even if the space is used exclusively for business purposes.

2. *Storage of inventory.* Section 280A(c)(2) exempts expenses allocable to space within the dwelling that is regularly used to store inventory for a business of selling products at retail or wholesale, but only if this is the sole fixed location of the business. This exception will frequently overlap the exception granted by IRC §280A(c)(1)(A); but it also covers door-to-door salesmen, whose homes are used for the storage of merchandise but arguably are not the taxpayer's "principal" place of business.

3. *Rental property.* Expenses attributable to the rental of dwelling units are exempted by IRC §280A(c)(3) but are subject to the special rules discussed below.[133]

---

for bookkeeping and kitchen used to prepare food for street vendor's hot-dog stand; food stand was principal place of business).

[132] Curphey v. CIR, 73 TC 766 (1980) (IRC §280A requires operation of business within meaning of IRC §162, not merely income-producing activity under IRC §212; but activities of dermatologist managing six rental units from home office qualify as business).

[133] Section 280A(c)(3) rules are discussed on the following page.

4. *Day care services.* Section 280A(c)(4) exempts items allocable to the regular use of a dwelling unit in the taxpayer's business of providing day care for children and persons who are over sixty-five or are physically or mentally unable to care for themselves. Exclusive use of the area for day care services is not required; but in the case of mixed uses, the expenses qualify for deduction only in the proportion that the hours of day care use bear to the number of hours that the space is available for all uses.

3. Rental Property. Items attributable to the rental of dwelling units are subject to special restrictions that do not apply to deductions attributable to other exempted uses of dwelling units. Because rental activity is subject to special rules whether it is profit-oriented or not, it is necessary to correlate IRC §280A's rules with those imposed by IRC §183 on hobbies and other activities that are not engaged in for profit. If, however, IRC §280A(a) is invoked to disallow deductions in a given taxable year, IRC §183 is inapplicable for that year.

The following four categories of dwelling units rented by the taxpayer can be examined separately:

1. *Dwelling units that are not used by the taxpayer for personal purposes at any time during the taxable year.* These units are not affected by IRC §280A. Ordinarily, the taxpayer can deduct all expenses under IRC §162, relating to trade or business expenses, or IRC §212, relating to property held for the production of income; but in the absence of a profit-oriented purpose (e.g., a vacation home that is rented simply to minimize the expense of having it available for personal use), the deductions are subject to IRC §183.

2. *Dwelling units used for personal purposes, but for less than the period prescribed by IRC § 280A(d)(1).* Expenses attributable to the rental period are deductible to the extent permitted by IRC §280A(e). This provision allows all deductions that are allowable without regard to the rental activity (e.g., mortgage interest, real property taxes, and casualty losses); but other deductions (e.g., accelerated cost recovery, utilities, repairs, and maintenance) must be allocated in the proportion that the number of rental days (counting only those for which a fair rental is charged) bears to the total number of days that the unit is used for all purposes. For example, if a summer cottage that is habitable for 100 days during the year is rented for ninety-five days and used by the owner for five days, the deductions cannot exceed (a) the expenses deductible without regard to the rental activity, plus (b) 95 percent of the other expenses.

3. *Dwelling units used for personal purposes for the period prescribed by IRC § 280A(d).* These units are subject to the allocation principles of IRC §280A(e), described in the preceding paragraph; and then the qualifying allocable amount is subjected to the overall limit prescribed by IRC §280A(c)(5), described below.

4. *Dwelling units rented for less than fifteen days.* If a dwelling unit is used by the taxpayer for the period prescribed by IRC §280A(d) but is rented for less than fifteen days during the same taxable year, IRC §280A(g) excludes the rent from gross income and disallows all deductions attributable to the rental use. This provision, which does not affect the taxpayer's right to deduct amounts allowable without regard to the rental activity (e.g., mortgage interest, real property taxes, and casualty losses), reflects an understandable de minimis principle if the rental activity is insignificant relative to the taxpayer's personal use of the property.

4. Overall Limit on Deductions. Under IRC §280A(c)(5), deductions attributable to exempted uses of dwelling units (other than rental dwelling units used for personal purposes for less than the period prescribed by IRC §280A(d)(1)) cannot exceed the gross income derived from the exempted use, reduced by the deductions allocable to the exempted use and allowable without regard to a business connection (e.g., interest on residential mortgages, real property taxes, and casualty losses).[134] The potential unfairness of restricting deductions to the rent actually received when a residence occupied for part of the year is converted in good faith to rental property is mitigated by IRC §280A(d)(4), exempting the taxpayer's principal residence from the overall limit if the deductions are attributable to a "qualified rental period" (ordinarily twelve consecutive months), as defined by IRC §280A(d)(4)(B). To prevent abuse, the exemption does not apply to vacation or other secondary homes but only to the taxpayer's principal residence.

¶9.12 EXPENSES RELATED TO TAX-EXEMPT INCOME

1. Exempt Income Other Than Interest. All otherwise deductible amounts are disallowed if allocable to exempt income other than interest. The disallowance applies not only to otherwise deductible trade or business expenses, such as educational expenses allocable to tax-exempt fellowships, and similar receipts,[135] but also to taxes otherwise deductible under IRC §164 and

[134] See Bolton v. CIR, 77 TC 104 (1981), which held that for this purpose, the allocation of interest and real property taxes to the exempted use should be ratable with time; if property was rented for three months, used for personal purposes for one month, and unused for eight months, the overall limit is reduced by 25 percent of the interest and taxes—three months out of twelve—rather than by 75 percent (3 months out of 4).

[135] Christian v. US, 201 F.Supp. 155 (E.D. La. 1962) (educational expenses financed by gift and fellowship), but see Rev. Rul. 62-213, 1962-2 CB 59 (education-

expenses otherwise deductible under IRC §212.[136] Premiums paid to purchase life insurance policies have also been disallowed under IRC §265(1).[137] The principal types of exempt income (other than interest) bringing IRC §265(1) into play seem to be gifts, scholarships and fellowships, exclududable foreign earned income, and life insurance proceeds.

Deductions attributable to income that is realized but not recognized by virtue of a nonrecognition provision are not disallowed by IRC §265(1), since the taxation of such income is ordinarily postponed rather than permanently exempted from tax. Deductions allocable to both exempt and taxable income must be apportioned between the two categories, since only the former portion is subject to disallowance under IRC §265(1).[138]

2. IRC §212 Deductions Allocable to Tax-Exempt Interest. Deductions allocable to tax-exempt interest are disallowed by IRC §265(1), but only if they arise under IRC §212. Thus, amortization deductible under IRC §167(a)(2) is not adversely affected by IRC §265(1).[139] The principal expenses disallowed by this part of IRC §265(1) are charges for safe-deposit boxes, investment advice, and custodial services incurred by investors in tax-exempt state and local bonds. Interest on debt incurred or continued to purchase or carry exempt obligations is also nondeductible by virtue of IRC §265(2), discussed earlier in this work.[140]

¶9.13 PRORATION OF COST OF PRODUCING FILMS, BOOKS, RECORDS, AND SIMILAR PROPERTY

Section 280(a) prohibits individuals and certain corporations from currently deducting the production costs of a film, sound recording, book or similar property (e.g., a play); the costs must instead be capitalized. They may then be deducted under IRC §280(b) over the useful life of the asset using the income forecast method, under which a fraction of the originally capitalized amount is deductible in each taxable year, determined by dividing the income received by the taxpayer from the asset in that year by the total amount of income that the taxpayer expects to receive from the asset over its useful life.

---

expense deduction of veterans not reduced by exempt payments received from Veterans Administration; IRC §265(1) not cited).

[136] Rev. Rul. 61-86, 1961-1 CB 41 (state income taxes allocable to exempt income other than interest); Rev. Rul. 62-9, 1962-1 CB 35 (legal fees to contest foreign tax on income exempt under tax convention, otherwise allowable under IRC §212(3)).

[137] Jones v. CIR, 25 TC 4 (1955), aff'd per curiam, 231 F.2d 655 (3d Cir. 1956).

[138] Treas. Regs. §1.265-1(c).

[139] Manufacturers Hanover Trust Co. v. CIR, 431 F.2d 664 (2d Cir. 1970).

[140] See supra ¶6.4.

The purpose of IRC §280 is to match the income and deductions from film-making and similar activities, which had been attractive tax shelters because all production expenses had previously been deducted in the early years of the asset's life.

SELECTED BIBLIOGRAPHY

Alvarez, The Deductibility of Reasonable Compensation in the Close Corporation, 11 Santa Clara L. Rev. 20 (1970).

Brawerman & Racine, Corporate Compensation: The Client's Compensation Is More Reasonable Than He Thinks, 1981 So. Calif. Tax. Inst. ¶1100.

Burns & Groomer, Effects of Section 183 on the Business/Hobby Controversy, 58 Taxes 195 (1980).

De Salvo, Final Regs. on Moving Expense Allowance: A Complex Area Clarified by New Rules, 38 J. Tax. 74 (1973).

Goff, Commingling Business and Personal Real Property: Severe Restrictions Under the 1976 Tax Reform Act, 13 Gonz. L. Rev. 493 (1978).

Griswold, New Light on "A Reasonable Allowance for Salaries," 59 Harv. L. Rev. 286 (1945).

Kaplan, Deduction for "Vacation Homes" Under the Tax Reform Act of 1976, 63 A.B.A.J. 1302 (1977).

Klein, The Deductibility of Transportation Expenses of a Combination Business and Pleasure Trip—A Conceptual Analysis, 18 Stan. L. Rev. 1099 (1966).

Knowles, The Tax Treatment of Entertainment Expenses Under §274: Results Reviewed and Revisions Recommended, 13 Harv. J. Legis. 845, 846–850 (1976).

Lang, When a House Is Not Entirely a Home: Deductions Under Internal Revenue Code §280A for Home Office, Vacation Homes, Etc., 1981 Utah L. Rev. 275 (1981).

Lee, A Blend of Old Wines in a New Wineskin: Section 183 and Beyond, 29 Tax L. Rev. 347 (1974).

Lee, Command Performance: The Tax Treatment of Employer Mandated Expenses, 7 U. Rich. L. Rev. 1, 29 et seq. (1972).

Milton, Logan & Tallant, The Travelling Taxpayer: A Rational Framework for His Deductions, 29 U. Fla. L. Rev. 119 (1976).

Mylan, Current Tax Treatment of Educational Costs, 32 U. Fla. L. Rev. 387 (1980).

Note, Daly v. Commissioner: Effect of the Tax Home Rule Under Section 162 on Two-Earner Families, 34 Tax Lawyer 829 (1981).

Postlewaite, Deductibility of Expenses for Conventions and Educational Seminars, 61 Minn. L. Rev. 253 (1977).

Ruffner, Deductibility of Entertainment Expenses, 60 A.B.A.J. 121 (1974).

Schoenfeld, The Educational Expense Deduction: The Need for a Rational Approach, 27 Villanova L. Rev. 237 (1982).

CHAPTER 10

Cost Recovery, Depreciation and Amortization

¶10.1 INTRODUCTORY

Section 167(a) authorizes taxpayers to deduct "a reasonable allowance for the exhaustion, wear and tear (including a reasonable allowance for obsolescence) of property used in the trade or business or held for the production of income." In *United States v. Ludey,* decided in 1927, the Supreme Court gave the following much-quoted explanation for the deduction:

> The depreciation charge permitted as a deduction from the gross income in determining the taxable income of a business for any year

> represents the reduction, during the year, of the capital assets through wear and tear of the plant used. The amount of the allowance for depreciation is the sum which should be set aside for the taxable year, in order that, at the end of the useful life of the plant in the business, the aggregate of the sums set aside will (with the salvage value) suffice to provide an amount equal to the original cost. The theory underlying this allowance for depreciation is that by using up the plant, a gradual sale is made of it.[1]

Until 1981, this theory, as reflected by IRC §167, governed the timing of deductions for the cost of most assets, both tangible and intangible, used in the taxpayer's trade or business or held for the production of income. For tangible property placed in service in a trade or business or for the production of income after December 31, 1980, however, the Economic Recovery Tax Act of 1981 instituted a new set of cost recovery rules departing dramatically from the basic principles of prior law. Under the Accelerated Cost Recovery System (ACRS) of IRC §168 the cost of tangible property placed in service in 1981 and thereafter is generally recovered over a period specified by statute for each of four broad classes of property.

Congress enacted ACRS to replace the old rules for depreciation because they were unnecessarily complicated and did not provide "the investment stimulus that is essential for economic expansion." [2] The preexisting depreciation rules, however, have not been entirely supplanted by ACRS. Depreciation under IRC §167 continues as the method for recovery of the cost of intangible property with a limited useful life (e.g., patents, contract rights, and franchises), since IRC §167(a) is concerned not only with physical wear and tear but also with the effect of exhaustion and obsolescence. Furthermore, because the tax benefits of ACRS are substantially greater than those allowed by prior law, IRC §168(e)(4) excludes from ACRS certain tangible property acquired by the taxpayer after 1980 in transfers involving related persons, nonrecognition transactions, and similar arrangements with a tax avoidance potential. These assets remain subject to depreciation under IRC §167, as do other tangible assets in certain limited circumstances. For these reasons, and because ACRS did not spring forth fully grown but is a child of depreciation, an understanding of depreciation under IRC §167 is a prerequisite to the study of ACRS.

The function of both depreciation under IRC §167 and accelerated cost recovery under IRC §168 is to permit the taxpayer to recover tax-free the cost

---

[1] US v. Ludey, 274 US 295, 300-301 (1927). In speaking of "capital assets," the Court used the term not in its technical tax sense (for which see infra ¶25.4), but rather as a synonym for business plant and equipment.

[2] S. Rep. No. 97-144, at 47 (1981).

(or other basis) of property exhausted in the process of generating business income. Thus, depreciation serves essentially the same function as the deduction for such business expenses as wages, rent, interest, and property taxes, except that the allowance is not deducted in a single year but is instead spread out over a number of years.

Neither depreciation nor cost recovery, however, reflects the asset's *actual* decline in value during any particular year; they are methods of cost allocation, not of valuation. Total depreciation is equal to the anticipated decline in an asset's value over the period of expected use, since the amount to be depreciated over the asset's useful life is the difference between its adjusted basis and its anticipated salvage value, but this amount, once determined, is allocated to the years of service by one of several allowable methods that do not purport to measure the actual decline in the asset's value from year to year. Depreciation deductions take into account neither fluctuations in value through market appreciation or depreciation, nor fluctuations in the cost of replacing the property.

Accumulated depreciation is not a reserve with which new machines can be purchased to replace worn-out equipment, because the amount that can be deducted is the old asset's *cost* (or other basis) less, in the case of depreciation (but not ACRS), its salvage value. Moreover, since the deduction is a bookkeeping entry rather than a bank deposit, it does not build up a replacement "fund." The deduction simply protects taxpayers against overstating their profits.

Finally, the theory of depreciation as an allowance matching the cost of business assets with the income generated by their use is more accurate when the entire useful life of the asset is taken into account than when the results of any particular year are examined in isolation, because neither ACRS nor depreciation deductions (except in rare instances) take into account income fluctuations during the life of the asset. Furthermore, under ACRS the cost of an asset may be charged entirely against the income realized during the early part of its useful life, and income realized thereafter is computed as though use of the asset in question were costless.

¶10.2 THE IMPORTANCE OF TIMING

The allowance of a deduction for depreciation or ACRS is an indispensable corollary of the basic tax principle forbidding taxpayers to deduct the cost of acquiring, rehabilitating, or improving a long-lived asset. Once capitalized, such an outlay can be recovered only by deductions over the asset's useful life (for assets subject to IRC §167) or its recovery period (for assets subject to IRC §168), as a loss on its abandonment, or as an offset against the proceeds in computing gain or loss on a sale or other disposition. Computed in the aggregate over the entire life of an enterprise, the taxpayer's income will be the same whether capital investments are deducted when made, depreciated over the asset's useful life, deducted over its recovery period, or deducted when the asset is disposed of. These alternative modes of accounting for the taxpayer's capital outlays will also produce the same year-to-year result if the enterprise reaches a level of complete equilibrium during a period of price stability by purchasing and retiring the same number of assets, with the same per-unit cost, every year. But during periods of expansion or contraction, expensing accelerates deductions more than does depreciation or cost recovery over the life of the asset and depreciation or cost recovery accelerates deductions more than does deducting the cost of the asset at retirement.

Prior to ACRS, taxpayers were almost always presented with a range of possibilities in computing depreciation, rather than a uniquely determined amount. There was some leeway in selecting both the asset's useful life and salvage value, as well as a variety of depreciation methods to choose from. Some of this leeway continues under ACRS. Offered a choice, taxpayers usually find it advantageous to depreciate assets as rapidly as possible because the resulting reduction in the current year's tax liability frees funds for business use. To be sure, large current deductions are offset over the long haul by smaller deductions in the future, which will mean that taxable income in later years will be correspondingly larger; but in the meantime, the taxpayer can enjoy the equivalent of a tax-free loan.

¶10.3 EFFECT OF DEPRECIATION AND ACRS ON BASIS

Section 167(g) provides that the basis for computing depreciation is the adjusted basis prescribed by IRC §1011 for the purpose of determining gain on the sale or other disposition of the property. In computing basis, the taxpayer ordinarily starts with the property's cost; but it may have to be adjusted upward or downward to reflect capitalized improvements, casualty losses, and other amounts chargeable to capital account. When the taxpayer depreciates the property, its basis must be reduced by the depreciation allowable, whether actually deducted or not. If an excessive amount of depreciation is deducted, the basis must also be reduced accordingly, unless the excess deduction was of no tax benefit. Thus, on a later sale or other disposition of the property, the taxpayer's gain or loss will reflect the amount of depreciation charged against the property's basis.

The basis for computing ACRS deductions is the unadjusted basis of the property, defined by IRC §168(d)(1) as the excess of the basis of the property used for computing gain—which is generally determined in the same manner as the basis for computing depreciation under IRC §167(g)—over the sum of the portion of the basis amortized under IRC §167(k)(relating to capital expenditures to rehabilitate low-income housing), the portion of the cost of the property that the taxpayer treated as a currently deductible expense under IRC

§179, and one half of the amount of the investment credit allowed with respect to the property. Just as with depreciation, the basis of the property is reduced by the deductions allowable under ACRS.

An additional adjustment to the basis of property qualifying for the investment credit is required by IRC §48(q), enacted in 1982. In general, the basis of the property must be reduced by 50 percent of the credit; but this requirement is subject to several exceptions, including an election to preserve the property's basis intact in return for a reduction of 2 percentage points in the credit.

¶10.4 DEPRECIABLE INTEREST

The person entitled to depreciation or ACRS deductions is ordinarily the owner of the property, whether it has been fully paid for or not.[3] This means the beneficial owner if title is vested in an agent or dummy as a matter of convenience. Conversely, mortgagees, vendors under conditional sales agreements, and others interested in property as security for a debt are not entitled to depreciation or ACRS deductions, even if they are indirectly adversely affected by wear and tear, exhaustion, and obsolescence of the property because the owner may fail to pay the debt at maturity.

In some circumstances, however, a person other than the owner is the one whose economic enjoyment of particular property is adversely affected by its deterioration or obsolescence. Thus, a taxpayer who installs equipment or pays for improvements on someone else's property is permitted to take depreciation or ACRS deductions, despite a lack of title, if the expenditure provides benefits to the taxpayer over an extended period and hence does not qualify for deduction in the year it is paid or incurred.[4]

Property held by a life tenant is depreciable or subject to ACRS deductions as though he were the absolute owner (i.e., over the property's useful life rather than over the tenant's expected life), and any unrecovered investment is depreciable by the remainderman when his interest falls in.[5] When depreciable or cost recovery property is held in trust, the allowable deduction is apportioned between the income beneficiaries and the trustee in accordance with the trust instrument; if the instrument does not apportion the allowance, it is allocated in proportion to the trust income. Depreciation and ACRS deductions allowable on property held by an estate are allocated, under IRC

---

[3] For the basis of property acquired subject to mortgages or other encumbrances, see infra ¶23.2.

[4] See D. Loveman & Son Export Corp. v. CIR, 34 TC 776, 806-807 (1960) (Acq.), aff'd per curiam, 296 F.2d 732 (6th Cir. 1961), cert. denied, 369 US 860 (1962) (cost of paving dead-end street leading to taxpayer's premises).

[5] IRC §167(h); Treas. Regs. §1.167(h)-1(a).

§167(h), among the estate, heirs, legatees, and devisees in proportion to their pro rata shares of the estate's income.

¶10.5 LEASED PROPERTY AND LEASEHOLDS

Lessors are entitled to depreciation or ACRS deductions for leased buildings, equipment, and other depreciable or cost recovery property over the asset's useful life or cost recovery period (regardless of the term of the lease) because, as owners, they bear the burdens of exhaustion, wear and tear, and obsolescence.[6] This general rule is subject to exceptions for such unusual situations as an agreement requiring the lessee to return property of equivalent value when the rental term ends [7] or if the purported lessor-owner is found, on the facts, to be the equivalent of a mortgagee.[8] If lessee-financed improvements constitute rent to the lessor (e.g., when the lessee is required to erect a building meeting prescribed standards, with an expected useful life in excess of the term of the lease), the lessor must include their value in gross income and hence acquires a basis in the improvements that qualifies for depreciation or ACRS allowances. If the improvements do not constitute rent, however, they are excluded from the lessor's gross income by IRC §109, even when the lease terminates. Since the lessor acquires no basis in the improvements, he cannot depreciate them.

Lessee-financed improvements can be written off by the lessee, even though ownership vests in the lessor on construction or installation, since the value of the lessee's investment is reduced by physical deterioration and obsolescence and ends when the lease terminates.[9] The regulations provide that the lessee's investment is recoverable through allowances for depreciation over the useful life of the improvements, if that is equal to or shorter than the remaining life of the lease, and through ratable deductions "in lieu of allowances for depreciation" otherwise.[10] For lessee improvements made in 1981 and thereafter, the lessee recovers the investment under ACRS if the recovery period (usually fifteen years) is less than the remaining term of the lease;

---

[6] Treas. Regs. §1.167(a)-4 (last sentence).

[7] See Royal St. Louis, Inc. v. US, 578 F.2d 1017 (5th Cir. 1978) (lessee of hotel furniture obligated to return furniture of same or better quality and age composition; held, lessor suffered no depreciation).

[8] See Helvering v. F. & R. Lazarus & Co., 308 US 252 (1939) (seller-lessee under ninety-nine-year leaseback allowed depreciation since transaction was in reality a financing device, not a sale; right to depreciate does not necessarily follow legal title but flows to person bearing "the burden of exhaustion of [the] capital investment").

[9] Treas. Regs. §1.167(a)-4.

[10] Id. Note that an appropriate part of the cost of the leasehold itself is deductible each year of the term of the lease. Treas. Regs. §1.162-11(a).

otherwise, the lessee's investment is recovered by equal annual deductions over the remaining term of the lease.[11]

Section 178(a) requires renewal periods to be included in the term of a lease if the remaining life of the lease on completion of the improvement is less than 60 percent of its useful life. When the lessor and lessee are related, IRC §178(b) treats the lease as having a term equal to at least the useful life of the improvement, even if not subject to a renewal option. In other cases, IRC §178(c) permits renewal periods to be disregarded unless the lease has been, or the facts show with reasonable certainty that it will be, renewed.

Section 168(f)(8) provides special rules to allocate ACRS deductions to the "owner-lessor" in certain transactions that have both "sale" and "lease" elements or are sophisticated financing transactions in which the nominal lessee bears more of the burdens of ownership. One set of rules, the so-called safe-harbor leasing rules, apply for transactions entered into after December 31, 1980 and before January 1, 1984. Another set of rules applies to so-called lease finance transactions entered into after December 31, 1983. Both rules are subject to numerous technical qualifications and limitations.

¶10.6 ELIGIBLE PROPERTY

1. Property Used in Business or Held for Production of Income. Section 167(a) restricts depreciation and ACRS deductions to (1) "property used in the trade or business" and (2) "property held for the production of income." The first category embraces the overwhelming bulk of depreciable assets—plant, machinery, and equipment used in business—along with most rental property. The primary reason for including the second category of depreciable property—"property held for the production of income"—is to permit investors to depreciate rental property entailing so little management or maintenance activity that it does not constitute property held in a trade or business, such as property leased under a net ("carefree") lease or a single-family residence temporarily rented by the taxpayer.[12]

Section 168 limits ACRS deductions to "recovery property," defined by IRC §168(c)(1) as tangible property of a character used in a trade or business or held for the production of income and subject to the depreciation allowance. This broad definition is qualified by (1) IRC §168(e)(1), which excludes property placed in service by the taxpayer before 1981; (2) IRC §168(e)(2), permitting the taxpayer to elect to depreciate qualifying property under the unit-of-production method or any other method not expressed in a term of years; and

[11] IRC §168(f)(6).

[12] See supra ¶8.5.

(3) IRC §168(e)(3), excluding certain property acquired by the taxpayer after 1980 in transfers involving related persons, nonrecognition transactions, and similar arrangements with a tax avoidance potential. Since the ACRS rules apply only to deductions allowed by IRC §167(a), they do not encompass property that is subject to amortization rather than depreciation, such as a lessee's outlay for leasehold improvements with a longer useful life than the lease or pollution control facilities subject to IRC §169. For "recovery property" as defined by IRC §168(c)(1), however, the rules of IRC §168 are exclusive, and the investment must be recovered through ACRS rather than by the depreciation methods described in IRC §167(b).

A business taxpayer's stock in trade, being held for sale, did not qualify for depreciation prior to 1981 and, accordingly, does not qualify for ACRS deductions.[13] Depreciation and ACRS deductions are also denied to equipment used by the taxpayer to construct long-lived property; in effect, the cost of using the construction equipment becomes part of the cost of the new structure, to be written off over the structure's useful life or recovery period.[14]

Depreciation and ACRS deductions are not allowed for property devoted to personal use, such as the taxpayer's residence or family car. If property originally serving a personal use is converted to a business use, the amount eligible for ACRS is the asset's unadjusted basis (as defined in IRC §168(a)(1)) or fair market value at the date of conversion, whichever is lower.[15] In the common situation of a personal residence vacated by the taxpayer and placed on the rental market, the requisite conversion occurs when the property is listed for rental, even though some time elapses before a tenant is found.[16] If a personal residence is listed for sale rather than rental, however, depreciation or ACRS is not allowable in the absence of a showing, which can seldom be made, that the taxpayer anticipated a post-conversion profit.[17]

[13] See Rev. Rul. 75-538, 1975-2 CB 34 (automobile dealer presumed to hold all cars, including company cars and demonstrators, for sale; presumption overcome only by clear showing "that the dealer looks to consumption through use of the vehicle in the ordinary course of business operation" to recover its cost); compare Nash v. CIR, 60 TC 503, 519 (1973) (Acq.) (taxpayer, engaged in building and selling apartment houses, held particular building for investment and may depreciate it).

[14] CIR v. Idaho Power Co., 418 US 1 (1974).

[15] See Treas. Regs. §§1.167(g)-1 (depreciation on pre-1981 conversion), 1.165-9(b) (basis for determining loss on sale of converted property).

[16] Robinson v. CIR, 2 TC 305 (1943) (Acq.); Odom v. CIR, ¶79,053 P-H Memo TC (1979) (property occupied rent-free by tenant not held for production of income).

[17] Newcombe v. CIR, 54 TC 1298 (1970) (property offered for sale not "held for production of income" in absence of anticipated increase in value after listing; earlier cases summarized); Riss v. CIR, 56 TC 388, 415 (1971), aff'd on other issues, 478 F.2d 1160 (8th Cir. 1973) (same principle applied to corporate property formerly held for shareholder's use); May v. CIR, 299 F.2d 725, 728 (4th Cir. 1962) (abandonment of

Property is often devoted to both personal and business or income-producing purposes, either simultaneously (e.g., a physician's personal residence with a wing used exclusively to receive patients) or successively (e.g., a salesman's car used to call on customers, as well as for family transportation). The business portion of such dual-purpose property qualifies for ACRS deductions, the amount allocable thereto being ordinarily estimated on a mileage, square-footage, or other reasonable basis.[18] Sporadic uses of a residence or other personal property for business activities, such as entertaining customers or typing business reports, however, do not give rise to depreciation or ACRS deductions for the space temporarily devoted to these uses, even if the business connection is clear enough to permit the taxpayer's out-of-pocket expenses to be deducted.

2. Home Offices, Vacation Homes, and Property Used in Hobby and Entertainment Facilities. Depreciation and ACRS deductions under IRC §§167 and 168 are subject to the special statutory limitations, discussed elsewhere in this work,[19] applicable to (1) dwelling units used for both profit-oriented and personal activities (including rental), (2) property used in activities not engaged in for profit, and (3) facilities used for entertainment, amusement, or recreation.

3. Commencement and Termination of Business Use of Depreciable and Cost Recovery Property. Under the rules applicable to all depreciable property placed in service prior to 1981 and still applicable to property not eligible for ACRS, assets can be depreciated from the time when they are "placed in service" until they are "retired from service." [20] Non-ACRS assets are considered as "placed in service" when acquired and available for business use, even though testing is required or actual use is delayed,[21] and the asset may be

---

personal use did not convert palatial yacht's status "from fun-making to money-making").

[18] In the case of a dual-purpose automobile, the taxpayer may deduct a specified amount per mile in lieu of itemizing expenses. See Taylor v. CIR, ¶80,376 P-H Memo TC (1980) (mileage allowances provide method of computing *dollar amount* of automobile expenses, but time, place, and business purpose must also be established).

[19] See supra ¶¶9.11, 9.13, and 9.3 respectively.

[20] Treas. Regs. §1.167(a)-10(b).

[21] See Sears Oil Co. v. CIR, 359 F.2d 191 (2d Cir. 1966) (barge ready for service in 1957 but not put to actual use until spring of 1958 due to ice in canal; depreciation for proportionate part of 1957 allowed); Rev. Rul. 79-98, 1979-1 CB 103 (utility plant placed in service when operational, although subsequently tested and not accepted from contractor until later date). For elective use of a half-year convention, based on the assumption that all additions and retirements occur in the middle of the taxable year, see Treas. Regs. §1.167(a)-10(b); Rev. Rul. 73-202, 1973-1 CB 81 (averaging conven-

depreciated until retired, sold, or abandoned, despite interruptions in actual use as a result of business exigencies.

Under ACRS, assets classified as three-year property, five-year property, ten-year property, or fifteen-year public utility property are treated as placed in service at mid-year of the year in which they are actually placed in service, even if the taxpayer elects one of the alternate rates or periods for recovery. Under IRC §168(d)(2)(B), however, no ACRS deduction is permitted with respect to any such recovery property in the year of sale, other disposition, or retirement from service. ACRS deductions on improvements to real property, which constitute fifteen-year recovery period property, on the other hand, are computed under IRC §168(b)(2) from the month the property is placed in service until the month of sale or retirement from service. The deductions in the initial and final years are equal to the deductions allowable if the property had been in service for the entire year multiplied by a fraction, the numerator of which is the number of months the asset was in service during the year and the denominator of which is 12. Unlike other property subject to ACRS, fifteen-year property may generate a deduction under IRC §168(a) in the year of disposition.

4. Wasting Investment Requirement. Property cannot be depreciated unless the taxpayer's investment will be partly or wholly destroyed by exhaustion, wear and tear, or obsolescence. Thus, the taxpayer cannot depreciate property whose basis has been reduced to zero by prior depreciation or ACRS deductions, or the cost of which was properly expensed, such as mailing lists, contract rights, industrial know-how, and similar property entailing no capitalized outlay. Depreciation and ACRS deductions are also denied to assets that are not adversely affected by the passage of time or by use in the taxpayer's business, such as works of art, antiques, and raw land,[22] since their value on retirement from use is likely to equal or exceed the taxpayer's original cost or other basis.

5. Real Property. The regulations provide that "land apart from the improvements or physical development added to it" does not qualify for depreciation deductions,[23] and the IRS has ruled that agricultural land cannot be depreciated even if there is evidence that it will subside and be abandoned within a foreseeable period because of an anticipated drop in the water

---

tion unavailable for large and unusual purchases, which must be depreciated separately).

[22] See Rev. Rul. 68-232, 1968-1 CB 79 (works of art generally not depreciable); Gudmundsson v. CIR, ¶78,299 P-H Memo TC (1978) (no evidence of probable remaining useful life of antique furniture).

[23] Treas. Regs. §1.167(a)-2.

table.[24] The severe view adopted by the regulations avoids troublesome disputes regarding the impact of traffic patterns, demographic changes, and other socioeconomic factors on the useful economic life of urban land and can be defended as a reasonable administrative interpretation of the statutory language. It is more dubious, however, as applied to land whose physical characteristics will be changed in the reasonably foreseeable future by erosion, loss of underground water, or similar causes.[25]

Man-made improvements to land qualified for depreciation prior to 1981 and qualify for ACRS deductions after 1980,[26] but if the improvement is not a building or other structure but a change in the physical nature of the land (effected, for example, by planting, excavating, or grading the property), its status under ACRS is problematical because the taxpayer would have encountered difficulties in establishing its useful life under IRC §167. This burden should be sustained by demonstrating that the improvement is subject to physical deterioration over a reasonably foreseeable period (e.g., a dam or canal), is so closely associated with a particular building that it lacks an independent value (e.g., an access road to a lumber camp that will be abandoned when an existing stand of timber is harvested), or will be destroyed when a building is replaced (e.g., trees and shrubbery immediately adjacent to an apartment building).[27] If so, the improvements should be classified as fifteen-year property. Expenditures to clear and grade a building site that will continue to be useful when the existing building is replaced, however, are no more subject to depreciation or ACRS than the cost of the raw land itself.[28]

Under special provisions applicable to farmers and railroads, a miscellany of expenditures for man-made improvements to land may either be deducted when made or amortized over a specified period of time. These provisions

---

[24] Rev. Rul. 55-730, 1955-2 CB 53.

[25] See Sexton v. CIR, 42 TC 1094 (1964) (taxpayer engaged in rubbish removal entitled to depreciate difference between cost of land with large pits and estimated lower value of land when filled in).

[26] When improved real estate is purchased for a lump sum, the purchase price must be allocated between the nondepreciable land and the depreciable improvements. See Treas. Regs. §1.167(a)-5.

[27] See Rev. Rul. 74-265, 1974-1 CB 56 (cost of shrubbery and trees immediately adjacent to garden apartments can be depreciated because they will be destroyed on replacement of building; contra for cost of clearing, grading, adding topsoil to the site, and planting around perimeter); Trailmont Park, Inc. v. CIR, ¶71,212 P-H Memo TC (1971) (grading and landscaping mobile-home park held depreciable over same period as pads, patios, and similar improvements, on evidence that any other business use would require reshaping land); Rudolph Inv. Corp. v. CIR, ¶72,129 P-H Memo TC (1972) (earthen water tanks and dams on ranch found to have useful life of ten years); Rev. Rul. 72-96, 1972-1 CB 66 (cost of building reservoir and dam depreciable over life of related generating facilities).

[28] Rev. Rul. 74-265, supra note 27.

include IRC §§175 (soil and water conservation expenditures), 180 (fertilizer, etc.), 182 (cost of clearing land for farming), and 185 (railroad grading and tunnel bores).

6. Intangible Property. In authorizing a deduction for exhaustion, wear and tear, and obsolescence, IRC §167(a) does not distinguish between tangible and intangible assets, but IRC §168(c)(1) limits ACRS to "tangible property." As a result, intangible assets used in a business remain subject to depreciation under IRC §167 even if first placed in service after 1980, provided their useful life is limited and can be estimated with reasonable accuracy. Intangibles are immune to physical forces, however, and unless limited in duration by statute or contract or so closely linked to a physical asset as to be rendered worthless by its retirement from service,[29] they are unaffected by the mere passage of time. The taxpayer must therefore establish that public taste or similar socio-economic forces—which are less susceptible to proof than physical forces—will cause the intangible to be retired from service and, what is even more difficult, establish a reasonable date for this event.

Intangible assets whose legal life is limited by statute (e.g., patents and copyrights) or contract (e.g., contracts not to compete, leaseholds, and life estates) constitute major exceptions to these generalizations.[30] The legal life of such an asset establishes an outer limit on its useful life, but this does not preclude proof of a shorter useful life, attibutable to foreseeable economic forces that will result in its earlier retirement. An intangible's limited legal life is an inappropriate measure of its useful life, however, if it can be renewed repeatedly at the taxpayer's option or if experience indicates that renewal applications will be granted more or less as a matter of course. In *Nachman v. CIR,* for example, a taxpayer who paid $8,000 for a one-year city liquor license that had cost the original licensee $750 was denied the right to depreciate the premium because new licenses were not available and an existing license "carried with it by established custom, if not by law, a valuable renewal privilege." [31] On the other hand, the IRS has ruled that renewable one-year professional football player contracts can be depreciated over their useful lives, which presupposes acceptance by the IRS of a method of estimating their

[29] See Panhandle E. Pipe Line Co. v. US, 408 F.2d 690 (Ct. Cl. 1969) (easements depreciable over useful life of related pipeline).

[30] See Treas. Regs. §1.167(a)-3 (patents and copyrights); Bell v. Harrison, 212 F.2d 253 (7th Cir. 1954) (purchased life estate); Treas. Regs. §1.162-11(a) (payment for leasehold); Rev. Rul. 68-636, 1968-2 CB 92 (covenant not to compete).

[31] Nachman v. CIR, 191 F.2d 934, 935 (5th Cir. 1951); see also Richmond Television Corp. v. US, 354 F.2d 410 (4th Cir. 1965) (costs incurred in anticipation of FCC license not depreciable, despite three-year legal life, because of high probability of renewal on request by licensee); but see Chronicle Publishing Co. v. CIR, 67 TC 964 (1977) (Nonacq.) (cable TV franchises depreciable despite potential renewal).

duration notwithstanding the many variables that enter into the annual renegotiation process.[32]

It is virtually impossible to establish a limited useful life for goodwill, and the regulations elevate this difficulty to the level of a rule of law by stating flatly that "no deduction for depreciation is allowable with respect to goodwill." [33] The uncertain scope of the term "goodwill" as used in the regulations clouds the right to depreciate lists of customers and other records, acquired when a going business is purchased even if the taxpayer can show that part of the purchase price is properly allocable to intangibles of this type.

If the price paid to acquire an enterprise exceeds the value of its physical assets, it is clear that an appropriate portion of the excess may be allocated to patents, copyrights, leaseholds, covenants not to compete, and similar identifiable assets that can be separated from the newly acquired goodwill. Although the IRS had long rejected attempts to depreciate lists of customers' subscription lists, patients' records, and similar materials, which it regarded as the documentary evidence of goodwill, this position was rejected by the Court of Appeals for the Fifth Circuit in *Houston Chronicle Publishing Co. v. United States.* [34] The court held that such intangibles could be depreciated if the taxpayer proved that the intangible involved had "an ascertainable value separate and distinct from goodwill" and had "a limited useful life, the duration of which can be ascertained with reasonable accuracy." Presumably, the "limited useful life" standard can be met by showing that the old customers will be lost within a predictable period of time, even though the taxpayer succeeds in getting new customers to replace them.

Following *Houston Chronicle Publishing Co.,* the IRS modified its earlier posture by ruling that customer and subscription lists, location contracts, insurance expirations, and so forth, can be depreciated if the taxpayer can satisfy the standards set out in that decision, but went on to announce that "generally" these assets "are in the nature of goodwill." [35] The courts, however, have been applying more liberal principles, allowing taxpayers to depreciate customer lists, business records, and similar intangibles if a limited useful life can be plausibly established.[36]

---

[32] Rev. Rul. 71-137, 1971-1 CB 104; see also Laird v. US, 556 F.2d 1224 (5th Cir. 1977), cert. denied, 434 US 1014 (1978) (useful life of 5.25 years held reasonable for particular team).

[33] Treas. Regs. §1.167(a)-3.

[34] Houston Chronicle Publishing Co. v. US, 481 F.2d 1240, 1250 (5th Cir. 1973), cert. denied, 414 US 1129 (1974).

[35] Rev. Rul. 74-456, 1974-2 CB 65.

[36] See Richard S. Miller & Sons v. US, 537 F.2d 446 (Ct. Cl. 1976) (insurance expirations separable from goodwill; limited useful life established); Los Angeles Cent. Animal Hosp., Inc. v. CIR, 68 TC 269 (1977) (Acq.) (medical records of veterinary hospital distinguished from goodwill embodied in location, trade name, and continued patronage of neighborhood customers; amount allocable to records, depreciable over

When property is acquired for a lump sum, the buyer must allocate the purchase price among the acquired assets in proportion to their respective market values in order to compute depreciation and ACRS deductions and gain or loss on subsequent sales and other dispositions. Because market quotations are rarely available, especially for the components of a going business, controversy with the IRS regarding the validity of the taxpayer's allocation is almost inevitable. Although a lump-sum payment must be allocated whether the acquired assets are tangible or intangible, the problem arises more frequently when intangibles are involved for two reasons. First, intangibles created by the taxpayer's own activities usually have an adjusted basis of zero because the asset came into being without a direct outlay of funds or as a result of deductible expenditures. Thus, there is ordinarily no basis to be depreciated unless the asset was purchased, usually as a component part of a going business, the cost being a debatable portion of a lump-sum purchase price. Second, intangibles like customer lists are similar to goodwill, which is not subject to depreciation, so that the allocation of a large amount to intangibles often stimulates the IRS to contend that most, if not all, of the amount so allocated represents the nondepreciable cost of goodwill.

Franchises, trademarks and trade names are accorded treatment different from other intangibles. Section 1253 generally denies capital gains treatment to amounts received on the transfer of these assets and, as a corollary of this adverse treatment of the transferor, the transferee can deduct periodic payments for the transferred item and can amortize lump-sum payments over a period of years.

¶10.7 USEFUL LIVES (DEPRECIABLE PROPERTY) AND RECOVERY PERIODS (ACRS)

1. Introductory. Section 167 contains several references to "the useful life" of depreciable property, but does not define this term. To fill the statutory gap, the regulations prescribe a "facts and circumstances" test under which the useful life is not the physical life of the asset, but the period it may reasonably be expected to be useful to the taxpayer, determined by the tax-

---

seven-year period); Computing & Software, Inc. v. CIR, 64 TC 223 (1975) (Acq.) (credit information files separable from goodwill since they had no relationship to preexisting business relationships and same information was sold to both old and new customers; six-year useful life); but see General Television, Inc. v. US, 449 F.Supp. 609, 612 (D.Minn. 1978), aff'd, 598 F.2d 1148 (8th Cir. 1979) (subscriber contracts of purchased cable TV companies constituted "customer structures which included the expectancy of continued patronage," not distinguishable from goodwill); Miami Valley Broadcasting Corp. v. US, 499 F.2d 677, 680 (Ct. Cl. 1974) ("going concern" value nondepreciable; indefinite duration).

payer's own experience or, if this is inadequate, the industry-wide experience. Among the factors to be considered are physical wear, tear and decay, the taxpayer's policy as to repairs, and economic obsolescence due to normal progress of technology and economic changes within the industry.[37]

The facts and circumstances standard, however, is not applicable to most tangible depreciable assets placed in service after 1980, which are instead subject to ACRS under IRC §168, requiring taxpayers to recover the cost of the asset over one of four designated recovery periods to which the asset is assigned by statutory standards, or one of the optional recovery periods available at the election of the taxpayer.

The useful life of intangibles continues to be determined under the facts and circumstances test, and the same is true of property depreciated under a system not expressed in terms of years, such as the unit-of-production method. When the facts and circumstances test is applicable, it is subject to modification under IRC §167(d), providing that an agreement between the taxpayer and the IRS shall be binding in the absence of facts or circumstances not taken into account in adopting the agreement.

2. Standardized Useful Lives. In 1942 and 1962, the IRS issued tables of estimated or "guideline" useful lives for tangible depreciable assets, which were replaced in 1971 by the asset depreciation range (ADR) system.[38] ADR was, in turn, repealed by the Economic Recovery Tax Act of 1981 for assets placed in service after 1980, which made ACRS under IRC §168 mandatory for almost all tangible assets. The normal recovery periods for ACRS assets, however, are based primarily on the class life to which such an asset would have been assigned under ADR, except that improvements to real property are assigned a fifteen-year recovery period. Both ACRS and ADR were spawned partly by administrative difficulties in determining useful lives under the facts and circumstances standard.

3. Changes in Useful Life and Assignment of Erroneous Recovery Period. For assets placed in service prior to 1980, if an erroneous useful life was originally assigned to an asset, the impact of a correction on the depreciation allowance for later years depended on whether the original estimate was too long or too short. If it was too long, the depreciation actually taken was less than the amount allowable; but the basis of the property was reduced by the full amount allowable, even if the earlier years were barred by the statute of limitations.[39] If the original life was too short, the taxpayer's basis was reduced

[37] Treas. Regs. §1.167(a)-1(b); 1.167(a)-9; see also Massey Motors, Inc. v. US, 364 US 92 (1960).

[38] See Rev. Proc. 72-10, 1972-1 CB 721.

[39] IRC §1016(a)(2).

by the deductions taken except to the extent that the excess over the proper amount was of no tax benefit.[40] The corrected rate of depreciation was then applied prospectively to the adjusted basis. These rules continue to apply to depreciable property excluded from ACRS, and should also govern ACRS recovery property to which an erroneous recovery period was assigned. The recovery period of assets placed in service after 1980 and subject to ACRS is not otherwise subject to change.

If the useful life of non-ACRS property was correctly estimated when the property was placed in service but is altered by subsequent events, the regulations permit a corresponding change for tax purposes, but "only when the change in the useful life is significant and there is a clear and convincing basis for the redetermination."[41]

4. Obsolescence. Obsolescence due to technological improvements, governmental action, and other factors may shorten the life of depreciable assets more than physical deterioration. If anticipated when property not subject to ACRS is placed in service, these factors are built into the initial depreciation rate.[42] If, however, obsolescence is more rapid than originally anticipated, the asset's useful life can be reduced to reflect the altered circumstances, provided the taxpayer proves that the asset will be retired sooner than expected.[43]

Anticipated obsolescence prior to the end of the physical life of an asset is not a factor, however, in determining an asset's recovery period under ACRS, although in extreme cases, unforeseen extraordinary obsolescence may bring the asset's useful life to an abrupt end during its recovery period. If the asset is abandoned or permanently withdrawn from service and consigned to the scrap heap, the rules governing losses on retirement are applicable,[44] even for ACRS assets.

5. Salvage Value. Section 167 permits taxpayers to deduct during a depreciable asset's useful life the difference between its cost (or other basis) and its "salvage value," the estimated amount for which it can be disposed of on retirement from service. Because ACRS deductions under IRC §168 are based on the unadjusted basis of recovery property, the need to take salvage value

[40] Id.

[41] Treas. Regs. §1.167(a)-1(b); see also Treas. Regs. §1.167(a)-9.

[42] Treas. Regs. §1.167(a)-9.

[43] See Zimmerman v. CIR, 67 TC 94 (1976) (construction of interstate highway, resulting in drastic change in traffic patterns; shorter life established for one motel but not for two others).

[44] Tanforna Co. v. US, 313 F.Supp. 796 (N.D.Cal. 1970), aff'd per curiam, 462 F.2d 605 (9th Cir. 1971) (racetrack became useless as a result of legislation and public pressure).

into account is eliminated by IRC §168(f)(9) for recovery property placed in service after 1980.

To the extent that salvage value remains relevant, it ordinarily is subtracted from the basis of the asset in fixing the amount to be depreciated; but intangible assets, which are the primary exception to ACRS, rarely have any salvage value to be considered.

¶10.8 DEPRECIATION METHODS AND RATES

1. Introductory. From 1913 to 1954, the federal revenue acts failed to describe any specific depreciation methods, and the regulations long provided that the proper allowance must reflect a reasonably consistent plan, but not necessarily a uniform rate.[45] During the formative years of the tax laws, the straight-line method of computing depreciation was almost universally used, except by public utilities, railroads, investors in rental real estate, and taxpayers in a few other industries. The straight-line method's popularity was due in large part to its simplicity: The asset's cost (or other basis), less the estimated salvage value (if any), is divided by its estimated useful life in years, and the resulting amount is the annual deduction. For example, if an asset costs $10,000, has an estimated salvage value of $2,000, and is expected to last for ten years, the annual deduction is $800 (i.e. $8,000/10). Expressed as a rate of depreciation, the annual deduction is 10 percent of the amount to be depreciated.

In 1954 Congress enacted IRC §167(b), which explicitly endorsed use of the straight-line method and two accelerated depreciation methods—the declining-balance and sum-of-the-years'-digits methods. The latter methods were particularly attractive to tax-conscious businessmen because they yield larger deductions in the early years of an asset's useful life than does the straight-line method. Section 167(b) also authorizes use of "any other consistent method" producing annual allowances that are consonant with the double declining-balance method, but this has been of minor importance.

Because Congress believed that the existing rules for depreciation did not provide sufficient investment stimulus for the national economy, the 1981 statutory schedules prescribing ACRS deductions on a year-by-year basis reflect the use of various methods of accelerated depreciation as the norm. Straight-line cost recovery is still available, however, at the election of the taxpayer.

Thus, the existing statutory framework comprises five components:

---

[45] Treas. Regs. §1.167(a)-1(a), which is identical in this respect with Treas. Regs. 111, §19.23(1)-1(1949).

1. The "normal" accelerated cost recovery for all tangible property placed in service after 1980 under IRC §168(b).
2. Optional straight-line cost recovery for tangible property placed in service after 1980.
3. The statutory endorsement by IRC §167(b)(1) of straight-line depreciation for all types of property excluded from ACRS.
4. The statutory endorsement by IRC §§167(b)(2), 167(b)(3), and 167(b)(4) of the double declining-balance, sum-of-the-years'-digits, and similar accelerated methods for property excluded from ACRS and described by IRC §167(c).
5. A residual right to use any other method for property excluded from ACRS, provided it produces a "reasonable allowance" within the meaning of IRC §167(a).

For the future, most property will be subject to the first two rules. Intangibles are generally governed by the third rule. The fourth rule will generally be applicable only to property placed in service before 1981, although it is essentially embodied in ACRS. The fifth rule will be applicable to tangible property depreciated under a method expressed in terms other than years, such as the unit-of-production method.

2. Straight-Line Depreciation. Unlike the other methods of depreciation listed in IRC §167(b), a variant of straight-line depreciation is allowable for tangible property placed in service after 1980. Under IRC §168(b)(3), the taxpayer may elect to recover the cost of recovery property (without any reduction for salvage value) under the straight-line method over the normal recovery period or any one of the specified optional recovery periods.

3. Double Declining-Balance, Sum-of-the-Years'-Digits, and Other Methods. As a result of the enactment of IRC §168 in 1981, the declining-balance and sum-of-the-years'-digits methods are not directly available for property placed in service after 1980, but normal cost recovery under ACRS incorporates them into the statutory tables.

1. *The declining-balance method.* Under the declining-balance method, the depreciation deduction is determined by multiplying the asset's adjusted basis at the beginning of the taxable year by a uniform rate, ordinarily expressed as a percentage (e.g., 125, 150, or 200 percent) of the straight-line rate. When applied, for example, to an asset with a cost of $10,000 and an estimated useful life of ten years (resulting in a straight-line rate of 10 percent), the double declining-balance method (i.e., 200 percent of the straight-line rate) produces a deduction in the first year of $2,000 (10% × 2 × $10,000). In the second year, the same rate (20 percent) is applied to the asset's then adjusted basis of $8,000, producing a deduction of $1,600. The label "declining balance"

refers to the fact that the asset's adjusted basis, to which the uniform rate is applied, declines from year to year.

The asset's salvage value does not enter directly into the computation of the depreciation deduction when a declining-balance method is used, but it operates as a floor below which the asset cannot be depreciated.[46] If the deduction otherwise computed under the declining-balance method would reduce the asset's remaining basis below its salvage value, the allowable deduction is limited to the amount of basis remaining in excess of salvage value.

Because the deduction produced by the declining-balance method is a percentage (never more than 66.7 percent and usually much less) [47] of the asset's adjusted basis at the beginning of each taxable year, the taxpayer's unrecovered investment at the end of the useful life of the asset may exceed its salvage value. To remedy this deficiency, IRC §167(e)(1) permits taxpayers using declining-balance depreciation pursuant to IRC §167(b)(2) to switch to the straight-line method. On making the change, the taxpayer spreads the asset's unrecovered cost or other basis, less its salvage value, over its estimated remaining useful life.[48]

2. *Sum-of-the-years'-digits method.* The sum-of-the-years'-digits method authorized by IRC §167(b)(3) resembles the declining-balance method in producing larger deductions in the early year of an asset's useful life than the straight-line method. Unlike the declining-balance method, however, it takes salvage value into account at the outset and, hence does not leave an unrecovered "tail" at the end of the asset's estimated useful life. The annual allowance is a constantly declining fraction of the asset's original cost (or other basis) less its salvage value, the numerator of the fraction being the number of remaining years in the asset's useful life and the denominator being the sum of the numbers making up its useful life (the "years' digits").

4. Pre-1981 Property Eligible for Accelerated Depreciation. The accelerated depreciation methods authorized by IRC §§167(b)(2), 167(b)(3), and 167(b)(4) can be used for pre-1981 property that meets two sets of statutory conditions.

1. *The restrictions of IRC § 167(c).* Section 167(c) limits the use of these methods to depreciable assets with a useful life of three years or more constructed or acquired by the taxpayer and first used by him after December 31,

---

[46] Treas. Regs. §1.167(a)-1(a) (third sentence).

[47] For an asset with an estimated useful life of three years (the minimum eligible under IRC §167(c) for the double declining-balance method), the straight-line rate is 33.3 percent and the double declining-balance rate is 66.7 percent.

[48] Treas. Regs. §1.167(e)-1(b).

1953.[49] Accelerated depreciation was limited to new assets to stimulate increased investment and because Congress believed that new assets, in fact, lost value more quickly than used assets in the early years of use. Used tangible personal property, however, was eligible for 150 percent declining-balance depreciation under IRS rulings because this was considered reasonable prior to the enactment of IRC §167(b).[50]

2. *The restrictions of IRC § 167(j) on Section 1250 property.* Section 167(j) further restricted the use of accelerated depreciation for "section 1250 property," a term that included almost all depreciable real property. Section 1250 property was classified into five categories, reflecting a diversity of legislative judgments about the propriety of tax incentives for the real estate activity in question. In order of the most favored to least favored, the categories were (a) new residential rental property, (b) property constructed (or under construction) before July 25, 1969, (c) new nonresidential property acquired after July 24, 1969, (d) certain used residential property acquired after July 24, 1969, and (e) used nonresidential property acquired after July 24, 1969.

5. Nonstatutory Methods. Section 167(b) permits the taxpayer to use a nonstatutory method of depreciation if it produces a "reasonable allowance" and, if the property was placed in service after 1980, IRC §168 is inapplicable. Because IRC §168(e)(2) permits taxpayer depreciating property under a unit of production method or any other method not expressed in a term of years to elect out of ACRS, some of these nonstatutory methods may be used for property placed in service after 1980.

The principal nonstatutory methods may be classified as follows:

1. *Depreciation based on production or use.* Under the unit-of-production method, the cost or other basis of the depreciable asset, less estimated salvage value, is divided by the number of units expected to be produced during its useful life; and the resulting unit cost is multipled by the actual production in each taxable year to yield that year's deduction. This method matches depreciation to actual operations, increasing or decreasing the deduction to take account of variations in the asset's use, and is especially suitable for transportation equipment whose life can be estimated in terms of miles and for extractive industries, where the volume of ore, timber, or other material processed by equipment may be a more important determinant of useful life than the mere passage of time.[51]

The so-called operating-day and machine-hour methods similarly spread

---

[49] See Treas. Regs. §§1.167(c)-1(a), 1.167(c)-1(a)(2).

[50] Treas. Regs. §1.167(b)-0(b).

[51] Treas. Regs. §1.167(b)-0(b); Treas. Regs. §§1.611-5(a), 1.611-5(b)(2) (use of unit-of-production method in extractive industries).

the cost of the depreciable asset, less its estimated salvage value, over its estimated productive life, computed in days or hours, based on the asset's actual use in the taxable year.

2. *Depreciation based on completed contracts.* Taxpayers using the completed-contract method in computing income from long-term construction and similar contracts do not depreciate the property used in performing the contract in annual installments, but instead deduct in the year of completion the difference between the asset's cost or other basis and its salvage value at that time.[52]

3. *Depreciation based on predicted income.* Motion-picture and TV films may be depreciated by an "income forecast" method.[53] The deduction in any given year is computed by multiplying the total production costs by a fraction, of which the numerator is that year's income and the denominator is the anticipated total income during the useful life of the film. The acceptability of this method resulted from evidence that the useful life of films is dependent not on the mere passage of time but on the income they produce.

¶10.9 ACCELERATED COST RECOVERY SYSTEM (ACRS)

Tangible property placed in service in 1981 and thereafter, subject to a few exceptions, is not eligible for the depreciation methods endorsed by IRC §167(b). Section 167(a) provides that "[i]n the case of recovery property . . ., the deduction allowable under section 168 shall be deemed to constitute the reasonable allowance provided by this section. . . ." The methods of computing deductions under the accelerated cost recovery system of IRC §168 are not revolutionary, since they employ the straight-line and accelerated depreciation methods discussed above. The distinctive features of ACRS are that an accelerated method is generally prescribed and that fixed recovery periods take the place of the asset's useful life.

1. Recovery periods. Assets subject to ACRS are assigned by IRC §168(c)(2) to a recovery class of three, five, ten, or fifteen years, based in part on the asset's classification under the superseded Asset Depreciation Range (ADR) system.

a. *Three-year property.* This class consists of personal property that had a pre-1981 ADR class life of four years or less (primarily automobiles and light-duty trucks) or that is used in connection with research and development).

[52] See Treas. Regs. §1.451-3(d)(5).

[53] See Rev. Rul. 60-358, 1960-2 CB 68 (leased or rented TV films, taped shows for reproduction, and similar property); Rev. Rul. 64-273, 1964-2 CB 62 (motion-picture films).

b. *Five-year property.* This class consists of almost all other personal property, except certain long-lived public utility assets.
c. *Ten-year property.* This class embraces real property with an ADR class life of twelve and one-half years or less (with rare exceptions buildings were not assigned class lives under ADR) and public utility personal property with an ADR class life of eighteen to twenty-five years.
d. *Fifteen-year property.* This class is composed of two subclasses: (1) real property with an ADR class life of more than twelve and one-half years, and (2) public utility property not assigned to a shorter period. Almost all real estate improvements fall in this class.

2. Depreciation Method. Section 168(b)(1) uses statutory tables to prescribe ACRS deductions in terms of percentages of the unadjusted basis of the relevant recovery property. The prescribed percentages are based on the 150 percent declining-balance method, shifting to the straight-line method.

The statutory tables do not cover fifteen-year real property, but the IRS has prescribed tables based on the 175 percent declining-balance method (200 percent for certain low-income housing), switching to the straight-line method.

3. Optional Recovery Periods and Depreciation Methods. Under IRC §168(b)(3), taxpayers may elect, with respect to one or more classes of recovery property placed in service during the taxable year, a longer recovery period as follows:

Three-year property—five or twelve years

Five-year property—twelve or twenty-five years

Ten-year property—twenty-five or thirty-five years

Fifteen-year property—thirty-five or forty-five years

If this election is made, it covers all property of the class in question put in service during the taxable year, and it is binding for these assets throughout the period elected, except that the election may be made on a property-by-property basis for fifteen-year real property. Taxpayers electing an extended recovery period can use only the straight-line method of cost recovery for the affected property. In the alternative, taxpayers can elect to apply the straight-line method to the regular three-, five-, ten-, or fifteen-year recovery period to which the property is assigned by IRC §168(c)(2).

4. Foreign Property. Reflecting the longstanding distinction between domestic and foreign property for investment credit purposes, IRC §168(f)(2) prescribes less generous allowances for recovery property used predominantly outside the United States during the taxable year. As a general rule, the recovery periods for foreign property are twelve years for personal property and thirty-five years for real property, and the depreciation methods used in computing the annual allowances are less accelerated than those applicable to domestic property.

5. Effect of Recapture of ACRS. All nonresidential real estate (e.g., office buildings, factories, warehouses, stores), the cost of which is recovered under the accelerated ACRS method, is subject to IRC §1245, under which the sum of ACRS deductions (or the taxpayer's gain, if less) is recaptured as ordinary income on a taxable disposition of the property. Section 168(b)(3), however, allows the taxpayer to escape this result by electing to recover the cost of real property on the straight-line basis. Three other classes of property are subject to the recapture rules of IRC §1250 rather than IRC §1245: (1) residential rental property as defined by IRC §167(j)(2)(B); (2) property used predominantly outside the United States, as described by IRC §168(f)(2); and (3) certain low-income and federally insured housing, as described in IRC §§1250(a)(1)(B)(ii) through 1250(a)(1)(B)(iv).

¶10.10 EXPENSING OF BUSINESS ASSETS

Section 179 permits taxpayers (other than estates and trusts) to deduct, subject to certain qualifications, the cost of property qualifying for the investment credit ("section 38 property") purchased for use in a trade or business, if it qualifies as recovery property under IRC §168. The deduction may not exceed $5,000 in 1982 and 1983, $7,500 in 1984 and 1985, and $10,000 in 1986 and thereafter. For married taxpayers filing separately, the dollar limit is cut in half. The term "purchase" is limited by IRC §179(d)(2) to exclude certain transactions, such as an acquisition from a person whose relationship to the taxpayer would result in a disallowance of loss on a transaction between them.

The election cannot be revoked unless the IRS consents, and it precludes an investment credit for the amount deducted. Under IRC §168(d)(1), the unadjusted basis of property for computing the ACRS deduction must be reduced by that portion of the cost that the taxpayer elected to expense under IRC §179.

¶10.11 WITHDRAWAL FROM SERVICE OF DEPRECIABLE ASSETS AND RECOVERY PROPERTY

If a depreciable asset or recovery property is withdrawn from use in the taxpayer's business and sold, exchanged, or abandoned, the taxpayer's gain or loss—the difference between the amount realized, if any, and the adjusted basis of the property—is recognized in accordance with the usual rules governing gain or loss on the disposition of property. Gains and losses from sales or exchanges ordinarily go into the "hotchpot" described in IRC §1231, except to the extent of depreciation or ACRS deductions recaptured by IRC §§1245 and 1250. On an abandonment, the taxpayer's unrecovered basis in the asset, if any, is ordinarily deductible under IRC §165.[54] Property retained for standby use in the event that replacement equipment breaks down is not "permanently withdrawn" from service and remains subject to depreciation or ACRS.

The taxpayer may shortcut these rules in the case of recovery property by electing under IRC §168(d)(2) to include as ordinary income all proceeds realized on the disposition, rather than just the gain. As a result of such election, the taxpayer will continue to be entitled to ACRS deductions for the remainder of the recovery period, on the unadjusted basis of the property, despite its retirement and disposition.

SELECTED BIBLIOGRAPHY

Blum, Accelerated Depreciation: A Proper Allowance for Measuring Net Income?!! 78 Mich. L. Rev. 1172 (1980).

Broenen & Reed, Amortizing Intangible Assets: Setting a Cost Basis and Determinable Life, 44 J. Tax. 130 (1976).

Broenen & Reed, Amortizing Intangible Assets: Effect of Going Concern Value and Abandonment, 44 J. Tax. 331 (1976).

Byrne, Conversion of a Personal Residence to a Business or Investment Use for Tax Purposes, 8 Rut.-Cam. L.J. 393 (1977).

Dubin, Allocation of Costs to, and Amortization of, Intangibles in Business Acquisitions, 57 Taxes 930 (1979).

Kahn, Accelerated Depreciation Revisited—A Reply to Professor Blum, 78 Mich. L. Rev. 1185 (1980).

Luscombe & Chevis, New Depreciation Rules, 55 J. Tax. 194 (1981).

Whitmire & Reynolds, Selecting the Optimum Depreciation Method for Real Estate Under the New ACRS System, 55 J. Tax. 360 (1981).

Wiener, Going Concern Value: Goodwill by Another Name?" 53 Tax Lawyer 183 (1979).

---

[54] For the possibility of an extraordinary obsolescence deduction for property that is no longer useful but has not been physically discarded, see Treas. Regs. §1.167(a)-9 (retirement rules govern where usefulness of depreciation property suddenly terminates).

CHAPTER 11

Depletion

¶11.1 DEPLETION—IN GENERAL

1. Introductory. Unlike land, mineral deposits are wasting assets, whose owners must be allowed to deduct their investments over the life of the property if they are to be taxed on net income rather than on gross income or gross receipts. Section 611(a) permits taxpayers to deduct "a reasonable allowance" for depletion of mines, oil and gas wells, other natural deposits and timber.

Taxpayers compute depletion allowances by whichever of two methods produces the larger deduction for the current taxable year. The first is cost depletion, which is allowed by IRC §612 for virtually all exhaustible natural resources. Since the taxpayer is allowed to deduct an appropriate portion of the property's adjusted basis for each unit that is extracted and sold, cost depletion is analogous to the right of merchants to deduct the cost of goods sold in computing gross income.

The second method—allowed for almost all hard minerals and, with certain exceptions, for oil and gas—is percentage depletion, which is a prescribed percentage of the taxpayer's gross income from the mineral property. Because percentage depletion is not restricted to the taxpayer's adjusted basis for the deposit but continues as long as production holds up, even though prior deductions exceed the taxpayer's entire investment, the analogy to the merchant's cost of goods sold breaks down when percentage depletion is used; and for this reason it has been a subject of intense controversy. The dispute, however, was abated somewhat by the enactment in 1975 of IRC §613A, which restricts the use of percentage depletion for oil and gas.

Neither cost nor percentage depletion is allowed unless the taxpayer owns an economic interest in a mineral property that is subject to exhaustion. The Code does not define "economic interest" or mark out a boundary between exhaustible and inexhaustible minerals; these issues have instead been left for administrative and judicial development. In application, the distinction between exhaustible and inexhaustible resources has led to depletion allowances for sand and gravel deposited in a riverbed by glacial action or similar nonrecurring cause and for underground reservoirs of water used for irrigation, but to the denial of allowances for land used for farming or grazing.[1] Soil, sod, dirt, turf, water, or mosses may qualify for cost depletion if extracted from an exhaustible source; but minerals from sea water, air, or similar inexhaustible sources qualify for neither cost nor percentage depletion.[2]

2. Economic Interest in Minerals. A taxpayer claiming a depletion deduction must establish ownership of an economic interest in the deposit; it is not enough to be adversely affected by the exhaustion of a deposit. Although it is a crucial factor in determining whether a taxpayer is entitled to depletion deductions, the concept of an "economic interest" in the mineral deposit does not appear in the relevant statutory provisions but owes its origin and most of its development to the courts. It was first explicitly enunciated by the Supreme Court in *Palmer v. Bender,* decided in 1933, which held that the lessees of certain oil and gas properties who engaged in drilling and then transferred their rights to other parties in return for a cash bonus, a payment from the first oil produced thereafter, and a continuing royalty of one-eighth of the oil were entitled to depletion without regard to whether they "owned" the mineral deposit under local law.[3] It was enough, according to the Court, that they acquired an "economic interest" in the oil in place by virtue of the original leases and retained such an interest when granting the subleases.

In a later case, *Helvering v. Bankline Oil Co.,* the Supreme Court denied depletion deductions to the operator of a refining plant that extracted gasoline from natural gas under contract with the producers.[4] Since the producers were obligated by contract to supply their natural gas to the taxpayer, it "obtained

---

[1] See Victory Sand & Concrete, Inc. v. CIR, 61 TC 407 (1974) (Acq.) (taxpayer engaged in extracting and selling sand and gravel from river on a tract of land owned by it; deposit was partly replenished by flow of river, but quantity and quality were reduced by upstream flood-control facilities; held, taxpayer had economic interest in wasting asset); for IRS view, see Rev. Rul. 76-484, 1976-2 CB 185; US v. Shurbet, 347 F.2d 103 (5th Cir. 1965) (underground water reservoirs not inexhaustible).

[2] Treas. Regs. §1.611-1(d)(5) (cost depletion); IRC §613(b)(7) (percentage depletion).

[3] Palmer v. Bender, 287 US 551 (1933).

[4] Helvering v. Bankline Oil Co., 303 US 362 (1938).

an economic advantage from the production of the gas," but the Court held that "the controlling fact is that [the taxpayer] had no interest in the gas in place [and hence] no capital investment in the mineral deposit which suffered depletion" as the gas was extracted.

Drawing primarily on the opinions in *Palmer v. Bender* and *Bankline Oil Co.,* the regulations summarize the "economic interest" concept as follows:

> An economic interest is possessed in every case in which the taxpayer has acquired by investment any interest in mineral in place or standing timber and secures, by any form of legal relationship, income derived from the extraction of the mineral or severance of the timber, to which he must look for a return of his capital. . . . A person who has no capital investment in the mineral deposit or standing timber does not possess an economic interest merely because through a contractual relation he possesses a mere economic or pecuniary advantage derived from production.[5]

As used in the regulations, the term "capital investment" does not require an investment of cash or property by the taxpayer but can consist of an economic interest acquired by gift, inheritance, personal effort, government permit, or other circumstances. A depletion deduction is not allowed if the taxpayer can look to a source other than the mineral deposit for payment. The leading case on this point is *Anderson v. Helvering,* holding that a taxpayer could not deplete amounts payable from the proceeds of oil produced by certain leases because the obligation was secured by the fee interest in the leased properties and hence could be satisfied by selling the nonmineral interests in the properties if necessary.[6]

Two later Supreme Court cases illustrate the difficulties in applying the concept of economic interest to less conventional mining operations. In *CIR v. Southwest Exploration Co.,* the Court held that the owners of coastal properties were entitled to depletion deductions with respect to royalties received under grants of drilling rights to an operator, who used their land for slant drilling in order to extract offshore oil from deposits below the adjacent ocean.[7] To bid for a state lease permitting extraction of the offshore oil, the operator needed the permission of the littoral landowners. The Court held that this requirement of state law, coupled with the landowner's proximity to the

---

[5] Treas. Regs. §1.611-1(b)(1). Although the regulations reject local property labels as controlling, the taxpayer's legal rights under local law are not immaterial. See, e.g., Harrington v. CIR, 404 F.2d 237 (5th Cir. 1968) (depletion denied as to oil pumped unlawfully from adjacent property); Rev. Rul. 77-341, 1977-2 CB 204 (oral contract between miner and landowner, terminable at will under state law, does not create economic interest in mineral property).

[6] Anderson v. Helvering, 310 US 404 (1940).

[7] CIR v. Southwest Exploration Co., 350 US 308 (1956).

shore, gave them an economic interest in the oil, even though none of it lay beneath their property. In *Parsons v. Smith,* however, the Supreme Court held that two companies engaged in strip-mining coal operations under contracts requiring them to deliver the coal to the landowners for a specified amount per ton were not entitled to depletion.[8] They claimed that their contractual right to mine the coal and the use of their equipment and skill constituted a capital investment giving them an economic interest in the coal in place; but this theory was described by the Court as a legal fiction, which was inconsistent with the facts that the contracts of the miners were terminable on short notice, they had no right to sell the coal after extraction and the miners looked for payment to the owner's promise, rather than to the sale of the coal.

The significance of the terminability of the taxpayer's rights on short notice, however, has recently been called into question. In *United States v. Swank,* the Supreme Court held that a lessee of coal rights under a lease terminable on thirty days notice held an economic interest in the mineral in place, rejecting the IRS' argument that the lessee's rights were rendered illusory by the termination clause.[9]

3. Allocation of Depletion Among Separate Owners. When the ownership of mineral deposits is split among two or more taxpayers, each of whom has an economic interest that will be exhausted by extraction, the depletion allowance must be allocated among them. Section 611(b) prescribes rules for allocation between (1) lessors and lessees, (2) life tenants and remaindermen, (3) trusts and their beneficiaries, and (4) estates and their beneficiaries. These statutory rules are obviously incomplete. They fail, for example, to provide a method of allocating depletion deductions among tenants in common of mineral properties, who undoubtedly are entitled to deduct depletion in proportion to their fractional interests in the property. Nor does the Code provide explicit standards for allocating the deduction among the multiplicity of other interests that have been developed in the extractive industries.

The major arrangements for the division of ownership, and their effects on the rights of the parties to deplete their interests, are summarized briefly below.

1. *Bonuses.* When the owner of a mineral deposit (other than oil and gas) leases the property for a royalty and a bonus, both are subject to cost or

[8] Parsons v. Smith, 359 US 215 (1959). See also Paragon Jewel Coal Co. v. CIR, 380 US 624 (1965) (same result for contract miners of coal under leases requiring them to mine substantially all recoverable coal for per-ton fee).

[9] US v. Swank, 451 US 571 (1981).

percentage depletion. The payor treats the bonus as a capital investment that is recoverable by depletion.[10] If, however, the lease terminates or is abandoned before any income is derived from production, the lessor must increase the basis of the property by the depletion deductions and take them back into income.[11] Because IRC §613A(c) conditions the continued use of percentage depletion for oil and gas on actual production, bonuses for oil and gas property generally cannot qualify for percentage depletion under the proposed regulations, at least if there is no production within the same taxable year.[12]

2. *Advanced royalties.* Advanced royalties can be deducted by the payor from the royalties that would otherwise be payable to the lessor when production occurs. The payee is entitled to deplete the advanced royalties, but not the income from the production that is retained by the payor to recoup the advance; and if the prepayment is not fully recouped by the payor, the payee must include the excess depletion in income, since the prior deductions presupposed a level of production that was not attained.[13] Under IRC §613A, the payee of advanced royalties for oil and gas properties is entitled to cost depletion, but not to percentage depletion, unless there is production in the year of receipt.[14]

3. *Delay rentals.* Delay rentals constitute rent in the hands of the payee, rather than compensation for diminution of the mineral deposit; and depletion is not allowed.[15]

4. *Net profits interest.* A net profits interest is a right to receive a share of gross production from a mineral property, measured by the net operating profits, which is either carved out of the working interest or retained when the working interest is transferred. Such an interest constitutes an economic interest in the mineral deposit, and the amounts received are subject to depletion.[16]

5. *Production payments.* The tax treatment of production payments is discussed below in the context of an examination of IRC §636.[17]

---

[10] See Treas. Regs. §§1.612-3(a)(1) (cost depletion), 1.612-3(d) (percentage depletion); Burnet v. Harmel, 287 US 103 (1932) (bonus subject to depletion).

[11] Treas. Regs. §1.612-3(a)(2); Herring v. CIR, 293 US 322 (1934).

[12] See Prop. Regs. §1.613A-7(f); Prop. Regs. §1.613A-3(a)(4), Example (4); but see Engle v. CIR, 677 F.2d 594 (7th Cir. 1982) (invalidating regulations).

[13] See Treas. Regs. §§1.612-3(b) (cost depletion), 1.612-3(d) (percentage depletion).

[14] See Prop. Regs. §1.613A-3(a)(4), Example (4); but see Engle v. CIR, supra note 12.

[15] Treas. Regs. §1.612-3(c).

[16] Kirby Petroleum Co. v. CIR, 326 US 599 (1946).

[17] Infra ¶11.4.

6. *Carried interests.* A carried interest is an arrangement, employed especially in the oil and gas industry, by which one party (the "carrying party" or "carrier") defrays the cost of drilling and other activities on a mineral lease in return for a portion of the working interest of the lessee (the "carried party"), usually consisting of a fraction of the interest plus a right to receive the production from the remaining part of the interest until recovery of the amount expended. At payout, the latter fraction of the working interest reverts to the carried party. The IRS ruled in 1975 that the carrier is the owner of the entire working interest during the pay-out period,[18] and the proposed regulations under IRC §613A provide that the carried party is entitled to percentage depletion under the independent producer exemption only when the carrying party has reached payout and the carried party is receiving a share of the production.[19]

7. *Farmouts.* The owner of a gas or oil lease who does not wish to bear the expense of drilling often "farms out" this burden to another operator under an agreement entitling the latter to an assignment of the lease or a fraction thereof on drilling the "obligation" well. Frequently the assignment covers the entire working interest in the drill site (possibly subject to an overriding royalty or production payment), plus a fractional working interest in the remainder of the leased acreage.

As traditionally viewed, a farmout arrangement entails a merger of resources by the lessee and driller, which creates a "pool of capital" but does not result in the realization of income by either party. But in 1977 the IRS limited this rationale to a grant of rights to the drill site, ruling that the value of any rights assigned to the driller in the rest of the acreage constituted compensation for his capital and services.[20] The "transfer" rationale would evidently preclude the deduction of percentage depletion on the driller's share of the production from the non-drill site if it is a "proven" property.[21] On the other hand, since the driller's rights to the drill site production are attributable to the hypothesized pooling of capital rather than acquired by a taxable transfer, the production from this property could qualify for percentage depletion under the small producer exemption of IRC §613A(c).[22]

8. *Sales.* A sale of mineral properties does not generate depletable income for the seller but instead results in gain or loss, computed by subtracting the taxpayer's adjusted basis from the amount realized (to be reported as capital gain or loss or ordinary income or loss, as the case may be).

In determining whether a transaction is a sale or a lease, the controlling

---

[18] See Rev. Rul. 75-446, 1975-2 CB 95.

[19] Prop. Regs. §1.613A-7(f)(3).

[20] Rev. Rul. 77-176, 1977-1 CB 77.

[21] See IRC §613A(c)(9).

[22] For IRC §613A(c), see infra ¶11.3.

factor is whether the transferor retained an economic interest in the mineral deposit. Thus, the IRS has ruled that a lump-sum payment received by a landowner for purportedly transferring fee simple title to all minerals under his land, subject to a reserved royalty interest, constitutes ordinary income, subject to depletion, rather than the proceeds of a sale of a capital asset.[23] On the other hand, if all of the payments to the grantor are fixed in amount and payable in all events, without regard to extraction or sale of the mineral, the transaction constitutes a sale, on which the grantor realizes either nondepletable gain or loss, subject to the capital gain and loss provisions if the transaction otherwise qualifies.[24]

4. Separate vs. Combined or Aggregated Properties. Whether the taxpayer uses cost or percentage depletion, the deduction is computed property by property, rather than by reference to all of the taxpayer's mineral properties, unless some or all of the properties are "combined" (operating oil and gas interest) or "aggregated" (other minerals and nonoperating oil and gas interests) under IRC §614. By defining the term "property" to mean "each separate tract or parcel of land," IRC §614(a) leans heavily toward the multiplication of units. The regulations give specific examples of situations giving rise to two properties rather than one, as well as situations in which previously separate properties will be combined in the hands of a transferee of the fee.[25] Section 614 also provides for elective aggregation or combination of two or more separate properties in certain limited situations.[26]

¶11.2 COST DEPLETION

1. Minerals. Cost depletion under IRC §612 entails a spreading of the taxpayer's adjusted basis for the depletion property over the entire number of recoverable units, resulting in a deduction of the cost attributable to the units sold in the current year. The basis used in computing cost depletion is the adjusted basis of the mineral property determined under IRC §1011. When mineral properties include land and depreciable equipment, the adjusted basis allocable to the mineral deposit itself is the only portion subject to depletion.[27] In the case of oil and gas wells, the taxpayer's basis includes intangible

[23] Rev. Rul. 69-352, 1969-1 CB 34 (lump-sum payment likened to bonus or advanced royalty, regardless of state law characterization).

[24] See Ima Mines Corp. v. CIR, 32 TC 1360 (1959) (Acq.) (fixed sum payable at minimum rate annually, with additional payments from net profits to be credited against purchase price; sale, despite buyer's limited power to abandon agreement by surrendering possession of property, etc.).

[25] Treas. Regs. §1.614-(a)(3); Treas. Regs. §1.614-1(a)(5).

drilling and development costs, unless—as usually occurs—the taxpayer elects to deduct these costs currently.[28] The taxpayer's adjusted basis for the property is reduced annually by the amount allowed or allowable as a depletion deduction, whichever is greater, even if the allowable depletion deductions were not claimed or resulted in no tax benefit. Once the basis has been reduced to zero, cost depletion terminates; but percentage depletion continues to be permissible.

The aggregate amount to be depleted is divided by the estimated number of recoverable units to obtain the per-unit deduction. If a material change in the estimate is warranted as a result of subsequent events, the revised estimate is used for the year of the change and thereafter.[29] Although the per-unit cost remains constant from year to year if cost depletion is consistently used, an intervening year in which a greater amount of percentage depletion is claimed will reduce the aggregate basis more than cost depletion would have, thereby requiring the per-unit cost to be recalculated, and lowered, for subsequent years in which cost depletion is claimed.

2. Timber. Timber qualifies only for cost depletion, not for percentage depletion. The amount qualifying for depletion is the taxpayer's adjusted basis for the timber property, excluding amounts allocable to the land, depreciable equipment and other property, and immature timber until it becomes merchantable. The depletable amount is increased by amounts paid or incurred for the preparation of timber sites for planting, for seedlings, and for planting, but not by current silvicultural expenses incurred for normal maintenance, which are deductible under IRC §162.

Because trees grow and reproduce themselves, the taxpayer must take account each year of changes in the quantity of depletable timber. The depletion deduction is determined on a per-unit basis (e.g. board feet, cords, etc.) under a formula prescribed by the regulations.[30]

Under IRC §631(a), taxpayers who own timber or have a contract to cut timber can treat the cutting of the timber, either for sale or for use in the taxpayer's business, as a sale or exchange of the timber. The disposal of timber under a contract by which an economic interest is retained by the owner or a person having cutting rights is similarly treated as a sale or exchange of the timber under IRC §631(b). When these provisions apply, the taxpayer is entitled to IRC §1231 treatment for the proceeds, but not to cost depletion.[31]

---

[26] IRC §§614(b), 614(c), 614(e).

[27] Treas. Regs. §1.612-1(b); see also Treas. Regs. §§1.611-2(d) and 1.611-2(e).

[28] IRC §263(c); Treas. Regs. §1.612-4.

[29] IRC §611(a) (last sentence); Treas. Regs. §1.611-2(c)(2).

[30] Treas. Regs. §1.611-(b)(2).

[31] See Treas. Regs. §§1.611-(b)(2), 1.611-3(b)(3); for IRC §1231, see infra ¶27.1.

¶11.3 PERCENTAGE DEPLETION

1. Introductory. Unlike cost depletion, percentage depletion is based on the taxpayer's income from the mineral property rather than on its adjusted basis; and the allowance continues for the property's entire economic life, even though its basis has been recovered many times over. When cost depletion produces a larger deduction for the current year, however, it is used instead of percentage depletion.

There are three basic steps in the computation of percentage depletion: (1) determination of whether the taxpayer's mineral qualifies for percentage depletion and, if so, the appropriate percentage; (2) application of the percentage rate to the taxpayer's "gross income from the property" (which for property other than an oil or gas well means "gross income from mining"); and (3) imposition of a limit of 50 percent of the taxpayer's "taxable income from the property." In the case of oil and gas wells, percentage depletion is also subject to the special limitations enacted in 1975, described below. Section 291(a)(2) requires corporate taxpayers to reduce the otherwise allowable percentage depletion deduction by 15 percent of the amount by which percentage depletion for the year exceeds the property's basis at the end of the year.

2. Qualifying Minerals. The rates for percentage depletion, ranging from 5 to 22 percent, are specified for scores of minerals by IRC §613(b), which in the case of some minerals depend on the use to which the minerals are put. A catchall rate of 14 percent is prescribed for "all other minerals" except: (1) soil, sod, dirt, turf, water or mosses, which do not qualify for percentage depletion but may, if exhaustible, qualify for cost depletion; (2) minerals from seawater, the air, or "similar inexhaustible sources," which do not qualify for either percentage or cost depletion; and (3) oil and gas wells, which are given special treatment under IRC §613A.

3. Oil and Gas. Section 613A(a) provides that, as a general rule, the depletion allowance for oil and gas wells shall be computed under IRC §611 without regard to IRC §613 (percentage depletion), but IRC §§613A(b) and 613A(c) then set out a series of complex exceptions for domestic oil and gas, which are briefly summarized below.

Percentage depletion is available to independent producers and royalty owners under IRC §613A(c) at the rate specified by IRC §613A(c)(5) (22 percent for 1975–1980, declining in stages to 15 percent for 1984 and subsequent years). Their income from domestic crude oil and natural gas qualifies for percentage depletion in an amount based on the taxpayer's average daily production, up to the taxpayer's "depletable oil quantity," 1,000 barrels per day. Taxpayers wishing to deplete domestic natural gas can elect to convert the applicable depletable oil quantity into an equivalent amount of depletable natural gas, at the ratio of 6,000 cubic feet of natural gas to one barrel of oil. Producers who exceed the prescribed depletable quantity are required by IRC

§613A(c)(7) to reduce their percentage depletion rate by a fraction based on the taxpayer's depletable oil or gas quantity and average daily production.

Percentage depletion that is otherwise allowable under these rules is limited by IRC §613A(d)(1) to 65 percent of the taxpayer's taxable income, computed without regard to percentage depletion under IRC §613A(c), net operating loss and capital loss carrybacks, and, in the case of individuals, the zero bracket amount. Disallowed amounts may be carried forward to future taxable years.[32]

If the taxpayer or a related person engages in the refining of crude oil and the refinery run exceeds 50,000 barrels on any day during the taxable year, percentage depletion is denied by IRC §613A(d)(4). Percentage depletion is also denied to retailers with gross receipts for all retail outlets of more than $5 million for the year. Section 613A(d)(2) defines the term "retailer" broadly, including trademark licensors.

Finally, percentage depletion is ordinarily denied by IRC §613A(c)(9)(A) with respect to oil and gas production from "proven" property transferred after December 31, 1974. Subject to a variety of detailed conditions, however, IRC §613A(c)(9)(B) exempts certain transfers between related persons and corporations, including transfers at death, from disqualification.

4. Gross Income From the Property. Section 613(a) provides that the depletion allowance shall be the percentage specified by IRC §613(b) of "the gross income from the property," after excluding rents or royalties paid or incurred by the taxpayer in respect of the property. Since rents and royalties are subject to depletion in the hands of the recipient, their exclusion in computing the payor's gross income from the property prevents double deductions for the same income.

The "gross income from the property" in the case of oil or gas is the amount for which the taxpayer sells the product "in the immediate vicinity of the well" or, if the taxpayer transports or refines the oil or gas before sale, the "representative market or field price" before transportation or conversion into a refined product.[33]

For minerals other than oil and gas, IRC §613(c)(1) provides that "gross income from the property" means "gross income from mining." "Mining" is defined for this purpose to include not merely the extraction of the minerals from the ground but also the treatment processes specified by IRC §613(c)(4) or necessary or incidental thereto. The term "mining" also includes transportation of the minerals from the point of extraction to processing plants up to 50 miles away, or farther if the IRC finds that "physical and other requirements" necessitate transportation for a greater distance.

---

[32] Prop. Regs. §1.613A-4(a)(2), Example (2) (perpetual carryover).

[33] Treas. Regs. §1.613-3(a).

If the taxpayer sells the minerals immediately after applying the processes specified by IRC §613(c)(4), gross income from mining ordinarily equals the sales proceeds. But if the taxpayer is an integrated producer and goes on to refine the product further, using processes that do not constitute "mining" as defined by IRC §613(c)(2), gross income from mining must be determined by use of a "representative market or field price" for the mineral prior to the application of nonmining processes, if such a price can be determined for minerals of like kind and grade.[34] In the absence of a representative market or field price, the regulations ordinarily require use of a "proportionate profits" method, under which gross income is reconstructed by multiplying the taxpayer's gross sales by a fraction whose numerator is mining costs and whose denominator is total costs.[35]

5. Taxable Income Ceiling. The percentage depletion deduction may not exceed 50 percent of the taxpayer's taxable income from the property, computed before deducting depletion. "Taxable income" for this purpose is computed by taking account of mining processes, as defined by IRC §613(c)(2), and using the representative market price or proportionate-profits method of computing income from mining if nonmining processes are applied before selling the minerals. To compute "taxable income from the property," therefore, the taxpayer starts with "gross income from the property" and then subtracts all allowable deductions (except depletion) attributable to mining processes, including operating expenses, selling expenses, administrative overhead, depreciation, deductible taxes, losses, etc.[36]

¶11.4 PRODUCTION PAYMENTS

1. Introductory. A production payment is a right to receive a share of the production from a mineral deposit (in kind or in money, usually free of operating expenses) when, as, and if produced, up to an aggregate amount specified in terms of money, quantity of mineral, or period of time, such as a right to receive the gross income from production until $100,000, plus interest at the rate of 6 percent per year, has been received. A production payment may be a charge against all production from the burdened property, or it may be limited to income from a specified portion (e.g., 50 percent of production). It may either be "carved out" of an existing mineral interest and transferred by the creator or be retained by him on disposing of the underlying interest.

While production payments can serve a variety of business purposes, their

[34] Treas. Regs. §1.613-4(c).

[35] Treas. Regs. §1.613-4(d)(4)(ii).

[36] Treas. Regs. §1.613-5(a).

use before 1969 for three tax-avoidance purposes generated controversy, led to litigation, and finally elicited the enactment of IRC §636.

1. *Transformation of ordinary income into capital gain.* One tax-avoidance use of carved-out production payments was the sale of a production payment that was virtually certain to pay out within a few years in the hope of reporting the amount received as long-term capital gain, although it served to anticipate receipts that would be taxed as ordinary income (subject to depletion) if received in due course. In *CIR v. P.G. Lake, Inc.*, decided in 1958, the Supreme Court held that such a transaction generated ordinary income, subject to depletion.[37]

2. *Acceleration of income.* Carved-out production payments were also used to accelerate income in situations where the taxpayer preferred to report the amount received currently rather than in later years. For example, a taxpayer with an expiring net operating loss carryforward could sell a production payment, report the proceeds currently, and use the carryforward to eliminate tax liability. Although the Supreme Court did not address itself in *Lake* to arrangements of this type, it virtually validated them by seemingly holding that the consideration for a production payment is ordinary income (subject to depletion) when received.

3. *ABC transactions. Lake* also tended to validate a third tax-avoidance technique entailing the use of retained production payments—so-called ABC transactions. This device can be illustrated by assuming that *A,* the owner of an interest in mineral property worth $1 million, sold it to *B* for $400,000, retaining a production payment of $600,000 (plus interest on the deferred payments), and then sold the production payment to *C* for $600,000. Since the two sales taken in combination terminated *A*'s entire interest in the property, they qualified for capital gain treatment. As the production payment paid out, *C* recovered his $600,000 investment plus interest. *B* acquired a $1 million property for $400,000 plus deferred payments of $600,000; but the production used to pay the latter amounts was not included in *B*'s income when generated by the property, since *C,* rather than *B,* was considered to be the owner of the production.

Had *B* purchased the mineral property in the conventional manner (i.e., by paying $400,000 down and giving *A* or *C* a $600,000 nonrecourse mortgage on the property), however, the income produced by the property would have been taxed to *B* even though used to pay off the loan. In effect, the ABC transaction permitted the purchaser of property to acquire it with pre-tax dollars, a bonanza that was not feasible in the case of ordinary real estate and other income-producing assets, whose acquisition must normally be financed with after-tax dollars.

---

[37] CIR v. P.G. Lake, Inc., 356 US 260 (1958).

2. Carved-Out Production Payments. To forestall these tax-avoidance arrangements, IRC §636(a) now treats carved-out production payments as mortgage loans that do not qualify as economic interests in the mineral property. The amount received by the transferor for the production payment is not includable in income, but the production used to pay off the transferee must be included, subject to depletion. If the property is sold or otherwise transferred before the production payment pays out, the unpaid balance is part of the amount realized by the transferor on the disposition.[38] The transferee of the payment, who is taxed on the interest component,[39] may not deplete his receipts.

These principles are not applicable to production payments that are sold by the creator under a pledge to use the proceeds to finance exploration or development of a mineral property. Transactions of this type are analogized to the commencement of a joint venture or partnership (a so-called pooling of capital), to which the transferee contributed developmental or exploratory activities (or the equivalent in case) in return for a prior claim on future income in the form of a production payment [40] and the transferee is permitted to deplete the payments as received. If a carved-out production payment is transferred to finance operations rather than exploration or development, however, the exception is inapplicable and the transaction is subject to the basic mortgage loan analogy.

3. Retained Production Payments. Section 636(b) treats a retained production payment as a purchase-money mortgage given by the buyer to the seller, which does not qualify as an economic interest in the property. This means that the seller of the underlying property must include the production payment in determining the amount realized (and hence the gain or loss) on the sale and cannot deplete the production income received by him as the payment pays out. Conversely, the buyer includes the production payment in his basis for the property, reports as income the production applied to pay off the production payment, and is entitled to cost or percentage depletion thereon.[41]

Production payments retained by a lessor are treated by IRC §636(c) as a bonus granted by the lessee to the lessor, payable in installments. Thus, the lessee must include in income the amounts used to satisfy the production payment as it is paid off; these amounts are capitalized and recovered by cost or percentage depletion.[42] The lessor's tax status is determined without regard

[38] See Treas. Regs. §1.636-1(c)(1)(i).

[39] See Treas. Regs. §1.636-1(a)(1)(ii).

[40] See G.C.M. 22730, 1941-1 CB 214, 221–222; Rev. Rul. 77-176, 1977-1 CB 77.

[41] Treas. Regs. §1.636-1(a)(1)(ii); Treas. Regs. §1.636-1(a)(3), Example (3).

[42] Treas. Regs. §§1.636-2(a), 1.636-2(c); Treas. Regs. §1.612-3(a).

to IRC §636(c): the production payment constitutes an economic interest in the mineral property and the receipts, as it pays out, are ordinary income to the lessor, subject to depletion.[43]

4. Scope of the Term "Production Payment." The regulations define production payment as:

> [A] right to a specified share of the production from mineral in place (if, as, and when produced), or the proceeds from such production. . . . Such right must have an expected economic life (at the time of its creation) of shorter duration than the economic life of one or more of the mineral properties burdened thereby. . . . A right to mineral in place has an economic life of shorter duration than the economic life of a mineral property burdened thereby only if such right may not reasonably be expected to extend in substantial amounts over the entire productive life of such mineral property.[44] The term includes any right that is "in substance economically equivalent to a production payment. . . ."[45] Rights whose expected life is not shorter than the economic life of the underlying property are excluded from the definition of production payments because they are not suitable vehicles for the tax avoidance schemes at which IRC §636 is aimed.

SELECTED BIBLIOGRAPHY

Baker & Griswold, Percentage Depletion—A Correspondence, 64 Harv. L. Rev. 361 (1951).

Casey, The Economic Interest—Play It Again, Sam, 24 Tax Lawyer 129 (1970).

Englebrecht & Hutchins, Section 613A: A Decision Tree Analysis of Percentage Depletion Deductions for Oil and Gas, 26 Oil & Gas Tax Q. 54 (1977).

Fiske, Gross Income From Mining Property, 36 J. Tax. 114 (1972).

Galvin, The "Ought" and "Is" of Oil and Gas Taxation, 73 Harv. L. Rev. 1441 (1960).

Joyce & Del Cotto, The AB (ABC) and BA Transactions: An Economic and Tax Analysis of Reversed and Carved Out Income Interests, 31 Tax L. Rev. 121 (1976).

Linden, Income Realization in Mineral Sharing Transactions: The Pool of Capital Doctrine, 33 Tax Lawyer 115 (1979).

McMahon, Defining the "Economic Interest" in Minerals After *United States v. Swank,* 70 Ky. L.J. 23 (1981).

---

[43] Treas. Regs. §§1.636-2(b), 1.636-2(c).

[44] Treas. Regs. §1.636-3(a)(1).

[45] Treas. Regs. §1.636-3(a)(2).

DEPLETION

Sneed, The Economic Interest—An Expanding Concept, 35 Texas L. Rev. 307 (1957).

Williams, Percentage Depletion Regulations: Let's Try It Again One *More* Time! 26 Oil & Gas Tax Q. 114 (1977).

CHAPTER 12

Losses and Other Business Deductions

¶12.1 INTRODUCTORY

Section 165(a) allows taxpayers to deduct "any loss sustained during the taxable year and not compensated for by insurance or otherwise." In its breathtaking simplicity, the phraseology of this fundamental provision of federal income tax law resembles IRC §61(a), defining gross income, and IRC §162(a), allowing business expenses to be deducted and, like these other basic provisions, it covers a vast miscellany of events and transactions and is subject to numerous statutory and administrative qualifications that belie its simple language.

Loss deductions may be claimed only by the taxpayer who sustained the loss for which the deduction is claimed. Usually nominal and beneficial ownership of property coincide, and losses are properly claimed by the person having title to property giving rise to the loss. If the property is held by a nominee, however, the beneficial owner is ordinarily entitled to the deductions.[1] But if the nominee or owner of record is held out to a government agency as the true owner, the parties may be held to their representations, either by way of estoppel or because the documentation is considered more reliable than their oral disclaimers.[2]

Taxpayers extending financial assistance to relatives and friends cannot deduct losses incurred in a business or investment financed with the funds if the advance is a gift or loan; the deductions belong instead to the transferee.[3] A beneficiary who is guaranteed against losses is not entitled to deductions under IRC §165(a) because the loss is "compensated for" within the meaning of IRC §165(a).[4]

The business affairs of family and one-man corporations are often conducted in disregard of formalities, but the corporation is a separate entity; and the shareholders are rarely entitled to deduct the losses on their own returns. If corporate expenditures are defrayed with personal funds, the payment is usually characterized as a contribution to the corporation's capital or as a loan,[5] and the individuals sustain no deductible losses unless and until their stock becomes worthless or the debt becomes uncollectible. Occasionally, however, a court is persuaded that the corporation was only a nominee or title-holding entity and the losses are deductible by the ostensible shareholders.[6]

---

[1] See Bloch v. CIR, 6 BTA 563 (1927) (Acq.) (husband filing individual return entitled to deduct loss on sale of stock held in wife's name to avoid creditors' claims).

[2] See, e.g., Moyer v. CIR, ¶50,282 P-H Memo TC (1950), aff'd per curiam, 193 F.2d 876 (3d Cir. 1952) (taxpayer's father treated as true owner of strip-mining business; representations to government lending agency reflected the true intention of the parties).

[3] Kamborian's Est. v. CIR, 469 F.2d 219 (1st Cir. 1972) (claim that transferee of funds was transferor's agent in making losing investment rejected on facts).

[4] Dunne v. CIR, 75 F.2d 255 (2d Cir. 1935) (taxpayer indemnified against loss by friend who recommended investments not entitled to deduction).

[5] See, e.g., Cooper v. CIR, 61 TC 599 (1974) (shareholders paid corporation's operating loss each year in proportion to stock holdings; held, contributions to capital).

[6] See, e.g., Blue Flame Gas Co. v. CIR, 54 TC 584, 598-600 (1970) (no stock issued and no assets transferred to corporation).

¶12.2 RELATION TO BUSINESS AND PROFIT-ORIENTED TRANSACTIONS

Losses incurred by individuals, including trusts, estates, and members of partnerships, can be deducted only if they satisfy the test prescribed by IRC §165(c), which permits losses to be deducted by individuals and other noncorporate taxpayers only if they are incurred in a trade or business or a transaction entered into for profit or are caused by fire, storm, shipwreck, other casualty, or theft. Casualty losses are examined in detail later in this work [7] and are not generally discussed further in this chapter. It should be noted, however, that if property damaged by casualty is used in an individual taxpayer's business or profit-oriented activities, the loss is deductible in full; but if the deduction rests solely on IRC §165(c)(3), relating to casualty losses, the first $100 is nondeductible and the balance is deductible only to the extent that the aggregate of such losses exceeds 10 percent of the taxpayer's adjusted gross income.[8]

1. Business Losses and Losses on Transactions Entered Into for Profit. The standards determining whether an individual's loss was "incurred in a trade or business" within the meaning of IRC §165(c)(1) are substantially identical with those determining whether expenses qualify for deduction under IRC §162(a).[9] Losses from activities lacking the regularity and continuity required to qualify as a "trade or business" can be deducted under IRC §165(c)(2) if incurred "in any transaction entered into for profit." [10] A transaction is not entered into "for profit" within the meaning of IRC §165(c)(2) if the sole potential benefit is a tax savings; but if there is also a reasonable prospect of economic gain, the transaction qualifies even though the taxpayer was motivated in part by knowledge that a loss, if incurred, would be deductible from income otherwise subject to high marginal tax rates.[11]

Since the disposition of depreciated property cannot produce a profit, the "transaction" to which IRC §165(c)(2) refers is obviously not the sale itself; it necessarily refers to the *inception* of an investment or other action under-

---

[7] See infra ¶18.1.

[8] See IRC §165(h)(1).

[9] See, e.g., McDowell v. Ribicoff, 292 F.2d 174 (3d Cir. 1961), cert. denied, 368 US 919 (1961) (nonprofessional executrix' part-time management of relative's estate did not constitute "business").

[10] See, e.g., Imel v. CIR, 61 TC 318, 327 (1973) (Acq.) (loss incurred by guarantor on guaranteeing obligation of taxpayer's corporation).

[11] See In re King, 545 F.2d 700 (10th Cir. 1976) (speculative oil and gas transactions entered into for profit, notwithstanding potential tax write-offs); compare Knetsch v. US, 348 F.2d 932 (Ct. Cl. 1965), cert. denied, 383 US 957 (1966) (IRC §165(c)(2) not satisfied by investment on which sole anticipated gain was tax reduction).

taken with the expectation of making a profit. Thus, an investor's sale of securities or other profit-oriented investments is a transaction entered into for profit, even though the taxpayer's only objective in taking the *final* step is to forestall a greater loss.[12] To be deductible, however, the loss must be bona fide, and this element may be questioned if the sale is for less than the property's fair market value.

Although losses incurred on the disposition of investment property acquired by gift or inheritance do not neatly fit the statutory language, since the property was not *acquired* by the taxpayer in a transaction entered into for profit, taxpayers may deduct losses on selling donated and inherited investment assets; in effect, the prior owner's profit-oriented objective runs with the property. If the inherited property was used by the decedent for personal purposes (e.g., as a residence), the courts have focused on the use to which it was put by the heir after acquiring it and have allowed losses to be deducted if attributable to a post-acquisition decline in value while the heir is endeavoring to rent or sell the property.[13] In general, if expenses are deductible under IRC §212(2) because paid or incurred for the management, conservation, or maintenance of property "held for the production of income," a loss on a sale or other disposition of the property is ordinarily deductible under IRC §165(c)(2).

2. Type of Deduction. Business losses under IRC §165(c)(1) are ordinarily deductible from gross income in computing adjusted gross income, but losses on transactions entered into for profit under IRC §165(c)(2) must be deducted from adjusted gross income unless attributable to the sale or exchange of property.

3. Mixed Profit-Personal Objectives. No deduction is allowed for losses incurred on the sale or other disposition of wholly personal property, like the taxpayer's residence or vacation home. But losses on property regularly devoted to both business or profit-oriented uses and personal uses, such as a physician's automobile or a family farm, can be bifurcated on a sale, thus permitting a deduction under IRC §165 for any loss attributable to the business or profit-oriented activities.[14]

If the taxpayer entertains simultaneous mixed motives with respect to

---

[12] See also Rev. Rul. 65-254, 1965-2 CB 50 (amounts repaid to victim by embezzler deductible because embezzlement was a transaction entered into for profit).

[13] See Marx v. CIR, 5 TC 173, 174 (1945) (Acq.) (loss on inherited yacht, never used by decedent's widow, allowed; fact that it was acquired by inheritance "is, by itself, neutral").

[14] See Rev. Rul. 72-111, 1972-1 CB 56 (dual-use automobile); see also Treas. Regs. §1.165-9(b); Treas. Regs. §1.165-9(c), Examples (1), (2).

the entire property, however, the primary motive is controlling in determining whether the loss is deductible [15] and, in the case of a residence, the IRS and courts are understandably skeptical of claims that the property was acquired primarily as an investment, rather than for personal occupancy.

4. Converted Property. Property acquired for personal reasons can be converted by the taxpayer to business or profit-oriented purposes; in the latter case, the "transaction entered into for profit" is the taxpayer's change of mind, as evidenced by such facts as termination of personal use, physical alterations, and renting the property. In the case of a personal residence, the regulations specify that a loss on a sale is allowable if, "prior to the sale, [the property is] rented or otherwise appropriated to income-producing purposes and is used for such purposes up to the time of the sale." [16] Any loss, however, is based on the property's adjusted basis or fair market value when converted, whichever is lower, plus or minus any adjustments for improvements, depreciation, or other items chargeable to capital account for the period subsequent to the conversion.[17]

If property acquired and used for business or profit-oriented purposes is converted to personal uses, a loss on a sale or other disposition cannot be deducted under IRC §165 even if it is wholly attributable to a decline in the value of the property while it was used in the taxpayer's business.

5. Corporations. Section 165(c) does not apply to corporations which are subject only to the general rule of IRC §165(a).

¶12.3 CLOSED TRANSACTION REQUIREMENT

1. Introductory. A loss may be deducted under IRC §165(a) only in the taxable year in which it is sustained; and the regulations require losses to be "evidenced by closed and completed transactions, fixed by identifiable events." [18] Except for attempts to deduct losses attributable to an individual's personal activities, the principal grounds asserted by the IRS for rejecting a claim are that the taxpayer sustained a loss, but in an earlier or later year, or that the taxpayer has not yet sustained a loss, though one may be sustained in a later year.

---

[15] Helvering v. National Grocery Co., 304 US 282, 289 n.5 (1938).

[16] Treas. Regs. §1.165-9(b)(1).

[17] Treas. Regs. §1.165-9(b)(2); Treas. Regs. §1.165-9(c), Examples (1), (2).

[18] Treas. Regs. §1.165-1(b).

2. Sales. The sale of listed securities in arm's-length transactions with anonymous outsiders on organized stock exchanges is a quintessential "closed transaction," betokening a bona fide loss. But sales of depreciated property can also be devices for realizing artificial tax losses. For example, a sale followed immediately by a repurchase of the same or similar property preserves the taxpayer's investment, except during the interval between the sale and the repurchase; and a sale to a member of the taxpayer's family can also perpetuate the taxpayer's investment in substance though terminating it in form. Accordingly, the Code disallows losses on so-called wash sales (IRC §1091) and on sales between related persons (IRC §267(a)), even if the sale is effected at the fair market value.

These statutory safeguards against the premature deduction of losses are neither comprehensive nor preemptive, however, and they leave room for administrative and judicial determinations that a particular sale is only a provisional step, rather than a "closed transaction" within the meaning of the regulations under IRC §165(a). The principal targets for disallowance are (1) sales subject to agreements or options to repurchase, which in appropriate circumstances can be disregarded as sham transactions or, in less pejorative language, as preserving the substance of ownership;[19] (2) matched transactions that are not technical wash sales, because they involve property other than stock or securities or a longer interval than the thirty days prescribed by IRC §1091;[20] and (3) sales to related persons who are not within the tainted circle described by IRC §167(a) but who nevertheless insure perpetuation of the taxpayer's financial interest in the property.

Taxpayers falling afoul of the nonstatutory common law that has developed under IRC §165(a) may be worse off than those whose losses are subject to automatic disallowance under IRC §1091 or §267(a), since the rigors of the latter two provisions are softened by explicit provisions taking the disallowed loss into account at a later time. By contrast, the courts have not developed a body of ancillary law to insure that taxpayers failing in an attempt to recognize losses prematurely will be able to recognize them when their economic interest in the property is finally terminated.

3. Abandonment. Another method of closing out a losing investment, especially business or income-producing physical property that is devoid of value, is abandonment. Because an abandonment is not a "sale or exchange" of the property within the meaning of IRC §1222 or §1231(a), the taxpayer's

---

[19] See Du Pont v. CIR, 118 F.2d 544 (3d Cir.), cert. denied, 314 US 623 (1941) (losses disallowed where friends sold stock to each other at the end of one year and by prearrangement repurchased the stock early in the following year).

[20] See Rev. Rul. 77-185, 1977-1 CB 48 (matched transactions in silver futures), and cases there cited; Rev. Rul. 78-715, 1978-2 CB 214 (same as to Treasury bills).

loss is not a capital loss, and it can therefore be deducted from ordinary income.

The most common bone of contention in abandonment cases is whether the property was actually discarded or only shelved temporarily in the hope that it would become useful again at some future time. Even if the asset has lost most of its value, the decline in value cannot be deducted until the taxpayer's investment is closed; halfway measures are not enough. The existence of any residual or potential value can be rebutted by consigning outworn assets to the city dump; but the regulations also allow a loss to be deducted if nondepreciable property "is permanently discarded from use," even without an "overt act of abandonment" or loss of title to the property. For depreciable property, a loss from "physical abandonment" is recognized if "the intent of the taxpayer [is] irrevocably to discard the asset so that it will neither be used again by him nor retrieved by him for sale, exchange, or other disposition" or when the assets are "retired" by being permanently withdrawn from use in the business or income-producing activity—an action that falls short of a physical abandonment, because it can be accomplished by transferring the property to a supplies or scrap account, even though the property is later cannibalized for spare parts or other salvageable items.[21]

A determination that the taxpayer abandoned an asset rests on an analysis of all the facts, including the taxpayer's intent; and this makes it impossible to extract much guidance from the welter of litigated cases. Retention of possession and title to property, however, invites a dispute no matter how clearly a decline in value is established, unless the taxpayer takes such drastic steps as junking the property, going out of business unequivocally, or, in the case of a building, boarding it up and letting it go to wrack and ruin.[22]

Abandonment claims involving intangible business assets, such as goodwill, lists of customers, or trade names, raise special problems, since these assets cannot be "physically" abandoned and mere nonuse does not preclude a revival of the intangible's value and usefulness. If the enterprise remains in business, the loss must be evidenced by alterations in its operations that clearly

---

[21] Treas. Regs. §1.167(a)-8(a)(4); Treas. Regs. §1.167(a)-8(a)(3) (loss based on difference between property's adjusted basis and its estimated salvage value or fair market value at retirement, subject to qualifications).

[22] Compare United Cal. Bank v. CIR, 41 TC 437 (1963); aff'd per curiam, 340 F.2d 320 (9th Cir. 1965) (building not abandoned despite nonuse and later demolition); Shoolman v. CIR, 108 F.2d 987 (1st Cir.), cert. denied, 310 US 637 (1940) (decision to invest no more money in real estate parcel and instructions authorizing secretary to release interest therein; held, insufficient to establish loss), with Tanforan Co. v. US, 313 F. Supp. 796 (N.D. Cal. 1970), aff'd per curiam, 462 F.2d 605 (9th Cir. 1972) (abandonment of racetrack occurred when racing operations were discontinued and all personalty was assigned; subsequent sale of property was "fortuitous"); Hanover v. CIR, ¶79,332 P-H Memo TC (1979) (building locked, boarded, and barricaded; utilities, insurance, maintenance, and heat discontinued; held, sufficient physical acts).

eliminate the intangible asset as an income-producing factor in the continuing activities. The cost of a list of customers or of a prime location, for example, may be rendered worthless if the company moves to a new territory; but its trademarks and trade names may continue to have some value even if they are less familiar to new customers than to the old ones.[23]

4. Worthlessness. When securities become worthless, there is ordinarily no way by which they can be "abandoned." For this reason, the "closed transaction" evidencing the taxpayer's loss is the event or concatenation of events resulting in worthlessness, rather than an explicit action by the taxpayer. Moreover, even in the case of real estate and other property that *can* be abandoned in the traditional sense, proof of worthlessness entitles the taxpayer to deduct the loss even if the property is not abandoned until a later year.[24]

To deduct a loss-from-worthlessness, the taxpayer does not have to wait until the last possible minute to write off an investment as worthless; on the other hand, he cannot be a "Stygian pessimist" [25] and write it off as soon as trouble looms on the horizon. Alas, most cases involving securities, which generate a large volume of loss claims, fall between these two extremes in a murky interval that may span a number of years.

Although the absence of any current liquidation value is a prerequisite to worthlessness, it is not determinative. Securities are generally considered worthless only when there is no reasonable hope and expectation that they will have any value at a future time. If the securities may acquire value in the future through the foreseeable operations of the enterprise, they are not worthless. Ordinarily, the loss of any potential value can be established "only by some 'identifiable event' in the corporation's life which puts an end to such hope and expectation." [26] Whether the potential value of an enterprise has been wiped

---

[23] See Massey-Ferguson, Inc. v. CIR, 59 TC 220 (1972) (Acq.) (move to new location; held, distributorship system, going concern value and one trade name abandoned, but another trade name and product line not abandoned); see also Beatty v. CIR, 46 TC 835 (1966) (no loss on change in liquor license law; held, mere diminution in value of single asset, not complete abandonment or worthlessness of distinct rights).

[24] Rev. Rul. 54-581, 1954-2 CB 112 (loss on worthlessness deductible despite postponement of sale, abandonment, and loss of title until later years).

[25] Ruppert v. US, 22 F.Supp. 428 (Ct. Cl.), cert. denied, 305 US 630 (1938) (debt not worthless where taxpayer continued to extend credit to debtor and later collected).

[26] Morton v. CIR, 38 BTA 1270, 1278-1279 (1938) (Nonacq.) aff'd, 112 F.2d 320 (7th Cir. 1940); Treas. Regs. §§1.165-5(b)(c) (requiring asset to be "wholly" worthless); Richards v. CIR, ¶76,380 P-H Memo TC (1976) (fair market value of assets exceeded balance sheet liabilities; held, stock not worthless); Rev. Rul. 77-17, 1977-1 CB 44 (stock not worthless as result of corporate bankruptcy proceeding where corporation had two sound subsidiaries and shareholders had prospect of receiving stock in reorganized entity).

out by an identifiable event is a question of fact, requiring all relevant circumstances to be examined. The occurrences that are most likely to qualify are cessation of business, receivership, foreclosure, sale of all assets, liquidation, and bankruptcy.[27] On the other hand, no single event is necessarily sufficient; even the cessation of operations and sale of all assets may not consitute a "closed transaction" if there is a possibility of recovering something by litigation.[28]

5. Demolition of Buildings. Demolition of a building is usually an identifiable event establishing a loss of the taxpayer's remaining adjusted basis in the property, increased by the cost of demolition or decreased by amounts received for salvageable items.[29] But if the property was purchased with the intent to demolish the building, whether immediately or at a later time, the taxpayer's entire basis must be allocated to the land and nothing may be deducted when the building is destroyed.[30] The regulations set out a list of factors to determine whether the intent to demolish the building existed when the property was acquired or arose subsequently.[31] Although the regulations concern themselves solely with the demolition of buildings, the same principles apply to the acquisition of a going business or other collection of assets with the intent to discard or abandon some of the items.[32]

Section 280B disallows any deduction for a loss from or an expense incurred for the demolition of any certified historic structure, as defined by IRC §48(g)(3)(A).

6. Tax Straddles. A tax straddle is a pair of transactions, such as the purchase of a contract for the delivery of a commodity at a future date and a simultaneous sale of a contract for delivery of the same commodity in a different month, which in conjunction enables the taxpayer to close out

---

[27] See, e.g., Scifo v. CIR, 68 TC 714 (1977) (Acq.) (strike, bankruptcy petition, and shutdown of plant).

[28] See Anderegg v. CIR, ¶78,509 P-H Memo TC (1978) (liquidation not controlling); Rev. Rul. 77-18, 1977-1 CB 46 (shareholder lawsuit to rescind merger negates worthlessness of stock); Ramsay Scarlett & Co. v. CIR, 521 F.2d 786 (4th Cir. 1975) (taxpayers had prospect of recovery from banks that cashed checks drawn by embezzlers).

[29] Treas. Regs. §1.165-3(b)(1); but see Treas. Regs. §1.165-3(b)(2) (no deduction for demolition pursuant to lease).

[30] Treas. Regs. §1.165-3(a)(1); for the provisional allocation of basis to the building for the purpose of computing depreciation between acquisition and demolition, see Treas. Regs. §1.165-3(a)(2).

[31] Treas. Regs. §1.165-3(c)(2).

[32] See Wood County Tel. Co. v. CIR, 51 TC 72 (1968) (acquisition of telephone company with intent to scrap outmoded manual equipment on conversion to dial phones).

the losing contract and offset the loss against ordinary income or capital gain from some other source, while holding the appreciated position open until a later year and matching it with another offsetting contract in order to protect the unrealized gain against evaporation. This technique was used by taxpayers to defer the recognition of income and to convert ordinary income into capital gain and short-term capital gain into long-term capital gain.

In 1981, Congress responded to this practice by enacting IRC §1256(a), a complex provision requiring regulated futures contracts (regardless of whether the taxpayer in fact has an offsetting matched contract) to be "marked to market" on the last business day of the taxable year.[33] Forty percent of the resulting gain or loss is then treated as short-term capital gain or loss and sixty percent as long-term gain or loss. When the gain or loss is actually realized, proper adjustment is made for the constructive gain or loss previously taken into account. As a result of these rules, realized losses on futures contracts are offset by unrealized gains, and only the net loss, if any, is deductible against other income.[34] Section 1212(c) permits unused losses to be carried back three years and applied against constructive gains.

Straddles involving property other than regulated futures contracts are not marked to market, but losses are allowed by IRC §1092 only to the extent that they exceed the unrealized gains of the taxpayer (or of certain related persons) on offsetting positions. Disallowed losses are deferred and treated by IRC §1092(a)(1)(B) as sustained in the following taxable year.

¶12.4 INSURANCE OR OTHER COMPENSATION

Losses can be deducted only if "not compensated for by insurance or otherwise." This restriction is most frequently encountered as a barrier to deductions when insured property is damaged by fire or other casualty, but it also prevents the deduction of other types of losses if covered by insurance, such as a business enterprise's liability to customers for injuries caused by defective products or the negligence of its employees.

There is some authority for the proposition that a loss cannot be deducted if the taxpayer fails to pursue a claim for reimbursement against another

---

[33] The mark-to-market rules do not apply to hedging transactions defined in IRC §1256(e).

[34] To prevent ordinary loss treatment, IRC §1234(a) requires sale or exchange treatment for the cancellation, lapse, expiration, or other termination of a future contract in certain instances.

party.[35] If the taxpayer waives a right to collect from a relative or friend, this theory is valid, since the waiver is an indirect gift; but a waiver in a business setting is another matter. Employers, for example, are constantly held liable for the negligence of their employees under the doctrine of respondeat superior; and they fail, with equal regularity, to sue the negligent employees for reimbursement. It would, however, fly in the face of economic reality to hold that the employer's payments to the injured parties cannot be deducted under IRC §165(a) because the employer has a theoretically valid claim to be reimbursed by the employee who is primarily responsible for the loss.

The principal problem in applying IRC §165(a) to insured losses involves timing. Taxpayers having "a reasonable prospect of recovery" cannot deduct the loss unless and until "it can be ascertained with reasonable certainty whether or not such reimbursement will be recovered," an issue that can be resolved by settlement, adjudication, or abandonment of the claim.[36] If the claim for reimbursement covers only part of the loss, however, the uninsured portion can be deducted when the casualty or other event generating the loss occurs. If the taxpayer is later reimbursed for a loss that was properly deducted when sustained (e.g., because the prospect of recovery was insubstantial at that time or the amount of coverage was underestimated), the recovery must be included in gross income when received, subject to the tax benefit doctrine of IRC §111.[37]

The compensation restriction also encompasses reimbursement of the taxpayer's loss by a tort-feasor, supplier, or other person liable under tort or contract law. Reimbursement can bar a deduction even if it does not take the form of a payment in cash. For example, if a defective machine purchased by the taxpayer is replaced by the supplier or accepted as part payment on another item, the taxpayer's loss is eliminated or reduced pro tanto.[38]

---

[35] See H.D. Lee Mercantile Co. v. CIR, 79 F.2d 391 (10th Cir. 1935) (failure to make claim against supplier of defective goods bars deduction); Rev. Rul. 78-141, 1978-1 CB 58 (same where lawyer paid client to rectify erroneous advice but failed to seek reimbursement under malpractice insurance policy); but see Hills v. CIR, 76 TC 484 (1981), aff'd, 691 F.2d 997 (11th Cir. 1982) (voluntary election not to file insurance claim for fear of cancellation of policy; loss not compensated by insurance).

[36] Treas. Regs. §§1.165-1(d)(2)(i), 1.165-1(d)(2)(ii).

[37] Treas. Regs. §1.165-1(d)(2)(iii); for IRC §111, see supra ¶1.10.

[38] See Holder v. US, 444 F.2d 1297 (5th Cir. 1971) (owner-lessor suffered no deductible loss when lessee demolished building under lease requiring replacement with other buildings meeting specified standards); see also Rev. Rul. 77-17, supra note 26 (victim of stock fraud not entitled to worthless stock or theft deduction where issuer was being reorganized in bankruptcy and taxpayer would receive stock in reorganized corporation).

¶12.5 AMOUNT DEDUCTIBLE

Out-of-pocket losses on discharging a liability incurred in business or in a transaction entered into for profit are fully deductible. In the case of property, however, IRC §165(b) limits the deductible amount to the adjusted basis of the property for determining loss as fixed by IRC §1011. For example, if property costing $1,000 increases in value to $1,500 and then becomes worthless, the loss is $1,000, not $1,500; not having been realized and included in income, the taxpayer's paper profit of $500 cannot be deducted when it evaporates. In the same vein, if business property costing $1,000 is depreciated down to $500 and then becomes worthless, the loss under IRC §165(a) cannot exceed the latter amount.

Similarly, deductions cannot be bottomed on the taxpayer's failure to collect an amount that would be taxable if received, unless it was includable in gross income in an earlier year when the taxpayer's rights accrued. If the taxpayer reports on the cash basis, as is almost universally true of nonbusiness taxpayers, items such as wages earned but not collected, unpaid rent owed by unreliable tenants, and the sales price of goods sold on credit to defaulting buyers, cannot be deducted since the uncollected amount was not previously included in income.[39] Although the taxpayer's financial detriment in these situations is real, it is adequately—and automatically—reflected by excluding the lost amount from gross income. The adjustment can be illustrated by comparing *A,* who earns and collects wages of $5,000, with *B,* who earns the same amount but fails to collect it because the employer disappears. The financial spread between *A* and *B* is $5,000, and it is reflected on their respective tax returns: *A* reports $5,000 more than *B.* Were *B* allowed to deduct $5,000, the spread between their reported incomes would be $10,000—twice the financial difference separating them.

¶12.6 DISALLOWED LOSSES

Because losses can be easily exaggerated and are sometimes fictitious, the Code restricts or disallows deductions for many categories of losses thought by Congress to be particularly susceptible to abuse. The principal restrictions, which are discussed elsewhere in this work, are:

---

[39] See, e.g., Alsop v. CIR, 290 F.2d 726 (2d Cir. 1961) (royalties embezzled by author's agent); Marks v. CIR, 390 F.2d 598 (9th Cir.), cert. denied, 393 US 883 (1968) (loss of income following revocation of teacher's credentials); Gertz v. CIR, 64 TC 598 (1975) (no bad-debt deduction on failure of employer to pay income earned).

1. IRC §183, restricting deductions incurred in hobbies and other activities not engaged in for profit to an amount determined by reference to the taxpayer's gross income from the activities.[40]
2. IRC §267(a), disallowing losses from sales or exchanges of property between related persons (as defined).[41]
3. IRC §271, disallowing deductions for worthless securities and bad debts if the debtor is a political party.[42]
4. IRC §274(a), disallowing deductions attributable to facilities used for entertainment, amusement, or recreation.[43]
5. IRC §280A, restricting deductions for a dwelling unit used by the taxpayer or certain other persons as a residence during the taxable year.[44]
6. IRC §465, permitting the excess of the taxpayer's deductions from each business or profit-oriented activity over the gross income produced by the activity to be deducted from other income only up to the amount that the taxpayer has at risk (as defined) in the loss activity.[45]
7. IRC §1091, disallowing deductions resulting from wash sales of stock or securities.[46]

These restrictions were augmented in 1982 by the enactment of IRC §165(j), denying any deduction for a loss sustained on a so-called registration-required obligation unless it is in registered form or was subject when issued to the excise tax formerly imposed by IRC §4701. This disallowance is part of a network of rules designed to prevent tax avoidance through the use of bearer bonds, whose owners cannot be ascertained. The other rules include IRC §163(f), denying any deduction for interest paid, and IRC §1232(d), requiring gain on a sale or other disposition to be reported as ordinary income rather than capital gain, if the obligation does not comply with the registration requirements. In addition to these statutory restrictions, the deduction of losses under IRC §165(a) is subject to disallowance under the judge-made frustration-of-public-policy doctrine.[47]

---

[40] Supra ¶9.10.

[41] Infra ¶33.1.

[42] Infra ¶17.9.

[43] Supra ¶9.3.

[44] Supra ¶9.11.

[45] See text following heading "Tax-Shelter Losses—Limitation of Deductions to Amounts at Risk," pages 12-16–12-22.

[46] Infra ¶24.6.

[47] Rev. Rul. 77-126, 1977-1 CB 48 (deduction of loss from forfeiture of unlawful gambling devices would frustrate public policy); Holt v. CIR, 69 TC 75 (1977), aff'd per curiam, 611 F.2d 1160 (5th Cir. 1980) (same as to confiscated truck used to transport marijuana).

¶12.7 ANCILLARY MATTERS

1. Ordinary vs. Capital Losses. Section 165(a) does not determine whether the deductible amount is an ordinary loss or a capital loss. The proper characterization of losses depends on other provisions.

1. *Sale or exchange of capital assets.* Section 165(f) provides that losses from the sale or exchange of capital assets are deductible only to the extent permitted by IRC §§1211 (limitation on deduction of capital losses) and 1212 (capital loss carrybacks and carryovers). To avoid IRC §165(f), taxpayers often argue that an ambiguous transaction created a loss from abandonment, demolition, or worthlessness, since these events give rise to ordinary losses even if the property is a capital asset.[48] But the conveyance of mortgaged property to the creditor is a sale, subject to IRC §165(f), even if the mortgagee is not personally liable and hence gets nothing in return, not even a release from liability.[49]

2. *Worthless securities.* Section 165(g) provides that if a security (as defined) is a capital asset and becomes worthless during the taxable year, the resulting loss shall be treated as a loss from the sale or exchange of a capital asset on the last day of the taxable year. This provision also affects the holding period of the worthless security.

2. Recoveries of Deducted Amounts. If a taxpayer properly claiming a loss under IRC §165(a) subsequently recovers part or all of the amount deducted, the recovery must be included in gross income in the later year. If the deduction did not generate a tax benefit, however, the recovery is excludable from gross income under IRC §111.[50]

3. Losses vs. Expenses and Bad Debts. It is sometimes necessary to determine whether a transaction produced (a) a "loss" under IRC §165, (b) an "expense" under IRC §162 or §212, or (c) a "worthless debt" under IRC §166. For example, IRC §267(a) disallows deductions for losses on sales and exchanges of property between related persons (as defined), but it does not apply to payments to a related person that are "expenses," nor to worthless debts owed by a relative. All bad debts are deductible. By contrast, losses sustained by individuals are deductible only if attributable to the taxpayer's business, a transaction entered into for profit, or casualty, while expenses can

---

[48] See, e.g., Industrial Cotton Mills Co. v. CIR, 43 BTA 107 (1940) (Acq.) (ordinary loss on discarding equipment, despite sale to secondhand dealer for salvage value).

[49] Rev. Rul. 78-164, 1978-1 CB 264, citing Millar v. CIR, 67 TC 656 (1977).

[50] For the tax benefit doctrine, see generally supra ¶1.10.

be deducted only if related to the taxpayer's business or income-producing activities.

Sometimes the borderline between losses, expenses, and bad debts is blurred because the event exhibits characteristics belonging to two or all three categories. An uncollectible advance belongs in the "bad debt" category and is simultaneously disqualified as a "loss" within the meaning of IRC §165(a).

In *Putnam v. CIR,* the Supreme Court held that because a guarantor, on paying a debt when the debtor defaults, becomes subrogated to the creditor's claim against the debtor, the guarantor's loss "is by its very nature a loss from the worthlessness of a debt"—with the result that the guarantor's claim for a deduction is governed by IRC §166, relating to bad debts, not by IRC §165, relating to losses.[51] The Tax Court, however, has held that *Putnam* does not apply if the guarantor pays the debtor's debt in circumstances creating no right of subrogation (e.g., if the guarantor pays only part of the underlying debt) and that a nonsubrogated guarantor sustains an ordinary loss under IRC §165(a).[52] But two courts of appeals have held that *Putnam* subjects the guarantor's loss to IRC §§166(a) and 166(d) even in the absence of subrogation.[53]

The distinction between "losses" and "expenses" is described—a trifle blithely, perhaps—as "self-evident" by the Tax Court in a 1977 case contrasting the unlawful use of liquor to entertain clients (an "expense," deductible only if permitted by IRC §162) with the confiscation of unlawful liquor by law-enforcement officials (a "loss," deductible only if permitted by IRC §165).[54] The distinction can also be illustrated by contrasting damage to business property by fire (a loss subject to IRC §165) with the cost of repairing the property (an expense subject to IRC §162).

4. Gambling Losses. Section 165(d) allows a deduction for losses from "wagering transactions" only to the extent of gains from such transactions.[55] Disallowed gambling losses die at the end of the taxable year in which they are sustained; they do not create net operating losses that can be carried over to other years. Individual taxpayers who are not engaged in the business of gambling cannot deduct gambling losses in computing adjusted gross in-

[51] Putnam v. CIR, 352 US 82, 85 (1956).

[52] Rietzke v. CIR, 40 TC 443, 450-453 (1963).

[53] Stratmore v. US, 420 F.2d 461 (3d Cir.), cert. denied, 398 US 951 (1970); US v. Hoffman, 423 F.2d 1217 (9th Cir. 1970).

[54] Holt v. CIR, 69 TC 75 (1977), aff'd per curiam, 611 F.2d 1160 (5th Cir. 1980) (forfeiture of truck used to transport marijuana generated loss, not expense; held, nondeductible under frustration-of-public-policy doctrine).

[55] See Presley v. CIR, ¶79,339 P-H Memo TC (1979) (IRC §165(d) covers all gambling, whether in business, recreation, or sport; gains and losses from all types of gambling netted).

come; hence, their gambling losses are deductible only if they itemize their personal deductions. In applying this principle, however, gains and losses can probably be netted to some extent (e.g., on a per-game or per-session basis).[56]

¶12.8 TAX SHELTER LOSSES—LIMITATION OF DEDUCTIONS TO AMOUNTS AT RISK

1. Introductory. To combat the dramatic increase in the use of tax shelters in the 1960's and early 1970's, IRC §465 was enacted in 1976, limiting the deduction of otherwise allowable losses to the amount that the taxpayer had "at risk" in each of four specified activities: farming, oil and gas exploration and exploitation, motion-picture films and video tapes, and equipment leasing. Section 465 was expanded in 1978 to cover losses from all business and profit-oriented activities except the holding of real property (other than mineral property) and equipment leasing by certain closely held corporations. Section 465(d) defines "losses" as the excess of the allowable deductions allocable to a covered activity over the income received or accrued by the taxpayer from the activity.

The tax shelters that Congress sought to curb took many forms but ordinarily had two features in common: (1) The investors put up relatively little cash and hence had little to lose if the venture failed; but (2) the venture borrowed heavily on a nonrecourse or other basis entailing no personal liability for the investor, so that the investor's deductions for depreciation, amortization, intangible drilling and development costs, business expenses, interest, or other items greatly exceeded the cash outlay. This leveraging aspect of virtually all classical tax shelters was based on the taxpayer's long-established right to deduct interest, business expenses, and other out-of-pocket items when paid or incurred, even if they are defrayed with borrowed funds, and on the fact that depreciation and amortization are computed on the full adjusted basis of property, even if it is purchased with funds borrowed on a nonrecourse basis. In addition to producing large deductions for minimal cash outlays, these deductions were not offset solely against income produced by the tax shelter itself, but could be applied against salaries, professional fees, dividends, interest, and business income of all types, resulting in dramatic reductions in the investor's current tax liabilities and corresponding large increases in spendable funds.

In theory, leveraged tax shelters could only defer tax liabilities, not eliminate them. If the investment was successful, it would in time generate net

---

[56] For proof of gambling gains and losses, see Rev. Proc. 77-29, 1977-2 CB 538 (re proper records).

income equaling or exceeding the expenditures deducted in the shelter's early years, and the inclusion of this income on the investor's return would increase taxable income by at least as much as the taxable income of the earlier years was reduced by the deductions. But since the cash reflecting this income would be used to pay off the borrowed funds that had financed the deducted expenditures, it could not be distributed to the investor. On reaching this crossover point, therefore, the investor would have to draw on other funds to pay the deferred taxes. On the other hand, if the investment failed before the borrowed funds were repaid, the unpaid debt would constitute an "amount realized" within the meaning of IRC §1001(a) on the termination of the shelter, producing phantom income of the same amount because the taxpayer's basis would have been reduced by the early deductions to either zero or a nominal amount. Therefore, the taxpayer would have taxable income equal to the prior deductions, but no new cash to pay the resulting tax liability.

In either event, however, the taxpayer would have had an opportunity in the interim to invest or spend the amount of taxes saved. Thus, even if a tax shelter's only effect was a deferral of taxes, it was attractive to many taxpayers. Furthermore, by entering into a new shelter when the original one began to generate income, taxpayers could avert the evil day; and, even if this was not feasible, the taxpayer might be in lower tax brackets (e.g., as a result of retirement) when deferral ended.

To eliminate this tax-avoidance potential of leveraged tax shelters, IRC §465 modifies the two structural features of the tax system on which pre-1976 tax shelters depended: (1) the aggregation of all ordinary income and deductions, regardless of source, in computing taxable income, and (2) the taxpayer's right to deduct expenditures even if financed with funds borrowed on a nonrecourse basis. Section 465 modifies the aggregation principle of prior law by segregating all income and deductions for each of certain specified activities. Within each segregated channel, deductions can be applied up to the full amount of the income produced by the same activity. If, however, the deductions attributable to the activity exceed the income from the activity, the net loss can be deducted against income from other activities only to the extent of the taxpayer's at-risk investment in the activity producing the loss. An at-risk investment requires either the commitment of the taxpayer's funds and property or the assumption of personal liability for borrowed funds. Underlying these modifications is a value judgment that a net loss in a covered activity should be deductible against income from other activities only to the extent that it entails a "true" loss.

Although these modifications of prior law by IRC §465 are of great importance, it is equally important to bear in mind that neither change is applied generally throughout the tax law. Channelization is an exception to the basic principle—still in force, despite IRC §465—that taxable income is computed on a global basis. For example, taxpayers who finance all business and profit-oriented activities with their own funds or with debt entailing personal liability continue to compute taxable income on a global rather than channelized basis. Second, IRC §465's at-risk principle does not supplant or repeal the basic rule that expenditures are deductible even if financed with nonrecourse debt. For example, taxpayers whose business or profit-oriented activities fall into a single channel can apply all deductions, regardless of how the expenditures are financed, against their income, and they can carry a net loss over to other taxable years under IRC §172, relating to net operating losses. Indeed, nonrecourse-financed expenditures are fully taken into account even by taxpayers investing in tax shelters, up to the income produced by the segregated activity, and excess deductions are carried forward for application in the same manner in later years.

2. Covered Taxpayers and Activities. Section 465 casts a shadow on transactions and activities far removed from the targeted area. It is especially important, therefore, to delineate the taxpayers and activities that it covers and, conversely, those exempted from its jurisdiction.

1. *Covered taxpayers.* Section 465(a)(1) limits the deduction of losses incurred by individuals (including trusts, estates, and noncorporate members of partnerships), Subchapter S corporations, and certain closely held corporations engaging in activities to which IRC §465 applies. The targeted corporations are those satisfying the personal holding company stock ownership rules of IRC §542(a)(2), which encompass any corporation more than 50 percent of whose stock (by value) is owned at any time during the last half of the taxable year by not more than five individuals. Since direct, indirect, and constructive ownership is taken into account in determining the number of individual shareholders owning the requisite amount of stock,[57] virtually all closely-held corporations satisfy the stock ownership test: if a corporation's outstanding stock is owned by fewer than ten individuals, the stock ownership test of IRC §465(a)(1)(C) will automatically be satisfied.

2. *Covered activities.* Section 465(c) covers (1) holding, producing, or distributing motion-picture films or video tapes; (2) farming, within the broad definition of IRC §464(e); (3) leasing Section 1245 property, as defined by IRC §1245(a)(3) (primarily business equipment but also some items of tangible realty other than buildings and their structural components); (4) exploring for or exploiting oil and gas resources; and (5) exploring for or exploiting geothermal deposits. Section 465(c)(3), enacted in 1978, expands the coverage to embrace any other activity engaged in by the taxpayer as a business or for the production of income. This covers virtually all profit-oriented activities, including such diverse fields as manufacturing, wholesale and retail trade, rendi-

---

[57] There is, however, no attribution from one partner to another in determining the ownership of stock.

tion of personal and professional services, and investing in marketable securities—no matter how remote from the rash of tax shelters that evoked the enactment of IRC §465.

3. *Separation and aggregation of covered activities.* The impact of IRC §465 depends heavily on whether a group of transactions constitutes one activity or more than one. For example, if two oil wells constitute a single activity, losses from one can be freely applied against income from the other, and the taxpayer may then have no net loss from the activity to be limited by IRC §465(a)(1). If, however, each well constitutes a separate activity, losses from an unprofitable well can be applied against income from a profitable one only to the extent of the taxpayer's at-risk investment in the loss well. Under IRC §465(c)(2), each oil and gas property, as defined by IRC §614, is a separate activity; thus, all wells on the same "property" constitute a single activity, but a taxpayer with wells on two or more properties is engaged in two or more separate activities for purposes of IRC §465.

When IRC §465 was expanded in 1978 to cover all other business and income-producing activities, Congress did not undertake to divide the multifarious activities covered by the new dragnet proviso into separate activities. Instead, it authorized the IRS to prescribe regulations for the segregation or aggregation of these newly covered activities and to take their "tax shelter characteristics" into account in prescribing the necessary rules.

4. *Excluded activities.* When enacting the 1978 dragnet proviso of IRC §465(c)(3), Congress imposed two limits on its otherwise unlimited scope.

Under IRC §465(c)(3)(D)(i), the holding of real property (other than mineral property) is treated as a separate activity and IRC §465(a) does not apply to losses from it. Personal property and services incidental to living accommodations (but not meals, nursing care, etc.) are treated as part of the activity of holding the underlying real property; for example, income from the ownership and operation of a hotel is covered by the exemption. The exemption does not apply to real property used in the five activities listed in IRC §465(c)(1) (farming, leasing Section 1245 property, etc.).

Section 465(c)(4) provides a similar, but much more restricted, exclusion for corporations actively engaged in leasing equipment subject to IRC §1245, such as computers and airplanes. The leasing activity is treated as a separate activity, and the deduction of losses attributable to the activity is not limited by IRC §465(a).

3. Losses Subject to At-Risk Limitation. Section 465 permits deductions incurred in an activity to be applied freely against income generated by that activity and intervenes only when a taxpayer attempts to use a loss incurred in a covered activity to reduce income from other sources. The amount subject to the at-risk limitation is defined by IRC §465(d) as the excess of (a) the deductions allowable for the taxable year that are allocable to a covered activity over (b) the income received or accrued by the taxpayer from the activity during the same taxable year. This is the net loss resulting from the covered activity. It should not be confused with a "loss" deductible under IRC §165(a), which is merely an item taken into account in determining whether the taxpayer incurred a loss from the activity within the meaning of IRC §465(d).

Any disallowed loss is carried forward to the next taxable year for application against the income (if any) from the loss activity and, if the taxpayer's at-risk investment increases, against income from other activities. In accordance with the manifest legislative intent, the proposed regulations allow the unlimited carryforward of disallowed amounts.

The proposed regulations prescribe rules that allocate specially treated items, such as tax preference items and long-term and short-term capital losses, between the loss year and the later years to which disallowed losses are carried and that determine the order in which items carried forward from two or more loss years are to be applied.[58]

4. Computation of At-Risk Amount. The heart of IRC §465—or, from the taxpayer's perspective, its fist—is IRC §465(b), prescribing the amount that taxpayers have "at risk" in a covered activity, since this limits the amount of loss allocable to a covered activity that can be used to offset income from other sources. Reflecting its function as a weapon against leveraged tax shelters, IRC §465(b) is designed to separate genuine losses of the taxpayer's investment in the covered activity from ostensible losses that have not yet pinched the taxpayer because the underlying expenditures were financed on a nonrecourse basis.

Computation of the "at risk" amount entails four steps:

1. *Contributions of money and property.* Under IRC §465(b)(1)(A), the taxpayer is at risk to the extent of the money and property contributed to the activity, including the cost of acquiring an interest therein.[59] Property is taken into account to the extent of its adjusted basis, regardless of its market value, since the adjusted basis reflects the taxpayer's investment in the property—the amount that can be deducted, for example, if the property becomes worthless in conducting the activity.

2. *Borrowed amounts.* The taxpayer is also at risk for amounts borrowed with respect to the activity to the extent of (a) the taxpayer's personal liability for repayment or (b) the net fair market value of property pledged as security for repayment of the debt. Pledged property cannot be counted if it is used in

[58] Prop. Regs. §1.465-38.

[59] See Prop. Regs. §1.465-22(d). For contributions of encumbered property, see Prop. Regs. §1.465-23(a)(2).

the activity or is directly or indirectly financed by debt secured by property contributed to the activity. For example, if the taxpayer borrows on a nonrecourse basis against his residence, contributes the funds to a covered activity, and pledges activity property as security for the nonrecourse debt, the latter is viewed as the true security for the debt; and the debt is therefore disqualified, just as it would have been if the funds had been borrowed solely on the security of the activity property.

Section 465(b)(3) disqualifies amounts borrowed from persons with an interest in the activity (other than creditors) or from persons related to the taxpayer (as defined in IRC §267(b)). For example, amounts borrowed by a limited partner in a tax shelter from the general partner or from the taxpayer's children are excluded from the at-risk computation by virtue of these limitations.[60]

3. *Protection against loss.* Under IRC §465(b)(4), no amount may be included in the taxpayer's at-risk investment if the taxpayer is protected against loss by nonrecourse financing, guaranties, stop-loss agreements, or similar arrangements. Although this provision is aimed primarily at funds borrowed on a nonrecourse basis, the regulations set forth numerous other arrangements that constitute protection against loss. Insurance against casualties or tort liabilities, however, does not ordinarily constitute protection against loss within the meaning of IRC §465(b)(4).[61] Nonrecourse financing, however, is disqualified by IRC §465(b)(4) even if it is so amply covered by the value of the pledged property that there is little or no likelihood of default.

4. *Changes in at-risk amount.* Section 465(b)(5) provides that losses incurred in a covered activity and deducted from another activity's income reduce the taxpayer's at-risk amount for later years. This provision is obviously required to prevent the same at-risk amount from being used year after year. The proposed regulations provide a complete network of at-risk accounting rules, including provisions for increasing the at-risk amount by the taxpayer's net income from the activity and for decreasing the amount by withdrawals of cash.[62]

5. Recapture of Losses If At-Risk Amount Drops Below Zero. Although the taxpayer's at-risk amount limits the extent to which losses incurred in a

[60] Under IRC §465(c)(3)(E), these restrictions apply to activities covered by IRC §465(c)(3), as distinguished from those listed in IRC §465(c)(1), only to the extent prescribed by the regulations.

[61] Prop. Regs. §§1.465-5, 1.465-6(b), 1.465-6(c).

[62] See, e.g., Prop. Regs. §§1.465-22(b) (withdrawal of money), 1.465-22(c) (income and loss), 1.465-23(a)(2)(ii) (reduction of encumbrances on property contributed to activity), 1.465-24(b) (repayment of debt for which taxpayer is personally liable), 1.465-25(a)(2) (repayment of nonrecourse debt).

covered activity can be applied against income from other activities, it is possible for the at-risk amount to drop below zero as a result of withdrawal of funds from the activity or the conversion of debt to a nonrecourse obligation. Under IRC §465(e), the taxpayer's below-zero at-risk amount must be included in gross income; and it is then treated as a deduction allocable to the activity, deductible in subsequent years subject to the at-risk limitations applicable to those years. The effect of IRC §465(e) is to recapture losses allocable to a covered activity if they exceed the sum of the taxpayer's at-risk amount and the income, if any, reported from the activity.

¶12.9 NET OPERATING LOSS CARRYBACKS AND CARRYOVERS

1. Introductory. Section 172 ordinarily permits net operating losses to be carried back to the three taxable years before the loss year and forward to the fifteen succeeding years, so that the expenses of earning income will be taken into account over a nineteen-year cycle. When carried back, a net operating loss (NOL) reduces the taxable income of the relevant earlier year, resulting in a recomputation of the tax liability and a refund or credit of the excess amount paid. Carryovers produce a similar reduction in the taxable income of later years, and this reduces the tax payable when the return is filed.

The primary purpose of the NOL deduction is to ameliorate the effect of the annual accounting period by treating businesses with widely fluctuating income more nearly in accord with steady-income businesses; without a carryover, firms experiencing loss years could not deduct the full cost of earning income during the entire business cycle. The deduction also serves to encourage investment in new ventures, because early losses can be deducted in future profitable years.[63]

2. Computation of Net Operating Loss. Section 172(c) defines "net operating loss" as the excess of deductions over the taxpayer's gross income, subject to the modifications prescribed by IRC §172(d). Because corporations are treated differently from other taxpayers by IRC §172(d), they are discussed separately below.

1. *Corporate taxpayers.* For corporations, the most significant modification is prescribed by IRC §172(d)(6), providing that the deduction for dividends received shall be computed without regard to the taxable-income limitation of IRC §246(b)(1).[64] The removal of this limit means that a corporation

---

[63] See US v. Foster Lumber Co., 429 US 32, 42 (1976).

[64] The dividends-received deduction is generally equal to 85 percent of the lower

can sustain an NOL even if it reported taxable income, provided there would have been an NOL if the dividends-received deduction had not been limited by IRC §246(b)(1).

2. *Other taxpayers.* In determining whether individuals and other noncorporate taxpayers sustained an NOL, IRC §172(d) prescribes elaborate rules to prevent investment expenses, itemized personal deductions, and personal and dependency exemptions from being carried from one year to another. First, personal and dependency exemptions are disregarded in determining whether noncorporate taxpayers have an excess of deductions over gross income.[65] Second, the deduction allowed by IRC §1202 (60 percent of net capital gain), a rate-reduction measure that does not reflect any economic loss to the taxpayer, is disregarded. Third, deductions not attributable to the taxpayer's trade or business (e.g., IRC §212 expense deductions) are ordinarily allowed only to the extent of nonbusiness gross income. If these items exceed the taxpayer's nonbusiness gross income, the excess cannot create or increase an NOL and hence cannot be used to reduce taxable income in other years. The zero bracket amount (ZBA) is also treated as a nonbusiness deduction, provided the taxpayer did not elect to itemize deductions; this permits nonitemizers to reduce nonbusiness income by their ZBA, in the same way that itemizers can reduce nonbusiness income by their itemized deductions.

3. Years to Which Net Operating Losses Are Carried. Section 172(b)(1) provides that an NOL is a "net operating loss carryback" to the three taxable years immediately preceding the year of the loss and a "net operating loss carryover" to the fifteen immediately succeeding years. Some classes of taxpayers, however, are subject to different carryback and carryforward periods.[66]

Under IRC §172(b)(3)(C), taxpayers may elect to relinquish the entire carryback period for an NOL sustained in any post-1975 taxable year, in which event the NOL is used only prospectively.

Section 172(b)(2) requires an NOL to be carried first to the earliest permissible year, and any unabsorbed amount is then carried forward year by year in chronological order until the NOL is fully absorbed or expires. In general, any period for which a tax return is required is a "year" that must be counted; for example, a short taxable year resulting from a change of the

---

of dividends received or taxable income (before this deduction). See IRC §§243(a); 246(b)(1).

[65] This modification also covers the analogous exemptions allowed to trusts and estates by IRC §642(b).

[66] See IRC §§172(b)(1)(C), 172(b)(1)(D), 172(b)(1)(E), 172(b)(1)(F), 172(b)(1)(G), 172(b)(1)(H), 172(b)(1)(I).

taxpayer's accounting period is a full year for this purpose.[67] If a taxpayer sustains NOLs in two or more years, the oldest loss is used first, which ordinarily increases the likelihood that NOLs will be used before they expire.[68]

Section 6511(d)(2) extends the statute of limitations for claiming credits and refunds for NOL carryback years from the normal three-year period to the period ending three years after the due date (including extensions) for the return for the *loss* year.[69]

4. Computation of NOL Deduction. Computing the net operating loss deduction is simple if the taxpayer has only one NOL and it is carried to the earliest year in the normal carryback-carryover cycle; the entire amount of the NOL is the deduction for that year. But if the NOL carryback exceeds the taxable income of the earliest carryback year, it must be reduced to determine the amount, if any, that can be carried to the second year in the cycle; and this adjustment process must be repeated for each year in the nineteen-year cycle, until the NOL either is fully absorbed or expires. If the taxpayer has two or more NOL carrybacks and/or carryovers to the same year by virtue of sustaining NOL losses in two or more years, the NOL deduction for the year to which they are carried is the sum of these amounts, unless the total cannot be fully absorbed, in which case the earliest NOL is absorbed first, and the balance is carried forward.

In recomputing an individual taxpayer's tax liability for a carryback year, all deductions dependent on adjusted gross income and taxable income are recomputed, with the exception of the charitable deduction, and credits must be recomputed if they are related to the amount of the tax liability.

5. Effect of Intervening Years on Unused Net Operating Losses. When NOL carrybacks and carryovers are carried through one or more intervening years to the next relevant year, they must be adjusted as prescribed by IRC §172(b)(2). The carryback or carryover is reduced in rotation by the taxable income of each intervening year, modified by some of the adjustments that were employed when the NOL was originally computed, except that the modifications are now applied to the correct taxable income of the intervening year, even if the statute of limitations bars the assertion of refunds or deficiencies. The modifications may result in a gain that "absorbs" part or all of the NOL, even if the intervening year originally showed a loss.[70]

---

[67] See Treas. Regs. §1.172-4(a)(2).

[68] See Treas. Regs. §1.172-4(a)(3) (second sentence).

[69] See Treas. Regs. §301.6511(d)-2.

[70] See Treas. Regs. §1.172-4(a)(3) (use of term "absorb"); Rubin v. CIR, 26 TC 1076 (1956), rev'd on procedural grounds, 252 F.2d 243 (5th Cir. 1958) (loss of about $11,000 turned into modified taxable income of about $67,000).

6. Changes of Taxpayer Status, Identity, and Ownership. During the nineteen-year carryback-carryover cycle, taxpayers sustaining NOLs can experience many changes of status, identity, and ownership—for example, individuals may marry, get divorced, or die, and corporations may be sold to new shareholders, merge, liquidate, or split up. The effect of many of these events is prescribed by statutory provisions and the regulations, some of which are summarized below:

1. *Joint/separate returns of married couples.* If a married couple files joint returns for every year in the nineteen-year cycle, they compute joint NOL carrybacks or carryovers in the same manner as individuals, but on the basis of their combined NOLs and combined taxable income.[70] If they file a joint return for the deduction year but separate returns for all other years in the cycle, their separate carrybacks and carryovers are combined into a joint carryback or carryover for the deduction year.[71]

2. *Bankruptcy.* An individual taxpayer's estate in bankruptcy succeeds to the taxpayer's NOL carryovers under IRC §1398(g)(1). If the estate in bankruptcy incurs an NOL, it may be carried back to a taxable year of the bankruptcy, but the refund generated by the carryback belongs to the estate.[72] Section 1398(i) provides that, upon termination of the bankruptcy proceedings, the debtor succeeds to all surviving unused NOLs generated either before or during the bankruptcy proceedings; but IRC §1398(d)(2)(B) prohibits the taxpayer from carrying back a post-bankruptcy NOL to a pre-bankruptcy year.

3. *Death.* NOLs cannot be carried forward from a deceased individual's returns to the estate's returns or back from the estate's returns to the deceased's returns.[73] But this principle does not preclude carrybacks and carryovers as between the decedent and the decedent's surviving spouse, if joint returns were filed for some or all of the pre-death years.[74]

¶12.10 INTANGIBLE DRILLING AND DEVELOPMENT COSTS—OIL AND GAS (IDC)

As an exception to IRC §263(a), prohibiting the deduction of capital expenditures, IRC §263(c) permits taxpayers to elect to deduct intangible drilling and development costs (IDC) for oil, gas, and geothermal wells. The Treasury first permitted taxpayers to deduct intangible drilling and development expenses for oil and gas wells in 1916, despite the absence of any express statutory authority for the deduction. In *F.H.E. Oil Co. v. CIR,* decided in 1945, the Court of Appeals for the Fifth Circuit held that the regulations

---

[71] Treas. Regs. §1.172-7(c).

[72] Treas. Regs. §1.172-7(b).

[73] Segal v. Rochelle, 382 US 375 (1966); IRC §1389(j)(2)(A).

[74] Rev. Rul. 74-175, 1974-1 CB 52.

authorizing this election were invalid under the statutory predecessor of IRC §263(a).[75] Shortly after this decision, however, Congress shored up the regulations by enacting House Concurrent Resolution 50, declaring that Congress "has recognized and approved" the disputed regulations.[76] In 1954, the regulations gained formal statutory approval with the enactment of IRC §263(c), and in 1978, similar treatment was extended to IDC for wells drilled for geothermal deposits, as defined by IRC §613(e)(3).

If a taxpayer does not elect to deduct IDC, they increase the basis of the affected property and are recovered by depreciation deductions if they relate to physical properties and by depletion otherwise. Since percentage depletion is unaffected by the adjusted basis of the property, taxpayers entitled to use this method of depleting oil and gas properties almost always benefit from electing to deduct IDC under IRC §263(c). If the taxpayer is an integrated oil company, fifteen percent of the amount otherwise deductible cannot be deducted currently but must instead be deducted ratably over the thirty-six months following the month in which the costs were incurred.

Only an "operator," a person with a working interest (even if temporary), may deduct IDC.[77] Qualified expenses undertaken directly or through contract are deductible, but only to the extent allocable to the operator's fractional interest. The balance of the expenses, which in effect constitutes the cost of acquiring the assigned rights, must be capitalized. Expenses fixed in amount and incurred under a turnkey contract by which the drilling contractor agrees to drill and equip a well can be deducted; but the contract price must be allocated between the intangibles and the depreciable equipment.

The option to deduct IDC applies to all expenditures by an operator for wages, fuel, repairs, hauling, supplies, etc., incident to and necessary for the drilling of wells and the preparation of wells for the production of oil or gas, if incurred for any of the following purposes:

1. Drilling, shooting, and cleaning wells.
2. Clearing ground, draining, road making, surveying, and geological work necessary in preparation for the drilling of wells.
3. Constructing derricks, tanks, pipelines, and other physical structures necessary for the drilling of wells and the preparation of wells for the production of oil or gas.[78]

Items with salvage value, however, may not be deducted; but labor, fuel, repairs, hauling, and supplies are not considered as having salvage value, even

[75] F.H.R. Oil Co. v. CIR, 147 F.2d 1002 (5th Cir.), rehearing denied, 149 F.2d 238, second rehearing denied, 150 F.2d 857 (1945).

[76] H.R. Con. Rec. No. 50, 59 Stat. (Part 2) 844 (1945).

[77] Treas. Regs. §1.612-4(a) (first sentence).

[78] Treas. Regs. §1.612-4(a).

though used in connection with the installation of physical property that does have salvage value. These items must be distinguished from expenditures for tangible property that ordinarily has a salvage value, such as materials used in structures in the wells or on the property, drilling tools, pipe, casing, tanks, engines, and other equipment, which must be capitalized and recovered by depreciation deductions over their useful lives.

Exploratory geological and geophysical expenditures to determine the existence, location, and extent of oil and gas are not subject to IRC §263(c), but are instead added to the basis of the property.[79] On the other hand, geological and geophysical expenditures required to prepare for the drilling of wells may be deducted.[80]

Although the election to deduct IDC is normally advantageous to the taxpayer, it can have some adverse tax consequences. Under IRC §263(c), IDC's can generate tax preference items subject to the minimum tax imposed by IRC §56. Furthermore, on the disposition of a property with respect to which IDC's were deducted, IRC §1254 may generate some recapture income.

¶12.11 MINING EXPLORATION AND DEVELOPMENT EXPENDITURES

Section 617 permits taxpayers to elect to deduct mining exploration expenditures instead of capitalizing them; and IRC §616 grants a similar election for expenditures for the development of mines and other natural deposits. Neither election applies to oil or gas wells. A third provision relating to mineral exploration and development is IRC §621, excluding from gross income payments and the forgiveness of loans by federal agencies to encourage exploration, development, or mining of critical and strategic minerals and metals under a program requiring the taxpayer to render an accounting to the appropriate agency. Excluded amounts cannot be deducted or taken into account in computing depletion, depreciation, or gain or loss on a disposition of the property unless repaid by the taxpayer, in which event the amount is either deductible or includable in the basis of the property at the time of the repayment.

Section 617 grants taxpayers an election to deduct expenditures "for the purpose of ascertaining the existence, location, extent, or quality of any deposit of ore or other mineral" if paid or incurred before the beginning of the development stage of the mine, and if the expenditures are not otherwise allowable as a deduction.[81] The election does not apply to expenditures for the

[79] See Rev. Rul. 77-188, 1977-1 CB 76.

[80] Treas. Regs. §1.612-4(a); see also Treas. Regs. §1.612-4(b)(1).

[81] For corporations, 15 percent of the amount otherwise currently deductible under IRC §616 or §617 is disallowed by IRC §291(b), and is instead recovered over

acquisition or improvement of depreciable property, but the depreciation itself, if allocable to exploration, is treated as an exploration expenditure. The exploration stage of the taxpayer's activities terminates and the development stage begins when considering all facts and circumstances, deposits are disclosed in sufficient quantity and quality so that commercial exploitation by the taxpayer is reasonably justified.[82]

Expenditures deducted under IRC §617 are subject to recapture. At the taxpayer's election, the adjusted exploration expenditures are includable in gross income when the mine reaches "the producing stage," [83] and the taxpayer then includes them in the depletable basis of the minerals.[84] If the taxpayer does not elect this method of recapture, the depletion deductions otherwise allowable with respect to the property (not merely those allocable to the particular mine) are disallowed until the expenditures have been fully recaptured.[85]

Upon a sale or other disposition of the mineral property, IRC §617(d) requires the taxpayer to recognize as ordinary income the lower of (a) the adjusted exploration expenditures or (b) the excess of the amount realized on the sale, exchange, or involuntary conversion (or the property's fair market value, in the case of other dispositions) over its adjusted basis.

Section 616(a) provides for the deduction of all expenditures for the development of a mine or other natural deposit, if paid or incurred after the existence of ores or minerals in commercially marketable quantities has been disclosed. It does not apply to expenditures for the acquisition or improvement of depreciable property; but the depreciation itself is considered a development expenditure. Instead of deducting development expenditures under IRC §616(a), taxpayers may elect under IRC §616(b) to treat them as deferred expenses, in which event they are includable in the basis of the property and can be deducted, in addition to depletion, on a ratable basis as the minerals benefited are sold. Unlike exploration expenses, development expenses are not subject to recapture.

Only expenditures paid or incurred *for development* of the mine or other natural deposit may be deducted under IRC §616. Thus, if a taxpayer agrees to pay all expenditures required to develop a deposit in return for a three-fourths interest in the mineral lease, only three-fourths of the expenditures can be deducted, since the remaining one-fourth is the cost of acquiring the taxpayer's interest in the lease.[86] Distinguishing development expenditures from

---

the next five years under statutory tables. The amount subject to deferred recovery is eligible for the IRC §38 investment tax credit under IRC §291(b)(2).

[82] Treas. Regs. §1.617-1(a).

[83] For this term, see Treas. Regs. §1.616-2(b).

[84] See IRC §617(b)(1)(A); Treas. Regs. §1.617-3(a)(2).

[85] IRC §617(b)(1)(B); Treas. Regs. §1.617-3(a)(1)(i).

[86] Treas. Regs. §1.616-1(b)(3).

operating expenses, the IRS describes the former as "expenditures that benefit an entire mineral deposit or large areas of a mineral deposit" by providing "benefits that extend over relatively long periods of extraction of the valuable ore or mineral," as contrasted with day-to-day operating expenses that are "integrally related to extraction of a limited area of the [mineral] to be mined." [87]

¶12.12 AMORTIZATION OF BOND PREMIUM

If an investor pays more for a bond than the amount payable on maturity or redemption, the interest ostensibly received by the investor represents in part a return of the premium. By permitting taxpayers to elect to amortize bond premium, IRC §171 matches the premium with the interest received and protects investors against sustaining only a capital loss after having reported the interest as ordinary income in its entirety. Tax-exempt securities are subjected to mandatory amortization to prevent the taxpayer from deducting the premium as a loss on maturity after having recovered the premium during the life of the bond as tax-exempt interest under IRC §103.

Both original-issue premium and market premium (arising from the purchase of a bond for more than par, reflecting an interest rate in excess of the market rate for obligations of similar quality) can be amortized. Moreover, purchase commissions and other capitalized expenses can ordinarily be included in the basis of the bond and may even be the sole reason why a premium exists.[88] Premiums attributable to a conversion privilege, however, do not quality for amortization.[89] The premium is normally amortized on a monthly basis; but some other methods are permitted.[90]

The amortizable premium reduces the basis of the bond each year by virtue of IRC §1016(a)(5). If the bond is held until maturity, therefore, the entire amount of the premium will have been amortized; and since the basis of the bond will equal the amount payable on maturity, there will be no gain or loss at that time. If the bond is sold before maturity, however, the unamortized premium will reduce the gain (or increase the loss) realized on the sale.

[87] Rev. Rul. 77-308, 1977-2 CB 208.

[88] See Treas. Regs. §1.171-2(d); see also Ades v. CIR, 38 TC 501 (1962), aff'd per curiam, 316 F.2d 734 (2d Cir. 1963) (unamortized premium on convertible bonds cannot be deducted on conversion; basis of bonds as of conversion is transferred from bonds to stock received in exchange).

[89] IRC §171(b)(1) (last sentence). The value of a conversion feature is computed by reference to the price of a comparable nonconvertible bond. See Treas. Regs. §§1.171-2(c)(2), 1.171-2(c)(3).

[90] Treas. Regs. §1.171-2(f); see also Treas. Regs. §1.171-1(c).

¶12.13 DEDUCTION AND AMORTIZATION OF CERTAIN CAPITAL OUTLAYS

1. Introductory. The general depreciation and amortization rules are supplemented by a number of special provisions allowing capital outlays to be deducted currently or amortized over a prescribed period shorter than the property's useful life. Some of these provisions apply to property that would otherwise be depreciable over its estimated useful life or subject to ACRS, but others apply even if the property does not qualify for any depreciation or ACRS deductions. In the latter situation, were it not for the special provisions, the taxpayer's investment would be held in abeyance, to be offset against the sales proceeds if the asset was sold or to be deducted as a loss if it became worthless and was abandoned. In general, the function of these provisions is to provide taxpayers with an incentive for investments that Congress views as socially desirable but not sufficiently profitable to be made without a subsidy, to alleviate inequalities among taxpayers, or to eliminate uncertainty by establishing a permissible period for the amortization of assets whose useful life is difficult to determine.

2. Research and Experimental Expenditures. At the taxpayer's election, IRC §174 allows research and experimental expenditures paid or incurred in connection with a trade or business to be deducted currently or deferred and amortized over a prescribed period of sixty months or more. Expenditures of this type that are neither deducted nor deferred and amortized are chargeable to capital account [91] and are (a) amortized over the estimated useful life of the asset generated by the expenditure, (b) held in abeyance and offset against the sales price of the asset if it does not have a limited useful life, or (c) deducted as losses if the assets are abandoned or the research project is a failure.

Section 174 was enacted in 1954 "to eliminate uncertainty and to encourage taxpayers to carry on research and experimentation." [92] The uncertainty that IRC §174 was designed to eliminate resulted from the fact that the only statutory authority under prior law for deducting research and experimental expenditures was IRC §162, relating to ordinary and necessary business expenses, which requires expenses incurred in carrying on an existing business to be distinguished from those with a sufficiently long-range impact to constitute capital outlays. In the latter situation, the capitalized amount can be amortized only if a limited useful life can be ascribed to the results of the research. It is also often difficult to determine when a line of research has ended in a blind alley, justifying an abandonment loss, and when it is only

---

[91] Treas. Regs. §1.174-1.

[92] S. Rep. No. 1622, 83d Cong., 2d Sess. 33 (1954).

temporarily stymied. By electing either to deduct the research and experimental expenditures under IRC §174(a) or to defer and amortize them under IRC §174(b), the taxpayer can avoid any need for these impalpable distinctions.

Section 174 applies only to expenditures paid or incurred "in connection with [the taxpayer's] trade or business." The Supreme Court observed in *Snow v. CIR* [93] that this phrase is broader than the standard language of IRC §162, relating to expenses paid or incurred "in carrying on" the taxpayer's trade or business, and that IRC §174 can be used by companies "that are upcoming and about to reach the market" as well as by existing businesses. Section 174 does not, however, embrace research conducted as a hobby or other not-for-profit project.

The regulations define "research and experimental expenditures" as research and development costs "in the experimental or laboratory sense," including all costs incident to the development of pilot models, processes, products, formulas, inventions, and similar property; the improvement of these items; and legal and other expenses in obtaining a patent.[94] Expenditures to acquire or improve land or depreciable property are not deductible under IRC §174, even though the property is to be used in connection with research or experimentation. The ACRS allowances on such property, however, are treated as research and experimental expenditures under IRC §174.[95]

3. Trademark and Trade Name Expenditures. Taxpayers can elect under IRC §177 to treat trademark and trade name expenditures as deferred expenses and amortize them ratably over a designated period of sixty months or more. In the absence of an election under IRC §177, these expenditures are ordinarily not currently deductible but must instead be capitalized; and they cannot ordinarily be depreciated because the useful life of most trademarks and trade names is not ascertainable.[96]

To be amortizable under IRC §177, expenditures must be (1) directly connected with the acquisition, protection, expansion, registration, or defense of a trademark or trade name; (2) chargeable to capital account; and (3) not part of the consideration paid for an existing trademark, trade name, or business. Typical qualifying expenses are legal fees paid to register a trademark, artists' fees and similar design expenses, and litigation expenses incurred

---

[93] Snow v. CIR, 416 US 500, 504 (1974); see also Rev. Rul. 71-162, 1971-1 CB 97 (IRC §174 encompasses expenditures to develop new products or processes, even if unrelated to taxpayer's current product lines or manufacturing processes).

[94] Treas. Regs. §1.174-2(a)(1).

[95] See Treas. Regs. §1.174-2(b)(1).

[96] See Medco Prods. Co. v. CIR, 523 F.2d 137 (10th Cir. 1975), and cases there cited (legal fees incurred in suit to compel competitor to terminate use of taxpayer's trademark must be capitalized and cannot be amortized under IRC §177 in absence of timely election); see also supra ¶10.6 (goodwill not ordinarily depreciable).

in infringement proceedings (excluding expenses for the recovery of damages).[97]

The taxpayer can select any amortization period of sixty months or more, beginning with the first month of the taxable year in which the expenditure is paid or incurred. The capitalized amount must be reduced by the amortization allowed or allowable under IRC §1016(a)(16);[98] and presumably any unamortized expenditure can be deducted under IRC §165, relating to losses, if the trademark or trade name becomes worthless and is abandoned.

4. Business Start-Up Expenditures. Section 195(a) authorizes taxpayers to elect to treat "start-up expenditures" paid or incurred after July 29, 1980 as deferred expenses to be deducted ratably over a period of not less than sixty months selected by the taxpayer. "Start-up expenditures" are defined by IRC §195(b) as expenses incurred to investigate the acquisition or creation of an active trade or business or to create an active trade or business, which would have been deductible if incurred by a taxpayer already active in the trade or business being investigated or created. Whether an activity constitutes an active trade or business is determined by the same standards that distinguish expenses deductible under IRC §162 (trade or business) from expenses deductible under IRC §212 (activity engaged in for profit). Expenditures that may not be deducted under IRC §162 because they are capital expenditures (e.g., the cost of acquiring property to be depreciated or whose cost is to be recovered under ACRS) are not amortizable under IRC §195.

Investigatory costs include only expenses incurred before the taxpayer decides to enter or acquire the business, such as the cost of analyzing potential markets and transportation facilities. Start-up costs include, for example, salaries paid to employees who are being trained and to their instructors, travel and other expenses incurred in lining up prospective customers, suppliers, and distributors, and fees paid to consultants. These expenditures are amortizable only if incurred to acquire assets or an interest in a partnership in which the taxpayer is active as a general partner; the acquisition of common stock is an investment.

Business investigatory expenses were neither deductible nor amortizable under prior law, but were viewed as either personal or capital expenses. It is still necessary to distinguish start-up expenditures from the ordinary and necessary expenses of expanding an existing business, however, because expenses of the latter type are currently deductible rather than amortizable under IRC §195.

---

[97] Treas. Regs. §1.177-1(b)(1).

[98] Treas. Regs. §1.1016-5(m) (reduction in basis to reflect amortization allowed unless of no tax benefit, but not less than amount allowable).

5. Specialized Provisions. Many other provisions authorize capital outlays for particular purposes to be deducted currently or amortized over a specified or elected period. These provisions include IRC §167(k) (rehabilitation of low-income rental housing), §169 (pollution-control facilities), §173 (newspaper and magazine circulation expenditures), §§175, 180, and 182 (certain farming expenses—soil and water conservation, clearing of land, etc.), §185 (railroad grading, tunnel bores, and rolling stock), §188 (child care facilities), §190 (removal of architectural and transportation barriers to handicapped and elderly), §191 (rehabilitation of certified historic structures), and §194 (reforestation).

SELECTED BIBLIOGRAPHY

Boyle, Net Operating Losses of Noncorporate Taxpayers, Parts I and II, 4 Tax Adviser 580, 667 (1973).

Broenen & Reed, Amortizing Intangible Assets, 44 J. Tax. 130, 331 (1976).

Campisano & Romano, Recouping Losses: The Case for Full Loss Offsets, 76 Nw. U.L. Rev. 709 (1981).

Epstein, The Consumption and Loss of Personal Property Under the Internal Revenue Code, 23 Stan. L. Rev. 454 (1971).

Fielder, Drilling Funds and Nonrecourse Loans—Some Tax Questions, 24 Inst. Oil & Gas L. & Tax. 527 (1973).

Fielder, The Option to Deduct Intangible Drilling and Development Costs, 33 Texas L. Rev. 825 (1955).

Ginsburg, The Leaky Tax Shelter, 53 Taxes 719 (1975).

Grossman & Johnson, The Distinction Between Exploration and Development Expenditures in the Hard Minerals Industry, 27 Tax Lawyer 119 (1973).

Henze, Transactions in Options: Some New Wrinkles and Old Risks, 4 Rev. Tax. Individuals 70 (1980).

Javaras, Nonrecourse Debt in Real Estate and Other Investments, 56 Taxes 801 (1978).

Martin, Living With the At-Risk Rules, 1982 So. Calif. Tax Inst. 100.

Meir, Tax Shelters and Real Estate: The Rehabilitation of Low Income Housing, 7 Suffolk U.L. Rev. 1 (1972).

Schapiro, Commodities, Forwards, Puts and Calls—Things Equal to the Same Things Are Sometimes Not Equal to Each Other, 34 Tax Lawyer 581 (1981).

Shapiro & Shaw, Start-Up Expenditures—Section 195: Clarification or More Confusion? 1982 So. Calif. Tax Inst. 1100.

Solomon & Weintraub, Business Start-Up Expenses and Section 195: Some Unresolved Problems, 60 Taxes 27 (1982).

Strauss, An Analysis of the Tax Straddle Provisions of the Economic Recovery Tax Act of 1981, 60 Taxes 163 (1982).

Weisner, Tax Shelters—A Survey of the Impact of the Tax Reform Act of 1976, 33 Tax L. Rev. 5, 7–39 (1977).

CHAPTER 13

Business Credits

¶13.1 THE INVESTMENT CREDIT

1. Introductory. In 1962, to encourage capital investment, Congress enacted the statutory predecessors of IRC §§38 and 46-48, providing a tax incentive in the form of an investment credit equal to 7 percent (now 10 percent) of the taxpayer's investment in qualifying property. Because the allowance is a credit rather than a deduction, its value does not depend on the taxpayer's tax bracket but is equal for all taxpayers, since it reduces tax liability dollar for dollar. Thus, the credit has substantially the same effect as a 10 percent reduction in the cost of the qualified property. Section 48(q), however, generally requires a reduction in the taxpayer's basis for the property equal to 50 percent of the amount of the credit claimed, to be taken into account in computing ACRS deductions and gain or loss on a sale or other disposition.

2. Investment Credit Property. The investment credit is allowed only for "section 38 property." This statutory term is defined by IRC §48(a)(1) to mean the following six classes of property, provided the asset qualifies for ACRS deductions, depreciation, or amortization in lieu thereof[1] and, in the case of

[1] If property is used for both business and personal purposes, the depreciable portion qualifies for the investment credit under IRC §48(a)(1); see Treas. Regs. §1.48-1(b)(2).

depreciable property, has a useful life when placed in service of three years or more: (1) tangible personal property (other than air conditioning and heating units), (2) other tangible property (not including buildings and their structural components) serving specified purposes, (3) elevators and escalators, (4) single-purpose agricultural or horticultural structures,[2] (5) rehabilitated buildings, and (6) storage facilities for petroleum or primary petroleum products. These basic categories are subject to a long list of exceptions. "Energy property" as defined by IRC §48(1) is treated as meeting the requirements of IRC §48(a)(1) even if not otherwise qualified. The principal interpretative problems in applying these principles are:

1. *Tangible personal property.* The regulations define "tangible personal property" to mean "any tangible property except land and improvements thereto," which disqualifies buildings and other inherently permanent structures and their structural components, such as swimming pools, paved parking areas, docks, bridges, and fences.[3] The term, however, includes "all property (other than structural components) which is contained in or attached to a building," such as production machinery, transportation and office equipment, display racks, shelves, and signs, as well as property "in the nature of machinery" outside the structure, even if affixed to the ground, such as gasoline pumps, car lifts, and automatic vending machines. Local law is not controlling in classifying property; thus, fixtures can be "tangible personal property" even though classified as real property by local law.

The vast bulk of business equipment is clearly on the qualified side of the boundary while buildings are clearly on the wrong side. A flood of rulings and judicial decisions classifying borderline assets inevitably turn on the physical and functional characteristics of particular assets and are of limited precedential value. The IRS has ruled that the distinction between "personal" and "inherently permanent" property "should be made on the basis of the manner of attachment to land or the structure and how permanently the property is designed to remain in place";[4] the fact that property serves the same function as an inherently permanent structure is not disqualifying. Property that is both "in the nature of machinery" and an "inherently permanent structure" is treated as equipment eligible for the investment tax credit.[5]

2. *Other tangible property.* Tangible property not qualifying as "personal" may qualify under IRC §48(a)(1)(B) if it passes two tests.

First, it must not be a building or structural component thereof. As

---

[2] For these structures, see IRC §48(p).

[3] Treas. Regs. §1.48-1(c).

[4] Rev. Rul. 75-178, 1975-1 CB 9, citing cases and revoking two earlier rulings.

[5] Weirick v. CIR, 62 TC 446 (1974) (IRS conceded terminal towers of commercial ski lift were "tangible personal property," though sunk in concrete foundations; held, intermediate line towers also "tangible personal property," though permanent).

illustrations of structures that pass the first test because they are essentially items of machinery or equipment and their closely related housing structures, the regulations list oil tanks, silos, blast furnaces, and brick kilns.[6] To illustrate the disqualification of structural components of a building, the regulations distinguish walls, windows, central air conditioning and heating systems, plumbing and plumbing fixtures, and sprinkler systems (disqualified) from machinery installed solely to meet temperature or humidity requirements essential to operate other machinery or to process materials or foodstuffs (qualified). While a separate facility serving the needs of the machinery qualifies, facilities serving "the overall needs . . . of the building system" are nonqualifying structural components of the building even though larger in capacity because they also service the machinery.[7]

Second, the property must constitute (a) an integral part of manufacturing, production, transportation, communication, electrical energy, or similar facilities; (b) research facilities used in connection with any of the foregoing qualifying activities; or (c) facilities for the bulk storage of fungible commodities, including liquids and gases, used in connection with any of the foregoing.

3. Intangible Property. Because intangible property is not explicitly listed by IRC §48(a)(1), it cannot qualify as Section 38 property. Thus, the costs of producing and obtaining patents, copyrights, subscription lists, and other intangible assets do not qualify for the investment credit.[8] The Court of Appeals for the Fifth Circuit, however, has held that the investment credit can be claimed for the cost of collecting seismic data recorded on tapes and films sold to the taxpayer's customers, since these items constitute tangible property.[9] This theory will undoubtedly stimulate a flood of claims by taxpayers engaged in gathering and publishing information, since the normal mode of transmission is almost invariably a tangible document or other "hard" copy rather than word of mouth. Moreover, IRC §48(k) explicitly permits expenses for movie and television video tapes to qualify, subject to a percentage limitation and other qualifications.

4. Ineligible Property. Even if property satisfies the standards of IRC §48(a)(1), it is disqualified if it falls within any of the following categories of assets, whose acquisition is not viewed by Congress as serving the economic objective of the investment credit.

---

[6] Treas. Regs. §1.48-1(c)(1).

[7] See Rev. Rul. 70-160, 1970-1 CB 7 (boilers supplying steam for furniture factory qualified, but not electrical system serving needs of both building and machinery); Rev. Rul. 68-405, 1968-2 CB 35 (heavy-duty insulation in refrigerated building not qualified).

[8] Treas. Regs. §1.48-1(f).

[9] Texas Instruments, Inc. v. US, 551 F.2d 599 (5th Cir. 1977).

1. *Foreign use or origin.* Property used predominantly outside the United States is disqualified by IRC §48(a)(2), with the exception of aircraft, ships, and certain other specified items. Section 48(a)(7) also generally disqualifies property "completed outside the United States" or having a basis less than 50 percent of which is attributable to value added within the United States.

2. *Lodging.* Property used predominantly for lodging is disqualified by IRC §48(a)(3), but this disqualification does not apply to nonlodging commercial facilities open to outsiders on the same basis as lodgers or to hotels and motels whose accommodations are used predominantly by transients.[10]

3. *Livestock.* Horses are disqualified by IRC §48(a)(6), but other livestock (including poultry) qualifies as Section 38 property, subject to a limitation if substantially identical livestock is sold or disposed of within a prescribed period in a transaction not subject to IRC §47(a).

4. *Boilers.* As an antipollution measure, IRC §48(a)(10) disqualifies boilers primarily fueled by oil or gas unless (a) the use of coal is precluded by federal or certain state air pollution regulations or (b) the boiler is to be used for a residential facility, office building, or certain other exempt uses set out in IRC §48(a)(10)(B).

5. Amount of Investment Credit. In most situations, the investment credit is equal to 10 percent of the cost of the qualified property, but the computation can be much more complicated.

1. *Applicable percentage.* The credit consists of three components, described by IRC §46(a)(2) as "the regular percentage" (10 percent of qualified investment), "the energy percentage" (10 percent of "energy property," as defined by IRC §48(1)), and "the ESOP percentage" (at the rate prescribed by IRC §46(a)(2)(E), limited to corporations with an ESOP plan under IRC §409A).[11] Usually only the regular credit is claimed. Section 46(a)(2)(F) provides a special three-tier credit for qualified building rehabilitation expenditures.[12]

Under IRC §48(q)(4), a taxpayer may avoid the basis reduction of qualified property required by IRC §48(q)(1) by electing an alternative, lower regular credit equal to 4 percent of the full cost of three-year property and 8 percent of the qualified investment in all other recovery property.

2. *Qualified investment.* For new Section 38 property, the taxpayer's "qualified investment" as defined by IRC §§46(c)(1) and 46(c)(7) is 100 percent of the property's basis if it has a five-year, ten-year, or fifteen-year public utility cost recovery period under ACRS and 60 percent of the property's basis

---

[10] For these distinctions, see Treas. Regs. §1.48-1(h).

[11] See IRC §48(a) (qualification for ESOP percentage).

[12] See infra ¶13.4.

if it has a three-year recovery period. The same percentages apply to used Section 38 property; but the base is the property's cost rather than its basis.

Under IRC §46(c)(8) the property's basis for investment credit purposes may not ordinarily exceed the amount by which the taxpayer is at risk under IRC §465(b) at the close of the taxable year. An exception is provided for certain loans from institutional lenders if, among other conditions, the taxpayer is at risk for at least 20 percent of the property's basis.

3. *New vs. used property.* "New Section 38 property" is defined by IRC §48(b) as property (a) the construction, reconstruction, or erection of which is completed by the taxpayer after December 31, 1961 or (b) that is acquired after December 31, 1961 if its original use commences with the taxpayer.[13] Section 48(c) treats all other section 38 property acquired after December 31, 1961 as "used section 38 property." Taxpayers who purchase and reconstruct used equipment may escape the "used property" limitation so far as their reconstruction expenses are concerned.[14] Used property qualifies for the credit only if it is (1) acquired by the taxpayer by purchase and (2) not used after the acquisition by a person who either used the property previously or is related to such a person.[15] In addition, the cost of used Section 38 property to be taken into account in computing the taxpayer's qualified investment is limited to $150,000 for any taxable year ($125,000 prior to 1985).[16] In the case of partnerships, the dollar limit applies to the firm itself as well as to each partner. The dollar limit is cut in half for married persons filing separate returns, unless the taxpayer's spouse has no qualifying used Section 38 property for the taxable year.

If the cost of the qualified used property placed in service in any year exceeds the dollar limitation, the taxpayer must designate the items to be taken into account for credit purposes.[17] The used property that is not selected cannot be carried over for use in a later year in which the property placed in service is less than the applicable dollar limit.

4. *Limitation based on tax liability.* Section 46(a)(3) limits the credit allowed for the taxable year to (a) the taxpayer's tax liability, but not in excess of $25,000, plus (b) 85 percent of the balance, if any, of the taxpayer's liability. Under §46(b), investment credits that cannot be used when earned because of this limitation can be carried back to the three preceding taxable years and forward to the fifteen following years.

---

[13] These requirements are elaborated by Treas. Regs. §1.48-2.

[14] See Treas. Regs. §1.48-2(b)(7).

[15] The term "purchase" is defined by IRC §48(c)(3)(A) by reference to IRC §179(d)(2), and the tainted relationships are listed in IRC §§179(d)(2)(A) and 179(d)(2)(B).

[16] For the meaning of "cost" as applied to used property, see IRC §48(c)(3)(B); Treas. Regs. §1.48-3(b).

[17] See Treas. Regs. §1.48-3(c)(4).

5. *Leased property.* The investment credit, like depreciation and cost recovery allowances, is ordinarily allowed only to the owner of qualifying property; but this general principle is subject to one exception and one quasi-exception.

The exception is IRC §48(d), which allows lessors of new Section 38 property to elect to have the lessee treated as having acquired the property for its fair market value, subject to various qualifications. This election makes it possible for the credit to be claimed by a lessee who can use it to better advantage than the lessor—because, for example, the lessor's tax liability is too low to absorb the credit in the year of acquisition or in the years to which unused credits can be carried.

The quasi-exception is IRC §168(f)(8), relating to so-called finance leases, a complex provision concerned with classifying certain transactions that have both "sale" and "lease" components, such as leveraged equipment leases. If IRC §168(f)(8) does not apply, it is necessary to determine whether the owner of the property is the purported lessor (as the parties normally would expect) or the purported lessee; and this issue is resolved by analyzing the agreement in its economic setting and deciding which party is entitled to more of the benefits, and bears more of the burdens, of ownership.[18] If, however, the conditions of IRC §168(f)(8) are satisfied and the parties so elect, the purported lessor is treated as the owner (and hence is entitled to the investment credit), without regard to any non-statutory factors that might otherwise require the lessee to be so treated. This makes it possible for loss companies and other taxpayers who cannot make use of any additional investment credits or cost recovery allowances when acquiring assets to "sell" these allowances to profitable companies through so-called finance leases, without facing an IRS contention that the loss company remains the "true owner" of the property. Section 168(f)(8) applies to leases entered into after December 31, 1983; it replaces a more lenient provision that gave similar effect to so-called safe harbor leases.

6. *Regulated utility companies.* Section 46(f) denies the investment credit to certain regulated utility companies if the credit will flow through to its customers by virtue of a reduction in rates or in the base to which the allowable rate of return is applied.

6. Recapture of Investment Credit. Because the taxpayer's "qualified investment," on which the credit is based, depends on the ACRS recovery period of the Section 38 property, IRC §47 provides for a recapture of the credit if property is disposed of, or otherwise ceases to be Section 38 property, before the end of the recovery period on which the credit was based. If Section

[18] See, e.g., Rev. Rul. 55-540, 1955-2 CB 39, and cases there cited; Rev. Proc. 75-21, 1975-1 CB 715.

38 property is disposed of before the end of the recovery period used in computing the credit, the credit is recomputed by allowing a 2-percent credit for each full year that the property was held. For example, if qualifying five-year property is sold during the fifth year, the allowable credit is reduced to 8 percent from the originally allowed credit of 10 percent. There is no recapture, however, if qualifying ten-year or fifteen-year property is held for at least five years, since the recomputed credit (10 percent) is the same as the credit originally allowed.

Section 47 covers not only sales, exchanges, gifts, abandonments, and other "dispositions," but also events by which the property "ceases to be section 38 property with respect to the taxpayer," such as the conversion of property from business to personal use or, in the case of dual-use property, an increase in the fraction of personal use.[19] Since investment credits are passed through when earned by Subchapter S corporations, trusts and estates, and partnerships to their shareholders, beneficiaries, and partners, these individuals are also subject to the recapture rules when the property is disposed of by the entity or ceases to be Section 38 property in its hands.[20]

The recapture rules are subject to a variety of exceptions: (1) If the taxpayer dies, the resulting transfer is not a disposition;[21] (2) transfers by corporations are exempt if subject to IRC §381(a); (3) transfers resulting from a "mere change" in the form of conducting the taxpayer's trade or business are exempt;[22] (4) sale-leaseback transactions do not ordinarily trigger recapture;[23] and (5) on a disposition of used property, a taxpayer who acquired other qualified used property in the credit year that was not selected for credit purposes can engage in a retroactive "re-selection" of the excess property, and, in effect, substitute it for the property disposed of.[24]

¶13.2 TARGETED JOBS CREDIT

Sections 44B and 51-53 provide a credit of 50 percent of the qualified first-year wages and 25 percent of the qualified second-year wages paid to members of seven "targeted groups," regarded by Congress as requiring special aid in finding employment. The credit, which is elective, covers only wages paid or incurred before 1984. The employer's deduction for wages is disallowed to the extent of the allowable credit.

---

[19] Treas. Regs. §§1.47-2(a)(1), 1.47-2(d); Treas. Regs. §1.47-2(e).

[20] See Treas. Regs. §§1.47-4 (Subchapter S corporations), 1.47-5 (trusts and estates), 1.47-6 (partnerships).

[21] IRC §47(b)(2); see Treas. Regs. §1.47-3(b).

[22] IRC §47(b); for the scope of this exemption, see Treas. Regs. §1.47-3(f).

[23] Treas. Regs. §1.47-3(g).

[24] Treas. Regs. §1.47-3(d).

¶13.3 RESEARCH AND EXPERIMENTAL EXPENDITURES

Section 44F allows a credit of 25 percent of the amount by which the current year's qualified research and experimental expenditures exceed the taxpayer's average research expenditures in a base period, which is generally the three preceding taxable years. Qualifying expenditures are the taxpayer's "in-house research expenses" (for wages, supplies, and certain charges for the research use of computeers, laboratory equipment, etc.) and 65 percent of its "contract research expenses" (certain amounts paid to research firms, universities, etc.). Section 44F(d) incorporates by reference the definition of "research" in IRC §174, with minor exceptions. The credit cannot exceed the tax otherwise due (after taking certain credits into account), but unused credits can be carried back for three years and forward for fifteen years.

¶13.4 REHABILITATION OF CERTIFIED HISTORIC STRUCTURES AND OLDER BUILDINGS

Section 46(a)(2)(F) grants a 25-percent credit for qualified rehabilitation expenditures for certified historical structures, 15 percent of such expenditures for thirty-year-old buildings, and 20 percent of such expenditures for forty-year-old buildings. The credit is conditioned on use of the straight-line method of cost recovery for the expenditures, and the basis of the property is reduced by 50 percent of the credit.

SELECTED BIBLIOGRAPHY

Black & Boyd, Research Expenditures Take on New Impetus Under Provisions in the 1981 Act, 55 J. Tax. 348 (1981).

Dorr, Working With the Investment Credit Recapture Rules: A Blend of the Old and the New, 56 J. Tax. 354 (1982).

Hoff, The Appropriate Role for Tax Credits in an Income Tax System, 35 Tax Lawyer 339 (1982).

Koffey, Safe Harbor Leasing, 1982 So. Calif. Tax Inst. 200.

Maples, When Will a Building Qualify for the Investment Credit: An Analysis, 51 J. Tax. 358 (1979).

Note, The Great Section 38 Property Muddle, 28 Vand. L. Rev. 1025 (1975).

Sunley, Towards a More Neutral Investment Tax Credit, 26 Nat'l Tax J. 209 (1973).

CHAPTER 14

Personal Exemptions and Itemized Deductions

Page

¶14.1 PERSONAL AND DEPENDENCY EXEMPTIONS: INTRODUCTORY

In computing taxable income, every individual taxpayer is allowed by IRC §151(b) to deduct a personal exemption of $1,000. If a joint return is filed, both spouses are "taxpayers" (even if one has no income), so two personal exemptions are allowed. If a married person files a separate return, however, a personal exemption is allowed for the taxpayer's spouse only if the spouse has no gross income and is not the dependent of another taxpayer. These allowances are augmented by an additional personal exemption of $1,000 if the taxpayer or spouse is over the age of sixty-five and by still another exemption of the same amount for blindness. The personal exemptions are cumulative, so that a total of $6,000 ($1,000 × 6) may be deducted if a joint return is filed by a married couple, both of whom are over sixty-five and blind.

In addition to the personal exemptions, IRC §151(e) authorizes a dependency exemption of $1,000 for each individual who (a) is related to the taxpayer in the manner specified by IRC §152 (ordinarily by blood, marriage, or adoption), (b) receives more than one-half of his or her support from the taxpayer or satisfies a special support requirement, and (c) either has less than $1,000 of gross income for the taxable year or is relieved of this requirement by IRC §151(e)(1)(B) (relating to certain children of the taxpayer).

Three technical features of the personal and dependency exemptions are worthy of note: (1) Regardless of births, deaths, and other changes during the taxpayer's taxable year, exemptions are not prorated over the year but are, instead, allowed in full if the requisite conditions are met at the time specified by IRC §§151 and 152 (ordinarily the close of the taxpayer's taxable year, though sometimes another date is controlling); (2) exemptions are never divided between two taxpayers but are instead awarded or disallowed in full to the qualifying claimant; and (3) unused exemptions cannot be carried over from one year to another. Beginning in 1985, the $1,000 amounts allowed by current law will be increased under §2151(f) to reflect a cost-of-living adjustment.

Most tax theorists agree on the desirability of a device to protect a basic amount of income from erosion by the income tax, but some liken the cost of government to the cost of food, shelter, and housing, arguing that income taxes should be paid by all and that persons in need should be protected by social welfare programs instead of by tax allowances. While this would entail some circular transfers of money from low-income taxpayers to the Treasury to social agencies to impoverished taxpayers, the buck would stop short in some circumstances. Some of those who now fall below the bottom tax-paying group are the children of well-to-do parents and wealthy persons with temporarily depressed incomes. They would be taxed if the exemptions and zero bracket amount of existing law were abolished but would almost certainly be excluded if an augmented social welfare program took the place of these tax allowances.

Another debate in this area concerns the function of personal exemptions at higher income levels. The "continuing exemption" system of existing law, under which exemptions are deductible regardless of income level, can be rationalized on the theory that the basic amount needed to sustain life provides no "tax-paying capacity" and that taxes should be imposed only on the excess above the basic amount, whether the taxpayer is a ditchdigger or a millionaire. In opposition to this theory, it is argued that exemptions are needed only to remove persons with no tax-paying capacity from the tax rolls and that persons above the statutory bench mark need no further protection. Advocates of an allowance for the bottom group only (a so-called initial exemption) buttress their criticism of existing law by pointing out that the continuing exemptions grow in value as income increases. A deduction of $1,000 is "worth" only $200 to taxpayers whose marginal tax rate is 20 percent, for example, but $700 to those subject to the top rate of 70 percent. Between the theoretical extremes of initial and continuing exemptions, there are many possible compromises, such as a "vanishing exemption" (declining in amount as income rises) and a credit of a fixed dollar amount, which would be worth the same amount to all taxpayers regardless of income level.

The additional personal exemptions for persons over sixty-five or blind were enacted in 1948 to compensate for the increased cost of living brought about by postwar conditions. The factual premise of increased expenses has been challenged as respects the elderly; as to the blind, it is not clear whether their expenses are significantly larger than those of other handicapped persons, who do not enjoy an additional exemption.

Like the personal exemptions, the dependency exemptions insulate a basic amount of income from the tax collector, insuring that this amount can be used for living expenses; and they simplify both compliance and enforcement by removing low-income families from the tax rolls. But they also serve to differentiate tax burdens by reference to family size, resembling in this respect the separate rate schedules for married persons, heads of households, and single persons. This is a worthy objective in the eyes of tax theorists who measure tax-paying capacity by reference to the income that is available after taxpayers have defrayed not only their own living expenses but also those of their dependents. Other theorists, however, view the cost of maintaining children and other dependents as outlets for personal preferences that deserve no more special consideration from the tax collector than the cost of vacations and hobbies.

¶14.2 DEPENDENCY EXEMPTIONS

1. Introductory. Section 151(e) allows individual taxpayers to deduct $1,000 for every dependent meeting three sets of requirements:

1. *Affinity and support.* To qualify as a "dependent," an individual must (a) be related to the taxpayer (by blood, marriage, or adoption) in the manner described by IRC §152(a) or be a member of the taxpayer's household with the taxpayer's home as his or her principal place of abode; (b) receive over half of his or her support from the taxpayer or be covered by a multiple-support agreement or special rule applicable to the children of divorced or separated parents; and (c) except for certain adopted children, be a citizen or national of the United States or a resident of the United States or of a contiguous country.

2. *Gross income.* Except in the case of a child of the taxpayer who is a student or under the age of nineteen, a dependent (as defined above) does not qualify for a dependency exemption if his or her gross income for the calendar year in which the taxpayer's taxable year begins is $1,000 or more.

3. *Certain married dependents.* Finally, the taxpayer is not entitled to a deduction for a dependent, even if otherwise qualified, who files a joint return with his or her spouse for the taxable year beginning in the calendar year in which the taxpayer's taxable year begins. This provision is aimed primarily at—but is not restricted to—married couples, one of whom is a student while the other is gainfully employed. In the absence of IRC §151(e)(2), they could claim two personal exemptions on a joint return and benefit from the lower

joint-return rates, even if the student is supported by his or her parents and hence qualifies for a dependency exemption on the parents' return. Under IRC §151(e)(2), if the parents want the dependency exemption on their return, the employed spouse must file a separate return, which is subject to higher tax rates than a joint return, and forgo a personal exemption for the student spouse.

There is no general rule, however, precluding children from claiming personal exemptions while their parents claim dependency exemptions for them. Unmarried students who are employed during the summer, for example, are entitled to personal exemptions on their individual returns, even though more than half of their support comes from parents who claim them as dependents on their returns.

It is important to note that an individual becomes a "dependent" of the taxpayer by meeting the first set of requirements (affinity and support) summarized above; the second and third requirements are additional hurdles that determine whether a *dependency exemption* can be deducted for the dependent in question. Taxpayers are entitled to a variety of tax allowances for "dependents" who do not qualify for the dependency exemption. A taxpayer who provides more than half of the support of elderly parents, for example, can deduct medical expenses paid for them under IRC §213(a)(1), even though they have more than $1,000 of gross income each and therefore do not give rise to dependency exemptions.

2. Affinity to Taxpayer. No matter how much support the taxpayer may supply to a particular individual, he or she can qualify as a "dependent" only if one of the relationships set out in IRC §152(a) exists between them. Except for IRC §152(a)(9), discussed below, the requisite affinity is defined by reference to blood, marriage, or adoption, limited to the following relatives of the taxpayer:

1. Children and descendants.
2. Stepchildren.
3. Brothers, sisters, stepbrothers, and stepsisters.
4. Parents and ancestors.
5. Stepparents.
6. Nieces and nephews.
7. Aunts and uncles.
8. Sons-in-law, daughters-in-law, fathers-in-law, mothers-in-law, brothers-in-law, and sisters-in-law.

In determining these relationships, the terms "brother" and "sister" include half-blood siblings; and legally adopted children, certain children awaiting adoption, and foster children are treated as children by blood. Exemptions can be claimed for children born out of wedlock if the parent proves the requirements for eligibility and, in the case of the father, acknowledges paternity.

Even if not related to the taxpayer by blood, marriage, or adoption as summarized above, persons supported by the taxpayer can qualify as dependents under IRC §152(a)(9) if, for the taxpayer's taxable year, they are members of his household and his home is their principal place of abode. The regulations provide that the taxpayer must "maintain" the household and that the taxpayer and dependent must occupy it for the entire taxable year, save for temporary absences by reason of illness, education, business, vacations, military service, and other special circumstances.[1]

Section 152(a)(9) was enacted in 1954, primarily to embrace foster children and children awaiting adoption. With the later enactment of IRC §152(b)(2), assimilating foster children to children by blood, the role of IRC §152(a)(9) was reduced. Its primary current importance is that it functions to enable friends and distant relatives, not listed by IRC §§152(a)(1)-152(a)(8), to qualify as dependents on meeting the "household" and "principal place of abode" tests. The Tax Court held in 1957 that IRC §152(a)(9) did not embrace illicit relationships, and this interpretation was codified in 1958 by the enactment of IRC §152(b)(5).[2] If the relationship creates a common-law marriage under local law, the parties are "spouses" and can file a joint return, but the parenthetical clause of IRC §152(a)(9) precludes a dependency exemption. If the relationship is unlawful, however, it is disqualified by IRC §152(b)(5) even if the parties hold themselves out as married and are so accepted by their neighbors.[3] In 1979, the Court of Appeals for the Fourth Circuit held that IRC §152(b)(5) is constitutional even though sexual relationships between unmarried consenting adults are lawful in some states but not in others.[4]

---

[1] Treas. Regs. §1.152-1(b); for discussion of the terms "household" and "principal place of abode," see infra ¶39.3, text at notes 76–80.

[2] Turnipseed v. CIR, 27 TC 758 (1957) ("member of household" not intended by Congress to include a married woman "whom the taxpayer is maintaining in an illicit relationship in conscious violation of the criminal law"); Buckley's Est. v. CIR, 37 TC 664, 673 (1962) (marriage void because divorce of prior spouse was ineffective; held, no dependency exemption, but mother of purported wife, who lived with and was supported by taxpayer, qualifies as dependent); Treas. Regs. §1.152-1(b) (second sentence).

[3] See Eichbauer v. CIR, ¶71,133 P-H Memo TC (1971).

[4] Ensminger v. CIR, 610 F.2d 189 (4th Cir. 1979) (affirming Tax Court determination that on disallowance by IRS of dependency exemption, based on state statute punishing lewd and lascivious cohabitation between man and woman, burden is on taxpayer and companion to disprove sexual association); query whether IRS could adopt the same tactic if two persons of the same sex live together in a state forbidding homosexual behavior; see also In re Shackelford, 45 AFTR2d 1074 (W.D. Mo. 1980) (not officially reported) (employed woman entitled to dependency exemption for unmarried man in household; sexual relationship does not violate Missouri law in absence of lascivious behavior, public indecency, etc.).

Since IRC §152(a)(9) is concerned with persons who are supported by the taxpayer "from motives of charity, affection, or moral obligation without thought of receiving in return a *quid pro quo,*" [5] it does not authorize a dependency deduction for live-in domestic servants, such as housekeepers and baby-sitters. Even if they are "members of the taxpayer's household," their meals and lodging constitute compensation rather than "support." On the other hand, the dependency exemption is not forfeited as to children merely because they receive allowances for performing household chores.

3. Support From Taxpayer. To qualify as a "dependent" of the taxpayer, an individual must not only satisfy the affinity test just described but must also (a) receive over half of his or her support from the taxpayer or (b) be covered by a multiple-support agreement or a special-support rule relating to the children of divorced or separated parents.[6]

Whether the taxpayer furnishes over half of the individual's support is measured by economic value rather than elapsed time. Thus, if a child lives with a parent for seven months of a calendar year and with a grandparent for the remaining five months but the parent provides less in economic terms for the child's support than the grandparent, the child is the grandparent's dependent, not the parent's. Moreover, since an individual can be a dependent of only one taxpayer, the term "over half" means just that; if the parent and grandparent each contribute *exactly* one-half of the child's support, the child is the dependent of neither rather than of both. This predicament can sometimes be avoided by a multiple-support agreement.[7]

Section 152(a) does not define the term "support"; and the regulations say only that it "includes food, shelter, clothing, medical and dental care, education, and the like," recreation, and transportation.[8] Despite the brevity of this list, it is misleading: the value of *public* education is disregarded in determining whether a taxpayer has supplied more than half of the support of a given individual. The vagueness of the statutory term "support" creates no problems, however, for the overwhelming bulk of dependency claims. In 1975, for example, 75.5 million dependency exemptions were claimed, of which about 94 percent were for children living at home. In most of these cases the parents undoubtedly supplied either all of their children's material needs or so large

[5] Hamilton v. CIR, 34 TC 927, 929 (1960); see also Protiva v. CIR, ¶70,282 P-H Memo TC (1970).

[6] For these alternatives to the over-half rule, see infra, text at notes 23–25 (multiple-support agreements), and infra, text at note 26 (divorced or separated parents).

[7] See infra, text at notes 23–25.

[8] Treas. Regs. §§1.152-1(a)(2)(i), 1.152-4(e)(3)(v). See also Gulvin v. CIR, ¶80,111 P-H Memo TC (1980) (taxpayer's alleged obligation to reimburse state for support of minor children did not exist, but would not in any event constitute support "received" by them).

a proportion, as compared with the children's outside earnings or assistance from grandparents and other relatives, as to leave no room for debate about the validity of the parents' claims.

On the other hand, there are also many situations in which it is necessary to determine whether particular items constitute "support" and to allocate the aggregate amount provided among two or more contributors. If, for example, a child lives at home with parents who supply $4,000 worth of conventional support (food, clothing, shelter, etc.) but receives a $5,000 sports car as a graduation present from his or her grandparents, is the car part of the child's "support"? The answer determines whether the parents or the grandparents supplied more than half of the child's support. After twenty years of opposition to including the cost of cars in "support," the IRS bowed to the times by ruling that, beginning in 1978, the cost of a car is included in the support of children.[9]

Areas that can be troublesome in close cases include the following:

1. *Scope of "support."* It was once thought that only "necessities" were covered by the concept of support, but that standard has been either abandoned or liberalized to fit an affluent society. Thus, in addition to food, shelter, clothing, and education, singing, dancing, and drama lessons are part of support, as are permanent waves, admission to swimming pools, toys, pets, Christmas gifts, vacation expenses, parking tickets, school lunch desserts, and allowances.[10]

The source of funds used to defray expenses for the claimed dependent sometimes affects whether they are properly included in support. For instance, welfare and social security benefits are included if spent on support items; although excluded from gross income, they are treated as support provided by the government or by the dependents on their own behalf. The local-law measure of a parent's obligation to support his or her children is relevant for some federal tax purposes (e.g., in determining whether a trust's distributions to children discharge their parents' legal obligations), but it is not relevant in applying IRC §152(a). Private school tuition, for example, is counted in determining the amount spent for a child's support even if the parent's obligations would be satisfied by public education, whether the tuition is paid by the

---

[9] Rev. Rul. 77-282, 1977-2 CB 52 (cost of car includable in support whether purchased by child with own funds or supplied as gift by parents, but not if title is retained by parents).

[10] See, e.g., Hastings v. CIR, ¶57,202 P-H Memo TC (1957); Taitt v. CIR, ¶78,264 P-H Memo TC (1978) (parking violations); Puckett v. CIR, ¶78,337 P-H Memo TC (1978) (extra charge for desserts with school lunches); Svendsen v. CIR, ¶78,503 P-H Memo TC (1978) (replacement of windows broken during play); Cramer v. CIR, 55 TC 1125 (1971) (Acq.) (electric organ included); McKay v. CIR, 34 TC 1080, 1082 (1960) (care of dog).

parents or by someone who has no obligation under local law to play Santa Claus, such as a grandparent.

2. *Valuation.* In general, support is computed by reference to the cost of the item in question to the person furnishing it, but the regulations provide that support supplied in the form of property or lodging should be taken into account at its fair market value.[11] Thus, the rental value of housing, rather than the homeowner's out-of-pocket expenses for taxes, interest, repairs, and utilities, is the relevant figure.[12] But the reference in the regulations to the value of "support furnished . . . in the form of property" is probably not intended to require or permit inclusion of unpaid family labor enhancing the property's value. In the case of home-cooked meals, for example, the controlling figure should be the cost of the ingredients, not the value of the finished product.

Because the regulations refer to "the amount of expense incurred" by the person furnishing support and make no mention of uncompensated personal services, it has been held that taxpayers caring for invalids cannot take the value of their services into account in determining the invalid's total support, even though wages paid to a nurse or attendant for similar services would qualify under the regulations. This principle is equally applicable to the care given by parents to their children. Conversely, it means that services performed by dependents for themselves are not counted in determining whether they received more than half from their parents or other persons.

The fact that a taxpayer furnishing an item to a dependent can deduct it (e.g., as a medical expense) does not prevent its inclusion in computing support, except for alimony payments that are deductible by one spouse and taxable to the other, which cannot be treated by the payor as support payments even if the recipient spouse and the children have no other resources.[13]

3. *Support furnished to a group.* Support furnished to a group of persons is often difficult to allocate among them, as in the case of food and lodging provided by parents to children and amounts paid by a divorced parent for the support of children in the ex-spouse's custody. These collective contributions are usually allocated equally among the recipients, although this administratively convenient rule of thumb gives way to evidence that they drew disparate portions from the common pot because of differences in age, medical needs, or other factors.[14] Thus, if *A* and *B* contribute $5,000 and $4,000, respectively,

---

[11] Treas. Regs. §1.152-1(a)(2)(i).

[12] See Carter v. CIR, 62 TC 20 (1974) (rental value of home furnished by divorced father allocated between ex-wife and two children); Tharp v. CIR, ¶77,036 P-H Memo TC (1977) (similar allocation among ex-wife, new spouse, and three children).

[13] IRC §152(b)(4).

[14] See Pierce v. CIR, 66 TC 840, 844 (1976) (equal allocation of household expenses, except for food and medical expenses); Edwards v. CIR, ¶75,072 P-H Memo TC (1975) (public ADC funds allocated equally among persons in recipient's household); Cameron v. CIR, ¶74,166 P-H Memo TC (1974) (divorcee and two children lived

for the support of four children, *A* is entitled to all four dependency exemptions in the absence of evidence that the contributions should be allocated unequally among the children, even though it is possible that *A*'s funds were used exclusively for one child and that *B* supported the other three.

4. *Allocating expenditures among payors.* It is often easy to trace particular living expenses back to the payor. Cancelled checks, for example, may prove that a medical or college bill was paid by a dependent's parents rather than grandparents. But if rival claimants for the dependency exemption both send cash to the dependent, who deposits the funds in a bank account and then writes checks to pay for living expenses as well as to purchase items that do not constitute "support" (e.g., investment securities), who gets credit for the support payments? In the same vein, if a college student commingles funds received from a parent with earnings from a part-time job, using only part of the total to defray the cost of living, has the parent contributed to the child's support or to the unspent balance?

One approach to these issues, which have not often surfaced in cases or rulings, is a presumption that the rival benefactors contributed to the recipient's support in the same proportion as their contributions. If the dependent commingles the gifts with personal funds, however, the IRS is likely to argue that the dependent contributed to his own support to the full extent of his own resources, and that only the balance of the support, if any, was supplied by the person claiming the dependency exemption. In the face of the currently uncertain legal rules and the burden of proof on the taxpayer to prove support, claimants foreseeing a problem may be able to enter into a multiple-support agreement,[15] instruct the dependent not to commingle funds, or explicitly designate the purpose of a contribution. The IRS has stated that it will give "great weight" to notations of purpose and recipient made when support funds are spent and that it will accept designations of recipients by the donor.[16]

5. *Self-support.* In determining whether a taxpayer has supplied more than one-half of an alleged dependent's support, the latter's contributions to his or her own support must be taken into account even if attributable to tax-exempt receipts or imputed income, such as borrowed funds, welfare and social security benefits, and the rental value of the dependent's own residence. In the case of public social welfare programs, the same result is sometimes reached by a different route, viz., by attributing part of the dependent's support

---

in her house; ex-husband successfully argued that housing costs of adult exceed costs for children; 60 percent of housing allocable to wife); Dunn v. CIR, ¶63,189 P-H Memo TC (1963) (housing and food divided equally among wife and three children, but two-thirds of automobile expenses attributed to wife, whose transit needs were greater).

[15] Infra, text at notes 23–25.

[16] Rev. Rul. 72-591, 1972-2 CB 84, 86.

to the state. Funds available to the dependent are disregarded, however, if they are banked or invested rather than *used* for self-support.

Moreover, the IRS has ruled that supplemental Medicare benefits, "being in the nature of medical insurance proceeds" because participation in the plan is voluntary and requires the payment of premiums, are not part of the insured individual's support, evidently on the theory that the insured is sheltered against the medical expense.[17] The same principle has been applied by the IRS to medical expenses defrayed by private insurance and tort-feasors [18] and, over IRS opposition, to basic medicare benefits.[19] These results are consistent with the universal assumption that the value of free public education is not counted as part of a child's support, but it is not clear why other social welfare benefits (e.g., the value of care in a public institution) are counted.[20]

6. *Scholarships.* Section 152(d) provides a special support rule for children of the taxpayer, excluding scholarships received by a student for study at an educational institution (as defined) in determining whether the student's parents supplied more than half of his or her support. The regulations provide that the term "scholarship" has the same meaning as in IRC §117, excluding scholarships from the recipient's gross income; hence, veterans' educational benefits, earnings from part-time employment, and similar receipts do not qualify.[21]

7. *Estimates.* While the taxpayer must shoulder the burden of proving both the total support of a dependent and his or her contribution to it, detailed records of all expenses are neither feasible nor necessary. Courts regularly accept reasonable estimates of support payments, especially of expenses that are difficult to keep track of, recognizing that not even the most meticulous and conscientious taxpayer can provide written proof or exact figures for some types of expenses.[22]

---

[17] Rev. Rul. 70-341, 1970-2 CB 31, revoked as to basic Medicare benefits by Rev. Rul. 79-173, 1979-1 CB 86; see infra note 19.

[18] See Rev. Rul. 64-223, 1964-2 CB 50 (payments by tort-feasor or his insurance company are not support, nor are benefits from dependent's own medical insurance policy; but premiums on medical insurance policy are included in support).

[19] Turecamo v. CIR, 554 F.2d 564 (2d Cir. 1977) (extensive discussion; implication that social security taxes financing basic Medicare program are includable in support); Rev. Rul. 79-173, supra note 17 (acquiescence in *Turecamo*); see also Archer v. CIR, 73 TC 963 (1980) (New York State Medicaid benefits excluded from support under *Turecamo*).

[20] Donner v. CIR, 25 TC 1043 (1956) (state welfare payments for institutional care deemed support); House v. CIR, ¶59,047 P-H Memo TC (1959) (cost of maintaining patient in state mental institution counted toward support).

[21] Treas. Regs. §1.152-1(c).

[22] See, e.g., Haley v. CIR, ¶76,374 P-H Memo TC (1976) (acknowledging "a large number of small day-to-day expenditures which go unrecognized"); Ree v. CIR, ¶63,125 P-H Memo TC (1963) (taxpayer's estimates used in determining support where income and expenses small); Hemingway v. CIR, ¶60,190 P-H Memo TC (1960)

4. Multiple-Support Agreements. If two or more taxpayers contribute equally to someone's support, as in the case of three children who split the cost of an institutionalized parent, the recipient is not the dependent of anyone, since no one has furnished the requisite "over half" of his or her support. This predicament can be avoided, without disturbing the desired equality of burden, by an astute rotation of the payments—for example, by having each child provide the lion's share of the support every third year. An alternative is provided by IRC §152(c), under which the parties may designate one of their number to claim their beneficiary as a dependent. The designation determines dependency status for the dependency exemption (assuming compliance with the gross income and other statutory requirements) as well as for other tax allowances turning on whether a given individual is the taxpayer's dependent, such as the right to deduct medical expenses under IRC §213.[23]

A multiple-support agreement is sanctioned by IRC §152(c) only if (1) no one person contributed more than half of the beneficiary's support [24] and (2) more than half of the support is contributed by persons who would have been entitled to claim the beneficiary as a dependent had he or she contributed more than one-half of the support.[25] If the statutory conditions are met, any member of the support group who contributes more than 10 percent of the beneficiary's support can claim the beneficiary as a dependent if the other over-10-percent members of the group waive their claims. Since the members of the support group have a free option each year, they can assign the dependency claim to the member who will derive the greatest tax benefit from it, judged in retrospect between the end of the taxable year and the due date of the return; and they can either rotate the claim or, if they wish, assign it to the same person year after year.

5. Children of Divorced or Separated Parents. The dependency status of children whose parents are divorced or separated is complicated both by a

---

(taxpayer's "clear and orderly recollection" accepted; "most of the expenditures which he made were not of the type customarily made by check or evidenced by receipts").

[23] For the distinction between "dependency status" and entitlement to a dependency exemption, see supra, at 14-3, 14-4.

[24] For purposes of IRC §152(c), the IRS has ruled that support provided by a community-property couple from community funds is equally allocable to each spouse. Rev. Rul. 61-52, 1961-1 CB 23. Thus, if a community-property couple provides 80 percent of the support of one of their children and a second child supplies 20 percent of the first child's support, the over-half restriction is not violated, and the parents and second child can allocate the dependency claim to the latter.

[25] Thus, the beneficiary must be related to each member of the support group within the meaning of IRC §152(a), discussed supra, text at note 1. It is not necessary, however, for the *same* relationship to exist between them; thus, if more than half of *A*'s support is provided by two children and a grandchild, they may enter into a multiple-support agreement. See Treas. Regs. §1.12-3(b), Example 2.

rule of law and by difficulties in proving the amount spent by the respective parents.

The rule of law is IRC §152(b)(4), under which alimony and similar amounts may not be treated by the payor as paid for the support of any dependent if the amount is taxable to the recipient under IRC §71 or §682.[26] As explained elsewhere in this work,[27] alimony payments that are not *explicitly* earmarked for the children of divorced parents are usually taxable to the ex-spouse who receives them; and if he or she then uses the funds to support the children, the payments are credited to the recipient spouse rather than the payor in determining the children's dependency status. In this situation, therefore, the payor is credited only with any additional support provided to the children, such as expenditures when exercising visitation rights or temporary custody and amounts that are explicitly earmarked for the children by the divorce decree or agreement or are paid voluntarily (e.g., school tuition and summer camp fees).

The complicating evidentiary problem is the difficulty encountered by the noncustodial parent in determining the amount spent by the custodial parent and, conversely, the custodial parent's lack of precise information about the noncustodial parent's expenditures when exercising visitation rights or enjoying temporary custody.

In 1967, to reduce the number of conflicting claims requiring the IRS to act as "an unwilling arbiter between the contending parents,"[28] Congress enacted IRC §152(e), under which the custodial parent is ordinarily entitled to claim the children as dependents and an exchange of information is authorized. Section 152(e) comes into play if (a) more than half of a child's support is provided by parents who are divorced, legally separated under a divorce or separation decree, or separated under a written separation agreement and (b) one or both of the parents has custody of the child for more than half of the calendar year. Thus, the special rules of IRC §152(e) do not apply if a grandparent or other third person supplies more than half of the child's support or has custody for more than half of the calendar year. Section 152(e)(4) is also inapplicable if a multiple-support agreement under IRC §152(c) is in effect.

When applicable, IRC §152(e) prescribes a special support rule, estab-

---

[26] IRC §152(b)(4), like IRC §§71 and 682, uses the terms "wife" and "husband" for the recipient and payor, respectively, but these terms are interchangeable when payments go in the opposite direction.

[27] For the principles determining when alimony and similar amounts are taxable to the recipient and deductible by the payor, see infra ¶¶32.1, 32.3.

[28] H. Rep. No. 102, 90th Cong., 1st Sess., reprinted in 1967-2 CB 590, 591 (principal issue in 5 percent of all income tax cases at informal conference level of administrative process was dependency status of children of divorced or separated parents).

lishes two exceptions to it, and provides for the exchange of information, as follows:

1. *Special support rule.* The basic principle laid down by IRC §152(e)(1) is that the child is the dependent of the custodial parent (i.e., the one with custody as defined above for a greater portion of the calendar year than the other parent), regardless of the amount of support actually supplied by either parent. It is possible, therefore, that the custodial parent will be entitled to the dependency exemption, even though the noncustodial parent supplies *all* of the child's support.

2. *Exception if noncustodial parent is designated by decree or agreement.* Notwithstanding the special support rule, the child is treated as the dependent of the noncustodial parent if he or she (a) provides at least $600 for the child's support and (b) is assigned the dependency exemption by the decree of divorce or separate maintenance or by a written agreement between the parents.

3. *Exception for actual support.* The special support rule of IRC §152(e)(1) is also displaced if the noncustodial parent supplies $1,200 or more for the support of the child. In this event, the noncustodial parent is entitled to treat the child as a dependent, unless the custodial parent "clearly" establishes that he or she provides more for the child's support than the noncustodial parent. The custodial parent need prove only that he or she provided more support than the noncustodial parent, not more than half of the total. The noncustodial parent is entitled to this presumption even if the dependency deduction is allocated to the custodial parent by the divorce decree or a written agreement between the parents.[29]

4. *Allocation of noncustodial parent's funds to support.* One of the evidentiary difficulties for a noncustodial parent is establishing that funds sent to the custodial parent for the support of children were actually so used, rather than saved by or for the children or diverted to other uses. This problem is exacerbated if the support money is commingled with the custodial parent's funds or the child's earnings. In applying the $600 and $1,200 exceptions to the special support rule, IRC §152(e)(2) remedies this problem by giving noncustodial parents the benefit of an irrebuttable presumption that amounts expended for a child's support are supplied by them to the extent of their contributions.

5. *Exchange of information.* Section 152(e)(3) provides for an exchange of itemized support statements between the parents at the request of either one, and the regulations authorize the IRS to demand such a statement from either parent and to make it available to the other.[30]

---

[29] Treas. Regs. §1.152-4(d)(3).
[30] Treas. Regs. §1.152-4(e).

6. Gross Income Restriction. To qualify for the $1,000 dependency-exemption deduction, an individual not only must be the taxpayer's "dependent" but also must either (a) have gross income of less than $1,000 for the calendar year in which the taxpayer's taxable year begins or (b) be exempted from the gross income restriction by virtue of being a child of the taxpayer who is under nineteen or a full-time student.

The gross income restriction is evidently intended to exclude persons who, though dependent on the taxpayer, can provide a modest amount of self-support. Because it looks to "gross income," however, the benchmark is ill suited to accomplish this purpose. It disqualifies persons with more than $1,000 of gross income from business activities or rental properties, for example, even if bona fide business expenses generate an operating loss. Moreover, if gross income exceeds the $1,000 limit by a single dollar, the entire dependency exemption is lost. On the other hand, the gross income test fails to disqualify persons with a substantial capacity for self-support from interest on state and municipal bonds, a personal residence, or other assets generating income that is excluded from gross income. This includes situations in which the dependent saves some or all of his or her exempt income and uses the taxpayer's contributions to defray the cost of living.

Because the gross income limit discouraged part-time employment by students, it was eliminated in 1954 for children and stepchildren of the taxpayer who have not attained the age of nineteen by the close of the calendar year in which the taxpayer's taxable year begins or who are students. For this purpose, the term "student" is defined by IRC §152(e)(4) to mean an individual who (a) is a full-time student at an "educational organization" or (b) is pursuing a full-time accredited on-farm training course during each of five calendar months of the calendar year in which the taxpayer's taxable year begins. The IRS has classified persons enrolled in vocational high schools and technical institutes as "full-time students" even if part of their training consists of jobs in private industries, but student status has been denied to interns and residents working in a general hospital.[31] To qualify as an "educational organization," an institution must normally maintain a regular faculty and curriculum and have a regularly enrolled body of students in attendance at the place where its educational activities are conducted.[32] The regulations state that the statutory definition includes "primary and secondary schools, colleges, universities, normal schools, technical schools, mechanical schools, and similar institutions," but not "noneducational institutions, on-the-job training, correspon-

---

[31] For definitions of "child," "student," and "educational organization," see Treas. Regs. §1.151-3.

[32] IRC §170(b)(1)(A)(ii), which is incorporated by reference by IRC §151(e)(4)(A).

dence schools, night schools, and so forth." [33] It should be borne in mind that children who are not exempted from the gross income limit and, consequently, fail to qualify for the dependency exemption may nevertheless be "dependents" for such purposes as the medical expense deduction.[34]

¶14.3 ITEMIZED DEDUCTIONS

Although substantially all expenses incurred in earning a living or in profit-oriented activities are deductible,[35] so-called personal expenses are not deductible unless explicitly allowed by a specific statutory provision. Referring to this distinction, the Supreme Court observed in *United States v. Gilmore* that "Congress has seen fit to regard an individual as having two personalities"—(1) "a seeker after profit who can deduct the expenses incurred in that search" and (2) "a creature satisfying his needs as a human and those of his family but who cannot deduct such consumption and related expenditures." [36]

The statutory framework for the disallowance of personal expenses is IRC §262, which provides: "Except as otherwise expressly provided in [the income tax provisions of the Internal Revenue Code], no deduction shall be allowed for personal, living, or family expenses." The precise function of IRC §262, however, is unclear. Since taxpayers cannot deduct *any* expenses unless allowed to do so by an identifiable statutory provision,[37] IRC §262 seems merely to repeat this basic principle; and it is not clear that the tax world would change if IRC §262 were repealed or, at the opposite extreme, broadened to read that "except as otherwise expressly provided, no deduction shall be allowed for any expenditure." For this reason, IRC §262 serves less as an operative rule of law than as a warning or reminder of a basic structural principle, viz., that the cost of living is ordinarily not deductible. Since IRC §262 explicitly gives way to other statutory provisions expressly allowing personal expenses to be deducted, however, it does not conflict with any deduction provisions.

---

[33] See Treas. Regs. §1.151-3(c).

[34] See Counts v. CIR, 42 TC 755 (1964); see also IRC §44A(c)(1)(B) (credit for certain employment-related expenses for care of dependents, without regard to dependency exemption); compare IRC §44A(c)(1)(A) ("dependent . . . with respect to whom the taxpayer is entitled to a deduction [i.e., dependency exemption] under section 151(e)").

[35] See generally supra ¶8.1.

[36] US v. Gilmore, 372 US 39, 44 (1963), quoting Surrey & Warren, Cases on Federal Income Taxation 272 (Foundation Press 1960).

[37] See New Colonial Ice Co. v. Helvering, 292 US 433, 440 (1934) ("Whether and to what extent deductions shall be allowed depends upon legislative grace; and only as there is clear provision therefor can any particular deduction be allowed").

While most "personal, living, or family expenses" are nondeductible, Congress has seen fit, for reasons of policy that vary from one provision to another, to exempt a few categories of expenses from the basic principle of nondeductibility. These provisions, which allow certain expenses to be deducted even though not incurred in a business or profit-oriented transaction, are usually referred to in the trade as "itemized" or "personal" deductions.

The term "personal deductions," however, leaves something to be desired, since some of the so-called personal deductions (e.g., IRC §§163 and 166, relating to interest and bad debts) are broad enough to embrace items arising in business or profit-oriented activities, as well as those wholly attributable to the taxpayer's personal life. For want of a better brief label, however, the terms "itemized deductions" and "personal deductions" are used interchangeably in later chapters of this work as a label for deductions that are allowed even if they are not attributable to business or profit-oriented activities and would be disallowed by IRC §262 as "personal, living, or family expenses" in the absence of a statutory provision explicitly allowing them to be deducted.

Four other aspects of the itemized deductions, discussed in more detail elsewhere in this work, should be noted here:

1. They are deductible from adjusted gross income (AGI) in computing taxable income (rather than from gross income in computing AGI) and, hence, cannot be deducted if the taxpayer takes advantage of the zero bracket amount.[38] This limitation does not apply to so-called direct charitable contributions, which can be deducted from gross income in computing the taxpayer's adjusted gross income by virtue of IRC §§63(i) and 170(i).[38.1]

2. Itemized deductions that are not used because they exceed AGI cannot be carried over for use in other years under IRC §172, relating to net operating losses, unless attributable to the taxpayer's trade or business.[39]

3. Some itemized deductions (e.g., for taxes, interest, and bad debts) cover items that can arise in the taxpayer's business and could, in the alternative, be deducted as business expenses under IRC §162. In general, these instances of overlapping jurisdiction are resolved by treating the items as deductible under IRC §162.[40]

---

[38] See infra ¶14.4.

[38.1] See infra ¶19.3.

[39] See supra ¶12.9.

[40] See Brown v. US, 434 F.2d 1065 (5th Cir. 1970) (ad valorem taxes must be deducted from gross income, rather than from AGI, with resulting impact on deduction allowed for charitable contributions); Dorminey v. CIR, 26 TC 940, 947 (1956) (interest and taxes); but see IRC §163(d)(4)(A)(i) (deductions taken into account only if allowable solely by reason of IRC §162).

4. Itemized deductions viewed as excessive in amount by IRC §57(b) constitute tax preference items taken into account in computing the alternative minimum tax imposed by IRC §55.[41]

¶14.4 THE ZERO BRACKET AMOUNT (ZBA)

1. ZBA vs. Election to Itemize Deductions. In 1944 Congress enacted a so-called standard deduction, designed to simplify the preparation and audit of individual tax returns by requiring taxpayers to choose between itemizing their personal deductions and deducting a flat allowance in lieu of any itemized deductions to which they were entitled. At the outset, the standard deduction (10 percent of adjusted gross income, but not more than $500) was elected by about 82 percent of individual taxpayers; but as incomes rose in later years the percentage of taxpayers preferring the standard deduction fell, leading Congress to liberalize its features from time to time in order to restore its patronage. In addition to raising the dollar amount of the optional allowance for most taxpayers, the 1977 revision converted the standard deduction into a "zero bracket amount" (ZBA). This change made it possible to incorporate the flat allowance into the tax schedules prescribed by IRC §1 and the tax tables promulgated by the Treasury pursuant to IRC §3.

The ZBA for 1979 and later taxable years is $3,400 for married couples filing joint returns and surviving spouses, $2,300 for individuals who are not married and do not qualify as surviving spouses, and $1,700 for married individuals filing separate returns.[42] These amounts (increased after 1984 by the cost-of-living adjustment mandated by IRC §§1(f) and 63(d)) are subject to a zero tax rate, which accounts for the statutory label "zero bracket amount." A taxpayer with itemized deductions in excess of the applicable ZBA amount may elect to deduct the excess in computing taxable income; and since the ZBA amount itself is incorporated in the tax tables authorized by IRC §3 and the rate schedules prescribed by IRC §1, such a taxpayer gets the full benefit of his or her itemized deductions. A taxpayer who fails to make this election is entitled only to the applicable ZBA and gets this benefit automatically.

The foregoing rules are qualified for (1) married couples filing separate returns if either spouse itemizes his or her deductions, (2) nonresident aliens, (3) citizens subject to IRC §931 (relating to income from sources within possessions of the United States), and (4) taxpayers for whom a dependency exemption is allowable to another taxpayer under IRC §151(e). The first three

---

[41] For the alternative minimum tax, see infra ¶39.3.

[42] IRC §63(d); the zero bracket amount is zero for "any other case" (e.g., trusts and estates).

groups are denied the benefit of the ZBA, but any itemized deductions to which they are entitled are taken into account in computing their taxable income; and the fourth group either gets the same treatment or can deduct the amount of their earned income, whichever is more favorable.

2. Effect of ZBA on Taxable Income. The 1977 conversion of the optional standard deduction into the zero bracket amount (ZBA) as defined by IRC §63(d) required the time-honored term "taxable income" to be redefined. Under pre-1977 law, taxable income was computed by subtracting the taxpayer's personal exemptions and either the standard deduction or the taxpayer's itemized deductions from adjusted gross income (AGI). Since the ZBA was incorporated into the tax schedules of IRC §1 and the tax tables authorized by IRC §3, it was necessary to redefine taxable income as AGI minus (a) the taxpayer's personal exemptions and (b) the excess of the taxpayer's itemized deductions over the applicable ZBA.[43]

The effect of the changed definition can be illustrated by comparing a married couple having $1,000 of taxable income as defined by pre-1977 law with a couple having $4,400 of taxable income as defined by IRC §63(b)(1) of 1980 law. Both couples paid a tax of $140—not because the rates were reduced in 1977 but because $4,400 of taxable income as redefined, less the ZBA applicable to married couples ($3,400), built into the new definition, equals $1,000 of taxable income as previously defined.

As was true of the pre-1977 choice between the standard deduction and the itemized deductions, the ZBA of current law reduces the value of the itemized deductions, since they are taken into account only if, and to the extent that, they exceed the zero bracket amount. Thus, a married couple will incur the same tax liability whether their itemized deductions aggregate $1, $3,400, or any amount between these extremes. And the taxable income of a couple with $3,401 of itemized deductions will be only $1 less than the taxable income of a couple with no deductions at all.

The ZBA can therefore be viewed as disallowing an equivalent amount of itemized deductions or as giving a free ride to taxpayers who have not incurred any expenses generating itemized deductions. Whether the itemized deductions are viewed as helping to define the taxpayer's economic income (e.g., the casualty deduction), as incentives to engage in socially useful conduct (e.g., the charitable contribution deduction), or as tailoring tax liabilities to the taxpayer's ability to pay (e.g., the medical expense deduction), the ZBA interferes pro tanto with the achievement of these objectives. Congress decided that

---

[43] IRC §63(b)(1). The additional adjustment mandated by IRC §63(b)(2) has the effect of eliminating the ZBA for the four special categories of taxpayers listed in IRC §63(e)(1), described supra, text in preceding paragraph.

this price is worth paying, however, since it serves to simplify preparation and audit of millions of tax returns.

On several occasions, however, Congress intervened to protect particular deductions against the erosion produced by the ZBA's statutory predecessor, the optional standard deduction. Alimony is deductible from gross income in computing AGI;[44] as a result, it is taken into account in full, whether the taxpayer elects to itemize his or her other deductions or not. By contrast, under prior law this allowance could be deducted only *from* AGI in computing taxable income and, hence, had to be waived by taxpayers claiming the standard deduction. By promoting alimony to "above the line" status in 1976, Congress enabled taxpayers to claim this deduction in addition to the zero bracket amount. A similar shield was conferred on the so-called child care allowance in 1976, when it was converted from an itemized deduction to a credit, whose amount is unaffected by the taxpayer's applicable ZBA.[45]

Conversely, demoting a deduction to below-the-line status is a way of increasing simplicity by requiring taxpayers to waive the deduction if they take advantage of the zero bracket amount. Certain employee business expenses have suffered this fate.[46] Because they do not qualify under IRC §§62(1) and 62(2) for deduction from gross income in computing AGI, they can be deducted only as itemized deductions as defined by IRC §63(f); and this inferior status means that they are taken into account only if, and to the extent that, the taxpayer's itemized deductions exceed his or her ZBA. Along with a few other categories of business and profit-oriented deductions, therefore, these employee expenses are exceptions to the general rule allowing business and profit-oriented deductions to be deducted from gross income in computing AGI, so that they are taken into account even by taxpayers who take advantage of the ZBA rather than itemize their deductions.

SELECTED BIBLIOGRAPHY

Bittker, Federal Income Taxation and the Family, 27 Stan. L. Rev. 1389 (1975).

Bittker, Income Tax Deductions, Credits, and Subsidies for Personal Expenditures, 16 J.L. & Econ. 193 (1973).

Brannon & Morss, The Tax Allowance for Dependents: Deductions Versus Credits, 26 Nat'l Tax J. 599 (1973).

---

[44] IRC §62(13) (alimony under IRC §215); see infra ¶32.1.

[45] See IRC §44A, discussed infra ¶21.1.

[46] See IRC §62(2), listing the only employee business deductions that can be deducted above the line in computing AGI.

Kelman, Personal Deductions Revisited: Why They Fit Poorly in an "Ideal" Income Tax and Why They Fit Worse in a Far From Ideal World, 31 Stan. L. Rev. 831 (1979).

Sander, Dependency Exemptions for Children of Divorced or Separated Spouses, 45 Taxes 710 (1967).

Schenk, Simplifying Dependency Exemptions: A Proposal for Reform, 35 Tax Lawyer 855 (1982).

Sjostrand, Why Not Go Back to the Standard Deduction? 56 Taxes 265 (1978).

Turnier, Evaluating Personal Deductions in an Income Tax—The Ideal, 66 Cornell L. Rev. 262 (1981).

CHAPTER 15

Interest Paid or Accrued on Indebtedness

Page

¶15.1 INTRODUCTORY

Section 163(a) provides that, as a general rule, the taxpayer may deduct "all interest paid or accrued within the taxable year on indebtedness." Since interest attributable to business or profit-oriented transactions would be deductible under IRC §162 (business expenses) or §212 (expenses incurred for the production of income, etc.) even in the absence of IRC §163(a), its principal function is to permit the deduction of interest arising in personal activities, such as the purchase on credit of private residences, automobiles, and consumer durable goods. In this respect, IRC §163(a) is an exception to IRC §262, which denies any deduction for "personal, living, or family expenses" unless expressly permitted.[1]

Although interest incurred in the taxpayer's personal activities has been deductible since the inception of the federal income tax, Congress has never announced its reasons for enacting or retaining this exception to the nondeductibility of personal expenditures. Its objective may be to equalize the tax status of persons who must borrow to pay for personal residences and other assets with that of taxpayers who pay for similar assets with funds that would otherwise yield income. The deduction allowed by IRC §163(a) to borrowers gives them a tax advantage that persons who pay cash obtain indirectly,

[1] For IRC §262, see supra ¶14.3.

because their gross income declines while the value of using the newly acquired property is not includable in income. This point can be illustrated by assuming that *A* and *B* each own marketable securities with a cost and market value of $5,000, producing $500 of income per year; that *A* sells his securities to purchase a $5,000 automobile; and that *B* retains his securities and borrows $5,000 at 10 percent to purchase an identical automobile. *A*'s gross income after these transactions will be zero, while *B*'s will continue to be $500. Unless *B* is allowed to deduct the $500 of interest paid by him (so that his taxable income will be zero), he will be worse off than *A,* although they have the same net worth and each has the use of a $5,000 automobile.

Whatever may have been the original objective of the interest deduction, its perpetuation may reflect a legislative desire to stimulate the national economy by encouraging the use of credit to purchase homes, automobiles, and other consumer durable goods. Congress may also have thought that the repeal of so deeply entrenched a deduction would inflict a loss on persons who incurred mortgages and other long-term debts expecting the interest to be deductible. Finally, it is difficult in some situations to determine whether debt is attributable to personal activities or to business and investment transactions, especially in the case of sole proprietors; and administrative convenience is served by allowing all interest to be deducted, rather than limiting the deduction to profit-oriented activities.

The general rule laid down by IRC §163(a), allowing a deduction for "all interest paid or accrued within the taxable year on indebtedness," can be applied with ease to the overwhelming bulk of periodic payments by ordinary taxpayers on their home mortgages, bank loans, and other run-of-the-mill obligations. But the beguilingly simple statutory language conceals a vast array of problems that the courts have had to decide with scant assistance from the statute's legislative history or the regulations. Thus, "interest" and "indebtedness" are often difficult to distinguish from other payments and financial arrangements, and this requires the courts to grapple with numerous elusive problems in classifying particular transactions. Moreover, the interest deduction lends itself to exploitation in tax-avoidance schemes, which in turn have been attacked by the IRS with its customary arsenal of judge-made weapons; and, when these have proved to be cumbersome or inadequate, Congress has sometimes come to the rescue with specific statutory restrictions. As is ordinarily true, however, these statutory hurdles have in turn stimulated the ingenuity of taxpayers, leading the IRS to respond with additional rounds of litigation and administrative countermeasures.

1. The Meaning of "Interest." The most commonly quoted definition of interest, enunciated by the Supreme Court on several occasions, is "compensation for the use or forbearance of money." [2] The Court's reference to "money"

[2] Deputy v. Du Pont, 308 US 488, 498 (1940); see also US v. Midland-Ross Corp.,

precludes a deduction under IRC §163(a) for compensation paid for the use of borrowed property. The charge made by an owner for allowing another person to use property other than money ordinarily has another name; thus, one pays "rent" for using land or a building, "royalties" for using a patent or copyright, etc. These amounts are not deductible as interest under IRC §163(a), but they may qualify as business expenses under IRC §162 or as expenses paid for the production of income under IRC §212. On the other hand, "interest" as used in IRC §163(a) is not restricted to payments for borrowed funds but is broad enough to include payments on overdue taxes and judgments. Interest is ordinarily fixed as a percentage of the unpaid principal; but, so long as the amount due is ascertainable, it can be related to some other standard, such as the borrower's profits.

In *Old Colony R.R. v. CIR,* decided in 1932, the Supreme Court held that the "interest" paid on long-term bonds issued at a premium before 1913 was the coupon or stated interest thereon, not the effective rate (i.e., the coupon rate less a ratable portion of the premium). Describing the "effective rate of interest" as an "esoteric concept derived from subtle and theoretic analysis," the Court said that the term "interest" was used by Congress in the statutory predecessor of IRC §163(a) in "the usual, ordinary, and everyday meaning of the term" and that "he who pays and he who receives payment of the stipulated amount conceives that the whole is interest." [3] Although this observation presaged a simplistic view of the meaning of interest, in later cases the Court shifted to a more sophisticated economic analysis, concluding that original-issue discount is the equivalent of stated interest from the viewpoint of both the lender and the borrower.[4] The Court's earlier fear that "esoteric concepts" would confuse the common man may have been dispelled by public familiarity with the discount bonds issued by the government to finance World War II; the practice of requiring mortgagors to pay "points" on home loans; and other financial devices that are regularly described in newspaper, radio, and TV advertisements.

2. Interest vs. Other Charges. Because borrowers often incur a variety of charges in addition to the stated interest on borrowed funds (e.g., the cost of appraisals, "points," prepayment penalties, delinquency charges, and commissions), it is frequently necessary to distinguish between "interest" and other payments that are directly or indirectly associated with the borrowed funds.

---

381 US 54, 57 (1965); CIR v. National Alfalfa Dehydrating & Milling Co., 417 US 134, 145 (1974); IRC §461(g) ("charge for the use or forbearance of money").

[3] Old Colony R.R. v. CIR, 284 US 552, 560-561 (1932). For current law, see Treas. Regs. §1.61-12(c)(2) (premium on bonds issued after 1913 is includable in lender's income ratably over the bond's life), discussed infra, text at note 55.

[4] US v. Midland-Ross Corp., supra note 2 (lender must treat original-issue discount as ordinary income, not capital gain); CIR v. National Alfalfa Dehydrating & Milling Co., supra note 2 (borrower).

Moreover, if the loan is incurred to finance a particular transaction, such as the purchase or construction of property, the process of separating the interest component from other charges buried in an integrated financial package may be quite complicated. The principal problem areas are discussed below.

Payments that can be classified as interest on indebtedness are deductible under IRC §163, either when paid or accrued or ratably over the life of the loan, while the tax consequences of other payments depend on their nature. Thus, the denial of "interest" status to a particular payment does not necessarily mean that it is nondeductible; it may qualify for deduction under IRC §162(a) (business expenses), §212 (expenses for production of income), or §165 (losses). On the other hand, a noninterest payment may be an additional cost of acquiring property, increasing its basis and thus affecting the taxpayer's depreciation deductions and gain or loss when the property is disposed of.

1. *Commitment fees, "points," service charges, etc.* Business taxpayers often pay commitment or standby fees to institutional lenders so that they can borrow funds if and when the occasion for doing so arises. Since the payment must be made whether the lender is actually called upon to make the loan or not, the IRS has ruled that the arrangement does not create a debt; consequently, the charge is not compensation for the use of money and hence does not constitute "interest" within the meaning of IRC §163(a), but it may be deducted as a business expense under IRC §162.[5]

In its approach to service charges paid by borrowers, the IRS, with some support in the case law, distinguishes between charges compensating the lender for the loan and those defraying "the cost of specific services performed in connection with a borrower's account," such as investigating the borrower's credit, appraising assets, preparing the loan documents, and similar activities.[6] Unless charges for such services are computed by reference to the amount and life of the loan, which is not customary, the IRS rules that they do not constitute interest within the meaning of IRC §163(a).[7] If the funds are used for business or investment purposes, the charges can be deducted ratably over the period of the loan under IRC §162 or §212; but if the debt is incurred for personal purposes, the charges cannot be deducted, nor can they be added to the basis of property purchased with the borrowed funds, since the charges are part of the cost of the loan rather than of the property.

Service charges must be distinguished from amounts that carry similar

---

[5] Rev. Rul. 56-136, 1956-1 CB 92; Rev. Rul. 70-362, 1970-2 CB 147.

[6] See Wilkerson v. CIR, 70 TC 240 (1978) (2 percent "initial service charges" or "financing fee" charged by mortgage banker divided by court between deductible interest and payment for services; latter amount capitalized and deducted over life of loan).

[7] Rev. Rul. 72-315, 1972-1 CB 49 (service charge is "a fixed charge having no relationship to the amount borrowed or the time given to pay whereas interest is based on the amount deferred and the time of deferral").

labels ("premiums," "loan origination fees," "points," etc.) but are computed by reference to the amount and duration of the loan. Since these amounts are paid by the borrower (or deducted by the lender from the funds made available to the borrower) in order to convert the nominal rate of interest to an effective rate reflecting the lender's risk, they clearly constitute "interest" within the meaning of IRC §163(a).[8] Since these charges are in substance prepaid interest, however, they may have to be deducted ratably over the life of the loan.[9]

Amounts paid by the borrower *to third parties* for legal, accounting, appraisal, printing, or other services do not constitute "interest" even though paid as a prerequisite to a loan, since the payees are not lenders. From the borrower's perspective, it makes little difference whether these services are procured directly by it, procured by the lender from third parties and paid for by the borrower, or supplied by the lender and buried in its overhead expenses and hence in the stated rate of interest; but IRC §163(a) is applicable only in the last of these three situations. If the funds are borrowed for business or investment purposes, however, amounts paid to third parties to facilitate the financing are deductible under IRC §162 or §212 over the life of the loan.

2. *Carrying charges on installment purchases.* If personal property or educational services are purchased under a contract calling for installment payments and the carrying charges are separately stated but the interest charge cannot be ascertained, IRC §163(b) provides that the annual payments shall be treated as interest to the extent of 6 percent of the unpaid balance (but not in excess of the carrying charges allocable to the particular taxable year).

With the enactment in 1969 of the Truth-in-Lending Act, charges for consumer credit must be disclosed and interest, investigation fees, carrying charges, loan fees, and similar items must be combined in a separately stated "finance charge" expressed in terms of an annual percentage rate. The IRS has ruled that this legislation does not convert noninterest charges by the lender into deductible interest; but this admonition has been watered down by rulings permitting finance charges on bank credit card plans, revolving charge accounts, and similar credit arrangements to be deducted if based on the amount deferred and the length of the deferral.[10]

---

[8] Rev. Rul. 69-188, 1969-1 CB 54 ("points" or "loan processing fee" constitutes deductible interest); see also Rev. Rul. 69-582, 1969-2 CB 29 (amplifying Rev. Rul. 69-188); Rev. Rul. 69-290, 1969-1 CB 55 ("premium for privilege of being granted a loan"; deductible as interest); L-H Heat Treating Co. v. CIR, 28 TC 894 (1957) ("negotiated bonus or premium to be paid the lender as a prerequisite to obtaining borrowed capital").

[9] See IRC §461(g), enacted in 1976, discussed infra ¶15.3.

[10] Rev. Rul. 71-98, 1971-1 CB 57 (bank credit card plan); Rev. Rul. 73-136, 1973-1 CB 68 (oil company's credit card plan); Rev. Rul. 73-137, 1973-1 CB 68 (retail installment contract, including prepayment charges); see also Rev. Rul. 77-417, 1977-2 CB 60 (bank credit card; flat one-time charges for cash advances, check advances, and overdraft advances qualify as interest).

Section 163(b) does not apply to loans of money, even if the proceeds are used by the borrower to purchase personal property, or to loans to finance the purchase of noneducational services or real property.[11] When interest is not separately stated in such a transaction, taxpayers claiming interest deductions have the burden, as under the pre-1954 case law, of separating the interest component from other charges made by the lender.

Section 163(b) is also inapplicable if there is no "separately stated" carrying charge. Thus, if the taxpayer purchases property for $50,000, to be paid in five equal annual installments without interest, IRC §163(b) does not permit the imputation of deductible interest. A financial analyst would insist that interest is necessarily embedded in the terms of this arrangement (unless the seller was induced by a family or similar relationship to make a gift to the buyer of the time value of deferring payment) and that, if the going rate of interest for comparable loans is 10 percent per year, the property can be worth only about $38,000, so that the balance of the payments constitutes interest. Despite this analysis, the courts have been unwilling to impute interest to the seller or to permit the buyer to take a deduction if their contract does not provide for interest, unless the surrounding circumstances supply a reason for disregarding the terms of the agreement—for example, that interest was bargained for and then buried in the deferred-payment schedule.[12]

In 1964, Congress stepped into this breach by enacting IRC §483, which ordinarily requires the seller of property to treat a prescribed part of any deferred payments as interest if the contract either fails to provide for stated interest or adopts an unrealistically low rate.[13] Although the principal objective of this legislation was to compel the seller to report an appropriate part of any gain on such a sale as ordinary income rather than long-term gain, a by-product of IRC §483 is an interest deduction for the purchaser.[14]

3. *Payments of interest vs. payments of principal.* A recurring problem under IRC §163(a) is to determine whether a particular payment by the borrower is a payment of interest or of principal, or whether it should be

---

[11] Treas. Regs. §1.163-2(a)(3); Treas. Regs. §1.163-2(d), Example (5).

[12] Elliott Paint & Varnish Co. v. CIR, 44 BTA 241 (1941) (parol evidence admissible to contradict terms of no-interest agreement, but evidence failed to establish that parties intended allocation of deferred payments between principal and interest); Hundahl v. CIR, 118 F.2d 349 (5th Cir. 1941) (taxpayer purchased divorced wife's share of community property for installment payments, whose amount was calculated by taxpayer on basis of present value plus interest on deferred payments, but interest was not mentioned in contract; held, no deduction for implicit interest is allowable, no matter "how petitioner in his own mind or in discussion with his attorney arrived at the amount he would agree to pay"); but see Berry's Est. v. CIR, 372 F.2d 476 (6th Cir.), cert. denied, 389 US 834, rehearing denied, 389 US 998 (1967) (Tax Court upheld in finding "interest in the contemplation of the parties," based on prepayment discount schedule).

[13] For IRC §483, see infra ¶27.6.

[14] See generally infra ¶27.6.

allocated between the two. If the parties agree when the debt is contracted at a later time that interest is to be paid before principal, or vice versa, their agreement will ordinarily determine the income tax consequences of later payments.[15]

In the absence of an agreement between the parties, the status of particular payments depends on state law, which usually provides that the debtor can specify whether a payment is to be applied to interest or to principal; that the creditor can make the allocation if the debtor fails to do so; and that if neither designates how the payment should be applied, it will apply to the delinquent interest in preference to principal and to the least secure or oldest debt if there are several obligations or a running account between the parties.[16]

4. *Interest vs. prepayment premiums, delinquency penalties, etc.* Amounts paid to creditors for the privilege of prepaying a debt or calling the taxpayer's bonds before maturity reflect the higher price that must sometimes be paid for short-term rather than long-term credit and constitute interest within the meaning of IRC §163(a).

If the creditor is a governmental agency, which can both charge for the use of money and exercise its sovereign prerogative to *punish* delinquent debtors, it becomes necessary to ascertain whether payments by a defaulting taxpayer fall in one category or the other. If it is determined that a charge is imposed not to compensate the government for extending credit but to punish the debtor, the payment is removed from the "interest" category and categorized as a "penalty," which cannot be deducted as interest or even as a business expense. Conversely, if the payment is properly classified as "interest," it can be deducted.

5. *Interest vs. cost of property purchased.* As seen earlier, the courts have been reluctant to sanction deductions for the implicit interest component of deferred payments if they are ostensibly payable without interest.[17] In the same vein, a taxpayer buying on credit from a merchant whose regular prices are inflated to reflect the risks and delays inherent in collection cannot ordinarily deduct the hidden interest charges.[18]

3. The Requirement of "Indebtedness." Section 163(a) allows a deduction for "interest paid or accrued . . . on indebtedness." The statutory terms "interest" and "indebtedness" usually refer to opposite sides of the same coin, so that the same criteria will establish either that a particular payment is

---

[15] See generally Mason v. US, 453 F.Supp. 845 (N.D. Cal. 1978) (review of principles, with citations).

[16] See Keith v. CIR, 35 TC 1130 (1961) (payment to IRS with no allocation by taxpayer; applied by IRS in succession to principal, penalties, and interest for earliest taxable years); Lincoln Storage Warehouses v. CIR, 189 F.2d 337 (3d Cir. 1950) (judicial allocation pursuant to state law).

[17] Supra note 12 and accompanying text.

[18] Erwin v. CIR, ¶45,121 P-H Memo TC (1945).

"interest" on "indebtedness" or that it does not constitute "interest" and is not paid on "indebtedness." Thus, in *Deputy v. Du Pont,* involving dividends paid by the taxpayer on borrowed stock, the Supreme Court held that IRC §163(a) permits a deduction for compensation for the use or forbearance of money; as applied to the taxpayer, this definition meant not only that the payments were not "interest" but also that there was no "indebtedness" within the meaning of IRC §163(a).[19]

To support an interest deduction, there must be an obligation to pay a money debt [20] that is not a sham or a disguise for another relationship. A frequently cited definition of "indebtedness" is "an existing, unconditional, and legally enforceable obligation for the payment of money." [21] The debt must be enforceable, but personal liability is not required; a nonrecourse purchase-money obligation, for example, qualifies under IRC §163(a) if the value of the property equals or exceeds the amount of the debt.[22] Promoters of tax shelters sometimes purport to lend funds on a nonrecourse basis to the investors, recouping part or all of the "advance" by charging excessive prices for services or property. If this aspect of the transaction is detected, the debt is disregarded to the extent of the overcharge, and only the balance qualifies as "indebtedness" within the meaning of IRC §163(a).

In application, the principal issues posed by the concept of "indebtedness" are the following:

1. *Gratuitous obligations.* Since a promise to make a gift is not ordinarily enforceable because of the absence of consideration, purported interest on an amount that the taxpayer promises to pay to a donee at a specified future time is as much a gift as the principal and is therefore not deductible. On the other hand, if the gratuitous promise is enforceable under local law (e.g., because made under seal or because other parties act in reliance thereon), the interest is deductible.

While alleged intra-family debts must be scrutinized closely to insure that they are not shams, there is no reason to deny an interest deduction for payments on such an obligation if it is enforceable and is shown to be what it purports to be. For example, a taxpayer who wishes to make a gift to a child can transfer cash, in which event the interest or other yield on the transferred funds will be excluded from the taxpayer's gross income; or the taxpayer can borrow the funds from a bank, donate them to the child, and deduct the interest on the bank loan. Still another method of accomplishing the same

---

[19] Deputy v. Du Pont, supra note 2.

[20] Id.

[21] First Nat'l Co. v. CIR, 289 F.2d 861 (6th Cir. 1961).

[22] Treas. Regs. §1.163-1(b) (first sentence); Franklin's Est. v. CIR, 544 F.2d 1045 (9th Cir. 1976) (payments on nonrecourse debt in excess of security's value were not compensation for use of money but were similar to cost of option to acquire property that may appreciate in value).

result is to execute an interest-bearing promissory note and give it to the child, who can discount or pledge it or enforce it at maturity. If the obligation can meet the rigorous standards employed to test the bona fides of intra-family transactions, the taxpayer's interest payments, though made to the child, are functionally equivalent to the interest that is excluded from income if the taxpayer transfers cash from a bank account to the child and to the interest payable on a bank loan if that method of making a gift is employed.

2. *Debt vs. equity.* One of the most frequently litigated form-substance issues is whether evidences of "indebtedness" issued by a closely held corporation to its shareholders constitute true debt (so that payments thereon can be deducted as interest) or should instead be classified as equity, in which event the payments are nondeductible distributions of the corporation's profits. A related issue is whether a withdrawal of corporate funds by a controlling shareholder is a loan to him or a taxable distribution of profits; if the former, the shareholder is not taxed on receiving the funds and can deduct periodic payments thereon as interest under IRC §163(a). In general, however, the very fact that the shareholder has made such payments will tend both to validate his claim that the advance was a loan and to establish that the validating payments constitute interest.

3. *Debt vs. sale with option to repurchase.* From time immemorial—or at least since medieval theologians began to analyze the Biblical condemnation of interest—attempts have been made to disguise loans secured by property by effecting a "sale" of the property subject to an option in the "seller" to repurchase at a higher price on or before a prescribed date. It should come as no surprise that the courts are able to pierce the veil and characterize the transaction as a loan by the "buyer" to the "seller" if the latter is virtually certain to exercise the option. If the transaction is so viewed, the spread between the amount received by the alleged seller and the amount paid to repurchase the property is interest, which can be deducted under IRC §163(a); and the same amount must be reported by the alleged buyer as interest income rather than capital gain on the purported resale of the property.[23]

4. *Debt vs. lease with option to purchase.* When equipment or other property is acquired on credit, the parties may wish to avoid conventional debt financing by structuring the transaction as a lease with option to buy. If the transaction is taken at face value, the lessee is not subject to any indebtedness; in this event, each periodic payment constitutes rent, which is deductible by the tenant if incurred in business but is not if the transaction involves a personal residence or other nonbusiness property. On the other hand, if the

[23] Green v. CIR, 367 F.2d 823 (7th Cir. 1966) (purported sale of stock treated as loan as to both parties); see also Comtel Corp. v. CIR, 45 TC 294 (1965), aff'd, 376 F.2d 791 (2d Cir.), cert. denied, 389 US 929 (1967) (loan in form of purchase and resale).

transaction is found to be a disguised purchase of the property on credit (e.g., because it can be acquired by the "lessor" at the end of the "lease" for a nominal consideration by exercising the option), the interest component of the periodic payments can be deducted by the purchaser under IRC §163(a) whether the property is acquired for business or personal use, but the balance of the payments constitutes nondeductible payments of principal.[24]

5. *Indebtedness of the taxpayer.* Although IRC §163(a) speaks of "interest . . . on indebtedness" and does not explicitly refer to *the taxpayer's* debt, it is well established that a taxpayer is not entitled to a deduction on paying interest on someone else's obligation. Another way of putting the same point is that the payment must be "interest" from the taxpayer's point of view; it is not sufficient that it constitutes interest as between the creditor and the third person on whose behalf the taxpayer makes the payment. Thus, IRC §163(a) does not authorize deductions for payments constituting indirect gifts to the debtor (e.g., a parent's payment of interest on the mortgage indebtedness of a child), investments by the taxpayer (e.g., a second mortgagee's payment of interest on the first mortgage), or rent (e.g., a tenant's payment of interest on the landlord's mortgage). Since the payments in these circumstances are ordinarily abbreviated methods of transferring funds to the debtor, who in effect pays the funds to the creditor, the debtor is entitled to an interest deduction.

If one of several joint obligors or joint owners of property pays more than his or her ratable share of the interest, the case law supports a deduction for the full amount paid, on the theory that the taxpayer is subject to the entire indebtedness.[25] Since, however, the taxpayer is entitled to reimbursement from the other joint obligors, much could be said for treating the excess payment as an implicit loan to the other obligors, so that each obligor would deduct an appropriate fraction of the interest. In any event, if the parties explicitly agree that the excess payment will be so treated, there is no reason not to honor their arrangement for tax purposes.

4. Tenant-Stockholders of Cooperative Housing Corporation. Section 216 permits the tenant-stockholders of a cooperative housing corporation (CHC) to deduct their ratable shares of the interest and real estate taxes paid by the CHC. Enacted in 1942 to reverse judicial determinations that the

---

[24] See Starr's Est. v. CIR, 274 F.2d 294 (9th Cir. 1959); Judson Mills v. CIR, 11 TC 25 (1948) (Acq.) (lease with option to purchase treated as purchase on credit; interest component deductible); Cal-Maine Foods, Inc. v. CIR, ¶77,089 P-H Memo TC (1977) (lease with option to purchase treated as such; extended discussion of applicable principles).

[25] See Mason v. US, supra note 15, and cases there cited; Finney v. CIR, ¶76,329 P-H Memo TC (1976) ("deduction in respect of payment of a joint obligation is allowable to whichever of the parties liable thereon makes the payment out of his own funds," including situations in which person supplying funds turns them over to other obligor who acts merely as conduit).

tenant-stockholders could not deduct their corporation's interest or real estate taxes, the provision achieves a rough tax equivalence among owner-occupied homes, condominiums,[26] and CHCs. In furtherance of this status of equality, IRC §216(c) permits the tenant-stockholder to deduct depreciation on his proprietary lease or tenancy if it is used in a trade or business or held for the production of income; and gain on selling stock in a CHC qualifies for nonrecognition under IRC §§121 and 1034, relating to sales of the taxpayer's principal residence.[27]

To qualify under IRC §216, the CHC and its tenant-stockholders must satisfy a series of tightly defined requirements. Subject to minor exceptions, the CHC may have only a single class of stock outstanding; its stockholders must be entitled solely by reason of their stock ownership to occupy for dwelling purposes a house or apartment owned or leased by the CHC; no stockholder can be entitled to receive distributions (other than from the CHC's earnings and profits), except on partial or complete liquidation; and 80 percent or more of the CHC's gross income for the taxable year in which the deductible taxes and interest are paid or incurred must be derived from its tenant-stockholders. The term "apartment" is defined by an IRS ruling as "an independent housekeeping unit . . . which contains facilities for cooking, sleeping, and sanitation normally found in a principal residence," thus excluding an arrangement for the ownership of separate rooms in a building whose cooking and sanitation facilities are shared by the occupants.[28]

¶15.2 NONDEDUCTIBLE INTEREST

1. Debt Incurred to Purchase or Carry Tax-Exempt Securities. The general rule of IRC §163(a), allowing "all interest paid or incurred during the taxable year" to be deducted, is qualified by IRC §265(2), disallowing any deduction for interest on indebtedness "incurred or continued to purchase or carry [tax-exempt] obligations." The restriction of IRC §265(2) is discussed elsewhere in this work in conjunction with the tax status of state and municipal securities—the only obligations to which it now applies.

2. Debt Incurred to Purchase or Carry Life Insurance, Endowment, or Annuity Contracts. Premiums on life insurance, endowment, and annuity

---

[26] For condominiums, see Rev. Rul. 64-31, 1964-1 (Part 1) CB 300 (owner of condominium apartment can deduct his share of mortgage interest and taxes).

[27] For IRC §§121(d)(3) (sale of principal residence by taxpayer fifty-five years of age or older) and 1034(f) (sale and repurchase of principal residence within prescribed time period), see infra ¶24.4.

[28] Rev. Rul. 74-241, 1974-1 CB 68.

contracts can often be paid in part or even in whole by borrowing against the contract's cash value. This arrangement ordinarily enables the taxpayer to take current deductions for the interest paid, although the corresponding increase in the contract's value will usually be either exempt from tax (in the case of life insurance proceeds paid on death) or realized in a later year (in the case of endowment and annuity contracts). But this practice is restricted by IRC §264(a)(2), which disallows deductions for amounts paid or accrued on indebtedness incurred to purchase or carry single-premium contracts, and by IRC §264(a)(3), which disallows similar payments with respect to other contracts if the plan of purchase contemplates systematic borrowing against increases in the contract's cash value.

Although interest on indebtedness incurred to purchase or carry life insurance, endowment, and annuity contracts is the subject of special legislation, there is nothing unique about the tax savings generated by borrowing to finance these categories of assets. For example, interest on debt incurred to purchase a personal residence or family automobile is deductible, even though the rental value of these assets is excluded from income. Conversely, a taxpayer with income-producing assets who borrows to finance the purchase can deduct the interest on the mortgage, even though he could avoid incurring the debt by selling the investment assets and using the proceeds to pay for the residence. If the same taxpayer buys a single-premium life insurance policy, however, he will be better off if he sells the investment assets and uses the proceeds to pay for the policy, thus eliminating the investment income, than if he borrows to finance the purchase, since in the latter case his investment income will continue to be taxed, with no offsetting deduction for the interest paid on the debt.

If the purpose of IRC §163(a) is to equalize the tax status of taxpayers who use income-producing assets to finance their expenditures and those who borrow for this purpose,[29] IRC §§264(a)(2) and 264(a)(3) interfere with the achievement of that objective; and there seems to be no sound reason for distinguishing between taxpayers who purchase residences with borrowed funds and those who borrow to buy life insurance.

1. *Single-premium policies.* Section 264(a)(2) rules out deductions for interest on debts incurred or continued to purchase or carry a "single premium" life insurance, endowment, or annuity contract. Debt is incurred or continued to "carry" a policy if it enables the taxpayer to retain a policy already purchased; as a 1979 ruling observes, "one who borrows to buy a single-premium annuity contract and one who borrows against such a contract already owned are in virtually the same economic position." [30] For example, if the taxpayer purchases a single-premium policy for cash and then pledges it for a loan, the debt will probably be treated as incurred to "carry" the policy.

---

[29] See supra ¶15.1, text following note 1.

[30] Rev. Rul. 79-41, 1979-1 CB 124 (use of insurance contract as collateral for indebtedness is direct evidence of purpose to "carry" policy).

2. *Systematic borrowing against cash value of policies.* To curb the sale of insurance "primarily on the grounds that the policies are tax-saving devices," [31] IRC §264(a)(3) disallows deductions for amounts paid or accrued on debt that is incurred or continued to purchase or carry life insurance, endowment, or annuity contracts "pursuant to a plan of purchase which contemplates the systematic direct or indirect borrowing of part or all of the increases in the cash value of such contract." The restriction applies whether the borrowing is from the insurer, a bank, or other lender and even if the policy is not pledged as security for the debt.

To protect the value of insurance policies as collateral for loans, IRC §264(c) sets out four exceptions to the disallowance principle, which permit interest to be deducted even if paid on debt incurred pursuant to a tainted plan. These safe harbor provisions cover (1) payments if for a seven-year period at least four annual premiums were paid without the note financed with indebtedness; (2) an annual $100 de minimis exemption; (3) debt incurred because of an unforeseen substantial loss of income or increase in financial obligations; and (4) debt incurred in connection with the taxpayer's trade or business.

3. Interest Charged to Capital Account. Under IRC §266, discussed elsewhere in this work,[32] taxpayers may elect to charge interest, taxes, and other carrying charges to capital account if incurred in a construction project or similar activity. If capitalized under IRC §266, interest cannot be deducted, since it increases the taxpayer's basis for the property.

4. Debt to Finance Corporate Acquisitions. In a belated attempt to curb the growth of conglomerates during the roaring sixties, Congress enacted IRC §279, disallowing a deduction for interest in excess of $5 million per year on "corporate acquisition indebtedness," defined as debt to acquire stock or two-thirds of the noncash operating assets of another corporation if (1) the debt is subordinated and either convertible into the issuing corporation's stock or issued as part of an investment unit including an option to acquire stock and (2) the issuing corporation's debt-equity ratio exceeds 2:1 or the projected earnings do not exceed three times the interest on the acquisition debt. But by the time Congress prescribed this remedy, conglomerate fever—at least the virulent strain characterized by equity-flavored, subordinated debt—had virtually disappeared.

5. Tax-Avoidance Transactions. From an early date, the interest deduction has spawned a variety of ingenious tax-avoidance transactions, to some of which Congress responded with protective legislation after the IRS and the

[31] S. Rep. No. 830, 88th Cong., 2d Sess., reprinted in 1964-1 (Part 2) CB 505, 582.

[32] See infra ¶23.8.

courts had grappled with the problem on their own for a period of years.[33] Since a new device appeared on the market whenever an old one collapsed under scrutiny, it is difficult to generalize about the formal characteristics of the tax-avoidance schemes to be discussed below; but they ordinarily sought to exploit, singly or in combination, three features of the tax law as it existed in the heyday of these devices. First, interest was deductible from ordinary income when paid or accrued, even though the borrowed funds were invested in property whose yield would be realized only at a later date, at the favorable capital gain rate, or both. Second, prepaid interest was deductible by cash-basis taxpayers when paid, rather than ratably over the period to which it was allocable.[34] Third, interest was deductible even if the debt was contracted on a nonrecourse basis secured solely by the assets purchased with the borrowed funds.

These principles (curtailed in important respects by subsequent law, as explained below [35]) encouraged taxpayers to engage in transactions that had little if any independent economic significance but that held out the hope of substantial tax savings. The problem can be illustrated by assuming that a taxpayer borrows $1 million at 5 percent per year, without personal liability but with no right to prepay the debt, in order to purchase an asset that will grow at the rate of 5 percent per year and cannot appreciate beyond that amount, pledging the asset as security for the loan. There is no possibility on these facts of an economic gain or loss, because the taxpayer must pay out in interest the same amount that will be received when the investment matures; but the taxpayer can nevertheless realize a profit if (1) the interest can be deducted when paid and (2) the increase in the investment's value will be taxed only when the transaction is closed. As will be seen, most tax-avoidance transactions are variations on this theme, though the documentation is usually more sophisticated, and sometimes the prospect of a true economic gain or loss can be discerned on the far horizon if remote possibilities are taken into account.

Despite their ingenuity, transactions of this type almost always collapsed when subjected to the scrutiny of the federal judiciary. But it is easier to list the cases lost by taxpayers than to extract useful principles of law from them; as was said in one of the leading decisions, the tax-avoidance area "is particularly full of black-letter maxims that prove singularly unhelpful when it comes to deciding cases." [36]

---

[33] See IRC §265(2), discussed supra ¶6.4; IRC §§264(a)(2) and 264(a)(3), discussed supra, text following heading "Debt Incurred to Purchase or Carry Life Insurance, Endowment, or Annuity Contracts," page 15-11.

[34] For restrictive 1976 legislation in this area, see infra ¶15.3, text preceding note 51.

[35] Infra ¶15.3, text preceding note 51.

[36] Goldstein v. CIR, 364 F.2d 734, 741 n.7 (2d Cir. 1966), cert. denied, 385 US 1005 (1967); see also supra ¶1.3.

Even so, it is convenient and may be helpful to classify tax-avoidance schemes by reference to the particular defect resulting in a disallowance of the claimed deduction. So classified, the transactions found wanting by the courts fall into three major groups: (1) arrangements failing to create a genuine debt between the taxpayer and the alleged lender, (2) transactions creating a debt but otherwise lacking in economic substance because the only potential gain was a tax reduction, and (3) transactions creating both a debt and a potential for economic gain but motivated solely by anticipated tax savings.

In reviewing the fate of these devices, it should be borne in mind that subsequently enacted statutory provisions weaken or destroy the assumptions on which some of them were built. For example, cash-basis taxpayers can no longer freely deduct prepaid interest in the year when it is paid but must instead usually deduct it ratably during the years to which it is allocable; and limitations have been imposed on the deduction of so-called excess investment interest.[37]

1. *No indebtedness.* From an early date, the courts have refused to allow deductions for "interest" under IRC §163(a) in the absence of a bona fide indebtedness between the purported borrower and lender, especially in the case of intra-family and corporate-shareholder transactions.[38] The inquiry in such cases is predominantly factual, ordinarily requiring the court to decide whether a transaction claimed by the taxpayer to be a loan was in fact a gift or an equity investment that did not create a genuine debtor-creditor relationship.

In *Goodstein v. CIR,* involving the prototype of numerous tax-avoidance transactions, a similar but more complicated inquiry was required to determine whether a purported debt actually existed.[39] Pursuant to a plan devised by a promoter, the taxpayer placed an order with the promoter's controlled corporation for $10 million of Treasury notes, to be financed by a down payment of $15,000 and the taxpayer's promissory note, secured by the same Treasury obligations, for the balance. The promoter's corporation executed the order; but, having no cash to pay for the securities, it ordered them to be sold within thirty minutes after delivery. The Tax Court found that the taxpayer did not give an order for the immediate sale of the securities and was not aware of the action at that time, but it also concluded that "it was the intention of all the three participants [the taxpayer, the promoter, and the latter's financing corporation] that the petitioner would not purchase the Treasury notes, that there would be no actual loan to the petitioner, and that he would not pay any interest" and that "any action taken [by the promoter and his corporation]

[37] For IRC §461(g) (prepaid interest), see infra ¶15.3, text preceding note 51; for IRC §163(d) (excess investment interest), see infra ¶15.3, text following heading "Excess Investment Interest," page 15-22.

[38] Supra ¶15.1.

[39] Goodstein v. CIR, 267 F.2d 127 (1st Cir. 1959).

must be considered to have been at least with [the taxpayer's] acquiescence." [40]

It should be noted that *Goodstein* did not hold that the taxpayer's dealings with the promoter were entirely fictional, but only that they did not create a borrower-lender relationship. In effect, the taxpayer purchased a call option,[41] whose exercise would have produced a genuine profit if the market for Treasury securities rose, assuming that the promoter was not judgment-proof. But this aspect of the transaction, though legally and economically significant, did not create a debt and hence did not give rise to an interest deduction.

2. *Absence of economic substance.* In a major pronouncement on the deductibility of interest, the Supreme Court held in *Knetsch v. United States* that the taxpayer could not deduct interest on a purported debt where "there was nothing of substance to be realized by [the taxpayer] from this transaction beyond a tax deduction." [42] The transaction involved the purchase of ten single-premium, thirty-year annuity contracts, financed by a nominal down payment in cash and a nonrecourse loan secured by the contracts for the balance, the interest on which was paid partly in cash and partly by borrowing against the increasing cash value of the contracts.[43]

Because the taxpayer's equity under the *Knetsch* plan (i.e., the excess of the cash value of the contracts over the escalating debt) could not exceed $1,000, the annuity to be received when the contracts matured was bound to be trivial. Despite this, the taxpayer was forced to pay out much more than he received back from the company—about $137,000 in four years—to keep the program alive, because the interest payable on the debt (3.5 percent) exceeded the rate of growth in the cash value of the contracts (2.5 percent annually). Thus, unless a drastic drop in the market rate of interest enabled the taxpayer to refinance the program for less than the guaranteed rate of growth in the investment (a possibility that the Court evidently thought too unlikely to deserve mention in its opinion), the taxpayer's out-of-pocket expenses were obviously incurred in the hope of getting tax deductions under IRC §163(a) that would be worth more than their cost.

3. *"Purposive activity" as essential.* In *Goldstein v. CIR,* the Court of Appeals for the Second Circuit was unwilling to describe a transaction as a "sham" and acknowledged that it created a genuine indebtedness, but the court nevertheless disallowed a deduction for interest paid on the debt because

---

[40] Goodstein v. CIR, 30 TC 1178, 1181, 1188 (1958).

[41] Goodstein v. CIR, supra note 39, at 131.

[42] Knetsch v. US, 364 US 361, 366 (1960); see also Knetsch v. US, 348 F.2d 932 (Ct.Cl. 1965), cert. denied, 383 US 957 (1966).

[43] Section 264(a)(2), precluding the deduction of interest on debts incurred or continued to purchase or carry single-premium annuity contracts (discussed supra, text preceding note 29), was not in force for the years before the Court in *Knetsch.*

it was contracted solely to generate the deduction itself.[44] Having won about $140,000 in the Irish Sweepstakes, the taxpayer in *Goldstein* sought to generate a large interest deduction to offset part of the gain by borrowing $945,000 from two banks to finance the purchase of $1 million of Treasury securities, which were pledged as collateral for the loans, on which she paid about $81,000 of prepaid interest. The purpose of the plan was to shield the sweepstakes winnings against the ravages of the progressive rate schedule in the year of receipt by reducing net income for that year, with the expectation that the profit when the investments were subsequently closed could be reported as long-term capital gain. To effect this self-help averaging device, the taxpayer incurred interest charges on the borrowed funds in excess of the interest payable on the pledged securities and paid substantial fees to her advisers. These out-of-pocket expenses were to be recouped solely through the anticipated tax savings.

In holding that the interest was not deductible, the Court summarized its reasoning as follows:

> [It] is fair to say that Section 163(a) is not entirely unlimited in its application and that such limits as there are stem from the Section's underlying notion that if an individual or corporation desires to engage in purposive activity, there is no reason why a taxpayer who borrows for that purpose should fare worse from an income tax standpoint than one who finances the venture with capital that otherwise would have been yielding income.
>
> In order fully to implement this Congressional policy of encouraging purposive activity to be financed through borrowing, Section 163(a) should be construed to permit the deductibility of interest when a taxpayer has borrowed funds and incurred an obligation to pay interest in order to engage in what with reason can be termed purposive activity, even though he decided to borrow in order to gain an interest deduction rather than to finance the activity in some other way. In other words, the interest deduction should be permitted whenever it can be said that the taxpayer's desire to secure an interest deduction is only one of mixed motives that prompts the taxpayer to borrow funds; or, put a third way, the deduction is proper if there is some substance to the loan arrangement beyond the taxpayer's desire to secure the deduction.

4. *Registration-required obligations.* Section 163(f), enacted in 1982, denies any deduction for interest paid on any so-called registration-required obligation unless it is in registered form. The purpose of this provision is to

---

[44] Goldstein v. CIR, supra note 36.

discourage the issuance of bearer bonds, whose owners cannot be ascertained and hence may neglect to report their interest receipts as taxable income.

¶15.3 TAXABLE YEAR WHEN INTEREST IS DEDUCTIBLE

1. Cash-Basis Taxpayers. Although IRC §163(a) allows a deduction for interest "paid *or* accrued" (emphasis added) during the taxable year, cash-basis taxpayers cannot deduct interest until it is *paid.*[45] In an important early case the Supreme Court held that a cash-basis taxpayer's promissory note did not constitute "payment" of an obligation, even though secured by collateral; and this principle is applied to notes given to "pay" interest, even if the creditor treats the notes as new obligations and regards the interest on the old debt as having been paid.[46]

In the same vein, when a cash-basis taxpayer borrows funds on a discounted basis, giving the creditor a note for the aggregate amount of principal and interest, the interest is not "paid" until the obligation is discharged in cash, since the note actually given is the equivalent of two notes—one for the principal and a second for the interest. On the other hand, taxpayers can deduct interest even if they use borrowed funds to make the payment—borrowing from Peter, for example, to pay Paul. More troublesome are transactions in which additional funds are borrowed from the creditor to whom the interest is payable and are commingled with the borrower's other funds for a brief period before the interest is paid. In several cases, funds obtained in this manner have been analogized to funds borrowed from third parties, resulting in deductions for the interest payments.[47] In applying the "commingled funds" rationale, ad hoc decisions based on the facts of each case are, unfortunately, unavoidable, since there can be no precise answer to the question, "How much control over the funds does the borrower have to have enough control?"

This perplexing question was demoted in importance in 1976, however, by the enactment of IRC §461(g), under which cash-basis taxpayers must prorate prepaid interest to the years to which it is properly allocable.[48] Thus,

---

[45] Even if "paid," the amount cannot be deducted unless it constitutes "interest," as distinguished from payments of principal, deposits, etc., under principles examined supra ¶15.1, text following note 2.

[46] Helvering v. Price, 309 US 409 (1940). For cash-basis accounting, see generally infra ¶35.2.

[47] See Wilkerson v. CIR, 70 TC 240 (1978), and cases there cited.

[48] See infra, text preceding note 51; see also Burck v. CIR, 533 F.2d 768 (2d Cir. 1976), reaching the same result under pre-1976 law: The interest was treated as paid from the additional loan, but the deduction for the year of payment was limited to one year's interest under IRC §446(b) in order to "clearly reflect income."

even if the borrower has effective control over the funds obtained by the new loan, the deduction in the year of payment is limited to the amount allocable to that year, and the balance must be deducted in installments over the appropriate later years. The distinction between funds *withheld from* the borrower to "pay" interest and funds *advanced to* the borrower that are used by him to pay interest can arise even after 1976, however, since withheld amounts are not paid until the loan matures and hence cannot be deducted until then, while amounts satisfying the commingled funds test constitute prepaid interest and can be deducted in installments over the life of the loan under IRC §461(g).

2. Prepayment of Interest by Cash-Basis Taxpayers. Cash-basis taxpayers have never been allowed to deduct the cost of business equipment or buildings when paid but must instead capitalize the outlay and recover it by annual deductions for depreciation.[49] Several early cases, however, allowed cash-basis taxpayers to deduct prepaid interest in full,[50] although arguably prepaid interest is a capital outlay whose cost should be allocated over its useful life and deducted accordingly. In an effort to cope with tax shelters entailing prepaid interest (some of which generated deductions without any cash outlay by permitting the investor to borrow not only the entire cost of the purported investment but also the amount to be prepaid as interest), the IRS counterattacked—with varied success—by denying deductions for prepaid interest if the amount would materially distort the taxpayer's income, characterizing some plans as shams lacking in economic substance and asserting in other situations that purported prepayments of interest were deposits, down payments of purchase price, repayments of principal, or payments for options to purchase the underlying property.

In 1976, Congress provided the IRS with a more comprehensive weapon against these manipulative devices by enacting IRC §461(g), requiring cash-basis taxpayers to determine their deductions for prepaid interest on an accrual basis. Section 461(g) explicitly provides that prepaid interest "shall be treated as paid" in the period to which it is allocable, thus sidestepping a pre-1976 argument that cash-basis taxpayers would be denied any deduction for prepaid interest incurred for personal expenditures, such as a residence, if it had been characterized as a capital outlay. This concern grew out of the fact that individuals can depreciate property used in business or other profit-oriented activities, but not property acquired for personal use. Section 461(g) applies whether or not a deduction of the full amount when paid would distort income, and it makes no exception for de minimis amounts.

---

[49] See supra ¶8.4.

[50] Fackler v. CIR, 39 BTA 395 (1939) (Nonacq.); see also Rev. Rul. 68-643, 1968-2 CB 76, withdrawing earlier acquiescences in *Fackler* and in a 1943 case to the same effect.

Although IRC §461(g) provides that prepaid interest shall be "treated as paid" in the period to which properly allocable, it does not insure that the allocated amount will qualify for deduction at that time. Like interest *actually* paid in the period in question, the allocated portion of prepaid interest will be subject to any relevant limitations, such as IRC §§189 (construction period interest) and 163(d) (excess investment interest).[51]

3. Accrual-Basis Taxpayers. Accrual-basis taxpayers are required to deduct interest allocated on a daily basis during the life of the loan, regardless of when the interest is due or paid. In the absence of a contractual provision, the interest is computed on a straight-line basis, even though the borrower makes level monthly or other periodic payments covering both principal and interest; but a different method (e.g., the "Rule of 78s," commonly used by commercial lenders) is permissible if the loan agreement so provides.

In accordance with the general rule applicable to accrual-method taxpayers, interest cannot be deducted until all events required to create a liability have occurred;[52] but if this condition is satisfied, current deductions are not precluded by the possibility that the interest rate might be reduced at a later date by agreement of the parties. If, however, the borrower's liability to pay interest is contingent on an event that may not occur (e.g., the availability of cash or payment of prior obligations), interest cannot be accrued until the contingency is eliminated.

4. Original-Issue Discount, Premium, and Issue Expenses. When borrowing funds, the borrower may receive either less or more than the amount to be repaid, rather than the ostensible principal amount. If the amount received is less than the stated principal, the shortfall ("discount") is functionally equivalent to an increase in the stated interest (or takes the place of interest entirely);[53] conversely, if the amount received exceeds the amount to be repaid, the excess ("premium") reduces the cost of borrowing below the stated interest. For the lender, discount and premium have the opposite effects: A discount increases the lender's profit, while a premium decreases it.[54]

The borrower may also incur expenses on floating a loan (e.g., commissions, service charges by the lender, legal and accounting fees, printing ex-

---

[51] For IRC §189, see infra, text preceding note 60; for IRC §163(d), see infra, text following heading "Excess Investment Interest," page 15-22.

[52] Treas. Regs. §1.446-1(c)(1)(ii); see infra ¶35.3 (re "all events" standard); Hollingsworth v. US, 568 F.2d 192, 202 (Ct.Cl. 1977) (meaning of "contest").

[53] See generally CIR v. National Alfalfa Dehydrating & Milling Co., 417 US 134 (1974), Union Pac. R.R. v. US, 524 F.2d 1343 (Ct. Cl. 1975) (Issues VIII and IX—extensive analysis of bond discount and expense).

[54] For tax treatment of lenders, see infra ¶27.4 (original-issue discount); supra ¶12.12 (amortization of bond premium).

penses, etc.) that are not paid to the lender for the use or forbearance of money and hence do not constitute "interest," but that nevertheless increase the cost of borrowing above the stated interest. Another expense often incurred by borrowers, albeit a voluntary one, is a penalty imposed by the lender for the privilege of prepaying a loan.

For the borrower, the principal tax effects of loan discounts, premiums, and expenses are the following:

1. *Original-issue discount.* In general, original-issue discount can be deducted as interest, but the time when the deduction is allowable depends on the borrower's status. Corporate borrowers amortize discount over the life of the loan, whether on the cash or accrual method of reporting income; noncorporate borrowers do the same if on the accrual method, but other noncorporate debtors are allowed to deduct the discount only when the principal amount is paid.

2. *Issue premium.* If the borrower receives more than the amount to be repaid, the premium, which reduces the cost of borrowing below the stated interest, is includable in income ratably over the life of the loan under longstanding regulations, whether the taxpayer reports on the cash or accrual method.[55]

3. *Borrowing expenses.* In a 1930 decision, the Board of Tax Appeals held that commissions, fees, and printing expenses paid by a cash-method taxpayer in connection with a bank loan to finance the construction of rental property enabled her to use the borrowed funds for a period of years and, hence, could not be deducted when paid.[56] Because of the long-term benefits derived from these expenses, they are allocable to the entire life of the loan; but since they are not viewed as "interest," they can be amortized only if they qualify as business or investor expenses under IRC §162 or §212; no deduction is allowable if the funds are used for personal purposes.[57]

4. *Prepayment.* If a debt is prepaid, refinanced, or, in the case of debt evidenced by marketable securities, purchased on the open market by the borrower for more than the sum of the issue price plus any previously amortized discount (or minus any amortized premium), the excess is deductible when paid,[58] along with any unamortized borrowing expenses. Conversely, if the borrower pays less than the issue price (adjusted for previously amortized discount or premium), the transaction produces cancellation-of-indebtedness

---

[55] Treas. Regs. §1.61-12(c)(2).

[56] Lovejoy v. CIR, 18 BTA 1179 (1930); Denver & R.G.W.R.R. v. CIR, 32 TC 43 (1959) (Acq.), aff'd on other grounds, 279 F.2d 368 (10th Cir. 1960) (expenses of authenticating and printing bonds).

[57] IRC §262; see also supra ¶15.1, text following note 7.

[58] See Treas. Regs. §1.163-4(c)(1).

income, unless the taxpayer elects to exclude it from income and reduce the basis of its assets under IRC §§108 and 1017.[59]

5. *Transfer of mortgaged property.* When property subject to a debt is transferred by sale or corporate dissolution, the transferor can deduct any unamortized discount and borrowing expenses, since the transfer terminates the period during which it had the use of the borrowed funds.

5. Excess Investment Interest. Section 163(d) permits interest on debt incurred to acquire or carry property held for investment to be deducted by noncorporate taxpayers only to the extent of $10,000 per year, plus the taxpayer's net investment income and, in special cases, certain additional amounts. Any disallowed interest can be carried forward indefinitely and deducted, subject to the same limitations, in later years. These restrictions were enacted to prevent taxpayers from sheltering business income by deducting large amounts of interest on debts to acquire investments that are not expected to produce income currently, especially if the profit will constitute long-term capital gain rather than ordinary income.

Section 163(d) applies to "investment interest," defined by IRC §163(d)(3)(D) as interest paid or accrued on indebtedness incurred or continued to purchase or carry property held for investment. Thus, IRC §163(d) does not apply, at one end of the spectrum, to interest paid to acquire property used in the taxpayer's trade or business, such as plant, equipment, and inventory; and, at the other end of the spectrum, it does not apply to property acquired for personal use, such as the family residence or automobile. The primary focus, therefore, is on debt incurred to acquire assets producing passive income, such as interest, royalties, dividends, and capital gains.

Sections 163(d)(4)(B) and 163(d)(4)(C) provide for the pass-through of investment interest, income, and expenses from partnerships and Subchapter S corporations to the partners and shareholders, pursuant to the regulations. The allocated items are then amalgamated on the returns filed by the partners and shareholders with similar amounts incurred in their personal capacity in applying the limitations of IRC §163(d).

6. Real Property Construction Period Interest and Taxes. In 1976, as part of a broad-based legislative campaign against tax shelters, Congress enacted IRC §189, requiring "real property construction period interest and taxes" to be capitalized and amortized over specified periods instead of being deducted when paid or accrued. Although much could be said for requiring these expenses to be written off over the property's useful life, IRC §189 permits them to be amortized over periods of four to ten years, depending on

[59] Treas. Regs. §1.61-12(c)(3); for IRC §§108 and 1017, see supra ¶2.4.

the nature of the property and the year in which the interest and taxes are paid or accrued. Section 189 applies to individuals, Subchapter S corporations, and personal holding companies, but not to other corporations, trusts, or estates. Partners are not expressly mentioned, but presumably they must pick up their distributive shares of the partnership's interest and taxes.

The restrictions of IRC §189 apply only to real property, but not to real property that is not, and cannot reasonably be expected to be, held in a trade or business or an activity conducted for profit. This exemption for personal residences, vacation homes, and the like will require an allocation of interest and taxes incurred during the construction of a multiple dwelling if one of the units is to be occupied by the taxpayer. The deduction of construction period interest or taxes on farm buildings or other borderline hobby-business property may be taken as an admission against interest if the taxpayer later asserts that the activity is carried on for profit and hence is not subject to IRC §183.[60]

SELECTED BIBLIOGRAPHY

Asimow, The Interest Deduction, 24 A.C.L.U. L. Rev. 749 (1977).

Blum, Knetsch v. U.S.: A Pronouncement on Tax Avoidance, 1961 S. Ct. Rev. 135, 137 n.8, reprinted in 40 Taxes 296, 297–298 n.8 (1962).

Congressional Budget Office, The Tax Treatment of Homeownership: Issues and Options (1981).

Cowan, Tax Reform on the Home Front: Cooperative Housing Corporations, Condominiums, and Homeowners Associations, 5 J. Real Est. Tax. 101 (1978)

Feder, Financing Real Estate Construction: The IRS Challenge to Construction Period Deductions, 8 J. Real Est. Tax. 3 (1980).

Joyce & Del Cotto, Interest-Free Loans: The Odyssey of a Misnomer, 35 Tax L. Rev. 459 (1980).

Keller, The Tax Treatment of Interest-Free Loans: A Two-Transaction Approach, 1 Va. Tax Rev. 241 (1981).

McIntyre, An Inquiry Into the Special Status of Interest Payments, 1981 Duke L.J. 765 (1981).

Molloy & Hayes, Deductibility of "Commitment Fees," 51 J. Tax. 278 (1979).

Schapiro, Prepayments and Distortion of Income Under Cash Basis Tax Accounting, 30 Tax L. Rev. 117 (1975).

[60] See IRC §183, discussed supra ¶9.10.

CHAPTER 16

Taxes

Page

¶16.1 INTRODUCTORY

Section 164(a) permits four categories of state, local, and foreign taxes to be deducted, whether incurred in the taxpayer's business or profit-oriented activities or not. Individuals, however, may deduct the enumerated taxes under IRC §164(a) only if they elect to itemize their personal deductions or are permitted by IRC §162 to deduct them in computing adjusted gross income.[1] Subject to certain restrictions, taxes can be deducted if they constitute ordinary and necessary expenses in carrying on the taxpayer's business or income-producing activities under IRC §162 or §212, whether listed in IRC §164(a) or not, and taxes that so qualify can be deducted whether taxpayers elect to itemize their personal deductions or not.[2] At the taxpayer's option, IRC §266 permits certain deductible taxes to be charged to capital account and included in the basis of the property with respect to which they were incurred.[3] Finally, taxpayers paying foreign income taxes can elect to credit these taxes against their federal income tax liability, instead of deducting them in computing taxable income, under complex rules discussed elsewhere in this work.[4]

---

[1] For the election to itemize personal deductions, see supra ¶14.3.

[2] For the deduction of taxes under IRC §§162 and 212, see infra ¶16.2. For certain taxes that cannot be deducted under any circumstances (e.g., federal income, estate and gift taxes), see IRC §275, discussed infra ¶16.2.

[3] See Treas. Regs. §1.266-1(b), discussed infra ¶23.8.

[4] For the foreign tax credit, see infra ¶16.2.

The statutory predecessor of IRC §164(a) dates from 1913, but the details of the allowance have varied from time to time. Because it allows taxpayers to deduct taxes constituting part of the cost of living (e.g., real property taxes on owner-occupied residences and sales taxes on articles for personal consumption), tax theorists have, on the whole, been hostile to the deduction. In its present form, IRC §164(a) can be regarded as a crude form of revenue-sharing, making state and local taxes somewhat more palatable (or, at least, less painful) by reducing their net cost to the citizenry.

The resulting amelioration of the federal tax burden is felt particularly by high-bracket taxpayers, who are more likely than their low-bracket counterparts to itemize their personal deductions.

In addition to authorizing a deduction for taxes incurred in personal pursuits, IRC §164(a) permits business taxpayers to deduct currently certain taxes that would otherwise be capitalized and deducted gradually over a period of years (e.g., sales taxes on the purchase of depreciable business equipment); but this feature of IRC §164 has not attracted much attention or criticism.

Because it rarely creates a problem, it is easy to overlook the threshold requirement of IRC §164(a), viz., that a charge must be a "tax" to qualify for deduction. A widely quoted distinction between taxes and other governmental fees and charges, enunciated on several occasions by the IRS, is the following:

> A tax is an enforced contribution, exacted pursuant to legislative authority in the exercise of taxing power, and imposed and collected for the purpose of raising revenue to be used for public or governmental purposes, and not as a payment for some special privilege granted or service rendered. Taxes are, therefore, distinguishable from various other contributions and charges imposed for particular purposes under particular powers or functions of the Government.[5]

This distinction is readily applied in some situations. Tuition and laboratory fees paid by students to a state university are obviously not "taxes"; on the other hand, it is equally clear that a state's retail sales tax qualifies as a tax under IRC §164(a). Among the many minor items that, it has been held, do not constitute "taxes" are fees paid for dog licenses, hunting and fishing licenses, automobile inspections, and the registration of automobile titles. Governmental fees and charges that do not qualify as deductible taxes may, of course, be deducted under IRC §162 or §212 if they constitute ordinary and necessary expenses of carrying on the taxpayer's business or profit-oriented

[5] Rev. Rul. 57-345, 1957-2 CB 132, 133, revoked on its facts by Rev. Rul. 60-366, 1960-2 CB 63; see also Campbell v. Davenport, 362 F.2d 624 (5th Cir. 1955) (Texas assessment on candidate in primary election constitutes a "tax").

activities; and charges for the late payment of taxes may be deductible as "interest" under IRC §163.

1. Identifying the "Taxpayer." To be deductible under IRC §164(a), an amount must be a "tax" from the perspective of the person making the payment, not a gift, loan, payment for goods or services, or other transaction. For example, local real property taxes cannot be deducted by the tenants of a rented apartment house, even though the rents paid by them obviously reflect the landlord's tax burden.

The person who can deduct the tax is the one on whom it is "imposed," who is not necessarily the person paying the tax or bearing its ultimate economic burden. This easily stated principle can be surprisingly difficult to apply, especially to taxable transactions between merchants and their customers. A sales tax, for example, may be imposed on the merchant, even though it is separately stated and passed on to the customer; on the other hand, the tax may be imposed on the customer, even though it must be paid by the merchant if he neglects to collect it from the customer. Controversy in this area was substantially reduced in 1942, when Congress enacted the predecessor of IRC §164(b)(5), providing that the consumer shall be treated as the taxpayer in the case of a separately stated general sales tax. A tax is "separately stated" for purposes of IRC §164(b)(5) if, for example, local law requires a posted notice that the tax will be added to the quoted price; the tax does not have to be separately stated on an invoice or sales slip. But this statutory designation does not apply to other taxes (or to sales taxes if not separately stated or if paid in connection with the consumer's trade or business); and in these situations it continues to be necessary to analyze the local law imposing the tax in order to determine which of several persons is the taxpayer.

2. Deductible Taxes. The following four categories of taxes can be deducted under IRC §164(a), even if not incurred in the taxpayer's business or profit-oriented activities, provided in the case of individuals that they itemize their deductions:

1. *State, local, and foreign real property taxes.* The term "real property taxes" is defined by the regulations to mean "taxes imposed on interests in real property and levied for the general public welfare," imposed "at a like rate against all property in the territory over which [the taxing] authorities have jurisdiction," [6] but excluding, by virtue of IRC §164(c)(1), "taxes assessed against local benefits of a kind tending to increase the value of the property assessed."

The restriction of IRC §164(c)(1), relating to taxes for benefits that

[6] Treas. Regs. §§1.164-3(b), 1.164-4(a).

increase the value of the assessed property (described in the regulations as "so-called taxes . . . more properly assessments"), denies a deduction if the tax is imposed only on the property benefited and applies even if "an incidental benefit may inure to the public welfare." [7] This restriction disqualifies assessments for street, sidewalk, and other improvements; but it does not prevent a deduction for maintenance, repairs, or interest charges resulting from the improvements if the taxpayer can establish the amount allocable to these charges.[8]

2. *State and local personal property taxes.* The regulations define "personal property tax" as a tax imposed (a) substantially in proportion to the value of the property ("ad valorem"), as distinguished from criteria like weight, horsepower, or model year; (b) on an annual basis, even if collected more or less frequently; and (c) in respect of personal property.[9] The third requirement does not disqualify a tax ostensibly imposed on the exercise of a privilege if it is in substance imposed on ownership of the property and based on its value (e.g., an annual ad valorem automobile registration or highway use tax).

3. *State, local, and foreign income taxes.* Section 164(a)(3) permits taxpayers to deduct state, local, and foreign income, war profits, and excess profits taxes.

4. *State and local general sales taxes.* The deduction allowed by IRC §164(a)(4) for state and local sales taxes has a tortuous history and a number of current complexities. To qualify as a "sales tax," the tax must be measured by the gross sales price, gross receipts from the sale, or stated sum per unit of property sold.[10] The reference to "general sales taxes" disqualifies taxes on a narrowly defined class of commodities or services, and IRC §164(b)(2)(A) explicitly limits the term to "a tax imposed at one rate in respect to the sale at retail of a broad range of classes of items."

The one-rate requirement, which is interpreted by the regulations to tolerate only a single general rate within any one taxing jurisdiction, disqualifies taxes imposed at a lower rate, except for (a) lower rates on food, clothing,

---

[7] Treas. Regs. §1.164-4(a).

[8] Treas. Regs. §1.164-4(b)(1). For other charges that the IRS views as nondeductible special assessments, see Rev. Rul. 77-29, 1977-1 CB 44 (fees earmarked for refuse disposal, varying with type of property, amount of refuse, etc.); Rev. Rul. 76-45, 1976-1 CB 51 (taxes for sewer, water, and waste-disposal systems, imposed by special utility districts that include only benefited property); Rev. Rul. 73-188, 1973-1 CB 62 (taxes to finance downtown pedestrian shopping mall, assessed against affected property; interest component allowed as deduction); Rev. Rul. 75-346, 1975-2 CB 66 (sewerage service charges, based on amount of water used); Rev. Rul. 75-455, 1975-2 CB 68 (front-foot benefit charges for water and sewer improvements).

[9] Treas. Regs. §1.164-3(c).

[10] Treas. Regs. §1.164-3(e).

medical supplies, and motor vehicles; (b) dollar exemptions (e.g., a tax that applies only to sales of more than 10 cents each), (c) competitive rates in areas adjacent to another taxing jurisdiction; and (d) higher rates on motor vehicles, in which event the general rate (but not the excess) is deductible.[11]

Although the amount of a taxpayer's state and local income and real property taxes can almost always be accurately established by cancelled checks or receipted bills, taxpayers ordinarily estimate their state and local sales taxes. If called upon to support their estimates, a few compulsive taxpayers could produce a shoe box full of cash register receipts; but most would have to rely on an honest face plus credit card records and cancelled checks for major purchases like automobiles and household furniture. The IRS reduces the role of guesswork and intuition by promulgating optional state sales tax tables, graduated by income and family size for each state.[12] The tables are based on spendable income (adjusted gross income plus such nontaxable receipts as social security and veterans' benefits, the untaxed part of long-term capital gains, etc.). Taxpayers employing these tables need not provide evidence of their taxable purchases, but a larger amount may be deducted if it is supported by the taxpayer's records.

¶16.2 SPECIAL PROBLEMS

1. Apportionment of Real Property Taxes Between Seller and Purchaser. When property is acquired subject to delinquent taxes, payment of the overdue obligations by the new owner is not a payment of "taxes" but a cost of acquiring or clearing title to the property. When the *current* year's taxes are divided between the seller and purchaser at the time of a closing, however, something can be said for treating each share as though it had been imposed on the party paying it. In 1942, however, the Supreme Court held in *Magruder v. Supplee* that the statutory predecessor of IRC §164(a) did not permit the purchaser to deduct his ratable share of the current taxes if the tax lien had attached and the seller had become personally liable before the sale.[13] A necessary consequence of this decision was that the purchaser's contractual share of the real property taxes was (a) an integral part of the cost of the property, taken into account in determining depreciation and gain or loss on an ultimate disposition of the property, and (b) part of the amount realized by the seller on the sale, thus increasing his gain (or decreasing his loss); and a corollary was that the seller was entitled to deduct the entire amount of the tax rather than merely his contractual share.

---

[11] IRC §164(b)(2)(E); Treas. Regs. §1.164-3(g).

[12] IRS Pub. No. 17, Your Federal Income Tax (revised annually).

[13] Magruder v. Supplee, 316 US 394 (1942).

These results were changed by the enactment in 1954 of IRC §164(d), which provides that the real property tax allocable to the part of the "real property tax year" ending on the day before the sale shall be treated as a tax imposed on the seller and that the balance (i.e., the amount allocable to the portion of the real property tax year beginning on the day of the sale) shall be treated as imposed on the purchaser. This allocation, which achieves the result sought by the purchaser in *Magruder v. Supplee,* applies whether the parties provide for an adjustment of taxes at the closing or not. In effect, IRC §164(d)(1) treats the tax as though it consisted of a series of daily charges throughout the real property tax year, rather than a lump-sum obligation imposed on the person owning the property on the assessment or lien date. For example, assume (a) that the real property tax year for property sold by *A* to *B* on June 30, 1982 is April 1, 1982 to March 31, 1983 and (b) that *A* owns the property from the beginning of the real property tax year to the date of the sale and *B* owns it for the balance of that period. Since *A* and *B* own the property for 90/365 and 275/365 of the real property tax year, respectively, a tax of $365 is treated under IRC §164(d)(1) as imposed on *A* to the extent of $90 and on *B* to the extent of $275.[14]

The apportionment rules of IRC §164(d) apply only to sales of real property. The deduction of taxes assessed on personal property, as well as on real property transferred by transactions other than sales (e.g., gifts) continues to be governed by the principles enunciated by *Magruder v. Supplee.*

2. Taxes Paid by Cooperative Housing Corporations. Although real estate taxes and mortgage interest on the property of a cooperative housing corporation are imposed on the corporation rather than on its shareholder-occupants, IRC §216 recognizes that they are the real parties in interest and permits them to deduct their proportionate shares of the entity's real estate taxes and mortgage interest. The standards that must be met by the corporation to qualify for conduit treatment are discussed elsewhere in this work.[15]

3. Taxes Incurred in Business or Profit-Oriented Activities. The four categories of taxes listed in IRC §164(a) are deductible whether or not they are incurred in the taxpayer's business or profit-oriented activities. Taxpayers are also allowed to deduct other federal, state, local, and foreign taxes if incurred in carrying on a trade or business (IRC §162) or an activity described in IRC §212 (relating to expenses for the production of income). To be deductible under IRC §162 or §212, a tax must clear two hurdles:

1. The tax must be an "ordinary and necessary expense" of the business

---

[14] See Treas. Regs. §1.164-6(b)(3), Example (1).

[15] Supra ¶15.1.

or profit-oriented activity. This criterion is met, for example, by state and federal unemployment compensation taxes paid by employers. But a tax paid to acquire a long-term asset (e.g., a sales tax paid by the purchaser of depreciable business equipment that does not qualify for deduction under IRC §164(a)(3) because imposed by a foreign country) is not an ordinary and necessary expense under either IRC §162 or §212. Such a tax must be capitalized and included in the asset's basis; like the cost of the property itself, it will be written off over the asset's depreciable life or taken into account in computing gain or loss when it is sold.

2. Section 275 prohibits any deduction for federal income taxes, estate, inheritance, legacy, succession, and gift taxes; foreign income taxes if the taxpayer elects the foreign tax credit; and a few more specialized taxes.

If a tax is neither included in the four categories described by IRC §164(a) nor incurred in the taxpayer's business or profit-oriented activities, it cannot be deducted. Familiar examples of nondeductible taxes are federal excise taxes on long-distance telephone calls, social security taxes on employers of domestic servants, and state and local taxes on consumers of cigarettes and alcoholic beverages. But if the tax is incurred to acquire property (e.g., a foreign sales tax or federal duty on imported household furniture), it is includable in the taxpayer's basis for the property and will be taken into account if and when the property is sold at a profit.

4. Foreign Tax Credit. In lieu of deducting foreign income taxes, taxpayers are permitted by IRC §§901-908 to take these taxes as a credit against the federal income tax that would otherwise be payable. In some circumstances, foreign income taxes paid by a foreign corporation are imputed to its shareholders when they receive dividends, entitling them to a so-called derivative or indirect foreign tax credit for their allocable shares of the taxes.

The foreign tax credit provisions in effect treat the foreign income tax paid by the taxpayer as a down payment on the federal income tax in order to avoid double taxation of the same income. The option is limited to foreign taxes on income, war profits, and excess profits (and certain taxes in lieu of such taxes) and does not apply to foreign taxes on sales, property, or other nonincome transactions or items.

When available, an election under IRC §§901-908 is ordinarily favorable to the taxpayer, since a credit reduces federal income tax liability dollar for dollar, while a deduction reduces only the taxpayer's taxable income. But in unusual circumstances, it is advantageous to deduct foreign income taxes rather than to elect the credit.

5. Tax Refunds. Tax refunds are includable in gross income if the tax was deducted in a prior year, unless the refund is covered by the "recovery exclusion" described by IRC §111(b)(4), relating to the recovery of amounts that were deducted without tax benefit.[16] If the refunded tax was not deducted (because, for example, the taxpayer used the zero bracket amount rather than itemizing personal deductions or because the tax was not of a deductible type), however, the recovery is excluded from gross income, since it merely restores an amount for which the taxpayer was not liable and hence does not increase the taxpayer's net worth.

SELECTED BIBLIOGRAPHY

Bittker, Income Tax Deductions, Credits, and Subsidies for Personal Expenditures, 16 J.L. & Econ. 193 (1973).

Bridges, Deductibility of State and Local Nonbusiness Taxes Under the Federal Individual Income Tax, 19 Nat'l Tax J. 1 (1966).

Cannon, The Apportionment of Real Estate Taxes Between Purchaser and Seller Under Section 164(d) of the 1954 Code, 12 Tax L. Rev. 433, 438 (1957).

[16] For IRC §111, see supra ¶1.10.

CHAPTER 17

Bad Debts

¶17.1 INTRODUCTORY

Section 166(a)(1) allows a deduction for "any debt which becomes worthless within the taxable year." When debts arising from the taxpayer's business or profit-oriented activities become worthless, a deduction is inherent in the concept of a tax on net income and might have been allowed as a business expense under IRC §162 or as an expense incurred in the production of income under IRC §212 even if IRC §166 had not been enacted. But IRC §166 applies to all bona fide debts, regardless of their origin, and it thus sanctions the deduction of uncollectible obligations growing out of family or other nonprofit transactions. Congress has never offered an explicit rationale for this aspect of IRC §166, though it can be defended as an allowance for losses outside the expected course of daily living, analogous to the deduction allowed by IRC §165(c)(3) for casualty losses. This justification would be strengthened, of course, if IRC §166 contained a nondeductible floor for such personal bad debts, similar to the floor on the deduction of casualty losses and medical expenses.[1]

[1] For these floors, see infra ¶¶18.4 (casualty losses), 20.1 (medical expenses). A

¶17.2 REQUIREMENTS OF "DEBT"

As will be seen, the general rule of IRC §166(a) is subject to many refinements and qualifications, relating to the deduction of partially worthless debts, reserves for bad debts, and nonbusiness debts; but all these special provisions, like the general rule, presuppose the existence of a bona fide debt—described by the regulations as "a debt which arises from a debtor-creditor relationship based upon a valid and enforceable obligation to pay a fixed or determinable sum of money." [2] This definition precludes deducting debts that cannot be enforced because they violate local usury laws or claims that are unliquidated and disputed, but it does not require that the debtor be personally liable on the obligation or prohibit deduction of a worthless debt that is not yet due or is payable only from specified funds.

Disputes over whether a transfer of funds created a debtor-creditor relationship, resulting in a bona fide debt, can arise in a wide variety of circumstances. Transfers within the family are a common source of disagreement between taxpayers and the IRS, since the transfer of a note or other evidence of indebtedness does not conclusively establish that the transferor intended to create a debtor-creditor status rather than to make a gift. Another much-litigated question is whether advances by shareholders to their corporations are loans or contributions to capital increasing the basis of their stock. These and other transactions between related parties are fruitful sources of litigation because characterization of the relationship often makes little if any difference to the parties, except as it affects their tax liability. Characterization issues can also arise in arm's-length transactions, however, since funds are often transferred in a business arrangement that clouds the relationship between the parties in ambiguity. If the purported creditor is found to be a joint venturer, for example, a failure to recover the amount advanced does not create a bad debt within the meaning of IRC §166, but a loss; and if the taxpayer is an individual, the loss can be deducted only if it occurred in the taxpayer's business or in a transaction entered into for profit.[3] When funds are advanced under an agreement for repayment only when and if a specified event occurs (e.g., successful termination of litigation or the realization of profit on a

---

partial corrective for the absence of a floor is provided by IRC §166(d), under which an individual's bad debts generate short-term capital losses rather than deductions for ordinary income; see infra ¶17.6.

[2] Treas. Regs. §1.166-1(c). See also IRC §385, authorizing regulations (not yet issued except in proposed form) to determine whether an interest in a corporation is to be treated as stock or indebtedness and stating that one of the factors that can be taken into account is the existence of "a written unconditional promise to pay on demand or on a specified date a certain sum in money in return for an adequate consideration in money or money's worth, and to pay a fixed rate of interest."

[3] See IRC §§165(c)(1) and 165(c)(2), discussed supra ¶12.2.

proposed sale of property), the advance does not create a "debt" within the meaning of IRC §166 unless the event occurs. If it never occurs, the taxpayer suffers a loss whose tax consequences are determined by IRC §165 rather than by IRC §166.

Depending on the circumstances, the taxpayer may be better or worse off if a transaction is classified as a bad debt under IRC §166 rather than as a loss under IRC §165. Section 166 is preferable for individual taxpayers if the transaction did not arise in a business or profit-oriented activity, since these are conditions to deducting a loss under IRC §165. On the other hand, if the transaction entails a nonbusiness debt arising out of an investment, IRC §166 restricts individual taxpayers to short-term capital losses,[4] while IRC §165 allows losses to be deducted from ordinary income even if attributable to an investment. Another difference between bad debts and losses is that the taxpayer can deduct additions to a reserve for bad debts under IRC §166(c), while IRC §165 does not sanction reserves for prospective losses.

When a bad-debt deduction is warranted, IRC §166(b) provides that the amount to be deducted is the debt's adjusted basis as prescribed by IRC §1011 for determining loss on a sale or other disposition.[5] This is ordinarily the amount advanced by the creditor, but if the debt was acquired by purchase or inheritance, for example, its adjusted basis is usually the purchase price or its value at the date of the decedent's death, as the case may be.

An important corollary of IRC §166(b) is that no deduction is allowable for a debt having a zero basis, such as a cash-basis taxpayer's claim for unpaid wages or rent.[6] Since these amounts would be includable in income if collected in due course, the taxpayer's loss when they become worthless is adequately reflected by their permanent exclusion from gross income; a deduction not only would be superfluous but would confer an unwarranted benefit.

¶17.3 WORTHLESSNESS

It is frequently impossible to determine with precision the date when a debt became partially or wholly worthless. The regulations virtually acknowledge this lamentable fact of life by providing for consideration of "all pertinent evidence" in determining whether a debt is worthless;[7] and the consequence of picking the wrong year is mitigated by IRC §6511(d)(1), extending the statute of limitations for refund claims based on worthless debts from the

---

[4] See infra ¶17.6.

[5] For IRC §1011, see infra ¶23.1. Ordinarily, property has the same adjusted basis for determining both gain and loss; for a situation in which they differ, see IRC §1015(a), relating to property acquired by gift, discussed infra ¶23.3.

[6] Treas. Regs. §1.166-1(e).

[7] Treas. Regs. §1.166-2(a).

normal span of three years to seven years. If the debtor's financial circumstances gradually deteriorate over a long period of time, the year of worthlessness is likely to occur sometime between the excessively early date that would be chosen by a "stygian pessimist" and the excessively late date that an "incorrigible optimist" would select.[8]

Among the numerous factors suggesting that a debt is worthless are the debtor's serious financial reverses, insolvency, lack of assets, persistent refusals to pay on demand, ill health, death, disappearance, abandonment of business, bankruptcy, and receivership, as well as the debt's unsecured or subordinated status and expiration of the statute of limitations. Factors pointing in the opposite direction are the creditor's failure to press for payment (especially if the debtor is a relative or friend), willingness to make further advances, availability of collateral or guaranties by third parties, the debtor's earning capacity, minor defaults, payment of interest, and sluggish business conditions. All these indicia are subject to rebuttal or explanation, however, and none is conclusive in itself. At first blush, one might think that expiration of the statute of limitations or a discharge in bankruptcy would at least establish the date beyond which a debt could have no value, but several cases comment adversely on the taxpayer's failure to show that the debtor would rely on these defenses.[9] There are, in short, no absolutes in this area.

¶17.4 PARTIAL WORTHLESSNESS

Section 166(a)(2) permits taxpayers to deduct partially worthless debts by charging off an appropriate amount if the IRS is satisfied that the debt is "recoverable only in part." While a deduction for *complete* worthlessness does not require action by the taxpayer (other than claiming the deduction on the return or in a claim for refund) and must be taken in the year in which the debt "becomes worthless," deductions for *partial* worthlessness are elective with the taxpayer and are conditioned on a "charge-off" of the uncollectible amount on the taxpayer's books and records.[10] The discretion over deductions for partial worthlessness vested in the IRS by IRC §166(a)(2) must be exercised in a reasonable fashion, but it has been held that the taxpayer's burden of proof is heavier under IRC §166(a)(2) than under IRC §166(a)(1), relating to total worthlessness, since the issue in a litigated case is not whether the debt

---

[8] For these terms, see US v. S.S. White Dental Mfg. Co., 274 US 398, 403 (1927) ("incorrigible optimist"); Ruppert v. US, 22 F.Supp. 428, 431 (Ct. Cl. 1938) ("stygian pessimist").

[9] See Schultz v. CIR, 30 TC 256, 266 (1953), rev'd on other grounds, 278 F.2d 927 (5th Cir. 1960) (running of statute of limitations does not necessarily render debt worthless).

[10] See Treas. Regs. §1.166-3(a).

became partially worthless but whether the IRS abused its discretion in holding to the contrary.[11]

¶17.5 RESERVES FOR BAD DEBTS

In lieu of deducting specific debts as partially or wholly worthless, taxpayers may establish a reserve for bad debts and deduct a "reasonable addition" thereto pursuant to IRC §166(c). The regulations require the taxpayer to choose between the specific charge-off and the reserve methods when filing a return for the first year for which a deduction under IRC §166 is permitted and to use the selected method consistently thereafter unless permission for a change is granted by the IRS.[12] The reserve method of providing for bad debts permits anticipated losses to be deducted before they are actually sustained, but it can nevertheless be used by cash-basis as well as accrual-basis taxpayers. Taxpayers electing to use the reserve method are required to advise the IRS of the volume of charge sales or other business transactions for the taxable year and the total amount of notes and accounts receivable; and the IRS contends that a significant level of such transactions and assets is a prerequisite to a valid election.[13]

On establishing a reserve, the taxpayer estimates the amount necessary to provide for existing debts that will prove to be uncollectible. In making this estimate, accounts receivable are usually "aged"—that is, classified by due date so that the amount added to the reserve can be graduated by reference to the various delinquency levels. When debts actually prove to be uncollectible, they reduce the reserve but are not deducted. If the existing reserve (built up by deductions in previous years and reduced by debts that have actually proved uncollectible) is insufficient in any year to cover the current estimate of uncollectible debts, however, the taxpayer adds an appropriate amount to the reserve, and deducts it in the taxable year.

Unduly pessimistic estimates in one year are corrected by adding less to the reserve in later years. For example, if on December 31, 1981 the taxpayer had $100,000 in accounts receivable outstanding, against which a reserve of $5,000 had been provided, and if $2,000 of these accounts proved uncollectible during the year 1982, the bad-debt reserve would have a balance of $3,000 at the end of 1982. If at that time the taxpayer had $90,000 of accounts, of which $4,000 could be expected to prove uncollectible, the addition to the reserve in 1982 would need be only $1,000 to give full protection against the anticipated

---

[11] See generally Brimberry v. CIR, 588 F.2d 975 (5th Cir. 1979) (disallowance upheld), and cases there cited.

[12] Treas. Regs. §1.166-1(b).

[13] Treas. Regs. §1.166-4(c).

losses. Conversely, an unduly optimistic estimate in an earlier year will be corrected by making a larger addition to the reserve in a later year. Recoveries of bad debts are similarly credited to the reserve and hence affect the amount to be added to the reserve.

When a taxpayer goes out of business or the balance in its reserve becomes superfluous for other reasons, the unneeded reserve must be taken into income, to reflect the fact that the amounts previously deducted from income have proved to be excessive or unnecessary.[14]

¶17.6 NONBUSINESS DEBTS

Section 166(d) provides that when nonbusiness debts held by taxpayers other than corporations become worthless, the loss shall be considered a short-term capital loss. Nonbusiness debts are subject to two other disabilities: they do not qualify for charge-off under IRC §166(a)(2) when partially worthless or for the reserve method of providing for bad debts allowed by IRC §166(c).

When the statutory predecessor of IRC §166(d) was enacted in 1942, the only explicit legislative statement of its purpose referred to claims for losses on "loans [for] which [taxpayers] do not expect to be repaid." [15] It was presumably thought that difficulties of proof made it impossible to rebut claims for "bad debts" that were in effect gifts to relatives or friends and that the next best thing was a mechanical rule subjecting all nonbusiness debts to the limited deductibility of capital losses. The Supreme Court held in *Putnam v. CIR,* however, that the 1942 amendment had another purpose: to put "nonbusiness investments in the form of loans on a footing with other nonbusiness investments."[15.1] The capital loss provisions had for many years provided that a taxpayer who acquired bonds, debentures, or other securities for investment realized a capital loss on worthlessness; and the *Putnam* case concluded that IRC §166(d) was designed in part to treat worthless loans that are not evidenced by a "security," as defined by IRC §165(g)(2)(C), consistently with those that are.

The term "nonbusiness debt" is defined by IRC §166(d)(2) by a process of exclusion to include any debt other than (a) a debt created or acquired in connection with a trade or business of the taxpayer or (b) a debt the loss from

[14] See supra ¶1.10 (re tax benefit); for the status of bad-debt reserves on a change of business form (e.g., the incorporation of a sole proprietorship or partnership, the liquidation or merger of a corporation, etc.), see Nash v. US, 398 US 1 (1970) (no recovery of reserve on incorporating sole proprietorship); Rev. Rul. 78-280, 1978-2 CB 139 (application of *Nash* principle).

[15] H. Rep. No. 2333, 77th Cong., 1st Sess., reprinted in 1942-2 CB 372, 408.

[15.1] Putnam v. CIR, 352 US 82, 92 (1950).

the worthlessness of which is incurred in the taxpayer's trade or business. Clause (a) was enacted in 1954 to overrule the pre-1954 regulations, which imposed nonbusiness status on debts generated by the taxpayer's business if the taxpayer was no longer engaged in business when the debt became worthless. A further change was made in 1958 to require the debt to have been originally created or acquired in connection with a business of the taxpayer, as distinguished from the business of the taxpayer's donor or other transferor.

Litigation under IRC §166(d) arises primarily from uncollectible advances by taxpayers to family corporations and other enterprises with which the taxpayer had a business relationship (e.g., employee-employer, landlord-tenant, or supplier-customer), stimulating claims that the loan was not an ordinary investment (generating a short-term capital loss as a worthless nonbusiness debt) but was integrally related to the taxpayer's business. But in *Whipple v. CIR,* the leading case on this subject, the Supreme Court crushed the hopes of innumerable taxpayers by holding that loans to the creditor's closely held corporation are nonbusiness debts even though the taxpayer's trade or business consists of working for the debtor. In a few cases, taxpayers have successfully claimed the mantle of "promoter" by showing, as required by *Whipple,* that they advanced funds to enterprises in the developmental stage to set the stage for profitable sales, but these cases are few and far between; and they may be Pyrrhic victories, since profits on selling any successful enterprises resulting from the taxpayer's self-styled business should be reported as ordinary income, rather than capital gains.[16]

Aside from the promoter cases, taxpayers have endeavored to escape nonbusiness classification for loans by establishing that the funds were advanced to establish or cement relationships with employers, clients, suppliers, tenants, and customers. But if the debtor is a corporation controlled by the creditor, it is difficult to establish that it was necessary to advance funds to achieve objectives of this type in view of the taxpayer's preexisting control; and an additional obstacle is *United States v. Generes,* in which the Supreme Court held that advances by a taxpayer who is both an investor in the borrowing corporation and its employee create nonbusiness debts unless the taxpayer can show that his *dominant* motive in making the loan was protection of his job.[17] Applying this test to a taxpayer who loaned more than $150,000 to a family corporation that employed him for a salary of only $12,000, the Court said that the taxpayer's assertion that the funds were advanced to preserve his job "falls of its own weight." [18]

The principal types of debts that may be able to avoid "nonbusiness" status are loans (a) in the course of promoting, financing, or lending activities

---

[16] Whipple v. CIR, 373 US 193, 202 (1963).

[17] US v. Generes, 405 US 93 (1972).

[18] Id. at 107.

that are so extensive as to constitute a business; (b) to create or preserve business relationships with employees, suppliers, clients, customers, and other business associates of the taxpayer; (c) to protect the taxpayer's business reputation or credit standing; and (d) to obtain or preserve a job, especially with an unrelated employer.

¶17.7 LOSSES FROM LOAN GUARANTIES

Losses attributable to guaranties of the debts of third persons have had a checkered tax history. Before 1956, when the Supreme Court decided *Putnam v. CIR,*[19] it was arguable that the guarantor's payment did not create a bad-debt deduction (and was deductible only pursuant to IRC §165, relating to "losses") if the guarantor's claim against the defaulting debtor was worthless on acquisition and hence did not "become worthless" during the taxable year. This worthless-on-acquisition notion was rejected by the *Putnam* case, which holds that the guarantor's loss is attributable to the *original* debt owed by the debtor to the principal, to which the guarantor succeeds by subrogation. As applied to the taxpayer in *Putnam,* this rationale meant that the deduction was a short-term capital loss under IRC §166(d) because the guaranty was not proximately related to the taxpayer's trade or business, rather than a loss under IRC §165 that could have been deducted from ordinary income if incurred in a transaction entered into for profit within the meaning of IRC §165(c)(2).

¶17.8 SECURED DEBTS—FORECLOSURES AND REPOSSESSIONS

On the foreclosure of a mortgage, the tax treatment of the mortgagee's underlying debt depends on whether the property is purchased by a third party or by the mortgagee and, in the latter situation, on whether the mortgagee was the vendor of the property or merely a lender. The effects of these variables, and of voluntary conveyances of the property by the mortgagor to the mortgagee, are summarized below.

1. *Purchase by third party.* If the mortgaged property is purchased by a third party at the foreclosure sale, the amount realized by the mortgagee (after expenses) is applied against the adjusted basis of the debt, and the unpaid balance can be deducted as worthless under IRC §166, subject to the capital loss restriction of IRC §166(d) if the mortgagee is not a corporation and the debt is a nonbusiness debt.[20]

---

[19] Putnam v. CIR, supra note 15.1.

[20] See Treas. Regs. §§1.166-6(a)(1) (deduction of deficiency in principal), 1.166-6(a)(2) (uncollectible accrued interest deductible only if previously included in income). For IRC §166(d), see supra ¶17.6.

2. *Purchase by mortgagee.* If a nonvendor mortgagee buys in the property at a foreclosure sale, the transaction has two aspects: (1) the mortgagee is entitled to a bad-debt deduction equal to the uncollectible difference between the unpaid balance and the bid price (less expenses), and (2) the mortgagee realizes gain or loss measured by the difference (if any) between the adjusted basis of the mortgage debt applied to the bid price and the property's fair market value. For both purposes, the property's fair market value and the bid price are presumed to be equal in the absence of "clear and convincing proof" to the contrary.[21]

3. *Voluntary conveyance to mortgagee.* If the mortgagor voluntarily conveys the property to a nonvendor mortgagee instead of insisting on formal foreclosure, the mortgagee applies the market value of the property (less expenses) against the adjusted basis of the debt, and any deficiency is deductible as a worthless debt.

4. *Reacquisition of real property by vendor mortgagee.* If the vendor mortgagee of real property reacquires the property in partial or full satisfaction of the debt (whether by foreclosure or voluntary conveyance), IRC §1038 obviates the necessity of determining the property's fair market value and, where the value of the property exceeds the adjusted basis of the debt, the necessity of recognizing gain and paying taxes on a transaction producing no cash. Section 1038, enacted in 1964, achieves these objectives by providing, subject to certain exceptions, that no gain or loss results to the vendor mortgagee from the reacquisition and that the debt does not become worthless, either in whole or in part. In effect, the vendor is restored to the *status quo ante,* except that (1) under IRC §1038(b), any consideration in money or other property received before the reacquisition generates gain if not previously included in income, but not in excess of the gain realized on the sale less any portion thereof already reported and less any money or property given up by the seller in connection with the reacquisition; and (2) under IRC §1038(d), any amount previously written off as a bad debt must be taken back into income, resulting in a corresponding increase in the mortgagee's adjusted basis for the property.

¶17.9 DEBTS OWED BY POLITICAL ORGANIZATIONS

Section 271 provides that, as a general rule, taxpayers are not entitled to deductions for the worthlessness of any debt owed by a political party. This prohibition covers both bad-debt deductions under IRC §166 and worthless-security deductions under IRC §165(g) but does not apply to banks functioning in accordance with usual commercial practices. The term "political party" is defined by IRC §271(b) to include not only federal, state, and local commit-

[21] Treas. Regs. §§1.166-6(a), 1.166-6(b).

tees of a political party but also any organization that accepts contributions or makes expenditures in seeking the election of an individual to federal, state, or local public office; but it does not encompass an organization whose sole function is to influence the passage of legislation.

An exception to the general rule is provided for certain accrual-basis taxpayers holding receivables attributable to bona fide sales of goods or services in the ordinary course of business. Under IRC §271(c), if such a taxpayer made substantial efforts to collect on the debt and if more than 30 percent of the receivables for the year in which the worthless receivables accrued was due from political parties, the taxpayer is not prohibited from taking a deduction. The exception is designed to protect businesses catering primarily to political campaigns, such as organizations conducting straw polls, which have accrued their sales and are then unable to collect the receivables.

SELECTED BIBLIOGRAPHY

Brown, Comment: *Putnam v. Commissioner*— The Reimbursable Outlay Under the Tax Law, 6 Buffalo L. Rev. 283 (1957).

Handler, Tax Consequences of Mortgage Foreclosures and Transfers of Real Property to the Mortgagee, 31 Tax. L. Rev. 193 (1976).

Natbony, Worthlessness, Debt-Equity, and Related Problems, 32 Hastings L.J. 1407 (1981).

Ohl, The Deduction for Bad Debts: A Study in Flexibility and Inflexibility, 22 Tax Lawyer 579, 584–598 (1969).

CHAPTER 18

Casualty Losses

¶18.1 INTRODUCTORY

Section 165(a) of the Internal Revenue Code provides as a general rule that "any loss sustained during the taxable year" may be deducted, if it is not compensated for by insurance or otherwise. But IRC §165(c) limits this broad rule by permitting individual taxpayers to deduct a loss if it is incurred in a trade or business or in a transaction entered into for profit, but, in the case of other property,[1] only if the loss arises "from fire, storm, shipwreck, or other casualty, or from theft," and then only to the extent of the excess over $100 per casualty or theft.

Since losses attributable to business and profit-oriented property can be deducted under IRC §165(c)(1) or §165(c)(2) regardless of the cause, the principal significance of the deduction allowed by IRC §165(c)(3) for casualty losses is that it encompasses personal residences, private automobiles, jewelry, home furnishings, and other property owned and used by individual taxpayers

[1] Section 165(c)(3) exempts only property "connected with a trade or business," thus implying that the restriction embraces property held for the production of income as well as property held solely for personal use; but Treas. Regs. §1.165-1(e)(3) interprets the provision as also exempting losses incurred in transactions entered into for profit.

for personal purposes. Property of this type does not qualify for depreciation deductions while the taxpayer owns it, and losses on the sale of such property are also nondeductible.[2]

Recognizing that the casualty loss deduction is an exception to the normal rule that personal, living, and family expenses cannot be deducted,[3] Congress has indicated that the exception should be confined to "extraordinary, nonrecurring losses [that] go beyond the average or usual losses incurred by most taxpayers in day-to-day living" and thus significantly reduce the taxpayer's ability to pay an income tax.[4] In 1963, this distinction between ordinary and extraordinary losses was achieved by providing that the first $100 of any casualty loss cannot be deducted; and the distinction was sharpened in 1981 by aggregating all casualty losses for the taxable year (after application of the $100 floor) and allowing a deduction only if and to the extent that they exceed 10 percent of the taxpayer's adjusted gross income.[5]

Section 165(c)(3) is restricted to losses "of property" and does not permit the taxpayer to deduct losses attributable to bodily injuries or similar personal misfortunes, consequential damages (e.g., hotel expenses incurred when a personal residence is destroyed by fire), or premiums on policies of fire insurance. Even if there is a loss of property, a deduction is not allowed if the lost item would have been includable in income had it been received in due course (e.g., an author's royalties, if embezzled by an agent). The fact that the amount was not taken into income adjusts for the taxpayer's loss, and a deduction under IRC §165(c)(3) would be duplicative.[6] Finally, the loss must be attributable to the damaged property. Thus, while the cost of clearing away debris qualifies for deduction, the taxpayer cannot deduct the cost of a general decline in the value of undamaged property reflecting public resistance to buying property in a casualty-damaged area, nor can the cost of fences, dams, or other protective devices be deducted.

The deduction for a casualty loss ordinarily belongs to the owner of the affected property; but if someone with custody of the property (e.g., a tenant or borrower) must make good the damage, the owner is not entitled to a deduction because his loss is "compensated for by insurance or otherwise" within the meaning of IRC §165(a). In these circumstances, the person who must repair or replace the property suffers the loss and is, therefore, entitled to the deduction. But an indirect interest in the damaged property is not

---

[2] Treas. Regs. §1.165-9(a); see also supra ¶10.6 (depreciation).

[3] IRC §262, discussed supra ¶14.3.

[4] S. Rep. No. 830, 88th Cong., 2d Sess., reprinted in 1964-1 (Part 2) CB 505, 561.

[5] IRC §165(h)(1).

[6] Alsop v. CIR, 290 F.2d 726 (2d Cir. 1961) (IRC §165(c)(3) "can hardly be read as permitting a deduction for the deprivation of income [a cash-basis] taxpayer has not received"); see also Treas. Regs. §§1.165-7(a)(4), 1.165-8(e) (similar result as to inventory assets).

sufficient, even if the taxpayer's own net worth is adversely affected, as in the case of shareholders whose stock reflects damage to corporate property or parents who feel impelled to replace damaged property belonging to their adult children.

¶18.2 DEFINITION OF "CASUALTY"

To be deductible under IRC §165(c)(3), the taxpayer's loss must "arise from fire, storm, shipwreck, or other casualty, or from theft." The terms "fire," "storm," and "shipwreck" are relatively straightforward, and "theft"—interpreted by the regulations to include, without being limited to, larceny, embezzlement, and robbery—is discussed below, along with losses resulting from fraud, misrepresentation, and similar commercial misconduct.[7]

In construing the term "other casualty," the courts have looked for characteristics similar to those inherent in fire, storm, and shipwreck, an approach that reflects both the canon of statutory construction "eiusdem generis" and the legislative policy of restricting the deduction to "extraordinary, nonrecurring losses" that "go beyond the average or usual losses incurred by most taxpayers in day-to-day living,"[8] such as the progressive deterioration of property through ordinary wear and tear and the mere passage of time.

In a 1972 ruling, the IRS described the essential elements of a "casualty" as follows:

> The courts have consistently upheld the Internal Revenue Service position that an "other casualty" is limited to casualties analogous to fire, storm, or shipwreck. The Service position has been that a casualty is the complete or partial destruction of property resulting from an identifiable event of a sudden, unexpected, and unusual nature. . . .
>
> To be "sudden" the event must be one that is swift and precipitous and not gradual or progressive.
>
> To be "unexpected" the event must be one that is ordinarily unanticipated that occurs without the intent of the one who suffers the loss.
>
> To be "unusual" the event must be one that is extraordinary and nonrecurring, one that does not commonly occur during the activity in which the taxpayer was engaged when the destruction or damage occurred, and one that does not commonly occur in the ordinary course of day-to-day living of the taxpayer.[9]

---

[7] Treas. Regs. §1.165-8(d); infra ¶18.3.

[8] S. Rep. No. 830, supra note 4, at 561.

[9] Rev. Rul. 72-592, 1972-2 CB 101.

Given the vagueness of these criteria and the manifold afflictions to which human beings are subject, it should be no surprise that the cases are difficult to reconcile "in result, theory, or language." [10]

As applied, the distinction between sudden and extraordinary calamities and those operating slowly has led to the classification of earthquakes, floods, lightning, and a "mass attack" of insects as "casualties" but to the exclusion of rust, corrosion, and Dutch elm disease.[11] The proper treatment of termite damage produced a split among the courts of appeals, an IRS ruling that the loss is due to casualty if it occurs within a short period of time, and finally a 1963 ruling, based on later scientific evidence, that the damage is never sufficiently sudden to qualify for deduction under IRC §165(c)(3).[12] Damage from drought has similarly elicited a variety of responses, depending on how sudden the event is perceived to be. The death of trees and shrubs from drought, even if unusually prolonged, is not regarded as a casualty by the IRS; but subsoil subsidence resulting from drought qualifies.[13] In both cases the damage is unusual, but it is "sudden" only in the latter situation.

---

[10] Heyn v. CIR, 46 TC 302, 309 (1966). For an extended review of the cases, see Keenan v. Bowers, 91 F.Supp. 771 (E.D.S.C. 1950) (no deduction for careless flushing of wife's diamond ring in toilet).

The many misfortunes for which IRC §165(c)(3) has been held to provide no balm include: Newton v. CIR, 57 TC 245 (1971) (Acq.) (burned-out auto engine); Schonhoff v. CIR, ¶63,213 P-H Memo TC (1963) (taxpayer paid $8,825 to a dancing studio on implied representation he could "date" the instructors; held, no theft loss even though he made no dates); Vance v. CIR, 36 TC 547 (1961) (taxpayer's household furniture repossessed by finance company when his ex-wife failed to keep up payments and wrongfully took property from house on her departure; held, neither event a casualty); Dyer v. CIR, ¶61,141 P-H Memo TC (1961) (taxpayer's cat broke a vase; taxpayer claimed that loss was attributable to cat's neurotic behavior rather than to her "ordinary perambulations"); Mann v. US, 40 AFTR2d 5708 (N.D. Ill. 1977) (not officially reported) (new car proved to be a "lemon").

Losses by governmental confiscation or seizure do not ordinarily constitute casualties; see Powers v. CIR, 36 TC 1191 (1961) (taxpayer's Volkswagen confiscated three days after purchase by East German authorities; held, a despotic act but not a casualty); Rev. Rul. 69-354, 1969-1 CB 58 (perishable food discarded due to postponement of social event on imposition of curfew).

[11] Grant v. CIR, 30 BTA 1028 (1934) ("underground disturbance" resulting in sudden subsidence of surface); Coburn v. CIR, ¶53,084 P-H Memo TC (1953) (storm resulting in flood); Nelson v. CIR, ¶68,035 P-H Memo TC (1968) (mass attack of beetles, capable of killing trees in five to ten days); Matheson v. CIR, 54 F.2d 537, 539-540 (2d Cir. 1931) (gradual deterioration from rust and corrosion not a casualty); Appleman v. CIR, 338 F.2d 729 (7th Cir. 1964), cert. denied, 380 US 956 (1965) (Dutch elm disease not sufficiently unexpected to constitute a casualty).

[12] Rev. Rul. 63-232, 1963-2 CB 97 (citing earlier cases and ruling). With the slow work of termites, compare Exodus 10:13 (plague of locusts).

[13] Rev. Rul. 66-303, 1966-2 CB 55; but see Rev. Rul. 54-85, 1954-1 CB 58 (damage to residential property from "relatively" rapid and severe subsoil shrinkage resulting from unusually severe drought; held, a casualty); Charno v. CIR, ¶71,022 P-H Memo TC (1971) (same).

When IRC §165(c)(3) was in its infancy, the IRS endeavored to confine its scope to losses attributable to natural forces similar to storms. When presented with a claim for damage to a taxpayer's automobile while his chauffeur was on a joyride, however, the Court of Appeals for the Second Circuit flatly rejected the "natural cause" limitation, pointing out that the statute referred not only to "storm" but also to "fire" and "shipwreck." [14] Since the latter events can be caused by careless Boy Scouts and drunken navigators, the court saw no reason to restrict the term "casualty" to acts of God. The IRS promptly accepted this decision, and the regulations now cover damage to the taxpayer's automobile, not only when caused by other vehicles but also when attributable to the taxpayer's own faulty driving, unless "due to the willful act or willful negligence of the taxpayer." [15]

¶18.3 THEFT

When enacted in 1913, the statutory predecessor of IRC §165(c)(3) referred only to fire, storm, and shipwreck; but it was amended in 1916 to embrace a loss from "other casualty, and from theft." Theft losses, however, are deductible by virtue of IRC §165(e) only when "discovered," and in some situations (e.g., embezzlement by a trusted employee) discovery may occur long after the loss occurred. Circumstances can be envisioned (e.g., fire, storm, or shipwreck followed by looting) in which the taxpayer would be unable to determine whether a loss of particular articles was caused by casualty (deductible when sustained) or by theft (deductible when discovered); and if discovery was delayed, the taxpayer could be whipsawed between the two years. Judging from the litigated cases, however, this possibility has not proved to be a problem.

The explicit statutory reference to theft has also served another function, since it implies that fraud, misrepresentation, and similar commercial misconduct do not give rise to deductions unless sufficiently flagrant to constitute "theft." The regulations construe the statutory term to include (without necessarily being limited to) larceny, embezzlement, and robbery.[16] This construction leaves room for expansion to embrace crimes of a similar character; a 1972 ruling, for example, provides that "theft" as used in IRC §165(c)(3) covers "any theft or felonious taking of money or property by which a taxpayer sustains a loss, whether defined and punishable under the penal codes of the states as larceny, robbery, burglary, embezzlement, extortion, kidnapping for

---

[14] Shearer v. Anderson, 16 F.2d 995 (2d Cir. 1927).

[15] I.T. 2408, VII-1 CB 85 (1928), declared obsolete by Rev. Rul. 69-43, 1969-1 CB 310; the ruling excluded the taxpayer's "willful act or negligence," but the 1931 regulations inserted the word "willful" before negligence. Treas. Regs. 74, Art. 171 (1931). For the current version of this provision, see Treas. Regs. §1.165-7(a)(3).

[16] Treas. Regs. §1.165-8(d).

ransom, threats, or blackmail." [17] By implication, this interpretation excludes noncriminal fraud.

In some of these situations, the denial of a theft loss under IRC §165(c)(3) is not final, since the taxpayer may be able to deduct the loss under IRC §165(c)(1) or §165(c)(2) (losses in trade or business or in transactions entered into for profit) if it is evidenced by a closed transaction or to treat the misconduct as creating a debt from the malefactor, which can be deducted (ordinarily as a capital loss) if and when it becomes worthless.

If the taxpayer's property disappears mysteriously, theft may be inferred if it is a more reasonable explanation for the loss than any other.[18] In this respect, the tax cases have adopted the "mysterious disappearance" concept used in screening claims for reimbursement under theft insurance policies.

¶18.4 AMOUNT DEDUCTIBLE

1. Introductory. To determine the amount of the casualty loss deduction, it is necessary to (1) compute the taxpayer's loss; (2) take account of any insurance recovery, other compensation, or salvage value; and (3) apply the $100 nondeductible floor and the 10 percent of adjusted gross income (AGI) limit.

2. Computation of Taxpayer's Loss. Section 165(b) provides that the basis for determining the amount to be deducted for any loss (including casualty losses) is the adjusted basis used under IRC §1011 for determining the taxpayer's loss from a sale or other disposition of the property. In the case of a personal residence, automobile, or other item purchased by the taxpayer and used exclusively for personal purposes, the adjusted basis is ordinarily cost, with adjustments for improvements, prior casualty deductions, and certain other receipts, expenses, and tax allowances. When there is a difference between the asset's basis for computing a gain and its basis for computing a loss (e.g., under IRC §1015(a), relating to property acquired by gift), IRC §165(b) requires use of the latter.

By limiting the deduction to the adjusted basis of the damaged or lost property, IRC §165(b) prevents the taxpayer from deducting any unrealized appreciation. For example, if an uninsured work of art costing $1,000 but

[17] Rev. Rul. 72-112, 1972-1 CB 60 (ransom extorted by kidnappers).

[18] See Jungert v. CIR, ¶68,116 P-H Memo TC (1968) (unexplained disappearance of $36,000 cash left on seat of taxpayer's auto; loss by theft inferred); Jones v. CIR, 24 TC 525 (1955) (Acq.) (same as to disappearance of jewelry from locked box to which taxpayer's maid had access, where loss coincided with maid's departure from employment).

worth $5,000 is totally destroyed by fire, the deduction is limited by IRC §165(b) to $1,000, before taking account of the $100 nondeductible floor. Since the unrealized appreciation has not been taken into income, it does not figure into the computation of the deduction.[19] Indeed, if the taxpayer recovered $5,000 from an insurance company or tort-feasor, the gain of $4,000 would be includable in income.

If the work of art was held solely for personal pleasure and was worth only $750 at the time of the fire, however, the taxpayer is not permitted to deduct its adjusted basis of $1,000 despite the reference to this amount in IRC §165(b), since the prefire decline in value of $250 was not attributable to the casualty. Under *Helvering v. Owens,* decided by the Supreme Court in 1939, the deduction in this situation is limited to the lesser of the property's adjusted basis and its value immediately before the casualty.[20] Thus, the deduction, before application of the $100 nondeductible floor, is $750, the property's pre-casualty value, rather than $1,000, its adjusted basis. Though not clearly delineated in the statute, this limitation is in harmony with the legislative intent to distinguish between extraordinary losses and the ordinary cost of living. Had the *Owens* case gone the other way, the taxpayer would be able to deduct the pre-casualty decline in value, which is attributable to ordinary wear and tear, merely because the property happened to be destroyed by a casualty; and in some situations it would be preferable to lose a depreciated asset by casualty than to sell it. In the *Owens* case, for example, a private automobile costing $1,825 was damaged in a collision when it was worth $225. If the car had been totally destroyed and the taxpayer were allowed to deduct the original cost, the resulting tax savings could easily have exceeded the amount he would have received had he sold it for $225 before the casualty, since the loss on the hypothetical sale would not have given rise to a deduction because of IRC §262.[21]

The *Owens* principle, however, is not applicable to the destruction of depreciated assets used in the taxpayer's trade or business or held for the production of income, however, since in this situation the full amount of the property's adjusted basis has been lost in a business or profit-oriented activity, justifying a deduction whether the loss precedes the casualty or not.[22]

---

[19] For parallel treatment of potential income or other items that were not taken into income before the casualty loss, see supra note 6.

[20] Helvering v. Owens, 305 US 468 (1939); Treas. Regs. §1.165-7(b)(1)(ii).

[21] For IRC §262, disallowing deductions for personal, living, or family expenses, including losses on the sale of property held solely for personal purposes, see supra ¶14.3.

[22] Treas. Regs. §1.165-7(b)(1) (last sentence). If property is converted from personal to business or income-producing uses, the lower of its value and adjusted basis at the time of conversion is used in computing a casualty loss, with adjustments for post-conversion events. See Treas. Regs. §1.165-7(a)(5); infra ¶23.9.

The regulations provide that in determining the amount of a casualty loss, the fair market value of the property immediately before and after the casualty shall "generally be ascertained by competent appraisal." [23] Supplemental instructions issued by the IRS stress the importance of the appraiser's knowledge of the conditions in the area and familiarity with the taxpayer's property, the value of photographs, and the use of industry "bluebooks" to establish the value of automobiles.[24]

The regulations also state that the cost of repairs is "acceptable evidence" of the loss in value if the repairs are necessary to restore the property to its precasualty condition, are not excessive in amount, and are confined to the damage in question, provided the value of the property after the repairs does not exceed its precasualty value.[25] The latter condition is easily satisfied in some circumstances (e.g., the replacement of a broken window), but some repairs almost inevitably add value to the property. When a used automobile is repainted after a collision, for example, the new paint job will usually last longer than the residual life of the old paint.

In some circumstances, on the other hand, repairs are far more expensive than the financial loss sustained by the taxpayer. A ten-year-old car may be worth $600 before and $500 after its fenders are damaged in a collision, and a $300 repair bill may add only $100 to its market value. In this situation, an estimate of the cost of repairs does little to establish the decline in value attributable to the casualty, and high actual expenditures may prove that the taxpayer is wallowing in nostalgia, not that he sustained a loss of $300.

Appraisers' fees and other expenses incurred to establish a deductible loss, it should be noted, are not part of the casualty loss itself, but they may be deducted under IRC §212(3) (expenses of establishing tax liability) by taxpayers who itemize their deductions.[26]

3. Insurance Recoveries, Other Compensation, and Salvage Value. Although a taxpayer can hardly be said to sustain a "loss" if casualty damage is fully covered by insurance or made good by a tort-feasor, IRC §165(a) makes this point crystal clear, rather than leaving it to be litigated, by permitting losses to be deducted only if "not compensated for by insurance or otherwise." Expenses incurred in obtaining reimbursement for a casualty loss are part of the loss or offset against the recovery.

If compensation for the loss or the property's salvage value is collected in the year of the casualty, these offsets are taken into account at that time in

[23] Treas. Regs. §1.165-7(a)(2)(i).

[24] IRS Pub. No. 547, Tax Information on Disasters, Casualty Losses, and Thefts 2 (1979).

[25] Treas. Regs. §1.165-7(a)(2)(ii).

[26] For IRC §212(3), see supra ¶8.5.

computing the remaining loss, if any. Conversely, if there is no reasonable prospect of a recovery, the entire loss is taken into account when sustained; and any unexpected subsequent recovery is taken into income when received, subject to the tax benefit doctrine discussed elsewhere in this work.[27] In a common intermediate situation—a reasonable prospect of reimbursement, falling short of certainty—the taxpayer can deduct the loss currently only if and to the extent it exceeds the potential recovery (e.g., in the case of a fire, the amount in excess of the taxpayer's insurance policy limit). The balance of the loss must be held in abeyance pending resolution of the uncertainty, to be deducted if it exceeds the amount collected or if the claim is abandoned.

Amounts received on the occasion of a casualty are not necessarily compensation for the damage or destruction of the taxpayer's property. Thus, insurance proceeds compensating the taxpayer for loss of the use and occupancy of business property or for additional living expenses do not ordinarily constitute compensation for property and, hence, do not reduce the taxpayer's casualty loss. Similarly, benefits paid to victims of disasters may or may not be allocable to damaged property.

4. The $100 Nondeductible Floor and Adjusted Gross Income Limit. By virtue of IRC §165(h)(1), casualty losses of property not used in the taxpayer's trade or business or held for income-producing purposes are nondeductible to the extent of the first $100 per casualty or theft. If the property is damaged in two or more separate casualties in a single taxable year, the $100 floor is applied independently to each casualty. If two or more assets are damaged in the same casualty, however, the $100 floor is applied to the entire loss.[28] When jointly owned property is damaged or destroyed, each owner's loss is subject to the $100 floor unless the owners are husband and wife, in which event there is only a single $100 disallowance if they file a joint return. If property serving both personal and business purposes is damaged by casualty, the floor is applied only to the part of the loss allocable to the personal element; thus, if an auto used fifty-fifty for business and pleasure suffers an otherwise deductible $150 loss, the $75 business loss is fully deductible, but the $75 personal loss is nondeductible.

After the $100 floor has been applied, the taxpayer's casualty losses for the taxable year are aggregated. Under IRC §165(h)(1)(B), enacted in 1982, the aggregated amount is deductible only if and to the extent that it exceeds

---

[27] See Treas. Regs. §§1.165-1(d)(2)(ii), 1.165-1(d)(2)(iii); for the tax benefit principle, see supra ¶1.10.

[28] Treas. Regs. §1.165-7(b)(4)(ii) (whether damage is from a single casualty or from two or more separate casualties is a question of fact; events closely related in origin, such as winds and flood caused by a hurricane, are treated as a single casualty).

10 percent of the taxpayer's adjusted gross income.[29] If married taxpayers file a joint return, their casualty losses are combined and the 10 percent limit is based on their joint adjusted gross income.

¶18.5 ANCILLARY PROBLEMS

1. Year of Deduction. Section 165(a) permits taxpayers to deduct "any loss sustained during the taxable year." This ordinarily means that the loss is to be deducted in the year of the casualty itself, but there are several qualifications and exceptions to this general principle.

1. *Delayed damage.* In unusual circumstances, the taxpayer may be unable to determine promptly whether a storm or other casualty has damaged his property or, if so, the extent of the loss. In such a case, the loss is not "sustained" until the effects of the casualty can be observed and evaluated.

2. *Reimbursement claims.* As explained earlier, if the taxpayer has a reasonable prospect of recovering the loss from an insurer or tort-feasor, the deduction must be postponed until the claim is resolved, settled, or abandoned.[30]

3. *Disaster losses.* To speed up economic recovery from widespread disasters, IRC §165(h) permits taxpayers, at their election, to deduct casualty losses in the taxable year immediately preceding the year of a disaster if it is officially declared to warrant federal assistance under the Disaster Relief Act of 1974. If the prior year's return has not yet been filed, this election reduces the cash required to pay the tax or results in a refund; if the return has already been filed, the taxpayer can file a claim for a refund.

4. *Theft losses.* By virtue of IRC §165(e), enacted in 1954, a loss from theft (interpreted by the regulations to include, without being limited to, larceny, embezzlement, and robbery) [31] is deductible when "the taxpayer discovers such loss." Ordinarily, discovery of the loss is contemporaneous with the crime, but it may be long delayed, as in the case of embezzlement by a trusted employee. Although IRC §165(e) refers to the taxable year "in which *the taxpayer* discovers [the] loss" (emphasis added), the cases hold that a loss "is considered to be discovered when a reasonable man in similar circumstances would have realized the fact that he had suffered a theft loss." [32]

---

[29] Adjusted gross income is defined by IRC §62. A similar floor, fixed at 5 percent of adjusted gross income, is imposed by IRC §213(a) on the deduction of medical expenses; see infra ¶20.1.

[30] Supra ¶18.4.

[31] Treas. Regs. §1.165-8(d); see supra ¶18.3.

[32] See McComb v. CIR, ¶77,176 P-H Memo TC (1977).

2. Basis of Casualty-Damaged Property. The basis of property damaged or destroyed by casualty must be reduced by the amount of the deduction allowable under IRC §165 and by the amount of any insurance or other compensation received or recoverable in the year the casualty loss is sustained. The adjusted basis is then increased by any capital expenditures made to repair or restore the damaged property.[33]

SELECTED BIBLIOGRAPHY

Comment, The Casualty Loss Deduction and Consumer Expectation: Section 165(c)(3) of the Internal Revenue Code, 36 U. Chi. L. Rev. 220 (1968).

Epstein, The Consumption and Loss of Personal Property Under the Internal Revenue Code, 23 Stan. L. Rev. 454, 463–467 (1971).

Feld, Appreciation Under the Casualty Loss, 59 Taxes 379 (1981).

U.S. Comptroller General, The Personal Casualty and Theft Loss Tax Deduction: Analysis and Proposals for Change (GGD-80-10, 1979).

[33] See, e.g., Rev. Rul. 71-161, 1971-1 CB 76; IRS Pub. No. 334, Tax Guide for Small Business 110 (1979) (examples).

CHAPTER 19

Charitable Contributions

¶19.1 CHARITABLE CONTRIBUTIONS—IN GENERAL

1. Introductory. Since 1917 Congress has permitted taxpayers to deduct contributions to religious, charitable, educational, and similar nonprofit organizations, up to a specified percentage of the taxpayer's income. In one of the few explicit legislative statements of the charitable deduction's purpose, the House Committee on Ways and Means observed in 1938:

> The exemption from taxation of money or property devoted to charitable and other purposes is based upon the theory that the Government is compensated for the loss of revenue by its relief from financial burden which would otherwise have to be met by appropriations from public funds, and by the benefits resulting from the promotion of the general welfare.[1]

The deduction has been both attacked and defended vigorously in the years since its enactment, and these controversies have stimulated the enactment of a variety of statutory qualifications, which have turned the two sentences that sufficed in 1917 into a complex web of phraseology.

---

[1] H. Rep. No. 1860, 75th Cong., 3d Sess. (1938), reprinted in 1939-1 (Part 2) CB 728, 742.

In general, to be deducted under IRC §170, a charitable transfer must (a) go to a qualified recipient; (b) constitute a "contribution" rather than payment for goods or services; (c) satisfy a "payment" requirement; (d) consist of cash or qualified property; (e) not exceed a specified percentage of the taxpayer's income in the year of payment or, when a carryover is permitted, in subsequent years; and (f) meet certain other standards. These governing principles, which are discussed in detail below, sometimes distinguish between corporations and other donors, as well as among various classes of charitable donees.

2. Qualified Recipients. Gifts to needy individuals and worthy causes are not automatically deductible under IRC §170. For example, in *Thomason v. CIR,* the Tax Court held that the taxpayer could not deduct payments to a school attended by a child who was under the legal guardianship of a public charitable organization and for whom the taxpayer "felt a keen fatherly and personal interest," stating that "charity begins where certainty in beneficiaries ends. . . . Whenever the beneficiary is designated by name and his merit alone is to be considered, the bequest is private and not public and ceases to have the peculiar merit of a charity." [2] This distinction between public and private generosity spawns close cases when charities solicit funds for designated beneficiaries or the gift is otherwise earmarked when received by the charity.[3]

To qualify for deduction, gifts must be made to or for the use of an organized body fitting into one of the following categories:

1. The United States, the District of Columbia, or a state or political subdivision thereof, provided the gift is made for exclusively public purposes, such as parks, museums, and public memorials.

2. A corporation, trust, community chest, fund, or foundation (a) created or organized in or under the laws of the United States, the District of Columbia, or a state; (b) organized and operated exclusively for religious, charitable, scientific, literary, or educational purposes, to prevent cruelty to children or animals, or to foster national or international amateur sports competition;

---

[2] Thomason v. CIR, 2 TC 441, 443-444 (1943); see also Dohrmann v. CIR, 18 BTA 66 (1929) (gifts to needy persons do not qualify for deduction in absence of organized charitable institution); Havemeyer v. CIR, 98 F.2d 706 (2d Cir. 1938) (contributions to association primarily for benefit of elderly family retainers; held, qualified; Hand, J., dissenting); Hunton v. CIR, 1 TC 821 (1943) (Acq.) (trust fund for relief of poor and sick persons in Richmond, Va., by direct contributions or gifts to established charitable organizations; held, qualified even though donor's spouse had exclusive power to designate recipients).

[3] For problems in determining whether a gift to an individual is intended as a gift to a qualified organization, see Winn v. CIR, 595 F.2d 1060 (5th Cir. 1979) (gift to support work of specified foreign missionary held deductible); Rev. Rul. 79-81, 1979-1 CB 107 (payments to religious organization to support students soliciting contributions from sponsors; held, nondeductible because earmarked for particular students).

(c) no part of whose net earnings inures to the benefit of any private shareholder or individual; and (d) that is not disqualified for tax exemption under IRC §501(c)(3) for attempting to influence legislation and that does not participate or intervene in political campaigns on behalf of candidates for public office.

These requirements are similar to those imposed by IRC §501(c)(3), exempting charitable and similar organizations from tax on their own income. It should be noted, however, that contributions do not qualify for deduction under IRC §170(c) merely because the recipient is itself a tax-exempt organization. Social welfare organizations, chambers of commerce, and social clubs, for example, qualify for tax exemption, but gifts to these groups are not deductible under IRC §170.

The requirement of IRC §170(c)(2)(A) that the recipient of deductible contributions be a domestic organization can be troublesome for domestic groups soliciting funds for foreign charitable projects. If the U.S. body is merely a conduit for a foreign entity, the latter will be treated as the true donee and the contribution will not satisfy the statutory condition. If, however, the domestic organization is an independent body that makes grants in its own discretion to foreign charitable agencies or that organizes a foreign subsidiary to facilitate its own operations, the domestic organization is the donee for purposes of IRC §170(c)(2).

3. Veterans' groups, charitable projects of fraternal lodges (gifts by individuals only), nonprofit cemetery companies, and a few organizations specified by nontax statutes, subject to a variety of special restrictions.

Contributions to the organizations listed above qualify under IRC §170(c) if made either "to" or "for the use of" the organization. The latter phrase encompasses gifts in trust for the benefit of the organization, as well as payments that further its charitable activities even though not made directly to it, such as the unreimbursed expenses of trustees and volunteer workers.[4]

3. Donative Intent. To qualify for a deduction under IRC §170(c), the taxpayer's transfer to the charitable recipient must be "a contribution or gift," as distinguished from a payment for goods or services. In specific litigated

---

[4] See Treas. Regs. §1.170A-1(g) (unreimbursed expenditures incident to rendition of services to charity; e.g., cost of special uniforms, out-of-pocket transportation expenses, and meals and lodging while away from home); McCollum v. CIR, ¶78,435 P-H Memo TC (1978) (expenses incurred during voluntary services to National Ski Patrol deductible, even though taxpayer enjoyed skiing and camaraderie of other members of patrol; otherwise, regulation permitting deduction of out-of-pocket expenses of volunteers "would be rendered virtually meaningless"); see also Hamilton v. CIR, ¶79,186 P-H Memo TC (1979) (cost of transporting children to Girl Scout meetings incurred for benefit of children rather than charity; nondeductible).

cases, the courts have both accepted and rejected the "detached and disinterested generosity" phraseology used by the Supreme Court in construing the term "gift" as used by IRC §102(a) (excluding gifts from the donee's gross income).[5] For example, in *Singer Co. v. United States,* decided in 1971, the Court of Claims commented that the "subjective approach of 'disinterested generosity' need not be wrestled with" and that the proper test is "if the benefits received, or expected to be received, are substantial, and meaning by that, benefits greater than those that inure to the general public . . . which benefits are merely incidental . . . then in such case we feel the transferor has received, or expects to receive, a *quid pro quo* sufficient to remove the transfer from the realm of deductibility under section 170." [6] Applying this test, the court in *Singer* denied a deduction for sewing machines sold to schools at a discount because the taxpayer's predominant purpose was to encourage students to use the taxpayer's machines in later years. It allowed deductions for bargain sales to churches, hospitals, the Red Cross, and government agencies, however, because the primary purpose was to foster the donees' charitable activities; maintaining the taxpayer's "favorable public image" was only an incidental purpose.

Abstract formulations, however, are likely to be no more successful in settling borderline cases under IRC §170 than they have been in resolving debatable cases under IRC §102. In particular, although the term "disinterested generosity" seems initially to disqualify gifts by a business enterprise if they serve to advertise its products or enhance its "image," on reflection it becomes clear that very few donors are so "detached and disinterested" as to cloak themselves in anonymity to avoid the plaudits of the public and the gratitude of their beneficiaries. Thus, the satisfaction of fostering a worthy cause, even if the donor's name is memorialized by a cornerstone or professorial chair, is not the kind of quid pro quo that disqualifies the contribution under IRC §170. Moreover, the fact that business corporations are explicitly permitted to deduct contributions is inconsistent with denying a deduction merely because the gift improves the enterprise's reputation.

The boundary between deductible contributions and nondeductible payments for services rendered can be difficult to locate and police. For example,

---

[5] See CIR v. Duberstein, 363 US 278, 285 (1960) ("detached and disinterested generosity"), discussed supra ¶3.2; Winters v. CIR, 468 F.2d 778 (2d Cir. 1972) (payments to fund for support of church school that taxpayers' children attended without charge were expected but not mandatory; held, nondeductible because not reflecting "detached and disinterested generosity"); see also Rev. Rul. 80-77, 1980-1 CB 56 (deductions allowed for contributions to Girl Scouts by parents of Girl Scout, to volunteer fire department by local resident, to Red Cross by person who received disaster aid, and to combined charity fund by taxpayer with dependent parent residing in home for elderly belonging to fund).

[6] Singer Co. v. US, 449 F.2d 413, 423 (Ct. Cl. 1971).

the IRS has ruled that membership fees and dues charged by charitable organizations are deductible only to the extent that the payments exceed the value of such rights and privileges as free concerts, discounts on the purchase of publications, and invitations to special events for members only. Overpriced tickets to charity balls and benefit performances raise substantially the same issue, except that it is ordinarily clear that part of the cost is a nondeductible payment for the evening's pleasure; and disallowance of the balance, even if warranted, may seem niggling when the amount is small. If there is a comparable commercial event, a 1967 ruling states that the established admission fee can be employed to determine whether the charity's charge includes a deductible component and that otherwise a reasonable estimate of the value accruing to the donor will be acceptable.[7] The common practice of representing that the full amount charged can be deducted is usually improper and may even border on fraud. The 1967 ruling also states that the value of admission is nondeductible even if the purchasers do not attend the event, since they have the right to do so, and that an intent to reject the privilege can be manifested by an outright gift of the amount in question coupled with a refusal to accept or keep the ticket.

Another recurring context requiring contributions to be distinguished from transfers for value is a gift of land to a municipality for a road, park, or other public facility, made by a real estate operator seeking a zoning change or approval of a subdivision plan. In unusual circumstances, dedication of the property to a public use can realistically be viewed as a contribution, but more frequently it is conditioned on public action that will enhance the value of the retained property. If a payment of this type fails to qualify as a charitable contribution because the transferor obtains an offsetting financial benefit, it may qualify for deduction under IRC §162 as an ordinary and necessary business expense. Taxpayers making otherwise deductible gifts in excess of the percentage limitations imposed by IRC §170, however, are prevented by IRC §162(b) from deducting them as business expenses.[8]

4. "Payment" Within Taxable Year. Section 170(a)(1) authorizes the deduction of a contribution "payment of which is made within the taxable year." The regulations provide that a contribution is made when "delivery is effected" and that delivery of a check is effected by mailing it to the charity, provided it clears in due course.[9] Since the statutory requirement of "payment" implies an irrevocable transfer of control over the property to the donee, a deduction is premature if the taxpayer has only made a pledge, credited

[7] Rev. Rul. 67-246, 1967-2 CB 104.

[8] See infra ¶19.4.

[9] Treas. Regs. §1.170A-1(b).

property on his books, or given the charity a postdated check.[10] Revoking an earlier contrary ruling, however, the IRS ruled in 1978 that a contribution charged to the donor's bank credit card is paid when the charge is made, regardless of when the donor pays the bank.[11]

The statutory requirement of "payment" has also been interpreted to deny a deduction if there is no "payment" of cash or property, even if the taxpayer's action confers a measurable economic benefit on the charity. Thus, taxpayers cannot deduct the value of services, donated blood, broadcast time, advertising space, and similar uncompensated assistance to charitable organizations.[12]

An alternative ground for these results may be that a sale of the services by the taxpayer would have produced taxable income and that exclusion of these hypothetical amounts from gross income when the services are furnished without charge to the charity is the equivalent of a deduction. In keeping with this rationale, taxpayers who refuse to accept compensation for services and direct that the earnings be paid instead to a charity are allowed a deduction if the renounced amount is taxed to them under *Lucas v. Earl,* as though it had been received and then paid over to the charity as a contribution.[13] But this rationale is not applied consistently, since deductions are allowed for the fair market value of appreciated property (including, in limited circumstances, inventory assets) even though the potential profit component is not includable in the donor's gross income.[14]

Charitable contributions are sometimes expressly or implicitly contingent on the donee's success in attracting additional funds, official approval of construction plans, continued use of the donated property for a specified purpose, or similar events and conditions. The regulations provide that if a gift when made is dependent on the performance of some act or the occurrence of an event, no deduction is allowable unless the possibility that the transfer will not become effective is negligible.[15] If a conditional gift is not deductible when made, it is treated as paid, and hence it becomes deductible, if and when

---

[10] See Mann v. CIR, 35 F.2d 873 (D.C. Cir. 1929) (unpaid charitable subscriptions not deductible); Christensen v. CIR, 40 TC 563 (1963) (book entries); Griffin v. CIR, 49 TC 253 (1967) (postdated check to pay interest; same principle would govern charitable gift).

[11] Rev. Rul. 78-38, 1978-1 CB 67.

[12] Treas. Regs. §1.170A-1(g) (services); Rev. Rul. 67-236, 1967-2 CB 103 (radio broadcast time); Rev. Rul. 162, 1953-2 CB 127 (blood donated to blood bank).

[13] For Lucas v. Earl, 281 US 111 (1930), and the troublesome distinction between donating services to a charity and assigning income to the organization, see infra ¶30.2.

[14] For the deduction of the fair market value of appreciated property, see infra ¶19.2; for the status of inventory property, see infra ¶19.2.

[15] Treas. Regs. §1.170A-1(e); Rev. Rul. 77-148, 1977-1 CB 63 (gift of timberland to United States for wildlife preserve subject to reverter if government offers timber for sale, etc.; held, immediately deductible because possibility of defeasance is negligible).

the condition is satisfied.[16] Conversely, the return to the donor of a deducted contribution (e.g., on breach of a condition by the donee) generates gross income unless the prior deduction was of no tax benefit.[17]

A special payment rule is prescribed by IRC §170(a)(3) for gifts of future interests in tangible personal property: The contribution is treated as made only on the expiration of all intervening interests to actual possession or enjoyment of the property that are held by the donor or any persons related to the donor.[18] Before 1964, when this provision became effective, donors could contribute remainder interests in an art collection to a museum, subject to life interests in themselves or members of their families, and deduct the value of the charitable remainder in the year of the gift, a practice enabling them to contemplate their tax savings while looking at the pictures. Under IRC §170(a)(3), a deduction is allowed when the intervening interests terminate, for the value of the contribution as of that date, provided this occurs during the donor's lifetime.

The postponed deduction principle of IRC §170(a)(3) does not apply to gifts of real estate (other than fixtures that are to be severed from the realty) or of undivided *present* interests, such as the contribution of a one-half interest in a painting entitling the donor and the donee to possession for six months each year.

¶19.2 CHARITABLE CONTRIBUTIONS OF PROPERTY

1. Introductory. If property is contributed to a charity, the amount of the contribution is the property's fair market value when the gift is made, whether this exceeds or is less than its adjusted basis.[19] Value is to be determined by the customary willing-buyer, willing-seller standard. If the contribution consists of property customarily sold by the taxpayer in the ordinary course of business, its fair market value for this purpose is the price in the market in which the property would have been sold; thus, wholesale rather than retail value may be controlling. Taken in conjunction with the basic principle that a gift is not a taxable event, the use of the property's fair market value to fix the amount that can be deducted means that a taxpayer is well advised to sell depreciated property in order to realize the loss and then to

---

[16] See Gagne v. CIR, 16 TC 498 (1951) (check delivered in 1942 subject to conditions on use was deductible in 1943, when charity accepted conditions).

[17] See Alice Phelan Sullivan Corp. v. CIR, 381 F.2d 399 (Ct. Cl. 1967), discussed supra ¶1.10 (re tax benefit doctrine).

[18] The tainted relationships are specified by IRC §267(b), for which see infra ¶33.3.

[19] Treas. Regs. §1.170A-1(c)(1).

donate the proceeds, while the shrewd strategy with appreciated assets is to contribute the property in kind, allowing the charity to sell if it prefers cash.

Although the use of appreciated property to satisfy the taxpayer's debts is ordinarily a taxable event, long-standing administrative practice exempts charitable pledges from this principle.[20] Thus, an exuberant donor who is inspired at a fund-raising event to pledge a specific dollar amount may use appreciated assets to discharge the liability without being taxed on the difference between the property's adjusted basis and the amount pledged.

The Treasury has sought in a few special situations to limit the taxpayer's right to deduct an asset's fair market value without taking the increase in its value into income. For example, if the donor is about to engage in a sale or other taxable disposition of the property but changes course in midstream in order to donate to a charity, a prompt sale by the charity to the proposed purchaser may be imputed to the donor, as though he had sold the property and then donated the proceeds to the charity.[21] If the charity assumes or takes subject to a liability in excess of the donated property's adjusted basis, the IRS has similarly sought to treat the transfer as a taxable event, especially if the debt was incurred in anticipation of the gift.[22] The previously mentioned disallowance of deductions for contributed services and facilities can also be viewed as limiting the taxpayer's right to deduct the fair market value of items that have not been taken into income.[23] In a similar vein, the IRS ruled in 1970 that a taxpayer receiving unsolicited merchandise who claims a deduction on contributing the goods to a charity must take their value into income, and its position has been upheld in a litigated case.[24]

These sporadic limits on the amount to be deducted under IRC §170 were buttressed in 1969 by the enactment of three statutory restrictions on the use of appreciated property for charitable contributions, discussed below.[25]

---

[20] Rev. Rul. 55-410, 1955-1 CB 297.

[21] See Rollins v. US, 302 F.Supp. 812 (W.D. Tex. 1969) (sales contract executed before gift; held, donor taxable on proceeds); Jones v. US, 531 F.2d 1343 (6th Cir. 1976) (gift of stock after corporation adopted plan of liquidation; donor must report liquidation proceeds on assignment-of-income grounds).

[22] See Rev. Rul. 70-626, 1970-2 CB 158 (pre-1969 gifts); for discussion of the effect of disposing of property subject to a liability in excess of its basis, see infra ¶23.16. If the transfer of property to a charity is treated as a sale to the extent of the liability, IRC §1011(b) (relating to bargain sales) comes into play, and the gain is not the excess of the liability over the taxpayer's adjusted basis (as before 1969, when IRC §1011(b) was enacted) but the excess of the liability over a ratable part of the adjusted basis; see also infra, text following note 28.

[23] Supra ¶19.1.

[24] Rev. Rul. 70-498, 1970-2 CB 6 (books received by newspaper book reviewer from publishers); Haverly v. US, 513 F.2d 224 (7th Cir.), cert. denied, 423 US 912 (1975).

[25] Infra, text at notes 26-28.

2. Ordinary-Income and Short-Term Capital Gain Property. If a sale of donated property for its fair market value would have generated ordinary income or short-term capital gain, IRC §170(e)(1)(A) requires the otherwise deductible amount to be reduced by the amount of the hypothetical gain. In effect, the taxpayer can deduct only the property's adjusted basis. The assets subjected to value reduction by IRC §170(e)(1)(A) include (a) items includable in the donor's inventory or otherwise held for sale to customers in the ordinary course of business (except for certain medical and similar supplies for the ill, needy, or infants); (b) works of art, literary compositions, etc., created by the donor or a person whose basis is used by the donor, and similar assets described by IRC §§1221(3) and 1221(6);[26] (c) short-term capital assets; and (d) certain other items. Because artists and authors can deduct only the adjusted basis of art objects and manuscripts—ordinarily the cost of the canvas, paints, or paper—contributions of their works to galleries, museums, and libraries have declined precipitously since 1969, when these restrictions were imposed.

3. Long-Term Capital Gain Property. In two limited situations, the deduction is reduced by IRC §170(e)(1)(B) even if the taxpayer's gain on a sale would be long-term capital gain rather than ordinary income or short-term capital gain. The first such case is a gift of appreciated tangible personal property, if the charitable donee's use is unrelated to its exempt purposes or functions, such as a contribution of antiques to be auctioned off at a charity ball. If the antiques are given to a museum, however, the regulations provide that it is reasonable for the donor to anticipate that they will not be put to an unrelated use (e.g., a sale) in the absence of actual knowledge to the contrary.[27] The other situation encompassed by IRC §170(e)(1)(B) is a contribution of appreciated property to a private foundation.

Capital gain property escaping the restriction imposed by IRC §170(e)(1)(B) is subjected by IRC §170(b)(1)(C) to a special limitation, described below, in computing the percentage ceiling on charitable deductions.[28]

4. Bargain Sales of Appreciated Property to Charities. Before 1969 a taxpayer who sold appreciated property to a charity for its adjusted basis did not realize gain (since the amount realized did not exceed the property's adjusted basis) and could deduct the difference between the sales price and the property's fair market value as a charitable contribution. In effect, therefore, taxpayers could make deductible gifts of "pure" appreciation. This privilege was curtailed by the enactment in 1969 of IRC §1011(b), requiring the prop-

---

[26] See infra ¶25.7 (re 1976 legislation—IRC §1221(3)).

[27] Treas. Regs. §1.170A-4(b)(3)(ii)*(b)*.

[28] Infra ¶19.3.

erty's adjusted basis to be allocated proportionately between the portion sold to the charity and the donated portion instead of assigned in its entirety to the sale part of the transaction. For example, if a taxpayer sells property worth $100 to a charity for its adjusted basis of $20, only $4 (20/100) of the basis is allocated to the sale, resulting in gain of $16. But the 1969 legislation did not alter the method of computing the amount of the charitable contribution. Thus, the gift in the preceding example is $80 (i.e., the excess of the property's value ($100) over the amount received by the taxpayer ($20)).

5. Remainders and Other Partial Interests. The Tax Reform Act of 1969 severely restricted the deductibility of charitable remainders, income interests, and other split interests in property, if the donor either retains the remaining interest or gives it to a nonexempt person. The elaborate restrictions imposed by IRC §§170(f)(2) and 170(f)(3) on such transfers are best examined in the perspective of pre-1969 law, under which a taxpayer who transferred property in trust, retaining the income for life and vesting the remainder in a charity, was entitled to deduct the actuarial value of the charitable remainder, computed on the assumption of a 3.5 percent yield on the property. In point of fact, however, the trustee often had investment and invasion powers that could be exercised to favor the income beneficiary at the expense of the charitable remainder without serious risk of surcharge. Conversely, if a charity was entitled to the income of a trust for a term of years and the members of the donor's family were to receive the remainder, the charity could be put on short rations in order to enrich the noncharitable beneficiaries.

In 1969 Congress took drastic action to revise the law in this area:

1. *Transfers in trust.* Under IRC §170(f)(2)(A), no deduction is allowed for contributions of remainder interests in trust unless the trust is a charitable remainder annuity trust, a charitable remainder unitrust, or a pooled income fund. To qualify, the trust must satisfy conditions insuring that the charity's interest will be appropriately protected. Comparable restrictions are imposed by IRC §170(f)(2)(B) on the deductibility of transfers of income interests in trusts.

2. *Nontrust transfers.* Contributions of partial interests in property are treated by IRC §170(f)(3) in a fashion similar to transfers in trust, but three types of contributions are exempted from the 1969 restrictions: (a) remainder interests in personal residences (including summer homes and cooperative apartments) or farms; (b) an undivided portion of the taxpayer's entire interest in the property (e.g., an undivided one-half interest, creating a tenancy in common); and (c) certain contributions for conservation purposes, including outdoor recreation, historically important property, and environmental protection.

¶19.3 PERCENTAGE LIMITATIONS ON DEDUCTION OF CHARITABLE CONTRIBUTIONS

1. Introductory. When enacted in 1917, the deduction for charitable contributions was limited to 15 percent of the donor's net income. Gradually relaxed over the years, the percentage limitation is now a web of intricate rules, which distinguish between individual donors and corporations, between so-called 50 percent charities and 20 percent charities, between gifts of certain capital gain property and gifts of cash and other types of property, and between contributions "to" and contributions "for the use of" the charitable donee. Contributions in excess of the applicable percentage limitation can be carried forward for use in later years under rules that depend on the donor, donee, and type of property.

Although individuals can ordinarily deduct their charitable contributions only if they itemize their personal deductions, IRC §§63(f)(3), 63(i), and 170(i) allow non-itemizers to deduct so-called direct charitable contributions from gross income in computing adjusted gross income. This allowance, encated in 1981, is limited to the lower of (a) 25 percent of the individual's contributions (50 percent of 1985 and 1986; 100 percent for 1986) or (b) $100 (1982 and 1983) and $300 (1984, 1985, and 1986).

2. Individual Donors. For individuals, IRC §§170(b)(1)(A) and 170(b)(1)(B) create a two-level hierarchy of charitable donees and gear the amount that can be deducted to the taxpayer's "contributions base"—defined as adjusted gross income before taking account of any net operating loss carrybacks. The deduction cannot exceed (a) 50 percent of the taxpayer's contribution base for contributions "to" (but not those that are "for the use of") so-called 50 percent charities (churches, schools and colleges, hospitals, medical research agencies, charitable organizations receiving substantial support from government or the general public, private operating foundations, and a few others) or (b) 20 percent of the contribution base (or, if lower, the unused portion of the taxpayer's quota for 50 percent charities) for other charitable contributions—that is, those (1) "for the use of" 50 percent charities and (2) to or for the use of other qualified donees (so-called 20 percent charities).

If the taxpayer's contributions to 50 percent charities exceed the applicable quota for any taxable year, the excess may be carried over to each of the five succeeding years, subject to certain qualifications.

The foregoing description of the percentage limitations must ordinarily be qualified if the taxpayer's contributions include any appreciated capital gain property. Unless the capital gain property is subject to IRC §170(e)(1)(B) (relating to certain gifts of tangible personal property and gifts to certain private foundations)[29], it may be taken into account and deducted (subject to the 50 percent and 20 percent limits) only to the extent that it does not exceed 30 percent of the taxpayer's contribution base. Any excess over the 30 percent limit may be carried forward for five years, subject to certain restrictions.

The seemingly insignificant distinction between contributions "to" a 50 percent charity and contributions "for the use of" such a donee, as indicated above, can determine whether a contribution is subject to the 50 percent limitation or the 20 percent limitation; and it also determines whether any nondeductible excess can be carried forward to the five succeeding years. Transfers of the donor's entire interest in cash and property, with no intervening trustee, are the clearest examples of contributions "to" the charity. Transfers in trust, on the other hand, are ordinarily "for the use of" the charity, except for remainder interests that will become possessory (rather than continue to be held in trust) on the termination of the prior interests. Other common examples of contributions for the use of a charity are out-of-pocket expenditures incurred by a volunteer worker in rendering services to the charity.[30]

3. Corporations. The limitation on corporate deductions is far simpler than the rules applicable to individuals. Section 170(b)(2) provides that a corporation's deductions may not exceed 10 percent of its taxable income, and IRC §170(d)(2) permits contributions in excess of this limit to be carried forward for use in the five succeeding taxable years. Unlike the percentage limitations applicable to individual taxpayers, the corporate percentage limitation does not vary with the character of the donee, nor is it reduced if the contribution consists of appreciated capital gain property. Corporate contributions to charitable organizations qualify for deduction, however, only if the gift is to be used within the United States.[31]

¶19.4 CHARITABLE CONTRIBUTIONS—MISCELLANEOUS MATTERS

1. Students Maintained as Members of the Taxpayer's Household. Amounts paid by the taxpayer to maintain a full-time elementary or secondary student, other than a dependent or relative, as a member of the taxpayer's household under a written agreement with certain charitable organizations are

---

[29] Supra ¶19.2.

[30] Rev. Rul. 58-279, 1958-1 CB 145; for the deduction of out-of-pocket expenditures incurred by members, trustees, and volunteer workers, see supra ¶19.1.

[31] See IRC §170(c)(2) (final sentence).

treated by IRC §170(g) as paid for the use of the charity, in an amount not in excess of $50 times the number of full calendar months of schooling. Amounts paid "to ensure the well-being of the [student] and to carry out the purpose for which the individual was placed in the taxpayer's home" qualify, including the cost of books, food, medical care, and recreation; but expenses that would have been incurred in any event, such as home repairs, depreciation, and insurance, do not qualify, nor does the value of services rendered by the taxpayer or other members of the household to the student.[32]

2. Substantiation. Taxpayers claiming deductions have the burden of establishing that the donee organization qualifies for the receipt of deductible contributions, but this burden is alleviated by a procedure for advance IRS rulings confirming an organization's exempt status. Rather than compel donors to rely on the organization's statements or to prove independently that it is a qualified recipient, the IRS issues a Cumulative List of Exempt Organizations, which is kept current by notices in the weekly *Internal Revenue Bulletin.*

If an organization has not received an IRS ruling confirming its tax-exempt status, the right of donors to deduct contributions under IRC §170 depends on when the donee was organized. If it was organized on or before October 9, 1969, the donor has the right to establish that the organization satisfies the requirements of IRC §170(c)—a showing that can call for a detailed analysis of the organization's charter, bylaws, and activities.[33] If, however, the donee was organized after October 9, 1969, it is subject to special rules, including IRC §508(a)(1), which provides that the organization shall not be treated as a Section 501(c)(3) organization unless it has given notice of its application for recognition of its exempt status. The notice requirement does not apply to certain charities—primarily churches and organizations that do not normally have gross receipts in excess of $5,000 per taxable year.

3. Charitable Contributions as Business Expenses. Section 162(b) provides that contributions and gifts cannot be deducted as business expenses if they would qualify as deductible charitable contributions were it not for the percentage limitations or time-of-payment requirements of IRC §170. Since this restriction applies only to "contributions or gifts," it does not prevent payments to charitable organizations from being deducted as business expenses if they are related to the taxpayer's business and are made with a reasonable expectation of financial benefit; and it is also inapplicable if the recipient

[32] Treas. Regs. §1.170A-2(a)(2).

[33] See S. Rep. No. 91-552, reprinted in 1969-3 CB 459 ("the nature of the organization itself," not IRS determination, is controlling).

organization does not qualify for the receipt of deductible contributions under IRC §170.[34]

SELECTED BIBLIOGRAPHY

Andrews, Personal Deductions in an Ideal Income Tax, 86 Harv. L. Rev. 309, 344–375 (1972).

Anthoine, Deductions for Charitable Contributions of Appreciated Property—The Art World, 35 Tax L. Rev. 239 (1980).

Bittker, Charitable Contributions: Tax Deductions or Matching Grants? 28 Tax L. Rev. 37 (1972).

Colliton, The Meaning of "Contribution or Gift" for Charitable Contribution Deduction Purposes, 41 Ohio St. L.J. 973 (1980).

Feld, Artists, Art Collectors and Income Tax, 60 B.U.L. Rev. 625 (1980).

Hambrick, Charitable Donations of Conservation Easements: Valuation, Enforcement and Public Benefit, 59 Taxes 347 (1981).

Hobbet, Charitable Contributions—How Charitable Must They Be? 11 Seton Hall L. Rev. 1 (1980).

McDaniel, Federal Matching Grants for Charitable Contributions: A Substitute for the Income Tax Deduction, 27 Tax L. Rev. 377 (1972).

Speiller, The Favored Tax Treatment of Purchasers of Art, 80 Colum. L. Rev. 214 (1980).

[34] For analysis of IRC §162(b), see supra ¶8.1.

CHAPTER 20

Medical and Dental Expenses

¶20.1 MEDICAL AND DENTAL EXPENSES—IN GENERAL

1. Introductory. Section 213 allows expenses paid for the medical care of the taxpayer and his or her spouse and dependents to be deducted if the expense is not compensated for by insurance or otherwise (e.g., by Blue Cross or a tort-feasor). Because the deduction is intended to assist taxpayers burdened by "unusual outlays for medical purposes" rather than "to take care of . . . ordinary medical expenses," qualified expenses can be deducted only if, and to the extent that, they exceed 5 percent of the taxpayer's adjusted gross income (AGI) and only if the taxpayer elects under IRC §63(g) to itemize his or her deductions.

2. The Scope of "Medical Care." From its inception in 1942, IRC §213 has provided that the term "medical care" means amounts paid "for the diagnosis, cure, mitigation, treatment, or prevention of disease, or for the purpose of affecting any structure or function of the body." This definition, which was augmented in 1954 and 1965 by provisions relating to transportation and insurance, is easily applied—indeed, it is hardly needed—in the overwhelming bulk of cases, involving run-of-the-mine payments to doctors, nurses, hospitals, medical laboratories, and pharmacies. But many expenses are close to the boundary between "medical care," as defined by IRC §213(e)(1), and "personal, living, or family expenses," which are nondeductible by virtue of IRC §262 unless otherwise expressly provided. In a nation obsessed by physical and mental health, whose young people patronize health food stores as religiously as their parents worship the sun, the borderline between ordinary expenses and medical care gets constantly fuzzier.

The regulations state that expenditures that are "merely beneficial to the general health of an individual," such as the cost of a vacation, are not deductible and that deductions "will be confined strictly to expenses incurred primarily for the prevention or alleviation of a physical or mental defect or illness." [1] While these are satisfactory guides to the first part of the statutory definition of medical care (relating to the diagnosis, cure, etc., of disease), the IRS has interpreted the second part of the definition (amounts paid "for the purpose of affecting any structure or function of the body") to embrace cosmetic surgery, even though its therapeutic effect may be limited to the taxpayer's self-image, as well as birth control pills, legal abortions, and vasectomies, whether or not a "physical or mental defect or illness" is thereby prevented or alleviated.[2]

The cases and rulings delineating the boundary between nondeductible personal expenses and deductible medical expenses can be grouped for review in the following major categories:

1. *Expenses of preserving general health.* The exclusion from IRC §213 of expenditures that are "merely beneficial to the general health of an individual, such as an expenditure for a vacation," [3] is well established; and the same principle disqualifies the cost of exercise devices and membership in athletic clubs. Even if the taxpayer's health is below par, expenses serving both medical and personal objectives are not deductible if the medical benefit is secondary or remote, the expenses would have been incurred even if the medical condition had not arisen, or the mode of achieving the medical benefit is needlessly expensive.[4]

---

[1] Treas. Regs. §1.213-1(e)(1)(ii).

[2] See Rev. Rul. 76-332, 1976-2 CB 81 (cost of face-lifting deductible even though not recommended by taxpayer's physician); Rev. Rul. 73-200, 1973-1 CB 140 (contraceptive pills); Rev. Rul. 73-201, 1973-1 CB 140 (legal abortions and vasectomies); Rev. Rul. 73-603, 1973-2 CB 76 (operation to render woman incapable of having children; held, deductible); Rev. Rul. 73-189, 1973-1 CB 139 (expenses incurred by kidney donor deductible).

[3] Treas. Regs. §1.213-1(e)(ii); Rev. Rul. 79-162, 1979-1 CB 116 (cost of participation in program to stop smoking not deductible if purpose is to improve general health rather than cure specific ailment); Haines v. CIR, 71 TC 644 (1979) (taxpayer requiring physical therapy for fractured leg denied deduction for cost of swimming pool; no showing that primary purpose was therapeutic rather than convenience and improvement of general health).

[4] See Havey v. CIR, 12 TC 409, 412 (1949) (improved climate did not alleviate heart condition and was no more beneficial to patient than to other vacationers); Altman v. CIR, 53 TC 487 (1969) (victim of emphysema needed light exercise; since benefit could be obtained by walking, cost of getting to and from golf course is not

2. *Meals, lodging, and education.* Meals, lodging, and education do not ordinarily constitute "medical care." Soon after the statutory predecessor of IRC §213 was enacted, however, the IRS ruled that it authorized a deduction for the cost of travel "primarily for and essential to . . . the prevention or alleviation of a physical or mental defect or illness," including the patient's meals and lodging while in a travel status.[5] When this interpretation came to include the entire cost of meals and lodging incurred, for example, by a taxpayer whose physician recommended a winter in Florida to alleviate a chronic illness that would be aggravated by unfavorable climatic conditions at home, Congress intervened by enacting the statutory predecessor of IRC §213(d)(1)(B). This provision, which explicitly defines "medical care" to include transportation essential to medical care, has been construed to forbid the deduction of meals and living expenses incurred by taxpayers while convalescing away from home in a more benign climate.[6]

This change, as indicated by the regulations, does not disqualify the cost of food and lodging while in a hospital, and the regulations go on to provide that the deductibility of living expenses in other institutions is "primarily a question of fact," which depends on the individual's condition and the services received rather than on the nature of the institution.[7] The regulations then provide that if "a principal reason"[8] for the individual's presence in the institution is the availability of medical care, the cost of meals and lodging while receiving medical care is deductible; otherwise, the amount allocable to medical care is deductible, but not the cost of meals and lodging.

The most litigated problem in the deductibility of institutional care concerns the expenses of sending handicapped children to special schools, whose charges ordinarily include the cost of education, meals, and lodging, as well as medical care and remedial services. If the institution's resources for alleviating the handicap or qualifying the individual for future normal education or normal life are a principal reason for attendance (e.g., a school teaching braille or lip reading), the regulations acknowledge that the expenses, including the cost of ordinary education incidental to the school's special services, are deductible in full.[9] Schools without special classses, facilities, or resources ordi-

---

deductible); Ende v. CIR, ¶75,256 P-H Memo TC (1975) (child with curvature of spine; expense of attending ballet school not deductible in absence of evidence she would not have been taking ballet lessons had she not been suffering from ailment).

[5] I.T. 3786, 1946-1 CB 75.

[6] See CIR v. Bilder, 369 US 499 (1962).

[7] Treas. Regs. §1.213-1(e)(1)(v).

[8] See Counts v. CIR, 42 TC 755, 764 (1964) (Acq.) (entire expense of maintaining aged person in nursing home qualified under IRC §213 where *a* principal reason was to receive nursing services, even if not *the* principal reason).

[9] Treas. Regs. §1.213-1(e)(1)(v)(*a*); for rulings recognizing particular types of institutions as qualified, see Rev. Rul. 58-533, 1958-2 CB 108 (psychiatric center); Rev. Rul. 70-285, 1970-1 CB 52 (special classes for mentally retarded children in public

narily fail to meet this test even if their handicapped children receive more attention than they would get in the public school system.[10] Moreover, parents who send their children to a school with a predominantly normal student body rather than to a segregated special school are more likely to be praised for their views than granted a deduction.[11] In time, however, increased public sensitivity to the needs of handicapped persons may induce the IRS or the courts to treat the extra cost of total immersion in a normal environment as an expense of alleviating the handicap.

Noninstitutional food qualifies as medical care under IRC §213, in the view of the IRS, if taken solely for the alleviation or treatment of illness, but not if it supplies the patient's nutritional needs and is a substitute for a normal diet.[12] A 1976 Tax Court decision, however, allowed a deduction for the excess cost incurred by a couple who purchased chemically pure food because of their allergic reaction to pesticides, even though the food supplied (rather than supplemented) their normal nutritional needs.[13] The "excess cost" rationale brings the noninstitutional food issue into line with decisions and rulings allowing taxpayers to deduct part of the cost of salt-free restaurant meals, books and magazines in braille, and specially equipped automobiles—all of which serve normal needs but at an additional cost attributable to physical handicaps or medical needs.[14]

3. *Domestic services.* Nursing services qualify for deduction under IRC §213 even if rendered in the patient's residence, but the cost of domestic or housekeeping services is a nondeductible living expense, even if incurred only because illness makes it impossible for the afflicted individual to perform the services in person.[15] An allocation of expenditures, therefore, is required if the

---

school system of neighboring community); Rev. Rul. 72-226, 1972-1 CB 96 (drug abuse center); Rev. Rul. 73-325, 1973-2 CB 75 (center for alcoholics).

[10] Sims v. CIR, ¶79,499 P-H Memo TC (1979) (emotionally disturbed child; allocation of expenses required); (extensive review of cases); compare Greisdorf v. CIR, 54 TC 1684 (1970) (Acq.) (school to provide supportive environment for children with emotionally caused learning disabilities held to be a "special school").

[11] See Martin v. CIR, ¶75,362 P-H Memo TC (1975), aff'd per curiam, 548 F.2d 633 (6th Cir. 1977), and cases there cited.

[12] Rev. Rul. 55-261, 1955-1 CB 307.

[13] Randolph v. CIR, 67 TC 481 (1976) (distinguishing earlier cases disallowing the cost of special foods where taxpayers did not claim that they were burdened with excess expenses); see also von Kalb v. CIR, ¶78,366 P-H Memo TC (1978) (same as to excess cost of high-protein diet required to counteract abnormally low blood sugar).

[14] Rev. Rul. 70-606, 1970-2 CB 66 (automobile modified to accommodate wheelchair); Rev. Rul. 75-318, 1975-2 CB 88 (Braille books and magazines); but see Cohn v. US, 240 F.Supp. 786 (N.D. Ind. 1965) (rented kitchen facilities in hotel to prepare salt-free diet not deductible).

[15] See Treas. Regs. §1.213-1(e)(1)(ii) (cost of nurse's services and board qualifies); Borgmann v. CIR, 438 F.2d 1211 (9th Cir. 1971) (cooking, cleaning, and other domestic services nondeductible, despite physician's advice to taxpayer with heart condition to hire live-in housekeeper).

same employee serves both functions. A fortiori domestic services are not deductible if the employee is hired not to render services to the patient but to take the patient's place in looking after *other* members of the household.[16] On the other hand, if the victim of illness is so totally disabled as to require constant attention and a choice must be made between institutional care and full-time assistance at home, the home may be assimilated to an "institution," in which event the attendant's expenses can be deducted even though domestic services as well as nursing care are provided.[17]

4. *Nonmedical personnel or treatment.* "Medical care" within the meaning of IRC §213 can be administered by persons who are not licensed to practice medicine or nursing in the conventional sense, such as chiropractors, psychologists, and Christian Science practitioners.[18] But expenditures for a trip to a religious shrine (Lourdes) and for Scientology "processing" have been disallowed by the Tax Court.[19] In both cases the expectation of improvement in a medical condition was somewhat remote, and the patient's purpose in seeking aid was not clearly established. Given the long-established qualification of Christian Science practitioners, however, First Amendment and due process problems would be raised if fees paid to other faith healers were systematically disallowed.

To qualify for deduction, the practitioner's services must be addressed to a physical or mental disability, not to the taxpayer's general well-being. In a post-Freudian world, this is obviously a difficult line to draw. The IRS has somehow persuaded itself, however, that psychiatric treatment for sexual inadequacy and incompatibility (deductible) can be distinguished from marriage counseling ("not for the prevention or alleviation of a physical or mental defect or illness, but rather to help improve the taxpayers' marriage"—not deductible).[20]

5. *Transportation.* Section 213(e)(1)(B) provides that the term "medical care" includes transportation "primarily for and essential to medical care."

---

[16] Van Vechten v. CIR, ¶73,282 P-H Memo TC (1973), aff'd by unpublished order (3d Cir., Jan. 7, 1975); see also Ochs v. CIR, 195 F.2d 692 (2d Cir. 1952) (cost of sending healthy children to boarding school to alleviate pain and suffering of wife, who was prevented by illness from caring for them; held, nondeductible).

[17] See Bye v. CIR, ¶72,057 P-H Memo TC (1972) (housekeeper also provided services to patient's children; allowance for this part of the expenses is problematical).

[18] Rev. Rul. 63-91, 1963-1 CB 54 (chiropractors and psychotherapists; services can qualify even if practitioner is not required to be licensed or, despite such a requirement, practitioner is in fact not licensed); Rev. Rul. 55-261, supra note 12 (Christian Science practitioners); Rev. Rul. 72-593, 1972-2 CB 180 (acupuncture).

[19] Ring v. CIR, 23 TC 950 (1955) (Lourdes); Brown v. CIR, 62 TC 551 (1974), aff'd per curiam, 523 F.2d 365 (8th Cir. 1975) (Scientology); see also Tautolo v. CIR, ¶75,277 P-H Memo TC (1975) (treatment by native Samoan healers; not oriented specifically toward patient's illness and given to all persons; nondeductible).

[20] Rev. Rul. 75-187, 1975-1 CB 92 (sexual inadequacy); Rev. Rul. 75-319, 1975-2 CB 88 (marriage counseling).

Thus, ambulance and taxi charges incurred in getting to and from a hospital or doctor's office are deductible, as are the out-of-pocket expenses of using a private automobile for these purposes.[21] Litigation in this area has primarily involved transportation to distant localities and institutions, the cost of which is deductible if the travel is undertaken to obtain relief from a specific ailment or to recuperate from an operation on a doctor's recommendation, but not if the taxpayer's purpose is to enjoy a benign climate, relax in a resort hotel, or obtain medical care in an institution chosen for its proximity to the patient's relatives.[22]

Transportation expenses incurred by a disabled person in pursuing the activities of ordinary life, such as visiting friends or commuting to work, rather than to obtain medical care are not deductible, though the added cost of a specially equipped vehicle can be deducted, as can the cost of a Seeing Eye dog or wheelchair.[23]

6. *Capital expenditures.* Section 263 ordinarily prohibits the deduction of capital outlays for long-lived property; but it is not applied to equipment and devices purchased for medical reasons, such as eyeglasses, crutches, wheelchairs, artificial teeth, and portable air-conditioners.[24] Thus, the cost of these items can be deducted when paid, even though they will be serviceable for some years and may have a salvage value when no longer needed. The deduction taken on acquisition of the article reduces its basis, however; and if it is

---

[21] Treas. Regs. §1.213-1(e)(1)(iv); Rev. Proc. 80-7, 1980-1 CB 590 (in lieu of proving actual out-of-pocket expenses for medical care, taxpayer may deduct 8 cents per mile for automobile, plus parking fees and tolls; prescribed amount is less than 18.5 cents allowed for business travel because depreciation, insurance, and general maintenance do not qualify for deduction under IRC §213).

[22] Treas. Regs. §1.213-1(e)(1)(iv); Rev. Rul. 58-110, 1958-1 CB 155 (transportation expenses of elderly heart patient in traveling to a specified area on physician's recommendation, together with nurse whose attendance was essential; held, deductible); Winderman v. CIR, 32 TC 1197 (1959) (Acq.) (transportation expenses incurred by Los Angeles resident in visiting New York City physician in whom he had special confidence; held, deductible).

[23] Donnelly v. CIR, 262 F.2d 411 (2d Cir. 1959) (cost of operating specially equipped car, used by polio victim who could not use public transportation to commute to work; held, nondeductible as either business or medical expense); Buck v. CIR, 47 TC 113 (1966) (epileptic taxpayer advised by physician to remain active in business but not to drive car; held, even if work was therapy, no deduction for chauffeur's salary in absence of showing that public transportation was not available); Rev. Rul. 70-606, supra note 14 (specially equipped car).

[24] Treas. Regs. §1.213-1(e)(1)(iii). For IRC §263, see supra ¶8.4. See also Rev. Rul. 75-302, 1975-2 CB 86, and Rev. Rul. 75-303, 1975-2 CB 87, allowing a lump-sum payment for lifetime medical care to be deducted in the year paid; compare Rev. Rul. 58-303, 1958-1 CB 61 (similar payment allocated year by year in determining payor's right to claim patient as a dependent).

ultimately sold for more than its adjusted basis, the taxpayer will realize gain at that time.[25]

If a medically required item is permanently attached to the taxpayer's residence or other property and can serve nonmedical purposes (e.g., an elevator or ramp), the restriction of IRC §263 on the deduction of "permanent improvements or betterments" is applied to the extent of the increase (if any) in the property's value, and only the excess of cost over the increase in value is deductible.[26]

3. Medicine and Drugs. For many years, expenditures for medicine and drugs were taken into account only if and to the extent that they exceeded one percent of the taxpayer's adjusted gross income. Commencing in 1984, the one percent floor will no longer be imposed; but, while the cost of insulin will continue to qualify as a deductible medical expense, other medicine and drugs will qualify only if prescribed.

4. Medical Insurance. Section 213(d)(1)(C), enacted in 1965, provides that the term "medical care" includes "insurance . . . covering medical care"; and this phrase includes premiums paid for insurance to cover medical care, prescription drugs, ambulance hire, or any other items that independently qualify as "medical care" within the meaning of IRC §§213(d)(1)(A) and 213(d)(1)(B). If a policy provides benefits for items other than medical care (e.g., lost income; loss of life, limb, or sight; waiver of premiums; etc.), the premiums do not qualify for deduction unless the portion allocable to medical care is separately stated and is reasonable in amount relative to the total charges. To encourage the use of insurance to protect against medical expenses in post-retirement years, IRC §213(d)(5) treats premiums paid by a taxpayer under sixty-five years of age as currently deductible even if the policy provides for benefits after sixty-five, provided certain conditions relating to level payments are met.

Before 1983, one-half of the amount paid for medical insurance was deductible (up to $150 per year) without regard to the AGI floor, and the

---

[25] See Rev. Rul. 78-221, 1978-1 CB 75.

[26] Treas. Regs. §1.213-1(e)(1)(iii); see also Rev. Rul. 70-395, 1970-2 CB 65 (cost of ground floor bath and shower installed in rented house); but see Wallace v. US, 439 F.2d 757 (8th Cir.), cert. denied, 404 US 831 (1971) (central air-conditioning system; no evidence of excess cost); Daniels v. CIR, 41 TC 324 (1963) (air raid shelter; risk of disease from radiation in nuclear attack too remote); Ferris v. CIR, 582 F.2d 1112 (7th Cir. 1978) (remand to determine difference between minimum reasonable cost of adequate swimming pool, recommended by physician for twice-daily use, and cost of pool with architectural features befitting taxpayer's sumptuous residence); Rev. Rul. 79-66, 1979-1 CB 114 (application of regulations to cost of removing lead-based paint from taxpayer's residence to protect child with lead poisoning).

balance was taken into account subject to the percentage limit; but this incentive was eliminated in 1982. For 1983 and later years, therefore, the cost of medical insurance will be included with doctors' bills and other expenses in determining whether the taxpayer's expenses exceed the 5 percent floor.

¶20.2 ANCILLARY PROBLEMS

1. Medical Care of Dependents. Section 213(a) permits the taxpayer to deduct expenses for medical care of dependents, as well as those incurred for the taxpayer and his or her spouse. To be a "dependent" of the taxpayer, an individual must (a) be related by blood, marriage, or adoption within the degrees specified by IRC §§152(a)(1)-152(a)(8) or meet the special test of IRC §152(a)(9) for members of the taxpayer's household and (b) receive more than one-half of his or her support from the taxpayer.[27] It is not necessary, however, to meet the additional gross income requirement imposed by IRC §151, denying dependency exemptions for dependents (except certain children) with gross income of more than $1,000.[28]

Following a divorce or legal separation, amounts for an ex-spouse's medical care do not qualify for deduction under IRC §213(a) since they are not paid for the taxpayer's "spouse," [29] but they may qualify as deductible alimony payments under principles examined elsewhere in this work.[30] Payments to the ex-spouse for medical care of the children can also qualify as deductible alimony payments. If payments are earmarked for a child, however, they cannot be deducted as alimony; and they are deductible as medical expenses only if the child is a dependent of the payor rather than of the payor's ex-spouse.[31]

Medical expenses for care of a dependent of the taxpayer may qualify as employment-related expenses under IRC §44A, relating to expenses for the care of dependents to enable the taxpayers to be gainfully employed, as well as under IRC §213. In this situation (e.g., wages paid to a nurse to care for

[27] For relaxation of the "support" rule by IRC §§152(c) and 152(e), relating to multiple support agreements and dependency exemption designations by separated or divorced parents, see supra ¶14.2.

[28] See supra ¶14.2.

[29] See Treas. Regs. §1.213-1(e)(3) (payments qualify if requisite status exists either when services were rendered or when expenses were paid, but status terminates on divorce or separation under decree of separate maintenance).

[30] Infra ¶32.1.

[31] See Rev. Rul. 76-344, 1976-2 CB 82 (children's medical expenses deductible by taxpayer when paid by taxpayer's former spouse with funds supplied by taxpayer, where former spouse had custody of children but taxpayer was entitled under IRC §151 to claim them as dependents).

an employed taxpayer's sick child during working hours), IRC §213(f) provides that expenses allowed under IRC §44A shall not be treated as paid for medical care. Any excess over the amount qualifying under IRC §44A can be used in computing the medical deduction under IRC §213, subject to the 5 percent nondeductible floor.

2. Timing Problems. Because it refers to "expenses paid during the taxable year," IRC §213 permits expenses to be deducted only in the year of payment, no matter when the injury or illness occurred and whether the taxpayer uses the cash or accrual method of accounting.[32] Taxpayers whose expenses would fall below the 5 percent floor for two or more consecutive years if paid when incurred may be able to create a deduction by postponing payment and concentrating all payments into a single year.

Prepayments are an alternative, but more precarious, way to cram medical payments into a single taxable year. If payment in advance of medical services is a prerequisite to their rendition (e.g., a lump sum paid for admission to a retirement home providing lifetime medical care), the payment defrays an "expense" within the meaning of IRC §213(a) and hence qualifies for deduction.[33] On the other hand, if the advance payment is no more than a refundable deposit, it cannot be deducted until the taxpayer incurs an "expense" and the deposit is applied against actual medical charges.[34]

For a decedent's estate, the requirement of payment is lifted by IRC §213(d), treating amounts paid by the estate within one year after death as though paid when the expense was incurred, thus permitting the expenses to be deducted on the decedent's income tax return for the year of death or the prior year, provided the estate waives the right to deduct the expenses as claims against the estate under IRC §2053.[35]

---

[32] Treas. Regs. §1.213-1(a)(1); see also Rev. Rul. 78-39, 1978-1 CB 73 (medical expense is paid when charged to bank credit card, regardless of when taxpayer pays bank); Rev. Rul. 78-173, 1978-1 CB 73 (taxpayer's medical expense paid by parent pursuant to prior agreement under which taxpayer issued negotiable promissory note to parent; deductible in year of parent's payment to doctor).

[33] Rev. Rul. 76-481, 1976-2 CB 82 (advance fee for lifetime care in retirement home, refundable on termination of membership but subject to a penalty; held, deductible when paid; any refund taxable when received); Rev. Rul. 75-302, supra note 24 (same).

[34] Rose v. CIR, 52 TC 521, 532 (1969), aff'd per curiam, 435 F.2d 149 (5th Cir. 1970), relying on Bassett v. CIR, 26 TC 619 (1956). The *Bassett* case involved a compulsory advance payment and is pro tanto weakened by the rulings cited supra note 32.

[35] See Treas. Regs. §1.213-1(d); Rev. Rul. 77-357, 1977-2 CB 328 (estate tax deduction denied for portion of medical expenses below percentage floor).

3. Married Couples. In unusual circumstances, married couples may find it advantageous to file separate rather than joint returns, since the one percent floor on drugs and medicines and the 5 percent AGI floor will then be based on the AGI of the spouse who pays the medical expenses, and the resulting increase in their medical expense deductions may outweigh the increased rates to which married couples are subject when they file separate returns.[36] Since IRC §213(a) allows taxpayers to deduct expenses for the medical care of their spouses, one spouse can pay their combined medical expenses if they so choose. To employ this gambit, however, the couple must maintain separate records and, probably, separate bank accounts,[37] and the bother may outweigh the tax advantage.

4. Reimbursed Expenses. Medical expenses cannot be deducted if compensated for by insurance or otherwise, but since the reimbursement is excluded from the taxpayer's gross income by IRC §104(a) or §105(b) when received,[38] the net effect is that the taxpayer is not taxed on amounts used to pay for qualified medical expenses, whether they are paid from personal resources or by an insurer, tort-feasor, or employer.[39] Damages compensating the taxpayer for pain and suffering, loss of earnings, or disfigurement, however, do not constitute compensation for medical expenses and hence do not affect the amount to be deducted under IRC §213.[40] When damages are collected from a tort-feasor by suit or settlement, it is necessary to allocate the recovery between medical expenses, pain and suffering, and other items.[41]

If the taxpayer's right to be compensated for medical expenses is contested or otherwise debatable when they are paid, they can be deducted; but if and

[36] See infra ¶39.3 (separate returns filed by married persons).

[37] Rev. Rul. 59-66, 1959-1 CB 60 (separate earnings of husband and wife in non-community-property state deposited in joint account; held, absent proof to the contrary, expenses are paid equally by each spouse in determining deductions on separate returns); Rev. Rul. 55-479, 1955-2 CB 57 (medical expenses paid with community funds by couple in community-property state; held, attributable one-half to each spouse when separate returns are filed).

[38] For IRC §§104(a) and 105(b), see supra ¶¶5.1 and 5.2, respectively.

[39] See also Rev. Rul. 76-144, 1976-1 CB 17 (grant pursuant to government disaster relief program treated as compensation for taxpayer's medical expenses); Litchfield v. CIR, 330 F.2d 509 (1st Cir. 1964) (in dictum, court expressed view that gift to person paying medical expenses is not "compensation" under IRC §213).

[40] IRC §§104(a), 105(f); Treas. Regs. §1.213-1(a)(3)(ii).

[41] See Rev. Rul. 75-230, 1975-1 CB 93 (recovery allocable first to medical expenses where complaint did not state amount claimed for each item and general release was executed, but allocation by parties will be presumed correct unless unreasonable); Morgan v. CIR, 55 TC 376 (1970) (explicit allocation in consent judgment to medical expenses); Rev. Rul. 79-427, 1979-2 CB 120 (medical expenses deductible only to extent they exceed portion of damages awarded by jury attributable to future medical expenses, determined by reference to taxpayer's claims in pleadings and appellate brief).

when the taxpayer is reimbursed, the receipts must be included in gross income to the extent attributable to the prior deductions.[42] In making this computation, the regulations allocate the compensatory receipts first to the amount allowed as a deduction rather than to the amount that was nondeductible because of the 5 percent floor.[43]

5. Medical Care as a Business Expense. Medical expenses attributable to occupational diseases or on-the-job accidents seem, at first blush, to qualify for deduction under IRC §162 as ordinary and necessary expenses incurred in the taxpayer's trade or business; but there are astonishingly few cases and rulings in this area.[44] This dearth no doubt reflects the fact that medical expenses incurred by employees are normally defrayed or reimbursed by the employer, but this is not a universal practice; and thousands of uninsured self-employed taxpayers must bear their own job-related medical expenses. If deductible under IRC §162, these expenses could be deducted in addition to the zero bracket amount by self-employed taxpayers who do not itemize their personal deductions, would avoid the 5 percent floor imposed by IRC §213 on the deduction of medical expenses, and would be taken into account in computing net operating loss carryovers from one taxable year to another.

The strangest case for allowing medical expenses to be deducted under IRC §162 arises in a few peripheral situations, such as the expenses of airline pilots who are required by their jobs to undergo more frequent medical examinations than ordinary citizens, blind persons who hire special readers to assist them in performing business duties, and invalids who require attendants only while on business trips.[45] These expenses are attributable to the taxpayer's job, and, unlike most medical expenditures, they do not improve the quality of the

---

[42] Treas. Regs. §1.213-1(g). For similar problems in dealing with debatable claims for compensation, see supra ¶¶18.4 (re casualty loss deduction), 12.4 (re IRC §165(a) losses).

[43] Treas. Regs. §1.213-1(g).

[44] See Denny v. CIR, 33 BTA 738 (1935) (Nonacq.) (replacement of actor's teeth, knocked out in making movie; deductible); Rev. Rul. 71-45, 1971-1 CB 51 (professional singer; treatment by throat specialist nondeductible even if amount expended is increased by occupation).

[45] Rev. Rul. 58-382, 1958-2 CB 59 (periodic medical examinations required to hold pilot's certificate deductible under IRC §162, but any additional expenses to enable taxpayer to maintain requisite physical fitness deductible only under IRC §213); Rev. Rul. 75-316, 1975-2 CB 54 (readers employed by blind employees); Rev. Rul. 75-317, 1975-2 CB 57 (attendant required by invalid on business trips but not while at home—expenses deductible under IRC §162); see also Greenberg v. CIR, 367 F.2d 663 (1st Cir. 1966) (cost of psychoanalytic training that included personal analysis deductible under IRC §162); but see Rev. Rul. 78-128, 1978-1 CB 39 (health spa expenses not deductible by law-enforcement officer required as condition of employment to be in excellent physical condition).

taxpayer's personal life after working hours. This rationale has not been applied to commuting expenses even when increased by a taxpayer's physical disability, however, but there are a few cases holding commuting expenses deductible as medical expenses because the work was prescribed by a physician as occupational therapy.[46]

SELECTED BIBLIOGRAPHY

Affonso, Medical Expense Deductions Under Section 213 of the Internal Revenue Code of 1954: The Definition of "Medical Care," 7 Golden Gate U.L. Rev. 535 (1977).

Feld, Abortion to Aging: Problems of Definition in the Medical Expense Tax Deduction, 58 B.U.L. Rev. 165 (1978).

Newman, The Medical Expense Deduction: A Preliminary Postmortem, 53 So. Calif. L. Rev. 787 (1980).

[46] Goldaper v. CIR, ¶77,343 P-H Memo TC (1977) (taxpayer with impaired eyesight hired driver to commute to work; expenses are nondeductible commuting expenses, not deductible medical expenses); Weinzimer v. CIR, ¶58,137 P-H Memo TC (1958) (contra where work was a form of occupational therapy).

CHAPTER 21

Personal Credits

¶21.1 CARE OF EMPLOYED TAXPAYER'S SPOUSE, DEPENDENTS, AND HOUSEHOLD

1. Introductory. In *Smith v. CIR,* the Tax Court held that a two-job married couple could not deduct, as a business expense under IRC §162, the cost of nursemaids employed to care for their young child during working hours.[1] Implying that the expenses bore only an "indirect and tenuous" relationship to the couple's employment, the court expressed fear that a deduction would take the IRS and the courts down a slippery slope, ending in tax deductions for the employed taxpayer's food, shelter, and clothing.

Because the taxpayers in *Smith* would not have been taxed on the value of their own household services if one or both of them had stayed at home to care for the child,[2] the denial of a deduction discriminates against working taxpayers who must pay for comparable services. Thus, if a taxpayer can earn $10,000 by working in an office or factory but must pay $4,000 a year for

[1] Smith v. CIR, 40 BTA 1038 (1939), aff'd per curiam, 113 F.2d 114 (2d Cir. 1940).

[2] For the exclusion of imputed income, see supra ¶1.6.

housekeeping or day care services, the net economic income from employment is only $6,000; but under *Smith* the taxable income is $10,000.

In 1954, Congress intervened by enacting a relief provision, permitting working women and widowers to deduct, up to a total of $600 per year, expenses incurred for the care of children under the age of 12 and other dependents who were incapable of caring for themselves. This modest deduction was successively liberalized, and in 1976 it was converted into a credit, IRC §44A. If, however, expenses for the care of children and other dependents do not satisfy the statutory standards of IRC §44A or exceed its dollar limits, they continue to be nondeductible under the doctrine of the *Smith* case.

2. Scope of the Credit. Section 44A creates a credit equal to 20 to 30 percent (depending on the taxpayer's adjusted gross income) of the taxpayer's "employment-related expenses" for household services and the care of "qualifying individuals," up to $2,400 of expenses if the taxpayer's household includes only one qualifying individual or $4,800 if it includes two or more qualifying individuals. The credit can be used only to offset the taxpayer's tax liability; if it exceeds the liability, the excess is not refunded, nor can it be carried over for use in another year. The salient requirements imposed by IRC §44A are:

1. *Status of taxpayer.* To claim a credit under IRC §44A, the taxpayer must "maintain a household" that includes one or more "qualifying individuals" (as defined). Section 44A(f)(1) provides that an individual "maintains a household" only if he or she (including the taxpayer's spouse in the case of a married couple) furnishes over half of the cost of maintaining the household during the relevant period.

2. *Qualifying individuals.* The household maintained by the taxpayer must include as a member at least one "qualifying individual," defined by IRC §44A(c)(1) to mean (a) a dependent of the taxpayer under the age of 15 for whom the taxpayer is entitled to a dependency exemption under IRC §151(e); (b) a dependent who is physically or mentally incapable of caring for himself, even if a dependency exemption is not allowed for the individual; or (c) the taxpayer's spouse, if physically or mentally incapable of caring for himself. Thus, the taxpayers who have only themselves to look after are not entitled to a credit, even though they may have expenses (e.g., for domestic servants, restaurant meals, etc.) that would not be incurred if they could stay at home and live on income from investments.

3. *Employment-related expenses.* The credit is based on the taxpayer's "employment-related expenses," defined by IRC §44A(c)(2) to mean expenses incurred (1) to enable the taxpayer to be gainfully employed and (2) for household services or for the care of a qualifying individual.[3] Thus, expenses

[3] See Warner v. CIR, 69 TC 995 (1978) (expenses of transporting child to day care

can qualify for the credit even though incurred for such domestic services as cleaning, preparing meals, etc., rather than actual care of a child or incapacitated person, *provided* the household includes a qualifying individual. Expenses for services outside the taxpayer's household, however, qualify only if incurred for services in a "dependent care center," as defined by IRC §44A(c)(2)(C).

4. *Earned income limit.* By requiring the expenses to be incurred to enable the taxpayer to be gainfully employed, IRC §44A(c)(2) suggests that it may be necessary to psychoanalyze the taxpayer to determine whether he or she hired a baby-sitter in order to work or worked in order to hire a baby-sitter. This potentially abrasive problem is explicitly addressed by IRC §44A(e), imposing an earned-income limit on the amount of the employment-related expenses that can be taken into account. For an unmarried taxpayer, the expenses cannot exceed his or her earned income; for a married couple, the limit is the lesser of their separate earned incomes.

To permit married couples to claim the credit if one spouse is a full-time student or is incapacitated, IRC §44A(e)(2) treats the spouse as if he or she were gainfully employed for at least $166 or $333 per month, depending on whether the household includes one, or more than one, qualifying individual.

5. *Payments to related individuals.* The pre-1976 version of IRC §44A precluded deductions for payments to members of the taxpayer's family; thus, neighbors could deduct amounts paid to each other's children for baby-sitting, but not amounts paid to their own children. In 1976, Congress decided to soften this prohibition because "relatives generally provide superior attention";[4] but it feared that lifting the restriction completely would tempt taxpayers to claim credits for amounts that were in fact gifts to other members of the same household. Section 44A(f)(6) reflects these competing concerns by disqualifying payments to related persons only if the payee is either (a) a person for whom the taxpayer or the taxpayer's spouse is entitled to a dependency exemption under IRC §151(e) or (b) a child of the taxpayer under the age of 19 at the end of the taxable year.

6. *Divorced or separated parents.* If over half of the support of a child who is incapacitated or under the age of 15 is provided by parents who are divorced or separated under a judicial decree or written separation agreement and who have custody of the child for more than one-half of the calendar year, the parent having the longer period of custody during the calendar year is entitled by IRC §44A(f)(5) to treat the child as a "qualifying individual." This rule permits a working custodial parent to claim a credit for employment-

---

center not incurred for "care" of child); Treas. Regs. §§1.44A-1(c)(2) (qualifying household services), 1.44A-1(c)(3) (qualifying care of children and others), 1.44A-1(c)(4) (services outside household), 1.44A-1(c)(5) (allocation of expenses).

[4] S. Rep. No. 94-938, reprinted in 1976-3 CB (Vol. 3) 171; see also Bryant v. CIR, 72 TC 757 (1979) (disqualification of payments to relatives held constitutional).

related expenses even if the other parent is entitled to the dependency exemption for the child.

7. *Computation of credit.* In computing the credit, the taxpayer's employment-related expenses for the taxable year are taken into account up to a limit of $2,400 (one qualifying individual) or $4,800 (two or more qualifying individuals). The credit is a percentage of these expenses that ranges on a sliding scale from 30 percent (adjusted gross income of $10,000 or less) to 20 percent (adjusted gross income of $28,000 or more). Thus, the credit cannot exceed $720 (30% of $2,400) or $1,440 (30% of $4,800), regardless of the amount of expenses actually incurred or the number of qualifying individuals.

8. *Joint returns.* Under IRC §44A(f)(2), married couples are entitled to the credit only if they file joint returns. This provision prevents couples with three or four qualifying individuals from piercing the dollar limits by filing separate returns and claiming aggregate employment-related expenses of $7,200 or $9,600. The joint-return requirement is not imposed, however, on certain married individuals who live apart and file separate returns (e.g., deserted spouses); although they are entitled to file a joint return, for practical purposes they are separate economic units. If they file separate returns, they are also viewed as unmarried for such other purposes as application of the earned-income limit of IRC §44A(e).

¶21.2 CREDIT FOR THE ELDERLY

Low-income taxpayers attaining age 65 before the end of the taxable year are granted a credit of 15 percent of their "section 37 amount," up to specified amounts depending on the type of return filed. The current version of IRC §37 is a much-modified descendant of a credit for retirement income, enacted in 1954 to equalize the tax burden on persons receiving federal social security benefits, which have always been tax-exempt, and those who provided for their own retirement with pensions, annuities, or investments, producing taxable income.

The 15 percent credit now allowed by IRC §37 is based on an "initial amount" of $2,500 (single individuals and joint returns with eligible spouse), $3,750 (joint returns if both spouses are eligible), or $1,875 (married individuals filing separate returns). Married couples must file a joint return to qualify unless they live apart throughout the taxable year. The applicable initial amount is reduced by social security, railroad retirement, and other tax-exempt pensions and annuities—a principle reflecting the equalization objective of the 1954 retirement income credit. Unlike 1954-1976 law, however, current law does not restrict the credit to taxpayers receiving passive "retirement income" but instead allows a credit for any type of income (except tax-exempt pensions), including compensation for personal services.

To confine the credit to low-income taxpayers, IRC §37(c)(1) reduces the taxpayer's "section 37 amount" (i.e., the applicable initial amount reduced by exempt benefits) by one dollar for every two dollars of adjusted gross income in excess of $7,500 (single persons), $10,000 (joint returns), or $5,000 (separate return filed by married individual). By virtue of this phaseout, no credit can be claimed if the taxpayer's AGI exceeds $12,500, $17,500, or $8,750, respectively, and a complete phaseout occurs at even lower levels if the taxpayer's initial amount is reduced by any exempt benefits.

¶21.3 EARNED INCOME CREDIT

To encourage low-income taxpayers with children to seek gainful employment, IRC §43 allows a credit of 10 percent of the first $5,000 of an eligible individual's earned income for the taxable year, subject to a phaseout if adjusted gross income exceeds $6,000. By increasing after-tax earnings, the credit helps to offset the social security taxes on wages. In keeping with its function as an incentive, the credit is refundable to the extent that it exceeds the individual's tax liability, and taxpayers can convert it in advance into increased wages by filing an earned income eligibility certificate with the employer.

To qualify for the credit, the taxpayer must have a child with the same place of abode in the United States as the taxpayer and in addition must be (a) married, (b) a surviving spouse within the meaning of IRC §2(a), or (c) a head of household within the meaning of IRC §2(b). If the taxpayer is married or a surviving spouse, the child must qualify for a dependency exemption; in the case of heads of households, a dependency exemption is essential only if the child is married. The credit is 10 percent of the first $5,000 of the taxpayer's "earned income"—defined by IRC §43(b)(2) as wages, salaries, tips, other employee compensation, and net earnings from self-employment.

¶21.4 POLITICAL CONTRIBUTIONS

Section 41 allows individual taxpayers to claim a credit—not in excess of $50 or, if a joint return is filed, $100—for one-half of their political contributions and newsletter fund contributions paid during the taxable year. The term "political contribution" is defined in detail by IRC §41(c) to include gifts and contributions of money to candidates for nomination or election to any public office; campaign committees; and national, state, and local committees of national political parties. Contributions of property or services do not qualify. "Newsletter fund contributions" are contributions or gifts of money to a fund established and maintained by an incumbent or a candidate for use in the preparation and circulation of a newsletter.

The credit is independent of IRC §6096, allowing taxpayers, by check-off on their tax returns, to allocate $1 ($2 on joint returns) of their taxes to the Presidential Election Campaign Fund, used to provide public financing for presidential political campaigns under IRC §§9001-9013.

¶21.5 RESIDENTIAL ENERGY CREDIT

To encourage homeowners and tenants to conserve energy by insulating their residences and installing solar devices and other sources of renewable energy, IRC §44C provides a credit for specified expenditures serving these objectives. The credit is allowed for two types of expenditures: (1) qualified energy conservation expenditures—for insulation and other energy-conserving components such as storm windows, thermostats, and improved furnace ignition systems—for which the credit is 15 percent of the first $2,000 of qualifying expenditures; and (2) qualified renewable-energy-source expenditures—for such heating and cooling devices as solar, geothermal, and wind systems—for which the credit is 40 percent of the first $10,000 of qualifying expenditures.

Expenditures of both types qualify only if the affected dwelling is located in the United States and is the taxpayer's principal residence; and prior expenditures on the same residence for which the taxpayer was allowed a credit reduce the dollar amount qualifying for the credit in later years. An additional condition, applicable only to conservation expenditures, is that construction of the dwelling must have been substantially completed before April 20, 1977. Without this limitation, IRC §44C would provide an incentive for the construction of poorly insulated houses, since the purchaser could then qualify for a subsidy by rectifying the deficiency.

¶21.6 FOREIGN TAX CREDIT

Section 33 allows taxpayers paying foreign income taxes to credit them against their U.S. income tax liability, subject to the rules of IRC §§901–908, instead of deducting them under IRC §164. Although the foreign tax credit is claimed primarily by large business corporations engaged in overseas operations, it is allowed to individuals as well as corporations; and can be classified as a "personal" credit because it is not restricted to foreign taxes imposed on business or profit-oriented activities.

SELECTED BIBLIOGRAPHY

Blumberg, Sexism in the Code: A Comparative Study of Income Taxation of Working Wives and Mothers, 21 Buffalo L. Rev. 49 (1971).

PERSONAL CREDITS

Feld, Another Word on Child Care, 28 Tax L. Rev. 546 (1973).

Manvel, The Residential Energy Tax Credit: Two Years' Experience, Tax Notes, March 29, 1982, at 854.

Parr, Section 504 of the Tax Reform Act of 1976: The New Credit for Child Care Expenses, 30 Tax Lawyer 456 (1977).

Schaffer & Berman, Two Cheers for the Child Care Deduction, 28 Tax L. Rev. 535 (1973).

Schaffer & Berman, The Child Care Deduction and the Progressivity of the Income Tax: A Reply to Professor Feld, 28 Tax L. Rev. 549 (1973).

CHAPTER 22

Realization of Gains and Losses—Taxable Events

¶22.1 "REALIZATION" AND "RECOGNITION" OF GAINS AND LOSSES

The most popular economic definition of income embodies an accretion principle, under which the taxpayer's unrealized gains and losses on property would be taken into account by periodic net worth computations,[1] but the Internal Revenue Code takes gains and losses into account only when they are "realized" by a sale, exchange, or other disposition of property. This well-entrenched principle emerges from the Code largely by indirection, however, since IRC §61(a)(3), providing that gross income includes "gains derived from dealings in property," neither defines the term "dealings" nor expressly announces that gains and losses are to be disregarded until the taxpayer engages in an act constituting "dealing" with the property.

---

[1] See Simons, Personal Income Taxation 50, 61–62, 206 (U. of Chicago Press, 1938).

Moreover, IRC §61(a)(3) does not specify how gains and losses from "dealings in property" are to be computed. That function is discharged by IRC §1001(a), which provides:

> The gain from the sale or other disposition of property shall be the excess of the amount realized therefrom over the adjusted basis provided in section 1011 for determining gain, and the loss shall be the excess of the adjusted basis provided in such section for determining loss over the amount realized.

The terms "amount realized" and "adjusted basis" are defined by IRC §§1001(b) and 1011, respectively, discussed in later chapters.[2] Ordinarily the same adjusted basis is used in computing both gain and loss; but in a few special situations there is a difference (e.g., IRC §1015(a), relating to the basis of property acquired by gift).

Section 1001(a) provides for the computation of realized losses as well as realized gains. If property with an adjusted basis of $1,000 is sold for $800, for example, the realized loss under IRC §1001(a) is $200. Having ascertained that a loss was realized on the sale, the taxpayer must determine whether the loss is deductible, a subject that is examined elsewhere in this work.[3] If the realized loss is deductible, the taxpayer must then determine whether the deduction is applied against ordinary income or constitutes a capital loss.

The balance of this section is concerned with three principal subjects: (1) whether particular transactions constitute "a sale or other disposition of property" so that gain or loss is "realized," (2) computation of the taxpayer's gain or loss, which in turn requires a determination of the property's unadjusted or original basis, its adjusted basis, and the "amount realized," and (3) whether the realized gain or loss is recognized in whole, in part, or not at all.

¶22.2 THE CONCEPT OF A "TAXABLE EVENT"

Although IRC §1001(a) does not say so explicitly, its reference to gain or loss "from the sale or other disposition of property" implies that increases and decreases in the value of property are not taken into account for tax purposes when they accrue, but only when they are realized by a taxable event; and this implication is buttressed by the reference in IRC §61(a)(3) to gains "derived from dealings in property." In the overwhelming bulk of transactions by investors, manufacturers, and merchants, no serious issue of interpretation arises under IRC §1001(a), because it is either perfectly clear that the property has been sold (so that the taxpayer's gain or loss has been realized) or equally

[2] Infra ¶¶23.12 (amount realized), 23.8 (adjusted basis).

[3] See supra ¶12.1.

clear that the taxpayer still owns the property and has only leased or licensed it, with the result that any increase or decrease in its value has not yet been realized. Occasionally, however, it is more difficult to determine whether the transaction is a "sale or other disposition" within the meaning of IRC §1001(a) or falls short of that standard. The principal categories of ambiguous transactions, which are discussed in more detail hereafter, are: (1) gratuitous transfers vs. satisfaction of claim; (2) sales vs. divisions of property; (3) pledges vs. sale-leasebacks; (4) sales vs. leases; (5) sales vs. changes in or exercises of contract rights; and (6) involuntary transactions.

As even this brief list of transactions indicates, the reference in IRC §1001(a) to "the sale or other disposition of property" is both over-inclusive and under-inclusive. It is over-inclusive in that a gift or bequest is a "disposition" of property in ordinary parlance and for some nontax legal purposes. The phrase "sale or other disposition," however, is primarily concerned with transactions producing a quid pro quo for the taxpayer. Since this is not a characteristic of gifts and bequests, they fall outside the jurisdiction of IRC §1001(a).

But the statutory phrase "sale or other disposition" is also under-inclusive in that it seems to omit some transactions that, under the cases and rulings, constitute taxable events. It strains language to say that there has been a "disposition" of property, for example, when the proceeds of insurance are collected for property destroyed by fire or when property becomes worthless and is retained rather than discarded; yet these events can produce taxable gain or deductible loss. This can be illustrated by assuming that the taxpayer owns business equipment with an adjusted basis of $10,000 that is damaged by casualty on two occasions, resulting in each instance in the receipt of $6,000 from the tort-feasor or insurer. The taxpayer would apply the first $6,000 against the property's basis, reducing it to $4,000, so that no gain would be realized at that time. On receiving the second recovery of $6,000, however, the taxpayer would reduce the property's basis from $4,000 to zero, and the remaining $2,000 would constitute realized gain under the regulations.[4]

¶22.3 GIFTS AND BEQUESTS

If asked whether the phrase "sale or other disposition" includes a gift or bequest of property, a lexicographer would almost certainly say that it does; a gift is obviously a "disposition" of property in the laymen's sense, and a bequest is a way of getting rid of property that cannot be taken to the Great Beyond. Under IRC §1001(a), however, gain or loss on a sale or other disposition of property is computed by subtracting its adjusted basis from the

[4] Treas. Regs. §1.1001-1(c).

"amount realized," and our lexicographer would probably concede that transferors do not ordinarily "realize" anything in monetary terms on making gratuitous transfers.

On the other hand, taxpayers making gifts and bequests *could* be viewed as receiving noneconomic satisfactions equal to the value of the transferred property. Indeed, this rationale is the foundation of many cases in the assignment-of-income area, which received its classic expression in Mr. Justice Stone's opinion in *Helvering v. Horst,* holding that the donor of negotiable interest coupons (detached from bonds owned by him) realized income when the donee collected the interest at maturity later in the year.[5]

Rather than analogize gifts and bequests to sales, however, Congress has consistently treated them as nontaxable events. The legislative intent is not explicitly set out in the Code, but it is nevertheless unmistakable. So far as gifts are concerned, the decision in 1921 to require donees to carry over the donor's basis, now embodied in IRC §1015(a), was premised on the assumption that a gift is not a taxable event from the donor's point of view. By contrast, property transferred at death receives a new basis equal to its date-of-death value, but the failure to tax the appreciation between the date of the decedent's acquisition of the property and the date of death has elicited frequent complaints by tax commentators.

Thus, gifts and bequests fail to qualify as taxable events less because of the words used in IRC §1001(a) than because of more fundamental and pervasive legislative decisions shaping the basic structural aspects of the Internal Revenue Code. The IRS has nibbled away at the edges of these principles, but it has had no success in taxing donors of appreciated property except in a few special situations. These peripheral areas in which the IRS has been successful in taxing transferors on gifts and bequests of appreciated property are (a) cases like *Horst,* applying assignment-of-income principles, usually because the transferor made a gift of income or of "pure appreciation" while retaining the underlying income-producing property;[6] (b) transfers of appreciated property after the donor has arranged a sale, if the donee is required or expected to go through with the sale;[7] (c) gifts of property subject to a debt that is assumed or paid by the donee, especially if the debt was incurred in contemplation of the gift;[8] and (d) a few situations covered by specialized statutory provisions.[9]

---

[5] Helvering v. Horst, 311 US 122 (1940), discussed infra ¶30.3.

[6] Infra ¶30.3.

[7] Infra ¶30.3.

[8] Infra ¶23.16.

[9] See IRC §453B(a) (gain on gift of installment obligation); IRC §691(a)(2) and Treas. Regs. §1.691(a)-4(a) (gifts of income in respect of a decedent); IRC §644 (grantor of trust taxed on gain realized by trust on sale of certain appreciated assets).

¶22.4 SATISFACTION OF CLAIMS

1. Introductory. When property is transferred in satisfaction of a debt, the transaction is functionally equivalent to a sale of property for cash, coupled with a use of the proceeds to pay the debt. For this reason, the shortcut device of transferring the property directly to the creditor ordinarily constitutes a "sale or other disposition" of the property within the meaning of IRC §1001(a), on which gain or loss is realized. Thus, a taxpayer who uses stock that cost $750 to pay a shopkeeper's bill of $1,000 must include the difference of $250 in gross income, just as though the stock had been sold for $1,000 and the proceeds used to pay the bill. This principle is simple enough; but in application it encounters a number of complications, of which the most important, discussed below, are the use of property to make a gift or pay a legacy and the effect of disputes regarding the amount or validity of the claim that is settled by the transfer.

2. Specific vs. Pecuniary Legacies. As far back as 1920, the IRS ruled that a decedent's estate did not realize gain on transferring property to the residuary legatees under the decedent's will, even though the property had increased in value between the date of death and the distribution date.[10] The same principle is applicable to a transfer in satisfaction of a legacy of specific property: although the legatee has a "claim" against the estate, the claim is not a right to a specified dollar amount but a right to receive the property itself, regardless of its value at the time of distribution.[11] Because the estate is not obligated to pay a predetermined amount but only to distribute the property, neither the estate nor the other beneficiaries are financially affected by fluctuations in the value of the property between the decedent's death and the date of distribution. The exemption of the estate from income tax when the property is distributed, however, does not result in permanent escape: since the legatee's basis for the property is the same as the estate's basis, any appreciation in the property's value after the decedent's death, if realized on a sale by the legatee, will be subsequently reflected on the legatee's tax return.

Unlike legacies of specific property, pecuniary bequests are ordinarily paid in money and hence entail neither gain nor loss to the estate or beneficiaries. But if the executor uses property rather than cash to satisfy a pecuniary bequest, the economic results are different from those produced by transfers of property to satisfy specific legacies, since changes in the value of the estate's property after the decedent's death are immaterial to the pecuniary legatee but

---

[10] O.D. 667, 3 CB 52 (1920), reaffirmed by Rev. Rul. 55-117, 1955-1 CB 233; see also Treas. Regs. §§1.1014-4(a)(3), 1.661(a)-2(f)(1).

[11] See Treas. Regs. §1.661(a)-2(f)(1).

inure to the benefit or detriment of the other beneficiaries. For this reason, it was held in *Suisman v. Eaton* that the transfer by a testamentary trustee of appreciated securities to pay a $50,000 legacy was a "sale or other disposition" within the meaning of IRC §1001(a), resulting in gain to the trust equal to the difference between the legatee's $50,000 claim and the trust's basis for the transferred property.[12]

The principle announced in *Suisman v. Eaton* was extended in *Kenan v. CIR* to a distribution of appreciated securities in part payment of a legacy of $5 million, which the decedent's testamentary trustees were authorized to pay *either* in cash *or* in marketable securities of like value.[13] Rejecting the taxpayer's argument that the legacy was in effect converted into a specific legacy of securities when the trustees exercised their authority to satisfy it with such assets, the court held that the transfer was a "sale or other disposition" of the appreciated securities even though effected by a unilateral exercise of the trustees' power under the decedent's will rather than by an agreement between the trustees and the legatee, as in *Suisman v. Eaton.*

3. Marital Deduction Bequests. With the enactment in 1948 of IRC §2056, creating a marital deduction for federal estate tax purposes, the distinction between pecuniary and specific legacies became a matter of acute concern to a much larger group of estates than previously. Between 1948 and 1981, the marital deduction for property passing to the decedent's surviving spouse was limited to the greater of $250,000 or one-half of the adjusted gross estate, defined by IRC §2056(c)(2) as the gross estate less funeral and administration expenses, claims against the estate, and losses.[14] Since the controlling amounts could rarely be accurately predicted before death, testators wishing to get the largest possible marital deduction ordinarily employed either a so-called pecuniary formula clause (e.g., "an amount equal to one-half of my adjusted gross estate") or a fractional residuary formula (e.g., "that fractional share of my residuary estate which, together with all other property qualifying for the marital deduction, is equal to one-half of my adjusted gross estate").

The estate is not taxed when appreciated property is distributed pursuant to a fractional residuary formula, since changes in the value of the property after the date of death inure to the benefit or detriment of the surviving spouse. On the other hand, a pecuniary formula bequest becomes a claim for a fixed dollar amount when the variables controlling its computation are fixed on or after the date of the decedent's death, and this brings *Suisman v. Eaton* into

[12] Suisman v. Eaton, 15 F.Supp. 113 (D.Conn. 1935), aff'd per curiam, 83 F.2d 1019 (2d Cir.), cert. denied, 299 US 573 (1936).

[13] Kenan v. CIR, 114 F.2d 217 (2d Cir. 1940).

[14] These limits were eliminated by the Economic Recovery Tax Act of 1981, P.L. No. 97-34, 95 Stat. 172.

play if appreciated or depreciated assets are used by the executor to satisfy the claim.[15]

4. Charitable Pledges. Although the distribution of appreciated property by an estate to satisfy a pecuniary bequest is a taxable event, the IRS ruled in 1955 that a transfer of appreciated or depreciated property to satisfy a charitable pledge does not give rise to taxable gain or deductible loss.[16] Pointing out that IRC §170 grants a deduction for charitable gifts only when "payment" is made, the IRS asserted that it would be inconsistent to treat the same event as both a gift and the satisfaction of a debt. A more persuasive justification is that a contrary rule would be merely a trap for taxpayers who impulsively fill out a charitable pledge card with a specific dollar amount rather than follow the more prudent course of promising to give specific property in kind.

5. Unliquidated or Disputed Claims. In the cases and rulings discussed above, appreciated or depreciated property was used to satisfy an admittedly valid claim to a fixed dollar amount. What if appreciated property is used to settle a claim against the taxpayer (e.g., for negligence) that is disputed as to liability, amount, or both? By itself, the existence of a dispute regarding the claim's validity or amount is in no way inconsistent with concluding that the taxpayer engaged in a "sale or other disposition" of the property within the meaning of IRC §1001(a), and that the amount realized was the fair market value of the property, since this was in effect the value placed by the parties on the claim. If the claim had been liquidated by a lawsuit, a transfer of property to discharge the judgment would be covered by IRC §1001(a); and there is no reason to reach a different result if the claim is settled.

¶22.5 SALE VS. NONTAXABLE DIVISIONS OF PROPERTY

1. Jointly Held and Community Property. When co-owners of property, such as members of a partnership or tenants in common of real estate, divide the property among themselves so they can go their separate ways, it has long been established that the transaction is a nontaxable division of the property,

---

[15] See Rev. Proc. 64-19, 1964-1 CB (Part 1) 682, discussed in detail by Covey, The Marital Deduction and the Use of Formula Provisions 99-122 (Bobbs-Merrill, 2d ed. 1978).

[16] Rev. Rul. 55-410, 1955-1 CB 297. In special circumstances, however, the appreciation may result in a reduction of the donor's charitable contribution deduction; see supra ¶19.2. See also IRC §84, taxing donors who contribute appreciated property to political organizations, even if no pledge precedes the gift.

rather than a taxable "sale or other disposition" by each co-owner of an undivided interest in the whole in exchange for separate ownership of a fractional share of the individual assets.[17] The same principle applies to the conversion of a joint tenancy into a tenancy in common, even though this action eliminates each owner's survivorship rights, presumably on the theory that each one had from the outset the unfettered right to get by severance one-half of the property free of the other's survivorship interest and hence has merely asserted—rather than "disposed of"—his or her rights.[18]

A conversion of community property into the separate property of each spouse is similarly a tax-free transaction; and this is true even in states that follow the traditional community-property principle vesting managerial authority in the husband, although, as a result of the conversion, the husband loses—and the wife gains—both the duty to manage and the right to control her half of the community property.[19] The theory of a nontaxable division, however, does not embrace situations in which a spouse exchanges an interest in community property for the separate property of the other spouse or the aggregate value of the assets received by one spouse exceeds the value of his or her one-half interest in the community property.

If co-owners do not divide their property in kind, the transaction is less easily classified. For example, if *A* and *B* are joint tenants of both Blackacre and Whiteacre, which are of equal value, and they agree that Blackacre will go to *A* and Whiteacre to *B*, the theory of a tax-free "partition" is less persuasive than if each gets one-half of each parcel. Although there are no cases directly in point, the transaction could be treated as though there had been a tax-free division of each parcel followed by a taxable exchange by *A* of one-half of Whiteacre for *B*'s one-half of Blackacre, and vice versa as to *B*. The courts, however, have recognized that a fifty-fifty division of every asset is ordinarily not feasible, and have held that the split is not a taxable event if, for example, a husband gets complete ownership of some assets and the wife gets others, provided their shares are of equal value.[20] It is not clear whether this result would be reached if a fifty-fifty split was entirely feasible (e.g., if the assets of the joint tenants or marital community consisted of $100,000 in cash and 1,000 shares of stock of a listed corporation).

While most of the cases in this area deal with divisions of community property, the IRS has indicated its intention to apply the same principles to the division of jointly owned property when a married couple domiciled in a

---

[17] See Rev. Rul. 55-77, 1955-1 CB 339 (partition sale of tenancy in common).

[18] Rev. Rul. 56-437, 1956-2 CB 507.

[19] Carrieres v. CIR, 64 TC 959 (1975) (Acq.), aff'd per curiam, 552 F.2d 1350 (9th Cir. 1977); see also Rev. Rul. 76-83, 1976-1 CB 213 (approximately equal division of community property held nontaxable, even though some assets went to one spouse or the other in their entirety).

[20] Walz v. CIR, 32 BTA 718 (1935); Rev. Rul. 76-83, supra note 19.

common-law-property state becomes divorced.[21] An antenuptial transfer of property in settlement of any later-arising marital rights, however, is a taxable event.[22]

2. Marital Property Settlements. Although the division of community property between husband and wife on divorce or separation has been treated as a nontaxable event by both the IRS and the courts for many years, this approach was not extended to marital property settlements in common-law states, since a transfer by one spouse to the other of separately owned common-law assets on separation or divorce seems more like a "disposition" of property than a division of assets between co-owners. On the other hand, the courts were troubled by the problem of determining the "amount realized" by the transferor, since the value of the rights ordinarily relinquished by the transferee spouse (common-law or statutory dower and sometimes support rights) depends on numerous unpredictable variables.

To resolve a conflict among the lower courts on the tax status of such settlements, in 1962 the Supreme Court decided *United States v. Davis,* involving a transfer of appreciated property by a husband to his estranged wife pursuant to a separation agreement, which was later incorporated into a divorce decree, in settlement and satisfaction "of any and all claims and rights against the husband whatsoever (including but not by way of limitation, dower and all rights under the laws of testacy and intestacy)." [23] The Court held that the theory of a nontaxable division applicable to community property could not be extended to common-law states:

> [T]he inchoate rights granted a wife in her husband's property by the Delaware law do not even remotely reach the dignity of co-ownership. The wife has no interest—passive or active—over the management or disposition of her husband's personal property. . . . Upon dissolution of the marriage she shares in the property only to such extent as the court deems "reasonable. . . ."
>
> This is not to say it would be completely illogical to consider the shearing off of the wife's rights in her husband's property as a division of that property, but we believe the contrary to be the more reasonable construction. Regardless of the tags, Delaware seems only to place a burden on the husband's property rather than to make the wife a part owner thereof. In the present context the rights of succession and reasonable share do not differ significantly from the husband's obligations of

---

[21] See Rev. Rul. 81-292, 1981-2 CB 158 (non-community-property state); Rev. Rul. 74-347, 1974-2 CB 26.

[22] See Farid-Es-Sultaneh v. CIR, 160 F.2d 812 (2d Cir. 1947) (recipient of property in antenuptial settlement receives cost basis therein).

[23] US v. Davis, 370 US 65, 67, rehearing denied, 371 US 854 (1962).

> support and alimony. They all partake more of a personal liability of the husband than a property interest of the wife. The effectuation of these marital rights may ultimately result in the ownership of some of the husband's property as it did here, but certainly this happenstance does not equate the transaction with a division of property by co-owners.[24]

Having concluded that the settlement was a "sale or other disposition" of property within the meaning of IRC §1001(a), the Court went on to hold that the "amount realized" by the husband was equal to the value of the property transferred by him:

> It must be assumed, we think, that the parties acted at arm's length and that they judged the marital rights to be equal in value to the property for which they were exchanged. There was no evidence to the contrary here. Absent a readily ascertainable value it is accepted practice where property is exchanged to hold . . . that the values "of the two properties exchanged in an arm's-length transaction are either equal in fact or are presumed to be equal."[25]

Like most leading cases, *Davis* marked the end of an important controversy but simultaneously left room for debate about other issues, both old and new. These loose ends include:

1. *Divorce settlements as gifts.* In *Davis* the Court rejected as "completely unrealistic" the claim that the property settlement before it was a gift by the husband so that he realized no gain: "Property transferred pursuant to a negotiated settlement in return for the release of admittedly valuable rights is not a gift in any sense of the term."[26] Although framed as a flat generalization, this comment may have been intended as a rebuttable presumption rather than as a rule of law. If so, some room is left for characterizing a transfer of property on separation or divorce as a gift on appropriate facts (so that the transferor would not realize gain or loss and the transferee would take a carryover basis for the property under IRC §1015), rather than as a "sale or other disposition" within the meaning of IRC §1001(a). The strongest case would be presented by a transfer of property to the couple's children, which might be motivated solely by affection or generosity even if formalized by a settlement agreement whose other terms were hotly contested.

2. *Divisions of jointly owned and partnership assets.* The appreciated property transferred by the taxpayer in *Davis* to his wife—corporate stock owned by him—was subject only to his wife's statutory right to a share of his property on divorce or death. In holding that the transfer of this property was

[24] Id. at 70–71.

[25] Id. at 72–73.

[26] Id. at 69 n.6.

a "sale or other disposition" within the meaning of IRC §1001(a), the Court did not undermine the established principle that a division of jointly held or partnership property is not a taxable event. A divorce settlement, therefore, might entail both a tax-free division of property owned jointly by husband and wife and a taxable disposition by one spouse to the other of individually owned property.[27]

3. *Common-law states recognizing "common ownership" of marital property.* In the *Davis* case, the Supreme Court refused to extend the "nontaxable division" theory to a Delaware resident, but it made no global assumption about the wife's rights in other common-law states. Rather, it examined Delaware law in some detail before holding that it did not vest the wife with interests analogous to those she would possess in "a typical community property jurisdiction." The Court did not, however, foreclose the possibility that the marital property law of other common-law states might be sufficiently similar to traditional community-property rules to justify identical federal tax treatment.

In the years since *Davis* was decided, this possibility has been intensively explored by taxpayers in a number of common-law states, and victory has been achieved—with the aid of the local courts—in Oklahoma and Colorado. The relevant Oklahoma statute provided that on divorce, the court "shall make such division between [husband and wife] respectively as may appear just and reasonable" of all property "acquired by the parties jointly during their marriage, whether title thereto be in either or both of said parties." The taxpayer successfully litigated the meaning of this statute before the Oklahoma Supreme Court, which interpreted the language to mean that "if property has been acquired by joint effort during marriage the wife has a vested interest therein which is not forfeited [on divorce] even though she may be at fault" and that "the wife's interest is similar in conception to community property . . . and is regarded as held by a species of common ownership." [28]

Armed with this interpretation of local law, the husband on remand convinced the federal court of appeals that the wife was "a part owner" of the marital property under Oklahoma law, so that his transfer of appreciated property to her under the settlement agreement was a nontaxable division of property between co-owners.[29] The IRS now accepts the result reached in *Collins* if co-ownership is created by local law.[30]

---

[27] See Carrieres v. CIR, supra note 19 (division and transfer of community property plus transfer of separate property; held, in part taxable and in part tax-free).

[28] Collins v. Oklahoma Tax Comm'n, 446 P.2d 290, 295 (Okla. 1968).

[29] Collins v. CIR, 412 F.2d 211 (10th Cir. 1969).

[30] Rev. Rul. 74-347, supra note 21. See also Imel v. US, 523 F.2d 853 (10th Cir. 1975) (same result under Colorado law via different procedural route); but see Wiles v. CIR, 60 TC 56 (1973) (Acq.), aff'd as to another issue, 499 F.2d 255 (10th Cir. 1974), cert. denied, 419 US 996 (1974) (Kansas law does not create co-ownership).

4. *Transfers to trusts.* When appreciated property is transferred to a trust for the benefit of the divorced or separated spouse, the transferor is subject to the *Davis* principle if the transfer discharges the transferor's legal obligation to the beneficiary spouse. If the trust arrangement is merely a security device, however, so that the transferor must make good any deficiency, the transfer is not a taxable event and the appreciation in value is not realized until the trustee sells or otherwise disposes of the property.[31]

5. *Deductibility of loss.* When depreciated property is transferred to a divorced or separated spouse in settlement of marital rights, the *Davis* principle indicates that the transferor realizes a loss, but IRC §267(a)(1) disallows deductions for losses from the sale or exchange of property, directly or indirectly, between spouses. Except when the Internal Revenue Code provides to the contrary, marital status is usually determined by state law;[32] and this suggests that the transferor's loss, though realized, will give rise to a deduction only if the transfer occurs after the marital relationship is terminated.[33]

6. *Tax treatment of the transferee.* In *Davis,* the Supreme Court pointed out a corollary of treating the transfer of the appreciated property as a taxable event, viz., that the market value of the property at the time of the transfer will become its basis in the hands of the transferee by virtue of IRC §1012. Thus, the transferee will realize gain or loss on a later disposition only to the extent that its value increases or decreases after the transfer.[34]

The *Davis* case has still other ramifications from the transferee's point of view. Since the husband in that case was treated as receiving the wife's marital rights as consideration for the stock, does it follow that her action in releasing those rights in exchange for the stock was a "sale or other disposition," so that she realized gain equal to the difference between her basis for the surrendered marital rights (presumably zero) and the value of the stock received by her? The Supreme Court was not required to decide this issue in *Davis,* but it referred to "the present administrative practice" as holding that such a settlement is not a taxable event as to the wife; and this position was subsequently formally confirmed by the IRS in Revenue Ruling 67-221.[35] If the marriage had continued, IRC §102 would have protected the wife against being taxed on property received as a bequest under her husband's will or as her statutory share under an election to take against the will; and a property settlement on the occasion of divorce can be properly regarded as a prepaid substitute for a transfer at death in discharge of her dower rights.[36]

---

[31] See Rev. Rul. 59-47, 1959-1 CB 198.

[32] See Deyoe v. CIR, 66 TC 904 (1976), and cases there cited.

[33] See Siewert v. CIR, 72 TC 326, 338-340 (1979) (IRC §267 applies to taxable exchange between husband and wife in a divorce situation).

[34] US v. Davis, supra note 23, at 73.

[35] Id. at 73 n.7; Rev. Rul. 67-221, 1967-2 CB 63.

[36] See Howard v. CIR, 447 F.2d 152 (5th Cir. 1971) (payment in lieu of dower tax-free).

¶22.6 SALE VS. MORTGAGE

1. Introductory. It is sometimes difficult to determine whether the taxpayer has "sold" property or has instead borrowed against it without personal liability, especially if he remains in possession and has an option to repurchase the property at a nominal or fixed price or if the "buyer's" rights in the property will terminate when he has recovered his investment plus a predetermined amount of profit thereon. For centuries, under both common law and statutory rules, transactions cast in the form of sales have been treated as devices to borrow against the property if the facts warrant;[37] and it should occasion no surprise that the same realism is exhibited in federal tax cases.

If the transaction is treated as a sale within the meaning of IRC §1001(a), the transferor realizes gain (or loss) if the amount realized is greater (or less) than the adjusted basis of the property, and the realized gain (loss) is recognized unless a nonrecognition provision applies to the transaction.[38] Conversely, the transferee, as the new owner, cannot deduct the payments to the transferor, since they constitute capital investments rather than business expenses, but is entitled to the tax allowances inherent in ownership (e.g., depreciation and the investment credit).

On the other hand, if the amount paid by the "buyer" is, realistically viewed, tantamount to a loan to the "seller," the transaction will be recast as a loan. In this event, its principal tax consequences from the purported transferor's point of view are that he is not taxed on the borrowed funds, continues to be recognized as the owner and hence can depreciate the property, and allocates the purported rent paid to the transferee between principal repayments and interest, deducting the latter portion. As for the transferee, he cannot depreciate the property because he has only a security interest, and the amounts collected by him must be bifurcated (as in the case of the transferor), the interest component being includable in income and the balance being excluded as a return of principal.

2. Sale and Leaseback vs. Loan. In *Helvering v. F. & R. Lazarus & Co.*, which was for many years the leading sale and leaseback case, the trial court found that the owner of real estate with a fair market value of about $6 million, wishing to refinance existing debt of about $3.2 million, accomplished its

---

[37] See Peugh v. Davis, 96 US 332, 336 (1878) ("a court of equity will treat a deed, absolute in form, as a mortgage when it is executed as a security for a loan of money"; held, "seller" did not lose equity of redemption).

[38] See, e.g., IRC §1031 (exchange of property for other property of a like kind), discussed infra ¶24.2, which may result in nonrecognition of a realized loss on a sale-leaseback arrangement because the right to occupy the property under a long-term lease is viewed as property of a like kind to the transferred realty under Treas. Regs. §§1.1031(a)-1(c).

objective by "selling" the property for that amount and leasing it back for ninety-nine years, subject to options to renew the lease or to repurchase the property at the call price of certificates issued by the purported purchaser to raise the necessary funds.[39] Since the property was worth almost twice the purported sale price, the court concluded that the "seller" would either renew the lease for a second ninety-nine-year period or exercise its repurchase option, and the Supreme Court upheld the trial court's conclusion that the deed "was in reality a mortgage" and that the original owner did not lose its right to depreciate the improvements over their useful life.[40]

The ineluctable difficulty in this area is that any investor, whether denominated a mortgagee or a buyer-lessor, must recover over the life of the arrangement the amount advanced at the outset plus a return commensurate with its risk. Conversely, the other party, whether a borrower or a seller-lessee, will be willing to repay the amount advanced with interest. In making their calculations, the parties to a long-term arrangement are not likely to attach much importance to ownership of the underlying property at the end of the financing period, because, when the agreement is negotiated, the probable value of this residual item is almost always minor relative to the other terms of the bargain. In *F. & R. Lazarus & Co.,* for example, the building (with an estimated useful life of forty or fifty years) was expected to be a heap of rubble when the ninety-nine-year lease terminated; and, when the ninety-nine-year lease was executed, the value of getting back the land, assuming no change in its $3.5 million value, was about $11,000 if discounted at 6 percent and only $280 at 10 percent.

When the Supreme Court faced its next sale-leaseback case, almost four decades after deciding *F. & R. Lazarus & Co.,* it was persuaded by a multiplicity of imponderables that the substance of the transaction accorded with its form, so that the lessor was a true owner, entitled to depreciate the property and to take other deductions compatible with ownership. The financing arrangement in the case, *Frank Lyon Co. v. United States,* was a complex three-party transaction, involving a bank (Worthen) needing a new building that could not be financed by a conventional mortgage loan because of state and federal banking restrictions, an entrepreneur (Frank Lyon Co., the taxpayer) prepared to construct the building and lease it to the bank, and an institutional lender (New York Life Insurance Co.).[41] In deciding in the taxpayer's favor, the Court announced no sweeping generalizations but, instead, stressed the factual nature of the judicial inquiry:

> Worthen's undercapitalization; Worthen's consequent inability, as a matter of legal restraint, to carry its building plans into effect by a conven-

[39] F. & R. Lazarus & Co. v. CIR, 32 BTA 633, 637 (1935).

[40] Helvering v. F. & R. Lazarus & Co., 308 US 252 (1939).

[41] Frank Lyon Co. v. US, 435 US 561 (1978).

> tional mortgage and other borrowing; the additional barriers imposed by the state and federal regulators; the suggestion, forthcoming from the state regulator, that Worthen possess an option to purchase; the requirement, from the federal regulator, that the building be owned by an independent third party; . . . the bona fide character of the negotiations; the three-party aspect of the transaction; Lyon's substantiality and its independence from Worthen; the fact that diversification was Lyon's principal motivation; . . . the reasonableness, as the District Court found, of the rentals and of the option prices; the substantiality of the purchase prices; Lyon's not being engaged generally in the business of financing; the presence of all building depreciation risks on Lyon; the risk, borne by Lyon, that Worthen might default or fail, as other banks have failed; . . . the inescapable fact that if the building lease were not extended, Lyon would be the full owner of the building, free to do with it as it chose; Lyon's liability for the substantial ground rent if Worthen decides not to exercise any of its options to extend; the absence of any understanding between Lyon and Worthen that Worthen would exercise any of the purchase options; the nonfamily and nonprivate nature of the entire transaction; and the absence of any differential in tax rates and of special tax circumstances for one of the parties—all convince us that Lyon has far the better of the case.[42]

After referring at length to the facts, the Supreme Court went on in *Frank Lyon Co. v. United States* to say that the case did not involve "manipulation by a taxpayer through arbitrary labels and dealings that have no economic significance" or "tax-avoidance features that have meaningless labels attached." [43] Taxpayers often use sale-leasebacks instead of mortgages in order to shunt deductions or other tax allowances to the party who can make the best use of them, but it is not clear whether this constitutes forbidden "manipulation" if the nontax consequences of the transaction are similar to those in *Frank Lyon Co.*

3. Nonrecourse Loans in Excess of Basis. If a taxpayer buys Blackacre for $10,000 and, after it has increased in value to $15,000, mortgages it for $12,000 without personal liability, the loan will not have to be repaid even if Blackacre becomes worthless. Thus, the taxpayer not only has recovered his investment but also has received an additional $2,000 that he can retain, come what may. To be sure, he has an incentive to repay the loan at maturity if Blackacre is worth more than $12,000 at that time, since he will forfeit his equity if he defaults; and if the debt is paid and Blackacre drops in value thereafter to less than $12,000, he will lose some or all of the previously secure

---

[42] Id. at 581–583.

[43] Id. at 583–584.

$2,000 profit. But these possibilities do not undermine the fact that a taxpayer who borrows $12,000 against property with an adjusted basis of $10,000 has nailed down a profit of $2,000 if the debt is contracted without personal liability. For this reason, a businessman or financial analyst might analogize the nonrecourse loan to a sale of the property for $12,000, generating a gain of $2,000, coupled with an option to repurchase it for $12,000.

For tax purposes, however, the courts have rejected the theory that a nonrecourse mortgage in excess of the property's basis is a "sale or other disposition" within the meaning of IRC §1001(a). In the leading case, *Woodsam Associates v. CIR,* the Court of Appeals for the Second Circuit held that a mortgage in these circumstances is a true loan rather than a disposition of the property, because the owner continues to manage the property, to receive the income it produces, and to be subject to market fluctuations so long as the property's value exceeds the amount of the lien.[44]

4. Sales of "Carved-out" Interests. There is ordinarily no difficulty in determining that a taxpayer has engaged in a "sale or other disposition" within the meaning of IRC §1001(a) on selling a portion of a larger whole, such as ten acres of a 100-acre tract, an undivided 50 percent interest in Blackacre, or ten shares of stock from a 100-share block. The basis of the whole is allocated proportionately to the units sold, and gain or loss is computed accordingly. But the proper classification of a transfer is more problematic if the transferred rights are limited in amount, duration, or physical volume—for example, the next $10,000 of dividends payable on the transferor's stock, the next two years' rent on a specified building, or the next 100 tons of gravel excavated from Blackacre. If the transfer of such a "carved out" interest is taken at face value and treated as a sale of a portion of the underlying property, part of the latter's basis would, under normal principles, be allocated to the interest being sold, and gain or loss would be computed accordingly. Conversely, if the transaction is a sale, the transferee gets a basis for the transferred rights and must include the rents or dividends in gross income, but can amortize the basis of the property against these receipts.

On the other hand, if the transaction is viewed as a nonrecourse loan secured by the assigned property, no gain or loss is currently realized by the "seller," the income from the property is taxed to him, and the transferee's receipts (dividends, rents, etc.) will be allocated between interest (deductible by the transferor and taxable to the transferee) and principal (nondeductible by the transferor and nontaxable to the transferee).

Sales of carved-out interests are common financial arrangements in the extractive industries, and their tax ramifications are affected by geophysical

---

[44] Woodsam Assocs. v. CIR, 198 F.2d 357 (2d Cir. 1952).

factors and a complex web of decisions, regulations, and statutes discussed elsewhere in this work.[45] In other industries, however, carved-out income interests are rarely encountered except as tax-avoidance devices; and this aura quite naturally evokes skepticism about the surface documentation and frequently leads the IRS and the courts to decide that things are not as they seem.[46]

¶22.7 SALE OR OTHER DISPOSITION—MISCELLANEOUS TRANSACTIONS

1. Modification of Contract Terms, Novation, Etc. A "sale or other disposition" of property can occur even though the taxpayer does not receive cash or tangible property in exchange. A transfer of appreciated marketable securities to an insurance company to pay for an annuity contract, for example, is a taxable event. Moreover, the property given up can consist of intangible rights; thus, a taxpayer who surrenders a franchise or employment contract for other property must report any gain realized on the transaction. These principles, however, do not lead to the conclusion that the modification of a contract or the substitution of a new contract for an old one between the same parties constitutes a "disposition" of each party's rights under the original contract in exchange for rights under the modified or replacement contract.

The major litigated case on this issue, *CIR v. Olmsted Inc. Life Agency,* involved an agreement between an insurance company and one of its general agents, by which the agent gave up the right to receive future renewal commissions (contingent on its customers' renewals of existing insurance policies) in exchange for a contract providing for fixed monthly payments for fifteen years.[47] The IRS claimed that the transaction was a taxable event from the point of view of the agent, on the theory that the agent disposed of its rights under the old contract within the meaning of IRC §1001, and that the amount realized was the fair market value of the new contract. The Court of Appeals for the Eighth Circuit, however, held that the transaction was a substitution of "one contract for another—in other words, a novation," which "merely provided for a different rate or manner of payment whereby the insurance company could discharge its liability under its agency contract."[48] Although the court relied heavily on the fact that the transferor was a cash-basis taxpayer, the no-disposition rationale, being based on IRC §1001, is equally

---

[45] See supra ¶¶11.1 (economic interest concept), 11.4 (production payments).

[46] See infra ¶25.12.

[47] CIR v. Olmsted Inc. Life Agency, 304 F.2d 16 (8th Cir. 1962).

[48] Id. at 22–23.

applicable to accrual-basis taxpayers; and the IRS has evidently not endeavored to construe the case narrowly.

2. Securities: Extensions of Due Date, Conversions, Etc. The exchange of defaulted bonds for new instruments in a refunding operation is a nontaxable event if the terms of the new bonds are substantially the same, save for the maturity date, as those of the old bonds.[49] But more substantial changes may trigger the realization of gain or loss, whether the refunding is effected by issuing new obligations or amending the old ones.[50]

3. Options. The granting of an option is not a "sale or other disposition" of the underlying property, resulting in a taxable event to the grantor in the year of the grant, whether the amount received for the option can be credited against the price to be paid for the property or not.[51] Instead, the taxable event occurs when the option is exercised or expires, because only then is it possible to determine whether the amount received by the taxpayer granting the option is ordinary income generated by the unexercised option or part of the amount realized for the underlying property, generating gain or loss after the adjusted basis is taken into account.[52]

4. Involuntary Transactions (Foreclosure, Etc.). When mortgaged property is auctioned off at a foreclosure sale or surrendered to a creditor to avoid foreclosure, the transaction is a "sale or disposition" within the meaning of IRC §1001, on which the debtor's gain or loss is the difference between the adjusted basis of the property and the amount of the cancelled debt.[53] The statutory phrase "sale or other disposition" does not necessarily imply a *voluntary* transfer; but even if it did, a volitional element can be found in the original transaction by which the debtor incurred the debt or acquired the property subject to the debt.

On the other hand, it is more difficult to find a "sale or other disposition" when property is destroyed by fire, stolen, or expropriated, especially if the owner is not compensated by insurance or otherwise for the calamity. Nevertheless, gain or loss can be realized on these events. In some cases, IRC §1001 is simply sidestepped—losses are deductible under IRC §165(a) when

---

[49] See West Mo. Power Co. v. CIR, 18 TC 105 (1952) (Acq.).

[50] Rev. Rul. 81-169, 1981-1 CB 429 (exchange of municipal bond subject to sinking fund for bond of same issuer with equal face amount but different interest rate and maturity date that is not subject to sinking fund; held, taxable exchange).

[51] See Koch v. CIR, 67 TC 71, 85-89 (1976) (Acq.).

[52] See Virginia Iron, Coal & Coke Co. v. CIR, 99 F.2d 919 (4th Cir. 1938), cert. denied, 307 US 630 (1939).

[53] See Helvering v. Hammel, 311 US 504 (1941) (foreclosure).

"sustained," whether evidenced by a sale or other disposition of the affected property or not; conversely, IRC §61(a)(3) provides that gross income includes "gains derived from dealings in property," without regard to whether there is a disposition of the property within the meaning of IRC §1001. Moreover, for many of these borderline transactions, the Code explicitly provides that the event shall be treated as a "sale or exchange" in determining the character of the taxpayer's gain or loss under IRC §1222 or §1231, relating to capital gains and losses;[54] and this necessarily implies that it is to be treated as a sale or other disposition in computing the *amount* of the taxpayer's gain or loss under IRC §1001.

5. Date of Sale or Disposition. Although the date when property was sold or disposed of is usually crystal clear, it can be veiled in ambiguity if the owner relinquishes his rights gradually. In the case of real property, if the transfer of legal title and the shift of the benefits and burdens of ownership are not simultaneous, the sale usually dates from the first of these events to occur, especially if passage of legal title is delayed to secure payment of the purchase price. In determining who has the benefits and burdens of ownership, the courts consider such factors as possession, the right to receive the income from the property, liability for expenses, payment of taxes and utility bills, and the exercise of managerial prerogatives.[55]

SELECTED BIBLIOGRAPHY

Bost, Christensen, & Nelson, Income Reservation in Real Estate Transactions, 1982 So. Calif. Tax. Inst. 900

Del Cotto, Basis and Amount Realized Under *Crane*: A Current View of Some Tax Effects in Mortgage Financing, 118 U. Pa. L. Rev. 69, 96–98 (1969).

Del Cotto, Sales and Other Dispositions of Property Under Section 1001: The Taxable Event, Amount Realized, and Related Problems of Basis, 26 Buffalo L. Rev. 219 (1977).

Del Cotto, Sale and Leaseback: A Hollow Sound When Tapped? 37 Tax L. Rev. 1 (1981).

Hjorth, Community Property Marital Settlements: The Problem and a Proposal, 50 Wash. L. Rev. 231, 244–256 (1975).

---

[54] For these "statutory" sales and exchanges, see infra ¶26.1.

[55] Deyoe v. CIR, supra note 32 at 910 (1976) (liability for operating expenses, transfer of books, assumption of managerial functions, etc.).

Joyce & Del Cotto, The AB (ABC) and BA Transactions: An Economic and Tax Analysis of Reserved and Carved Out Income Interests, 31 Tax L. Rev. 121 (1976).

Kaney, Federal Income Taxation of Exchanges in Partition of Commonly Owned Property: Realization vs. Realism, 8 Fla. St. U.L. Rev. 629 (1980).

Kaney, Tax Planning for Division of Jointly-Held Property in a Divorce Made Easier by Ruling, 57 J. Tax. 174 (1982).

New York State Bar Association, Personal Income Committee, Report on the *Davis* Rule Regarding Property Settlements in Divorce or Separation, 3 Rev. Tax. Individuals 30 (1979).

Note, Problems of Judicial Interpretation of Real Estate Sale and Leaseback Taxation: Description, Analysis, and Proposed Revision, 33 Tax Lawyer 237 (1979).

Schapiro, Commodities, Forwards, Puts and Calls—Things Equal to the Same Things Are Sometimes Not Equal to Each Other, 34 Tax Lawyer 581 (1981).

Shurtz, A Decision Model for Lease Parties in Sale-Leasebacks of Real Estate, 23 Wm. & Mary L. Rev. 385 (1982).

Solomon & Fones, Sale-Leasebacks and the Shelter-Oriented Investor: An Analysis of *Frank Lyon Co.* and *Est. of Franklin,* 56 Taxes 618 (1978).

Turley, Divorce and Taxes—A Decade Later, 20 S. Tex. L.J. 407 (1981).

Wolk, Federal Tax Consequences of Wealth Transfers Between Unmarried Cohabitants, 27 U.C.L.A. L. Rev. 1240 (1980).

CHAPTER 23

Sales of Property—Basis and Amount Realized

¶23.1 BASIS—INTRODUCTORY

On a sale of property, gain or loss is the difference between the amount realized by the taxpayer and his adjusted basis for the property. This fundamental principle, embodied in IRC §1001(a), permits the taxpayer's investment to be recovered tax-free before he is charged with gain on the sale; conversely, the transaction generates a loss if the amount realized is less than the taxpayer's investment.[1]

The starting point in determining the taxpayer's adjusted basis for property is his "basis" (sometimes called "original" or "unadjusted" basis), which is ordinarily the cost of the property but in some situations (e.g., property received by gift or bequest, as compensation, or in a tax-free exchange) is fixed by a special statutory, administrative, or judicial rule. Transactions that occurred long in the past, involving other property or other taxpayers, sometimes determine the basis of recently acquired property. For example, stock acquired in a tax-free corporate merger takes a "substituted" basis equal to the basis of the stock surrendered by the taxpayer, and property acquired by gift has a "carryover" basis for determining the donee's gain[2] that depends on the donor's cost, depreciation, and other tax allowances. Although IRC §1016(b) defines "substituted basis" to include both a basis carried over from a prior owner and a basis carried over from other property owned by the taxpayer in question, the former situation is usually denoted in common tax parlance by the term "carryover basis" or "transferred basis" and only the latter by the term "substituted basis"; and this distinction is ordinarily preserved in this treatise.

Once determined, the taxpayer's original (or unadjusted) basis must be adjusted downward from time to time to take account of depreciation, cost recovery, and similar tax allowances, and upward to reflect improvements or other capital outlays. The adjusted basis of some types of assets (e.g., business equipment) may change from year to year to reflect depreciation, major alterations, and other events chargeable to capital account.

Example 23-1 illustrates how these principles, which are discussed in detail below, determine the taxpayer's adjusted basis for property. Assume that the taxpayer purchased improved real property on January 1, 1981 for $50,000, payable in five annual installments of $10,000 each with interest on the outstanding balance, and that (1) $30,000 of the purchase price was allocable to the building and $20,000 to the land; (2) the taxpayer elected to depreciate the building on a straight-line basis over fifteen years; (3) the taxpayer paid

---

[1] Treas. Regs. §1.1001-1(a).

[2] But in computing *loss* on disposing of the property, the donee's original or "unadjusted" basis is either (1) the donor's basis or (2) the fair market value of the property at the time of the gift, whichever is less. See infra ¶23.3.

$10,000 to a neighbor in 1982 to eliminate an easement to the land; and (4) the taxpayer sold a one-half interest in the property on January 1, 1983 for $35,000. On these facts, the taxpayer's gain on the sale is $7,000 and his adjusted basis in the retained half-interest is $28,000, computed as shown in Example 23-1. As indicated, the fact that the purchase price of property is payable in installments over a period of time does not affect the purchaser's right to use the full purchase price as his cost basis.

Example 23-1

Computation of Adjusted Basis and Gain on Sale

1. Unadjusted basis for entire property (cost)	$50,000
2. Less: Depreciation for 1981 and 1982 (2 × 1/15 × $30,000—portion of line 1 allocable to building) (not less than amount allowable)	4,000
3. Basis adjusted for depreciation	$46,000
4. Plus: Adjustment for price paid for easement	10,000
5. Adjusted basis as of January 1, 1983	$56,000
6. Sales price	35,000
7. Less: Portion of line 5 allocable to one-half interest (½ of $56,000)	28,000
8. Gain on sale of one-half interest	$7,000
9. Adjusted basis in remaining property (line 5 minus line 7)	$28,000

In general, the taxpayer has the burden of proving the adjusted basis of property in computing such matters as gain or loss on a sale, the amount subject to depreciation, and casualty losses. It is customary, however, to apply the *Cohan* rule, allowing reasonable approximations when the absence of original documents creates difficulties in valuations.[3] Moreover, if a crucial transaction occurred long in the past or other circumstances exacerbate the taxpayer's burden of proof, the courts have allowed taxpayers to claim a minimum basis in property where it is probable that some basis exists but the correct amount is unknown.[4]

---

[3] Cohan v. CIR, 39 F.2d 540 (2d Cir. 1930), discussed supra ¶8.1; for application, see Cinelli v. CIR, 502 F.2d 695 (6th Cir. 1974) (basis in Italian villa inherited during World War II).

[4] See Jones v. CIR, 24 TC 525 (1955) (Acq.) (theft of diamond pin appraised at $3,000 shortly after receipt as gift; no evidence of donor's basis or when or how he acquired it; held, donor's basis was $1,500 and fair market value at gift was not less than this); Burr v. CIR, ¶66,112 P-H Memo TC (1966) (bank account withdrawals prior to purchase of merchandise used as guide to cost).

¶23.2 UNADJUSTED BASIS—COST

1. Introductory. In determining gain or loss from the sale or other disposition of property, the taxpayer's "adjusted basis" is controlling,[5] but to compute this amount, the taxpayer must first ascertain the property's unadjusted or original basis and then make the adjustments prescribed by IRC §1016. Section 1012 provides that the basis of property is its cost, except as otherwise prescribed by the Code. Although there are many important exceptions (e.g., for property acquired by gift or bequest or in a tax-free exchange), the basis of property in the overwhelming number of cases is its "cost."

In general, the cost of property within the meaning of IRC §1012 is the amount paid for it, regardless of its true value, provided the transaction is at arm's length and does not encompass an extraneous element like a gift or compensation for services. Thus, the fact that the buyer got a bargain—or a lemon—does not create current gain or loss for him;[6] but the amount actually paid becomes the basis of the property, and the inchoate gain or loss will be recognized if the property is disposed of at its true value. When an excessive amount is paid, however, the burden of proving that the transaction was negotiated at arm's length rests on the taxpayer; and a failure to sustain this evidentiary burden will result in a reduction of his basis to the fair market value of the property at acquisition.[7] In such a case, the excess payment cannot be treated as part of the cost of the property, though in appropriate circumstances it may be otherwise deductible (e.g., as compensation paid by the buyer for services performed by the seller).

2. Inclusion of Debt in Purchaser's Cost Basis. Called upon to interpret the term "cost" as used in IRC §1012, a businessman or investor would no doubt point to the purchase price of property, whether the transaction was consummated on an all-cash or credit basis. In general, the courts and the IRS follow the same principle, so that property purchased for $10,000 has a cost basis of that amount, even if part or all of the purchase price is to be paid at a later time.

Moreover, a mortgage to which the acquired property is subject is includable in the purchaser's basis even if he does not assume personal liability for the debt. This doctrine stems from the concern of the Supreme Court, expressed in *Crane v. CIR,* that if the mortgage is not included in the buyer's basis, his depreciation deductions will not reflect actual physical exhaustion

---

[5] IRC §1011(a).

[6] See CIR v. LoBue, 351 US 243 (1956) (dictum, bargain purchase not ordinarily a taxable event).

[7] See, e.g., Majestic Sec. Corp. v. CIR, 120 F.2d 12 (8th Cir. 1941) (unexplained excessive payment).

and, accordingly, income will be distorted.[8] In *Mayerson v. CIR,* the Tax Court expanded on this point:

> Taxpayers who are not personally liable for encumbrances on property should be allowed depreciation deductions affording competitive equality with taxpayers who are personally liable for encumbrances or taxpayers who own unencumbered property. The effect of such a policy is to give the taxpayer an advance credit for the amount of the mortgage. This appears to be reasonable since it can be assumed that a capital investment in the amount of the mortgage will eventually occur despite the absence of personal liability.[9]

Although this premise is realistic if the purchaser makes a substantial cash payment above the debt, it is debatable when there is no such cash investment and the debt does not have to be amortized promptly. In these circumstances, the purchaser is claiming depreciation on property that he will probably drop rather than pay for, unless its market value goes up. Concerned with this problem, the IRS has announced that it will "review transactions . . . designed to improperly create or inflate depreciation deductions" and "disallow unwarranted depreciation deductions." [10]

Under a major qualification to the *Crane* principle, liabilities are not included in the purchaser's cost basis if they are "contingent and indefinite in nature." [11] Thus, purchasers of business assets have been denied the right to increase the cost basis of an acquired business to reflect contingent liabilities for mortgage bonds of doubtful enforceability, obligations contingent on future profits, and severance pay that is dependent on the number of employees remaining on the payroll in the event of a future closing of the plant.[12]

As pointed out above, liabilities are usually included in the buyer's cost basis for property on the implicit assumption that he will ultimately pay off the debt so that, over the long haul, the basis with which he was credited will not exceed his cash investment. If, instead of paying in full, the purchaser succeeds in discharging the debt for less than its face amount, the difference is ordinarily either includable in income under *United States v. Kirby Lumber Co.* [13]

---

[8] Crane v. CIR, 331 US 1 (1947), discussed infra ¶23.16.

[9] Mayerson v. CIR, 47 TC 340, 352 (1966) (Acq.).

[10] Rev. Rul. 69-77, 1969-1 CB 59, acquiescing in Mayerson v. CIR, supra note 9, "on the particular facts in the case."

[11] See Mayerson v. CIR, supra note 9, at 353, and cases there cited.

[12] Albany Car Wheel Co. v. CIR, 40 TC 831 (1963), aff'd per curiam, 333 F.2d 653 (2d Cir. 1964) (severance pay); Columbus & G. Ry. v. CIR, 42 TC 834 (1964), aff'd per curiam, 358 F.2d 294 (5th Cir.), cert. denied, 385 US 827 (1966) (mortgage bonds); Lemery v. CIR, 52 TC 367, 377 (1969), aff'd per curiam, 451 F.2d 173 (9th Cir. 1971) (covenant contingent on profits); see also Gibson Prods. v. US, 637 F.2d 1041 (5th Cir. 1981) (contingent nonrecourse debt incurred in oil drilling venture).

[13] US v. Kirby Lumber Co., 284 US 1 (1931), discussed supra ¶2.4.

or applied under IRC §1017 to reduce the basis of the taxpayer's assets.[14] Either of these adjustments will bring the purchaser's tax position into harmony with economic reality, thus validating the premise on which the original cost basis was computed.

3. Purchase Commissions, Legal Fees, and Other Acquisition Expenses. The cost basis of property includes such expenses of acquisition as brokers' commissions on the purchase of securities or real estate and the cost of defending or perfecting title (e.g., legal fees paid in a suit to quiet title to land).[15] Expenses of this type are included in the taxpayer's basis for the property as a corollary of the principle that they may not be deducted under IRC §162 as business expenses or under IRC §212 as expenses paid or incurred for the maintenance of income-producing property.[16]

If property is acquired by exercising an option, the transaction is not a taxable disposition of the option itself, but the cost or other basis of the option is added to the amount paid on exercising it in computing the taxpayer's cost basis for the underlying property.[17]

4. Barter Transactions—Disparities in Value. When property is acquired in exchange for other property in an arm's-length transaction, their values are ordinarily identical; but if there should be a disparity, the layman would probably say that the cost of the property received was the fair market value of the property with which it was purchased.

As pointed out above, if a taxpayer buying for cash pays more (or less) than the value of the property received, the amount paid becomes the cost basis of the property, and the disparity simply shows that he was careless (or shrewd). An extension of this principle to property acquired with other property rather than cash, however, would create a gap in the treatment of the buyer, which can be illustrated by assuming that *A* exchanges Blackacre (adjusted basis $8,000, fair market value $11,000) for an Oriental rug worth only $10,000, the disparity being attributable to *A*'s distaste for protracted negotiations. Since the amount realized by *A* for Blackacre, determined under IRC §1001(b), is the value of the property received ($10,000), his gain, com-

---

[14] See IRC §108 (election to exclude income from cancellation of indebtedness on condition that basis of assets is reduced), discussed supra ¶2.4.

[15] See Treas. Regs. §1.263(a)-2(e).

[16] See, e.g., CIR v. Idaho Power Co., 418 US 1 (1974) (depreciation incurred by utility company on construction equipment used to build its own capital facilities is not deductible but must be capitalized as part of cost of facilities); Woodward v. CIR, 397 US 572 (1970) (same as to cost of appraisal proceeding to establish value of dissenting shareholder's stock, purchased pursuant to state law).

[17] See Rev. Rul. 67-96, 1967-1 CB 195 (cost of property acquired by exercising testamentary option is basis of latter under IRC §1014(a) plus cash paid; extensive discussion of prior cases).

puted under IRC §1001(a), is $2,000 (the amount realized, $10,000, less the adjusted basis of Blackacre, $8,000). If *A* were allowed to treat the rug as costing $11,000 on a later sale for $12,000, he would report only $3,000 of gain on the two transactions, though his economic gain would be $4,000 (i.e., $12,000 of cash received less $8,000 paid for Blackacre). To forestall this result, the courts have rejected the layman's conception of "cost," construing the term as used in IRC §1012 to mean the value of the property *received* rather than the value of the property *given up.*[18] The transaction just described, therefore, would result in a cost basis of $10,000 for the rug, rather than $11,000; and *A* would realize gain of $2,000 on selling it for $12,000.

If the value of the property given up cannot be determined with reasonable accuracy but the property received has a readily ascertainable value, the latter becomes the cost basis of the property on the assumption that an arm's-length exchange betokens equality.[19] On rare occasions, however, it may be impossible to place a realistic value on *either* asset in a property-for-property exchange, compelling use of the so-called open transaction doctrine as the only way out of the dilemma.[20]

5. Property Received as Compensation or in Other Taxable Transactions—"Tax Cost." Property received as compensation for services, as a dividend, or in other taxable transactions takes a basis equal to its fair market value, since this is the amount includable in the taxpayer's income for the year of receipt. If the taxpayer had received an equivalent amount of cash as compensation or as a dividend and had then used the cash to buy the property, its basis under IRC §1012 would be its cost; and a different basis is not justified merely because the stock was acquired in a less roundabout manner. In recognition of this principle, the term "tax cost" is often used as a descriptive label for the basis of the property that was not purchased in the conventional sense but whose fair market value was includable in the taxpayer's gross income.

¶23.3 PROPERTY ACQUIRED BY GIFT

1. Introductory. When property is acquired by gift, IRC §1012's general rule prescribing a "cost" basis for property cannot be applied; and IRC §1015 provides instead that the donee must use the donor's basis, subject to

---

[18] Philadelphia Park Amusement Co. v. US, 126 F.Supp. 184 (Ct. Cl. 1954).

[19] See US v. Davis, 370 US 65 (1962) (principle of equal-value exchange applies in determining wife's basis for stock received by her in divorce settlement in exchange for release of marital rights, giving her basis equal to value of the stock received); but see Mitchell v. CIR, 590 F.2d 312 (9th Cir. 1979) (*Davis* principle applicable only when required as last resort to prevent gain from escaping taxation, not when valuation can be postponed until determinable with precision).

[20] For the open transaction doctrine, see infra ¶23.13.

several qualifications discussed below. The requirement of a carryover basis is a corollary of the structural principle, in force since 1913, that donors do not realize gain on transferring appreciated property to their donees. From 1913 to 1921, however, when there was no statutory provision prescribing the donee's basis, the Treasury permitted donees to use the fair market value of the property on the date of the gift when computing gain or loss on a later sale, with the result that appreciation during the donor's ownership escaped tax. To pinch off this source of "serious abuse" by intra-family gifts of highly appreciated property, the Revenue Act of 1921 required the donee to use the donor's basis in computing gain on selling or otherwise disposing of the property.[21] By virtue of IRC §102(a), relating to property acquired by gift, the donee is not taxed on receiving the property. In effect, this exclusion is permanent as respects the donor's *investment* in the property, but so far as *appreciation* is concerned, it lasts only until the donee sells the property.

The donor's basis for the property must be adjusted to take account of depreciation, capital improvements, and similar items during the period of his ownership, so that the basis carried over by the donee under IRC §1015(a) is the amount that the donor would have used in computing gain or loss had he sold the property on the date of the gift. If the donor in turn had acquired the property by gift from a prior owner, the final donee uses the basis of the last preceding owner who did not acquire it by gift. Thus, if *A* purchases property and gives it to *B,* and *B* gives it to *C, C*'s basis is *A*'s basis, adjusted for depreciation, improvements, and similar items during both *A*'s and *B*'s ownership.

While the donee uses the donor's basis in determining *gain* on the eventual sale of the property, the donee's basis for determining *loss* is a bit more complicated. This reflects a congressional desire to prevent the shifting of potential losses from donor to donee. The barrier consists of the qualification in IRC §1015(a), providing that if the donor's basis is greater than the fair market value of the property at the time of the gift, the donee must use the latter amount in computing loss. Thus, if property with a basis of $100 and a fair market value of $90 at the time of gift is sold for $85, the donee's loss is only $5. The result of this rule is that the $10 decline in value during the donor's ownership will not be recognized by either the donor or the donee, even though it reflects a genuine decline in the value of the family's assets. A foresighted donor can avoid this result, however, by selling the property if he wishes to use the loss on his own tax return, and then giving the proceeds to the donee.

If the property just described is sold by the donee for an amount between $90 (its value on the date of the gift) and $100 (the donor's basis), the donee

[21] See Taft v. Bowers, 278 US 470, 479-480 (1929).

realizes neither gain nor loss.[22] This seems curious at first blush, but it is entirely reasonable. If the sales price were $101, the donee would realize $1 of gain; and it would be unreasonable to impute *more gain* to him on selling for *less* than $101. On the other hand, a sale for $89 would generate $1 of loss and it would be unreasonable to allow him to deduct a larger amount on selling for more than $89. Hence there is a no-man's-land between $90 and $100.

2. Increase in Basis for Federal Gift Tax. The foregoing basis rules are modified by IRC §1015(d), enacted in 1958 and amended in 1976, for property whose transfer to the donee was subject to federal gift tax. The 1958 rules, which continue to apply to pre-1977 gifts, treat the gift tax as though it were a cost incurred by the donee in acquiring the donated property. The basis of property acquired between September 2, 1958 and January 1, 1977 is increased by the amount of the gift tax paid with respect to the gift.

In 1976 Congress abandoned the 1958 theory that the federal gift tax is a cost to the donee of acquiring the donated property, and replaced the 1958 rules by an adjustment based on the more limited theory that the gift tax allocable to any *appreciation* in the property at the time of the gift is a cost of acquiring that component of the donated property. In keeping with this theory, IRC §1015(d)(6) provides for an increase in the basis of property acquired by gift after December 31, 1976 by an amount bearing the same ratio to the gift tax as the net appreciation in the value of the gift when made bears to the total value of the gift. This adjustment, which cannot exceed the gift tax actually paid, is illustrated by Example 23-2, involving a taxable gift of property with an adjusted basis of $5,000 in the hands of the donor and a fair market value of $20,000 on the date of the gift.

Example 23-2

Adjustment Under IRC §1015(d)(6) for Federal Gift Tax on Appreciated Donated Property

1. Taxable gift	$20,000
2. Federal tax	2,000
3. Fair market value on date of gift	20,000
4. Less: Donor's adjusted basis	5,000
5. Net appreciation	$15,000
6. Increase in basis ($15,000/$20,000 × $2,000)	$ 1,500
7. Basis to donee (line 4 plus line 6)	$ 6,500

[22] See Treas. Regs. §1.1015-1(a)(2), Example.

3. Donor's Basis Unknown. The donee of property is often unable to determine the donor's basis with precision.

The calculation prescribed by IRC §1015(d)(6) is relatively simple if the donor made only one gift during the relevant period, as in Example 23-2. It is more complex if two or more gifts were made in the same quarterly period, since the gift tax paid must then be allocated among all gifts before computing the amount allocable to the appreciation on any particular gift.[23] Ordinarily taxpayers against whom a deficiency is assessed have the burden of disproving it and will lose on failing to establish the relevant facts, regardless of difficulties in excavating and proving them. But IRC §1015(a) relaxes the usual rules of proof, if the facts "necessary to determine the basis in the hands of the donor" are unknown to the donee, by requiring the IRS to obtain the facts from the donor or any other informed person. If the donee cannot establish the donor's actual basis and the IRS is unable to make a finding of value pursuant to this statutory mandate, it has been held that neither gain nor loss is realized when the donee sells the property.[24]

4. Part-Gift, Part-Sale Transactions. When property is acquired partly by purchase and partly by gift, it would be unreasonable to assign a basis as though it had been acquired solely by purchase, producing a cost basis under IRC §1012, or solely by gift, producing a carryover basis under IRC §1015. If property with a basis of $60,000 and a fair market value of $90,000, for example, purchased for $30,000 from the taxpayer's parents, it would be inappropriate to saddle the recipient with a $30,000 cost basis, since he would have been entitled to a $60,000 carryover basis had the property been transferred to him as an outright gift. On the other hand, if he paid $75,000, a carryover basis of only $60,000 would be inappropriate, since he parted with $75,000 in cash to get the property.

Under the current regulations, the transferor is viewed as selling the entire property for the amount received, and the transferee's basis is the amount paid for the property or the transferor's adjusted basis at the time of the transfer, whichever is greater, plus any increase for federal gift tax paid on the transfer authorized by IRC §1015(d).[25] The treatment under the current regulations is illustrated in Example 23-3, which assumes (a) a sale by *A* to *B* for $60,000 of property with an adjusted basis to *A* of $30,000 and a fair market value of $90,000, followed by (b) a sale by *B* to *C* of the property for its fair market value of $90,000.[26]

---

[23] See IRC §1015(d)(2); Treas. Regs. §1.1015-5(b)(1)(ii).

[24] Caldwell & Co. v. CIR, 234 F.2d 660 (6th Cir. 1956).

[25] Treas. Regs. §1.1015-4(a).

[26] Example 23-3 is based on Treas. Regs. §1.1001-1(e)(2), Example (1) (transferor's gain), and Treas. Regs. §1.1015-4(b), Example (2) (transferee's basis).

Example 23-3

Part Gift, Part Sale Under Current Regulations
(Dollars in Thousands)

1. Amount realized by *A*	$60
2. Less: *A*'s adjusted basis	30
3. Gain realized by *A*	$30
4. Basis of gift portion in *A*'s hands ($30 less line 2)	0
5. *B*'s basis	
a. Cost of purchased portion	60
b. Carryover basis of gift portion (line 4)	0
c. Total	$60
6. *B*'s gain on sale to *C*	
a. Amounts realized	90
b. Less: *B*'s basis (line 5c)	60
c. Gain	$30

Note: Computation assumes that transfer was not subject to federal gift tax (e.g., because amount was below donor's available credit).

In harmony with the usual treatment of property acquired by gift, the regulations qualify the foregoing basis rule in determining loss to the transferee. In this situation, the transferee's unadjusted basis cannot exceed the property's fair market value at the time of the gift. For example, if property with an adjusted basis of $90,000 and a fair market value of $60,000 is transferred for $30,000 in a part-gift, part-sale transaction, the transferee's basis is $90,000 in computing gain, but only $60,000 in computing loss.[27]

While the part-gift, part-sale regulations do not allocate the donor's basis between the sale and gift portions, IRC §1011(b) applies a different principle to bargain sales to charitable organizations generating charitable deductions under IRC §170. The problem addressed by IRC §1011(b) can be illustrated by assuming that *B* in Example 23-3 is a tax-exempt charitable organization. In this event, *A* would be entitled to a charitable contribution deduction of $30,000—the excess of the property's fair market value ($90,000) over the amount realized by *A* on the sale ($60,000). Because of its exempt status, however, the charitable organization—unlike *B* in the example—would not be taxed on selling the property, and this would mean not only that the $10,000 of appreciation on the *donated* one-third of the property would be untaxed (the

[27] See Treas. Regs. §1.1015-4(a) (second sentence); Treas. Regs. §1.1015-4(b), Example (4). For the result if the property is sold by the transferee for between $60,000 and $90,000, see principle illustrated supra, text at note 22.

normal result of donating appreciated property to a taxexempt organization), but also that $20,000 of *A*'s appreciation on the portion *sold* by him would escape taxation. To forestall the latter result, IRC §1011(b) requires *A* to allocate the adjusted basis of the property to the fraction sold to the charity in the ratio that the amount realized bears to the property's fair market value ($60,000/$90,000). The result is that *A* must recognize $40,000 of gain on the transfer and can deduct $30,000 as a charitable contribution—the same outcome that would have been reached by dividing the property, contributing one-third (worth $30,000) to the charity, and selling the other two-thirds to an outsider in an unrelated transaction (amount realized of $60,000 less allocated basis of $20,000).

¶23.4 PROPERTY ACQUIRED FROM DECEDENTS—DATE-OF-DEATH BASIS

1. Introductory. Under IRC §1014, the basis of property acquired from a decedent is its fair market value on the date of death (or on the optional valuation date authorized by IRC §2032, if the estate was subject to federal estate tax and the executor elected to value it as of that date). To avoid needless repetition, the term "date-of-death basis" is used hereafter to denote a basis equal to the property's value either at the decedent's death or on the optional valuation date, when applicable. The date-of-death value is commonly called a stepped-up basis because the fair market value of property held until death is usually greater than the decedent's cost or other basis. Property can decline in value even in an era of inflation, however, resulting in a stepped-down basis; but being perennial optimists, tax practitioners like to accentuate the positive by using "stepped-up basis" as a generic label, whether the property has gone up or down in value.

The date-of-death basis mandated by IRC §1014 is sometimes defended as a device to protect property transferred at death from subjection to both the federal estate tax and the federal income tax. But this rationale does not hold water, since the estate tax takes account solely of the aggregate value of the transferred assets, without regard to whether their value rose, declined, or remained the same during the decedent's ownership. For this reason, the estate tax does not cover the same ground as the income tax, which is concerned with increases and decreases in economic worth. In this respect, the federal estate tax resembles the federal gift tax, which has never been thought inconsistent with requiring the donee to carry forward the donor's basis so that appreciation arising during the donor's ownership will not be permanently immunized against income taxation.

2. Probate Assets. In prescribing a date-of-death basis for inherited property, IRC §1014(a) lays down a general rule that seemingly embraces all property "acquired" or "passing" from a decedent, but it has been held that these phrases have no independent force and encompass only the specific situations set out in the nine paragraphs of IRC §1014(b).[28] The core of IRC §1014 is IRC §1014(b)(1), providing a date-of-death value for property acquired from the decedent "by bequest, devise, or inheritance," a term that in effect encompasses the decedent's probate estate, except for assets used to pay claims, administration expenses, taxes, and the decedent's debts.

3. Inherited Property Encumbered by Debt. In *Crane v. CIR,* involving inherited property encumbered by a $250,000 mortgage and having a date-of-death value of the same amount, the Supreme Court held that the basis of the inherited property was not the zero-value equity but the full economic value of the property, including the mortgage.[29] Thus, the heir was entitled under IRC §1014 to use $250,000 as her basis for the inherited property and to compute depreciation allowances by reference to that amount. This principle, which may be qualified if the mortgage exceeds the date-of-death value, is discussed elsewhere in this work [30] in connection with the computation of gain or loss on sales of property subject to a mortgage for which the owner is not personally liable.

4. Nonprobate Assets. Sections 1014(a) and 1014(b)(9) confer a date-of-death value not only on property acquired by bequest, devise, or inheritance but also on substantially all property includable in the decedent's gross estate for federal estate tax purposes.

Because IRC §1014(b)(9) is as broad as the federal estate tax, it largely overlaps the coverage of IRC §§1014(b)(1)–1014(b)(5), 1014(b)(7), and 1014(b)(8). However, IRC §1014(b)(9) requires a reduction in basis for depreciation, amortization, and depletion deducted by the donee before the decedent's death. This limitation was enacted to avoid giving the donee double deductions by stepping up the basis of the property to its date-of-death value after he had already deducted part or all of its original carryover basis, determined under IRC §1015. But the date-of-death value may itself reflect the physical wear and tear, depletion, etc., that gave rise to the prior deductions by the donee, in which event the adjustment prescribed by IRC §1014(b)(9) is a case of overkill.

Section 1014(b)(6) confers a date-of-death value on the surviving spouse's one-half share of community property if the other one-half was includable in the deceased spouse's gross estate. This provision differs from the other paragraphs of IRC §1014(b) in that the property in question was never owned by the decedent, at least not in community-property theory, and was not includ-

[28] Collins v. US, 318 F.Supp. 382 (C.D. Cal. 1970), aff'd per curiam, 448 F.2d 787 (9th Cir. 1971) (payments received by widow from deceased husband's employer as compensation not "acquired from decedent" within meaning of IRC §1014).

[29] Crane v. CIR, 331 US 1 (1947).

able in his gross estate. Section 1014(b)(6) analogizes the surviving spouse's half of the community property to the amount that, in common-law states, qualifies for the marital deduction but nevertheless gets a date-of-death value. In keeping with this statutory objective, the courts have restricted the application of IRC §1014(b)(6) to property that would have received a stepped-up basis in a non-community-property state.[31]

5. Relation of Estate Tax Value to Income Tax Basis. The regulations provide that the value of property as appraised for federal estate tax purposes (or state inheritance tax if no federal estate tax return is required) "shall be deemed to be its fair market value" in applying IRC §1014,[32] but the IRS has announced the more flexible principle that, "except where the taxpayer is estopped by his previous actions or statements, such value is not conclusive but is a presumptive value which may be rebutted by clear and convincing evidence."[33]

6. Life Estates, Remainders, and Other Divided Interests—"Uniform Basis." Property acquired from a decedent takes a date-of-death basis regardless of when the taxpayer's interest becomes possessory. Thus, if property is bequeathed to the testator's children for life, then to the grandchildren for their lives, and then outright to a great-grandchild, the latter's basis on coming into possession is the value of the property at the date of the testator's death, adjusted for such postmortem events as improvements and depreciation deductions, regardless of its value when the ultimate heir's interest become possessory. In the same vein, the date-of-death basis is controlling despite changes in the value of the property between that date and the date of distribution.

This so-called uniform-basis concept is concerned with the property as a whole; and while the prescribed amount may have to be divided among the taxpayers interested in the property, this is rarely necessary. First, in the normal situation involving a life tenant who receives the income from the inherited property throughout his or her life, the basis of the life interest is irrelevant since the amount received is includable in gross income in its entirety, without any offset for the gradually declining basis. This principle is promulgated by IRC §273, disallowing any deduction "for shrinkage (by whatever name called) in the value of such interest due to the lapse of time," if a life or terminable interest is acquired by gift, bequest, or inheritance.

---

[30] See infra ¶23.16.

[31] See Collins v. US, supra note 28 (no step-up for widow's half of community-property-contract right to payments from deceased husband's employer).

[32] Treas. Regs. §1.1014-3(a).

[33] Rev. Rul. 54-97, 1954-1 CB 113; see also Feldman v. CIR, ¶68,019 P-H Memo TC (1968), and cases there cited.

Second, the remainderman receives the property tax-free when the life estate or other intervening interests terminate, whether it is then worth more or less than the basis of his or her remainder. Thus, while the life estate exists, the life tenant is treated as the absolute owner in computing depreciation and depletion; and these allowances are determined by reference to the property's uniform basis, not the basis of the life tenant's interest.

For these reasons, an apportionment of the property's uniform basis among the divided interests is required only when one of the parties sells his or her rights in the property (as distinguished from a sale of the underlying property itself); and even when a divided interest is sold, its basis is sometimes disregarded under IRC §1001(e). This provision, enacted to restrain tax-fostered transactions in this area, provides that the apportioned basis of a life estate or other terminable interest (but not the basis of a remainder) must be disregarded unless the sale or other disposition is a part of a larger transaction transferring the entire interest in the property. Thus, if the life tenant joins with the remainderman in a sale, she can offset her basis against her share of the sales price; but if the life tenant acts alone, her apportioned basis is disregarded, and the entire amount received (whether it exceeds or is less than the basis) constitutes gain on the sale.[34] Sales of life interests to remaindermen, who are often the most likely purchasers, are thus deprived of their principal tax advantage by IRC §1001(e).

7. Property Not Qualifying for Date-of-Death Basis. Certain assets are denied a date-of-death value by IRC §1014, even though includable in the decedent's gross estate for federal estate tax purposes:

1. Property passing directly or indirectly from a decedent to a donor (or donor's spouse) if the donor made a gift to the decedent within one year of death. The donor (or donor's spouse) must use the basis of the property in the decedent's hands immediately before death.[35] This 1981 change prevents the holder of appreciated property from engaging in a grisly tax-avoidance scheme: giving the property to a parent or other relative who is about to die, in order to get it back by inheritance—with a stepped-up basis.

2. Property received from the decedent during his lifetime but sold, exchanged, or otherwise disposed of before the decedent's death.[36] On selling property of this type (e.g., gifts in contemplation of death), the donee uses a carryover basis determined under IRC §1015, relating to property acquired by gift; and if a date-of-death basis were retroactively assigned to the property on the donor's death, it would be necessary to recompute gain or loss on transactions that were closed in earlier years.

3. Items constituting "income in respect of a decedent" under IRC

---

[34] For illustrations of the operation of IRC §1001(e), see Treas. Regs. §1.1014-5(c).

[35] IRC §1014(e).

[36] IRC §1014(a); for the phrase "sold, exchanged, or otherwise disposed of," see

§691, such as the decedent's final paycheck, uncollected professional fees, and similar items that would have been includable in his income had he survived. These items are taxed to the estate or heirs on collection, and a date-of-death value would be inconsistent with this treatment.[37]

4. Property purchased by an executor with funds obtained by selling property acquired from the decedent. Since the fiduciary would have used the date-of-death value on selling the original property, the new investment has a cost basis under IRC §1012, which is carried forward by the legatee.[38]

¶23.5 SUBSTITUTED, CARRYOVER, AND OTHER SPECIAL BASIS RULES

Section 1012 establishes the general rule that the basis of property is its cost, except as otherwise provided. The special rules just examined (IRC §1015, relating to property acquired by gift, and IRC §1014, relating to property acquired from a decedent) are only two of numerous exceptions to the cost basis prescribed by IRC §1012. The Code's many "nonrecognition" provisions, under which gain or loss is not recognized when appreciated or depreciated property is exchanged in specified circumstances, are ordinarily supplemented by a basis rule requiring that the taxpayer transfer his basis for the property surrendered to the property received or carryover the property's previous basis. As a result of this substituted or carryover basis, the untaxed gain (or undeducted loss) on the exchange will be reflected in determining the taxpayer's gain (or loss) when the new property is sold. For example, if the taxpayer exchanges a building with an adjusted basis of $75,000 and a fair market value of $100,000 for a similar building in a tax-free exchange under IRC §1031, relating to exchanges of "like kind" property, the new building has a basis of $75,000 in the taxpayer's hands, and the taxpayer's unrecognized gain on the old building will be taxed if the new building is sold for $100,000 or more.

¶23.6 ALLOCATION OF BASIS

If property is bought in a large parcel and sold piecemeal, its basis must be allocated among the separate components. Every investor, for example, knows that if he buys a 100-share block of stock and later sells some of the shares, he can compute his cost basis for those that are sold by simple arithme-

---

Treas. Regs. §1.1015-5(a)(1)(ii).

[37] IRC §1014(c).

[38] Treas. Regs. §1.1014-3(c).

tic; the basis of each share is 1/100 of the price paid for the entire block. When the units are not interchangeable, however, the process of allocating a lump-sum purchase price is more complicated. Familiar examples requiring an allocation that cannot be computed by simple division include:

1. Rental real estate, whose cost must be allocated between the depreciable building and the nondepreciable land.

2. A home office, requiring allocation of the taxpayer's basis for the residence between the depreciable business area and the nondepreciable personal portions.

3. A subdivider's sale of building lots, if part of the tract is unsuitable for residential construction and hence is worth less than other areas.

4. The purchase of a going business, including inventory that will be sold promptly, machinery and equipment that can be depreciated over a short useful life, depreciable buildings with a long useful life, and intangibles (franchises, trade names, lists of customers, covenants not to compete, etc.), of which some can be amortized and others represent nondepreciable goodwill.

The regulations provide a starting point in this area by requiring an "equitable" apportionment of basis among the larger property's components.[39] If a ratable apportionment of basis would be inequitable or impossible, the apportionment must usually take account of location, economic potential, and other elements of value. For example, in a leading case involving land acquired by a taxpayer interested primarily in strip-mining coal from a portion of the tract, the Court of Appeals for the Sixth Circuit rejected a per-acre apportionment of the tract's cost for purposes of computing depletion of the coal and held that an equitable apportionment required assigning an above-average part of the cost to the land overlying the coal.[40]

If it is impossible or impracticable to allocate an aggregate basis among the property's components, a taxpayer who sells a single item could be relegated to a zero basis for failure to establish the proper amount and required to include in gross income the entire amount realized; this would leave the entire original basis intact, to be offset when the balance of the property is sold. A more generous principle, however, sanctioned by the leading case in this area, has been accepted by the IRS. In *Inaja Land Co. v. CIR,* the taxpayer received about $50,000 for an easement to divert polluted waters into a stream bordering on the taxpayer's fishing preserve, which had a cost basis of $61,000.[41] Because it was impossible to allocate the taxpayer's cost basis between the adversely affected property and the rest of the land, the Tax Court treated the amount received as a return of capital in its entirety, rather than taxing it in full on failure-of-proof grounds. The excluded amount reduced the

---

[39] Treas. Regs. §1.61-6(a).

[40] Beaver Dam Coal Co. v. US, 370 F.2d 414 (6th Cir. 1966).

[41] Inaja Land Co. v. CIR, 9 TC 727 (1947) (Acq.).

taxpayer's basis for the property from $61,000 to $11,000, thus increasing the potential gain (or reducing the potential loss) on a future disposition of the property.

To employ the cost recovery principle sanctioned by *Inaja Land Co.,* the taxpayer must show that the aggregate basis of the entire property exceeds the amount received but cannot be apportioned among its components. If, however, the taxpayer's aggregate basis can be allocated among several components and the amount received is paid for rights or damage to only one component, the latter's share of the aggregate basis must be used in applying the cost recovery principle. In a 1968 ruling, for example, the IRS held that a taxpayer receiving $5,000 from a power company for an easement to construct and maintain electric poles across a 600-acre farm with a basis of $60,000 could use only $2,000—the portion of the cost basis allocable to the 20 acres directly affected by the easement—(20/600 × $60,000)—in applying the *Inaja Land Co.* principle.[42] As a result, the taxpayer realized $3,000 of gain. Had the amount received been less than $2,000, however, it would have been excludable from gross income in its entirety.

In *Inaja Land Co.,* the cost recovery principle was applied to an amount received by the taxpayer for rights carved out of a larger integrated whole. The same principle has been employed in several cases involving lump-sum payments for a grab bag of assets not integrally linked to each other, such as the assets of an insolvent bank, consisting of "hundreds of items of various kinds such as notes, judgments, accounts, mortgages, and other evidences of debt." [43]

Taxpayers holding claims with a basis less than their face amounts allocate the basis among all payments due on the debt, so that each payment is divided between a return of capital and income.[44] For example, if a promissory note for $1,000 payable in ten installments of $100 each (plus 6 percent on the unpaid principal) is purchased from its holder for $900, each installment has a basis of $90, and the payment when received constitutes a $90 return of capital and $10 of interest income. The market discount constitutes interest income even though the purchaser is an investor and holds the obligation as a capital asset.[45] The stated interest is also taxable, when collected, as interest income.

The litigated cases are primarily concerned with an important exception to this pro rata principle, under which the basis of speculative claims that may

---

[42] Rev. Rul. 68-291, 1968-1 CB 351.

[43] United Mercantile Agencies, Inc. v. CIR, 23 TC 1105 (1955) (Acq.), mdf'd as to other issues sub nom. Drybrough v. CIR, 238 F.2d 735 (6th Cir. 1956).

[44] See Smith v. CIR, 48 TC 872 (1967), aff'd on this issue, 424 F.2d 219 (9th Cir. 1970), and cases collected in the Tax Court opinion at 879.

[45] Ehlers v. Vinal, 382 F.2d 58 (8th Cir. 1967) (collecting earlier cases).

not be collected in full can be recovered before any income is realized.[46] A conventional explanation for the cost recovery exception is that the ultimate realization of gain by the purchaser of speculative claims at a discount is conjectural. An alternative rationale is that early installments of doubtful claims are more likely to be paid than later installments and that the differential is so uncertain that an equitable apportionment of the taxpayer's basis is not feasible. The allocation of basis in part-gift, part-sale transactions involving both noncharitable and charitable donees is discussed elsewhere.[47]

¶23.7 IDENTIFICATION OF PROPERTY SOLD

If the owner of Blackacre and Whiteacre sells Blackacre, he must use its own adjusted basis (and, if relevant, its holding period) in computing gain or loss, even if the two tracts are similar in physical characteristics and equal in value. What if the taxpayer sells one out of two or more fungible assets (e.g., merchandise or securities) to a purchaser who may not know, and does not care, which unit is delivered to consummate the contract of sale?

In the case of property includable in inventory, IRC §1013 provides that the taxpayer's basis is the "last inventory value." Elaborating on this brief provision, a set of statutory, administrative, and judicial rules disregards the cost of the particular unit sold and computes gain or loss by reference to accounting conventions (e.g., FIFO, LIFO, or average cost).[48] On the other hand, taxpayers owning fungible assets that are not includable in inventory (the most important examples are securities held for investment) are permitted—and ordinarily required—to match their actual costs with the units actually delivered.

When a taxpayer purchases two or more lots of identical securities at different dates or prices and then sells part of his holdings, the regulations lay down two basic principles for matching the securities sold to the various lots held by the taxpayer: (a) If a particular lot can be "adequately identified" as the one that was sold, its cost and holding period are controlling; but (b) in the absence of adequate identification, the securities sold are charged against the earliest lots acquired on a FIFO basis.[49]

If the taxpayer rather than a broker or other agent has custody of the

---

[46] See, e.g., Liftin v. CIR, 36 TC 909 (1961), aff'd, 317 F.2d 234 (4th Cir. 1963); cases cited in Smith v. CIR, supra note 44.

[47] See supra ¶23.3.

[48] Infra ¶35.4.

[49] Treas. Regs. §1.1012-1(c)(1), applying not only to stock but also by virtue of Treas. Regs. §1.1012-1(c)(6), to a sale or transfer of bonds after July 13, 1965.

securities and if the taxpayer is not a trustee, executor, or administrator, delivery of the certificate for a particular lot of securities is controlling.[50] If the taxpayer's records disclose the cost of the securities represented by each certificate, this basic principle enables a careful investor with several lots of identical securities to pick and choose among them and thus to control the amount of gain or loss realized when reducing his portfolio. The IRS and the courts have addressed the problem of adequate identification in a number of specific areas including: (a) several lots of securities represented by a single certificate; (b) stock splits and stock dividends; and (c) securities exchanged in corporate reorganizations.[51]

When securities are left in the custody of a broker or other agent, the investor can satisfy the "adequate identification" requirement by notifying the agent (not necessarily in writing) of the securities to be sold and obtaining, within a reasonable time thereafter, a written confirmation of the specification. (An extensive but unsystematic survey by the author suggests that written confirmations are not a common practice.) If this procedure is followed, the taxpayer's designation is controlling, even if the agent delivers the wrong certificates to the buyer.[52] In a 1961 ruling, the IRS sanctioned a blanket designation of the sequence in which a number of lots of securities are to be sold over a long period, provided the requisite written confirmation is furnished by the broker or agent.[53]

Although fungible assets other than securities are often acquired at different times and prices (e.g., stamps and coins accumulated by a collector) and create identification problems similar to those discussed above, the regulations neither extend the rules applicable to securities to other interchangeable assets nor prescribe special rules; and the issue has not stimulated a body of litigation or IRS rulings. To fill the void, it would be reasonable to apply analogous principles, permitting the assignment of actual costs to particular items by appropriate entries on the taxpayer's records or instructions to custodians and resorting to the FIFO principle when identification is not feasible.

---

[50] Treas. Regs. §1.1012-1(c)(2). Special rules applicable to trustees and executors or administrators of estates are set out in Treas. Regs. §1.1012-1(c)(4); they can identify the lot sold or distributed by a written notation in the books and records of the trust or estate plus, in the case of the distribution, a written notification to the distributee. When securities are so identified, it is irrelevant whether one certificate or another is delivered to the transferee.

[51] Treas. Regs. §1.1012-1(c)(3)(ii) (single certificate); Rev. Rul. 56-653, 1956-2 CB 185 (stock splits and dividends); Bloch v. CIR, 148 F.2d 452 (9th Cir. 1945) (reorganizations).

[52] Treas. Regs. §1.1012-1(c)(3)(1).

[53] Rev. Rul. 61-97, 1961-1 CB 394.

¶23.8 ADJUSTMENTS TO BASIS

1. Introductory. After the taxpayer's original (or unadjusted) basis for property has been ascertained in the manner described above, it must be adjusted as prescribed by IRC §1016, since the property's "adjusted basis" is controlling in determining gain or loss on a sale, as well as depreciation and many other tax allowances.[54] The adjustments to basis mandated by IRC §1016 are ancillary to a structural principle of the Internal Revenue Code, viz., that in computing taxable income, the taxpayer is entitled to write off his investment in business or income-producing property (represented by its unadjusted basis)—but neither more nor less than that amount by depreciation, cost recovery, amortization, deduction of damage caused by casualty, etc., during the asset's productive period or when his interest is terminated by sale, abandonment, physical destruction, or similar event. In rare circumstances, however, the taxpayer is allowed to write off more than his investment; thus, percentage depletion continues even after the entire investment has been recovered tax-free, and the basis of property is only partially reduced by the investment credit.

In order to measure the taxpayer's gain or loss accurately, his original investment in the property (represented by its unadjusted basis) must be increased by any additional capital outlays (e.g., the cost of adding a new wing to a building, clearing title to land, or modernizing a machine) and reduced by tax deductions (e.g., depreciation, cost recovery, or casualty losses) and any tax-free receipts generated by the property.[55]

Given its mission, IRC §1016 is, in effect, the opposite face of the tax deduction coin. Thus, if an expenditure to repair property can be deducted as a business expense under IRC §162, it cannot be added to the property's basis under IRC §1016; but if a deduction is denied because the outlay adds to the value of the property or substantially prolongs its life, an increase in basis is ipso facto warranted. Similarly, if property qualifies for a depreciation of cost recovery deduction under IRC §§167 or 168, its basis must be correspondingly reduced under IRC §1016; but if deductions are denied because the property, like land, is immune to exhaustion, wear and tear, or obsolescence, its basis remains intact and can be written off when the property is ultimately sold or disposed of.

2. Taxes, Interest, and Other Carrying Charges. Section 266 permits otherwise deductible taxes, interest, and other carrying charges to be charged

---

[54] See, e.g., IRC §§1001(a) (gain or loss on sale or other disposition), 167(g) (depreciation), 165(b) (losses), and 170(e)(2) (charitable contributions).

[55] Tax-free receipts are uncommon, but see Inaja Land Co. v. CIR, supra note 41 (payment for easement and damages to land not taxable on receipt).

at the taxpayer's election to capital account and thus to be included in the basis of the affected property. The logic of IRC §266 implies that the deduction of carrying charges is ordinarily inconsistent with a proper matching of costs and revenues and hence does not clearly reflect income. But since Congress has deliberately preserved the statutory provisions explicitly permitting taxes and interest to be deducted even if incurred during the construction of business property or while unproductive property is being brought to an income-producing threshold,[56] taxpayers can either compute income in accordance with these rules or elect under IRC §266 to disregard these statutory aberrations and compute income accurately.

The regulations sanction elections under IRC §266 to capitalize four categories of expenses:

1. In the case of unimproved and unproductive real property, annual taxes, mortgage interest, and other carrying charges.[57]

2. In the case of real property, whether improved, unimproved, productive, or unproductive: (a) interest on a loan; (b) payroll taxes; (c) taxes on the purchase, storage, use, or consumption of materials; and (d) other necessary expenditures. To qualify, these expenditures must be paid or incurred for development or improvement of the property before development or construction is completed; but the work qualifies whether the property will produce taxable income (e.g., a factory) or not (e.g., a personal residence).[58]

3. As to personal property, expenses paid or incurred up to the date of installation or first use by the taxpayer, whichever is later, for (a) payroll taxes on compensation for services in transporting or installing machinery or other fixed assets; (b) interest on loans to purchase, transport, or install the property; and (c) taxes on the purchase, storage, use, or consumption of the property.[59]

4. Any other taxes and carrying charges that in the opinion of the IRS are chargeable to capital account "under sound accounting principles." [60]

3. Depreciation, Amortization, and Depletion. By all odds, the most important adjustments reducing the taxpayer's basis for property are mandated by IRC §1016(a)(2), requiring basis to be adjusted for depreciation,

---

[56] Section 189, restricting current deductions for real property construction-period interest and taxes, which is discussed supra ¶15.3, does not apply to amounts that the taxpayer properly elects to capitalize under IRC §266.

[57] Treas. Regs. §1.266-1(b)(1)(i).

[58] Treas. Regs. §1.266-1(b)(1)(ii); but see Megibow v. CIR, 218 F.2d 687 (3d Cir. 1955) (taxes and interest on mortgage encumbering previously constructed personal residence not chargeable to capital account).

[59] Treas. Regs. §1.266-1(b)(1)(iii).

[60] Treas. Regs. §1.266-1(b)(1)(iv).

amortization, and depletion to the extent "allowed" or "allowable" (whichever is greater) as deductions in computing taxable income in current or prior years. (By virtue of IRC §167(a), cost recovery deductions under IRC §168 are allowances for exhaustion, wear and tear, and obsolescence, and hence are embraced by IRC §1016(a)(2)'s requirements.) Although these deductions do not generate any cash for the taxpayer (except indirectly in the form of reduced income tax payments), they must be applied to reduce basis because, pro tanto, the taxpayer's investment has been written off. If the property's original basis remained intact despite the deduction of depreciation, amortization, or depletion, there would be a second write-off of the investment when the property was sold, since gain or loss is computed under IRC §1001(a) by deducting the property's adjusted basis from the amount realized.

The double-barreled reference in IRC §1016(a)(2) to depreciation, amortization, and depletion "allowed" or "allowable" prevents a taxpayer having no current use for a depreciation deduction from refraining to claim it in the hope of preserving the property's basis intact for write-off in a later year. Since in uncontested cases there is no formal procedure by which the IRS allows deductions, the Supreme Court held in *Virginian Hotel Corp. v. Helvering* that (a) depreciation was "allowed" within the meaning of the 1932 law if it was claimed by the taxpayer and not challenged by the IRS and (b) a reduction in basis was required when depreciation was allowed in this sense, even if it did not reduce the taxpayer's taxable income because he had an excess of other valid deductions for the year in question.[61] Four Justices dissented, arguing that the term "allowed" should not be interpreted to include depreciation that did not in fact reduce the taxpayer's gross income. Although their point of view did not carry the judicial day, it was accepted by Congress in 1952, when the statutory predecessor of IRC §1016(a)(2) was amended to provide that basis must be reduced by the greater of (a) the amount "allowable" (whether claimed or not, and without regard to whether it had or would have produced a tax benefit)[62] and (b) the amount that was "allowed" and resulted in a tax reduction.

The rules determining whether a deduction that was "allowed" (i.e., claimed and not challenged by the IRS) resulted in a reduction of taxes are illustrated by the regulations and resemble the rules developed under

---

[61] Virginian Hotel Corp. v. Helvering, 319 US 523, rehearing denied, 320 US 810 (1943).

[62] See Gardiner v. US, 536 F.2d 903 (10th Cir. 1976) (IRC §1311, mitigating statute of limitations, not applicable where taxpayer failed to claim allowable depreciation, even though basis was reduced by allowable amount in computing gain on sale of depreciable asset).

the general tax benefit principle embodied in IRC §111.[63] Because depreciation deducted in a loss year can reduce taxes if it enters into a net operating loss and is carried over to an earlier or later year, a taxpayer must sustain a long streak of losses to get any benefit from the 1952 limitation.

4. Other Adjustments to Basis. In addition to the broad rule of IRC §1016(a)(1), requiring the basis of property to be adjusted for all expenditures, receipts, losses, and other items "properly chargeable to capital account" and the equally fundamental rules of IRC §§1016(a)(2) and 1016(a)(3) for adjustments to reflect depreciation, amortization, and depletion, IRC §1016(a) lays down a number of more specialized rules. For example, taxpayers deducting or amortizing the following expenditures (which would be capitalized under ordinary financial accounting) are required to reduce the basis of the property involved by the greater of (a) the amount allowed as deductions and resulting in a tax reduction and (b) the amount allowable: (1) deferred expenses under IRC §616(b), relating to the development of mines and natural deposits; (2) deferred research and experimental expenditures amortized under IRC §174(b)(1); (3) trademark and trade name expenditures amortized under IRC §177; and (4) amounts paid for purchased franchises, trademarks, or trade names, if deducted under IRC §1253(d)(2).[64]

Two other adjustments, which are the converse of the above, permit the taxpayer to increase the basis of property to reflect the disallowance of deductions for the following: (1) expenses and depreciation attributable to unharvested crops when sold with the land, to the extent disallowed under IRC §168; and (2) expenses relating to contracts for the disposal of coal or iron ore, to the extent disallowed under IRC §272.[65]

One other basis adjustment deserves special mention. IRC §1016(a)(24) requires a downward adjustment by an amount equal to 50 percent of the investment tax credit taken, before a taxpayer can compute depreciation or cost recovery deductions.[66] Taxpayers can avoid this downward adjustment by reducing the investment tax credit taken by two percentage points.[67] In the event of recapture of the tax credits taken, an upward adjustment in basis is mandated to reflect the fact that the taxpayer received no benefit from the recaptured credit.[68]

---

[63] Treas. Regs. §§1.1016-3(e), 1.1016-3(h); for the tax benefit doctrine, see supra ¶1.10.

[64] IRC §§1016(a)(9), 1016(a)(14), 1016(a)(16), 1016(a)(20).

[65] IRC §§1016(a)(11), 1016(a)(15).

[66] See IRC §48(q)(1); supra ¶13.1

[67] See IRC §48(q)(4).

[68] IRC §48(q)(2).

¶23.9 BASIS OF PROPERTY DEVOTED TO PERSONAL USE WHEN SOLD OR CONVERTED TO BUSINESS USE

Since property devoted to personal use, such as the taxpayer's home, cannot be depreciated for tax purposes, its basis remains intact despite physical deterioration. A taxpayer selling a home costing $50,000 for $75,000, for example, realizes gain of only $25,000, even though a similar house on the rental market might have generated $10,000 of depreciation deductions during the same period, reducing its basis to $40,000 at the time of sale and thereby producing a gain on sale of $35,000. By exempting personal residences from analogous treatment, existing law buttresses the long-entrenched exemption of imputed income. Homeowners are not taxed on the rental value of their homes during occupancy,[69] and the implicit depreciation during this period is also exempted from tax when the property is sold. In effect, the portion of the taxpayer's original basis that is "consumed" during personal occupancy is applied against the sales proceeds in determining whether the taxpayer has realized a gain and, if so, its amount.

On the other hand, no loss is allowable under IRC §263, disallowing deductions for personal, living, or family expenses, even if the property's value is depressed by market forces and it is sold for less than its original cost minus the implicit depreciation attributable to physical deterioration during the period of personal occupancy. For example, if a residence is bought for $50,000 and sold for $30,000, no deduction is allowed, even if only $5,000 of the $20,000 decline in value is attributable to wear and tear inflicted by the family during its occupancy and the entire balance of the loss results from outside market forces arising shortly before the sale.

If personal property is converted to business or profit-oriented purposes, the regulations provide that its basis in computing depreciation and loss on a later sale is either its adjusted basis for loss at the time of conversion or its fair market value at that time, whichever is lower.[70] There is no explicit statutory authority for this change in basis on a conversion, but the rationale of the regulations is evidently that depreciation and loss after the conversion are incurred in a business or profit-oriented activity only to the extent of the value of the property when devoted to that function. The operation of the principle promulgated by the regulations is illustrated by Example 23-4, which assumes that the taxpayer (1) purchased a residence in 1976 for $100,000, of which $60,000 was allocable to the building; (2) used the property as a personal residence until December 31, 1980; (3) converted the property to rental use on January 1, 1981, when it was worth $90,000; (4) depreciated the building on a straight-line basis during the three-year rental period, based on an es-

[69] See supra ¶1.6.

[70] Treas. Regs. §§1.167(g)-1 (depreciation), 1.165-9(b)(2) (losses).

timated useful life of fifteen years; and (5) sold the property for $70,000 on January 1, 1984. Of the property's fair market value when converted to rental use ($90,000), Case *A* assumes that $50,000 was allocable to the building, while Case *B* assumes that $65,000 was allocable to the building.

Example 23-4

Loss on Sale of Residence Converted From Personal to Rental Use

	Case A	*Case B*
1. Basis of property at conversion (lesser of $100,000 cost and $90,000 value)	$90,000	$90,000
2. Less: Depreciation at 6.67 percent per year for three years, based on lesser of building's value when converted (Case *A,* $50,000; Case *B,* $65,000) and cost ($60,000)	10,000	12,000
3. Adjusted basis for determining loss	$80,000	$78,000
4. Less: Amount realized on sale	70,000	70,000
5. Loss	$10,000	$ 8,000

¶23.10 ADJUSTMENTS TO SUBSTITUTED OR CARRYOVER BASIS

When property has a substituted or carryover basis, IRC §1016(b) requires two sets of adjustments for depreciation, improvements, and other items properly affecting basis,[71] which can be illustrated by assuming that the taxpayer is about to sell rental property received as a gift from one of his parents. Since the taxpayer has a carryover basis for the property determined under IRC §1015(a) by reference to its basis in the hands of the donor, the taxpayer must start with the donor's cost or other unadjusted basis and then adjust it, in the manner described above,[72] for all items affecting basis that occurred during the donor's ownership. The result of these adjustments is the adjusted basis of the property in the donor's hands at the time of the gift. The second

[71] Section 1016(b) uses "substituted basis" as a generic term to denote both carryover basis and substituted basis. See supra ¶23.1, text following note 2.

[72] If a loss is incurred, the second set of adjustments is applied to the property's adjusted basis at the time of the gift (determined as described in the text) or its fair market value at that time, whichever is lower. See supra ¶23.3.

set of adjustments is then made to reflect similar items during the period of the taxpayer's ownership and this determines the adjusted basis to be used in computing gain or loss on the sale.

Similar principles are controlling if the property has a substituted basis, as in the case of property acquired in a tax-free exchange of property for other property of a like kind under IRC §1031. The basis of the property given up in the exchange must be adjusted to the date of the exchange; its adjusted basis is then transferred to the new property, and appropriate additional adjustments are then made to reflect depreciation and other items from the date when the new property was acquired until its sale or other disposition.

¶23.11 NEGATIVE BASIS

Although occasionally discussed by commentators, the possibility that property can have a "negative basis" (i.e., a basis that is less than zero) has usually encountered surprise and skepticism. Resistance to the concept stems from two sources. First, under existing law, the unadjusted or original basis of property can almost always be traced back to the amount paid for the property by the taxpayer or a predecessor in title. Since cost must be a positive amount and since reductions in basis ordinarily reflect deductions for depreciation, cost recovery, casualty losses, and similar items that in the aggregate cannot ordinarily exceed the property's basis, reduction of the original basis to a subzero level is not normally possible. Second, even when loopholes or anomalies in existing law create the theoretical possibility of a negative basis (such as percentage depletion, which can exceed the taxpayer's basis for the mineral deposit), recognizing its existence could result in gain exceeding the selling price of the property. For example, if property with a basis of minus \$50 were sold for \$100, the gain would be \$150.

¶23.12 AMOUNT REALIZED—INTRODUCTORY

Under IRC §1001(a), the taxpayer's gain or loss on a sale or other disposition of property is the difference between the adjusted basis of the property and the "amount realized." This provision is purely computational; it determines the *amount* of the taxpayer's gain or loss but leaves to other provisions the task of determining whether the amount so computed is taxable or deductible, recognized or not recognized, and capital or ordinary. The term "amount realized" is defined by IRC §1001(b) as the sum of any money received plus the fair market value of the property (other than money) received. By referring to "the amount realized therefrom"—that is, from the sale or other disposition of property—IRC §1001(a) implicitly requires amounts received for other reasons to be excluded in computing gain or loss and to be treated in accordance with their nature. For example, deferred payments for property may have to be allocated in part to unstated interest under IRC §483 and excluded from the "amount realized," if the credit arrangement does not provide an appropriate rate of interest.[73]

Although IRC §1001(b) makes no reference to expenses incurred in selling the property, such as sales commissions, advertising expenses, and attorneys' fees, they cannot be deducted under IRC §162 (business expenses) or §212 (expenses of managing income-producing property, etc.) unless incurred by dealers in disposing of inventory property. Instead, they serve to reduce the "amount realized" by the seller.[74] Computation of the "amount realized" by the seller when real estate taxes are adjusted at a closing, once dependent on the niceties of local law, is now controlled by the second sentence of IRC §1001(b). To the extent that the seller is reimbursed by the buyer for taxes allocable to the period beginning on the date of sale, the payment is not part of the "amount realized" by the seller, but instead reduces his deduction for taxes under IRC §164; on the other hand, real property taxes paid by the buyer that are allocable to the period of the seller's ownership increase the "amount realized" by the latter on the sale.[75]

¶23.13 PROPERTY OF INDETERMINATE VALUE: "OPEN" TRANSACTIONS

If the amount realized by the seller on disposing of an asset includes property, its fair market value must be determined by reference to stock market quotations, appraisals, assessments, recent transactions, or other evidentiary sources. The regulations state that fair market value is "a question of fact, but only in rare and extraordinary cases will property be considered to have no fair market value." [76] The government's track record in establishing that almost all assets can be valued is particularly impressive, in light of the fact that the Supreme Court in *Burnet v. Logan,* the leading case in this area, expressed distaste for the computation of gain based on "mere estimates, assumptions and speculation." [77]

The taxpayer in *Burnet v. Logan* sold stock in a closely held corporation, whose principal asset was stock in a second corporation that owned a valuable

[73] See infra ¶27.6.

[74] Treas. Regs. §1.263(a)-2(e).

[75] See Treas. Regs. §1.1001-1(b); IRC §164(d).

[76] Treas. Regs. §1.1001-1(a).

[77] Burnet v. Logan, 283 US 404, 412 (1931).

lease on an iron mine, for cash plus the buyer's promise to pay additional amounts when and as ore was extracted from the mine under an agreement allocating the output to the lease-holding company's shareholders in proportion to their holdings. The government valued the buyer's promise by estimating its proportionate share of the total amount of ore in the mine, assuming that the ore would be extracted in equal amounts over its estimated life, and computing the discounted value in the year of sale of the estimated future payments. On the theory that this amount had to be taken into account in computing the seller's gain or loss in the year of sale (1916) and hence became her basis for the contract, the government then determined that the royalties received by her in later years should be divided between tax-free returns of capital (i.e., recovery of the basis of the contract) and taxable income. The Supreme Court, however, held that the 1916 transaction was not "closed," with the result that the seller was entitled to apply all cash receipts against her basis for the stock until that amount was recovered tax-free, whereupon all subsequent receipts would be includable in income.

The difference between open and closed transaction treatment of a sale is illustrated by Example 23-5, involving (a) a sale in 1979 of a capital asset with an adjusted basis of $10 for a claim of debatable value and (b) collections in 1980-1982 of either $40 (Case *A*) or $5 (Case *B*) in full payment of the claim. The "closed transaction" columns assume that the claim is valued at $20 when received; the "open transaction" columns assume that it cannot be valued when received.

Example 23-5

Closed vs. Open Transactions

	Case A (\$40 Collected)		*Case B (\$5 Collected)*	
	Closed	*Open*	*Closed*	*Open*
1. Amount realized, 1979 sale	$20	N.A.	$20	N.A.
2. Less: Adjusted basis of property sold	10	N.A.	10	N.A.
3. Gain (loss) on 1979 sale	$10	N.A.	$10	N.A.
4. Basis of claim received in 1979 sale	$20	N.A.	$20	N.A.
5. Amount Collected, 1980–1982	$40	$40	$ 5	$ 5

6. Less: Adjusted basis of claim (closed transaction—line 4) or of property sold (open transaction—line 2)	20	10	20	10
7. Gain (loss) on 1980-1982 collections	$20	$30	($15)	($ 5)
8. Net gain (loss), 1979-1982 (line 3 plus line 7)	$30	$30	($ 5)	($ 5)

N.A. = Not applicable

As Example 23-5 illustrates, the aggregate amount of gain or loss realized by the taxpayer is the same, whether closed or open transaction treatment applies, since it is the difference between the adjusted basis of the property sold ($10) and the aggregate amount received in 1980–1982 ($40 in Case *A*, $5 in Case *B*); but there are differences in the years when the aggregate amount is reportable.

Moreover, the 1979 transaction is a "sale or exchange" for capital gain and loss purposes, so that closed transaction treatment results in capital gain or loss in 1979 in both Case *A* and Case *B*. Since the collection of a claim does not usually qualify as a "sale or exchange," however, the 1980-1982 results in the closed transaction situation are ordinary income of $20 (Case *A*—$40 collected) or ordinary loss of $15 (Case *B*—$5 collected). By contrast, open transactions are viewed as amounts belatedly realized from the capital asset sold in 1979, resulting in capital gain of $30 (Case *A*—$40 collected) or capital loss of $5 (Case *B*—$5 collected).

The result in *Burnet v. Logan* is seldom encountered in practice; and the statement in the regulations that property received by the seller must be valued in computing the "amount realized" on a sale except "in rare and extraordinary cases" is a fair summary of current law.[78] Moreover, under IRC §453, as amended in 1980, the open transaction theory faces an uncertain future. The temporary regulations all but eliminate cost recovery, and it is not

[78] See Rev. Rul. 58-402, 1958-2 CB 15 (extensive review of litigated cases); Waring v. CIR, 412 F.2d 800 (3d Cir. 1969) (rights under royalty contract; held, valuation adopted by taxpayer but later withdrawn was admission properly treated by Tax Court as evidence in finding rights could be valued); McCormac v. US, 424 F.2d 607 (Ct. Cl. 1970) (right to receive percentage of cash receipts from sale of cemetery land and services; held, subject to reasonable valuation); but see Dorsey v. CIR, 49 TC 606 (1968) (royalty agreement lacked ascertainable market value); Wiggins' Est. v. CIR, 72 TC 701 (1979) (land contracts lacked ascertainable fair market value; cost recovery method allowed).

clear if taxpayers can elect out of installment sales treatment into open transaction treatment.[79]

Even if a transfer does not result in an open transaction under *Burnet v. Logan,* however, the consideration received may not be taxable currently to cash-basis taxpayers, who are ordinarily not taxed on the value of a transferee's promises unless the promises are secured or evidenced by negotiable or marketable instruments. The interplay between the open transaction doctrine and cash-basis accounting is acutely raised by transfers of appreciated real estate or securities to private persons, usually younger members of the transferor's family, in exchange for an agreement to pay specified periodic amounts for the balance of the transferor's life—so-called private annuities. The early cases held that because of uncertainties regarding the transferee's ability to make the payments when due, (1) the transferor was not taxable at the time of the transfer even if the actuarial value of the annuity exceeds the adjusted basis of the transferred property, and (2) the payments themselves were not taxable until the taxpayer had fully recovered the basis of the transferred property. In 1969, the IRS rejected the latter aspect of the case law, ruling instead that the transferor's realized gain (the excess of the actuarial value of the annuity over the adjusted basis of the property) must be reported in installments as the payments are received, usually as capital gain.[80] There is some recent authority for confining this principle to unsecured annuities, however, and for taxing the gain at the time of the transfer if the annuity agreement is secured by a pledge of the transferred property.[81]

¶23.14 DEFERRED PAYMENT SALES

Although nothing could be more familiar than a sale of property for an agreed price to be paid over a period of years, the courts have never resolved the seemingly elementary issue of when the "amount realized" by the seller includes the value of the buyer's obligations to make the future payments. Taxpayers often sidestep the issue by reporting the gain on such sales on the installment method under IRC §453,[82] and this popular alternative probably accounts for the paucity of litigation on the basic issue. The problem arises because IRC §1001(b) defines "amount realized" as "the sum of any money received plus the fair market value of the property (other than money) re-

---

[79] See Temp. Regs. §15A.453-1(c) (contingent payment sales); but see IRC §453(d) (election out); see also ¶36.2 (installment sales).

[80] See, e.g., Lloyd v. CIR, 33 BTA 903 (1936) (Acq.) (cost recovery principle applied); Rev. Rul. 69-74, 1969-1 CB 43.

[81] Bell's Est. v. CIR, 60 TC 469 (1973).

[82] See infra ¶36.1.

ceived," which is a poor way to describe the buyer's promise to pay the balance due, especially if it is not evidenced by a negotiable instrument or secured by a mortgage.

The irrepressible conflict between the "fair market value" language of IRC §1001(b), buttressed by the theory of the regulations that property has a fair market value except "in rare and extraordinary cases," and the cash equivalency requirement of cash-basis accounting came to a head in *Warren Jones Co. v. CIR.*[83] There the Tax Court held (with three judges dissenting) that a land contract was not includable in the amount realized by a cash-basis taxpayer, even though there was a local market in which it could have been sold, because he would have had to accept a discount of almost 50 percent from the contract's face amount. In the Tax Court's view, it was unfair to close the transaction on the basis of such a low market value, which would allow only about half of the taxpayer's potential profit to qualify for capital gain treatment. Furthermore, if the taxpayer was financially pressed, he might have to sell the contract at a great sacrifice to meet his tax liability.

The Court of Appeals for the Ninth Circuit reversed, pointing out that taxpayers can ordinarily protect themselves against both of these hardships by employing the installment method of reporting gain on deferred payment contracts. It then held that the existence of a fair market value for the contract compelled its inclusion in the seller's amount realized, despite the severity of the discount from its face amount. The court went on, however, to acknowledge that some contracts might be so unmarketable, contingent, or speculative as to lack a fair market value, citing with approval the reference in the regulations to such "rare and extraordinary" situations.

¶23.15 SERVICES AND OTHER BENEFITS AS "AMOUNTS REALIZED"

Because IRC §1001(b) refers only to money and "property (other than money)" in defining the term "amount realized," it leaves uncertain the status of a transfer of property if the quid pro quo received by the taxpayer on a transfer is not "property" in the traditional sense, but services (performed or to be performed), good will, anticipated improvements in employee morale, or similar benefits. If the taxpayer expects to get his money's worth rather than to make a gift, it is reasonable to interpret IRC §1001(b) as encompassing these benefits. This construction strains the statutory language a bit, but no more than the well-established practice of treating claims as generating an "amount realized" when paid with appreciated or depreciated property.[84]

[83] Warren Jones Co. v. CIR, 60 TC 663 (1973), rev'd, 524 F.2d 788 (9th Cir. 1975).
[84] Supra ¶22.4.

In *International Freighting Corp. v. CIR,* the leading case in this area, the Court of Appeals for the Second Circuit held that a corporate taxpayer realized gain on transferring appreciated property to employees pursuant to a stock bonus plan, designed to reward those who had contributed to the corporation's success, even though the taxpayer was not obliged to make the payment and hence did not discharge an indebtedness thereby.[85] The court also held that the taxpayer was entitled to deduct the value of the transferred property as a business expense under IRC §162; but that was not the opinion's ratio decidendi, and the amount of gain under IRC §1001(b) was in no way related to the tax benefit produced by the deduction. It was, rather, the fact that the taxpayer received its money's worth in the form of services that brought IRC §1001(b) into play.

¶23.16 RELIEF FROM LIABILITY AS AN AMOUNT REALIZED

1. Relief From Personal Liability. If the owner of mortgaged property is personally liable on the bond and sells the encumbered property under a contract requiring the purchaser to pay off the debt at the closing, the resulting relief from liability is treated as equivalent to a payment of money to the mortgagor and is includable in the "amount realized" by him under IRC §1001(b). In *Old Colony Trust Co. v. CIR,* decided in 1929, the Supreme Court held that an employer's payment of an employee's federal and state income taxes was tantamount to a payment of the same amount directly to the employee [86] and this hoary principle was later applied by the Court in *United States v. Hendler* to a buyer's assumption and payment of the bonded indebtedness of a predecessor company pursuant to a merger agreement: "[The seller] was the beneficiary of the discharge of its indebtedness. Its gain was as real and substantial as if the money had been paid it and then paid over by it to its creditors." [87]

The same principle has long been applied if the buyer assumes the debt or takes subject to it, rather than paying it off at the closing, though this action may be substantially less beneficial to the seller than an immediate discharge from the liability. Since the seller's continuing secondary liability is a sword of Damocles, which will fall on him if the property declines in value and the

[85] International Freighting Corp. v. CIR, 135 F.2d 310 (2d Cir. 1943), cited with approval in US v. Davis, 370 US 65, 72 (1962); see also US v. General Shoe Corp., 282 F.2d 9 (6th Cir. 1960), cert. denied, 365 US 843 (1961) (transfer of appreciated property to employee pension trust); Riley v. CIR, 328 F.2d 428 (5th Cir. 1964) (gain realized by subdivider on transferring forty lots to contractor for services in improving the subdivided tract).

[86] Old Colony Trust Co. v. CIR, 279 US 716 (1929), discussed supra ¶1.11.

[87] US v. Hendler, 303 US 564 (1938).

buyer becomes insolvent, only a gullible taxpayer would accept at full value the judicial assurance that an assumption of the debt (let alone a transfer subject to the debt) is tantamount to payment. On the other hand, if the seller does not worry about secondary liability because it is minimized or eliminated by local anti-deficiency legislation or because he is and expects to remain insolvent, he is even less likely to regard the buyer's action of assuming or taking subject to the debt as the equivalent of cash.

Despite these shortcomings in the theory that the seller of mortgaged property gets the equivalent of cash whether the buyer pays off the debt at the closing or merely assumes or takes subject to it, there are good reasons for not attempting to distinguish among these alternatives in applying IRC §1001(b). The economic value to the seller of the buyer's action in assuming or taking subject to the debt is a function of many variables: the amount of cash paid at the closing, the improvements that the buyer may make to the property, the probable value of the property when payments of interest and principal are due, the likelihood that the buyer will be able to make good on a deficiency judgment if there should be one, the seller's probable financial status if the mortgagee proceeds against him in the event of default by the buyer, and other elusive imponderables. If these uncertainties had to be weighed in determining the "amount realized" by the seller, the computation of gain or loss on every routine sale of mortgaged property would be plunged into uncertainty.

In applying IRC §1001(b), therefore, the courts have in effect employed the simplifying and comforting premise that the buyer will pay the debt when it matures, so that the seller's secondary liability can be disregarded when computing his gain or loss. If this optimistic premise proves to be erroneous and the seller is compelled to rectify a default by the buyer, the amount paid by the seller to the mortgagee (if not reimbursed by the buyer) can be deducted when paid—usually as a capital rather than ordinary loss.

2. Relief From Nonrecourse Liability. The principles just described require further analysis if the seller of mortgaged property is not personally liable for the debt, having either acquired the property subject to the debt or borrowed against it on a nonrecourse basis. The problem of fitting nonrecourse debt into the statutory framework can be illustrated by a simple example. Assume that a taxpayer purchased Blackacre for $10,000, paying $2,000 in cash and taking subject to an existing mortgage of $8,000, and later sold the property for $11,000 to a buyer who paid $3,000 in cash and took subject to the mortgage, which had not been amortized and hence still amounted to $8,000. A businessman knowing nothing of the Internal Revenue Code would unhesitatingly compute the seller's gain as $1,000, either by subtracting the purchase price of $10,000 from the sales price of $11,000 or—more likely—by subtracting the cash paid out ($2,000) from the cash received ($3,000). Turning to IRC §1001(b), however, it is not easy to see how the "amount realized" by the seller—defined as "the sum of any money received plus the fair market value of the property (other than money) received"—amounts to $11,000.

Since the seller has no liability on the debt and will not care whether the buyer pays the mortgage at maturity or defaults, he is not likely to think that he got the equivalent of $8,000 in cash when the buyer took subject to the mortgage. On the other hand, the seller could not have effected a sale and thereby converted the value of his equity ($3,000, in our example) into cash except by finding a buyer who would either pay off the debt or take subject to it. For this reason, the buyer's decision to take subject to the mortgage is as beneficial to the seller as actual payment of the debt, since one or the other is an indispensable condition to his getting the $3,000 of cash from the buyer. Thus, something can be said in favor of describing the "amount realized" by the seller as $11,000, since this reaches a rational result, even though it strains the words used in IRC §1001(b).

In *Crane v. CIR,* a seminal case decided in 1947, the Supreme Court bent the statutory language to meet the perceived need.[88] The facts, somewhat simplified, were that the taxpayer inherited an apartment building worth $250,000, subject to a mortgage of the same amount; held it for seven years, during which she took $25,000 of depreciation deductions (based on a date-of-death basis under IRC §1014 of $250,000); and then sold it, subject to the unamortized mortgage, for $2,500 in cash. She reported $2,500 of gain on the sale, based on the theory that (a) the inherited property was not the building but only the decedent's equity therein, which had a value at his death of zero, entitling her to a zero basis under IRC §1014, and (b) the amount realized for the equity when she sold it was $2,500. The zero-basis claim was manifestly inconsistent with her use of a basis of $250;000 in computing depreciation on the building.

The government computed the taxpayer's gain in *Crane* as follows:

1. Amount realized		
a. Cash		$ 2,500
b. Mortgage		250,000
c. Total		$252,500
2. Less: Adjusted basis		
a. Unadjusted basis	$250,000	
b. Less: Adjustment for depreciation	25,000	
c. Adjusted basis		$225,000
3. Gain (line 1c less line 2c)		$ 27,500

---

[88] Crane v. CIR, supra note 8 (three Justices dissenting).

The Supreme Court upheld the IRS' theory of the transaction. It agreed that the property inherited by the taxpayer was the real estate, not the equity, giving three reasons for this conclusion. First, the Court noted that the "ordinary, everyday" dictionary meaning of "property" is either "the physical thing which is a subject of ownership" or "the aggregate of the owner's rights to control and dispose of that thing." [89] Second, the IRS had consistently interpreted IRC §1014 as using the term "property" in this familiar sense. Finally, the Court concluded that if "property" referred only to the taxpayer's equity, the allowable depreciation deductions would be based on this amount and would seriously understate the actual physical exhaustion of the property; moreover, since the taxpayer's equity changes whenever the mortgage is amortized, the depreciation basis would have to be repeatedly recomputed.

Having concluded that the taxpayer's unadjusted basis for the property under IRC §1001(b) was $250,000, the Court turned to the taxpayer's claim that, her equity being worth nothing, she incurred no economic loss when the property deteriorated. Reserving judgment on the validity of this claim if the property had been worth less than the mortgage (so that economic loss from deterioration would fall on the mortgagee), the Court held that, in the absence of such a showing, the burden of deterioration fell on the taxpayer, thus entitling her to depreciate the property. This in turn required her date-of-death basis to be reduced under IRC §1016 by the amount of the depreciation allowed or allowable.

Finally—"at last," in its words—the Court turned to the phrase "amount realized," as used in IRC §1001(b). Since the taxpayer's "property" consisted of a building worth more than $250,000, the Court observed that limiting the amount realized to the $2,500 of cash received by the seller would require accepting "the absurdity that she sold a quarter-of-a-million-dollar property for roughly one percent of its value, and took a 99 percent loss." [90] The Court's interpretation of IRC §1001(b)—that the "amount realized" included the nonrecourse mortgage—was, in essence, a by-product of the taxpayer's $250,000 date-of-death basis for the property and her concomitant right to compute depreciation on that basis.

The Court in *Crane* relied heavily on an economic benefit theory in including the relief from nonrecourse indebtedness as part of the amount realized.[91] Relief from a nonrecourse debt, however, is not an economic benefit if it can obtained only by giving up the mortgaged property. It is analogous to the relief one obtains from local real property taxes by disposing of the property: Like nonrecourse debt, the taxes must be paid to retain the property;

---

[89] Id. at 6.

[90] Id. at 13.

[91] Id. at 13–14.

but no one would suggest that the disposition of unprofitable property produces an economic benefit equal to the present value of the taxes that will not be paid in the future. Although the economic benefit rationale of *Crane* is unpersuasive, the result reached by the Court was justifiable because it brought the tax consequences of the taxpayer's dealings with her property into harmony with economic reality by recapturing her depreciation deductions to the extent that they exceeded her investment in the encumbered property. The value ascribed to the alleged "relief" she obtained from a liability for which she was not liable was, at bottom, a balancing entry that was appropriate when viewed in its tax context.

The facts giving rise to *Crane* were unusual: Not many taxpayers inherit property worth the same amount as the debt by which it is encumbered, and still fewer succeed in selling this type of property at a gain. But *Crane*'s reverberations belie its modest origin. By holding that nonrecourse liabilities are includable in the taxpayer's basis for property, *Crane* laid the foundation stone for most tax shelters, while the corollary of this basis rule—that the termination of nonrecourse liability is an "amount realized" when the property is sold or disposed of—became a booby trap for tax-sheltered investors when their venture is wound up. Thus, tax shelters enable investors to deduct depreciation, drilling expenses, and similar items as rapidly as the expenditures are made, even though they are financed by nonrecourse borrowing and hence exceed their current cash outlay. But when the investment is sold, nonrecourse liabilities are includable in the amount realized in computing gain, so that the deductions taken in the earlier years are—or should be—recaptured at the end of the road.

In *Crane,* the taxpayer closed out her investment by a sale that produced cash above the nonrecourse liability, and the Court did not address itself to several major issues, discussed below, that are encountered if the investment is terminated in some other way.

1. *Transfer by gift or at death.* Had the taxpayer in *Crane* given the property to a relative or a charity during her lifetime or held it until death so that it passed by testate or intestate succession, there would have been no "taxable event" as that term is ordinarily interpreted. Does a gift or bequest become a taxable event if the property is subject to a nonrecourse liability in excess of its basis? *Crane* itself does not speak to this issue, but it is hard to escape the conclusion that the $2,500 of cash received by the taxpayer on selling the property was not the best reason for holding that she realized $27,500 of gain on the transaction. In the last analysis, her depreciation deductions were recaptured because the debt encumbering the property exceeded its adjusted basis; and the significance of the sale was simply that it terminated any prior likelihood that she would eventually pay off the debt. But the same could have been said if she had transferred the property by gift or at death. For this reason, much can be said for treating such a transfer as a

constructive realization to the extent that the debt exceeds the property's basis.[92] This principle could be established as a corollary of the tax benefit doctrine,[93] an approach that would not require stretching the concept of "taxable event" to embrace gratuitous transfers.

2. *Foreclosure.* In *Parker v. Delaney,* one of the few cases dealing with the ultimate disposition of excessively mortgaged property, the Court of Appeals for the First Circuit held that the owner of property with an adjusted basis of about $228,000, subject to nonrecourse debt of about $259,000, realized gain of $31,000 (the excess of the debt over basis) on transferring the property to his creditors in lieu of foreclosure at a time when the debt was in default.[94] The court relied on *Crane* when including the unassumed debt in the amount realized by the taxpayer on disposing of the property. In *Crane,* the taxpayer received $2,500 of cash from the transferee of the property, but the court commented in *Parker v. Delaney* that this merely established that the debt in *Crane* did not exceed the value of the property transferred. In the absence of evidence that the debt in *Parker v. Delaney* exceeded the value of the property, the court held that the *Crane* principle applied.[95]

3. *Value of property below amount of debt.* In *Crane,* the taxpayer did not contend that the unpaid debt exceeded the value of the encumbered property at the time of the sale, and her receipt of $2,500 in cash from the purchaser would have refuted such a claim. In the most extensively discussed footnote in tax history, however, the Supreme Court observed:

> 37. Obviously, if the value of the property is less than the amount of the mortgage, a mortgagor who is not personally liable cannot realize a benefit equal to the mortgage. Consequently, a different problem might be encountered where a mortgagor abandoned the property or transferred it subject to the mortgage without receiving boot [i.e., cash or other property]. That is not this case.[96]

Like the basic theory of *Crane,* the rationale of this footnote is faulty. If "relief" from a nonrecourse debt is an amount realized when the value of the property exceeds the debt, there is no reason to treat differently debt that

---

[92] See Levine's Est. v. CIR, 634 F.2d 12 (2d Cir. 1980) (transfer of property subject to debt in excess of adjusted basis to trust for taxpayer's grandchildren treated as a sale); Guest v. CIR, 77 TC 9 (1981) (same for charitable contribution).

[93] For the tax benefit doctrine, see supra ¶1.10.

[94] Parker v. Delaney, 186 F.2d 455 (1st Cir. 1950).

[95] See Freeland v. CIR, 74 TC 970 (1980) (reconveyance of property to seller to avoid foreclosure resulted in amount realized equal to nonrecourse debt even though in excess of fair market value at time of conveyance); but see Tufts v. CIR, 651 F.2d 1058 (5th Cir. 1981), cert. granted,—US—(1982) (amount realized limited to fair market value of property).

[96] Crane v. CIR, supra note 8, at 14 n. 37.

exceeds the property's value. In both cases, the taxpayer has enjoyed the benefit of the depreciation deductions, gives up any chance of profiting from future increases in the value of the property, and will be unaffected by whether the debt is paid or not.

If the suggestion of Footnote 37 were converted into a rule of law, it would produce some startling results, which can be illustrated by assuming that a taxpayer purchases Blackacre for $100,000, making a down payment of $25,000 and giving the seller a nonrecourse purchase-money mortgage of $75,000 for the balance; that the value of the property rises to $300,000, enabling the taxpayer to increase the face amount of the mortgage from $75,000 to $250,000 (the increase of $175,000 being received by him in cash); that Blackacre's value (unencumbered) then drops to $40,000; and, finally, that the taxpayer transfers it to an optimist subject to the unpaid mortgage of $250,000. If the amount realized by the taxpayer is only $40,000 (the value of the property), as implied by *Crane,* he will realize a loss of $60,000 (Blackacre's cost of $100,000 less amount realized of $40,000), although his economic gain over the years was $150,000 ($175,000 of cash received on increasing the mortgage less $25,000 of cash paid as a down payment).

These indefensible tax results arise only because Footnote 37 of *Crane* attaches weight to something that cannot possibly affect the taxpayer once he has decided to abandon or otherwise dispose of the property—viz., its value. Whether the value of the property at that time is just barely sufficient to pay off the debt or falls short of that amount, and what happens to its value thereafter, are matters of concern to the mortgagee and the new owner; but the old owner has no reason to worry about these matters. Thus, the result in *Crane* can be justified only if the "amount realized" by a taxpayer who disposes of property encumbered by nonrecourse debt in excess of its basis is viewed as a balancing entry, which brings the tax results into conformity with economic reality. If this is its function, the amount realized should be computed by reference to the taxpayer's adjusted basis, the amount of the nonrecourse debt, and the cash or other property (if any) received by him. If it falls out that the property is worth less than the debt, that is the lender's misfortune; but this should no more affect the taxpayer's tax returns than it affects his economic position.

The mystery and uncertainty that have swirled around Footnote 37 may be stilled once and for all when the Supreme Court decides *Tufts v. CIR.*[97] There, the taxpayer's partnership purchased depreciable property for $1.8 million financed in full by a nonrecourse loan; and, after taking depreciation deductions of $400,000, the partners sold the property for a token cash payment subject to the unamortized $1.8 million loan. The fair market value and

---

[97] Tufts v. CIR, supra note 95.

the adjusted basis of the property at the time of sale were both $1.4 million. The taxpayers reported no gain even though they had enjoyed $400,000 of depreciation deductions with virtually no cash outlay, contending that the amount realized was bounded by the fair market value of the property. The Fifth Circuit, relying on Footnote 37, upheld their position.[98]

3. Gifts Subject to Gift Tax Liability ("Net Gifts"). For some years, the status of gifts of appreciated property on condition that the donee pay the federal gift tax was clouded in uncertainty.[99] Pointing to the well-established principle that the tax liability reduced the value of the gift to a net amount for gift tax purposes, donors argued that a so-called net gift was not a taxable event for income tax purposes, even if the tax liability discharged by the donee exceeded the adjusted basis of the property. The government, on the other hand, argued that a net gift should be viewed as a part-sale, part-gift transaction, and that the donee's payment of the gift tax is an "amount realized" on the part-sale component, taxable if and to the extent that it exceeds the donor's adjusted basis for the property. This theory was accepted by the Supreme Court in *Diedrich v. CIR,* decided in 1982:

> The fact that the gift tax obligation was discharged by way of a conditional gift rather than from funds derived from a pre-gift sale [of the donated property] does not alter the underlying benefit to the donors.[100]

¶23.17 CARVED-OUT RIGHTS: RETAINED INTERESTS OR AMOUNTS REALIZED?

If a taxpayer sells an undivided two-thirds fractional interest in Blackacre (fair market value $90,000, basis $33,000) for $60,000, and if there are no extraneous circumstances establishing that the sale is not what it purports to be, the amount realized by the seller is $60,000, and the gain is $38,000 ($60,000 less $22,000, the portion of Blackacre's basis allocable to the two-thirds sold). There is no reason to restructure the transaction as a sale of the

---

[98] With *Tufts,* compare Millar v. CIR, 577 F.2d 212 (3d Cir.), cert. denied, 439 US 1046 (1978) (gain realized on surrender of stock in discharge of nonrecourse debt, regardless of stock's fair market value); Delman's Est. v. CIR, 73 TC 15 (1979) (extensive analysis); Prop. Regs. §1.1001-2(b) (value of encumbered property not relevant in determining amount of liabilities treated as discharged).

[99] See Owen v. CIR, 652 F.2d 1271 (6th Cir. 1981) (divided court); Evangelista v. CIR, 629 F.2d 1218 (7th Cir. 1980) (net gifts distinguished from transfers subject to preexisting liabilities).

[100] Diedrich v. CIR, 102 S. Ct. 2414 (1982).

entire fee in which the amount realized is $60,000 of cash and property worth $30,000 (viz., a one-third interest in Blackacre), producing gain of $57,000 ($90,000 less basis of $33,000).

In the same vein, a sale of Blackacre for $60,000, subject to a retained life estate worth $30,000, is ordinarily taken at face value—that is, a sale of the remainder (allocated basis of $22,000) for $60,000, producing gain of $38,000, rather than as a sale of the fee for $90,000—$60,000 in cash and $30,000 in property (the life estate).[101] But if the parties set the transaction up as an outright sale of the fee with a transfer back of occupancy rights, the IRS and the courts may take them at their word. For example, in *Alstores Realty Corp. v. CIR,* a sale of property for cash, with a simultaneous grant by the buyer to the seller of the right to occupy part of the premises rent-free for two and one-half years under a leaseback arrangement, was held to generate rental income for the buyer on the theory that the value of the leasehold was implicitly received by the buyer and used to pay for the property.[102] In a companion case involving the seller, the Tax Court applied the same rationale in holding that the value of the occupancy rights was part of the amount realized by the seller, to be taken into account in computing gain or loss on the sale, and that the same amount could be amortized by the seller as rental expense over the two- and one-half-year period, since the premises were occupied for business purposes.[103]

SELECTED BIBLIOGRAPHY

Adams, Exploring the Outer Boundaries of the *Crane* Doctrine: An Imaginary Supreme Court Opinion, 21 Tax L. Rev. 159 (1966).

Bittker, Tax Shelters, Nonrecourse Debt, and the *Crane* Case, 33 Tax L. Rev. 277 (1978).

Burford, Basis of Property After Erroneous Treatment of a Prior Transaction, 12 Tax L. Rev. 365 (1957).

Cooper, Negative Basis, 75 Harv. L. Rev. 1352 (1962).

Del Cotto, Basis and Amount Realized Under *Crane:* A Current View of Some Tax Effects in Mortgage Financing, 118 U. Pa. L. Rev. 69 (1969).

Del Cotto, Sales and Other Dispositions of Property Under Section 1001: The Taxable Event, Amount Realized and Related Problems of Basis, 26 Buffalo L. Rev. 219, 279–281 (1977).

---

[101] See Rev. Rul. 77-413, 1977-2 CB 298 (amount realized on the sale of property does not include the value of a retained twenty-year possessory interest).

[102] Alstores Realty Corp. v. CIR, 46 TC 363 (1966) (Acq.).

[103] Steinway & Sons v. CIR, 46 TC 375 (1966) (Acq.).

Del Cotto & Joyce, Inherited Excess Mortgage Property: Death and the Inherited Tax Shelter, 34 Tax L. Rev. 569 (1979).

Epstein, The Consumption and Loss of Personal Property Under the Internal Revenue Code, 23 Stan. L. Rev. 454, 457–462 (1971).

Halpern, Liabilities and Cost Basis: Some Fundamental Considerations, 7 J. Real Est. Tax. 307 (1980).

Jackson, The New Rules Governing Bargain Sales to Charitable Organizations Under the Tax Reform Act of 1969, 24 Tax Lawyer 279 (1971).

Kanter, Recent Tax Court Decisions Shed Further Light on Private Annuity Transactions, 42 J. Tax. 66 (1975).

Litwin, Apportionment of Date of Death Basis; Analyzing the Anomalies of Uniform Basis, 27 Tax L. Rev. 303 (1972).

Osgood, Carryover Basis Repeal and Reform of the Transfer Tax System, 66 Cornell L. Rev. 297 (1980).

Perry, Limited Partnerships and Tax Shelters: The *Crane* Rule Goes Public, 27 Tax L. Rev. 525 (1972).

Rose, *Warren Jones Co.*: The Ninth Circuit Distills the Legal Quagmire of Code Sec. 1001(b), 54 Taxes 410 (1976).

Stern, Premature Deductions for Taxes and Carrying Charges, 22 U.C.L.A. L. Rev. 1342, 1359–1362 (1975).

CHAPTER 24

Nonrecognition Transactions

¶24.1 NONRECOGNITION OF REALIZED GAIN OR LOSS

1. Introductory. Gain or loss realized by a taxpayer on the sale or exchange of property, as determined under IRC §1001(a), must be "recognized" in full by virtue of IRC §1001(c) unless a "nonrecognition" provision prescribes otherwise. In the case of gain, this means that the taxpayer's profit is includable in gross income; but IRC §1001(c) does not determine whether it will be taxed as ordinary income or as capital gain, nor, in the case of a loss, whether it can be deducted. The Code's numerous nonrecognition provisions cover a wide range of transactions that have little in common except that they have elicited a legislative judgment that the taxpayer's realized gain or loss should not be taxed when the exchange or other event occurs, since "the new property is substantially a continuation of the old investment still unliquidated." [1]

The nonrecognition provisions can be viewed as refinements of the pervasive concept of realization, which postpones the taxation of appreciation in the value of property (and the deduction of a decline in value) until the taxpayer sells or otherwise disposes of the property. In effect, the nonrecognition provisions mandate a further deferral of tax consequences if the disposition is a

[1] Treas. Regs. §1.1002-1(c).

transaction vesting the taxpayer with a continuing interest in similar property. In addition, the nonrecognition provisions are undoubtedly influenced by a legislative belief that taxing transactions producing no cash may impose hardships in some instances, even though the receipt of cash is not ordinarily a prerequisite to taxability.

2. Receipt of Nonqualified Property ("Boot"). When nonrecognition of gain or loss is accorded to an exchange of property, the statutory language ordinarily permits the taxpayer to receive solely property meeting specified standards;[2] and in some instances the receipt of cash or other nonqualified property in addition to the qualified (or "nonrecognition") property renders the nonrecognition provision wholly inapplicable to the transaction.[3] More frequently, however, the Code provides that the receipt of nonqualified property ("boot" in tax jargon, since along with the qualified property, the taxpayer has received nonqualified property "to boot") is not fatal but will simply result in a pro tanto recognition of any realized gain.[4] On the other hand, if the taxpayer realizes a loss on the exchange, the receipt of boot in addition to qualified property does not authorize him to deduct the loss, either in whole or in part.[5] This seemingly inconsistent treatment of gains and losses when boot is received is evidently based on the theory that, since the qualified property may increase in value after its acquisition, the taxpayer's original investment has been perpetuated so that the transaction is not sufficiently closed to warrant a deduction.

3. Benefits and Burdens of Nonrecognition—Avoidance Transactions. When a taxpayer realizes gain on a sale or other disposition of property, nonrecognition treatment is ordinarily welcome, because it defers the day when the gain is taxable; and it may also permit the gain to be recognized in a later year when the taxpayer is subject to a lower marginal tax rate or has offsetting losses. Moreover, if the nonrecognition property is held until death, it will receive a stepped-up basis under IRC §1014 equal to its fair market value at the date of death.

Occasionally, however, taxpayers are adversely affected by the nonrecognition of realized gain, particularly if current recognition would be offset by loss carryovers that are about to expire.[6] In the case of realized losses, as

---

[2] See, e.g., IRC §1031(a) (like-kind exchanges).

[3] See IRC §§368(a)(1)(B) and 354(a)(1).

[4] See, e.g., IRC §1031(b), discussed infra ¶24.2.

[5] See, e.g., IRC §1031(c), discussed infra ¶24.2.

[6] Excess personal deductions (e.g., for medical expenses, taxes, etc.) ordinarily expire with the taxable year in which they arise, but net operating losses and capital losses can be carried forward under provisions discussed supra ¶12.9 (net operating losses) and infra ¶25.2 (capital losses—individuals).

distinguished from gains, taxpayers usually prefer current recognition; but in unusual circumstances (e.g., a superfluity of current deductions), postponed recognition of the loss may be preferable.

Although nonrecognition treatment is sometimes elective, it is more frequently mandatory—provided, of course, the transaction meets the statutory standards. But since the taxpayer can often control the nature of a transaction within limits dictated by the relevant financial and business parameters, he can often shape it to fit, or fall outside, the prescribed nonrecognition pattern.

¶24.2 EXCHANGES OF PROPERTY FOR PROPERTY OF A "LIKE KIND"

1. Introductory. Under IRC §1031(a), gain or loss is not recognized on exchanges of business or investment property (other than stock in trade, other property held primarily for sale, and stock and securities) solely for other property "of a like kind" to be held for business use or investment. Gain or loss realized on such an exchange is subject to nonrecognition under IRC §1031(a) only if the taxpayer transfers property that (a) is "held for productive use in trade or business or for investment" and (b) is not disqualified by the parenthetical exclusion of stock in trade, other property held primarily for sale, stock, bonds, notes, choses in action, securities, and similar intangibles.

The phrases used by IRC §1031(a) to describe the property that can be transferred by the taxpayer have evoked few administrative or judicial interpretations, but they are similar to terms used by Congress in provisions that have been extensively litigated; and one can reasonably expect substantially the same principles to apply under IRC §1031. Thus, the terms "productive use in trade or business," "stock in trade," and "held primarily for sale" seem intended to cover the same ground as their analogues in IRC §§1221(1) and 1221(2).[7] It is important to note, however, that the phrase "property held primarily for sale" as used in IRC §1031(a) is substantially broader than the phrase "property held by the taxpayer primarily for sale to customers in the ordinary course of his trade or business," which has been much litigated under IRC §1221(1).[8]

When qualified property is exchanged for like-kind property with a greater value, the transferor ordinarily equalizes the bargain by transferring cash, securities, or other unqualified property along with the qualified property. This does not taint the exchange, but any gain or loss realized on the

[7] For IRC §§1221(1) and 1221(2), see infra ¶25.5.

[8] See Griffin v. CIR, 49 TC 253 (1967); Black v. CIR, 35 TC 90 (1960) (property held for sale does not qualify for tax-free exchange, even if it was not held primarily for sale to customers in the ordinary course of the taxpayer's trade or business for purposes of IRC §1221(1)); see also infra ¶25.5.

unqualified property (i.e., the difference between its adjusted basis and market value at the time of the exchange) is recognized by the transferor.[9]

2. "Like Kind" Property. Under IRC §1031(a), the transferred property must be exchanged solely for "property of a like kind" to be held either for productive use in a trade or business or for investment.

Four preliminary points regarding this requirement should be noted.

First, since the property received by the taxpayer qualifies only if it is "to be held" for productive use or investment, the *taxpayer's* intentions, rather than the prior owner's, are controlling. Thus, the exchange can qualify if the taxpayer holds the new property for the prescribed purpose, even though he acquired it from a dealer who held it for sale to customers; conversely, the exchange is outside of IRC §1031(a) if the taxpayer intends to sell the property, even though the prior owner held it for investment or productive business use.[10]

Second, the regulations interpret IRC §1031(a) as permitting property held for productive business use to be exchanged for property to be held for investment, and vice versa.[11]

Third, although the parenthetical disqualification of stock and securities is explicitly applicable only to the property transferred by the taxpayer, the same disqualification evidently attaches to the property *received,* since the two must be "of a like kind."

Finally, if the transferred property was held *by the taxpayer* for productive use in a trade or business or for investment, the *transferee's objective* in acquiring it is irrelevant. Thus, an exchange of properties can qualify under IRC §1031(a) so far as the transferor is concerned, even if the transferee intends to sell the property received by him, contracted to sell it before the exchange, or is assisted by the taxpayer in finding a buyer—unless the transferee can be properly classified as the taxpayer's agent, so that the sale can be imputed to the taxpayer.[12]

The central requirement of IRC §1031(a)—an exchange of qualified property for other property "of a like kind"—is interpreted by the Treasury regulations as follows:

---

[9] Treas. Regs. §1.1031(a)-1(a) (last two sentences); Treas. Regs. §1.1031(d)-1(e), Example.

[10] See Rev. Rul. 75-291, 1975-2 CB 332 (nonrecognition as to taxpayer acquiring real estate from a corporation that constructed it in order to effect an exchange, but not as to the latter taxpayer).

[11] Treas. Regs. §1.1031(a)-1(a).

[12] See Woodbury v. CIR, 49 TC 180, 197-199 (1967) (Acq.) (IRC §1031 applied even though taxpayer assisted transferee in finding a purchaser for transferred property).

> As used in section 1031(a), the words "like kind" have reference to the nature or character of the property and not to its grade or quality. One kind or class of property may not, under that section, be exchanged for property of a different kind or class. The fact that any real estate involved is improved or unimproved is not material, for that fact relates only to the grade or quality of the property and not to its kind or class.[13]

As applied to real estate, this interpretation of "like kind" is extraordinarily liberal, not to say lax, given the legislative and administrative theory that IRC §1031 is concerned with exchanges that do not substantially alter the taxpayer's economic status. The regulations go on to illustrate the Treasury's interpretation of "like kind" by endorsing the exchange of (1) urban real estate for a ranch or farm, (2) a leasehold of a fee with thirty years or more to run for real estate (presumably of any type), and (3) improved real estate for unimproved real estate.[14] Except for interests that are restricted to an individual's life or to a specified quantity or dollar value of production (e.g., an oil payment), the cases and rulings seem to treat all real property as a single class,[15] thus sanctioning drastic changes in the taxpayer's investment status provided he does not venture outside the real estate field.[16]

A substantial body of litigation focusing on IRC §1031 has been stimulated by sale-leaseback transactions, in which the owner of depreciated realty sells it for cash, simultaneously entering into a long-term lease with the new owner. For practical purposes, these arrangements may have substantially the same consequences for both parties as a mortgage coupled with the original owner's renunciation of the property when the lease expires, which is usually so far in the future that the reversion is of trivial value. When this analysis is accepted for tax purposes, the original owner realizes neither gain nor loss on

---

[13] Treas. Regs. §1.1031(a)-1(b).

[14] Treas. Regs. §1.1031(a)-1(c).

[15] See Rev. Rul. 68-331, 1968-1 CB 352 (exchange of leasehold interest in producing oil lease for an improved ranch qualifies under IRC §1031); Rev. Rul. 55-749, 1955-2 CB 295 (exchange of perpetual water rights for fee interest in land qualifies, but right to a specified amount of water does not); Rev. Rul. 72-601, 1972-2 CB 467 (exchange by seventy-year-old taxpayer of remainder interest in real property for a life interest in another parcel; held, not qualified); Rev. Rul. 68-363, 1968-2 CB 336 (exchange of domestic realty for foreign realty qualifies); Rev. Rul. 73-476, 1973-2 CB 300 (exchange of fractional undivided interest in three parcels of real property for 100 percent ownership of one parcel; held, qualified).

In Rev. Rul. 67-255, 1967-2 CB 270, however, the IRS ruled that land and improvements thereon are not properties of a like kind, even though both constitute "real estate"; see also, to the same effect, Rev. Rul. 76-390, 1976-2 CB 243; but see Davis v. US, 411 F.Supp. 964 (D.Hawaii 1976), aff'd on another ground, 589 F.2d 446 (9th Cir. 1979) (rejecting Rev. Rul. 67-255).

[16] To the effect that real estate and personal property are not of a like kind, see Oregon Lumber Co. v. CIR, 20 TC 192 (1953).

the "sale" (since the amounts received are treated as borrowed funds) but may deduct an appropriate portion of the "rent" as interest on the loan, and the balance is treated as amortization of the debt. Most litigated cases have not pursued this approach, however, but have instead treated the transaction as a bona fide transfer of the realty to the new owner. If the transaction is so viewed, it becomes necessary to determine whether it is a simple sale of the property, on which gain or loss is recognized to the extent realized, or an exchange of the realty for a leasehold plus cash, subject to IRC §1031. The "exchange" approach then requires a further determination, viz., whether the realty and the leasehold are properties of a like kind (an issue that the regulations decide in the affirmative if the leasehold has thirty years or more to run); if so, IRC §1031 comes into play, with the result that the taxpayer must recognize any realized gain to the extent of the cash received but cannot recognize a realized loss.[17]

The treatment of personal property is more problematical. In sharp contrast to their latitudinarian view of real estate exchanges, the regulations illustrate the exchange of personal property under IRC §1031 with two narrowly circumscribed instances: the exchange of a truck used in business for another truck and the exchange of a passenger automobile used in business for another passenger automobile to be used for a like purpose.[18] The IRS has ruled that the exchange of all the assets of a telephone company (except inventory and securities) for similar assets of another operating telephone company qualifies as a "like kind" exchange,[19] but it is not clear whether the same ruling would have been forthcoming if the companies had been engaged in different lines of business. In another ruling, however, the IRS held that a transfer of "multiple assets" must be fragmented in applying IRC §1031(a) even if the assets constitute a going business or an integrated economic investment.[20] So analyzed, the transaction—entailing an exchange of rental property consisting of land and a house for farmland and improvements and associated farm machinery—was treated as tax-free so far as the exchange of realty was concerned, but the taxpayer's realized gain was held taxable to the extent of the value of the farm machinery received.

In keeping with this focus on the separable assets of a business, the IRS has argued that partnership interests are "choses in action" that do not qualify

---

[17] Compare Jordan Marsh Co. v. CIR, 269 F.2d 453 (2d Cir. 1959) ("sale" of property at fair market value held independent of simultaneous leaseback at fair rental for thirty years and three days with options to renew; loss upon sale recognized), with Century Elec. Co. v. CIR, 192 F.2d 155 (8th Cir. 1951), cert. denied, 342 US 954 (1952) (transfer of foundry for cash and 95-year leasehold held to be an exchange; leasehold was "like kind" property with a capital value; loss not recognized); see also Rev. Rul. 60-43, 1960-1 CB 687 (IRS will not follow *Jordan Marsh*).

[18] Treas. Regs. §1.1031(a)-1(c).

[19] Rev. Rul. 57-365, 1957-2 CB 521.

[20] Rev. Rul. 72-151, 1972-1 CB 225.

for a tax-free exchange under IRC §1031(a); but this theory has been rejected by the courts, and the exchange of a 50 percent partnership interest in a tavern for a 25 percent interest in an auto supply business has been held to satisfy the "like kind" requirement.[21]

3. Receipt of Nonqualified Property ("Boot"). Although IRC §1031(a) provides for nonrecognition of gain or loss only if qualified property is exchanged "solely" for other property of a like kind, this ostensibly draconic requirement is moderated by IRC §1031(b), which provides that if an exchange would qualify save for the receipt of money or nonqualified property ("boot") along with the qualified property, the transferor's realized gain (if any) is recognized only to the extent of the money and the fair market value of the nonqualified property. By virtue of IRC §1031(c), however, the receipt of boot does not entitle the transferor to deduct a realized loss on the transferred property.

These principles are illustrated by Example 24-1, in which it is assumed that the taxpayer exchanged Blackacre (with an adjusted basis of $50 in Case *A*, $85 in Case *B*, and $100 in Case *C*) for Whiteacre (value $75) plus $10 in cash.

Example 24-1

Receipt of Boot in Like-Kind Exchange Under IRC §1031

	A	*B*	*C*
1. Amount realized under IRC §1001(b):			
a. Whiteacre	$75	$75	$75
b. Cash	10	10	10
c. Total	$85	$85	$85
2. Less: Adjusted basis of Blackacre	50	85	100
3. Gain (loss) realized under IRC §1001(a)	$35	-0-	($15)
4. Gain (loss) recognized under IRC §1031(b) or §1031(c)	$10	-0-	-0-
5. Unrecognized gain (loss)	$25	-0-	($15)
6. Basis of Whiteacre under IRC §1031(d)	$50	$75	$90

As explained below, the correlative basis rules prescribed by IRC §1031(d).

[21] See Pappas v. CIR, 78 TC 1078 (1982), and cases there cited (exchange of general partnership interest for interest as general partner in another partnership); query whether *limited* partnership interests are "securities" within meaning of IRC §1031.

insure that the taxpayer's unrecognized gain of $25 in Case *A* and the unrecognized loss of $15 in Case *C* will be taken into account when Whiteacre is sold.

If mortgaged property is exchanged for unencumbered property, the amount of the debt must be treated as boot, whether the transferee assumes the liability or merely takes subject to it. If both properties are encumbered, the liabilities are netted out; and the liability assumed by the transferee (or to which the property received by him is subject) constitutes boot only if, and to the extent that, it exceeds the liability attaching to the property received by the transferor.[22]

In the same vein, if the taxpayer transfers money or other nonqualified property along with mortgaged nonrecognition property, the nonqualified property can be offset against the amount of the mortgage in determining the amount of boot received. Thus, if the taxpayer transfers Blackacre (subject to a mortgage of $15,000) plus $5,000 in cash for Whiteacre (unencumbered), the boot is not $15,000 but only $10,000—the same result that would be reached if the taxpayer had used the cash to reduce the mortgage to $10,000 before making the transfer and had then exchanged Blackacre for Whiteacre in an even exchange.[23] On the other hand, if the taxpayer *receives* money or other boot, he cannot reduce it to reflect liabilities assumed by him (or to which the property received by him is subject), even though he would have received no boot (but would have occupied a substantially similar economic position) if the money or other property had been used by the transferee to reduce the liabilities before the exchange.[24]

4. Exchanges vs. Sales. To qualify for nonrecognition of gain or loss under IRC §1031(a), a transaction must constitute an "exchange" of like-kind properties. The principal issue arising under this requirement is the distinction between (a) an exchange and (b) a sale coupled with a reinvestment of the proceeds in like-kind property, since only the first transaction qualifies. The regulations formerly stated that "ordinarily, to constitute an exchange the transaction must be a reciprocal transfer of property, as distinguished from a transfer of property for a money consideration only." [25] But if Smith agrees to sell Blackacre to Jones and concurrently agrees to buy Whiteacre from Jones, under a plan calling for an exchange of checks (or for the issue of one check, to be endorsed by the drawee back to the drawer), it does not require

---

[22] IRC §1031(d) (last sentence); Treas. Regs. §1.1031(b)-1(c); Treas. Regs. §1.1031(d)-2, Examples (1), (2).

[23] See Treas. Regs. §1.1031(d)-2, Example (2)(c).

[24] Id., Examples (2)(b) (involving *D*), (2)(c) (second sentence of parenthetical explanation); but see Barker v. CIR, 74 TC 555 (1980) (cash received can be offset if liability is paid off contemporaneously with the exchange).

[25] Treas. Regs. §1.1002-1(d) (under prior law).

much imagination to envision the transaction as an exchange rather than as two bona fide sales, despite the transitory use of money. If the transaction is an exchange in substance, it is subject to IRC §1031 whether it is the IRS or the taxpayer who would prefer it to be treated instead as a sale.

Thus, the step transaction doctrine has been applied to a taxpayer's sale of used equipment to a dealer coupled with a purported purchase of new equipment of a like kind, where the two transactions were "reciprocal and mutually dependent," even though there were two separate contracts rather than a single contract with a trade-in allowance.[26] If the old equipment was sold to one person and the new equipment purchased from an independent party, however, the transaction would not be an "exchange" within the meaning of IRC §1031(b), even if the taxpayer entered into the two contracts concurrently because he was not willing to sell the old equipment without knowing that he could obtain the new equipment, and vice versa. Since the contracts are with unrelated persons, the breach of one would not release the taxpayer from his obligations under the other.

Although IRC §1031(a) requires an "exchange" of properties, it is not restricted to two-party arrangements; and the like-kind property received by the taxpayer does not have to come from the transferee of his property. Thus, a round robin transaction in which *A* transfers Blackacre to *B, B* transfers Whiteacre to *C,* and *C* transfers Greenacre to *A* would qualify as an exchange for all three participants if the other conditions prescribed by IRC §1031(a) (business or investment use, like-kind character, etc.) were satisfied.[27]

Three parties may also figure in the arrangement if *A* wishes to swap Blackacre for Whiteacre, while *B,* who owns Whiteacre, wants to sell it and *C,* who wants to acquire Blackacre, has no property to swap. An agreement under which *C* agrees to buy Whiteacre from *B* and transfer it to *A* in exchange for Blackacre can qualify as an "exchange" under IRC §1031 so far as *A* is concerned.[28] A transaction of this type qualifies even if *A* was about to sell Blackacre to *C* and then suggests that *C* acquire Whiteacre in order to effect a swap in lieu of the contemplated sale.[29]

Similar to these triangular arrangements are two-party contracts under which the taxpayer agrees to exchange property for like-kind property to be

---

[26] Rev. Rul. 61-119, 1961-1 CB 395; Redwing Carriers, Inc. v. Tomlinson, 399 F.2d 652 (5th Cir. 1968) (accord, where old equipment was sold by parent of subsidiary purchasing like-kind property; "buying and selling were synchronous parts meshed into the same transaction").

[27] See Rev. Rul. 57-244, 1957-1 CB 247.

[28] See Biggs v. CIR, 632 F.2d 1171 (5th Cir. 1980) (three-cornered transaction qualified); Barker v. CIR, supra note 24 (four-party exchange qualified; transactions mutually interdependent); Brauer v. CIR, 74 TC 1134 (1980) (multi-party exchange part of "overall plan").

[29] See Coupe v. CIR, 52 TC 394, 405 (1969).

constructed by the other party or purchased by the latter from someone else. The taxpayer's exchange can qualify under IRC §1031(a) even though the other party to the contract must recognize any realized gain or loss because the property transferred by him is not held for business use or investment, as required by IRC §1031(a), but is instead acquired or constructed to the taxpayer's specifications in order to effect the exchange.[30]

In the transactions just described, the replacement property was identified by the taxpayer before disposing of the original property, and the two properties were transferred simultaneously. In an important case decided by the Court of Appeals for the Ninth Circuit, three taxpayers sought the shelter of IRC §1031 even though the replacement property had not been identified when the original transfer occurred. To meet this business problem, they transferred their property under a so-called land exchange agreement to the transferee, a publicly owned corporation, for an "exchange balance" of about $1.5 million, to be used by the transferee (with a "growth factor" of 6 percent of the outstanding balance) to acquire suitable replacement property as designated by the transferor taxpayers within five years, or to pay them any outstanding balance in cash. Since it was not possible at the time of the original transfer to determine whether the taxpayers would eventually acquire qualified replacement property or draw down the unexpended credits in cash, the transferee acted as a kind of savings bank in the interim. The court, however, held that the transaction qualified under IRC §1031 on a showing that the taxpayers preferred replacement property to cash both before and throughout the executory period and that only like-kind property was ultimately received.[31] The "growth factor," however, was held to constitute disguised interest, taxable as such when received.

5. Basis of Property Received. Like almost all other nonrecognition provisions, IRC §1031(a) is intended to defer recognition of the taxpayer's realized gain or loss, not to eliminate it. To achieve this objective, IRC §1031(d) provides that the property received by the taxpayer shall have the same basis as the property given up, with appropriate adjustments if the transaction entails more than a simple exchange of one parcel of unencumbered property for a parcel of unencumbered like-kind property. If the taxpayer transfers money or other nonqualified property along with the qualified property, the basis assigned to the property received is the basis of the qualified property, plus the money or basis of the nonqualified property, plus any gain or minus any loss recognized on transferring the latter.[32] This computation is illustrated by Example 24-2, which assumes that *A* exchanges Blackacre with an adjusted basis of $10,000 and a fair market value of $11,000, plus stock with

---

[30] See Rev. Rul. 75-291, supra note 10.

[31] Starker v. US, 602 F.2d 1341 (9th Cir. 1979).

[32] Treas. Regs. §1.1031(d)-1(e).

an adjusted basis of $4,000 and a fair market value of $2,000, for Whiteacre, with a fair market value of $13,000.[33] As shown by Example 24-2, *A* realizes and recognizes a loss of $2,000 on the transfer of the stock, but *A*'s realized gain of $1,000 on Blackacre is not recognized because Blackacre is exchanged for Whiteacre, property of a like kind. The basis of Whiteacre, as shown by Example 24-2, is $12,000 (line 6).

Example 24-2

Computation of Basis on Exchange of Qualifying Property Plus Nonqualifying Property for Qualifying Property in Like-Kind Exchange Under IRC §1031

1. Loss of transfer of stock	
a. Adjusted basis	$ 4,000
b. Less: Amount realized	2,000
c. Loss realized and recognized	$ 2,000
2. Adjusted basis of Blackacre	$10,000
3. Plus: Adjusted basis of stock transferred	4,000
4. Subtotal	$14,000
5. Less: Loss recognized on transfer of stock (line 1c)	2,000
6. Basis of Whiteacre	$12,000

Computation of the basis to be allocated and its assignment to the properties received become more complex if the taxpayer receives boot (including relief from liabilities) along with the nonrecognition property. First, the aggregate amount of basis to be assigned is (a) decreased by any money received (including, for this purpose, any liabilities assumed by the transferee or to which the transferred property is subject) and (b) increased by any gain recognized (or decreased by loss recognized) on the exchange. The amount thus computed is then allocated to the boot received (other than cash) to the extent of its fair market value at the time of the exchange, and the balance is assigned to the nonrecognition property received. These principles are illustrated by Example 24-3, which assumes that *A* transfers Blackacre (adjusted basis $500,000, fair market value $800,000) to *B,* subject to a mortgage of $150,000, for Whiteacre (worth $600,000), plus $30,000 in cash and an oil painting worth $20,000. *A*'s realized gain on the exchange is $300,000, of which $200,000 is recognized, and the basis of Whiteacre is $500,000, computed as shown in Example 24-3:

If *A* then sells Whiteacre for $600,000 and the oil painting for $20,000,

[33] Example 24–2 is based on Treas. Regs. §1.1031(d)-1(e), Example.

their respective fair market values, he will realize and recognize $100,000 of gain on Whiteacre and no gain or loss on the painting. Thus, he will have reported a gain of $300,000 over the long haul—$200,000 (Example 24-3, line 4) at the time of the exchange and $100,000 on selling Whiteacre and the painting. This corresponds to his aggregate profit.

Example 24-3

Allocation of Basis on Receipt of Boot in Like-Kind Exchange Under IRC §1031

(Dollars in Thousands)

1. Amount realized:		
a. Whiteacre		$600
b. Cash		30
c. Oil painting		20
d. Liabilities subject to which Blackacre is transferred		150
e. Total amount realized		$800
2. Less: Adjusted basis of property (Blackacre) transferred		500
3. Gain realized		$300
4. Gain recognized (sum of lines 1b, 1c, and 1d)		$200
5. Adjusted basis of property transferred (line 2)		$500
6. Less:		
a. Money received	$ 30	
b. Liabilities to which transferred property is subject	150	
c. Total reduction		180
7. Balance		$320
8. Plus: Gain recognized (line 4)		200
9. Total to be allocated		$520
10. Amount allocable to oil painting (fair market value)		$ 20
11. Amount allocable to Whiteacre (line 9 less line 10)		$500

¶24.3 GAIN ON INVOLUNTARY CONVERSIONS OF PROPERTY

1. Introductory. By virtue of IRC §1033, gain on an "involuntary conversion" of property (including destruction in whole or in part, theft, condemnation, sale under threat or imminence of condemnation, and certain similar events) is not recognized if the owner replaces it within a prescribed period of time with other property that is "similar or related in service or use" or with stock representing control of a corporation owning such property. If the old property is converted directly into qualified replacement property (e.g., by an exchange of real estate threatened with condemnation for similar property in another locality), IRC §1033 makes nonrecognition of gain mandatory; but if the taxpayer receives money (e.g., the proceeds of fire insurance or a condemnation award) or other dissimilar property for the involuntarily converted property and acquires qualified replacement property within the prescribed time period, nonrecognition of the gain is optional.

In keeping with the "deferral" rationale for nonrecognition provisions, IRC §1033(b) prescribes a basis for the replacement property that is designed to take the taxpayer's gain on the involuntary conversion into account when the replacement property is sold. Thus, if under threat of condemnation, *A* sells Blackacre (adjusted basis of $20,000) for $25,000, buys Whiteacre for $27,000 in a transaction qualifying under IRC §1033, and elects not to recognize the $5,000 of gain realized on the sale of Blackacre, *A*'s basis for Whiteacre is not its purchase price ($27,000), but $22,000 (i.e., $27,000 less $5,000 of nonrecognized gain).[34] If *A* then sells Whiteacre for $27,000, its fair market value, *A* will realize gain of $5,000—which corresponds to *A*'s economic gain over the long haul.

If condemned, destroyed, or otherwise involuntarily converted, partial interests in property, such as undivided fractional interests, remainders, leaseholds, easements, and mineral rights, qualify as "property" as that term is used by IRC §1033(a);[35] but payments for temporary interferences with the taxpayer's right to use his property and other receipts in the nature of income must be reported as such, even if promptly reinvested.[36]

2. Scope of Term "Involuntary Conversion." The events bringing IRC §1033 into play, assuming acquisition by the taxpayer of qualified replacement property, include:

1. *Destruction in whole or in part.* The legislative history of IRC §1033 associates the term "destruction" with the concept of a "casualty," denoting an accident or mishap that occurs by chance and unexpectedly and is attributable to an unknown cause or an unusual known cause. Thus, it

---

[34] IRC §1033(b) (third sentence).

[35] Rev. Rul. 71-567, 1971-2 CB 309 (remainder interest); Rev. Rul. 71-519, 1971-2 CB 309 (leasehold); Rev. Rul. 72-433, 1972-2 CB 470 (perpetual easement to flood taxpayer's farm).

[36] Rev. Rul. 57-261, 1957-1 CB 262 (under threat of condemnation, taxpayer leased property to city for three years, with option to purchase; held, gain on sale when option was exercised qualifies for nonrecognition under IRC §1033, but not the rental payments); Treas. Regs. §1.1033(a)-2(c)(8) (compensation for loss of profits under business use and occupancy insurance does not qualify).

encompasses events constituting casualties within the meaning of IRC §165(c)(3), such as fire, shipwreck, hail, and lightning.[37] The IRS has ruled, however, that the term "destruction" as used in IRC §1033 does not incorporate the element of "suddenness," which has been a persistently troublesome requisite to casualty losses under IRC §165(c)(3); thus, pollution of an underground water supply by the gradual seepage of salt water qualifies as an involuntary conversion.[38] The progressive deterioration of property attributable to other slowly operating causes (e.g., termites, drought and disease) should also qualify as "destruction" under this ruling if unusual and unexpected;[39] but the ruling clearly does not expand the concept to include ordinary wear and tear, obsolescence, and other normal consequences of the sad fact that assets, like taxpayers, eventually wear out.

If, however, the taxpayer's gain is generated by a *sale* of the damaged property rather than by the receipt of damages, insurance, or other reimbursement, the IRS holds that IRC §1033(a) does not apply if the property can be readily repaired but is replaced because of the owner's preference for the new property, since then the old property has not been "involuntarily" converted into money as a result of destruction.[40]

2. *Theft.* The term "theft," which is also employed by IRC §165(c)(3), seems to have engendered few problems of construction under IRC §1033. Since thieves are seldom apprehended and even less frequently solvent, a taxpayer is likely to receive more than the adjusted basis of the stolen property, so as to realize a gain, only if he is compensated by an insurer or negligent custodian.[41] In these circumstances, recognition of the gain can be avoided by an election under IRC §1033(a)(2) if the taxpayer purchases qualified replacement property within the prescribed period of time.

3. *Seizure.* As contrasted with "requisition" and "condemnation," which are used by IRC §1033(a) to denote an exercise of the power of eminent

---

[37] For IRC §165(c)(3), see supra ¶18.1.

[38] Rev. Rul. 59-102, 1959-1 CB 200 (modifying earlier rulings adopting the "suddenness" concept); Rev. Rul. 66-334, 1966-2 CB 302 (contamination of water supply by seepage of salt water, produced as a by-product of oil wells on same property).

[39] See Rev. Rul. 63-232, 1963-2 CB 97 (termites); Rev. Rul. 66-303, 1966-2 CB 55 (drought); Rev. Rul. 57-599, 1957-2 CB 142 (disease).

[40] Compare C.G. Willis, Inc. v. CIR, 41 TC 468 (1964), aff'd per curiam, 342 F.2d 996 (3d Cir. 1965) (gain on sale of ship damaged by collision does not qualify under IRC §1033 where ship could have been repaired; sale did not result from partial destruction but from desire to reinvest proceeds in new vessel), with Rev. Rul. 80-175, 1980-2 CB 230 (proceeds from sale of timber downed by high winds, earthquake, or volcanic eruption qualify for nonrecognition under IRC §1033 if used to buy other standing timber).

[41] See Rev. Rul. 66-355, 1966-2 CB 302 (unauthorized pledge of taxpayer's securities by employee as collateral for personal loan constituted theft; damages paid by bank for unlawful sale of pledged securities qualify for reinvestment under IRC §1033).

domain, seizure seems to encompass the confiscation of property by a public agency without compensation, an event that can generate a gain only if the taxpayer is insured or reimbursed by some private arrangement. Seizure also differs from requisition and condemnation in that a sale under threat or imminence of seizure does not constitute an involuntary conversion, while a sale under threat or imminence of requisition or condemnation does qualify. This distinction does not emerge clearly from the phraseology of IRC §1033(a) but is sanctioned by its historical lineage and adopted by the regulations.[42]

4. *Requisition or condemnation.* From the practitioner's point of view, the core of IRC §1033 is the deferral of gain when property is involuntarily converted "as a result of . . . requisition or condemnation or threat or imminence thereof"; and these terms also account for most of the litigation and administrative rulings under IRC §1033.

The statutory phrase "requisition or condemnation" is linked to the Fifth Amendment's prohibition on taking private property for public use without just compensation,[43] thus excluding an enormous body of regulatory legislation that renders property useless for its accustomed purpose but that constitutes an exercise of the police power rather than the power of eminent domain and, hence, gives rise to no right of compensation even though the taxpayer can no longer use the property or can do so only if he is prepared to make expensive changes. For example, IRC §1033 has been held inapplicable when property violating a municipal building code was sold after the threat of criminal proceedings; the taxpayer could have brought the building into compliance with the law, but this would have reduced the usable space and made the property unsuited to its business needs.[44] In the same vein, property disposed of pursuant to legislation designed to settle private disputes is not "condemned" even if the owner is compelled to sell. Thus, sales of property in a foreclosure action or pursuant to a deadlocked-shareholder provision of state corporate law are not involuntary conversions within the meaning of IRC §1033(a).[45] Although sales under actual or threatened judicial or administrative orders or pursuant to statute do not qualify as involuntary conversions under IRC §1033, Congress has supplied specific statutory relief for a few such transactions.[46]

---

[42] See Treas. Regs. §1.1033(a)-1(a) (referring to "the threat or imminence of requisition or condemnation of property").

[43] See American Natural Gas Co. v. US, 279 F.2d 220, 225 (Ct. Cl.), cert. denied, 364 US 900 (1960).

[44] Dorothy C. Thorpe Glass Mfg. Corp. v. CIR, 51 TC 300 (1968).

[45] Cooperative Publishing Co. v. CIR, 115 F.2d 1017 (9th Cir. 1940) (foreclosure sale); Dear Publication & Radio, Inc. v. CIR, 274 F.2d 656 (3d Cir. 1960) (state deadlock statute).

[46] See IRC §1071 (sales made to effect FCC policies), IRC §1081 (sales made

5. *Threat or imminence of requisition or condemnation.* From its inception, IRC §1033 has accorded relief not only when there is an actual requisition or condemnation, but also when the involuntary conversion occurs "as a result of . . . threat or imminence" of such action. Were such anticipatory transactions not covered, negotiated sales to the condemning authority in advance of a formal taking of the property would be discouraged. But IRC §1033 simplifies the task of the condemning agency by complicating life for the tax collector, who must determine in particular cases whether condemnation was threatened or imminent and whether the sale occurred "as a result . . . thereof." Under current IRS rulings, these conditions are satisfied if, prior to the execution of a binding contract to sell the property,

> the property owner is informed, either orally or in writing by a representative of a governmental body or public official authorized to acquire property for public use, that such body or official has decided to acquire his property, and from the information conveyed to him has reasonable grounds to believe that his property will be condemned if a voluntary sale is not arranged.[47]

3. Acquisition of Property "Similar or Related in Service or Use." Gain realized by the taxpayer when property is compulsorily or involuntarily converted is not recognized under IRC §1033(a) if the taxpayer acquires property "similar or related in service or use" to the converted property in circumstances satisfying prescribed conditions. Neither the Code nor the regulations defines the phrase "similar or related in service or use." Summarizing the cases interpreting the statutory concept, the Tax Court said in *Maloof v. CIR* that the "reinvestment must be made in substantially similar business property," that the statute requires a "reasonably similar business continuation of the [taxpayer's] prior commitment of capital and not a departure from it," that "it is not necessary to acquire property which duplicates exactly that which was converted [but that] the fortuitous circumstance of involuntary conversion does not permit a taxpayer to change the character of his investment without tax consequences," and that IRC §1033 is "a means by which a taxpayer whose enjoyment of his property is interrupted without his consent may arrange to have that interruption ignored for tax purposes, by returning as closely as possible to his original position."[48]

The taxpayer in the *Maloof* case acquired a complete manufacturing plant, with more than half of his investment going into fixed assets, following an involuntary conversion of a business involving the acquisition of raw

---

under the Public Utility Holding Company Act); IRC §1101 (distributions under Bank Holding Company Act).

[47] Rev. Rul. 74-8, 1974-1 CB 200, 200.

[48] Maloof v. CIR, 65 TC 263, 269-270 (1975).

materials and the design and marketing of finished products in which inventory and accounts receivable comprised more than 99 percent of his investment. The Tax Court held that IRC §1033 did not apply to such a disproportionate shift from current to fixed assets, reflecting a fundamental change in the nature of the business itself, except to the extent of the replacement inventory.

The most persistently litigated issue in interpreting the phrase "similar or related in service or use" concerns property held by the taxpayer for rental income. For many years the IRS and the Tax Court maintained that the physical characteristics and end uses of the converted and replacement properties had to be similar. Thus, property rented to the operator of a retail grocery business, for example, could not be replaced by property rented to an automobile sales agency, since such a shift from one business to another would be fatal if the old and new properties were both occupied and used by the taxpayer itself for such divergent activities.[49] As applied to rental property, however, this "functional" or end-use test was rejected by a series of appellate decisions, which accepted the less exacting requirement of a "similar economic relationship," which was promulgated by the Court of Appeals for the Second Circuit in *Liant Record, Inc. v. CIR* and later endorsed by other courts.[50]

Using the "similar economic relationship" test to determine whether the old and new properties are "similar or related in service or use" within the meaning of IRC §1033, the courts have held that Illinois property leased as a filling station can be replaced by a fractional interest in Florida real estate to be leased for the construction of apartments; that property leased to a shoe manufacturer can be replaced by property leased to a wholesale grocery business for office and warehouse space; and that property rented for the production, transportation, and distribution of gas can be replaced by property to be leased to a company that is to build and operate a motel.[51] On the other hand, the replacement of an office building by a hotel was denied the benefits of IRC §1033, although both properties produced rental income, on the ground that the services rendered by the taxpayer to the tenants of the two properties were totally different, requiring a shift from a two-employee maintenance staff for the office building to a 130-employee staff for the hotel by which it was replaced.[52]

---

[49] See Rev. Rul. 64-237, 1964-2 CB 319.

[50] Liant Records, Inc. v. CIR, 303 F.2d 326 (2d Cir. 1962); see also Johnson v. CIR, 43 TC 736 (1965) (Acq.), and cases there cited.

[51] Pohn v. CIR, 309 F.2d 427 (7th Cir. 1962) (filling station converted; Florida real estate acquired); Loco Realty Co. v. CIR, 306 F.2d 207 (8th Cir. 1962) (replacement property leased to wholesale grocery company); Capitol Motor Car Co. v. CIR, 314 F.2d 469 (6th Cir. 1963) (motel).

[52] Clifton Inv. Co. v. CIR, 312 F.2d 719 (9th Cir. 1963), cert. denied, 373 US 921 (1963); see also Rev. Rul. 70-399, 1970-2 CB 164 (IRC §1033 not satisfied by replace-

Section 1033(a)(2) requires the replacement property to be "purchased" by the taxpayer, but the IRS has risen above literalism by ruling that remodeling or improving property already owned by the taxpayer satisfies this requirement.[53] The "purchase" requirement, however, serves to disqualify property acquired by a gift, tax-free exchange, or other transaction that does not entail an expenditure by the taxpayer offsetting the amount realized for the old property.

4. Acquisition of Corporation Owning Qualified Replacement Property. Instead of purchasing replacement property directly, the taxpayer is permitted by IRC §1033(a)(2) to purchase stock to acquire control of a corporation owning qualified replacement property, "control" being defined as ownership of stock with at least 80 percent of the total combined voting power of all clases of stock entitled to vote and at least 80 percent of the total number of shares of all other classes. The language of IRC §1033(a)(2) seems to imply that the entire amount paid for the stock qualifies as a reinvestment of the proceeds of the conversion, even if the acquired corporation owns both qualified replacement property and other assets.

5. Special Rule for Condemned Realty. Because the "similar or related in service or use" test of IRC §1033(a) is in most cases more stringent than the "like kind" test of IRC §1031, Congress enacted IRC §1033(g) to permit certain involuntarily condemned realty to be replaced by other real property of a "like kind."[54] This special rule applies only to real property, and it resembles IRC §1031 in using the term "like kind" and in requiring both the original and the replacement property to be held either for business use or for investment (thus excluding stock in trade, other property held primarily for sale, and property held for personal use, such as owner-occupied residences).

Section 1033(g) applies only if the property is involuntarily converted by reason of seizure, requisition, or condemnation or the threat or imminence thereof; thus, it does not apply to other involuntary conversions, of which the most important is destruction by fire, flood, or other catastrophe. Moreover, the "like kind" standard does not apply if the taxpayer acquires stock of a corporation owning the replacement property.

In unusual circumstances (e.g., an exchange of farm property held for

---

ment of resort hotel by another resort hotel, where taxpayer leased first hotel on net lease but operated second hotel in its own right).

[53] Rev. Rul. 67-254, 1967-2 CB 269 (proceeds of involuntary conversion used to rearrange facilities on property that was not condemned and to build new facilities on nearby property already owned by taxpayer); Davis v. US, 589 F.2d 446 (9th Cir. 1979) (improvements on existing property qualified).

[54] See Biedermann v. CIR, 68 TC 1 (1977), holding that condemned unimproved realty can be replaced with improved realty under IRC §1033(g) even though such an improved-unimproved transaction does not qualify under IRC §1033(a).

investment for farm property held primarily for sale), the replacement property may satisfy the traditional "similar or related in service or use" test of IRC §1033(a)(2), but not the "like kind" test of IRC §1033(g). In this event, the enactment of IRC §1033(g) as a relief measure should not be interpreted to preclude nonrecognition under the more general rule of IRC §1033(a)(2).[55]

6. Elective Nonrecognition of Gain. If the taxpayer receives money or nonqualified property when appreciated property is involuntarily converted, the realized gain qualifies for nonrecognition under IRC §1033(a)(2) if (1) qualified replacement property is purchased with a cost equaling or exceeding the amount realized on the conversion, (2) the purchase occurs within a prescribed period, and (3) nonrecognition treatment is elected pursuant to the regulations.

The taxpayer's realized gain, however, must be recognized if, and to the extent that, the amount realized for the converted property exceeds the cost of the replacement property.[56] If mortgaged property is converted, amounts paid to the mortgagee by the condemning authority are included in the "amount realized" whether the taxpayer is liable on the debt or not.[57] The same principle should apply to a payment of fire insurance proceeds to a mortgagee. On the other hand, the regulations sanction a reduction of the amount realized for condemned property to take account of amounts retained by the government to satisfy special assessments levied against related property owned by the taxpayer for benefits accruing to it by reason of the condemnation.[58]

Amounts received as rent, interest, or compensation for loss of profits are not part of the "amount realized" for the converted property. Thus, they need not be reinvested; conversely, they must be included in income regardless of the amount paid for qualified replacement property. On the other hand, amounts received to defray relocation and moving expenses have been held to qualify for reinvestment under IRC §1033(a); and the courts have reached the same conclusion as to severance damages.[59]

These principles are illustrated by Example 24-4, which assumes that (a) the taxpayer received a condemnation award of $10,000 in cash for Blackacre

---

[55] See Rev. Rul. 71-41, 1971-1 CB 223 (replacement of a warehouse with a gas station held not to qualify under §1033(g) but did under §1033(a)).

[56] See Rev. Rul. 71-476, 1971-2 CB 308 (condemnation award reduced by legal, engineering, and appraisal fees in computing "amount realized upon . . . conversion").

[57] Treas. Regs. §1.1033(a)-2(c)(1).

[58] Treas. Regs. §§1.1033(a)-2(c)(10), 1.1033(a)-2(c)(11).

[59] See Graphics Press, Inc. v. CIR, 523 F.2d 585, 589 (9th Cir. 1975) (IRC §1033 applicable to lump-sum award in excess of taxpayer's adjusted basis, even if part compensated for moving heavy machinery from condemned realty; "[f]rom the taxpayer's viewpoint, he is being compensated for a loss due to the condemnation of his property").

which had a $10,000 adjusted basis; (b) the condemning authority paid an additional $15,000 to a bank to discharge a mortgage on Blackacre; (c) the taxpayer incurred legal expenses of $2,000 in the condemnation proceeding; and (d) the taxpayer purchased qualified replacement property for $5,000 in cash, taking the property subject to a mortgage of $15,000 and paying purchase commissions of $1,000. The taxpayer's realized gain on Blackacre was $13,000, of which $2,000 is recognized and $11,000 unrecognized, computed as shown in Example 24-4.

Example 24-4
Computation of Nonrecognized Gain on Replacement of Condemned Mortgaged Property With Qualifying Mortgaged Property

1. Amount realized for Blackacre:		
a. Cash	$10,000	
b. Mortgage discharged	15,000	
c. Gross amount realized	$25,000	
d. Less: Expenses	2,000	
e. Amount realized		$23,000
2. Less: Adjusted basis of Blackacre		10,000
3. Gain realized on condemnation		$13,000
4. Gain recognized:		
a. Amount realized (line 1e)	$23,000	
b. Less: Cost of replacement property (cash, $5,000; mortgage, $15,000; purchase commissions, $1,000)	21,000	
c. Excess of amount realized for converted property (line 1e) over cost of replacement property (line 4b)	$ 2,000	
d. Recognized gain (lower of lines 3 and 4c)		2,000
5. Unrecognized gain (line 3 less line 4d)		$11,000

Under IRC §1033(a)(2)(B), the period during which the taxpayer must purchase the qualified replacement property (a) begins on the date the converted property was disposed of or the earliest date when requisition or condemnation was threatened, whichever is the earlier, and (b) ends two years after the close of the first taxable year in which any part of the taxpayer's gain on the conversion was realized or at the close of such later date as may be specified by the IRS on timely application by the taxpayer. The replacement property is "purchased" when the taxpayer becomes its owner, not when he contracts to purchase it.[60] The permissible period was extended to three years by IRC §1033(g)(4) for involuntarily converted realty satisfying the like-kind rule of IRC §1033(g)(1).

If a taxpayer shows "reasonable cause" for being unable to replace the converted property within the statutory period, the IRS can extend it.[61] But an extension must be requested before the replacement period has expired, unless the application is made within a reasonable time after the original deadline and the taxpayer can show reasonable cause for not having filed a timely application.[62]

7. Basis of Replacement Property. If the involuntarily converted property is converted directly into replacement property, the basis of the old property carries over and becomes the basis of the replacement property.[63] If the conversion is into money or dissimilar property and the taxpayer purchases qualified replacement property and elects nonrecognition of the gain under IRC §1033(a)(2), the replacement property's basis is its cost less the unrecognized gain.[64]

If the taxpayer purchases two or more items of replacement property, the basis must be allocated among them in proportion to their respective costs. For example, if the taxpayer (a) received $100,000 on the condemnation of Blackacre (adjusted basis $60,000), (b) replaced Blackacre with Whiteacre (cost $50,000) and Greenacre (cost $25,000), and (c) elected under IRC §1033(a)(2) to recognize the realized gain ($40,000) only to the extent of the uninvested cash of $25,000, his $60,000 basis for the replacement properties (cost of $75,000 less $15,000 of unrecognized gain) would be allocated $40,000 to Whiteacre and $20,000 to Greenacre.

¶24.4 GAIN ON SALE OR EXCHANGE OF TAXPAYER'S PRINCIPAL RESIDENCE

1. Introductory. The Internal Revenue Code contains two provisions for the nonrecognition of gain on a sale or exchange of the taxpayer's principal residence.

The first, IRC §1034, which is of the greatest general interest, provides that gain on the sale or exchange of a principal residence shall not be recog-

---

[60] See Fort Hamilton Manor, Inc. v. CIR, 445 F.2d 879 (2d Cir. 1971).

[61] IRC §1033(a)(2)(B)(ii); Treas. Regs. §1.1033(a)-2(c)(3); Rev. Rul. 60-69, 1960-1 CB 294 (extension of time depends on facts and circumstances of each case).

[62] Treas. Regs. §1.1033(a)-2(c)(3).

[63] IRC §1033(b) (first sentence).

[64] IRC §1033(b) (last sentence). The holding period of the replacement property includes the holding period of the old property if the latter was a capital asset at the time of the conversion. See Rev. Rul. 72-451, 1972-2 CB 480.

nized if replacement property is purchased and used as a principal residence within the period beginning two years before and ending two years after the sale of the old residence, except to the extent that the adjusted sales price of the old residence exceeds the cost of the replacement property. Section 1034 is a typical nonrecognition provision, requiring the basis of the new residence to be reduced by the unrecognized gain so that the gain will be recognized if and when the new residence is sold for more than its basis.

The second of the Code's principal-residence provisions is IRC §121, applicable only to taxpayers over the age of fifty-five, which excludes gain on the sale or exchange of a principal residence from gross income, whether the taxpayer purchases a replacement residence or not. Section 121 differs from IRC §1034 in important respects: It is not mandatory but applies only if the taxpayer so elects; it excludes gain only up to $125,000 ($62,500 in the case of a separate return by a married individual); it permanently excludes the gain from income rather than merely postponing its recognition; and it can be used only once in a lifetime.

2. Sale and Replacement of Principal Residence. To qualify for nonrecognition under IRC §1034, gain must be realized on the sale or exchange of the taxpayer's "principal residence," and property must be purchased and used as the taxpayer's "principal residence" within the period beginning two years before and ending two years after the sale or within an extended period if certain conditions are met.[65] Ordinarily it is not difficult to determine whether the old and new properties constitute the taxpayer's "residences" or to determine, when the taxpayer either owns or purchases two dwelling places, which is the "principal" one. The distinction is crucial, since IRC §1034 does not apply to gain realized on selling a summer cottage or other second home, even if the proceeds are invested in a home for year-round occupany, or to gain realized on selling the taxpayer's principal residence if the proceeds are invested in a secondary home. In disputed cases the regulations look to "all the facts and circumstances," including "the good faith of the taxpayer."[66]

---

[65] For an extension of time if the new residence is constructed by the taxpayer, see Rev. Rul. 57-234, 1957-1 CB 263; see IRC §1034(h) (extension for armed forces).

[66] Treas. Regs. §1.1034–1(c)(3)(i); see also Evans v. CIR, ¶62,061 P-H Memo TC (1962) (taxpayer vacated his principal residence in 1952, though it continued to be occupied until sale in 1956 by his mother; new residence purchased in 1956 was occupied regularly by his mother; held, neither residence qualified as taxpayer's principal residence despite weekend and holiday visits); Stolk v. CIR, 40 TC 345, 350-356 (1963) (Acq.), aff'd per curiam, 326 F.2d 760 (2d Cir. 1964) (taxpayer vacated suburban principal residence, lived for two years in a rented apartment in New York City, then sold old residence and invested proceeds of sale

In practice, the most troublesome issue in applying the "principal residence" concept is identifying the time when the property must be "used" as the taxpayer's principal residence. So far as the old residence is concerned, IRC §1034 leaves this issue open; but it was clearly not intended to embrace gain on a home that is converted from personal use to rental property held for income-producing purposes for many years while the taxpayer lives elsewhere, and then sold, even if the sales price is invested in property that the taxpayer moves into and occupies as his principal residence. On the other hand, it is equally clear that the taxpayer's principal residence does not lose its status merely because the taxpayer moves into the new residence and the old place remains vacant or is rented for a few weeks or months while he endeavors to find a buyer. The happy medium between these two extremes, according to the Tax Court, is reached by requiring the taxpayer to occupy the old residence either when it is sold or when the new residence is purchased, unless "exceptional and unusual" [67] circumstances are present, such as (a) vacating the old residence with an intent to return after a temporary absence (which, if shown, will permit the old residence to qualify even if the taxpayer does not in fact return to it) or (b) economic conditions, such as a poor real estate market or a shortage of mortgage funds requiring the taxpayer to lease the old residence while endeavoring to sell it.[68]

Although the failure of IRC §1034(a) to pinpoint the time when the old property must have been used as the taxpayer's principal residence introduces elements of both flexibility and uncertainty, the statutory language is more precise, and hence less malleable, as respects the replacement property, which must be purchased *and used* as the taxpayer's principal residence *within* the

---

in a country home that he furnished and occupied on weekends and holidays; held, the apartment was the taxpayer's principal residence, both before and after the sale).

[67] See Houlette v. CIR, 48 TC 350, 354 (1967).

[68] See Treas. Regs. §1.1034-1(c)(3)(i) ("mere fact that property is, or has been, rented is not determinative that such property is not used by the taxpayer as his principal residence").

For the "intent to return" principle, see Trisko v. CIR, 29 TC 515 (1957) (Acq.) (old residence vacated when taxpayer accepted temporary government position in Europe, intending to return; because repossession seemed impractical on termination of foreign assignment, taxpayer sold old residence and purchased new one; held, qualified); Rev. Rul. 59-72, 1959-1 CB 203 (acquiescence in *Trisko* case). But see Stucchi v. CIR, ¶76,242 P-H Memo TC (1976) (insufficient evidence of intent to return to property rented for several years when taxpayers moved to another state, where they lived in rented quarters). The source of the "adverse economic conditions" principle is Clapham v. CIR, 63 TC 505 (1975), where the taxpayers vacated their residence because the husband's employer transferred him from San Francisco to Los Angeles, leased it for three years while trying to sell it for a reasonable price, and sold it about nine months after buying a new residence.

statutory period. It has been held that physical occupany of the new residence within the statutory period is essential.[69]

The most celebrated delay in occupying a replacement residence in the annals of IRC §1034 occurred in 1969, when ex-President Nixon purchased the "Western White House" at San Clemente as a replacement for his New York City dwelling place. The staff of the Joint Committee on Internal Revenue Taxation concluded that occupany on weekends and holidays, coupled with an intent to occupy the residence permanently on leaving the White House, was insufficient to qualify it as Nixon's principal residence and that there was no statutory basis for an exception for taxpayers whose official duties require their presence elsewhere.[70] Though San Clemente became Nixon's principal residence earlier than anticipated, the statutory period had already run.

3. Computation of Unrecognized Gain and Basis of Replacement Residence. If the conditions prescribed by IRC §1034 are satisfied, the taxpayer proceeds to determine (a) the amount of gain realized on the sale of the old residence; (b) the amount, if any, of the realized gain that is not recognized; and (c) the basis of the replacement residence.

The taxpayer's realized gain is determined under general principles that are not altered by IRC §1034. In general, the realized gain is the excess of the "amount realized" for the old residence (i.e., any money received plus the fair market value of any property received) over its adjusted basis. Mortgages and other liabilities that are assumed by the buyer or to which the property is subject are treated as money received in computing the amount realized by the seller, but selling commissions and other sales expenses are deducted.[71]

The gain realized by the taxpayer on selling the old residence is recognized

---

[69] US v. Sheahan, 323 F.2d 383 (5th Cir. 1963) (contract of sale for new residence signed on last day of statutory period; taxpayer's daughter supervised construction, installed mailbox, etc., before purchase and moved in two days after contract of sale, but taxpayer and his wife did not spend time there until later; held, despite undisputed intent to make the property their principal residence, taxpayers did not so use it within the prescribed period).

[70] Joint Comm. on Internal Revenue Taxation, Examination of President Nixon's Tax Returns for 1969 Through 1972, H. Rep. No. 93-966, 93d Cong., 2d Sess. 117-118 (1974).

[71] See Treas. Regs. §1.1034-1(b)(4). Expenses that are deducted under IRC §217(b)(2) (moving expenses of employee or self-employed person) cannot be deducted a second time in computing the amount realized.

by IRC §1034(a) only if and to the extent that the "adjusted sales price" of the old residence exceeds the taxpayer's cost of purchasing the new residence. The term "adjusted sales price" is defined by IRC §1034(b) as the amount realized less so-called fixing-up expenses incurred for work performed on the old residence to assist in its sale, such as painting. Thus, to avoid recognizing gain, the taxpayer need not reinvest the entire amount realized for the old residence, but only the amount realized less the fixing-up expenses.

To qualify, fixing-up expenses must be (a) for work performed during the ninety-day period ending when the contract to sell the old residence is entered into and (b) paid on or before the thirtieth day after the sale of the old residence. To avoid double counting, fixing-up expenses do not include amounts that are (1) otherwise deductible in computing taxable income (e.g., repairing storm damage), (2) taken into account in computing the amount realized, or (3) included in the old residence's adjusted basis (e.g., the cost of a new furnace).[72]

In computing the "cost" of the new residence, the taxpayer can include not only its purchase price (including purchase commissions and similar acquisition expenses, as well as mortgages that the taxpayer assumes or to which the property is subject),[73] but also additional expenditures for reconstructing or improving the property within the statutory period, such as the cost of remodeling a kitchen, installing new plumbing, or adding a room.[74] Since the expenditures must be "properly chargeable to capital account," routine repairs are not counted, but a mass of minor items may constitute, in the aggregate, a capital outlay.[75]

These principles are illustrated by Example 24-5, in which none of the taxpayer's gain on selling the old residence is recognized. Example 24-5 assumes that *A* (1) sells a principal residence with a basis of $15,000 for $60,000 ($10,000 in cash over an assumed mortgage of $50,000), (2) incurs fixing-up expenses of $5,000 and selling expenses of $5,000, and (3) purchases a new principal residence for $85,000 ($10,000 in cash and a mortgage of $75,000).[76]

---

[72] IRC §1034(b)(2); Treas. Regs. §1.1034-1(b)(6).

[73] Treas. Regs. §1.1034-1(c)(4)(i).

[74] IRC §1034(c)(2); Treas. Regs. §§1.1034-1(b)(7), 1.1034-1(c)(4)(ii).

[75] See supra ¶8.4, text at note 116 (aggregation of minor expenses incurred in large-scale rehabilitation).

[76] For other illustrations of the operation of IRC §1034, including situations in which part or all of the taxpayer's realized gain must be recognized, see Treas. Regs. §1.1034-1(c)(2).

Example 24-5

Nonrecognition of Gain Under IRC §1034 on Replacement of Principle Residence

1. Sales price of old residence (cash of $10,000 plus mortgage of $50,000)	$60,000
2. Less: Selling expenses	5,000
3. Amount realized	$55,000
4. Less: Basis of old residence	15,000
5. Gain realized	$40,000
6. Amount realized (line 3)	$55,000
7. Less: Fixing-up expenses	5,000
8. Adjusted sales price	$50,000
9. Less: Cost of new residence ($10,000 cash plus mortgage of $75,000)	85,000
10. Gain recognized (not less than zero)	-0-
11. Gain realized (line 5)	$40,000
12. Less: Gain recognized (line 10)	-0-
13. Gain realized but not recognized	$40,000
14. Cost of new residence (line 9)	$85,000
15. Less: Gain realized but not recognized (line 13)	40,000
16. Basis of new residence	$45,000

As is customary when the acquisition of replacement property results in the nonrecognition of gain on the old property, the replacement property's holding period for capital gain purposes includes the holding period of the old property.[77]

4. Sale of Principal Residence by Taxpayer Over Fifty-five Years of Age. When a taxpayer who is over fifty-five years of age sells his or her principal residence, gain up to $125,000 ($62,500 for a married individual filing a separate return) can be excluded from gross income under IRC §121 at the taxpayer's election. Because IRC §121 does not require a reduction in the basis of any property held by the taxpayer, it serves to exclude the nonrecognized gain from gross income permanently, not merely to postpone its recognition; but it can only be elected once in a lifetime.

Though qualified by numerous limitations, the basic principle of IRC §121(a) is quite straightforward. It permits gain on the sale or exchange of property to be excluded from gross income, at the taxpayer's election, if (a) the taxpayer has attained the age of fifty-five before the date of the sale or

[77] IRC §1223(7).

exchange and (b) the property was owned and used by the taxpayer as his principal residence for periods aggregating three years or more during the five-year period ending on the date of the sale or exchange. Section 121 resembles IRC §1034 in requiring personal ownership of the residence, so that property owned by trusts, estates, and corporations does not qualify; but, unlike §1034, it includes principal residences that the taxpayer vacated and converted to rental purposes, provided the three-out-of-five-years requirement is met.[78]

By virtue of IRC §121(d)(1), if (1) a residence is owned by husband and wife as joint tenants, tenants by the entirety, or community property, (2) they file a joint return for the year of the sale, and (3) one of them satisfies the age, holding, and use requirements with respect to the residence, then both of them are treated as satisfying these requirements. (Marital status is determined as of the date of the sale, and persons legally separated under a decree of divorce or of separate maintenance are not "married" for purposes of IRC §121.[79]) Thus, their combined gain, rather than only the gain attributable to the one-half ownership of the qualifying spouse, is eligible for exclusion. If, however, a residence is owned jointly by any other persons (or by a married couple filing separate returns), the gain realized by each co-owner is computed separately and can be excluded under IRC §121 only by an owner who personally meets the statutory age, use, and holding requirements and only to the extent of $62,500 in the case of a separate return by a married individual.[80]

5. Replacement of Principal Residence by Taxpayer Over Fifty-five Years of Age. If gain on the sale of a principal residence by a taxpayer who attains the age of fifty-five before the sale or exchange is excluded only in part under IRC §121 because the gain exceeds $125,000, the balance of the gain may qualify for nonrecognition if the taxpayer purchases a qualified replacement residence within the time period prescribed by IRC §1034. When both IRC §§121 and 1034 apply, the amount that must be invested in the replacement residence is not the full adjusted sales price of the old residence but only that amount less the gain excluded under IRC §121.[81]

---

[78] See Treas. Regs. §1.121-1(d), Example (1); re IRC §1034, see Treas. Regs. §1.1034-1(c)(3)(i) (only limited rental status permitted).

[79] See IRC §121(d)(6).

[80] Rev. Rul. 67-234, 1967-2 CB 78 (qualified unmarried individual owning principal residence as joint tenant or tenant in common can elect under IRC §121 to exclude portion of gain attributable to his undivided interest in residence).

[81] IRC §121(d)(7); Treas. Regs. §1.121-5(g)(2), Example (1).

¶24.5 MISCELLANEOUS NONRECOGNITION PROVISIONS

1. Exchanges of Life Insurance, Endowment, and Annuity Contracts. Under IRC §1035(a), neither gain nor loss is recognized on the exchange of (1) a contract of life insurance for another contract of life insurance or for an endowment or annuity contract, (2) an endowment contract for another endowment contract providing for regular payments at a date no later than payments would have begun under the old contract or for an annuity contract, or (3) an annuity contract for another annuity contract. As under IRC §1031, if the taxpayer receives not only nonrecognition property but also money or other property ("boot") in the exchange, his gain must be recognized to the extent of the boot. The basis of the nonrecognition property received is prescribed by IRC §1031(d).

2. Exchanges of U.S. Obligations. The Treasury is authorized by IRC §1037 to provide by regulations for the nonrecognition of gain and loss on the exchange of obligations issued under the Second Liberty Bond Act for other obligations issued under the same act.[82] This provision was originally enacted as part of a bill to stem the redemption of savings bonds in favor of nongovernmental investments with higher yields. By allowing an increase in maximum interest rates on Series E and H bonds and providing for nonrecognition on exchanges, the bill was "intended to aid the Government in its attempts to achieve a better balance in the debt structure by facilitating the refinancing of outstanding securities in advance of their final maturities."[83]

3. Reacquisitions of Real Property on Buyer's Default. Section 1038 prescribes a set of special rules governing the seller's reacquisition of real property after a sale giving rise to indebtedness secured by the property. The provision is mandatory rather than elective. It applies only to the seller, however, and only to sales of real property giving rise to indebtedness secured by the property. Thus, IRC §1038 does not apply to (a) sales in which the buyer's obligation to pay part or all of the sales price is unsecured, (b) reacquisitions of property by the seller's assignee,[84] or (c) sales of personal property.

1. *Seller's gain or loss.* Under the general rule of IRC §1038(a), no gain or loss results to the seller from a qualified reacquisition of real property and

---

[82] See Treas. Regs. §1.1037-1(a).

[83] S. Rep. No. 909, 86th Cong., 1st Sess., reprinted in 1959-2 CB 895.

[84] See Rev. Rul. 69-83, 1969-1 CB 202 (IRC §1038 not applicable to repossession by seller's estate).

no debt becomes worthless or partially worthless for tax purposes as a result of the reacquisition, except as provided in IRC §1038(b) or §1038(d). Under IRC §1038(b)(1), however, gain results to the seller, despite this general rule, if and to the extent that any money and the fair market value of any property received by the seller before the reacquisition (other than the purchaser's obligations) were not previously taken into income. To prevent the seller from being taxed on a return of capital, this amount is limited by IRC §1038(b)(2) to the excess of the sale price over the adjusted basis of the property, less (a) any gain previously reported and (b) any money and other property (except the purchaser's obligations) paid by the seller in connection with the reacquisition.

Another limitation on the general no-gain-or-loss rule of IRC §1038(a) is imposed by IRC §1038(d), which requires a seller who wrote off the debt secured by the reacquired property as partially or wholly worthless to treat the amount of the write-off as the recovery of a bad debt. This rule, which is a variation of the tax benefit doctrine, is consistent with the legislative objective of restoring the *status quo ante,* since otherwise the seller could deduct part or all of the unpaid debt in addition to repossessing the property. If the deduction did not produce a tax benefit for the seller, however, the amount written off does not have to be taken back into income.[85]

2. *Basis of reacquired property.* The function of IRC §1038(c) is to place the taxpayer in the position he occupied before the sale, with proper adjustments for any gain recognized on the reacquisition. This legislative objective is accomplished by assigning a basis to the repossessed property equal to the adjusted basis of the debt secured by the property (determined at the time of repossession) plus (a) any gain recognized on repossession, (b) any expenses incurred by the seller in repossessing the property, and (c) any money or property (except the buyer's obligations) transferred by the seller in connection with the reacquisition.[86]

3. *Character of gain.* Because Congress did not intend when enacting IRC §1038 to change the "type of income" resulting from the reacquisition of real property, the character of gain recognized under IRC §1038 depends on factors that are irrelevant in determining the *amount* of the gain or loss, such as whether title was transferred to the buyer or not, whether the reacquisition was by foreclosure or voluntary conveyance, and whether the buyer's obligations are "securities" as defined by IRC §165(g)(2)(C) or not. The effect of these distinctions is set out in the regulations.[87]

---

[85] See Treas. Regs. §1.1038-1(f)(2); for the tax benefit doctrine and its statutory codification by IRC §111, see supra ¶1.10.

[86] See Treas. Regs. §1.1038-1(g)(1) (basis of debt owed by buyer to seller).

[87] Treas. Regs. §1.1038-1(d).

4. Corporate-Shareholder Transactions. Many of the most important nonrecognition provisions, which are beyond the scope of this work, concern transactions between shareholders and their corporations (e.g., transfers of appreciated and depreciated property to controlled corporations in exchange for stock) or between one corporation and another (e.g., transfers of property in mergers and liquidations).

¶24.6 WASH SALES OF STOCK AND SECURITIES

1. Introductory. To prevent the deduction of paper losses, IRC §1091 provides that losses from the sale or other disposition of stock or securities cannot be deducted if the taxpayer acquires, or enters into a contract or option to acquire, substantially identical stock or securities within the period beginning thirty days before the sale and ending thirty days thereafter. Section 1091(d) provides for a basis adjustment to the securities whose acquisition caused the loss on the wash sale to be disallowed; and this adjustment permits the disallowed loss to be recognized when the taxpayer's investment is finally closed out, unless the loss is recouped because the securities go up in value. Thus, IRC §1091 serves to *postpone* the recognition of losses rather than to disallow them permanently. This deferral function is buttressed by IRC §1223, permitting the period during which the taxpayer held the original securities to be included ("tacked") in determining, for capital gain and loss purposes, the holding period for the reacquired securities.

Section 1091 applies only to wash sales of stock and securities, and not to commodity futures, foreign currency, or other assets.[88]

The operation of IRC §1091 is illustrated by Example 24-6, involving a purchase of 100 shares of *X* Company's Class A stock (lot A) for $10,000 on January 1, 1976; their sale on December 1, 1982 for $7,500; the purchase of 100 shares of the same company's Class B stock (lot B) on December 15, 1982 for $6,000; and the sale of the Class B shares on January 15, 1983 for $6,500. If IRC §1091 were inapplicable because the Class B shares were not "substantially identical" to the Class A shares, the taxpayer would recognize a long-term capital loss of $2,500 on selling the Class A shares and a short-term capital gain of $500 on selling the Class B shares. On the other hand, if the Class B shares are substantially identical to the Class A shares, the loss of $2,500 on selling lot A is disallowed by IRC §1091(a); but the Class B shares have a basis of $8,500 (cost of $6,000 plus the disallowed loss of $2,500), and their holding period includes the three-year period during which the taxpayer held the Class A shares. Thus, on selling the Class B shares for $6,500, the

---

[88] Rev. Rul. 71-568, 1971-2 CB 312 (commodity futures); Rev. Rul. 74-218, 1974-1 CB 202 (foreign currency; definition of "security" in IRC §1236 cited as relevant).

taxpayer sustains a long-term capital loss of $2,000. This corresponds to the taxpayer's economic gain since, over the long haul, he invested a total of $16,000 ($10,000 for lot A and $6,000 for lot B) and received a total of $14,000 ($7,500 for lot A and $6,500 for lot B). These results are summarized in Example 24-6.

Example 24-6

Wash Sale of Securities

Date	*Taxpayer's Action*	*Tax Results* *IRC § 1091 Inapplicable*	*IRC § 1091 Applicable*
1/01/76	Buys lot A for $10,000	Basis—$10,000	Basis—$10,000
12/01/82	Sells lot A for $7,500	$2,500 LTCL (1982)	$2,500 loss disallowed
12/15/82	Buys lot B for $6,000	Basis—$6,000	Basis—$8,500
1/15/83	Sells lot B for $6,500	$500 STCG (1983)	$2,000 LTCL (1983)

By its terms, IRC §1091(a) applies to individual taxpayers if the loss would otherwise be deductible under IRC §165(c)(2), relating to losses on transactions entered into for profit; but not if the loss qualifies for deduction under IRC §165(c)(1), relating to losses incurred in the taxpayer's trade or business, as in the case of a securities dealer. Section 1091(a) is more explicit with respect to corporate taxpayers, who are exempted from the wash sale provision only if the loss is incurred by a securities dealer in the ordinary course of business. The exemption of dealers in securities presumably reflects a legislative judgment that they sell and replenish their merchandise as rapidly as possible without attempting to create tax losses.

Because losses are disallowed only if "substantially identical" securities are acquired within the specified time period, sophisticated investors wishing to deduct losses on depreciated securities can often replace them with securities of other issuers (or even with another class of the same issuer's securities) that are not "substantially identical," as that term has been construed, even though the replacement securities are subject to similar market influences and hence serve substantially the same investment objective. This gambit is not ordinarily feasible if the depreciated securities were issued by a closely held corporation, however, for want of a suitable investment alternative.

By laying down a mechanical rule, which takes no account of the taxpayer's motive, IRC §1091 can result in the disallowance of losses incurred by taxpayers who have no tax-avoidance objective or who are forced into a transaction by circumstances beyond their control. For example, a taxpayer who pledges a block of securities for a loan and purchases another block in the belief that the issue will increase in value cannot deduct the loss if there is a precipitous drop in the market and the pledged securities are sold by the creditor within thirty days after the second block was purchased.[89]

2. Transactions Constituting "Wash Sales." Losses on sales and other dispositions of securities are disallowed by IRC §1091(a) if the taxpayer acquires substantially identical securities, or enters into a contract or option to acquire such securities, "within a period beginning thirty days before the date of [the] sale or disposition [of the securities sold] and ending thirty days after such date." In computing the statutory sixty-one-day period, the crucial date is the date when the first block of securities was sold or disposed of, not the date when the taxpayer agreed to sell or was paid for it. Since IRC §1091(a) specifies a period of thirty days, not one month, a sale on January 29 is a wash sale if replacement securities are acquired on February 28, even though the events are separated by more than a calendar month. A short sale is ordinarily not consummated for tax purposes until the securities are delivered by the short seller, but the regulations provide that the day when the sale was entered into is controlling if on that day the taxpayer owned (or held a contract or option to acquire) the securities used to close the short sale.

A transaction is a wash sale not only if the taxpayer acquires substantially identical securities within the statutory sixty-one-day period but also if, within the period, he "has entered into a contract or option" to acquire such securities. To be sure, a seller with an option to reacquire property occupies a significantly different economic position than a seller who reacquires, or is obligated to reacquire, the property; an option enables the seller to recoup if the depreciated securities rise in value, but, unlike a repurchase, it does not subject him to the risk of a further decline in value, because he is not obligated to exercise the option. Since he will benefit from an increase in the value of the securities, however, it is reasonable to postpone recognition of the loss until the option expires or the securities obtained by exercising it are sold.

3. "Substantially Identical" Securities. Section 1091(a) disallows losses not merely if the taxpayer reacquires the same securities within the statutory sixty-one-day period, but also if the original securities are replaced with "substantially identical" securities. A number of cases and rulings have wrestled

---

[89] See Rev. Rul. 71-316, 1971-2 CB 311.

with the statutory language, as applied to different call and maturity dates, interest rates, and types of security;[90] but no precise standards have emerged, nor is this likely to occur, unless the IRS chooses to announce a set of mechanical guidelines to govern its audit practices.

When one class of stock must be compared with another, the features determining whether the shares are "substantially identical" are their respective voting, liquidation, and dividend rights. If the replacement securities are convertible back into the original securities, however, they should qualify as substantially identical to the original securities even though they may have some additional features, since they enable the taxpayer to restore the *status quo ante* by exercising the conversion privilege and thus to nullify the economic effect of the sale.[91]

If the original and replacement securities were issued by different corporations, they can rarely be characterized as substantially identical, even if the two companies are engaged in the same industry and their securities are responsive to the same winds of economic change.[92] While this enables astute investors to sell their depreciated securities at a loss without relinquishing a position in a particular industry or business area, a broader interpretation of "substantially identical," requiring the future internal policies of the two companies to be compared, would invite, if not require, expert testimony between investment counselors that would degenerate into a battle of words about hopelessly imponderable business prospects. Securities issued by different obligors may become fungible in special circumstances, however, as in the case of an impending corporate merger if the target company's securities fluctuate directly with the securities of the acquiring corporation for which they will be exchanged.[93] Similarly, securities issued by different but affiliated corporations may be substantially identical if the replacement securities can be converted into those that were sold.

4. Allocating Replacement Securities to Particular Losses. If the taxpayer sells depreciated securities in several lots and/or purchases several lots of replacement securities, it is necessary to match the replacement securities with particular losses in order to identify both the losses to be disallowed and the replacement securities whose basis is to be adjusted under IRC §1091(d). Pursuant to IRC §§1091(b) and 1091(c), the regulations prescribe rules for matching the original and replacement securities on a chronological basis,

---

[90] Hanlin v. CIR, 108 F.2d 429, 430 (3d Cir. 1939) (bonds of same issuer were substantially identical despite minor differences in maturity dates).

[91] Rev. Rul. 77-201, 1977-1 CB 250 (convertible security is an "option" to acquire securities into which it is convertible).

[92] See Rev. Rul. 59-44, 1959-1 CB 205 (bonds of different local housing authorities are not substantially identical, despite federal guaranty of all bonds).

[93] See Treas. Regs. §1.1233-1(d)(1).

starting with the earliest loss and the earliest acquisition of replacement securities.[94]

5. Wash Sales Not Covered by IRC §1091. Section 1091 is not the IRS' sole weapon against wash sales, which can be disregarded in appropriate circumstances under IRC §267(a)(1) (disallowing losses on sales of property to or exchanges of property between "related persons," whether the seller reacquires the property or not)[95] or, when the transaction lacks economic substance or can be characterized as a sham. If a wash sale runs afoul of these vague but ubiquitous principles, it may be ineffective for tax purposes even though it falls outside the statutory boundaries of IRC §1091 when additional factors (e.g., sale to an intermediary or pursuant to a repurchase agreement) testify to a lack of substance.[96] Moreover, when a loss incurred on a *sham* transaction is disregarded, the taxpayer may be worse off than under either IRC §1091 or §267(a)(1), both of which take account of the disallowed loss in certain circumstances when the property is ultimately sold by the taxpayer or by the related person.

SELECTED BIBLIOGRAPHY

Cook & Owen, Swaps and Wraps: Dispositions of Real Estate by Partnerships, Application of the "At Risk" Rules and Other Considerations, 58 Taxes 227 (1980).

Goldstein & Lewis, Tax Treatment of Like-Kind Exchanges of Property Used in a Trade or Business or for Investment, 5 Rev. Tax. Individuals 195 (1981).

Guerin, A Proposed Test for Evaluating Multiparty Like Kind Exchanges, 35 Tax L. Rev. 545 (1980).

Handler, Tax Consequences of Mortgage Foreclosures and Transfers of Real Property to the Mortgage, 31 Tax L. Rev. 193 (1976).

Harroch, Employing Section 1031 Exchanges: New Opportunities, New Problems and Continuing Risks, 58 Taxes 136 (1980).

---

[94] Treas. Regs. §§1.1091-1(b) through 1.1091-1(d).

[95] For IRC §267(a)(1), see infra ¶33.1.

[96] See Shoenberg v. CIR, 77 F.2d 446, 449 (8th Cir.), cert. denied, 296 US 586 (1935) (sale and repurchase outside the period specified by IRC §1091; loss disallowed because, "for all practical purposes, [taxpayer] used the [vendee, a controlled corporation] as an agency for purchasing, holding, and selling to him, stocks identical with those he sold to establish the claimed loss"); Rev. Rul. 72-225, 1972-1 CB 59 (sale subject to oral repurchase option not bona fide, without regard to IRC §1091); Brochon v. CIR, 30 BTA 404 (1934) (sale by husband and repurchase by wife, with payment guaranteed by husband; held, sale not bona fide, or, if it was, then taxpayer was both seller and purchaser within meaning of IRC §1091).

NONRECOGNITION TRANSACTIONS

Henning, Personal Residences—Planning for Tax-Free and Tax-Deferred Sales and Exchanges, 4 Rev. Tax. Individuals 22 (1980).

Huskins, Section 1031 Like-Kind Property Exchanges; Possibilities and Pitfalls, 1978 So. Calif. Tax Inst. 459.

Huskins & Saddington, Tax Aspects of Creative Equity Participation Real Estate Financing, 1982 So. Calif. Tax Inst. 1900.

Iredale, Creative Dispositions of Real Estate, 1982 So. Calif. Tax Inst. 400.

Solomon, Multi-Party Exchanges and Other Recent Developments in Section 1031, 1981 So. Calif. Tax Inst. 100.

CHAPTER 25

Taxation of Capital Gains and Losses—Basic Structure and Definitions

¶25.1 INTRODUCTORY

Since 1921, capital gains have been taxed more leniently than ordinary income, and as a corollary, the deductibility of capital losses has been subjected to special limitations since 1924. These principles have been controversial throughout their history; and the statutory details, which have varied widely from time to time, are the product of compromises among strongly held economic and political views, rather than the logical outgrowth of basic premises. From this maelstrom of contending theories, the following main features of current law have emerged:

1. A reduced rate of tax on long-term capital gains, achieved directly for corporations by the 28 percent alternative tax on net capital gain imposed by IRC §1201(a) and indirectly for individuals and other noncorporate taxpayers by IRC §1202(a), permitting 60 percent of the taxpayer's net capital gain to be deducted from gross income.
2. Limits on the deduction of capital losses, applicable to both corporate and noncorporate taxpayers, that permit capital losses to be deducted only from gains plus, in the case of individuals and other noncorporate taxpayers, a maximum of $3,000 of ordinary income.
3. The carryover of unused capital losses—in the case of corporations, back to the three taxable years preceding the loss year and forward to the five succeeding years; in the case of individuals and other noncorporate taxpayers, forward indefinitely until used.

Essential to this basic structure is a method of separating capital gains and losses from ordinary income and ordinary losses. The boundary between these concepts cannot be found in the world of business and industry but is instead established by the Internal Revenue Code, as interpreted by the courts and the IRS. The principal landmarks are created by IRC §1222, which refers to gains and losses "from the sale or exchange of a capital asset," and IRC §1221, which defines the term "capital asset." From these provisions it is clear enough that listed securities held by an investor give rise to capital gain or loss when sold and, conversely, that a mercantile or manufacturing company realizes ordinary income or loss on selling its products. But between these polar extremes lie numerous categories of assets whose classification, which depends on the activities of the taxpayer who owns the property as well as on the nature of the property itself, is often more difficult. Moreover, by requiring that the capital asset be disposed of in a "sale or exchange," IRC §1222 creates interpretative problems when an asset is transferred pursuant to a foreclosure, corporate liquidation, or other unusual event.

The assignment of gains and losses to the "capital" or "ordinary" side of the boundary line is sometimes simplified, and in other instances complicated, by a series of statutory qualifications to the general pattern established by IRC §§1221 and 1222. Under these ancillary rules, capital gain or loss treatment is accorded to gain or loss on the disposition of many items that do not constitute "capital assets" within the meaning of IRC §1221 or that are disposed of in transactions not constituting a "sale or exchange" under IRC §1222. Thus, profit on the sale of business machinery and equipment is often treated as capital gain even though the property is not a capital asset under IRC §1221(2), and investors are allowed to report certain patent royalties as capital gain even though the payments are received under a license that does not constitute a "sale or exchange" so far as IRC §1222 is concerned. Transactions like these may be brought within the shelter of the capital gain provisions because they closely resemble capital gain transactions or simply because Congress was persuaded, for extraneous reasons, that liberalized tax treatment was appropriate. In the latter situation (involving so-called statutory capital gains, to distinguish them from what are sometimes called "true" capital gains), the capital gain rules serve as a convenient and familiar repository for "tax relief."

On the other hand, some transactions that meet the "capital asset" and "sale or exchange" standards of IRC §§1221 and 1222, respectively, are nevertheless removed by statute from the capital gain and loss side of the dividing line, and give rise instead to ordinary income or ordinary loss. When a taxpayer sells a depreciable capital asset to his or her spouse, for example, any gain is taxed as ordinary income, even though the transaction would generate capital gain if the purchaser were an unrelated person. Another example of this phenomenon is a loss on so-called Section 1244 stock, which is treated as an ordinary loss even though incurred on a sale of a capital asset. Still another instance of special legislation is IRC §1232(d), which denies capital gain treatment to profits on the sale or other disposition of so-called registration-required obligations, unless they are in registered form or were subject when issued to the excise tax imposed by IRC §4701. This provision was enacted in 1982 to discourage the issue of bearer bonds, which serve as tax-avoidance devices because the owners cannot be readily identified and the interest coupons can be cashed at foreign banks.

In combination, the capital gain and loss provisions are a leading source of tax complexity, comparable in this respect to the realization concept and the separate taxation of corporate income.

Although governed by an elaborate web of statutory provisions, capital gains and losses do not occupy a tax world of their own. The term "gross income," for example, includes both capital gains and ordinary income, so that provisions that refer to a dollar amount of gross income (e.g., IRC §6012(a), relating to the filing of tax returns) apply whether the income is ordinary or capital. There are many other statutory, administrative, and judicial rules that apply equally to capital and ordinary transactions in determining the amount of gain or loss, the time when gains and losses are taken into account, the deductibility of losses, and the recognition of gains and losses. Thus, the sale of a personal residence for less than its cost would produce a capital loss so far as IRC §§1221 and 1222 are concerned; but the homeowner will find that this is useless information since the loss, not having occurred in a trade or business or a transaction entered into for profit, cannot be deducted.[1] Because

---

[1] See supra ¶12.2.

the actual tax treatment of transactions creating capital gains and losses always depends on provisions of more general import, it is essential that they be viewed in this larger context.

¶25.2 INDIVIDUALS AND OTHER NONCORPORATE TAXPAYERS

For individuals, trusts, and estates, the special rules governing capital gains and losses consist primarily of (a) a reduced rate of tax on the taxpayer's net capital gain (effected by IRC §1202, which permits 60 percent of the net capital gain to be deducted from gross income); (b) limitations prescribed by IRC §1211(b) on the taxpayer's right to deduct capital losses in the year sustained; and (c) the carryover of unused capital losses to later years, authorized by IRC §1212(b). The applicable rules are described below following a summary of IRC §1222, which defines the relevant terms.

1. Definitions. Section 1222(1) defines "short-term capital gain" as gain from the sale or exchange of a capital asset held for not more than one year, if and to the extent that the gain is taken into account in computing gross income. "Long-term capital gain" is defined by IRC §1222(3) in the same way, except that the asset must be held for more than one year. "Short-term capital loss" and "long-term capital loss" are defined by IRC §§1222(2) and 1222(4), respectively, in a parallel fashion.

Since the definitions of IRC §§1222(1)–1222(4) apply to gains only "if and to the extent such gain is taken into account in computing gross income" and to losses only "if and to the extent such loss is taken into account in computing taxable income," gains and losses are disregarded if they are not recognized (e.g., gains and losses on tax-free corporate mergers); and nondeductible losses (e.g., losses on sales of personal residences or on sales of property to related persons within the meaning of IRC §267(a)(1)), are also disregarded.

The terms defined by IRC §§1222(1) through 1222(4) apply to individual transactions, and these amounts are then aggregated into net amounts by IRC §§1222(5)–1222(8). The taxpayer's net short-term capital gain is the excess of short-term capital gains over short-term capital losses; the taxpayer's net short-term capital loss is the excess of short-term capital losses over short-term capital gains. A similar matching process generates the taxpayer's net long-term capital gain and net long-term capital loss.

For present purposes, one other aggregate is relevant: "net capital gain," defined by IRC §1222(11) as the excess of the taxpayer's net long-term capital gain for the taxable year over the net short-term capital loss for the same year. In the absence of a net short-term loss, the net capital gain is equal to the taxpayer's net long-term capital gain. Since 60 percent of the taxpayer's net capital gain can be deducted from gross income under IRC §1202(a), it is crucial to note that net capital gain does not include the taxpayer's short-term capital gains. A taxpayer whose only relevant transaction is a short-term capital gain of $100,000, for example, does not have a net capital gain.

2. Capital Gain Deduction. Section 1202(a) permits noncorporate taxpayers to deduct 60 percent of their net capital gain from gross income. Although formulated as a deduction, this has the same effect as taxing the taxpayer's net gain at the rate of 40 percent of the normal rate. For example, if the net capital gain would have been taxed at the top marginal rate of 50 percent, it is in effect taxed instead at 20 percent (40% × 50%) when the deduction is taken into account.

Since the IRC §1202 deduction is applied against gross income (rather than adjusted gross income), it can be taken whether the taxpayer itemizes personal deductions or not.[2]

3. Short-term Capital Gains. Since short-term capital gains are not included in the taxpayer's "net capital gain" as defined by IRC §1222(11), they do not qualify for the 60 percent deduction allowed by IRC §1202 but are instead subject to the same tax rate as ordinary income. Despite this, short-term capital gains enjoy three subsidiary tax advantages over ordinary income.

First, they can be wiped out by capital losses; by contrast, capital losses can be applied against only $3,000 of ordinary income. For example, if a taxpayer's only relevant transactions are a short-term capital gain of $100,000 and a short-term capital loss of $90,000, taxable income (disregarding personal exemptions, deductions, etc.) is $10,000; but if the first transaction had produced $100,000 of ordinary income rather than a short-term capital gain of $100,000, taxable income would be $97,000. Although the undeducted portion of the short-term capital loss ($87,000) can be carried forward under IRC §1212(b), it can be deducted in later years only to the extent of capital gains and $3,000 per year of ordinary income.

Second, short-term capital gains are also preferable to ordinary income because they absorb short-term capital losses, which erode the taxpayer's right to deduct 60 percent of net capital gain under IRC §1202. For example, if the taxpayer's only relevant transactions are (1) a long-term capital gain of $100,000, (2) a short-term capital gain of $100,000, and (3) a short-term capital loss of $100,000, his net short-term capital loss as defined by IRC §1222(6) is zero and his net capital gain as defined by §1222(11) is $100,000, of which $60,000 can be deducted under IRC §1202, resulting in $40,000 of taxable

[2] See IRC §62(3).

income. If, however, the second transaction had generated ordinary income of $100,000 rather than short-term capital gain, the taxpayer's net capital gain would be zero (net long-term capital gain of $100,000 minus net short-term capital loss of $100,000), there would be no deduction under IRC §1202, and taxable income would be $100,000.

Third, short-term capital gains absorb excess long-term capital losses dollar for dollar, while, as explained below, it takes $2 of long-term capital losses to offset $1 of ordinary income.

4. Limitation on Deduction of Capital Losses. The right of noncorporate taxpayers to deduct capital losses is governed by IRC §1211(b), under which capital losses (whether short- or long-term) can be deducted to the full extent of the taxpayer's capital gains (whether short- or long-term). If the capital losses in the aggregate exceed the capital gains, the excess can be deducted only to the extent of the smallest of the three amounts described below.

1. *$3,000.* The simplest and most important of the three ceilings, imposed by IRC §1211(b)(1)(B), prevents taxpayers with capital losses from applying them against ordinary income except to the extent of $3,000 ($1,500 on a married person's separate return). This limitation can be viewed as a quid pro quo exacted by Congress as an offset to the reduced effective rate on net capital gains.

2. *$2 gets you $1.* The second ceiling, imposed by IRC §1211(b)(1)(C), is the sum of (a) the excess of the net short-term capital loss over the net long-term capital gain and (b) one-half of the excess of the net long-term capital loss over the net short-term capital gain. If the only relevant transactions for the year are a long-term capital loss of $8,000 and a short-term capital gain of $3,000, for example, the taxpayer can reduce taxable income by $2,500 (one-half of $5,000, the excess of $8,000 over $3,000), provided neither of the other two ceilings is lower than $2,500. Even though the $5,000 excess of loss over gain can be deducted to the extent of only $2,500, it is treated as consumed in full, so nothing can be carried forward to later years under IRC §1212(b).

The $2-for-$1 principle is a rough offset to the deduction allowed by IRC §1202 to taxpayers with a net long-term capital gain in excess of net short-term capital loss. The limiting fraction was fixed at one-half of excess capital loss when taxpayers were allowed to deduct 50 percent of net capital gain under IRC §1202, but it was not changed when the deduction was increased to 60 percent in 1978. The $2-for-$1 rule is not imposed by IRC §1211(b)(1)(C) on excess short-term capital losses because short-term capital gains do not qualify for the deduction allowed by IRC §1202.

3. *Taxable income.* The final ceiling, imposed by IRC §1211(b)(1)(A), which is applicable only to taxpayers with low taxable income relative to their capital losses, limits the reduction of ordinary income by capital losses to the taxpayer's taxable income (as specially defined).

The operation of the three ceilings imposed by IRC §1211(b)(1), the lowest of which is controlling, is illustrated by a series of examples in the regulations.[3]

5. Carryover of Capital Losses. Capital losses that are not used to reduce capital gains or ordinary income in the taxable year in which they are sustained can be carried forward indefinitely by noncorporate taxpayers by virtue of IRC §1212(b). As explained above, capital losses are "used" in the sense of being reduced or exhausted even if they produce no tax benefit, for example, because of the $2-for-$1 rule of IRC §1211(b)(1)(C).

Although the carryover rules of IRC §1212(b) are formidable, they boil down to a few sequential rules: Starting with all capital losses for the given year, (1) the losses are reduced to the extent of any capital gains for the year (first, long-term gains reduce long-term losses; then, short-term gains reduce short-term losses; and then any excess gains reduce any excess losses); (2) any short-term losses that remain are reduced by the applicable amount or other ceiling provided in IRC §1211(b)(1); and (3) if any applicable amount or other ceiling remains after step 2, any remaining long-term losses are reduced by using $1 of the applicable amount or other ceiling to wipe out $2 of long-term loss. Any short-term and/or long-term capital losses remaining after these steps are carried over to the next year.

When carried forward, capital losses retain their short- or long-term character; are treated as sustained in the year to which they are carried; are amalgamated with the losses actually sustained in that year in determining the taxpayer's net capital gains and losses and the amount to be deducted from ordinary income; and, like losses actually sustained, must be used to the extent possible even if it would be more advantageous to hold them in abeyance for use in a later year.[4] Unused capital loss carryovers expire with the death of the individual taxpayers by whom the losses were sustained.

¶25.3 CORPORATIONS

1. Capital Gains. The tax concession for capital gains realized by corporations is an alternative tax, computed under IRC §1201(a) (payable if it is less than the tax computed in the regular manner), which consists of the sum of (a) a tax computed in the regular manner on the corporation's taxable income, reduced by its net capital gain and (b) a tax of 28 percent of the net capital gain. For corporations subject to the regular corporate rates prescribed by IRC §11(a), the alternative tax can produce a savings at 1982 rates only if the

---

[3] Treas. Regs. §1.1211-1(b)(8).

[4] Rev. Rul. 76-177, 1976-1 CB 224.

corporation's taxable income (including its net capital gain) exceeds $50,000, since the regular rate is only 16 or 19 percent on amounts below that level.

2. Capital Losses. Corporations sustaining capital losses can deduct them only to the extent of capital gains; unlike individuals, they are wholly prohibited by IRC §1211(a) from using capital losses to reduce ordinary income. The corporation's net capital loss, defined by IRC §1222(10) as the excess of capital losses over the amount deductible under IRC §1221,[5] can be carried back to the three taxable years preceding the loss year and forward to the five succeeding taxable years. The carryback or carryover is treated as a short-term capital loss in the year to which it is carried and is applied in order of time to that year's capital gain net income (i.e., capital gains not already offset by that year's capital losses).[6]

¶25.4 DEFINITION OF "CAPITAL ASSET"—INTRODUCTORY

Capital gains and losses are generated primarily by the "sale or exchange" of a "capital asset"; but they also arise from some less common transactions that Congress chose to qualify for capital gain and loss treatment even though they do not entail either a "sale or exchange" of a "capital asset." The crucial term "capital asset" is defined by IRC §1221 to mean "property held by the taxpayer (whether or not connected with his trade or business)," with the exception of the items described by IRC §§1221(1) through 1221(5). Given the legislative objective of providing special treatment for a limited class of transactions, it is surprising—and a source of confusion—that IRC §1221's definition confers "capital asset" status on all assets except those that are explicitly disqualified, rather than singling out those that are to enjoy special treatment.

This roundabout method of defining capital assets often generates a misapprehension by leaving in the residue—seemingly qualified for liberal treatment—some items that are clearly outside the legislative target. For example, an employee's right to be paid in advance for work to be performed at some future date is "property" for many legal purposes, and it is not expressly disqualified from "capital asset" status by IRC §§1221(1)–1221(5). But it is evident that Congress did not expect the sale of claims of this nature to generate capital gains; and one can be certain that, if the issue were raised, a rationale for denying capital gain treatment would be found (e.g., that the

[5] Capital loss carrybacks and carryovers are excluded from the corporation's net capital loss by the second sentence of IRC §1222(10); otherwise they would get a new lease on life annually and could be carried to years outside the nine-year span prescribed by IRC §1212(a)(1).

[6] See IRC §§1212(a)(1), 1222(9). Capital loss carrybacks and carryovers cannot be "saved" for use in more advantageous years. See Rev. Rul. 76-177, supra note 4.

claim is not "property" within the meaning of IRC §1221 or that the sale is in substance an anticipatory assignment of income).[7] These and other judicial theories that close the gaps left by the draftsmen of IRC §1221 are discussed below, following an examination of the specific statutory limitations imposed by IRC §§1221(1) through 1221(5) on the "capital asset" concept.

¶25.5 PROPERTY HELD FOR SALE TO CUSTOMERS

1. In General. The first, and the most important, qualification on the broad language of IRC §1221 is imposed by IRC §1221(1), providing that stock in trade, property includable in inventory if on hand at the end of the taxable year, and property held primarily for sale to customers in the ordinary course of the taxpayer's trade or business do not constitute "capital assets." This brief exclusion carries an enormous amount of freight since, by denying capital gain and loss treatment to the regular business operations of merchants and manufacturers, it puts into effect the basic legislative distinction between investment and business. As summarized by the Supreme Court, the function of IRC §1221(1) "is to differentiate between the 'profits and losses arising from the everyday operation of business' on the one hand . . . and 'the realization of appreciation in value accrued over a substantial period of time' on the other."[8]

In application, the three categories of assets listed by IRC §1221(1)—stock in trade, inventory property, and property held primarily for sale to customers in the ordinary course of business—often overlap. A retail shop's merchandise, for example, fits into all three categories. But the categories, though sometimes loosely described as interchangeable, are not always identical. For example, a manufacturer's raw materials and work in process constitute inventory property, though not themselves held for sale to customers in the ordinary course of business; conversely, building lots in the hands of a real estate subdivider are held for sale to customers in the ordinary course of business but are not customarily inventoried.

Because the first two categories of assets described by IRC §1221(1) (stock in trade and other inventory property) are held almost entirely by easily identifiable merchants and manufacturers, they have created few problems of interpretation. The third category, however, has been very difficult to apply

---

[7] See Vaaler v. U.S., 454 F.2d 1120 (8th Cir. 1972) (denying capital gain treatment to payment terminating insurance agent's contract); IRC §1221(4), excluding claims arising in the ordinary course of business for "services rendered," seems to apply only to completed services, though it might be pressed into service and interpreted to embrace claims for future services.

[8] Malat v. Riddell, 383 US 569, 572 (1966).

and has generated a vast body of litigation and even more disputes at the administrative level. Each of the phrases held by IRC §1221(1) to describe this third category of property ("held . . . primarily for sale," "to customers," and "in the ordinary course of [the taxpayer's] trade or business") is a source of difficulty.

First, the statutory reference to "property held . . . primarily for sale" is troublesome. If it is to have any operative significance, it must require something more than the fact that the property was sold in the transaction that actually occurred; viewed just before the sale, the property was obviously held primarily for sale. The statutory reference to "held . . . primarily for sale" also implies more than the fact that in a mercantile society virtually all economic assets are "held for sale" in the sense that the owner will sell if offered a high enough price. The assets of even the most conventional investor, interested solely in long-term appreciation, are held "primarily for sale" in the sense that a sale is the normal method of realizing gain when the targeted level of appreciation has been attained.

As will be seen, the term "primarily for sale" is interpreted by the courts to require a purpose that is comparable to a conventional merchant's attitude toward his merchandise, and this judicial approach entails a distinction between "investors" (including, in the case of securities, "traders") and "dealers." The line of demarcation is especially difficult to establish in the real estate field when, for example, a tract of land acquired for investment or farming is subdivided and sold in small parcels, since the courts recognize that an "investor" can become a "dealer" if the purpose for which his assets are held changes in midstream. The term "primarily" is also difficult to apply if the property is held for two or more purposes simultaneously (e.g., for rent or sale) depending on which offers the greater opportunity for profit.

Second, IRC §1221(1)'s requirement that property be held primarily for sale "to customers" seems to imply that the taxpayer must have an identifiable body of customers, like a retail store's clientele. In fact, however, the term has been construed to embrace anyone who purchases the taxpayer's assets, with the result that it has virtually no operative significance except in the case of "traders" in securities and commodities, who are distinguished from dealers in these assets on the theory that traders do not sell to "customers."

Third, the term "ordinary course of [the taxpayer's] trade or business" is ambiguous, partly because the concept itself is vague, but also because the term "trade or business" appears in many other provisions of the Internal Revenue Code (both with and without the qualifying phrase "ordinary course of") [9]; and the relationship of these numerous statutory references is uncertain.

---

[9] E.g., IRC §§162(a) (expenses "in carrying out any trade or business"), 167(a)(1) ("property used in the trade or business"), 512(b)(5)(B) ("property held primarily for sale to customers in the ordinary course of the trade or business").

In applying the term, the courts have looked to a variety of factors that are thought to separate investment activities from "business." [10] A basic premise of these cases, more often unarticulated than explicit, is that the statutory phrase can embrace the process of liquidating a commercial venture even though the taxpayer does not intend to replenish his stock when the assets on hand are exhausted.[11] This is often true when a large tract of land, acquired for farming or as an investment, is subdivided and sold; if the transactions attain a critical mass in terms of number, frequency, subdivision and improvement activities, and sales efforts, the taxpayer will be treated as a dealer holding the lots for sale in the ordinary course of business, even though he does not intend to repeat the process with another tract. The same is true of a one-shot venture consisting of the purchase of quantity of assets for prompt resale;[12] if anything, this is an easier case for the IRS than when it must show a change from an investment purpose to a business objective.

2. Securities, Commodities, and Commodity Futures. Although the capital gain and loss rules were enacted primarily for the benefit of investors who seek long-term profits and engage in relatively few transactions in a given year, they also apply to traders in securities, commodities, and commodity futures, who devote all their time to the security and commodity markets, watching the quotations like hawks and responding to daily or even hourly fluctuations in prices. This tax phenomenon is attributable to a series of crucial decisions holding that IRC §1221(1), which denies "capital asset" status to stock in trade, inventory property, and property held for sale to customers, applies to "dealers" in securities and commodities but not to "traders," no matter how active they may be.[13] The boundary between these two groups, which is all-important though occasionally hazy, owes its origin to a 1934 amendment which added the phrase "to customers" to the statutory predecessor of IRC §1221 in order to prevent speculators whose securities had declined in value during the 1930's from deducting their losses from ordinary income.[14] The

---

[10] See Higgins v. CIR, 312 US 212 (1941) (investor not engaged in trade or business).

[11] See Grace Bros. v. CIR, 173 F.2d 170 (9th Cir. 1949) (stock in trade sold in bulk; held, taxpayer realized ordinary income); Lawrie v. CIR, 36 TC 1117 (1961) (liquidation by contractor of twenty-one subdivided lots and one unsubdivided parcel of real estate in one sale did not change fact that holding was for sale to customers in the ordinary course of business).

[12] Hollis v. US, 121 F.Supp. 191 (N.D. Ohio 1954) (syndicate to purchase and resell Japanese art objects); but compare Reese v. CIR, 615 F.2d 226 (5th Cir. 1980) (single venture not ordinarily trade or business in absence of expectation of continuing in field of endeavor).

[13] See, e.g., CIR v. Burnett, 118 F.2d 659 (5th Cir. 1941) (securities and commodities).

[14] See Wood v. CIR, 16 TC 213, 225–226 (1951) (Acq.).

terms "dealer" and "trader," which do not appear in IRC §1221(1) itself, are simply labels—"dealer" referring to a taxpayer who holds securities for sale to customers in the ordinary course of his trade or business; "trader," to a taxpayer who does not have "customers" even though he buys and sells securities with great frequency during the taxable year.

Although enacted to restrict deductions (some of which, it was suspected by Congress, reflected paper losses by taxpayers who had not actually closed out their investment positions), the 1934 provision also applies to profitable transactions. Successful traders in securities and commodities, therefore, can report their income as capital gains, however much they resemble ordinary businessmen. Like other human institutions, federal income taxation suffers from cultural lag: enacted as a shield for the Treasury, the 1934 change has remained in force, even though it now is primarily a sword in the hands of taxpayers.

Although transactions by traders invariably give rise to capital gains and losses because the securities or commodities are not held for sale "to customers" in the ordinary course of trade or business, the converse is not necessarily true for "dealers." Because IRC §1221(1) is concerned not only with whether the taxpayer is engaged in a trade or business but also with the purpose for which particular assets are held, it is possible for a dealer to hold some assets for sale to customers in the ordinary course of business while holding other assets of the same type for investment.[15] This possibility, in turn, opens the door to manipulation, since the taxpayer is tempted to claim in retrospect that securities sold at a profit were held for investment and constituted capital assets but that those sold at a loss were noncapital assets generating deductions from ordinary income. Hindsight classifications by dealers in securities, however, are restrained by IRC §1236, requiring investment securities to be identified as such on the taxpayer's books when acquired.

3. Real Estate. As applied to real estate, IRC §1221(1) has a much broader reach than when securities are involved, so that real estate is far more likely than securities to be treated as held "primarily for sale to customers in the ordinary course of [the taxpayer's] trade or business." Persons whose real estate transactions are comparable in scale and frequency to those of a conventional trader in securities are almost certain to be classified as dealers subject to ordinary income and loss treatment. The Court of Claims, for example, has held that two lawyers who invested in real estate as minority members of certain syndicates realized ordinary income on the sale of thirty-two such

[15] Carl Marks & Co. v. CIR, 12 TC 1196 (1949) (Acq.) (securities held to be capital assets, though held by dealer); Frank v. CIR, 321 F.2d 143 (8th Cir. 1963) (taxpayer held to be dealer with respect to certain securities, despite substantial private investments).

interests during a three-year period.[16] The properties were not developed, subdivided, or otherwise altered by the syndicates but were sold in substantially the same condition as when acquired, save for depreciation in the interim. The court's conclusion that the taxpayers held their interests for sale to customers in the ordinary course of business within the meaning of IRC §1221(1) was evidently based solely on the frequency and continuity of their transactions and on the fact that their income from these sales exceeded their income from the practice of law during the seven-year period including the taxable years before the court.

In applying IRC §1221(1) to real estate, the most troublesome and extensively litigated problem is the proper classification of real estate that is being subdivided by a taxpayer who did not acquire it with this in mind. When property purchased for agricultural use or as a long-term investment or inherited from a farmer or investor is not sold as a single tract but is instead subdivided so that small plots can be sold, the courts customarily refer to a long list of factors to be weighed in determining whether the property is held for sale; and they often gloomily observe that no one factor is conclusive, that relative weights cannot be assigned to individual factors, and that each case depends on its own facts.[17]

The factors that are most frequently mentioned, with comments on their relevance, are the following:

1. *Purpose of acquisition.* Section 1221(1) is concerned with the purpose for which property is held, rather than the purpose for which it was acquired; but the latter may be significant in the absence of evidence of a change of purpose, and it may have a bearing on the quantum of evidence required to establish a change of purpose. If a tract of land is purchased with a view of subdividing it and selling the separate lots, for example, the burden of proving that this purpose was abandoned and the property converted to investment status is a heavy one. Conversely, it is ordinarily a reasonable inference that property acquired for investment continues to enjoy this status in the absence of evidence of a changed purpose. Moreover, a taxpayer forced by unanticipated and involuntary events (e.g., a zoning change) to abandon an investment purpose is less likely to run afoul of IRC §1221(1) than one who voluntarily subdivides the property in order to exploit an opportunity for greater profits.

2. *Number and regularity of sales.* The more numerous, frequent, and regular the sales, the more likely it is that the property is held for sale to

[16] Goodman v. US, 390 F.2d 915 (Ct. Cl.), cert. denied, 393 US 824 (1968); but see Adam v. CIR, 60 TC 996 (1973) (Acq.) (contra on similar facts).

[17] See, e.g., Maddux Constr. Co. v. CIR, 54 TC 1278, 1284 (1970); Biedenharn Realty Co. v. US, 526 F.2d 409 (5th Cir.), cert. denied, 429 US 819 (1976).

customers in the ordinary course of business; conversely, sales that are few in number and that occur at irregular intervals are more characteristic of investors than of dealers. The "substantiality" of sales is often mentioned as a factor; but if this refers to the dollar size of particular transactions, it is not clear why a large average dollar amount per sale, or even a large aggregate amount for all sales, is more typical of dealers than of investors.

3. *Subdividing and improvements.* If the property is subdivided and/or improved by grading, paving, installing drainage or utilities, or similar activity, the taxpayer inevitably gravitates toward dealer status,[18] since these changes are comparable to the functions performed by a manufacturer of personal property. Subdividing or improving property before its sale may result in taxation of the gain as ordinary income even in the absence of other facts demonstrating the seller's dealer status, particularly if the gain is primarily attributable to subdivision status or the improvement rather than to appreciation in the value of the raw land.[19] But if the cost of improvements to the property represents an insignificant contribution to the gain involved, capital gain treatment may be allowed in the absence of other tainting factors;[20] and some courts have minimized the importance of improvements that were essential to liquidating and investment in an orderly fashion.[21]

Since the purpose for which property is *held* controls under IRC §1221(1), an intention to subdivide or improve property may prove as fatal to capital gain treatment as actually subdividing or improving it.[22]

4. *Sales effort.* Extensive advertising, active solicitation, and promotional activities, whether by the taxpayer in person or by employees and brokers on his behalf,[23] are inconsistent with investor status and are evidence

---

[18] Biedenharn Realty Co. v. US, supra note 17, at 422; Bynum v. CIR, 46 TC 295 (1966); Jersey Land & Dev. Co. v. US, 539 F.2d 311 (3d Cir. 1976) (filling and grading).

[19] See Hansche v. CIR, 457 F.2d 429 (7th Cir. 1972) (ordinary income where gain was due to substantial subdivision and development activities by taxpayers); Gates v. CIR, 52 TC 898, 906 (1969) (when taxpayer "bought the land, subdivided it, installed improvements, and immediately sold lots therein she went into the business of selling lots in that addition, irrespective of any of her other activities").

[20] See Huey v. US, 504 F.2d 1388 (Ct. Cl. 1974); Brodnax v. CIR, ¶70,164 P-H Memo TC (1970) (capital gain on sale of twenty-eight parcels over three years despite partitioning and construction of access road, where appreciation was due to planned freeway construction nearby).

[21] See Barrios' Est. v. CIR, 265 F.2d 517 (5th Cir. 1959), described in Biedenharn Realty Co. v. US, supra note 17, as enunciating a "liquidation plus integrally related improvements theory."

[22] See, e.g., Philhall Corp. v. US, 546 F.2d 210 (6th Cir. 1976) (intent to subdivide or develop shown by option purchase contract, testimony before local planning commission, and listing tract on books as inventory; held, ordinary income); Sapphire Lands, Inc. v. CIR, ¶73,023 P-H Memo TC (1973), aff'd per curiam, 33 AFTR2d 610 (5th Cir. 1974).

[23] Biedenharn Realty Co. v. US, supra note 17.

that the property is held for sale to customers in the ordinary course of the taxpayer's business. The absence of sales efforts is not determinative of the issue, however, since a dealer can sometimes sit back and wait for the public to beat a path to his door.[24]

5. *Relation of activity to taxpayer's primary occupation.* In the case of taxpayers with occupations separate from their real estate activities, the courts often compare the amount of time devoted to, or the percentage of income derived from, each area, on the assumption that the greater the fractional time or income allocable to real estate ventures, the more appropriate it is to treat the taxpayer as a dealer.

6. *Miscellaneous.* Other factors that are sometimes treated as relevant, but that are often ambiguous, are:

a. Use of sales proceeds to replace the property. Replenishing a stock of goods is characteristic of merchants, but capital asset classification is also frequently denied to taxpayers engaged in selling off property that they do not intend to replace.
b. Duration of ownership, on the assumption that a short term is more characteristic of merchants than of investors. A long holding period is not necessarily inconsistent with dealership, however, since the taxpayer may have abandoned an investment purpose at some point before sale.[25]
c. The reason for the sale, especially if this betokens a change in the purpose for which the property was held.
d. Pre-purchase investigation or other activity regarding a property's potential for development, which may evidence that it was acquired for resale in the ordinary course of business.[26]

7. *Purpose at time of sale.* Although sometimes listed as a relevant "factor," [27] the purpose for which the property was held at the time of sale is actually one of the ultimate facts to be determined. Unless the property is held

---

[24] See Thompson v. CIR, 322 F.2d 122 (5th Cir. 1963) (certain lots held for sale even though there was no organized sales program, advertising, use of agents, or haggling over price); see also International Shoe Mach. Corp. v. US, 491 F.2d 157 (1st Cir.), cert. denied, 419 US 834 (1974) (shoe machines held primarily for sale to customers in ordinary course of business, although taxpayer preferred to lease machines, had no sales force, and made sales "only as a last resort, after attempts to dissuade the customer from purchasing had failed").

[25] See Scheuber v. CIR, 371 F.2d 996 (7th Cir. 1967) (long holding period as indicative of investment status); Harper v. CIR, ¶76,058 P-H Memo TC (1976) (short holding period as indicating property held for sale).

[26] Philhall Corp v. US, supra note 22 (agreement to purchase conditioned on taxpayer's effort to obtain permission to subdivide).

[27] See, e.g., Maddux Constr. Co. v. CIR, supra note 17, at 1284.

for sale (and, in the case of several purposes, unless the sale is the "primary" purpose), it is not removed from the "capital asset" category by the last clause of IRC §1221(1). Thus, unlike the other factors listed above, which are only evidentiary, the "primarily for sale" factor is a necessary condition to denial of capital gain status under this part of IRC §1221(1). It is not a sufficient condition, however, since the "ordinary course of business" requirement must also be satisfied.

In the hope of clarifying the status of subdivided property and reducing the volume of litigation in this area, Congress enacted IRC §1237 in 1954. This provision provides, subject to a number of conditions, that real property shall not be deemed to be held primarily for sale to customers in the ordinary course of business solely by reason of the taxpayer's subdividing and sales activities. Even when the complex conditions imposed by IRC §1237 are satisfied, its scope is rather narrow. Other important provisions affecting the status of real property so far as capital gain and loss treatment is concerned are:

1. IRC §1221(2), providing that real property used in the taxpayer's trade or business (e.g., a factory, warehouse, apartment house, or hotel) is not a capital asset.[28]
2. IRC §1231, providing that gain or loss on the sale, exchange, condemnation, and certain other transactions involving real property used in the taxpayer's trade or business and held for more than one year shall be treated as ordinary or capital, depending on the outcome of a "hotchpot" that includes all such transactions during the taxable year.[29] Realty that is otherwise a capital asset and that is condemned or involuntarily converted also goes into the hotchpot.
3. IRC §1237, permitting gain on certain subdivided property to be reported as capital gain.[30]
4. IRC §1239, providing that gain on a sale or exchange of depreciable property between husband and wife or certain related business entities shall be treated as ordinary income.[31]
5. IRC §§1245 and 1250, providing for the recapture of depreciation on the sale or other disposition (including some transactions that are not ordinarily taxable events) of depreciable real property.[32]

4. Dual-Purpose, Change-of-Purpose, and Liquidating Ventures. Section 1221(1) speaks of property held "primarily" for sale to customers in the ordinary course of the taxpayer's business, but taxpayers sometimes hold

---

[28] Infra ¶25.6.
[29] Infra ¶27.1.
[30] Infra ¶27.10.
[31] Infra ¶27.11.
[32] Infra ¶28.5.

property for several purposes, planning to take advantage of future developments as they fall out. In *Malat v. Riddell,* involving a tract of land acquired by a joint venture whose members intended "either to sell the property or develop it for rental, depending upon which course appeared to be most profitable," the Supreme Court held that, as used in IRC §1221(1), "primarily" means "of first importance" or "principally." [33]

The Supreme Court decided *Malat v. Riddell* on the premise that the taxpayers held their land for two purposes (sale in bulk or development of residential and commercial buildings for rental) that they regarded as alternatives. This feature of *Malat* distinguishes it from a series of cases involving manufacturers who are willing to sell or rent their products, depending on the customer's preference, and who are properly regarded as engaged simultaneously in two businesses—selling equipment and renting identical equipment—especially if both entail promotional activity. Although an individual unit cannot be rented once it is sold or be sold without terminating its rental status, the manufacturer has (or can produce) a virtually unlimited supply of fungible units; and it is not surprising that the courts have held that sales of this type of merchandise produce ordinary income and loss even if the taxpayer would prefer to rent its products and is compelled to offer them for sale by an antitrust decree or other outside pressure.[34]

Dual-purpose cases like *Malat* must also be distinguished from change-of-purpose cases. In the latter situation, which is often characteristic of real estate subdivisions, a taxpayer holding a large tract solely for investment or agricultural purposes decides, usually in response to a marked increase in value, to sell it off in small parcels. As pointed out above, the promotional activity inherent in the marketing process is often treated as terminating the taxpayer's investment purpose, so that the property is held thereafter for sale to customers in the ordinary course of business. *Malat* is inapplicable in these circumstances because the two purposes are not entertained simultaneously; instead, the taxpayer's investment purpose has been displaced by a business purpose. When the liquidation of an investment entails such a change of purpose, the taxpayer's entire gain is taxed as ordinary income no matter how much of it is attributable to a gradual increase in value during the period when the property was held solely as an investment.

In the absence of a statutory mechanism to separate the investment part

---

[33] Malat v. Riddell, supra note 8. On remand, the district court held that the property was held primarily for rental and therefore not within the scope of IRC §1221(1). See Malat v. Riddell, 275 F.Supp. 358 (S.D. Calif. 1966).

[34] Continental Can Co. v. US, 422 F.2d 405 (Ct. Cl.), cert. denied, 400 US 819 (1970); International Shoe Mach. Corp. v. US, supra note 24. Cases of this type usually involve IRC §1231(b)(1)(B), discussed infra ¶27.1, rather than IRC §1221(1); but both provisions use the same language, and the legal issues thereunder are identical.

of a taxpayer's gain from the portion attributable to promotional and marketing activities after a change of purpose, the courts have developed an "orderly liquidation" theory, under which sales efforts are sometimes treated as the final stage in realizing the taxpayer's investment gain rather than as the inception of a new business. Pursuant to this rationale, taxpayers have occasionally been held to realize capital gains even though the liquidating process continued for several decades and involved numerous sales.[35] In recent years, however, the orderly liquidation theory has commanded less support. Faced by an all-or-nothing choice between ordinary income and capital gain (regardless of the relative sizes of the two components), the courts have usually opted for the former result by employing the change-of-purpose theory.[36]

A variation of the change-of-purpose theme involves taxpayers who acquire property with the intent to use it for business purposes for a period of time and then to sell it.[37] If the business use can be characterized as "temporary," such as the use by an automobile dealer of new cars as demonstrators, the property will be treated as held primarily for sale to customers in the ordinary course of business.[38] If the business use is more substantial, however, the property may be treated as held primarily for business *use* rather than for *sale.*[39]

5. Development and Sales Activities by Related Parties. Substantially appreciated investment property, especially raw land, is sometimes sold to a related party (e.g., a controlled corporation or a member of the taxpayer's family) in the hope that the taxpayer will be able to report the pre-transfer

---

[35] Alabama Mineral Land Co. v. CIR, 250 F.2d 870 (5th Cir. 1957); Chandler v. US, 226 F.2d 403 (7th Cir. 1955).

[36] See Biedenharn Realty Co. v. US, supra note 17; see also Huxford v. US, 441 F.2d 1371, 1376 (5th Cir. 1971) (referring to Alabama Mineral Land Co. v. CIR, supra note 35, with something less than enthusiasm).

[37] Since depreciable property used in the trade or business is removed from the capital asset category by IRC §1221(2), this situation usually involves quasi-capital asset status under IRC §1231. Business use property may qualify for such status, but property held primarily for sale in the ordinary course of the trade or business cannot. See infra ¶27.1.

[38] See W.R. Stephens Co. v. CIR, 199 F.2d 665 (8th Cir. 1952) (automobiles used by auto dealer as demonstrators or as company cars pending sale); R.E. Moorhead & Son v. CIR, 40 TC 704 (1963) (similarly as to company cars held an average of less than ten months).

[39] See, e.g., Latimer-Looney Chevrolet, Inc. v. CIR, 19 TC 120, 123 (1952) (Acq.) (enumerating a wide variety of uses for auto dealer's company cars). For the current IRS position on automobiles used in the business of an auto dealer, see Rev. Rul. 75-538, 1975-2 CB 34 (dealer presumed to hold all vehicles, including demonstrators and company cars, primarily for sale to customers unless vehicles are actually used in business and dealer intends to recover their cost through such use).

profit as capital gain, even though the related transferee will engage in development and sales activities and hold the property primarily for sale in the ordinary course of business. These arrangements presuppose that the "ordinary income" activities of the transferee will not be retrospectively imputed to the transferor, thereby subjecting him to the change-of-purpose cases that require ordinary income to be reported if an investor becomes a dealer before disposing of his property.

If property is held for investment purposes until the transfer and the sales price correspond to the fair market value of the property when transferred, there is in theory no reason for refusing to allow capital gain treatment for the pre-transfer investment property, since the post-transfer business profits will be taxed as ordinary income. But the line of demarcation between pre-transfer investment gain and post-transfer business profits is not easily drawn when property is sold in a non-arm's-length transaction to a related party, and the self-serving valuation chosen by the parties cannot be verified by comparison with an independent market price. It should occasion no surprise, therefore, that both the IRS and the courts view such transfers with skepticism, and that they sometimes impute the transferee's dealer status back to the transferor, view the two as engaged in a joint venture, or treat the transferee as the transferor's agent.[40]

As a result, capital gain on the sale of property to a controlled corporation that will become a dealer can be safely anticipated only when property that the transferor has made no effort to improve is transferred in an isolated transaction. As the taxpayer's pre-transfer activity with respect to the property increases, so does the likelihood of his being held a dealer on transferring it to a controlled corporation.[41]

---

[40] See Tibbals v. US, 362 F.2d 266 (Ct. Cl. 1966) (some personal development activities plus use of and sale to controlled corporation to continue development); Boyer v. CIR, 58 TC 316 (1972) (agency or alter ego relationship); but see Gordy v. CIR, 36 TC 855 (1961) (Acq.) (no evidence that taxpayer who made two isolated sales to 60-percent-controlled real estate development corporation was dealer). For transfers between controlled corporations under common ownership, see H-H Ranch, Inc. v. CIR, 357 F.2d 885 (7th Cir. 1966) (agency theory; series of sales by one corporation imputed to related corporations, which subdivided tracts and built houses thereon).

[41] See Harbour Properties v. CIR, ¶73,134 P-H Memo TC (1973); Lakin v. CIR, 28 TC 462 (1957), aff'd per curiam, 249 F.2d 781 (4th Cir. 1957) (land purchased over ten-year period, subdivided into 240 lots and sold to controlled home-building corporation and to third parties agreeing to buy building materials from another controlled corporation); Burgher v. Campbell, 244 F.2d 863 (5th Cir. 1957) (sale of large tract to controlled corporation by taxpayer regularly engaged in real estate); Brown v. CIR, 448 F.2d 514 (10th Cir. 1971) (real estate developer engaged in subdivision arrangements before transferring land to controlled corporation).

¶25.6 PROPERTY USED IN THE TRADE OR BUSINESS

Section 1221(2) denies "capital asset" status to property used in the taxpayer's trade or business if it is either (a) depreciable or (b) real property. Thus, machinery and other depreciable business items are not capital assets, nor are factories, warehouses, and similar buildings or the land on which they stand. Section 1221(2) also embraces apartment houses, office buildings, and other property held for rental, unless the landlord's management activities are too minimal to constitute a "trade or business." [42]

Section 1221(2) was enacted in 1938 to permit taxpayers selling depreciable business property to deduct any loss on a sale from ordinary income, presumably because the depreciation that would have been sustained, had the property been retained in use, would have been deducted from ordinary income, and possibly also to encourage taxpayers to modernize by selling their old equipment and buying new items at a time when the economy badly needed a shot in the arm.[43] The right to deduct losses was appealing to taxpayers sustaining losses, but for those with gains the 1938 provision resulted in a denial of the capital gain treatment they had previously enjoyed. In 1942, however, Congress reconciled the conflicting interests of these two categories of taxpayers by enacting the statutory predecessor of IRC §1231, an extraordinary provision that gives each group what it prefers: Taxpayers incurring losses on the sale of business property can usually deduct them from ordinary income, while taxpayers with gains qualify for the preferential capital gain rate.

Taken in combination, therefore, IRC §§1221(2) and 1231 have the following effect on depreciable property and real property used in the taxpayer's trade or business:

1. By virtue of IRC §1221(2), these items are not capital assets, with the result that a disposition produces ordinary income or ordinary loss, except as provided by IRC §1231.
2. Under IRC §1231, if an asset has been held for more than one year, it usually produces capital gain if sold at a profit but a deduction from ordinary income if sold at a loss.

The principal interpretative issues in applying IRC §1221(2) have concerned three statutory phrases:

1. *Trade or business property.* Section 1221(2) covers real and depreciable property used in the taxpayer's "trade or business" but not property devoted to personal use, such as the taxpayer's residence and personal effects, which qualify as capital assets. A distinction must also be drawn between

---

[42] For this possibility, see infra note 45.

[43] S. Rep. No. 1567, 75th Cong., 3d Sess. (1938), reprinted in 1939-1 (Part 2) CB 779, 783.

"trade or business" property and investment property, since the latter category—embracing most securities and similar assets—is the very heart of the capital asset concept. Locating this dividing line has been troublesome in the case of rental real estate, especially if it is owned by an individual or other noncorporate taxpayer. In *Fackler v. CIR,* the leading case in this area, it was held that a lawyer who owned a leasehold interest in an apartment house was engaged in a trade or business because of the level of managerial and maintenance activity—furnishing of elevator service, heat, light, and water, employment of labor, purchases of material, and repairs and alterations.[44] In a few cases, the *Fackler* principle has been held inapplicable to property requiring only a trivial amount of managerial activity (e.g., the rental of an inherited single-family residence).[45]

2. *Use of property in trade or business.* Occasionally it is necessary to determine whether property *acquired* for a business purpose that has either not yet been placed in service or has been retired from active service is "used" in the trade or business within the meaning of IRC §1221(2). The Tax Court has held that real estate purchased with a view to constructing a place of business but sold when a requisite zoning variance could not be procured was a capital asset, outside the scope of IRC §1221(2), on the ground that it was never put to a business use.[46]

Once actual business use of property has commenced, the prevailing view is that the property is "used" in the trade or business so far as IRC §1221(2) is concerned even if it is retired from active service and put up for sale.[47]

3. *Depreciable property.* Section 1221(2) embraces all real property used in the trade or business, whether depreciable or not, but it covers other business property only if it is "of a character which is subject to the allowance for depreciation provided in section 167." Section 167, to which IRC §1221(2) refers, grants a depreciation allowance for "exhaustion, wear and tear (including a reasonable allowance for obsolescence)" and thus applies to all property

---

[44] Fackler v. CIR, 133 F.2d 509, 511-512 (6th Cir. 1943); see also Elek v. CIR, 30 TC 731 (1958) (Acq.).

[45] Grier v. US, 120 F.Supp. 395 (D.Conn. 1954), aff'd per curiam, 218 F.2d 603 (2d Cir. 1955) (one-family house, inherited by taxpayer; upon examination of taxpayer's subsequent activities, held, capital asset); but see Hazard v. CIR, 7 TC 372 (1946) (personal residence rented by taxpayer when he moved to another city; held, used in trade or business).

[46] Davis v. CIR, 11 TC 538 (1948) (Acq.); but see Carter-Colton Cigar Co. v. CIR, 9 TC 219 (1947) (Acq.) (although construction plans abandoned, some use of the lot had been made; capital asset status denied).

[47] See Wilson Line, Inc. v. CIR, 8 TC 394 (1947) (Acq.) (dismantled equipment held used in trade or business under IRC §1231 when sold five years later); Wright v. CIR, 9 TC 173 (1947) (Acq.) (rental property destroyed by hurricane; held, land was used in trade or business when sold five years later); Wofac Corp. v. US, 269 F.Supp. 654 (D.N.J. 1967) (premises and equipment of business that was discontinued because unprofitable).

that is adversely affected by use or the passage of time. This includes almost all tangible property, including assets subject to the cost recovery allowances of IRC §168, but not art objects and antiques, which do not deteriorate with time.

As to intangibles, some have a limited useful life (e.g., leaseholds, patents, copyrights, and franchises for a specified term of years) and therefore qualify for the depreciation allowance of IRC §167, which in turn brings them within the scope of IRC §1221(2), even though it is customary to apply the term "amortization" rather than "depreciation" to the process of writing off the cost of intangibles. Other intangibles, however, have an unlimited or perpetual life (e.g., corporate charters and franchises of indefinite duration) so that they cannot be depreciated under IRC §167; hence, they are not covered by IRC §1221(2) and can qualify as capital assets. The most important business asset in this category is goodwill, whose commercial life can almost never be predicted with enough accuracy to qualify for a depreciation allowance.

¶25.7 COPYRIGHTS, WORKS OF ART, LETTERS, ETC.

Section 1221(3) denies capital asset status to copyrights; literary, musical, and artistic compositions; and letters, memoranda, and similar property—in each case, if the property was created by the taxpayer's personal efforts. In the case of letters, memoranda, and similar property, however, the disqualification applies not only to the author, but also to any taxpayer for whom the property was prepared and produced. The items listed in IRC §1221(3) are also noncapital assets if held by a taxpayer whose basis for computing gain on a sale or exchange is determined by reference to the basis of the property in the hands of a disqualified taxpayer, such as a corporation to which the author transferred the property in exchange for its stock, or a member of the author's family who received the property by gift. In addition to being treated as a noncapital asset, property described by IRC §1221(3) cannot qualify as a "quasi-capital asset" under the hotchpot rules of IRC §1231,[48] and, if contributed to a charity, can be deducted only to the extent of its cost or other basis,[49] which is usually nominal (e.g., the cost of the paper, canvas, paints etc., used by the author or artist, if not already deducted as a business expense).

Before 1950, when the statutory predecessor of IRC §1221(3) was enacted, copyrights, literary compositions, and similar property qualified as capital assets unless held for sale to customers or used in the taxpayer's business within the meaning of IRC §§1221(1) or 1221(2). During this early period, therefore, amateur authors and artists could realize capital gains by

---

[48] See IRC §1231(b)(1)(C), discussed infra ¶27.1.

[49] See IRC §170(e)(1)(A), discussed supra ¶19.2.

selling their works even though the property was the embodiment of their personal efforts. This possibility attracted a great deal of public attention in 1948, when the financial arrangements for the publication of General Eisenhower's World War II memoirs, Crusade in Europe, were discussed in the press, including a rumor that the manuscript was being "aged" after completion to satisfy the holding period for long-term capital gain treatment.

Spurred by this and other events, in 1950 Congress enacted the statutory predecessor of IRC §1221(3), sometimes called "the Eisenhower Amendment," denying capital gain treatment to copyrights; literary, muscial, and artistic compositions; and similar property, if held by the creator of the item or by a taxpayer with a basis carried over from the creator. In 1969, IRC §1221(3) was expanded to include letters, memoranda, and similar property, whether held by the author or by the person for whom they were prepared or produced. Although primarily intended to prevent public officials from deducting the value of their collected papers on contributing them to public libraries, universities, and other tax-exempt institutions, the provision also serves to tax gain on the sale of the papers as ordinary income. An appropriate label for this part of IRC §1221(3) would be "the Nixon Amendment" because it was enacted during Nixon's presidency and helped to bring about his impeachment inquiry when it was discovered that a gift of his papers to the National Archives, for which he took a deduction under IRC §170, involved a backdated deed of gift purportedly executed before the effective date of the amendment.[50]

The reference in IRC §1221(3) to "similar property" includes theatrical productions, radio programs, newspaper cartoon strips, and other property eligible for copyright protection, but not patents, inventions, or designs that can be protected under the patent law but not under the copyright law.[51] The term "similar property" has also been applied to the format of a radio quiz program *(Double or Nothing),* on which participants could progressively double their winnings by electing to answer an additional question.[52] Even if not entitled to copyright protection, the idea was held to be similar to the items explicitly listed in IRC §1221(3) because it was a type of artistic work resulting from personal effort and skill. The same fate befell "Francis," a talking army mule figuring in a series of novels, when the author sold all his rights to the character and the novels to a motion-picture company.[53]

---

[50] See House Comm. on the Judiciary, Impeachment of Richard M. Nixon, President of the United States, H. Rep. No. 93-1305, 93d Cong., 2d Sess. 221-223 (1974).

[51] Treas. Regs. §1.1221-1(c)(1).

[52] Cranford v. US, 338 F.2d 379 (Ct. Cl. 1964).

[53] Stern v. US, 164 F.Supp. 847 (E.D. La. 1958), aff'd per curiam, 262 F.2d 957 (5th Cir.), cert. denied, 359 US 969 (1959); see also Glen v. CIR, 79 TC 208 (1982) (interview tapes for oral-history research are "similar property").

When items described by IRC §1221(3) are held by persons other than (a) a taxpayer whose personal efforts created the property; (b) in the case of letters, memoranda, and similar property, a taxpayer for whom the document was prepared; or (c) a taxpayer whose basis for computing gain is determined by reference to the property's basis in the hands of one of the foregoing taxpayers, the property can qualify for capital asset status. Thus, investors in manuscripts and collectors of art are unaffected by IRC §1221(3).[54] The same is true of dealers in works of art; but this immunity from IRC §1221(3) is cold comfort, since their wares are held for sale to customers in the ordinary course of business and therefore generate ordinary income under IRC §1221(1).[55] An enterprise holding copyrights or similar property for use in its business (e.g., a publisher) is also outside the scope of IRC §1221(3) (unless its personal efforts created the works or the copyrights have a carryover basis), and the copyrights qualify for the unusually favorable treatment accorded to "quasi-capital assets" by IRC §1231. Finally, property acquired from a decedent is outside the scope of IRC §1221(3), since it has a basis equal to its fair market value on the date of the decedent's death by virtue of IRC §1014 and hence does not satisfy the carryover-basis condition of IRC §1221(3)(C).

¶25.8 ACCOUNTS AND NOTES RECEIVABLE ACQUIRED IN THE ORDINARY COURSE OF BUSINESS

Section 1221(4) denies capital asset classification to accounts and notes receivable if acquired by the taxpayer in the ordinary course of business for services rendered or for the sale of property described in IRC §1221(1) (relating to property held for sale to customers, etc.). The principal function of IRC §1221(4) is to permit accrual-basis taxpayers who realize ordinary income on credit sales of merchandise and subsequently sell the accounts receivable for less than their adjusted basis (viz., the amount taken into income when the merchandise was sold) to deduct the resulting loss from ordinary income. In the less common situation of a sale for more than the adjusted basis of the accounts, IRC §1221(4) has the effect of taxing the profit as ordinary income.

Although primarily concerned with accrual-basis taxpayers, IRC §1221(4) applies without regard to the taxpayer's method of reporting income. Thus, a cash-basis physician who performs services on credit would realize

---

[54] See Fidler v. CIR, 231 F.2d 138 (9th Cir. 1956) (literary property held to be a capital asset when held by an investor; decided under pre-1950 law, but principle is unaffected by subsequent enactment of IRC §1221(3)).

[55] See Griffin v. CIR, 33 TC 616 (1959) (sale by motion-picture producer of one-half interest in a story in conjunction with contract to produce a film based on story; held, property held for sale to customers in ordinary course of taxpayer's business of producing films).

ordinary income on selling the resulting claims against patients; and since no income would have been reported when the bills were sent out, the entire amount received would be taxed as ordinary income. While this result would no doubt have been reached even if IRC §1221(4) had not been enacted,[56] it now rests on an explicit legislative foundation.

¶25.9 FEDERAL PUBLICATIONS ACQUIRED FOR LESS THAN REGULAR SALES PRICE

Section 1221(5) denies capital asset status to any federal publication received from the government, except by purchase at the publication price, if held by the recipient or by a person whose basis for computing gain is computed by reference to the recipient's basis. Although this provision was added to the definition of "capital asset" and therefore characterizes gain on a sale of such publications as ordinary income, its principal function is to deny a charitable contribution deduction for gifts of government publications to public libraries, universities, or similar tax exempt institutions by persons receiving the documents without charge (e.g., Congressmen) or members of their families. The denial of a deduction occurs because IRC §170(e)(1)(A) permits donors to deduct only the basis of property if a sale would have generated ordinary income.[57]

¶25.10 OPTIONS TO BUY OR SELL PROPERTY

In determining whether sales and exchanges of options to buy or sell property give rise to capital gains and losses or to ordinary income and ordinary losses, IRC §1234(a) provides that the character of the underlying property in the hands of the taxpayer (or the character it would have if acquired by the taxpayer) is controlling. The tax treatment of losses attributable to the failure to exercise an option is also determined by looking to the optioned property.

Section 1234(a) does not apply:

1. To options held for sale to customers in the ordinary course of the taxpayer's trade or business, which generate ordinary income and ordinary loss regardless of the character of the underlying property.[58]

---

[56] See O'Neill v. CIR, ¶64,003 P-H Memo TC (1964) (lawyer's sale of claim for compensation for finding distributor for client's products held to produce ordinary income).

[57] See IRC §170(e)(1)(A), discussed supra ¶19.2.

[58] IRC §1234(a)(3)(A).

2. To the extent that gain on the sale or exchange of the option generates ordinary income without regard to IRC §1234 (e.g., compensatory options governed by IRC §83).[59]
3. To losses attributable to the failure to exercise options described in IRC §1233(c), relating to certain options to sell property at a fixed price if the option and the property are acquired on the same day.[60]

Because the term "option" is not defined by IRC §1234, its application to a variety of contractual privileges, such as a right of first refusal, is veiled in uncertainty.[61] It seems clear, however, that it does not encompass bilateral contracts, even though each party can be viewed as vested with an option to perform or pay damages for breach.[62]

Being concerned with sales and exchanges of options and with losses attributable to the failure to exercise options, IRC §1234(a) has no direct bearing on amounts paid for *exercised* options. In general, on exercising an option to purchase property, the buyer adds the amount paid for the option to the cost of the property itself in computing its basis,[63] so that the character of any gain or loss on a subsequent sale of the property depends on the purpose for which the property—rather than the option—was held by the taxpayer. Conversely, the amount paid by the owner of property for an option to sell it at a specified price (a "put") is offset against the sale price if the option is exercised; the cost of the option, therefore, reduces the taxpayer's gain (or increases the loss) on the sale, and the gain or loss will be capital or ordinary depending on the nature of the property.[64]

Writers of options ("optionors") on property other than stock, securities, commodities, and commodity futures realize ordinary income equal to the premium received if the option lapses without exercise.[65] This amount is includable in the optionor's income when the option lapses, rather than when received.[66] Under IRC §1234(b), however, options on stock, securities, com-

---

[59] IRC §1234(a)(3)(B); Mitchell v. CIR, 590 F.2d 312 (9th Cir. 1979) (IRC §1234 inapplicable to disposition of compensatory option); for IRC §83, see infra ¶29.2.

[60] IRC §1234(a)(3)(C).

[61] For discussion, see Anderson v. US, 468 F.Supp. 1085 (D.Minn. 1979) (right of refusal not subject to IRC §1234; payment received for release constituted capital gain).

[62] See U.S. Freight Co. & Subsidiaries v. US, 422 F.2d 887 (Ct. Cl. 1970) (forfeiture of down payment on breach of contract to buy stock not subject to IRC §1234).

[63] See Realty Sales Co. v. CIR, 10 BTA 1217 (1928) (Acq.).

[64] Rev. Rul. 58-234, 1958-1 CB 279.

[65] Treas. Regs. §1.1234–1(b).

[66] See Koch v. CIR, 67 TC 71 (1976) (Acq.) (quarterly payments to keep five-year option effective not includable in optionor's income when received). The IRS unsuccessfully argued in *Koch* that the arrangement was a series of three-month options, each producing income on termination.

modities, or commodity futures produce short-term capital gains and losses with respect to (a) gain on the lapse of such an option or (b) gain or loss from a "closing transaction" with respect to the option. In either case, the length of the option's life is irrelevant. This provision does not apply to options issued by the taxpayer in the ordinary course of an option-writing trade or business.

¶25.11 FRAGMENTATION VS. UNIFICATION OF COLLECTIVE ASSETS (SOLE PROPRIETORSHIPS, PARTNERSHIP INTERESTS, ETC.)

1. In General. In defining the term "capital asset," IRC §1221(1) refers to "property" and then specifies a number of items that are not to be treated as capital assets; but it does not deal directly with the status of assets that are sold in a single transaction because they are functionally interrelated and would lose some of their value if sold separately. In *Williams v. McGowan,* the Court of Appeals for the Second Circuit addressed itself to this problem, holding that a going business (originally operated as a two-man partnership but subsequently conducted as a sole proprietorship following the death of one partner) could not be treated as a unified "capital asset." [67] In an opinion by Judge Learned Hand, the court held that the definition of IRC §1221(1) must be applied separately to each asset, with the result that some were capital assets and others were not.

The "fragmentation" approach of *Williams v. McGowan* requires a going business to be treated as a group of separate assets not only if the enterprise is conducted by a sole proprietorship but also if it is owned and sold by a partnership or a corporation.[68] In the case of partnerships and corporations, however, this area is complicated by the fact that the sale or exchange of a partner's interest in the partnership or a shareholder's stock in the corporation generally produces capital gain or loss, while a sale by the partnership or corporation of its business is governed by the fragmentation principle enunciated by *Williams v. McGowan.*

2. Allocation of Lump-Sum Sales Price. When negotiating the sale of a going concern or other group of assets, the parties often agree on a lump-sum sales price and make no effort to allocate it among the components of the package. After the transaction is consummated, however, the seller must make an allocation in order to comply with the fragmentation principle of *Williams*

---

[67] Williams v. McGowan, 152 F.2d 570 (2d Cir. 1945).

[68] See US v. Woolsey, 326 F.2d 287 (5th Cir. 1963) (fragmentation of partnership assets); United States Mineral Prods. Co. v. CIR, 52 TC 177, 199 (1969) (Acq.) (same, corporate assets).

v. McGowan, and the buyer must do the same in order to compute gain or loss on selling the inventory, depreciation on depreciable assets, and such other tax allowances as depletion and the investment credit. For both parties, the proper objective is an allocation of the aggregate amount paid among the various assets in proportion to their relative fair market values.

The most frequently disputed allocations concern covenants not to compete and commercial goodwill. If the seller of a business agrees not to compete with the purchaser, the latter ordinarily seeks to allocate as much of the lump sum to the covenant as possible, since this portion of the purchase price can be amortized by annual deductions over the life of the covenant; conversely, the seller customarily seeks to minimize the significance of the covenant, since payments thereunder are taxed to the recipient as ordinary income rather than capital gain. The same conflict can arise if the seller agrees to provide consulting services rather than merely to refrain from competing with the buyer.

The roles are reversed when goodwill is involved, however, since its adusted basis to the seller is usually zero and the resulting profit is capital gain; conversely, the buyer cannot deduct or amortize the amount paid but must instead treat it as a capital outlay that has a useful life of indefinite duration and that has no tax effect until it is sold or becomes worthless. Hence, the seller typically seeks to magnify the value of the goodwill, and the buyer to minimize it.

Rather than entrust allocation of lump sum payments to the ex post facto vagaries of the administrative and judicial processes, the parties sometimes agree on an allocation in advance and incorporate it in the sales contract. Since an agreed allocation ordinarily resolves opposing views about the way the aggregate amount to be paid should be distributed among the various assets, it is often accepted by the IRS; and taxpayers seeking to escape from an agreed allocation may be required to establish that it was fictitious by unusually persuasive evidence—"strong proof," or even proof of mistake, fraud, or duress.[69] But if the tax circumstances of the contracting parties are substantially divergent (e.g., because one is subject to higher marginal rates than the other), a particular allocation may save one party far more than it costs the other. In this event, the latter taxpayer may be induced to accept an artificial division in return for an increase in the amount to be paid to him, or a reduction in the amount to be paid by him. Rather than permit the parties to gang up on the IRS in this way, the courts have held that "the parties cannot contractually preclude the Commissioner from attacking an allocation which has no basis in economic reality." [70] In dealing with this problem, as well as

[69] See Forward Communications Corp. v. US, 608 F.2d 485 (Ct. Cl. 1979), and cases there cited.

[70] Dixie Finance Co. v. US, 474 F.2d 501, 504 (5th Cir. 1973).

with contracts that do not contain an allocation, the courts have developed two principal rival standards—"severability" and "economic reality."[71]

If the sole purpose of the covenant not to compete is to protect the goodwill by assuring the buyer that his enjoyment of the goodwill will not be impaired by the seller's activities, the "severability" test precludes assigning any portion of the sales price to the covenant.[72] The alternative economic reality test "seeks to determine whether the parties to the agreement intended to allocate a portion of the purchase price to the covenant not to compete and whether such allocation establishes that the covenant had an independent basis in fact or some relationship to business reality."[73]

Because of its special history, mention should be made here of the problem of goodwill on the sale of a professional practice by a physician, accountant, or other person engaged in furnishing personal services to the public. In 1957, the IRS ruled that goodwill could be recognized on the sale of a professional practice if the buyer acquired the exclusive right to use the firm name, but it implied that goodwill will rarely if ever be recognized in the absence of such a transfer of the firm name.[74] If intended as a description of the real world, this implication was manifestly defective, since the buyer of a professional practice can benefit from the firm's location, supporting staff, patient and client records, and other factors that ordinarily contribute to goodwill, even if the practice is conducted under the buyer's name rather than the seller's and, in some circumstances, even if the seller continues to practice in the same community. Having encountered little success in the courts with its 1957 theory, the IRS pared it down in stages by later rulings;[75] and there now seems to be no difference in legal theory between personal-service enterprises and other business firms in determining whether goodwill is present.

¶25.12 JUDICIAL RESTRICTIONS ON CAPITAL GAIN AND LOSS TREATMENT

1. Introductory. Although IRC §1221 defines the term "capital asset" in some detail, its categories are far from watertight, and the bulkheads between them are subjected to constant pressure by taxpayers and revenue

---

[71] See Proulx v. US, 594 F.2d 832 (Ct. Cl. 1979).

[72] See Michaels v. CIR, 12 TC 17 (1949) (Acq.).

[73] Bacon v. CIR, ¶77,052 P-H Memo TC (1977).

[74] Rev. Rul. 57-480, 1957-2 CB 47.

[75] See Rev. Rul. 60-301, 1960-2 CB 15 (transferable goodwill can be recognized if practice is not dependent solely on seller's personal characteristics, even without assignment of exclusive use of firm name); Rev. Rul. 70-45, 1970-1 CB 17 (earlier rulings modified to remove implication that partial transfer of goodwill cannot be made on admission of new partners to continuing practice).

agents. Moreover, the form of the definition is curious for a provision that grants preferential tax treatment to gains, since, instead of specifying the assets or transactions that are to qualify, IRC §1221 begins by conferring capital asset status on *all* property held by the taxpayer, and "then withdraws a few classes of property from this otherwise universal state of grace."[76] As a result, some transactions seem at first blush to qualify for the capital gain rate, although they are clearly outside the spectrum of intended beneficiaries.

The effort to confine capital gain treatment to transactions meeting the dimly expressed legislative standards, as perceived by the courts, has generated a body of judicial interpretation that amounts to a common law of capital gains and losses. These glosses on the statutory language are discussed below under descriptive rubrics that divide the principal cases into separate categories, but it should be noted that they often overlap and that several principles are sometimes cited in support of the same conclusion.

2. Scope of the Term "Property." Section 1221 defines the term "capital asset" to mean "property held by the taxpayer" (except for certain specified items), and it contains nothing to suggest that "property"—a term that is frequently used in legal discourse—should be given a restricted or technical meaning. Building on this, a taxpayer argued in *CIR v. Gillette Motor Transport, Inc.* that compensation paid by the United States for temporary seizure of its business facilities during World War II was taxable as capital gain because the seizure was a taking of its "property" under the just compensation clause of the Fifth Amendment.[77] The Supreme Court, however, held that neither the taxpayer's right to use its premises nor its right to be compensated by the government for the temporary taking of its premises constituted "property" within the meaning of IRC §1221:

> While a capital asset is defined in [IRC §1221] as "property held by the taxpayer," it is evident that not everything which can be called property in the ordinary sense and which is outside the statutory exclusions qualifies as a capital asset. This Court has long held that the term "capital asset" is to be construed narrowly in accordance with the purpose of Congress to afford capital-gains treatment only in situations typically involving the realization of appreciation in value accrued over a substantial period of time. . . .
>
> In the present case, respondent's right to use its transportation facilities was held to be a valuable property right compensable under the

[76] The source of this comment has been lost by the author, who offers the first reader to supply the missing citation a copy of this work, autographed or not, at his/her option.

[77] CIR v. Gillette Motor Transp., Inc., 364 U.S. 130 (1960).

requirements of the Fifth Amendment. However, that right was . . . simply an incident of the underlying physical property, the recompense for which is commonly regarded as rent . . . and the fact that the transaction was involuntary on respondent's part does not change the nature of the case.[78]

Although the restricted interpretation of "property" enunciated in *Gillette* distinguished between the "underlying physical property" and "the right to use" the underlying property, the decision has been applied most frequently to deny capital gain treatment to intangible assets created largely or solely by the taxpayer's personal efforts. In *Vaaler v. United States,* for example, where the taxpayer's general agency contract with an insurance company was terminated by a payment for "all his claims, interests and rights in policies in force in his territory on the date of termination and any renewals thereof," the court cited *Gillette* in holding that the taxpayer realized ordinary income rather than capital gain, because he was paid for "the extinguishment of the right to render [personal] services and to earn . . . commissions" that would have been taxed as ordinary income if the agency contract had remained in force.[79] In reaching this conclusion, the court distinguished several cases that were only marginally different, where taxpayers succeeded in establishing that part or all of the amount received was paid for files, lists of customers, or transferable goodwill.[80]

Another problem arising under IRC §1221 is whether the taxpayer has any "property" rights to convey. In an important opinion involving this issue, the Court of Appeals for the Second Circuit held that a payment by a motion-picture company to the widow of Glenn Miller, allegedly for her property rights in her deceased husband's name, image, and reputation, was taxable as ordinary income rather than capital gain, since there had been no authoritative decision holding, as a matter of local law, that a deceased entertainer's successors possessed any rights in his reputation.[81]

---

[78] Id. at 134-136; see also Carter's Est. v. CIR, 298 F.2d 192 (8th Cir.), cert. denied, 370 US 910 (1962) (payments received in settlement of antitrust suit for interference with theater business held ordinary income since paid for interrupted use rather than destruction of property); Republic Automotive Parts, Inc. v. CIR, 68 TC 822 (1977) (ordinary income on transfer of right to receive royalties for period less than useful lives of underlying assets), Turner v. CIR, 47 TC 355 (1967) (lump sum received by restaurateur to surrender occupancy of leased premises held ordinary income; paid for right to do business on premises in which he had no "investment").

[79] Vaaler v. US, supra note 7 at 1121-1123.

[80] CIR v. Killian, 314 F.2d 852 (5th Cir. 1963); Nelson Weaver Realty Co. v. CIR, 307 F.2d 897 (5th Cir. 1962). These cases have been rejected, at least to some extent, by another panel of the same court. See Bisbee-Baldwin Corp. v. Tomlinson, 320 F.2d 929 (5th Cir. 1963).

[81] Miller v. CIR, 299 F.2d 706 (2d Cir.), cert. denied, 370 US 923 (1962).

The *Miller* case also affects transfers of secret formulas, industrial know-how, and similar intangibles, whose legal protection depends on local rules that vary from one jurisdiction to another. If the taxpayer is permitted by local law to transfer the material by contract and can prevent uses in violation of the agreement, it evidently qualifies as "property" under IRC §1221, but the authority is meager.[82]

Finally, it should be noted that the term "property" may have different meanings as between one taxpayer and another. When an identifiable amount is paid for a covenant not to compete in conjunction with the sale of a going business, for example, the rights relinquished by the seller do not constitute "property" within the meaning of IRC §1221. Yet the correlative rights received by the buyer can be depreciated by him under IRC §167(a)(1) (relating to "property used in the trade or business"), and they also constitute "property" held by him within the meaning of IRC §§1221(2) and 1231, so that these provisions will dictate the tax treatment of gain or loss realized by him if he sells the business together with the covenant before the latter expires.

3. Ordinary Business Operations—The *Corn Products* Doctrine. In *Corn Products Refining Co. v. CIR,* the Supreme Court held that a company engaged in converting corn into starch, syrup, and other products realized ordinary income and loss on the sale of corn futures even though they were not denied capital asset status by the exclusions set out in IRC §1221, relating to stock in trade, property held for sale to customers, depreciable property used in the trade or business, etc.[83] Because the taxpayer's transactions in corn futures were designed to protect its manufacturing operations against increases in the cost of its principal raw material and to assure a ready supply of corn if needed, the resulting profits and losses were held to come within a congressional intent "that profits and losses arising from the everyday operation of a business be considered as ordinary income or loss rather than capital gain or loss." [84]

The result in *Corn Products* could have been reached with less strain by a narrower rationale, viz., that the future contracts were removed from the capital asset category by IRC §1221(1), relating to "property of a kind which would properly be included in the inventory of the taxpayer if on hand at the close of the taxable year." It may not be customary to inventory futures contracts per se, but when held by a taxpayer whose decisions to buy, sell or take delivery under the contracts are determined by its manufacturing needs,

---

[82] See Nelson v. CIR, 203 F.2d 1 (6th Cir. 1953); United States Mineral Prods. Co. v. CIR, 52 TC 177, 198 (1969) (Acq.); Commercial Solvents Corp. v. CIR, 42 TC 455, 467 (1964).

[83] Corn Products Refining Co. v. CIR, 350 US 46 (1955).

[84] Id. at 52.

they could easily be viewed as surrogates for the raw material itself. Section 1234 provides that options shall be treated as having the same character as the underlying property; and the case for assimilating futures contracts to the commodity is even stronger, since the owner of such a contract is subject to both upside and downside fluctuations in the commodity's value, while an optionee can lose no more than the cost of the option, no matter how much the value of the optioned property drops.

Because the taxpayer in *Corn Products* realized a net gain on its futures transactions during the years before the Court, the Court's narrow construction of the term "capital assets" was favorable to the government. But it is clear that the Court, though focusing on gains, intended an evenhanded application of the *Corn Products* doctrine, so that it can be invoked by taxpayers as well as by the IRS. For taxpayers realizing losses, therefore, the "narrow construction" enunciated by *Corn Products* is a blessing in disguise, since it permits losses to be deducted from ordinary income free of the restrictions that frequently make capital losses useless.

Corn Products has been extensively cited and applied, but only a few of these subsequent cases involve repetitive, everyday transactions like those that evoked the *Corn Products* doctrine. The principal instance of such a situation is *Mansfield Journal Co. v. CIR,* holding that a newspaper publisher entitled to purchase paper from a manufacturer under a favorable long-term contract realized ordinary income, rather than capital gain, on assigning its rights from time to time to other publishers for payments equal to the difference between the contract price and the higher current price for paper.[85] Although there were far fewer transactions in the *Mansfield Journal* case than in *Corn Products,* the circumstances were otherwise analogous, since the taxpayer entered into the long-term contract to assure itself a source of newsprint at a specified price and the assignments were made because the paper was not required in its own business.

Rather than involving recurring transactions of this type, however, most of the litigated cases applying *Corn Products* arise from sporadic or even once-in-a-lifetime losses on stock that was purchased by the taxpayer to serve a business purpose, such as insuring a source of raw materials or preserving a valued customer, and that was sold when no longer needed. On demonstrating that the stock was acquired and held for a business purpose rather than as an investment, taxpayers in these cases have been allowed to deduct the loss from ordinary income. This result had been presaged by a few cases even before *Corn Products* was decided,[86] but the Supreme Court's imprimatur unleashed

---

[85] Mansfield Journal Co. v. CIR, 274 F.2d 284 (6th Cir. 1960).

[86] See, e.g., Western Wine & Liquor Co. v. CIR, 18 TC 1090 (1952) (Acq.) (liquor wholesaler bought stock of national distiller that allowed shareholders to purchase liquor at cost, held, stock not "capital asset" for excess profits tax purposes); CIR v.

a horde of additional decisions. A much-cited illustration is *Booth Newspapers, Inc. v. United States,* holding that two newspaper publishers who purchased the stock of a paper manufacturer in order to have a dependable source of newsprint were entitled to ordinary deductions when they sold the stock at a loss on entering into long-term contracts with an unrelated supplier.[87] Later cases have allowed taxpayers to deduct from ordinary income their losses on selling stock acquired for such varied purposes as assisting a major customer to survive a financial crisis, obtaining the right to occupy leased property, and getting access to a team of electronic technicians to avoid the expense of developing its own in-house staff.[88] In some instances, the taxpayers were individuals who acquired stock of an employer or customer in order to cement their business relationship.[89]

Among these source-of-supply and analogous cases, there are few if any in which the IRS succeeded in taxing a gain realized on a sale of stock as ordinary income. It is possible that taxpayers rarely realize profits on selling stock purchased for business reasons, but a more plausible explanation for the prevalance of losses in the litigated cases is that losses supply an incentive for disclosing the business objective if a plausible rationale can be conjured up. By contrast, if a profit is realized, mum's the word; and since capital gain is the normal outcome when stock is sold at a profit, the IRS is not likely to scratch beneath the face of the return. To reduce this type of fence-straddling, Con-

---

Bagley & Sewell Co., 221 F.2d 944 (2d Cir. 1955) (government bonds purchased to be posted as collateral by taxpayer to insure performance of manufacturing contract; held, loss deductible from ordinary income).

[87] Booth Newspapers, Inc. v. US, 303 F.2d 916 (Ct. Cl. 1962); see also FS Servs., Inc. v. US, 413 F.2d 548 (Ct. Cl. 1969) (same for stock of oil refinery purchased by cooperative to insure supply of petroleum products needed in taxpayer's business).

[88] Waterman, Largen & Co. v. US, 419 F.2d 845 (Ct. Cl. 1969), cert. denied, 400 US 869 (1970) (commission agent's purchase of stock of company using its services); John J. Grier Co. v. US, 328 F.2d 163 (7th Cir. 1964) (lessee corporation acquired to avoid difficulty in acquiring consent of lessor to assignment of lease to taxpayer in connection with asset acquisition); Schlumberger Technology Corp. v. US, 443 F.2d 1115 (5th Cir. 1971) (access to technical staff).

For cases holding that an investment motive was either paramount or sufficiently weighty to result in capital asset status, see Dearborn Co. v. US, 444 F.2d 1145 (Ct. Cl. 1971) (investment motive inferred); Agway, Inc. v. US, 524 F.2d 1194 (Ct. Cl. 1975); see also W.W. Windle Co. v. CIR, 550 F.2d 43 (1st Cir.), cert. denied, 431 US 966 (1977), where the IRS disputed the "predominant motive" test, arguing that the taxpayer's motive in acquiring stock is immaterial; Rev. Rul. 78-94, 1978-1 CB 58 (existence of "substantial investment motive" for acquiring or holding stock requires capital gain or loss treatment, despite existence of "predominant" business motive).

[89] Steadman v. CIR, 424 F.2d 1 (6th Cir.), cert. denied, 400 US 869 (1970) (stock of employer bought by general counsel); Hagan v. US, 221 F.Supp. 248 (W.D. Ark. 1963) (commission salesman—stock of company with which he had exclusive contract).

gress might appropriately require taxpayers to declare their "business" objectives when the stock is acquired, under penalty of losing the right to claim an ordinary deduction if it is later sold at a loss.[90]

The broad construction of *Corn Products* adopted by the source-of-supply cases encounters an acute doctrinal difficulty when gain is realized on a sale of the taxpayer's own business property, such as a factory, machinery and equipment, or patents. Since 1942, IRC §1231 has accorded capital gain treatment to assets "used in the trade or business" if the taxpayer has a net gain from such transactions during the taxable year. Being derived from property used in the trade or business, however, these gains are clearly linked to the taxpayer's ordinary business operations, and, indeed, they often reflect excess depreciation deducted in prior years in computing ordinary income. Were *Corn Products* to be applied across the board to gains of this type, however, almost nothing would be left of IRC §1231. For this reason, and perhaps also because the capital gain opportunities created by IRC §1231 have been well known to Congress for many years,[91] the IRS has never claimed that IRC §1231 was obliterated by the *Corn Products* doctrine. Thus, taxpayers regularly report profits realized on run-of-the mine sales of IRC §1231 property as capital gains without challenge by the IRS.

In a few cases, however, the IRS has invoked the *Corn Products* doctrine in an effort to nibble around the edges of IRC §1231. This endeavor was successful in *Hollywood Baseball Association v. CIR,* holding that ordinary income was realized by a minor league baseball team on selling its player contracts.[92] Although the taxpayer's franchise required it to sell these contracts to major league teams under the so-called player draft, the sales were involuntary; and this led the court to hold that the contracts were not held *primarily* for sale to customers in the ordinary course of business. But they were *used* in the taxpayer's trade or business and hence came within IRC §1231, and this in turn raised the *Corn Products* issue.

4. Income From Personal Services. Being concerned primarily with increases and decreases in the value of investments, the capital gain and loss provisions do not ordinarily encompass income from personal services. For

---

[90] See IRC §1236, discussed infra ¶27.9, requiring dealers in securities to identify securities held for investment (rather than sale) on acquisition.

[91] For statutory palliatives to this phenomenon, see IRC §§1245 and 1250 (relating to the recapture of depreciation), discussed infra ¶¶28.1–28.5.

[92] Hollywood Baseball Ass'n v. CIR, 423 F.2d 494 (9th Cir.), cert. denied, 400 US 848 (1970); see also Norton v. US, 551 F.2d 821 (Ct. Cl. 1977) (gain on sale by logging company of timber-cutting contract excluded from IRC §1231 hotchpot under *Corn Products* doctrine); but see Deltide Fishing & Rental Tools, Inc. v. US, 279 F.Supp. 661, 666 (E.D. La. 1968) (IRC §1231 creates "fence of immunity" protecting property used in trade or business from *Corn Products* doctrine).

example, an employee or self-employed person with a claim against an employer or customer for unpaid personal services who sells the claim to a third party must report the proceeds as ordinary income. Capital gains in this situation is explicitly barred by IRC §1221(4), which provides that accounts acquired in the ordinary course of business for services rendered do not constitute capital assets, even if the amount payable is contingent on future profits—a feature that could be characterized as an investment. Thus, a lawyer who was entitled to receive compensation for finding a foreign distributor for a client's products was held to realize ordinary income on disposing of the claim for a fixed amount, even though the amounts payable under the compensation agreement could not be ascertained with reasonable accuracy because they were contingent on the future results of the distributorship.[93] The same result is reached even if the taxpayer's claim for personal services is contingent on fluctuations in the value of another person's capital assets, as in the case of an investment counselor who is to receive a percentage of a client's capital gains.[94]

Ordinary income is also the order of the day if the claim involves services to be rendered in the future, though here the courts have suggested an additional barrier to capital gain treatment, viz., that the right to be paid for future services cannot qualify as a capital asset because it is not "property" within the meaning of IRC §1221.[95]

Though formidable, these barriers to reporting the fruits of personal services as capital gain are not insurmountable, and a few categories of taxpayers are positioned to meet the challenge. The key to success is an occupation or activity culminating in "property" of a more traditional sort than a mere claim for services rendered or to be rendered. By hard work, long hours, and luck, for example, the sole proprietor of a business may create goodwill or a trade name that will constitute a capital asset when the business enterprise is sold, even though its value reflects past personal efforts. Personal services preformed in a business context may also culminate in agreements, lists of customers, business records, and other items whose status as "property" permits the profit on a sale to be reported as capital gain under either IRC

---

[93] O'Neill v. CIR, supra note 56; see also Turner v. CIR, 38 TC 304 (1962) (sale of fractional interest in rights to receive future commissions on renewal of insurance policies previously written by taxpayer; held, ordinary income).

[94] See Smith's Est. v. CIR, 313 F.2d 724 (8th Cir. 1963) (investment adviser); Pounds v. US, 372 F.2d 342 (5th Cir. 1967) (real estate broker).

[95] McFall v. CIR, 34 BTA 108, 110 (1936) (employee's profit-sharing contract is "property in the constitutional sense" but "is not the sort of property which is susceptible of ownership for a length of time as is a share of stock, a bond, or a thing"); Furrer v. CIR, 566 F.2d 1115 (9th Cir. 1977) (same for damages received by insurance agent for company's breach of contract giving taxpayer right to earn future commission income).

§1221 or §1231.[96] Similarly, the stock of an incorporated business is ordinarily a capital asset in the hands of the shareholders, even if they augmented its value by working for the corporation without compensation; and the same is true of a partner's interest in a partnership.

5. Substitutes for Ordinary Income. In two far-reaching cases, the Supreme Court has held that a taxpayer who disposes of the right to receive payments that would be taxed as ordinary income if received in due course (e.g., real estate rentals and mineral royalties) must report the "substitute" payment as ordinary income rather than as capital gain. The first of these cases, *Hort v. CIR,* involved a taxpayer who inherited an office building subject to a long-term lease that, because of the collapse of real estate values in the early 1930s, was burdensome to the tenant and correspondingly valuable to the taxpayer.[97] The taxpayer agreed to cancel the lease in return for a payment by the tenant of $140,000, which the Court taxed as ordinary income on the theory that it was a substitute for ordinary income, viz., the future rental payments specified by the lease. It would have been more accurate to describe the tenant's payment as compensation for the fact that the taxpayer, on leasing the property to another tenant, would be able to charge only the current rental value of the property, rather than the higher rent stipulated in the lease. Even so, the payment was a substitute for a *portion* of the stipulated rent, viz., the excess over the fair current rental value.

The "substitute for ordinary income" theory was again used by the Supreme Court in *CIR v. P.G. Lake, Inc.,* holding that the disposition of certain mineral payments carved out of established deposits yielded ordinary income rather than capital gain:

> Lake is a corporation engaged in the business of producing oil and gas. It has a seven-eighths working interest in two commercial oil and gas leases. In 1950 it was indebted to its president in the sum of $600,000 and in consideration of his cancellation of the debt assigned him an oil payment right in the amount of $600,000, plus an amount equal to the interest at 3 percent a year on the unpaid balance remaining from month to month, payable out of 25 percent of the oil attributable to the taxpayer's working interest in the two leases. At the time of the assignment it could have been estimated with reasonable accuracy that the assigned oil pay-

[96] For problems in distinguishing between "a contract right to earn ordinary income in the future by the performance of personal services," which is not "property" within the meaning of IRC §1221, and "an exclusive right to use or possess specific property," which qualifies, see Kingsbury v. CIR, 65 TC 1068 (1976) (Acq.).

[97] Hort v. CIR, 313 US 28 (1941).

ment right would pay out in three or more years. It did in fact pay out in a little over three years. . . .

> We do not see here any conversion of a capital investment. The lump sum consideration seems essentially a substitute for what would otherwise be received at a future time as ordinary income. The pay-out of these particular assigned oil payment rights could be ascertained with considerable accuracy. . . . The substance of what was received was the present value of income which the recipient would otherwise obtain in the future. In short, consideration was paid for the right to receive future income, not for an increase in the value of the income-producing property.[98]

Despite *Hort* and *Lake,* sales of income-producing assets regularly serve to convert the present value of income streams into capital gains. If, for example, the taxpayer in *Hort* had sold the building, the sales price would include the value of the favorable lease; similarly, if the taxpayer in *Lake* had sold its working interests, the sales price would reflect the present value of the periodic payments anticipated during the remaining life of the mineral deposit. In both cases, therefore, the sales proceeds could be viewed as a substitute for ordinary income; yet, it is clear that neither *Hort* nor *Lake* intended to deny capital gain treatment in these routine sale situations.

Unless and until Congress establishes an arbitrary line on the otherwise seamless spectrum between *Hort-Lake* transactions and conventional capital gain transactions,[99] therefore, the courts must locate the boundary in a case-by-case process, which can yield few useful generalizations because there are so many relevant but imponderable criteria. In establishing an appropriate boundary for the "substitute for ordinary income" concept, the following transactions are of major importance.

1. *Functional and geographical divisions.* It is not uncommon for taxpayers owning intellectual property to dispose separately of interests that are defined in functional or geographical terms. The owner of a copyright, for example, may transfer the book, magazine, motion-picture, and TV rights to different buyers, and the owner of a patentable idea may transfer the exclusive right to use the invention in a specified country or industry. Assuming that the property is a capital asset in the hands of the taxpayer,[100] the "substitute for ordinary income" doctrine does not ordinarily bar capital gain treatment on the sale of such divided interests, even though ordinary income would have been realized if the taxpayer had retained the property and granted a series of

---

[98] CIR v. P.G. Lake, Inc., 356 US 260, 261–262, 265–267 (1958).

[99] In a few special situations, Congress has laid down a statutory line. See IRC §1235 (relating to certain transfers of patents), discussed infra ¶27.8; IRC §1241 (relating to cancellations of leases or distributor's agreements), discussed infra ¶26.4; IRC §1253 (relating to transfers of franchises, trademarks, and trade names), discussed infra ¶26.5.

[100] See supra ¶25.7 (copyrights); infra ¶27.8 (patents).

nonexclusive licenses permitting it to be used on a royalty basis.[101] In effect, a functional or geographical division that is coextensive with the life of the property is likened to a fractional division, which generates capital gain rather than ordinary income.

2. *Temporal divisions.* In applying the "substitute for ordinary income" theory the murkiest area encountered by the courts is composed of situations in which the taxpayer disposes of rights that are not coextensive with the life of the property but are, instead, limited to a period of years. *Hort* itself illustrates a temporal division, since the taxpayer there disposed of rights under a lease with about thirteen years to run.[102]

Distinguishing *Hort* because of the limited time period there involved, the Court of Appeals for the Second Circuit held in *McAllister v. CIR* that the income beneficiary of a trust who sold her entire interest to the remainderman realized capital gain or loss even though she thereby obtained, in a lump sum, the present value of amounts that would have constituted ordinary income if received in due course during the remainder of her life.[103] Unlike the taxpayer in *Hort,* however, she transferred everything she owned; and the court observed that "the distinction seems logically and practically to turn upon anticipation of income payments over a reasonably short period of time and an out-and-out transfer of a substantial and durable property interest, such as a life estate at least is." [104]

3. *Anticipatory transactions.* The "substitute for ordinary income" rationale is especially appropriate if the taxpayer, on the eve of an ordinary-income transaction, makes a sale for the principal or sole purpose of transmuting the income into capital gain. In *Rhodes' Estate v. CIR,* where the taxpayer sold the right to receive a corporate dividend, already declared though not yet payable, the court held that the proceeds constituted ordinary income.[105] On the other hand, anticipatory sales sometimes do the trick. In *International*

---

[101] See infra ¶26.1; but note the limitation on functional and geographical divisions under IRC §1235 (relating to certain transfers of patents), discussed infra ¶27.8.

[102] For decisions involving limited temporal divisions, see Pickren v. US, 378 F.2d 595 (5th Cir. 1967) (amount received for exclusive right and license to use secret formulas and trade names for twenty-five years held ordinary income since all substantial rights were not transferred); Griffith v. US, 403 F.Supp. 705 (S.D.Tex. 1975) (proceeds from sale of minerals in tract held ordinary income, where minerals remaining after twelve years reverted to seller); Rev. Rul. 69-471, 1969-2 CB 10 (payments received by wife over three-year period in exchange for release of community-property interest in one-half of husband's first sixty-nine monthly retirement payments; held, ordinary income).

[103] McAllister v. CIR, 157 F.2d 235 (2d Cir. 1946), cert. denied, 330 US 826 (1947).

[104] Id. at 235, 237; see also Blair v. CIR, 300 US 5 (1937), using the "transfer of all one owns" rationale in the assignment-of-income context, infra ¶30.3.

[105] Rhodes' Est. v. CIR, 131 F.2d 50 (6th Cir. 1942); see also Treas. Regs. §1.61-9(c); infra ¶30.3.

Flavors & Fragrances, Inc. v. CIR, for example, a short sale of a contract to deliver foreign currency produced long-term capital gain for the taxpayer although it was effected shortly before maturity (at which time the taxpayer's gain would have been ordinary income) and the buyer promptly neutralized its residual risk by purchasing the currency required to comply with its contractual obligations on the due date.[106]

4. *"Income items."* In *United States v. Midland-Ross Corp.,* the Supreme Court said that "this Court has consistently construed 'capital asset' to exclude property representing income items or accretions to the value of a capital asset themselves properly attributable to income." [107] The reference to "accretions" to a capital asset that constitute income presumably refers to such items as accrued dividends and interest sold along with the stock or bond to which they adhere. The reference to "income items" seems to encompass more ground, however, implying that the right to receive amounts constituting ordinary income cannot be treated as a capital asset. If so, the theory overlaps the "substitute for ordinary income" rationale of *Hort* and *Lake;* and it must be similarly qualified lest it collide with the inconvenient fact that when capital assets are unbundled, they almost always consist of a series of potential income items.

5. *Accrued income.* The references in *Midland-Ross* to "income items" and "accretions to the value of a capital asset" may imply endorsement of an ill-defined doctrine under which income that has already been earned but has not yet been recognized under the taxpayer's accounting method cannot be converted from ordinary income into capital gain by a sale. An illustration of this doctrine is the principle that a sale of a bond or other debt with accrued interest produces ordinary income to the extent that the proceeds are allocable to the interest accruing during the taxpayer's ownership.[108] If the taxpayer bought the instrument when it was in default and sells it "flat," the sale price must be allocated between (a) principal and pre-acquisition interest (generating capital gain or loss) and (b) post-acquisition interest, which gives rise to ordinary income.[109]

---

[106] International Flavors & Fragrances, Inc. v. CIR, ¶77,058 P-H Memo TC (1977).

[107] US v. Midland-Ross Corp., 381 US 54, 57 (1965). *Midland-Ross* involved original-issue discount, an area that is now largely covered by legislation, for which see infra ¶27.4.

[108] See Treas. Regs. §1.61-7(d) (interest income realized on sale of bonds between interest dates); Fisher v. CIR, 209 F.2d 513 (6th Cir.), cert. denied, 347 US 1014 (1954) (sale of notes in default for more than face value produced ordinary income to extent sale price exceeded face value).

[109] Treas. Regs. §1.61-7(c); Jaglom v. CIR, 303 F.2d 847 (2d Cir. 1962) (discussion and citation of analogous cases, including sale of stock with accrued dividends and sale of interest in movie rights with accrued royalties).

¶25.13 CORRELATION WITH PRIOR RELATED TRANSACTION

Although each taxable year normally stands on its own footing, sometimes the tax consequences of a transaction are determined by reference to a prior related transaction. An example of this occasional triumph of transactional over annual accounting is the tax benefit principle, taxing a receipt that would not ordinarily constitute income if it is a recovery of an expenditure deducted with tax benefit in an earlier year.[110] In *Merchants National Bank v. CIR,* a transactional approach was employed by the Court of Appeals for the Fifth Circuit to deny capital gain treatment to a bank's profit on selling loans receivable that had been previously charged off and deducted as worthless.[111] The bank conceded that the receipts were taxable, since they constituted recoveries of amounts previously deducted (from ordinary tax income) with tax benefit; but it argued that the dispositions satisfied the statutory requirement of a "sale or exchange" of a "capital asset." The court, however, insisted on impressing the receipts with the character of the earlier deductions, requiring the receipts to be reported as ordinary income.

Although *Merchants National Bank* is often cited with approval,[112] its rationale must be severely curtailed to avoid a collision with other principles that are even more deeply entrenched in the tax law. The sale of goodwill, for example, routinely produces capital gain, even though the expenses of creating it are deducted from ordinary income when paid or incurred.[113] Unfortunately, the decisions have not established clearly when zero-basis assets can generate capital gain on a sale (as in the case of goodwill) and when the profit is ordinary income (as in *Merchants National Bank*).

In *Merchants National Bank,* the tax status of a transaction was determined by an earlier *ordinary*-loss transaction. The converse—a transaction whose status is determined by an earlier *capital* gain or loss transaction—is also possible and, indeed, has broader judicial support. The leading case is *Arrowsmith v. CIR,* holding that taxpayers who reported capital gain on the complete liquidation of a closely held corporation could not deduct from ordinary income their subsequent payment of unpaid corporate obligations that had been neglected at the time of liquidation.[114] Since payment of these

---

[110] For the tax benefit principle, see supra ¶1.10.

[111] Merchants Nat'l Bank v. CIR, 199 F.2d 657 (5th Cir. 1952). The same result would now be reached via IRC §1221(4). Compare Rev. Rul. 80-56, 1980-1 CB 154 (gain on acquisition of mortgaged property at foreclosure offsets bad-debt deduction and is ordinary income).

[112] E.g., Bresler v. CIR, 65 TC 182, 187 (1975) (Acq.); Mayfair Minerals, Inc. v. CIR, 456 F.2d 622 (5th Cir. 1972).

[113] See supra ¶8.4.

[114] Arrowsmith v. CIR, 344 US 6 (1952); see also Brown v. CIR, 529 F.2d 609 (10th Cir. 1976) (payments under Section 16(b) of Securities Exchange Act of 1934 relating to insider's profits); Kimbell v. US, 490 F.2d 203 (5th Cir.), cert. denied, 419

liabilities by the corporation before its liquidation would have reduced the liquidating distributions received by the taxpayers, they would have realized less capital gain in the earlier year; and the Supreme Court held that this fact required treating their subsequent payment as a capital loss, although, viewed in isolation, it was not a sale of a capital asset.

SELECTED BIBLIOGRAPHY

Andrews & Freeland, Capital Gains and Losses of Individuals and Related Matters Under the Tax Reform Act of 1969, 12 Ariz. L. Rev. 627, 638–645 (1970).

Beghe, Income Tax Treatment of Covenants Not to Compete, Consulting Agreements and Transfers of Goodwill, 30 Tax Lawyer 587 (1977).

Bernstein, "Primarily for Sale": A Semantic Snare, 20 Stan. L. Rev. 1093 (1968).

Brown, Individual Investment in Real Estate: Capital Gains vs. Ordinary Income; Attaining Nondealer Status; Structuring Disposition of Investment; Dealer as Investor; Implications of Investor-Dealer Partnership, 34 NYU Inst. on Fed. Tax. 189, 231B (1976).

Chirelstein, Capital Gain and the Sale of a Business Opportunity: The Income Tax Treatment of Contract Termination Payments, 49 Minn. L. Rev. 1, 3–5 (1964).

Del Cotto, "Property" in the Capital Asset Definition: Influence of "Fruit and Tree," 15 Buffalo L. Rev. 1 (1965).

Guerin, Condominium Conversions: An Analysis of Alternative Routes to Capital Gain Treatment, 1 Tax. L.J. 1 (1982).

Henze, Transactions in Options: Some New Wrinkles and Old Risks, 4 Rev. Tax. Individuals 70 (1980).

Javaras, Corporate Capital Gains and Losses—The *Corn Products* Doctrine, 52 Taxes 770 (1974).

Schenk, *Arrowsmith* and Its Progeny: Tax Characterization by Reference to Past Events, 33 Rutgers L. Rev. 317 (1981).

US 833 (1974) (capital loss on payment made to settle claim based on taxpayer's alleged misconduct in earlier transaction that generated capital gain).

For treatment of an earlier event as a closed transaction, so that property received in later years produces ordinary income unless the statutory conditions for capital gain or loss treatment are independently present, see Waring v. CIR, ¶68,126 P-H Memo TC (1968), aff'd per curiam, 412 F.2d 800 (3d Cir. 1969) (royalties under license agreement distributed to taxpayer in complete liquidation of wholly owned corporation; held, receipts in excess of value placed on agreement at time of liquidation are taxable as ordinary income).

CAPITAL GAINS AND LOSSES—IN GENERAL

Surrey, Definitional Problems in Capital Gains Taxation, 69 Harv. L. Rev. 985 (1956).

Warren, The Deductibility by Individuals of Capital Losses Under the Federal Income Tax, 40 U. Chi. L. Rev. 291 (1973).

Zinicola, Note—Real Estate and Section 1221: Business as a Pattern of Activity in the Definition of a Capital Asset, 35 Tax Lawyer 225 (1981).

CHAPTER 26

Capital Gains and Losses—"Sale or Exchange" and Holding Period Requirements

¶26.1 "SALE OR EXCHANGE" VS. "SALE OR OTHER DISPOSITION"

1. Introductory. By virtue of IRC §1222, capital gains and losses arise from "the sale or exchange" of capital assets. Because this statutory requirement is clearly satisfied by most routine dispositions of investment assets, such as sales of securities on a securities exchange or over the counter, it is easily overlooked in peripheral situations that do not fit the layman's conception of a "sale or exchange," such as loss of the property by theft, fire, abandonment, or condemnation. Moreover, Congress has dispensed with the technical requirement of a "sale or exchange" in many of these peripheral situations, so that its residual importance in a few remaining circumstances can be a trap for the unwary.

Interpreting the phrase "sale or exchange" in these residual situations is made difficult by the absence of any legislative explanation of its function. At first blush, the phrase seems to specify the circumstances in which the taxpayer must compute gain or loss, thus distinguishing *realized* from *unrealized* capital gains and losses. This cannot be the function of IRC §1222, however, because IRC §1001(a), providing that gain or loss is to be computed on "the sale or other disposition" of property, applies to both capital and noncapital assets.

In the absence of a cogent reason for requiring the taxpayer's interest in capital assets to be terminated in a special way in order to qualify for capital gain or loss treatment—and none has been suggested—it would be appropriate to interpret "sale or exchange" as used in IRC §1222 as coextensive with "sale or other disposition" as used in IRC §1001(a). Evidence that the difference in phraseology is accidental can be found in IRC §1001(c), which uses the phrase "sale or exchange" but is intended to apply to all closed transactions and thus to cover the same ground as IRC §1001(a). In *Helvering v. William Flaccus Oak Leather Co.,* however, the Supreme Court held that the taxpayer did not engage in a "sale or exchange" within the meaning of IRC §1222 when its business plant was destroyed by fire and it was compensated for the loss by insurance.[1] Since the events in *William Flaccus Oak Leather Co.* constituted a "sale or other disposition" within the meaning of the statutory predecessor of IRC §1001(a), the case created a rift between that phrase and "sale or exchange" that has continued to this day. As a result, some transactions generate ordinary income or ordinary loss, although a sale of the same property prior to the event would have produced capital gain or loss.

Congress, however, has intervened in many situations to provide that a particular method of terminating the taxpayer's investment should be treated as a "sale or exchange," even though the "ordinary meaning" principle enunciated in the *William Flaccus Oak Leather Co.* case might lead to a different conclusion. These so-called statutory sales are described below, following an examination of the status of borderline transactions that have not been the subject of special legislation.

2. Foreclosure, Condemnation, Destruction, and Other Involuntary Events. In *Helvering v. Hammel,* the Supreme Court held that a foreclosure sale was a "sale or exchange" within the meaning of the statutory predecessor of IRC §1222, even though it did not result from the taxpayer's voluntary

[1] Helvering v. William Flaccus Oak Leather Co., 313 US 247, 249 (1941). The result in this case was subsequently changed by IRC §1231(a) for some assets (e.g., capital assets held for more than one year) but not for others (e.g., capital assets held for one year or less). See infra ¶27.2.

action and hence was not a "sale" for some private-law purposes (e.g., a property owner's covenant against sale or assignment of his interest).[2] *Hammel* has been applied even when the mortgagor is not liable on the debt.[3]

In reliance on *Hammel,* it has been held that property taken by eminent domain is sold or exchanged within the meaning of IRC §1222, even though for some purposes the event is often described as a "taking" rather than a "sale" and the payment as "damages" rather than "consideration."[4] If, however, the government takes not the property itself but only the right to use it for a limited period, the compensation is a substitute for rent, taxable as ordinary income.[5] Ancillary payments, such as severance damages and interest to compensate the taxpayer for a delay in awarding or paying damages, similarly constitute ordinary income rather than payment for the property.[6]

When property is destroyed by fire, however, it has been held that the event does not constitute a "sale or exchange" even if the taxpayer is compensated for the loss by an insurance company.[7] This judicial refusal to extend the "forced sale" rationale of *Hammel* to destruction of property by fire would presumably also encompass losses from tortious or criminal conduct (e.g., negligence, theft, or embezzlement), as well as the unexplained disappearance of property as a result of the taxpayer's failure to keep it under lock and key.

3. Worthless and Abandoned Property. When property becomes worthless, the taxpayer suffers a loss equal to the property's adjusted basis; but the loss does not arise from a "sale or exchange" within the meaning of IRC §1222. In the case of worthless securities, however, several special provisions ordinarily require the loss to be treated as though it resulted from a sale or exchange.[8] When these provisions are not applicable (e.g., bonds issued by an individual and property other than securities), the taxpayer suffers an ordinary loss rather than a capital loss.[9]

Even if property not only becomes worthless but is abandoned by the taxpayer, the additional step does not constitute a "sale or exchange" within

---

[2] Helvering v. Hammel, 311 US 504 (1941); see also Helvering v. Nebraska Bridge Supply & Lumber Co., 312 US 666 (1941) (tax sale; same result).

[3] Freeland v. CIR, 74 TC 970 (1980) (reconveyance of property subject to nonrecourse purchase-money mortgage treated as sale, generating capital loss).

[4] Hawaiian Gas Prods., Ltd. v. CIR, 126 F.2d 4 (9th Cir.), cert. denied, 317 US 653 (1942).

[5] CIR v. Gillette Motor Transp., Inc., 364 US 130 (1960).

[6] CIR v. Kieselbach, 127 F.2d 359 (3d Cir. 1942), aff'd on another issue, 317 US 399 (1943).

[7] Helvering v. William Flaccus Oak Leather Co., supra note 1.

[8] See IRC §§165(g), 166(d)(1)(B), 1244; infra ¶26.3.

[9] It should be remembered, however, that a deduction can be taken only if authorized by IRC §165, discussed supra ¶12.2; in particular, property devoted to personal use does not give rise to a deduction on becoming worthless.

the meaning of IRC §1222. If, however, mortgaged property is "abandoned" by a voluntary conveyance to the creditor, the transfer is treated by the IRS as a sale or exchange even if the taxpayer is not personally liable on the debt.[10]

4. Collection of Claims. In *Fairbanks v. United States,* the Supreme Court held that the redemption of a corporate bond was not a sale or exchange and that the taxpayer's gain, though attributable to an increase in the value of a capital asset, constituted ordinary income.[11] When *Fairbanks* was decided, Congress had already enacted the predecessor of IRC §1232, providing that amounts paid on the retirement of certain bonds and other obligations "shall be considered" as paid in exchange therefor. This "statutory sale" provision did not apply to the taxable year before the Court, however, and its limited scope continues to leave a good deal of room for the *Fairbanks* principle. Open-account and noncorporate debts, for example, are not covered by IRC §1232(a); consequently, the collection of such an obligation produces ordinary income or loss under *Fairbanks* even if the claim itself is a capital asset. The same principle holds true for compromise settlements of claims and judgments.[12]

At first blush, it would seem that foresighted investors could avoid *Fairbanks* by selling their claims to third parties rather than waiting for payment by the obligors. But since merchants and employees might also seek to avoid *Fairbanks* by selling their claims against customers and employers, the courts developed a series of doctrines designed to prevent such transactions from being treated as sales of capital assets;[13] and these obstacles (especially the theory that a "naked" contract claim is not "property" within the meaning of IRC §1221) may also apply to bona fide investors.

5. Surrender, Cancellation, and Termination of Contract Rights. The scope of the term "sale or exchange" is also uncertain as applied to transactions that cancel, terminate, surrender, rescind, or otherwise extinguish the taxpayer's rights under a contract with another person. In common parlance, "sale or exchange" connotes a transfer of property to a person who will make use of it, rather than an event that not only terminates the taxpayer's interest but also simultaneously extinguishes the "property" itself. These "disappearing asset" cases, in which the courts have held or intimated that there was no

---

[10] Middleton v. CIR, 77 TC 310 (1981).

[11] Fairbanks v. US, 306 US 436 (1939).

[12] Ogilvie v. CIR, 216 F.2d 748 (6th Cir. 1954) (satisfaction of judgment debt); Hale v. Helvering, 85 F.2d 819 (D.C. Cir. 1936) (compromise payment to settle mortgage notes).

[13] See supra ¶25.12; infra, text at and preceding note 16; text at notes 32-33.

"sale or exchange," include decisions denying capital gain treatment when a musical booking agent assigned his management contracts to another booking agent as a prelude to their cancellation so that the transferee could enter into new contracts with the performers,[14] when a distributor was paid for terminating its exclusive contract with a manufacturer,[15] and when a taxpayer was paid to surrender rights under an exclusive contract to purchase coal.[16]

In *CIR v. Ferrer,* however, the Court of Appeals for the Second Circuit described the line between "a sale to a third person that keeps the 'estate' or 'encumbrance' alive, and a release that results in its extinguishment" as a "formalistic distinction," asserting that the tax law should not be concerned with whether the taxpayer's rights are "passed to a stranger or to a person already having a larger 'estate.' "[17] *Ferrer,* a carefully reasoned case gaining additional authority because it came from the court that was the major source of the "disappearing asset" cases, proved to be a turning point in this area; and in deciding whether a contract or other business relationship was sold or exchanged, later decisions have played down or wholly disregarded the fact that it was "terminated" rather than kept alive.[18] In a number of other post-*Ferrer* disappearing asset cases, capital gain treatment has been denied on the ground that the transferor's rights did not constitute "property" within the meaning of IRC §1221 or represented only an opportunity to earn income from personal services or because the payment was a substitute for future income.[19] Thus, the "formalistic distinction" between two-party and three-party transactions that was criticized in *Ferrer* is fast becoming a footnote to history.

Moreover, if a gain or loss is attributable to the cancellation, lapse, expiration, or other termination of the taxpayer's rights or obligations with respect to "actively traded" personal property other than stock (e.g., com-

---

[14] General Artists Corp. v. CIR, 205 F.2d 360 (2d Cir.), cert. denied, 346 US 866 (1953).

[15] CIR v. Starr Bros., 204 F.2d 673 (2d Cir. 1953). As to distributors with a substantial capital investment in the distributorship, this result was later altered by IRC §1241, discussed infra ¶26.4.

[16] CIR v. Pittston Co., 252 F.2d 344 (2d Cir.), cert. denied, 357 US 919 (1958).

[17] CIR v. Ferrer, 304 F.2d 125, 131 (2d Cir. 1962).

[18] See, e.g., Turzillo v. CIR, 346 F.2d 884 (6th Cir. 1965) (proceeds received in settlement of litigation over rights in employment contract and stock options; held, sale or exchange to extent received for options); Anderson v. US, 468 F. Supp. 1085 (D.Minn. 1979) (amount received for release of taxpayer's right of first refusal qualified as capital gain); Sirbo Holdings, Inc. v. CIR, 509 F.2d 1220 (2d Cir. 1975) (payments received by landlord to release tenant from obligation to restore leased premises to former condition held ordinary income; no mention of disappearing asset theory).

[19] See Vaaler v. US, 454 F.2d 1120 (8th Cir. 1972) (payment for cancellation of general insurance agency contract constituted compensation for right to earn income from personal services); Furrer v. CIR, 566 F.2d 1115 (9th Cir. 1977), cert. denied, 437

modities, futures, and options), IRC §1234A, enacted in 1982, treats the gain or loss as though incurred on the sale of a capital asset if the underlying property is (or on acquisition would be) a capital asset in the taxpayer's hands. Thus, if the taxpayer realizes a capital gain on selling a contract for the future *delivery* of German marks, and suffers a loss on settling a similar contract to *purchase* German marks by making a cash payment to the other party, the loss is a capital loss even though the transaction effected a "termination" rather than a "sale" of the purchase contract.

6. "Sale or Exchange" vs. License or Lease. When property is transferred subject to a reservation of rights in the transferor, the transaction's tax status may be ambiguous. If it is classified as a sale or exchange, the transferor's adjusted basis is offset against the amount realized, and the difference can qualify for capital gain or loss treatment if the transferred property is a capital asset or qualifies for the hotchpot established by IRC §1231. If, on the other hand, the transaction is classified as a license or lease, the transferor must report the amount received as ordinary income, subject to depreciation or amortization if the property qualifies for such deductions. Similar problems in classifying borderline transactions are encountered in other areas of the tax law,[20] but the distinction between sales and licenses is especially troublesome when taxpayers claim capital gain treatment for amounts received from transferees of patents, copyrights, franchises, or other intangible assets, if the payments are dependent on the transferee's use of the property and are not limited in amount.

The principal litigated issues can be grouped under three headings, though the facts of many cases overlap these categories:

1. *Contingent payments.* At an early date, the IRS regularly argued that capital gain treatment for payments contingent on the transferee's sales or profits from the transferred property was inconsistent with the anti-bunching function of the capital gain provisions, since these payments—royalties, in common usage—were by their nature spread out over a period of years. Had this theory carried the day, virtually no transfers of patents, copyrights, franchises, or similar assets would have qualified for capital gain treatment since the difficulty of ascribing a value to these intangibles usually impels the parties to employ a royalty arrangement. Largely for this reason, the courts regularly rejected the IRS position; and the IRS now acknowledges that patent and copyright royalties can qualify for capital gain treatment.[21]

US 903 (1978) (damages awarded to sales manager for breach of agency contract by insurance company not paid for "property").

[20] See, e.g., supra ¶22.6 (sale vs. mortgage).

[21] Rev. Rul. 60-226, 1960-1 CB 26, 27 (copyrights); Rev. Rul. 58-353, 1958-2 CB 408 (patents).

Although the issue is settled for conventional royalty payments received for the use of patents and copyrights, less common arrangements may be characterized as licenses rather than sales. In 1969, for example, the Tax Court held that a purported sale of a going business for installment payments plus a "license royalty" based on the transferee's sales, to be paid annually for ninety-nine years, perpetuated the transferor's interest in the business and therefore required the annual payments to be reported as ordinary income.[22]

The IRS' concession that the transfer of a patent or copyright on a royalty basis can qualify as a "sale or exchange" for capital gain purposes is less important than might appear at first glance, however, because of two explicit statutory provisions, both discussed elsewhere in this work: (1) IRC §1235, under which most patent royalties received by inventors (and certain other persons) qualify for capital gain treatment even if the patent is not a capital asset in the taxpayer's hands; and (2) IRC §1221(3), denying capital gain status to copyrights, literary and musical compositions, and similar assets if held by the person whose personal efforts created the property or by certain other persons.[23]

2. *Geographical and field-of-use restrictions.* Taxpayers owning patents, copyrights, and other intangibles often grant licenses that are limited to specified geographical areas (e.g., the United States) and/or fields of use (e.g., book publication or motion-picture production). The IRS' original position was that geographical and functional divisions were hallmarks of a license, producing ordinary income; but this theory was rejected by the courts, which held that the transfer of exclusive rights to a patent, copyright, or trademark could be a sale for tax purposes even if restricted to a geographical area or prescribed field of use.[24]

3. *Reservations of control.* Geographical and field-of-use restrictions are often accompanied by provisions requiring the assignee to adhere to quality and other standards prescribed by the assignor, designed both to insure the continued flow of income from the assigned rights and to prevent debasement of the assignor's name, symbols, and product. In the litigated cases, the courts had difficulty finding "a legitimate place to draw the line between the reservation of sufficient rights and restrictions to protect [the taxpayer's] continuing financial interest and the reservation of rights to continuing participation in the business on such a scale that it cannot properly be said that there was a sale." [25] But this area is now largely preempted by the statutory rules of IRC

---

[22] Nassau Suffolk Lumber & Supply Corp. v. CIR, 53 TC 280 (1969) (Acq.).

[23] Infra ¶27.8; supra ¶25.7.

[24] See, e.g., Rainier Brewing Co. v. CIR, 7 TC 162 (1946) (Nonacq. as to this issue) (geographical division of trade names), aff'd per curiam, 165 F.2d 217 (9th Cir. 1948).

[25] US v. Wernentin, 354 F.2d 757, 766 (8th Cir. 1965) (transfer of Dairy Queen franchise resembled lease more than sale, as indicated by agreement and conduct of parties; lessor's active continuing interest in development and guidance of lessee's

§1235, relating to patents, and IRC §1253, relating to franchises, trademarks, and trade names.[26]

7. Bootstrap Sales—Prices and Payment Contingent on Future Profits. Capital assets are ordinarily sold for a fixed price, and if credit is extended by the seller, the buyer is usually personally liable for the unpaid balance. In commercial contexts, however, property is sometimes sold for a price determined in part by the buyer's future profits or the productivity of the transferred asset, to a buyer who assumes no personal liability for the unpaid balance or has no assets other than the transferred property. Carried to its logical extreme, a bootstrap purchase may entail a price wholly dependent on future profits to a buyer who makes no down payment, assumes no personal liability for the scheduled payments, and either supplies no managerial skill or is to be compensated before computation of the profits from which the payments are to be made. When the seller reports the profits on a transaction of this type as capital gain, the IRS is understandably restive, since there is no bunching of income, the seller remains fully subject to downside risks, and the arrangement resembles a joint venture between two parties to exploit the transferred property and share the profits.

In the fountainhead of learning on this subject, however, the Supreme Court held that a once-popular type of bootstrap sale to a tax-exempt organization generated capital gain for the sellers. In *CIR v. Brown*—usually known as the *Clay Brown* case, in honor of the lead plaintiff in the Tax Court—the transaction entailed the sale of a closely held corporation to a tax-exempt organization for $1.3 million (which was found by the Tax Court to be "within a reasonable range" in light of the corporation's earnings and net worth), of which $5,000 was payable from the company's assets and the balance was to be paid within ten years solely from earnings.[27] As prearranged, the exempt buyer liquidated the corporation and leased its assets to a newly organized corporation, owned by the seller's attorneys, for 80 percent of the operating profits, computed before depreciation and taxes. The exempt organization was required to pay 90 percent of the amount received by it to the selling shareholders to apply to the sales price.

---

business held incompatible with capital gain treatment of payments; extensive review of cases); see also Condé Nast Publications, Inc. v. US, 38 AFTR2d 5796 (S.D.N.Y. 1976) (not officially reported) (payments received by assignor from assignee of dress pattern business qualified only in part as capital gains), rev'd in part and remanded, 575 F.2d 400 (2d Cir. 1978) (on facts, taxpayer did not have any significant continuing interest or participation in assignee's business, but only the right to protect value of retained rights).

[26] For IRC §§1235 and 1253, see infra ¶¶27.8 and 26.5, respectively.

[27] CIR v. Brown, 380 US 563 (1965).

Under this arrangement, the business profits realized by the lessee operating company were offset in large part, if not entirely, by its deductions for depreciation and the rent paid to the exempt lessor; the rents were received tax-free by the lessor; and the selling shareholders, who received the lion's share of the business profits, offset the basis of their stock against the payments and reported the balance as long-term capital gain. Because the business profits were virtually untouched by taxation while traveling through the lessee and lessor, the selling shareholders were paid off faster (and paid their taxes sooner) than would have been possible under a similar arrangement with a taxable buyer.

The down payment in *Brown* was not only nominal but came from the transferred company's assets; the purchase price was evidenced by a nonrecourse promissory note; and the business was to be managed by the principal selling shareholder (the famous Clay Brown) at a specified salary. Thus, the transaction was as close to a perfect bootstrap for the buyer as could be devised. For practical purposes—and aside from taxes—the arrangement resembled an announcement by the selling shareholders that they would draw $1.3 million out of the business and then donate the husk to the exempt organization as a charitable contribution.

The Supreme Court, however, held that the shareholders in *Clay Brown* could report their profit as long-term capital gain. In so holding, the Court stressed the factual finding by the Tax Court that the sale price was "within a reasonable range" in the light of the company's earnings and net worth; pointed out that the shares had in fact appreciated in value over a period of years, as contemplated by the capital gain provisions; held that the term "sale" was used by IRC §1222(3) in its common and ordinary meaning; and concluded that the transaction in the case was a "sale" in which the shareholders realized gain "upon the enhanced value of a capital asset." [28] The Court also observed that requiring "a financially responsible buyer who undertakes to pay the purchase price from sources other than the earnings of the assets sold or to make a substantial down payment seems to us at odds with commercial practice and common understanding of what constitutes a sale" and that if such a rule was to be imposed, Congress was the proper governmental agency to do so.[29]

Although a 1969 statutory change eliminated the appeal of *Clay Brown* transactions to tax-exempt organizations,[30] it did not undercut the Court's decision; and *Clay Brown* transactions are still feasible with buyers who have operating loss carryovers that can be applied against the business profits or who are subject for other reasons to low tax rates. If the purchase price is

---

[28] Id. at 573.

[29] Id. at 575.

[30] See IRC §§512(b)(3)(B)(ii), 514.

excessive, however, it has been held that *Clay Brown* applies only to the reasonable portion and that the excess must be reported as ordinary income.[31]

8. Transaction Related to Prior Sale or Exchange. In two categories of transactions, both important though of uncertain scope, the courts related current receipts to an earlier sale or exchange, so that capital gain or loss treatment results even though the current transaction, if viewed in isolation, does not satisfy the "sale or exchange" requirement of IRC §1222.

1. *Open transaction cases.* The first category consists of so-called open transaction cases, in which the taxpayer sells or exchanges property under a contract calling for a series of variable or contingent payments, usually geared to the gross receipts, profits, or production generated by the transferred property. If the contract rights cannot be valued with reasonable accuracy, the seller's gain or loss cannot be computed in the year of the sale; but when the payments are received, they enjoy the same status—usually capital gain—that they would have occupied if received in the earlier year.[32]

2. *Relation back to earlier transaction.* In the second category of cases, a sale or exchange in an earlier year determines how a later transaction is to be characterized; in effect, the courts dispense with the requirement of a technical sale or exchange in the later year in order to relate its events to the earlier capital gain/loss transaction. The leading case in this area is *Arrowsmith v. CIR,* in which the Supreme Court held that taxpayers who reported capital gain on the liquidation of a closely held corporation were required to treat their subsequent payment of unpaid corporate obligations as a capital loss (despite the absence of a sale or exchange at that time), since payment of the obligations by the corporation before liquidation would have reduced the taxpayer's capital gain on the liquidation.[33]

¶26.2 RETIREMENT OF BONDS AND OTHER OBLIGATIONS

Section 1232(a)(1) provides that amounts received on the retirement of certain bonds and other evidences of indebtedness "shall be considered" as having been received in exchange for the bonds, with the result that the taxpayer realizes capital gain or loss if the obligation is a capital asset in his

---

[31] Berenson v. CIR, 507 F.2d 262 (2d Cir. 1974) (remanding case to divide purchase price between amount attributable to accumulated value of transferred property when sold and amount attributable to buyer's "extra purchasing power" by virtue of tax-exempt status); for the proceedings on remand, see 612 F.2d 695 (2d Cir. 1980).

[32] See supra ¶23.13 (open vs. closed transactions).

[33] Arrowsmith v. CIR, 344 US 6 (1952), supra ¶25.13.

hands. By giving the retirement the status of a "statutory sale," IRC §1232(a)(1) dispenses with the need for a technical sale or exchange, thus avoiding an anomalous disparity between a bond that is sold by the holder just before retirement and one that is held until retirement. Retirements that are outside the scope of IRC §1232(a)(1), however, are subject to *Fairbanks v. United States,* holding that the redemption of a bond is not a "sale or exchange" thereof.[34] Because the *Fairbanks* rule applies when IRC §1232(a)(1) is inapplicable, the following self-contained limits on IRC §1232(a)(1) should be noted:

1. Section 1232(a)(1) applies only to evidences of indebtedness issued by corporations and governmental bodies, not to those issued by individuals and partnerships.
2. Even in the case of corporate and governmental debtors, IRC §1232(a)(1) applies only to "evidences of indebtedness," not to open-account loans and similar claims.
3. Section 1232(a)(1) applies only to amounts received on the "retirement" of a bond or other evidence of indebtedness. In *McClain v. CIR,* the Supreme Court held that the term "retirement" is broader than "redemption," so that it includes payments by a financially embarrassed obligor to retire its bonds for less than their face amount, as well as payments to redeem obligations in accordance with their terms.[35] The difference in *McClain* between the adjusted basis of the bonds and the amount received in settlement, therefore, gave rise to a capital loss rather than to a deduction from ordinary income under the statutory predecessor of IRC §166, relating to bad debts.

¶26.3 WORTHLESS SECURITIES

When property becomes worthless, the taxpayer's loss is usually an ordinary loss, even if the property is a capital asset, because the property has not been "sold or exchanged" within the meaning of IRC §1222. For this reason, a taxpayer who holds deteriorating property until it becomes totally worthless may be better off than if he sells the property for a nominal consideration. Section 165(g)(1) eliminates disparities of this type for an important category of capital assets by providing that if a "security" becomes worthless during the taxable year, the resulting loss shall be treated as a loss from the sale or exchange of the security on the last day of the taxable year.[36] The term

---

[34] Fairbanks v. US, 306 US 436 (1939), discussed supra ¶26.1.

[35] McClain v. CIR, 311 US 527 (1941).

[36] Backstopping IRC §163(g)(1), IRC §166(e) provides that the general rule of

"security" is broadly defined by IRC §165(g)(2) to mean (a) corporate stock; (b) the right to subscribe for or receive corporate stock; and (c) bonds, debentures, notes, certificates, or other evidences of indebtedness issued by a corporation or by a government or political subdivision thereof, with interest coupons or in registered form.

The following limits on the scope of IRC §165(g)(1) should be noted:

1. Section 165(g)(1) applies only to securities issued by corporations or political bodies. A loan to an individual or to a partnership will give rise to a bad-debt deduction from ordinary income when it becomes worthless, although a sale before it became worthless would have produced a capital loss. This disparity is eliminated for taxpayers other than corporations if the worthless obligation is a "nonbusiness debt," since IRC §166(d) then imposes short-term capital loss treatment; but even in this situation there is a residual disparity, since a sale of the claim would have produced either a long-term or short-term capital loss, depending on the holding period.

2. Even if the borrower is a corporation or a political body, IRC §165(g)(1) does not apply to loans if there is no evidence of indebtedness or if the evidence of indebtedness is not coupon-bearing or in registered form. When IRC §165(g)(1) is inapplicable, the taxpayer's deduction on worthlessness is governed by IRC §166(a) (relating to bad debts), subject to the restriction of IRC §166(d) described in the preceding paragraph.

3. When IRC §165(g)(1) applies, the worthless security is treated as though it had been sold on the last day of the taxable year in which it became worthless, which may give the taxpayer a long-term capital loss even if a sale a few days earlier would have resulted in a short-term capital loss.

4. By virtue of IRC §165(g)(3), the general rule of IRC §165(g)(1) is ordinarily inapplicable if the taxpayer is a domestic corporation and the worthless securities were issued by an "affiliated" corporation (as defined). The restriction of IRC §165(g)(3) serves to approximate the treatment that would have been accorded to the loss if it had been incurred directly by the taxpayer.

5. Section 165(g)(1) is also limited by IRC §1244, which allows losses on so-called small-business stock to be deducted from ordinary income, up to $50,000 ($100,000 for husband and wife filing a joint return) per taxable year.

¶26.4 CANCELLATION OF LEASES AND DISTRIBUTORSHIPS

When a contract is terminated or cancelled in exchange for a payment by one contracting party to the other, it is at least arguable that the recipient of

---

IRC §166, permitting a reduction for bad debts, does not apply to debts evidenced by "securities" as defined by IRC §165(g)(2)(C).

the payment has not engaged in a "sale or exchange" of his rights under the rescinded contract, since they do not survive the transaction. Section 1241 gets the taxpayer over the "sale or exchange" hurdle in this situation if the payment is received by (a) a lessee for the cancellation of a lease or (b) a distributor of goods for the cancellation of a distributor's agreement, provided he has a substantial capital investment in the distributorship.

Section 1241 is now of minor importance, since the "disappearing asset" theory that it supersedes has been significantly curtailed by the courts;[37] and payments to lessees for the cancellation of leases have been held by the courts to qualify for capital gain or loss treatment independently of IRC §1241.[38] Moreover, being addressed only to the "sale or exchange" prerequisite to capital gain or loss treatment, IRC §1241 does not prevent the IRS from relying on the "substitute for ordinary income" ground for denying capital gain treatment when appropriate.[39] Finally, since IRC §1241 is explicitly limited to payments received by lessees and distributors, it has no bearing on contract termination payments received by lessors and manufacturers from their lessees and distributors, which are likely to be treated as substitutes for ordinary income.[40]

¶26.5 FRANCHISES, TRADEMARKS, AND TRADE NAMES

1. Introductory. When a taxpayer receives periodic payments contingent on the productivity or use of transferred property, the IRS has traditionally argued that the payments do not constitute capital gains because they do not entail a bunching of income into a single year. If the transferor not only arranges for payment in installments over a period of years but also retains supervisory authority over the transferee's business practices in the interim, resistance by the IRS to capital gain treatment is ordinarily even stiffer, on the theory that the continuing relationship is typical of a license or joint venture and correspondingly antithetical to the statutory requisite of a "sale or exchange" of the property.

After a series of inconclusive skirmishes involving these issues in the courts, Congress intervened in 1969 by enacting IRC §1253, which deals separately with retained powers and contingent payments. As to retained powers, IRC §1253(a) provides that a transfer of a franchise, trademark, or

---

[37] See CIR v. Ferrer, 304 F.2d 125 (2d Cir. 1962), discussed supra ¶26.1.

[38] CIR v. Golonsky, 200 F.2d 72 (3d Cir. 1952), cert. denied, 345 US 939 (1953); CIR v. McCue Bros. & Drummond, Inc., 210 F.2d 752 (2d Cir.), cert. denied, 348 US 829 (1954); Miller v. CIR, 48 TC 649 (1967) (Acq.).

[39] See supra ¶25.12, 26.1.

[40] See Hort v. CIR, 313 US 28 (1941), discussed supra ¶25.12.

trade name shall not be treated as a sale or exchange of a capital asset if the transferor retains "any significant power, right, or continuing interest" (as defined) with respect to the subject matter of the transferred property. As for contingent payments, IRC §1253(c) provides that amounts received on account of a transfer, sale, or other disposition of a franchise, trademark, or trade name shall be treated as received from the sale or other disposition of a noncapital asset if contingent on the "productivity, use, or disposition" of the transferred property.

Section 1253(b)(1) defines the term "franchise" to include agreements giving one of the parties the right to distribute, sell, or provide goods, services, or facilities within a specified area. Transfers of franchises to engage in professional sports are excluded by IRC §1253(e), but franchises to operate sports facilities for the public are within the statutory coverage. The term "trademark" means "any word, name, symbol, or device or any combination thereof adopted and used by a manufacturer or merchant to identify his goods and distinguish them from those manufactured or sold by others." [41] The Senate Finance Committee's report on IRC §1253 states that the term "trade name" includes a "trade brand." [42]

2. Retained Powers. If the transferor of a franchise, trademark, or trade name retains "any significant power, right, or continuing interest," the transaction does not qualify for capital gain or loss treatment under IRC §1253(a), even if some or all of the payments are fixed in amount, rather than contingent, and are paid in a lump sum. Under IRC §1253(b)(2), the forbidden rights include (1) a right to disapprove assignments of the interest; (2) a right to terminate the transfer at will; (3) a right to prescribe quality standards for the products, services, and promotional equipment and facilities; (4) a right to require the transferee to sell or advertise only the transferor's service and products; (5) a right to require the transferee to purchase substantially all supplies and equipment from the transferor; and (6) a right to payments contingent on productivity, use, or disposition of the subject matter of the transferred interest if they are a substantial element of the transfer agreement.[43] In addition to these specific instances of a forbidden "significant power, right, or continuing interest," attention must be given to the reference in the Senate Finance Committee's report to participation by the transferor in the transferee's business operations by sales promotion, management training, "and other forms of continuing assistance." [44]

---

[41] Trademark Act of 1946, §45, 60 Stat. 427, 443.

[42] See S. Rep. No. 91-552, reprinted in 1969-3 CB 423, 557.

[43] See Prop. Regs. §1.1253-1(d).

[44] S. Rep. No. 91-552, supra note 42, at 555; see Prop. Regs. §§1.1253-1(d)(8), 1.1253-1(d)(9).

3. Contingent Payments. Even if the transferor of a franchise, trademark, or trade name escapes the ordinary-income rule of IRC §1253(a) by relinquishing all significant powers, rights, and interests, IRC §1253(c) provides that amounts contingent on "productivity, use, or disposition" of the transferred interest are to be treated as received from the sale or other disposition of a noncapital asset. Section 1253 does not define the phrase "contingent on the productivity, use, or disposition," but the Senate Finance Committee explains the statutory language as follows:

> Contingent payments would include continuing payments (other than installment payments of a principal sum agreed upon in the transfer agreement) measured by a percentage of the selling price of products marketed or based on the units manufactured or sold, or any other similar method based upon production, sale or use, or disposition of the franchise, trademark, or trade name transferred.[45]

4. Transfers Outside the Scope of IRC §1253. Section 1253 denies capital gain/loss treatment on the transfer of franchises, trademarks, and trade names if the transferor retains significant powers or receives contingent payments, but it does not explicitly deal with other transfers of such interests. To qualify for capital gain/loss treatment, therefore, transfers that are outside the scope of IRC §1253 are subject to the general capital gain and loss rules requiring a "sale or exchange" of a "capital asset."

5. Tax Treatment of the Transferee. Section 1253(d) provides rules for the transferee of a franchise, trademark, or trade name that are roughly parallel to the rules governing the transferor. First, amounts paid or incurred that are contingent on the productivity, use, or disposition of the transferred interest can be deducted by the transferee under IRC §162, relating to trade or business expenses. Second, if the transfer is subject to IRC §1253(a), noncontingent payments discharging a principal sum agreed upon in the transfer agreement are, in general, deductible over an appropriate period of years. This result is accompanied by three rules: (1) A single payment made in discharge of the principal sum is deductible ratably over a ten-year period or the life of the agreement, whichever is shorter; (2) payments that are part of a series of approximately equal payments over either the life of the agreement or a period of more than ten years are deductible when made; and (3) other payments are deductible in the years specified by the regulations, consistent with the preceding principles.

---

[45] S. Rep. No. 91-552, supra note 42, at 556; see also Prop. Regs. §1.1253-1(e). Although IRC §1253(c) disqualifies only contingent payments, IRC §§1253(b)(2)(F) and 1253(a) seem to disqualify *all* payments unless the contingent payments, if any, are modest when compared to any fixed payments.

¶26.6 MISCELLANEOUS "STATUTORY SALES"

The Code contains many other "statutory sale" provisions, requiring certain transactions to be treated as sales or exchanges, whether or not they are encompassed by the normal meaning of these terms. Provisions of this type that are discussed elsewhere in this work, either because of their specialized character or because they not only create "statutory sales" but also provide for capital gain or loss treatment even if the transferred property is not a capital asset, cover (1) involuntary conversions,[46] (2) short sales,[47] (3) lapse of options to buy or sell property,[48] (4) transfers of all substantial rights to patent,[49] and (5) timber, coal, and iron ore.[50]

¶26.7 HOLDING PERIOD FOR CAPITAL GAIN AND LOSS TREATMENT

1. Introductory. On the sale or exchange of a capital asset, the taxpayer realizes long-term capital gain or loss if the asset was held for more than one year and short-term capital gain or loss if it was held for one year or less.[51] The one-year dividing line between long-term and short-term transactions was established by the Tax Reform Act of 1976, supplanting a six-month bench mark that had existed from 1942 to 1976. The six-month period was retained, however, for transactions in commodities futures subject to the rules of an organized exchange.[52] When recommending adoption of the current one-year holding period, the House Ways and Means Committee said:

> A distinction is made between short-term and long-term capital gains with respect to two major considerations. . . .
>
> First, the special capital gains treatment is provided for long-term gains in recognition of the fact [that] the gain on the sale of an asset which is attributable to the appreciation in value of the asset over a long period of time otherwise would be taxed in one year, and, in the case of an individual, at progressive rates.
>
> Second, it is argued that there should be special tax treatment for

---

[46] For IRC §1231, see infra ¶¶27.1, 27.2 (preliminary hotchpot), 27.3 (regular hotchpot).

[47] For IRC §1233, see infra ¶27.7.

[48] For IRC §1234, see supra ¶25.10.

[49] For IRC §1235, see infra ¶27.8.

[50] For IRC §631, see infra ¶27.3.

[51] IRC §§1222(1), 1222(2) (short-term capital gain and loss); IRC §§1222(3), 1222(4) (long-term capital gain and loss).

[52] IRC §1222, final sentence.

> gains on assets held for investment but not on those held for speculative profit. The underlying concept is that a person who holds an investment for only a short time is primarily interested in obtaining quick gains from short-term market fluctuations which is a distinctively speculative activity. In contrast, the person who holds an investment for a long time probably is basically interested fundamentally in the income aspects of his investment and in the long-term appreciation in value.[53]

Since corporate income above $100,000 is not subject to a progressive rate schedule, the anti-bunching function of the holding period is primarily concerned with individual taxpayers and small corporations; and individuals get the benefit of the capital gain deduction of IRC §1202 even if the tax on any bunched income is moderated by the general income-averaging provisions of IRC §§1301–1305.[54] Moreover, capital gains qualify for the reduced rate whether they accrue gradually, result from a sudden spurt in value, or reflect the final outcome of a series of ups and downs occurring at irregular intervals during the taxpayer's holding period.

2. Computation of Holding Period. An easily forgotten aspect of the holding period specified by IRC §1222 is that property must be held for *more than* one year to qualify for long-term treatment. In computing the elapsed time, the day of acquisition is disregarded but the day of sale is included.[55] Thus, property purchased on January 1, 1983 cannot be sold until January 2, 1984 if a long-term transaction is desired. Since fractions of a day are not counted, a sale on January 1, 1984 would not qualify even if it occurred at a later hour than the purchase on the previous January 1.

Property is generally treated as acquired and disposed of when title passes or the benefits and burdens of ownership are transferred, whichever occurs first, even though payment is deferred to a later date.[56] In the case of transactions effected through brokers on an organized stock exchange, for example, the customer's order is executed on the "contract" or "trade" date, but delivery and payment take place on the "settlement date," currently five business days later. It is the former date that controls for holding period purposes: The period begins the day after the purchase order is executed and ends on the day the sale order is executed. In the case of sales on the last few days of a calendar year, the holding period may end on or before December 31; but if the taxpayer is on the cash basis, gain will not be *realized* until January, since that is when the broker credits the proceeds to the taxpayer's account. A taxpayer who

[53] H. Rep. No. 94-658, reprinted in 1976-3 CB (Vol. 2) 695, 1033.

[54] For IRC §§1301–1305, see infra ¶39.5.

[55] Fogel v. CIR, 203 F.2d 347 (5th Cir. 1953).

[56] See generally supra ¶22.2.

wants to recognize the transaction in December, however, can instruct the broker to make a "cash" or "next day" sale (so that payment is available on or before December 31) rather than a "regular way" sale. A cash-basis taxpayer who sells at a *loss* on December 31, however, sustains the loss in that year within the meaning of IRC §165(a) even though the payment is not made until January.[57]

3. Split Holding Period. If a number of assets are sold at the same time, as in the case of a going business, the holding period must be computed separately for each asset.[58] On a sale of recently constructed property, a split holding period is appropriate, derived by allocating the gain either on a percentage basis or, if the components have appreciated or depreciated at different rates, among the components so as to take account of their divergent contributions to the aggregate gain or loss.[59]

4. Identification of Property Sold. When a taxpayer sells part of a mass of fungible assets acquired on different dates and at different prices (e.g., 100 shares from a 1,000-share holding), the shares to be transferred can be designated by reference to the date of acquisition or other identifying characteristics. When identification is impossible, the principles employed in determining the cost or other basis of the transferred shares are also applicable in determining their holding period.[60]

5. Short Sales. To cope with tax-avoidance transactions, IRC §1233 prescribes three special rules, summarized below,[61] for determining whether certain short sales result in short-term or long-term treatment.

¶26.8 OPTIONS, SALES AGREEMENTS, AND ESCROWS

The holding period for an asset does not ordinarily terminate when the owner grants an option on the property, even if exercise of the option is probable and actually occurs; similarly, the optionee's holding period for the property does not ordinarily commence until the option is exercised.[62]

---

[57] Rev. Rul. 70-344, 1970-2 CB 50.

[58] See Williams v. McGowan, 152 F.2d 570 (2d Cir. 1945), discussed supra ¶25.11.

[59] See Aagaard v. CIR, 56 TC 191, 207 (1971) (Acq.) (allocation based on percentage of completion in absence of evidence of other factors, such as cost); Rev. Rul. 75-524, 1975-2 CB 342 (percentage of cost).

[60] Treas. Regs. §1.1223-1(i).

[61] Infra ¶27.7.

[62] See Helvering v. San Joaquin Fruit & Inv. Co., 297 US 496 (1936).

A contract to sell property is sometimes accompanied by an escrow agreement, under which the seller deposits a deed, stock certificates and stock transfer powers, or other documents to effect the transfer against the buyer's certified check and evidences of indebtedness for any deferred payments. If the postponed closing is subject to genuine conditions, such as a government agency's approval or a lender's consent, the seller's holding period ends (and the buyer's begins) only when the condition is satisfied and the transfer is consummated.[63] The seller's holding period may terminate earlier, however, if an escrow arrangement serves only as a security device, or is a mere attempt to extend the seller's holding period, since the arrangement is then analogous to a sale with payment deferred to a future time.[64]

The principles applicable to escrow arrangements also apply to contracts to sell that call for postponed closings, especially in real estate transactions, where it is important to distinguish between options and unconditional contracts to sell land. Under state law, the execution of a land sale contract often passes equitable title to the purchaser, notwithstanding conditions requiring the seller to discharge liens or provide title abstracts; in these circumstances, and especially if the buyer takes immediate possession, the buyer's holding period starts (and the seller's ends) when the contract is executed.[65] If, however, under state law the contract is an option or is wholly executory or the burdens and benefits of ownership do not pass until the closing, the holding period's commencement or termination is correspondingly delayed.[66]

¶26.9 INHERITED PROPERTY

Prior to 1971, a person receiving property from a decedent was deemed to have acquired the property on the date of the decedent's death for purposes of determining whether a subsequent sale generated long-term or short-term capital gain or loss. In order to minimize the estate's income taxes, therefore, executors sometimes held property until capital gains could be treated as long-term gains, even though the property would otherwise have been sold earlier to meet estate tax liabilities or other debts.

Congress eliminated this problem in 1971 by enacting IRC §1223(11), which provides that when property acquired from a decedent has a basis in the recipient's hands determined under IRC §1014 (usually its date-of-death value), the recipient will be considered to have held the property for more than

---

[63] Dyke v. CIR, 6 TC 1134 (1946) (Acq.) (ICC approval required; later escrow delivery date controlling).

[64] Hoven v. CIR, 56 TC 50 (1971) (Acq.).

[65] Boykin v. CIR, 344 F.2d 889 (5th Cir. 1965).

[66] Borrelli v. CIR, ¶72,178 P-H Memo TC (1972) (agreement was option or executory contract until buyer made down payment).

one year, regardless of the actual length of the holding period. Thus, a sale immediately after the decedent's death will generate long-term capital gain or loss if the property is a capital asset.

¶26.10 "TACKED" HOLDING PERIOD

In computing the holding period for an asset, the taxpayer is often allowed by IRC §1223 to add ("tack on") the time he held other property or the time another taxpayer held the same or other property, ordinarily because the property disposed of has a "substituted" or "carryover" basis.[67]

The extremely diverse circumstances resulting in a tacked holding period can be grouped in the following categories:

1. Property With Substituted Basis. Section 1223(1) provides that, in determining the holding period of property *received* in an exchange, the taxpayer may include the period for which he held the property *surrendered* in the exchange if (1) the property received has, for the purpose of computing gain or loss, the same basis in whole or in part as the property exchanged and (2) the latter property was either a capital asset or an IRC §1231 asset at the time of the exchange. Thus, IRC §1223(1) usually permits use of a tacked holding period for stock received in tax-free merger, spin-off, or other corporate reorganization; property received in an exchange for property of a like kind pursuant to IRC §1031 (relating to exchanges of property held for investment or productive use); property into which similar property was involuntarily converted pursuant to IRC §1033 (relating to condemnations and certain other involuntary conversions), and property received in many other types of tax-free exchanges resulting in a substituted basis.

If the taxpayer sells a personal residence at a profit and avoids recognition of some or all of the gain by acquiring another residence within the time prescribed by IRC §1034, IRC §1223(7) provides that the holding period of the new residence shall include the holding period of the old one.[68]

2. Property With Carryover Basis. Section 1223(2) authorizes a tacked holding period that includes the holding period of the taxpayer's predecessor in title if the taxpayer's basis for the property is the same, in whole or in part, as the transferor's basis. A common example is property received by gift, where the taxpayer uses a carryover basis under IRC §1015. The reference in IRC §1223(2) to "the same basis in whole or in part" as that of the transferor clearly embraces situations in which the transferor's basis is increased pursuant to

[67] For substituted and carryover basis, see supra ¶¶23.1, 23.5.

[68] For IRC §1034, see supra ¶24.5.

IRC §1015(d) to take account of the gift tax paid on the transfer, as well as a basis that has been adjusted during the donee's ownership by capital outlays or depreciation deductions.

If, however, the donee incurs a loss on the transaction and is required by IRC §1015(a) to use the fair market value of the property at the time of the gift in determining the amount of the loss, an IRS ruling takes the position that the donor's holding period cannot be tacked to the donee's own holding period because the donee in this situation does not use a carryover basis.[69] Property acquired in a part-sale part-gift transaction has been held to qualify for tacking, however, notwithstanding the fact that the regulations sometimes determine the transferee's basis in such circumstances by the price paid rather than by the statutory measure of IRC §1015(b), viz., the transferor's basis increased (decreased) by any gain (loss) recognized in the transfer;[70] and this rejection of the regulations is based on a rationale that could also apply to the gift situation described in the previous sentence.

3. Miscellaneous Transactions in Securities and Commodities. Section 1223 also authorizes a tacked holding period for stock or securities received in tax-free distributions and other nontaxable transactions.[71] If stock or securities are acquired by the exercise of rights, however, IRC §1223(6) explicitly provides that the taxpayer's holding period begins on the date the rights are exercised, so that the holding period of the rights cannot be tacked on to that of the stock or securities.

SELECTED BIBLIOGRAPHY

Hall, Tax Aspects of Franchising Operations, 20 Tul. Tax Inst. 102 (1971).

Morreale, Patents, Know-How and Trademarks: A Tax Overview, 29 Tax Lawyer 553 (1976).

Waggoner, Eliminating the Capital Gains Preference, Part I: The Problem of Inflation, Bunching, and Lock-In, 48 U. Colo. L. Rev. 313 (1977).

---

[69] See I.T. 3453, 1941-1 CB 254, declared obsolete by Rev. Rul. 69-43, 1969-1 CB 310.

[70] See Treas. Regs. §1.1015-4; Citizens Nat'l Bank of Waco v. US, 417 F.2d 675 (5th Cir. 1969) (questioning validity of Treas. Regs. §1.1015-4).

[71] IRC §§1223(3), 1223(4), 1223(5), 1223(8), and 1223(10).

CHAPTER 27

Quasi-Capital Assets, Unstated Interest, and Other Specially Treated Items

¶27.1 QUASI-CAPITAL ASSETS—THE IRC § 1231 HOTCHPOT

1. Introductory. Section 1231, a provision that is unusually favorable to taxpayers, ordinarily permits gains on the sale or exchange of property used in the taxpayer's trade or business and held for more than one year to be reported as capital gains, even though this type of property is described by IRC §1221(2) and hence does not constitute a capital asset. On the other hand, if the taxpayer realizes losses on the sale or exchange of assets of this type, they are usually treated as ordinary losses under IRC §1231. Similar best-of-both-worlds treatment is accorded to gains and losses from the involuntary conversion of property used in the taxpayer's trade or business and of capital assets held for more than one year (after being tested in a preliminary hotchpot) [1] and, by virtue of IRC §1231(b), to certain transactions in timber, coal, iron ore, livestock, and unharvested crops.

Although the result of the hotchpot calculation for practical purposes is often a net capital gain (or ordinary loss) in the aggregate, IRC §1231 does not explicitly call for netting the hotchpot transactions against each other; and individual items may require separate treatment after their nature has been determined by the hotchpot. An individual's casualty losses, for example, can be deducted only if itemized, even if the loss transaction goes into the hotchpot. Moreover, all hotchpot gains, rather than the net amount of the hotchpot computation, enter into gross income in determining whether a return must be filed and other issues geared to the amount of gross income realized by the taxpayer.

The origin of IRC §1231 lies in the congressional response to problems of the shipping industry in the early days of World War II. Because many companies were realizing involuntary profits when their vessels were requisitioned for military use or destroyed in action while heavily insured, Congress was persuaded that it was unfair to tax these unsolicited profits at the high wartime rates. While the capital gains rate seemed appropriate in the gain situation, it was thought desirable to preserve the ordinary loss deduction for taxpayers not benefiting from wartime inflation. From this specific rationale, IRC §1231 was expanded beyond involuntary conversions, and it continued in force long after its wartime impetus disappeared.

2. Included Items. The IRC §1231 hotchpot includes the taxpayer's recognized gains and losses on two categories of assets, provided the property was held for more than one year.

1. *Depreciable and real property used in the taxpayer's trade or business, if sold, exchanged, requisitioned, or condemned.* Land goes into the hotchpot; but assets other than real property are included only if "of a character which is subject to the allowance for depreciation," a phrase that includes property subject to cost recovery allowances under IRC §168. This phrase also embraces fully depreciated property,[2] but not goodwill or other nondepreciable business assets. The term "property used in the trade or business" is specially defined by IRC §§1231(b)(2) through 1231(b)(4) to encompass timber, coal, iron ore, livestock, and unharvested crops in certain circumstances. Property

[1] See infra ¶27.2.

[2] For the inclusion of fully depreciated property, see Treas. Regs. §1.1231-1(c)(1).

used in the trade or business is also included in the hotchpot if the gain or loss results from partial or complete destruction or from theft (whether the property is insured or not), unless the outcome of a preliminary hotchpot consisting solely of these items is a net loss.[3]

2. *Capital assets, if requisitioned, condemned, or involuntarily converted as a result of destruction, in whole or in part, or theft.* Inclusion of casualty and theft gains and losses in the IRC §1231 hotchpot, however, depends on the outcome of the "preliminary hotchpot" described below.

Gains and losses on both the foregoing types of assets go into the IRC §1231 hotchpot only if they are "recognized" and "taken into account" in computing gross or taxable income. These restrictions have the effect of excluding (a) nondeductible losses (e.g., losses on the sale of the taxpayer's personal residence and losses incurred in transactions between related taxpayers subject to IRC §267); (b) nonrecognized gains and losses (e.g., on "like kind" exchanges under IRC §1031 and on tax-free corporate reorganizations); and (c) gains on sales reported on the installment method under IRC §453, except to the extent reported during the current year. But losses are included in the hotchpot even if the taxpayer's right to deduct them is restricted by IRC §1211, limiting the extent to which capital losses can be deducted from ordinary income.

Once the items going into the IRC §1231 hotchpot have been identified, the gains and losses are separately totalled. If the gains exceed the losses, all hotchpot gains and losses are considered as gains and losses from the sale or exchange of capital assets held for more than one year. If the gains are equal to or less than the losses, the hotchpot gains and losses are treated as ordinary income and ordinary losses. Although IRC §1231 consistently refers to "gains and losses" in the plural, the hotchpot may include only a single item, which will result in either long-term capital gain or ordinary loss, as the case may be.

After the taxpayer's hotchpot gains and losses are characterized as capital or ordinary by IRC §1231, their role in computing gross and taxable income is prescribed by the Code's more general operating rules. Thus, capital gains and losses resulting from IRC §1231 are aggregated with the taxpayer's other capital gains and losses in determining the amount to be deducted under IRC §1202 (deduction of 60 percent of net capital gain) or §1211 (limitation on deductibility of capital losses); conversely, if the hotchpot items result in ordinary income and loss, these amounts are aggregated with the taxpayer's other income and deductions in computing gross and taxable income.

---

[3] See infra ¶27.2.

3. Excluded Items. In keeping with the basic principle that ordinary business profits cannot be reported as capital gains, IRC §§1231(b)(1)(A) and 1231(b)(1)(B) exclude from the IRC §1231 hotchpot inventory property and property held primarily for sale to customers in the ordinary course of the taxpayer's business. Being excluded from capital asset status by IRC §1221(1) and from quasi-capital asset status by IRC §1231(b)(1), these assets generate ordinary income and loss on a sale or exchange except in the rare case of a conversion to investment or business-use status.[4]

Section 1231(b)(1)(C) also excludes from the IRC §1231 hotchpot copyrights; literary, musical, or artistic compositions; letters; memoranda; and similar property, if held by a taxpayer described in IRC §1221(3) (relating to property held by the author, donees of the author, and certain other persons). Like a merchant's stock in trade, items of this type cannot constitute either capital assets under IRC §1221 or quasi-capital assets under IRC §1231. Since, however, they are excluded from the hotchpot only if held by the persons specified by IRC §1221(3), IRC §1231 encompasses copyrights, musical compositions, and similar assets used by motion-picture companies, theatrical producers, publishers, and other taxpayers in their businesses.

4. Effect of Timing. Because the IRC §1231 hotchpot includes all qualified gains and losses recognized during the taxable year, a hotchpot is computed separately for each year. As a result, the tax treatment of hotchpot items is often dramatically affected by whether two or more transactions occur in the same year or are instead spread out over time. For example, an individual taxpayer with a $10,000 gain on the condemnation of a personal residence by a public agency and a $10,000 loss on the sale of a business warehouse would report the profit as a long-term capital gain and the loss as an ordinary loss if they occurred in separate years, assuming that both assets were held for more than one year and that there were no other hotchpot transactions in either year. But if the profit and the loss are incurred in the same year, both go into the IRC §1231 hotchpot; and since the gain does not exceed the loss, both are treated as noncapital transactions.

5. Exclusion of Recaptured Gain From Hotchpot. The regulations provide that the recapture rules of IRC §§1245 and 1250 apply to gain on the disposition of assets that otherwise constitute IRC §1231 property.[5] This means that only the residual gain (if any) that is not converted into ordinary income by the recapture provisions goes into the hotchpot. Thus, if a taxpayer

---

[4] For difficulties distinguishing assets "used in the trade or business" from those "held for sale to customers," see supra ¶25.5.

[5] See Treas. Regs. §§1.1245-6(a), 1.1250-1(c)(1). For other recaptured gain, see Treas. Regs. §§1.1251-1(e)(1), 1.1252-1(d)(1); and see generally IRC §64.

realizes a gain of $1,000 on the sale of depreciable business property held for more than one year, $600 of which is recaptured as ordinary income by IRC §1245, only the remaining $400 of gain goes into the IRC §1231 hotchpot, not the full $1,000.

¶27.2 INVOLUNTARY CONVERSIONS—THE "PRELIMINARY HOTCHPOT"

Section 1231 provides for a preliminary hotchpot, limited to recognized gains and losses from the involuntary conversion—as a result of casualty or theft, but not condemnation—of property used in the taxpayer's trade or business and capital assets held for more than one year. Section 165(h)(1) imposes two floors on the deduction of casualty losses relating to personal property owned by individuals ($100 per casualty and 10 percent of adjusted gross income), both of which must be applied before the loss is put into the preliminary hotchpot, since it encompasses only recognized losses.[6] The casualties bringing the preliminary hotchpot into play are identical with those listed in IRC §165(c)(3), viz., "fire, storm, shipwreck, or other casualty" and theft. Because destruction by fire is probably the most common occasion for a preliminary hotchpot, it is called "the firepot" by aficionados of New York University Law School's LL.M. program in taxation—a crowd much addicted to insider code words.

The items going into the preliminary hotchpot are aggregated in order to determine their fate, pursuant to the final sentence of IRC §1231(a). If the recognized gains on preliminary hotchpot items equal or exceed the losses, both are promoted from the preliminary hotchpot to the main event, where they are aggregated with all other IRC §1231 hotchpot items. Thus, if a taxpayer realized a gain of $5,000 on collecting insurance for damage by fire to a summer cottage in the same year as a $10,000 loss on the sale of a warehouse used for business purposes and a $10,000 gain on condemnation of a personal residence, the $5,000 gain on the summer cottage would move from the preliminary hotchpot into the final hotchpot; and the latter would show an excess of recognized gains ($15,000) over losses ($10,000). As a result, all three transactions would be treated as sales of capital assets.

---

[6] See Treas. Regs. §1.1231-1(g), Example (4). For the floors, see infra ¶18.4. The 10 percent floor on the deduction of the nonbusiness casualty losses, enacted in 1982, can create a circularity problem, since the amount going into the preliminary hotchpot depends on the taxpayer's adjusted gross income; but if the loss comes out of the preliminary and final hotchpots as a long-term capital loss, the resulting deduction allowed by IRC §1202(b) affects the amount of adjusted gross income by virtue of IRC §62(3), and then in turn alters the 10 percent AGI floor on the amount going into the hotchpot, and so on.

On the other hand, if the recognized losses in the preliminary hotchpot exceed the gains, the final sentence of IRC §1231 excludes both from the regular hotchpot. Since these items are outside its scope, IRC §1231 does not prescribe their actual tax treatment, and it is necessary to look elsewhere for the governing principles. Business property used in the trade or business is a noncapital asset by virtue of IRC §1221(2), so gains and losses thereon are ordinary rather than capital items. Gains and losses on the involuntary conversion of capital assets by casualty or theft will also generate ordinary income and ordinary loss if excluded from the IRC §1231 hotchpot, since these events do not constitute "sales or exchanges" within the meaning of IRC §1222.[7]

¶27.3 TIMBER, COAL, IRON ORE, LIVESTOCK, AND UNHARVESTED CROPS

1. Timber. The general rules of IRC §1221 or §1231 apply to the sale or exchange of standing timber and timberlands, provided the property is a capital asset or a hotchpot asset in the taxpayer's hands and is not held for sale to customers in the ordinary course of the taxpayer's business.[8]

In addition to these standard rules, IRC §631(a) permits taxpayers who own timber or a contract to cut timber to treat the cutting of the timber, either for sale or for use in the taxpayer's trade or business, as a sale or exchange, provided the timber or cutting contract has been owned for more than one year; and IRC §631(b) permits the disposition of timber under a contract by which the taxpayer retains an economic interest in the timber to be treated as a sale or exchange. By conferring "sale or exchange" status on transactions of these types, IRC §§631(a) and 631(b) lay the foundation for capital gain and loss treatment under IRC §1231, provided the taxpayer's hotchpot transactions in the aggregate show a net gain.

2. Coal and Iron Ore. If an owner of coal (including lignite) held for more than one year disposes of it by a contract under which an economic

---

[7] See Helvering v. William Flaccus Oak Leather Co., 313 US 247 (1941), discussed supra ¶26.1.

[8] For sales of timber qualifying under IRC §1221 or §1231, see Rev. Rul. 62-82, 1962-1 CB 155 (sale by landowner for lump sum); Rev. Rul. 62-81, 1962-1 CB 153 (sale by landowner for payments over a period of sixty years); Rev. Rul. 78-267, 1978-2 CB 171 (IRC §483, relating to unstated interest, applicable to Rev. Rul. 62-81). For cases determining whether timber was held for sale to customers in the ordinary course of the taxpayer's business, see Kirby Lumber Corp. v. Phinney, 412 F.2d 598 (5th Cir. 1969) (lumber company's sale of hardwood, incidental to development of pine forest, qualified for capital gain under IRC §1231).

interest in the coal is retained, the transaction is treated by IRC §631(c) as a sale, with the result that the gain or loss enters into the IRC §1231 hotchpot.[9] Applicable even if the coal is held for sale to customers in the ordinary course of the taxpayer's business,[10] IRC §631(c) thus creates the possibility of capital gain treatment for royalty payments that would otherwise constitute ordinary income. In general, royalties under leases failing to meet the standards of IRC §631(c) constitute ordinary income, subject to depletion.[11]

The benefits of IRC §631(c) are also enjoyed by lessors of iron ore mined in the United States.

3. Livestock and Unharvested Crops. Section 1231(b)(3) throws gains and losses from certain cattle, horses, and other livestock into the hotchpot and unharvested crops sold with a farm held by the taxpayer for more than one year qualify as "property used in the trade or business" in applying IRC §1231, by virtue of IRC §1231(b)(4).

¶27.4 ORIGINAL-ISSUE DISCOUNT (OID)

1. Introductory. When a non-interest-bearing obligation is issued at a discount, the difference between the amount payable at maturity and the issue price—usually labeled original-issue discount (OID)—is the economic equivalent of interest to both the borrower and the lender. In 1965, the Supreme Court ruled in *United States v. Midland-Ross Corp.* that an investor could not report gain on selling a discount obligation as capital gain where the profit was concededly equal to the earned discount as of the date of sale, unaffected by market fluctuations.[12] By the time the issue in *Midland-Ross* reached the Supreme Court, Congress had already intervened to achieve the same result for taxable years subject to the 1954 Code by enacting the predecessor of IRC §§1232(a)(2) and 1232A. This legislation, which was in force from 1954 to 1969, segregated the interest component of an investor's gain on the sale, exchange, or retirement of a discount obligation (using a formula based on the amount of OID and the elapsed time from the date of issue) and required it to be treated as ordinary income. The balance (if any) of the taxpayer's gain qualified for capital gain treatment.

---

[9] See IRC §1231(b)(2).

[10] See Treas. Regs. §1.631-3(a)(2).

[11] For examples, see Rev. Rul. 77-84, 1977-1 CB 173.

[12] US v. Midland-Ross Corp., 381 US 54 (1965).

2. OID on Corporate Obligations Issued Between May 27, 1969 and July 2, 1982. The 1954 approach to OID, which did not require earned discount to be taken into income until the obligation was sold, exchanged, or retired, was superseded in 1969 by the enactment of an annual accrual system. This provision, applicable to corporate bonds and other evidences of indebtedness issued after May 27, 1969,[13] requires the holder (even if on the cash basis) to report a ratable share of the OID in each taxable year. Since the investor has not received the amount that must be reported, his basis is correspondingly increased;[14] thus, gain on disposing of the obligation will not be taxed to the extent that it reflects the discount previously taken into income. In computing a subsequent purchaser's ratable share of earned discount, an appropriate adjustment is made if he pays more than the issue price plus the discount includable in the income of any previous holder. If the buyer pays par or more for the obligation, he will not have to report any OID.

3. OID on Bonds Issued After July 1, 1982. Under the 1969 ratable amortization rules, discount obligations offered tax advantages to both issuers and holders, when compared with interest-bearing bonds, under which interest accrues at a constant rate. To eliminate this disparity, Congress adopted the constant-interest principle, embodied in IRC §1232A, for discount bonds issued after July 1, 1982. The 1982 rules are illustrated by Examples 27-1 through 27-3, based on a "zero coupon" bond with an issue price of $1,000, a 30-year term, and a stated redemption price at maturity of $66,212, which reflects a yield to maturity of 15 percent of the issue price, compounded annually. The OID, determined under IRC §1232A, is $65,212, which must be amortized by the investor annually at the rate of 15 percent of the "adjusted" issue price. The adjusted issue price, which increases each year, is the original issue price, plus the previous year's OID. (If the discount bond were not a *zero* coupon obligation but instead paid some interest before maturity, the amounts actually paid would be subtracted in determining computing the adjusted issue price.) As indicated by Example 27-1, the amount of OID includable in the original holder's gross income rises annually, because the investment grows at the rate of 15 percent per year, applied to the issue price plus the unpaid but implicit yield during prior years. For convenience, Example 27-1 omits the details for years 4 through 29.

---

[13] For the status of corporate bonds issued after 1954 but before May 28, 1969, as well as that of federal and foreign governmental bonds issued after 1954 but before July 1, 1982, see IRC §1232(a)(2)(B), which is similar to the 1954 rules.

[14] IRC §1232A(c)(5).

Example 27-1

Inclusion of Original-Issue Discount in Original Investor's Income

Year	*Issue Price*	*Previous OID Inclusion*	*Adjusted Issue Price*	*OID Inclusion (15% of adjusted issue price)*
1	$1,000	$ 0	$1,000	$ 150
2	1,000	$150	$1,150	173
3	1,000	$323	$1,323	198
24–29	1,000	(Details omitted)		55,755
30	1,000	$56,576	$57,576	8,636
				$65,912

If the investor sells the bond for $18,000 at the end of the third year, his basis, determined under IRC §1232A(c)(5), is $1,521, and the gain is $279, computed as shown in Example 27-2.

Example 27-2

Sale of Discount Obligation

1. Unadjusted basis (cost)	$1,000
2. Plus: Amount included in income (OID for Years 1–3: $150 + $173 + $198, from Example 27-1)	521
3. Adjusted basis (end of third year)	$1,521
4. Gain:	
a. Sales price..	$1,800
b. Less: Adjusted basis (line 3)	1,521
c. Long-term capital gain under IRC §1232(a)(2)(A)	$ 279

In accordance with IRC §1232A(a)(6), the purchaser's yearly portion of OID is reduced ratably by the amount the purchase price exceeds the issue price plus the previously included OID, as shown in Example 27-3.

Example 27-3

Inclusion of Original-Issue Discount in Subsequent Purchaser's Income

1. Cost of bond to purchaser	$1,800
2. Less: Issue price ($1,000) plus previously included OID of prior holder ($521)	1,521
3. Balance	$ 279
4. Line 3 divided by number of years (27) from date of purchase to stated date of maturity	$10.33
5. Purchaser's portion of OID for year 4 (adjusted issue price (line 2) × 15%) minus reduction (line 4)	$217.82

Similar calculations are required for later years to determine the amount of OID includable in the purchaser's gross income so that, at maturity, the purchaser has fully amortized the amount shown on line 3 of Example 27-3.

4. Gain on Disposition of Corporate Obligations Issued After May 27, 1969. In conjunction with the 1969 legislative decision requiring investors to include OID in gross income ratably during the term of the debt, Congress enacted IRC §1232(a)(2)(A), which provides that gain realized on the sale or exchange (including, by virtue of IRC §1232(a)(1), retirement) of corporate bonds issued after May 27, 1969 (and government bonds, issued after July 1, 1982) is to be considered long-term capital gain if the obligation was held by the taxpayer for more than one year. Since the investor must now include OID in income as it accrues, any gain realized on the sale of the obligation reflects market fluctuations rather than earned discount.

Because the capital gain result prescribed by IRC §1232(a)(2)(A) presupposes that the taxpayer is required to report OID ratably by IRC §1232A, obligations that are not subject to the latter provision are also outside the scope of IRC §1232(a)(2)(A). These obligations include (a) post-1954 but pre-July 1, 1982 securities issued by a government or political subdivision and corporate obligations issued after 1954 but before May 28, 1969, which are subject to IRC §1232(a)(2)(B), and (b) obligations issued by private individuals and other noncorporate persons and pre-1955 corporate obligations, which are wholly outside the scope of IRC §1232 and remain subject to the nonstatutory case law, including the *Midland-Ross* case.

5. Intent to Call Before Maturity. The capital gain principle established by IRC §1232(a)(2)(A) for sales and exchanges of corporate obligations and post-July 1, 1982 government obligations is not fully applicable if at the time of original issue the obligor intended to call the obligation before maturity. In this event, the investor's gain on disposition must be reported as ordinary income to the extent of any OID not previously taxable to him or other holders.[15] In the absence of a restriction of this type, an obligor might cooperate with related investors to issue discount obligations with a long term, subject to an understanding that the debt would be called before maturity; the investors would then be able to report part of the OID as capital gain.

6. Restrictions on Scope of IRC § 1232. Except for bonds with interest coupons detached, IRC §1232 is wholly inapplicable to obligations that (a) are not capital assets in the taxpayer's hands; (b) are issued by individuals and other noncorporate and nongovernmental obligors; or (c) do not constitute "bonds, debentures, notes, or certificates or other evidences of indebtedness," such as open-account indebtedness. Restriction (a) is primarily applicable to dealers in securities, who are not concerned with IRC §1232's distinction between ordinary income and capital gain because their transactions generate ordinary income in any event. Restrictions (b) and (c) have the effect of remanding the taxpayer, for a determination of tax treatment, to the nonstatutory case law, the most important features of which are that the retirement of an obligation does not qualify as a "sale or exchange" within the meaning of IRC §1222 [16] and that the *Midland-Ross* case denies capital gain treatment when earned discount is realized on a sale of the obligation.[17]

7. Optional Inclusion in Income of Increasing Redemption Value of Discount Obligations. Cash-basis taxpayers who own non-interest-bearing obligations issued at a discount that are redeemable for fixed amounts increasing at stated intervals can elect under IRC §454 to report the increase in the redemption price as income in the taxable year of the increase. Series E United States savings bonds are now the principal subject of this provision.

¶27.5 BONDS WITH UNMATURED COUPONS DETACHED

The purchaser of a coupon bond from which some of the unmatured coupons have been detached occupies, for practical purposes, the same position as an investor who buys a discount obligation from the issuer: No interest

[15] See Treas. Regs. §§1.1232-3(a)(3) through 1.1232-3(a)(5).

[16] See Fairbanks v. US, 306 US 436 (1939), discussed supra ¶26.1.

[17] US v. Midland-Ross Corp., supra note 12.

will be received on the stripped bond for the period represented by the detached coupons, but the difference between the price paid by him and the redemption price at maturity will compensate the bondholder for the use of his capital during the interim. Thus, a stripped bond is a do-it-yourself discount obligation, and gain realized on its disposition is the functional equivalent of interest for the period covered by the detached coupons. For this reason, IRC §1232B(a) treats the excess of the redemption price over the purchase price as original issue discount which must be periodically included in the purchaser's income. Section 1232B(b) requires the seller to (1) include any accrued interest to the date of sale in income; (2) increase his basis accordingly; (3) calculate gain by allocating the basis between the bond and the retained coupons; and (4) treat the retained coupons as OID bonds. Similar rules apply if the seller retains the bond and sells the coupons.

¶27.6 UNSTATED INTEREST ON DEFERRED PAYMENT SALES

1. Introductory. When property is sold or exchanged under a contract deferring some or all of the payments for more than one year, IRC §483 imputes interest at a rate to be determined by the Treasury (currently 10 percent compounded semiannually) if the contract itself does not provide for interest equaling or exceeding the so-called test rate (currently 9 percent simple interest).

Before 1964, when IRC §483 was enacted, it was ordinarily possible to sell a capital asset under a contract for deferred payments without stated interest and to report the excess of the sales price over the adjusted basis of the property as long-term capital gain in its entirety, even though part of the amount received was the functional equivalent of interest. Thus, if a capital asset with an adjusted basis of $40,000 and a fair market value of $50,000 was sold for $100,000, to be paid at the end of ten years without interest, the seller could ordinarily report the $60,000 profit as long-term capital gain even though the arrangement was tantamount to selling the property for its fair market value of $50,000, to be paid at the end of ten years with interest at 7 percent compounded semiannually. If the transaction had been cast in this alternative form, however, the taxpayer would have realized $10,000 of capital gain and $50,000 of ordinary income. The pre-1964 advantage to the seller of using the "no interest" device was accompanied by a loss of any interest deduction so far as the buyer was concerned; but if the property was depreciable, this disadvantage was in turn counterbalanced by the buyer's right to depreciate the entire purchase price ($100,000).

These anomalies of pre-1964 law impelled Congress to enact IRC §483, under which a portion of the $100,000 payment in the example described above is treated as interest, taxable as ordinary income to the seller and deductible by the buyer under IRC §163.

2. Included Transactions. Section 483 applies to sales and exchanges of property, but it does not cover loans of money, deferred-compensation arrangements, or other nonproperty transactions, even if the terms of payment contain a hidden interest factor. These transactions are presumably excluded from IRC §483 because they ordinarily lack any capital gain potential for the recipient of the deferred payments. Since "exchanges" of property, as well as sales, are subject to IRC §483, interest may be imputed to the transferor even though no cash is paid and the exchange is otherwise nontaxable, such as an exchange of stock for other stock in a tax-free merger if part or all of the new stock is to be paid at a future time.[18]

Section 483(f) establishes five exceptions to the principles set out above:

1. *De minimis transactions.* To avoid the imputation of interest in relatively small transactions, IRC §483 is inapplicable to any payment if the sales price of the property, determined at the time of the sale or exchange, cannot exceed $3,000.
2. *Ordinary-income transactions.* The seller is exempted if the entire gain on the transaction would be considered as ordinary income.
3. *Carrying charges.* To avoid a collision with IRC §163(b), an older provision recognizing the hidden interest in certain installment sales, the buyer is not subject to IRC §483 if IRC §163 applies.
4. *Patent royalties.* Section 483(f)(4) exempts payments pursuant to a transfer "described in section 1235(a)," permitting amounts received for certain transfers of patents to be reported as long-term capital gain.
5. *Annuities.* If liability for a payment depends on an individual's life expectancy and is subject to IRC §72, relating to annuities, IRC §483(f)(5) removes it from IRC §483's jurisdiction.

3. Unstated interest. Once it has been determined that a contract is subject to IRC §483, a "test rate" of interest is applied to determine whether "total unstated interest" exists. If application of the test rate discloses the presence of total unstated interest, its amount is recomputed by reference to a higher rate of interest (which might be termed the "imputation" rate), and the recomputed amount is then used to determine the portion of each payment that is to be treated as interest under IRC §483.

1. *Total unstated interest—the test rate.* Since the ultimate goal of IRC §483 is to impute interest only if the parties to the contract failed to provide for adequate interest on their own motion, Congress had to prescribe a method for separating the sheep from the goats. The chosen method was to authorize the Treasury to prescribe a test rate of interest to determine whether unstated

[18] See Solomon v. CIR, 570 F.2d 28 (2d Cir. 1977) (tax-free merger; IRC §483 applied to additional stock paid under formula relating to future value of acquiring corporation's stock).

interest was implicit in the contract. Thus, if the parties provide for interest at (or above) the test rate, currently 9 percent simple interest per year, no additional interest is imputed by IRC §483. But if the rate chosen by the parties is below the test rate, additional interest is imputed in order to bring the rate up to the imputation rate, currently 10 percent compounded semiannually.

Sometimes, a mathematical computation is required to determine whether the threshold test is satisfied. For example, property is sold for $4,000, to be paid at the rate of $1,000 annually for four years with a balloon interest payment of $900 with the final installment of principal, the effective rate of interest implicit in the balloon payment is not apparent to the naked eye, and hence it cannot be readily compared with the test rate. Instead of computing the effective rate, however, the taxpayer can follow the shortcut method set out in the regulations, under which the present value of the deferred payments of principal and interest is computed by reference to discount tables based on the test rate. In making this computation, principal payments due not more than six months after the date of the sale or exchange are excluded and interest payments due within the six-month period are taken at face value.

If the present value as thus determined equals or exceeds the face amount of the deferred payments of principal, the effective rate buried in the contract equals or exceeds the test rate; and no imputation of interest is warranted. On the other hand, if the present value of the deferred payments is less than the face amount of the deferred principal payments, the implicit contract rate is inadequate; and the taxpayer must then move on to the second computation, involving the imputation rate.

Use of the test rate illustrated by Example 27-4, which is based on the facts described above ($4,000, to be paid in four equal annual installments, with interest of $900 payable with the fourth installment) (Case A), as well as with a contract for identical deferred payments of principal but with a balloon interest payment of $1,000 (Case B).

Example 27-4

Unstated Interest—Application of Test Rate

	Case A	*Case B*
1. Sum of payments to which IRC §483 applies	$4,000	$4,000
2. Present value of deferred payments:		
a. Present value of line 1 payments—$1,000 × 3.28758 (Table IX, Col. (a), factor for 4 years)	$3,288	$3,288

	Case A	*Case B*
b. Present value of stated interest—$900 (Case A) or $1000 (Case B) × 0.73529 (Table VII, Col. (a), factor for 45-51 months)	662	735
c. Sum of lines 2a and 2b	$3,950	$4,023
3. Total unstated interest (line 1 less line 2c)	$ 50	$ -0-

Note: Tables VII and IX are set out in Treas. Regs. §1.483-1(g).

As the computation in Example 27-4 indicates, the stated interest in Case A ($900) reflects an effective rate that is below the test rate, so that the contract is subject to the imputation of interest. The *amount* of the total unstated interest (line 3) is not material; the test rate is applied only to determine whether there is *some* total unstated interest.

In Case B, the rate implicit in the stated interest of $1000 exceeds the test rate, so that the contract in Case B is not subjected to the imputation rate.

2. *Total unstated interest—the imputation rate.* If the test rate computation discloses any "total unstated interest" (as in Example 27-4, Case A above), the amount thereof is computed using the imputation rate—currently 10 percent compounded semiannually. The recomputed amount is determined by the same principles used in applying the test rate; but since the imputation rate is higher than the test rate, the second computation necessarily results in an increase in the total unstated interest. When the imputation rate is applied to Case A of Example 27-4, for example, the total unstated interest rises from $50 to $238, as shown by Example 27-5.

Example 27-5
Unstated Interest—Application of Imputation Rate to Example 27-4, Case A

1. Sum of payments to which IRC §483 applies		$4,000
2. Less:		
a. Present value of line 1 payments—$1,000 × 3.15279 (Table IX, Col. (b), factor for 4 years)	$3,153	
b. Present value of stated interest—$900 × .67684 (Table VII, Col. (b), factor for 45–51 months)	609	
c. Sum of lines 2a and 2b		3,762
3. Total unstated interest		$ 238

3. *Allocation of total unstated interest.* The third step in applying IRC §483 is to spread the total unstated interest, computed by reference to the imputation rate, over the deferred payments in order to identify the amount of interest hidden in each payment. The allocation is effected on a pro rata basis,[19] although it would be more accurate to use a method reflecting the discounted value of each deferred payment. Using the pro rata method prescribed by the regulations, each of the four deferred payments in Case A of Example 27-5 is treated as interest to the extent of $59.50, computed as follows:

$$\$1{,}000 \times \$238/\$4{,}000 = \$59.50$$

Over the life of the contract, therefore, the aggregate amount treated as interest will be $1,138 (total unstated interest of $238 plus $900 stated interest).

4. Indefinite Payments. The computations described above and illustrated by Examples 27-4 and 27-5 assume that the deferred payments are fixed as to time, liability, and amount when the sale or exchange occurs, since their present value as of that date must be determined in order to apply the test and imputation rates. To avoid the difficult valuation problems that would arise if transactions involving indefinite payments (e.g., contingent on the buyer's attainment of a specified earnings level) had to be fitted into this framework, IRC §483(d) segregates indefinite payments and treats them as though payable under a separate contract.

For example, if the sellers in Cases A and B of Example 27-4 were entitled to receive an additional payment of $1,000 five years after the sale provided the buyer's earnings exceeded those realized during a specified base period, the calculations as to the definite payments would be unaffected; but the additional payment, if earned and paid, would be subjected to the test and imputation of interest as of the payment date.

5. Changes in Contract Terms. Because any interest that is imputed to a series of definite deferred payments is determined and allocated at the time of the sale or exchange, allowance must be made for subsequent changes in the terms of the contract. Pursuant to IRC §483(e), the Treasury has issued a set of complex rules for the recomputation and allocation of the unstated interest if there is a change in liability for any payment of either principal or interest or a change in the relevant amounts or due dates.[20]

6. Transfers of Deferred Payments or Property. Section 483 says nothing about the treatment of the buyer, seller, or transferee if the seller transfers

---

[19] See Treas. Regs. §1.483-1(a)(2).

[20] Treas. Regs. §1.483-1(f); Rev. Rul. 68-247, 1968-1 CB 199.

the right to receive deferred payments under an IRC §483 contract (e.g., by gift, sale, or corporate liquidation) or if the buyer transfers the duty to make the payments (e.g., by selling encumbered property to an assuming transferee); but the regulations contain a set of rules to govern these situations.[21] Briefly summarized, they are as follows:

1. *Transfer by seller.* If the seller transfers the right to receive deferred payments under a contract with total unstated interest, the transfer is treated as the final payment under the seller's contract with the buyer, requiring a recomputation of total unstated interest as though the transfer constituted a change in the terms of the original contract.

2. *Transfer by buyer.* If the buyer transfers the obligation to make deferred payments under a contract with total unstated interest (e.g., by selling the property to a transferee who assumes or takes subject to the obligations), the transferee steps into the shoes of the buyer-transferor and is entitled to the deductions for unstated interest that would have been taken by the buyer-transferor had the transfer not occurred. The buyer-transferor, therefore, cannot take these deductions unless he makes the deferred payments because of a default by the transferee.

7. Ancillary Effects of Unstated Interest. Although primarily intended to prevent unstated interest from being reported as long-term capital gain by the seller of a capital asset, IRC §483 characterizes portions of the deferred payments as interest "for all purposes of the Internal Revenue Code." Being so persuasive, the impact of IRC §483 cannot be exhaustively catalogued;[22] but the following are its principal areas of application:

1. *Impact on seller.* When a portion of a deferred payment is characterized as unstated interest, the seller must not only report it as such but also treat it as interest income in determining personal holding company and Subchapter S status and in determining whether the item constitutes domestic or foreign-source income in computing the foreign tax credit. Since the unstated interest component of the deferred payments is treated as interest, it must be excluded in computing the amount realized for the property; and this in turn will affect the amount of gain or loss on the sale or exchange for such purposes as depreciation recapture under IRC §§1245 and 1250 and the outcome of the IRC §1231 hotchpot.

2. *Impact on buyer.* In addition to permitting deductions under IRC §163, relating to interest, the characterization of part of the deferred payments as interest by IRC §483 affects the buyer by reducing the "cost" of the

[21] Treas. Regs. §1.483-1(f)(6).

[22] See generally Treas. Regs. §§1.483-1(a)(3), 1.483-2(a).

property, which in turn affects the buyer's investment credit, depreciation deductions, gain or loss on a later sale, loss on abandonment, and other tax allowances related to the property's basis.

¶27.7 SHORT SALES OF SECURITIES AND OTHER PROPERTY

1. Introductory. By dealing explicitly with gains and losses from short sales, IRC §1233 clears up several difficulties in fitting short sales into the general capital gain and loss framework. A frequently quoted definition of a short sale by the Supreme Court is:

> As the phrase indicates, a short sale is a contract for the sale of shares which the seller does not own or the certificates for which are not within his control so as to be available for delivery at the time when, under the rules of the [New York Stock] Exchange, delivery must be made.[23]

In point of fact, however, tax-oriented short sales are often made even if certificates for identical securities are in the hands of the taxpayer's broker.

It is not clear that the delivery of securities to close a short sale is a "sale or exchange" within the meaning of IRC §1222, but IRC §1233(a) eliminates this interpretative problem by providing that gains and losses on short sales are to be considered as gains and losses from the sale or exchange of a capital asset if the property used to close the short sale is a capital asset in the taxpayer's hands.

Sections 1233(b) and 1233(d) deal with a number of problems created by tax-oriented short sales of stock, securities, and commodity futures, such as a short sale of securities by a taxpayer with a long position in the same securities (a "sale against the box"), designed to convert a short-term capital gain into a long-term capital gain without running any economic risk in the interim. Manipulations of this type are controlled by three rules (a short-term capital gain rule, an abbreviated holding period rule, and a long-term capital loss rule). These rules come into play only if the taxpayer making a short sale owns (or acquires after the short sale but before it is closed) "substantially identical property"—a term that is limited by IRC §1233(e)(2)(A) to stocks, securities, and commodity futures that are capital assets in the taxpayer's hands.[24]

2. Short-Term Capital Gain Rule. The purpose and operation of the short-term capital gain rule prescribed by IRC §1233(b)(1) are best explained with an example.

---

[23] Provost v. US, 269 US 443, 450-451 (1926).

[24] See Treas. Regs. §1.1233-1(d)(1), which incorporates by reference the concept of "substantially identical stock or securities" as used in IRC §1091 (relating to wash sales), discussed supra ¶24.6.

If stock purchased on January 1 for $100 a share increases in value to $250 a share by December 1 of the same year, a sale to nail down the profit will constitute a short-term transaction. An alternative way of protecting the profit against erosion, however, is to sell the stock short on December 1. The taxpayer will then be unaffected by fluctuations in the market after the short sale, since a decline in the market will improve his short position at the expense of his long position, while a rise in the market will have the opposite effect. Were it not for IRC §1233(b)(1), the taxpayer could claim a long-term capital gain on using the securities purchased on January 1 to close the short sale on January 2 (or later) of the following year, on the theory that this transaction constitutes a sale or exchange of shares held for more than one year.

Section 1233(b)(1), however, provides that a taxpayer making a short sale when he has held substantially identical property for not more than one year must treat any profit on closing the short sale as a short-term capital gain, regardless of the actual holding period for the property delivered to close the sale. The taxpayer described above, therefore, must treat the gain as short-term even though the stock transferred to close the sale was held for more than one year when delivered.

Section 1233(b)(1) applies not only to sales against the box, but also to short sales by a taxpayer acquiring substantially identical securities after the short sale but on or before the closing date. Even if the securities are acquired more than one year after the short sale, so that the taxpayer has been at the risk of the market for that period, any profit on closing the sale is a short-term capital gain. In effect, the taxpayer is not regarded as holding a capital asset until the securities are acquired, and from that date forward he is immune to market fluctuations because of his open short position.

Options to sell stock, securities, or commodity futures at a fixed price ("puts") are also covered by the short-term capital gain rule of IRC §1233(b)(1). If they were exempt, a taxpayer with an unrealized short-term capital gain could protect it by purchasing a put, hold the securities until the one-year period had run, pick up the previously assured profit by exercising the put, and report the gain as long-term capital gain. To forestall this maneuver, the final sentence of IRC §1233(b) provides that the acquisition of an option to sell property at a fixed price shall be considered as a short sale, which is closed either by exercising the option or by failing to exercise it before expiration.

3. Abbreviated Holding Period Rule. In the example above of a short sale against the box, the taxpayer used his long shares to close the short sale. If he had instead purchased additional shares to close the short sale, the holding period of the original shares would commence with the closing of the short sale, by virtue of IRC §1233(b)(2). The purpose of this rule is to eliminate the period during which the taxpayer is immune to market fluctuations in determining whether gain or loss on the ultimate sale of the original shares is attributable to a long-term or short-term investment. To achieve long-term capital gain or loss status, therefore, the taxpayer must expose the original securities to the vagaries of the market for more than one year after *closing* the short sale. The taxpayer gets no credit for the period between acquisition of the securities and the short sale, even though they were subject to market fluctuations during that period.

Like the short-term capital gain rule of IRC §1233(b)(1), the abbreviated holding period rule of IRC §1233(b)(2) applies not only if the taxpayer holds substantially identical securities when making the short sale but also if the securities are acquired after the short sale, but before it was closed. Like the short-term capital gain rule, the abbreviated holding period rule is buttressed by the final sentence of IRC §1233(b), treating the acquisition of a put as a short sale and the exercise or failure to exercise the option within its life-span as closing the sale.

4. Long-Term Capital Loss Rule. To prevent taxpayers with unrealized long-term gains from creating artificial short-term losses by selling short, IRC §1233(d) establishes a long-term capital loss rule. Its function can be illustrated by assuming that a taxpayer holds securities purchased on January 1, 1982 for $100 and that their market value on January 2, 1983 is $250, so that a sale would generate a long-term capital gain of $150. By selling short on January 2, 1983, the taxpayer gains immunity to subsequent market fluctuations; but if the securities rise thereafter to $300, he could—in the absence of the long-term capital loss rule of IRC §1233(d)—purchase securities for $300 to close the short sale (claiming a short-term capital loss of $50) and realize a long-term capital gain of $200 by selling the long shares for $300. Thus, his economic gain of $150 (total proceeds of $250 plus $300, less total paid out of $100 plus $300), which was attributable to the original shares and frozen on January 2, 1983, would be reflected by a long-term capital gain of $200 and a short-term capital loss of $50.

To prevent this manipulation, IRC §1233(d) requires a taxpayer making a short sale when he owns substantially identical property with a holding period of more than one year to report any loss on the short sale as a long-term capital loss, regardless of the holding period of the property used to close the sale. Thus, the taxpayer in the example above would realize a long-term capital loss of $50 on the short sale and a long-term capital gain of $200 on selling the original shares, or a net long-term capital gain of $150.

5. Exceptions. Section 1233 is made inapplicable to hedging transactions in commodity futures by IRC §1233(g).[25] More limited exceptions are created

[25] See Treas. Regs. §1.1233-1(b).

by IRC §§1233(e)(3) and 1233(f) for certain arbitrage operations in commodity futures and securities, by IRC §1233(e)(4) for certain transactions by dealers, and by IRC §1233(c) for certain options to sell property ("puts") acquired on the same day as the property to be used in exercising the option.

¶27.8 TRANSFERS OF PATENT RIGHTS

1. Introductory. In 1950, when Congress enacted IRC §1221(3) to deny "capital asset" status to copyrights and literary compositions held by the author, a similar fate was proposed for inventions and patents by the House of Representatives. But the Senate Finance Committee recommended excising this part of the House bill because "the desirability of fostering the work of [occasional] inventors outweighs the small amount of additional revenue which might be obtained under the House bill," and the legislation as enacted conformed to this recommendation.[26] As a result, inventors continued to qualify for capital gain treatment, provided the invention or patent was a capital asset and the method of disposition constituted a sale or exchange. The "capital asset" category is open primarily to amateur inventors, since professionals usually hold their inventions for sale to customers in the ordinary course of business, though sometimes a professional's invention or patent is used in the taxpayer's trade or business (e.g., a patent-licensing business) and can qualify for quasi-capital asset status under IRC §1231.

Not content with preserving the general provisions of capital gain law for inventors, in 1954 Congress enacted IRC §1235, which provides that a transfer by a "holder" of all substantial rights to a patent shall be considered to be a sale or exchange of a capital asset held for more than one year, whether or not the amounts received are payable periodically during the transferee's use of the patent or are contingent on the productivity, use, or disposition of the transferred property. While IRC §1235 guarantees capital gain treatment to anyone who can meet its condition, including professional inventors, other taxpayers are entitled to capital gain treatment for patents and inventions if they come within the general provisions of law, without any adverse inference from their failure to satisfy the conditions of IRC §1235.[27]

2. Transfers by "Holders" to Unrelated Persons. Section 1235 applies only to transfers of patent rights by a "holder" to a person who is not related to the holder within the meaning of IRC §1235(d). The crucial term "holder" is defined by IRC §1235(b) as an individual (a) whose efforts created the

[26] See S. Rep. No. 2375, 81st Cong., 2d Sess., reprinted in 1950-2 CB 483, 515.
[27] Treas. Regs. §1.1235-1(b).

invention or (b) who acquired an interest therein for money or money's worth, paid to the creator prior to the invention's reduction to practice, and who is neither the creator's employer nor a related person when the rights to be acquired are determined and the amount to be paid is fixed. Even if the taxpayer is a holder, however, the transfer does not qualify for IRC §1235's benefits if it occurs directly or indirectly between "related persons," determined (as of the time of the transfer) by reference to the rules of IRC §267(b), as modified by IRC §1235(d). Section 1235(d) is presumably aimed at such tactics as the conversion of the transferee's manufacturing profits into capital gain for a related transferor by excessively generous royalty terms.

The holder's employer can qualify as a transferee, but then the IRS will scrutinize the transaction closely to determine whether the payments are for transferred patent rights or instead constitute compensation for services.[28] The IRS has attacked sales of patent rights by employees to employers on two grounds: that the employee was hired to invent, so that any patents belonged to the employer and the payments were compensation for the employee's services as an inventor,[29] and that the payments were compensation for general personal services, not conditioned on the transfer of patent rights.[30] In general, payments conditioned on the continued employment of the employee by the employer and/or labeled "compensation" or the like are treated as compensation, while payments that are separable from the employee's regular compensation and conditioned on transfers of inventions or patents qualify for capital gain treatment under IRC §1235, even if the employee agreed in the contract of employment to assign to the employer any patents arising out of his employment.[31]

3. Transfer of "All Substantial Rights." To qualify for preferential treatment under IRC §1235, the holder must transfer "all substantial rights to a patent, or an undivided interest therein which includes a part of all such rights." The regulations provide that "all substantial rights to a patent" means all rights (whether or not then held by the grantor) that are of value at the time of the transfer, that a security interest to secure performance or payment may be retained with impunity, and that all the circumstances must be examined

---

[28] See Treas. Regs. §1.1235-1(c)(2).

[29] See, e.g., Downs v. CIR, 49 TC 533 (1968) (Acq.) (taxpayer hired to reduce employer's concept to practical application; held, compensation); Goldman v. CIR, ¶75,138 P-H Memo TC (1975) (taxpayer hired to improve patents previously acquired from him by employer; he was paid "for his labor and not for the product").

[30] See, e.g., Komarek v. CIR, ¶67,112 P-H Memo TC (1967) (payments were compensation, since made irrespective of whether patents were transferred and conditional on continued employment).

[31] Chilton v. CIR, 40 TC 552 (1963) (Acq.); Melin v. US, 478 F.2d 1210 (Ct. Cl. 1973) (employee not hired to invent).

to determine whether retention of the right to prohibit sublicenses or subassignments or a failure to convey the right to use or sell the patent is substantial.[32]

It is well established that an assignment of an exclusive right to exploit a patent in a single field of use or geographical area may constitute a sale or exchange of a capital asset if IRC §1235 does not apply to the transaction,[33] but the regulations expressly provide that such an assignment is not a transfer of "all substantial rights to a patent." [34] In other respects, however, the principles determining whether all substantial rights have been transferred follow those used to ascertain the existence of a sale or exchange, as opposed to a license, in situations not subject to IRC §1235.

4. Treatment of Payments by Transferee. Although the primary function of IRC §1235 is to permit the *transferor* of a patent to report royalties or other receipts as capital gains when the statutory conditions are satisfied, a by-product is that the *transferee* must treat the payments as the cost of acquiring the patent rather than as royalties.[35] As capital outlays, the payments cannot be deducted currently but must instead be depreciated over the life of the patent.

¶27.9 DEALERS—IDENTIFICATION OF INVESTMENT SECURITIES

Because the status of property under IRC §1221 depends on the purpose for which it is held rather than on the occupation or other characteristics of the owner, it is possible for a taxpayer to hold a particular asset for investment purposes while holding identical property for sale to customers in the ordinary course of business. To prevent self-serving hindsight classifications by dealers in securities, IRC §1236 denies capital gain treatment on the sale or exchange of a security unless it was "clearly identified in the dealer's records as a security held for investment" by the end of the day of acquisition.[36]

Even if properly identified, however, the security cannot qualify for capital gain treatment if it was in fact held for sale at any time after acquisition.

---

[32] Treas. Regs. §1.1235-2(b).

[33] See supra ¶26.1, text at notes 20-26.

[34] Treas. Regs. §1.1235-2(b); Kueneman v. CIR, 68 TC 609 (1977), aff'd, 628 F.2d 1196 (9th Cir. 1980) (extensive review of legislative history and earlier decisions, concluding that geographically limited transfer may or may not qualify under IRC §1235, depending on relative values of rights transferred and retained).

[35] Treas. Regs. §1.1235-1(d).

[36] Floor traders are allowed seven business days to designate stock in which they are registered specialists.

On the other hand, once a security is identified as held for investment, its sale or exchange cannot give rise to an ordinary loss.

¶27.10 REAL PROPERTY SUBDIVIDED FOR SALE

1. Introductory. Section 1237 prescribes a special rule for determining whether a taxpayer holds real property primarily for sale to customers in the ordinary course of his trade or business, under which qualified taxpayers can realize capital gains on selling lots or parcels from a tract held for investment, even though they subdivided the tract and made active efforts to sell the property. To qualify, the taxpayer must establish that (1) the real property in question was never previously held by him primarily for sale in the ordinary course of business (unless it would have been covered by IRC §1237 when so held), (2) no other realty was so held in the year of the sale, (3) no substantial improvements substantially enhancing the value of the lots sold were made to the property by the taxpayer or certain related persons, and (4) the property was either inherited or held by the taxpayer for a period of five years. In more detail, these conditions are as follows:

1. *Property sold—nondealer status.* The first condition, imposed by IRC §1237(a)(1), concerns the tract from which the lot or parcel in question was sold. The taxpayer must show that neither it nor any lot or parcel thereof was ever held by the taxpayer primarily for sale to customers in the ordinary course of business, unless the tract would have been covered by IRC §1237 when so held. In effect, the taxpayer's activities with respect to the tract in all prior years must have been consistent with reporting any profits on sales as capital gains, either under the general capital gain/loss rules or under IRC §1237.

2. *Other real property.* In addition to negating dealer status for the tract from which the lots or parcels were sold, the taxpayer must also show—but only for the year of sale—that he holds no other realty primarily for sale to customers in the ordinary course of his trade or business. In determining whether a taxpayer satisfies this condition, the regulations provide that he is considered as holding property owned individually, jointly, or as a member of a partnership (but not property owned by members of his family, estates, trusts, or corporations) and that the purpose of a prior owner may be indicative of the purpose for which the taxpayer holds a lot.[37]

3. *The substantial-improvement, substantial-enhancement rule.* The most restrictive condition of IRC §1237(a) is that the taxpayer must not have made any "substantial improvement [on the tract] that substantially enhances the value of the lot or parcel sold." This prohibition applies not only to

[37] Treas. Regs. §1.1237-1(b)(3).

improvements made by the taxpayer himself, but also to those made during his ownership (or during a prior period imputed to him by IRC §1232(2), relating to "tacked" holding periods) by (a) members of the taxpayer's family, as defined by IRC §167(c)(4); (b) a corporation controlled by the taxpayer; (c) a partnership of which the taxpayer is a partner; (d) a lessee, if the improvement constitutes income to the taxpayer; or (e) a governmental body, if the improvement constitutes an addition to basis, as in the case of special assessment for paving sidewalks, streets, sewers, etc.[38]

Since improvements are often preconditions to local zoning or subdivision changes, the no-substantial-improvement rule frequently makes it impossible for taxpayers to avail themselves of IRC §1237's benefits. To prevent sidestepping the prohibition by arranging for improvements to be installed by the buyer, the latter's improvements are imputed to the taxpayer by IRC §1237(a)(2) if made pursuant to the contract of sale.

An improvement precludes the use of IRC §1237 only if it (a) is substantial and (b) substantially enhances the value of the lots sold. The regulations provide that the term "substantial improvement" includes, but is not limited to, shopping centers; other commercial or residential buildings; hard-surface roads; sewers; and water, gas, or electric lines; but that it does not include temporary field offices; surveying, filling, draining, levelling, and clearing operations; and minimum all-weather access roads.[39] As to when a substantial improvement "substantially enhances" the value of the lots sold by the taxpayer, the regulations establish a 10 percent bench mark: If the improvements increase the value of the lot by 10 percent or less, they can be disregarded; otherwise, "all relevant factors" determine whether the increase is substantial.[40]

The rigors of the substantial-improvement, substantial-enhancement rule are relaxed by IRC §1237(b)(3) if the affected lot or parcel is held by the taxpayer for at least ten years, a period that includes the holding periods of prior owners if "tacked" by IRC §1223 to the taxpayer's period, as in the case of gifts. If the taxpayer meets this requirement, otherwise substantial improvements can be disregarded if (a) they consist of the building or installation of roads or water, sewer, or drainage facilities; (b) it is shown to the satisfaction of the IRS that, save for the improvement, the benefited lot would not have been marketable at the prevailing local price for similar building sites; and (c) the taxpayer elects not to add the cost of the improvement to the basis of the lot (or any other property owned by the taxpayer) or to deduct it.

4. *Five-year holding period.* Unless the lot or parcel was acquired by inheritance or devise, it must have been held by the taxpayer for a period of

[38] See Treas. Regs. §1.1237-1(c)(2)(i).

[39] Treas. Regs. §1.1237-(c)(4).

[40] Treas. Regs. §1.1237-1(c)(3).

five years. The five-year holding period includes any "tacked" holding period of a prior owner, but this concession may simultaneously disqualify the taxpayer by attributing the prior owner's improvements or dealer status to him.[41]

2. Effect of Subdividing and Sales Activities. If the taxpayer meets the condition set out above, IRC §1237 provides that the lots sold by him "shall not be deemed to be held primarily for sale . . . solely because of the taxpayer having subdivided [the tract that includes the lots] for purposes of the sale or because of any activities incident to such subdivision or sale." This guarded language does not guarantee capital gain treatment; it protects the taxpayer only if his subdividing and related activities are the *sole* basis for denying capital gain treatment. If there is *other* substantial evidence that the property was held primarily for sale, the taxpayer's subdividing and sales activities are no longer neutralized by IRC §1237, and the taxpayer's status then depends on the general capital gain/loss provisions, unaided by IRC §1237.[42]

3. Characterization of Gain. When its conditions are satisfied, IRC §1237 provides that qualified lots or parcels "shall not be deemed" to be held primarily for sale. Although this language could be interpreted to require losses on qualified property to be reported as capital losses, the regulations flatly provide that IRC §1237 does not apply to realized losses,[43] whose status therefore depends on the general rules distinguishing between capital and ordinary losses.

As to gains, IRC §1237 results in capital gain treatment (or inclusion in the IRC §1231 hotchpot) unless more than five lots or parcels are sold or exchanged from the same tract. Starting with the taxable year in which the sixth lot is sold or exchanged, gains on all qualified lots (including the first five, if sold in the same taxable year as the sixth) constitute ordinary income to the extent of 5 percent of the selling price under IRC §1237(b)(1), an amount analagous to a sales commission; the balance is capital gain or goes into the IRC §1231 hotchpot. In computing the ordinary-income component of the taxpayer's gain, IRC §1237(b)(2) in effect marshals the expenses actually incurred in selling each lot against the hypothetical 5 percent sales commission.[44]

---

[41] For attribution of a prior owner's improvements, see Treas. Regs. §1.1237-1(c)(2)(ii), Example; for the imputation of dealer status, see Treas. Regs. §1.1237-1(b)(3), Example.

[42] Treas. Regs. §1.1237-1(a)(3).

[43] Treas. Regs. §1.1237-1(a)4)(i).

[44] See Treas. Regs. §1.1237-1(e)(2)(ii), Example (2).

¶27.11 TRANSFERS OF DEPRECIABLE PROPERTY BETWEEN RELATED TAXPAYERS

Under IRC §1239(a), gain recognized on a sale or exchange of depreciable property between husband and wife, an individual and a controlled corporation, or two corporations controlled by the same individual constitutes ordinary income, even if it otherwise qualifies as capital gain. This provision, which covers indirect as well as direct sales between the specified related parties, was enacted to frustrate the practice of selling depreciable assets with a low basis to a related person, reporting the profit as long-term capital gain and thus enabling the transferee to depreciate the property's stepped-up basis against ordinary income. Such a fresh start is still feasible if the buyer-seller relationship is outside the reach of IRC §1239, but the seller's depreciation deductions may be recaptured as ordinary income by IRC §1245 or §1250.[45]

Section 1239 applies to property that, in the hands of the transferee, is "subject to the allowance for depreciation provided in Section 167," including property that can be either depreciated under IRC §167 or amortized under some other provision, at the taxpayer's election.

SELECTED BIBLIOGRAPHY

Carlson, Income Tax Blue Law: Imputation of Interest Under Section 483, 34 Tax L. Rev. 187 (1979).

Chandler, The Failure of Section 1237 in Dealing With Sales of Subdivided Realty, 60 Minn. L. Rev. 275 (1976).

Landis, Original Issue Discount After the Tax Reform Act of 1969, 24 Tax Lawyer 435 (1971).

Postlewaite, Timber Capital Gains—The Option Rule of Section 631(b), 29 Hastings L.J. 451 (1978).

Whiteside & Gillig, Coal and Conservation—Tax Policy, 64 Ky. L.J. 573 (1976).

---

[45] For the recapture of depreciation by IRC §§1245 and 1250, see infra ¶¶28.2 and 28.5, respectively.

CHAPTER 28

Recapture of Depreciation and Other Tax Allowances

¶28.1 RECAPTURE—INTRODUCTORY

Because gain on the disposition of depreciable assets often represents the recoupment of depreciation and cost recovery deductions that were applied against ordinary income and that, it turns out, exceeded the property's loss of value while in use, IRC §§1245 and 1250 require taxpayers to report gains of this type as ordinary income rather than as capital gains. Although IRC §§1245 and 1250 are concerned with "excess" depreciation and cost recovery deductions, neither provision requires any change in the deductions actually taken; the corrective mechanism is to require taxpayers to report a specified portion of their profit on disposing of the property as ordinary income, even if it would otherwise qualify as a capital gain under IRC §1221 or §1231.

To prevent tax avoidance, IRC §§1245 and 1250 apply to certain dispositions of property even if the taxpayer receives nothing in exchange, such as distributions of depreciated property by corporations to their shareholders. Since there is no "amount realized" in these cases, the property's fair market value is used to determine the amount to be recaptured. Because gain is not ordinarily realized or recognized on these transactions, the resulting tax liability can come as an unpleasant surprise to the taxpayer, particularly since the transaction generates no cash with which to pay the taxes. On the other hand, some transfers (e.g., gifts) are exempt from recapture, but the excess depreciation or cost recovery deductions are held in abeyance and charged against the transferee if and when he or she disposes of the property in a nonexempt transaction. Moreover, some exempt transactions (e.g., an exchange of depreciated property for like-kind property in a transaction qualifying for nonrecognition under IRC §1031) result in shifting the taint from the excessively depreciated property to the replacement property, whose later disposition can generate ordinary income under IRC §1245 or §1250 even though, viewed in isolation, the new property is not itself responsible for any excess depreciation.

Finally, to put IRC §§1245 and 1250 into perspective, the phenomenon of ordinary deductions that can be recouped at a later time as capital gains is by no means confined to depreciation, amortization, and cost recovery deductions, although they are probably the most important examples of this interplay between ordinary income and capital gain. Other examples include advertising and promotional expenses that create goodwill; research expenses that create secret processes and industrial know-how; investment expenses; the cost of materials, supplies, and small tools; and many farm improvement expenditures, to say nothing of misclassified items, such as capital outlays deducted as repairs, acquisition expenses deducted as overhead expenses, and premature claims for abandonment and worthlessness losses.

Congress, however, has not prescribed a comprehensive remedy for this problem, but has instead dealt with it in fits and starts. Specialized recapture provisions requiring taxpayers to report gain on the disposition of property as ordinary income rather than capital gain or to take other remedial steps reflecting particular tax allowances include: (1) IRC §47 (premature dispositions of investment credit property); (2) IRC §1251 (deduction of abnormally large farm losses from nonfarm income); (3) IRC §1252 (deduction of farm expenditures for soil and water conservation, anti-erosion measures, or land clearing under IRC §§175 and 182); (4) IRC §1254 (intangible drilling and development costs); (5) IRC §617 (mine exploration expenditures); and (6) IRC §465(e) (negative at-risk amounts).

¶28.2 RECAPTURE OF DEPRECIATION ON PERSONAL AND CERTAIN OTHER TANGIBLE PROPERTY

1. Introductory. Subject to qualifications set out below, IRC §1245 requires taxpayers to report gain on the sale, exchange, or involuntary conversion of so-called Section 1245 property and Section 1245 recovery property as ordinary income to the extent of the depreciation or cost recovery deductions allowed or allowable since 1962 (or specified later years in the case of certain classes of property), even though the profit otherwise qualifies as capital gain. A similar requirement applies to "any other disposition," including some transactions on which gain is not ordinarily realized or recognized, such as corporate distributions to shareholders, except that the recaptured gain must be computed by reference to the property's fair market value in these situations since there is no "amount realized" on the disposition. The application of these rules entails three basic steps: (1) identification of Section 1245 property and Section 1245 recovery property; (2) determination of whether the property was disposed of in a transaction subject to IRC §1245; and (3) if so, determination of the amount of depreciation or cost recovery deductions subject to recapture.

2. Section 1245 Property. The phrase "Section 1245 property" is defined by IRC §1245(a)(3) to encompass any property of a character subject to the depreciation allowance provided by IRC §167 if it is either (a) personal property or (b) other property (not including buildings or their structural components) that is intangible and meets the additional conditions described below, as well as certain more specialized classes of property, viz., elevators and escalators, and real property amortized under IRC §169, §185, §188, or §190 (relating, respectively, to pollution-control facilities, railroad grading and tunnel bores, child care facilities, and expenditures to remove architectural and transportation barriers to the handicapped and elderly).

1. *Depreciable "character."* The reference in IRC §1245(a)(3) to "property which is or has been property of a character subject to the allowance for depreciation provided in section 167" embraces not only property that is depreciable in the conventional sense but also property that, at the taxpayer's election, can be either depreciated or amortized (e.g., pollution-control facilities subject to IRC §169). The statutory phrase does not cover property subject to neither depreciation nor amortization (e.g., goodwill). Because property is embraced by IRC §1245(a)(3) if it is *or has been* of a depreciable character, depreciation deductions can be recaptured even if the property is converted to a personal use and is no longer depreciable when disposed of; and if the taxpayer holds property with a carryover basis (e.g., property received by gift), this is true, even if the only depreciation deductions were taken by a prior owner.[1]

2. *Personal property.* Section 1245(a)(3)(A) covers "personal property," whether tangible or intangible—provided, of course, it meets the "depreciable character" test just described. To define tangible personal property, the regulations incorporate the definitions used in determining eligibility for the investment credit, summarized elsewhere in this work.[2]

3. *Investment credit realty.* Section 1245(a)(3)(B) covers tangible real property (not including buildings or their structural components), but only if

---

[1] See Treas. Regs. §1.1245-3(a)(3).

[2] Treas. Regs. §§1.1245-3(b)(1), 1.48-1(c); see supra ¶13.1 (investment credit property).

the property's adjusted basis reflects depreciation or amortization while it (or other property by reference to which its basis is determined) was used for the purposes listed in IRC §1245(a)(3)(B)(i) or §1245(a)(3)(B)(iii)—primarily manufacturing, production, extraction, or furnishing transportation or utility services.[3]

3. Section 1245 Recovery Property. The phrase "Section 1245 recovery property" was enacted along with IRC §168 as part of the Economic Recovery Tax Act of 1981 to cover property depreciable pursuant to IRC §§168(a) and 168(c)(1), starting in 1981.[4] The term reaches tangible property of a character subject to the allowance for depreciation, used in a trade or business or held for the production of income. Section 1245 recovery property is broader than Section 1245 property because it includes real as well as personal property. The most important exceptions to the inclusion of real property are residential real property and real property depreciated under the straight-line method.[5]

¶28.3 DISPOSITIONS TRIGGERING RECAPTURE

Unless one of the exceptions on limitations prescribed by IRC §1245(b) applies, IRC §1245 comes into play whenever Section 1245 property or Section 1245 recovery property "is disposed of," although the computation of the amount to be recaptured depends on whether the transaction is "a sale, exchange, or involuntary conversion" or "any other disposition." Because of the extreme breadth of the term "disposition," taxpayers seeking to escape from IRC §1245 focus more on the hole in the doughnut than on the edible ring. The hole, which is described by IRC §1245(b), consists of four escape hatches:

1. Gifts. Transfers by gift, which are exempted by IRC §1245(b)(1), result in a carryover of the tainted depreciation to the donee, who will be subject to recapture on disposing of the property in a nonexempt transaction. Gifts to charitable organizations do not trigger recapture any more than gifts to private individuals, but the donor's charitable contribution deduction is reduced under IRC §170(e)(1)(A) by the recapture potential in the donated property.

---

[3] Treas. Regs. §1.1245-3(c)(2); see supra ¶13.1.

[4] See IRC §1245(a)(5); supra ¶10.9.

[5] See IRC §§1245(a)(5)(A) (residential rental property), 1245(a)(5)(C) (straight-line method). Section 1245 recovery property also does not include property used predominantly outside the United States, IRC §1245(a)(5)(B), or specified low-income housing, IRC §1245(a)(5)(D).

2. Death. Transfers at death are exempt dispositions so far as the decedent is concerned by virtue of IRC §1245(b)(2). In addition, the transferee is not saddled with the recapture potential in the property if it acquires a date-of-death basis under IRC §1014, since the decedent's depreciation deductions are then not reflected in the property's adjusted basis.[6] There are two significant exceptions to this forgive-and-forget policy: (1) if the property was transferred during the decedent's life but was nevertheless included in the decedent's gross estate for federal estate tax purposes, the transferee's depreciation deductions are reflected in the property's basis by virtue of IRC §1014(b)(9) and hence continue to taint the property; and (2) when amounts constituting income in respect of a decedent under IRC §691 (e.g., the unpaid balance due on a sale by the decedent of Section 1245 property) are collected, the proceeds are subject to recapture.

3. Tax-free Transfers With Carryover Basis. If property with recapture potential is transferred to a transferee whose basis is determined by reference to the transferor's basis under one of the provisions listed in IRC §1245(b)(3), relating to transfers to corporations and partnerships, there is no recapture if the transaction is wholly tax-free. If gain is recognized by the transferor (e.g., because boot is received or the transferred property is subject to liabilities in excess of its basis), the transferor's recapture obligation cannot exceed the amount of gain recognized. In either case, the transferee's basis for the property will reflect any tainted deductions that escape recapture at the time of the transfer.

4. Tax-free Rollovers With Substituted Basis. If gain on the transfer of Section 1245 property is not recognized by virtue of IRC §1031 or §1033, relating to like-kind exchanges and involuntary conversions respectively, IRC §1245(b)(4) provides that the gain taken into account in applying the recapture rules shall not exceed the sum of (a) the gain otherwise recognized on the transfer and (b) the fair market value of any property received that is not Section 1245 property and that is not already taken into account under (a) in determining the gain on the transfer. For example, if *A* exchanges a truck used in a business for another truck in a like-kind exchange under IRC §1245, *A* is not subject to recapture; but since the basis of the second truck in *A*'s hands is the same as that of the first truck, the depreciation deductions taken by *A* on both trucks will be subject to recapture under IRC §1245 if and when *A* disposes of the second truck at a gain.[7]

[6] See IRC §1245(a)(2) (recapture limited to deductions reflected in adjusted basis).

[7] For other transactions subject to IRC §1245(b)(4), see Treas. Regs. §§1.1245-4(d), 1.1245-5 (adjustments to basis).

¶28.4 AMOUNT SUBJECT TO RECAPTURE

Under IRC §1245(a)(1), the amount recaptured as ordinary income on a disposition of Section 1245 property or Section 1245 recovery property is the amount (if any) by which the lower of (a) the property's "recomputed basis" or (b) the amount realized in the case of a sale, exchange, or involuntary conversion (or the property's fair market value in the case of any other disposition) exceeds the property's adjusted basis. This computation is illustrated for a variety of situations by Example 28-1, in which the recomputed basis of the property subject to Section 1245 recapture is $12,000 (adjusted basis of $10,000 plus depreciation subject to recapture of $2,000).

Example 28-1

Amount Recaptured as Ordinary Income Under IRC §1245

	A	*B*	*C*	*D*
1. Amount realized on sale, exchange, or involuntary conversion..............	$15,000	—	$11,000	—
2. FMV on other disposition (e.g., distribution by corporation to shareholder)	—	$15,000	—	$ 9,000
3. Less: Adjusted basis	10,000	`10,000	10,000	10,000
4. Gain (loss)	$ 5,000	$ 5,000	$ 1,000	($ 1,000)
5. Recomputed basis: Adjusted basis ($10,000) plus depreciation ($2,000)..................	$12,000	$12,000	$12,000	$12,000
6. Lower of (a) line 1 or 2 and (b) line 5 ..	$12,000	$12,000	$11,000	$ 9,000
7. Amount recaptured: Excess of line 6 over adjusted basis of $10,000 (line 3) ..	$ 2,000	$ 2,000	$ 1,000	-0-

"Recomputed basis," whose central role in the recapture mechanism is indicated by Example 28-1, is defined by IRC §1245(a)(2) as the adjusted basis of Section 1245 property or Section 1245 recovery property plus all adjustments reflected in the adjusted basis by reason of deductions allowed or allowable for depreciation [8] or for amortization under the statutory provisions listed in IRC §1245(a)(2).

Section 1245(a)(1) provides that recaptured gain "shall be recognized notwithstanding any other provision of this subtitle," and IRC §1245(d) announces even more broadly that "this section shall apply notwithstanding any other provision of this subtitle." The strong-arm principle embodied in these provisions is powerful, but it is not invincible. Recaptured gain must be recognized, for example, despite IRC §§311(a), 336, and 337, under which corporations do not ordinarily recognize gain on ordinary or liquidating distributions of appreciated property to their shareholders,[9] and such provisions as IRC §1231 (hotchpot for gains and losses on sales of business assets, etc.) come into force only if and to the extent that the taxpayer's gain exceeds the amount subject to IRC §1245(a)(1).[10] On the other hand, the regulations provide that on an installment sale of property subject to Section 1245, the amount to be included in income as installments are collected is determined by IRC §453 but that the amount so determined is deemed to consist of recaptured gain until the amount subject to IRC §1245(a) has been reported in full.[11]

¶28.5 RECAPTURE OF DEPRECIATION ON BUILDINGS AND OTHER REAL PROPERTY

Under IRC §1250, gain on the disposition of certain depreciable buildings and other depreciable property ("section 1250 property," as defined) must be reported as ordinary income, rather than as capital gain, to the extent of any so-called additional depreciation—roughly speaking, part or all of the excess of depreciation taken after 1975 over the deductions allowable under the straight-line method. Although IRC §1250 ordinarily applies only to taxpayers using an accelerated method of depreciating realty (e.g., cost recovery under IRC §168(b), the declining-balance or sum-of-the-years'-digits method), it reaches depreciation computed on a straight-line basis if the property was held for one year or less or, regardless of the holding period, if the taxpayer ascribed an unjustifiably short useful life or low salvage value to the property.

The coverage of IRC §1250 is described in residuary terms by IRC §1250(c), which defines Section 1250 property as real property—other than Section 1245 property—that is or has been property of a character subject to

---

[8] See Treas. Regs. §1.1245-2(a)(3).

[9] Treas. Regs. §1.1245-6(b).

[10] Treas. Regs. §1.1245-6(a).

[11] Treas. Regs. §1.1245-6(d).

depreciation under IRC §167.[12] Before 1981, this definition meant that the principal targets of IRC §1250 were (1) buildings and their structural components, with certain exceptions; (2) improvements to land, such as earthen dams, pipelines, and orchards; and (3) intangible real property, such as leaseholds. These assets continue to be subject to IRC §1250 if acquired before 1981. For post-1980 acquisitions, however, the scope of IRC §1250 is much narrower, because Congress, on extending the liberal ACRS rules to nonresidential buildings,[13] concurrently subjected these assets to the recapture rules of IRC §1245 rather than IRC §1250. As a result, the principal classes of real property subject to IRC §1250 if acquired after 1980 are apartment buildings and other residential real estate.[14]

The principal differences between IRC §1245 and IRC §1250 are that (a) except for property held for less than one year, IRC §1250 recaptures depreciation only to the extent that the deductions exceeded the amount that would have been allowed had the taxpayer used the straight line method, while IRC §1245 recaptures almost all depreciation and cost recovery deductions, and (b) IRC §1250 reduces the amount to be recaptured on dispositions of certain classes of property on a sliding scale that depends on the length of the taxpayer's holding period for the property. Because IRC §1250 has been amended repeatedly since its enactment in 1964, computations of the recaptured amount can be inordinately complicated, as even a cursory examination of IRC §§1250(a)(1)(B), 1250(a)(2), and 1250(a)(3) will reveal.

Section 1250 resembles IRC §1245 in covering all dispositions, including many transactions that are ordinarily tax-free, except for transfers at death and certain transactions resulting in a carryover or substituted basis. The two recapture provisions are also similar in applying only if (and to the extent that) the amount realized by the taxpayer on a sale or exchange (or the property's fair market value, in the case of other dispositions) exceeds the taxpayer's adjusted basis for the property.

SELECTED BIBLIOGRAPHY

Halperin, Capital Gains and Ordinary Deductions: Negative Income Tax for the Wealthy, 12 B.C. Indus. & Com. L. Rev. 387 (1971).

Horvitz, Sections 1245 and 1250: The Puddle and the Lake, 20 Tax L. Rev. 285, 322–328 (1965).

---

[12] IRC §125(a) does not apply to Section 1245 recovery property. See IRC §1250(d)(11).

[13] For cost recovery deductions under ACRS, see supra ¶10.9.

[14] See ¶10.19 for real property items subject to IRC §1250 if acquired after 1980.

CHAPTER 29

Deferred Compensation–Contracts and Other Nonqualified Arrangements

¶29.1 INTRODUCTORY

Deferred compensation can be paid in many different ways, but for federal income tax purposes the myriad of arrangements can be divided into two principal classes—qualified employee retirement plans, such as qualified pension, profit-sharing, and stock bonus plans, and nonqualified arrangements. Qualified plans, which are subject to a network of complex statutory provisions beyond the scope of this work, have three major characteristics: The employee is not taxed when the benefits are earned, but only when they are received or made available in cash or its equivalent; the employer can deduct contributions to funded plans currently; and earnings on funded plans are not subject to tax as realized, but only when distributed to the beneficiaries. By contrast, nonqualified types of deferred compensation are subject to much less detailed statutory rules; the employee may or may not be taxed currently, depending on factors discussed later in this chapter; and the employer ordinarily is entitled to deduct contributions, payments, or benefits only when they are taxed to the employee, even if the employer's method of accounting would otherwise permit or require the employer's liability to be deducted when the benefits are earned and the liability to pay becomes fixed and determinable.

As explained below, the employee's tax status when nonqualified deferred compensation is earned depends primarily on the doctrine of constructive receipt, augmented by the basic principle that cash-basis taxpayers—the class to which virtually all employees belong—are taxed when they receive cash or its equivalent.[1] The employer's right to deduct contributions, benefits, and payments under nonqualified arrangements can be described as secondary or derivative, since it depends largely on the tax treatment of the employee.[2] After these interrelated subjects are discussed, the special rules relating to the transfer of property for services and to stock options are examined.[3]

¶29.2 DEFERRED COMPENSATION ARRANGEMENTS

1. Revenue Ruling 60-31. The fountainhead of learning on the subject of nonqualified deferred compensation is Rev. Rul. 60-31, which sets out the IRS' conclusions about the taxable year in which employees in a series of hypothetical cases must report various types of deferred compensation if they use the cash receipts and disbursements method of reporting income from services.[4]

The first case described by Rev. Rul. 60-31 is an employment contract under which a cash-basis corporate executive is to receive a stated annual salary plus additional compensation of a specified amount per year, which is to be credited by the employer to a bookkeeping reserve account, accumulated, and paid in five annual installments starting when the employee leaves the company's employ, becomes a part-time employee, or becomes partially or totally incapacitated. Under the agreement, the employer's duty to pay the deferred amounts is "a merely contractual obligation to make the payments when due," and the amounts in the reserve are not held by the employer in trust for the employee. The contract does not provide for forfeiture of the taxpayer's right to receive the prescribed distributions, and in the event of death before receipt in full of the amount in the account, the balance is distributable in installments to the employee's personal representatives.

On these facts, the IRS ruled in Rev. Rul. 60-31 that the deferred compensation is taxable to the employee not when earned but only when actually received in cash or other property.[5] The ruling rests on two major points. First,

---

[1] Infra ¶29.2.

[2] Infra ¶29.2.

[3] Infra ¶¶29.3 (transfers of property for services), 29.4 (stock options).

[4] Rev. Rul. 60-31, 1960-1 CB 174, modified by Rev. Rul. 70-435, 1970-2 CB 100, to delete one of the examples and substitute an alternative one.

[5] For the tax status of deferred compensation paid to a deceased employee's

a promise to pay in the future is not includable in a cash-basis taxpayer's gross income if it is not represented by notes or secured in any way.[6] Second, although the constructive receipt doctrine requires taxpayers to report amounts that they can have for the asking,[7] the agreement in Rev. Rul. 60-31 does not give the employee the right to receive the deferred amount currently; and, even if the employer might have been willing to enter into a different agreement, "the statute cannot be administered by speculating whether the payor would have been willing to agree to an earlier payment." [8]

In holding that this arrangement does not generate income currently, Rev. Rul. 60-31 concentrates on the constructive receipt aspect of cash-basis accounting, but it necessarily holds, albeit by implication, that the employee received neither cash *nor its equivalent* until the deferred compensation is distributed to him.[9] In a later ruling, the IRS held that an employee was not taxable currently on deferred compensation even though the employer funded its liability by purchasing an annuity contract.[10] Since the agreement provided for distributions only on the employee's death or retirement, he did not receive, actually or constructively, any cash; and because he acquired no rights to the annuity contract, he did not receive any "property" constituting the equivalent of cash. If, however, the deferred amount had been used by the employer to purchase an annuity contract naming the employee as the annuitant, the employee would have been taxed currently, even if the employer retained possession of the contract and thereby prevented the employee from exercising a right under the policy to accelerate payments.[11]

Another aspect of Rev. Rul. 60-31, clarified by a later ruling, is the status of an agreement under which the employee has an option, exercisable annually, to receive or defer payment for services to be rendered in the next taxable year. In Rev. Rul. 69-650, involving an employment contract permitting employees earning a specified amount in any taxable year to elect to defer receipt of either 5 or 10 percent of their scheduled salaries for the twelve-month period following the election year, the IRS held that amounts deferred under this year-by-

---

beneficiaries, see IRC §691 (income in respect of a decedent). Collins v. US, 318 F.Supp. 382 (C.D. Calif. 1970), aff'd per curiam, 448 F.2d 787 (9th Cir. 1971).

[6] For the cash receipts and disbursements method of reporting, see generally infra ¶35.2.

[7] For the constructive receipt principles, see generally infra ¶35.2.

[8] Rev. Rul. 60-31, supra note 4, citing Amend v. CIR, 13 TC 178 (1949) (Acq.).

[9] For the "cash equivalent" aspect of cash-basis accounting, see infra ¶35.2.

[10] Rev. Rul. 72-25, 1972-1 CB 127; see also Rev. Rul. 68-99, 1968-1 CB 193 (same result for contract funded by insurance contract purchased and owned by the employer).

[11] See US v. Drescher, 179 F.2d 863 (2d Cir.), cert. denied, 340 US 821 (1950) (prior law); for current law, see IRC §83, discussed infra ¶29.3.

year election were not taxable until paid to the employees or otherwise made available to them.[12]

2. 1978 Standstill Legislation. Rev. Rul. 60-31, as refined and elaborated by later rulings, reigned supreme in the nonqualified deferred compensation area until 1978, when the IRS proposed to amend the regulations by providing that "if under a plan or arrangement . . . payment of an amount of a taxpayer's basic or regular compensation fixed by contract, statute, or otherwise (or supplements to such compensation, such as bonuses, or increases in such compensation) is, at the taxpayer's individual option, deferred to a taxable year later than that in which such amount would have been payable but for his exercise of such option, the amount shall be treated as received by the taxpayer in such earlier taxable year." [13] Under this proposal, year-to-year deferral elections would be ineffective if applicable to long-term employment contracts, but the impact of the new principles on agreements executed by new employees was uncertain.

Congress promptly intervened, however, by enacting Section 132(a) of the Revenue Act of 1978, providing that "the taxable year of inclusion in gross income of any amount covered by a private deferred compensation plan shall be determined in accordance with the principles set forth in regulations, rulings, and judicial decisions relating to deferred compensation which were in effect on February 1, 1978." [14] Despite the reference to "judicial decisions" in this standstill legislation, the accompanying committee reports eschew any intent "to restrict judicial interpretation of the law relating to the proper tax treatment of deferred compensation or interfere with judicial determinations of what principles of law apply in determining the timing of income inclusion." [15]

3. Current Law. The main features of pre-1978 law that are preserved, at least for the time being, by the 1978 legislation can be summarized as follows:

1. *Timing of deferral.* Under Rev. Rul. 60-31 and later rulings based thereon, a deferral is effective for tax purposes if made before the services are rendered, without regard to whether the employer would have been willing to pay the deferred amount currently. An agreement to defer amounts that are

---

[12] Rev. Rul. 69-650, 1969-2 CB 106; see also Rev. Rul. 71-419, 1971-2 CB 220 (same result for amounts deferred under contract allowing deferral election to be rescinded as to amounts earned thereafter).

[13] 43 Fed. Reg. 4638 (1978).

[14] Revenue Act of 1978, P.L. No. 95-600, §132(a), 92 Stat. 2782.

[15] See Joint Comm. on Taxation, 95th Cong., 2d Sess., General Explanation of the Revenue Act of 1978, at 76 (1979).

already due and payable is not necessarily ineffective, but it is clearly more vulnerable. If the obligor is ready, willing, and able to pay, the amounts are almost certainly constructively received by the employee; on the other hand, if the employer is in financial difficulties, a deferral agreement by a cash-basis taxpayer does not require the postponed amounts to be reported currently.

2. *Forfeiture clauses.* Deferred compensation agreements often condition the employee's right to receive the deferred payments on abstaining from competition with the employer, performing post-retirement consulting services on request, and/or refraining from transferring or encumbering his interest or benefits under the plan. Before Rev. Rul. 60-31 was issued, tax advisers often included no-competition and consulting clauses of these types in deferred compensation agreements in order to add an additional argument to their forensic bow—that the deferred amounts were not fully earned currently because dependent on future events.

Although Rev. Rul. 60-31 attaches no importance to these safeguards, they continue to be used by some cautious practitioners. They also serve ancillary functions in special circumstances. For example, if the employee's rights to the deferred compensation are secured by an escrow arrangement or other device, a forfeiture clause may neutralize an otherwise fatal arrangement by establishing that the deferred amount is not yet fully earned.[16] It should be noted, however, that formal forfeiture provisions may be disregarded if perfunctory, depending on the facts and circumstances of the particular case.[17]

3. *Acceleration in emergency.* Because employees encountering an unexpected need for cash may regret the decision to defer the receipt of compensation, they may wish to include a clause in the employment contract permitting or requiring distributions before the prescribed due date in specified circumstances. If the criteria are loosely defined (e.g., maintenance of the employee's standard of living) or embrace events within the employee's control (e.g., purchase of a new residence) or if the employee can unilaterally determine whether the criteria are satisfied, the amounts subject to acceleration may well be taxed to the employee when earned, on the ground that, for practical purposes, they are placed at his disposal at that time.

4. *Escrows and other security devices.* A basic presupposition of the favorable rulings in Rev. Rul. 60-31 on deferred compensation agreements is that the employee cannot draw down deferred amounts until the prescribed due date and will be only a general creditor of the employer at that time. If, however, the employee is protected by an escrow arrangement, trust, or other device, the secured amount may be constructively received under the regula-

[16] See Harrison's Est. v. CIR, 62 TC 524 (1974) (employee not taxed on amounts placed in irrevocable trust by employer; benefits not fully earned because of consulting services and no-competition clauses in agreement).

[17] See Treas. Regs. §1.83-3(c)(2).

tions, which refer to an amount that "is credited to [the taxpayer's] account, set apart for him, or otherwise made available so that he may draw upon it at any time, or so that he could have drawn upon it during the taxable year if notice of intention to withdraw had been given." [18]

5. *Transferable rights.* Under the cash equivalent or economic benefit principle, cash-basis taxpayers are taxable if amounts owing to them are satisfied by the transfer of promissory notes or other negotiable evidences of indebtedness. On the other hand, a so-called naked promise to pay does not generate income currently, even though the common law has for centuries permitted choses in action to be assigned. The uncertain boundary line between these two principles is discussed elsewhere in this work; to obtain an extra margin of safety, deferred compensation agreements often explicitly prohibit assignments of the employee's rights.

6. *Earnings on deferred amounts.* Except for the anticipated tax savings, the present value of a deferred payment is less than the value of getting the same amount currently; and if the deferral is protracted, the tax savings must be very substantial to compensate the employee for waiting. For example, the present value of $100,000 payable in twenty years is only $20,511 if discounted at 8 percent quarterly. The possibility that taxpayers seeking to outsmart the IRS will outsmart themselves is illustrated by the following incident:

> For appearing in *Bridge on the River Kwai,* William Holden agreed to 10 percent of the gross, but for tax reasons wanted it paid to him at the rate of only $50,000 a year. The picture has already made so much money (between $20 and $30 million) that Holden's share now stands at between $2,000,000 and $3,000,000. Not only will it take 40-year-old Holden at least 40 years to get the last of his money, but [the producer] can in the meantime invest it and make well over $50,000 a year, thus in effect having got Holden's services in *Kwai* for nothing.[19]

To reflect the time value of money, deferred payment agreements often inflate the amount to be paid, either implicitly (by designating a sum larger than would be reasonable if the compensation were paid immediately) or explicitly (by crediting the employee's account with interest at a specified

---

[18] Treas. Regs. §1.451-2(a), discussed infra ¶35.2; see also Rev. Rul. 60-31, supra note 4 (taxable escrow example); IRC §402(b) (employer contributions to nonexempt trust taxable to employee pursuant to IRC §83).

[19] Time, Jan. 19, 1959, at 66. See also "The Hite Report" Author Sues Publisher, New York Times, May 30, 1979, at B-3, reporting a suit by an author against a publisher alleging that an agreement to restrict royalties to $25,000 per year would require thirty-two years for payout of the royalties earned in the first few years after publication ($875,000) and that this amount would produce an annual yield for the publisher in the interim in excess of the $25,000 payable under the agreement.

annual rate). Other possibilities are credits based on the consumer price index, the Dow-Jones average, or the gains and losses actually incurred by the employer on investing the balance in the employee's account.

If, however, the employee retains control over the investment decisions rather than leaving them to the employer's discretion or specifying an objective external standard (e.g., the Dow-Jones average), the arrangement resembles an investment account, even though distributions are deferred and the employee is only a general creditor of the employer. The earnings are especially vulnerable, since the employer can be realistically viewed as the employee's agent, whose receipt of the earnings is tantamount to receipt by the employee.[20]

7. *IRC § 83.* A potential jurisdictional conflict between the general principles governing the tax status of compensation and the specific rules of IRC §83, relating to the transfer of property for services, is largely avoided by the regulations under IRC §83, which provide that the term "property" does not include "an unfunded and unsecured promise to pay money in the future." [21] This exclusion, however, carries the implication that funded and secured promises are subject to the rules of IRC §83, which distinguishes between rights that are subject to a substantial risk of forfeiture and those that are not.[22]

4. Employer Deductions. Deferred compensation is not deductible by employers using the cash receipts and disbursements method of computing income until paid. By contrast, compensation is ordinarily deductible by accrual-basis employers when it is earned and the liability arises, whether payment is made currently or not.[23] Since 1942, however, accrual-basis taxpayers have been allowed, with some exceptions, to deduct deferred compensation only when it is includable in the employee's gross income, which is ordinarily when paid. When enacted, this departure from the customary rules of accrual accounting may have been intended to prevent accrual-basis employers from deducting compensation under nonqualified pension and other deferred payment plans in computing income subject to abnormally high World War II tax rates, since their cash-basis employees could defer reporting their earnings until the anticipated return of lower peacetime rates. The principle was retained, however, even when the tax system resumed its peacetime footing.

As currently phrased, IRC §404(a) provides that "compensation . . . paid or accrued on account of any employee under a plan deferring the receipt of such compensation," if otherwise deductible under IRC §162 or §212, can be deducted only subject to the limitations of IRC §404. Section 404 imposes very

---

[20] For an analogy, see Rev. Rul. 77-85, 1977-1 CB 12 (taxpayer taxed on earnings under annuity arrangement because of retained control over investments).

[21] Treas. Regs. §1.83-3(e).

[22] For IRC §83, see infra ¶29.3.

[23] See infra ¶35.3 (expenses).

elaborate restrictions on the deduction of employer contributions to qualified pension, profit-sharing, and stock bonus plans; but for nonqualified plans the limitation is briefly stated. Under IRC §404(a)(5), the deduction is allowable when the amount is includable in the gross income of the employee participating in the plan. As summarized by the regulations, "deductions under section 404(a) are generally allowable only for the year in which the contribution or compensation is paid, regardless of the fact that the [employer] may make his return on the accrual method of accounting." [24]

Section 404(a)(6) establishes a grace period by providing that payments attributable to a taxable year shall be deemed made on the last day of that year if actually made not later than the due date of the return for the next succeeding year. If a calendar year accrual-basis employer does not pay salaries earned in December until January or defers the payment of year-end bonuses based on net earnings until the books are closed at the beginning of the following year, cash-basis employees are not taxed until the later year, when they receive the payments; but IRC §404(a)(6) permits the employer to deduct the payments for the taxable year in which the compensation is earned.

Section 404(a) refers to compensation paid by employers to or for the account of employees; but IRC §404(d), enacted in 1978, subjects plans deferring the compensation of independent contractors to the same rules.

¶29.3 TRANSFERS OF PROPERTY FOR SERVICES

1. Introductory. Stripped of its refinements, IRC §83 provides that a taxpayer who performs services in return for property realizes income and that the amount realized is the fair market value of the property or, if the transfer takes the form of a bargain purchase, the excess of its value over the amount paid. Since these propositions are as self-evident as any ideas in the law of taxation, their ratification by an explicit statutory provision was hardly necessary. In point of fact, IRC §83 was enacted in 1969 primarily to deal with a limited but troublesome problem in applying these basic propositions—the tax status of compensation paid in property subject to restrictions making it difficult to value the property at the time of transfer, such as stock transferred subject to an option in the employer to repurchase the stock at a specified price on termination of employment.

The "restricted property" problem can be illustrated by reference to two seminal Tax Court decisions, both decided in the early 1950s. In *Kuchman v. CIR,* the Tax Court held (1) that stock issued to an employee for $5 a share, under an agreement prohibiting a sale or other disposition for one year and

[24] Treas. Regs. §1.404(a)-1(c); see also Treas. Regs. §1.404(a)-12(b)(1).

requiring resale at the employee's cost if his employment terminated during that period, did not have an ascertainable fair market value, although identical shares free of restrictions were sold at $37 a share about four months later, and (2) that "acquisition of the stock [did] not justify charging [the taxpayer] in the year of its receipt with income in any amount." [25] As for a tax when the restrictions expired, the Tax Court held in *Lehman v. CIR* that the pea was not under that shell either:

> Termination of the restrictions was not a taxable event such as the receipt of compensation for services or the disposition of property. Values fluctuate from time to time and the value on a later date might be out of all proportion to the compensation involved in the original acquisition of the shares.[26]

This rationale meant that any profit realized by the employee on ultimately selling the liberated stock was, a fortiori, noncompensatory; in point of fact, the taxpayer in *Lehman* sold the stock shortly after the restrictions expired, and the court held that his profits were long-term capital gains rather than ordinary income.[27]

Taken in combination, *Kuchman* and *Lehman* meant that ordinary income was not realized at any time by the participants in a carefully designed employee stock purchase plan, despite its unmistakable compensatory flavor. In 1976, the Tax Court concluded that this result could not be reconciled with the Supreme Court's 1956 decision in *CIR v. LoBue,* which recognized the compensatory nature of employee stock options; and the Tax Court overruled *Lehman.* [28] This belated action did not restore the *status quo ante,* however, because Congress had enacted IRC §83 in the meantime.

2. The "Transfer" of "Property" in Connection With "The Performance of Services." Section 83 is brought into force if (1) "property" (2) is "transferred" (3) "in connection with the performance of services." Although these three statutory phrases are readily applied in most circumstances, they are fuzzy around the edges.

The term "property" is defined by the regulations to include both personal and real property but to exclude money and unfunded and unsecured promises to pay deferred compensation.[29] The exclusion of money, however,

[25] Kuchman v. CIR, 18 TC 154, 163 (1952) (Acq.).

[26] Lehman v. CIR, 17 TC 652, 654 (1951), acq. on this issue withdrawn and nonacq. substituted, 1962-2 CB 7.

[27] Id. at 654.

[28] CIR v. LoBue, 351 US 243 (1956), discussed infra ¶29.4; Lighthill v. CIR, 66 TC 940 (1976) (overruling *Lehman*).

[29] Treas. Regs. §1.83-3(e).

does not embrace contracts for the payment of money that are commonly regarded as "property," such as life insurance and endowment contracts; and the exclusion of unfunded and unsecured promises preserves the long-standing principle that these commitments are not taxed currently to cash-basis taxpayers [30] and implies, by negative inference, that notes, bonds, and similar evidences of indebtedness are currently taxed.[31]

A third threshold problem is the scope of the requirement that property be "transferred" as compensation for services. Section 83 specifies in some detail whether income is realized when the transfer occurs or on one of several subsequent dates, but it does not flesh out the "transfer" concept itself. The regulations step into the breach by stating that "a transfer of property occurs when a person acquires a beneficial ownership interest in such property." [32] Factors tending to establish that no present transfer has occurred, so that there is no current realization of income, are (a) that the arrangement resembles an option, (b) that the transferee is not subject to a risk of loss if the property declines in value, and (c) that the transferee is obligated to resell the property at a price that does not approach its fair market value at the time of resale.[33]

Since the grant of an option is not a transfer of the underlying property,[34] it is necessary to deal with nonrecourse obligations to purchase property, which may be the functional equivalent of options unless the employee makes a down payment large enough to induce payment of the balance when due. Where nonrecourse liability is involved, the regulations hold that the existence of a transfer depends on all the facts and circumstances, taking into account such factors as the nature of the property, the extent to which the risk of loss has been transferred, and the likelihood that the purchase price will be paid.[35]

If a transaction satisfies these threshold requirements—a *transfer* of *property* in connection with the *performance of services*— the main features of IRC §83, discussed in more detail below, are:

---

[30] See supra ¶29.2.

[31] See Treas. Regs. §§1.61-2(d)(4) (notes and other evidences of indebtedness received as payment for services includable in gross income at fair market value), 1.83-4(c) (effect of cancellation or satisfaction at less than face amount).

[32] Treas. Regs. §1.83-3(a)(1). See also Treas. Regs. §1.421-7(g) (defining "transfer" in connection with stock options); Rev. Rul. 70-335, 1970-1 CB 111 (time of transfer); Treas. Regs. §1.61-2(d)(2)(i) (transfer for IRC §61 purposes); Rev. Rul. 71-34, 1971-1 CB 31 (same).

[33] Treas. Regs. §§1.83-3(a)(3) through 1.83-3(a)(6).

[34] Treas. Regs. §1.83-3(a)(2). If the option has a readily ascertainable fair market value, however, the grant is a transfer *of the option,* though not of the underlying property. See Treas. Regs. §1.83-7; infra, text preceding note 46.

[35] Treas. Regs. §1.83-3(a)(2); Treas. Regs. §1.83-3(a)(7), Example (2).

1. The transfer is covered by IRC §83(a) whether there is an employer-employee relationship between the parties or not. Thus, IRC §83 applies to property transferred by a parent, controlling shareholder, or subsidiary of the employer, as well as property transferred to independent contractors for services rendered or to be rendered by them.

2. The person performing the services is taxed, even if the property is transferred to someone else, such as a member of an employee's family.

3. The amount includable in gross income is the excess of the property's fair market value (determined without regard to restrictions, unless they will never lapse) over the amount (if any) paid, determined as of the first taxable year in which the recipient's rights in the property are either transferable or free of a substantial risk of forfeiture.[36] Thus, the receipt of nonforfeitable property is taxable even though it cannot be sold, pledged, or otherwise disposed of.

4. Restrictions that by their terms will never lapse are taken into account in valuing the property; but if such a restriction is cancelled, the resulting increase in the property's value is taxed in the year of cancellation unless the taxpayer establishes that the cancellation was not compensatory.

5. The employer is allowed to deduct compensation paid in property only when, and to the extent that, the person performing the services is required to include the property in gross income.

6. Section 83 also prescribes rules for a number of ancillary situations, including an election by the taxpayer to accelerate the recognition of income, gifts, and sales of restricted property before the restrictions expire, and tax-free exchanges of restricted property.

3. Restricted Property. Section 83(a) requires the excess of the fair market value of property transferred in connection with the performance of services over the amount (if any) paid for the property to be included in the gross income of the person performing the services. If the property is freely transferable and is not subject to a substantial risk of forfeiture (e.g., on termination of employment before a specified date), computation of the amount includable in income is ordinarily straightforward, but valuation may be difficult if the property is unique and there are no comparable market transactions between willing sellers and willing buyers.

If the property is subject to a restriction that by its terms will never lapse (a "nonlapse restriction"), the restriction is ordinarily determinative of the

---

[36] For the constitutionality of taxing the employee on the unrestricted value of restricted property, see Sakol v. CIR, 574 F.2d 694 (2d Cir. 1978). See also Alves v. CIR, 79 TC No. 55 (1982) (employee taxed on spread between price paid for stock and value when restrictions lapsed, even though there was no spread when option was exercised; divided court).

property's fair market value. Thus, if the transferee of stock is required to resell it to the issuer at book value pursuant to a restriction that is enforceable against subsequent holders, the formula price will ordinarily be controlling under IRC §83(a). "Nonlapse" restrictions are given this effect, according to the Senate Finance Committee's report on IRC §83, because they "are not tax motivated" and impose "an inherent limitation on the recipient's property rights." [37]

By contrast with nonlapse restrictions, which are ordinarily determinative of the property's fair market value but do not result in the deferral of income, other restrictions are disregarded in valuing the property; but if they create a substantial risk of forfeiture, they postpone the time when the transfer generates income. Under IRC §83(a), if the recipient's rights to the restricted property are nontransferable and are subject to a substantial risk of forfeiture, income is not realized until the first taxable year in which the rights *either* become transferable *or* are no longer subject to a substantial risk of forfeiture. As a shorthand expression for this date, the regulations describe it as the taxable year in which the transferred property becomes "substantially vested." [38]

The regulations discuss the phrase "substantial risk of forfeiture" at some length and illustrate the concept with several examples.[39] At one extreme, a requirement that an employee must return the transferred property unless he completes an additional period of substantial services creates a substantial risk of forfeiture, and it simultaneously renders the recipient's rights to the property nontransferable, thus deferring the taxable date until the condition is satisfied.[40] At the other end of the spectrum, the regulations state that a substantial risk of forfeiture is not created by a requirement that the employee return the property upon commission of a crime;[41] thus, even though the restriction might chill bidding by potential buyers, it would neither affect the fair market value of the property nor defer recognition of the income.

The most troublesome situations fall between these two extremes—for example, conditions requiring surrender or resale of the property if the employee accepts a position with a competing firm or, on retirement, fails to render consulting services at the ex-employer's request. Since conditions of this type may be no more than camouflage, the regulations require a factual show-

---

[37] S. Rep. No. 91-552, reprinted in 1969-3 CB 501.

[38] Treas. Regs. §1.83-1(a) (second sentence).

[39] Under Treas. Regs. §1.61-2(d)(5), issued in 1959 following the *Kuchman* and *Lehman* cases, restrictions with "a significant effect on value" have the effect of deferring the recognition of income. As used in IRC §83, "substantial risk of forfeiture" was obviously intended to impose a more stringent standard; see Sakol v. CIR, supra note 36.

[40] See Treas. Regs. §§1.83-3(c)(1), 1.83-3(c)(2); Treas. Regs. §1.83-3(c)(4), Example (1) (two-year employment requirement).

[41] Treas. Regs. §1.83-3(c)(2); see Burnetta v. CIR, 68 TC 387 (1977).

ing that the risk of forfeiture is serious.[42] The regulations are also skeptical of conditions imposed by corporations on property transferred to an employee who owns, directly or indirectly, more than 5 percent of the corporation's stock—or even less, if the rest of the stock is so widely diversified that the employee subject to the restriction controls the corporation for practical purposes.[43] The regulations also provide that "investment letter" restrictions on the resale of stock do not create a substantial risk of forfeiture.[44]

Because a substantial risk of forfeiture not only defers the *recognition* of income until the risk terminates but also requires the *amount* of income to be measured at that time, IRC §83(a) differs from deferral provisions that simply postpone the date for recognizing a fixed amount of income. By contrast, IRC §83(a) is both a shield for the taxpayer and a sword for the IRS; and if the value of the restricted property rises between the transfer and the date when the restriction expires, deferral may prove to be a Pyrrhic victory for the employee.

This danger can be avoided by an election under IRC §83(b), which permits taxpayers to compute their tax liability when the property is transferred by including in gross income in that year the excess of its fair market value (determined without regard to restrictions that can lapse) over the amount (if any) paid for the property. Having made an election under IRC §83(b), the taxpayer does not have to report any additional income if and when the risk of forfeiture terminates. Thus, by giving up the deferral shield, the taxpayer deprives the IRS of the deferral sword. But there is a cost to this tactic: If the property is subsequently forfeited, the taxpayer may not deduct the amount previously included in income.[45] If the current value of the property is comparatively low, however, the gamble may be worthwhile, since it eliminates the open-ended risk of an unpredictably large amount of income when the risk of forfeiture evaporates.

---

[42] Treas. Regs. §1.83-3(c)(2). See Richardson v. CIR, 64 TC 621 (1975) (requirement of post-retirement consulting services inserted at employee's instance, rather than employer's; no showing of employee's ability to perform services or of employer's need for them; held, no substantial risk of forfeiture).

[43] Treas. Regs. §1.83-3(c)(3) (ownership of more than 5 percent of total combined voting power or value of all classes of stock of employer or its parent or subsidiary, including stock owned by members of employee's immediate family).

[44] Treas. Regs. §1.83-5(c), Example (3); see also IRC §83(c)(3), enacted in 1982 to overrule Horwith v. CIR, 71 TC 932 (1979) (restrictions on insider trading imposed by Section 16(b) of Securities Exchange Act of 1934 do not create substantial risk of forfeiture).

[45] Section 83(b) states that "no deduction shall be allowed in respect of such forfeiture," but Treas. Regs. §1.83-2(a) takes into account the amount paid for the property (if any), as distinguished from the amount included in income as a result of the election, in determining loss on a forfeiture or sale.

4. Options to Acquire Property. When options to acquire property are transferred to employees and independent contractors in a compensatory context, restrictions (e.g., relating to continued employment) are often attached to the option, to the property subject to the option, or to both. If the option itself does not have a "readily ascertainable fair market value" (a standard that is more stringent than the customary fair market value test), it is excluded from IRC §83's coverage by IRC §83(e)(3), with the result that the tax effect of the transfer depends upon other statutory provisions—primarily the general principles established by IRC §61(a), as interpreted by the regulations. When such an option is exercised, however, the transfer of the property is subject to IRC §83.

Conversely, the transfer of an option *with* a readily ascertainable fair market value is subject to IRC §83. Since the compensatory element in the arrangement is taxed to the employee or independent contractor by IRC §83, the optionee is viewed thereafter as an investor, whose exercise of the option is not a compensatory event.

These principles are discussed in more detail below, in conjunction with the tax status of employee stock options.

5. Deduction by Employer. Section 83(h) links together the employer and the employee—more precisely, the person for whom the services are performed and the person performing the services—by allowing the employer to deduct the amount "included" in the employee's gross income under IRC §83(a) (transfer of property), §83(b) (election to accelerate income), or §83(d)(2) (compensatory cancellation of nonlapse restriction). As used by IRC §83(h), the phrase "included . . . in the [employee's] gross income" means, under the regulations, the amount properly *includable,*[46] a construction that preserves the employer's deduction even if the employee neglects to report the amount as required.

The taxpayer entitled to deduct property transferred as compensation under IRC §83(h) is the person for whom the services were performed. If property is transferred to the employee by a parent or other shareholder of the employer, the regulations provide that the transaction is to be treated as a contribution to the employer's capital followed by a transfer of the property by the employer to the employee.

6. Ancillary Problems. Section 83 and the regulations thereunder deal with a number of ancillary problems created by the transfer of property in recognition of services, including:

---

[46] Treas. Regs. §1.83-6(a).

1. *Disposition before transfer is complete.* If property is acquired subject to a substantial risk of forfeiture, the transfer is not "complete," and the recipient's rights are not "transferable" if a subsequent transferee's rights are subject to forfeiture; but these tax rules do not preclude an effective transfer so far as local law is concerned. Thus, property may be transferred, despite the continuing risk of forfeiture, for example, to a donee (who will not look the gift horse in the mouth, since it is better than nothing).

Under the regulations, an employee who disposes of restricted property in an arm's-length transaction before the transfer becomes complete must treat the excess of the amount realized over the amount (if any) paid for the property as compensation.[47] If the disposition is not at arm's length, the employee realizes compensation in the amount of any money or other property received, subject to his accounting method, but not in excess of the value of the property (less the price, if any, paid for it), determined without regard to any restrictions other than those that will never lapse. If and when the transfer becomes complete, the employee realizes additional compensation in the manner provided by IRC §83(a) (i.e., as though the property had not been disposed of), the amount included in gross income at the time of the disposition being treated as an amount paid for the property. Thus, the impact of IRC §83(a) cannot be avoided by a gift of restricted property to a member of the employee's family, since the compensation will have to be recognized by the employee when the donee's rights become nonforfeitable.

2. *Death.* If a transfer of restricted property becomes complete at or after the employee's death, the income realized under IRC §83(a) is income in respect of a decedent, subject to IRC §691.[48]

3. *Basis and holding period.* The basis of IRC §83 property in the hands of the recipient (or any person acquiring the property in a subsequent transfer that is not at arm's length) is the amount, if any, paid for the property plus any amount included in the gross income of the person performing the services; and the holding period begins when the transfer becomes complete or, if an election was made under IRC §83(b), when the transfer occurred.[49] So far as an arm's-length subsequent transferee is concerned, the basis of the property is determined under IRC §1012 (cost, unless another basis provision is applicable) and the holding period begins when the property is acquired.[50]

4. *Tax-free exchanges.* Section 83(g) provides that an exchange of restricted property for property subject to similar restrictions, pursuant to cer-

---

[47] Treas. Regs. §1.83-1(b). If the forfeiture condition materializes, the property's adjusted basis can be deducted as a capital loss if the property is a capital asset in the transferee taxpayer's hands.

[48] Treas. Regs. §1.83-1(d).

[49] Treas. Regs. §§1.83-4(a), 1.83-4(b).

[50] Treas. Regs. §§1.83-4(a), 1.83-4(b); for IRC §1012, see supra ¶23.2.

tain nonrecognition provisions (such as IRC §354, relating to corporate reorganizations), does not trigger the realization of income but that the property received is subject to IRC §83(a). Thus, restricted stock can be exchanged for similarly restricted stock of a corporation acquiring the original employer in a merger.

¶29.4 EMPLOYEE STOCK OPTIONS

1. Introductory. No legal device has been more buffeted about by turbulent administrative, judicial, and legislative tax currents than the employee stock option, whose tax history began in 1923, when the Treasury ruled that the value of stock issued to an employee on exercising a stock option, less the option price, constituted income when the option was exercised.[51] Fifteen years later, however, the Tax Court distinguished between stock options intended to compensate employees and those designed to inculcate a "proprietary attitude" toward the employer, holding that only the former type generated taxable income when exercised.[52]

This unpersuasive distinction gained ground for a period of years, resulting in amended regulations that accepted the tax-free status of so-called proprietary stock options; but the theory was rejected by the Supreme Court in *CIR v. Smith,* decided in 1945, and again, more conclusively, in *CIR v. LoBue,* decided in 1956.[53] After holding that the employee stock options in *LoBue* "bore none of the earmarks of a gift" stimulated by detached and disinterested generosity, the Court administered a coup de grace to the "proprietary" stock option theory:

> It is true that our taxing system has ordinarily treated an arm's length purchase of property even at a bargain price as giving rise to no taxable gain in the year of purchase. . . . But that is not to say that when a transfer which is in reality compensation is given the form of a purchase the Government cannot tax the gain under [IRC §61(a)]. The transaction here was unlike a mere purchase. It was not an arm's length transaction

---

[51] T.D. 3435, II-1 CB 50 (1923); Treas. Regs. 86, Art. 22(a)-1 (1935).

[52] Geeseman v. CIR, 38 BTA 258 (1938). The court's opinion in *Geeseman* was less conclusive than subsequent generalizations, since it was based on an examination of the facts, which led the court to decide that the IRS had failed to establish "definitely and clearly . . . that a transaction, which in form is nothing more than a purchase and to an obvious and substantial extent is unquestionably a purchase, is in fact to some extent the payment of compensation for services rendered or to be rendered." Id. at 264.

[53] CIR v. Smith, 324 US 177, opinion on rehearing, 324 US 695 (1945); CIR v. LoBue, 351 US 243 (1956).

> between strangers. Instead it was an arrangement by which an employer transferred valuable property to his employees in recognition of their services. We hold that LoBue realized taxable gain when he purchased the stock.[54]

By holding that the employee in *LoBue* realized taxable gain on exercising the options to purchase the stock, the Court necessarily rejected two alternative theories of taxation, viz., (1) that the employee realized income when the options were issued to him, in an amount equal to their fair market value at that time, and (2) that income was realized only if and when the stock was sold, in an amount equal to the amount realized less the amount paid for the stock when the options were exercised.

Congress intervened in this area in 1950 by conferring on "restricted stock options" the tax status unsuccessfully sought by the taxpayers in the *Smith* and *LoBue* cases (i.e., no taxable income on exercising the option; capital gain or loss on selling the stock). To qualify as a "restricted stock option," an option had to meet a series of statutory conditions (e.g., the option price had to be at least 85 percent of the stock's fair market value when the option was issued), which were intended to keep employee stock options from being too much of a good thing. Options not meeting these standards, which came to be known as "nonstatutory stock options," were left to their fate under existing law. The 1950 "restricted stock option" rules were replaced in 1964 by provisions for "qualified stock options," which were required to meet a somewhat different set of elaborate conditions;[55] once again, nonstatutory stock options remained subject to the developing case law. In 1976, the statutory qualified stock option provisions were repealed, subject to a grandfather clause to preserve certain existing rights,[56] on the grounds that there was no reason to treat the incentive feature of stock options any differently from any other compensatory device and that the asserted incentive effect was in any event doubtful because the value of options is subject to the uncertainties of the stock market.[57]

2. Incentive Stock Options—Definition. Like a troop of whirling dervishes, Congress changed direction again in 1981, when it reinstated the favorable pre-1976 treatment of employee stock options by enacting IRC §422A, under which "incentive stock options" are not taxable when granted or exercised, and the employee is taxed at capital gains rate when and if the stock received on exercise is sold. According to the Senate Finance Committee, "reinstitution of a stock option provision will provide an important incentive

---

[54] CIR v. LoBue, supra note 53, at 247-248.

[55] See IRC §§422(b)(1) through 422(b)(7).

[56] See IRC §§422(b), 422(c)(7).

[57] S. Rep. No. 94-938, reprinted in 1976-3 CB (Vol. 3) 49, 199.

device for corporations to attract new management and retain the service of executives who might otherwise leave" and encourage management "to expand and improve the profit position of [their] companies," without reviving "the alleged abuses which arose with the restricted stock option provision of prior law." [58]

The term "incentive stock option" is defined by IRC §422A(b) as an option granted to an individual, for any reason connected with his or her employment, by the employer corporation (or its parent or subsidiary) to purchase stock of any such corporation, provided the following eight conditions, set out in IRC §422A(b), are satisfied:

1. *Shareholder-approved plan.* The option must be granted under a plan specifying the number of shares of stock to be issued and the employees or class of employees to receive the options. The plan must be approved by the shareholders of the corporation within twelve months before or after the plan is adopted.

2. *Grant within ten years of plan.* The option must be granted within ten years of the date the plan is adopted or the date the plan is approved by the shareholders, whichever is earlier.

3. *Ten-year life.* The option must by its terms be exercisable only within ten years of the date it is granted.

4. *Option price.* The option price must equal or exceed the fair market value of the stock at the time the option is granted. Section 422A(c)(1) provides that this requirement shall be deemed satisfied if there was a good-faith attempt to value the stock accurately.

5. *Non-transferability.* The option by its terms must be nontransferable by the employee except by will or the laws of descent and distribution and must be exercisable during the employee's lifetime only by the employee.

6. *Stock ownership limit.* The employee must not, immediately before the option is granted, own stock representing more than 10 percent of the voting power or value of all classes of stock of the employer corporation or its parent or subsidiary. This limitation is waived by IRC §422A(c)(8) if the option price is at least 110 percent of the fair market value of the stock subject to the option and the option by its terms is not exercisable more than five years from the date it is granted.

7. *Outstanding earlier options.* The option by its terms must not be exercisable while there is outstanding any incentive stock option that was granted to the employee at an earlier time. Under IRC §422A(c)(7), an option that was not exercised in full is treated as outstanding for the period during which, under its initial terms, it could have been exercised. Thus, the cancella-

[58] S. Rep. No. 97-144, at 98-99 (1981).

tion of an option will not accelerate the date when a subsequent option can be exercised.

8. *Per-employee annual dollar limit.* The plan must limit the aggregate fair market value of the stock (determined at the time of the grant of the option) for which any employee may be granted incentive stock options in any calendar year to not more than $100,000 plus a carryover amount permitting 50 percent of underutilized amounts to be carried forward to the three succeeding calendar years. For example, if no options are issued to an employee during 1981, 1982, and 1983, the limit for 1984 would be $250,000 ($100,000 plus 50 percent of $300,000).

Section 422A applies to qualifying options exercised in 1981 or thereafter, including options granted before its enactment if they satisfy the conditions of IRC §422A(b). If granted before 1981, however, options are subject to IRC §422A only if the granting corporation elects this treatment, and the election cannot apply to stock with a fair market value per employee (determined as of the date when the option was granted) of more than $50,000 per calendar year and $200,000 in the aggregate. Section 251(c)(2) of the Economic Recovery Tax Act of 1981 (not incorporated into the Internal Revenue Code) permitted options granted on or after January 1, 1976 and outstanding when IRC §422A was enacted to be amended within one year thereafter (i.e., by August 12, 1982) to permit them to qualify as incentive stock options. Thus, a 1980 option with an excessive term (e.g., twelve years) or too low an exercise price (e.g., 90 percent of the stock's value when the option was granted) could be amended to satisfy the 1981 rules.[59]

3. Incentive Stock Options—Exercise, Disposition, Etc. If an option satisfies the foregoing definitional conditions, the following operational rules come into play.

1. *Tax-free exercise of option.* On exercise of the option, the employee realizes no income by virtue of IRC §421(a)(1) provided (1) the stock is held for two years or more from the date when the option was granted and one year or more from the date when it was exercised, and (2) at all times from the grant of the option until three months before exercise, the individual was an employee of the corporation granting the option or of a related corporation as specified by IRC §422A(a)(2).

2. *Disposition below fair market value at exercise.* If stock acquired by exercising an incentive stock option is disposed of within the forbidden two-year period described above, the amount of ordinary income includable in

[59] Temporary Regulations in question-and-answer form have been promulgated to provide guidance to taxpayers seeking incentive stock option treatment for existing stock options. T.D. 7799, 1982-1 CB 67.

gross income is limited to the excess of the amount realized over the share's adjusted basis. Thus, if an option to buy stock for $5 a share is exercised when it is worth $35 and the stock is sold three months later for $20, the employee is taxed on $15 ($20 less $5), regardless of the value of the option when granted or the spread between the option price and the stock's value when the option was exercised.

3. *Tax preference.* The bargain element enjoyed by an employee on exercising an incentive stock option is an item of tax preference under IRC §57(a)(10), which must be taken into account in computing the base on which the alternative minimum tax of IRC §55 is imposed.[60]

4. *Employer deduction.* Under IRC §421(a)(2), the employer is denied any deduction under IRC §162, relating to business expenses, for stock transferred pursuant to an incentive stock option if the employee's exercise of the option is tax-free.

4. Nonstatutory Options With a Readily Ascertainable Value. Section 83, the basic statutory provision prescribing the tax effect of transfers of property in connection with the performance of services, encompasses options only if they have "a readily ascertainable fair market value." [61] This phrase was taken by Congress from the opinion in *CIR v. LoBue.*[62] It is elaborated on by the regulations under IRC §83, which provide that an option has a readily ascertainable fair market value if it is actively traded on an established market—a truism of little practical use, since options with the duration of compensatory options (e.g., two years or more) are seldom traded. In the absence of an active market, the regulations provide that an option qualifies if its value can be measured "with reasonable accuracy," a standard that is satisfied only if (1) the option is transferable and is immediately exercisable in full by the optionee; (2) neither the option nor the underlying property is subject to restrictions or conditions having a significant effect on the option's fair market value, other than a lien or other condition to secure payment of the purchase price; and (3) the fair market value of the "option privilege" (i.e., the opportunity to benefit from appreciation in the underlying property during the life of the option without risking any capital) can be measured with reasonable accuracy.[63] If an option succeeds in running this gauntlet, the

[60] For the alternative minimum tax, see infra ¶39.4.

[61] IRC §83(e)(3); see supra ¶29.3.

[62] CIR v. LoBue, supra note 53, at 249.

[63] Treas. Regs. §1.83-7(b). For difficulties in ascribing a fair market value to stock options issued by closely held corporations, see Swenson v. CIR, ¶71,088 P-H Memo TC (1971) ("an inexact, time-consuming, complex analytical determination based upon a derived value of the stock would be necessary to arrive at an estimated date of grant value of the option and option privilege," precluding a "readily ascertainable" value); for cases in which taxpayers succeeded in establishing the value of options, see McNamara v. CIR, 210 F.2d 505 (7th Cir. 1954) (options constituted income

employee is treated by IRC §83(a) as though his salary had been increased by the value of the option, requiring this amount to be included in gross income. Having paid his way, the employee thereafter has the status of an ordinary investor who purchased the option for cash at its fair market value. This means that exercise of the option is a nontaxable event and that any other disposition of the option—sale, gift, transmission at death, etc.—is governed by the rules applicable to investors, rather than by the rules of IRC §83.

5. Nonstatutory Options Without a Readily Ascertainable Fair Market Value. Options without a readily ascertainable fair market value when granted are not subject to IRC §83; but when the option is exercised, the transfer of the underlying property is subject to IRC §83. This is, in effect, the mirror image of the treatment of options with a readily ascertainable fair market value, whose transfer to the optionee is subject to IRC §83 while the subsequent transfer of the underlying property on exercise of the option is outside the aegis of IRC §83.

By rendering IRC §83 inapplicable to options without a readily ascertainable fair market value, IRC §83(e)(3) leaves their tax status to be determined under the *LoBue* case.[64] This means that the grant of the option is not a taxable event; but when the option is exercised, the excess of the fair market value of the underlying property (determined without regard to any restrictions that can lapse) over the amount paid is includable in the gross income of the person who performed the services. The inclusion in gross income is required in the taxable year of the transfer or in the first year thereafter when the recipient's rights in the transferred property become transferable or are free of any substantial risk of forfeiture—the same rule that applies to other types of restricted property subject to IRC §83.

The general rules of IRC §83 also cover dispositions of the restricted property (by sale, gift, transmission at death, or otherwise) before it becomes transferable or the risk of forfeiture terminates, compensatory cancellations of restrictions that by their terms will never lapse, exchanges of restricted property in nonrecognition transactions, and the employer's right to deduct the amounts taxable to the person who performed the services.[65]

Although IRC §83 prescribes a comprehensive network of rules govern-

---

when granted); CIR v. Stone's Est., 210 F.2d 33 (3d Cir. 1954) (same); but see Union Chem. & Materials Corp. v. US, 296 F.2d 221 (Ct. Cl. 1961) (same transaction as in *Stone's Estate;* held, option lacked readily ascertainable market value when granted).

See also H. Rep. No. 94-1515 (1976) (IRS to make every reasonable effort to determine fair market value if employee elects to have option valued when granted); Prop. Regs. §1.83-6 (reporting required if employer contends that option has readily ascertainable fair market value).

[64] See CIR v. LoBue, supra note 53.

[65] Supra ¶29.3.

ing the receipt and disposition of the property received by *exercising* an option that does not have a readily ascertainable fair market value, it has nothing to say about dispositions of *unexercised* options. The regulations fill in this gap by specifying the amount of compensation realized by the employee if an unexercised option is transferred, whether in an arm's-length transaction or not, or if the employee dies before the option is exercised or transferred.[66]

SELECTED BIBLIOGRAPHY

Anspach, Marlin & Muller, Deferred Compensation: A Case Study of Purposeful Negation of Supreme Court Jurisdiction Over Income Tax Laws, 59 Taxes 691 (1981).

Colvin, Incentive Stock Options, 55 J. Tax. 202 (1981).

Greene, Compensating the Executive in Cash: Payment Now or Payment Later, 1978 So. Calif. Tax Inst. 193.

Irwin & Zimmerman, Incentive Stock Options, 1982 So. Calif. Tax Inst. 500.

Nolan, Deferred Compensation and Employee Options Under the New Section 83 Regulations, 57 Taxes 790 (1979).

Sollee, Final Section 83 Regs. Endanger Employer Deductions, Premium on Employee Elections, 49 J. Tax. 342 (1978).

Tritt, An Evaluation of Deferred Compensation Plans, 56 Taxes 787, 789–791 (1978).

[66] Treas. Regs. §§1.421-6(d)(3) through 1.421-6(d)(6).

CHAPTER 30

Assignments of Income

¶30.1 TRANSACTIONS BETWEEN RELATED TAXPAYERS: IN GENERAL

This chapter focuses on assignments of income and similar transactions shifting, or attempting to shift, deductions or other tax allowances from one person to another within a family or economic unit. These arrangements often exude an aura of tax avoidance, either because the parties are seeking to reduce their aggregate tax liability or because, whatever the motivation of the taxpayer before the court, the device, if successful, will be exploited by others. The resulting legislative and judicial countermeasures, though responding to taxpayer-initiated plans to reduce the aggregate tax liability of a closely knit family or other economic collectivity, have come to permeate the tax law so completely that they sometimes determine which of several parties to an ordinary business transaction must report a particular receipt or can deduct an expense.

The principal features of current income tax law that encourage income splitting and similar tax tactics are (a) the right of every individual to report his or her own income on a personal return, (b) the exemption of a prescribed amount from tax by the personal exemptions and the "zero bracket amount" of IRC §63(d), and (c) the progressive rate structure. Individual returns are the infrastructure making income splitting worth the candle. If married couples or families were taxed on their consolidated income, there would be no advantage in shifting items from one member of the taxpaying group to another. As will be seen, the joint tax return authorized by Congress in 1948 for married couples, though optional, has virtually eliminated any income tax incentive to shift income or tax allowances from one spouse to the other,[1] but it does not affect the tax advantages of splitting parental income with children. Moreover, even if Congress went further by mandating a consolidation of family income, any politically acceptable definition of "family" would undoubtedly omit some persons (e.g., adult children living away from home), to whom income might then be assigned even if all *other* members of the family were taxed as a single unit.

The tax advantages obtained by a successful division of income within the family are complicated by other features of existing law. For example, fixed-dollar limits on tax allowances are usually computed on a per-taxpayer basis and can sometimes be sidestepped by transfers within the family;[2] the adverse tax impact of particular items can often be avoided by shifting them to less vulnerable members of the family,[3] and it may be possible to convert property from an ordinary asset to a capital asset by transferring it from a "dealer" to a related person who is an "investor."[4]

The Internal Revenue Code tells us a great deal about *what* is taxable and deductible and *when* these items are to be taken into account, but it says almost nothing about *who* is to report these elaborately defined items. Forced to write on this virtually blank statutory slate, the courts recognized at the outset that transfers within the family, if honored by federal tax law, could diminish the effect of the progressive rate schedule. This realization led to skepticism about transfers of income and property within the family, especially between husband and wife; and this judicial attitude frequently culminated in decisions holding that "bedchamber" transactions, however effective under local law, did not relieve the transferor of federal tax liability for the transferred item. The seminal cases in this area, all predating World War II, are replete with such observations as "the tax [can] not be escaped by anticipatory arrangements and contracts however skillfully devised," "taxation is not so much concerned with the refinements of title as it is with actual command over the property taxed," and "where the head of the household has income in excess of normal needs, it may well make but little difference to him (except income-tax-wise) where portions of that income are routed—so long as it stays in the family group."[5]

---

[1] Infra ¶39.3.

[2] See, e.g., IRC §116, excluding $100 of dividends from gross income, which can be multiplied by transferring stock from parents to children.

[3] For example, capital gains on appreciated property may be shifted to members of the family who are less vulnerable to the alternative minimum tax imposed by IRC §55 than the transferor. For IRC §55, see infra ¶39.4.

[4] See supra ¶25.5.

[5] Lucas v. Earl, 281 US 111 (1930) ("anticipatory arrangements"); Corliss v.

In the light of hindsight, one senses in the growth of these doctrines an assumption of marital stability tinctured with touches of what today would be called male and parental chauvinism—the belief that if "the head of the household" (invariably assumed to be male) transfers property to his wife, she will deal with it as he recommends, and that children to whom property is transferred will also dutifully comply with their daddy's wishes. These social presuppositions were never followed to the logical extreme of disregarding *all* gifts of property within the family.[6] But by and large, when donors failed to cut all their ties to the transferred property, there was a marked judicial tendency to require them to continue to report the income despite the "reallocation of income within the family group";[7] and if the transfer involved income attributable to personal services, the courts almost always refused to permit "the fruits [to be] attributed to a different tree from that on which they grew." [8]

This early "common law" of income splitting was also influenced, to an extent that can hardly be overstated, by the fact that the joint return of current law, now filed by virtually all married couples, was not authorized by Congress until 1948.[9] For this reason, the effort to reduce taxes by transfers between spouses accounted for the most important litigated cases of the 1930s and early 1940s. These early formative cases were concerned primarily with two types of assignments.

The first category consists of anticipatory transfers of earned income—primarily wages, salaries, and fees charged by self-employed taxpayers for personal services. Their tax treatment is governed by what the Supreme Court has described as "the first principle of income taxation: that income must be taxed to him who earns it." [10] For married couples in common-law jurisdictions, the first principle *is* controlling. As will be seen, however, a different conception of the ownership of income prevails in community property states, and this dramatically affected the development of the federal income tax law.[11]

The second major category of assignments to be examined in this chapter consists of transfers of investment income, where the applicable tax rules are more lenient than those governing earned income. A transfer of stocks, bonds, real estate, or other income-producing assets will effectively shift tax liability

---

Bowers, 281 US 376 (1930) ("actual command"); Helvering v. Clifford, 309 US 331 (1940) ("little difference").

[6] See, e.g., CIR v. Culbertson, 337 US 733, 747 (1949).

[7] CIR v. Sunnen, 333 US 591, 610 (1948).

[8] Lucas v. Earl, supra note 5, at 115. For the provenance of this insidiously seductive horticultural metaphor, see Waring v. Mayor of Savannah, 60 Ga. 93 (1878).

[9] See infra ¶39.3.

[10] CIR v. Culbertson, supra note 6, at 739-740, quoted with approval in US v. Basye, 410 US 441, 449 (1973).

[11] See infra ¶31.1.

for subsequent investment income to the new owner. But the transfer must ordinarily be without strings; when taxpayers retain the right to revoke the gift or otherwise benefit from the transferred property, the income is usually taxed to the transferor rather than the donee.[12]

A final point to be noted here is that when the assignment-of-income doctrine was in its infancy, both the IRS and the courts evidently assumed that if assigned income was reallocated back and taxed to the assignor, the assignee was entitled to a correlative exclusion from income and refund of tax paid on that income. This one-tax presupposition is still accepted.[13] If, however, the assignment is held invalid, the resulting tax liability must be paid by the assignor from personal funds, unless the assignment can be rescinded under local law or the assignee is willing to help out and is not subject to a legal disability (e.g., minority) barring the extension of financial assistance to the assignor.

¶30.2 ASSIGNMENTS OF EARNED INCOME

1. Anticipatory Assignments. By an irony of fate, *Lucas v. Earl,* the most influential of the early cases on income splitting, was concerned with the division of income between husband and wife under an agreement that was innocent of any tax-avoidance purpose.[14] Executed in 1901, after the 1894 income tax was held unconstitutional by the Supreme Court,[15] and long before the Sixteenth Amendment was submitted to the states for ratification, the agreement provided that Mr. and Mrs. Earl would hold as joint tenants with right of survivorship all property then owned by them or thereafter acquired "in any way, either by earnings (including salaries, fees, etc.), or any rights by contract or otherwise, during the existence of our marriage, or which we or either of us may receive by gift, bequest, devise, or inheritance, and all the proceeds, issues, and profits of any and all such property." When the agreement was made, both owned property of substantial value in their own right, and Mr. Earl was a corporate officer and practicing attorney. The trial court's opinion does not disclose whether Mrs. Earl was or expected to be employed.[16]

In a much-quoted opinion by Mr. Justice Holmes, the Supreme Court gave short shrift to the taxpayer's claim that only one-half of his salary and fees was taxable to him because the other half belonged to his wife by virtue of their agreement:

---

[12] See infra ¶30.3.

[13] See Treas. Regs. §1.102-1(e); infra ¶¶30.4, 41.9.

[14] Lucas v. Earl, supra note 5.

[15] Pollock v. Farmers' Loan & Trust Co., 157 US 429 (1895), discussed supra ¶1.1.

[16] Earl v. CIR, 10 BTA 723 (1928).

> There is no doubt that the statute could tax salaries to those who earned them and provide that the tax could not be escaped by anticipatory arrangements and contracts however skillfully devised to prevent the salary when paid from vesting even for a second in the man who earned it. That seems to us the import of the statute before us and we think that no distinction can be taken according to the motives leading to the arrangement by which the fruits are attributed to a different tree from that on which they grew.[17]

As initally interpreted by the lower courts, *Lucas v. Earl* was confined to income arising *after* an anticipatory assignment. Judge Learned Hand, for example, thought that the only plausible explanation for the decision was that the assignment was in effect conditioned on future performance by the assignor, who retained a negative control or veto power over the flow of income to the assignee by virtue of his power to refuse to work.[18] But the "veto" rationale for *Lucas v. Earl* would have permitted assignments of income *already* earned (e.g., claims for unpaid salaries), and this possibility was soon rejected by the Supreme Court in *Helvering v. Eubank,* holding that an insurance agent was taxable on renewal commissions on policies written by him, although he assigned the commissions to a trustee after they were earned but before they became payable.[19]

Rarely has a judicial decision shaped an entire area of tax practice as conclusively as *Lucas v. Earl.* For practical purposes, it prevents ordinary wage earners and salaried employees from assigning their earned income to members of their families, and it is almost equally effective against similar assignments by self-employed persons and partners engaged in occupations in which capital is not a material income-producing factor, such as the practice of law and medicine.

Lucas v. Earl, however, has not been applied to employees in community-property states. Instead, when required to face the issue in *Poe v. Seaborn* (decided only eight months after *Lucas v. Earl*), the Supreme Court held that the earnings of community-property couples must be reported one-half by each spouse, rather than in full by the spouse whose employment created the income.[20] *Lucas v. Earl* was distinguished on the ground that, in a community-property state, "by law the earnings are never the property of the husband, but that of the [marital] community." [21]

Whether *Lucas v. Earl* and *Poe v. Seaborn* can be persuasively reconciled

---

[17] Lucas v. Earl, supra note 5, at 114-115.

[18] Matchette v. Helvering, 81 F.2d 73 (2d Cir.), cert. denied, 298 US 677 (1936); see also Helvering v. Horst, 311 US 112, 118 (1940), discussed infra ¶30.3; Corliss v. Bowers, 281 US 376, 378 (1930).

[19] Helvering v. Eubank, 311 US 122 (1940).

[20] Poe v. Seaborn, 282 US 101 (1930).

[21] Id. at 117.

or not, they have coexisted as major landmarks for almost fifty years. The effects of the momentous distinction between income splitting under state community-property laws and income splitting by private arrangement, including its role in inducing Congress to authorize the 1948 joint return for married couples, are described below.[22]

2. Assignment of Income or Partnership? The marital agreement that was described as an "anticipatory assignment" of income in *Lucas v. Earl* required *both* parties to put their property and earned income into the pool. If Mrs. Earl were a lawyer and she and her husband had organized a two-member law firm, it is clear that the partnership income would be split between them in the ratio dictated by their agreement, unless the agreed ratio was so disproportionate to the value of their services that the agreement could be brushed aside as tantamount to a gift rather than a bona fide business arrangement. In making this judgment, however, the long-run effect of the agreement would be controlling, and its validity for tax purposes would not be impaired by year-to-year fluctuations in the relative value of each partner's services. Given an agreement that would be honored if the partners were unrelated, nothing in *Lucas v. Earl* requires the agreement to be rejected simply because the partners are married to each other.

An agreement to share salaries does not fit the usual conception of a partnership as a combination of individual talents to provide a joint service. Even so, it is difficult to see why two unrelated employees should be taxed on their individual salaries if they enter into an arm's-length agreement to pool and divide their individual earnings. If a metaphor is needed, one could say that the pooled income is the fruit of a single grafted tree, owned jointly by the parties to the agreement. In the absence of precedent, however, one cannot be confident about the tax consequences of this hypothetical arrangement. Moreover, if the parties are members of the same family rather than unrelated individuals, doubts about the outcome of litigation increase, especially since the initial hurdle—proof that the partnership ratio is reasonable—would have to be surmounted to the satisfaction of judges imbued with well-founded skepticism respecting intra-family agreements.

The taxpayer's difficulties proliferate if another modification is introduced into the equation, by assuming a "marital partnership" for the equal sharing of all money income attributable to work outside the home, in consideration of the respective contributions of the spouses to maintenance of the household. In effect, this marital partnership would be a homemade community-property arrangement, and the Supreme Court has made it clear that under existing law a community-property system will be honored only if "made an

[22] Infra ¶¶31.1, 39.3.

incident of marriage by the inveterate policy of the State," but not if it is a "consensual community [arising] out of contract." [23] In the absence of action by Congress, therefore, it must be concluded that a "marital" partnership will be recognized for federal income tax purposes if it resembles a conventional partnership in rendering personal service to customers or clients but that otherwise it will be treated as an anticipatory assignment of income under *Lucas v. Earl.*

3. Assignment of Income or Gratuitous Rendition of Services? It is familiar learning that parents and children are not taxed on the value of unpaid household services even if they work harder than the law of domestic relations requires.[24] The immunity of so-called imputed income, moreover, extends to gratuitous activities that are of direct financial aid to the beneficiary, such as investment advice to children or actual management of their assets.[25] It is inconceivable that Congress intended to impute management fees or a share of the resulting profits to parents who supply these financial services. Another common example of uncompensated services is the labor of parents who work for corporations owned by their children without compensation or for a modest salary, thereby increasing the value of the children's stock.[26]

Although *Lucas v. Earl* does not undermine the well-established tax immunity of persons who render services without charge to relatives, friends, or nonprofit organizations, good Samaritans must make their role clear in advance. If a taxpayer engaged in business waits until a transaction is consummated before announcing that its benefits are to inure to a donee, this belated action will be treated as an assignment of earned income, comparable to an employee's endorsement of a salary check over to a beneficiary. In short, he who hesitates is lost.

4. Refusal to Accept Compensation—Waivers, Renunciations, and Disclaimers. Taxpayers frequently render services without charge to nonprofit organizations without being taxed, even if the value of the donated services can be readily ascertained because the donee organizations would otherwise have had to employ an outsider. What if the organization "sells" the benefactor's services to the public, as in the case of an entertainer who performs at a charity's benefit night? The status of a benefactor who refuses in advance to

---

[23] CIR v. Harmon, 323 US 44, 45 (1944), discussed infra ¶31.1.

[24] See supra ¶1.6.

[25] See, e.g., Alexander v. CIR, 190 F.2d 753 (5th Cir. 1951) (child's cattle business managed by parent without compensation; held, income taxable to child).

[26] If the family business is conducted in partnership form, a salary may be imputed to the parent under IRC §704(e). For the impact of IRC §482 (reallocation of income among related taxpayers to clearly reflect income), see infra ¶30.4.

accept compensation for services that the charity can sell to the outside world was the subject of a spirited exchange in 1937 between Assistant Attorney General (later Mr. Justice) Jackson and members of a joint congressional committee, following a Treasury ruling that the proceeds of Eleanor Roosevelt's radio broadcasts, which were paid by the sponsor to charities, were not taxable to her. The ruling was defended by Mr. Jackson as follows:

> One who earns a salary or wages or has income from invested property cannot assign that income nor order it to be paid to a person or corporation so as to avoid a tax merely by routing his income so as not to pass through his hands. But this doctrine of constructive receipt of income cannot be used to create income when there is no income, and has never been used to justify a tax on services devoted to charity. Mrs. Roosevelt declined to work for money and was only willing to serve for charity's sake. It was and is my opinion that such benefit broadcasts do not result in taxable income.[27]

If the earnings that Mrs. Roosevelt refused to accept personally had been taxed to her, she would have been entitled to a deduction of an equal amount under IRC §170 (relating to charitable contributions) provided her contributions for the taxable year in question did not exceed the percentage limit then in force.[28] But if part or all of the earnings cannot be deducted, either because of the percentage limit or because contributions to the recipient (e.g., a social welfare organization) are not deductible, including the earnings in the taxpayer's gross income is a more serious matter.[29]

Two decades after the controversy over Mrs. Roosevelt's broadcasts, the regulations were amended to provide that if, "pursuant to an agreement or understanding, services are rendered to a person for the benefit of [a tax-exempt] organization . . . and an amount for such service is paid to such organization by the person to whom the services are rendered, the amount so paid constitutes income to the person performing the services."[30] This regulation and the ruling in Mrs. Roosevelt's case can be reconciled by interpreting the regulation to tax performers if *they* enter into an agreement or understanding with the third party, but not if their dealings are confined to the charity and it has unfettered power to make the performers' services available to the ticket-buying audience or other consumers. This approach, if accepted, seems to immunize performers against taxable income if the tax-exempt organization

---

[27] Hearings, Joint Comm. on Tax Evasion and Avoidance, 75th Cong., 1st Sess. 426 (1937).

[28] Supra ¶19.3.

[29] Including the earnings in gross income may have minor ancillary consequences, even if they are fully deductible. See, e.g., IRC §213, discussed supra ¶20.1.

[30] Treas. Regs. §1.61-2(c), added by T.D. 6272, 1957-2 CB 18, 21.

takes the initiative in proposing and organizing the event, unless the taxpayer responds to the charity's request by earmarking the proceeds of a previously scheduled event or otherwise fitting the charity into a prearranged series of performances.

Since charity begins at home, could the children of a professional entertainer take advantage of these rulings by organizing a "family benefit night" at which the parent would perform without compensation, thus enabling the children to sell tickets and report the profits on their personal tax returns? At a formal level, there is nothing to distinguish this arrangement from a benefit for a charity, political party, or other organization; and the rulings, if applicable, would relieve the parent of tax liability if the event is "planned, organized, promoted, and scheduled" [31] by the children and the entertainer performs at their request. Some ideas are too good to be true, however, and one can predict with confidence that this one would not hold up when attacked by the IRS; which verbal weapon would be selected from the judicial arsenal of tax-avoidance doctrines [32] is uncertain, but the scheme's fate is clear.

The distinction between gratuitous services and attempted income shifting is not confined to the world of entertainment. In a series of rulings, the IRS has addressed itself to the taxability of executors who waive their claims to statutory fees and commissions. In general, the executor is not taxed on the foregone fees if an "intention to serve on a gratuitous basis" is adequately manifested, either explicitly (e.g., by a formal waiver within six months of the fiduciary's initial appointment) or implicitly.[33]

An analogous problem is posed by a delayed waiver of compensation under an existing employment contract. The leading case in this area is *Giannini v. CIR,* involving the president of a corporation who was entitled to receive a percentage of its business profits as compensation.[34] In 1927, he advised the corporation that he would not accept any more compensation for that year and "suggested that the corporation do something worthwhile with the money"; early in 1928 the corporation contributed the refused amount to

---

[31] Rev. Rul. 68-503, 1968-2 CB 44.

[32] Supra ¶1.3; infra ¶30.4; see also Rev. Rul. 75-257, 1975-2 CB 251 (grantor of "Family Estate Trust" who assigned his "lifetime services," including all remuneration earned by him regardless of its source, for units of beneficial interests in the trust, held grantor taxable on outside earnings despite assignment).

[33] Rev. Rul. 66-167, 1966-1 CB 20; see also Rev. Rul. 70-237, 1970-1 CB 13. For the status of members of religious orders bound by vows of poverty, whose earnings inure to the benefit of the order, see, e.g., Rev. Rul. 77-290, 1977-2 CB 26 (income received as agent of order is not taxable to individual; contra for income from outside employment); Minckler v. CIR, ¶81,343 P-H Memo TC (1981) (petitioner taxable on earnings as electronics technician, assigned under vow of poverty to church without regularly scheduled functions, of which petitioner and father were trustees; petitioner did "nothing more than rearrange the form of his financial affairs").

[34] CIR v. Giannini, 129 F.2d 638 (9th Cir. 1942).

the University of California to establish a foundation in his honor. The court held that "we cannot say as a matter of law that the money was beneficially received by the taxpayer." [35] The date of the waiver in *Giannini* was not clearly identified by the trial court. This ambiguity later led the Court of Appeals for the Second Circuit, in a case taxing a retired employee on a series of pension checks that he refused to cash because he feared that as a pensioner he would find it difficult to obtain other employment, to observe that if *Giannini* cannot be distinguished on the facts, "we are not persuaded that it should be followed." [36]

5. Assignment of Income Under Legal or Contractual Compulsion. Observing that "the assignment-of-income doctrine assumes that the income would have been received by the taxpayer had he not arranged for it to be paid to another," the Supreme Court held in *CIR v. First Security Bank of Utah* that a taxpayer is not taxable on "income that he did not receive and that he was prohibited from receiving." [37] The taxpayer, a national bank prohibited by law from acting as an insurance agent, was affiliated with an insurance company that wrote policies of credit life insurance for individuals borrowing funds from the taxpayer. The IRS imputed a portion of the premiums to the taxpayer on the ground that it originated the insurance business and had "diverted" income to its affiliate by failing to claim an appropriate share of the premiums as compensation for its role in the transaction. Had the government prevailed in *First Security Bank of Utah,* the affiliated insurance company would have been allowed a deduction for the income taxed to the taxpayer bank; but this would not have produced a "wash," since the bank's tax rate was higher than that of its affiliate.[38] If the taxpayer in *First Security Bank* had been qualified by law to act as an insurance agent, it is quite likely that an imputation to it of an agent's normal commission would have been upheld on the theory that a failure to charge the customary fee was an anticipatory assignment of earned income. Stressing the legal prohibition, however, the Court, with three Justices dissenting, held that none of the affiliated insurance company's premium income could be attributed to the taxpayer.

Shortly after deciding the *First Security Bank* case, the Supreme Court limited it to deflections of income compelled by law, holding in *United States v. Basye* that it does not apply to "an assignment [of income] arrived at by the consensual agreement of two parties acting at arm's length." [39] In *Basye* the Court held that a partnership of physicians, which provided services under a

---

[35] Id. at 641.

[36] Hedrick v. CIR, 154 F.2d 90, 91 (2d Cir. 1946).

[37] CIR v. First Security Bank of Utah, 405 US 394, 403-404 (1972).

[38] Id. at 399, n.6.

[39] US v. Basye, 410 US 441, 453 n.13 (1973).

contract with a nonprofit corporation to members of a prepaid medical plan, was required to treat as partnership income certain payments by the nonprofit corporation to a trust established to pay retirement benefits to the partnership's professional partners and employees. Since the contributions were clearly compensation for services rendered by the partnership, the Court held that they were includable in its income under *Lucas v. Earl,* even though the firm had no right under its contract to receive these amounts directly. Since the partners were required to include their distributive shares of the firm's income on their individual income tax returns, their returns would reflect the contributions to the retirement fund, even though any particular partner might not receive retirement benefits commensurate with the amounts taxed to him or her.

Though crucial on the facts before the Court, the distinction in *Basye* between an assignment of income by "consensual agreement" and "a deflection of income imposed by law" should not be carried to a dryly logical extreme. *Basye* obviously does not mean that employees of a personal-service enterprise are taxable on amounts paid by customers to the employer for their services rather than on their salaries, or that entertainers are taxable on the amounts paid by the public for admission rather than on their fees.[40]

The effect of a contractual arrangement designating the recipient of income is more problematical if the beneficiary is a child or friend of the person performing the services. In *Teschner v. CIR,* for example, the taxpayer was the winner of an essay-writing contest sponsored by a business enterprise, whose rules required any entrant over seventeen years of age to designate a younger person to receive the award (an annuity contract) if the entrant's essay was successful.[41] Although the taxpayer could not have received the prize in his own right, the exercise of his unrestricted power to designate the beneficiary might well have been treated as an anticipatory assignment of income under *Lucas v. Earl.* The Tax Court held otherwise, however, and the Supreme Court later cited *Teschner* with approval in *First Security Bank of Utah.*[42] It did not repeat this testimonial in *Basye,* however, and *Teschner* is not easily reconciled with *Basye.*

6. Gifts of Property Created by Donor's Personal Efforts. Although *Lucas v. Earl* makes it virtually impossible for wage earners and salaried employees to assign earned income to members of their families or other donees, a few self-employed persons enjoy a markedly different status. If personal services culminate in an income-producing asset, such as a literary composition, invention, copyright, or patent, a gift is not treated as an anticipa-

---

[40] See Rev. Rul. 69-274, 1969-1 CB 36.

[41] Teschner v. CIR, 38 TC 1003 (1962).

[42] CIR v. First Security Bank of Utah, supra note 37, at 406 n.22.

tory assignment of income but as a transfer of property, so that income from its exploitation is taxable to the donee rather than the donor.

To have this effect, the transfer must be complete in the sense that the donor cannot retain the power to revoke or alter his disposition; but the IRS has ruled that the donor may with impunity contribute services to assist the donee in preparing the transferred property for publication.[43] Moreover, if the asset can be split into separate properties, the donor can select one of the divided interests (such as the TV rights to a novel) for transfer, retaining the other interests in his own right or transferring them to other donees.[44]

Although the created-product escape from *Lucas v. Earl* is important, its scope should not be exaggerated. Taxpayers with unpaid claims against employers, clients, and customers for personal services cannot transfer their rights;[45] nor can lawyers and doctors treat wills or prescriptions as literary compositions that can be donated to members of their families and sold by the donees to the client or patient.

7. Transfers of Income Generated by Closely Held Businesses. The taxpayers who are best positioned to escape the rigors of *Lucas v. Earl* with respect to income from personal services are those engaged in family business enterprises. If the parents transfer part or all of the stock of a family corporation to their children, the parents can work for less than the value of the services performed, or without compensation; the corporation's dividends and net worth will be increased by these personal exertions and the resulting increase in the income or capital gains realized by the children is ordinarily taxed to them, despite *Lucas v. Earl,* rather than to the parents.[46]

This gambit is not feasible if the business is conducted as a partnership, since IRC §704(e) ordinarily imputes reasonable compensation to the donor of an interest in a family partnership who continues to work for the firm if the partnership agreement does not provide for an adequate salary. If the donor of a family business does not continue as a partner, however, IRC §704(e) is not applicable, and services performed gratuitously for the firm do not ordinar-

[43] Rev. Rul. 71-33, 1971-1 CB 30. For problems in applying the distinction between the assignment of income and the transfer of an income-producing asset that was created by the transferor's services, see Siegel v. US, 464 F.2d 891, 894 (9th Cir. 1972) (income earned by corporation before liquidating distribution to shareholders); Strauss v. CIR, 168 F.2d 441 (2d Cir.), cert. denied, 335 US 858, rehearing denied, 335 US 888 (1948) (taxpayer held not transferor of process, but mere assignor of royalties).

[44] Rev. Rul. 54-599, 1954-2 CB 52.

[45] See Rev. Rul. 55-2, 1955-1 CB 211.

[46] For the possibility of a contrary result in extreme situations, see CIR v. Laughton, 113 F.2d 103 (9th Cir. 1940); Borge v. CIR, 405 F.2d 673 (2d Cir. 1968), cert. denied sub nom. Danica Enterprises, Inc. v. CIR, 395 US 933 (1969).

ily result in the imputation of income but instead are treated as a rendition of gratuitous services to the donee.

Finally, a taxpayer engaged in business can ordinarily relinquish business opportunities in favor of other members of the family without being taxed on the income when it is realized, if the transfer occurs before embarking on the venture and the beneficiaries perform whatever services are required to turn the opportunity into actuality.[47] Strictly speaking, steering of business in their direction is not a *transfer* of earned income; but if the donor could readily reap the benefits personally, the waiver has substantially the same practical effect as an assignment of earned income but not its adverse tax results.

8. Salaries to Children and Other Members of Taxpayer's Family. If parents employ their children in a family business, deducting the salaries, the tax result may be similar to an assignment of income. Although the employment of the taxpayer's child for a reasonable salary has the same tax impact as the employment of an outsider, if the salary exceeds the value of the child's services, deducting the full amount paid is tantamount to an anticipatory assignment of the parents' income to the extent of the overpayment. For this reason, salaries paid to children and other members of the taxpayer's family are subjected to close scrutiny to determine whether the relative is a bona fide employee, and excess deductions are frequently disallowed.

Although payments by parents to children for services are rather common, occasionally the compensation trickles up rather than down. In *Hundley v. CIR,* for example, a talented high school athlete paid his father, a former semiprofessional baseball player and coach, half of a bonus received in 1960 on signing a professional baseball contract, under a 1958 oral agreement to compensate his father, for his services as coach, agent, and business manager. On finding that the services rendered by the father were instrumental in improving the taxpayer's skills and in obtaining an exceptionally large bonus, the court held that he could deduct his father's share of the bonus as a business expense.[48]

¶30.3 TRANSFERS OF INCOME-PRODUCING PROPERTY

1. Introductory. When taxpayers transfer cash, real estate, securities, or other income-producing property to members of their families, the tax consequences are totally different from those attached to assignments of income

---

[47] See Crowley v. CIR, 34 TC 333 (1960) (Acq.).

[48] Hundley v. CIR, 48 TC 339 (1967) (Acq.); see also Goodrich v. CIR, 20 TC 323 (1953).

created by personal services. Income from the latter source is almost always taxed to the wage earner, salaried employee, or self-employed taxpayer under *Lucas v. Earl;* but if income-producing property is transferred, the dividends, interest, rents, or other "fruits" of the "tree" are usually taxed to the new owner rather than to the donor. The principal issues concern not this accepted bias in favor of investment income but rather whether (a) the assignor has retained so much control that he or she should continue to be treated as the owner of the property; (b) the subject of the assignment is the income-producing property (the "tree") or only the income (the "fruit"); and (c) the assignment should be disregarded either because it followed, rather than preceded, realization of the income in question or because it was interposed immediately before income was to be realized in the normal course of events. These issues are discussed below.

To be honored for federal income tax purposes, a transfer of income-producing property must be effective under the applicable state law. In the discussion that follows, validity of the transfer under local law is assumed, and attention is focused on whether the transfer is also effective for federal income tax purposes or falls short of its objective.

2. Retention of Control. The taxpayer's right to shift the tax liability for income by transfering the income-producing property presupposes a completed gift. If the transfer is subject to a retained right to revoke the gift, the income generated by the property is taxed to the donor just as though he had kept the property and merely transferred the income from time to time to suit his pleasure.[49] What if the gift cannot be revoked, but the donor prescribes in advance, or retains discretionary control over, the way the donee must deal with the property or the uses to which the income may be put?

If the transfer is in trust, the tax consequences of reserved rights are specified by an elaborate network of statutory, judicial and administrative rules, painfully worked out over a period of several decades.[50] But for nontrust transfers there is no parallel body of statutory provisions, and relatively few judicial and administrative rulings examine the amount of control that the donor can retain without being taxed on the income.

In *CIR v. Sunnen,* an inventor transferred to his wife all his rights in certain royalty contracts with a family corporation licensed to use his inventions. Although he reserved no direct rights under the contracts themselves, the Court found that he was taxable on the royalties received by his wife for a variety of reasons, including his power as the dominant shareholder to control the corporation's production policies and to cause it to cancel the

---

[49] See Corliss v. Bowers, 281 US 376 (1930).

[50] Infra Ch. 34.

contracts without liability, the failure of the contracts to specify minimum royalties, and the fact that the royalty income remained within the family group. As the Court tartly observed, the assignments "left him with something more than a memory." [51]

The standards for determining whether a nontrust transfer is sufficiently complete to relieve the transferor of tax liability are extremely vague. For planning purposes, therefore, the taxpayer who wants to be sure of tax immunity is well advised either to cut all strings to the transferred property or else to transfer the property in trust and stay within the safe harbors laid down by the statutory provisions governing so-called grantor trusts.[52] If the assignor retains controls over a nontrust transfer that are comparable to those generating tax liability when retained by the grantor of a trust, he is inviting a lawsuit that he will almost certainly lose;[53] and even if the retained nontrust controls are more restricted, the absence of any statutory safe harbors means that the assignor is embarking on a perilous voyage.

3. Transfers of Income-Producing Property vs. Transfers of Income. To be relieved of income tax liability, the assignor must transfer the income-producing property itself, not merely the income that it will generate. This requirement is satisfied by the overwhelming bulk of intra-family gifts of real estate, securities, and other investment assets; but it creates problems for offbeat transactions. If, for example, the owner of rental real estate transfers to his children the right to receive the gross rents for a period of time, the assignor must continue to report the income just as though he had collected the rents in due course and then endorsed the tenants' checks over to the beneficiaries of his bounty from month to month. After such an assignment, a donor can sabotage the assignment by refusing to repair the premises, renew expiring leases, rebuild after a fire, or similar acts of retaliation; thus, the donee's continued enjoyment of the gift depends on retaining the donor's goodwill.[54]

Even if an assignment effectively deprives the donor of a continuing veto power (e.g., by forbidding the donor to interfere with the donee's right to reap the harvest as it matures), the transaction is analogous to a transfer of the income-producing property in trust for a specified period; and the donor's

---

[51] CIR v. Sunnen, 333 US 591, 608 (1948).

[52] See infra Ch. 34.

[53] But the income tax consequence to the lender of a "Crown" loan has not yet been determined. See CIR v. Crown, 585 F.2d 234, 236 n.3 (7th Cir. 1978), holding that interest-free demand loans impose no gift tax liability on the lender; Dickman v. CIR, 690 F.2d 812 (11th Cir. 1982) (contra).

[54] For an extended discussion of the tenuous status of the assignee of rents, see Galt v. CIR, 19 TC 892, 902-908 (1953), aff'd, 216 F.2d 41 (7th Cir. 1954), cert. denied, 348 US 951 (1955).

right to resume control over the property at the end of this period could be viewed as tantamount to a retention of "sufficient power and control over the assigned property"[55] to justify taxing the donor on the income produced during the temporary hiatus in his direct enjoyment of the property. If the transfer is analogized to a trust, the IRS might pursue the analogy further by applying the ten-year benchmark prescribed by IRC §673 for determining whether trust income is taxable to the grantor of a reversionary trust.[56]

The distinction between an assignment of income-producing property and an assignment of income is especially troublesome if the assignor's rights consist solely of a series of items that would constitute income if collected by him in the normal course of events, since in this situation the two concepts coalesce. In *Blair v. CIR*, the Supreme Court addressed itself to this problem, which arose when the life beneficiary of a trust created by his father's will assigned to his children specified annual amounts of the trust income that he would otherwise receive for the rest of his life.[57] The Court held that the taxpayer as life beneficiary of the trust was "the owner of an equitable interest in the [trust] corpus," entitling him to enforce the trust and to be redressed for any breach; that this interest "was present property alienable like any other"; and that the obligation to report the income was effectively shifted from him to his assignees.

Lest its holding be construed to permit claims for unpaid salaries, accounts receivable generated by personal services to customers, and similar ordinary-income items to be effectively assigned for tax purposes on the theory that they also embody a legal right to proceed against the debtor, the Court in *Blair* drew a distinction between the assignment of "a chose in action" and the assignment of the "right, title, and estate in and to property." Only assignments of the latter class, such as the interest of the life beneficiary in *Blair,* are protected by the Court's decision.

The assignments validated by *Blair* were coextensive with the assignor's interest in the trust—that is, each assignee was to receive a specified dollar amount of the trust income that the assignor would otherwise be entitled to receive for the rest of his life. Such a "horizontal" division of the assignor's rights is similar to the transfer of an undivided fractional interest in real estate or other property, and must be contrasted with a "vertical" division, under which the assignee's rights can terminate before the assignor's death, such as a transfer of the trust income for the next five years or of the first $10,000 of trust income to become due. A division of the latter type is comparable to a

---

[55] See CIR v. Sunnen, supra note 51, at 604.

[56] See Rev. Rul. 55-38, 1955-1 CB 389. For the treatment of grantor trusts, see infra ¶34.1.

[57] Blair v. CIR, 300 US 5 (1937).

temporary alienation of the income-producing property, since the assignor will resume his pre-assignment status when the assignee's rights terminate.

In keeping with this distinction, the Supreme Court refused in *Harrison v. Schaffner* to apply *Blair* to the income beneficiary of a testamentary trust who assigned to her children specified amounts to be paid from the trust income for the following year.[58] The Court's suggestion in *Harrison v. Schaffner* that an authoritative temporal line could be drawn by Congress or the Treasury has not been heeded. In a 1955 ruling, however, the IRS analogized a life beneficiary's vertical division of trust income to the creation of a trust, holding that an income beneficiary's irrevocable assignment of the trust income for a period of not less than ten years will be treated as "a disposition of a substantial interest in the trust property" (immunizing him from tax under *Blair*) if the assignor does not retain the type of control that would subject him to tax under the "grantor trust" rules if he were the grantor of a trust.[59] Although directly concerned only with the assignment of trust income by a life beneficiary, this sensible approach could appropriately be extended by the IRS to all comparable transactions; but as of this writing, there are no other published rulings on point.

The hazy boundary between income-producing property and "mere income" is also exemplified by the facts in another celebrated assignment-of-income-case, *Helvering v. Horst.*[60] The issue in *Horst* was whether the taxpayer, who gave his son $25,000 (face amount) of interest coupons detached from negotiable bonds owned by him, was taxable on the interest collected by the donee when the coupons matured later in the same year. Because the coupons were payable to bearer and separately negotiable, the taxpayer retained no power to negate the gift by settling up the debt with the obligor; in this respect the transfer of the coupons differed from a transfer of future rents or dividends that a donor who later regrets his generosity can sabotage by disposing of the underlying property or letting it fall into disrepair. Even so, the Court, referring to the fruit-and-tree analogy, held that the interest was taxable to the donor rather than to the donee.

So far as the fruit-and-tree analogy is concerned, the taxpayer's investment in *Horst* could have been fragmented for analysis into a series of separate coupons plus a naked bond, with each of these instruments being viewed as an independent discount obligation, purchased for an amount equal to the present value of its face value at maturity. Had the Court in *Horst* treated each

---

[58] Harrison v. Schaffner, 312 US 579 (1941).

[59] Rev. Rul. 55-38, supra note 56; see also Hawaiian Trust Co. v. Kanne, 172 F.2d 74 (9th Cir. 1949) (same result for assignments for minority of children aged nine and ten and for unmarried life of divorced wife); contra Galt v. CIR, supra note 54 (rents assigned for twenty-year period).

[60] Helvering v. Horst, 311 US 112 (1940).

coupon as a separate income-producing asset, the amount taxed to the donor would have been only the difference between its cost (viz., its allocable share of the cost of the bond with all coupons attached) and its value at the time of the gift or the amount collected at maturity by the donee. The Court, however, taxed the father on the face amount of the donated interest coupons.

4. Transfers of Property With Accrued Income or Immediately Before Sale. Although a gift of income-producing property usually shifts the tax liability for subsequently accruing income to the donee, the donor must ordinarily report any income that accrued before the gift, even though the gift encompasses both the underlying property and the accrued income. For example, parents who give stock to a child must report any dividends declared before the gift, even if they are cash-basis taxpayers and the transfer is consummated before the dividends are payable.[61] The donor of a debt instrument has been similarly taxed when interest accruing before the gift was paid to the donee, though several courts have refused to apply this principle to past-due interest if payment was dubious when the gift was made because of the debtor's financial condition or uncertain liability,[62] possibly on the unarticulated ground that the principal source of value in such claims is the favorable resolution of the prior contingencies *after* the assignment.

In contrast to these cases of past-due interest and dividends declared before the date of the gift, the *Horst* case involved a gift of interest coupons *before* their due date.[63] In holding that the interest was taxable to the donor when paid to the donee later in the same year, the Court said:

> [T]he donor . . . has . . ., by his act, procured payment of the interest as a valuable gift to a member of his family. Such a use of his economic gain, the right to receive income, to procure a satisfaction which can be obtained only by the expenditure of money or property, would seem to be the enjoyment of the income whether the satisfaction is the purchase of goods at the corner grocery, the payment of his debt there, or such non-material satisfactions as may result from the payment of a campaign or community chest contribution, or a gift to his favorite son.[64]

In a 1965 decision pushing the "non-material satisfactions" theory of

---

[61] Smith's Est. v. CIR, 292 F.2d 478 (3d Cir. 1961), cert. denied, 368 US 967 (1962); Rev. Rul. 74-562, 1974-2 CB 28.

[62] See, e.g., Rev. Rul. 55-278, 1955-1 CB 471 (donor of Series E U.S. savings bonds taxable on interest accrued at time of transfer, unless interest previously reported as income); but see, e.g., CIR v. Timken, 141 F.2d 625 (6th Cir. 1944) (debtor's ability to pay uncertain; donor not taxed).

[63] Helvering v. Horst, supra note 60.

[64] Id. at 117.

Horst to its outer limit, the Court of Appeals for the Eighth Circuit held that a generous but dishonest bank cashier was taxable on bank funds improperly transferred by her to the accounts of friends, who thought these increases in their bank balances were gifts or loans.[65]

The *Horst* statement quoted above is frequently cited in assignment-of-income cases, but its rationale is far from precise. Everything that the Court says about "non-material satisfactions" would be equally valid if the taxpayer had given appreciated stock or real estate to the donee; but it is entirely clear that *Horst* does not require a donor of such property to treat the gift as a constructive realization of the unrealized economic gain.

The Court may have based its decision on the ground that a gift of bond coupons "shortly before their due date" [66] is for practical purposes tantamount to collecting the income and then giving it to the donee. The case was tried on a stipulation of facts stating that the intervals varied from about one to four months.[67] Analyzed as a transfer of income on the eve of a taxable receipt, the transaction in *Horst* raises primarily a question of judgment: When is a transfer too late? Conversely, how soon is soon enough? The courts have wrestled with this issue in numerous cases involving sales of property, where the owner decides at the last minute to call off a proposed transaction in order to give the property to a related person, who then makes a sale in his or her own name. In general, if the terms of the sale are fluid when the transfer is made and the donee has some elbow-room, the transaction is taken at face value and the gain is taxed to the donee. On the other hand, if the donee is expected to step into the donor's shoes and consummate a transaction previously negotiated by the donor, the donee's role is disregarded as mere camouflage and the sale is attributed to the donor.[68]

If the terms of the transaction are tailor-made, the degree of pre-arrangement before a gift is a feasible criterion, albeit an uncertain one, in deciding whether the gift occurred too late to shift the resulting gain from the donor to the donee. But the concept of prearrangement is irrelevant in situations like *Horst,* where neither the donor nor the donee negotiates with the obligor and

---

[65] Geiger's Est. v. CIR, 352 F.2d 221 (8th Cir. 1965).

[66] Helvering v. Horst, supra note 60, at 114.

[67] See Record at 23-24, Helvering v. Horst, supra note 60.

[68] The leading cases involve corporations liquidated in order to permit their assets to be sold by their shareholders. Compare CIR v. Court Holding Co., 324 US 331 (1945) (sale imputed to corporation), with US v. Cumberland Pub. Serv. Co., 338 US 451 (1950) (sale treated as a shareholder transaction). Although IRC §337, enacted in 1954, displaces these decisions as respects most corporate liquidations, they remain controlling in other contexts.

For special legislation taxing trusts at the transferor's rate on built-in appreciation if property is sold at a gain within two years after the transfer in trust, see IRC §644.

the income ripens into maturity solely because of the passage of time. In these circumstances, the courts must draw an arbitrary line based on the elapsed time between the gift and the receipt of the income.[69] For planning purposes, the ten-year safe harbor created by IRC §673 for grantor trusts may be a useful analogy; but the IRS has never promulgated any temporal guidelines for *Horst*-type transactions,[70] and the courts have exonerated the donor from tax liability in a number of cases involving much shorter periods, especially where the value of the transferred property was uncertain when the gift was made.[71]

5. Gift-Leasebacks of Income-Producing Property. The IRS has litigated a large number of gift-leaseback transactions involving transfers of office buildings by parents to their children, usually in trust, followed by a lease of the property back to the transferor, who occupies the space for business or professional purposes and deducts the rent paid to the transferee. If accepted at face value, the transaction shifts the amount paid as rent from the transferor's gross income to the transferee's.

It is not entirely clear why the IRS pursues these transactions so implacably, since, if the amount paid equals the fair rental value of the leased property, the transferor's deductions equal the amount that would be deductible if he or she leased the same or equivalent space from an outsider; and, conversely, the children include in gross income the same amount that they would realize by renting the space to outsiders. Moreover, if the children sold the building, it seems clear that the parents could deduct the rent paid by them to its new owner.

Despite the existence of these functionally equivalent alternatives, the IRS has persistently contended that rents paid under gift-leaseback arrangements are not "ordinary and necessary" business expenses because they can be traced back to a transfer that served no business purpose. Some courts have upheld the IRS position, but the prevailing judicial view is that the rents are deductible under IRC §162 if the lease is negotiated with an independent trustee obligated to demand a fair rental for the space and if the leaseback (as distinguished from the gift) serves a bona fide business purpose.[72] The latter condition is satisfied

---

[69] See, e.g., Friedman v. CIR, 346 F.2d 506 (6th Cir. 1965) (sale of endowment policies at cost to charities a few days before maturity; held, vendor-donor taxable on difference between cost and proceeds collected by charities).

[70] See Rev. Rul. 55-38, supra note 56.

[71] See, e.g., Braunstein v. CIR, ¶62,210 P-H Memo TC (1962) (gift of Irish Sweepstakes ticket with guaranteed minimum prize of $2,147 one day before race; held, guaranteed prize taxable to donor, but not balance of prize actually won, about $136,000); Morgan Guar. Trust Co. v. US, 585 F.2d 988 (Ct. Cl. 1978) (extensive review of case law).

[72] For a review of the cases, see Quinlivan v. CIR, 599 F.2d 269 (8th Cir.), cert.

if the transferor needs and uses the space for business or professional purposes.

¶30.4 RELATED PROBLEMS

1. Year When Ineffectively Assigned Income Is Taxable. If income is the subject of an ineffective assignment, the assignor is ordinarily taxed when the assigned item is collected by the assignee, rather than in the year of the assignment. In *Colby v. CIR,* for example, the court rejected an attempt by the IRS to tax the assignor of past-due interest in the year of the assignment (1935), indicating that the years of collection (1936 and 1937, not before the court) were the proper years.[73]

To be sure, the Supreme Court in *Horst* suggested that the gift itself constituted a taxable realization of the assignor's gain.[74] But this hint is neutralized by the fact that the assignor was taxed on the amount collected, not on the somewhat lower value of the assigned coupons at the time of the gift. Imputing income to the assignor when it is collected by the assignee rather than when the assignment is made creates enforcement and legal problems if there is a long delay, since the assignor may become insolvent or die in the interim; but the alternative—taxing the assignor when the assignment is made—is often equally impractical.

2. Treatment of Assignee Under Ineffective Assignment. If income is taxed to an assignor because the transfer is revocable or otherwise ineffective for federal income tax purposes, the transferee is entitled to a refund for any tax paid by him on the income, since the transaction is treated as though the assignor had collected the income and then transferred it to the assignee by gift. A refund is in order even if the statute of limitations has run on the taxable year for which the assignee reported the income, since IRC §1312 mitigates the statute of limitations in this situation.[75]

3. Earnings of Minor Children. Under IRC §73, amounts received in respect of a child's services are includable in the child's gross income rather than in the parents', even if the earnings belong to the parents under local law

---

denied, 444 US 996 (1979) (deduction allowed); May v. CIR, 76 TC 7 (1981) (concurring opinion by Judge Goffe).

[73] Colby v. CIR, 45 BTA 536, 539 (1941) (Acq.); see also Rev. Rul. 58-275, 1958-1 CB 22 (donor of past-due bond coupons taxable in year of collection).

[74] Helvering v. Horst, supra note 60.

[75] For IRC §1312, see infra ¶41.9.

and are paid directly to them.[76] Travel expenses, union dues, charitable contributions, and other business and personal items are deductible by the child even if paid by the parent, provided they are attributable to earnings taxed to the child solely by reason of IRC §73(a).[77] By virtue of the latter qualification, the parent's expenditures evidently do not qualify for deduction by the child if the child would be taxed on his or her earnings in the absence of IRC §73(a) (i.e., if under local law the income belongs to the child rather than to the parent). Thus IRC §73(b) carries forward, rather surprisingly, the variations in local law rejected by IRC §73(a).

4. Custodianships for Minors. In one form or another, statutes permitting gifts to be made to minors by means of custodianship arrangements are in force in every state. The statutes typically permit the principal and income to be applied by the custodian for the minor's benefit until majority, when the property and any undistributed income are turned over to the minor. Since the transfer vests ownership of the property in the minor under local law, the income is taxable to the minor unless it is used by the custodian to satisfy the parents' (or someone else's) legal obligation to support the minor.[78] In this event, the income so used is taxable to the person whose legal duty is discharged, whether he or she is the donor, the custodian, or a third party.

Like any other legal device, however, a custodianship can be disregarded as a sham if its substance does not accord with its form, as when a purported donor-custodian deals with the property in a manner inconsistent with his custodial duties.[79]

5. Ancillary Statutory and Judicial Barriers to the Assignment of Income—IRC §§446, 482, Etc. The pioneering Supreme Court decisions in the assignment-of-income area, which remain dominant although they are almost forty years old, rest on the statutory predecessors of IRC §1 (imposing a tax on the income of "every individual") and §61(a) (defining "gross income"), whose language is so general and inconclusive that the opinions constitute a veritable "common law" of taxation. In the intervening years, the IRS has occasionally relied on additional statutory provisions and judicial doctrines when taxing assigned income to the assignor rather than to the assignee. The principal sources that have been exploited by the government are the following:

---

[76] For the legislative history of IRC §73, see Allen v. CIR, 50 TC 466, 475 (1968), aff'd per curiam, 410 F.2d 398 (3d Cir. 1969).

[77] Treas. Regs. §1.73-1(b).

[78] See Rev. Rul. 59-357, 1959-2 CB 212.

[79] See e.g., Beirne v. CIR, 52 TC 210 (1969) (transfers under Alaska Gifts of Securities to Minors Act ineffective where donor-custodian continued to exercise dominion over alleged gifts).

1. *IRC § 446(b) (accounting method must clearly reflect income).* If a taxpayer's accounting method "does not clearly reflect income," the IRS is empowered by IRC §446(b) to substitute a more accurate method. In some circumstances, this authority overlaps the power vested in the IRS by the more general assignment-of-income principles. If, for example, a cash-basis physician systematically assigns accounts receivable arising from the rendition of professional services to a child, it is arguable (a) that the cash method of accounting fails to "clearly reflect income" within the meaning of IRC §446(b) and (b) that the taxpayer can be compelled to switch to accrual accounting, which would require amounts owed by patients to be included in income when billed rather than when paid.[80]

2. *IRC § 482 (allocation of gross income among taxpayers under common control).* If two or more organizations, trades, or businesses are owned or controlled by the same interests, IRC §482 permits the IRS to distribute, apportion, or allocate gross income, deductions, credits, or allowances among them in order to prevent evasion of taxes or clearly to reflect their respective income. This sweeping provision, discussed later in this work,[81] permits the IRS to compute the income of affiliated corporations or other taxpayers as though it resulted from arm's-length bargaining among them. Thus, if a manufacturing corporation markets its products through a subsidiary that promotes and distributes the goods without compensation, the IRS can invoke IRC §482 to impute a reasonable commission to the subsidiary for its services.[82]

3. *Form vs. substance and related doctrines.* When more specific remedies fail, the IRS often resorts to the substance-over-form and step transaction doctrines in order to frustrate a family-oriented tax-avoidance device or to establish that a purported assignment is a sham. These amorphous judge-created principles are discussed elsewhere in this work,[83] whose pages also record innumerable attacks, successful and unsuccessful, of this type in examining the tax consequences of specific transactions.

---

[80] See Rev. Rul. 73-157, 1973-1 CB 213 (denial of installment-basis accounting on sale by father to son, who then sold the same property by prearrangement to third party on terms not qualifying for installment election); Rev. Rul. 73-536, 1973-2 CB 158 (same, even in absence of prearrangement); Idaho First Nat'l Bank v. US, 265 F.2d 6 (9th Cir. 1959) (cash-basis liquidating corporation taxed on accrued interest on note receivable, in reliance on IRC §446(b)).

[81] Infra ¶33.4.

[82] See Treas. Regs. §1.482-2(b)(1); see also Borge v. CIR, 405 F.2d 673 (2d Cir. 1968) (allocation under IRC §482 of compensation to entertainer from wholly owned corporation, which hired out his services to promoters of TV, stage, and other public performances).

[83] See supra ¶1.3.

SELECTED BIBLIOGRAPHY

Bittker, Federal Income Taxation and the Family, 27 Stan. L. Rev. 1389, 1401 (1975).

Brown, The Growing "Common Law" of Taxation, 1961 So. Calif. Tax Inst. 1, 13–31.

Eustice, Contract Rights, Capital Gain, and Assignment of Income—The *Ferrer* Case, 20 Tax L. Rev. 1 (1964).

Kauder, The Service Corporation as the Taxpayer's Alter Ego: Variations on the *Borge* Theme, 28 NYU Inst. on Fed. Tax. 1109 (1970).

Lyon & Eustice, Assignment of Income: Fruit and Tree as Irrigated by the *P.G. Lake* Case, 17 Tax L. Rev. 293 (1962).

McMahon, Expanding the Taxable Unit: The Aggregation of the Income of Children and Parents, 56 NYU L. Rev. 60 (1981).

Note, Federal Tax Aspects of the Obligation to Support, 74 Harv. L. Rev. 1191, 1211–1213 (1961).

Rice, Judicial Trends in Gratuitous Assignments to Avoid Federal Income Taxes, 64 Yale L.J. 991 (1955).

Shapiro, The *Basye* Decision One Year Later: Judging Its Effect Upon Related Areas, 39 J. Tax. 376 (1973).

Soll, Intra-Family Assignments: Attribution and Realization of Income, 6 Tax L. Rev. 435, 7 Tax L. Rev. 61 (1951).

Surrey, Assignments of Income and Related Devices: Choice of the Taxable Person, 33 Colum. L. Rev. 791 (1933).

Surrey, The Supreme Court and the Federal Income Tax: Some Implications of the Recent Decisions, 35 Ill. L. Rev. 779 (1941).

Teschner, *First Security Bank of Utah:* Taxpayer Disability and the Supreme Court, 50 Taxes 260 (1972).

Worthy, Problems of Jointly Owned Property, 22 Tax Lawyer 601 (1969).

Ziegler, Gifts to Minors—Three Variations, 24 Tax Lawyer 297 (1971).

CHAPTER 31

Effect of Community-Property System

Page

¶31.1 RECOGNITION OF COMMUNITY-PROPERTY SYSTEM FOR FEDERAL INCOME TAX PURPOSES

1. Introductory. From its earliest days, the federal income tax had to come to terms with the community-property system, that as a legacy of Spanish law, governs the legal rights of married couples in Arizona, California, Idaho, Louisiana, Nevada, New Mexico, Texas, and Washington. Although the details vary from one state to another, the basic principle of marital property law in these states is that marriage is a partnership vesting each spouse with a present interest in one-half of the couple's joint income, whether derived from personal services or from their community property, subject until recently to the husband's managerial authority.[1] A married couple may also realize community income if either spouse or both are domiciled in a foreign country with a community-property system.[2]

---

[1] For recent legislative changes substituting joint management and control for the husband's traditional control, see Reppy & Samuel, Community Property in the United States, Ch. 14 (Michie, 2d ed. 1982).

[2] For special legislation applicable to such couples if one spouse is a nonresident alien, see IRC §879.

In 1930 the Supreme Court decided *Poe v. Seaborn,* which rejected the government's theory that the husband's power to manage community property warranted taxing all the community income to him, holding instead that one-half was taxable to each spouse. *Lucas v. Earl* was distinguished as involving an assignment (under an agreement made by a married couple domiciled in a common law state) of earnings that would have belonged to the husband in the absence of the assignment, while "here, by law, the earnings are never the property of the husband, but that of the community." [3]

From the decision in *Poe v. Seaborn* until 1948, when Congress authorized the now-familiar joint return,[4] the tax status of a married couple in a community-property state (assuming no noncommunity income) differed from that of a married couple in a common-law state in two fundamental ways. First, each community-property spouse paid the same tax as an unmarried person with one-half the aggregate community income. This result obtained in common-law states only in the unusual case of a married couple whose earned income was generated one-half by each spouse and whose investment income, if any, was also equally divided between them. Second, the federal tax burden for equal-income married couples was identical in community-property states, whether the income was attributable to one spouse or to both. In common-law states, by contrast, the tax liability of equal-income married couples could vary widely, since it depended on the amount attributable to each spouse. Although a common-law couple could reduce or eliminate this disparity by an equal division of their income-producing property, *Lucas v. Earl* prevented them from effecting a similar division of their earned income. Since *Poe v. Seaborn* was not rooted in constitutional law but merely reflected the Supreme Court's interpretation of the applicable revenue act, these geographical differences could have been eliminated by Congress whenever the political climate favored a change.[5]

Because *Poe v. Seaborn* does not create an option to split community income but imposes an *obligation* to do so, the Supreme Court held in *United States v. Mitchell* that a community-property wife was liable for the taxes on her share of her husband's earnings for years in which no returns were filed

---

[3] Poe v. Seaborn, 282 US 101, 117 (1930); for discussion of Lucas v. Earl, see supra ¶30.2.

[4] Infra ¶39.3.

[5] For disregard of community-property for some purposes, see, e.g., IRC §1402(a)(5) (for self-employment tax, trade or business income is taxed to spouse who manages the business; partnership trade or business income is taxed to the spouse who is the partner), §879 (if one spouse is U.S. citizen or resident and other is nonresident alien, income earned by each spouse and community income from his or her separate property are taxed to that spouse; trade or business and partnership income is taxed in accordance with IRC §1405), §66 (separated couple's community-property income is taxed in accordance with IRC §879 under certain circumstances).

by him, although she had little knowledge of his finances and relied on his assurances that he was filing timely returns and paying the taxes due.[6]

2. Adoption of Community-Property System by Common-Law States. As federal income tax rates increased before and during World War II, the tax advantages of the community-property system became more and more attractive to the common law states. In 1944, however, the Supreme Court decided in *CIR v. Harmon* that Oklahoma and Oregon do-it-yourself community-property laws, which permitted married couples to elect to be governed by the newly enacted community property system of these two states, were substantially the same as the income-splitting contract between husband and wife that was held ineffective for federal tax purposes in *Lucas v. Earl.*[7] The Court went on in *Harmon* to announce that only a nonelective system of community property, "made an incident of marriage by the inveterate policy of the State," could qualify for income splitting under *Poe v. Seaborn.*[8]

The result of the *Harmon* case was that the community-property system was effective for federal income tax purposes if under local law the couple could "opt out" of it (as permitted in most traditional community-property states), but not if they had to "opt in." Oklahoma and Oregon promptly replaced their optional community-property systems with mandatory ones, which were accepted as effective by the IRS. Hawaii, Nebraska, Michigan, and Pennsylvania also joined the community-property parade, and by 1948 similar action was under discussion in states as far removed from the civilizing mission of Spanish law as Massachusetts and New York.[9]

Congress responded to the community-property epidemic in 1948 by authorizing married couples to file joint returns, under which their separate incomes, deductions, and other tax allowances are aggregated, with the result that the division of income and property between them was no longer crucial. With the tax disparity between community property and common-law property largely eliminated, the new community-property states lost their taste for Spanish law and repealed their statutes.[10]

---

[6] US v. Mitchell, 403 US 190 (1971). The "innocent spouse" principle of IRC §6013(e) (infra ¶39.3) was not in force for the years before the Court in *Mitchell,* and in any event, it applies only to joint returns; IRC §66 (infra ¶31.3) was also not then in force.

[7] CIR v. Harmon, 323 US 44 (1944).

[8] Id. at 46.

[9] The Pennsylvania statute was held unconstitutional in Willcox v. Penn Mutual Life Ins. Co., 357 Pa. 581, 55 A.2d 521 (1947).

[10] For more recent proposals to bring community-property concepts to common-law states for non-tax reasons, see the Uniform Marital Property Act (Nat'l Conference of Commissioners on Uniform State Laws).

¶31.2 SEPARATE VS. COMMUNITY INCOME

The advent of the joint return in 1948 not only eliminated the geographical disparity between community-property and common-law states except in rare situations, but also made it unnecessary for married couples in community-property states to distinguish between separate income and community income, since all income of both spouses is aggregated if they file a joint return. When, however, community-property couples file separate returns (usually because they are too hostile to cooperate in executing an instrument generating joint and several liability),[11] the distinction between separate income and community income retains its pre-1948 significance. Each separate return must include one-half of the community income plus all of the taxpayer's separate income.

Disputes between taxpayers and the IRS in applying the distinction between community and separate income must be resolved by the federal courts; but the boundary is ultimately fixed by local law, which varies from one jurisdiction to another. For this reason, it is not feasible in this work to do more than summarize the principal problem areas.

1. *Domicile.* In general, local law determines whether a couple is domiciled in a community-property state, whether the earnings of a domiciliary spouse constitute community income when the other spouse is a nondomiciliary, and whether the income from real property owned by nondomiciliaries is community income.[12]

2. *Agreements negating community-property principles.* Most community-property states permit a married couple to agree that community property will be held in separate ownership, and vice versa; but the requisite formalities, scope, and other features of such agreements vary from one state to another.[13]

3. *Community vs. separate property and income.* The basic principle of community-property law is that property, earnings and gains acquired during marriage by labor, skill, or industry constitute community property. On the other hand, property acquired before marriage retains the character of separate property, at least if it was fully paid for before marriage and is not improved thereafter with community funds. Gifts and bequests to either spouse during marriage become community or separate property, depending on whether the

---

[11] For the use of separate returns by married persons, see infra ¶39.3.

[12] See de Funiak & Vaughn, Principles of Community Property 217-232 (U. of Arizona Press, 2d ed. 1971); Lay, Estate Planning Considerations Involved With Community Property and the Migrant Client, 11 J. Fam. L. 255 (1971).

[13] See de Funiak & Vaughn, supra note 12, at 337-354; Rev. Rul. 73-390, 1973-2 CB 12 (California separate-earnings agreement effective for federal income tax purposes).

donor intended to benefit both spouses or only one. The community property states are divided on whether income from separate property belongs and is taxed to the owner of the property, or to the community.[14]

4. *Commingling of separate and community property.* If community and separate property are so commingled that they resist identification, the presumption is that the property belongs to the community. This can result in an undesirable division between the spouses of the income from the property or the deductions generated by it.[15]

5. *Purchases on credit.* Money borrowed after marriage is presumed to be for the purpose of acquiring community property, but the presumption can be rebutted by proof that only one spouse was liable on the loan.[16]

6. *Improvement of separate property with community property, and vice versa.* If separate property is improved by the labor of either spouse or the expenditure of community funds, the resulting improvements belong to the community. An addition to community property financed with separate property should give its owner a corresponding claim on the value of the addition, but the presumption in favor of the community status of all property works against separate status, unless the facts demonstrate an intent to preserve it.

7. *Income from a business purchased with separate property.* When the labor of one or both spouses is applied to an enterprise acquired with separate property, the business income must be allocated between the contributing components. The portion generated by the invested separate property must ordinarily be assigned to the individual owner, while the balance of the income belongs to the marital community.[17]

8. *Effect of divorce, legal separation, etc.* Divorce terminates the community, and subsequent income is taxed to whichever spouse earned it or owns the property producing it. While not fully terminating the community, a legal separation may have a similar effect if it is viewed as partitioning the community property; but an "innocent" spouse often has a right under local law to share in postseparation income produced by the other spouse.[18]

---

[14] Idaho, Louisiana, and Texas follow the traditional view that the income from separate property is community property; see de Funiak & Vaughn, supra note 12, at 160-163; Prager, The Persistence of Separate Property Concepts in California's Community Property Systems, 24 U.C.L.A. L. Rev. 1 (1976).

[15] See, e.g., Nutt's Est. v. CIR, 447 F.2d 1109 (9th Cir. 1971) (illustrating complexity of allocation problems where separate issues exist as to ownership of funds used to buy stock, stock itself, gain produced by business, etc.).

[16] See, e.g., Weeks v. CIR, 31 BTA 627 (1934) (Acq.).

[17] See Rev. Rul. 73-391, 1973-2 CB 12.

[18] IRC §66, enacted in 1980 as a response to the plight of abandoned spouses who must pay the tax on, without receiving the benefit of, their share of the other spouse's earnings, permits community-property laws to be disregarded in certain situations. See infra ¶13.3.

9. *Effect of informal liaisons.* When a man and woman enter into a relationship short of marriage, they are not subject to the community-property system.[19]

¶31.3 SEPARATED COUPLES—SPECIAL ALLOCATION OF COMMUNITY INCOME

Responding to the plight of abandoned spouses who are taxed even though they do not receive their share of the other spouse's earnings, Congress enacted IRC §66 in 1980, disregarding the applicable community-property laws if (1) one or both spouses has earned income as defined by IRC §911(b) for the calendar year; (2) they live apart during the entire calendar year; and (3) no portion of the earned income is transferred directly or indirectly between them before the close of the calendar year. The Senate Finance Committee's report provides that de minimis transfers between the spouses are not to be taken into account, and that transfers to or for their dependent children are not to be treated as indirect transfers by one spouse to the other merely because they satisfy the abandoned spouse's duty of support.[20] If the statutory conditions are satisfied, the community income is allocated between them as provided by IRC §879(a)—earned income is allocated to the spouse performing the services and community income from separate property is allocated to the spouse who owns the property.

SELECTED BIBLIOGRAPHY

Bittker, Federal Income Taxation and the Family, 27 Stan. L. Rev. 1389, 1404–1414 (1975).

Lay, Tax and Estate Planning Considerations Involved With Community Property and the Migratory Client, 11 J. Fam. L. 255 (1971).

MacDonald, The Impact of Equal Management Upon Community Property Businesses, 13 Idaho L. Rev. 191 (1977).

Note, Epilogue to the Community Property Scramble: Problems of Repeal, 50 Colum. L. Rev. 332 n.4 (1950).

Pascal, Louisiana's 1978 Matrimonial Regimes Legislation, 53 Tul. L. Rev. 191 (1977).

---

[19] See Marvin v. Marvin, 557 P.2d 106, 134 Cal. Rptr. 815 (1976).

[20] H. Rep. No. 96-1278 (1980), reprinted at 1980-2 CB 709, 713.

CHAPTER 32

Alimony and Other Marital Support Payments

¶32.1 ALIMONY, SEPARATE MAINTENANCE, AND SUPPORT

1. Introductory. Alimony and separate maintenance payments are ordinarily taxable to a wife who is divorced or legally separated from her husband under IRC §71, and the payments are ordinarily deductible by the husband under IRC §215. Both provisions refer to payments by the "husband" to the "wife," and this usage is followed below; but the same rules are applicable, mutatis mutandis, to payments made by the wife to the husband.[1] Substantially the same rules apply to payments under a written separation agreement and to court-ordered support payments even if there is no decree of divorce or separate maintenance, provided the couple does not file a joint return.[2] The wife is also taxed under IRC §682 on the income of certain alimony trusts. Payments that are explicitly earmarked by the decree, instrument or agreement for the support of the husband's minor children, however, are not taxed to the wife even if she has custody of the children.[3]

[1] IRC §7701(a)(17).

[2] For the rules governing joint returns, see infra ¶39.3.

[3] See infra ¶32.2.

When their requirements are satisfied, these provisions place a stamp of legislative approval on income splitting between the divorced or separated spouses. This relationship to assignment-of-income principles is evidenced by their explicit statutory safeguards—now largely anachronistic, as will be seen [4]—against the use of spurious separation agreements for the unauthorized division of income between two amicable spouses.

In 1917, before the enactment of the statutory predecessors of IRC §§71 and 215, the Supreme Court held in *Gould v. Gould* that alimony paid to a divorced wife under a judicial decree was not encompassed by the phrase "gains or profits and income derived from any source whatever" as used in the Revenue Act of 1917. [5] During this early period, if the husband created a trust whose income was payable to the wife as alimony, he remained taxable on the trust income because it was applied to pay his legal obligations.[6] He could avoid being taxed on the income from transferred property only by making a lump-sum payment in complete discharge of his support obligation, provided such a final discharge was permissible under local law.[7] In 1942, to eliminate variations in the taxability of alimony attributable to differences in local law and to moderate the effect of wartime tax rates on the husband, Congress enacted the statutory predecessors of IRC §§71(a)(1) and 215, taxing alimony and separate maintenance payments to the wife and granting the husband a corresponding deduction.[8]

To be taxed to the wife under IRC §71 and deducted by the husband under IRC §215, payments of alimony, separate maintenance, and support must (a) be formalized by a decree of divorce or separate maintenance, a written instrument incident to such a decree, a written separation agreement, or a support decree; (b) serve to discharge the husband's obligation of support, as contrasted with gifts and payments settling the spouses' property rights; (c) constitute "periodic payments," as contrasted with a lump-sum settlement; and (d) not be earmarked for support of the husband's minor children. These requirements are discussed in detail below.[9]

2. Requirement of Decree or Written Instrument. Congress enacted the statutory predecessors of IRC §§71 and 215 in 1942, before the 1948 joint

---

[4] See infra, text at notes 10–12.

[5] Gould v. Gould, 245 US 151 (1917).

[6] See infra ¶34.4 (re grantor trusts).

[7] Helvering v. Fuller, 310 US 69 (1940); Helvering v. Fitch, 309 US 149, 156 (1940); see also Douglas v. Willcuts, 296 US 1 (1935).

[8] See Mahana v. US, 88 F.Supp. 285 (Ct. Cl.), cert. denied, 339 US 978, rehearing denied, 340 US 847 (1950) (1942 legislation held constitutional).

[9] For sample clauses that, subject to certain assumptions, will be treated by the IRS as satisfying the statutory requirements, so that the amounts paid will be deductible by the payor and taxed to the recipient, see Rev. Proc. 82-53, 1982-36 IRB 10.

return legislation, and the 1942 rules were restricted to couples who were divorced or legally separated under a decree of separate maintenance. From 1942 to 1948, therefore, a married couple with only one breadwinner could reduce their tax liability by getting a divorce, since their income would then be reported on two returns and hence be subject to lower marginal rates. To prevent exploitation of this opportunity by spurious informal separations, the 1942 legislation applied only to payments received after an actual *decree* of divorce or legal separation.

With the advent of the income-splitting joint return in 1948, the danger of collusive arrangements evaporated because no informal split of income between spouses could produce a lower tax than a joint return,[10] and this led Congress to enact IRC §71(a)(2) in 1954, extending the 1942 rules to payments received after the execution of a written separation agreement, even if it was not formalized by a judicial decree.[11] At the same time, Congress enacted IRC §71(a)(3), relating to judicial support orders, which encompasses not only payments in abandonment cases but also temporary alimony and separate maintenance payments, which did not qualify under IRC §71(a)(1) before 1954 because they did not entail a divorce or legal separation.[12] Thus, a decree of divorce or of separate maintenance is no longer essential.

If IRC §§71(a)(2) and 71(a)(3) are inapplicable, however, the "decree" requirement of IRC §71(a)(1) remains crucial. In practice, the principal problem arising under this requirement is the status of an ex parte decree whose validity is disputed. In *Borax's Estate v. CIR,* involving the deduction of payments by the husband, the Court of Appeals for the Second Circuit held that a Mexican divorce decree satisfied the requirements of IRC §71(a)(1) even though the ex-wife obtained a declaratory judgment in New York, where the husband was domiciled, holding that the divorce and his later marriage were invalid.[13]

The IRS announced in 1967 that it will not follow the *Borax* case as to a divorce decree held invalid by a state court of competent jurisdiction but that it generally will not on its own initiative question the validity of a divorce.[14] The issue is quiescent, as to the IRC §71(a)(1) requirement of a decree, because IRC §71(a)(2) (relating to post-1954 written separation agreements)

---

[10] Infra ¶39.3.

[11] Treas. Regs. §1.71-1(b)(2). If the parties to such an agreement file separate returns, they are subject to the rate schedule prescribed by IRC §1(d) for married persons filing separate returns, unless IRC §143(b) (married individuals living in a household with certain dependents) applies.

[12] See infra, text at notes 31-32.

[13] Borax's Est. v. CIR, 349 F.2d 666 (2d Cir. 1965), cert. denied, 383 US 935 (1966).

[14] Rev. Rul. 67-442, 1967-2 CB 65; see also 1968-1 CB 3 n.4 (acquiescence in *Borax* as respects taxability of wife on amounts deducted by husband).

ordinarily comes into play even if IRC §71(a)(1) is inapplicable for want of a judicial decree.[15]

Another formerly troubled aspect of IRC §71(a)(1), also now largely sidestepped by IRC §71(a)(2), is the requirement that periodic payments discharge a legal obligation imposed on or incurred by the husband "under the decree or under a written instrument *incident* to such divorce or separation" (emphasis added). With the enactment in 1954 of IRC §71(a)(2), payments under a written separation agreement are now taxed to the wife and deductible by the husband whether the agreement is followed by a divorce or legal separation or not.[16] However, a post-divorce agreement for support payments does not qualify under either IRC §71(a)(1) or §71(a)(2) if no obligation to support survives the dissolution of the marriage.[17] This ruling is a reminder that IRC §71(a) presupposes legal compulsion and does not embrace voluntary payments.[18]

3. Discharge of Support Obligation. To qualify under IRC §§71 (alimony taxable to wife) and 215 (deductible by husband), periodic payments not only must be formalized by a judicial decree or written agreement but also must be made in recognition of an obligation of support. Neither IRC §71(a)(1) (divorce or judicial separation) nor §71(a)(2) (written separation agreement) explicitly uses the term "support," but they require that the payments be made "because of the marital or family relationship," a phrase interpreted by the regulations to refer to "the general obligation to support" and not to payments settling the couple's property rights, such as the repayment of funds lent by one to the other.[19] This line may not be easy to discern.

---

[15] For cases where the IRS questioned the validity of a divorce where the issue was filing status, see Gersten v. CIR, 267 F.2d 195 (9th Cir. 1959) (husband obtained ex parte Mexican divorce and remarried; held, joint return with new wife not permissible, because former wife could annul divorce in California, where all parties resided); Rev. Rul. 76-255, 1976-2 CB 40 (year-end divorce to avoid taxes, followed by prompt remarriage, disregarded as sham; parties cannot file as unmarried); Boyter v. CIR, 668 F.2d 1382 (4th Cir. 1981) (remanding "sham divorce" question to Tax Court).

[16] Treas. Regs. §1.71-1(b)(2)(i).

[17] Rev. Rul. 60-142, 1960-1 CB 34.

[18] See Baker v. CIR, ¶78,103 P-H Memo TC (1978) (no evidence of legal compulsion; deduction by husband disallowed).

[19] Treas. Regs. §§1.71-1(b)(4), 1.71-1(c)(4); see also Warnack v. CIR, 71 TC 541, 550 (1979) (focus is not on support in isolation, but on "whether payments are for support in contradistinction to being in exchange for wife's release of some property interest"; extensive review of facts and cases); Hoffman v. CIR, 54 TC 1607 (1970), aff'd per curiam, 455 F.2d 161 (7th Cir. 1972) (wife not taxed on payments for period after remarriage, since husband's legal support obligation terminated under Illinois law); but see Engelhardt v. CIR, 58 TC 641 (1972) (IRC §71(a)(2) applies even if separation agreement is not enforceable under state law and payments are made after wife's remarriage).

If the wife brought property to the marriage, received gifts or bequests during the marriage, worked outside the home or in a family business, held assets in her own name, or otherwise acquired rights to property that the husband also claims, a resolution of their rights on termination of the marriage will usually include both property division and support components. Moreover, an increase in the frequency and validity of property claims is likely as the common-law states increasingly recognize joint interests in marital property.[20]

In effecting the separation between support and property settlements, the courts look at all relevant facts, since neither the labels used by state law nor those affixed by the parties are controlling. Among the circumstances that warrant classifying payments as "support" are the absence of a ceiling on the aggregate amount to be paid, termination of the obligation on the wife's remarriage or death, the wife's failure to claim ownership of any property, and the husband's agreement to reimburse the wife's income taxes on the payments.[21] Conversely, a property settlement is suggested if property was held jointly, the wife contributed capital or services to a family enterprise, a balloon payment is due when the payments commence, or the payments are to continue until a specified aggregate amount is paid, regardless of the wife's remarriage or death.[22] No one factor is conclusive, however, and the courts have on occasion found that payments were for support even though they had some of the earmarks of a property settlement (e.g., a specified dollar ceiling and an absence of contingencies)[23] and, conversely, that a property settlement was effected with payments resembling an ordinary support arrangement.[24] If the decree or agreement calls for a single series of payments, there is a judicial tendency to assign them in full either to support or to a property settlement. But if two sets of payments are to be made, the courts are likely to infer that one effects a property settlement and the other constitutes a support arrangement, especially if one set specifies an aggregate amount to be paid in all events and the other will terminate on the wife's remarriage or death.[25]

---

[20] See Mills v. CIR, 442 F.2d 1149 (10th Cir. 1971) (Oklahoma statute re property acquired during marriage); supra ¶22.5.

[21] See, e.g., Gerlach v. CIR, 55 TC 156 (1970) (Acq.) (labels not determinative); Thoda's Est. v. CIR, ¶79,219 P-H Memo TC (1979) (testimony re intent of parties less important than objective facts).

[22] McCombs v. CIR, 397 F.2d 4 (10th Cir. 1968); Bernatschke v. US, 364 F.2d 400 (Ct. Cl. 1966); Capodanno v. CIR, 69 TC 638 (1978).

[23] West v. US, 332 F.Supp. 1102 (S.D. Tex. 1971), aff'd per curiam, 477 F.2d 563 (5th Cir. 1973); Hesse v. CIR, 60 TC 685, 693 (1973) (Acq.), aff'd, 511 F.2d 1393 (3d Cir.), cert. denied, 423 US 834 (1975).

[24] Weiner v. CIR, 61 TC 155 (1973); Hall v. CIR, ¶82,604 P-H Memo TC (1982).

[25] See, e.g., Bartsch v. CIR, 18 TC 65 (1952), aff'd per curiam, 203 F.2d 715 (1953) (payment of $45,000 in installments held separate from periodic payments).

4. "Periodic" Payments. An additional condition imposed by IRC §71 is that payments must be "periodic." Section 71(a) goes on to provide that they need not be paid "at regular intervals," however, and there is no requirement that the payments be equal in amount. Thus, payments under an agreement to defray the wife's medical expenses or income taxes are "periodic payments" even though the amounts and due dates fluctuate and nothing is payable in some taxable years. The payment of arrearages is a "periodic payment" if the original amounts, had they been paid on time, would have qualified.[26]

The phrase "periodic payments" is qualified by IRC §71(c), providing that installment payments discharging an obligation whose "principal sum" is specified in terms of either money or property do not qualify as "periodic payments" unless the principal sum is to be (or may be) [27] paid over a period ending more than ten years from the date of the decree, instrument, or agreement, and then only to the extent of 10 percent of the principal sum for any one taxable year. For example, if the husband is to pay $10,000 in five equal annual installments, the payments do not qualify as periodic. If, however, the principal sum of $10,000 is to be paid at the rate of $1,500 annually for four years and $500 annually for the following eight years, $1,000 (10% of the principal sum) of each of the first four payments and all of the remaining payments would be "periodic" under the ten-year, ten-percent rule.[28]

The "periodic payment" requirement is readily satisfied by most alimony arrangements, which require payments to be made at intervals until the wife's death or remarriage and do not specify a principal sum. Moreover, following an important series of litigated cases, the Treasury promulgated a "contingency" standard under which payments qualify as "periodic" if they are subject to any one of several contingencies—death of either spouse, the wife's remarriage, or a change in either spouse's economic status—even if (a) the aggregate amount to be paid if the contingency does not occur is explicitly stated in, or can be calculated from the face of the decree, instrument, or agreement or (b) the total amount can be calculated actuarially.[29] The prescribed contingencies exist for this purpose whether they are set out in the decree, instrument, or agreement or are imposed by local law.[30]

---

[26] See Rev. Rul. 55-457, 1955-2 CB 527.

[27] See Wallace v. CIR, 485 F.2d 422, 426 (10th Cir. 1973).

[28] For the relationship of IRC §483 (imputed interest), discussed supra ¶27.6, to installment payments of a lump-sum obligation, see Rev. Rul. 76-146, 1976-1 CB 144; Fox v. US, 510 F.2d 1330 (3d Cir. 1975).

[29] Treas. Regs. §§1.71-1(d)(3) (payments for a period of ten years or less), 1.71-1(d)(4) (payments for more than ten years). For the origin of the contingency test, see Baker v. CIR, 205 F.2d 369 (2d Cir. 1953).

[30] Treas. Regs. §1.71-1(d)(3)(ii)(a); Rev. Rul. 59-190, 1959-1 CB 23. For cases involving payments not subject to contingencies under the agreement, decree, or local

The contingency standard classifies the overwhelming bulk of alimony payments as "periodic." Since the tax savings to the husband from deducting the payments is usually greater than the tax cost to the wife of including them in her gross income, the result is a net saving that can be divided between them if they or their advisers are well informed. This means that the contingency standard ordinarily produces the result that the parties desire. If they wish to avoid the "periodic" classification, however, they must fix the aggregate amount to be paid in all events and then either settle the liability with a single payment or, if local law does not permit modification of the agreement or decree on a change of economic status, provide for installment payments over a period of ten years or less.

5. Support Decrees. Under IRC §71(a)(3), enacted in 1954, periodic payments by the husband are includable in the wife's income if paid under a decree requiring the husband to make the payments for the wife's support and maintenance; and payments satisfying IRC §71(a)(3) are deductible by the husband under IRC §215. These payments—encompassing not only payments in abandonment cases but also temporary alimony and separate maintenance payments—did not qualify under IRC §71(a)(1) before 1954 in the absence of a decree of divorce or separate maintenance.

Husband and wife are "separated" for purposes of IRC §71(c)(3) if they live apart; this status need not be formalized by a legal decree or a written separation agreement.[31] Moreover, on facts worthy of a novel by Hawthorne, the Court of Appeals for the Eighth Circuit held in *Sydnes v. CIR* that the taxpayer and his wife were separated for purposes of IRC §71(a)(3) even while living in the same house, where the record showed that they virtually "never met face-to-face."[32]

¶32.2 PARTICULAR ITEMS

1. Real Estate. If a family residence is owned by the husband or jointly by husband and wife, financial arrangements for the dissolution of a marriage often provide for its transfer to the wife or for rent-free occupancy by her. A transfer of the husband's interest in the residence is not a "periodic payment,"

---

law, see Kent v. CIR, 61 TC 133 (1973); Martin v. CIR, 73 TC 255 (1979) (accepting contingency principle, but with dictum questioning its validity because dependence on variations in state law frustrates legislative intent to achieve uniform national standard).

[31] Treas. Regs. §1.71-1(b)(3).

[32] Sydnes v. CIR, 577 F.2d 60 (8th Cir. 1978); but see Washington v. CIR, 77 TC 601 (1981) (contra).

and hence its value is not taxable to the wife or deductible by the husband.[33] If, however, he is required by the divorce decree or agreement to pay for utilities, insurance, repairs, property taxes, or mortgage interest on the wife's residence, the payments are "periodic" under IRC §§71 and 215, assuming the other statutory requirements are satisfied.

If the husband retains ownership of the family residence and the wife is permitted to occupy it rent-free, the courts hold that the husband is not entitled to deductions under IRC §215 because there is a single transfer of the right to occupy the property for the stipulated period rather than a series of "periodic payments";[34] and this rationale also protects the wife against being taxed on the rental value of the residence under IRC §71. Payments by the husband of utility bills and current repairs during the wife's occupancy, however, qualify as periodic payments; but mortgage payments, property taxes, insurance premiums, and improvements do not, since they protect the husband's interest in the property more than they increase the value of the wife's right to occupy it.[35]

If the wife retains or is given ownership of the family residence, payments by the husband to amortize the mortgage are taxable to the wife if they are not part of a property settlement.[36] If, however, the wife receives the family residence in trust for the children, the husband's mortgage payments increase the children's equity in the house, and the incidental benefit to the wife does not render the payments taxable to her.[37] If the husband and wife retain ownership jointly, the treatment of mortgage payments depends on the nature of the joint ownership. Where property is held as tenants in common, payments of the mortgage by the husband are taxable to the wife to the extent of her ownership interest in the property.[38] Where property is held as joint tenants with right of survivorship, the wife is ordinarily not taxable if the husband makes payments on a mortgage for which he alone is liable; but if both are liable, one-half of the payments are taxable to the wife.[39]

2. Life Insurance. If the husband is required to maintain an ordinary life insurance policy on his life, of which the wife is both the owner and the irrevocable beneficiary, the premiums are taxable to her under IRC §71 and deductible by him under IRC §215.[40] The contrary result was reached, rather

[33] For realization of gain or loss by the transferor, see infra ¶32.4.

[34] See Pappenheimer v. Allen, 164 F.2d 428 (5th Cir. 1947); but see Marinello v. CIR, 54 TC 577 (1970).

[35] Bradley v. CIR, 30 TC 701 (1958); Gentry v. US, 283 F.2d 702 (Ct. Cl. 1960).

[36] See Rev. Rul. 62-39, 1962-1 CB 17.

[37] See Isaacson v. CIR, 58 TC 659 (1972) (Acq.).

[38] See Rev. Rul. 62-39, supra note 36.

[39] See Rev. Rul. 67-420, 1967-2 CB 63.

[40] Stevens v. CIR, 439 F.2d 69 (2d Cir. 1971).

surprisingly, in a case involving a term insurance policy because of the absence of any cash surrender or loan value and because the wife's rights, though exclusive, were limited to the right to collect the proceeds if her husband predeceased her within the period for which he was required to pay the premiums.[41] The transfer of an existing policy to enable the husband to deduct the future premiums has disadvantages, since the husband may realize taxable gain on the transfer and the wife will be a transferee for value who cannot exclude the insurance proceeds when collected on the husband's death under IRC §101.[42]

If the husband possesses any incidents of ownership in the policy, premiums paid by him are ordinarily not deductible by him or taxable to the wife, on the theory that they increase the value of his retained rights.[43]

3. Medical Expenses. If the husband is obligated to defray the wife's future medical expenses or medical and hospitalization insurance premiums, the payments qualify as "periodic."[44]

4. Income Taxes—Tax Reimbursement Agreements. If the husband is obligated to defray the wife's income taxes on the basic alimony payments so as to assure her of a net amount after taxes, the taxes paid by him are "periodic payments" that are taxable to her and deductible by him.[45] If the resulting "tax on a tax" must in turn be reimbursed by the husband under the tax reimbursement agreement, there is a second round of income to her and second deduction for him; and this process will continue for as many rounds as the agreement requires.[46]

5. Payments for Child Support. Section 71(b) provides that the wife is not taxable on any part of a payment that the terms of the decree, instrument, or agreement fix (in terms of an amount of money or part of the payment) as payable for the support of the husband's minor children. If the husband pays less than the full amount due for the support of the wife and the children, the payment is allocated to nondeductible child support up to the amount fixed for this purpose, so that only the excess is deductible under IRC §71(a).

In CIR v. Lester, the Supreme Court held that a divorce agreement

---

[41] Wright v. CIR, 62 TC 377 (1974), aff'd, 543 F.2d 593 (7th Cir. 1976); but see Turpin v. US, 240 F.Supp. 171 (W.D. Mo. 1965) (husband allowed to deduct premiums on both whole life and term policies).

[42] See infra ¶32.4 (gain on transfer); supra ¶4.2 (transferees for value).

[43] Kiesling v. US, 349 F.2d 119 (3d Cir.), cert. denied, 382 US 939 (1965).

[44] Rev. Rul. 62-106, 1962-2 CB 21.

[45] Mahana v. US, supra note 8; Rev. Rul. 58-100, 1958-1 CB 31.

[46] For the drafting and pyramiding problems of these agreements, see supra ¶1.11.

providing for a reduction in the amount payable by the husband to the wife when their children married, were emancipated, or died did not "fix" an amount for child support within the meaning of IRC §71(b), even though such an allocation could be inferred from the arrangement and state law might compel the wife to use that portion for the support of the children.[47] The Court read the provision as "in effect giving the husband and wife the power to shift a portion of the tax burden from the wife to the husband by the use of a simple provision in the settlement agreement," but only if it *explicitly* earmarked a specific portion of the periodic payment for child support.[48] In so holding, the Court stressed the congressional intent to "eliminate the uncertain and inconsistent tax consequences resulting from the many variations in state law." [49] This emphasis on national uniformity may also imply that a federal standard rather than local law determines whether children are "minors" for purposes of IRC §71(b).[50]

6. Payments To or For Third Persons. The regulations provide that "periodic payments described in Section 71(a) received by the wife for herself and any other person or persons [except their minor children] are includable in whole in the wife's income, whether or not the amount or portion for such other person or persons is designated." [51] What if the husband is required by the decree or separation agreement to make payments to the wife for the support of her parents or other relatives? The Tax Court has held that the wife is taxable on such payments if she feels a legal or moral obligation to provide for the beneficiaries of the payments.[52]

¶32.3 DEDUCTIONS FOR ALIMONY AND OTHER MARITAL SUPPORT PAYMENTS

Section 215(a) provides that, in general, a husband may deduct alimony, separate maintenance, and support payments to his wife if they are includable in her gross income under IRC §71. In permitting the husband to deduct these amounts in the taxable year when they are paid, IRC §215 requires only that they be "includable" in the wife's gross income; the husband does not lose the

---

[47] CIR v. Lester, 366 US 299 (1961); Treas. Regs. §1.71-1(e) (amount must be "specifically designated").

[48] CIR v. Lester, supra note 47, at 304.

[49] Id. at 301.

[50] See Borbonus v. CIR, 42 TC 983, 990 (1964).

[51] Treas. Regs. §1.71-1(e) (last sentence).

[52] Christiansen v. CIR, 60 TC 456 (1973) (Acq.); but see Faber v. CIR, 264 F.2d 127 (3d Cir. 1959); Emmons v. CIR, 36 TC 728 (1961), aff'd per curiam, 311 F.2d 233 (6th Cir. 1962).

deduction if the wife has no taxable income or fails to file a return. Moreover, the IRS has ruled that the husband can deduct payments described by IRC §215 even if the wife is exempt from tax under IRC §933 (relating to residents of Puerto Rico).[53]

Unlike most other personal deductions, IRC §215 is best viewed as a mode of designating the proper taxpayer for a given amount of income, rather than a tax allowance for particular expenditures. In combination, IRC §§71 and 215 treat part of the husband's income as though it were received subject to an offsetting duty to pay it over to the wife, so that he acts as a conduit who cannot make an independent judgment about the destination of these funds. In harmony with this rationale, alimony payments are deducted from gross income in computing adjusted gross income under IRC §62(13) and hence are allowed even if the husband does not itemize his personal deductions. The conduit analogy is also reflected by the fact that a husband who funds his obligation to his wife by a transfer of property, in trust or otherwise, is not entitled to deduct the subsequent periodic payments. Since they are excluded from his income by virtue of either IRC §71(d) (income from transferred property) or §682(a) (income from alimony trusts), a deduction under IRC §215 would be duplicative.

Although it is ordinarily easy to determine whether particular payments are includable in the wife's gross income under IRC §71, there are many problem areas, involving both interpretations of the statutory requirements and conflicting versions of the underlying facts. For this reason, it is not uncommon for the husband to claim a deduction under IRC §215 for payments that the wife asserts are not taxable to her under IRC §71. Fortunately, inconsistent results rarely materialize in practice, though the area evokes more litigation than would be required if a whipsaw effect were not an ever-present possibility.[54]

¶32.4 ANCILLARY PROBLEMS

1. Legal Expenses. Fees and other costs paid in connection with a divorce, separation, or decree for support are not ordinarily deductible by either the husband or the wife.[55] But this general principle, based on the disallowance by IRC §262 of deductions for "personal, living, or family expenses" unless otherwise expressly permitted, is qualified by IRC §212, which permits expenses for producing or collecting income and for tax advice to be deducted.

---

[53] Rev. Rul. 56-585, 1956-2 CB 166.

[54] See Final Report, Special Committee on Whipsaw, Section of Taxation, American Bar Association, 30 Tax Lawyer 127, 141 (1976).

[55] Treas. Regs. §1.262-1(b)(7).

Thus, the wife's legal expenses allocable to periodic payments that are taxed to her by IRC §71(a) are deductible under IRC §212, but not the expense of contesting a divorce petition, obtaining custody of children, or establishing her interest in marital property.[56] If, however, the husband defrays the wife's legal expenses, whether by reimbursing her or by direct payment to her attorney, the payment does not qualify as periodic; hence it is not taxable to her under IRC §71 or deductible by him under IRC §215.[57]

As for the husband's legal expenses, the Supreme Court held in *United States v. Gilmore* that legal expenses incurred in a divorce action are personal or living expenses that cannot be deducted under IRC §212(1) (expenses of collecting income) or §212(2) (expenses of conserving income-producing property), even though the husband's overriding concern was to protect his income-producing assets against the wife's claims, rather than to forestall the divorce itself.[58] However, the cost of tax advice sought by the husband in connection with a divorce or separation is deductible under IRC §212(3).[59]

2. Gain or Loss on Transfer of Property. On transferring appreciated or depreciated property in connection with a legal separation or divorce, the transferor realizes gain or loss under *United States v. Davis* if he thereby discharges a legal duty for support or obtains a release of marital rights, but not if the transaction is a division of jointly owned property.[60]

3. Payments Attributable to Transferred Property. If the husband's support obligation is funded by a transfer of property to the wife, periodic payments therefrom (if otherwise qualified) are taxable to her in full even if they come in whole or in part from the husband's capital rather than income. Thus, if the transferred property consists of an annuity contract, the payments to the wife are taxable to her without regard to the usual allocation of each annuity payment between income and return of capital. In these circumstances, the income from the property is not taxed to the husband, and he cannot deduct the amounts paid to the wife.[61]

---

[56] E.g., Wild v. CIR, 42 TC 706 (1964) (Acq.); Hesse v. CIR, 60 TC 685 (1973) (Acq.), aff'd by order, 511 F.2d 1393 (3d Cir.), cert. denied, 423 US 834 (1975).

[57] Baer v. CIR, 196 F.2d 646, 649 (8th Cir. 1952); US v. Davis, 370 US 65, 74–75 (1962).

[58] US v. Gilmore, 372 US 39 (1963), discussed supra ¶8.5; but see Gilmore v. US, 245 F.Supp. 383 (N.D. Cal. 1965) (husband allowed to add legal expenses to cost of stock in determining basis on later sale).

[59] Rev. Rul. 72-545, 1972-2 CB 179.

[60] US v. Davis, supra note 57, discussed supra ¶22.5.

[61] See Treas. Regs. §1.71-1(c); IRC §§71(d), 215(a) (second sentence); Treas. Regs. §1.215-1.

4. Alimony Trusts. If payments are made to the ex-wife under an alimony trust created at the time of divorce or legal separation, their status is determined by IRC §§71(a) and 71(d); and the status of distributions by a preexisting trust utilized to discharge the husband's obligations is determined by IRC §682(a), enacted in 1942 as a companion piece to the statutory predecessor of IRC §71.

SELECTED BIBLIOGRAPHY

Davies, The Taxation of Alimony: Policies, Problems and a Proposal, 31 Miami L. Rev. 1356 (1977).

Harris & Ravikoff, Controlling the Tax Effects of Transfers of Life Insurance or Annuities in Divorces, 47 J. Tax. 92 (1977).

Hjorth, Tax Consequences of Post-Dissolution Support Payment Arrangements, 51 Wash. L. Rev. 233, 239–240 (1967).

Kuntz, Simplification of the Definition of Periodic Payments in Internal Revenue Code Section 71, 47 U. Cin. L. Rev. 213 (1978).

Quaglietta, Minimizing Taxes in Separation and Divorce, 58 Taxes 531 (1980).

Turley, Divorce and Taxes—A Decade Later, 20 S. Texas L.J. 407 (1981).

Wenig, Use of Life Insurance in Divorce and Separation Agreements, 28 NYU Inst. on Fed. Tax. 837 (1970).

CHAPTER 33

Reallocation of Income and Deductions and Disallowance of Deductions

¶33.1 LOSSES ON SALES BETWEEN RELATED PERSONS

Section 267(a)(1) prohibits the deduction of losses on sales and exchanges of property between specified related persons, such as parents and their children and corporations and their controlling shareholders. Section 267(a)(1) is partly duplicative of existing judge-made law, which disallows fictitious losses in any case if the transaction is a sham;[1] but it also reaches out and disallows losses on transactions between related parties that either are bona fide or, at worst, are dubious but not demonstrably improper. Moreover, if some assets are sold at a profit at the same time that others are sold at a loss, the losses are not offset against the gains; instead, the gains must be recognized in full

[1] See, e.g., supra ¶12.3 (deductions under IRC §165 limited to bona fide losses).

but the losses cannot be deducted.[2] Finally, IRC §267(a)(1) is not a postponement provision under which losses incurred in transactions between related parties are held in abeyance until realized by sales to outsiders. Instead, the disallowed loss is not recognized by either of the related parties, although the severity of this result is relaxed by IRC §267(d), which takes the disallowed loss into account as an offset against any gain realized by the related buyer on a later sale of the property to a third party.

Voluntary transfers that "shuttle assets back and forth between members of a related group" [3] are the principal targets of IRC §267(a)(1), but an early line of cases exempting involuntary sales (e.g., by foreclosure) is now discredited.[4] In *McWilliams v. CIR,* the Supreme Court applied IRC §267(a)(1) to losses incurred by a taxpayer on selling marketable securities on a national stock exchange, where he concurrently instructed his broker to purchase for his wife's account the same number of shares of the same stock at as nearly the same price as possible.[5] These transactions were held to be sales "directly or indirectly" between the taxpayer and his wife, although the investors purchasing from the husband and selling to the wife were unknown strangers and the shares, though fungible, were not identical. Later cases shed little light on the proper treatment of stock market transactions when the buy and sell orders are not placed simultaneously but are instead separated by a sufficient interval so that the prices may differ significantly.[6] The loss should be recognized if the interval exceeds thirty days, since a seller of depreciated securities can recognize the loss even if he himself repurchases identical securities, provided he does so more than thirty days before or after the loss sale.[7] A time interval between the sale and purchase has little if any significance, however, if the related parties are separated only by an accommodating intermediary rather than by an impersonal stock market whose prices fluctuate in response to conditions that the parties cannot control.

Although the theory of IRC §267(a)(1) is that sales of property between related persons do not result in economically genuine realizations of loss, the group's loss is not merely postponed until the property is sold to an outsider. Since the related party whose acquisition of the property caused the original owner's loss to be disallowed must use his or her own cost (rather than the original owner's cost) in computing gain or loss on a later sale to an outsider,

---

[2] See Morris Inv. Corp. v. CIR, 156 F.2d 748 (3d Cir.), cert. denied, 329 US 788 (1946), and cases there cited.

[3] Merritt v. CIR, 400 F.2d 417, 419 (5th Cir. 1968).

[4] Id., and cases there cited; Hassen v. CIR, 599 F.2d 305 (9th Cir. 1979).

[5] McWilliams v. CIR, 331 US 694 (1947).

[6] See US v. Norton, 250 F.2d 902 (5th Cir. 1958); Shethar v. CIR, 28 TC 1222 (1957) (IRC §267(a)(1) applied—purchases preceded sales by one day).

[7] See supra ¶24.6 (re wash sales). The wash sale analogy was noted by the Supreme Court in *McWilliams* but was neither endorsed nor rejected.

the original owner's economic loss may never be recognized. Thus, if *A* sells property (cost, $100; value, $75) to *B,* a related party, for $75, and *B* later sells the property to *X,* an unrelated person, for $70 (its then value), *B* can deduct only $5 (the difference between *B*'s cost and the final sales price), even though *A* and *B* together incurred a genuine economic loss of $30.

To this draconic rule, IRC §267(d) provides a limited exception. If the property increases in value after its acquisition by *B*, *B*'s gain is recognized only if, and to the extent that, it exceeds the loss disallowed to *A.* Thus, *B* will realize no gain on selling the property for an amount between $75 and $100, and a sale at $110 will result in recognized gain of only $10. Section 267(d) does not, however, affect *B*'s holding period for the property, which begins for capital gain purposes only when *B* acquires the property, nor does it permit the disallowed loss to be taken into account in computing *B*'s depreciable basis for the property.[8] If *B* does not sell the property but instead disposes of it in a nonrecognition transaction (e.g., by trading it for property of a "like kind" within the meaning of IRC §1031), the relief accorded by IRC §267(d) is applicable to any gain recognized on a later sale of the property received in the IRC §1031 transaction.[9]

¶33.2 UNPAID EXPENSES AND INTEREST OWED TO RELATED PERSONS

1. Introductory. Section 267(a)(2) provides that expenses and interest owed by a taxpayer to a related person cannot be deducted in certain circumstances—primarily when the obligor uses the accrual method of computing income and the related obligee uses the cash method—unless the debt is paid within 2½ months after the close of the obligor's taxable year. This provision was enacted in 1937 to deal with such tax-avoidance devices as a loan by a cash-basis taxpayer to a related accrual-basis taxpayer, following which the debtor would accrue and deduct the interest annually but would not pay the accrued interest to the cash-basis creditor until the latter had offsetting losses. Substantially the same procedure could be employed with salaries, rents, and other expenses owed by an accrual-basis corporation to a related cash-basis individual. In some situations, the accrued liability went unpaid for many years. While this gambit would eventually empower the IRS to require the obligor to restore the deducted amounts to income, either on the tax benefit

---

[8] See Treas. Regs. §§1.267(d)-1(c)(1), 1.267(d)-1(c)(3); see also Treas. Regs. §§1.267(d)-1(a)(3) (IRC §267(d) applicable only to original transferees who purchased property), 1.1245-6(b) (depreciation recapture provisions override IRC §267(d)).

[9] See Treas. Regs. §1.267(d)-1(a)(2); for IRC §1031, see supra ¶24.2.

principle or on the theory that the debt had been cancelled,[10] the taxpayer would have benefited in the interim from the tax savings generated by the deduction.

Since the abuse to be prevented stemmed from a disparity between the accounting methods used by the related taxpayers, Congress might have remedied the problem either by requiring the cash-basis payee to report the accrued compensation or other item as soon as it was deducted by the related accrual-basis taxpayer or by postponing the latter's deduction until the year of payment, when the item was includable in the payee's gross income. But the remedy actually adopted was more severe—a permanent denial of the deduction to the obligor, even though the amount is later paid and taxed to the payee.[11] Moreover, the obligor loses the deduction even if the delay in paying the accrued liability to the related obligee is innocent of any tax-avoidance purpose.[12]

2. Conditions Requiring Disallowance of Deductions. Section 267(a)(2) prohibits a deduction for expenses and interest, if otherwise allowable under IRC §162 or §212 (expenses) or IRC §163 (interest), when the following three conditions exist:

1. *Nonpayment.* The deductible item is neither paid nor includable in the obligee's gross income within the period consisting of the obligor's taxable year and the following two and one-half months.[13]
2. *Relationship.* At the close of the obligor's taxable year or within the following two and one-half months, the obligor and obligee are related in a manner specified by IRC §267(b).[14]
3. *Obligee's accounting method.* Under the obligee's tax accounting method, the amount, unless paid, is not includable in gross income for the taxable year in which or with which the obligor's taxable year ends.[15] An actual inclusion, if erroneous, is ineffective.[16]

---

[10] See supra ¶¶1.10 (tax benefit principle), 2.4 (income from cancellation of debt for less than face amount).

[11] Treas. Regs. §1.267(a)-1(b)(2).

[12] See Radom & Neidorff, Inc. v. US, 281 F.2d 461 (Ct. Cl. 1960), cert. denied, 365 US 815 (1961).

[13] When originally prescribed, the two-and-one-half-month period corresponded to the time allowed for filing income tax returns for the preceding taxable year.

[14] For IRC §267(b), see infra ¶33.3.

[15] Both IRC §§267(a)(2)(A)(ii) and 267(a)(2)(B) are concerned with whether the amount in question is "includable" in the payee's gross income during the specified period, but the latter provision now serves no independent function, since it is automatically satisfied if an item is neither paid nor includable in the payee's income within the meaning of IRC §267(a)(2)(A)(ii); see Geiger & Peters, Inc. v. CIR, 27 TC 911 (1957).

[16] See Century Transit Co. v. US, 124 F.Supp. 148, 153 (D.N.J. 1954), rev'd on other grounds sub nom. Fiorentino v. US, 226 F.2d 619 (3d Cir. 1955).

These conditions can disallow deductions in circumstances that are devoid of a tax-avoidance purpose and do not in fact result in any deferral of the payee's tax liability. But IRC §267(a)(2) can be easily avoided by a foresighted and well-advised taxpayer; all that is required is payment of the accrued liability in the year of accrual or within the two-and-one-half-month grace period thereafter, and if cash is short, payment by a promissory note in negotiable form will do the trick. Most of the litigated cases arising under IRC §267(a)(2) concern efforts by taxpayers to escape its grasp by establishing that the disputed amount, though not paid in cash, was nevertheless includable in the payee's gross income during the statutory period because constructively received or evidenced by a cash equivalent (e.g, a negotiable promissory note).[17]

In several cases, amounts have been treated as "paid" notwithstanding a concurrent return of the amount paid by the payee as a "loan" to the obligor.[18] While something could be said for permitting the obligor to deduct any amount, whether "paid" or not, that the obligee agrees to include in gross income, IRC §267(a)(2) is not explicitly elective; and this means that payment-loanback transactions should be scrutinized with skepticism.[19]

¶33.3 RELATIONSHIPS REQUIRING DISALLOWANCE OF DEDUCTIONS

In order to avoid case-by-case determinations of whether the parties to a transaction are joined by a significant emotional or financial chain, IRC §267(b) specifies the relationships that bring the disallowance rules of IRC §§267(a)(1) and 267(a)(2) into play. Enacted in 1934 along with IRC §267(a)(1), IRC §267(b) was expanded in 1937 when IRC §267(a)(2) was enacted, and its list of tainted relationships has been adopted either intact or with minor variations by a number of other statutory restrictions and prohibitions.[20]

The most important relationships set out in IRC §267(b) can be summarized as follows:

1. *Members of a family.* Sections 267(b)(1) and 267(c)(4) provide that the family of an individual shall include only his or her brothers and sisters

---

[17] See Treas. Regs. §§1.267(a)-1(b)(1)(iii), 1.267(a)-1(b)(3). For taxability of a cash-basis taxpayer who receives the equivalent of cash, see infra ¶35.2; for constructive receipt, see infra ¶35.2.

[18] Walsh Food Serv., Inc. v. CIR, ¶66,057 P-H Memo TC (1966); Island Gas, Inc. v. CIR, 30 TC 787 (1958) (Acq.).

[19] See, e.g., H & H Drilling Co. v. CIR, 15 TC 961 (1950).

[20] See, e.g., IRC §§318, 544, 1563; see also Miller v. CIR, 75 TC 182 (1980) (IRC §267 applied to sale between two brothers despite hostile relationship).

(whether by the whole or the half blood), spouse, ancestors, and lineal descendants. Thus, transactions between an individual and his or her in-laws are not covered by IRC §267, nor are transactions between an individual and a stepchild or stepparent.[21] Because in-laws are not part of the "family" as defined by IRC §267(c)(4), transactions between parents and their married children must be carefully analyzed. For example, a sale to the taxpayer's child and his or her spouse as tenants in common must be fragmented, IRC §267(a)(1) being applicable to the half sold to the child but not to the half sold to the child's spouse.[22]

2. *Shareholder-corporate relationships.* By virtue of IRC §267(b)(2), a shareholder and a corporation are related if the shareholder owns, directly or indirectly, more than 50 percent in value of the corporation's stock. Section 267(b)(2) specifies *more* than 50 percent, and the base on which the fraction is computed is the value of the corporation's outstanding stock, not its voting power. The scope of IRC §267(b)(2) is much broader than initially appears, since ownership of the requisite amount of stock is determined by reference to a series of constructive ownership rules, which in a bewildering variety of circumstances treat taxpayers as owning stock that is actually owned by other persons and entities.

3. *Trust relationships—grantor, fiduciary, and beneficiary.* Under IRC §§267(b)(4) and 267(b)(6), the grantor of a trust and its beneficiaries are related to the fiduciary.[23] These grantor-fiduciary-beneficiary rules are buttressed by IRC §§267(b)(5) and 267(b)(7); if two trusts are established by the same grantor, the trusts are related to each other, and the beneficiaries of each are related to the fiduciary of the other. Finally, IRC §267(b)(8) provides that the fiduciary of a trust is related to a corporation if more than 50 percent in value of its outstanding stock is owned directly or indirectly by or for the trust or its grantor.

Section 267(b) does not, however, provide that a decedent's estate and its beneficiaries are related persons.

¶33.4 SECTION 482 REALLOCATIONS—INTRODUCTORY

Section 482 authorizes the IRS to distribute, apportion, or allocate gross income, deductions, credits, or allowances among two or more organizations, trades, or businesses under common ownership or control on determining that

[21] Rev. Rul. 71-50, 1971-1 CB 106; DeBoer v. CIR, 16 TC 662 (1951), aff'd per curiam, 194 F.2d 289 (2d Cir. 1952). Relationships by adoption are considered lineal; see Treas. Regs. §1.267(c)-1(a)(4).

[22] Simister v. CIR, 4 TC 470 (1944) (Acq.).

[23] See Dillard Paper Co. v. CIR, 341 F.2d 897 (4th Cir. 1965) (IRC §267(a)(1) applies to losses on sales by corporation to employee benefit trust).

this action is necessary "in order to prevent evasion of taxes or clearly to reflect the income of any of such organizations, trades, or businesses." Some early cases view manipulative "milking" of a profitable organization in order to shift income to affiliated organizations subject to lower rates or having offsetting losses as the only evil to be prevented, but later decisions make it clear that the IRS can compel each of the controlled taxpayers to report the taxable income that would have resulted from dealing at arm's length with the other members of the group. Thus, the IRS can place the "controlled taxpayer on a tax parity with an uncontrolled taxpayer,"[24] even if this disturbs legally enforceable arrangements that were established for business reasons and without any tax-avoidance motive.

The IRS has employed IRC §482 most extensively in recent years to question transfer prices and expense allocations between domestic corporations and their foreign affiliates, since the latter are ordinarily not subject to U.S. income taxes on their foreign-source income.[25] When these intercompany arrangements are subjected to the arm's-length standard enunciated by the regulations under IRC §482, the prices at which the parent's products are transferred to the foreign subsidiary must be revised to reflect a reasonable profit, and deductions attributable to the cost of conducting the foreign operations must be allocated to the subsidiary in an appropriate fashion. Although IRC §482 has particularly dramatic results when applied to transfer prices and other arrangements between domestic corporations and their foreign affiliates, it is by no means confined to these relationships. Thus, IRC §482 can be invoked to prevent the shifting of income from an individual to a corporation that is subject to a lower marginal tax rate or from a profitable corporation to an affiliated enterprise with unused deductions or loss carryovers. Indeed, IRC §482 can be invoked by the IRS to insure that each of the two related enterprises reports its true taxable income, even if they are both subject to the *same* marginal tax rate, since the reallocation can have such ancillary effects as increasing the earnings and profits of one of the corporations in order to characterize its distributions to shareholders as taxable dividends rather than tax-free returns of capital.

¶33.5 PREREQUISITES TO IRC §482 REALLOCATIONS

There are three statutory prerequisites to a reallocation under IRC §482: (a) two or more organizations, trades, or businesses; (b) common ownership or control; and (c) an IRS determination that a reallocation is necessary.

---

[24] Treas. Regs. §1.482-1(b)(1), quoted with approval by the Supreme Court in CIR v. First Security Bank of Utah, 405 US 394, 400 (1972).

[25] See IRC §881(a).

1. Two or More Organizations. Section 482's threshold condition is the existence of "two or more organizations, trades, or businesses (whether or not incorporated, whether or not organized in the United States, and whether or not affiliated)." The regulations give this language the broadest possible meaning—"organization" is defined to include sole proprietorships, partnerships, trusts, estates, associations, and corporations, whether domestic, foreign, taxable, or exempt; and "trade" and "business" are defined to include "any trade or business *activity of any kind*" (emphasis added), which may be broader than the familiar term "trade or business" as used in IRC §162, relating to business expenses.[26] In several recent cases, activities conducted by shareholders were held to be "organizations, trades, or businesses" separate from corporations controlled by them or members of their family, so that income realized by the corporation could be reallocated to them under IRC §482.[27] The unanswered question in this area is whether a shareholder-employee's failure to take a reasonable salary for services to a controlled corporation can trigger a corrective adjustment. Although the shareholder-employee is engaged in the trade or business of acting as a corporate executive,[28] the practice of under-compensating shareholder-employees may be so entrenched as to warrant an inference of legislative acquiescence; if so, a statutory amendment would be required to compel the allocation of an increased salary under IRC §482.

2. Common Ownership or Control. The second jurisdictional prerequisite for a reallocation under IRC §482—that the organizations, trades, or businesses are "owned or controlled directly or indirectly by the same interests"—is also construed in a broad fashion. The regulations state that "the reality" of control is decisive, not its form or mode of exercise; and that a presumption of control arises if income or deductions are arbitrarily shifted.[29] Section 482 has frequently been applied to enterprises owned by different members of the same family or in different proportions by the same persons;[30] and it has also been held that if two unrelated corporations own a third corporation equally, reallocations between the controlled corporation and each of its owners are permissible.[31]

---

[26] Treas. Regs. §§1.482-1(a)(1), 1.482-1(a)(2).

[27] See, e.g., Borge v. CIR, 405 F.2d 673 (2d Cir. 1968); Ach v. CIR, 358 F.2d 342 (6th Cir. 1966); but see Foglesong v. CIR, 691 F.2d 848 (7th Cir. 1982) (Tax Court's allocation of 98 percent of personal-service corporation's income to controlling shareholder-employee reversed on ground that IRC §482's requirement of two businesses is not satisfied if employee works *exclusively* for corporation receiving the income). Cobb v. Comm'r, 77 TC 1096 (1981).

[28] See, e.g., Trent v. CIR, 291 F.2d 669 (2d Cir. 1961).

[29] Treas. Regs. §1.482-1(a)(3).

[30] See, e.g., Ach v. CIR, supra note 27 (mother and son).

[31] B. Forman Co. v. CIR, 453 F.2d 1144 (2d Cir.), cert. denied, 407 US 934, rehearing denied, 409 US 899 (1972) (extensive analysis).

3. IRS Determination of Necessity. The final threshold condition to the application of IRC §482 is an IRS determination that a reallocation is "necessary" to prevent evasion of taxes or clearly to reflect the income of any member of the group. For practical purposes, "necessary" probably means "helpful" or "appropriate." The fact that the IRS determines that a reallocation is necessary does not mean that the determination is correct, although the courts have repeatedly stated that IRS determinations in this area will be upheld unless shown to be arbitrary or capricious.[32] Because of this heavy burden of proof, the taxpayer is entitled to notice that the IRS intends to rely on IRC §482.[33]

Since IRC §482 requires an IRS determination, taxpayers cannot resort to it on their own initiative, nor can they compel the IRS to take action.[34] Once the IRS invokes IRC §482, however, the regulations require the district director to make "correlative adjustments" to the income of other members of the group affected by the allocation and to "consider" the effect of reimbursement agreements and setoffs arising from other non-arm's length transactions between the parties.[35] Thus, IRC §482 is a one-way street at the outset; but when the IRS starts down this route, there is some room for taxpayer traffic in the opposite direction.

¶33.6 CHARACTER AND EFFECTS OF ADJUSTMENTS

When applicable, IRC §482 authorizes the IRS "to distribute, apportion, or allocate gross income, deductions, credits, or allowances" among or between the related organizations, trades, or businesses. For years, the power of the IRS to "create income where none is realized" was ardently debated; but this power is now widely conceded.[36] The IRS can impose an arm's-length price on an intercompany sale of goods, for example, even though the result is a profit to the seller before the related buyer has sold the goods to an outsider; and a profit can similarly be forced on the seller even if the buyer disposes of the goods at a loss or in a transaction in which it recognizes no income, such as a distribution to its shareholders. The miracle of income without gain, which obviously occurs every day in transactions between unrelated parties, is an inevitable consequence of the arm's-length standard enunciated by the IRC §482 regulations.

---

[32] See, e.g., Liberty Loan Corp. v. US, 498 F.2d 225 (8th Cir.), cert. denied, 419 US 1089 (1974), and cases there cited.

[33] See CIR v. Transport Mfg. & Equip. Co., 478 F.2d 731 (8th Cir. 1973).

[34] Treas. Regs. §1.482-1(b)(3).

[35] Treas. Regs. §§1.482-1(d)(2) (correlative adjustments) and 1.482-1(d)(3) (reimbursement agreements and setoffs), discussed infra ¶33.6.

[36] See Latham Park Manor, Inc. v. CIR, 69 TC 199, 215-216 (1977), and cases there cited; see also Treas. Regs. §1.482-1(d)(4).

Another battle ending with a victory for the IRS concerned its right to allocate the group's entire income to a single member, when appropriate, even though the statutory language—"distribute, apportion, or allocate"—seems to imply a division.[37]

These expansive features of IRC §482 are counterbalanced by four pro-taxpayer features of the regulations and IRS procedures thereunder:

1. Reimbursement Agreements. A proposed adjustment can be avoided or mitigated if an agreement between the affected parties for reimbursement, within a reasonable period before or after the taxable year, was in effect during the relevant taxable year. If the agreement provides adequate consideration for the services, judged as of the time when they were performed, no allocation is required.[38]

2. Offsetting Transactions. Taxpayers can ordinarily avoid or mitigate a proposed adjustment by establishing that they participated in *other* non-arm's-length transactions that, if taken into account, would result in a setoff against the proposed allocation.

3. Correlative Adjustments. If an adjustment is made, the regulations establish a "correlative adjustment" procedure, under which adjustments increasing the income of a member of the controlled group ("primary adjustments") are to be accompanied by appropriate correlative adjustments to the income of the related party if its tax liability would be affected by the change, currently or in a later year.[39] Section 482 itself does not explicitly sanction, let alone require, these offsetting adjustments in the taxpayer's favor; but they are obviously appropriate, and their inherent fairness may increase the willingness of the courts to enforce IRS actions under IRC §482.

4. Payments. Allocations under IRC §482 impute income to taxpayers receiving less than an arm's-length consideration for goods and services supplied to a related taxpayer, and the correlative adjustment procedure allows the latter to deduct the imputed amount or add it to the basis of its property when appropriate; but the resulting changes in tax liabilities do not alter the legal rights of the parties *inter sese.* Under Revenue Procedure 65-17, however, the imputed amount can be paid by one party to the other (or reflected on their books by accounts payable and receivable) without additional tax consequences, substantially as though the price had conformed at the outset to an

---

[37] See Your Host, Inc. v. CIR, 58 TC 10, 24 (1972), and cases there cited.

[38] Treas. Regs. §1.482-1(d)(3); for the procedure to be followed in establishing a reimbursement agreement, see Rev. Proc. 70-8, 1970-1 CB 434.

[39] Treas. Regs. §1.482-1(d)(2).

arm's-length standard, provided tax avoidance was not one of the principal purposes of the transaction and certain procedural requirements are satisfied.[40]

¶33.7 RELATIONSHIP OF IRC §482 TO OTHER TAX-AVOIDANCE PROVISIONS AND DOCTRINES

1. Assignment-of-Income Doctrine. Section 482 has much in common with the more pervasive assignment-of-income doctrine, and adjustments sometimes rest on both grounds; but each has areas of application that are beyond the reach of the other. For example, the results in two leading assignment-of-income cases—*Helvering v. Clifford* and *Helvering v. Horst*—could not have been reached under IRC §482, because neither case involved two "organizations, trades, or businesses," a prerequisite to the invocation of IRC §482.[41]

2. Substance Over Form. Because the principle that substance controls over form has no clearly identifiable limits,[42] this protean doctrine may encompass all of IRC §482 in the sense that any adjustment sanctioned by IRC §482 could instead rest on the principle that substance controls in applying the federal income tax to business arrangements. Indeed, allocations under IRC §482 have been judicially described as the substitution of substance for form.[43] On the other hand, the substance-over-form principle embraces transactions that are beyond the reach of IRC §482 because, for example, the parties are not under common ownership or control or do not constitute "organizations, trades, or businesses."

3. Section 269. Section 269 sanctions the disallowance of deductions, credits, and other tax allowances if control of a corporation is acquired for the principal purpose of avoiding federal income taxes and certain other conditions are satisfied. Section 269 is more sweeping than IRC §482 because it permits the total disallowance of tax benefits, not merely their reallocation between

---

[40] See Rev. Proc. 65-17, 1965-1 CB 833; Rev. Proc. 72-53, 1972-2 CB 833 (same as to adjustments under IRC §61 if they could have been made under IRC §482).

[41] For Helvering v. Clifford, 309 US 331 (1940), and Helvering v. Horst, 311 US 112 (1940), see infra ¶34.1 and supra ¶30.3, respectively. As defined by Treas. Regs. §1.482-1(a)(1), the term "organization" includes sole proprietorships; but individuals as such are pointedly omitted.

[42] For the substance-over-form doctrine, see supra ¶1.3.

[43] Simon J. Murphy Co. v. CIR, 231 F.2d 639, 644 (6th Cir. 1956).

two or more related parties; on the other hand, IRC §269 is triggered only by a tax-avoidance purpose, while IRC §482 can apply even if there is an inadvertent distortion of income. Moreover, IRC §269 defines "control" in a much more restricted fashion than IRC §482 and applies only to corporate tax allowances, while IRC §482 also applies to sole proprietorships, partnerships, and other unincorporated enterprises.

4. Section 446(b). If the taxpayer's accounting method does not "clearly reflect income," IRC §446(b) permits the IRS to compute taxable income by a method that will remedy this defect.[44] Since IRC §§446(b) and 482 are aimed at practices that do not clearly reflect income, it should not be surprising that they can overlap.

5. Section 162, Etc. Since IRC §482 is concerned with *distortions* of income, it necessarily incorporates by reference all provisions governing the computation of *true* taxable income. Given this relationship, it is obvious that some IRC §482 adjustments could rest solely on the governing substantive provision. If, for example, a parent company pays an excessive amount to a subsidiary for goods or services, the excess would not be deductible under IRC §162 even if IRC §482 were repealed; in the same vein, the parent's deduction of salaries and other expenses properly attributable to the business of a subsidiary can be disallowed under IRC §162 without reference to IRC §482.

SELECTED BIBLIOGRAPHY

Fuller, Section 482 Revisited, 31 Tax L. Rev. 475, 476–478 (1976).

O'Connor, Side Effects of Section 482 Can Be More Serious Than Original Allocation, 31 J. Tax. 194 (1969).

Ricketts, An Outline of the Four Major Attribution Rules: How They Operate, 26 J. Tax. 26 (1967).

Ringel, Surrey & Warren, Attribution of Stock Ownership in the Internal Revenue Code, 72 Harv. L. Rev. 209 (1958).

---

[44] For IRC §446(b), see infra ¶35.1.

CHAPTER 34

Grantor Trusts

¶34.1 GRANTOR TRUSTS: INTRODUCTORY

1. In General. During the period 1913 to 1921, Congress gradually worked out the basic pattern of taxing trust income to either the fiduciary or the beneficiaries, depending on whether it was accumulated or distributed. These early tax laws made no provision for taxing the grantor of a trust, however, no matter how extensive his control over the trust's corpus and income; and this omission created a golden opportunity for tax avoidance. By transferring securities, real estate, or other investments into a revocable trust and allowing the income to accumulate, a wealthy taxpayer could apparently shift income from his high tax brackets to the fiduciary's lower brackets, even though he retained economic control over the corpus and income and could get both back by a stroke of a pen.

For a time this maneuver was successful. Although for all practical purposes the grantor of a revocable trust is the owner of the trust assets, the validity of such trusts under local law was generally regarded by the courts, and on occasion by the Treasury, as decisive for income tax purposes.[1] In 1924, however, Congress enacted the statutory predecessor of IRC §676, taxing the income of a revocable trust to the grantor, whether it is distributed to the beneficiaries or accumulated by the trustee, and this provision was buttressed by protective provisions enacted from 1924 to 1934.[2]

These restrictions on tax avoidance (now embodied in IRC §§676 and 677), however, did not reach trusts whose corpus would revert to the grantor at the end of a specified period but that were irrevocable in the interim, nor did they affect trusts over which the grantor retained so-called nonbeneficial powers, such as the right to add new beneficiaries or to sprinkle the income among the named beneficiaries in such proportions as he might decide from year to year. In the 1930s, taxpayers began to make extensive use of these short-term trusts and nonbeneficial powers, and the IRS responded by arguing in numerous cases that these features constituted a sufficient degree of retained dominion and control over the income-producing property to justify taxing the trust income to the grantor, even though he could not use it for personal purposes and hence was not within the reach of the statutory predecessors of IRC §§676 and 677. Having no specific statutory provision to rely on, the IRS argued that the catchall definition of income in Section 22(a) of the 1939 Code [3] was broad enough to tax a grantor on the income of a short-term trust for members of his immediate family, especially if he reserved the power to manage the corpus and to decide when and in what proportions the designated beneficiaries would receive distributions.

This theory was accepted by the Supreme Court in *Helvering v. Clifford,* decided in 1940, which sustained the IRS in taxing trust income to the grantor of a trust over which he retained extensive managerial powers, which was to terminate in five years or on the earlier death of either the grantor or his wife, and the income of which was payable to his wife currently or at the termination of the trust at his discretion.[4] In an opinion whose importance to the tax law can scarcely be exaggerated, the Court said:

> So far as [the grantor's] dominion and control were concerned it seems clear that the trust did not effect any substantial change. . . . There were, we may assume, exceptions, such as his disability to make a gift of the corpus to others during the term of the trust and to make loans to himself. But this dilution in his control would seem to be insignificant and immaterial, since control over investment remained. If it be said that such

---

[1] Warden v. Lederer, 24 F.2d 233 (E.D. Pa. 1927); L.O. 1102, I-2 CB 50 (1922), declared obsolete by Rev. Rul. 69-31, 1969-1 CB 307, 308.

[2] See, e.g., Revenue Act of 1924, P.L. No. 176, §219(g), 43 Stat. 253, 277.

[3] The predecessor of IRC §61(a).

[4] Helvering v. Clifford, 309 US 331 (1940).

> control is the type of dominion exercised by any trustee, the answer is simple. We have at best a temporary reallocation of income within an intimate family group. . . . It is hard to imagine that respondent felt himself the poorer after this trust had been executed or, if he did, that it had any rational foundation in fact.[5]

Because the Court did not enunciate any specific criteria of taxability but instead held that all the facts and circumstances were relevant, the *Clifford* opinion set both the IRS and taxpayers adrift in a turbulent sea devoid of lighthouses; and the case was followed by a tidal wave of continued litigation.

In *Clifford,* the Supreme Court virtually invited the Treasury to issue regulations by referring to the "absence of more precise standards or guides supplied by statute or appropriate regulations;" and in 1946 the Treasury issued the so-called Clifford Regulations, embodying its view of the circumstances in which the grantor of a trust should be taxed on the basis of retained dominion and control. These regulations were codified with minor exceptions in 1954, when Congress enacted IRC §§671–678 (often called the "Clifford rules"). These provisions, whose details are discussed hereafter, tax the grantor of a trust on its income if he has (a) a reversionary interest that is likely to take effect within ten years, (b) certain powers to affect beneficial enjoyment of the corpus or income, or (c) specified managerial powers of a broad and unusual character.[6]

When the grantor trust rules were first enacted, Congress recognized that they would be ineffective if the grantor could avoid being taxed by entrusting an otherwise fatal power to an employee, friend, or other third person who could be expected to exercise the power if and when requested by the grantor to do so. To eliminate this escape route, the statutory rules provide, in most but not all cases, that a power vested in a third person shall be treated the same as a power retained by the grantor himself, unless the third person has a beneficial interest in the trust that would be adversely affected by exercising the power in the grantor's favor.[7]

The grantor trust rules normally result in taxing the trust income to the grantor. Since 1954, however, they have provided that the grantor "shall be treated as the owner" of the affected trust property, so that deductions, net operating and capital losses, tax credits, and other allowances attributable to the trust property can be claimed by the grantor on his individual tax return.[8]

---

[5] Id. at 335–336.

[6] See IRC §§673–675, discussed infra ¶¶34.2, 34.6, 34.7.

[7] Infra, text at notes 11-22.

[8] Treas. Regs. §1.671-3.

As a postscript to the legislation in this area, it is worth noting that the term "Clifford trust," historically applied to a trust whose income was imputed to the grantor, is now often used to denote the precise opposite, viz., a trust whose grantor is immune to tax because the retained powers come within the safe harbors left by the statutory rules.

2. Identifying the Grantor: Reciprocal Trusts. In the early years of federal taxation, taxpayers sometimes employed reciprocal trusts in an effort to obfuscate economic reality. Thus, *A* would create a trust whose income was to be accumulated for the benefit of *B* (who might be *A*'s spouse or business associate), while *B* would simultaneously create an identical trust for *A*'s benefit. Their hope was that each trust would be viewed in isolation, in which event *A* and *B* would each be treated as the grantor of a trust in which he or she had no interest, even though each enjoyed a financial status that would have resulted in tax liability under the statutory predecessor of IRC §677 [9] if achieved by creating a trust for his or her own benefit.

When litigated, however, the reciprocal trust device soon came unstuck. In *United States v. Grace's Estate,* the leading case to "uncross" reciprocal trusts created by a married couple, the Supreme Court held that the decedent husband should be treated as the grantor of the trust that was created, in form, by his spouse where the trusts were "interrelated" and "the arrangement, to the extent of mutual value, leaves the settlors in approximately the same economic position as they would have been in had they created trusts naming themselves as life beneficiaries." [10] In reaching this result, the Court held that the fact of interrelationship was controlling and that it was not necessary for the government to establish that the grantors entertained a tax-avoidance intent or that either trust was created "as a quid pro quo for the other." Although concerned with the federal estate tax status of reciprocal trusts, the doctrine enunciated in *Grace's Estate* also determines their income tax consequences.

3. Adverse and Nonadverse Parties. The original version of the grantor trust provisions, enacted in 1924, taxed the grantor if he reserved, "either alone or in conjunction with any person not a beneficiary of the trust," the power to revoke or revest in himself any part of the trust corpus or to receive all or part of the trust income.[11] This rudimentary legislative effort to deal with powers shared by the grantor with persons selected for their subservience seemed to invite other evasive tactics, such as vesting sole authority to act in

---

[9] For IRC §677, see infra ¶34.4.

[10] US v. Grace's Est., 395 US 316, 325 (1969).

[11] Revenue Act of 1924, §§219(g), 219(h), 43 Stat. 253, 277, upheld as constitutional, Reinecke v. Smith, 289 US 172, 177-178 (1933).

the chosen person or bestowing on him an interest of trivial value and thus converting him into a "beneficiary." These escape routes were closed in 1932, when powers held by a person "not having a substantial adverse interest" in the corpus or income—either alone or with the grantor—were given the same treatment as powers held by the grantor.[12]

In 1954, the statutory phraseology was given its current form by the enactment of IRC §§672(a) and 672(b), which define the terms "adverse party" and "nonadverse party." Under the grantor trust provisions, powers held by a nonadverse party, either alone or with the grantor, ordinarily have the same tax effect as powers held by the grantor alone.[13] A power is not imputed to the grantor, however, if it is held by an adverse party, defined by IRC §672(a) as a person having a substantial beneficial interest in the trust that will be adversely affected by the exercise or nonexercise of his power.[14]

The legislative theory for exempting such powers from attribution to the grantor is that the holder will probably act independently of the grantor because compliance with the grantor's wishes would damage his own financial interests. Thus, the grantor of a trust that can be revoked only if an adverse party consents is analogized to a donor of property who can get it back only if the donee chooses to sacrifice his own financial interest by relinquishing the property. Although its income tax consequences are similar to those of an outright gift, a trust whose corpus can be recovered if a person having an adverse interest consents to the revocation is not entirely analogous to such a gift. The difference lies in the fact that a completed gift can be recovered by the donor only if *all* persons with an interest in the donated property consent, whereas in many situations the grantor is relieved by IRC §§674–677 of responsibility for an otherwise tainted power if it is vested in *any* person with a substantial beneficial interest that would be adversely affected by an exercise of the power, even though this action would also penalize other beneficiaries whose consent is not required. If, for example, a number of beneficiaries have adverse interests (e.g., three alternative remaindermen, each of whom has a substantial chance to inherit the corpus), a grantor who retains the power to revoke the trust with the consent of any one of them will not be taxed.

This disparity between the "adverse party" concept employed by the grantor trust provisions and the status of donees of completed gifts is broadened by the regulations, which define "substantial interest" to mean one whose

---

[12] Revenue Act of 1932, §§166, 167, 47 Stat. 169, 221.

[13] Analogous rules apply under the federal estate and gift taxes, but there are some important differences. See infra, text following note 28.

[14] Under IRC §677(a), however, a *spouse's* adverse interest in the income of a trust is irrelevant pro tanto, since income that is or may be distributed to the grantor's spouse is taxed to the grantor.

value in relation to the total value of the property is "not insignificant." [15] This construction of the statutory phrase enables the grantor to avoid tax liability even though a power that would be fatal if held by the grantor or a nonadverse party is entrusted to someone with a comparatively modest (but "not insignificant") stake in the trust property.

The regulations state that a contingent income beneficiary may be an adverse party,[16] which necessarily implies that a contingent interest can be "substantial" within the meaning of IRC §672(a). Presumably the likelihood that the interest will become possessory must be estimated in determining whether the interest is "not insignificant" in relation to the property subject to the power. When a beneficiary's interest depends on mortality, its substantiality can be estimated by using actuarial tables;[17] but if the right to receive income or corpus is conditioned on such events as emergency medical needs, supervening poverty, or the approval of a third person, the likelihood of occurrence is difficult or impossible to estimate. The case law on the subject is sparse and not very helpful in predicting the effect of particular clauses;[18] it would, therefore, be perilous, from a planning perspective, to assume that a beneficiary's interest is "substantial," unless an estimate of its value can be supported by reliable evidence.

In addition to being "substantial," a beneficial interest qualifies its holder for "adverse party" status under IRC §672(a) only if it would be adversely affected by exercise or nonexercise of the power in question.

From time to time, it is suggested that a beneficiary of a trust cannot be an "adverse party" if he is linked to the grantor by family or emotional ties or if, as a prospective heir or legatee of the grantor, he would be unlikely to jeopardize his expectations by resisting the grantor's wishes. Although these pressures may destroy the suppositious independence attributed to the beneficiary's financial interest in the trust, the weight of authority supports the conclusion that relatives and close friends can be adverse parties within the meaning of IRC §672(a).[19] This conclusion was strengthened by the addition

---

[15] Treas. Regs. §1.672(a)-1(a) (last sentence).

[16] Treas. Regs. §1.672(a)-1(c) (last sentence).

[17] See IRS Pub. No. 723A, Actuarial Values II: Factors at 6 Percent Involving One and Two Lives (1970); Chase Nat'l Bank v. CIR, 225 F.2d 621 (8th Cir. 1955), cert. denied, 350 US 965 (1956) (to recover portion of trust, powerholder would have to survive one of two children and the child's issue within six or seventeen years; held, interest too remote).

[18] Compare Fulham v. CIR, 110 F.2d 916 (1st Cir. 1940) (beneficiary's right to receive income on falling into "necessitous circumstances" treated as insubstantial) with Phipps v. CIR, 137 F.2d 141 (2d Cir. 1943) (despite reference to trustee's "uncontrolled discretion," facts established that grantor intended beneficiary to receive substantial part of trust income).

[19] See Laganas v. CIR, 281 F.2d 731, at 735-736 (1st Cir. 1960).

in 1954 of the "related or subordinate party" concept of IRC §672(c), which for certain other purposes establishes a rebuttable presumption that specified family members are subservient to the grantor.[20] Congress refrained from extending this tainted circle approach to the concept of an "adverse party," and, while not conclusive, this legislative restraint buttresses the prevailing pre-1954 judicial view that members of a family are to be treated as independent persons, each standing on his or her own feet, in applying the substantial adverse interest test. A contrary theory would plunge the courts into a never-ending inquiry into the strength of emotional relationships, since most beneficiaries of trusts are related to the grantor by family or other close ties.

4. Related or Subordinate Parties. The "adverse party" concept as used throughout the grantor trust provisions was modified in 1954 by the enactment of IRC §672(c), defining the term "related or subordinate party," which is used as the antonym of an independent trustee by IRC §§674(c) (powers to distribute or accumulate income and corpus) and 675(3) (loans by trust to grantor).[21] In effect, these provisions permit some powers to be vested in persons who, lacking a beneficial interest in the trust, are not "adverse parties" within the meaning of IRC §672(b), but who nevertheless are regarded as sufficiently independent to permit them to hold certain limited powers without attribution to the grantor. A related or subordinate party cannot qualify for this status, however, if he is subservient to the grantor's wishes.

The term "related or subordinate party" is defined by IRC §672(c) to mean a nonadverse party who is the grantor's spouse if living with the grantor; a parent, descendant, sibling, or employee of the grantor; a corporation in which the grantor and the trust have a significant voting interest, or an employee thereof; or a subordinate employee of a corporation of which the grantor is an executive. The persons selected for this legislative taint are presumed to be subservient to the grantor unless the contrary is shown by a preponderance of the evidence. Most prudent draftsmen assume that all related or subordinate parties are subservient and go outside this tainted circle to find the requisite number of independent trustees. This rarely requires much of a search, since trust companies, business partners, lawyers, accountants, and most relatives are not proscribed by IRC §672(c)(2) and thus can qualify as independent, even though more cynical eyes may view them as the grantor's agents or instrumentalities.[22]

---

[20] See infra, text at note 21.

[21] For IRC §§674(c) and 675, see infra ¶¶34.6 and 34.7, respectively.

[22] See Goodwyn's Est. v. CIR, ¶76,238 P-H Memo TC (1976) (trustee treated as independent despite practice of acquiescing in grantor's decisions; grantor not treated as "true" trustee).

5. "Dominion and Control." Section 671, enacted in 1954, provides that the grantor of a trust shall not be taxed on trust income "solely on the grounds of his dominion and control over the trust under Section 61 (relating to definition of gross income) or any other provision of this title, except as specified" in the grantor trust provisions (i.e., IRC §§673–677).[23] This is a roundabout way of saying that if a grantor's powers over a trust are not condemned by the explicit terms of IRC §§673–677, the IRS cannot treat him as its owner on the theory that his powers, though individually innocent, have the effect when combined of preserving his dominion and control over the transferred property. Thus, IRC §671 is intended to forestall a repetition of *Helvering v. Clifford,* where the Supreme Court held that the grantor of a trust could be taxed on its income even though his powers over the trust property were not fatal under the specific grantor trust provisions then in effect, because the trust did not "effect any substantial change" in his "dominion and control" over the transferred property.[24]

But this does not mean that everything goes. In recommending enactment of IRC §671, the Senate Finance Committee explained its purpose and scope as follows:

> [T]his subpart has no application in situations involving assignments of future income to the assignor, as in *Lucas v. Earl* (281 US 111), *Harrison v. Schaffner* (312 US 579), and *Helvering v. Horst* (311 US 112), whether or not the assignment is to a trust; nor are the rules as to family partnerships affected by this subpart. This subpart also has no application in determining the right of a grantor to deductions for payments to a trust under a transfer and leaseback arrangement.[25]

Another aspect of IRC §671, not mentioned by the legislative committee reports, is its impact on trusts that are "shams," lack "economic reality," or are operated in a slipshod fashion in disregard of the trust agreement. The courts have held that the grantor can be taxed in situations like these;[26] since the defects are more fundamental than the retention of dominion and control found objectionable in the *Clifford* case, these decisions do not contravene IRC §671. On the other hand, trusts surviving the explicit statutory obstacles have

---

[23] For the effect of this part of IRC §671 on a person who, though not the grantor of a trust, has a power to vest the corpus or income in himself, see infra ¶34.8.

[24] See supra, text at notes 5 and 6.

[25] S. Rep. No. 1622, 83d Cong., 2d Sess. 365 (1954). For *Lucas v. Earl, Harrison v. Schaffner,* and *Helvering v. Horst,* cited by the Committee, see supra ¶¶30.2 and 30.3.

[26] Compare Furman v. CIR, 45 TC 360 (1966), aff'd per curiam, 381 F.2d 22 (5th Cir. 1967) with Goodwyn's Est. v. CIR, supra note 22 (grantor's de facto management of trust does not require disregarding IRC §671).

been upheld in some cases even though the grantor-trustee overstepped the bounds set by the trust instrument.[27]

6. Alimony Trusts. A trust created or utilized at the time of divorce or legal separation to support an ex-spouse or children may be a grantor trust, but its tax status is affected by specialized provisions relating to alimony.

7. Foreign Trusts. By virtue of IRC §679, enacted in 1976, U.S. persons who transfer property, directly or indirectly, to a foreign trust with at least one U.S. beneficiary are treated as owning the portion of the trust attributable to the transferred property. When recommending enactment of IRC §679, the Senate Finance Committee summarized the reasons for imposing grantor status on so-called offshore trusts as follows:

> The rules of present law permit U.S. persons to establish foreign trusts so that funds can be accumulated free of U.S. tax. Further, the funds of these foreign trusts are generally invested in countries which do not tax interest and dividends paid to foreign investors, and the trusts generally are administered through countries which do not tax such entities. Thus, these trusts generally pay no income tax anywhere in the world.[28]

8. Estate and Gift Tax Consequences of Grantor Trusts. The grantor trust provisions (IRC §§671–677) have as their objective the delineation of a distinction between those transfers that are sufficiently complete so that it is appropriate to relieve the grantor of tax liability for the income produced thereafter by the transferred property and those involving retained benefits or controls warranting his continued tax liability. The federal gift tax law also draws a line between those transfers that are complete enough to justify imposing a gift tax and those to which the transferor has attached so many strings that the property should continue to be regarded as owned by him. The federal estate tax, in turn, also draws a line between property transferred at death (or in a quasi-testamentary manner), which should be included in the decedent's gross estate in computing estate tax liability, and transfers completed during the decedent's life, on which an estate tax is not appropriate.

Although each of these three taxes distinguishes for its own purposes between complete and incomplete transfers, they establish quite different boundaries. As a result, a transfer that is complete enough to relieve the grantor of the obligation to report the income from the transferred property during the remainder of his life may nevertheless be treated as a transfer at

---

[27] See, e.g., Buehner v. CIR, 65 TC 723 (1976).

[28] S. Rep. No. 94-938, reprinted in 1976-3 CB (Vol. 3) 254-255.

death in computing his estate tax liability. Conversely, even though a transfer is too tentative to relieve the grantor of income tax liability, it may be complete enough to require payment of a gift tax on the transferred property. From a planning perspective, therefore, the tax consequences of each of these three taxes must be separately examined when creation of a trust is being considered, with an awareness that each has its own standards for testing the "completeness" of the transfer.

¶34.2 SHORT-TERM TRUSTS WITH REVERSION TO GRANTOR

1. In General. Section 673(a) treats the grantor as the owner of any portion of a trust (without regard to the identity of the beneficiaries) in which he has a reversionary interest in either corpus or income if the interest will, or may reasonably be expected to, take effect in possession or enjoyment within ten years commencing with the date of the transfer of that part of the trust. No matter how short the trust's life may be, the grantor is not taxable under IRC §673 unless he (or his estate) has a reversionary interest in a corpus or income. A reversionary interest in the grantor's spouse, however, is not subject to IRC §673(a), despite the fact that a married couple is treated as a single economic unit by IRC §677(a), relating to interests in the income of a trust.

If the trust is coextensive with the life of the income beneficiary or beneficiaries, it is not subject to IRC §673 even if it is expected to, and in fact does, last for less than ten years. If, however, the trust will terminate on the death of any other person with a life expectancy of less than ten years, the income is taxable to the grantor under IRC §673, no matter how long the measuring life turns out to be.[29]

Section 673(a) taxes grantors of short-term trusts by virtue of their reversionary interests, even if they have no control over beneficial enjoyment of the corpus or income, administrative authority, power to revoke, or other incidents of dominion and control. The rationale of this statutory emphasis on the trust's duration is that a trust whose corpus will revert to the grantor within a short period of time is tantamount to an assignment of income and is similar to transfers that, in a wide range of nontrust contexts, are ineffective to deflect taxation from the assignor to the assignee of the income.[30]

Although IRC §673 does not explicitly create a safe harbor for trusts with a duration of ten years or more, the grantor of such a trust cannot be taxed solely on the theory that its duration is unreasonably short; but he must still run the gauntlet of IRC §§674–677 and will be taxed on trust income if he has

[29] See Rev. Rul. 73-251, 1973-1 CB 324 (application of principle to creation and additions to trust terminating on grantor's death).

[30] See, e.g., Helvering v. Horst, 311 US 112 (1940), discussed supra ¶30.3.

any of the powers prohibited by these provisions. An easily overlooked aspect of the relationship between IRC §673 and these other provisions is that the allocation of capital gains to corpus, as is customary, means that they are accumulated for distribution to the grantor when the trust terminates. For this reason, the trust's capital gains and losses will be attributed to the grantor by IRC §677(a)(2), even though his reversionary interest will not become possessory within the ten-year period proscribed by IRC §673.[31] To avoid this result, trust instruments sometimes provide for the allocation of capital gains to income rather than principal, but this generates adverse gift tax consequences.[32]

In the absence of any rights or powers described by IRC §§674–677, however, the grantor gets the benefit of a safe harbor from tax if the trust is for ten years or more. The Code does not create a comparable durational haven for ordinary assignments of income, such as a gift of interest coupons from a coupon bond or of the rentals to be received from property retained by the donor. But in one analogous situation the IRS uses the time period prescribed by IRC §673 as a standard in ruling on the validity of nontrust assignments.[33]

Although IRC §673(a) reaches a reversionary interest only if it will (or may reasonably be expected to) take effect "within ten years commencing with the date of the transfer" of the relevant portion of the trust, grantors wanting to take advantage of this safe harbor often specify a somewhat longer life, such as ten years plus a day or a month. The additional period, though unnecessary from a technical point of view, provides some leeway in completing the formalities required to transfer property into the trust.

Trusts are subject to IRC §673(a) not only if the grantor's reversionary interest *will* take effect in possession or enjoyment within ten years of the transfer (e.g., a trust to terminate in eight years), but also if it *may reasonably be expected* to take effect within the ten-year period. The most common arrangement triggering this part of IRC §673 is a reversionary interest in the grantor taking effect on the death of a person (other than a life beneficiary) with a life expectancy of less than ten years.[34]

---

[31] See Treas. Regs. §1.671-3(b)(2); Treas. Regs. §1.673(a)-1(a) (third and fourth sentences); Treas. Regs. §1.677(a)-1(g), Example (2); Rev. Rul. 66-161, 1966-1 CB 164 (grantor of ten-year trust with power to withdraw capital gains as realized is also taxable on ordinary income attributable to gains that he allows to accumulate).

[32] See Rev. Rul. 77-358, 1977-2 CB 342.

[33] Rev. Rul. 55-38, 1955-1 CB 389 (irrevocable assignment of trust income by life beneficiary; held, comparable to creation of a trust; assignor will not be taxed on income if term of assignment is at least ten years); but see Rev. Rul. 58-337, 1958-2 CB 13 (grantor taxable under IRC §61 on rentals from ten-year leasehold transferred to trust).

[34] Treas. Regs. §1.673(a)-1(c).

2. Additions to and Extensions of an Existing Trust. When property is added to an existing trust, the ten-year period described by IRC §673(a) is measured from the "inception of that portion of the trust," not from the date when the trust was created. If the life of a trust is extended, the resulting postponement of the time when the grantor's reversionary interest will take effect is treated by IRC §673(d) as a new transfer in trust in determining whether the ten-year rule is satisfied; but this will not cause the grantor to be taxed on any income that would not have been taxed to him had the trust not been extended.[35]

The extension of a trust can also be used to convert the post-extension years of a short-term trust into the initial years of a nontaxable long-term trust. Thus, if during the third year of a five-year trust its life is extended by eight years, the last two years of the initial term would be amalgamated with the eight years of the extended term, and the grantor would not be subject to IRC §673(a) for the ten-year period following the extension.

¶34.3 REVOCABLE TRUSTS

1. In General. Under IRC §676(a), the grantor of a trust is treated as its owner if a power to revest title thereto is exercisable at any time by him, a nonadverse party,[36] or both. This rule comes into play not only when the power to revest is expressly reserved by the grantor in the trust indenture but also when it arises by operation of law (e.g., because the instrument does not explicitly provide for irrevocability and hence is revocable under state law). Section 676(a) also embraces a power that is functionally equivalent to a "power to revest," even though the label is different, such as an unrestricted power to invade corpus.[37] If the grantor's power is limited to a portion of the trust, he is treated as owner of that part rather than of the whole.

As originally enacted in 1924, IRC §676(a) taxed trust income of a particular year to the grantor only if he had a power to revoke during *that taxable year.* This feature of the 1924 legislation stimulated creation of "year and a day" revocable trusts, under which the grantor's power to revoke was exercisable in a given year only if notice was given during the *preceding* year of intent to exercise the power. To reach year-and-a-day trusts, the 1924 legislation was amended in 1934 to tax the grantor if "at any time the power

[35] Treas. Regs. §1.673(d)-1.

[36] For the term "nonadverse party," see supra ¶34.1.

[37] See Cox v. CIR, 110 F.2d 934 (10th Cir.), cert. denied, 311 US 667 (1940) (grantor's power to pay out principal for own "comfort, maintenance and/or education" treated as equivalent to power to revest under statutory predecessor of IRC §676).

to revest . . . is vested" in him.[38] This language was buttressed in 1954 by the enactment of IRC §672(d), explicitly stating that a person shall be considered to have a power even if it takes effect only on the expiration of a period of time after exercise or can be exercised only after notice.

Congress has never dealt explicitly with powers to revoke that take effect or can be exercised only on the occurrence of an event that the grantor has little or no power to control. If the condition (e.g., the death within ten years of an eighteen-year-old remainderman) cannot reasonably be expected to occur, if at all, until at least ten years after the property in question is transferred to the trust, the power to revoke can be disregarded by virtue of IRC §676(b), discussed below.[39] Conversely, if the event can reasonably be expected to occur within the ten-year period (e.g., the grantor's survival for three years), a power to revoke is for practical purposes the equivalent of a reversionary interest in a short-term trust.

If a power to revoke is contingent on an event whose occurrence is highly uncertain (e.g., a beneficiary's marriage, divorce, business failure, or disability), with the result that one cannot predict with assurance whether it may (or may not) reasonably be expected to occur within ten years of the transfer, its status under current law is not wholly clear. On balance, it seems probable that the exemption granted by IRC §676(b) for powers that cannot affect beneficial enjoyment until expiration of the ten-year or other period permitted by IRC §673 is the exclusive escape route from the general rule of IRC §676(a). To make use of IRC §676(b), the taxpayer must bear the burden of establishing that the power "can only" affect beneficial enjoyment after a period specified by IRC §673.

2. Postponed Power to Revoke. Section 676(b) exempts a power to revoke from the general rule of IRC §676(a) if its exercise can affect beneficial enjoyment of the income only after the expiration of a period of time such that the grantor would not be taxed under IRC §673 if the power were a reversionary interest. This exception to IRC §676(a) was enacted in 1954 to correlate the treatment of revocable trusts under IRC §676 with the treatment of reversionary interests under IRC §673.[40] If it were not qualified by IRC §676(b), the general rule of IRC §676(a) might be construed to treat a grantor who could revoke a trust at the end of a specified period of time more severely than the same grantor would be treated by IRC §673 if the trust instrument had provided for automatic (rather than discretionary) termination at the end of the same period.

---

[38] Revenue Act of 1934, §166, 48 Stat. 680, 729.

[39] See infra, text at note 40.

[40] For IRC §673, see supra ¶34.2.

¶34.4 POTENTIAL USE OF TRUST INCOME FOR GRANTOR'S BENEFIT

1. In General. Section 677(a) treats the grantor as the owner of any portion of a trust whose income is (or, in the discretion of the grantor, a nonadverse party, or both, may be) distributed or held or accumulated for future distribution to the grantor or the grantor's spouse if such action can occur without the approval or consent of any adverse party.[41] If capital gains can be distributed to the grantor (usually as part of an ultimate distribution of corpus), but not ordinary income, he is taxed only on the capital gains (and can deduct any capital losses); conversely, he is taxed on ordinary income (and can deduct ordinary losses) if the ordinary income, but not capital gains, can be distributed to him.[42]

Section 677(a) also treats the grantor as the owner of any portion of a trust whose income is or may be applied to pay premiums for insurance on the life of the grantor or the grantor's spouse, with an exception for policies payable to certain charitable beneficiaries.[43]

Section 677(a) supplements IRC §676 (relating to revocable trusts) by taxing the grantor on trust *income* that is or may be distributed to him, even if he has no power to get back the *corpus.*

In applying IRC §677(a), income is treated as distributed or held or accumulated for future distribution to the grantor or his spouse not only if it is paid or payable directly to them but also if it is paid or payable to another person on their behalf and in obedience to their instructions.[44] At an early date it was held that the statutory predecessor of IRC §677(a) also embraced income used to discharge the grantor's legal liabilities, since he thereby enjoys the benefit of the income "as though he had received the income personally."[45] This principle was applied by the Supreme Court in *Helvering v. Stuart* to a trust whose income *could be used* (in the discretion of nonadverse trustees) to support the grantor's minor children and thereby relieve him of his parental obligation, whether it was *actually used* for this purpose or not.[46] Although

---

[41] For the term "adverse party," see supra ¶34.1.

[42] Treas. Regs. §1.671-3(b); Treas. Regs. §1.673(a)-1(a) (third and fourth sentences).

[43] See infra ¶34.5.

[44] Treas. Regs. §1.667(a)-1(c).

[45] Douglas v. Willcuts, 296 US 1, 9 (1935) (trust to pay alimony to taxpayer's ex-wife). Rev. Rul. 64-240, 1964-2 CB 172, holds that trust income paid to a charity is not taxable to the grantor even if the payment satisfies a pledge. The exclusion of the income from the grantor's tax return takes the place of the deduction that would otherwise have been allowed under IRC §170, but the transfer is not charged against the taxpayer's percentage limit. See supra ¶19.3.

[46] Helvering v. Stuart, 317 US 154 (1942).

Congress subsequently enacted IRC §677(b),[47] changing this rule as to most so-called support trusts, it remains in force for trusts that do not come within this statutory exception.[48] Moreover, since IRC §677(a) includes income that is distributed or distributable to the grantor's spouse, the grantor is taxed on income that may be used to discharge his spouse's legal obligations as well as his own.[49]

The attribution to the grantor of income that is, or may be, used to discharge his legal obligations (or those of his spouse) is a reasonable interpretation of IRC §677(a); indeed, a contrary result would nullify that statutory rule by opening an escape hatch as wide as a barn door. In a more debatable line of cases, however, the courts have taxed the grantor on trust income used to pay off a debt to which the trust property was subject when transferred to the trust,[50] even though he retains no reversionary interest and the payments, like any reinvestment of trust income, inure primarily to the benefit of the named beneficiaries. The attribution of trust income to the grantor in this situation contrasts sharply with the treatment the grantor would have received on an outright gift of the encumbered property, viz., no income from the donee's subsequent payments to amortize or discharge the debt to which the donated property is subject.[51]

The impact of IRC §677(a) is also debatable when property is transferred to a trust subject to an obligation to pay the grantor's federal gift tax on the transfer. Since the donor is the primary obligor, despite the government's right to collect the tax from the donee if necessary, the gift tax is in effect a cost of creating the trust. Much can be said, therefore, for viewing the amount needed to pay the gift tax as property retained, rather than transferred, by the grantor. Indeed, this approach is employed in computing the gift tax itself, which is levied on the net amount of property transferred rather than on its gross value.[52] The courts treat the grantor as transferring the full value of the

---

[47] Infra, text at notes 59-64.

[48] Vreeland v. CIR, 16 TC 1041 (1951); Koehrer v. CIR, ¶45,068 P-H Memo TC (1945) (all trust income taxable to grantor where applicable to discharge his tax liabilities and limit on potential liability was not proved).

[49] Treas. Regs. §1.677(a)-1(d).

[50] See Wiles v. CIR, 59 TC 289, 300-301 (1972) (Acq.), aff'd without published opinion, 491 F.2d 1406 (5th Cir. 1974), taxing the grantor on income *actually* used to pay the debt without commenting on the status of income that "may be" but is not so used; cf. Furman v. CIR, 45 TC 360, 366-367 (1966), aff'd per curiam, 381 F.2d 22 (5th Cir. 1967), observing that "whether one has a legal obligation within the meaning of section 677(a)(1) of the Code . . . after he transfers to a trust property burdened by a debt and requires the trust to pay the debt, is difficult to fathom in view of the imprecise rationale of prior decisions."

[51] For special problems in this area if the debt exceeds the grantor's adjusted basis in the transferred property, see supra ¶23.16.

[52] See Rev. Rul. 75-72, 1975-1 CB 310 (formula for computing gift tax on net gift).

corpus, however, so that the grantor is taxable under IRC §677(a) on trust income that is or may be used to pay the gift tax under the trust instrument.[53] On the other hand, if the tax is paid with the proceeds of a loan procured by the *trustee* before the trust has any income, the grantor is not taxable on trust income used later to pay interest and principal on the loan.[54]

2. Income Payable to Grantor or Spouse Only in Contingencies. Because the grantor is taxable not only if trust income is actually distributed or held or accumulated for future distribution to him or his spouse but also if it "may be" so used, IRC §677(a) seems to embrace income that is payable only in a specified contingency, such as marriage, divorce, medical emergency, or bankruptcy, no matter how remote its occurrence may be;[55] but the case law, all based on an earlier version of IRC §677(a), is divided on this point.[56]

3. Effect of Postponed Power to Pay Income to Grantor or Spouse. If the income of a trust can be distributed or accumulated for future distribution to the grantor, he has the equivalent of a reversionary interest in the trust income. For this reason, the enactment in 1954 of IRC §673(a), taxing the grantor on trust income if he has a reversionary interest in income or corpus that will or may reasonably be expected to take effect within ten years of the trust transfer, created a potential conflict with IRC §677(a). The second sentence of IRC §677(a), added in 1954, avoids this conflict by protecting the grantor against tax liability if a power to distribute income (or to accumulate income for future distribution) to him can affect beneficial enjoyment of the income only after the term prescribed by IRC §673 for taxable reversionary

---

[53] Shaeffer's Est. v. CIR, 37 TC 99 (1961), aff'd, 313 F.2d 738 (8th Cir.), cert. denied, 375 US 818 (1963); see also Diedrich v. CIR, 102 S. Ct. 2414 (1982) (on gift of appreciated property on condition that donee pay gift tax, donor realizes gain to extent tax liability exceeds adjusted basis of property).

[54] Morgan's Est. v. CIR, 37 TC 981 (1962), aff'd per curiam, 316 F.2d 238 (6th Cir.), cert. denied, 375 US 825 (1963); but see Krause v. CIR, 56 TC 1242 (1971) (trust instrument permitted payment of grantor's gift tax; held, income realized by trust up to date of payment is taxable to grantor notwithstanding use of loan proceeds to pay taxes; but grantor is not taxable on trust income realized thereafter).

[55] See Treas. Regs. §1.677(a)-1(c).

[56] CIR v. Willson, 132 F.2d 255, 257 (6th Cir. 1942) (grantor taxed where income would be paid to her if she survived her husband); see also Barker v. CIR, 25 TC 1230 (1956) (income payable to grantor in event of need caused by "accident, sickness, or other emergency, or unusual condition of any kind"); Ward v. CIR, 40 BTA 225 (1939), rev'd on other grounds, 119 F.2d 207 (3d Cir. 1941) (grantor not taxable on accumulated income that would be distributed to him if his spouse and children predeceased him without issue); Boeing v. CIR, 37 BTA 178, 185 (1938) (same where grantor or his heirs would get income if his son died before thirty).

interests. Like IRC §676(b), which performs a similar harmonizing function between IRC §§676(a) and 673,[57] the second sentence of IRC §677(a) is also applicable to trust income arising after the death of an income beneficiary.

The second sentence of IRC §677(a) does not apply, however, if income or capital gains realized during the first ten years of a trust's life can be accumulated for the grantor's benefit, even though distribution is postponed until the expiration of ten years from the transfer or until the life beneficiary dies.[58]

The impact of the second sentence of IRC §677(a) on powers to distribute income to the grantor or his spouse only if a stated contingency occurs is not wholly clear. It would be appropriate to tax the grantor on the trust income if the contingency will or can reasonably be expected to occur within ten years of the transfer, but not if there is reliable evidence that it will occur, if at all, after that period (or after the death of the income beneficiary). The impact of contingencies whose occurrence is not susceptible to a reasonable estimate is more problematical, but it seems likely that the trust income in such circumstances is taxable to the grantor because (a) it "may be" distributed to him and (b) he cannot establish that the contingency is within the ambit of the second sentence of IRC §677(a).

4. Trust for Support of Grantor's or Spouse's Legal Dependents. As pointed out earlier, in *Helvering v. Stuart,* decided in 1942, the Supreme Court construed the language of IRC §677(a) (income that "may be" distributed to the grantor) to include trust income that could be used to relieve the grantor of the obligation to support his legal dependents, whether the income was so used or not.[59] Congress responded to this decision by enacting the predecessor of IRC §677(b), providing that trust income is not taxable to a grantor merely because it *may be* used (in the discretion of another person, the trustee, or the grantor acting as trustee or co-trustee) for the support or maintenance of a beneficiary whom the grantor is legally obligated to support.[60]

This statutory concession is the foundation of a common type of trust, under which the income is accumulated for the benefit of the grantor's children until majority, marriage, enrollment in a professional school, commencement of a business venture, or similar event, but can be diverted before then for current support in the trustee's discretion. By virtue of IRC §677(b), the grantor is taxed only if, and to the extent that, the trust income is *actually* used

[57] Supra ¶34.3.

[58] See Treas. Regs. §1.677(a)-1(f); Humphrey v. CIR, 39 TC 199, 202-203 (1962); Humphrey v. US, 245 F.Supp. 49 (D.Kan. 1965).

[59] Helvering v. Stuart, supra note 46.

[60] The protection accorded by IRC §677(b) applies only if use of the income for

to discharge a legal duty to support the beneficiaries. If under local law there is no duty to support dependents who have sufficient resources of their own, the obligation can be ignored for tax purposes so long as their resources are adequate. Moreover, if the creation of a trust whose income is sufficient to support the dependent on a scale appropriate to the family's circumstances eliminates the support obligation, distributions thereafter are presumably not imputed to the grantor.[61]

The exemption granted by IRC §677(b) does not embrace income that (a) can be used to discharge the grantor's legal obligation to support a spouse, (b) is subject to a discretionary power exercisable by the grantor in a nonfiduciary capacity, or (c) is available to discharge legal obligations other than the duty to support or maintain a beneficiary.[62] But the regulations read enough into IRC §677(b) to protect the grantor against tax liability for income that may be (but is not) used to relieve the grantor's spouse of the obligation to support the spouse's children, whether or not the grantor shares that duty.[63]

If trust income can be used solely to provide the grantor's dependents with luxuries or other items for which the grantor is not contractually liable and that are beyond his or her support obligation under local law, the income is not taxed to the grantor under the general rule of IRC §677(a).[64] Since IRC §677(b) imposes no liability on its own, but merely relieves the grantor of tax liability on income that would otherwise "be considered taxable" under IRC §677(a), it seems clear that trust income used to support dependents at a level above that mandated by state law is not taxable to the grantor under the first sentence of IRC §677(b). The scope of the parental obligation to support children under state law is so vague, however, that it is often difficult to determine whether a particular payment relieves the parents of a legal obligation or, instead, provides the beneficiary with an item that the grantor is not legally required to supply.

---

the beneficiary's support is discretionary, not if it is mandatory; see Treas. Regs. §1.677(b)-1(f).

[61] See Treas. Regs. §1.662(a)-4 (legal obligation to support arises only if obligation is not affected by adequacy of child's resources); see also R.I. Gen. Laws §33-15-1 (1970) (no parental obligation to provide children with private school or college education if this expense can be defrayed by child's property or by income or corpus of a trust).

[62] In Morrill v. US, 228 F.Supp. 734 (D.Me. 1964), the grantor of a trust was taxed on income used to relieve him of his own *contractual* liability to private schools for his children's tuition.

[63] Treas. Regs. §1.677(b)-1(a) ("maintenance of a beneficiary . . . whom the grantor *or his spouse* is legally obligated to support") (emphasis added).

[64] Brooke v. US, 468 F.2d 1155 (9th Cir. 1972); Wyche v. US, 36 AFTR2d 5816 (Ct. Cl. Trial Judge 1974); see also Rev. Rul. 56-484, 1956-2 CB 23.

¶34.5 LIFE INSURANCE TRUSTS

Section 677(a)(3) provides that the grantor of a trust shall be treated as the owner of any portion of the trust whose income is or may be (in the discretion of the grantor, a nonadverse party, or both, and without the consent of any adverse party)[65] applied to the payment of premiums on policies insuring the life of the grantor or the grantor's spouse, subject to an exception for policies irrevocably payable for certain charitable purposes. By contrast to IRC §§676, 677(a)(1), and 677(a)(2), which are concerned with trusts whose corpus or income can inure to the grantor's financial benefit, IRC §677(a)(3) taxes the grantor on income used to pay for insurance on his or his spouse's life even if he has no other interest in the trust property and the insurance policy is irrevocably assigned to the beneficiaries. Thus, life insurance trusts are treated more severely than trusts whose income must be, is, or may be used for such purposes as enabling children to get a college or professional education, start a business, purchase a home, or defray medical expenses. Even if beyond the grantor's legal obligation of support, these objectives no doubt rank as high on the priority list of many grantors as the maintenance of insurance on their lives; yet only the latter expense requires the trust income to be taxed to them.

In seeming defiance of its broad language (income that "may be . . . applied to the payment of premiums"), however, IRC §677(a)(3) is interpreted by the courts to apply only if an insurance policy whose premiums can be paid with trust income is in existence during the taxable year; the grantor is not taxable merely because the trustee, in the exercise of ordinary investment discretion, could apply for and maintain such a policy.[66] The IRS has acquiesced in this result[67] but has not explicitly embraced it in any published ruling. Even though neither silence nor boiler plate investment clauses permitting the purchase of insurance on the life of the grantor or his spouse will automatically bring IRC §677(a)(3) into play, however, cautious draftsmen often explicitly forbid the use of trust income for this purpose.

¶34.6 POWER TO CONTROL BENEFICIAL ENJOYMENT

1. In General. Section 674(a) provides that the grantor shall be treated as the owner of any portion of a trust whose "beneficial enjoyment" is subject to "a power of disposition" excercisable by the grantor, a nonadverse party,

---

[65] For the term "nonadverse party," see supra ¶34.1.

[66] Corning v. CIR, 104 F.2d 329, 333 (6th Cir. 1939); Weil v. CIR, 3 TC 579 (1944) (Acq.).

[67] Weil v. CIR, supra note 66; see also Moore v. CIR, 39 BTA 808 (1939) (Acq.).

or both, without the approval or consent of any adverse party. This language obviously taxes the grantor who can effect such major changes in the enjoyment of a trust's income and corpus as the addition and elimination of beneficiaries; but, if taken in isolation, it also would tax the grantor if an independent trustee possesses such minor and customary powers as the authority to withhold income temporarily from a beneficiary who is subject to a legal disability. But IRC §674(a) is qualified by a lengthy series of detailed exceptions; as a result, as will be seen, its "general rule" comes in like a lion but goes out like a lamb.

Unlike IRC §§673 (short-term trusts with reversion to grantor), 676 (revocable trusts), and 677 (trusts whose income can inure to grantor's benefit), the elaborate rules of IRC §674 are concerned with trusts whose income and corpus cannot inure to the grantor's direct personal benefit; it focuses instead on so-called nonbeneficial powers, which enable the grantor or a nonadverse party to alter the beneficiaries' enjoyment of the income or corpus. The legislative decision to tax grantors on powers that cannot be exercised in their own favor was foreshadowed by the *Clifford* line of cases, which held that powers to determine who will enjoy trust property constitute a type of dominion and control that warranted treating the grantor as the owner of the trust under Section 22(a) of the Internal Revenue Code of 1939.[68]

To qualify the general rule of IRC §674(a), which taxes the grantor whenever beneficial enjoyment of the trust income or corpus is subject to a power of disposition exercisable by the grantor, a nonadverse party, or both, without the approval or consent of any adverse party, IRC §§674(b), 674(c), and 674(d) establish a tripartite hierarchy of exempted powers. These protected powers, discussed below, consist of (1) certain powers that are exempted regardless of who holds them; (2) a broader power that is exempt if limited by "a reasonably definite external standard" and if exercisable only by a trustee or trustees other than the grantor or a spouse living with the grantor; and (3) two still broader powers that are exempt if vested in trustees other than the grantor, no more than half of whom are related or subordinate parties who are subservient to the grantor's wishes.

Because of the breadth of the general rule of IRC §674(a) and the particularity of the exceptions, it is impossible to compile an exhaustive list of powers generating tax liability for the grantor. The only important power that invariably is fatal is a right to add additional beneficiaries to those designated (by name or by class) in the trust instrument, except to provide for after-born or after-adopted children. With this exception, substantially all powers that are customarily desired in a normal trust instrument can be vested in either the grantor or an independent trustee without rendering the income taxable to the

---

[68] Supra ¶34.1.

grantor. Moreover, the exemptions granted by IRC §§674(b), 674(c), and 674(d) are not mutually exclusive, but instead may be cumulated by grantors who want to get the maximum freedom allowed by law; and the grantor can also retain a reversionary interest if it will not take effect until after the period prescribed by IRC §673.[69] Since the 1954 provisions relating to grantor trusts were intended by Congress to replace the "facts and circumstances" approach of the *Clifford* doctrine with precise landmarks, there is no room for a judicial determination that the synergistic aggregation of two or more independently exempt powers constitutes the reservation of excessive dominion and control over the trust property for tax purposes.[70]

Neither the Code nor the regulations attempt to prescribe the outer limits of the general rule of IRC §674(a) by setting out the circumstances in which "the beneficial enjoyment of the corpus or the income therefrom is subject to a power of disposition." According to the regulations, this statutory language reaches "every case in which [the grantor] or a nonadverse party *can affect* the beneficial enjoyment of a portion of a trust," [71] unless the power is explicitly exempted by IRC §674(b), §674(c), or §674(d).

2. Powers Exempted Regardless of Holder. Section 674(b) commences the process of qualifying the broad general rule of IRC §674(a) by listing eight powers that can be vested in anyone, including the grantor himself, without causing him to be treated as the owner of the affected property.

The first two of these exemptions serve to correlate IRC §674(a) with two other provisions relating to grantor trusts, so that the Code does not take away with one hand what it gives with the other. Thus, since IRC §677(b) relieves the grantor of tax liability on the income of a trust for the support of his legal dependents to the extent that the income is not in fact so used,[72] IRC §674(b)(1) provides that the unexercised power will not generate tax liability under IRC §674(a). In the same vein, IRC §674(b)(2) correlates the scope of the general rule of IRC §674(a) with the operation of IRC §673, relating to short-term trusts with reversion to the grantor.[73]

The remaining paragraphs of IRC §674(b) exempt the following powers to affect beneficial enjoyment of a trust's income or corpus:

1. *Power over corpus exercisable only by will.* Section 674(b)(3) grants immunity to a power exercisable only by will, unless it permits the grantor to appoint trust income that is or may be accumulated in the discretion of the grantor, a nonadverse party, or both, without the consent of an adverse party.

---

[69] For IRC §673, see supra ¶34.2.
[70] Supra ¶34.1.
[71] Treas. Regs. §1.674(a)-1(a) (emphasis added).
[72] For IRC §677(b), see supra ¶34.4.
[73] See Treas. Regs. §1.674(b)-1(b)(2).

In effect, this permits the grantor to reserve (or entrust to a nonadverse party) a testamentary power to appoint the corpus as he sees fit, no matter how drastically this dispositive plan differs from the provisions in the trust instrument.[74] This immunity, however, does not embrace testamentary powers over accumulations of ordinary income or capital gains, unless the accumulation requires the consent of an adverse party.

2. *Power to allocate corpus or income among charitable beneficiaries.* Section 674(b)(4) exempts the power to determine beneficial enjoyment of trust corpus or income if the affected item is irrevocably payable for a purpose specified in IRC §170(c), relating to charitable contributions.

3. *Power to distribute corpus if limited by standard or charged against income beneficiary's share of corpus.* Section 674(b)(5) exempts the power to distribute corpus (a) to any beneficiary or beneficiaries [75] if the power is limited by a "reasonably definite standard" set forth in the trust instrument or (b) to a current income beneficiary if the distribution is chargeable against the proportionate part of the corpus held for payment of that beneficiary's income as though it constituted a separate trust. In neither case, however, is a power exempt under IRC §674(b)(5) if it permits additional beneficiaries to be named or a class of beneficiaries to be expanded by amending the instrument, except to provide for after-born and after-adopted children. For practical purposes, the powers exempted by IRC §674(b)(5) are among the most important powers than can be retained by the grantor himself with tax impunity.

The scope of the "reasonably definite standard" exception to IRC §674(a) is described at some length by the regulations. They bestow a seal of approval on powers to distribute corpus "for the education, support, maintenance, or health of the beneficiary; for his reasonable support and comfort; or to enable him to maintain his accustomed standard of living; or to meet an emergency" and then go on to state that the phrase "pleasure, desire, or happiness of a beneficiary" does not supply a reasonably definite standard.[76] A grantor wishing to retain the power to advance corpus to trust beneficiaries without being limited by a reasonably definite standard may do so under IRC §674(b)(5)(B), exempting the power to make advances to current income beneficiaries if they are chargeable against the part of the corpus held for payment of the recipient's income as though it constituted a separate trust. It is not necessary, however, that the income beneficiary also be the remainderman.[77]

4. *Power to withhold income temporarily.* Section 674(b)(6) exempts a power to distribute or apply ordinary income to or for current income benefici-

---

[74] See Treas. Regs. §1.674(b)-1(b)(3).

[75] The regulations imply that the beneficiary to whom corpus is distributable must be either an income beneficiary or a remainderman; Treas. Regs. §1.674(b)-1(b)(5)(i).

[76] Treas. Regs. §1.674(b)-1(b)(5).

[77] See Treas. Regs. §1.674(b)-1(b)(5)(iii), Example (3).

aries or to accumulate trust income (but not to add new beneficiaries, except to provide for after-born and after-adopted children) if the accumulated income must ultimately be paid to (a) the beneficiary from whom the income was withheld; (b) the beneficiary's estate; (c) the beneficiary's appointees, provided the power of appointment does not exclude any person other than the beneficiary himself, his estate, his creditors, or the creditors of his estate; [78] or (d) on termination of the trust or in conjunction with a distribution of corpus that is augmented by the accumulated income, to the current income beneficiaries in shares that are irrevocably specified in the trust instrument.

5. *Power to withhold income during beneficiary's disability or minority.* Section 674(b)(7) exempts from the general rule of IRC §674(a) a power, exercisable only during the legal disability of a current income beneficiary or the period when an income beneficiary is under twenty-one, to distribute or apply income to or for the beneficiary or to accumulate the income and add it to corpus. This power is similar to the power to withhold income temporarily that is exempted by IRC §674(b)(6), but there is no requirement that the withheld income ultimately be subject in whole or in part to the income beneficiary's disposition.

6. *Power to allocate receipts and disbursements between corpus and income.* Section 674(b)(8) exempts a power to allocate trust receipts and disbursements between corpus and income ("even though expressed in broad language"), despite the obvious impact this power can have on the relative benefits of income beneficiaries and remaindermen.

3. Trustee's Power to Allocate Income Subject to Standard. Under IRC §674(d), a power to distribute or allocate income to or among beneficiaries, subject to a "reasonably definite external standard" set out in the trust instrument, may be vested in a trustee or trustees, other than the grantor or a spouse living with the grantor. The power must be exercisable by the trustees without the approval or consent of any other person; thus, neither the grantor nor anyone else may retain a veto over their decisions. Unlike the power to distribute income or withhold it temporarily, which is exempted by IRC §674(b)(6), IRC §674(d) permits distributions to remaindermen as well as current income beneficiaries, and it makes no effort to insure that accumulated income will eventually be placed at the disposition of the beneficiary from whom it was withheld. Subject to the requirement of a reasonably definite external standard (e.g., "the education, support, maintenance, or health" of the beneficiary),[79] IRC §674(d) permits the grantor to create a "spray" trust whose income can be shifted from one beneficiary to another.

---

[78] See IRC §§2041(b)(1) and 2514(c) ("general power of appointment" defined).

[79] The phrase "reasonably definite external standard" has the same meaning as "reasonably definite standard" as used in IRC §674(b)(5). See Treas. Regs. §1.674(d)-1.

4. Independent Trustee's Power to Allocate Income and Distribute Corpus. The most drastic relaxation of the general rule of IRC §674(a) is IRC §674(c), exempting powers to distribute, apportion, or accumulate income or to pay out corpus to beneficiaries or within a class of beneficiaries if the power is solely exercisable by a trustee or trustees, other than the grantor, no more than one-half of whom are related or subordinate parties who are subservient to the grantor's wishes.[80] Since the trustees must be able to act without the approval or consent of any other person, the grantor cannot reserve a veto over their decisions. Unlike IRC §674(d), IRC §674(c) does not require that the trustee's discretion be limited by a standard, and it embraces corpus as well as income.

Thus, if at least half of the trustees are independent, they can be given broad discretionary authority to sprinkle income and corpus among the beneficiaries (subject to the obligation of fairness implicit in their trusteeship), provided only that additional beneficiaries cannot be added to those designated by name or by class in the instrument, except to provide for after-born and after-adopted children. To take advantage of IRC §674(c), a grantor can appoint his or her spouse and a trust company as co-trustees.

¶34.7 ADMINISTRATIVE POWERS

Section 675 treats the grantor of a trust as the owner of any portion that is subject to certain administrative powers exercisable (a) primarily in the grantor's interest, rather than for the benefit of the beneficiaries, or (b) in a nonfiduciary capacity. Section 675, enacted in 1954, replaces the open-ended approach of the *Clifford* case with a detailed compilation of the administrative controls and circumstances that will cause the grantor to be treated as the owner of the trust property. In general, it gives the grantor carte blanche to retain (or assign to a nonadverse party) normal powers to administer the trust, while proscribing nonfiduciary powers and the borrowing of corpus or income from the trust.[81]

¶34.8 NONGRANTORS WITH POWER TO DEMAND TRUST INCOME OR CORPUS—"MALLINCKRODT TRUSTS"

1. Taxation of Income of Demand Trust to Nongrantor. Subject to certain exceptions, IRC §678(a) provides that a person who is not the grantor of

[80] See IRC §672(c), discussed supra ¶34.1.

[81] For the possibility that some administrative powers, though not listed by IRC §675, are fatal under IRC §674, see supra ¶34.6, text at note 71.

a trust shall be treated as its owner if (1) he has a power, exercisable solely by himself, to vest the corpus or the income therefrom in himself or (2) he has partially released or modified such a power, retaining such control over the trust as would, if he were its grantor, cause him to be treated as its owner under the grantor trust provisions (IRC §§671–677). A typical arrangement subject to this provision is a trust whose income is payable to the grantor's child at the latter's request, with the corpus and accumulated income to be distributed to the grantor's grandchildren when they become of age or their parents die. Trusts of this type are often called "demand trusts" (because of the power vested in the intermediate generation to obtain the corpus on demand) or "Mallinckrodt trusts," because in *Mallinckrodt v. Nunan* the Court of Appeals for the Eighth Circuit affirmed a pioneering Tax Court decision holding that the *Clifford* doctrine required a trust's income to be reported by a person who could get it on demand, even though he refrained from exercising his power.[82]

The taxpayer can be treated as the owner under IRC §678 only if he can exercise the power "solely by himself," not if the consent of a third party is required. Grantors are taxed under IRC §§674–677 on powers vested in them jointly with a nonadverse third party because they have the power to select cooperative co-holders of otherwise taxable powers; but since nongrantors do not have the same freedom to choose their fellow powerholders, they are not taxed by IRC §678(a) on jointly held powers.

Although the grantor trust rules were amended in 1969 to tax grantors of trusts whose income or corpus can be distributed to their spouses, this decision to treat married couples as a unit was not extended to IRC §678. As a result, a husband with unfettered power to pay trust income or corpus to his wife is not subject to IRC §678, because he cannot "vest the corpus or the income therefrom in *himself,*" while the wife is equally immune because she does not have a power exercisable solely by herself to reach the income or corpus.[83]

2. Exceptions. The basic principle adopted by IRC §678(a) of taxing the income of a "demand trust" to a person who can vest the corpus or income in himself is subject to four statutory exceptions:

1. *Income taxable to grantor.* By virtue of IRC §678(b), if the trust's grantor is treated as the owner under the grantor trust provisions (IRC §§671–677), these rules take precedence over IRC §678(a). For example, if the grantor reserves a reversionary interest that causes him to be treated as owner of the trust property under IRC §673, such as a reversionary interest that will

[82] Mallinckrodt v. Nunan, 146 F.2d 1 (8th Cir.), cert. denied, 324 US 781 (1945).

[83] Rev. Rul. 67-268, 1967-2 CB 226.

become possessory in eight years, a person having the right to withdraw the income for himself in the interim is not taxed, even though his power is otherwise within the reach of IRC §678(a)(1).

2. *Renunciation or disclaimer.* Under IRC §678(d), a person holding an otherwise taxable power over a demand trust is exempt if he renounces or disclaims the power within a reasonable time after becoming aware of its existence. Even in the absence of this exemption, he would not be taxed on income realized by the trust after a legally effective release of the power; but IRC §678(d) serves to protect him against liability for income realized between the date his power arose and the date of renunciation or disclaimer.

3. *Partial release or modification.* If the holder of a tainted power releases or modifies it only in part, his liability thereafter depends on whether his remaining control would subject the grantor of a trust to tax liability under the grantor trust provisions of IRC §§671–677. Thus, if the holder of an unrestricted power to allocate current income between himself and other beneficiaries whittles it down by excluding himself as a potential beneficiary and providing that his power to allocate income among the remaining beneficiaries may be exercised only by will, he will not thereafter be treated as owner of the trust under IRC §678(a)(2), because IRC §674(b)(3) permits a similarly limited power to be retained with impunity by the grantor of a trust.

4. *Support trusts.* Finally, to harmonize IRC §678 with IRC §677,[84] IRC §678(c) exempts a power permitting the holder, as trustee or co-trustee, to use trust income to discharge his obligation to support a dependent, except to the extent that the income is actually so used.

SELECTED BIBLIOGRAPHY

Alexandre, A Case Method Restatement of the New Clifford Regulations, 3 Tax L. Rev. 189 (1947).

Berge, *U.S. v. Estate of Grace*: The Reincarnation of the Reciprocal Trust Doctrine, 17 U.C.L.A. L. Rev. 436 (1969).

Cohan, Drafting California Irrevocable Inter Vivos Trusts (Appendix F—Chart of Federal Tax Consequences to Settlor of Powers of Permanent Trust) (Cal. Cont. Educ. Bar 1973).

Del Cotto & Joyce, Taxation of the Trust Annuity: The Unitrust Under the Constitution and the Internal Revenue Code, 23 Tax L. Rev. 257, 312–358 (1968).

Heckerling, Tax Aspects of Power to Remove, Substitute and Appoint Trustees, 8 Real Prop., Prob. & Tr. J. 545, 558–560 (1973).

[84] For IRC §677(b), see supra ¶34.4.

GRANTOR TRUSTS

Henning, Treatment of the Grantor Trust as a Separate Entity, 32 Tax L. Rev. 409 (1977).

Lewis, Powers Retained by the Settlor of a Trust: Their Income, Estate and Gift Tax Treatment, 5 Real Prop., Prob. & Tr. J. 1 (1970).

Magill, What Shall Be Done With the *Clifford* Case? 45 Colum. L. Rev. 111 (1945).

Nitzburg, The Obligation of Support: A Proposed Federal Standard, 23 Tax L. Rev. 93 (1967).

Peschel, The Impact of Fiduciary Standards on Federal Taxation of Grantor Trusts: Illusion and Inconsistency, 1979 Duke L.J. 709.

Schmolka, Selected Aspects of the Grantor Trust Rules, 9 U. Miami Inst. on Est. Plan. ¶¶1403–1407 (1975).

Turley, Section 674: Mr. Clifford's Enigmatic Progeny, 9 Hous. L. Rev. 928 (1972).

Ward, Taxation of Gratuitous Transfers of Encumbered Property: Partial Sales and Section 677(a), 63 Iowa L. Rev. 823 (1978).

Westfall, Trust Grantors and Section 674: Adventures in Income Tax Avoidance, 60 Colum. L. Rev. 326 (1960).

Yohlin, The Short-Term Trust—A Respectable Tax Saving Device, 14 Tax L. Rev. 109 (1958).

Zimmerman, Using Foreign Trusts in the Post-1976 Period: What Possibilities Remain? 47 J. Tax. 12 (1977).

CHAPTER 35

Cash and Accrual Accounting

¶35.1 BASIC PRINCIPLES

1. Introductory. Sections 441 through 483 prescribe the statutory rules governing accounting periods and methods of accounting. In general, taxable income is computed on the basis of the taxpayer's regular accounting period, which is usually either the calendar year or the fiscal year used by the taxpayer in keeping his books.[1] The method of accounting regularly used by the taxpayer to compute income in keeping his books is also ordinarily used to compute taxable income, provided it clearly reflects income.[2] In practice, most employees and self-employed persons providing personal services to the public use the cash receipts and disbursements method of computing taxable income, but merchants and manufacturers must usually use an accrual method. Once the taxpayer has chosen an accounting period and an accounting method, they must ordinarily be used in subsequent taxable years unless the IRS consents to a change, which is usually conditioned on appropriate transitional ad-

---

[1] See IRC §§441–443, discussed infra, text at notes 5–20.

[2] See IRC §§446–472, discussed infra ¶¶35.3, 35.4.

justments.[3] Although the taxpayer's books and records exert a powerful influence on the accounting period and accounting method used in computing taxable income, they are not controlling, and there are important differences between tax and financial accounting.[4]

2. Taxable Year. Taxable income is computed on the basis of the taxpayer's "taxable year," which means (a) the taxpayer's annual accounting period on the basis of which he regularly computes income in keeping his books,[5] if it is either a calendar or a fiscal year; (b) the calendar year, if the taxpayer keeps no books, does not have an annual accounting period, or has an annual accounting period that does not qualify as a fiscal year; or (c) the period for which the return is made, if it is less than twelve months.[6] To qualify as a "fiscal year," the period employed by the taxpayer must end on the last day of a month other than December.[7] An exception to these rules is provided by IRC §441(f), which permits a 52-53 week year to be used if the annual period always ends on the same day of the week (e.g., the last Saturday in June or the Saturday closest to the last day of June).

If a taxpayer's business year includes both hectic and slack periods, a fiscal year ending in the slow season may be advantageous. It is important to choose the appropriate fiscal year when the first tax return is filed,[8] since a change of accounting period at a later time is usually effective only if approved by the IRS under IRC §442. Moreover, since the initial fiscal year can be a short period, a one-time advantage may be obtained by segregating a particular transaction or limited amount of income in the initial period.[9]

If rates are changed during a taxable year, IRC §21 apportions the tax according to the length of the taxable periods before and after the effective date

---

[3] See IRC §§442 (change of accounting period) and 481 (adjustments on change of accounting method); infra ¶35.6.

[4] See infra, text at notes 37–47.

[5] For the meaning of "books and records," see infra, text at notes 48–54.

[6] IRC §§441(a)–441(e), 441(g); see also C.H. Leavell & Co. v. CIR, 53 TC 426 (1969) (joint venture computing all income under completed-contract method had no annual accounting period and hence must use calendar year).

[7] IRC §441(e); see also Treas. Regs. §1.411-1(e)(2) (fiscal year permissible only if used in keeping taxpayer's books); Rev. Rul. 54-273, 1954-2 CB 110 (regularly employed period ending exactly twelve months after day on which business was begun does not qualify; calendar year must be used).

[8] Under Treas. Regs. §1.411-1(b)(3), a new taxpayer's first taxable year must be adopted on or before the time prescribed for filing the return for that year, excluding extensions of time; see also Rev. Rul. 68-125, 1968-1 CB 189 (failure to file return on time does not vitiate choice of fiscal year); Wilson v. US, 267 F.Supp. 89 (E.D. Mo. 1967) (fiscal year claimed on timely amended return effective despite different year claimed on original return).

[9] But see Resnik v. CIR, 66 TC 74 (1976) (unsuccessful effort to use initial taxable year of one day).

of the change.[10] The tax for a taxable period straddling a rate change is determined by computing tentative taxes on the taxable income under both the old rate and the new rate. The tentative taxes so determined are then apportioned on a daily basis, according to the proportion of the taxable year to which IRC §21 applies, to any change in the rate of tax imposed by Chapter 1.

A taxpayer wishing to change his annual accounting period and adopt a new taxable year must obtain prior approval from the IRS, unless the regulations authorize a change without permission.[11] If a change is made without approval, the IRS can either hold the taxpayer to the change (thereby in effect, approving it) or require the taxpayer to reinstate the old period.[12]

After stating that a change of the taxpayer's annual accounting period will be approved if the taxpayer establishes "a substantial business purpose" for making the change, the regulations expand on the applicable principles and requirements as follows:

> In determining whether a taxpayer has established a substantial business purpose for making the change, consideration will be given to all the facts and circumstances relating to the change, including the tax consequences resulting therefrom. Among the nontax factors that will be considered in determining whether a substantial business purpose has been established is the effect of the change on the taxpayer's annual cycle of business activity. The agreement between the taxpayer and the Commissioner under which the change will be effected shall, in appropriate cases, provide terms, conditions, and adjustments necessary to prevent a substantial distortion of income which otherwise would result from the change.[13] These rules are relaxed for a newly married husband or wife, who can change to the other spouse's annual accounting period without prior approval in order to file a joint return for the first or second taxable year ending after the date of marriage;[14] and in a few other situations.

3. Short Taxable Periods. Although a taxable year cannot exceed twelve months (except for taxpayers electing a 52-53 week accounting period), a so-called short period is authorized by IRC §443(a) if a change of the taxpayer's annual period is approved by the IRS or if the taxpayer is in existence

---

[10] IRC §21 does not apply to changes relating to deductions, exclusions, inclusions, credits or limitations on amount of tax. Treas. Regs. §1.21-1(h).

[11] IRC §442.

[12] Williamson v. CIR, 22 TC 684 (1954).

[13] Treas. Regs. §1.442-1(b)(1); see also Rev. Rul. 76-407, 1976-2 CB 127 (Subchapter S shareholder wanted to change from calendar to fiscal year to coincide with availability of dividend information when making fourth-quarter estimated tax payment; held, not substantial business purpose); Rev. Proc. 74-33, 1974-2 CB 489 (method of establishing taxpayer's "natural business year").

[14] Treas. Regs. §1.442-1(e) (change conditioned on prompt filing of return for resulting short period, etc.).

during only part of what would otherwise be his taxable year.[15] In the case of a corporation or other artificial entity, a partial-existence short return can result from creation or dissolution on a day other than the first or last day of the chosen taxable year; for individuals, the corresponding events are birth and death.[16] Marriage does not create a short period unless the taxable year of one spouse must be changed in order to conform to the other spouse's taxable year.

The tax for a short period is ordinarily computed by placing the taxable income on an annual basis, computing a hypothetical tax thereon, and taking the same fraction of the annualized tax as the number of months in the short period bears to twelve months.[17] In making this computation, individuals must reduce their personal and dependency exemptions appropriately if the short period results from a change in the annual accounting period, but they are entitled to the full amount if the short period reflects birth or death during what would otherwise be the taxpayer's taxable year.[18]

The annualization method prescribed by IRC §443(b)(1) can produce an inordinately high tax if a nonrecurring profit is isolated in a very short period, since annualizing it catapults the taxpayer into high brackets. As an alternative, therefore, IRC §443(b)(2) permits the taxpayer to pay the greater of (a) the tax for the short period without annualizing his taxable income or (b) the tax for a hypothetical twelve-month period beginning on the first day of the short period multiplied by a fraction whose numerator is the short period income and whose denominator is the income for the hypothetical twelve-month period.[19]

Although encompassing less than twelve months, a short taxable period is a "taxable year" under IRC §§441(b)(3) and 7701(a)(23). It must be counted, therefore, in determining the number of years to which net operating loss carrybacks and carryovers are carried and may result in an unexpectedly early expiration of these tax allowances.[20]

4. Annual vs. Transactional Accounting. In a seminal early case, *Burnet v. Sanford & Brooks Co.,* the Supreme Court contrasted the statutory imposition of the income tax "on the basis of annual returns showing the net result of all the taxpayer's transactions during a fixed accounting period" with a hypothetical alternative method "by which the tax could be assessed, wholly

[15] IRC §443(a)(2).

[16] See Nico v. CIR, 565 F.2d 1234 (2d Cir. 1977) (alien's change of status from nonresident to resident did not create short period; individual was in "existence" throughout entire year).

[17] IRC §443(b)(1).

[18] IRC §443(c).

[19] For examples, see Treas. Regs. §1.443-1(b)(2).

[20] See Treas. Regs. §1.172-4(a)(2).

or in part, on the basis of the finally ascertained results of particular transactions." [21] The Court held that a recovery arising out of an earlier transaction in which the taxpayer had sustained a loss was taxable even though "it equalled, and in a loose sense was a return of, expenditures made in performing the contract"; that it is not necessary to postpone taxation "until the end of a lifetime, or for some other indefinite period, to ascertain more precisely whether the final outcome of the period, or of a given transaction, will be a gain or a loss"; and that taxing the interim results on an annual basis is permissible under the Sixteenth Amendment.

Congress subsequently alleviated the problem in *Sanford & Brooks* by enacting the statutory predecessor of IRC §172, permitting net operating losses to be carried over to a specified number of prior and subsequent taxable years.[22] But the principle enunciated in *Sanford & Brooks* continues to apply if the operating loss cannot be fully utilized during the carryover period established by IRC §172; and the Court's emphasis on the annual accounting period has been influential in many other areas.

Although annual rather than transactional accounting is thus the norm, *Sanford & Brooks* does not tell the whole story, since there are numerous circumstances in which the tax results of a particular receipt or expenditure depend on earlier or later installments in the same transaction. The collection of a debt, for example, does not ordinarily produce income, but if it was previously deducted as worthless, a recovery is a taxable event unless the prior deduction produced no tax benefit.[23] Another example is the taxpayer's right to hold an amount (e.g., an amount received or paid under a lease with option to purchase) in abeyance until its status is clarified by later events.[24]

5. Permissible Accounting Methods. Taxable income is ordinarily computed by the accounting method regularly used by the taxpayer in keeping his

---

[21] Burnet v. Sanford & Brooks Co., 282 US 359, 365 (1931).

[22] For IRC §172, see supra ¶12.9.

[23] For the tax benefit rule, see supra ¶1.10.

[24] See Virginia Iron, Coal & Coke Co. v. CIR, 99 F.2d 919 (4th Cir. 1938), cert. denied, 307 US 630 (1939) (payments for option to be applied in reduction of option price are not taxed until option expires, when it can be determined whether the payments are option income or return of capital). For judicial exceptions to the annual accounting period concept, see Arrowsmith v. CIR, 344 US 6 (1952) (transaction relates back to a prior related transaction for its character); Burnet v. Logan, 283 US 404 (1931) (open transaction); US v. Skelly Oil Co., 394 US 678 (1969) (items received under claim of right and repaid in a later year are not deductible to extent not previously included in income); Bowers v. Kerbaugh-Empire Co., 271 US 170 (1926) (gain on repayment of debt not taxable because borrowed funds were lost in prior years). For legislative exceptions, see IRC §§111 (tax status of recoveries related to tax treatment of related payments in prior years), 1341 (special tax computation on repayment of amounts previously received under claim of right).

books.[25] This obligation is somewhat watered down by the regulations, under which adjustments reconciling the taxpayer's books and the return are themselves part of the taxpayer's accounting records.[26]

The regulations state that the term "method of accounting" denotes not only the "overall method" (e.g., the cash receipts and disbursements method or an accrual method), but also the accounting treatment of any item, such as depreciation, research and experimental expenditures, and soil and water conservation expenditures.[27] If, however, no method has been regularly used by the taxpayer or if the method used does not clearly reflect income, the taxpayer is required by IRC §446(b) to use the method that in the opinion of the IRS clearly reflects income. Because the regulations construe "method of accounting" to include the treatment of "any item," IRC §446 overlaps many statutory provisions allowing special treatment of particular items, such as the election granted by IRC §174 to deduct or amortize research and experimental expenditures.

Subject to these principles, a taxpayer is permitted by IRC §446(c) to use (a) the cash receipts and disbursement method, (b) an accrual method, (c) any other method allowed by the income tax chapter of the Code (e.g., the installment, percentage-of-completion, or completed-contract methods),[28] or (d) a combination of the foregoing as permitted by the regulations. The contrast between the statutory reference to "the" cash receipts and disbursements method and its reference to "an" accrual method implies that the latter label embraces a range of related methods. The regulations acknowledge this diversity by providing that an accrual-basis manufacturer may account for sales of merchandise when the goods are shipped, when they are delivered, or when title passes to the customer, depending on the method regularly employed in keeping his books.[29] As for hybrid methods, the regulations illustrate this possibility by sanctioning use of an accrual method for accounting for purchases and sales in combination with the cash method in computing other items of income and expense.[30]

The most fundamental accounting distinction is between (a) the cash receipts and disbursements method, under which cash, property, and services constituting gross income are reported in the taxable year of actual or con-

---

[25] IRC §446(a). For difficulties in determining the method employed, see Consolidated Tea Co. v. Bowers, 19 F.2d 382 (S.D.N.Y. 1927) (use of "accounts receivable," "accounts payable," and inventories indicates accrual method used, although minor items were kept on cash basis and taxpayer's return used cash method).

[26] For year-end adjustments, see Treas. Regs. §1.446-1(a)(4).

[27] Treas. Regs. §1.446-1(a)(1).

[28] For these methods, see IRC §453 (installment method); Treas. Regs. §1.451-3 (percentage-of-completion and completed-contract methods).

[29] Treas. Regs. §1.466-1(c)(1)(ii).

[30] Treas. Regs. §1.446-1(c)(1)(iv).

structive receipt and expenditures are deducted when actually made, and (b) accrual accounting, under which income is included (and deductions are allowed) in the taxable year in which all events fixing the taxpayer's right to receive the income (or the taxpayer's liability to pay) have occurred and the amount can be determined with reasonable accuracy. Because merchants and manufacturers are ordinarily required to inventory their merchandise, they must use an accrual method rather than the cash receipts and disbursements method; the latter, however, is almost universally used by employees and investors. Taxpayers engaged in more than one trade or business are permitted by IRC §446(d) to use a different method (if otherwise appropriate) for each business, provided separate sets of books are maintained and profits or losses are not shifted between the enterprises.[31]

Once a method of accounting has been adopted, prior IRS consent is ordinarily required to compute taxable income under a different method; and if the change is permitted, it is usually conditioned on transitional adjustments, as explained below.[32]

The broad methods of accounting mentioned above are qualified by numerous specialized provisions assigning particular items to different taxable years than the taxpayer's overall accounting method would require;[33] and it is far from clear whether these rules prescribe or sanction mini-methods of accounting or should be viewed instead as rules of substantive tax law.

While the taxpayer's accounting method determines the taxable year for which income and deductions are taken into account in computing taxable income, the aggregate amount of taxable income realized over the long haul is ordinarily the same regardless of the method of accounting. Despite this neutrality as respects the taxpayer's aggregate *taxable income,* the chosen accounting method can significantly affect aggregate *tax liability* in the following circumstances, among others:

1. Changes from year to year in the taxpayer's marginal tax rate, resulting from varying amounts of taxable income.

2. Changes in tax rates.

---

[31] See Treas. Regs. §1.466-1(d); see also Rev. Rul. 74-280, 1974-1 CB 121 (bank using accrual method and inventories in bond department may use cash method for other business activities if separate books are kept and income is clearly reflected); Stern v. CIR, 14 BTA 838 (1928) (Acq.) (different methods may be used for separate and distinct businesses within the same partnership).

[32] See infra ¶35.6.

[33] See, e.g., IRC §§174 (permitting research and experimental expenditures to be deducted or amortized), 170(a) (charitable contributions deductible in year of "payment"), 213 (medical expenses deductible when paid), 215 (same for alimony), 165 (losses allowed when sustained), 83(a)(1) (income realized when restrictions on restricted property expire or beneficial owner's rights become transferable).

3. Changes of taxpayer status (e.g., from nonresident to resident alien or from unmarried to married) if the taxpayer's right to a deduction, credit or other allowance depends on whether he occupies one status or the other during the taxable year when the item is taken into account.

4. Losses, which can be carried over to other years for only a specified number of years.

5. Annual dollar or percentage limits on deductions and credits, especially if the excess cannot be carried over to other years.

6. Clear Reflection of Income. Taxpayers are ordinarily permitted (indeed, required) to compute taxable income under the accounting method used in regularly computing income in keeping their books, unless the method used "does not clearly reflect income."[34] Expanding on this qualification, the regulations provide:

> A method of accounting which reflects the consistent application of generally accepted accounting principles in a particular trade or business in accordance with accepted conditions or practices in that trade or business will ordinarily be regarded as clearly reflecting income, provided all items of gross income and expense are treated consistently from year to year. . . .
>
> The Commissioner may authorize a taxpayer to adopt or change to a method of accounting permitted by this chapter although the method is not specifically described in the regulations in this part if, in the opinion of the Commissioner, income is clearly reflected by the use of such method. Further, the Commissioner may authorize a taxpayer to continue the use of a method of accounting consistently used by the taxpayer, even though not specifically authorized by the regulations in this part if, in the opinion of the Commissioner, income is clearly reflected by the use of such method.[35]

The latter option—authorizing continued use of an otherwise unsanctioned method—does not mean that the mere fact that a taxpayer has used an offbeat or erroneous method consistently for many years without IRS objection, "makes it right" or justifies its perpetuation on grounds of "tenure."[36]

7. Tax vs. Financial Accounting. In an important 1979 decision, the Supreme Court observed that, "in most cases, generally accepted accounting

---

[34] IRC §446(b).

[35] Treas. Regs. §§1.446-1(a)(2), 1.446-1(c)(2)(ii).

[36] Coors v. CIR, 60 TC 368, 395 (1973).

practices will pass muster for tax purposes," but that they do not enjoy a presumption of accuracy and that, if the Commissioner of Internal Revenue, "in the exercise of his discretion, determines that they do not [clearly reflect the taxpayer's income], he may prescribe a different practice without having to rebut any presumption running against the Treasury." [37] This supervisory power vested in the IRS by IRC §446(b), has been described by the Supreme Court as leaving "much latitude for discretion," which "should not be interfered with [by the courts] unless clearly unlawful." [38]

These judicial testimonials to the broad powers of the IRS must be qualified in one fundamental respect: An accounting method that is explicitly authorized or prescribed by Congress cannot be rejected even if the IRS, on a sober evaluation of its impact, concludes that it does not clearly reflect income. The preemptive character of such statutory provisions as IRC §174, permitting taxpayers to deduct research and experimental expenditures even if income would be more clearly reflected by capitalizing these outlays and depreciating them over their useful lives, is obvious.[39]

The principle of conformity between the taxpayer's tax and financial or business accounting methods [40] is subject to important qualifications, since numerous items can or must be treated one way for tax purposes but differently in preparing financial statements for management, creditors, investors, and regulatory commissions. In preparing financial statements for creditors and investors, for example, it would obviously be misleading to omit tax-exempt interest or to neglect to deduct disallowed expenses;[41] and the assignment of items to the years specified by the Internal Revenue Code [42] can also produce misleading income statements or balance sheets. Thus, although "keeping two sets of books" may imply fraud to the layman, the practice not only is permissible but may even be mandatory.

Pointing out that financial and tax accounting have "vastly different objectives," the Supreme Court commented in *Thor Power Tool Co. v. CIR,* decided in 1979:

> The primary goal of financial accounting is to provide useful information to management, shareholders, creditors, and others properly interested; the major responsibility of the accountant is to protect these parties from being misled. The primary goal of the income tax system, in

---

[37] Thor Power Tool Co. v. CIR, 439 US 522, 540 (1979).

[38] Lucas v. American Code Co., 280 US 445, 449 (1930), quoted with approval in Thor Power Tool Co. v. CIR, supra note 37, at 541.

[39] For IRC §174, see supra ¶12.13.

[40] See IRC §446(a) and Treas. Regs. §1.446-1(a)(2).

[41] IRC §§274 (nondocumented travel and entertainment expenses); 267 (accrued salaries not paid to related parties within specified period).

[42] Infra ¶¶35.3 (prepaid income), 36.2 (installment method under IRC §453).

contrast, is the equitable collection of revenue; the major responsibility of the Internal Revenue Service is to protect the public fisc. Consistently with its goals and responsibilities, financial accounting has as its foundation the principle of conservatism, with its corollary that "possible errors in measurement [should] be in the direction of understatement rather than overstatement of net income and net assets." In view of the Treasury's markedly different goals and responsibilities, understatement of income is not destined to be its guiding light. . . .

This difference in objectives is mirrored in numerous differences of treatment. Where the tax law requires that a deduction be deferred until "all the events" have occurred that will make it fixed and certain . . . accounting principles typically require that a liability be accrued as soon as it can reasonably be estimated. Conversely, where the tax law requires that income be recognized currently under "claim of right," "ability to pay," and "control" rationales, accounting principles may defer accrual until a later year so that revenues and expenses may be better matched. Financial accounting, in short, is hospitable to estimates, probabilities, and reasonable certainties; the tax law, with its mandate to preserve the revenue, can give no quarter to uncertainty.[43]

Despite the Court's comments, tax and financial accounting principles overlap far more often than they diverge; and the important residual disparities are not always justified by the different objectives served by the two systems. A study published by the American Institute of Certified Public Accountants classifies the major timing difference between financial and tax accounting in the following four categories:

1. Revenues or gains taxed later than they are accrued for financial accounting purposes (e.g., profits on installment sales if deferred under IRC §453)
2. Expenses or losses deducted for tax purposes later than accrued for financial accounting purposes (e.g., estimated cost of guaranties and warranties recorded in financial accounts when products are sold but deducted for tax purposes only when paid)
3. Revenues or gains taxed before accrued for financial accounting purposes (e.g., advance rents and royalties and unearned fees and dues).
4. Expenses or losses deducted for tax purposes before accrued for financial accounting purposes (e.g., accelerated depreciation and research and development costs).[44]

[43] Thor Power Tool Co. v. CIR, supra note 37, at 542-544, citing numerous discussions of the differences between tax and financial accounting.

[44] Black, Interperiod Allocation of Corporate Income Taxes 8-10 (AICPA Accounting Research Study No. 9, 1966); see also AICPA Statement on Conformity of Tax and Financial Accounting (1971), reprinted in 132 J. Accountancy 75 (Dec. 1971).

A similar dichotomy exists between tax accounting and the accounting principles prescribed by federal and state regulatory agencies to serve their legislative functions, such as the protection of investors, consumers, or bank depositors.[45] In the event of a conflict, the Supreme Court has made it clear that the tax rules take precedence.[46] Although taxpayers are bound by tax accounting principles, the accounting rules prescribed by regulatory agencies are occasionally accepted in computing taxable income if the discrepancy is slight and no substantial distortion of income is perceived.[47]

8. Taxpayer Books and Records. Although IRC §§441 and 446 ordinarily require the taxpayer to compute taxable income by reference to the taxable year and accounting method "on the basis of which the taxpayer regularly computes his income in keeping his books," [48] these provisions do not explicitly require taxpayers to keep books or records. That function is performed by IRC §6001 and the regulations issued thereunder.[49] Although "no particular form" is prescribed for the "permanent" records required by this section and the regulations, they must be kept accurately in "forms and systems of accounting" enabling the district director to ascertain whether liability for tax is incurred and, if so, the amount thereof.[50]

This general rule sheds virtually no light on the scope and detail of the taxpayer's record-keeping obligations, because taxpayers, their transactions, and the applicable legal rules are so diverse that a code of explicit record-keeping guideposts is simply not feasible. There are, however, a few specific rules requiring special records in prescribed situations, such as IRC §274, relating to travel and entertainment expenses, and IRC §170(a)(1), relating to charitable contributions.[51] In addition, the regulations under IRC §446 require

---

[45] See, e.g., Gulf Power Co. v. CIR, 10 TC 852 (1948) (deduction denied for write-down of excess cost of public utility assets although required by Federal Power Commission).

[46] Old Colony R.R. v. CIR, 284 US 552 (1932) (bond premium required to be amortized by ICC is not income in year to which it relates; it was income in pre-1913 years, when received).

[47] Cincinnati, N.O. & T.P. Ry. v. US, 424 F.2d 563 (Ct. Cl. 1970) (deduction allowed for purchases of property costing less than $500 that were treated as operating expenses in accordance with ICC rules even though the items had useful lives in excess of one year; method was in accord with generally accepted accounting principles).

[48] See supra, text at notes 6, 7, and 25-33.

[49] Treas. Regs. §1.6001-1(a).

[50] Id.; Treas. Regs. §31.6001-1(a). For the meaning of "books," see Stryker v. CIR, 36 BTA 326 (1937) (Acq.) (informal records with summary sheets are not "books" entitling use of fiscal year); Brooks v. CIR, 6 TC 504 (1946) (check stubs, rent receipts, and dividend statements are not "books").

[51] For IRC §274, see supra ¶9.5; for IRC §170(a)(1), see Treas. Regs. §1.170A-1(a)(2). See also Treas. Regs. §1.6001-1(d), authorizing the district director by notice to require taxpayers to keep "specific records" establishing whether or not they are liable to tax.

taxpayers to maintain "accounting records" enabling them to file correct returns, defining the term to mean "the taxpayer's regular books of account and other such records and data as may be necessary to support the entries on his books of account and on his return, as for example, a reconciliation of any differences between such books and his return." [52] The record-keeping standard is relaxed for farmers and employees so far as formality is concerned, but it is difficult to discern in these rules any significant reduction of the information that must be recorded and preserved.[53]

In addition to being distressingly vague about the information to be preserved, the regulations do not amplify the reference to "permanent" books of accounts or records, except to state that records required by the regulations must be preserved (1) for at least four years after the due date of the return for the period to which the records relate or, if later, four years from the date when the tax is paid and (2) for "so long as the contents thereof may become material in the administration of any internal revenue law." [54] Since the cost of a capital outlay or investment may become relevant when the asset is sold or abandoned, the taxpayer may be called upon to prove, many years after its acquisition, its cost and the amount of depreciation or amortization deducted, as well as to prove that the cost was capitalized rather than deducted. This makes it virtually impossible to generalize about when records will lose any residual importance in determining the taxpayer's tax liability.

¶35.2 THE CASH RECEIPTS AND DISBURSEMENTS METHOD

1. Introductory. The cash receipts and disbursements method of accounting requires "all items which constitute gross income (whether in the form of cash, property, or services) . . . to be included [in income] for the taxable year in which actually or constructively received," while expenditures "are to be deducted for the taxable year in which actually made." [55] As will

[52] Treas. Regs. §1.466-1(a)(4) (illustrated by reference to inventory records, classification of expenditures between capital and expense, and the cost of improvements to depreciable property).

[53] Treas. Regs. §1.6001-1(b); see also Treas. Regs. §§31.6001-1(d) (advising employees to keep permanent records of employers, dates of employment, amounts of compensation, etc.), 1.446-1(b)(2) (taxpayer whose sole source of income is wages need not keep formal books in order to have an accounting method; tax returns or other records may be sufficient to establish method of accounting used in preparing returns); Meneguzzo v. CIR, 43 TC 824, 832-833 (1965) (restaurant employee obligated to keep records of tips; doubtful that weekly estimates satisfy regulations); see also Chippi v. CIR, ¶71,236 P-H Memo TC (1971) ("any systematic method of documentation satisfies section 6001 and the regulations promulgated thereunder").

[54] Treas. Regs. §§31.6001-1(e)(1) and 31.6001-1(e)(2).

[55] Treas. Regs. §1.446-1(c)(1)(i); see also IRC §451; Treas. Regs. §§1.451-1, 1.451-2.

be seen, the latter principle is subject to a very important qualification: Expenditures attributable to more than one taxable year (e.g., the cost of business equipment) cannot be deducted when made but must be capitalized and depreciated or amortized.

The literal implications of the term "cash method" must be qualified in another respect, since some items are includable in income though not "received" in a conventional sense (e.g., income from the discharge of the taxpayer's indebtedness for less than its face amount). Conversely, items that do not entail an out-of-pocket expense (e.g., depreciation, bad debts, and losses) are deductible even though there is no "payment" in the taxable year to which they are allocable—or even in a prior year if they related to property purchased on credit.[56] It should also be noted that amounts received under a claim of right, without restrictions on disposition by the recipient, are includable in income when received, even if the taxpayer may ultimately have to repay part or all of the amount received.[57]

Tax theorists regard cash-basis accounting as less accurate than accrual accounting, which takes into account the taxpayer's rights and liabilities; but the cash basis is explicitly sanctioned by IRC §446(c)(1), subject to the IRS' power to require taxable income to be computed under a different method if the cash method does not clearly reflect income (e.g., because inventories are a significant income-producing element in the taxpayer's trade or business). The cash method is almost universally employed by wage earners and employees; and it is almost equally popular among taxpayers engaged in furnishing personal services, such as doctors and lawyers.

2. Cash Equivalents. The cash receipts and disbursements method requires gross income to be reported when actually or constructively received, whether the item takes the form of cash, property, or services.[58] Benefits that are the equivalent of cash, whether or not transferable,[59] must also be reported when received by a cash-basis taxpayer even if they do not fit snugly within the phrase "cash, property, or services" as used by the regulations.[60]

Application of the cash equivalent standard is difficult if the item received

---

[56] See Treas. Regs. §1.461-1(a)(1) (expenditures not involving cash disbursements during taxable year); infra, text at note 87.

[57] For the claim of right doctrine, see supra ¶2.3.

[58] Treas. Regs. §1.446-1(c)(1)(i); see also Rev. Rul. 80-52, 1980-1 CB 100 (cash-basis members of barter club realize income when amounts credited to their accounts can be used to purchase goods or services or be transferred for value to other members).

[59] For example, the value of meals and lodging, though not transferable, might be treated as compensation, if not furnished for the convenience of the employer; see supra ¶7.5.

[60] See IRC §83, discussed supra ¶29.3; see also CIR v. LoBue, 351 US 243 (1956) (cash-basis employee taxed in year of purchase on excess of fair market value of stock over option price).

is a promise, since the basic difference between cash and accrual accounting is that the latter method requires accounts receivable and similar claims to be reported when they arise from a credit transaction. The difference would be obliterated if cash basis taxpayers were required to treat all claims against employers, clients, and customers as "property," to be valued and taken into income when the services are rendered, rather than when the claims are paid. On the other hand, if a cash-basis employee receives his employer's marketable bonds as compensation for services, they are no less equivalent to cash than the employer's stock, an alternative mode of payment that would be taxable on receipt.

In resolving this conflict, the courts have been far from consistent. There is some authority for all the following propositions: (1) The debtor's promise to pay is not the equivalent of cash unless it possesses "the necessary element of negotiability"; (2) a note or other instrument is the equivalent of cash if taken as payment for the goods or services supplied by the taxpayer, but not if received only as evidence of an underlying claim; (3) any promise is the equivalent of cash if it can be sold by the taxpayer; (4) a claim is not the equivalent of cash unless it can be sold at a discount not substantially greater than the generally prevailing premium for the use of money; and (5) two or more of these factors must coexist for the claim to constitute the equivalent of cash.[61]

3. Constructive Receipt. Cash-basis accounting would play hob with the progressive rate structure and the concept of annual accounting periods if it

---

[61] See, e.g., Ennis v. CIR, 17 TC 465 (1951) ("necessary element of negotiability" lacking; promise to pay was not equivalent of cash); Western Oaks Bldg. Corp. v. CIR, 49 TC 365 (1968) (Nonacq.) (rights were not equivalent of cash because "not easily negotiable and freely exchanged in commerce"); Heller Trust v. CIR, 382 F.2d 675 (9th Cir. 1967) (deferred payment contracts with fair market value of 50 percent of face; taxable although not negotiable); Cowden v. CIR, 289 F.2d 20 (5th Cir. 1961) (non-negotiable promise of solvent obligor taxable to cash-basis taxpayer because "unconditional and assignable, not subject to set-offs, and . . . of a kind that is frequently transferred to lenders or investors at a discount not substantially greater than the generally prevailing premium for the use of money"); Warren Jones Co. v. CIR, 524 F.2d 788 (9th Cir. 1975) (fair market value of deferred payment obligation received in sale must be included as amount realized under IRC §1001(b)).

For the distinction between notes taken in payment for services and notes taken as evidence of the underlying claim, see Dial v. CIR, 24 TC 117, 122-123 (1955) (cash-basis taxpayers not taxed on value of mortgage bonds evidencing claim for unpaid salaries), relying on Treas. Regs. §1.61-2(d)(4); Rev. Rul. 76-135, 1976-1 CB 114 (cash-basis lawyer received and discounted client's note in 1973, note payable in 1974 and 1975; held, fair market value of note taxable in 1973, when accepted as payment for services).

For the treatment of installment obligations if the vendor elects out of IRC §453, see infra ¶36.3.

permitted taxpayers to cash their salary checks or present their savings bank passbooks for the entry of interest in the year of their choice, which might be long after the funds could have been obtained on request. To prevent this type of manipulation, the regulations provide that cash, property, or services are taxable to cash-basis taxpayers when "actually or constructively received." [62] As summarized by a much-quoted metaphor, constructive receipt means that "a taxpayer may not deliberately turn his back upon income and thus select the year for which he will report it." [63] Despite its function as an obstacle to tax avoidance, the doctrine of constructive receipt is not reserved for use by the IRS, but can be invoked by taxpayers to assign items to years prior to actual receipt, even if the statute of limitations has run on the year of constructive receipt.[64]

The most obvious candidates for constructive receipt treatment are uncashed dividend and salary checks, matured interest coupons, interest on savings accounts, and similar items that could be turned into cash with a stroke of the pen but that the taxpayer deliberately or inadvertently fails to present for payment or otherwise process in the normal fashion.[65] The same is true of an open-account indebtedness if the obligor is ready, willing, and able to pay on demand.[66] Whether an account has been constructively received is more problematic, however, if the taxpayer's control over the date of payment is less complete, as in the following common situations:

1. *Due date fixed by contract.* In general, the date specified for payment by a contract is controlling, and the payment is not constructively received before then, even if the obligor would have agreed at the outset to an earlier

---

[62] Treas. Regs. §§1.446-1(c)(1)(i) and 1.451-2(a).

[63] Hamilton Nat'l Bank of Chattanooga v. CIR, 29 BTA 63, 67 (1933). Income constructively received by the taxpayer is sometimes likened to the income of a revocable trust, as to which the Supreme Court said in Corliss v. Bowers, 281 US 376, 378 (1930): "The income that is subject to a man's unfettered command and that he is free to enjoy at his own option may be taxed to him as his income, whether he sees fit to enjoy it or not."

[64] See Ross v. CIR, 169 F.2d 483 (1st Cir. 1948) (doctrine can be asserted by taxpayer to defeat IRS attempt to tax amount in later year; taxpayer not estopped by failure to report item when constructively received, in absence of misstatement of fact).

[65] See, e.g., Baker v. CIR, 81 F.2d 741 (3d Cir. 1936) (taxpayer taxable on stock sales although profits remained in margin account with stockbroker); Loose v. US, 74 F.2d 147 (8th Cir. 1934) (taxpayer constructively received interest reflected by mature bond coupons despite illness preventing access to safe-deposit box).

[66] Fetzer Refrigerator Co. v. US, 437 F.2d 577 (6th Cir. 1971) (rentals owed to controlling shareholder); Rev. Rul. 72-317, 1972-1 CB 128 (salary owed to controlling shareholder); but see Young Door Co. v. CIR, 40 TC 890 (1963) (commissions owed to controlling shareholders under directors' resolution requiring payment ninety days after close of taxable year; held, not constructively received before due date even though shareholders had legal power to accelerate date).

contract date or would have paid before the due date on request.[67] In exacerbated circumstances, however (e.g., an announcement by a savings bank that new depositors can specify the years when accumulated interest will be credited to their accounts and become available for withdrawal), the contractual date might be disregarded if the choice of one date rather than another has no adverse consequences because interest is credited on all accounts at the same rate. Less freakish contracts for the deferral of earnings are frequently employed with success by authors, entertainers, pugilists, and other taxpayers to avoid bunched income when they expect to strike it rich, as explained earlier in this work.[68]

2. *Deferral of payment by amending agreement after due date.* Once the sales proceeds for goods or payments for services are due and the obligor is ready, willing, and able to pay, the amount due is ordinarily constructively received by the obligee, even if he agrees to a delay in actual payment.[69] If, however, a contract modification is not a mere postponement of an amount already due but a revision of the parties' obligations to each other, the amounts originally payable are not constructively received when the original due dates occur.[70] Moreover, a unilateral decision by the taxpayer to defer billing a client or customer is ordinarily effective for tax purposes if rendition of the bill is a condition precedent to the other party's obligation to pay.

3. *Forfeiture of alternative rights.* Under the regulations, an amount is not constructively received if the taxpayer's control over the amount "is subject to substantial limitations or restrictions." [71] Cash or property that can be obtained only by satisfying a condition is not constructively received unless the condition is inconsequential.[72] Thus, taxpayers are not in constructive receipt

---

[67] See Amend v. CIR, 13 TC 178 (1949) (Acq.); Robinson v. CIR, 44 TC 20, 36 (1965) (bona fide contract providing for deferred payments given effect, notwithstanding that obligor might have been willing to contract to make payments at an earlier time; boxer did not constructively receive deferred payments for participation in championship bout before due dates); Schniers v. CIR, 69 TC 511 (1977) (farmer who sold crops under contract calling for payment on January 2 of year following delivery did not constructively receive payment before then, notwithstanding tax motive for deferral; execution of contract did not constitute change in accounting method or cause distortion of income).

[68] See supra ¶29.2 (deferred compensation agreements).

[69] Frank v. CIR, 22 TC 945 (1954), aff'd per curiam, 226 F.2d 600 (6th Cir. 1955) (lump-sum settlement deferred at request of taxpayer was constructively received); Holden v. CIR, 6 BTA 605 (1927) (sale proceeds held in escrow were constructively received in year escrow completed, despite fact that proceeds, at taxpayer's request, were not paid until following year).

[70] See CIR v. Oates, 207 F.2d 711 (7th Cir. 1953) (Acq.) (insurance agent's assignment of future renewal commissions for annuity of fixed amount; held, commissions due under original contract not constructively received).

[71] Treas. Regs. §§1.446-1(c)(1)(i), 1.451-2(a).

[72] See Patterson v. CIR, ¶73,039 P-H Memo TC (1973) (farmer's agreement with

of the cash surrender value of insurance policies or severance pay conditioned on retirement if they choose not to satisfy the condition on which immediate payment depends.[73]

4. *Escrows, security arrangements, third-party promises, etc.* Cash-basis taxpayers who wish to defer income but who are worried about the obligor's financial stability often try to eat their cake and have it too by contracting for segregated accounts, deposits in escrow, and other security arrangements. The more financial protection, however, the greater the likelihood that the arrangement will be viewed as the equivalent of cash or as a constructive receipt.[74] An alternative way of reducing the taxpayer's risk—bringing in a third party, such as an insurance company, to guarantee or assume the primary obligor's commitment—is also inconsistent with tax immunity, since the third party's liability may be viewed as the equivalent of cash.[75]

5. *Year-end checks.* A check that is received on December 31 and honored in due course when presented to the drawee bank in January is treated as includable in income when received, on the theory that it is the equivalent of cash.[76] On the other hand, the regulations state that dividends payable on

---

purchaser of crops provided for payment of three-fourths of proceeds on demand, subject to repayment if crops deteriorated between date of payment and delivery date; held, amount available on demand was constructively received notwithstanding potential repayment, since no deterioration had occurred before end of that taxable year).

[73] See, e.g., Griffith v. CIR, 35 TC 882 (1961) (cash surrender value of insurance policy not constructively received by taxpayer who would have to surrender interest in policy); Hale's Est. v. CIR, 40 BTA 1245 (1939) (same as to dividends on building and loan shares, obtainable only by surrendering shares before maturity).

[74] Harris v. CIR, 477 F.2d 812 (4th Cir. 1973) (sale proceeds due incompetent placed in escrow at direction of court; held, constructively received); Bell's Est. v. CIR, 60 TC 469 (1973) (gain on sale of property for private annuity taxed to seller because annuity promise was secured by escrow of property and cognovit judgment); Watson v. CIR, 613 F.2d 495 (5th Cir. 1980) (cotton farmer constructively received sales proceeds when cotton gin arranged for irrevocable letter of credit insuring compliance with deferred payment arrangement); but see Busby v. US, 679 F.2d 48 (5th Cir. 1982) (jury verdict in taxpayer's favor on similar facts upheld).

[75] See US v. Drescher, 179 F.2d 863 (2d Cir.), cert. denied, 340 US 821 (1950); Goldsmith v. US, 586 F.2d 810 (Ct. Cl. 1978) (under agreement with anesthesiologist, hospital withheld agreed amounts from compensation otherwise payable, promising to pay annuity and death and disability benefits; held, amounts withheld not constructively received even though hospital purchased insurance contract to fund its obligations, since policy was owned by hospital except to extent of economic benefits attributable to life, disability, and accidental-death features; extensive analysis).

[76] Kahler v. CIR, 18 TC 31 (1952) (two judges concurring because taxpayer did not negate possibility of cashing check after banking hours on December 31 at a place other than a bank or negotiating it to pay a debt); but see Fischer v. CIR, 14 TC 792 (1950) (contra for check received under oral agreement to hold until January because drawer's account was short of funds). See also Rev. Rul. 68-126, 1968-1 CB 194 (retirement check available for personal delivery to taxpayer on last working day of December was constructively received then, although mailed and delivered in January);

December 31 are not constructively received in December if the corporation customarily pays the dividends by checks arriving in January; but it is not clear whether this rule is applicable if shareholders can obtain their checks in person on December 31.[77]

6. *Losses.* If the taxpayer incurs a loss on selling property under a deferred payment arrangement, the constructive receipt doctrine does not fix the year in which the loss is deductible, since IRC §165(a) requires losses to be deducted in the year "sustained," even if the taxpayer reports on a cash basis and does not actually or constructively receive the proceeds until a later year.

4. Deductions. Section 461(a) provides that deductions "shall be taken for the taxable year which is the proper taxable year under the method of accounting used in computing taxable income." This platitude is fleshed out a bit, but not very much, by the regulations, which provide that taxpayers using the cash receipts and disbursements method of accounting ordinarily take deductions into account "when paid," unless (a) the expenditure results in the creation of an asset with a useful life substantially longer than the taxable year (in which event it may be deductible only in part, or not at all, in the year of payment) or (b) the deduction does not entail a cash disbursement (e.g., depreciation, depletion, and losses), in which event the deduction is taken in the year specified by the relevant statutory provision.[78] Another point to be noted in this area is that a transfer of funds, such as a payment into a mortgagee's real estate tax escrow, is not necessarily a "payment" of the obligation to which the funds are to be applied.[79]

A cash-basis taxpayer can "pay" a business expense or other deductible item by transferring cash or property or by rendering services; but the use of property or services generates not only a deduction for the amount paid but also gain or loss (if the obligation is greater or less than the adjusted basis of the property) or income (if payment is made by the rendition of services).[80] A cash-basis taxpayer's check constitutes payment when issued to the payee if honored on presentation, even if that does not occur until the following year

---

but see CIR v. Fox, 218 F.2d 347 (3d Cir. 1954) (contra as to dividends on savings and loan accounts, of which taxpayer had more than 100 in geographically dispersed locations).

[77] Treas. Regs. §1.451-2(b) (third sentence); see also Treas. Regs. §1.301-1(b) (corporate distribution to shareholders includable in gross income when cash or other property "is unqualifiedly made subject to their demands").

[78] Treas. Regs. §1.461-1(a)(1).

[79] See Rev. Rul. 78-103, 1978-1 CB 58, and cases there cited.

[80] See Rev. Rul. 69-181, 1969-1 CB 196 (fair market value of securities transferred by an employer to employee for services rendered may be deducted as business expense; excess of fair market value over adjusted basis is capital gain if securities are capital assets), and cases there cited.

and despite the taxpayer's ability to stop payment in the interim.[81] A promissory note, however, does not constitute "payment" of a deductible item when issued, even if negotiable in form and secured by collateral, but only when, as, and if paid.[82] On the other hand, deductions are regularly allowed for business expenses paid with borrowed funds, provided the funds are not borrowed from the person to whom payment is made; indeed, the taxpayer *must* take the deduction when the borrowed funds are used to pay the deductible item, rather than when the loan is repaid.[83] In 1978 the IRS concluded that a credit card charge was more than "a mere promise to pay" because the taxpayer "became immediately indebted to a third party (the bank) in such a way" that the transaction was tantamount to making the payment with borrowed funds.[84]

While cash-basis taxpayers cannot deduct an unpaid expense in the year the obligation is incurred, even if the debt is evidenced by a negotiable or secured instrument,[85] the obligee must include it in gross income because it is the equivalent of cash. A similar disparity exists between cash-basis obligors and obligees if funds are made available by the obligor to the obligee but are not actually paid: Even if the funds must be included in the obligee's gross income because constructively received, they are not "paid" by the obligor and hence do not support a deduction until the obligee actually draws down the funds.[86]

5. Prepaid Expenses. Cash-basis taxpayers who purchase deductible items on credit may cram deductions attributable to many years into the year when the debts are finally paid. It cannot be categorically said that cash-basis taxpayers can play this game with complete impunity, but there are no reported rulings or cases in which deductions were denied (or prorated to earlier years) on the theory that income is not clearly reflected when an accumulation of obligations is paid and deducted in a single year.

---

[81] Spiegel's Est. v. CIR, 12 TC 524 (1949) (Acq.); Rev. Rul. 54-465, 1954-2 CB 93 (same); see also Griffin v. CIR, 49 TC 253 (1967) (contra for postdated check, which has effect of a promise to pay).

[82] Helvering v. Price, 309 US 409 (1940) (taxpayer's own note not equivalent of cash); see also Eckert v. Burnet, 283 US 140 (1931) (bad-debt deduction not allowed when endorser of corporate note issued new note to creditor in payment of old note; no loss sustained by mere substitution of primary liability for prior secondary liability).

[83] Granan v. CIR, 55 TC 753 (1971), and cases there cited.

[84] Rev. Rul. 78-38, 1978-1 CB 73.

[85] Note, however, that depreciation, casualty losses, and similar items that do not entail out-of-pocket expenditures can be deducted when incurred, even if they relate to property purchased on credit by a cash-basis taxpayer.

[86] See Massachusetts Mut. Life Co. v. US, 288 US 269, 275 (1933) (cash-basis insurance company cannot deduct interest credited to policyholders' accounts but not paid; "constructive payment theory is, we think, untenable"); see also Vander Poel, Francis & Co. v. CIR, 8 TC 407, 410-412 (1947).

On the other hand, the converse of a delayed deduction—viz., the deduction of prepaid expenses—is a common feature of tax shelter transactions, frequently involving the use of funds borrowed on a nonrecourse basis, which in recent years have evoked a flood of cases, rulings, and statutory restrictions. The regulations provide that an expenditure by a cash-basis taxpayer resulting "in the creation of an asset having a useful life which extends substantially beyond the close of the taxable year" may not be deductible when made or may be deductible only in part.[87] The language of the regulations could be interpreted to encompass prepaid rent, insurance premiums, compensation, and supplies that will be used gradually over an extended period of time.[88] Although there is some authority for allowing the entire cost of such items to be deducted by cash-basis taxpayers when paid,[89] the prevailing and better view requires an allocation of the payment among the years benefited by the expenses.[90]

In 1976 Congress enacted IRC §461(g), which for practical purposes puts cash-basis taxpayers on an accrual basis so far as prepaid interest is concerned.[91] Prepayments for feed, fertilizer and other supplies used in farming that are not refundable deposits and that serve such business purposes as insuring preferential treatment or an adequate supply of a scarce product have been held deductible when made, but otherwise the payment is deductible only as the supplies are consumed.[92] Congress attached two more locks to the barn door in 1976 by enacting (1) IRC §464, permitting members of farming syndicates (as defined) to deduct amounts paid for feed, seed, fertilizer, and similar supplies only when they are used or consumed, and (2) IRC §447, requiring certain large corporations to use the accrual method of accounting for farm operations.[93]

---

[87] Treas. Regs. §1.461-1(a)(1).

[88] But see Zaninovich v. CIR, 616 F.2d 429 (9th Cir. 1980) (prepayment of rent for twelve-month period straddling two taxable years deductible when made; allocation not required because benefits did not extend *substantially* beyond close of taxable year). As to materials and supplies, see Treas. Regs. §1.162-3 (ordinarily deductible when consumed, but incidental materials and supplies that are not inventoried or recorded as consumed may be deducted when purchased if taxable income is clearly reflected).

[89] See, e.g., Waldheim Realty & Inv. Co. v. CIR, 245 F.2d 823 (8th Cir 1957) (cash-basis taxpayer allowed to deduct prepaid insurance in accordance with consistent practice, which did not substantially distort income because over time it yielded results comparable to annual deduction of pro rata amount).

[90] See CIR v. Lincoln Sav. & Loan Ass'n, 403 US 345 (1971) (premiums paid into secondary reserve fund of Federal Savings and Loan Insurance Corporation created nondeductible capital asset); CIR v. Boylston Mkt. Ass'n, 131 F.2d 966 (1st Cir. 1942) (three-year prepaid insurance premium allocable one-third to each year).

[91] See supra ¶15.3.

[92] See Rev. Rul. 79-229, 1979-2 CB 210 (IRS tripartite test: Payment must be a purchase rather than deposit, serve a business purpose, and not materially distort income), and cases there cited.

[93] See infra ¶35.5.

6. Refunded Expenditures. Cash-basis taxpayers are, in general, permitted to deduct taxes, business expenses, and similar items when paid, even if part of the payment may be and in fact, is refunded in a later year.[94] The disparity is remedied by including the refund in income when received, unless the prior deduction was of no tax benefit or unless an election is made under IRC §111.[95]

¶35.3 ACCRUAL ACCOUNTING

1. Introductory. Taxpayers using an accrual method of accounting, as authorized by IRC §446(c)(2), include income items in gross income "when all the events have occurred which fix the right to receive such income and the amount thereof can be determined with reasonable accuracy" and similarly deduct expenses when "all the events have occurred which determine the fact of the liability and the amount thereof can be determined with reasonable accuracy." [96] As with cash-basis taxpayers, however, expenditures creating an asset whose life extends substantially beyond the close of the taxable year must be capitalized.[97]

The "all events" test was first enunciated by the Supreme Court in *United States v. Anderson,* decided in 1926, which held that an accrual-basis taxpayer was required to deduct a federal tax on its 1916 business profits in that year, when the amount of the liability could be determined, rather than in 1917, when the tax was due, payable, and assessed:

> The [taxpayer's] true income for the year 1916 could not have been determined without deducting from its gross income for the year the total cost and expenses attributable to the production of that income during the year. . . . In a technical legal sense it may be argued that a tax does not accrue until it has been assessed and becomes due; but it is also true that in advance of the assessment of a tax all the events may occur which fix the amount of the tax and determine the liability of the taxpayer to pay it. . . . In the economic and bookkeeping sense . . . the taxes had accrued [in 1916].[98]

---

[94] See Lowenstein v. CIR, 12 TC 694 (1949) (Acq.), aff'd sub nom. First Nat'l Bank of Mobile v. CIR, 183 F.2d 172 (5th Cir. 1950), cert. denied, 340 US 911 (1951) (deduction allowed cash-method taxpayer on paying estimated state taxes even though refunded in a subsequent year, because payment made in good faith).

[95] See supra ¶1.10.

[96] Treas. Regs. §§1.451-1(a) (income), 1.461-1(a)(2) (deductions).

[97] See Treas. Regs. §1.461-1(a)(2), supra ¶8.4.

[98] US v. Anderson, 269 US 422, 440-441 (1926).

The accrual method of accounting, according to the Supreme Court in *Anderson,* was authorized by Congress "to enable taxpayers to keep their books and make their returns according to scientific accounting principles, by charging against income earned during the taxable period, the expenses incurred in and properly attributable to the process of earning income during that period." [99] In another formulation—*CIR v. South Texas Lumber Co.,* decided in 1948—the Supreme Court described accrual-method accounting as a method "under which all obligations of a company applicable to a year are listed as expenditures, whether paid that year or not, and all obligations to it incurred by others applicable to the year are set up as income on the same basis." [100]

Like all generalizations, these descriptions must be used with caution. In particular, the Supreme Court itself has refused to allow costs to be matched with revenues in the systematic manner implied by its descriptions of accrual accounting, since, as will be seen, payments for goods and services to be supplied in future years are ordinarily includable in the accrual-basis taxpayer's income when received rather than when earned, and deductions are not ususally allowed for the estimated cost of repairing or servicing the taxpayer's product under guaranties.[101] Moreover, these infusions of cash-basis features into accrual accounting are augmented by statutory provisions explicitly requiring charitable gifts, medical expenses, contributions to qualified pension and profit-sharing plans, and some other items to be deducted when paid, rather than when the liability to pay arises.[102] Even if these deliberate erosions of the accrual concept were reversed in favor of a single-minded matching of costs with revenues, the process would require the exercise of judgment in the application of imprecise rules, guaranteeing a choice among outcomes rather than a unique solution. To make a match, we need not only costs and revenues but also a matchmaker—and accounting matchmakers, alas, belong to competing religions, and their ranks even include a few agnostics.

Since income and expenses must be accrued when the relevant amounts can be determined "with reasonable accuracy," [103] rather than postponed until they are known to a certainty, subsequent adjustments are inevitable. In the case of accrued income, the taxpayer may later receive an additional amount or be required to refund part or all of the amount accrued; conversely, in the

---

[99] Id. at 440.

[100] CIR v. South Texas Lumber Co., 333 US 496 (1948); see also Spring City Foundry Co. v. CIR, 292 US 182 (1934).

[101] See infra, text at notes 125–159.

[102] See IRC §§170(a)(1) (charitable contributions "payment of which is made within the taxable year"), 213(a) (medical expenses "paid during the taxable year"), 404(a) (pension and profit-sharing plans).

[103] Treas. Regs. §§1.451-1(a), 1.461-1(a)(2).

case of accrued expenses, it may turn out that the taxpayer owes more than was accrued or that the accrued amount will be paid only in part, or not at all. Discrepancies of this type are corrected not by amending the returns for the taxable year in which the original accrual was made (unless it was erroneous as of that time under the "all events" standard) but by inclusions in income or by deductions, as the case may be, when the amount of the adjustment becomes determinable. This date may precede or coincide with the year in which the correction is made by an actual payment or refund.

In applying the all-events test, it should be borne in mind that it does not automatically require income to be accrued when a contract specifying the amount is executed. On renting property, for example, accrual-basis landlords are not required to accrue the present value of the stream of rent to be received under the lease, since the events generating the lessee's liability have not yet occurred. Interest to be received under a long-term loan is also accrued only when earned (unless collected in advance);[104] accrual of the interest as it is earned over the life of the loan is the best way to reflect income clearly.[105]

Accrual accounting is widely used by taxpayers engaged in business operations and is ordinarily compulsory if inventories are an income-producing factor, as in the case of merchants and manufacturers.[106]

2. The Accrual of Income. Although the "all events" standard ostensibly fixes a unique point in time for the accrual of income, in actuality it is less than precise even if the amount of the taxpayer's claim is known with exactitude, as the regulations properly acknowledge:

> The method used by the taxpayer in determining when income is to be accounted for will be acceptable if it accords with generally accepted accounting principles, is consistently used by the taxpayer from year to year, and is consistent with the Income Tax Regulations. For example, a taxpayer engaged in a manufacturing business may account for sales of his product when the goods are shipped, when the product is delivered or accepted, or when title to the goods passes to the customer, whether

---

[104] See Lake Charles Naval Stores v. CIR, 25 BTA 173, 176 (1932) (three years' interest not properly accrued in one year).

[105] See Security Flour Mills Co. v. CIR, 321 US 281, 285 (1944), stating that the "clearly reflect income" language of the statutory predecessor of IRC §446(b) was intended "to take care of fixed liabilities payable in fixed installments over a series of years" and that it protects tenants against the need to accrue in the first year of a lease the rental liability for the entire team—an explanation that is equally applicable to the lessor. For the accrual of interest, see Rev. Rul. 70-540, 1970-2 CB 101.

[106] For the use of inventories by taxpayers engaged in the manufacture, purchase, or sale of merchandise, see Treas. Regs. §1.471-1; infra ¶35.4.

or not billed, depending upon the method regularly employed in keeping his books.[107]

Accrual as of the time when title to fungible goods in the taxpayer's warehouse passed to its customers has also been judicially approved, even though the goods were to be labeled, packed, and shipped at a later date, where the practice was followed consistently and conformed to the custom and usage of the trade; and, by dictum, the court also approved accrual of the sales price when billed to customers even if title remained in the taxpayer-seller.[108]

Although consistency goes a long way to validate the taxpayer's choice among plausible alternative accrual dates, it is not available as a buttress if the transaction is unique or otherwise outside the ordinary course of business. In general, however, the amount payable under a contract is accrued when the transaction is a taxable event for income-realization purposes.[109] The operation of the "closed transaction" standard is illustrated by *Lucas v. North Texas Lumber Co.,* decided by the Supreme Court in 1930, which held that gain on the sale of property was not includable in an accrual-basis taxpayer's gross income in the year when the buyer gave notice of its exercise of an option to purchase (thereby creating an executory contract of sale), but only in the following year, when the documents transferring title and possession were executed.[110] Although primarily concerned with the time when the transaction was closed for income-realization purposes, *North Texas Lumber Co.* can be properly construed as holding that the all-events test for accrual accounting purposes was not satisfied by the executory contract since it did not impose "unconditional liability [on the] vendee for the purchase price."

The holding of part or all of the sales price of property in escrow will not affect accrual-basis taxpayers selling property on credit, who must include the sales price in gross income when the sale is consummated; the intervention of an escrow does not by itself preclude an accrual of the contract price.[111] A

---

[107] Treas. Regs. §1.466-1(c)(1)(ii); the explicit requirement of consistency with the regulations was added in 1973 by T.D. 7285, 1973-2 CB 163, which also substituted the current phrase "generally accepted accounting principles" for "generally recognized and accepted income tax accounting principles."

[108] Pacific Grape Prods. Co. v. CIR, 219 F.2d 862 (9th Cir. 1955); see also US v. Utah-Idaho Sugar Co., 96 F.2d 756 (10th Cir. 1938) (sale price properly accrued when contracts of sale were executed, consistency and trade custom stressed); but see Webb Press Co. v. CIR, 3 BTA 247 (1925) (Acq.) (income did not accrue until expiration of buyer's thirty-day period for testing and acceptance).

[109] See CIR v. Union Pac. R.R., 86 F.2d 637 (2d Cir. 1936); see also supra ¶22.2 (re taxable events).

[110] Lucas v. North Texas Lumber Co., 281 US 11 (1930).

[111] Clark v. Woodward Constr. Co., 179 F.2d 176 (10th Cir. 1950) (construction company required to accrue contract price when work was completed and accepted by

different principle applies, however, if the funds are deposited in escrow pending satisfaction of conditions to which the sale or other transaction is subject, since until then, the events fixing the taxpayer's right to receive the income have not occurred.[112]

Three-party transactions—a prominent feature of our credit economy—often resemble escrow arrangements, in that the seller's right to collect the full contract price is postponed to a future date and is subordinated to the rights of the seller's creditor, who financed the transaction. In *CIR v. Hansen,* the Supreme Court passed on the income tax consequences of a typical financing arrangement under which an accrual-basis automobile dealer endorsed and discounted its customer's installment notes with a finance company, which paid the dealer 95 percent of their face value and credited the remaining 5 percent to a reserve account as collateral security for the dealer's obligation to make good if the customer defaulted.[113] The Court held that the retained amounts had to be accrued when the notes were discounted since the dealer has "received" his reserve account whether it is applied, as he authorized, to the payment of his obligations to the finance company, or is paid to him in cash."[114]

3. Income—Doubts re Collectibility, Liability, or Amount. Under the all-events test for the accrual of income, it is arguable that a claim must be accrued if the *fact* of liability is established and the *amount* of the claim is undisputed, no matter how dubious its collectibility may be; and this theory derives some support from the taxpayer's statutory right to create a bad-debt reserve, which could be viewed as the exclusive method of providing in advance for uncollectible claims.[115] It has been held, however, that rights to income need not be accrued if the debtor's financial circumstances create a reasonable doubt as to collectibility.[116] If the debtor's financial condition

state, despite withholding of 15 percent under contract pending publication of notice of claimants).

[112] See Big Lake Oil Co. v. CIR, 95 F.2d 573 (3d Cir. 1938), cert. denied, 307 US 638 (1939) (escrowed stock not taxable until escrow terminated, since amount earned by taxpayer not determinable until then); Leedy-Glover Realty & Ins. Co. v. CIR, 13 TC 95, 105 (1949) (Acq.), aff'd per curiam, 184 F.2d 833 (5th Cir. 1950) (commissions due on policies requiring servicing by taxpayer over extended future period accruable only as taxpayer became entitled to withdraw amounts from escrow).

[113] CIR v. Hansen, 360 US 446 (1959).

[114] Id. at 465-466.

[115] See Spring City Foundry Co. v. CIR, supra note 100. For IRC §166(c), relating to bad-debt reserves, see supra ¶17.5.

[116] See Clifton Mfg. Co. v. CIR, 137 F.2d 290 (4th Cir. 1943); Commercial Solvents Corp. v. CIR, 42 TC 455 (1964) (Acq.) (accrual not required where taxpayer agreed to postpone collection until bank loan was repaid by debtor); but see Koehring

subsequently improves, however, the claim must be accrued when its collectibility reaches the degree of assurance that would warrant the accrual of a new-born claim.[117] The cases do not attempt to describe the level of doubt precluding accrual (or, conversely, consistent with accrual); but, to avoid a ping-pong game every time a debtor's financial condition fluctuates, it seems appropriate to require claims to be accrued at their face amounts rather than fair market values,[118] unless the prospect of total default is quite substantial, especially since taxpayers can take account of uncollectible items in an orderly fashion by deducting partially worthless business debts under IRC §166(a)(2) or by creating a reserve for uncollectible debts under IRC §166(c).

Turning from doubts about a claim's collectibility to doubts about its validity, we find that accrual-basis taxpayers are not required to accrue income if the obligor disputes the validity of the taxpayer's claim.[119] As applied, this sensible principle requires the income to be accrued when the dispute is terminated by a compromise settlement, a final judgment of the highest court with jurisdiction in the premises, or a final judgment by a lower court once the time for appeal has expired—or earlier, under the claim of right doctrine, if payment is actually received.[120] An amount offered in compromise need not be accrued if rejected, however, since the proffered amount can be obtained only by abandoning the right to sue for the full amount of the claim; but if the obligor admits liability for part and contests only the balance, the amount conceded to be due must be accrued.[121]

Under the all-events standard, a claim must be accrued only when its

---

Co. v. US, 421 F.2d 715 (Ct. Cl. 1970) (accrual required despite debtor's temporary financial embarrassment, where no real doubt existed re ultimate payment).

[117] Clifton Mfg. Co. v. CIR, supra note 116.

[118] See Schlude v. CIR, ¶63,307 P-H Memo TC (1963), distinguishing between accrual-basis and cash-basis taxpayers in this respect; if a cash-basis taxpayer is required to take a claim into gross income because it is the equivalent of cash, its fair market value is controlling rather than its face amount. See supra ¶35.2.

[119] North Am. Oil Consol. v. Burnet, 286 US 417 (1932); see also Cold Metal Process Co. v. CIR, 17 TC 916, 932 (1951) (when adverse claims "are not advanced frivolously and are made in good faith, a taxpayer is not required to evaluate his chances of success for the purpose of determining whether an item is to be accrued"), and cases there cited.

[120] H. Liebes & Co. v. CIR, 90 F.2d 932 (9th Cir. 1937) (income subject to accrual when time for appeal from judgment expired). For the inclusion of disputed amounts in income when received, regardless of the taxpayer's method of accounting, see supra ¶2.3 (claim of right doctrine).

[121] Maryland Shipbuilding & Drydock Co. v. US, 409 F.2d 1363 (Ct. Cl. 1969) (amount offered by insurer not accruable where settlement would have to be "purchased" by relinquishing rights under another policy; extensive discussion and citations); Johnson v. CIR, ¶47,057 P-H Memo TC (1947) (amount of admitted liability accruable when conceded, rather than in later year when litigation re balance terminated).

amount "can be determined with reasonable accuracy." [122] Thus, if the claim is subject to setoffs or other adjustments to be determined at a later time or arises under a contract providing that the price or other material terms are to be negotiated and agreed upon, an accrual is not warranted until the missing elements are supplied.[123] On the other hand, if the basis for computing the amount is undisputed, it must be accrued even though the computation remains to be made, unless the amount cannot be ascertained with reasonable accuracy.[124]

4. Advance Receipts for Goods or Services. When an accrual basis taxpayer is paid for goods or services to be furnished in the future, it is arguable that the receipts should not be accrued until the taxpayer performs its side of the bargain, since deferral until then is more likely to match the revenue against the taxpayer's expenses than accruing the funds when received. Although deferral of such advance receipts until earned by performance of the taxpayer's obligations conforms to generally accepted accounting principles, it was resoundingly rejected for federal income tax purposes by the Supreme Court in three cases, decided in rapid succession between 1957 and 1963.[125] In all three cases, the payments were nonrefundable and were freely available to the taxpayer for use in its general business operations upon receipt.

In *Automobile Club of Michigan,* the first of the Big Three, the Court seemingly endorsed the government's reliance on the claim of right doctrine to require annual membership dues to be included in income because they were received without restriction on their disposition.[126] The Court went on to state that the taxpayer's pro rata allocation of membership dues in monthly amounts over the membership year "is purely artificial and bears no relation

[122] Treas. Regs. §§1.451-1(a), 1.461-1(a)(2).

[123] US v. Harmon, 205 F.2d 919 (10th Cir. 1953) (setoffs and deductions to be established by audit); Globe Corp. v. CIR, 20 TC 299 (1953) (Acq.) (quantum meruit claim to be liquidated by later negotiations; held, too uncertain for accrual).

[124] Frost Lumber Indus., Inc. v. CIR, 128 F.2d 693 (5th Cir. 1942) (accrual proper where per-acre price was fixed, although survey determining number of acres remained to be made); Continental Tie & Lumber Co. v. US, 286 US 290 (1932) (accrual required of claim against government for reimbursement of deficit in operating income attributable to wartime period when railroad was under governmental control); but see Henry Hess Co. v. CIR, 16 TC 1363 (1951) (accrual not required of claim for compensation arising from requisition of property by government until amount fixed by judicial proceedings or parties' agreement).

[125] Automobile Club of Mich. v. CIR, 353 US 180 (1957) (three Justices dissenting); American Auto Ass'n v. US, 367 US 687 (1961) (four Justices dissenting); Schlude v. CIR, 372 US 128 (1963) (four Justices dissenting); see also Schlude v. CIR, supra note 118 (result on remand).

[126] Automobile Club of Mich. v. CIR, supra note 125, at 188-190; for the claim of right doctrine, see supra ¶2.3.

to the services which [the taxpayer] may in fact be called upon to render for the member," holding that in these circumstances the exercise of the government's discretionary authority under IRC §446(b), requiring use of an accounting method clearly reflecting income, did not exceed permissible limits.[127]

The "artificial accounting method" ground of decision stimulated hopes among some taxpayers that prepaid income could be deferred if their allocation methods could withstand this criticism. In *American Automobile Association v. United States,* the taxpayer endeavored to rehabilitate the monthly allocation rejected in *Automobile Club of Michigan* with expert testimony indicating that the allocation accorded with generally accepted accounting principles and correlated with experience when judged on a statistical basis, even though it did not match any individual member's demand for services. The Supreme Court, however, brushed aside the trial court's finding that the taxpayer's method conformed to generally accepted accounting principles and held that the membership dues were required to be included in income in the year of receipt since it was uncertain when, and even if, the taxpayer would be called upon to furnish services to its members.[128]

In *Schlude v. CIR,* a dance studio calculated a per-lesson charge and reported advance receipts as income when the customer took lessons, crediting any balance as income if and when the student's right to the remaining lessons terminated by the passage of time. In the Court's view, this allocation suffered from the same defect that was fatal to the taxpayers in the two automobile club cases. At the end of each fiscal period "the studio was uncertain whether none, some or all of the remaining lessons would be rendered." Therefore, the services were rendered on demand, as in the automobile club cases.[129]

Following the government's success in the Big Three prepaid income cases, taxpayers hoping to avoid the "artificial accounting method" barrier continued to litigate their cases; but, as will be seen, most fell by the wayside. In a remarkable volte-face, however, the IRS amended the regulations in 1971 and issued rulings in 1970 and 1971, surrendering many of the fruits of its judicial victories by permitting the deferral, subject to certain conditions, of prepaid income for goods and services.[130] In addition, Congress enacted IRC §455, authorizing the deferral of prepaid-subscription income, and IRC §456, permitting membership organizations (like the automobile clubs in the first two of the Big Three cases) to defer prepaid income from dues.

As a result of these developments, the post-*Schlude* landscape can be summarized as follows:

---

[127] Id. at 189.

[128] American Auto. Ass'n v. US, supra note 125.

[129] Schlude v. CIR, supra note 118, at 135-136.

[130] See Rev. Proc. 71-21, 1971-2 CB 549.

1. *Deposits, loans, trust funds, etc.* The all-events standard fixes the time when "income" must be accrued, and hence it takes hold of receipts only if they constitute "income." It does not encompass amounts received as deposits, loans, or trust funds, even if the taxpayer may become entitled to retain the funds by performing services or furnishing goods in the future.[131] Similarly, an amount received for an option to purchase the taxpayer's property that is applicable against the purchase price if the option is exercised is held in abeyance until its dual status is terminated.[132]

2. *Post-*Schlude *litigation.* In the litigated cases after *Schlude* and the other Big Three cases, a few taxpayers have succeeded in surmounting the "artificial accounting method" obstacle by demonstrating a certainty of performance of the obligations or services agreed to be provided or a certainty of the date at which the receipt would be earned. For example, advance payments for tickets which could be allocated to particular baseball games,[133] advance charges for mandatory future engineering services,[134] and prepaid interest in certain limited situations,[135] do not have to be taken into income upon receipt.

3. *Prepaid-service income—Rev. Proc. 71-21.* A 1971 ruling permits accrual-basis taxpayers receiving payments in one taxable year for services to be performed before the end of the next taxable year to include the payments in gross income as earned, rather than when received.[136] If for any reason the services are not completed by the end of the second taxable year, however, the amount allocable to the unperformed services must be reported at that time, regardless of when, if ever, the services are actually performed. The ruling (1) applies to services with respect to property sold, leased, built, installed, or constructed by the taxpayer (or a related person, as defined) only if in the ordinary normal course of business the taxpayer sells, leases, etc., the property without a related contingent service agreement; (2) does not apply to amounts received under guaranty or warranty contracts or to prepaid rent or prepaid

---

[131] See Angelus Funeral Home v. CIR, 407 F.2d 210 (9th Cir.), cert. denied, 396 US 824 (1969) (trust fund), and cases there cited; see also supra ¶¶2.2 (trust funds), 2.3 (claim of right doctrine).

[132] See CIR v. Dill Co., 294 F.2d 291 (3d Cir. 1961) (amount held in abeyance pending exercise or termination of option); but see Kitchin v. CIR, 353 F.2d 13 (4th Cir. 1965) (payments under lease-option contract taxable as rent); see also supra ¶22.7.

[133] Artnell Co. v. CIR, 400 F.2d 981 (7th Cir. 1968) (remanding to determine whether allocation clearly reflected income); for the decision on remand, see ¶70,085 P-H Memo TC (1970) (taxpayer's allocation reflected income more clearly than accrual on receipt).

[134] Boise Cascade Corp. v. US, 530 F.2d 1367 (Ct. Cl. 1976).

[135] Morgan Guar. Trust Co. of New York v. US, 585 F.2d 988 (Ct. Cl. 1978); but see Union Mut. Life Ins. Co. v. US, 570 F.2d 382 (1st Cir. 1978), and similar cases in other circuits (requiring the accrual of prepaid interest).

[136] Rev. Proc. 71-21, supra note 130.

interest; and (3) requires the amount included in gross income for financial accounting purposes for the year of receipt to be no less than the amount included in gross income for federal tax purposes for that year.

4. *Advance payments for goods.* Treasury Regs. §1.451-5, issued in 1971 and amended in 1976, permits taxpayers using an accrual or long-term contract method of accounting to defer, subject to certain qualifications, amounts received (a) for the sale or other disposition in a future taxable year of goods held for sale to customers in the ordinary course of business or (b) for building, installing, constructing, or manufacturing property if the agreement is not completed within the taxable year of receipt.[137]

5. *Prepaid subscription income.* Section 455, enacted in 1958, authorizes prepaid subscription income for newspapers, magazines, and other periodicals to be allocated over the subscription's life at the taxpayer's option and permits other established and consistent methods of accounting for prepaid subscription income to be continued in force for future years.[138]

6. *Prepaid dues.* Section 456 authorizes nonprofit membership organizations to elect to include prepaid dues in gross income ratably during the taxable years in which they are obligated to render services or to provide membership privileges, up to a maximum of thirty-six months. Transitional rules under IRC §456 reduce or eliminate the one-shot advantage which might be obtained by making an election under IRC §456 in a year when deferral would be abnormally advantageous.[139] In effect, the revenue loss from an election under IRC §456 is spread over a five-year period.

5. Expenses and Other Deductions. Under the all-events test, expenses are deductible when "all the events have occurred which determine the fact of the liability and the amount thereof can be determined with reasonable accuracy."[140] It has been held that liabilities satisfying this standard can be deducted even if payment is doubtful because the taxpayer is in straitened financial circumstances.[141] If, however, an accrued liability is ultimately forgiven in whole or in part or becomes unenforceable because of the statute of

[137] For long-term contract methods of accounting, see infra ¶36.4.

[138] For an explanation of IRC §455, see S. Rep. No. 1893, 85th Cong., 2d Sess., reprinted in 1958-3 CB 922, 963.

[139] For the transitional rules, see Treas. Regs. §1.456-7(c).

[140] Treas. Regs. §1.461-1(a)(2).

[141] Zimmerman Steel Co. v. CIR, 130 F.2d 1011 (8th Cir. 1942); Rev. Rul. 70-367, 1970-2 CB 37 (taxpayer in bankruptcy proceeding may accrue interest on obligations until debt is extinguished by reorganization exchange); but see Mooney Aircraft, Inc. v. US, 420 F.2d 400, 410 n.38 (5th Cir. 1969) (*Zimmerman Steel* "rather dubious"); Putoma Corp. v. CIR, 601 F.2d 734 (5th Cir. 1979) (compensation payable when directors determine that corporation's finances permit may not be accrued before then).

limitations, the taxpayer must report the unpaid amount as income from the cancellation of indebtedness.[142]

Although the all-events standard ordinarily insures that the accrual will clearly reflect the taxpayer's income under IRC §444(b), in unusual circumstances the IRS may be justified in disallowing an accrual under IRC §446(b) even if it passes the all-events test.[143]

Because it focuses on "the fact of the liability," the all-events test seems to imply that expenses can be deducted by accrual-basis taxpayers when the liability arises, even if they are properly allocable to future operations. This implication is rejected by the regulations, however, which provide that an expenditure creating "an asset having a useful life which extends substantially beyond the close of the taxable year" may be deductible only in part, or not at all, for the taxable year in which it is incurred.[144] The reference in the regulations to "the fact of the liability" is misleading in another respect, since it seems to imply that a liability can or must be deducted if owing as a matter of objective fact, even if the taxpayer denies liability and the dispute is not resolved until a year later. The Supreme Court, however, has held that a taxpayer cannot accrue a contested liability, even though the liability was in fact paid when assessed against the taxpayer.[145] Congress subsequently enacted IRC §461(f) to permit a contested liability to be deducted when money or other property is transferred "to provide for the satisfaction of the asserted liability," provided a deduction would be allowed for that year or an earlier year but for the contest. To qualify under IRC §461(f), the taxpayer must put the funds or other property beyond his control by a transfer to the person asserting the liability, an escrow agent or trustee, or a court or other public agency.[146] If the

---

[142] For the effect of a discharge of debt for less than the amount owing, see supra ¶2.4.

[143] Mooney Aircraft, Inc. v. US, supra note 141 (aircraft manufacturer could not accrue $1,000 "bonds" issued to purchasers of aircraft; bonds were not payable until planes were retired from service).

[144] Treas. Regs. §1.461-1(a)(2). See, e.g., Shelby Salesbook Co. v. US, 104 F.Supp. 237 (N.D. Ohio 1952) (commissions credited to salesmen's accounts on sales of goods to be shipped in later year not accruable until then); Security Flour Mills Co. v. CIR, supra note 105 (tenant not permitted to deduct prepaid rent as expense of current year); for prepaid interest, see supra ¶15.3; for the nondeductibility of capital outlays, see supra ¶8.4.

[145] Dixie Pine Prods. Co. v. CIR, 320 US 516 (1944); US v. Consolidated Edison Co., 366 US 380 (1961).

For the meaning of "contest" in this connection, see Dravo Corp. v. US, 348 F.2d 542 (Ct. Cl. 1965) (filing tax return admitting liability for state tax in amount reported does not constitute a "contest" as to any additional amount; hence, deficiency determined on audit relates back to year for which tax was imposed); Rev. Rul. 68-631, 1968-2 CB 198 (acquiescence in *Dravo*); see also Treas. Regs. §1.461-2(b)(2) (meaning of "contest" under IRC §461(f)).

[146] Treas. Regs. §1.461-2.

taxpayer is ultimately relieved of liability for the deducted amount, the refund is includable in gross income when received or in an earlier year if properly accruable then, subject to the recovery exclusion authorized by IRC §111.[147]

6. Contingent Liabilities and Estimated Expenses. In requiring the taxpayer's liability to be fixed and the amount to be ascertainable with reasonable accuracy, the all-events standard for deductions does not make complete certainty a prerequisite to the accrual of expenses. In commercial practice, innumerable expenses are accrued or paid in circumstances entailing a residual possibility that the liability will be cancelled or the payment refunded because, for example, the goods or services do not meet specifications or the supplier engaged in a misrepresentation or breach of a warranty. If accrual were postponed until these dormant possibilities evaporated, any hope of matching expenses against revenues would also disappear.

The courts have used a rule of reason to govern whether the accrual of expenses should be permitted;[148] have held that the propriety of an accrual "must be judged by the facts which [the taxpayer] knew or could reasonably be expected to know at the closing of its books for the taxable year"; and have rejected as "totally unrealistic" the government's theory that "where there is no change in pertinent law or facts after the end of the taxable year, the true liability and only that is accruable because as a matter of law it is *ascertainable.*"[149]

In several cases involving a taxpayer's liability in an ascertainable aggregate amount to a group of potential claimants, the courts have allowed the amount to be accrued even though the ultimate recipients were not currently identifiable;[150] but the IRS construes the all-events test as permitting an accrual only "when the fact of the liability to a specified individual . . . has been clearly established and the amount of the liability to each individual can be

[147] For IRC §111, relating to the recovery of taxes and certain other items that were deducted without tax benefit, see supra ¶1.10.

[148] Ohmer Register Co. v. CIR, 131 F.2d 682 (6th Cir. 1942); for later cases to the same effect, see North Am. Life & Cas. Co. v. CIR, 63 TC 364 (1974), and cases there cited.

[149] Baltimore Transfer Co. v. CIR, 8 TC 1, 7-8 (1947) (Acq.) (emphasis in original) (taxpayer entitled to accrue liability asserted by state, which it did not contest, even though amount was later reduced on reconsideration of legal issue).

[150] Washington Post Co. v. US, 405 F.2d 1279 (Ct. Cl. 1969) (liability to dealers under profit-sharing plan accrued when amount was allocated to plan, under which participants retiring before age 55 would lose a portion of credit but forfeited amounts would inure to benefit of other participants and nothing could revert to taxpayer); Lukens Steel Co. v. CIR, 442 F.2d 1131 (3d Cir. 1971) (same result as to employer's contributions to unemployment benefit fund under union contract); Rev. Rul. 72-34, 1972-1 CB 132 (rejecting *Lukens Steel*); Rev. Rul. 76-345, 1976-2 CB 134 (rejecting *Washington Post*).

determined with reasonable accuracy."[151] If the taxpayer's liability is contingent on future events, however, the courts agree with the IRS in disallowing an accrual before the contingency occurs.[152]

Although the taxpayer's ability to pay is not ordinarily a "contingency" precluding accrual of an undisputed liability, accrual is not permissible if the taxpayer can defer payment until it decides that its financial circumstances permit.[153]

The prohibition on accruing contingent liabilities creates a major disparity between tax and financial accounting in the treatment of estimated expenses, such as a manufacturer's obligation to repair its products for a specified number of years, an insurance company's obligation to pay renewal commissions if policies sold by an agent are renewed in future years by the policyholders,[154] and a self-insured taxpayer's estimated liabilities to persons injured by the negligence of its employees. During the 1950's, the courts seemed disposed to allow taxpayers to establish reserves for estimated expenses;[155] but the taxpayer's inability to determine in advance whether and when particular customers would request performance of the promised services suggests that accruing the estimated expenses is an "artificial accounting method" of the type condemned in the *Automobile Club of Michigan* and *American Automobile Association* cases.[156] This conclusion is buttressed by the fact that in 1954 Congress enacted a provision, former IRC §462, explicitly allowing taxpayers to deduct additions to reserves for certain estimated expenses, but repealed this provision in 1955.[157]

---

[151] Rev. Rul. 76-345, supra note 150.

[152] Union Pac. R.R. v. US, 524 F.2d 1343, 1351 (Ct. Cl. 1975) (amount of liability need not be precisely known and can be established by estimate, but "liability for the tax must have attached and cannot be approximated or estimated"); see also Eastman Kodak Co. v. US, 534 F.2d 252 (Ct. Cl. 1976) (*Union Pacific* applied to payroll taxes on year-end wages, but not to bonuses or vacation pay; extended analysis, with equally extended dissent).

For the complicated related issue of the accrual of vacation pay, see infra ¶36.5.

[153] See Putoma Corp. v. CIR, supra note 141.

[154] See Brown v. Helvering, 291 US 193 (1934).

[155] Schuessler v. CIR, 230 F.2d 722 (5th Cir. 1956); see also Pacific Grape Prods. Co. v. CIR, supra note 108 (estimated cost of labeling and preparing goods for shipment and related brokerage fees; held, deductible in the year of sale, although shipment and payment of fees would occur in the following years).

[156] For the automobile club cases, see supra note 125; see also Milwaukee & Suburban Transp. Corp. v. CIR, 293 F.2d 628 (7th Cir. 1961) (self-insurer's estimated liability to claimants not subject to accrual under *American Automobile Association* and *Consolidated Edison* cases).

[157] For the enactment and repeal of IRC §462, see American Auto. Ass'n v. US, supra note 125; Mr. Justice Stewart's dissent, id. at 698. In repealing IRC §462, Congress stated that it did not intend to "disturb prior law as it affected permissible

On the other hand, by prohibiting the deferral of prepaid income in the Big Three prepaid income cases, the Supreme Court insured that the taxpayer's entire profit from sales and other transactions will usually be taken into account at the earliest opportunity; and this suggests that income will be more clearly reflected by allowing the associated expenses, if they can be estimated with reasonable accuracy, to be deducted when the income is accrued.[158] So far as the record of litigation is concerned, however, attempts by taxpayers to deduct estimated expenses since the Big Three cases have been uniformly unsuccessful.[159]

¶35.4 INVENTORIES

1. Introductory. Just as taxpayers cannot deduct the cost of buildings and business equipment in the year of acquisition, but must instead spread the cost over the property's useful life by taking annual depreciation deductions, so merchants cannot deduct the cost of merchandise when it is purchased but must instead offset the cost against the sale price when the goods are sold. In effect, the cost of merchandise is capitalized and held in abeyance until it can be matched against the revenue produced by sales; and the same is true of raw materials and factory expenses incurred by manufacturers in producing finished goods for sale. These tax results are achieved by including the cost of merchandise, raw materials, manufacturing expenses, and other appropriate items in the taxpayer's inventory account and by deducting in each taxable year only the costs allocable to goods sold in that year. Expressed in a formula:

Opening inventory *plus* purchases during taxable year
minus closing inventory *equals* cost of goods sold.

---

accrual accounting provisions for tax purposes" (id. at 695), but this admonition did not prevent the Court from drawing such an adverse inference in *American Automobile Association.*

[158] See Hagen Advertising Displays, Inc. v. CIR, 407 F.2d 1105, 1110 (6th Cir. 1969) (accrual-basis taxpayer required to report advance payments for signs to be manufactured for customers; no attempt to estimate cost of complying with contract obligations).

[159] See, e.g., Simplified Tax Records, Inc. v. CIR, 41 TC 75 (1963) (reserve for estimated expenses of preparing tax returns for clients not deductible); Bell Elec. Co. v. CIR, 45 TC 158 (1965) (Acq.) (reserve denied for warranty service to be provided on appliances sold).

Under Rev. Proc. 75-25, 1975-1 CB 720, however, real estate subdividers are permitted to take estimated future development expenses into account in determining the basis of lots sold; see also Haynsworth v. CIR, 68 TC 703 (1977) (Rev. Proc. 75-25

Because the cost of goods sold is a residual amount, it includes not only the inventory prices of goods that are actually sold during the year, but also the cost of goods lost during the year because of pilferage, casualty, physical shrinkage, and similar causes. Since the inventory prices of these missing items do not appear in the closing inventory, they automatically in-crease the cost of goods sold; and a separate deduction for the casualty or other loss is not warranted. The cost of goods sold also includes any reductions in the closing inventory to reflect not only losses of value in subnormal goods (e.g., damaged and out-of-style items), but also, if the taxpayer elects to value the closing inventory at the lower of cost or market, unrealized depreciation in the value of normal goods attributable to market fluctuations. Strictly speaking, therefore, the term "cost of goods sold" is a misleading narrow label for the amounts that are charged against current sales.

Example 35-1 compares the tax effect of using inventories with the results that would be produced if taxpayers were permitted to deduct the cost of merchandise on acquisition, for the simplified case of a taxpayer beginning in year 1 and terminating operations at the end of year 3, if (1) $100 of goods are purchased for sale each year; (2) sales are $75, $150, and $225 for years 1, 2, and 3, respectively; and (3) wholesale and retail prices are unchanged throughout the period. Since the taxpayer's gross profit on these facts is 33.3 percent of sales (aggregate cost, $300; aggregate sales, $450; profit, $150), the use of inventories results in gross income from sales that is proportionate to each year's sales—$25 in year 1 on sales of $75, $50 in year 2 on sales of $150, and $75 in year 3 on sales of $225. By contrast, the hypothetical deduction method of computing income produces a loss of $25 in year 1, solely because purchases exceed that year's sales, and income of $50 and $125 for years 2 and 3, respectively. Over the three-year period, however, the aggregate profit is the same whichever method is used: $150.

It will be noted that the results for year 2 are the same under both methods of computing income, because the taxpayer's purchases in year 2 equal the depletion in inventory during that year. If tIf the taxpayer continued on this "steady state" plateau for a period of years—which assumes that the taxpayer's operations remain stable and that prices do not change—the two accounting methods would produce identical tax results indefinitely. In real life, however, steady-state conditions are rarely encountered; and for companies whose sales are either expanding or contracting, the contrast between the two methods shown by Example 35-1 is typical. Indeed, as will be seen, the differences would be accentuated if the volume of purchases varied from year to year and if wholesale or retail prices also fluctuated.

---

valid in light of early case law; if expenses are overestimated, inclusion of excess in income is required).

Example 35–1

Inventory Method vs Hypothetical Deduction of Inventory Costs

	Inventory Methods			*Hypothetical Deduction Method*		
	Year			*Year*		
	1	*2*	*3*	*1*	*2*	*3*
1. Opening inventory	0	50	50	—	—	—
2. Plus: Purchases.............	100	100	100	100	100	100
3. Equals: Goods available for sale	100	150	150	—	—	—
4. Less: Ending inventory	50	50	0	—	—	—
5. Equals: Cost of goods sold (COGS).................	50	100	150	—	—	—
6. Sales	75	150	225	75	150	225
7. Less:						
a. COGS (inventory method)	50	100	150			
b. Purchases (deduction method)				100	100	100
8. Gross income from sales..............................	25	50	75	(25)	50	125

The basic statutory authority for the use of inventories is IRC §471, providing that if the use of inventories is necessary in the opinion of the Treasury in order to determine income clearly, the taxpayer must take inventories on the basis prescribed by the IRS "as conforming as nearly as may be to the best accounting practice in the trade or business and as most clearly reflecting the income." A similar but more explicit message is conveyed by the regulations under IRC §61(a), which provide that "gross income" in the case of manufacturing, merchandising, and mining enterprises means "the total sales, less the cost of goods sold," plus income from investments and other sources.[160] The term "cost of goods sold" (COGS) is not defined by the regulations, but its well-established meaning is summarized by the formula above.

Pursuant to the authority vested in the Treasury by IRC §471, the regulations provide:

> It follows [from IRC §471] that inventory rules cannot be uniform but must give effect to trade customs which come within the scope of the best accounting practice in the particular trade or business. In order to

[160] Treas. Regs. §1.61-3(a).

> clearly reflect income, the inventory practice of a taxpayer should be consistent from year to year, and greater weight is to be given to consistency than to any particular method of inventorying or basis of valuation so long as the method or basis used is in accord with [Treas. Regs.] §§1.471-1 through 1.471-11.[161]

In *Thor Power Tool Co. v. CIR,* decided in 1979, the Supreme Court said "that as between the two statutory requirements—conformity to the best accounting practice in the business [IRC §471] and clearly reflecting income [IRC §446(b)]—the latter is 'paramount.' "[162]

The primary targets of these regulations are taxpayers engaged in manufacturing, merchandising, and mining, but service enterprises using significant amounts of parts, supplies, or components in serving their customers must maintain inventories even if these items are neither billed nor sold separately from the services.[163] Exceptions are recognized if inventories are impractical or contrary to accepted accounting practice;[164] and if small amounts are involved, taxpayers who consistently account for income without inventories may be allowed to continue unless the IRS can show that the established practice distorts income, a contention that can ordinarily be supported only if there are year-to-year fluctuations in the taxpayer's stock of merchandise or other inventoriable assets.[165]

The fact that particular identifiable items held for sale to customers are not customarily includable in inventory, however, does not ipso facto entitle the taxpayer to deduct the cost of the assets in question. If income will be more clearly reflected by capitalizing the outlay than by deducting it currently (as in the case of land held by a real estate subdivider), the taxpayer can be required to hold the amount in abeyance until the proper year—for example, the year in which the capitalized item is sold.[166]

---

[161] Treas. Regs. §1.471-1.

[162] Thor Power Tool Co. v. CIR, supra note 37.

[163] See Wilkinson-Beane, Inc. v. CIR, ¶69,079 P-H Memo TC (1969), aff'd, 420 F.2d 352 (1st Cir. 1970) (undertaker must inventory caskets, which constitute "merchandise" even though sold only in conjunction with services); Rev. Rul. 74-279, 1974-1 CB 110 (optometrist's supply of glasses and frames).

[164] See, e.g., Seigle v. CIR, 281 F.2d 372 (4th Cir. 1960) (dealer in surplus aircraft parts who bought from one to more than a million items of each of 1,500–2,000 classifications allowed to deduct fixed percentage of sales prices, based on industry experience, as cost of goods sold because taking inventories would be prohibitively expensive); Atlantic Coast Realty Co. v. CIR, 11 BTA 416 (1928) (inventories not appropriate for dealer in real estate).

[165] Ezo Prods. Co. v. CIR, 37 TC 385, 392 (1961) (on facts, fluctuations in inventory found to require accrual accounting).

[166] See Shaw Constr. Co. v. CIR, 35 TC 1102, 1120 (1961).

The scope of the inventory rules may arise indirectly, particularly in applying the capital gain and loss provisions, since IRC §1221(1) denies "capital asset" status to property that "would properly be included in the inventory of the taxpayer if on hand at the close of the taxable year." [167]

The required use of inventories when the production, purchase, or sale of "merchandise" is an income-producing factor must be contrasted with the more lenient treatment by the regulations of "incidental" materials and supplies, which can be deducted when purchased if the taxpayer does not keep records of consumption or physical inventories, provided taxable income is clearly reflected by this practice.[168] This rule of reason does not apply, however, if it is not followed consistently or if the taxpayer buys an excessive quantity of supplies in a single year.[169]

When inventories are required, the taxpayer must use an accrual method of accounting for purchases and sales of merchandise.[170] This is because income would be distorted if the cost of goods sold (which reflects the *cost* of the taxpayer's merchandise, whether paid for or not) were offset against the amount that happened to be *collected* during the taxable year, rather than against the sales price of the goods removed from inventory. The compulsory use of an accrual method for purchases and sales, however, does not preclude use of the cash method for such noninventory items as investment income and interest expense.[171]

If inventories are required in order to reflect income clearly, the principal problems encountered in computing the taxpayer's cost of goods sold are (1) determining the expenses includable in inventory; (2) if the goods available for sale were acquired at two or more different prices, allocating the prices between the goods sold during the year and goods on hand at the end of the year; and (3) valuing the closing inventory.

2. Items and Costs Includable in Inventory. The regulations summarize the items includable in inventory as follows:

> The inventory should include all finished or partly finished goods and, in the case of raw materials and supplies, only those which have been

---

[167] See supra ¶25.5. A parallel exclusion appears in IRC §1231(b)(1)(A); see Thor Power Tool Co. v. CIR, supra note 37.

[168] Treas. Regs. §1.162-3.

[169] See Smith Leasing Co. v. CIR, 43 TC 37 (1964) (leasing company allowed to deduct parts and supplies purchased during year and on hand at end of year, in accordance with consistent practice, where purchases were not excessive or abnormal in amount, even though unconsumed items were sold in capital gain transactions in the following year).

[170] Treas. Regs. §1.466-1(c)(2)(i).

[171] See Treas. Regs. §1.466-1(c)(1)(iv); Stoller v. US, 320 F.2d 340 (Ct. Cl. 1963); Ed Smithback Plumbing, Inc. v. US, 37 AFTR2d 1368 (Ct. Cl. 1976) (not officially reported).

acquired for sale or which will physically become a part of merchandise intended for sale, in which class fall containers, such as kegs, bottles, and cases, whether returnable or not, if title thereto will pass to the purchaser of the product to be sold therein. Merchandise should be included in the inventory only if title thereto is vested in the taxpayer. Accordingly, the seller should include in his inventory goods under contract for sale but not yet segregated and applied to the contract and goods out upon consignment. . . . A purchaser should include in inventory merchandise purchased (including containers), title to which has passed to him, although such merchandise is in transit or for other reasons has not been reduced to physical possession.[172]

By focusing on "merchandise," these rules exclude machinery and equipment that are exhausted through use but are not incorporated in the products manufactured by the taxpayer; conversely, materials that become part of the manufactured goods must be included in inventory even though the taxpayer maintains a constant stock of the materials in question and likens this stable quantity to its machinery or equipment.[173]

The distinction in the regulations between goods to which the taxpayer has title, which are includable in closing inventory, and goods "title to which has passed to the purchaser," which are excludable from inventory, is applied flexibly, provided the taxpayer adheres to a consistent practice in determining the goods includable in inventory.[174] In any event, it is essential to accrue the sales price for goods that are not included in closing inventory.

After identifying the physical items includable in inventory, it is necessary to determine their applicable costs. For merchandise on hand at the beginning of the taxable year, "cost" means the inventory price assigned to the goods at the end of the preceding year. For goods purchased during the year, "cost" means the invoice price less trade or other discounts (e.g., for quantity purchases).[175] Cash discounts for prompt payment, approximating a reasonable interest charge, can be either excluded from the price of the merchandise

---

[172] Treas. Regs. §1.471-1; see also Treas. Regs. §1.471-2(f)(5) (title-passage test).

[173] See Morris & Bailey Steel Co. v. CIR, 9 BTA 205 (1927) (materials or supplies that become "a part or ingredient of the manufactured article" includable in inventory, but not machinery used in producing the article); Lucas v. Kansas City Structural Steel Co., 281 US 264 (1930).

[174] See Pacific Grape Prods. Co. v. CIR, 219 F.2d 862, 866-867 (9th Cir. 1955) (title passed to customers on billing date, which preceded segregation, packing, and labeling of goods; but billing date was appropriate date to exclude goods from inventory even if title did not pass on that date, since taxpayer's practice conformed to industry practice and clearly reflected income); Amalgamated Sugar Co. v. CIR, 4 BTA 568 (1926) (under industry-wide practice, sugar treated as sold to customers on execution of sales contract).

[175] For black market and other unlawful costs, see Treas. Regs. §1.61-3(a); supra ¶1.7, note 112; ¶8.3.

or included in income, at the taxpayer's option, provided a consistent practice is used.[176] Transportation and other charges in acquiring possession of the goods ("freight-in") are also included.[177] Selling expenses, on the other hand, do not enter into the inventory cost of goods. Expenses excluded from inventory prices are often described as "period costs," since they can be deducted when paid or incurred, unlike inventory costs, which can be deducted only when the goods are sold.

Because department stores and other retail outlets usually take a physical inventory by adding up the prices on the sales tags affixed to merchandise, the regulations provide a method of converting these retail prices into an acceptable cost figure. Under this "retail method" of pricing inventories, the total of the selling prices of goods for each class of goods or department is reduced to approximate cost by a formula set out in the regulations.[178]

Whether the retail method or a more direct computation is made, the cost of goods entering into a merchant's inventory can be determined with moderate ease; but the task of pricing the inventory of manufacturers is far more complex, since it usually requires the allocation of a vast number of diverse expenses between the taxpayer's manufacturing process and such other operations as sales, research, and general administration. In assessing the significance of the allocation, it should be borne in mind that expenses includable in inventory do not reduce taxable income until the corresponding goods are sold, while other expenses ("period costs") are deductible when paid or incurred. Whether the delay in taking account of the inventoried expenses is long or short depends on how rapidly the taxpayer turns over its inventory and on whether the stock of unsold goods grows or declines in the interim.

3. The Flow of Goods and Costs—FIFO and LIFO. Because the goods available for sale by a taxpayer almost always reflect divergent per-unit costs, depending on when they were purchased or manufactured, it is necessary to allocate inventory costs between the goods removed from inventory for sale during the taxable year and those on hand in the closing inventory at the end of the year. For identifiable "big ticket" items, such as automobiles held by dealers and specially manufactured products, invoices and cost sheets may disclose the inventory prices of specific items. A taxpayer with records of this type can reach into inventory, select for sale high-cost or low-cost items in the

---

[176] See Rev. Rul. 73-65, 1973-1 CB 216 (if inventory is valued at net purchase price, discounts missed through late payment are deductible expenses).

[177] Treas. Regs. §1.471-3.

[178] See Treas. Regs. §1.471-8; Rev. Rul. 55-285, 1955-1 CB 69 (retail prices may not be used without reduction). The retail method may be used whether inventories are valued at cost or at the lower of cost or market.

way an investor can identify securities for sale by delivering the appropriate certificates, and compute gain or loss accordingly.[179]

With fungible and intermingled goods, however, unit identifications are ordinarily not feasible, and an accounting convention must be used to allocate inventory prices between the sold and unsold items. The rules allocating inventory costs between goods sold during the year and the taxpayer's closing inventory are methods of *identifying* inventory costs, rather than methods of *pricing* inventory; but, since the identification method used by the taxpayer may have an effect on inventory pricing (e.g., taxpayers using LIFO must value inventory at cost, rather than the lower of cost or market), this distinction is blurred in practice.

The identification principle ordinarily employed is first in, first out (FIFO), under which the oldest goods are treated as sold first—an allocation that can be likened to the careful housekeeper's practice of putting newly laundered sheets at the bottom of the pile and drawing from the top of the pile as sheets are put into use. It should be borne in mind, however, that the "flow of goods" for inventory purposes does not refer to their *physical movement,* but to the order in which *costs* are assigned in computing closing inventory and cost of goods sold, and this order is unaffected by whether the taxpayer draws from the bottom of the pile or the top when shipping goods to customers. Moreover, the cost of goods sold is not computed directly by assigning inventory costs to the goods as sold, but by a process of elimination; costs are assigned to the closing inventory, which is then deducted from the cost of goods available for sale (opening inventory plus additions during the taxable year) to ascertain the cost of goods sold. The size of the hole in the doughnut, in short, is determined by measuring the ring.

Instead of valuing closing inventory on the FIFO basis, the taxpayer may elect to use the opposite convention, viz., last in, first out (LIFO), which assigns the cost of the most recently acquired goods to the cost of goods sold and, conversely, assigns the cost of the oldest goods to the taxpayer's closing inventory.[180] The difference between FIFO and LIFO is illustrated by Example 35-2, which assumes that the taxpayer's opening inventory consists of 100 items costing $1 each, that 100 items are purchased during the taxable year for $1.20 each, and that 100 items remain on hand at the end of the year. On these assumptions, the cost of goods sold is $100 or $120, depending on whether FIFO or LIFO is used in valuing the closing inventory.

---

[179] See supra ¶23.7.

[180] Taxpayers are not explicitly limited to FIFO and LIFO, discussed in the text, but there is little authority for other methods.

Example 35-2

FIFO vs. LIFO

	FIFO	*LIFO*
1. Opening inventory (100 items at $1.00 each)	$100	$100
2. Plus: Goods purchased during the year (100 items at $1.20 each)	120	120
3. Equals: Goods available for sale	$220	$220
4. Less: Closing inventory (100 items priced at $1.20 (FIFO) or $1.00 (LIFO))	120	100
5. Equals: Cost of goods sold	$100	$120

It should be noted that the use of LIFO in Example 35-2 results in a cost of goods of $120 even if all sales occurred before the $1.20 items were purchased, so that the only goods physically available for sale were the $1 items in the taxpayer's opening inventory.

As Example 35-2 discloses, when replacement costs are rising, the use of FIFO decreases the cost of goods sold relative to LIFO; and this in turn increases taxable income, because the rising cost of replenishing the taxpayer's stock of goods is allocated to the closing inventory rather than to the cost of goods sold. These high costs will come out of the accounting closet, increasing the cost of goods sold and hence reducing income, only if and when replacement prices fall or the taxpayer sells off its merchandise faster than it is replaced; and these mitigating events, if they occur at all, may be long postponed. By contrast, LIFO takes account of rising replacement costs promptly, leaving the earlier low-cost inventory in the closet until the later high-priced items have been exhausted. The difference in response time between FIFO and LIFO is accentuated if the taxpayer increases its aggregate stock of goods in a period of rising costs, since this increase in the taxpayer's investment remains in the taxpayer's closing inventory under FIFO until the old low-cost goods have been cleared out. Under LIFO, on the other hand, the increasing stock of high-cost goods is a buffer that postpones the time when gain on the old low-cost items must be taken into account.

The effects of FIFO and LIFO are reversed, however, if replacement costs are declining. Since FIFO taxpayers include the newly acquired low-cost goods in closing inventory, the old high-cost goods enter into the cost of goods sold, thus reducing current income from sales. LIFO taxpayers, on the other hand, must report gain currently on the new low-cost goods and cannot take the old high-cost inventory into account until all later-acquired goods have been disposed of.

Under IRC §472, LIFO may be used, subject to regulations prescribed by the IRS, on three conditions: (1) Inventories must be valued at cost regardless of market value; (2) for taxable years beginning after 1981, taxpayers electing to use LIFO must take any previously deducted inventory markdowns into income in three equal annual installments beginning with the first LIFO year; and (3) LIFO must be used in financial reports to investors and creditors. The first of these conditions precludes use of cost or market, whichever is lower, an option permissible in valuing FIFO inventories.[181] The third condition, which compels taxpayers to report lower earnings in periods of rising prices than would be reported under FIFO, may restrain taxpayers to some extent; but this damper is mitigated by regulations and rulings permitting footnotes, interim financial reports, and other supplemental documents comparing the LIFO results as reported with the results had FIFO been used, as well as a disclosure that the market value of the taxpayer's inventory differs from cost.[182]

4. Cost vs. Market Value. After determining the costs includable in inventory and identifying the costs includable in closing inventory, the taxpayer must value the closing inventory. Under the regulations, the basis of valuation can be either (a) cost or (b) the lower of cost or market.[183] These two "bases of valuation"—the term used by the regulations—are somewhat less sharply distinguished than the labels imply, since, whichever is elected, goods that are unsalable at normal prices or unsalable in the normal way because of damage, imperfections, shop wear, style changes, broken lots, or similar causes should be written down to bona fide selling prices less the estimated direct cost of disposition.[184]

Taxpayers electing the cost-or-market option can write down not only subnormal goods but also normal goods that have declined in value below their inventory cost because of market fluctuations.[185] The decline in value below inventory cost is thus treated as an expense of the current period, even though the goods are still on hand—an important exception to the usual principle that declines in the value of the taxpayer's assets cannot be taken into account for

---

[181] See supra, text following note 183.

[182] See Treas. Regs. §1.472-2(e) (general rules re LIFO conformity requirement); Rev. Rul. 73-66, 1973-1 CB 218, amplified by Rev. Rul. 75-50, 1975-1 CB 152 (footnote to balance sheet); Rev. Proc. 75-10, 1975-1 CB 651, amplified by Rev. Proc. 76-3, 1976-1 CB 542 (types of footnotes or commentary permissible on annual reports and financial statements).

[183] Treas. Regs. §1.471-2(c).

[184] Id. (bona fide selling prices are established by actual offerings not later than thirty days after the inventory date); see also Hertz v. CIR, ¶53,109 P-H Memo TC (1953) (insufficient evidence that goods were out of style or damaged).

[185] Treas. Regs. §1.471-2(d).

tax purposes until realized by sales or other dispositions. The cost-or-market option (which cannot be elected for LIFO inventories) is an advantageous one-way street for taxpayers, in that goods with a market value above inventory cost are not marked up in value, even if the increase reflects the recovery of a previous write down.

Interpreting the valuation rules prescribed by the cost-or-market regulations strictly, the Supreme Court held in *Thor Power Tool Co. v. CIR* that goods cannot be written down below their replacement cost unless the taxpayer has actually offered merchandise for sale for less than that amount in the normal course of business.[186] If the decline in value is not established in accordance with the regulations, it is only a "paper loss," according to the Court, which cannot be deducted until realized by a sale or other disposition of the merchandise.

In sanctioning the valuation of inventories at either cost or the lower of cost or market, the regulations describe these options as the "most commonly used" methods.[187] Dealers in securities, however, are explicitly granted a third option, viz., to value their inventories at market, provided this method is consistently used for all securities in keeping their accounts.[188]

5. Inventory Manipulations. Since each year's closing inventory becomes the opening inventory for the succeeding year, undervaluations of inventory (e.g., because of an error in counting the items on hand or an unwarranted write-down to alleged market value) are self-adjusting if the closing inventory of the following year is correctly determined, since the second year's cost of goods sold will be reduced (and taxable income correspondingly increased) by the first year's inventory error. The taxpayer's gross income from sales for the two-year period will be correct in the aggregate, but part of the first year's income will not be reported until the second year.

If, however, the closing inventory of the following year is not correctly determined, the error might be carried forward for many years, to be corrected only when the company installs a new inventory system or sells its assets, so that the one-year deferral would be converted into a deferral for the extended period. This possibility has not gone unnoticed by unscrupulous taxpayers, who sometimes understate their closing inventories year after year in order to inflate the cost of goods sold for the current year and correspondingly reduce gross income from sales.

To exploit this tactic systematically, the taxpayer must understate closing

---

[186] Thor Power Tool Co. v. CIR, supra note 37, at 535.

[187] Treas. Regs. §1.471-2(c).

[188] Treas. Regs. §1.471-5; see also Rev. Rul. 74-227, 1974-1 CB 119 (market value option for dealers in commodities); see also supra ¶¶25.5 (dealers and investors), 27.9 (designation of investment securities by dealers under IRC §1036).

inventories by an *additional* amount each year, so that the fraud is compounded; but they may hope to avoid the day of reckoning when the deferred income is taken into account by disposing of the business in a tax-free merger or by holding the inventory until death so that it will obtain a stepped-up basis under IRC §1014.[189] Neither of these tactics is entirely satisfactory. An acquiring corporation will inherit the transferor's low basis for the inventory and will therefore be unwilling to pay full value for the inventory;[190] and in the case of death, a stepped-up basis can be obtained only by accurately valuing the inventory for estate tax purposes, which may bring on an audit of the decedent's income tax returns. In addition, alert revenue agents can sometimes detect disparities between reported and actual inventories by scrutinizing the taxpayer's inventory records and comparing the reported physical quantities and values with warehouse charges, the amount of fire insurance carried by the taxpayer, and other business data. Discrepancies can also be detected by comparing the taxpayer's operations with those of others in the same industry, a process that is facilitated by computer-generated data.[191]

¶35.5 FARMERS AND RANCHERS

1. Introductory. The Internal Revenue Code and regulations contain several important provisions exhibiting special solicitude for farmers, raisers of livestock, and other bucolic taxpayers, including the right of farmers to report income on the cash receipts and disbursements method without taking account of their inventories, to use special inventory pricing methods if they so desire, and to deduct currently certain expenditures that are normally capitalized. These tax concessions have naturally been exploited by the promoters of tax shelters; and Congress in turn has enacted a series of restrictions on the use of agricultural tax allowances by corporate executives, orthodontists, and other city slickers.

Because farmers qualify for special tax allowances, they must be distinguished from other taxpayers. The regulations provide that the term "farmers" includes all individuals, partnerships, or corporations "that cultivate, operate, or manage farms for gain or profit, either as owners or tenants," and that the term "farm" is used "in the ordinarily accepted sense" to include stock, dairy,

---

[189] For IRC §1014, see supra ¶23.4.

[190] See IRC §381(c)(5); Treas. Regs. §1.382(c)(5)-1 (carryover of inventories by distributee or transferee corporation).

[191] For IRS instructions to revenue agents regarding audit procedures to detect inventory manipulations, see IRM 4233(322.17), 4233(520.18) (industry comparisons, significant gross profit percentage variations, comparison of inventory balances with balances for prior and subsequent years, checking accuracy of inventory sheets and other records, and tracing totals to taxpayer's books and returns).

poultry, fruit, and truck farms, as well as plantations, ranches, and all land used for farming operations.[192] Investors in agricultural ventures are "farmers" even though they contribute money rather than sweat, because they profit from bountiful harvests and bear the risk of crop failures.[193]

2. Unharvested Crops Sold With Land. Under IRC §1231(b)(4), if unharvested crops on land used in the taxpayer's business and held for more than one year are sold with the land at the same time and to the same person, the crops and the land are treated as a unitary asset in applying IRC §1231; but the expenses incurred in producing the crops must be capitalized rather than deducted.[194] The result is that gain attributable to the unharvested crops can qualify for long-term capital gain treatment. In situations outside the scope of IRC §1231(b)(4), however, such as a sale of unharvested crops apart from the land or a sale of land held for one year or less with the growing crops, the profit allocable to the unharvested crop must be reported as ordinary income.[195]

3. Special Deductions. Cash basis farmers can deduct expenditures incurred in raising crops and livestock, although under normal tax accounting, expenses of this type are includable in inventory and deductible only when the resulting products are sold.[196] The same is true of accrual-basis farmers using the farm-price or unit-livestock-price method of valuing their inventories; but the net result in these cases is less dramatic because the deductions are at least partially offset by the inventory prices, and in some circumstances the deductions may be less than the value of the resulting inventory.

In addition to these departures from normal tax accounting principles, the Internal Revenue Code contains three more specialized provisions which permit taxpayers engaged in the business of farming to deduct expenditures to improve farmland, instead of capitalizing these outlays. The provisions are (1) IRC §182, covering expenditures to clear land to make it suitable for use in

---

[192] Treas. Regs. §1.61-4(d). For related concepts, see IRC §§175(c)(2) ("land used in farming"), 180 ("business of farming" and "land used in farming"), 464(e) ("farming"), 1251(e) ("trade or business of farming"), 6420(c) ("farm" and "farming purposes"); Treas. Regs. §1.6073-1(b)(2) ("gross income from farming"); Treas. Regs. §1.175-3 (fish farm defined as "an area where fish are grown or raised, as opposed to merely caught or harvested"); see also Rev. Rul. 76-241, 1976-1 CB 131 (oyster farms). For gentlemen farmers, see supra ¶9.10.

[193] See Maple v. CIR, 440 F.2d 1055 (9th Cir. 1971) (limited partners in firm owning citrus orchard); Duggar v. CIR, 71 TC 147 (1978) (physician-investor in cattle venture).

[194] See IRC §§268, 1016(a)(11).

[195] See Treas. Regs. §1.1231-1(f) (sale of unharvested crop with option to reacquire land not subject to IRC §1231).

[196] Treas. Regs. §1.162-12(a).

farming; (2) IRC §175, relating to expenditures for soil or water conservation or the prevention of erosion; and (3) IRC §180, covering expenditures for fertilizer and other material to enrich, neutralize, or condition land used in farming. All three provisions are confined to taxpayers "engaged in the business of farming," a term that does not require getting one's hands dirty. If land is sharecropped, for example, both the owner and the tenant qualify, and partners qualify if their firm is engaged in the business of farming. But persons receiving a fixed rental, unrelated to production, qualify only if they participate to a material extent in operating or managing the farm; and hobby farms, operating for recreation or pleasure rather than profit, do not qualify. Although plantations and orchards constitute farms, the regulations disqualify persons engaged in forestry or the growing of timber.[197]

4. Tax Shelter and Recapture Provisions. The relaxed tax rules applicable to farmers and raisers of livestock, especially the right to use the cash method of accounting without inventories and to deduct expenditures that, under normal accounting principles, would be capitalized, have elicited a series of offsetting statutory limitations, which are summarized below. Some of these counterweights are applicable to all farmers, but others are aimed primarily at tax shelter operations and apply only to specially designated taxpayers, often termed "white-collar cowboys." This derogatory term is always good for a headline, but taxonomists have never satisfactorily explained why the term "farmer" is not properly applied to anyone who invests in an agricultural venture.[198]

1. *Recapture of depreciation on livestock.* Pursuant to IRC §1245(a)(2)(C), recaptured depreciation on livestock is reported as ordinary income rather than capital gain on disposition of the livestock. Section 1245 recaptures only *depreciation* deductions, not deductions taken under IRC §162 for the cost of raising the animals.[199]

2. *Recapture of deductions for soil and water conservation, anti-erosion and land clearance expenditures.* If a taxpayer deducts expenditures under IRC §175 (relating to soil and water conservation and anti-erosion expenditures) or §182 (relating to land clearance expenditures), any gain realized on a disposition of the farmland (including certain otherwise nontaxable trans-

---

[197] For these principles, see Treas. Regs. §§1.175-3, 1.182-2, 1.180-1(b); see also Rev. Rul. 59-12, 1959-1 CB 59 (nursery specializing in ornamental plants is engaged in business of farming).

[198] For general discussion of tax shelters involving agricultural and livestock operations, see Joint Comm. on Taxation, 94th Cong., 2d Sess., General Explanation of the Tax Reform Act of 1976, reprinted in 1976-3 CB (Vol. 2) 40-46; S. Rep. No. 91-552, reprinted in 1969-3, CB 423, 484-488.

[199] For IRC §1245, see generally supra ¶28.2.

fers) is recaptured as ordinary income under IRC §1252, subject to rules similar to those applied under IRC §1245.[200]

3. *Twenty-four-month holding period for cattle and horses.* On the theory that a one-year holding period is not sufficiently long to determine whether cattle and horses are held for breeding, draft, or dairy purposes or for sale to customers in the ordinary course of the taxpayer's business, IRC §1231(b)(3)(A) requires the animal to be held for twenty-four months or more to qualify for hotchpot treatment under IRC §1231.[201]

4. *Like-kind exchanges of livestock of different sexes.* Section 1031(e) precludes the tax-free exchange of livestock of different sexes. According to the Senate Finance Committee, tax shelter promoters were erroneously advertising that such exchanges were tax-free, representing that investors in livestock operations could trade male calves, which would ordinarily constitute about half of the offspring and be sold in the ordinary course of business, for female calves and thus build up a breeding herd quickly on a tax-free basis.[202]

5. *Citrus and almond groves.* Amounts attributable to the planting, cultivation, maintenance, or development of citrus and almond groves must be capitalized under IRC §278(a) if incurred before the end of the fourth taxable year beginning with the year in which the trees were planted, even if otherwise deductible.

6. *Farming syndicates.* Farming syndicates, as defined by IRC §464(c), are subject to three sets of restrictions: (1) Otherwise deductible amounts attributable to the planting, cultivation, maintenance, or development of a grove, orchard, or vineyard must be capitalized if incurred before the first taxable year with a crop or yield in commercial quantities; (2) expenditures for feed, seed, fertilizer, and other supplies can be deducted only for the taxable year in which the supplies are actually used or consumed, or for a later year if the year of use or consumption is too early (e.g., because the supplies are consumed in an orchard's pre-productive period and must be capitalized under IRC §178(b));[203] and (3) the cost of poultry purchased for use in a trade or business must be capitalized and deducted ratably over twelve months or their useful life in the business, whichever is less, while the cost of poultry purchased

---

[200] For details, see Treas. Regs. §§1.1252-1, 1.1252-2; for the legislative background of IRC §1252, see S. Rep. No. 91-552, supra note 198, at 491 ("high-income taxpayers purchase farm land, make expenditures . . . in order to obtain current deductions [under IRC §§175 and 182] against their high-bracket, nonfarm income, and then receive capital gain income when the farm is sold, usually within a short period of time").

[201] See S. Rep. No. 91-552, supra note 198 at 488.

[202] Id. at 488–489.

[203] IRC §464(a); see also IRC §§464(d)(1), 464(d)(2) (exceptions for casualty, drought, etc., and for amounts capitalized under IRC §278).

for sale must be deducted in the taxable year of the sale or other disposition.[204]

7. *Corporations and partnerships with corporate partners—accrual accounting and capitalization of pre-productive expenses.* Corporations (and partnerships with one or more corporate partners) engaged in the trade or business of farming are required by IRC §447(a), with some exceptions, to (1) compute taxable income on an accrual method of accounting and (2) capitalize certain pre-productive period expenses. The purpose of IRC §447 is to match the taxpayer's agricultural expenses with the resulting products, as is required of merchants and manufacturers.

¶35.6 CHANGES OF ACCOUNTING METHODS

1. Introductory. Changes of accounting methods create the risk of duplications and omissions of taxable and deductible items unless effected by a dormant taxpayer with no transactions in progress at the time of the change. If, for example, an active cash-basis taxpayer changes to an accrual method, accounts receivable that were not reported when they arose in prior cash-basis years would not be reported when collected in the later accrual-basis years, and the cost of raw materials deducted as business expenses in cash-basis years and used in manufacturing goods that are on hand when the taxpayer switches to an accrual method would be included in the taxpayer's opening inventory. A solution to these anomalies is provided by IRC §446(e), which requires taxpayers changing their accounting methods to obtain the consent of the IRS before computing taxable income under the new method. By conditioning consent on an agreement by the taxpayer to make appropriate transitional adjustments to prevent omissions and duplications, the IRS is able to police taxpayer-initiated changes in accounting methods.

If the change is initiated by the IRS or permitted or compelled by statute, IRC §446(e) is inapplicable. Section 481, however, is designed to eliminate omissions and duplications when the change in accounting method is involuntary, as well as to ease the transition if the corrective adjustments bunch a large amount of income into the year of the change.

2. IRS Consent to Changes of Accounting Methods. Pursuant to IRC §446(e), requiring IRS consent to a change of accounting method, the IRS requires taxpayers to file an application disclosing all classes of items that would be treated differently under the new method, all amounts that would be duplicated or omitted as a result of the proposed change, and a computation

---

[204] IRC §464(b).

of the adjustments required to take these duplications and omissions into account.[205] Applications are processed under Rev. Proc. 70-27, which provides that requests to change to an accounting practice or method consistent with the regulations will ordinarily receive favorable consideration, provided the taxpayer agrees to take the necessary transitional adjustments into account ratably over an appropriate period, usually ten years.[206] Rev. Proc. 70-27 ordinarily applies whether the taxpayer is seeking to change from one permissible method to another or from an erroneous to a permissible method.

Although the overwhelming bulk of voluntary accounting changes can be accommodated within the framework established by IRC §446(e), the regulations thereunder, and Rev. Proc. 70-27, this standard operating procedure is fuzzy around the edges. The principal areas of uncertainty are the following:

1. *Scope of "accounting method."* The regulations provide that a change in accounting method includes "a change in the overall plan of accounting for gross income or deductions or a change in the treatment of any material item used in such overall plan."[207] A material item is "any item which involves the proper time for the inclusion of the item in income or the taking of a deduction."[208] Changes of the taxpayer's overall plan of accounting and of the treatment of material items within the overall plan are contrasted by the regulations with the correction of arithmetic, posting, and computational errors and with changes resulting from a change in the underlying facts.[209] Changes in "accounting method" usually occur when the proper time for reporting income or taking deductions is changed, but timing changes are not necessarily changes in accounting methods.[210]

---

[205] Treas. Regs. §1.446-1(e)(3)(i) (application to be filed within first 180 days of year of change); see also Rev. Proc. 70-27, 1970-2 CB 509 (180-day period may be extended in appropriate circumstances).

[206] Rev. Proc. 70-27, supra note 205; see also Rev. Proc. 75-18, 1975-1 CB 687. Consents under Rev. Proc. 70-27 may require taxpayers who cease to engage in business within the ten-year period to take the balance of the adjustments into account in the final year.

[207] Treas. Regs. §1.446-1(e)(2)(ii)(a).

[208] For the term "material item," see Connors, Inc. v. CIR, 71 TC 913 (1979) (change of accounting method occurred when cash-basis taxpayer that had been accruing bonus compensation payable to officer shifted to deductions when paid, because change concerns proper time for deductions).

[209] Treas. Regs. §1.446-1(e)(2)(ii)(b); see also Korn Indus., Inc. v. US, 532 F.2d 1351 (Ct. Cl. 1976) (adding amounts erroneously omitted in valuing inventory was correction of error, not change in method).

[210] See Schniers v. CIR, 69 TC 511, 519–520 (1977) (sale of farm products under deferred payment contracts rather than for cash not a change of accounting method); Treas. Regs. §1.446-1(e)(2)(ii)(b) (adjustment of additions to bad-debt reserves and changes in useful life of depreciable assets, affecting timing of deductions, are not changes in accounting methods); Decision, Inc. v. CIR, 47 TC 58 (1966) (taxpayer's change in contracts with customers, under which they were billed for advertisements

Although the regulations are helpful in identifying changes requiring IRS consent under IRC §446(e), they obviously leave room for debate about many adjustments. If a particular adjustment does not require consent, the IRS' power to compel consistency by opening up relevant earlier years depends on whether the statute of limitations has run or is mitigated by IRC §§1311-1314.[211]

2. *Adoption vs. change of method.* Section 446(e) does not ordinarily require consent to the *adoption* of an accounting method, as opposed to *changing* an existing method. In general, the adoption of a method of accounting is manifested by its use on the taxpayer's first return; but a taxpayer whose first return uses an improper method of accounting does not need consent if an amended return using a permissible method is filed before the return for the following year is due, or if the IRS disallows the accounting method employed by the taxpayer's first return and thereby "prevents its adoption." [212]

3. *No change in keeping books.* Section 446(e) provides that a taxpayer changing the method of accounting "on the basis of which he regularly computes his income in keeping his books" must obtain consent before computing taxable income on the new method. This seems to suggest that a taxpayer who has been computing taxable income on a method other than the method used in computing book income does not need IRS consent to *conform* the computation of taxable income to the method regularly used in keeping his books. In defining and illustrating the term "change of accounting method," however, the regulations refer to income as reported by the taxpayer's tax returns, not as computed on the taxpayer's books,[213] and this interpretation of IRC §446(e) is at least plausible.

4. *Changes from erroneous to proper method.* Consent is required to change from an erroneous method to a proper one; [214] but it is not clear that the IRS, by refusing to consent to a change, can compel taxpayers to use an erroneous method of accounting from here to eternity.

---

when published rather than when orders were placed, was not a change in accounting method requiring IRS consent).

[211] Infra ¶41.9.

[212] See Treas. Regs. §1.446-1(e)(1); see also Treas. Regs. §1.446-1(d)(1) (adoption of different methods for two or more businesses); Rev. Rul. 72-491, 1972-2 CB 104 (amended return).

[213] Treas. Regs. §1.446-1(e)(2)(iii), Examples (1)–(8). See also Pursell v. CIR, 38 TC 263, 268–269 (1962), aff'd per curiam, 315 F.2d 269 (3d Cir. 1963) (IRC §481 applicable on change of method of reporting income, even if method of keeping books is unchanged).

[214] Treas. Regs. §1.446-1(e)(2)(i) (last sentence); Treas. Regs. §1.446-1(e)(2)(iii), Examples (7), (8); see also Witte v. CIR, 513 F.2d 391 (D.C. Cir. 1975) (consent requirement as a method of preventing omissions and duplications is equally important whether old method is proper or erroneous), and cases there cited.

3. Adjustments on Changes of Accounting Methods. Section 481 provides that if a taxpayer's taxable income for any taxable year is computed under a different method of accounting from the method used in the preceding taxable year, the taxable income for the year of the change must take into account adjustments necessary to prevent any duplications or omissions that would otherwise result from the change.[215] Since these duplications and omissions must in any event be taken into account by taxpayers changing their accounting methods with IRS consent (because the IRS conditions its consent on appropriate transitional adjustments), the principal function of IRC §481 is to provide an orderly transition on *involuntary* changes of accounting methods. Like the consent procedure of IRC §446(e), IRC §481 comes into play only on a change of "accounting method," and the regulations under IRC §481 incorporate by reference the definition of "accounting method" issued under IRC §446(e).[216] In addition to being triggered only by a change of accounting method, IRC §481 requires duplications and omissions to be taken into account in the year of the change only if they were caused *solely* by the change.[217]

When applicable, IRC §481 requires the transitional adjustments (netted pursuant to the regulations) to be taken into account in the year in which the accounting method is changed, unless the IRS and taxpayer agree under IRC §481(c) to take them into account for other years.[218] If the adjustments increase taxable income for the year of the change by more than $3,000, however, the impact of the transition is moderated by two statutory limitations:

1. *Three-year allocation.* Section 481(b)(1) provides that if the old method of accounting was used in the two taxable years preceding the year of the change, the tax attributable to the increased taxable income is allocated evenly over the same three-year period.

2. *Recomputation of prior years.* A more complex limitation is imposed by IRC §481(b)(2), which permits the taxpayer to recompute taxable income for one or more consecutive taxable years preceding the year of the change by using the new method of accounting. Under this limitation, the adjustments

---

[215] For adjustments under IRC §481, see Western Cas. & Sur. Co. v. CIR, 571 F.2d 514 (10th Cir. 1978) (commissions deducted in prior years for policies expected to be renewed in future years must be taken into income in year of change to commissions-paid basis, although duplications would not otherwise occur until years after the year of change).

[216] Treas. Regs. §1.481-1(a)(1).

[217] Schuster's Express, Inc. v. CIR, 66 TC 588 (1976), aff'd per curiam, 562 F.2d 39 (2d Cir. 1977) (IRC §481 is not a vehicle by which all errors of past years during which a different method of accounting was used may be corrected).

[218] See Treas. Regs. §§1.481-1(c) (consolidation of adjustments), 1.481-5 (consents).

are allocated so far as possible to the appropriate prior years within this consecutive period.[219]

Since these limitations are *ceilings,* they apply only if they reduce the tax attributable to the adjustments; and if both apply, the operative limitation is the one producing the lowest tax.

SELECTED BIBLIOGRAPHY

Adinoff & Lopata, Section 461 and Accrual-Method Taxpayers: The Treatment of Liabilities Arising From Obligations to Be Performed in the Future, 33 Tax Lawyer 789 (1980).

Allington & Bravenec, Some Problems of Accrual Method Farmers, 31 Tax Lawyer 781 (1978).

Balter, Problems Relating to Taxpayer's Obligation to Retain Adequate Records for Federal Income Tax Purposes, 8 J. Tax. 207 (1958).

Bravenec, Guyton & Olsen, How 1978 Tax Laws Will Affect Farmers and Ranchers: A Harvest of Tax Benefits, 51 J. Tax. 46 (1979).

Comment, Taxpayer Initiated Change From Improper to Proper Method of Accounting, 1975 Wash. U.L.Q. 1083.

Hahn, Methods of Accounting: Their Role in the Federal Income Tax Law, 1960 Wash. U.L.Q. 1.

Hawekotte, Accrual and Unusual Punishment—The Reasonable Accuracy Requirement of the All Events Test, 25 U.C.L.A. L. Rev. 70 (1977).

Malman, Treatment of Prepaid Income—Clear Reflection of Income or Muddied Waters, 37 Tax L. Rev. 103 (1981).

McDaniel, Tax Expenditures in the Second Stage: Federal Tax Subsidies for Farm Operations, 49 So. Calif. L. Rev. 1277 (1976).

Metzer, Constructive Receipt, Economic Benefit and Assignment of Income: A Case Study in Deferred Compensation, 29 Tax L. Rev. 525 (1974).

Mihalov, Inventory Write-Downs and *Thor Power Tool,* 57 Taxes 384 (1979).

Moser & Lam, Tax Accounting Methods Available to Small Business Operations Including Elections, 1976 So. Calif. Tax Inst. 467, 483–491.

Mullin, Inventories: LIFO and FIFO Methods: Which Method to Use: Consideration of Some of the Problems, 30 NYU Inst. on Fed. Tax. 1757 (1972).

Opatrny, Handling Problems in Inventory Pricing and Valuation, 32 NYU Inst. on Fed. Tax. 489 (1974).

Penick & Siegel, Relationship of Federal Taxation to New Financial Reporting Requirements, 32 NYU Inst. on Fed. Tax. 403 (1974).

---

[219] For the recomputation limitation, see Treas. Regs. §§1.481-2(b) through 1.481-2(d).

Pinney, Agricultural Real Estate as a Tax Shelter, 1982 So. Calif. Tax Inst. 2000.

Schapiro, Prepayments and Distortion of Income Under Cash Basis Tax Accounting, 30 Tax L. Rev. 117, 138–140 (1975).

Seago, What Chance for Prepaid Income Deferrals Based on Statistical Estimates After RCA? 54 J. Tax. 16 (1981).

Smith, What Are Adequate Records for the Preparation of Income Tax Returns? 11 NYU Inst. on Fed. Tax. 1235 (1953).

Stanger, Vander Kam & Polifka, Prepaid Income and Estimated Expenses: Financial Accounting Versus Tax Accounting Dichotomy, 33 Tax Lawyer 403 (1980).

Swan & Marcus, Current Developments in Tax Accounting: Inventories (Now You See Them, Now You Don't), 1976 So. Calif. Tax Inst. 493.

Warren, Tax Accounting in Regulated Industries: Limitations on Rate Base Exclusions, 31 Rutgers L. Rev. 187 (1978).

Watts, Some Problems of Constructive Receipt of Income, 27 Tax Lawyer 23 (1973).

CHAPTER 36

Installment and Other Deferred Payment Sales, Long-Term Contracts, and Other Special Problems

¶36.1 INSTALLMENT AND DEFERRED PAYMENT SALES

For many years, taxpayers selling property on credit have been allowed to report gain on installment sales (variously defined over the years) as the deferred payments are collected. Until enactment of the Installment Sales Revision Act of 1980, taxpayers wishing this treatment had to make an affirmative election, and this is still true for installment sales by dealers in personal property; but other taxpayers are now automatically subject to the installment method unless they elect out under IRC §453(d). If a deferred payment transaction does not qualify as an installment sale under IRC §453(b)(1) or if it qualifies but the taxpayer elects out of installment treatment, the gain must ordinarily be reported in the year of sale, as explained later in this chapter.[1]

---

[1] Infra ¶36.3.

¶36.2 INSTALLMENT SALES

1. Introductory. The installment method of reporting income, which was extensively revamped by the Installment Sales Revision Act of 1980, spreads the taxpayer's profit on qualifying sales over the collections by requiring the payments actually received to be included in income in the proportion that the anticipated gross profit on the sale bears to the contract price. For dealers selling personal property on the installment plan, the installment method is a method of accounting that, once adopted, cannot be abandoned without permission from the IRS.[2] In the case of other installment sales of property, the installment method applies automatically, unless the taxpayer elects not to use it, whether the taxpayer ordinarily reports on the cash or accrual method.[3] Interest on the deferred payments, however, must be reported in the year that is appropriate under the taxpayer's regular accounting method.[4]

For accrual-basis taxpayers, as well as cash-basis taxpayers receiving obligations on a sale that are the equivalent of cash and would ordinarily be taken into income on receipt,[5] the installment method results in postponing the recognition of income.

In *CIR v. South Texas Lumber Co.,* the Supreme Court described the installment method as a "modified cash receipts basis" and summarized its purpose as follows:

> The installment basis of reporting was enacted . . . to relieve taxpayers who adopted it from having to pay an income tax in the year of sale based on the full amount of anticipated profits when in fact they had received in cash only a small portion of the sales price.[6]

The installment method also enables taxpayers anticipating lower marginal tax rates or offsetting losses to postpone the recognition of income to take advantage of these favorable circumstances. If, however, the installment sale produces a loss because the sales price is less than the property's adjusted basis, the installment method cannot be used to postpone recognition of the loss until the deduction will be more useful.[7]

---

[2] See supra ¶35.6.

[3] IRC §453(d). Before enactment of the 1980 legislation, the installment method had to be affirmatively elected.

[4] See Rev. Rul. 75-171, 1975-1 CB 140 (real estate developer deducting business expenses on accrual basis must accrue interest income on sales contracts for sale of building lots, even though profit on lots is reported on installment basis).

[5] See supra ¶35.2.

[6] CIR v. South Tex. Lumber Co., 333 US 496, 503 (1948).

The installment method applies only to sales and other dispositions contemplating the receipt of at least one payment after the close of the taxable year in which the sale or disposition occurs.[8] This probably excludes transactions in which a deferred payment is made in violation of the agreement—such as sales in which the buyer agrees to make all payments in the year of the sale, but breaches this obligation and makes one or more payments in the following year.

The installment method determines the *time* when income from installment sales is taxable, but the character of the asset and the mode of disposition determine whether the income is ordinary income or capital gain.

2. Personal Property Sold by Dealers. Under IRC §453A(a), a taxpayer who "regularly sells or otherwise disposes of personal property on the installment plan" may report the income proportionately as payments are received. The regulations refer to such a taxpayer as a "dealer." [9] In the handful of cases construing the term "regularly," the criteria have been the number of installment sales, their frequency, the ratio of installment sales to total sales, and whether the taxpayer holds itself out to the general public as a seller of goods on the installment plan.[10] If, however, a taxpayer is unable to qualify as a dealer under IRC §453A(a)(1), the sale may nevertheless qualify as an installment sale under IRC §453(b) if the property is not includable in inventory.

By referring to the sale or other disposition of "personal property," IRC §453A(a)(1) disqualifies persons who render services for payment on an installment basis; but it includes transactions involving labor that is embedded in a standardized product,[11] as well as unaccrued *claims* sold to *third parties* on the installment plan, even if the claims represent the right to be paid for personal services rendered by the taxpayer.[12]

The regulations state that "traditional" installment plans ordinarily entail a separate installment contract for each sale of personal property and the retention by the dealer of a security interest in the property;[13] but neither

[7] Rev. Rul. 70-430, 1970-2 CB 51; Martin v. CIR, 61 F.2d 942 (2d Cir. 1932), cert. denied, 289 US 737 (1933).

[8] IRC §453(b)(1).

[9] See, e.g., Treas. Regs. §1.453-1(a)(1). For the dealer/investor distinction under IRC §1221(1), see supra ¶25.5.

[10] See Greenspon v. CIR, 23 TC 138, 152-155 (1954), aff'd in part and rev'd in part on other issues, 229 F.2d 947 (8th Cir. 1956), and cases there cited.

[11] See Rev. Rul. 73-437, 1973-2 CB 156 (prefabricated houses whose components are produced in taxpayer's factory and "shell homes" whose components are produced at construction site with precut lumber materials qualify), and cases there cited.

[12] Realty Loan Corp. v. CIR, 478 F.2d 1049 (9th Cir.1973) (contractual right to fees for servicing mortgages).

[13] Treas. Regs. §1.453-1(a)(1); see also Treas. Regs. §1.453-2(a) (security interest not essential).

characteristic is essential. It is crucial, however, that the plan satisfy a two-payment test, set out in the regulations, providing that the plan must contemplate (a) that each sale under the plan will be paid for in two or more payments or (b) that the particular sale will be paid for in two or more payments.[14] The first alternative is satisfied even if payment is not made in installments as anticipated, but in a lump sum. The second alternative embraces plans under which some sales are to be paid for in a single installment but others entail two or more payments. Only sales of the latter category qualify, and then only if there are in fact two or more payments.[15]

Taken literally, neither alternative would ordinarily encompass sales under conventional revolving credit plans, requiring customers to pay a portion of the current outstanding monthly balance in their accounts; since payments are not allocable to particular sales, it is not possible to describe any particular sale as involving two or more payments. This deficiency is remedied, however, by the regulations, which permit the taxpayer to apply IRC §453A(a) to a percentage of its charges under a revolving credit plan, determined by a statistical study of its experience estimating the number of sales that in fact will be paid for in two or more installments.[16]

On electing under IRC §453A(a), the dealer includes in income a specified fraction of the total payments received in each taxable year from qualified installment sales. The fraction is ordinarily the ratio of (a) gross profit realized or to be realized on the total installment sales in the year to which the payments are allocable, to (b) the total contract price of all installment sales during that year.[17]

3. Real Property and Casual Sales of Personal Property. Section 453 requires taxpayers (other than dealers in personal property) to use the installment method of reporting income on sales or other dispositions of real property and personal property (other than inventory) [18] if at least one payment is

---

[14] Treas. Regs. §1.453-2(b).

[15] Treas. Regs. §1.453-2(b)(2)(ii); Rev. Rul. 71-595, 1971-2 CB 223 (plan permitting payment in deferred installments, with a 2 percent discount for prompt payment in full, if there are in fact two or more payments).

[16] See Treas. Regs. §1.453-2(d); see also Treas. Regs. §1.453-1(a)(1) (IRC §453A elections may be made for taxpayer's conventional installment plan, revolving credit plan, or both).

[17] Treas. Regs. §1.453-2(c)(1); for computation of "gross profits" and "total contract price," see Treas. Regs. §§1.453-2(c)(2) and 1.453-2(c)(3), respectively. Business expenses relating to installment sales are deductible when paid or accrued, depending on the taxpayer's regular accounting method.

[18] For the meaning of the terms "real property" and "personal property," which can include intangibles but not compensation, see Rev. Rul. 234, 1953-2 CB 29 (sale of manuscript by nonprofessional author qualifies); Rev. Rul. 55-374, 1955-1 CB 370 (sale of distributorship rights qualifies). For the "sale or other disposition" require-

to be received after the close of the taxable year in which the sale or disposition occurs, unless the taxpayer elects out.[19] Although the installment method is ordinarily used primarily for *sales* of qualifying property, it is also available for other dispositions, such as an exchange under IRC §1031 of real estate for property of a like kind plus a specified amount of cash to be paid in installments.[20]

In using the installment method, the taxpayer computes the ratio of (a) the gross profit realized or to be realized to (b) the total contract price, and then applies this ratio to each installment payment when received to determine its taxable component. Assume, for example, that Blackacre (adjusted basis $30,000) is sold for $100,000, payable $20,000 at the closing and $80,000 in four equal annual installments commencing one year after the closing, with interest at 10 percent on the deferred payments, and that the taxpayer incurs $10,000 of selling expenses.[21] On these facts, the gross profit is $60,000 (contract price of $100,000 less expenses of $10,000 and adjusted basis of $30,000), resulting in an applicable ratio of 60 percent ($60,000/$100,000). Applied to the payments, this ratio requires income of $12,000 (60 percent of $20,000) to be reported for the year of sale and a like amount to be reported when each of the four installments is received, resulting in aggregate income of $60,000.

If a cash-basis taxpayer elected out under IRC §453(d) for the transaction just described, the fair market value of the debt would be taken into account in the year of sale, resulting in a profit of $60,000 (assuming that the debt is worth its face amount) reportable in that year.[22]

In applying IRC §453, the "selling price" of property (roughly speaking, "the total amount that the purchaser agrees to pay") [23] consists of the cash to be paid by the purchaser; the face amount of the purchaser's evidences of indebtedness; the fair market value of any other property to be received; any obligations of the seller that are assumed, paid, or cancelled by the buyer; and

---

ment, see Barnsley v. CIR, 31 TC 1260 (1959) (notes received as advance royalty on oil and gas lease did not qualify for installment sale treatment—not a sale of property); but see Rev. Rul. 68-226, 1968-1 CB 362 (sale of oil and gas leasehold interest qualifies).

[19] IRC §§453(b), 453(d).

[20] See Rev. Rul. 65-155, 1965-1 CB 356; for IRC §1031, see generally supra ¶24.2.

[21] If the selling expenses are not deducted from the selling price but added to the basis of the property, as required by Kirschenmann v. CIR, 488 F.2d 270 (9th Cir. 1973), the method of computing the gain, but not its amount, would be altered; but see Rev. Rul. 74-384, 1974-2 CB 152 (*Kirschenmann* not followed; selling expenses reduce selling price).

[22] Temp. Regs. §15.453-1(d)(2); S. Rep. No. 96-1000, reprinted in 1980-2 CB 494, 506-507.

[23] Frizzelle Farms, Inc. v. CIR, 61 TC 737, 742 (1974) (buyer's obligations taken at face amount rather than fair market value), aff'd per curiam on other issues, 511 F.2d 1009 (4th Cir. 1975).

any debt to which the property is subject, whether the buyer assumes or takes subject to it.[24] The selling price is not reduced by commissions or other selling expenses paid or incurred by the seller.[25] If interest is not explicitly payable on the deferred payments, so that there is "unstated interest" within the meaning of IRC §453, the ostensible selling price must be adjusted to exclude the unstated interest.[26]

A later renegotiation of the amount to be paid does not result in a retroactive recomputation of the "selling price" for IRC §453 purposes, but only in an adjustment of the amount of income to be reported when the remaining installments are collected.[27] The definition of "installment sale"—any disposition in which at least one payment is to be received after the year of the disposition—does not distinguish between a payment whose amount is fixed and one whose amount is contingent on future events. Confirming this implied application of the installment method to contingent-payment sales, IRC §453(j)(2) directs the IRS to issue regulations providing for the ratable recovery of the taxpayer's adjusted basis even if the gross profit, total contract price, or both cannot be readily ascertained. The longest single section of the proposed regulations endeavors to discharge this mandate.[28]

In determining the amount of gain recognized in the taxable year of sale and whether the agreement contemplates deferred payment, the taxpayer must take account of all payments in that year, whether received before or at the closing or later in the same year.[29] Evidences of the buyer's indebtedness (even if payment is guaranteed by another person) are ordinarily not treated as payments, since the central feature of the installment method of accounting is postponement of the seller's tax liability until the deferred payments are received. Evidences of the buyer's indebtedness are "payments," however, if (1) the debt is payable on demand or (2) the instrument is issued by a corporation, government, or political subdivision either (a) with interest coupons attached or in registered form (except registered instruments that will not be readily tradable in an established securities market) or (b) in any other form

[24] See Temp. Regs. §15.453-1(b)(2)(ii); Treas. Regs. §1.453-4(c) (mortgage on property included, whether buyer assumes or takes subject to it); Burnet v. S. & L. Bldg. Corp., 288 US 406 (1933) (mortgage on property included in selling price but excluded from "contract price"). For the possibility that a mortgage loan obtained by the seller in anticipation of a sale will be treated as a down payment, see Denco Lumber Co. v. CIR, 39 TC 8 (1962) (mortgage treated as bona fide on analysis of facts).

[25] Temp. Regs. §15.453-1(b)(2)(ii); Treas. Regs. §1.453-4(c) (last sentence).

[26] For IRC §483, see supra ¶27.6.

[27] See Rev. Rul. 72-570, 1972-2 CB 241; Cox v. CIR, 62 TC 247, 255 (1974), and cases there cited.

[28] Temp. Regs. §15.453-1(c).

[29] Warren Nat'l Bank v. CIR, 22 BTA 759 (1931), aff'd, 61 F.2d 325 (3d Cir. 1932) (deposit received before year of sale); Riss v. CIR, 368 F.2d 965 (10th Cir. 1966) (cancellation of seller's debt to buyer is payment in year of sale).

designed to render the instrument readily tradable in an established securities market.[30] Obligations of third parties, however, constitute payments to the extent of their fair market value, regardless of their form or marketability.[31]

On a sale of mortgaged property to a buyer who assumes or takes subject to the debt, the buyer's action constitutes a "payment" only if and to the extent that the debt exceeds the seller's basis for the property.[32] The same excess-of-basis principle is applied to the buyer's assumption of the seller's liabilities if incurred in the ordinary course of business, even if they are paid by the buyer in the year of sale.[33] The buyer's assumption and payment of liabilities incurred by the seller in effecting the sale, however (e.g., brokerage fees and legal expenses), are treated as payments.[34] In a similar vein, if part of the consideration received by the seller is the cancellation of an existing unrelated obligation to the buyer, the discharge counts as a payment pro tanto.[35]

If the sale qualifies for installment reporting and an election out is not made, the seller includes as income the same proportion of the installment payments actually received in each taxable year that the gross profit realized or to be realized when payment is completed bears to the total contract price.[36] The controlling elements in this computation are (1) "installment payments actually received," (2) "gross profit," and (3) "total contract price." For this purpose, the term "payments" has the same meaning as discussed above. The seller's gross profit is the selling price less the property's adjusted basis as defined by IRC §1011;[37] the total contract price is the same as the selling price, except that liabilities are included in the contract price only to the extent they exceed the seller's adjusted basis for the property.[38] If the sales agreement requires the *seller* to pay the mortgage debt (an unusual arrangement), the buyer takes subject to the mortgage in the sense that his rights to the property are subordinate to the morgagee's; but such a "seller to pay" case

---

[30] IRC §453(f)(4); see generally Treas. Regs. §1.453-3. For securities convertible into disqualified obligations, see Treas. Regs. §1.453-3(e) (tainted unless convertible only at substantial discount, as defined).

[31] Holmes v. CIR, 55 TC 53 (1970) (third-party note not an evidence of purchaser's indebtedness even though guaranteed by purchaser).

[32] Treas. Regs. §1.453-4(c); Temp. Regs. §15.453-1(b)(3); but see Rev. Rul. 71-515, 1971-2 CB 222 (amount of mortgage treated as "payment" on sale of mortgaged property to mortgagee).

[33] Temp. Regs. §15.453-1(b)(2)(iv); Rev. Rul. 73-555, 1973-2 CB 159, and cases there cited.

[34] Bostedt v. CIR, 70 TC 487 (1978), and cases there cited.

[35] Riss v. CIR, supra note 29; see also Rev. Rul. 71-515, supra note 32.

[36] IRC §453(c).

[37] Temp. Regs. §15.453-1(b)(2)(v); Treas. Regs. §1.453-1(b)(1); for adjusted basis, see supra ¶23.8.

[38] See supra note 32.

must be distinguished from the usual arrangement under which, as between the seller and buyer, the latter must pay the mortgage debt ("buyer to pay").[39]

4. Sales to Related Persons. Prior to 1980, taxpayers contemplating an all-cash sale to an unrelated buyer could sometimes get the benefit of installment reporting by (1) a sale of the property to a related person or financial intermediary, such as a trust for the taxpayer's children or an accommodating bank, on terms satisfying the technical requirements of an installment sale, coupled with (2) a prearranged all-cash sale by the trust or intermediary to the outside buyer. Since the second sale generated little if any gain, its failure to qualify for installment reporting was irrelevant. The plan, approved by the courts in several important cases,[40] enabled the original seller to report the lion's share of the gain on the installment method, even though any credit risk was almost entirely eliminated because the intermediate purchaser received full payment in cash.

This gambit is restricted by two provisions of the 1980 legislation:

1. *Depreciable property.* Section 453(g) denies installment treatment to an installment sale of depreciable property between related persons as defined by IRC §1239(b)—spouses, the taxpayer and an 80-percent-owned entity (as defined), or two 80-percent-owned entities. This disqualification does not apply if the IRS is satisfied that the disposition did not have the avoidance of federal income tax as one of its principal purposes. When applicable, IRC §453(g) requires the seller to treat the deferred payments as received in the year of the disposition.

2. *Double-disposition transactions.* Section 453(e) prescribes a bitter pill for certain double-disposition transactions by providing that if a disposition of property by one person (*F*) to a related party (*S*) is followed by a second disposition of the property by *S* before *F* has received all payments with respect to the first disposition, the amount realized by *S* on the second disposition is treated as received at that time by *F*. The effect of this imputed receipt by *F* of the amount actually realized by *S* is that *F*'s installment sale to *S* must be recognized to the extent that cash or other property flows into the related group as a result of *S*'s disposition of the property. In applying this rule, the term "related party" is defined by IRC §§453(f)(1) and 318(a) to encompass

[39] See Stonecrest Corp. v. CIR, 24 TC 659 (1955) (property is "taken subject to mortgage" within meaning of regulations if as between buyer and seller, latter has no obligation to satisfy the debt and debt is to be satisfied out of the property); but see Temp. Regs. §15.453-1(b)(3)(ii) (for taxable year of sale "seller to pay" mortgage debt treated the same as "buyer to pay").

[40] See Rushing v. CIR, 441 F.2d 593 (5th Cir. 1971); Weaver v. CIR, 71 TC 443 (1978).

a much longer list of relationships than is applicable under the depreciable property rule of IRC §453(g).

If a transaction fits within both remedial rules, IRC §453(g) is controlling.

5. Dispositions of Installment Obligations. After an installment sale under IRC §453, sellers ordinarily collect the deferred payments in due course and report the resulting income in full as contemplated by IRC §453(c). If this orderly process—the premise underlying the privilege of postponing recognition of the taxpayer's gain—is interrupted by a sale, gift, bequest, or other transfer of some or all of the installment obligations, rules are required to prevent the unreported gain from going untaxed. On the theory that the installment method of accounting is a personal privilege, confined to the seller, IRC §453B(a) ordinarily requires the seller to report any previously unreported income on disposing of an installment obligation, even if the transfer is not a taxable event for other purposes. In a few situations, however, the transfer does not detonate these "explosive rights," and the transferee takes the obligations over at the transferor's basis and with the same duty to report the income component when the claims are collected. Since gain or loss would be realized with respect to sales, exchanges, and collections even in the absence of explicit legislation, the crux of IRC §453B(a) is that gain or loss must be reported on transfers that are not ordinarily taxable events.

The amount of gain or loss is the difference between the obligation's basis (defined by IRC §453B(b) as its face amount less the income returnable if it were satisfied in full) and either (a) the amount realized, if the obligation is sold, exchanged, or satisfied at an amount other than its face value, or (b) its fair market value when distributed, transmitted, or disposed of, if the transfer is not a sale or exchange.[41] The obligation's basis, which is equivalent to the taxpayer's unrecovered cost, is the reciprocal of the ratio used to determine its income component. In determining whether gain or loss on a disposition of installment obligation is capital or ordinary, the character of the original transaction creating the installment obligation is controlling.[42]

The principal categories of transactions bringing the disposition rules of IRC §453B into play are (1) sales and exchanges (including the discounting of an obligation, but not its use as collateral for a loan); (2) gifts, including transfers to nongrantor trusts), even if the donee is the obligor on the install-

---

[41] For problems in determining whether a disposition is a sale or exchange under IRC §453B(a)(1), requiring use of the amount realized in computing gain or loss, or is subject to IRC §453B(a)(2), so that the obligation's fair market value is controlling, see Smith v. CIR, 56 TC 263 (1971) (Acq.) (transfer of obligations for private annuity subject to fair market value standard).

[42] IRC §453B(a) (last sentence).

ment debt;[43] (3) distributions by trusts and estates to their beneficiaries, if the obligation arose from an installment sale by the trust or estate (as distinguished from obligations received by the trust or estate from a transferor who made the installment sale);[44] and (4) most corporate distributions, which are covered either by IRC §453B or by more explicit provisions in Subchapter C.[45] If an installment obligation is sold for an amount to be paid in installments, the gain determined under IRC §453B(a) must be reported at the time of the sale; it cannot be deferred by a second election under IRC §453(b)(1).[46]

The general rule of IRC §453B(a) is qualified by IRC §453, which provides that the transmission of installment obligations at death is not a taxable disposition, except as provided by IRC §691, relating to income in respect of decedents. Under IRC §691, the deferred income is not accelerated by the seller's death but continues to be deferred until the payments are collected by the seller's estate or distributees.[47] If, however, the obligation is bequeathed or transferred to the obligor, cancelled by the executor, or becomes unenforceable, any previously unreported gain must be recognized.[48]

¶36.3 ELECTION OUT OF INSTALLMENT METHOD

As pointed out above, IRC §453(d), enacted by Congress in 1980, permits taxpayers to elect out of IRC §453. The 1980 legislation says nothing explicit about the tax treatment of deferred payment sales that either do not qualify for installment sale treatment under IRC §453 or that, though qualified, are taken out of its jurisdiction by an election under IRC §453(d). This omission would ordinarily imply that the pre-1980 law continues to govern these transactions.[49] The Senate Finance Committee's report on the 1980 legislation, however, states that

> [I]t is the Committee's intent that the cost-recovery method not be available [in the future] in the case of sales for a fixed price (whether the seller's obligation is evidenced by a note, contractual promise, or other-

---

[43] Rev. Rul. 55-157, 1955-1 CB 293 (gifts of installment obligations to obligor); Rev. Rul. 67-167, 1967-1 CB 107 (gift to nongrantor trust taxed as disposition).

[44] Rev. Rul. 55-159, 1955-1 CB 391 (distribution by trust of installment obligations arising from its sale of trust property).

[45] See Treas. Regs. §1.453-9(b)(3), Example (2) (dividend distribution); IRC §311(a) (nonrecognition of corporate income on distributions not applicable to installment obligations); for exemptions from IRC §453B, see IRC §453B(d) (certain corporate liquidations).

[46] See Krist v. CIR, 231 F.2d 548 (9th Cir. 1956).

[47] IRC §453B(c); Treas. Regs. §§1.453-9(e), 1.691(a)-5.

[48] IRC §691(a)(5).

[49] Supra ¶23.14.

wise), and that its use be limited to those rare and extraordinary cases involving sales for a contingent price where the fair market value of the purchaser's obligation cannot reasonably be ascertained.[50]

The temporary regulations under IRC §453 accept this suggestion and provide that cash-basis taxpayers must treat the fair market value of fixed-amount installment obligations as part of the amount realized for the property in the year of sale and that accrual-basis taxpayers must do the same with the obligation's face amount.[51]

¶36.4 LONG-TERM CONTRACTS

1. Introductory. Income from a building, installation, construction, or manufacturing contract that is not completed within the taxable year in which it is entered (a "long-term contract") may be reported, at the taxpayer's option, under the percentage-of-completion method or the completed-contract method.[52] Under the percentage-of-completion method, the taxpayer's expenses are deducted currently, but income is reported in installments as the work progresses. By contrast, taxpayers using the completed-contract method hold expenses allocable to the contract in abeyance and deduct them when the contract is completed and the income is taken into account.[53] Because use of these special methods of accounting is restricted to "building, installation, construction, or manufacturing" contracts, contracts for the performance of services or the sale of goods do not qualify even though performance may require an extended period of time.[54]

A manufacturing contract qualifies for a long-term accounting method only if the contract covers either (a) "unique" items not ordinarily carried in the taxpayer's inventory or (b) items normally requiring more than twelve

---

[50] S. Rep. No. 96-1000, reprinted in 1980-2 CB 494, at 506–507.

[51] Temp. Regs. §15.453-1(d)(2).

[52] Section 229 of the Tax Equity and Fiscal Responsibility Act of 1982 (not incorporated in the Internal Revenue Code) directs the IRS to modify the regulations relating to accounting for long-term contracts to clarify the time when contracts are to be treated as completed and when two or more contracts should be treated as a single contract (or vice versa), and also to alter the rules governing the allocation of costs to long-term contracts. The latter mandate envisions stricter limits on current deductions by requiring more expenses to be attributed to the long-term contracts and thus to be held in abeyance until the taxpayer recognizes the income from the contract.

[53] Treas. Regs. §1.451-3.

[54] See Rev. Rul. 70-67, 1970-1 CB 117 (architect not qualified); Rev. Rul. 80-18, 1980-1 CB 103 (same for engineer); Deer Island Logging Co. v. CIR, 14 BTA 1027 (1929) (same for long-term contract under which logging company agreed to buy, cut, and sell timber).

calendar months to complete. The first category is exemplified by an industrial machine specifically designed to meet a customer's needs; the second, by a contract to manufacture a machine requiring more than twelve months to complete.[55]

Whichever of the two long-term accounting methods is chosen must be applied consistently to all long-term contracts "within the same trade or business." [56] The regulations water down this requirement, however, by allowing taxpayers to distinguish between long-term contracts "of substantial duration" and those of "less than substantial duration" and to use either the completed-contract or the percentage-of-completion method for the first category but not for the second, even though both types arise in the same trade or business.[57] Moreover, the completed-contract and percentage-of-completion methods are concerned only with income and expenses attributable to qualifying contracts, so that another proper method must be used to account for other business expenses (including the cost of servicing property constructed under a long-term contract), investment income, etc.[58]

If a long-term contract is transferred by a distribution, corporate liquidation, or other similar transaction before completion, the taxpayer's obligation to report the deferred income depends on general assignment-of-income principles and the clear-reflection-of-income requirements of IRC §446(b), as modified by specific statutory provisions in certain areas.[59] The completed-contract method is especially vulnerable, since none of the potential income will have been reported before the distribution; but percentage-of-completion contracts also invite attack if a disproportionately large portion of the aggregate anticipated costs has been deducted or if substantial progress is made on the contract during the year in which the distribution occurs.

2. Percentage-of-Completion Method. The percentage-of-completion method requires that a portion of the gross contract price be included in gross income for each taxable year, determined by one of two ratios, at the taxpayer's option: (a) the ratio of total costs incurred with respect to the contract as of the end of the taxable year to the estimated total contract costs or (b) the ratio of work performed on the contract as of the end of the taxable year to the

---

[55] Treas. Regs. §1.451-3(b)(1)(ii).

[56] Treas. Regs. §1.451-3(a); see also IRC §446(d) (sanctioning the use of different accounting methods for different businesses conducted by the same taxpayer), discussed supra ¶35.1, text at note 31.

[57] Treas. Regs. §1.451-3(a)(1); Rev. Rul. 78-180, 1978-1 CB 136 (taxpayer classifying long-term contracts by reference to duration cannot use completed-contract method for one category and percentage-of-completion method for the other).

[58] Treas. Regs. §1.451-3(a)(3).

[59] See generally supra ¶¶30.3 (assignment-of-income principles), 35.1 (accounting method must clearly reflect income).

estimated total work to be performed.[60] Whether the percentage of completion is determined by reference to incurred costs of physical completion, the resulting ratio is applied only to the gross contract price, not to the taxpayer's expenses, since they are deductible when incurred.[61]

3. Completed-Contract Method. Under the completed-contract method of accounting, the gross contract price for each contract is included in the taxpayer's gross income for the taxable year in which the contract is completed, whether the amounts due are collected in advance, on completion, or subsequently. Since all costs properly allocable to the contract are accumulated while the work progresses and are deducted in the year of completion when the contract price is reported, the taxpayer's revenues and expenses are closely matched by this transactional exception to normal accrual accounting.[62] While accrual-basis taxpayers can value inventories at the lower of cost or market, the completed-contract method does not permit the taxpayer's accumulated costs to be written down even if a loss on the contract is anticipated.[63]

¶36.5 SPECIAL PROBLEMS

1. Introductory. The Internal Revenue Code contains many provisions prescribing tax accounting rules for special problems and classes of taxpayers. Because the term "accounting method" is extremely broad, however, it is impossible to compile an exhaustive list of these special rules, especially since many of them have both accounting and substantive aspects. Some of these rules are summarized below, and others are discussed elsewhere in this work, in conjunction with the substantive principles to which they are ancillary.[64]

2. Vacation Pay. Section 463 permits accrual-basis employers to elect to deduct vacation pay as earned by their employees, even though payment is

---

[60] Treas. Regs. §1.451-3(c); Lord v. US, 296 F.2d 333 (9th Cir. 1961) (percentage of completion determined by visual inspection and engineer's certificate; held, taxpayer cannot shift to cost-comparison method by amended return). For the costs that may be used in determining the cost ratio, see Treas. Regs. §1.451-3(c)(2).

[61] Treas. Regs. §1.451-3(c)(3).

[62] For the rejection of transactional accounting except in special circumstances, see supra ¶35.1.

[63] For the cost-or-market option in valuing inventory, see supra ¶35.4; for completed contracts, see Rev. Rul. 59-329, 1959-2 CB 138 (deferred expenses not inventoriable).

[64] See, e.g., supra ¶¶12.12 (amortization of bond premium), 12.13 (deduction and amortization of certain outlays), 27.4 (original-issue discount).

subject to contingencies, provided the conditions of IRC §162(a), relating to business expenses, are otherwise satisfied. An election under IRC §463 is not a change of accounting method and hence does not require IRS consent or transitional adjustments under IRC §481; but the election cannot be revoked without consent.[65]

An electing employer must establish a vacation pay account, with an opening balance equal to the largest closing balance that such an account would have had during any of the three taxable years preceding the year in which it is established. Having established the account, the taxpayer can accrue annually a reasonable addition to reflect its liability for vacation pay earned by employees during the taxable year and payable during the same year or the twelve-month period thereafter. As vacation pay is paid, the account is reduced; but no further deduction is allowed.

Section 463(c) provides for a suspense account, with the same opening balance as the vacation pay account, which measures the extent to which the initial opening balance in the vacation pay account is actually used in any taxable year thereafter. When the balance in the suspense account exceeds the balance in the vacation pay account, the excess can be deducted under IRC §463(a)(2); on the other hand, when the vacation pay account balance exceeds the suspense account balance, the excess is included in gross income under IRC §81(2).[66]

3. Trading Stamps and Premium Coupons. Accrual-method taxpayers that issue redeemable trading stamps or premium coupons with sales or that sell stamps or coupons to other businesses to be issued with sales, in the initial year are allowed to reduce gross receipts by the cost of redeeming stamps during that year plus the expected cost of redeeming outstanding stamps in the future, based on the number of stamps or coupons outstanding at the end of the year that can reasonably be expected to be redeemed.[67] In subsequent years, only the actual cost of redemptions is deductible, unless the estimate of the cost of future redemptions changes. If the estimate is increased, the increase can be subtracted from gross receipts. If the estimate decreases, the amount of the decrease reduces the allowable deduction.

The cost of redeeming stamps or coupons includes only the cash paid out plus the cost of acquiring the necessary merchandise.[68]

---

[65] IRC §463(e)(1); Temp. Regs. §10.2(b)(3).

[66] For detailed explanation of the suspense account, see S. Rep. No. 93-1357 (1974), reprinted in 1975-1 CB 521.

[67] See Treas. Regs. §1.451-4(a); see also Rev. Rul. 78-212, 1978-1 CB 139 (method not applicable to discount coupons). For the normal rule, precluding deductions for estimated future expenses, see supra ¶35.3.

[68] Treas. Regs. §1.451-4(b)(1)(iii).

4. Discount Coupons. Accrual-method taxpayers issuing coupons that offer a discount of up to $5 on the purchase price of merchandise can elect under IRC §466 to deduct both (1) the redemption cost of coupons actually redeemed during the taxable year and (2) the redemption cost of coupons outstanding at the close of the taxable year that are redeemed within the following six months. The costs that can be deducted by an electing taxpayer include only the amount of the discount listed on the coupon (or, if less, the actual cost to the taxpayer of providing the discount), plus any amount paid to the retailer redeeming the coupon from the consumer if the coupon provides for such a payment.

For purposes of this election, discount coupons do not qualify unless they are redeemed indirectly by the taxpayer through a retailer of the product being discounted.

5. Periodicals, Paperbacks, and Records Returned to Seller. Accrual-method taxpayers who publish or distribute magazines, paperbacks, or records must ordinarily include the sales price of these items in income when they are shipped to retailers under the "all events" standard for the accrual of income and may reduce income for returns only in the year the items are returned unsold.[69] Section 458, however, allows these taxpayers to exclude from gross income the amounts refunded for goods returned within a specified merchandise return period or a shorter period selected by the taxpayer. The taxpayer must have a legal obligation to adjust the sales price of the returned goods if they are not resold and can exclude only the lesser of the amount covered by this legal obligation or the adjustment agreed to before the end of the merchandise return period.

SELECTED BIBLIOGRAPHY

Auster, Tax Aspects of Trading Stamps, Discount Coupons and Gift Certificates, 57 Taxes 379 (1979).

Cuff, Avoiding the Tax Impact of the Temporary Installment Sale Regs. on Wraparound Debt, 55 J. Tax. 144 (1981).

Emory, Disposition of Installment Obligations: Income Deferral, "Thou Art Lost and Gone Forever," 54 Iowa L. Rev. 945, 947 (1969).

Emory & Hjorth, An Analysis of the Changes Made by the Installment Sales Revision Act of 1980—Part I, 54 J. Tax. 66 (1981).

---

[69] See, e.g., Readers Publishing Corp. v. US, 40 F.2d 145 (Ct. Cl. 1930) (deduction denied publisher for magazines delivered to distributor during year and expected to be returned as unsold); for the all-events test standard for the accrual of income and expenses, see US v. Anderson, 269 US 422 (1926), discussed supra ¶35.3.

Ginsberg, Future Payment Sales After the 1980 Revision Act, 39 NYU Inst. on Fed. Tax. Ch. 43 (1981).

Ginsburg, Taxing the Sale for Future Payment: A Proposal for Structural Reform and an Outline of Present Law, 30 Tax L. Rev. 469 (1975).

Goldberg, Open Transaction Treatment for Deferred Payment Sales After the Installment Sales Act of 1980, 34 Tax Lawyer 605 (1981).

Ledlie, Letters of Credit or Escrow Accounts Used as Security in Installment Sale Transactions, 60 Taxes 130 (1982).

Miller, Installment Sales of Mortgaged Realty—Another View, 6 J. Real Est. Tax. 5 (1978).

Schneider, Tax Accounting for Contractors: Planning Under the New Regulations, 35 NYU Inst. on Fed. Tax. 29 (1977).

Sullivan, Tax Accounting for Returned Magazines, Paperbacks and Records—An Examination of Code Section 458, 58 Taxes 279 (1980).

CHAPTER 37

Indirect Methods of Computing Income

¶37.1 INTRODUCTORY

If a taxpayer fails to comply with the obligation to keep books and records as required by the regulations or if the records are incomplete or inaccurate, taxable income must be computed by other methods.[1] Evidence of the taxpayer's receipts may be available from information returns filed or records maintained by the taxpayer's employer, customers, stockbrokers, and others.[2] Once the IRS has reconstructed the taxpayer's gross income with direct evidence of this type, it ordinarily leaves proof of deductions to the taxpayer. If direct evidence of income is not available or is too fragmentary, the IRS "proceeds by indirection to overcome the absence of direct proof,"[3] resorting

[1] For the obligation to keep books and records, see supra ¶35.1; see also Ramsey v. CIR, ¶80,059 P-H Memo TC (1980) (IRS has "great latitude" in reconstructing income if taxpayer files inaccurate returns or fails to file and does not have records from which true income can be determined).

[2] For the obligation of third parties to file information returns in certain cases and to make their records available to the IRS on demand, see infra ¶39.1.

[3] Taglianetti v. US, 398 F.2d 558, 562 (1st Cir. 1968), aff'd on other grounds, 394 US 316 (1969) (referring to net worth and cash expenditures methods of reconstructing income).

to any evidence acceptable under the rules of evidence. In most cases, the IRS uses the so-called net worth, cash expenditures, and bank deposit methods, but other methods can be employed when necessary.[4]

It is sometimes said that indirect methods cannot be used if the taxpayer's records establish the amount of taxable income directly. But since the net worth and other methods can be used to test the accuracy of the books and records,[5] the choice between direct and indirect computations of taxable income rests, in the last analysis, on their respective persuasive weights; superficially meticulous books can be displaced by a reconstruction of the facts based on indirect evidence. As the Supreme Court observed in *Holland v. United States,* a leading case on the propriety of the net worth method in criminal cases, the IRS and the courts can infer from a persuasive net worth computation that the taxpayer's books "were more consistent than truthful, and that many items of income had disappeared before they had even reached the recording stage."[6]

Indirect methods of reconstructing income are sometimes used to reconstruct the taxable income of ignorant, sloppy, or negligent taxpayers and of taxpayers whose records were destroyed by accident; but the IRS makes use of indirect proof of taxable income most frequently in civil fraud cases and criminal prosecutions. These indirect methods are inherently inexact; and "the taxpayer may be ensnared in a system which, though difficult for the prosecution to utilize, is equally hard for the defendant to refute."[7] Since litigants in all kinds of cases are regularly subjected to decisions based on circumstantial evidence, the weight attached to the possibility of error when indirect proof is used should depend on whether the case involves a simple deficiency, a penalty for negligence or fraud, or a criminal prosecution and on whether the taxpayer has a valid excuse for the absence of the records required by law.[8]

---

[4] See Bolton v. CIR, ¶75,373 P-H Memo TC (1975) (IRS can choose any reasonable method of reconstructing income), and cases there cited.

[5] See, e.g., Lipsitz v. CIR, 21 TC 917, 931 (1954), aff'd without discussion of this issue, 220 F.2d 871 (4th Cir. 1955) (net worth method may be "cogent evidence . . . that the books and records are inadequate, inaccurate, or false"); but see Bushnell v. CIR, 49 TC 296 (1967) (Acq.) (net worth method inappropriate where taxpayer's books were accurate and complete, even though some amounts shown on books were not included on return).

[6] Holland v. US, 348 US 121, 132 (1954).

[7] Id. at 129; see also id. at 124 (net worth method involves "something more than the ordinary use of circumstantial evidence in the usual criminal case").

[8] For more on the burden of proof in deficiency, negligence, civil fraud, and criminal cases, see infra ¶42.4.

¶37.2 NET WORTH METHOD

The net worth method (more accurately, the net worth and expenditures method) is probably the most common technique for reconstructing income by inference from indirect evidence. The IRS starts by establishing the taxpayer's opening and closing net worth for the taxable period, and then assumes that any increase in the taxpayer's net worth during the taxable period plus the taxpayer's living expenses and other nondeductible expenses must have been financed with either taxable income or such nontaxable receipts as social security benefits, gifts, and bequests. After any nontaxable explanations for the taxpayer's expenditures have been taken into account, along with such statutory deductions as personal and dependency exemptions, the balance of the net worth increase and expenses can be attributed to taxable income. These principles are illustrated by Example 37-1.

Example 37-1

Net Worth Computation—Taxable Year 1980

	12/31/80	12/31/81
1. Assets		
a. Cash in banks	$10,000	$ 8,000
b. Undeposited cash	5,000	-0-
c. Securities (at cost)	10,000	30,000
d. Residence (at cost)	50,000	50,000
e. Swimming pool (at cost)	-0-	15,000
f. Total assets	$75,000	$103,000
2. Liabilities		
a. Bank loan	$15,000	$ 5,000
b. Mortgage-residence	25,000	23,000
c. Total liabilities	$40,000	$ 28,000
3. Change in net worth		
a. Net worth (line 1f minus line 2c)	$35,000	$ 75,000
b. Net worth at end of preceding year		35,000
c. Increase in net worth—1981		$ 40,000
4. Plus: Nondeductible expenses		
a. Living expenses paid by check		10,000

b. Other living expenses (estimated)		5,000
c. Federal income tax withheld	5,000	
d. Subtotal		$ 60,000
5. Adjustments		
a. Less: Bequest (nontaxable)		5,000
b. Taxable income—before exemptions		$ 55,000
c. Less: Exemptions claimed on return		4,000
d. Corrected taxable income	$51,000	
e. Less: Taxable income reported on return		30,000
6. Unreported income		$ 21,000

Example 37-1 illustrates a simple net worth computation, which would require adjustments to take account of more complex facts. Thus, if some of the securities owned at the beginning of 1981 (cost basis of $5,000) were sold for $15,000 but all other facts were unchanged (including the ownership of $30,000 of securities at the end of the year), the taxpayer would be entitled to a capital gain deduction under IRC §1202 of $6,000 (60 percent of the $10,000 profit); and this amount would reduce the corrected taxable income (line 5d) and the unreported income (line 6) by $6,000. If the taxpayer's home was damaged by fire, he would be entitled to a casualty loss deduction under IRC §165(c), and unreported income (line 6) would be correspondingly reduced. Many other adjustments may be required by the circumstances of a particular case, especially if business assets or expenses must be taken into account.[9] Sometimes most of the elements in the net worth statement are stipulated, leaving only a few crucial items to be determined at a trial.[10]

If two or more years are involved, the same principles are applied year by year. The computation may reflect a decrease in net worth for one of the years in the period, indicating that some or all of that year's living expenses could have been financed, in whole or in part, with assets on hand at the beginning of the year; and it is also possible that the corrected taxable income

[9] For examples, see Logan v. CIR, ¶76,143 P-H Memo TC (1976), aff'd per curiam, 595 F.2d 365 (6th Cir. 1979); Sporck v. CIR, ¶78,079 P-H Memo TC (1978); Coleman v. CIR, ¶79,139 P-H Memo TC (1979).

[10] See, e.g., Cenedella v. CIR, ¶62,039 P-H Memo TC (1962).

for one or more years will be less than the amount reported, because the taxpayer was careless or the IRS failed to discover all the taxpayer's assets or expenditures.[11]

In building or refuting a net worth computation, attention usually focuses on four principal issues:

1. Opening Net Worth. The taxpayer's opening net worth is crucial in a net worth computation, since assets on hand at the beginning of the taxable period can be used to finance the taxpayer's investments and living expenses during the period. A "cash hoard" (i.e., undeposited cash—described by the Supreme Court in the *Holland* case as "this favorite defense") is especially useful because, if its existence at the outset can be established,[12] it is difficult for the IRS to refute the taxpayer's claim that it was fully used during the period. The IRS occasionally concedes that a cash hoard actually existed (usually in an amount smaller than claimed by the taxpayer), but ordinarily it seeks to discredit the claim by introducing inconsistent financial statements or other documents prepared by the taxpayer or by showing that in the recent past the taxpayer was a virtual pauper who had to borrow small amounts from personal finance companies or friends, failed to pay debts on time, went through bankruptcy proceedings, lived like a church mouse, or filed no tax returns. These refutations may be persuasive, but it is of course possible that the taxpayer was a rich miser rather than a bona fide beggar.[13]

Astute revenue agents often ask taxpayers at the inception of an investigation whether they had a large amount of cash on hand, rented a safe-deposit box, or received any gifts or bequests; and the target often responds—sometimes falsely—in the negative, perhaps thinking that this will terminate the investigation. Recognizing, however, that taxpayers are often "more con-

---

[11] See, e.g., Stratton v. CIR, 54 TC 255, 276 (1970) (reported income exceeded "corrected" income in two out of eight years).

[12] For such claims, see, e.g., Kashat v. CIR, 229 F.2d 282 (6th Cir. 1956) ($40,000 accumulated in small village in Iraq by taxpayer's mother; deficiencies upheld, but not fraud penalties); Barsky v. US, 339 F.2d 180, 181 (9th Cir. 1964) (Russian rubles brought to United States before 1917 Revolution, converted into cash and precious stones, allegedly still owned thirty years later; "story was possible, but . . . one would have to search far and wide before finding anyone who would believe it"); Page v. CIR, ¶51,147 P-H Memo TC (1951) (cash allegedly received in 1894 and kept for fifty years); Goddard v. CIR, ¶62,083 P-H Memo TC (1962) (government employee claimed marriage while a student at Yale Law School to widow more than fifty years older than he for $200,000; claim accepted "with doubt").

[13] See, e.g., Holland v. US, supra note 6 (claimed cash hoard inconsistent with unpaid debts, small default judgment, loss of household furniture on failure to pay balance due of $92, etc.); Friedberg v. US, 348 US 142 (1954), rehearing denied, 348 US 932 (1955) (financial history of defendant disclosed no tax returns for many years, judgment for $13.76 returned nulla bona, deficiency judgment in mortgage foreclosure, financial statement showing negligible cash on hand, etc.).

cerned with a quick settlement than an honest search for the truth" and that the IRS may pick and choose from among their statements,[14] the courts sometimes discount these admissions against interest rather than accept them as proof that there was no opening cash hoard.[15]

The deficiencies of the net worth method are mitigated by requiring the government to negate "reasonable explanations by the taxpayer inconsistent with guilt" (such as a claimed cash hoard), by tracking down "relevant leads furnished by the taxpayer—leads reasonably susceptible of being checked, which, if true, would establish the taxpayer's innocence." [16] If not discharged, this obligation entitles the trial court to consider the taxpayer's explanations as true, and it is especially weighty in criminal cases, though it also arises in civil cases.[17]

2. Closing Net Worth. Once a reliable opening net worth is established, increases during the period are usually established by documentary evidence; and the taxpayer's closing net worth is therefore not ordinarily controversial, except for two matters.

First, if there was an opening cash hoard, the taxpayer's claim that it was depleted during the period in order to finance living expenses and investments may be attacked by the IRS, since a stable cash hoard cannot account for these expenditures. Courts sometimes avoid passing on whether a cash hoard existed by ruling that there was insufficient evidence that the same amount was not on hand at the end of the period.[18]

Second, taxpayers sometimes claim that their investments and living expenses during the taxable period were financed with borrowed funds, which should be listed as liabilities at the end of the period. Thus, if the taxpayer in Example 37-1 borrowed $21,000 from a friend, the taxpayer's net worth increase (line 3c) would be only $19,000 ($40,000 less additional liability of $21,000), and the corrected taxable income (line 5d) would be $30,000—exactly the amount reported on the return (line 5e). Claims of this type—especially if the lender is identified only as "Big Joe," who is, alas, de-

---

[14] Holland v. US, supra note 6, at 128.

[15] See, e.g., US v. Calderon, 348 US 160 (1954) (admissions procured on understanding that case would then be closed must be independently corroborated); Smith v. US, 348 US 147 (1954) (corroboration requirement—extensive analysis).

[16] Holland v. US, supra note 6, at 135–136.

[17] See Thomas v. CIR, 232 F.2d 520, 526 (1st Cir. 1956) (evidence of likely source viewed "as an indispensable element of the net worth method in any of its applications rather than as an additional safeguard superimposed upon the net worth method for the sole benefit of defendants in criminal cases"); but see the same case on rehearing, 261 F.2d 643 (1st Cir. 1958) (instead of likely source of taxable income, IRS can prove nonexistence of likely sources of nontaxable income).

[18] See, e.g., Beard v. US, 222 F.2d 84, 89 (4th Cir.), cert. denied, 350 US 846, rehearing denied, 350 US 904 (1955) (nothing to show change in amount of cash on hand).

ceased—are the mirror image of cash hoards. The IRS typically seeks to discredit the existence of the alleged loans and, as a second line of defense, argues that if any funds *were* borrowed, they were repaid during the same taxable year.[19] If so, the taxpayer's closing net worth is not reduced by the alleged liability.

3. Personal Expenditures. In a modest case, the IRS may posit a minimal standard of living. On the other hand, the taxpayer's cash expenditures may be extrapolated from the standard of living portrayed by known charges on credit cards or from the amount available from cashing salary checks or withdrawing cash from the bank.[20] To avoid an extensive IRS investigation into their personal affairs, taxpayers sometimes stipulate to their living expenses.

4. Likely Taxable Source. Although the IRS cannot be expected to "negate every possible source of nontaxable income, a matter peculiarly within the knowledge of the defendant," it cannot disregard explanations proffered by the taxpayer that are reasonably susceptible of being checked.[21] On the other hand, the Supreme Court has held that, "should all possible sources of nontaxable income be negatived, there would be no necessity for proof of a likely source."[22] As applied, this principle dispenses with proof of a likely source of taxable income if the taxpayer points to specific nontaxable sources and the claims are exploded by the IRS, since it is reasonable to assume that a taxpayer making such claims did not have access to any *other* nontaxable sources.

5. Year-to-Year Allocations. Even if a net worth computation establishes with reasonable accuracy that there was an unexplained net worth increase over a period of years, the aggregate amount must be allocated to the appropriate taxable years. In *Cox v. CIR,* the Tax Court upheld an equal annual allocation of the unreported income as computed over a thirteen-year period on the ground that, in the absence of proof by the taxpayer of a more

---

[19] See, e.g., Mecca v. CIR, ¶68,258 P-H Memo TC (1968) (taxpayer's claim of loans of approximately $34,000 from his wife prior to marriage, from her premarital savings, rejected).

[20] For cases from opposite ends of the spectrum, compare US v. Costello, 221 F.2d 668 (2d Cir. 1955), aff'd, 350 US 359, rehearing denied, 351 US 904 (1956) (gambler's living expenses of $60,000–$90,000 per year determined by circularizing department stores, nightclubs, etc.), with McCarthy v. CIR, ¶57,194 P-H Memo TC (1957) (taxpayer's statement of living expenses scaled down by trial court because he exaggerated to suppress fact he was a cheapskate).

[21] Holland v. US, supra note 6, at 138.

[22] US v. Massei, 355 US 595 (1958).

accurate allocation, this was the best that could be expected of the IRS under the circumstances.[23]

¶37.3 CASH EXPENDITURES METHOD

The IRS may compute the taxpayer's income by the so-called cash expenditures (or application-and-source-of-funds) method, which—summarized briefly—calls for a determination of the taxpayer's nondeductible expenditures for living expenses, investments, and other items; the deduction from this amount of the income reported on the taxpayer's return; and the attribution of any balance to unreported income. This procedure is better viewed as a variant of the net worth method than as a separate method, since increases in the taxpayer's assets and decreases in liabilities during the period represent funds expended, while decreases in assets and increases in liabilities are nontaxable sources of funds. Thus, the net worth and cash expenditures methods are functionally equivalent, differing only in the presentation of data. As a result, suggestions that the cash expenditures method dispenses with the need for an opening net worth or entails a different burden of proof are unreliable generalizations, though they may be warranted because of the special circumstances of a particular case.[24] Conversely, any safeguards necessary to avoid abuse of the net worth method are equally necessary in applying the cash expenditures method.

¶37.4 BANK DEPOSIT METHOD

The bank deposit method has been described as follows by the Court of Appeals for the Fourth Circuit:

> [It] involves the estimation of the gross receipts of a business by ascertaining the bank deposits made during the tax year, together with any other income shown to have been received but not placed in [the] bank. To the total thus shown it is necessary to make numerous deductions and adjustments, such as, for example, eliminating amounts deposited as the proceeds of bank loans . . . From the amount thus found there is deducted all proper business expenses in order to arrive at the adjusted gross income. This, in turn, is subject to deduction for such items as contributions, interest paid, taxes, medical expenses, etc. The result, after allowance for the exemptions for the taxpayer and his dependents, represents the taxable income.[25]

---

[23] Cox v. CIR, 54 TC 1735 (1970).

[24] See US v. Marshall, 557 F.2d 527 (5th Cir. 1977); Mundy v. CIR, ¶55,270 P-H Memo TC (1955); Singleton v. CIR, ¶77,098 P-H Memo TC (1977).

[25] Morrison v. US, 270 F.2d 1, 2–3 (4th Cir. 1959).

Once it is determined by the bank deposit method that the taxpayer's gross receipts exceeded the reported amount, there is a corresponding increase in taxable income, unless the taxpayer incurred business expenses in excess of those claimed on the tax return—and the taxpayer has the burden of proving this offset.[26]

The elements of a bank deposit case, as summarized by the Court of Appeals for the First Circuit, are; "(1) that, during the tax years in question, the taxpayer was engaged in an income producing business or calling; (2) that he made regular deposits of funds into bank accounts; and (3) that an adequate and full investigation of those accounts was conducted in order to distinguish between income and non-income deposits." [27] Use of the bank deposit (or bank deposit and expenditures) method is not confined to taxpayers engaged in ordinary businesses, but is equally appropriate for gamblers, corrupt public officials, and others if they foolishly keep their funds in bank accounts rather than under mattresses.

Viewed superficially, the bank deposit method differs from the net worth method in dispensing with opening and closing net worth computations; but since deposits reflecting the liquidation of assets on hand at the beginning of the taxable year or funds borrowed and not repaid during the period are nontaxable sources that must be eliminated, the methods have much in common. Aside from claims that cash on hand at the beginning of the period was deposited during the period and hence did not constitute current income,[28] the most common defense in bank deposit cases is that the IRS failed to eliminate duplications, such as the deposit of checks that the taxpayer cashed as an accommodation for customers with cash withdrawn from the same account at an earlier time.[29] Another conventional defense is that the deposited funds were not owned by the taxpayer but were held as trustee, agent, or intermediary for other persons.[30]

¶37.5 MISCELLANEOUS METHODS

Gross and taxable income can also be reconstructed indirectly by applying percentage markups and other ratios to amounts that can be proved. For example, if a liquor store has no records of gross receipts but its purchases can be determined from the records of suppliers, industry-wide ratios can be used

---

[26] See Rivera v. CIR, ¶79,343 P-H Memo TC (1979) (on taxpayer's failure to prove additional deductions, fraud can be inferred).

[27] US v. Morse, 491 F.2d 149, 152 (1st Cir. 1974).

[28] See Kirsch v. US, 174 F.2d 595 (8th Cir. 1949) (conviction reversed).

[29] See Sindler's Est. v. CIR, ¶79,229 P-H Memo TC (1979) (reasonable on facts to believe that shortly after robbery at home, elderly physician deposited cash accumulated from reported earnings of prior years).

[30] Steinberg v. US, 162 F.2d 120 (5th Cir.), cert. denied, 332 US 808 (1947).

to estimate gross receipts, as well as to estimate credit losses, inventory pilferage, delivery and advertising expenses, etc.[31] In some circumstances, net income can be estimated directly from the number of units handled by an enterprise, because the dollar or percentage profit per item does not vary with volume.[32]

It is impossible to provide an exhaustive list of these and less conventional methods of reconstructing income, since the process is bounded only by the ingenuity of revenue agents and the persuasive force of the inferences required to generalize from whatever scraps of evidence can be established with reasonable assurance.[33]

SELECTED BIBLIOGRAPHY

Duke, Prosecutions for Attempts to Evade Income Tax: A Discordant View of a Procedural Hybrid, 76 Yale L.J. 1 (1966).

Schmidt, Reconstruction of Income, 18 Tax L. Rev. 23 (1962).

---

[31] For the use of percentage markups and industry-wide ratios, see, e.g., Kurnick v. CIR, 232 F.2d 678 (6th Cir. 1956) (liquor dealer); Seagraves v. CIR, ¶61,007 P-H Memo TC (1961) (rural grocery store).

[32] See, e.g., Roberts v. CIR, 176 F.2d 221 (9th Cir. 1949) (taxi driver's tips estimated at 10 percent of gross receipts); Meneguzzo v. CIR, 43 TC 824 (1965) (restaurant waiter's tips estimated as twice taxpayer's wages).

[33] See, e.g., D & H Bagel Bakery, Inc. v. CIR, ¶55,100 P-H Memo TC (1955) (retail bakery income reconstructed by applying average price per dozen bagels to number manufactured, computed by formula based on amount of flour purchased, with allowance for shrinkage from waste, personal consumption by employees, returns of stale merchandise, etc.); Jackson v. CIR, ¶53,240 P-H Memo TC (1953) (income of used car dealer who sold for cash above invoice price constructed by ascertaining average amount of cash paid by some customers and assuming this amount was received on every sale); see also Glitter Starts to Wear Off the Sex Business Along Hamburg's Boardwalk of Bordellos, New York Times, April 5, 1980, at 5 (German tax inspectors determine income of bordellos by posing as garbagemen and checking number of empty champagne bottles).

CHAPTER 38

The Internal Revenue Service

¶38.1 INTERNAL REVENUE SERVICE—ORGANIZATION, FUNCTIONS, AND PROCEDURE

Sections 7801 and 7802 provide that the "administration and enforcement of [the Internal Revenue Code] shall be performed by or under the supervision of the Secretary of the Treasury" and that "there shall be in the Department of the Treasury a Commissioner of Internal Revenue who . . . shall have such duties and powers as may be prescribed by the Secretary of the Treasury." [1] By referring to the Internal Revenue Service,[2] the Code assumes the agency's existence; but its statutory status stems not from the Code but from an 1862 statute creating the Bureau of Internal Revenue and the Office of the Commissioner of Internal Revenue, to assume duties formerly assigned to the Commissioner of Customs.[3]

---

[1] IRC §§7801(a) (administration and enforcement), 7802(a) (Commissioner of Internal Revenue). Many provisions of the Internal Revenue Code vest authority in the Secretary of the Treasury; for the delegation of authority to the Commissioner in these circumstances, see IRC §§7701(a)(11), 7701(a)(12); Treas. Regs. §301.7701-9. The Commissioner and Chief Counsel are appointed by the President with the advice of the Senate; IRC §§7802(a) (Commissioner), 7801(b)(2) (Chief Counsel).

[2] E.g., IRC §7802(b).

[3] 12 Stat. 432 (1862).

Figure 38-1

IRS Organization Chart

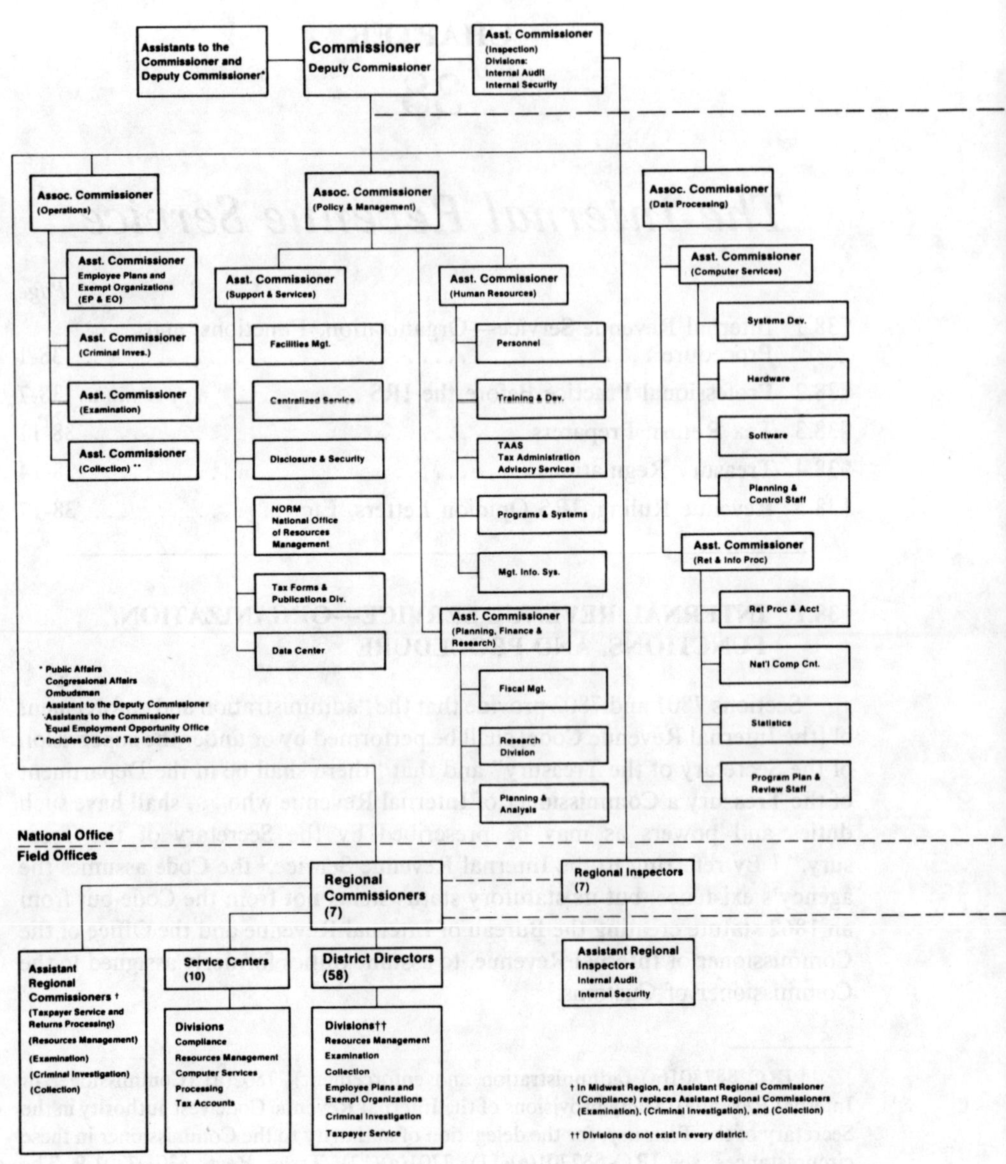

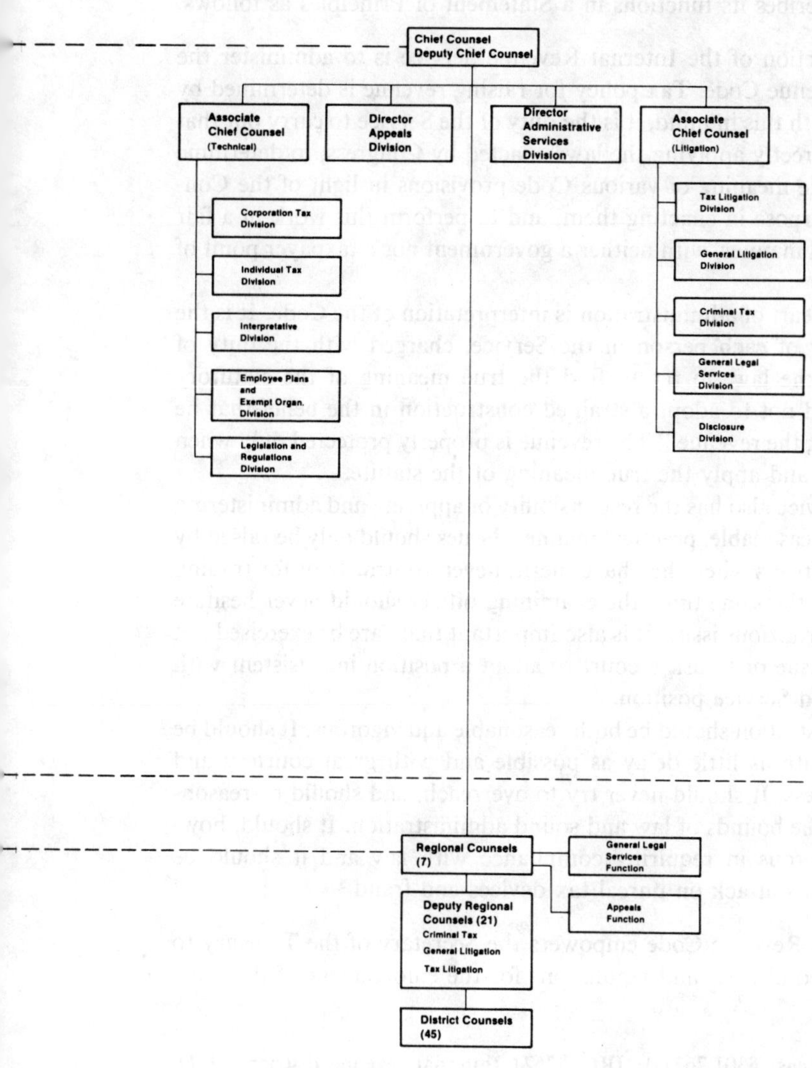
Chief Counsel
Deputy Chief Counsel
Associate Chief Counsel (Technical)
Director Appeals Division
Director Administrative Services Division
Associate Chief Counsel (Litigation)
Corporation Tax Division
Individual Tax Division
Interpretative Division
Employee Plans and Exempt Organ. Division
Legislation and Regulations Division
Tax Litigation Division
General Litigation Division
Criminal Tax Division
General Legal Services Division
Disclosure Division
Regional Counsels (7)
General Legal Services Function
Appeals Function
Deputy Regional Counsels (21)
Criminal Tax
General Litigation
Tax Litigation
District Counsels (45)

The IRS' current organizational framework, shown by Figure 38-1, is incorporated by reference by IRC §7804(a). In addition to this plan of organization, the Code authorizes the President to establish and alter "convenient internal revenue districts" without regard to state lines—authority that has been delegated by the President to the Secretary of the Treasury and by the Secretary to the Commissioner of Internal Revenue.[4]

The IRS describes its functions in a Statement of Principles as follows:

> The function of the Internal Revenue Service is to administer the Internal Revenue Code. Tax policy for raising revenue is determined by Congress. With this in mind, it is the duty of the Service to carry out that policy by correctly applying the laws enacted by Congress; to determine the reasonable meaning of various Code provisions in light of the Congressional purpose in enacting them; and to perform this work in a fair and impartial manner, with neither a government nor a taxpayer point of view.
>
> At the heart of administration is interpretation of the Code. It is the responsibility of each person in the Service, charged with the duty of interpreting the law, to try to find the true meaning of the statutory provision and not to adopt a strained construction in the belief that he is "protecting the revenue." The revenue is properly protected only when we ascertain and apply the true meaning of the statute.
>
> The Service also has the responsibility of applying and administering the law in a reasonable, practical manner. Issues should only be raised by examining officers when they have merit, never arbitrarily or for trading purposes. At the same time, the examining officer should never hesitate to raise a meritorious issue. It is also important that care be exercised not to raise an issue or to ask a court to adopt a position inconsistent with an established Service position.
>
> Administration should be both reasonable and vigorous. It should be conducted with as little delay as possible and with great courtesy and considerateness. It should never try to overreach, and should be reasonable within the bounds of law and sound administration. It should, however, be vigorous in requiring compliance with law and it should be relentless in its attack on unreal tax devices and fraud.[5]

The Internal Revenue Code empowers the Secretary of the Treasury to "prescribe all needful rules and regulations for the enforcement of this title,

---

[4] See Treas. Regs. §301.7621-1; IRC §7621 (internal revenue districts); E.O. 10289, 1951-2 CB 50; E.O. 10574, 1954-2 CB 732; Internal Revenue Manual 1141.1–1141.3.

[5] Rev. Proc. 64-22, 1964-1 CB 689, regularly published in the *Cumulative Bulletin.* See also Statement of Organization and Functions, 1974-1 CB 440.

including all rules and regulations as may be necessary by reason of any alteration of law in relation to internal revenue"; and this authority (which is augmented by provisions authorizing the promulgation of regulations covering a myriad of specialized areas) has been delegated by regulation to the "Commissioner, with the approval of the Secretary." [6] In exercising its rule-making powers, the IRS is subject not only to the Internal Revenue Code but also to the Administrative Procedure Act of 1946 (APA), as well as the more general principles of administrative and constitutional law.[7]

The regulations rank highest in the hierarchy of IRS rules because they can be issued by the Commissioner only with the imprimatur of the Secretary, and they are binding on the IRS as well as on taxpayers provided they are not inconsistent with the Internal Revenue Code. When the validity of a regulation is challenged, the courts distinguish between "legislative" and "interpretative" regulations, subjecting the latter to more critical scrutiny, at least in theory; but in practice this dichotomy is ephemeral, and taxpayers rarely succeed in upsetting regulations of either type.[8] In addition, the IRS issues revenue rulings—defined as "an official interpretation by the Service . . . for the information and guidance of taxpayers, Internal Revenue Service officials, and others concerned" [9]—and their unpublished and less weighty counterparts, described as "rulings," "determination letters," "opinion letters," and "information letters." [10]

Although the IRS' oral and written announcements are often taken as gospel by laymen, they are not binding on taxpayers; nor, as taxpayers often learn to their chagrin, do they bind the IRS. Except in rare circumstances, these informal sources of information are merely expressions of opinion, which do not waive any of the government's rights or estop the IRS from collecting a tax that is rightfully due, even if the taxpayer had no reason to question the advice and accepted it in good faith. In most situations of this type, the taxpayer is simply taxed on a transaction already frozen when the erroneous advice was received, so that the result is disappointment rather than a lost opportunity; but the same principle applies even if the taxpayer changed his position in reliance on the advice. Moreover, taxpayers sustaining losses cannot hold the IRS or its employees responsible for the consequences of their mistakes.[11]

---

[6] IRC §7805(a); Treas. Regs. §301.7805-1(a).

[7] For the Administrative Procedure Act's constraints, see infra ¶38.4.

[8] Infra ¶38.4.

[9] Statement of Procedural Rules, 26 CFR §601.601(d)(2)(i)(a). See also infra ¶38.5.

[10] Infra ¶38.5.

[11] See, e.g., Green v. CIR, 59 TC 456, 458 (1972) (sources of authoritative law are statute and regulations, not such informal IRS publications as *Your Federal Income Tax*); Wilkerson v. US, 304 F.2d 469 (Ct. Cl. 1962) (revenue agent's advice re future

Erroneous IRS advice, however, can protect taxpayers under statutes exempting delinquencies attributable to reasonable cause, and reliance on the advice is obviously relevant in applying provisions that turn on the taxpayer's intent or motive. In these situations the taxpayer is not seeking to hold the IRS to the erroneous position as a matter of substantive law, but only to establish that his conduct was not blameworthy, even though it failed to satisfy a statutory requirement.

Taxpayers seeking to escape a tax to which they have no substantive defense sometimes point to the IRS' mistaken failure to impose the tax on *other* similarly situated taxpayers. If racial, political, or similar constitutional overtones are absent and the taxpayer is simply the random victim of an unusually thorough audit, the claim that others got away scot-free usually gets nowhere. A few decisions, however, support the proposition that "the Commissioner cannot tax one and not another without a rational basis for the difference." [12] In time, these cases may turn out to be the thin edge of a powerful equal-protection wedge; but so far, they do not seriously undermine the government's theory that "taxpayers can never avoid liability for a proper tax by showing that others have been treated generously, leniently, or erroneously by the Internal Revenue Service." [13]

The IRS is required by the Administrative Procedure Act of 1946 to publish a Statement of Procedural Rules in the *Federal Register;*[14] and it also publishes many less august revenue procedures. In addition, the *Internal Revenue Manual,* prescribing internal IRS practices and procedures, is available to the public under the Freedom of Information Act.[15]

Most of these procedural rules are "directory" instructions to IRS employees designed to promote efficient administration; and this means that taxpayers derive no legal rights from an IRS employee's breach of instructions and cannot compel compliance. If, however, a particular rule is intended to confer procedural rights on taxpayers (a "mandatory" rule) or if the failure

---

transaction not binding even if the taxpayer changed position in reliance), and cases there cited. IRS employees are not liable for mistakes; see 28 USC §§1346(b) (sovereign immunity waived for injury or loss of property caused by negligent acts and omissions by government employee while acting within the scope of employment, under circumstances where United States, if a private person, would be liable), 2680(b) (no liability for any claim "arising in respect of the assessment or collection of any tax").

[12] US v. Kaiser, 363 US 299, 308 (1960) (Frankfurter, J., concurring); see also IBM Corp. v. US, 343 F.2d 914 (Ct. Cl. 1965), cert. denied, 382 US 1028 (1966); Vesco v. CIR, ¶79,369 P-H Memo TC (1979).

[13] IBM Corp. v. US, supra note 12, at 919. For cases rejecting "why only me?" as a defense, see Bookwalter v. Brecklein, 357 F.2d 78 (8th Cir. 1966), and cases there cited.

[14] Administrative Procedure Act of 1946 (APA), 5 USC §552(a)(1)(C).

[15] Hawkes v. CIR, 467 F.2d 787 (6th Cir. 1972) (APA applicable to IRM); Hawkes v. CIR, 507 F.2d 481 (6th Cir. 1974) (specifying portions to be disclosed).

to comply is arbitrary, the courts sometimes undertake to compel IRS compliance.[16]

The IRS' failure to follow its own procedural rules is usually raised by taxpayers; but occasionally the shoe is on the other foot, and the IRS seeks to repudiate action by an employee in violation of instructions. Although the government is ordinarily not bound when employees act outside the scope of their authority, it may be estopped by action that violates internal procedures, at least if the taxpayer has no reason to believe that the action is irregular.[17]

¶38.2 PROFESSIONAL PRACTICE BEFORE THE IRS

1. Introductory. The basic rules governing practice before the Internal Revenue Service are prescribed by Treasury Department Circular No. 230 and by the IRS' Statement of Procedural Rules.[18] "Practice" is defined as follows by Circular No. 230:

> "Practice before the Internal Revenue Service" comprehends all matters connected with presentation to the Internal Revenue Service or any of its officers or employees relating to a client's rights, privileges, or liabilities under laws or regulations administered by the Internal Revenue Service. Such presentations include the preparation and filing of necessary documents, correspondence with and communications to the Internal Revenue Service, and the representation of a client at conferences, hearings, and meetings. Neither the preparation of a tax return, nor the appearance of an individual as a witness for the taxpayer, nor the furnishing of information at the request of the Internal Revenue Service . . . is considered practice before the Service.[19]

---

[16] See, e.g., Trapp v. Baptist, 43 AFTR2d 956 (N.D. Ala. 1978) (not officially reported) (IRS ordered to provide conference and disclosure, as contemplated by IRS procedural rules); but see Rosenberg v. CIR, 450 F.2d 529 (10th Cir. 1971) (breach innocuous); Luhring v. Glotzbach, 304 F.2d 560 (4th Cir. 1962) (failure to issue thirty-day letter and advise taxpayer of right to file protest does not invalidate later deficiency notice or assessment of tax).

[17] See, e.g., Johnson v. CIR, 68 TC 637 (1977).

[18] For Circular No. 230, see 31 CFR Pt. 10; for the Statement of Procedural Rules, see 26 CFR Pt. 601. For the statutory foundation for these rules, see 31 USC §1026 (Treasury may prescribe rules governing recognition of agents, attorneys, and other persons representing claimants before the Department).

[19] Circular No. 230, supra note 18, §10.2(a); but see id. §10.22(a) (practitioner must use due diligence in preparing returns; query whether this is intended as a principle of general applicability or is concerned only with amended and delinquent returns supplied when practicing before the IRS within the meaning of Section 10.2(a)).

The Statement of Procedural Rules similarly defines practice.[20] Persons preparing tax returns or claims for refund for compensation ("tax return preparers") are subject to detailed regulations enacted in 1976, even though they are not engaged in "practice." [21]

2. Persons Qualified to Practice. Any attorney may represent other persons before any federal agency upon filing a written declaration of his or her current qualifications and authority to represent the party; and a similar provision is applicable to persons qualified to practice as certified public accountants.[22] These rules neither add to nor derogate from the agency's power to discipline or disbar persons appearing in a representative capacity, nor do they prevent the agency from requiring a power of attorney as a condition to the settlement of any controversy involving the payment of money.[23]

Persons who do not meet the attorney or CPA requirements for automatic admission can qualify to practice before the IRS as "enrolled agents" on demonstrating "special competence in tax matters" by written examination.[24] In addition, Circular No. 230 authorizes enrollment without examination, or appearance without enrollment, in a limited number of cases.[25]

A phenomenal increase in the use of tax preparers led the IRS in 1968 to authorize enrolled persons who sign returns as preparers to act as the taxpayer's representative at the audit level if accompanied by the taxpayer or on filing a written authorization from the taxpayer, subject to restrictions recognizing that preparers are not required to be attorneys or certified public accountants or to pass the special enrollment examination.[26]

3. Power of Attorney or Tax Information Authorization. The IRS conference and practice rules require persons appearing in a representative capacity to furnish evidence of their "recognition to practice" in the case of attorneys, certified public accountants, and enrolled agents (or satisfactory identification in the case of other persons) and, in addition, to file a power of attorney or tax information authorization in certain circumstances. A power

---

[20] Statement of Procedural Rules, supra note 9, §601.501(a).

[21] Rev. Proc. 68-29, 1968-2 CB 913 (preparer of tax return may appear as a witness to assist in factual development of case).

[22] P.L. No. 89-332, 79 Stat. 1281 (1965); see also S. Rep. No. 755, 89th Cong., 1st Sess. (1965), reprinted in 1965-2 CB 855.

[23] 5 USC §§500(d)(2), 500(d)(4), 1(c); see also 5 USC §500(f) (any notice shall be given to the representative, in addition to any other service specifically required by statute); Statement of Procedural Rules, supra note 9, §601.506(a) (failure to send notice or other communication to taxpayer's representative will not affect its validity).

[24] Circular No. 230, supra note 18, §10.4(a); see also IRS Pub. No. 486, Enrollment and Special Enrollment Examination; IRM 4052-4053.

[25] Circular No. 230, supra note 18, §10.5(c).

[26] Rev. Proc. 68-20, 1968-1 CB 812, modified and superseded by Rev. Proc. 81-38, 1981-2 CB 592.

of attorney is required to perform any of the following acts on behalf of the client: (a) receive a check in payment of a refund, (b) execute a waiver of restrictions on assessment or collection of a deficiency or a waiver of notice of disallowance of a claim for credit or refund, (c) execute a consent to extend the statutory period for assessment or collection of a tax, (d) execute a closing agreement under IRC §7121, or (e) delegate authority or substitute another representative.[27] Form 2848 is commonly used for powers of attorney, but unofficial forms are also satisfactory if they specify the acts that the representative is authorized to perform.

A tax information authorization permits the representative to inspect the taxpayer's return at a conference, receive information disclosing the position of the IRS with respect to the taxpayer's liability, discuss the merits of a request for a ruling or determination letter, and receive thirty-day and ninety-day letters;[28] as a result in many cases it is a satisfactory substitute for a power of attorney.

4. Standards of Professional Conduct, Disciplinary Proceedings, and Disbarment. Circular No. 230 imposes a variety of obligations on persons authorized to practice, including a duty (1) to submit records or information promptly upon proper request by the IRS and to refrain from interfering with IRS efforts to obtain records or information, unless the representative "believes in good faith and on reasonable grounds" that the information is privileged or that the IRS action is of "doubtful legality";[29] (2) upon learning that a client has not complied with the tax laws or has made an error in or omission from any return or other document that the client is required to execute, to advise the client promptly of the noncompliance, error, or omission;[30] (3) to exercise due diligence in preparing papers relating to IRS matters and in determining the accuracy of his oral or written representations to the Treasury or to clients with respect to IRS matters;[31] and (4) not to charge "unconscionable" fees.[32] The rules forbid the representation of conflicting interests and the solicitation of business, and restrict practice by former government employees and their partners and associates.[33]

The record-submission and compliance-advice duties draw the practitioner into the enforcement process in a way that is, if not unique, at least unusual for agencies in the executive branch of government; and since the IRS is not a judicial tribunal but a law-enforcement agency, lawyers are bound to

[27] Statement of Procedural Rules, supra note 9, §§601.502(b)(1) (recognition to practice), 601.502(c)(1) (power of attorney), 601.504(a) (delegation and substitution).

[28] Id. §601.502(c)(2).

[29] Circular No. 230, supra note 18, §10.20(a).

[30] Id. §10.21.

[31] Id. §10.22.

[32] Id. §10.28.

[33] Id. §§10.25, 10.26; see also id. §10.3(e).

be restive about certain aspects of these rules that may seem inconsistent with their normal professional role as advocates for clients. The American Bar Association's Committee on Professional Ethics, addressing the lawyer's obligations when practicing before the IRS has expressed these views:

> Negotiation and settlement procedures of the tax system do not carry with them the guarantee that a correct tax result necessarily occurs. . . . [C]ounsel will always urge in aid of settlement of a controversy the strong points of his case and minimize the weak; . . . Nor does the absolute duty not to make false assertions of fact require . . . disclosure of [the client's] confidences, unless the facts in the attorney's possession indicate beyond reasonable doubt that a crime will be committed. A wrong, or indeed sometimes an unjust, tax result in the settlement of a controversy is not a crime.
>
> Similarly, a lawyer who is asked to advise his client in the course of the preparation of the client's tax returns may freely urge the statement of positions most favorable to the client just as long as there is reasonable basis for those positions. . . . [T]he lawyer has no duty to advise that riders be attached to the client's tax return explaining the circumstances.
>
> The foregoing principle necessarily relates to the lawyer's ethical obligations—what he is *required* to do. Prudence may recommend procedures not required by ethical considerations. Thus, . . . the lawyer . . . *may,* as a tactical matter, advise his client to disclose the transaction in reasonable detail by way of a rider to the return. This occurs when it is to the client's advantage to be free from either a *claim* of fraud (albeit unfounded) or to have the protection of a shorter statute of limitations . . .
>
> [T]he lawyer is under a duty not to mislead the Internal Revenue Service deliberately and affirmatively, either by misstatements or by silence or by permitting his client to mislead. . . . [If] the client has in fact misled but without the lawyer's knowledge or participation, . . . the lawyer must advise the client to correct the statement; if the client refuses, the lawyer's obligation depends on all the circumstances.
>
> If for example, under all the circumstances, the lawyer believes that the Service relies on him as corroborating statements of his client which he knows to be false, then he is under a duty to disassociate himself from any such reliance unless it is obvious that the very act of disassociation would have the effect of violating Canon 37. Even then, however, if a direct question is put to the lawyer, he must at least advise the Service that he is not in a position to answer.[34]

---

[34] ABA Committee on Professional Ethics, Opinion 314, 51 A.B.A.J. 671 (1965); see also Committee on Standards of Tax Practice, American Bar Association, Tax Section, Guidelines to Tax Practice, 31 Tax Lawyer 551 (1978).

For opinions on the tax practice responsibilities of certified public accountants, reflecting the absence of an advocate's perspective and reaching somewhat different

Upon engaging in "disreputable conduct," a representative is subject to disciplinary proceedings by the Treasury Department's Director of Practice.[35] Disciplinary proceedings are also authorized if the practitioner is shown to be inconsistent, refuses to comply with the rules governing practice, or deceives a claimant orally or in writing with intent to defraud. The procedures to be followed in the proceedings, which can terminate in suspension or disbarment, are prescribed in great detail by Circular No. 230.[36]

¶38.3 TAX RETURN PREPARERS

1. Introductory. Responding in 1976 to problems created by rapid growth in the tax preparer industry, which was then subject to only sketchy regulation, Congress enacted an elaborate web of disclosure and penalty rules to bring the major abuses under control.[37] The 1976 legislation does not require income tax return preparers to meet any educational, experience, or other standards. Regardless of personal or vocational background, anyone can set up shop as a tax return preparer, subject to three sets of regulatory rules: (1) disclosure rules, requiring preparers to sign all returns prepared by them and to retain either copies of the returns or a list of the taxpayers; (2) penalties for negligent or intentional disregard of rules and regulations, for willful understatement of a client's tax liability, and for certain other infractions of law; and (3) authority in the IRS to apply for a federal court injunction forbidding the preparer to engage in particular types of misconduct or to continue to practice.

2. Scope of Term "Income Tax Return Preparer." The crucial term "income tax return preparer" is defined by IRC §7701(a)(36) as any person who prepares for compensation [38] an income tax return or claim for refund or who employs one or more persons for this purpose, excluding persons (a) furnishing typing, reproducing, or other mechanical assistance; (b) preparing returns or claims for refund for the employer (or officers or employees of the

---

conclusions from the ABA statement quoted in the text, see AICPA, Statements on Responsibilities in Tax Practice §§141 (recognition of administrative proceedings in prior years), 151 (use of estimates), 161 (knowledge of errors on returns), 171 (knowledge of errors—administrative proceedings), 181 (advice to clients) (CCH 1976).

[35] Circular No. 230, supra note 18, §§10.50–10.54. In flagrant cases, misconduct may warrant criminal prosecution. See infra ¶42.4 (substantive and conspiracy prosecutions of aiders and abettors, advisers, etc.). For standards of conduct the IRS expects of tax attorneys participating in the promotion of tax shelters, see the proposed amendments to Circular 230, 45 Fed. Reg. 58,594 (1980). For the standards adopted by the American Bar Association, see Revised Ethics Rule 346, 68 A.B.A.J. 471 (1982).

[36] Circular No. 230, supra note 18, §§10.54–10.75.

[37] For an explanation of the need for this legislation, see Joint Comm. on Taxation, 94th Cong., 2d Sess., General Explanation of the Tax Reform Act of 1976, reprinted in 1976-3 CB (Vol. 2) 346-347.

[38] For what constitutes compensation, see Treas. Regs. §301.7701-15(a)(4).

employer) by whom they are regularly and continuously employed; (c) preparing returns or claims for refund for trusts or estates of which they are fiduciaries; or (d) preparing claims for refund in connection with notices of deficiency or waivers of restrictions after commencement of an audit. To prevent obvious evasion, the regulations provide that persons furnishing sufficient information and advice to taxpayers or tax preparers so that "completion of the return or claim for refund is largely a mechanical or clerical matter" are preparers, even though they have no physical contact with the return.[39] Section 7216, enacted in 1971, makes it a criminal offense for any person engaged in the business of preparing returns (or providing services in connection with the preparation of returns) to disclose any taxpayer information or use the information for any purpose other than preparing returns.[40]

The regulations provide that persons are preparers within the meaning of IRC §7701(a)(36) only if they prepare all "or a substantial portion of a return or claim for refund." [41] If the portion of the return or claim involves gross income, deductions, or amounts on the basis of which credits are determined that are either (a) less than $2,000 or (b) less than $100,000 and also less than 20 percent of the gross income (or adjusted gross income if the taxpayer is an individual) as shown on the return or claim, the contribution made by the preparer is not considered substantial.[42] Advice on specific issues of law does not constitute the preparation of a return or claim for refund unless the advice concerns past events, is directly relevant in determining an entry on a return or claim, and the entry meets the "substantiality" standard described above.[43]

Finally, a person preparing one return may be considered to be a preparer of another return if an entry on the first return is directly reflected on, and constitutes a substantial portion of, the second. The preparer of a partnership or Subchapter S corporate return, for example, may be considered as the preparer of the return of an individual partner or shareholder if the substantiality standard is met.[44]

3. Obligations and Penalties. Income tax return preparers are subject to penalties for failure to sign returns prepared by them, with their identifying numbers and places of business.[45] In addition, the preparer must (1) furnish

---

[39] Treas. Regs. §301.7701-15(a)(1).

[40] Treas. Regs. §1.7216-1(b)(2); see Rev. Rul. 79-114, 1979-1 CB 441 (consent of clients required by IRC §7216 to use tax information to solicit loans, prepare statistical data, etc.).

[41] Treas. Regs. §301.7701-15(b)(2).

[42] Id.

[43] Treas. Regs. §§301.7701-15(a)(2), 301.7701-15(b).

[44] Treas. Regs. §301.7701-15(b)(3).

[45] IRC §§6695(b), 6695(c). The obligation to sign returns prepared for compensa-

the taxpayer with a completed copy of the return or claim for refund at or before the time it is presented for signature;[46] retain for three years completed copies of all returns and claims or a list of the taxpayers for whom they were prepared, and make them available for inspection by the IRS on request;[47] and (3) file an annual report with the IRS reporting the names, identification numbers, and places of work of all preparers employed during the applicable period or retain records of this information for three years.[48]

Civil penalties are imposed on preparers who are responsible for, or aid and abet, an understatement of a client's tax liability. First, if any part of the understatement is due to the preparer's negligent or intentional disregard of rules and regulations, a penalty of $100 is imposed by IRC §6694(a). The term "rules and regulations" includes published revenue rulings, but if a preparer "in good faith and with reasonable basis" takes the position that a rule or regulation does not accurately reflect the Code, the action does not constitute negligent or intentional disregard of the rule or regulation.[49] Second, a penalty of $500 per return is imposed by IRC §6694(b) if any part of the understatement "is due to a [preparer's] willful attempt in any manner to understate the liability for a tax." Third, IRC §6701, enacted in 1982, imposes a penalty of $1,000 for each return or other document ($10,000 in the case of a corporate return or document) on any person aiding in its preparation knowing that it will be used in connection with a material matter arising under the tax laws and will result, if used, in an understatement of another person's tax liability. The penalty can be imposed on anyone; but if imposed on an income tax return preparer, it displaces any otherwise applicable penalty under IRC §6694 with respect to the same document.

The regulations provide that in preparing returns preparers "may in good faith rely without verification upon information furnished by the taxpayer" and that they are not required "to examine or review documents or other evidence in order to verify independently the taxpayer's information." [50] Draining these remarks of their comforting assurance, however, the regula-

---

tion under the penalties of perjury arises under a long-standing regulation, but an explicit penalty for failure to sign was enacted in 1976; see Treas. Regs. §1.6065-1(b) (duty to sign); IRC §6695(b) ($25 penalty); see also IRC §6695(c) ($25 penalty for failure to provide identifying number); Treas. Regs. §1.6109-2 (identifying numbers of both preparer and employer must be given). The penalties under IRC §§6695(b) and 6695(c) are not imposed if the failure is due to reasonable cause and not willful neglect.

[46] IRC §§6107(a) (furnishing copy to taxpayer), 6695(a) ($25 penalty unless failure is due to reasonable cause and not willful neglect).

[47] IRC §§6107(b), 6695(d) (failure to retain copies of returns or list of taxpayers—$50 penalty for each failure unless due to reasonable cause and not willful neglect, up to a maximum of $25,000 for each return period).

[48] IRC §§6060(a), 6695(e).

[49] Treas. Regs. §1.6694-1(a)(4) (same test to be applied as under IRC §6653).

[50] Treas. Regs. §1.6694-1(b)(2)(ii).

tions go on to state that a preparer "may not ignore the implications of information furnished" and, in areas where documentation is specially required (e.g., IRC §274, relating to travel and entertainment expenses), "shall make appropriate inquiries of the taxpayer to determine the existence of facts and circumstances required by a code section or regulations incident to claiming a deduction." [51]

¶38.4 TREASURY REGULATIONS

1. Introductory. Section 7805(a) provides that the Secretary of the Treasury "shall prescribe all needful rules and regulations for the enforcement of [the Internal Revenue Code], including all rules and regulations as may be necessary by reason of any alteration of law in relation to internal revenue," and IRC §7805(b) provides that the Secretary may prescribe "the extent, if any, to which any ruling or regulation . . . shall be applied without retroactive effect." These powers have been delegated by the Secretary to "the Commissioner [of Internal Revenue], with the approval of the Secretary," [52] so that formal authority is divided between the Commissioner and the Secretary. The Code authorizes the issuance of regulations—ordinarily by the Secretary, who in turn almost invariably delegates the statutory power to the Commissioner—covering many specialized subjects.[53]

The Administrative Procedure Act of 1946 requires all government agencies to give notice of "proposed rule making" in the *Federal Register* and to provide an opportunity for "interested persons" to participate in the rulemaking process.[54] These requirements do not apply, however, to "interpretative rules, general statements of policy, or rules of agency organization, procedure, or practice" or if the agency "for good cause finds . . . that notice and public procedure thereon are impracticable, unnecessary, or contrary to the

---

[51] Id.

[52] Treas. Regs. §§301.7805-1(a), 301.7805-1(b); for retroactivity, see infra text appearing at and following note 67. See also the general governmental "housekeeping" provision of 5 USC §301, authorizing the head of every executive department to "prescribe regulations for the government of his department, the conduct of its employees, the distribution and performance of its business, and the custody, use, and preservation of its records, papers, and property."

[53] See Davenport v. CIR, 70 TC 922, 927 (1978) (describing IRC §1244(e) as "an extraordinary provision specifically delegating to the Secretary the authority to 'prescribe such regulations as may be necessary to carry out the purposes of [IRC §1244],' " which implies that they deserve even greater deference than is ordinarily accorded to regulations).

[54] Administrative Procedure Act of 1946, 5 USC §§553(b), 553(c), 553(e); Statement of Procedural Rules, supra note 9, §601.601(c).

public interest." [55] Despite this exemption, the Treasury ordinarily follows a notice-and-hearing procedure (including an opportunity for oral argument, which is discretionary under the Administrative Procedure Act), even for regulations of an interpretative character.[56] The "impracticable" exception is used most commonly by the IRS to dispense with notice and hearing when issuing "temporary" regulations under new legislation, on the theory that taxpayers and revenue agents require immediate guidance.[57]

2. Legal Effect of Regulations. In verbalizing the legal effect of regulations, conventional legal analysis distinguishes between "legislative" and "interpretative" regulations. Legislative regulations (e.g., regulations issued under IRC §1502, authorizing the Secretary to "prescribe such regulations as he may deem necessary" to determine the consolidated income of affiliated groups of corporations) are often said to have the force of law, because they entail an exercise of power delegated by Congress to the agency, as though it were a deputy legislature.[58] By contrast, interpretative regulations purport only to interpret, explain, and apply the rules prescribed by Congress, rather than to fill gaps deliberately left open by Congress; and this limited function seems to leave more room for judicial review to determine whether the agency's interpretation is a distortion of the legislation.[59] Even so, interpretative regulations are entitled to great weight, particularly if issued contemporaneously with the legislation;[60] and they can gain additional force if Congress

---

[55] Administrative Procedure Act of 1946, 5 USC §§553(b)(A), 553(b)(B).

[56] For the exemption of IRS "interpretative rules" from the requirements of the APA with respect to proposed rulemaking, thus avoiding the need for an "initial regulatory flexibility analysis" under the Regulatory Flexibility Act of 1980 (the "Paperwork Reduction Act"), P.L. No. 96-354, 94 Stat. 1164, 5 USC §§601-612, see, e.g., LR 50-81, 1981-16 IRB 28. For an example of an initial regulatory flexibility analysis, see the proposed regulations under the Installment Sales Revision Act, LR 73-80, 1981-10 IRB 45. For Treasury and IRS practice, see generally Schmidt, The Tax Regulations Making Process—Then and Now, 24 Tax Lawyer 541, 542-546 (1971).

[57] See, e.g., Temp. Reg. §§7.465 (relating to at-risk provisions of the Tax Reform Act of 1976), 7.48 (investment credit for movie films). Since temporary regulations are often interpretative, they could also be excluded from the APA application on that ground.

[58] See, e.g., Allstate Ins. Co. v. US, 329 F.2d 346, 349 (7th Cir. 1964) (legislative regulations have "force and effect of law, so long as they were reasonably adapted . . . to the administrative and enforcement of the act and did not contravene some statutory provision").

[59] Koshland v. Helvering, 298 US 441 (1936). For a recent citation of *Koshland,* see Caterpillar Tractor Co. v. US, 589 F.2d 1040, 1045 (Ct. Cl. 1978) ("no room for Treasury interpretation" of statute that is unambiguous on its face; sole purpose of interpretative regulations is to "reconcile ambiguities in the statute with reasoned interpretation").

[60] CIR v. South Tex. Lumber Co., 333 US 496 (1948).

subsequently reenacts the applicable statutory provision without change, amends other portions of the provision, or leaves the provision intact in circumstances suggesting knowledge of the interpretation, since action of this type is sometimes viewed as an acceptance or endorsement of the agency's interpretation.[61]

In practice, the distinction between legislative and interpretative regulations is often blurred,[62] and the supposedly diverse standards of judicial review tend to converge and even to coalesce.[63] On the one hand, legislative regulations must conform to the legislative intent to the extent that it can be discerned.[64] On the other hand, interpretative regulations "must be sustained unless unreasonable and plainly inconsistent with the revenue statutes."[65]

When all is said and done, for practical purposes there is only a single standard of judicial review, which requires *all* regulations to be reasonable relative to whatever criteria or guideposts were enacted by Congress. If the legislative standards are vague or general, the judicial oversight must perforce be limited; in this situation, regulations have the force of law not because they are "legislative" but because it is difficult or impossible to show that they are inconsistent with the only available legislative criteria.[66] But if Congress left more ample clues to its objectives, the regulations must be consistent with them; and they are subject to stricter judicial review not because they are "interpretative" but because Congress supplied more detailed standards, to which the agency was expected to conform.

---

[61] See Helvering v. Winmill, 305 US 79, 83 (1938) ("Treasury regulations and interpretations, long continued without substantial change, applying to unamended or substantially reenacted statutes, were deemed to have received congressional approval and have the effect of law"); see also US v. Correll, 389 US 299, 305-306 (1967); Cammarano v. US, 358 US 498, 511 (1959); but see CIR v. Glenshaw Glass Co., 348 US 426, 431 (1955) (reenactment without evidence that Congress was aware of a decision of Board of Tax Appeals is "unreliable indicium" of legislative endorsement).

[62] See US v. Cartwright, 411 US 546 (1973), invalidating as "unrealistic and unreasonable" a regulation that might have been viewed either as "interpretative" (construing the meaning of "value" as used in IRC §2031) or as "legislative" (prescribing a method of determining the value of mutual fund shares). In seeming confirmation of this ambiguity, neither the Supreme Court nor the two lower courts ascribed a definitive label to the regulation.

[63] See Anderson, Clayton & Co. v. US, 562 F.2d 972, 985 n.30 (5th Cir. 1977), cert. denied, 436 US 944 (1978).

[64] Manhattan Gen. Equip. Co. v. CIR, 297 US 129, 134 (1936); Service Life Ins. Co. v. US, 293 F.2d 72, 77 (8th Cir. 1961) ("elementary that . . . Treasury Regulations are without force if they are in conflict with the statute").

[65] CIR v. South Tex. Lumber Co., supra note 60, at 501.

[66] This assumes, of course, that the statutory standards are not so vague that the statute is an unconstitutional delegation of legislative power; the issue examined in the text is the validity of regulations issued under a *valid* statute.

3. Amended and Retroactive Regulations. Section 7805(b) authorizes the Treasury to prescribe "the extent, if any, to which any ruling or regulation, relating to the internal revenue laws, shall be applied without retroactive effect." [67] Unless this power to negate retroactive application is exercised, a regulation should ordinarily be construed to apply to past as well as future years, at least if it purports to do no more than interpret the statute.[68] But retroactive application can be negated by the context or the character of the regulation; indeed, the application of a new and unexpected rule to past years might be arbitrary or even unconstitutional if it departs too far from the reasonable expectation of taxpayers.

If the regulation not only is new but also reverses a prior regulation or settled administrative practice, retroactive application may be said to violate the reenactment principle.[69] If the original statute is susceptible of several interpretations, however, why does reenactment of the statute imply anything more than that the Treasury selected a permissible—as distinguished from *the sole* permissible—interpretation and why is a change in a regulation more offensive than a reversal of a line of earlier cases? Whatever might be the answer at the level of theory, the cases have in effect converted the reenactment doctrine as applied in this context into a more limited principle, akin to due process, under which retroactive application of an amended regulation is permissible unless it upsets reasonable expectations or is otherwise arbitrary and harsh.[70]

¶38.5 REVENUE RULING, IRS OPINION LETTERS, ETC.

1. Introductory. Pursuant to its practice of answering inquiries from individuals and organizations "whenever appropriate in the interest of sound tax administration, as to their status for tax purposes and as to the tax effects of their acts or transactions," [71] as well as to advise the public and its own staff,

---

[67] For the history of IRC §7805(b), see Helvering v. Griffiths, 318 US 371, 398 n.49 (1943) (purpose to permit Treasury to negate retroactive application of regulations, not to increase its power to make retroactive rulings).

[68] For the "declaratory" theory of interpretative regulations, now rather outmoded, see Anderson, Clayton & Co. v. US, supra note 63, at 985 n.30 (interpretative regulation "in theory merely elucidates a meaning that has resided in the statute since its enactment" and is no more "retroactive" than a judicial construction to the same effect). Changes in laws also ordinarily apply both retroactively and prospectively; see US v. Donnelley's Est., 397 US 286 (1970).

[69] See Helvering v. R.J. Reynolds Tobacco Co., 306 US 110 (1939).

[70] See Automobile Club of Mich. v. CIR, 353 US 180 (1957) (involving revocation of a ruling rather than an amended regulation, but treating issues interchangeably).

[71] Rev. Proc. 79-45, §4.01, 1979-2 CB 508.

the IRS issues numerous rulings and similar documents. These administrative rulings rest on the same statutory foundation as regulations;[72] but since they emanate from the IRS without formal approval by the Secretary of the Treasury, they are more readily issued, amended and withdrawn than regulations and do not evoke the same judicial deference when challenged by taxpayers.[73]

The principal current categories of IRS rulings, opinion letters, and similar documents are:

1. *Ruling.* "A written statement issued to a taxpayer or his authorized representative by the National Office that interprets and applies the tax laws to the taxpayer's specific set of facts."[74]

2. *Revenue ruling.* "An interpretation by the Service that has been published in the Internal Revenue Bulletin . . . for the information and guidance of taxpayers, Internal Revenue Service officials, and others concerned."[75] Revenue rulings are usually "rulings" that have been selected for publication; to distinguish the two, unpublished rulings are usually called "taxpayer letter rulings."

3. *Revenue procedure.* A statement of procedure affecting the rights or duties of taxpayers or other members of the public under the Code and related statutes, or information "that should be a matter of public knowledge" even though it does not affect anyone's rights and duties.[76]

4. *Determination letter.* A written statement by a district director in response to an inquiry by a taxpayer, applying "principles and precedents previously announced by the National Office to a specific set of facts," used particularly to rule on the qualification of pension, profit-sharing, and stock bonus plans and of exempt organizations.[77]

5. *Opinion letter.* A statement by the National Office regarding the acceptability of master plans under IRC §§401 and 501(a), relating to pension, profit-sharing, and stock bonus plans and to exempt organizations.[78]

6. *Information letter.* A statement by the National Office or a district director calling attention "to a well-established interpretation or principle of tax law, without applying it to a specific set of facts," when it appears that

---

[72] See supra ¶38.4.

[73] For publication of revenue rulings pursuant to the Administrative Procedure Act of 1946, see Rev. Proc. 72-1, §6.02, 1972-1 CB 693; see also id. §6.01(6) (comments and suggestions re proposed revenue rulings may be solicited "if justified by special circumstances").

[74] Rev. Proc. 79-45, supra note 71, §4.04.

[75] Id. §4.07.

[76] Rev. Proc. 78-24, 1978-2 CB 503, §3.02.

[77] Rev. Proc. 79-45, supra note 71, §4.05.

[78] Rev. Proc. 72-8, 1972-1 CB 716.

general information rather than a particularized application of the rules will be helpful.[79]

7. *Technical advice.* "Advice or guidance as to the interpretation and proper application of internal revenue laws, related statutes, and regulations, furnished by the National Office upon request of a district office in connection with the examination of a taxpayer's return or consideration of a taxpayer's claim for refund or credit." [80]

In addition to these rulings and other announcements, the IRS issues several series of more specialized rulings,[81] as well as a constant stream of press releases, pamphlets, and other documents.

2. Taxpayer Letter Rulings. The National Office issues rulings to taxpayers on the effect of prospective transactions and on completed transactions before the return is filed, but ordinarily not if the identical issue is present in a prior return of the taxpayer and is under examination in a district office or the Appeals Office.[82] Rulings may be sought voluntarily by taxpayers as guides to action or to the preparation of returns and to protect themselves against an adverse change in IRS policies or interpretations of law, but often they are requested because a statutory provision requires the taxpayer to obtain the consent or approval of the IRS as a condition to a tax allowance or change in the treatment of an item.[83]

1. *Procedure.* Rev. Proc. 79-45 prescribes in a general way the facts, documents, and data that must be included in requests for rulings, and these instructions are supplemented by detailed rules governing requests for rulings on recurring issues.[84] The application should include a statement of relevant authorities, even if the taxpayer is merely asking for advice without urging a particular determination, and it may contain a request for a conference.[85] The taxpayer is entitled to only one conference with the National Office and has no formal right to an appeal, but the National Office may invite the taxpayer to additional conferences; and in certain cases involving adverse action, a second conference is standard operating procedure.[86] On concluding that an

---

[79] Rev. Proc. 79-45, supra note 71, §4.06.

[80] Statement of Procedural Rules, supra note 9, §601.105(b)(5); see also Rev. Proc. 79-46, §4.04, 1979-2 CB 521.

[81] E.g., Commissioner delegation orders (C.D.O.'s), prohibited transactions exemptions (P.T.E.s), and technical information releases (T.I.R.s).

[82] Rev. Proc. 79-45, supra note 71, §5.01.

[83] See, e.g., IRC §367(a) (certain transfers to foreign corporations, etc.); IRC §§442 and 446(e) (changes of accounting periods or accounting methods), discussed supra ¶¶35.1 and 35.6, respectively.

[84] See Rev. Proc. 79-45, supra note 71, §9.

[85] Id. §§9.08, 9.14.

[86] Id. §§11.02, 11.06.

adverse ruling will be issued (and assuming, in the case of a prospective transaction, that the proposal cannot be reformulated to elicit favorable action), taxpayers often withdraw their requests for rulings. This does not, however, preclude the National Office from furnishing its views to the district director with audit jurisdiction over the taxpayer's return for consideration when the return is subsequently audited.[87]

2. *No-ruling areas.* Except when required by the Code or the regulations, rulings are issued as a matter of discretion "whenever appropriate in the interest of sound tax administration." [88] As a matter of policy, however, the IRS will not issue rulings on some issues and will not ordinarily rule on certain others, either because of the inherently factual nature of the problem or for other reasons. These no-ruling areas include (1) determinations of fact, such as the market value of property; (2) the tax effect of hypothetical situations and transactions to be consummated at an indefinite future time; (3) transactions lacking in bona fide business purpose or having tax reduction as their principal purpose; (4) alternate plans for proposed transactions; (5) matters as to which a judicial decision adverse to the government has been handed down, if the IRS has not yet decided whether to follow the decision or litigate the issue further; and (6) provisions not yet covered by temporary or final regulations, unless a business emergency exists or unusual hardship will result from a failure to obtain a ruling.[89]

Finally, rulings typically conclude with a disclaimer of the following type:

> No opinion is expressed as to the tax treatment of the transaction under the provisions of any of the other sections of the Code and Regulations [not mentioned in the body of the ruling] which may also be applicable thereto or to the tax treatment of any conditions existing at the time of, or effects resulting from, the transaction which are not specifically covered by the above rulings.[90]

3. *Checklists for requests on recurring subjects.* To guide taxpayers requesting rulings on particular subjects, the IRS issues numerous special instructions, including checklists, questionnaires, and percentage and other quantitative bench marks.

---

[87] Id. §15.

[88] Id. §§4.01, 5.

[89] For issues on which the IRS will not rule, see Rev. Proc. 81-10, 1981-1 CB 647 (questions of fact and transactions to be consummated at indefinite future dates); id. §3.02 (absence of bona fide business purposes, matters being litigated, alternate proposals, and hypothetical situations).

[90] For a case holding that a private ruling did not bind the IRS on an issue that was not explicitly addressed, see Jeffers v. US, 556 F.2d 986 (Ct. Cl. 1977) (ruling on status of proposed reorganization did not pass on impact of IRC §483).

3. Revenue Rulings. A revenue ruling is defined by Rev. Proc. 78-24 as "an official interpretation by the Service that has been published in the Internal Revenue Bulletin." [91] Since revenue rulings ordinarily originate in taxpayer letter rulings, the major difference between them is that revenue rulings are published "for the guidance of taxpayers, Internal Revenue Service officials, and others concerned," while rulings are denied this precedential force by Rev. Proc. 79-45, which provides that "a taxpayer may not rely on a ruling issued to another taxpayer." [92]

Only a small fraction of all private letter rulings is published. While an IRS rule provides that no unpublished ruling "will be relied on, used, or cited, by any officer or employee of the Service as a precedent in the disposition of other cases," [93] the *Internal Revenue Manual* advises IRS personnel that private letter rulings "may be used as a guide with other research material in formulating a district office position on an issue." [94]

Revenue rulings apply retroactively unless they explicitly provide otherwise, but rulings that revoke or modify previously published rulings ordinarily include a prospective-only qualification.[95]

4. Reliance on and Revocation of Rulings. There are important differences between taxpayer letter rulings and revenue rulings as respects the related issues of reliance by taxpayers and revocation by the IRS. Taxpayer letter rulings can be safely relied on by the taxpayer to whom they are issued, even though they are not vested by statute with the finality of closing agreements and compromises.[96] This is because Rev. Proc. 79-45 provides that, except in rare or unusual circumstances, a ruling will not be retroactively modified or revoked as to the taxpayer to whom it was issued or whose tax liability was directly involved in the ruling if (1) there was no misstatement or omission of material facts, (2) the facts as subsequently developed are not materially different from those on which the ruling was based, (3) the applicable law has not been changed, (4) the ruling was issued with respect to a prospective or proposed transaction, and (5) the taxpayer relied on the ruling in good faith and retroactive revocation would be to his detriment.[97]

---

[91] Rev. Proc. 78-24, supra note 76, §4.07.

[92] Rev. Rul. 79-45, supra note 71, §17.01. See also IRC §6110(j)(3) (written determinations may not be used or cited as precedents except as otherwise provided by regulations).

[93] Rev. Proc. 78-24, supra note 76, §7.01(4).

[94] IRM 4245.3, MT 4200-352 (April 27, 1979).

[95] Rev. Proc. 78-24, supra note 76, §7.01(3).

[96] For closing agreements and compromises, see infra ¶40.1.

[97] See Rev. Proc. 79-45, supra note 71, §17.05; see also id. §§17.06, 17.07 (distinction between retroactive and prospective application of revocation or modification). For cases in which grounds for retroactive revocation were established, see Stevens

Taxpayers who learn of a private ruling issued to another taxpayer are cautioned by Rev. Proc. 79-45 against reliance thereon,[98] but this caveat may be ineffective if applying different rules to the two classes of taxpayers would be an abuse of discretion, akin to a violation of the due process clause of the Fifth Amendment.[99]

By contrast with private letter rulings, revenue rulings are published so that taxpayers can rely on them "in determining the tax treatment of their own transactions and need not request specific rulings applying the principles of a published revenue ruling to the facts of their particular cases." [100] This invitation is accompanied by a warning against reaching the same conclusion in other cases unless the facts and circumstances of the particular case are substantially the same and a statement that the effect of subsequent legislation, regulations, court decisions, and revenue rulings should be considered.[101]

The IRS has almost untrammeled authority to amend or revoke a revenue ruling, at least prospectively, on concluding that it erroneously interprets the applicable law and regulations. When a published ruling is revoked or modified, however, the IRS ordinarily exercises its authority under IRC §7805(b) to provide that the change will not be applied retroactively to the detriment of taxpayers.[102]

Although revenue rulings are binding on IRS officials until revoked, their effect when challenged by taxpayers in judicial proceedings is another matter. The IRS itself acknowledges that they "do not have the force and effect of Treasury Department Regulations," [103] an admission that seems to reflect the

---

Bros. Foundation, Inc. v. CIR, 324 F.2d 633 (8th Cir. 1963), cert. denied, 376 US 969 (1964) (disqualifying facts not disclosed in request for ruling); Wisconsin Nipple & Fabricating Corp. v. CIR, 67 TC 490 (1976), aff'd, 581 F.2d 1235 (7th Cir. 1978) (change in facts in later years), and cases there cited.

[98] Rev. Proc. 79-45, supra note 71, §17.01; see also Goodstein v. CIR, 267 F.2d 127 (1st Cir. 1959).

[99] See IBM Corp. v. US, supra note 12; the case, which involved application of manufacturer's excise tax differently to two business competitors, both of which requested rulings, was directly concerned with the exercise of discretion under IRC §7805(b), but it has wider implications; see also Ogiony v. CIR, 617 F.2d 14 (2d Cir.), cert. denied, 449 US 900 (1980) (concurring opinion—"consistency over time and uniformity of treatment among taxpayers are proper bench marks from which to judge IRS actions," but, on facts, insufficient evidence of inconsistent treatment).

[100] Rev. Proc. 78-24, supra note 76, §7.01(5); this revenue procedure also provides that published revenue rulings do not have the force and effect of Treasury regulations but "are published to provide precedents to be used in the disposition of other cases, and may be cited and relied upon for that purpose." Id. §7.01(4).

[101] Id. §7.01(5); a similar warning appears in every issue of the *Internal Revenue Bulletin.*

[102] See Rev. Proc. 78-24, supra note 76, §7.01(3) (exercise of this authority requires "affirmative action").

[103] 1981-1 CB iii.

fact that rulings are issued, amended, and revoked with less formality than regulations. The issue ordinarily is whether a revenue ruling's interpretation of an ambiguous statute should be given weight in deciding the disputed issue. As considered expressions of the IRS' views, revenue rulings and regulations differ more in degree than in kind, and it is not clear that a sharp distinction in their weight is warranted.[104]

5. Public Inspection of Rulings and Other IRS Documents. Section 6110, enacted in 1976, provides that the text of all rulings, determination letters, and technical advice memoranda and any "background file document" (the request, material submitted in support thereof, and communications between the IRS and non-IRS personnel relating thereto) shall be open to public inspection, subject to elaborate conditions and qualifications to insure anonymity for the applicant and certain other persons, to safeguard trade secrets and confidential financial data, and to avoid clearly unwarranted invasions of personal privacy.[105] Section 6110 prescribes administrative procedures to deal with requests for additional disclosures and to restrain disclosures. On exhausting these administrative remedies, a petition can be filed in the Tax Court (anonymously, if appropriate) pursuant to IRC §6110(f)(3) to restrain disclosure. Conversely, IRC §6110(f)(4) allows suit to be brought in either the Tax Court or the District Court for the District of Columbia to open the requested document for public inspection. Section 6110(f)(4) provides for a trial de novo of the request for disclosure, in which the burden of proof is on the IRS, the private person or any other person, seeking to restrain disclosure.

Another category of actions is authorized by IRC §6110(d), which is concerned with so-called third-party contacts—oral or written communications, before a written determination is issued, from persons other than IRS employees and the person to whom the determination pertains. Any person may sue in the Tax Court or the District Court for the District of Columbia for disclosure of the third person's identity; and the court is directed by IRC §6110(d)(3) to order disclosure if there is evidence in the record reasonably warranting an inference of impropriety or undue influence.

Section 6110(1) provides that the Treasury shall not be required by any court to disclose, or refrain from disclosing, any written determination or

---

[104] See Industrial Valley Bank & Trust Co. v. CIR, 66 TC 272, 280 (1976) ("in the usual case we do not consider revenue rulings as having any particular legal significance other than as a statement of [the IRS] position . . . [but] in the field of bad debt reserves of banks, the applicable rules appear to have been customarily laid down by revenue ruling rather than by regulation"; since the parties treated the issue as whether the requirements of the revenue ruling were satisfied, the court did not raise the question of the ruling's validity on its own motion).

[105] See S. Rep. No. 94-938, reprinted in 1976-3 CB (Vol. 3) 49.

background file document except pursuant to IRC §6110, other provisions of the Code, or a judiciary discovery order, thus ousting the Freedom of Information Act (FOIA) from jurisdiction over this field.[106] But many other documents of potential interest to taxpayers, such as legal memoranda and explanations and summaries of past decisions, are outside the scope of IRC §6110; and these remain subject to the FOIA disclosure rules.[107]

6. Acquiescence and Nonacquiescence in Tax Court Decisions. When a decision of the Tax Court, other than a memorandum decision, decides an issue adversely to the government, it is IRS policy to announce "at the earliest practicable date" whether it acquiesces or does not acquiesce in the decision.[108] An acquiescence means that the conclusion reached by the Tax Court should be accepted by IRS personnel in disposing of similar cases, provided the facts and circumstances are substantially the same and after giving consideration to the effect of later legislation, regulations, rulings, and court decisions.[109] An announcement that the IRS acquiesces only in the result in a Tax Court case signals disagreement with some or all of the reasons given by the court for its conclusions. In some cases, the IRS announces acquiescence in the result reached in one issue and nonacquiescence as to others. From time to time, notices of acquiescence are withdrawn and nonacquiescences are substituted, and vice versa.[110]

The IRS does not invite taxpayer reliance on notices of acquiescence in

---

[106] See Grenier v. IRS, 449 F.Supp. 834 (D.Md. 1978) (FOIA displaced by IRC §6110).

[107] For FOIA litigation involving IRS documents, see Taxation With Representation Fund v. IRS, 485 F.Supp. 263 (D.D.C. 1980), aff'd in part and remanded, 646 F.2d 666 (D.C.Cir. 1981) (ordering disclosure of certain IRS General Counsel's memoranda, technical memoranda, and actions on decisions representing final policy statements); Falcone v. IRS, 479 F.Supp. 985 (E.D.Mich. 1979) (General Counsel's memoranda); Pies v. IRS, 484 F.Supp. 930 (D.D.C. 1979) (drafts of technical memoranda and of proposed regulations—disclosure ordered).

See also Long v. IRS, 596 F.2d 362 (9th Cir. 1979), cert. denied, 446 US 917 (1980) (computer printout used in measuring taxpayer compliance; IRS ordered to disclose after sanitizing data by deleting names, addresses, and social security numbers), which was remanded by the Supreme Court for further consideration in the light of a 1981 amendment of IRC §6103(b)(2), which permits the IRS to deny disclosure of the standards used for the selection of returns for audit or the data used in determining these standards. On remand, the requested disclosure was denied, Long v. IRS, 50 AFTR2d 5523 (W.D.Wash. 1982).

[108] See, e.g., Cumulative List of Announcements Relating to Decisions of the Tax Court, 1981-1 CB 1.

[109] Id.

[110] See Dixon v. US, 381 US 68 (1965) (IRS has authority under IRC §7805(b) to withdraw acquiescence in an erroneous decision retroactively, even if taxpayer relied on original notice).

the way it invites reliance on published revenue rulings; and, except in unusual circumstances, it is unlikely that an acquiescence estops the IRS.

The formal acquiescence/nonacquiescence policy applies only to Tax Court decisions; but the IRS also announces, though much more rarely, whether it accepts particular decisions of the federal district courts, courts of appeals, or Claims Court as precedents for the disposition of similar cases.[111]

SELECTED BIBLIOGRAPHY

Asimow, Public Participation in the Adoption of Interpretive Rules and Policy Statements, 75 Mich. L. Rev. 521 (1977).

Banks, Accountants in the Tax Practice, 5 Tul. L. Rev. 298 (1973).

Bittker, Does Tax Practice by Accountants Constitute the Unauthorized Practice of Law? 25 J. Tax. 184 (1966).

Brown, Regulations, Reenactment, and the Revenue Acts, 54 Harv. L. Rev. 377 (1941).

Caplin, Taxpayer Rulings Policy of the Internal Revenue Service: A Statement of Principles, 20 NYU Inst. on Fed. Tax. 1 (1962).

Collie & Marinis, Ethical Considerations on Discovery of Error in Tax Returns, 22 Tax Lawyer 455 (1969).

Comment, Limits on Retroactive Decision Making by the Internal Revenue Service: Redefining Abuse of Discretion Under Section 7805(b), 23 U.C.L.A. L. Rev. 529, 530–531 (1976).

Committee on Standards of Tax Practice, American Bar Association, Tax Section, Guidelines to Tax Practice, 31 Tax Lawyer 551 (1978).

Cooper, The Avoidance Dynamic: A Tale of Tax Planning, Tax Ethics, and Tax Reform, 80 Colum. L. Rev. 1553 (1980).

Darrell, Conscience and Propriety in Tax Practice, 17 NYU Inst. on Fed. Tax. 1 (1959).

Emory, Private Rulings: What May Practitioners Expect From the New Procedure? 47 J. Tax. 322 (1977).

Filpi, Problems in the Release of IRS Ruling Letters, GCMs, AODs and TMs: Impact on the IRS and on Tax Practitioners, Tax Notes, April 26, 1982, at 274.

Fisher & Griffith, The Section of Taxation and the Small Taxpayer: The Commitment to Volunteer Income Tax Assistance, 33 Tax Lawyer 107 (1979).

Garbis, New Rules Regulating Income Tax Return Preparers Affect All Tax Practitioners, 46 J. Tax. 152 (1977).

Griswold, A Summary of the Regulations Problem, 54 Harv. L. Rev. 398 (1941).

---

[111] See, e.g., Rev. Rul. 75-83, 1975-1 CB 112 (reasons for not following a decision of the court of appeals); Rev. Rul. 70-101, 1970-1 CB 278 (decision not to litigate further the validity of professional service corporations).

Johnston, Civil and Criminal Enforcement Weapons Available to the IRS Against Preparers and Other Practitioners, 1981 So. Calif. Tax Inst. 600.

Kovey & Winslow, Supreme Court's Citation of Letter Rulings: What Does It Mean to Practitioners? 55 J. Tax. 166 (1981).

Lynn & Gerson, Quasi-Estoppel and Abuse of Discretion as Applied Against the United States in Federal Tax Controversies, 19 Tax L. Rev. 487 (1964).

Note, The Commissioner's Non-Acquiescence, 40 So. Calif. L. Rev. 550 (1967).

Osimitz, Revenue Rulings and the Federal Administrative Procedure Act, 1975 Wis. L. Rev. 1135.

Parnell, The Internal Revenue Manual: Its Utility and Legal Effect, 32 Tax Lawyer 687 (1979).

Paul, The Responsibilities of the Tax Adviser, 63 Harv. L. Rev. 377 (1950).

Pennell & Stevens, The Professional as a Tax Return Preparer: From the Perspective of the Accountant and the Lawyer, 56 Taxes 726 (1978).

Report, Statement on Proposed Rule Amending Circular 230 With Respect to Tax Shelter Opinions, 34 Tax Lawyer 745 (1981).

Rogovin, The Four R's: Regulations, Rulings, Reliance and Retroactivity, 43 Taxes 756, 758 n.3 (1965).

Roth, New Penalty Provisions and Their Effect on Aggressive Tax Planning, 61 Taxes 52 (1983).

Sax, Lawyer Responsibility in Tax Shelter Opinions, 34 Tax Lawyer 5 (1981).

Schmidt, The Tax Regulations Making Process—Then and Now, 24 Tax Lawyer 541 (1971).

Smith, Tax Rulings, Their Use and Abuse, 1970 So. Calif. Tax Inst. 663

Sugarman, Drafting Clauses of Escape in Agreements With Uncertain Tax Consequences, 1960 So. Calif. Tax Inst. 131.

Surrey, The Scope and Effect of Treasury Regulations Under the Income, Estate, and Gift Taxes, 88 U. Pa. L. Rev. 556 (1940).

Surrey, A Comment on the Proposal to Separate the Bureau of Internal Revenue From the Treasury Department, 8 Tax L. Rev. 155 (1953).

Walter, The Battle for Information: Strategies of Taxpayers and the IRS to Compel (or Resist) Disclosure, 56 Taxes 740 (1978).

Weber, Latcham & Hyde, The Responsibilities and Liabilities of Tax Advisors, 1977 So. Calif. Tax Inst. 605.

Wright, Inadequacies of Freedom of Information Act as Applied to IRS Letter Rulings, 28 Okla. L. Rev. 701 (1975).

CHAPTER 39

Tax Returns, Rates, and Payments

¶39.1 TAX RETURNS

1. Introductory. The importance of the tax return as the basic document on which the self-assessment system rests is attested by the number of statutory provisions requiring returns to be filed; specifying their filing dates; attaching legal consequences to the fact of filing, the date of filing, and the information included; and imposing penalties for filing negligent or fraudulent returns and for failing to file.

2. Individual Returns. Section 6012, which prescribes the rules governing the filing of returns, starts out by requiring every individual with a gross income of $1,000 or more to file; but it then establishes higher thresholds for virtually all citizens and resident aliens, equal to the applicable zero bracket amount plus one personal exemption.[1]

[1] Gross income is computed for filing purposes without regard to the exclusions provided by IRC §911 (certain income earned abroad by individuals) and §121 (sale of residence by person over 55). See IRC §6012(c).

The regulations permit individual returns to be made by an agent in certain circumstances.[2] Minors may make their own returns; otherwise, the obligation falls on the minor's guardian.[3] In the case of decedents, insane persons, and others under disability, the obligation to file the individual's return is placed on the appropriate fiduciary by IRC §§6012(b)(1) and 6012(b)(2).[4]

Section 6020(a) provides that the IRS may prepare a return for a person who fails to file as required but who consents to disclose the necessary information; and if signed by the taxpayer, such an IRS-prepared return is treated the same as if it had been prepared personally.[5] Section 6020(b) and the regulations thereunder authorize an IRS officer or employee to make a return "from his own knowledge and from such information as he can obtain through testimony or otherwise" for a taxpayer failing to make a timely return or making a false or fraudulent return. Although such a return is "prima facie good and sufficient for all legal purposes," it does not start the running of the statute of limitations, and the amount shown as due cannot be assessed until a statutory notice of deficiency ("ninety-day letter") has been sent to the taxpayer and the time for filing a petition in the Tax Court has expired.[6]

3. Returns for Estates and Trusts. An income tax return must be filed for an estate with gross income for the taxable year of $600 or more, for a trust with gross income of $600 or any taxable income, and for estates and trusts with nonresident alien beneficiaries regardless of the amount of gross or taxable income.[7] Executors, trustees, and other fiduciaries filing on behalf of estates and trusts file *fiduciary* income tax returns.

4. Corporation Returns. Section 6012(a)(2) requires a return for every corporation subject to taxation, regardless of the amount (if any) of its gross or taxable income for the taxable year.[8] The regulations require a return if a

---

[2] Treas. Regs. §1.6012-1(a)(5) (taxpayer unable to file because of disease or absence from country, or district director determines good cause exists).

[3] Treas. Regs. §§1.6012-1(a)(4) (minor may file), 1.6012-3(b)(3) (guardian obligated to file if minor does not).

[4] See also Rev. Rul. 67-191, 1967-1 CB 318 (guardian may file joint return with ward's spouse); Heasley v. CIR, 45 TC 448, 460–462 (1966); Treas. Regs. §1.6012-3(b)(5) (appointment of receiver of an individual's property does not place individual under disability; receiver must file only if individual does not).

[5] Treas. Regs. §301.6020-1(a)(2).

[6] See Treas. Regs. §§301.6020-1(b)(1), 301.6020-1(b)(2), 301.6020-1(c); IRC §6501(b)(3) (return under IRC §6020(b) does not start running of statute of limitations on assessment and collection).

[7] IRC §§6012(a)(3), 6012(a)(4), 6012(a)(5).

[8] As elsewhere in the Code, the term "corporation," as used by IRC §6012(a)(2), includes unincorporated "associations" having sufficient corporate characteristics; see IRC §7701(a)(3).

corporation is "in existence" during any part of the taxable year.[9] A corporation's existence for income tax purposes may be determined differently than for the purposes of local law.[10]

5. Partnership Returns. Although partnerships are not taxable entities, it is necessary to determine a partnership's income, deductions, credits, and other items in order to prepare and audit the separate returns of the partners; and some elections (e.g., depreciation methods) are made at the partnership level rather than by the partners individually. For these reasons, partnership returns have both informational and operational aspects.[11] Section 6031 and the regulations thereunder require any partnership engaged in a U.S. trade or business or having income from sources within the United States to file a return, even if its principal place of business is outside the United States and all the partners are nonresident aliens.[12]

Sections §§6221–6231, enacted in 1982, permit the IRS to conduct audits and determine deficiencies at the partnership level (except in the case of certain "small partnerships"), require consistency between the treatment of an item by the partnership and by a partner or an explanation of the inconsistency, set up an elaborate procedure for keeping the partners informed of the progress of an audit and the administrative and judicial actions taken at the partnership level, and permit judicial review of adjustments made at the partnership level.

6. Filing Dates. In general, returns for individuals, estates, trusts, and partnerships must be filed on or before April 15 of the year following the taxable year, in the case of calendar year taxpayers, or on or before the fifteenth of the fourth month following the close of the taxpayer's fiscal year.[13] For corporations, the corresponding dates are March 15 or the fifteenth day of the third month following the close of the fiscal year.[14] If the due date is a Saturday, Sunday, or legal holiday, a return is timely if filed on the next succeeding day that is not a Saturday, Sunday, or legal holiday.[15]

Under the timely-mailing, timely-filing principle established by IRC §7502(a), a return sent by U.S. mail in a properly addressed envelope, postage prepaid, postmarked on or before the prescribed filing date (including exten-

---

[9] Treas. Regs. §1.6012-2(a)(2).

[10] Id.

[11] For the effect of an election under IRC §761(a) (joint ventures electing to be excluded from partnership status), see Treas. Regs. §§1.6031-1(a)(2), 1.6031-1(d)(2).

[12] Treas. Regs. §1.6031-1.

[13] See IRC §6072(a) (general rule).

[14] See IRC §6072(b).

[15] IRC §7503. The term "legal holiday" includes the federal holidays listed in Treas. Regs. §301.7503-1(b)(1) and, in the case of returns filed in an IRS office outside the District of Columbia, any statewide legal holiday. See Treas. Regs. §301.7503-1(b)(2).

sions of time) [16] is treated as delivered to the IRS on the postmark date.[17] If registered or certified mail is used, the date of registration or of the sender's certified mail receipt is controlling.[18] These rules apply only if the return is actually delivered to the IRS office where it is required to be filed.[19]

Extensions of time for the filing of returns, either automatic or by application, are granted in a variety of circumstances, but do not automatically extend the time for payment, for which there are separate procedures.[20]

7. Amended Returns. Although not explicitly authorized by statute, amended returns are a familiar custom, serving two principal functions: to modify, supplement, or supplant the taxpayer's original return, and to claim a refund.[21]

1. *Corrective returns.* The regulations provide that taxpayers ascertaining that items should have been included in gross income in prior taxable years "should, if within the period of limitation, file an amended return and pay any additional tax due." [22] When filed on or before the due date, a corrective amended return usually supersedes the original return.[23] If filed thereafter, an amended return correcting a mathematical or other error or an omission is usually accepted by the IRS; but it is ordinarily not accepted if it seeks to

---

[16] See Treas. Regs. §301.7502-1(c)(3).

[17] Section 7502 covers claims for refund, elections, and other documents, as well as returns, but not delinquent returns. See Rev. Rul. 73-133, 1973-1 CB 606. For extended analysis of IRC §7502, see Hotel Equities Corp. v. CIR, 65 TC 528 (1975), aff'd, 546 F.2d 725 (7th Cir. 1976) (statute of limitations on assessing deficiency commenced to run when the return was postmarked, rather than three days later when it was received by IRS).

[18] IRC §7502(c); Treas. Regs. §301.7502-1(c)(2).

[19] Treas. Regs. §301.7502-1(d)(1) (proof that return was sent by registered or certified mail in properly addressed envelope prima facie proof of delivery). When these statutory rules are inapplicable, other evidence can be used to establish filing. See, e.g., Kralstein v. CIR, 38 TC 810, 820 (1962) (taxpayer's testimony that return was filed before due date accepted when IRS failed to produce envelope); Workman v. CIR, ¶65,003 P-H Memo TC (1965) (testimony of taxpayer and accountant made out prima facie case of timely filing, which IRS failed to rebut).

[20] For individuals, see Treas. Regs. §§1.6081-4 (automatic two-month extension on application), 1.6081-2 (taxpayers outside United States), 1.6081-1 (discretionary extensions of time). See infra ¶39.6.

[21] A few statutory provisions authorize amended returns in special circumstances; see, e.g., IRC §6013(b) (change from separate to joint return), discussed infra ¶39.3.

[22] Treas. Regs. §1.451-1(a); see also Treas. Regs. §1.461-1(a)(3)(i) (same for belated discovery of erroneous deductions).

[23] See Haggar Co. v. Helvering, 308 US 389 (1940) (timely amended return is "first return" under prior statutory provision); Rev. Rul. 56-67, 1956-1 CB 437 (timely amended return treated as substitute for original return).

change a method of accounting or reporting, unless the method used in the original return was improper.[24] Whether an amended return will be accepted if it reflects a change of mind with regard to an election depends on the presumed intent of Congress in authorizing the election or on the meaning of the regulations specifying the method by which an election is to be made.[25]

2. *Claims for refund.* Amended returns are the principal documents by which taxpayers can apply for a credit or refund of income taxes.[26]

8. Deficient, Skeleton, and Tentative Returns. Occasionally a document's status as a "return" is ambiguous because, for example, the taxpayer uses the wrong form, omits crucial data, fails to sign, or describes the document as tentative or as an estimate. Although errors, even if the product of fraud, do not vitiate a document's status as a return,[27] a document may be so deficient that it is not even a "return." If so, it does not cause the normal three-year statute of limitations on the assessment of taxes to run; the taxpayer is liable for a delinquency penalty for failure to file a return by the prescribed filing date, unless the failure is due to reasonable cause and not willful neglect; and the taxpayer subjects himself to criminal prosecution if the failure to file is "willful." [28]

The regulations state that returns "shall include therein the information required by the applicable regulations or forms" and that "[e]ach taxpayer should carefully prepare his return and set forth fully and clearly the information required to be included therein." [29] The courts have in the main held that substantial compliance is sufficient; a document constitutes a "return" for all purposes if the taxpayer, under the penalties of perjury, represents it as a final statement of gross income, deductions, and credits for the pertinent taxable period. The courts require the purported return to evince an "honest and

---

[24] As examples of items that can be changed by amended returns, the *Internal Revenue Manual* refers to filing status, tax computation methods, and additional income or deductions. See, e.g., IRM 4121.1.

[25] See, e.g., Youngblood v. US, 388 F.Supp. 152 (W.D. Tex. 1974), aff'd per curiam, 507 F.2d 1263 (5th Cir. 1975) (belated amended return changing from installment to accrual method properly rejected by IRS).

[26] See infra ¶40.3.

[27] The Code itself inferentially recognizes some deficient documents as "returns" by imposing explicit penalties—for example, IRC §6501(e), extending the normal statute of limitations on assessments if the return omits more than 25 percent of the taxpayer's gross income, IRC §6653(b), imposing a 50 percent penalty for underpayment based on a fraudulent return, and IRC §6702, imposing a civil penalty of $500 for filing a "frivolous" income tax return.

[28] See infra ¶¶41.2 (statute of limitations on assessments), 42.3 (civil penalty for failure to file), 42.4 (prosecution for willful failure to file).

[29] Treas. Regs. §§1.6011-1(a), 1.6011-1(b).

genuine effort to satisfy the law,"[30] and they take into account three principal factors—the document's form, content, and finality—in deciding whether it is a statutory return.

1. *Form.* The substantial-compliance principle protects taxpayers who use the wrong form or who mistakenly believe they are not taxable and file an information return, provided the return furnishes the IRS with the information necessary to compute and assess the tax due.[31] Moreover, the regulations permit the use of homemade forms in limited circumstances and for limited purposes,[32] but they leave open at least three questions: (1) whether a homemade form can be used only if the prescribed form was unavailable to the taxpayer; (2) whether a homemade form can be rejected by the IRS if not supplemented by a proper form, even if it is submitted under the penalties of perjury and contains sufficient information to constitute a statutory return if submitted on the proper form; and (3) whether, if supplemented by a return on the proper form, the homemade return starts the statute of limitations running when filed or only when supplemented. The litigated cases do little to clarify these ambiguities.[33]

2. *Content.* The most glaring examples of documents failing to qualify as returns because their content is deficient are so-called skeleton returns—signed documents (usually Form 1040) that contain the taxpayer's name and address, but nothing more. Although "perfect accuracy and completeness" are not required,[34] such a document is not a "return"—not even if it contains an impassioned essay on the unconstitutionality of the federal income tax, the country's war crimes, the ravages of inflation, or the evils of demonetizing gold.[35]

---

[30] Zellerbach Paper Co. v. Helvering, 293 US 172, 180 (1934).

[31] See, e.g., Werbelovsky v. CIR, 8 BTA 442 (1927) (executor used Form 1041 for decedent's estate instead of Form 1040; statute of limitations required *a* return to be filed, but not necessarily *the prescribed* return).

[32] Treas. Regs. §1.6011-1(b).

[33] Parker v. CIR, 365 F.2d 792 (8th Cir. 1966), cert. denied, 385 US 1026 (1967) (delinquency upheld where sophisticated taxpayer used home-made form and did not explain failure to file proper form when notified of error); see also Houston v. CIR, 38 TC 486 (1962) (statute of limitations not started by letter reporting gross income but not itemizing deductions and credits and not clearly labeled as a return); but see Denman v. Motter, 44 F.2d 648 (D.Kan. 1930) (home-made form, submitted after diligent effort to obtain proper form, supplied requisite information and was clearly labeled; held, return started statute of limitations).

[34] Zellerbach Paper Co. v. Helvering, supra note 30, at 180.

[35] See, e.g., Cupp v. CIR, 65 TC 68, 79 (1975); Hatfield v. CIR, 68 TC 895 (1977) (delinquency penalty upheld for purported return asserting that Federal Reserve notes are nonreportable accounts receivable, with strong warning to future protesters that frivolous litigation will result in damages under IRC §6673). For documents satisfying the substantial compliance requirement despite deficiencies, because they enabled the

Skeleton returns are sometimes accompanied by statements claiming that the privilege against compulsory self-incrimination justifies a refusal to supply any information. The courts have regularly rejected blanket refusals to file,[36] and the governing principles have been summarized as follows: "(1) the privilege must be claimed specifically in response to particular questions, . . . (2) the claim is to be reviewed by a judicial officer who determines whether the information sought would tend to incriminate; [and] (3) the witness or defendant himself is not the final arbiter of whether or not the information sought would tend to incriminate." [37]

Returns occasionally are deficient because they cover the wrong taxable period or cover only part of the right period. Neither type is a statutory "return," [38] but if two documents are submitted that cover the proper period when pieced together, they constitute a return, dating from the filing date of the second document.[39]

3. *Finality.* Taxpayers are required to sign their returns under the penalties of perjury,[40] a requirement that implicitly disqualifies a "tentative return" that can be later disowned by the taxpayer as a mere estimate or guess.[41] An unsigned return, or a return signed but not under the penalties of perjury, does not start the running of the statute of limitations or preclude a failure-to-file penalty, since the taxpayer cannot be prosecuted for perjury—"one of the principal sanctions available to assure that honest returns are filed." [42]

The regulations sanction proxy signatures in narrowly defined situations, but require the agent's authority to be evidenced by a power of attorney in writing (the original or a copy of which must be attached to the return). Joint returns, however, can be signed by one spouse with the oral consent of a physically incapacitated spouse, provided an explanatory rider is attached by

---

IRS to compute and assess the taxpayer's tax liability, see General Mfg. Corp. v. CIR, 44 TC 513, 523 (1965), and cases there cited; Lohman's Est. v. CIR, ¶72,027 P-H Memo TC (1972) (estate tax return—extensive analysis, with citations).

[36] US v. Sullivan, 274 US 259 (1927); see also Heligman v. US, 407 F.2d 448 (8th Cir.), cert. denied, 395 US 977 (1969) (blanket refusal to respond to revenue agent's questions not within scope of privilege).

[37] US v. Johnson, 577 F.2d 1304, 1311 (5th Cir. 1978); see also cases there cited.

[38] See, e.g., August Belmont Hotel Co. v. CIR, 18 BTA 643 (1930) (return for January 1, 1918 to April 30, 1918, where taxpayer erroneously claimed to have ceased operations on latter date); Gensinger v. CIR, 18 TC 122 (1952), aff'd, 208 F.2d 576 (9th Cir. 1953).

[39] See, e.g., Atlas Oil & Ref. Corp. v. CIR, 22 TC 552 (1954) (three fiscal-year returns for years ending November 1942 to 1944 yielded calendar-year returns for 1942 and 1943).

[40] IRC §§6061–6063, 6065.

[41] See, e.g., Lucas v. Pilliod Lumber Co., 281 US 245 (1930).

[42] Vaira v. CIR, 52 TC 986, 1005 (1969).

the spouse who signs for both.[43] In the litigated cases, however, the courts have held that a purported return meets the statutory requirements if the taxpayer's name is signed by a person with actual authority to do so, even if the conditions prescribed by the regulations are not satisfied.[44]

9. Information. In addition to regular tax returns, the IRS receives millions of information returns under statutes and regulations requiring persons paying wages, dividends, interest, and other items to report these amounts so the IRS can ascertain whether they have been properly reported by the payees. The backbone of these reporting requirements is IRC §6041(a), requiring persons engaged in a trade or business to report all "rent, salaries, wages, premiums, annuities, compensations, remunerations, emoluments, or other fixed or determinable gains, profits, and income" of $600 or more in any taxable year if the amount is paid in the course of business, except for items covered by the more specialized reporting provisions or exempted by the regulations.[45] The exemptions include payments to corporations, income earned outside the United States if reasonably believed to be excludable from the recipient's gross income under IRC §911, salaries and profits distributed by partnerships to their partners, and reimbursed travel and business expenses if the employee accounts to the employer. Numerous other information returns are required by the Code or regulations, including reports on corporate dissolutions and liquidations; patronage dividends; foreign personal holding companies; qualification as executor, receiver, or similar fiduciary; stock options; and the receipt of tips.

10. Taxpayer Identification Numbers. The advent of automatic data processing by computers made it possible to use information returns more efficiently, but only if John Miller and John T. Miller could be instantly recognized by the IRS as the same person and distinguished from the thousands of other John Millers across the land. To achieve this result, IRC §6109(a) requires the use, pursuant to regulations, of taxpayer identification numbers on all returns and other documents filed with the IRS.[46]

---

[43] Treas. Regs. §1.6012-1(a)(5); see also infra ¶39.3 (requisites of joint return).

[44] See, e.g., Booher v. CIR, 28 TC 817 (1957) (wife signed joint return for husband of limited mental capacity, with oral authority); but see Hamilton v. CIR, ¶54,224 P-H Memo TC (1954), aff'd per curiam, 232 F.2d 891 (6th Cir. 1956) (no evidence of authority of person signing for taxpayer; since signing someone else's name is not a verification, document does not qualify as return).

[45] See Treas. Regs. §§1.6041-1 (general coverage), 1.6041-2 (payments to employees), 1.6041-3 (payments not required to be reported), 1.6041-4 (foreign items), 1.6041-5 (information as to actual owner of reported payments). For the items covered by IRC §6041(a) ("fixed or determinable gains," etc.), see Treas. Regs. §1.6041-1(c).

[46] See IRS Pub. No. 459 (1962 ed.), reprinted in [1963] P-H Fed. Taxes ¶54,630 (re reasonable cause).

For individuals, the identifying number is the taxpayer's social security number.[47] Employers, corporations, trusts, estates, partnerships, and exempt organizations are assigned "employer identification numbers" by the IRS, whether they have employees or not.[48]

¶39.2 CONFIDENTIALITY AND DISCLOSURE OF TAX RETURNS AND RETURN INFORMATION

1. Introductory. The Tax Reform Act of 1976 completely overhauled the rules governing the privacy of tax returns, increasing their protection against disclosure by specifying in great detail the types of information that can be made available to persons and agencies seeking access to returns and associated information for tax administration, law enforcement, and other purposes.[49] The 1976 confidentiality and disclosure rules, embodied in IRC §6103, define the protected area ("returns" and "return information") in detail, establish a basic rule of confidentiality, and prescribe different disclosure rules, as explained in more detail below, for each of three groups: (1) private persons, (2) government agencies concerned with tax administration, and (3) other government agencies. There is also a complex interplay between the Freedom of Information Act, which insures public access to IRS rulings and other determinations, and the confidentiality of information supplied by the taxpayers to whom these determinations are issued.[50] Another component of the privacy-disclosure interplay is the Right to Financial Privacy Act of 1978, regulating the confidentiality of records bearing on the relationship of customers to banks, savings and loan associations, credit unions, consumer finance companies, and other financial institutions. Finally, a totally different balance between privacy and disclosure is struck by IRC §6104, permitting public inspection of the applications for exemption, supporting documents, and information returns submitted to the IRS by charitable and other exempt organizations, private foundations, and qualified pension trusts.

2. Protected Information. Section 6103(a) commences by mandating confidentiality as the general rule: "Returns and return information shall be confidential, and except as authorized by this title [federal officers, employees, and certain other persons shall not] disclose any return or return informa-

---

[47] See IRC §6109(d).

[48] See Treas. Regs. §§301.6109-1(a), 301.6109-(1)(d)(2).

[49] See generally Joint Comm. on Taxation, 94th Cong., 2d Sess., General Explanation of the Tax Reform Act of 1976, reprinted in 1976-3 CB (Vol. 2) 1, 325; Joint Comm. on Taxation, 95th Cong., 2d Sess., General Explanation of the Revenue Act of 1978, at 396-398 (1979).

[50] See supra ¶38.5.

tion. . . . " The rest of IRC §6103 consists of exceptions to the no-disclosure principle and safeguards to insure compliance with the basic principle.

In prescribing the types of information that may be disclosed, IRC §6103 distinguishes among three categories of material: "returns," "return information," and "taxpayer return information." The term "return" is defined by IRC §6103(e)(1) as "any tax or information return, declaration of estimated tax, or claim for refund required by, or provided for or permitted under, the provisions of this title," including supporting schedules, supplements, and amendments. "Return information" is defined by IRC §6103(b)(2) to include the taxpayer's identity; the nature, source, and amount of income, deductions, and other data on the return; and off-return information received, prepared, recorded, or collected by or furnished to the IRS with respect to the return or the taxpayer's tax liability. The term does not, however, include data in a form that cannot be associated with or otherwise used to identify a particular taxpayer. The third category, "taxpayer return information," is defined by IRC §6103(b)(3) as "return information" (as just defined) filed with or furnished to the IRS by or on behalf of the taxpayer to whom it relates, such as data supplied by a taxpayer's accountant to support a deduction claimed on the return. This type of return information is specially defined, as a prelude to according it a higher degree of confidentiality than return information collected by the IRS from third persons.

3. Disclosure to Private Persons. Section 6103(e) authorizes the inspection of tax returns by, or their disclosure to, such persons as the taxpayer himself, beneficiaries in the cases of returns of estates and decedents, executors and guardians, both spouses in the case of joint returns, shareholders owning one percent or more of a corporation's stock in the case of corporate returns, and other persons with similar relationships to the taxpayer whose return is sought. If a person is entitled to inspect a taxpayer's return under IRC §6103(e), "return information" with respect to the same taxpayer is also subject to disclosure under IRC §6103(e)(7) if the Treasury determines that "disclosure would not seriously impair Federal tax administration.

4. Federal and State Tax Administration. Section 6103(h) authorizes the disclosure of returns and return information to Treasury employees whose official duties require inspection or disclosure for "tax administration" purposes, defined by IRC §6103(b)(4) to include the development and formulation of federal tax policy, as well as such obvious enforcement activities as the assessment and collection of taxes.[51] Disclosure of returns and return informa-

[51] For the use of tax returns and return information in the examination of the returns of unrelated taxpayers, see Special Committee on Confidentiality of Tax Returns, Section of Taxation, American Bar Association, Special Study of the Use by the

tion to officers and employees of the Department of Justice is also authorized, but only for grand jury and other judicial proceedings involving tax administration; and the Department of Justice is entitled to be advised in cases of this type whether prospective jurors have been the subject of audits or other tax investigations by the IRS. Returns and return information may also be disclosed in federal or state judicial or administrative proceedings relating to tax administration, subject to prescribed conditions.

Section 6103(k) authorizes the disclosure of returns, return information, and certain other data for other federal tax administration purposes, including correction of a published misstatement of fact with respect to a taxpayer's return (but only following approval by the Joint Committee on Taxation); and compliance with the terms of a tax treaty.[52]

Returns and return information can be disclosed to state tax authorities to the extent necessary to administer state tax laws, subject to certain restrictions. States with federally based income taxes often require their taxpayers to attach copies of their federal returns, in whole or part, to their state returns as an aid to piggy-back enforcement. Section 6103(p)(8) provides that no return or return information will be disclosed to such a state unless it adopts laws protecting the confidentiality of the federal return or return information included on the state tax return.

5. Federal Nontax Agencies. Section 6103(i) deals in great detail with disclosures to federal officers and employees in connection with the administration of federal laws not related to taxes, distinguishing among the three categories of protected data (returns, return information, and taxpayer return information) in regulating this area.

1. *Court orders.* In the case of nontax criminal investigations (e.g., by the Department of Justice), returns and taxpayer return information may be disclosed pursuant to an ex parte judicial order if a federal district judge or magistrate is satisfied that certain conditions have been met.[53] In the case of other federal investigations and proceedings, return information (but not returns or taxpayer return information) may be supplied, subject to certain threshold conditions and safeguards. Section 6103(i)(2) permits the disclosure of return information (including in this case the taxpayer's identity) for the preparation of a judicial or administrative proceeding pertaining to the enforcement of a federal criminal statute, an investigation that may result in such

---

Internal Revenue Service of Third Party Returns and Return Information, 33 Tax Lawyer 717 (1980).

[52] See IRC §6013(k) for a list of "tax administration purposes."

[53] See IRC §6103(i)(1) for a description of the preconditions to the issuance of a judicial order; IRC §6103(i)(5) permits such an order to be issued for the purpose of locating federal fugitives from justice.

a proceeding, or a grand jury proceeding pertaining to the enforcement of such a statute.

Section 6103(i)(3), which was extensively amended and elaborated in 1982, regulates the important area of data supplied by the Treasury to other federal agencies to apprise them of possible criminal activities, and of circumstances involving an imminent danger of death or physical injury to any individual or flight from federal prosecution, by permitting return information, such as information supplied by informants or collected by the IRS from third persons (but not returns or taxpayer return information) to be supplied voluntarily by the Treasury to the appropriate federal agency.

2. *White House.* Under IRC §6103(g), returns and returns information may be supplied in response to a request signed "personally" by the President, which must identify the taxpayer and specify the reason for the requested disclosure or inspection. Section 6103(g) also authorizes the Treasury to disclose certain return information about potential appointees to high-level executive or judicial posts.[54] The restraints on White House fishing expeditions are buttressed by the requirement, imposed by IRC §6103(g)(5), that the Joint Committee on Taxation be informed, with limited exceptions, of these requests.

3. *Congressional committees.* Returns and return information may be obtained on written request pursuant to IRC §6103(f) by the chairmen of the House Ways and Means Committee, the Senate Finance Committee, and the Joint Committee on Taxation or by the chief of staff of the Joint Committee on Taxation; but material that can be associated with particular taxpayers is to be furnished to the appropriate committee only in closed executive session. Other committees of Congress, upon the chairman's written request, may obtain returns and return information for use in closed executive session, if the committee is authorized to inspect returns or return information by a resolution of the Senate or the House or, in the case of joint committees, by concurrent resolution.

4. *Miscellaneous disclosures.* Section 6103 also contains provisions authorizing disclosure for certain limited nontax purposes, such as statistical use by federal agencies, audits of the IRS by the Comptroller General, administration of the federal social security system (including enforcement of child support obligations), notification of persons entitled to unclaimed tax refunds, collection of defaulted government loans to students, location of persons exposed to occupational hazards, and numerous other specialized activities.

6. Effect of Freedom of Information Act. The Freedom of Information Act, requiring certain governmental records and proceedings to be made

[54] IRC §6103(g)(2).

public on request, does not apply to "matters . . . specially exempted from disclosure by statute." [55] Before §6103 was amended in 1976, it provided that tax returns "shall constitute public records," but it permitted disclosure only to specified persons and agencies. When IRC §6103 was rewritten in 1976, the term "return information" was defined by IRC §6103(b)(2) to exclude "data in a form which cannot be associated with, or otherwise identify, directly or indirectly, a particular taxpayer." The reason for removing material of this type from the protected area was described as follows by the staff of the Joint Committee on Taxation:

> [T]he addition by the IRS of easily deletable identifying information to the type of statistical study or compilation of data which, under its current practice, has been subject to disclosure, will not prevent disclosure of such study or compilation under the newly amended section 6103. In such an instance, the identifying information would be deleted and disclosure of the statistical study or compilation of data could be made.[56]

Section 6103(b)(2) was amended again in 1981 to permit the IRS to deny disclosure of the standards used for the selection of returns for audit and the data used in determining these standards.

¶39.3 TAX RATES

1. Introductory. Sections 1(a)–1(d) prescribe separate tax rate schedules for four classes of individual taxpayers, whose statutory qualifications are discussed below: (1) married individuals filing joint returns and surviving spouses, (2) heads of households, (3) unmarried individuals (other than surviving spouses and heads of households), and (4) married individuals filing separate returns. Each schedule is graduated by reference to the taxpayer's taxable income, starting with an initial bracket that is subject to no tax (the so-called zero bracket amount) [57] and proceeding in a series of steps to impose marginal tax rates that rise from 11 percent to 50 percent (1983 rates). In lieu of the tax imposed by the applicable rate schedule, however, taxpayers with taxable income within brackets prescribed by the IRS from time to time are subject to the tax liability set out in the tax tables.

---

[55] 5 USC §552(b)(3).

[56] Joint Comm. on Taxation, 94th Cong., 2d Sess., supra note 49, at 328; see also Long v. IRS, 596 F.2d 362 (9th Cir. 1979) (analysis of IRS' obligation to segregate nonexempt material); Zale Corp. v. IRS, 481 F.Supp. 486 (D.D.C. 1979) (relationship between FOIA and IRC §6103).

[57] For the zero bracket amount, see supra ¶14.4.

A rate schedule is prescribed by IRC §1(e) for estates and trusts, which is similar to the schedule applicable to married individuals filing separate returns except that, since the zero bracket amount does not apply, the first bracket of taxable income is taxed at 11 percent.

Corporations are subject to the rates prescribed by IRC §11, which differ from the graduated rates applicable to individuals, estates, and trusts in consisting of only five steps, ranging (as of 1983) from 15 percent on taxable income of $25,000 or less to 46 percent of taxable income in excess of $100,000.

In addition to these basic rates, certain classes of taxpayers and types of income are subject to special rates, such as nonresident aliens and foreign corporations not engaged in a U.S. trade or business, which are subject under IRC §§871 and 881 to a 30 percent flat rate (or lower treaty rate) on certain types of income from U.S. sources.

Changes in tax rates are ordinarily made effective by Congress as of the first day of a calendar year. When the rates change during a taxpayer's taxable year, as in the case of fiscal year taxpayers, the rates are prorated by IRC §21 under principles illustrated at some length by the regulations.[58]

Section 1(f), enacted in 1982, mandates cost-of-living adjustments in the rate schedules applicable to individuals, estates, and trusts, starting with 1985. Increases in the Consumer Price Index are to be reflected by increases in the dollar amounts subject to the first-bracket zero tax rate, and the higher brackets are to be adjusted by changes in the minimum and maximum amounts included in each bracket.

2. Married Couples—Joint vs. Separate Returns

1. *Income splitting by joint returns.* Under IRC §1(a), married couples filing joint returns are subject to the same tax that they would pay if their taxable income were equally divided between them and they filed separate returns under IRC §1(d). For example, the 1983 rate schedule prescribed by IRC §1(a) imposes a tax of $16,014 on $60,000 of taxable income reported on a joint return, which is twice the tax imposed by IRC §1(d) on a separate return filed by a married individual with $30,000 of taxable income ($8,007 × 2 = $16,014). With exceptions mentioned below, therefore, married couples have no incentive to engage in income-splitting devices to shift income from one spouse to the other; the joint return itself is an efficient income-splitting device, which produces the same tax result as an actual equal division of their taxable income between the two spouses.

The "income splitting" joint return was first authorized in 1948, primarily to end prior tax disparities between community-property and common-law

[58] For fiscal and short taxable years, see supra ¶35.1.

states.[59] Before 1948, the community income of a married couple in a community-property state was divided equally between them for federal income tax purposes,[60] while the income of married couples in common-law states had to be reported by the spouse whose personal services or invested capital produced the income. Since 1948, however, it has not been possible for married couples to derive a federal income tax benefit by moving from a common-law state to a community-property state or by shifting income from one spouse to the other, except in a few circumstances.

The 1948 principle of tax equality for all married couples with equal amounts of taxable income, regardless of their residence or the proportions in which the spouses contribute to their aggregate income or deductions, would be undermined if their dollar-limited deductions could be increased by filing separate returns. Many tax allowances are, therefore, cut in half or denied if married persons file separate returns.[61] Under the separate schedules prescribed by IRC §§1(a) and 1(d) for joint returns and separate returns, buttressed by these adjustments to dollar-limited deductions, separate returns almost never offer any tax advantage over joint returns. For married persons with relatively equal amounts of income, however, the amount deductible for medical expenses may be larger if one spouse pays the lion's share of the expenses and they file separate rather than joint returns, since the 5 percent nondeductible floor of IRC §213(a) will then be applied to a smaller amount of adjusted gross income. A similar possibility is created by the 10 percent nondeductible floor applicable to casualty losses under IRC §165(h)(1).

When married individuals file separate instead of joint returns, however, they ordinarily are subject to a higher aggregate tax burden, a price that ordinarily is attributable to marital estrangement, so that one spouse does not want to disclose his or her income to the other, is unwilling to sign a joint return because of hostility or vindictiveness, or fears the resulting joint and several liability for the tax, which covers the amount actually due, not merely the amount reported on the return.

2. *Filing requirements.* A joint return may be filed by husband and wife, even though one has neither gross income nor deductions, provided (1) they are married at the close of the taxable year or, if one dies before the close of the taxable year, at the time of the decedent's death; (2) neither spouse is a

---

[59] See supra ¶31.1.

[60] Poe v. Seaborn, 282 US 101 (1930), discussed supra ¶31.1.

[61] See, e.g., IRC §§1211(b)(2) (capital losses deductible against ordinary income to extent of $3,000 on joint return, but only $1,500 on separate returns of married taxpayers), 121(b)(1) (dollar limit on exclusion of gain from sale of principal residence reduced from $125,000 to $62,500 in case of separate return by married individual), 44A(f)(2) (household and dependent care credit denied if married taxpayers file separate returns).

nonresident alien at any time during the taxable year;[62] and (3) husband and wife have the same taxable year, with an exception for different taxable years resulting from death.[63] Although the filing of a *joint* return bars the later filing of separate returns (unless a joint return made by a surviving spouse is disaffirmed by the deceased spouse's executor or administrator),[64] taxpayers filing *separate* returns may substitute a joint return even after the normal filing time has expired, provided they pay the full amount shown as due on the joint return and satisfy the other conditions set out in IRC §§6013(b)(1) and 6013(b)(2).

A joint return is ordinarily signed by both spouses, though in certain circumstances one can sign for the other.[65] Moreover, a nonsigner's consent can be inferred from the facts—for example, if his or her income is reported on the disputed joint return rather than on a separate return.[66] Conversely, occasionally a spouse signing a joint return under mental or physical duress is allowed to repudiate the return, usually after a divorce or the other spouse's death, when the IRS asserts liability for a deficiency against the victimized spouse.[67] To establish that a signature was affixed to a joint return under duress, the Tax Court requires a showing that the taxpayer was unable to resist the other spouse's demands to sign the return and would not have signed but for the constraint.[68]

When a joint return is filed, the couple's income and deductions are computed on an aggregate basis since, although there are two taxpayers, there is only one taxable income.[69]

3. *Joint liability—"innocent spouse" exception.* Since both parties to a joint return are "taxpayers," they are jointly and severally liable for the tax

---

[62] This restriction, however, is lifted for certain nonresident aliens by IRC §§6013(g) (election to treat nonresident alien as resident) and 6013(h) (nonresident alien who becomes a resident during taxable year).

[63] See IRC §6013(a)(2) (exception for death not applicable in cases of remarriage or short taxable years); see also IRC §6013(c) (different taxable years because of either spouse's death treated as though both years ended when surviving spouse's taxable year ended).

[64] IRC §6013(a)(3); Treas. Regs. §§1.6013-1(a)(1), 1.6013-1(d)(5).

[65] See supra, text at note 43.

[66] See, e.g., Klayman v. CIR, ¶79,408 P-H Memo TC (1979) (whether one-signature return is a joint return depends on intent of parties; taxpayer as well as IRS can invoke "tacit consent" principle; on facts, non-signing spouse—a calligrapher!—consented to joint return by entrusting filing to other spouse); Lane v. CIR, 26 TC 405 (1956) (Acq.) (non-signing spouse agreed to sign joint return as part of property settlement; held, joint return).

[67] See, e.g., Brown v. CIR, 51 TC 116 (1968) (wife not bound by joint return that she signed under duress); but see Stanley v. CIR, 45 TC 555 (1966) (wife's signature voluntary despite domineering husband). For the possibility of limited liability on a joint return, even if it was signed voluntarily, see infra, text at notes 70-72.

[68] See Brown v. CIR, supra note 67.

[69] See Treas. Regs. §1.6013-4(b); IRC §6013(d)(3).

due (not merely for the amount shown on the return), including interest, additions for negligence, and fraud penalties if applicable.[70] This principle, though regarded by Congress "as an important adjunct to the privilege of filing joint returns," [71] is mitigated by two exceptions.

First, if the return omits from gross income an amount attributable to one spouse that exceeds 25 percent of the reported gross income, the other spouse is excused by IRC §6013(e) from liability for the tax (including interest, penalties, etc.) attributable to the omitted amount, provided (1) he or she did not know and had no reason to know of the omission when signing the return and (2) it would be inequitable to hold the innocent spouse liable for the deficiency, taking into account all relevant circumstances, including whether he or she "significantly benefited" from the omitted items. Factors tending to establish that the innocent spouse had reason to know of the omission include unusual or lavish expenditures, participation in business affairs or bookkeeping, and the other spouse's refusal to be forthright about their income.[72]

The innocent-spouse provision does not convert the return into a separate return of the blameworthy spouse. For example, the innocent spouse remains jointly and severally liable for deficiencies attributable to matters other than the omitted amount, such as erroneous or fraudulent deductions;[73] moreover, IRC §6013(e) provides no protection to a taxpayer who innocently omits his or her share of community income from a separate return or fails to file a return, even if the income is attributable to the other spouse's personal services and the taxpayer's share was not made available to him or her.[74]

Second, a similar but more limited escape hatch is afforded by IRC §6653(b), under which the 50 percent civil fraud penalty is not imposed on a party to a joint return unless some part of the underpayment was due to his or her fraud.[75]

4. *Separate returns.* When married individuals file separate returns, a deductible item paid for with community income or jointly owned property is ordinarily divided between them; but the use of personal funds entitles the payor to take the entire deduction. A different result may occur if the amount

---

[70] IRC §6013(d)(3).

[71] Sonnenborn v. CIR, 57 TC 373, 381 (1971).

[72] Sanders v. US, 509 F.2d 162, 168 (5th Cir. 1975) ("reason to know" construed in line with Restatement (Second) of Agency §9); Vesco v. CIR, ¶79,374 P-H Memo TC (1979) (wife of big-time spender benefited from his practice of using company plane for personal travel, charging restaurant bills and club dues to company, etc.); Mysse v. CIR, 57 TC 680 (1972) (relief granted to wife where husband managed affairs and their standard of living was not noticeably higher by reason of the omitted income).

[73] See Treas. Regs. §1.6013-5(d).

[74] See Galliher v. CIR, 62 TC 760 (1974), aff'd by order, 512 F.2d 1404 (5th Cir.), cert. denied, 423 US 988 (1975) (omission of community income from separate return of married spouse).

[75] See infra ¶42.3.

was paid with joint funds but charged wholly against one spouse's share or, conversely, if it was paid with separate funds but was to be reimbursed in whole or in part by the other spouse. Moreover, if an item like interest or local taxes is paid by the "wrong" spouse, the item might not be deductible by either.[76]

3. Surviving Spouses. Under IRC §§1(a)(2) and 2(a), a return filed by a surviving spouse is subject to the joint return rates for two taxable years following the year of the other spouse's death if the survivor (1) is entitled to a dependency exemption for a child, (2) maintains a home constituting the child's principal place of abode as a member of the surviving spouse's household, and (3) furnishes over half the cost of maintaining the household. Under IRC §2(a)(2)(B), surviving spouse status arises only if a joint return could have been made for the year of the other spouse's death, and remarriage terminates the surviving spouse privilege, even if the other conditions of IRC §2(a) are satisfied.

4. Heads of Households. Although the special joint return rate schedule was enacted in 1948 to give married couples living in common-law states the tax advantages previously enjoyed by community-property couples, the resulting reduction in their tax liability came to be viewed by the public as a tax allowance for family responsibilities. So viewed, it was assailed as unfair to divorced, widowed, and unmarried persons with dependent children or parents, who argued that their tax-paying capacity was no greater than that of a married couple with the same amount of income and the same number of dependents. In 1951, Congress responded to these complaints by creating a new rate schedule for heads of households, with rates about midway between the joint return and separate return rates.

For convenience, persons qualifying for the special tax rates imposed by IRC §1(b) on heads of households can be divided into two classes—those living in their own households with a relative meeting prescribed conditions and those maintaining a dependent parent in a separate household. In either case, the taxpayer can qualify if, and only if, he or she is not (a) married at the close of the taxable year, (b) a surviving spouse as defined by IRC §2(a), or (c) a nonresident alien at any time during the taxable year.

1. *Taxpayer's own household.* A taxpayer can qualify as a head of household under IRC §2(b)(1)(A) by maintaining as his or her home a household constituting the principal place of abode, as a member of the household, of (a) a child (by blood or legal adoption), stepchild, or descendant of a child, but

[76] See e.g., Johnson v. CIR, ¶80,009 P-H Memo TC (1980) (husband cannot deduct taxes or mortgage interest paid on house owned by wife), and cases there cited.

if the qualifying relative is married at the close of the taxpayer's taxable year, only if the taxpayer is entitled to a dependency exemption for the relative under IRC §151;[77] or (b) any other dependent for whom the taxpayer is entitled to a dependency exemption under IRC §151, except a person who is a dependent solely by reason of IRC §152(a)(9) (certain unrelated persons) or §152(c) (persons covered by multiple-support agreements).[78]

2. *Separate household for parent.* Head of household status can be attained under IRC §2(b)(1)(B) if the taxpayer maintains a household constituting the principal place of abode of a mother or father for whom the taxpayer is entitled to a dependency exemption.[79]

3. *Maintenance of household.* To maintain a household, whether it is the taxpayer's own or a parent's, the taxpayer is required by IRC §2(b)(1) to furnish more than half of its maintenance cost—defined by the regulations as "the expenses incurred for the mutual benefit of the occupants [of the household] for [the] taxable year." [80] The regulations impliedly exclude the rental value of an owner-occupied residence; this exclusion is ordinarily disadvantageous to taxpayers owning the residence that constitutes the household, but it is advantageous to taxpayers supporting a parent who lives in the latter's own residence.[81]

4. *Principal place of abode.* Under both IRC §2(b)(1)(A) (taxpayer's household) and §2(b)(1)(B) (household of taxpayer's parent), the household maintained by the taxpayer must be "the principal place of abode" for the qualifying relative; and under IRC §2(b)(1)(A) it must also be the taxpayer's "home." [82] In general, these conditions require occupancy for the taxpayer's entire taxable year; but temporary absences are not fatal.[83]

---

[77] If the qualifying relative is unmarried, it does not matter that he or she is the dependent of another person. See Rev. Rul. 55-329, 1955-1 CB 205.

[78] For persons qualifying as "dependents" and the distinction between a dependent and a person for whom the taxpayer is entitled to a dependency exemption, see supra ¶14.2.

[79] See Robinson v. CIR, 51 TC 520 (1968), aff'd per curiam, 422 F.2d 873 (9th Cir. 1970) ("household" can be a nursing home or similar institution); Rev. Rul. 70-279, 1970-1 CB 1 (acquiescence in *Robinson;* ruling to contrary revoked).

[80] Treas. Regs. §1.2-2(d).

[81] See Glogowski v. CIR, ¶67,236 P-H Memo TC (1967) (taxpayer cannot count fair rental value of own personal residence in computing expenses of household occupied by him and his son, daughter-in-law, and grandchild); Teeling v. CIR, 42 TC 671 (1964) (taxpayer supporting parents, who lived in their own home, qualified as head of household because rental value of parent's home was excluded in determining whether he defrayed more than half of their household expenses).

[82] See Smith v. CIR, 332 F.2d 671 (9th Cir. 1964) (taxpayer can have two "homes" for this purpose); Rev. Rul. 72-43, 1972-1 CB 4 (contra); Treas. Regs. §1.6031(c)-1.

[83] See Treas. Regs. §§1.2-2(c)(1) (taxpayer's household), 1.2-2(c)(2) (separate household for taxpayer's parent). See also Blair v. CIR, 63 TC 214 (1974), aff'd on another issue, 538 F.2d 155 (7th Cir. 1976) (taxpayer's household was principal place

5. *Marital status.* A head of household return cannot be filed by a person who is married at the close of his or her taxable year.[84] Although legal separation under a decree of divorce or separate maintenance terminates the marriage for this purpose, a separation agreement does not, and neither do certain interlocutory or provisional legal orders, such as decrees for support.[85] Under IRC §§2(c) and 143(b), however, a married person can file a head of household return if (1) he or she maintains an otherwise qualifying household with a child or stepchild for whom a dependency exemption is allowable and furnishes over half of the cost of the household during the taxable year and (2) the other spouse is not a member of the household for the entire taxable year.[86] This so-called deserted spouse rule permits a qualifying taxpayer to file either a joint return (if the other spouse, though absent from the household, is willing to sign) or a head of household return.

5. Marriage Penalties and Bonuses. Unmarried individuals who do not qualify for surviving spouse or head of household rates are subject to the rate schedule prescribed by IRC §1(c).[87] This rate schedule produces a lower aggregate tax for two single persons with relatively equal amounts of taxable income than they would pay on the total amount if married; and there have been some widely publicized cases of tax-motivated divorces, followed by the filing of single-person returns under IRC §1(c). Such a divorce is probably effective for tax purposes even if the ex-spouses continue to live together, but the IRS refuses to recognize a divorce that is followed by a prearranged remarriage.[88] The relationship of the single-person rate schedule to the joint return rates has been controversial since 1948, and the issues are best examined in historical context.

---

of abode for child who was at boarding school, although other parent had custody under divorce decree); Stanback v. US, 39 AFTR2d 805 (M.D.N.C. 1977) (not officially reported) (father's household was not children's principal place of abode, although they spent more than half the year with him, since part of the time reflected visits pursuant to separation agreement giving permanent custody to their mother); Hein v. CIR, 28 TC 826 (1957) (taxpayer's household was principal place of abode of dependent sister, despite absence throughout the taxable year while in mental institution and even though return might be prevented by death, where no new permanent place of abode was established).

[84] IRC §2(b)(1); but see IRC §§2(b)(2)(C) (taxpayer considered as not married if spouse is nonresident alien at any time during taxable year), 2(b)(2)(D) (taxpayer considered as married at end of year if spouse died during year).

[85] IRC §2(b)(2)(B); see also Lebowitz v. CIR, ¶78,155 P-H Memo TC (1978) (spouse receiving temporary alimony is still married); Donigan v. CIR, 68 TC 632 (1977) (spouses separated under written separation agreement are still married).

[86] See infra, text at note 91.

[87] For problems in determining marital status, see infra, text at notes 91-95.

[88] Rev. Rul. 76-255, 1976-2 CB 40.

The 1948–1969 tax benefit resulting from marriage, which rose with taxable income and was greatest when one spouse was the sole breadwinner, was quickly viewed by the public as a "tax" on single persons. So characterized, it was attacked on the intertwined but independent grounds that (1) taxes should be independent of marital status ("marriage neutral"); (2) the disparity, even if partially justified by the increased cost of supporting the breadwinner's marital partner, was excessive, particularly if account was taken of the economic value of the second spouse's untaxed household services;[89] and (3) similar benefits should be granted to other persons such as widows and widowers, whose income also had to support two persons rather than one. Congress responded to the third of these complaints in 1951 and 1954 by enacting the special rate schedule for heads of households and allowing surviving spouses to use the joint return rates for two years following the deceased spouse's death,[90] and in 1969 it responded to the continuing complaints of other unmarried persons.

This remedy was a new rate schedule for unmarried taxpayers, under which their liability would not exceed a married couple's tax by more than 20 percent at any taxable income level. Recognizing that the use of separate returns by married persons to take advantage of this reduced rate schedule would revive the pre-1948 geographical disparity between community-property and common-law states, as well as the opportunity to reduce taxes by inter-spousal gifts of income-producing property, Congress rounded out the 1969 reform by denying use of the new single-person rate schedule to married taxpayers filing separate returns.

Because married persons who file separate returns must use the special rate schedule prescribed by IRC §1(d), rather than the rates imposed by IRC §1(c) on unmarried persons, the 1969 reform imposes a "marriage penalty" on persons with relatively equal amounts of income who get married and continue to have the same amount of income thereafter. If, for example, John and Martha have taxable income of $30,000 each from investments, their premarriage tax liability (at 1983 rates) is $6,477 each, or a total of $12,954. If they get married and file a joint return, however, their liability on $60,000 of taxable income will be $16,014—an increase of $3,060. They are entitled to file separate returns if they wish, but that will not restore the *status quo ante,* since they are no longer eligible for the single-person rates but must instead use the special rate schedule of IRC §1(d) for married persons filing separate returns, which imposes a tax of $8,007 each, for a total of $16,014—the same amount as a joint return. At any given level, the marriage penalty is most

---

[89] For untaxed imputed income, see supra ¶1.6.

[90] See supra, text following note 76 (surviving spouses); text at notes 77-78 (heads of households).

pronounced if the couple's aggregate income is equally divided between them, but it is not inconsiderable even if the division is 60-40.

Viewed in isolation, the marriage penalty seems capricious and indefensible. But it is the unavoidable result of pursuing three policies, all of which have vigorous advocates, viz., (1) equal taxes for all equal-income married couples; (2) a smaller differential between single and married persons than was provided by "pure" income splitting from 1948 to 1969; and (3) a progressive rate schedule. The first of these policies was qualified in 1981 by the enactment of IRC §221, allowing married couples filing joint returns to deduct 10 percent of the lesser of (1) $30,000 or (2) the qualified earned income (as defined) of the spouse with the lower amount of such income for the taxable year. If, for example, one spouse earns $20,000 and the other $15,000, they are allowed a deduction (from gross income in computing adjusted gross income) of $1,500. This deduction, which mitigates but does not necessarily eliminate the marriage penalty that exists for some two-job married couples, means that married couples with equal aggregate amounts of income no longer pay the same tax, as they did from 1948 to 1982. Moreover, since it is limited to earned income, IRC §221 does not reduce the marriage penalty for couples with income from investments or other nonqualifying sources.

6. Marital Status for Filing Purposes. As explained above, marital status is controlling in determining the type of return that individuals can file. There being no federal law of marriage and divorce (except in the District of Columbia), the cases often state that the marital status of taxpayers is governed by local law. Though true, this is not the whole truth because the Code contains three provisions relating to martial status that, when applicable, take precedence over local law:

1. The determination of whether a person is married is made as of the close of the person's taxable year unless his or her spouse died during that year, in which event the determination is made as of the time of the death.[91]
2. Persons legally separated from their spouses under decrees of divorce or separate maintenance are not considered as married, regardless of status under state law.[92] Since a decree is required, separation agreements do not terminate the marriage for tax purposes, nor do support

[91] See IRC §143(a)(1).

[92] See IRC §§143(a)(2), 601(d)(2), 2(b)(2)(B); see also Boyer v. CIR, 79 TC 143 (1982) (Massachusetts decree enjoining taxpayer from restraining spouse's personal liberty or entering marital home was equivalent to legal separation under decree of separate maintenance).

orders and other decrees that do not grant a divorce or provide for separate maintenance.[93]

3. In determining the taxpayer's entitlement to personal exemptions and to file a head of household return, IRC §§143(b) and 2(c) treat certain married taxpayers filing separate returns as unmarried if the taxpayer's spouse is not a member of the household throughout the entire taxable year.[94]

Marital status issues not governed by these statutory rules are ordinarily determined by local law. For example, local law determines whether a relationship constitutes a common-law marriage, annulment wipes out the marriage ab initio, divorce in another jurisdiction terminates a marriage, or remarriage after divorce is valid.[95]

7. Tax Tables. To promote accuracy in the computation of tax liabilities by reducing the arithmetic skill required, the Treasury is authorized by IRC §3 to promulgate tax tables for individuals, which must be used by persons covered by the tables, unless they are subject to income averaging or are making a return for a short year because of a change in the annual accounting period.[96] Since the zero bracket amount is built into the tables, the tax is technically imposed on "tax table income," as defined by IRC §3(a)(4). For 1982, the tables are graduated by increments of $25 and $50 of taxable income, starting at zero and terminating at $50,000, and contain separate columns for single taxpayers, married couples filing joint returns, married couples filing separate returns, and heads of household.

Taxpayers whose taxable income exceeds the tax table limits use the rate schedules, as do estates and trusts and individuals subject to income averaging or filing short-period returns.

8. Estates and Trusts. Estates and trusts are subject to the rate schedule prescribed by IRC §1(e), which is identical with the schedule prescribed by IRC §1(d) for married persons filing separate returns, except for the zero bracket amount.

---

[93] See also Treas. Regs. §1.6013-4(a) (interlocutory divorce decree does not terminate marital status); Rev. Rul. 57-368, 1957-2 CB 896 (same for interlocutory divorce decree).

[94] Section 143(b) is made applicable to IRC §§1–5 by IRC §2(c).

[95] For the effect of local law on marital status, see Lee v. CIR, 64 TC 552 (1975), aff'd per curiam, 550 F.2d 1201 (9th Cir. 1977) (purported marriage after invalid Mexican divorce not valid under local law; joint filing of return not permissible), and cases there cited, refusing to follow Borax's Est. v. CIR, 349 F.2d 666 (2d Cir. 1965), cert. denied, 383 US 935 (1966) (uniform federal standard favored).

[96] For income averaging and short-period returns, see infra ¶39.5 and supra ¶35.1, respectively.

By virtue of IRC §1398(c)(2) estates of bankrupt individuals are subject to the rate schedule prescribed by IRC §1(d), rather than to the schedule prescribed by IRC §1(e) for trusts and other estates. This qualifies bankrupt estates for the zero bracket amount applicable to married persons filing separate returns.

9. Corporations. Corporations are subject to the rate schedule of IRC §11, imposing rates (in 1983) that rise in five steps from 15 percent of the first $25,000 of taxable income to 46 percent of taxable income above $100,000. Income splitting among affiliated corporations is checked by IRC §1561, which in effect amalgamates the income of corporations under common control in applying the five-step rate schedule. On the other hand, affiliated corporations are allowed to file consolidated returns, which, roughly speaking, eliminate the tax consequences of intercompany transactions.

¶39.4 ALTERNATIVE MINIMUM TAX

In 1966, one hundred fifty-four individuals with adjusted gross incomes in excess of $200,000 succeeded in entirely eliminating any income tax liability by extensive use of tax allowances authorized by the Internal Revenue Code—the most popular combination being the exclusion (under existing law) of one-half of long-term capital gains and the offset of itemized deductions against the taxpayer's remaining income.[97] Judged from the Treasury's macroeconomic heights, the revenue loss from these high-income, low-tax individuals was not overwhelming, but Congress thought that their immunity threatened taxpayer morale. In the words of the Senate Finance Committee:

> The fact that present law permits a small minority of high-income individuals to escape tax on a large proportion of their income has seriously undermined the belief of taxpayers that others are paying their fair share of the tax burden. It is essential that tax reform be obtained not only as a matter of justice but also as a matter of taxpayer morale. Our individual and corporate income taxes, which are the mainstays of our tax system, depend upon self-assessment and the cooperation of taxpayers. The loss of confidence on their part in the fairness of the tax system could result in a breakdown of taxpayer morale and make it far more difficult to collect the necessary revenues.[98]

Congress responded to this situation with legislation that, as amended from time to time, now consists of the so-called add-on tax on tax preferences

[97] See S. Rep. No. 91-552, reprinted in 1969-3 CB 423, 430.
[98] Id. at 431.

of IRC §56, which is applicable only to corporations and must be paid in addition to the corporation's regular income tax, and the alternative minimum tax of IRC §55, imposed on other individuals, trusts and estates, which is payable only if it exceeds the amount of the taxpayer's regularly computed tax liability.

1. Minimum Tax Base. The minimum tax base is, roughly speaking, the taxpayer's adjusted gross income, increased by the tax preferences listed in IRC §57 and reduced by the itemized deductions listed in IRC §55(e). The tax preferences that must be added back to the taxpayer's adjusted gross income include such items as the excess of percentage depletion over cost depletion, accelerated depreciation and ACRS cost recovery deductions to the extent they exceed straight-line depreciation on the taxpayer's real property, the bargain element in certain tax-favored employee stock options, dividends excluded from gross income under IRC §116, and the deduction allowed by IRC §1202 for capital gains. The itemized deductions that can be deducted in computing the minimum tax base include the allowances for casualty losses, charitable contributions, medical deductions (but subject to a 10 percent nondeductible floor rather than the normal 5 percent floor), and "qualified interest" (elaborately defined by IRC §55(e)(4) to restrict the amount of investment income that can be deducted).

2. Alternative Tax Liability. The minimum tax base (computed as summarized above, but with certain other adjustments) is subject to an exemption of $40,000 (joint returns and surviving spouses), $30,000 (unmarried persons), or $20,000 (married persons filing separate returns, trusts, and estates). As a practical matter, the alternative minimum tax is 20 percent of the balance, payable if, but only if, it exceeds the taxpayer's regular tax. Technically speaking, however, the taxpayer's regular tax is imposed, and the alternative minimum tax is the excess (if any) of 20 percent of the minimum tax base over the regular tax.

¶39.5 INCOME AVERAGING

1. Introductory. To moderate the impact of the progressive individual rates on taxpayers with fluctuating incomes, IRC §§1301–1305 prescribe an elective method of computing the tax liability of taxpayers with "averagable income" in excess of $3,000 for the computation year. Subject to qualifications described below, averageable income is the excess of taxable income for the computation year over 120 percent of the taxpayer's average income during the four-year base period immediately preceding the computation year. The tax on averageable income is computed by applying the taxpayer's rate for the computation year to one-fifth of the averageable income and multiplying the resulting amount by five. Taxpayers electing to average their income under IRC §§1301–1305 cannot take advantage of two other tax allowances in the computation year—IRC §§911 (foreign earned income) and 931 (income from U.S. possessions).[99]

The announced objective of IRC §§1301–1305 is "to treat everyone as nearly equally for tax purposes as possible, without regard to how their income is spread over a period of years and without regard to the type of income involved."[100] This objective is attained only for taxpayers experiencing a substantial increase in income above their average base period income, however, since the provisions do nothing for taxpayers whose income rises and falls from year to year like a roller coaster, nor for those whose high-bracket years precede, rather than follow, a series of lean years.[101]

2. Eligibility. To be eligible for income averaging, the taxpayer (both taxpayers, if a joint return is filed) must be a citizen or resident alien throughout the computation year and must not have been a nonresident alien at any time during the base period.[102] In addition, IRC §1303(c)(1) provides, subject to certain exceptions, that an individual is ineligible if he and his spouse furnished less than one-half of his support during any base period year.[103] Dependent children are presumably the principal targets of the self-support requirements, but it applies even if the taxpayer was not a dependent of any other taxpayer during the base period.

3. Averageable and Base Period Income. To employ income averaging, an eligible taxpayer must have averageable income of more than $3,000 in the computation year. Averageable income is defined by IRC §1302(a)(1) as the amount by which taxable income for the computation year exceeds 120 percent of the taxpayer's average base period income.[104] Base period income for each of the four base period years is ordinarily the taxable income for that year.

---

[99] IRC §1304(b).

[100] S. Rep. No. 830, 88th Cong., 2d Sess., reprinted in 1964-1 (Part 2) CB 505, 644.

[101] If the taxpayer incurs operating or capital losses, however, they can be carried over to other years, as explained supra ¶¶12.9 (net operating losses), 25.2 (capital losses).

[102] IRC §§1303(a), 1303(b).

[103] For the meaning of "support," see Sharvy v. CIR, 67 TC 630 (1977), aff'd per curiam, 566 F.2d 1118 (9th Cir. 1977) (funds from fellowship and teaching assistantship under National Defense Education Act did not constitute self-support), and cases there cited.

[104] See Unser v. CIR, 59 TC 528 (1973) (correct taxable income for base period year is controlling, regardless of amount reported, even if statute of limitations bars assessment of deficiency or refund of overpayment for that year); Treas. Regs. §1.1302-2(b) (income of base period year may not be less than zero).

Because proof of this amount is essential to a computation under IRC §§1301–1305, taxpayers whose income during one or more of the base period years was too low to require them to maintain records or file tax returns may find it difficult to establish their right to an election when their fortunes improve.

4. Computation of Tax. The tax relief resulting from income averaging is illustrated by Example 39-1, which assumes that an unmarried individual with average base period income of $10,000 realized $52,000 of taxable income in the computation year (1983), resulting in averageable income (line 3) of $40,000. Under IRC §1301, the tax on the averageable income is limited to the amount that would have been due if it had been received in five equal annual installments, each stacked on top of 120 percent of the taxpayer's average base period income. The taxpayer's tax liability for the computation year, therefore, is the sum of $1,485 (the tax on $12,000 of nonaverageable income—line 8) and $9,420 (the tax on $40,000 of averageable income—line 10), or a total of $10,905 (line 11).

Since the tax on $52,000 without regard to income averaging is $15,638 the election reduces the taxpayer's liability by $4,733 (line 13).

Example 39-1

Computation of Tax Under IRC §§1301-1305, Relating to Income Averaging— Unmarried Individual, 1983 Rates

1. Taxable income in computation year	$52,000
2. Less: 120 percent of average base period income ($10,000)	12,000
3. Averageable income (must exceed $3,000 to qualify)	$40,000
4. 120 percent of average base period income (line 2)	$12,000
5. Plus: One-fifth of averageable income	8,000
6. Tentative taxable income	$20,000
7. Tentative tax (1983 rate applied to line 6)	$ 3,369
8. Less: Tax on $12,000 (line 2) not subject to averaging	1,485
9. Tax on one-fifth of averageable income	$ 1,884
10. Tax on entire averageable income (line 9 times 5)	$ 9,420
11. Tax liability—tax on $12,000 of nonaverageable income plus tax on $40,000 of averageable income (i.e., line 8 plus line 10)	$10,905
12. Tax on line 1 without income averaging	$15,638
13. Tax savings from income averaging (line 12 minus line 11)	$ 4,733

¶39.6 PAYMENT OF TAXES

1. Basic Principles. In general, income taxes are due and payable at the time and place fixed for filing returns, even if the time for filing the return is extended.[105] Individuals electing under IRC §6014 to have their taxes computed by the IRS, however, are not required to pay until thirty days after the IRS notifies them of the amount due and demands payment. This option is limited by IRC §6014(a) to persons with gross income of less than $10,000, derived entirely from services as an employee, dividends, and interest, whose income from sources other than wages (as defined for withholding purposes) does not exceed $100, and who do not itemize their deductions.

The IRS is authorized by IRC §6161(a)(1) to extend the time to pay the tax shown on the return for "a reasonable period," not to exceed six months (or longer if the taxpayer is abroad). To qualify for an extension (which does not stop the running of interest on the tax due), the taxpayer must show that payment on the due date will result in "undue hardship," such as substantial financial loss from the sale of property at a sacrifice price.[106]

2. Withholding of Taxes From Wages. Sections 3401–3404 require income taxes to be collected by employers at the source by withholding prescribed amounts from the employee's compensation. In determining their tax liabilities, employees are credited with the amounts withheld, even if the employer fails to pay them over to the Treasury.[107] In recent years, the wage withholding system has accounted for about 80 percent of the individual income and employment taxes collected by the IRS.

Withholding at the rates prescribed by IRC §3402 is required for "wages," a term that is defined by IRC §3401(a) as "all remuneration (other than fees paid to a public official) for services performed by an employee for his employer," including noncash remuneration.[108] Although "fees" paid to public officials are excluded, their salaries are subject to withholding.[109]

The extremely broad statutory definition of "wages" is subject to numerous specialized exceptions, the most important of which cover (1) agricultural labor (as defined); (2) domestic services in a private home; (3) services not

---

[105] IRC §6151(a).

[106] See Treas. Regs. §1.6161-1(b) (sale at current market price not ordinarily considered to be undue hardship); Treas. Regs. §1.6161-1(c) (application for extension must be accompanied by financial statements); IRC §6165 (IRS may require bond to secure payment).

[107] See Sladov v. US, 436 US 238, 243 (1978).

[108] See Treas. Regs. §31.3401(a)-1; Rev. Rul. 80-124, 1980-1 CB 212 (preretirement leave payments constitute "wages"); Rowan Cos. v. US, 452 US 247 (1981) (value of meals and lodging furnished for convenience of employer excluded from "wages").

[109] Treas. Regs. §31.3401(a)-2(b).

performed in the course of the employer's trade or business, if the remuneration satisfies the conditions set out in IRC §3401(a)(4) (cash remuneration not exceeding $50 per calendar quarter, etc.) or IRC §3401(a)(11) (noncash remuneration); (4) services for a foreign government or international organization; (5) services qualifying for the exclusion provided by IRC §911, relating to certain income earned abroad; (6) payments for services performed by nonresident aliens outside the United States, exempt from tax under a treaty, or meeting certain other conditions; (7) services performed by clergymen and members of religious orders in the exercise of their religious duties; and (8) certain types of excluded compensation, such as meals and lodging furnished for the convenience of the employer, group term life insurance, employee moving expenses, and some other reimbursed expenses.

The terms "compensation for services" as used by IRC §61(a)(1) in defining gross income, "wages" as defined by IRC §3401(a) for withholding purposes, and "wages" as defined by IRC §3121(a) for social security purposes overlap in large part and include the overwhelming bulk of wages and salaries in the layman's sense. There are, however, peripheral differences in coverage among these three statutory concepts.[110]

Because employers who fail to withhold the prescribed amounts from wages are liable for an employee's taxes if the employee fails to pay them,[111] the employer's obligation must be "precise and not speculative" unless Congress specifically decides otherwise.[112] To determine whether remunerated services are "performed by an employee for his employer"—a crucial part of the definition of "wages"—the regulations adopt conventional common-law principles:

> Generally the relationship of employer and employee exists when the person for whom services are performed has the right to control and direct the individual who performs the services, not only as to the result to be accomplished by the work but also as to the details and means by which that result is accomplished. . . . The right to discharge is also an important factor indicating that the person possessing that right is an employer. . . . In general, if an individual is subject to the control or direction of another merely as to the result to be accomplished by the work and not

---

[110] For example, while clearly taxable to the recipient, wages paid to domestic servants are not subject to withholding, IRC §3401(a)(3). For a table comparing the withholding and social security concepts, see [1983] 7 CCH Stand. Fed. Tax. Rep. ¶4934.1803.

[111] See IRC §§3402(d), 3403; Treas. Regs. §§31.3403-1, 31.3402(d)-1; see also infra ¶42.3 (liability for withheld taxes).

[112] Central Ill. Pub. Serv. Co. v. US, 435 US 21, 31 (1978); see also Rev. Proc. 80-53, 1980-2 CB 848.

as to the means and methods of accomplishing the result, he is not an employee.[113]

The regulations go on to provide that physicians, lawyers, contractors, "and others who follow an independent trade, business, or profession, in which they offer their services to the public, are not employees"—a distinction that in effect incorporates the common-law concept of an independent contractor.[114] On the other hand, a few classes of compensation for services are subjected to withholding even in the absence of an employer-employee relationship, such as tips received from customers, pensions, annuities, certain deferred income, and certain supplemental unemployment compensation benefits.[115]

The IRS has issued numerous rulings determining whether the requisite employer-employee relationship exists,[116] but the issue continues to be troublesome in the extreme, especially if purported independent contractors are unexpectedly reclassified as employees by the IRS or the courts, and the new ruling is applied retroactively.[117] As a temporary measure pending further legislative action, the Revenue Act of 1978 prohibits the issuance of regulations and revenue rulings on common-law employment status and allows taxpayers who had a reasonable basis for not treating workers as employees in the past to continue their practice.[118]

The amount to be withheld from an employee's wages is prescribed by tables promulgated by the Treasury under IRC §3402(a),[119] which reflect the number of withholding exemptions claimed by the employee under IRC

---

[113] Treas. Regs. §31.3401(c)-1(b).

[114] Treas. Regs. §31.3401(c)-1(c); see also Treas. Regs. §31.3401(c)-1(f) (corporate officers "generally" are employees, but directors as such are not).

[115] For tips, see IRC §§3401(a)(16), 3401(f); Treas. Regs. §31.3401(f)-1; for payments by pension trusts, etc., see IRC §§3401(d)(1), 3405; for annuities and certain other forms of deferred income, see IRC §3405; for supplemental unemployment compensation benefits, see IRC §3402(o).

[116] See, e.g., Rev. Rul. 73-591, 1973-2 CB 337 (beautician leasing space but required to work specified number of hours and to furnish reports to owner of premises; held, employee); Rev. Rul. 73-592, 1973-2 CB 338 (contra where free to work as beautician pleases); Rev. Rul. 71-571, 1971-2 CB 347 (drivers operating cabs under conditional sales agreement requiring daily payments but giving no control over operations; held, not employees); Rev. Rul. 71-572, 1971-2 CB 347 (contra where subject to taxicab company's controls).

[117] For the legal propriety of retroactive changes in the status of payments, see Central Ill. Pub. Serv. Co. v. US, supra note 112, at 3, 38 (concurring opinions); see generally supra ¶38.4. (retroactive rulings).

[118] For discussion, see Conf. Rep., H. Rep. No. 97-760, 650–652 (1982).

[119] Amounts to be withheld are usually computed by the wage bracket or percentage method, but other methods can be used. See Treas. Regs. §§31.3402(b)-1 (percentage method), 31.3402(c)-1 (wage bracket method); IRC §3402(h); Treas. Regs. §§31.3402(h)-1 et seq.

§3402(f), as reported to the employer by a signed withholding exemption certificate. An employee who anticipates no income tax liability for the current year is exempted from withholding on filing an appropriate certificate with the employer, provided the employee incurred no tax liability for the prior taxable year.[120] On the other hand, by agreement between employers and employees, withholding can be increased above the mandatory amount or extended to payments not otherwise subject to withholding (e.g., compensation for agricultural and domestic services).[121]

The employer is liable for amounts required to be deducted and withheld from wages, is protected by IRC §3403 against liability to the employee for these amounts, and is required to report and remit the withheld amounts to the Treasury.[122]

3. Withholding of Taxes From Interest and Dividends. Sections 3451-3456, enacted in 1932, provide a system of withholding a tax at the 10 percent rate on the payment of interest and dividends (including patronage dividends of certain cooperatives) after June 30, 1983. No withholding is required on interest paid by an individual, such as payments on a home mortgage; but virtually all other payors of interest or dividends, including the United States, are required to withhold. In addition, certain middlemen, such as custodians, nominees, and corporate trustees, are considered payors.

A few classes of payees are exempt from the withholding requirements, primarily (1) individuals with a tax liability of $600 or less ($1,000 on a joint return) for the preceding year; (2) individuals aged 65 or over with a tax liability of $1,500 or less ($2,500 on a joint return) for the preceding year; (3) simple trusts currently distributing all income to individual beneficiaries who are exempt from withholding; and (4) "exempt recipients," defined to include financial intermediaries, such as brokers and custodians, who are themselves required to withhold the requisite amount when passing the interest or dividends on to their customers and clients. Payees claiming exemption from withholding may be required by the payor to provide exemption certificates.

Section 3451 does not apply to various forms of tax exempt interest, interest subject to withholding under other provisions of the Code, and interest paid by certain foreign governments and corporations, except as otherwise provided by the regulations. Certain classes of dividends are also exempted, including dividends reinvested in public utility stock as part of a qualified

---

[120] IRC §3402(n).

[121] IRC §§3402(i), 3402(p); Treas. Regs. §§31.3402(i)-1, 31.3402(p)-1.

[122] IRC §3501. A periodic deposit procedure may be required, see IRC §6302(c); Treas. Regs. §31.6302(c)-1. Violations of the employer's obligations are subject to penalties for negligence and fraud, and a 100 percent penalty of any unpaid amounts can also be assessed against any "responsible officer," see infra ¶42.3.

dividend reinvestment plan and capital gain dividends of regulated investment companies and real estate investment trusts.

4. Withholding of Taxes From Gambling Winnings. Section 3402(q) requires withholding of taxes from certain gambling winnings at a 20 percent rate; but, on the theory that most gamblers end up the year with no net gains, the requirement is limited to transactions involving large gains of a windfall character. Withholding was first required by the Tax Reform Act of 1976, when Congress concluded that prior rules requiring racetracks to report payouts of $600 or more were ineffective because successful bettors often used intermediaries to cash their winning tickets for a 10 percent fee. These so-called ten-percenters, in turn, often claimed offsetting losses when reporting their fictitious gains, or simply evaporated at the end of the racing season.

5. Withholding of Taxes From Payments to Nonresident Aliens and Foreign Corporations. Persons having "the control, receipt, custody, disposal, or payment" of dividends, interest, wages, salaries, and certain other items payable to nonresident aliens and foreign corporations are required by IRC §§1441–1442 to withhold taxes therefrom. As a further precaution against tax avoidance, an alien (whether resident or nonresident) is required by IRC §6851(d) to obtain a "sailing permit" from the IRS before departing from the United States.

6. Payments of Estimated Tax by Individuals. Individuals are required by IRC §6153 to estimate their tax for the current year and to pay the estimated amounts in quarterly installments if they are not covered by wage withholding and certain other estimated credits. Estimated tax must be paid by every individual whose gross income can reasonably be expected (a) to include more than $500 from sources other than wages subject to withholding or (b) to exceed $5,000, $10,000, or $20,000, depending on marital status.[123] These conditions are relaxed, however, by a small taxpayer exemption determined by the amount of estimated tax (after allowing for taxes to be withheld from wages, etc.).

A married couple can make a joint estimate (resulting in joint and several liability for the estimated tax), unless one of them is a nonresident alien, they are separated under a decree of divorce or separate maintenance, or they have different taxable years.[124] A joint estimate does not bind the couple to filing

---

[123] IRC §§6015(a)(1), 6015(c).

[124] IRC §6015(c). For similar, but not identical, conditions governing the filing of joint tax returns, see supra ¶39.3.

a joint tax return; and if they file separate returns, the estimated tax may be allocated entirely to one spouse or divided as they may agree.[125]

Calendar year taxpayers must pay the first installment of estimated tax on April 15, unless the filing requirements are met for the first time at a later date, in which event the first installment date is June 15, September 15, or January 15 of the following year, as the case may be.[126] These dates are changed correspondingly for fiscal year taxpayers by IRC §6073(e). An amended estimate may be made pursuant to IRC §6015(b) if the taxpayer estimates that his gross income, deductions, or credits will differ from those reflected on the previous declaration.

Payments of estimated tax may be made in four equal installments if the first installment is paid on April 15, or in fewer installments if it is made later.[127] Taxpayers filing their tax returns on or before January 31 and paying in full the amount shown as payable on the return are not required to pay the January 15 installment of the estimated tax.[128]

The assumptions to be used by taxpayers in estimating their tax are described by the regulations as follows:

> For the purpose of making the [estimate], the amount of gross income which the taxpayer can reasonably be expected to receive or accrue, depending upon the method of accounting upon which taxable income is computed, and the amount of the estimated allowable deductions and credits to be taken into account in computing the amount of estimated tax shall be determined upon the basis of the facts and circumstances existing at the time [when the estimate] is made as well as those reasonably to be anticipated for the taxable year. . . . In the case of a taxpayer engaged in business on his own account, there shall be made an estimate of gross income and deductions and credits in the light of the best available information affecting the trade, business, or profession.[129]

Section 6654(a) imposes an "addition" for an underpayment of estimated income tax, which is computed without reference to the taxpayer's good faith; and it is not excused by evidence that the estimated amount accurately reflected the facts as known and reasonably projected when made.[130] The underpayment is defined by IRC §6654(b), in objective after-the-fact terms, as the

---

[125] See Treas. Regs. §1.6015(b)-1(b) for the method of allocating payments if the spouses do not agree on a division.

[126] IRC §§6073(a), 6153(a).

[127] IRC §§6015(c), 6153(a).

[128] See Treas. Regs. §1.6015(f)-1(a)(1).

[129] Treas. Regs. §1.6015(d)-1(a)(1).

[130] See Treas. Regs. §1.6654-1(a)(1); Ruben's Est. v. CIR, 33 TC 1071 (1960) (reasonable cause and extenuating circumstances irrelevant).

excess of (a) the amount that would have been payable if the estimated tax were 80 percent (66⅔ percent for farmers and fishermen) of the tax actually shown on the return over (b) the amount actually paid. The imposition of a penalty on taxpayers making the best estimate feasible under the circumstances is superficially oppressive, but the addition charged by IRC §6654 is equivalent to an interest charge on the underpayment for the period that funds remained available to the taxpayer.[131]

Section 6654(d) creates four safe harbors, which protect the taxpayer against the penalty imposed by IRC §6654(a) on underpayments if the total amount of estimated tax (including, for this purpose, taxes withheld from wages)[132] paid on or before a quarterly installment date equals or exceeds the amount that would have been payable on or before that date if the estimated tax had been computed by the most favorable of the four statutory methods. The taxpayer is not required to use any one safe harbor consistently but can instead seek shelter for each installment under a different method.

1. *Prior year's tax.* The simplest source of protection is IRC §6654(d)(1), which applies if the amount paid, together with the prior installments, equals or exceeds the amount that would have been due if the estimate had been based on the tax shown on the preceding year's return.[133]

2. *Prior year's income.* Section 6654(d)(4) protects the taxpayer if the amount paid is based on the "facts" shown on the prior year's return and on that year's tax law, but using the current year's rates and exemption status.[134] In effect, the taxpayer determines the tax that would be due for the current year, based on the prior year's reported income and the current year's rates and exemptions.

3. *Current income annualized.* A more complex safe harbor is IRC 6654(d)(2), requiring payment of 80 percent (66⅔ percent for farmers and fishermen) of the tax for the current year, computed by annualizing the taxable income for the months before the particular installment is required to be paid.[135]

4. *Actual current income.* Section 6654(d)(3) also looks to the taxpayer's current income; but instead of annualizing the income already received, it

---

[131] The penalty, however, is not deductible as "interest" under IRC §163.

[132] Amounts withheld from wages are allocated equally to the four installments by IRC §6654(e), regardless of when they are actually withheld.

[133] See Schwarzkopf v. CIR, 246 F.2d 731, 734 (3d Cir. 1957) (underpayment excused where installment payments exceeded tax shown on prior year's return, even though income on prior return was fraudulently understated).

[134] See Steiner v. CIR, 25 TC 26, 29 (1955) ("facts" are elements entering into tax computation, such as income, deductions, gains, losses, and credits, with adjustment for nonrecurring items); see also Rev. Rul. 69-307, 1969-1 CB 304 ("facts" include adjustments under income averaging).

[135] Treas. Regs. §§1.6654-2(a)(2), 1.6654-2(d).

creates a hypothetical short taxable year and exempts the taxpayer from penalties if the installments paid by the relevant date equal at least 90 percent of a hypothetical tax based on the actual taxable income and self-employment tax for the months ending before the installment is due.[136] In addition to the safe harbors of IRC §6654-2(a), IRC §6654(h) exempts an individual who was a citizen or resident of the United States throughout the preceding 12-month taxable year, but had no liability for tax for that year.

¶39.7 COLLECTION OF UNPAID TAXES

1. Introductory. If taxpayers do not pay their income taxes by the prescribed date, the government can sue for the unpaid amount and then exercise the usual rights of a judgment creditor.[137]

Instead of pursuing this conventional debt-collection route, the government can, and usually does, invoke its sovereign power to assess the unpaid taxes and seize the taxpayer's property to satisfy the assessment without any judicial proceeding. This summary procedure does not determine that the assessed taxes are actually due; but it distinguishes the tax collector from other creditors, who must ordinarily establish the validity of their claims before grabbing the alleged debtor's property. The summary assessment-levy-seizure procedure, authorized by IRC §6331 ("levy and distraint"), is a time-honored (or, at least, time-sanctioned) method of collecting taxes, because they are "the life-blood of government."[138]

The exercise of the government's authority to collect the tax by seizure, is not final, however, since the taxpayer can sue for a refund and obtain repayment if the assessed amount was not legally owing. Thus, an assessment is like a provisional or default judgment that can be reopened by the judgment debtor but is final until then.

If the unpaid taxes are attributable to a deficiency (e.g., the disallowance of a deduction or credit on audit), the government's right to employ summary collection procedures is also subject to the taxpayer's right (1) to pursue the administrative remedies within the IRS that are discussed elsewhere in this work,[139] (2) to receive a statutory notice of deficiency ("ninety-day letter"),[140] and (3) to petition the Tax Court for a redetermination of the deficiency. These remedies are protected by IRC §6213(a), which forbids the IRS

---

[136] For the short-period computation, see Treas. Regs. §1.6654-2(a)(3); Treas. Regs. §1.6654-2(c), Examples (4), (5).

[137] See IRC §6502(a) (proceeding in court).

[138] Bull v. US, 295 US 247, 259-260 (1935).

[139] See infra ¶40.1.

[140] For the requisites of a ninety-day letter, see infra ¶40.1.

to assess a deficiency until expiration of the ninety-day period allowed for filing a petition to the Tax Court and, if a petition is filed, until the Tax Court's decision becomes final.[141] Taxpayers can waive their right to litigate deficiencies in the Tax Court by consenting under IRC §6213(d) to an immediate assessment,[142] in which event the IRS can proceed to levy on the taxpayer's property if the assessed amount is not paid on notice and demand.

The taxpayer's right to postpone payment of a deficiency until its validity has been determined by the Tax Court is qualified by IRC §§6851 and 6861, authorizing termination and jeopardy assessments if the IRS believes that ultimate collection will be jeopardized by delay.[143] An immediate assessment is also authorized by IRC §6871(a) for taxpayers in bankruptcy or state or federal receivership proceedings.

The government's right to collect unpaid taxes by summary procedures is buttressed by two other weapons, both of which distinguish the tax collector from ordinary creditors. First, an unpaid assessment generates a lien against all property belonging to the taxpayer, valid against some of the taxpayer's transferees and creditors even before it is filed.[144] Second, in pursuing donees and other transferees of the taxpayer's property, the IRS can assess their liability in the same manner as a tax without resorting to a plenary action.[145]

2. Assessments and Abatements. Pursuant to IRC §§6201–6204, assessments are made by an assessment officer signing a summary record, which is augmented by supporting records identifying the taxpayer, the character of the liability assessed, the taxable period, and the amount assessed.[146] The date of the assessment, which determines the validity and priority of the resulting tax lien and starts the running of the statute of limitations, is the date on which the summary record is signed by the assessment officer.[147]

The amount of tax shown on the taxpayer's income tax return, whether paid or not, can be assessed by the IRS without any preliminary procedural steps.[148] Assessments based on deficiencies, however, are subject to IRC §6213, which protects the taxpayer's right to petition the Tax Court before

[141] Infra ¶40.1; the period is 150 rather than 90 days if the statutory notice of deficiency is addressed to a person outside the United States.

[142] See infra ¶40.1.

[143] See infra, text preceding note 150.

[144] See infra, text at notes 154-165.

[145] See infra, text at note 180.

[146] See Treas. Regs. §301.6203-1.

[147] Treas. Regs. §301.6203-1; see also IRC §§6322 (federal lien arises when assessment is made), 6501(a) (taxes must ordinarily be assessed within three years after filing of return).

[148] IRC §§6201(a)(1), 6213(b)(4); Treas. Regs. §301.6201-1(a)(1).

paying the amount claimed, as explained above. If a "mathematical or clerical error" [149] in the taxpayer's favor appears on the return, the IRS can proceed to assess the additional amount due under IRC §6213(b)(1), but the assessment must be abated if the taxpayer so requests within sixty days after notice of the correction. The IRS must then revert to the regular deficiency procedure, including a ninety-day letter.

Interest, additions to tax, additional amounts, and assessable penalties are assessed in the same manner as taxes, but a statutory notice of deficiency under IRC §6212(a), which protects the taxpayer's right under IRC §6213(a) to petition the Tax Court before assessment, is appropriate only if there is an underlying deficiency in tax. If there is none, the sue-now, pay-later principle does not apply, and the taxpayer can challenge these charges only by paying them and suing for a refund.

The term "abatement" is used to describe the reduction of an assessment, as in the case of an assessment based on the correction of an alleged mathematical or clerical error to which the taxpayer objects under IRC §6213(b)(2). Abatements are also authorized by IRC §6404 if the unpaid part of an assessment is excessive in amount or is too small to warrant collection, or if the assessment was made after the expiration of the statute of limitations or was otherwise erroneous or illegal. Section 6404(b), providing that a taxpayer may not file a "claim for abatement" of income, estate, or gift taxes, means only that the proper way to attack the assessment is a claim for refund or credit of any alleged overpayment.

3. Termination and Jeopardy Assessments. The IRS is authorized to cut short the normal procedures governing the filing of tax returns, payment of the reported tax, and collection of any deficiency by resorting to a summary "termination" assessment under IRC §6851 or a "jeopardy" assessment under IRC §6861, either of which can be followed up by a levy on the taxpayer's property if the assessed amount is not paid promptly. These summary assessments neither determine the amount actually owed by the taxpayer nor preclude administrative and judicial review of any question of liability, but they do deprive the taxpayer of the normal right to pursue the review process within the IRS and to litigate the amount due in the Tax Court without paying in advance.

1. *Termination assessments.* A termination assessment is authorized by IRC §6851 if the IRS finds that "a taxpayer designs quickly to depart from the United States or to remove his property therefrom, or to conceal himself

[149] IRC §6213(g)(2). The term "mathematical or clerical error" encompasses more than errors in arithmetic; see Joint Comm. on Taxation, 94th Cong., 2d Sess., General Explanation of the Tax Reform Act of 1976, reprinted in 1976-3 CB (Vol. 2) 371-375.

or his property therein, or to do any other act . . . tending to prejudice or to render wholly or partially ineffectual proceedings to collect the income tax for the current or the immediately preceeding taxable year." The taxable year is closed by IRC §6851(a)(2) as of the date of the termination assessment; but the resulting short period is treated as an entire year for the sole purpose of computing and assessing a hypothetical tax, and amounts collected as a result of the termination assessment are treated by IRC §6851(a)(3) as payments of tax to be applied against the amount due for the full, normal taxable year when it ends.

Termination assessments cannot be made for a taxable year after the due date for filing the taxpayer's return (determined with regard to extensions of time, if any), but the government's interest in assessing and collecting any unpaid taxes for the year in question is fully protected by its power (1) to assess and collect any amount reported on the return as due, if it is not paid when the return is filed, and (2) to make a jeopardy assessment under IRC §6861 of any deficiency if the return is not filed by the due date or if the return understates the taxpayer's liability.

2. *Jeopardy assessments.* If the IRS believes that the assessment or collection of a deficiency (as defined by IRC §6211) will be "jeopardized by delay," it is directed by IRC §6861 to assess the deficiency immediately (together with interest and civil penalties) and to give notice and demand for payment. Being based on a "deficiency," a jeopardy assessment cannot be made before the due date for the taxpayer's return; but it can be made at any time thereafter, even if the taxpayer is pursuing administrative remedies within the IRS or is litigating the liability in the Tax Court.

Section 6861 does not define the phrase "jeopardized by delay," but the regulations incorporate by reference the circumstances mentioned by IRC §6851 as grounds for a termination assessment, such as the concealment of assets and threat of imminent departure from the country.[150] Moreover, IRC §6867, enacted in 1982, creates a presumption—presumably aimed at gamblers and drug dealers—that collection will be jeopardized by delay if a person in physical possession of cash in excess of $10,000 does not claim ownership in himself or in another person whose identity the IRS can readily ascertain and who acknowledges ownership.

Once a jeopardy assessment is made, the IRS is authorized to demand immediate payment of the tax and tó seize the taxpayer's property if payment is not made. Unless a statutory notice of deficiency ("ninety-day letter") has

---

[150] Treas. Regs. §301.6861-1(a). For IRS instructions to agents regarding the existence of jeopardy, see Joint Comm. on Taxation, 95th Cong., 2d Sess., supra note 49, at 356; IRM 4584.7(2) ("well-known major operators in the criminal field, irrespective of present financial condition"; heavy gamblers; persons against whom large damage suits are pending or threatened; alien "border hoppers"; etc.).

already been mailed to the taxpayer under IRC §6212(a), the IRS must send one within sixty days after the jeopardy assessment, thus enabling the taxpayer to petition the Tax Court for redetermination of the deficiency.

3. *Procedural restraints.* On making a termination or jeopardy assessment, the IRS is subjected to the following restrictions:

a. Section 7429 requires the IRS to give the taxpayer a written statement of the information on which it relied in making the assessment and to offer a prompt administrative review of the assessment on request; and it authorizes the taxpayer to bring a civil action in a federal district court to determine whether it was reasonable to make the assessment and whether its amount is "appropriate."[151] The burden of proof on the former issue is placed by IRC §7429(g)(1) on the IRS; the burden on the latter issue falls on the taxpayer, but the IRS must supply the taxpayer with "any information" on which the amount of the assessment was based. Judicial inquiry into the amount assessed should—but may not—restrain exaggerated or arbitrary determinations. The enactment of IRC §7429 presupposes that the IRS will not pluck its figures out of the sky.[152]

The judicial review authorized by IRC §7429 is expedited by IRC §7429(b)(2), requiring a decision on the assessment's validity within twenty days after the action is commenced, unless an extension, which may not exceed forty days, is granted under IRC §7429(c). If the court finds that the assessment is unreasonable or excessive, it can order an abatement, a redetermination of the amount, or other appropriate action.[153] The IRS is also authorized by IRC §6861(g) to abate a jeopardy assessment on its own motion on determining that jeopardy does not exist.

b. The IRS may not sell any property seized pursuant to a jeopardy or termination assessment within the period allowed for a Tax Court petition and, if a petition is filed, until the expiration of the period during which nonjeopardy assessments are prohibited, unless the taxpayer consents to the sale,

---

[151] For inquiries into the facts under the expedited procedure prescribed by IRC §7429, see Bremson v. US, 459 F.Supp. 121 (W.D. Mo. 1978). For current IRS procedures, see Rev. Proc. 78-12, 1978-1 CB 590 (jeopardy and termination assessments "are made sparingly," and care "is taken to assure that the assessments are reasonable in amount in the light of existing facts and that they are necessary to protect the Government"; post-assessment review provided for; taxpayer has right to administrative appeal; whether filing of tax lien based on assessment is sufficient or levy on taxpayer's assets is required "will depend upon the type of property involved and the conditions existing in each particular case").

[152] See Loretto v. US, 440 F.Supp. 1168 (E.D. Pa. 1977) (reasonable to treat cash found under drug dealer's mattress as taxable income); Lace v. US, 45 AFTR2d 367 (D.Vt. 1979) (not officially reported) (assessment based on drug dealer's record of sales and costs upheld).

[153] IRC §7429(b)(3).

maintenance expenses will greatly reduce the net proceeds, or the property is perishable.

c. Collection of amounts assessed under IRC §6851 or §6861 can be stayed, in whole or in part, if the taxpayer posts a bond to insure payment of the taxes when due.

4. *Bankruptcy and receivership.* Section 6871(a) provides for an immediate assessment of any deficiency (with interest, additional amounts, or additions to the tax, as owing) upon the adjudication of bankruptcy of any taxpayer, or the appointment of a receiver in any federal or state receivership proceeding.

4. Federal Tax Liens. If a person neglects or refuses to pay any tax after demand, IRC §6321 provides that the unpaid amount, including any interest or civil penalties, becomes a lien in favor of the United States "upon all property and rights to property, whether real or personal, belonging to such person." Although IRC §6321 refers to the nonpayment of any "tax," the lien cannot arise until the tax has been assessed and notice and demand for payment have been made. The IRS is directed by IRC §6303(a) to give the taxpayer notice as soon as practicable and within sixty days after making an assessment, and the taxpayer is ordinarily allowed ten days for payment after notice and demand; but immediate payment can be demanded if the IRS finds that collection is in jeopardy.[154] If payment is not made within the allotted time, the lien created by IRC §6321 takes effect retroactively as of the date of the assessment and continues until liability for the assessed amount (or a judgment based thereon) is satisfied or becomes unenforceable by reason of lapse of time.[155]

The effect of federal tax liens, which depends in part on whether they are filed or not, is governed by the Internal Revenue Code, but it is also indissolubly intertwined with the Uniform Commercial Code, the Bankruptcy Act, and state law regulating the rights of secured creditors. It is, therefore, impossible in a work focusing on federal taxation to do more than summarize the governing principles.

1. *Property covered by lien.* The lien reaches "all property and rights to property, whether real or personal," belonging to the taxpayer, including property exempt under state law. Whether rights, privileges, etc., constitute "property" is often litigated under IRC §6331, authorizing the IRS to levy

[154] IRC §6331(a); see also Treas. Regs. §301.6303-1(a) (failure to give notice within sixty days does not invalidate notice).

[155] IRC §6322; under IRC §6502(a), liens ordinarily last for six years, but this period may be extended by agreement or other circumstances, as provided by IRC §§6502(a)(2) and 6503.

"upon all property and rights to property" belonging to the taxpayer; and the same principles seem applicable in determining whether the IRS is entitled to a lien under IRC §6321.[156]

In two landmark cases, the Supreme Court held that IRC §6321 "creates no property rights but merely attaches consequences, federally defined, to rights created under state law" [156.1] and that "once the tax lien has attached to the taxpayer's state-created interests, we enter the province of federal law, which we have consistently held determines the priority of competing liens asserted against the taxpayer's "property" or "rights to property." [157] As a corollary of these principles, the government's rights can rise no higher than those of the taxpayer to whom the property belongs.[158] Conversely, the lien covers all property belonging to the taxpayer at any time during the lien's life, including property acquired after the assessment.[159]

2. *Filing.* When the lien first arises, it is a "secret" lien, unrecorded except as a concomitant to the assessment, so that creditors and other persons dealing with the taxpayer have no way of ascertaining its existence or amount unless the taxpayer chooses to inform them. Although it is nevertheless valid against some third parties, the lien gains additional force if notice thereof is filed pursuant to IRC §§6323(a) and 6323(f).[160]

3. *Priority of unfiled tax liens.* On attaching to the taxpayer's property within the meaning of IRC §6321, the federal tax lien's status vis-a-vis other

---

[156] See, e.g., US v. Hubbell, 323 F.2d 197 (5th Cir. 1963) (unliquidated tort claim); In re Rosenberg, 308 NYS2d 51 (N.Y. 1979) (contingent remainder); Rev. Rul. 54-154, 1954-1 CB 277 (options); US v. Balanovski, 236 F.2d 298 (2d Cir. 1956) (partnership interest); Carter v. US, 399 F.2d 340 (5th Cir. 1968) (jointly held property); In re Lackey, 30 AFTR2d 5357 (M.D.N.C. 1972) (not officially reported) (reversionary interest in trust); US v. Bess, 357 US 51 (1958) (life insurance policy, including cash surrender value, despite exemption from creditors' claims under state law).

[156.1] US v. Bess, supra note 156, at 55.

[157] Aquilino v. US, 363 US 509, 512-514 (1960) (amounts owed to subcontractor by general contractor under construction contract; remanded for determination of state law).

[158] First Nat'l Bank of Cartersville v. Hill, 412 F.Supp. 422 (N.D. Ga. 1976) (tax lien on embezzled funds inferior to owner's rights, since embezzler holds funds as constructive trustee for victim); Rev. Rul. 68-57, 1968-1 CB 553 (purchase-money mortgagee protected regardless of when transaction occurs because taxpayer's interest in mortgaged property is limited to his equity); Carolina Apartment Investors "A" v. US, 39 AFTR2d 1045 (E.D. Cal. 1977) (not officially reported) (taxpayer's interest in ground lease terminated by state court judgment quieting title; tax lien on interest extinguished).

[159] Treas. Regs. §301.6321-1; see also Glass City Bank v. US, 326 US 265 (1945) (lien covered taxpayer's claim for services rendered five years after lien arose).

[160] Filing is made in a state or local office properly designated by state law, otherwise with the clerk of the federal district court. For details of the filing procedures, see Treas. Regs. §301.6323(f)-1.

liens and claims is determined by IRC §6323, which provides that it is not valid (a) as against four classes of claimants (purchasers, holders of security interests, mechanic's lienors, and judgment lien creditors) until notice has been filed in accordance with IRC §6323(f), or (b) as against ten other classes, even after notice has been filed. Other claimants are subject to unfiled tax liens unless their liens became "choate" before the tax lien arose.[161]

4. *Priority of filed tax liens.* Ten classes of claimants are protected against federal tax liens even if notice thereof has been filed. These super-priority classes are defined and qualified by IRC §6323(b) and the regulations, which in some cases distinguish between persons with knowledge of the lien and others. Subject to these qualifications, the protected persons, items and lienholders are (1) purchasers, pledgees, etc., of corporate and other securities; (2) purchasers of motor vehicles; (3) personal property purchased at retail in the ordinary course of the seller's business; (4) household goods, personal effects, and other tangible personal property purchased for less than $250 in a casual sale; (5) tangible personal property subject to a possessory lien to secure the reasonable cost of repairs or improvements; (6) certain real property liens for taxes, special assessments, and charges for utilities or public services; (7) mechanic's liens not exceeding $1,000 for repairs or improvements to owner-occupied personal residences with no more than four dwelling units; (8) attorney's liens on judgments and settlements subject to the tax lien; (9) claims by insurance companies under life insurance, endowment, and annuity contracts for automatic advances to keep a policy in force; and (10) passbook loans by savings institutions.[162] Two other classes of claimants entitled to super-priority status are (1) persons making "disbursements" (additional loans and advances) under a security interest agreement entered into before the tax lien was filed, if the payment is made not more than forty-five days after filing and is secured solely by preexisting collateral, and (2) certain financing agreements meeting the elaborate standards prescribed by IRC §6323(c).[163]

5. *Release of lien or discharge of property.* Section 6325(a) requires the IRS to issue a certificate releasing any tax lien not later than 30 days after the day on which the liability for the amount assessed (including interest thereon) is satisfied or becomes legally unenforceable, or if the taxpayer posts an acceptable bond. A less complete remedy for the taxpayer is provided by IRC

[161] See US v. City of New Britain, 347 US 81 (1954) (liens for local taxes and water rents not choate); US v. Scovil, 348 US 218 (1955) (landlord's distress for rent not choate).

[162] For detailed explanations of these super-priorities, see Treas. Regs. §301.6323(b)-1.

[163] See IRC §6323(d); Treas. Regs. §§301.6323(c)-1 (commercial transactions financing agreements), 301.6323(c)-2 (real property construction or improvement financing agreements), 301.6323(c)-3 (obligatory disbursement agreements).

§6325(b), authorizing the discharge of part of the property from the lien in specified circumstances.

6. *Insolvency.* Under Section 3466 of the Revised Statutes, when a person indebted to the United States becomes insolvent, "the debts due to the United States shall be first satisfied." [164] It is not clear whether claimants with priority or super-priority status under IRC §6323 vis-a-vis the federal tax lien lose their place in line by virtue of Section 3466.[165] The importance of the issue, however, is reduced by the fact that Section 3466 ordinarily comes into play only in circumstances warranting administration of the insolvent taxpayer's assets in bankruptcy; and the distribution priorities established by the Bankruptcy Act then take precedence over both Section 3466 and IRC §§6321–6323.

5. Levy, Seizure, and Distraint. Section 6331(a) authorizes the IRS to collect delinquent taxes "by levy upon all property and rights to property . . . belonging to [the taxpayer] or on which there is a lien provided [by IRC §6321] for the payment of such tax." [166] A levy is permissible under IRC §6331(d) if the taxpayer fails to pay the tax within the ten-day period after notice in writing of intention to levy, unless the IRS finds that collection is in jeopardy, in which event it can demand immediate payment and proceed to levy on the taxpayer's property without regard to the normal ten-day grace period.

The term "levy" is defined by IRC §6331(b) to include "the power of distraint and seizure by any means"; but "levy" is ordinarily used to describe the process of reaching amounts owing to the taxpayer by third persons, while "seizure" usually refers to the process of taking possession of the taxpayer's tangible property. Interference with a seizure is a criminal offense.[167]

Section 6334(a) exempts nine categories of property from levy, including personal effects, tools of the trade, unemployment benefits, workmen's compensation, child support payments, and a minimum subsistence allowance.[168] "Arms for personal use" are also exempt (National Rifle Association, please

---

[164] 31 USC §191. This provision is also triggered by death if the estate in the hands of the executor or administrator is insufficient to pay all the deceased debtor's debts.

[165] See Kentucky v. US, 383 F.2d 13 (6th Cir. 1967).

[166] A levy must ordinarily be made within six years after the assessment, but the period may be extended by consent or other circumstances. See IRC §§6502(a) and 6503.

[167] See IRC §7212(b) (forcible rescue of seized property).

[168] For details, including dollar limits on several of the exemptions, see IRC §§6334(a)(2), 6334(a)(3), 6334(d)(1); Treas. Regs. §301.6334-1(a); see also Treas. Regs. §301.6334-1(c) (property exempt under state exemption or homestead laws subject to federal tax levy).

take note), along with "undelivered mail" (American Civil Liberties Union, ditto). Subject to these meager exemptions, IRC §6331(a) authorizes a levy on all the taxpayer's property and property rights, using virtually the same language as IRC §6321, which creates a lien for unpaid taxes.[169] Unlike a tax lien, however, a levy does not capture after-acquired property; the IRS must instead make successive levies, except to reach salaries and wages, as to which IRC §6331(e)(1) authorizes a continuing levy that is good until the liability is satisfied or becomes unenforceable by lapse of time.[170]

If property seized under IRC §6331(a) is paid to the IRS in cash, it can be readily applied, as required by IRC §6342, to the expenses of the proceeding and then to the unpaid taxes, and any surplus can be returned to the persons entitled thereto. When other types of property are seized, the IRS is required by IRC §6335 to sell the property upon notice to the taxpayer in the manner prescribed by IRC §§6335 and 6336, and to apply the proceeds as required by IRC §6342.[171] The taxpayer can get the seized property back by paying the amount due plus the expenses of the levy at any time before the sale; and real property can be redeemed at any time within 180 days after a sale.[172]

If property is wrongfully levied upon, IRC §6343(b) authorizes the IRS to return the amount of money seized, the specific property, or the amount received from a sale of the property. If the IRS is recalcitrant, the claimant (other than the taxpayer subject to the assessment on which the levy was based) can sue the United States under IRC §7426 in a federal district court, which can prohibit enforcement of the levy, prohibit a sale, order a return of specific property in the possession of the United States, or take other action as specified by IRC §7426(b).[173] In such a suit, the assessment is conclusively presumed to be valid, and claims that the IRS wrongfully levied on property held by the delinquent taxpayer's relatives, friends, or family

[169] For the breadth of IRC §6321, see supra, text preceding note 154; for similar cases under IRC §6331, see Dimmit & Owens Financial, Inc. v. US, 35 AFTR2d 1117 (E.D. Pa. 1975) (not officially reported) (accounts receivable); Campbell v. Campbell, 210 A.2d 644 (N.J. Super. 1965) (alimony, even if public welfare would be required to maintain family intact); Spectator Casuals, Inc. v. US, 35 AFTR2d 1435 (M.D. Pa. 1975) (not officially reported) (artisan's lien).

[170] See Treas. Regs. §§301.6331-1, 301.6331-2(c).

[171] For the rights of the purchaser of seized property, see IRC §§6338, 6339. Junior lienors are protected by IRC §7425(b) when seized property is sold; see also IRC §6325(b)(3) (proceeds of sale substituted for seized property on sale).

[172] IRC §6337; see also IRC §6343; Treas. Regs. §301.6343-1(a) (release of levy upon making satisfactory escrow arrangement, posting bond, agreeing to pay delinquent amount in installments, consent to extension of statute of limitations, etc.).

[173] For the statute of limitations on such actions, see IRC §6532(c) (period is ordinarily nine months from the date of the levy, subject to extension if request for return of property is made under IRC §6343(b)).

corporations are ordinarily received with skepticism.[174] In addition to the remedies explicitly authorized by IRC §7426, persons injured by a wrongful levy may be compensated under the Tucker Act, relating to claims against the United States.[175]

6. Foreclosure of Tax Liens, Suits for Taxes, and Setoff. Instead of resorting to levy and seizure under IRC §6331, or in addition to a levy, the government can proceed under IRC §§7401 and 7403 to bring a civil action to enforce its tax lien or to subject any property of the delinquent taxpayer to the payment of taxes. An action under IRC §7403 can be brought upon the taxpayer's refusal or neglect to pay any tax, but not later than six years after the assessment unless the six-year period is extended by consent under IRC §6502(a)(2) or suspended by IRC §6503. Unlike a levy, a suit under IRC §7403 determines the validity of the assessment and the priority of other lienors and claimants.[176] Although the United States is the plaintiff in a suit under IRC §7403, the taxpayer has the burden of proving that the assessment is erroneous.[177] If the taxpayer has no visible property on which to levy, the government can use a suit under IRC §7403 to get a judgment that can be enforced for the indefinite future against the taxpayer's after-discovered or after-acquired property.[178]

Under an administrative setoff procedure, the government sometimes collects delinquent taxes by withholding amounts owed to the taxpayer, such as tax refunds or amounts due under a contract. Since this procedure does not constitute a "levy" within the meaning of IRC §6331, the rights of other lienors are not protected by IRC §7426, and the setoff may benefit the government at the expense of third parties with valid claims against the amounts owed by the government to the taxpayer.[179]

---

[174] IRC §7426(c) (assessment presumed valid).

[175] 28 USC §1346(a)(1). For the possibility of recovering damages from IRS agents violating the taxpayer's constitutional rights when seizing property, see G.M. Leasing Corp. v. US, 560 F.2d 1011 (10th Cir. 1977), cert. denied, 435 US 923 (1978) (agents acting in good faith not liable for search without proper warrant).

[176] See, e.g., US v. Cotier, 403 F.Supp. 397 (D.N.J. 1975) (suit to foreclose tax lien against jewelry purchased on credit by delinquent taxpayer).

[177] See US v. O'Connor, 291 F.2d 520 (2d Cir. 1961); US v. Janis, 428 US 433 (1976) (semble).

[178] See US v. Overman, 424 F.2d 1142 (9th Cir. 1979) (tax liability for 1946–1947 taxes merged into 1961 judgment in IRC §7403 action, which preserved tax liens indefinitely; enforcement in 1967 against taxpayer's share of community property not barred by statute of limitations, laches, or equitable estoppel).

[179] See IRC §6402 (overpayments may be credited against unpaid taxes); Treas. Regs. §301.7426-1(a)(1) (setoff does not constitute levy); but see United Pac. Ins. Co. v. US, 320 F.Supp. 450 (D.Ore. 1970) (setoff treated as levy by United States).

7. Transferee Liability

1. *Introductory.* When unable to collect from a delinquent taxpayer, the IRS can assert so-called transferee liability against persons who are secondarily liable for the taxpayer's debts by contract or state statute or by virtue of having received property from the taxpayer without adequate consideration in circumstances rendering the taxpayer insolvent. In the case of successive transfers, liability may be imposed on a transferee of a transferee.[180] Construing IRC §6901(a), which provides that "the liability, at law or in equity, of a transferee of property" of a taxpayer subject to income taxes shall "be assessed, paid, and collected in the same manner and subject to the same provisions and limitations as in the case of the taxes with respect to which the liabilities were incurred," the Supreme Court in *CIR v. Stern* held that it "neither creates nor defines a substantive liability but provides merely a new procedure by which the Government may collect taxes" and that "the existence and extent of liability should be determined by state law." [181] *Stern* leaves the impact of state statutes of limitations unclear—in particular, whether transferee liability can be assessed after the liability becomes unenforceable under state law, if that event occurs before the time fixed by IRC §6901(c) has run.[182]

Section 6901(a) does not define the "liabilities" of the transferor for which the transferee is liable, but it is well established that transferee liability includes not only the underlying tax but also any related interest and civil penalties owed by the transferor taxpayer.[183]

Although transferee liability can be assessed and collected under IRC §6901(a) in the same manner as the underlying tax, there are two significant procedural distinctions between tax liability and transferee liability. First, the period of limitations for assessing transferee liability does not run until one year after expiration of the time for an assessment of the underlying taxes against the transferor, and this period is extended for another year if the target is a transferee of a transferee.[184] Second, in proceedings before the Tax Court, the IRS is required by IRC §6902(a) to carry the burden of proving that the petitioner is "liable as a transferee of property of a taxpayer" (but not that the

---

[180] See Fibel v. CIR, 44 TC 647, 658-660 (1965) (several layers of intra-family transfers).

[181] CIR v. Stern, 357 US 39, 42-45 (1958) (under Kentucky law, beneficiary of life insurance is liable to creditors of deceased insured only to extent of premiums paid by him in fraud of creditors).

[182] See generally US v. West Tex. State Bank, 357 F.2d 198 (5th Cir. 1966), which does not discuss the effect of the *Stern* case; Chevron Oil Co. v. Huson, 404 US 97, 104 (1971) (relation between state statutes of limitations and rights under federal statutes).

[183] See, e.g., Ruderman v. US, 355 F.2d 995 (2d Cir. 1966) (transferee liable for transferor's taxes and fraud penalties).

[184] See IRC §§6901(c)(1), 6901(c)(2).

transferor taxpayer was liable for the tax). It has been held, however, that this reversal of the normal burden of proof does not apply when transferee liability is challenged in the federal district courts.[185]

Section 6901(a)(1)(A) is customarily construed to limit the transferee's liability to the fair market value of the property received from the taxpayer.[186] In the wake of the *Stern* case, however, the extent of liability—assuming that the target is a transferee of *some* property—probably depends on state rather than federal law.[187] The extent to which the transferee is credited with any amounts paid to the transferor for the property should also be governed by state law.[188]

Section 6901(h) defines "transferee" to include donees, heirs, legatees, devisees, and distributees, and the regulations extend this list by adding shareholders of a dissolved corporation, assignees and donees of an insolvent person, the successor of a corporation, and parties to a corporate reorganization, as defined by IRC §368.[189] Transferee status can also arise from a bona fide business relationship between the transferor and transferee if the amount received by the transferee for goods or services exceeds their value, provided the excess generates liability under state law for the transferor's debts.[190] Indeed, even if the transferee gave full value for the taxpayer's property, liability under IRC §6901 can arise if the transfer did not satisfy the requirements of a creditor protection statute, such as a law requiring a proposed bulk sale of business assets to be advertised in a prescribed fashion.[191]

2. *Liability in equity—trust fund theory.* Transferee liability is ordinarily based on common-law principles, which were summarized by the Tax Court in 1975 as requiring that (1) a transfer of assets to the transferee without consideration or for an inadequate consideration took place; (2) the transferee was either insolvent at the time of the transfer or was rendered insolvent

---

[185] Wehby v. Patterson, 6 AFTR2d 5122 (N.D. Ala. 1960) (not officially reported).

[186] See, e.g., C.D. Constr. Corp. v. CIR, 451 F.2d 470 (4th Cir. 1971), cert. denied, 405 US 988, rehearing denied, 406 US 911 (1972).

[187] See CIR v. Stern, supra note 181 ("existence and extent of [transferee] liability should be determined by state law").

[188] See Nader v. CIR, 323 F.2d 139 (7th Cir. 1963) (transferee credited with amount paid to transferor); Mendelson v. CIR, 52 TC 727 (1969) (transferee credited with amounts returned to transferor, but not with amounts allegedly used to pay transferor's debts, in absence of proof that debts had priority over tax claim).

[189] Treas. Regs. §301.6901-1(b); see also Atlas Tool Co. v. CIR, 70 TC 86 (1978) (circumstances in which purchaser of corporation's assets becomes transferee; extended analysis).

[190] See, e.g., Nader v. CIR, supra note 188 (excess payment for property); Charles E. Smith & Sons Co. v. CIR, 184 F.2d 1011 (6th Cir. 1950) (excessive compensation).

[191] See Noltze Motor Co. v. Burrows-Moore Pontiac, Inc., 157 F.Supp. 593 (N.D. Iowa 1958); US v. Goldblatt Bros., 128 F.2d 576 (7th Cir.), cert. denied, 317 US 662 (1942).

thereby; and (3) reasonable efforts were made by the IRS to collect the amount due from the transferor.[192]

3. *Liability under statute.* Transferee liability can also arise under creditor protection statutes, such as the Uniform Fraudulent Conveyance Act, even though the transferee paid full value for the transferred property—for example, if the statute's procedural requirements were not satisfied.

4. *Liability by contract.* Transferee liability can also arise by contract, a common example being the sale of assets to a purchaser who agrees to assume the seller's liabilities.

8. Liability of Fiduciaries. Section 6903(a) provides that on notifying the IRS that he or she is acting for another person "in a fiduciary capacity," the fiduciary "shall assume the powers, rights, duties, and privileges of such other person in respect of [federal taxes] until notice is given that the fiduciary capacity has terminated." The term "fiduciary" is defined by IRC §7701(a)(6) to mean "a guardian, trustee, executor, administrator, receiver, conservator, or any person acting in any fiduciary capacity for any person." [193] If a fiduciary fails to give the notice contemplated by IRC §6903(a), the IRS is entitled under the regulations to send notices of deficiencies to the taxpayer's last known address or to the last known address of a transferee, even if the addressee is deceased or under a legal disability or, in the case of a corporation, has terminated its existence.[194]

The rights and obligations devolving on a fiduciary under IRC §6903(a) concern the fiduciary's *representative* capacity, and any resulting liabilities bind the estate only, not the fiduciary's personal assets. The function of IRC §6903(a), therefore, is not to create an additional source of funds that can be tapped by the IRS, but to permit the IRS to proceed against the fiduciary, in his representative capacity, in the same manner that it can proceed against *taxpayers.*

The procedural features of IRC §6903(a) are powerfully augmented, however, by Sections 3466 and 3477 of the Revised Statutes—provisions that predate the Internal Revenue Code by many years,[195] which provide that (1) if any person indebted to the United States is insolvent or if the estate of a deceased debtor is insufficient to pay all the deceased's debts, the debts to the United States shall be satisfied first; and (2) any executor, administrator, assignee, or other person who pays any debt in a representative capacity before paying the debts due to the United States "shall become answerable in his own

[192] Bellin v. CIR, 65 TC 676, 683 (1975).

[193] See also Treas. Regs. §301.6903-1(d); Grimm v. CIR, 43 TC 623 (1965) (owner of life estate not a "fiduciary" as to remainder interest).

[194] Treas. Regs. §301.6903-1(c).

[195] 31 USC §§191, 192; for background, see US v. Moore, 423 US 77, 80-83 (1975).

person and estate" to the extent of the amount paid to the improperly preferred creditors.

Prudent fiduciaries can minimize this exposure to personal liability by (1) applying for a discharge under IRC §6905 (income or gift taxes) or §2204 (estate taxes); (2) requesting the prompt assessment of income, gift and estate tax liabilities under IRC §6501(d);[196] and (3) giving prompt written notice of the termination of the fiduciary relationship under IRC §6903(a).

SELECTED BIBLIOGRAPHY

Barndt, Transferee Liability: Burden of Proof, Extent of Liability, and Defenses to Liability, 11 Gonz. L. Rev. 505 (1976).

Barron, The Processing Cycle: What Happens From Filing Date to Action Date, 24 J. Tax. 306 (1966).

Bittker, Federal Income Taxation and the Family, 27 Stan. L. Rev. 1389 (1975).

Borison, Section 6901: Transferee Liability, 30 Tax Lawyer 433 (1977).

Caplin, The Taxpayer-Identifying Number System: The Key to Modern Tax Administration, 49 A.B.A.J. 1161 (1963).

Emory, Tax Return Confidentiality, in Administrative Procedures of the Internal Revenue Service, Report to the Administrative Conference of the United States, S. Doc. No. 94-266, 94th Cong., 2d Sess. 821 (1976).

Feld, Divorce, Tax-Style, 54 Taxes 608 (1976).

Ferguson & Hood, Income Averaging, 24 Tax L. Rev. 53 (1968).

Frazer & Goldberg, Independent Contractor Status: Leading Up to the 1978 Revenue Act Changes and Beyond, 57 Taxes 374 (1979).

Gann, Abandoning Marital Status as a Factor in Allocating Income Tax Burdens, 59 Texas L. Rev. 1 (1980).

Garlock, An Analysis of the Alternative Minimum Tax and the Planning Possibilities It Offers, 52 J. Tax. 206 (1980).

Marmoll, Employer-Employee Relations: Independent Contractor or Employee Status, 37 NYU Inst. on Fed. Tax., Ch. 29 (1979).

McGregor & Davenport, Collection of Delinquent Federal Taxes, 1976 So. Calif. Tax Inst. 589.

McIntyre, Prolegomena to Future Arguments for Individual Filing in the Personal Income Tax, Tax Notes, June 18, 1979, at 763.

McIntyre & Oldman, Taxation of the Family in a Comprehensive and Simplified Income Tax, 90 Harv. L. Rev. 1573 (1977).

Miller, The Fiduciary's Personal Liability for Deficiencies in Federal Income, Estate, and Gift Taxes of a Decedent or a Decedent's Estate, 11 Gonz. L. Rev. 431 (1976).

---

[196] See infra ¶41.2.

Note, The Case for Mandatory Separate Filing by Married Persons, 91 Yale L.J. 363 (1981).

Panny & Faust, The Innocent Spouse Provisions of the Internal Revenue Code: In Search of Equity, 32 U. Miami L. Rev. 137 (1977).

Saltzman, IRS as a Creditor: Liens and Levies Preferences, Other Creditors, Tax Levy Authority, Discharge and Removal of Levy; Informal Arrangements, 34 NYU Inst. on Fed. Tax. 433 (1976).

Smith, Influence of the Tax Reform Act of 1976 on the Minimum Tax, 55 Taxes 4 (1977).

Special Committee on Confidentiality of Tax Returns, Section of Taxation, American Bar Association, Special Study of the Use by the Internal Revenue Service of Third Party Returns and Return Information, 33 Tax Lawyer 717 (1980).

Steuerle, McHugh & Sunley, Who Benefits From Income Averaging? 31 Nat'l Tax J. 19 (1978).

U.S. Comptroller General, IRS Seizure of Taxpayer Property: Effective, But Not Uniformly Applied (GGD 78-42, 1978).

Weisbard, Amended Returns: When, How to File; Rule Not Clear; Ethical Problems Arise, 16 J. Tax. 370 (1962).

CHAPTER 40

Audits, Deficiencies, and Refunds

¶40.1 EXAMINATION AND AUDIT OF RETURNS

1. Selection of Returns for Audit. On being filed with the district director or regional service center, tax returns are checked first for form, execution, and mathematical accuracy. If there is a mathematical or clerical error, a correction notice is sent to the taxpayer with a demand for payment of the shortage or a refund of the overpayment; in the former case, remittance within ten days from the date of notice and demand is considered timely.[1] The correction notice sets out "the error alleged and an explanation thereof" but is not considered a notice of deficiency for such purposes as petitioning the Tax Court.[2]

A similar summary procedure, the Unallowable Items Program, is used by the IRS when the return is first processed to identify items that appear to be unallowable (e.g., the deduction of a loss on the sale of a personal residence or the cost of maternity clothing), which the IRS tries to correct by correspondence with the taxpayer.[3] Since these mistakes are not "mathematical or clerical errors," the taxpayer may refuse to accept the proposed adjustment and force the IRS to follow the normal audit and deficiency notice procedures.

---

[1] Treas. Regs. §301.6601-1(f)(4).

[2] See IRC §6213(b)(1); but see IRC §6213(b)(2) (taxpayer may request abatement of assessment in notice within sixty days, thus bringing deficiency procedure into force).

[3] See IRM 4(13)21, 4(13)(20-21) (list of "unallowables").

Returns are then classified for audit at the IRS Service Center. Of the returns chosen for audit, the great majority are selected pursuant to the discriminant function system (DIF), which employs mathematical formulas developed from intensive examination of returns selected at random to identify those with a high probability of error. During the processing of returns at the Service Centers, significant items are weighted by the computer, resulting in an index score indicating the return's "audit potential"—the higher the score, the greater the probability of a significant tax change. The Service Centers also operate other programs that may result in the selection of a return for audit, based on matching information returns with the tax return, the coordinated examination of members of the same partnership and of taxpayers in the same industry, and other techniques.[4] In addition, the IRS often allocates resources to particular areas thought to entail special abuse, audit potential, or public interest. In a 1979 case, the Tax Court responded to a taxpayer's claim that he was denied deductions that were allowed to similarly situated taxpayers by asserting that "mere selectivity in enforcement of the tax laws against petitioners while not against others is not a violation of their constitutional right to due process, unless such selectivity is based on an unjustifiable criterion such as race, religion, or expression of unpopular views." [5]

Although the IRS denies that revenue agents are expected to meet quotas or that promotions depend on "production," [6] it is hard to believe that pussycats are as highly respected by their colleagues as tigers. On the other hand, one can hardly take exception to the standards formulated by the IRS in stating the agency's mission:

> The function of the Internal Revenue Service is to administer the Internal Revenue Code. Tax policy for raising revenue is determined by Congress. With this in mind, it is the duty of the Service to carry out that policy by correctly applying the laws enacted by Congress; to determine

[4] See U.S. Dep't of Treasury, The President's 1978 Tax Program, Detailed Description and Supporting Analysis of the Proposals 121–131 (1978); H. Rep. No. 95-1445, reprinted in 1978-3 CB (Vol. 1) 181, 248–252; IRM 42(11)1 et seq.; Subcomm. on Oversight, House Ways and Means Comm., 95th Cong., 2d Sess., A Review of the Coordinated Examination Program—IRS Methods (Committee Print 1978). For partnership audits, see infra ¶41.2.

[5] Ranheim v. CIR, ¶79,502 P-H Memo TC (1979); see also Teague v. Alexander, 45 AFTR2d 495 (D.D.C. 1980) (not officially reported) (selective investigation and prosecution of war protesters upheld, extensive analysis).

[6] See IRM P-1-20 ("records of tax enforcement results shall not be used to evaluate [IRS employees or to] impose or suggest production goals or quotas"; subject to this prohibition, "a manager may raise questions with an individual about the number of cases he has processed, the amount of time he has been spending on individual cases, or the kind of results he has been obtaining"); similar provisions are contained in the contract between the IRS and the National Treasury Employees Union.

the reasonable meaning of various Code provisions in light of the Congressional purpose in enacting them; and to perform this work in a fair and impartial manner, with neither a government nor a taxpayer point of view.

The Service also has the responsibility of applying and administering the law in a reasonable, practical manner. Issues should only be raised by examining offices when they have merit, never arbitrarily or for trading purposes. At the same time, the examining officer should never hesitate to raise a meritorious issue. It is also important that care be exercised not to raise an issue or to ask a court to adopt a position inconsistent with an established Service position.

Administration should be both reasonable and vigorous. It should be conducted with as little delay as possible and with great courtesy and considerateness. It should never try to overreach, and should be reasonable within the bounds of law and sound administration. It should, however, be vigorous in requiring compliance with law and it should be relentless in its attack on unreal tax devices and fraud.[7]

2. Office and Field Audits. Office audits of returns are conducted by correspondence or interview and are distinguished from field audits, which involve an examination of the taxpayer's books and records at the taxpayer's premises when a more thorough analysis is required. In either case, the taxpayer may be represented by an attorney, certified public accountant, or other representative.[8] The IRS advises taxpayers to notify it if their returns were examined in either of the two prior years for the items checked in the initial contact letter, since if no change resulted, the audit will be suspended pending a review of the files to determine whether it should be resumed.[9]

Office audits are conducted by correspondence "when information concerning questionable items can be readily furnished by mail and information indicates that the taxpayer can effectively correspond with the Service." [10] Office audits are generally either treated initially as office interview audits or converted to that status when "the criteria for selecting the correspondence technique become invalid or the taxpayer requests an interview examination." [11] When warranted by the circumstances, an office audit may be con-

---

[7] This statement appears regularly in the *Internal Revenue Bulletin* and the *Cumulative Bulletin.* See, e.g., 1977-2 CB ii.

[8] Statement of Procedural Rules, 26 CFR §601.105(b).

[9] IRM 4253.7(2).

[10] IRM 4252(2)(a). For example, in a correspondence examination the taxpayer may be asked for supporting material for a claimed deduction, which, if accepted by the Service, can remove the need for personal contact.

[11] IRM 4252(2)(c). During an interview the taxpayer "has the right to point out

verted to a field audit. Returns are assigned to field agents when it is expected they will "require the application of professional accounting skills and knowledge in verifying books and records." [12] If the audit involves an engineering or appraisal problem, the revenue agent may call upon an engineer agent.[13] The revenue agent may also refer a matter to the National Office for technical advice.[14] Taxpayers may also initiate requests for technical advice "on the grounds that a lack of uniformity exists as to the disposition of the issue, or that the issue is so unusual or complex as to warrant consideration by the National Office," and they may appeal to the Examination Division if the revenue agent declines to refer the matter to Washington.[15]

At the conclusion of either an office or a field audit, a taxpayer who agrees with the proposed adjustments will be asked to execute a waiver of restrictions on assessment and collection of the deficiency or an acceptance of the proposed overassessment (Form 870).[16] Agents are obligated to advise taxpayers of their right to appeal a proposed adjustment.[17] If the taxpayer disagrees with the proposed adjustments, he receives a so-called thirty-day letter, advising him of his appeal rights and stating that if he does not respond within thirty days a statutory notice of deficiency ("ninety-day letter") [18] will be issued or other definitive action (e.g., denial of a refund claim) will be taken. Agreement may be reached as to some issues but not others, in which event the agreed ones can be settled while the others are appealed.[19]

3. Unnecessary and Repetitive Examinations. Section 7605(b) provides that taxpayers shall not be subjected to "unnecessary examination or investigations" and that "only one inspection of a taxpayer's books of account shall be made for each taxable year" unless the taxpayer requests a reexamination or the IRS, "after investigation, notifies the taxpayer in writing that an additional inspection is necessary." [20] Because it is concerned with duplicative inspections

---

to the examiner any amounts included in the return which are not taxable or any deductions which the taxpayer failed to claim on the return." Statement of Procedural Rules, 26 CFR §601.105(b)(2)(ii).

[12] IRM 4214(1).

[13] Statement of Procedural Rules, 26 CFR §601.105(b)(3).

[14] Id. §601.105(b)(5). For the technical advice procedure, see Rev. Proc. 79-46 1979-2 CB 521.

[15] Statement of Procedural Rules, 26 CFR §601.105(b)(5).

[16] For the effect of an executed Form 870, see infra, text at note 33.

[17] IRM 4(22)30(6).

[18] For ninety-day letters, see infra, text at notes 52–61.

[19] For restricted consents, limited to specified issues, see infra ¶41.5. For the possibility of reopening settled issues when the case goes to the Appeals Office, see Statement of Procedural Rules, 26 CFR §601.106(d).

[20] For a detailed analysis of IRC §7605(b), see US v. Kendrick, 518 F.2d 842 (7th Cir. 1975) (original inspection not completed; provision does not prevent separate

of the same taxpayer's books of account, IRC §7605(b) is not violated by an inspection of a different person's records, even if the two are related.[21]

Since the IRS "may investigate merely on the suspicion that taxes are owed," the prohibition of "unnecessary" examinations is violated only by arbitrary or oppressive action.[22] Moreover, a violation of either aspect of IRC §7605(b) probably does not undermine the validity of an ensuing notice of deficiency.[23]

As a matter of internal administration, the IRS has a policy of reopening closed cases to make an adjustment unfavorable to the taxpayer only if (a) there is evidence of fraud or similar misconduct, (b) the closing involved a substantial error based on an established IRS position, or (c) failure to reopen would otherwise be a serious administrative omission.[24]

4. IRS Appellate Procedure. A taxpayer who disagrees with an examining agent's proposed adjustments receives a copy of the agent's report with a thirty-day letter, which offers a second opportunity to accept the findings and sets out the taxpayer's right to appeal to the Appeals Office.[25] A conference with the Appeals Office is available on request and without the filing of a written protest, except in a field audit case in which the proposed additional tax or overassessment or the refund claimed exceeds $2,500, in which case it is necessary to file "a written protest . . . setting forth the facts, law and arguments on which the taxpayer relies." [26]

Proceedings before the Appeals Office are informal and the taxpayer may appear in person or by a qualified representative.[27] All aspects of the case can be explored; but the appellate conferee does not have investigative authority to gather new data or information.[28] The introduction of evidence at the appellate conference, however, is not rigidly prohibited; indeed, the IRS rules provide that matters "alleged as facts may be submitted in the form of affida-

---

inspections re two different taxes); US v. Interstate Tool & Eng'r Corp., 526 F.2d 59 (7th Cir. 1975) (original inspection not terminated when case was referred by original agent to special agent).

[21] See US v. Bass, 33 AFTR2d 1164 (M.D. Fla. 1974) (not officially reported) (corporation and controlling shareholder).

[22] Collins v. CIR, 61 TC 693, 699 (1974).

[23] See id. at 700 n.4, citing cases; but see Reineman v. US, 301 F.2d 267 (7th Cir. 1962) (deficiency assessment set aside).

[24] See IRM 4023.2; for the definition of a "closed case," see IRM 4023.4; see also Rev. Proc. 68-28, 1968-2 CB 912. Judicial enforcement of this policy is unlikely unless the violation raises a due process issue. See Collins v. CIR, supra note 22.

[25] Statement of Procedural Rules, 26 CFR §601.105(c).

[26] Id.

[27] Id.

[28] Statement of Procedural Rules, 26 CFR §601.106(f)(6). Taxpayers offering new evidence may find their cases referred back to the district director for reconsideration.

vits or declared as true under the penalties of perjury." [29] Conferees are instructed not to reopen previously agreed-upon issues or to raise new issues "unless the ground for such action is a substantial one and the potential effect upon the tax liability is material." [30] Appellate conferees are affirmatively instructed by the IRS to be realistic:

> [The Appeals Office] will ordinarily give serious consideration to an offer to settle a tax controversy on a basis which fairly reflects the relative merits of the opposing views in the light of the hazards which would exist if the case were litigated. . . . If the taxpayer makes an unacceptable proposal of settlement [in] good-faith . . . the Appeals officer generally should give an evaluation of the case in such a manner as to enable the taxpayer to ascertain the kind of settlement that would be recommended for acceptance.[31]

This extract reflects the official IRS position that the taxpayer must take the initiative to settle a case, but experienced negotiators can sense when the conferee is likely to respond favorably to a proposal.

IRS procedures for the consideration of settlement proposals depend on whether the case is in a "docketed" or "nondocketed" status while before the Appeals Office—for example, whether the taxpayer has or has not filed a petition with the Tax Court. Nondocketed cases can be settled by the Appeals Office without the participation or concurrence of the Chief Counsel's office. If, however, the case is docketed, the Appeals Office has exclusive settlement authority for only four months. Thereafter (or earlier if it is concluded that settlement is unlikely), the Chief Counsel's office, which has responsibility for preparing the case for trial, has exclusive settlement jurisdiction. The Chief Counsel's office also has settlement authority over cases docketed in the Tax Court following issuance of a statutory notice of deficiency by the Appeals Office, but in this situation the latter's views may be solicited before a proposed settlement is accepted.[32]

5. Settlements—Form 870, Closing Agreements, and Compromises. The overwhelming bulk of tax returns is accepted as filed, and, although there is no legal barrier to the subsequent assertion of a deficiency until the statute of limitations has run, unexamined returns rarely see the light of day again unless the taxpayer goes on the offensive by claiming a refund. Returns that

---

[29] Id. §601.106(c).

[30] Id. §601.106(d)(1).

[31] Id. §601.106(f)(2); see also Rev. Rul. 64-22, 1964-1 CB 689 (principles of tax administration).

[32] Rev. Proc. 78-9, 1978-1 CB 563, modified by Rev. Proc. 79-59, 1979-2 CB 573.

are examined and then accepted as filed are also settled for practical purposes so far as the IRS is concerned.

Less important so far as sheer numbers are concerned—but more important to the practitioner—are four formal ways of settling tax cases, each involving a different set of procedures and legal consequences: Form 870, Form 870-AD, closing agreements under IRC §7121, and compromises under IRC §7122.

1. *Form 870.* To implement IRC §6213(d), permitting taxpayers to "waive the restrictions provided in [IRC §6213(a)] on the assessment and collection" of deficiencies, Form 870 is used to settle cases, in whole or in part, in the district director's office. By signing Form 870 ("Waiver of Restrictions on Assessment and Collection of Deficiency in Tax and Acceptance of Overassessment"), the taxpayer authorizes the IRS to assess the agreed deficiency and collect the resulting taxes without issuing a statutory notice of deficiency ("ninety-day letter") under IRC §6213(a).[33] Without a statutory notice, a taxpayer who later changes his mind about the deficiency cannot attack the assessment in the Tax Court but must instead sue for a refund in a district court or the Claims Court. On the other hand, if notice and demand for payment are not made within thirty days after the taxpayer signs Form 870, the IRS cannot charge interest for the period between the end of the thirty-day period and the date of notice and demand.[34] Form 870 is effective when signed by the taxpayer; it does not require acceptance by the IRS, except when special conditions are added to the normal documents.[35]

2. *Form 870-AD.* To settle a nondocketed case in the Appeals Office, the IRS uses Form 870-AD.[36] Unlike Form 870, it is an "offer" by the taxpayer to waive the restrictions of IRC §6213(a) and to consent to the assessment and collection of the agreed deficiency, and it is not effective unless and until accepted by the IRS.[37] Moreover, Form 870-AD provides that, on acceptance, "the case shall not be reopened in the absence of fraud, malfeasance, concealment or misrepresentation of material fact, an important mistake in mathematical calculation, or excessive tentative allowances of carrybacks . . . and no

---

[33] Form 870 is also used to accept a proposed overassessment, in which case the refund will be processed without further formality. For an extended examination of the function of Form 870, see US v. Price, 361 US 304 (1960) (rejecting taxpayer's theory that Form 870 is valid only if executed after notice of deficiency).

[34] See IRC §6601(c).

[35] See, e.g., Godchaux v. US, 102 F.Supp. 266 (E.D. La. 1952) (time limit added to standard form); Steiner v. Nelson, 259 F.2d 853 (7th Cir. 1958) (taxpayer agreed not to sue for refund).

[36] Docketed cases are settled by filing a stipulation of the agreed deficiency or overpayment in the Tax Court, so as to obtain a judicial order terminating the case. See Statement of Procedural Rules, 26 CFR §601.106(d)(3)(i).

[37] See US v. Goldstein, 189 F.2d 752 (1st Cir. 1951).

claim for refund or credit shall be filed or prosecuted for the year(s) [involved] other than for amounts attributed to carrybacks provided by law." [38] After this statement of quasi-finality, however, Form 870-AD goes on to state that it is not a final closing agreement under IRC §7121.

The explicit renunciation in Form 870-AD of the status of a statutory closing agreement echoes the holding of the Supreme Court in *Botany Worsted Mills v. United States* that the analogous compromise procedure now embodied in IRC §7122 was, for the taxable years there involved, the exclusive method of settling a tax matter with finality.[39] While it does not preclude binding agreements by taxpayers, *Botany Worsted Mills v. United States* has been construed to allow taxpayers as well as the IRS to repudiate an informal settlement unless estopped to do so.

Since the IRS rarely repudiates a settlement incorporated in Form 870-AD, the issue of estoppel arises primarily when a taxpayer sues for a refund in violation of the commitment in Form 870-AD. The conditions necessary to estop the taxpayer, however, are hopelessly unclear. Some cases require the IRS to establish the conventional elements of a common-law, equitable estoppel—which are rarely present.[40] Other cases hold that the taxpayer is estopped if the suit for refund is brought after the statute of limitations bars the IRS from assessing the deficiency originally proposed by it, at least if only a single issue is involved or if the settlement involved two or more taxpayers.[41]

3. *Closing agreements.* Most administrative settlements are evidenced by Form 870 or 870-AD, but greater finality can be achieved by a "closing agreement." Sanctioned by IRC §7121, a closing agreement is an agreement between the IRS and the taxpayer "relating to the liability of such person . . . in respect of any internal revenue tax or any taxable period," which is "final and conclusive . . . except upon a showing of fraud or malfeasance, or misrepresentation of a material fact." [42] The regulations provide that closing agree-

---

[38] See also Statement of Procedural Rules, 26 CFR §601.106(h), which contains similar provisions for nondocketed cases closed by the Appeals Office on the basis of reciprocal concessions.

[39] Botany Worsted Mills v. US, 278 US 282 (1929).

[40] Lignos v. US, 439 F.2d 1365, 1368 (2d Cir. 1971) (elements necessary to establish estoppel); see also McGraw-Hill, Inc. v. US, 44 AFTR2d 5463 (Ct. Cl. Trial Judge 1979) (review of equitable estoppel theories).

[41] See Stair v. US, 516 F.2d 560 (2d Cir. 1975), which cites and reviews the principal cases, affirming the summary dismissal of a refund action by a taxpayer who signed a 870-AD settling a single-issue case by a 50-50 compromise; the refund action was brought when the IRS could no longer assert the full amount of the original deficiency, so the taxpayer risked nothing by repudiating the settlement except counsel fees in the refund action.

[42] For circumstances permitting closing agreements to be set aside, see Rev. Rul. 72-486, 1972-2 CB 644 (fraud by officer against employer corporation does not permit

ments with respect to taxable periods ending after the date of the agreement are subject to any post-agreement change in the law and that every closing agreement shall contain a recital to this effect.[43]

Although the execution of closing agreements is discretionary with the IRS, the regulations provide that an agreement may be executed "in any case in which there appears to be an advantage [presumably to the IRS] in having the case permanently and conclusively closed, or if good and sufficient reasons are shown by the taxpayer for desiring a closing agreement and it is determined by the Commissioner that the United States will sustain no disadvantage through consummation of such an agreement." [44] Examples of "acceptable reasons" for entering into closing agreements include:

1. The taxpayer wishes to establish its tax liability to facilitate a transaction, such as a sale of stock or distribution of the assets of an estate or trust, or to satisfy a creditor's demands for evidence of the status of its tax liability.
2. The fiduciary of an estate desires a closing agreement in order that he may be discharged by the court.
3. A taxpayer wishes to assure itself that a controversy between it and the IRS is conclusively disposed of.[45]

4. *Compromises.* Section 7122(a) authorizes the IRS to compromise "any civil or criminal case arising under the internal revenue laws" prior to reference of the matter to the Department of Justice for prosecution or defense; thereafter, compromise authority is vested in the Department of Justice.[46] Unlike closing agreements under IRC §7121, compromises can settle criminal as well as civil liabilities; but this distinction is narrower than it initially seems, since the regulations provide that criminal liabilities will be compromised only if the violation involves a regulatory statute and was not deliberately committed with intent to defraud.[47] On the other hand, closing agreements can clearly

---

closing agreement between corporation and IRS to be set aside); Rev. Rul. 72-487, 1972-2 CB 645 (unintentional error in revenue agent's report does not constitute misrepresentation of material fact). See generally Statement of Procedural Rules, 26 CFR §§601.202(c)(2)–601.202(c)(7); see also Dorl v. CIR, ¶73,145 P-H Memo TC (1973), aff'd per curiam, 507 F.2d 406 (2d Cir. 1974) (letter signed by IRS official not entitled to execute closing agreements does not constitute such an agreement).

[43] Treas. Regs. §301.7121-1(c). For what constitutes a "change" in applicable law, see Treas. Regs. §301.7121-1(b)(4), Example (closing agreement determining fair market value of stock on March 1, 1913 for basis purposes binding "unless or until the law is changed to require the use of some other factor to determine basis").

[44] Treas. Regs. §301.7121-1(a); and see Statement of Procedural Rules, 26 CFR §601.202(a)(2).

[45] Rev. Proc. 68-16, §4.01, 1968-1 CB 770, 773.

[46] See generally Statement of Procedural Rules, 26 CFR §601.203; IRM 5700 et seq.

[47] Treas. Regs. §301.7122-1(b).

affect future years, while the authority to compromise "cases" under IRC §7122 may not include the power to determine the effect of future transactions.[48]

The regulations provide for the use of compromises in cases involving doubt as to either "liability" or "collectibility." [49] In actual practice, however, compromises are used principally in cases involving doubts about the collectibility of an assessed liability.[50] An offer in compromise based on doubts regarding collection must be accompanied by financial statements, including information regarding the value of the taxpayer's interests in life insurance, pension and profit-sharing plans, business licenses, real estate, and community property. Moreover, "the liquidating or quick sale value of the taxpayer's assets is ordinarily the starting point in the consideration of an offer." [51]

6. Statutory Notice of Deficiency ("Ninety-Day Letter"). If a disputed income tax case cannot be settled, the IRS issues, pursuant to IRC §6212, a statutory notice of deficiency ("ninety-day letter"), which is a crucial document for the following intertwined reasons:

1. In the absence of such a notice, the deficiency cannot be assessed or collected, unless the taxpayer consents to assessment and collection under IRC §6213(d) [52] or the IRS closes the taxpayer's taxable year under IRC §6851 (relating to flight or concealment) or makes a jeopardy assessment under IRC §6861.[53]

2. The notice is the taxpayer's "ticket to the Tax Court," permitting him to petition the Tax Court for a redetermination of the deficiency within ninety days after the notice is mailed (hence the term "ninety-day letter") or, if it is addressed to a person outside the United States, 150 days.[54]

---

[48] See Barnes v. US, 34 AFTR2d 5146, 5162–5164 (Ct. Cl. 1974) (not officially reported).

[49] Treas. Reg. §301.7122-1(a).

[50] IRM 5752.1 (compromise precluded if a definite determination of tax liability may be made through regular channels); see also Treas. Regs. §301.7122-1(a) (liability established by valid judgment cannot be compromised in absence of doubt as to collectibility); IRM 5712(1) (compromise not warranted by sympathy, equitable considerations, or mere possibility of doubt as to amount legally due). See also Statement of Procedural Rules, 26 CFR §601.203(a)(2) (offers in compromise usually arise when payments of assessed liabilities are demanded, ad valorem penalties for delinquency in filing returns are asserted, or specific civil or criminal penalties are incurred).

[51] IRM 5753.11(3).

[52] If a statutory notice is not sent as required by IRC §6213(a), the taxpayer can enjoin assessment or collection of the tax; see IRC §§6213(a) (last sentence), 7421(a).

[53] For termination and jeopardy assessments, see supra ¶39.7.

[54] For the Tax Court's lack of jurisdiction in deficiency cases if a notice of deficiency has not been issued or if the petition is filed after the statutory ninety-day or 150-day period, see infra ¶43.2.

3. Section 6213(a) prohibits assessment and collection of the deficiency until the expiration of the ninety-day or 150-day period and, if a petition is filed, until the Tax Court's decision become final.

4. The statute of limitations on assessment and collection is suspended during the ninety-day or 150-day period and during the Tax Court proceedings but commences to run again sixty days thereafter.[55]

5. The deficiency asserted in the statutory notice is an administrative determination that is presumptively correct when challenged by the taxpayer in the Tax Court; but if the IRS asserts an increased deficiency, it must bear the burden of proof with respect to the additional amount.[56]

The requirement of IRC §6212(b)(1) that the ninety-day letter be mailed to the taxpayer's "last known address" is fulfilled if the notice is sent to "the address which, in the light of [all relevant] circumstances, the [IRS] reasonably believes the taxpayer wishes to have the [IRS] use in sending mail to him." [57] An erroneously addressed notice, however, is valid if actually received.[58] The taxpayer can designate an attorney's address for IRS communications, in which event it will be treated as the taxpayer's last known address. In the case of a joint return, a single joint notice is authorized by IRC §6212(b)(2) unless either spouse notifies the IRS that "separate residences have been established," in which event a duplicate original of the joint notice must be sent by certified or registered mail to each spouse at his or her last known address.[59]

The Tax Court has held that it lacks jurisdiction over a petition based on a ninety-day letter sent by regular mail, even if the taxpayer is willing to waive the defect.[60] The Tax Court's theory that certified or registered mail is mandatory is not universally accepted, however, and in jurisdictions rejecting it a taxpayer may be told that a ninety-day letter sent by regular mail or by hand is effective if received.[61]

---

[55] See infra ¶41.6.

[56] See infra ¶43.2. For the definition of "deficiency," see IRC §6211(a).

[57] Lifter v. CIR, 59 TC 818, 821 (1973), citing and summarizing numerous earlier cases in this area. See also IRC §6212(b)(1) (in event fiduciary fails to give notice under IRC §6903, notice to taxpayer's last known address is sufficient despite death, legal disability, or, in the case of corporations, dissolution); Treas. Regs. §301.6903-1(b) (method of giving notice of fiduciary relationship and of termination thereof).

[58] See Lifter v. CIR, supra note 57, at 823; Brzezinski v. CIR, 23 TC 192 (1954) (notice sent by registered mail to wrong address but received by taxpayer in due course).

[59] For the "separate residence" requirement, see Camous v. CIR, 67 TC 721 (1977) (insufficient knowledge by IRS of separate residences); *Camous* also holds that the 150-day period is applicable to both spouses if either one is outside the United States.

[60] See Williams v. CIR, 13 TC 257 (1949) (unnecessary to decide whether document was ninety-day letter, because use of regular mail is fatal).

[61] See Boren v. Riddell, 241 F.2d 670 (9th Cir. 1957) (regular mail); Tenzer v. CIR, 285 F.2d 956 (9th Cir. 1960) (hand delivery).

¶40.2 IRS INVESTIGATIVE AUTHORITY

1. Introductory. In auditing income tax returns, the IRS can turn to many sources of data, provided voluntarily or under compulsion, including the taxpayer's, related parties', customers', and suppliers' returns and information returns filed by entities of which the taxpayer is a member or which make payments to him. More sporadic sources include newspaper articles, complaints by disgruntled former employees and spouses, local law-enforcement officials, and leads supplied by informers seeking a reward.[62]

The IRS can issue an administrative summons under IRC §7602(a)(2) to compel both the taxpayer and third persons with relevant information to produce their books and records and to testify in the inquiry.[63] Since once a deficiency is asserted by the IRS, it is presumptively correct when litigated,[64] taxpayers usually lose more than they gain by dragging their feet when asked for information.

If the IRS wants to obtain data in the hands of third persons, it can approach them directly; and it often encounters cooperation rather than resistance. Neither the IRS nor the persons interviewed are obligated to notify the taxpayer of these contacts. If the third person refuses to supply the information until served with a summons, this may entitle the taxpayer to notice and an opportunity to intervene in the subsequent proceeding,[65] but if the third person is willing to supply the data voluntarily, the taxpayer usually has no remedy, except an injunction action if disclosure would breach an attorney-client or other privileged relationship.[66] The Right to Financial Privacy Act of 1978, however, establishes special rules for financial records maintained by certain financial institutions, which restrict voluntary disclosure of these sources of information.[67]

If the desired information is not supplied voluntarily, the IRS can resort

---

[62] For provisions requiring banks and other financial institutions to report large currency transfers and other unusual transactions to the Treasury, see the Currency and Foreign Transactions Reporting Act of 1920, 31 USC §1051; 45 Fed. Reg. 37,818 (1980).

[63] For IRC §7602(a)(2), see infra, text at note 71.

[64] See infra ¶43.2.

[65] See infra, text at note 90.

[66] See Kirshenbaum v. Beerman, 376 F.Supp. 398 (W.D. Pa. 1974), holding that the taxpayer cannot challenge a summons unless an enforcement proceeding under IRC §7604(a) ensues; a fortiori, the taxpayer would be unable to intervene at a voluntary interview between the IRS and a witness; but see the debatable holding in Kemlon Prods. & Dev. Co. v. US, 44 AFTR2d 5381 (S.D. Tex. 1979) (not officially reported) (IRS enjoined because irreparable damage would result from contacting taxpayer's customers and inquiry threatened disclosure of confidential return information).

[67] See infra, text at note 96.

to compulsion under IRC §§7601 and 7602. In *United States v. Bisceglia,* a 1975 analysis of these provisions, the Supreme Court commented:

> [Section] 7601 gives the Internal Revenue Service a broad mandate to investigate and audit "persons who *may be* liable" for taxes and §7602 provides the power to "examine any books, papers, records, and other data which may be relevant . . . [and to summon] any person having possession . . . of books of account . . . relevant or material to such inquiry." Of necessity, the investigative authority so provided is not limited to situations in which there is probable cause, in the traditional sense, to believe that a violation of the tax laws exists. . . . The purpose of the statutes is not to accuse, but to inquire.[68]

In more detail, IRC §§7601 and 7602 provide as follows:

1. *Canvass of districts for taxable persons and objects.* Section 7601 authorizes the Secretary of the Treasury, "[to] cause officers or employees of the Treasury Department to . . . inquire after and concerning all persons . . . who may be liable to pay any internal revenue tax, and all persons owning or having the care of and management of any objects with respect to which any tax is imposed." In point of fact, IRC §7601 has not played a significant role in the enforcement of the income tax, though its reference to an IRS canvass of "persons who *may* be liable" for a tax was cited by the Supreme Court in *United States v. Bisceglia* as evidence that the authority to issue administrative summonses under IRC §7602 is not restricted to "investigations which have already focussed upon a particular return, a particular named person, or a particular potential tax liability."[69]

2. *Examination of books and witnesses.* Section 7602 authorizes the IRS (1) to examine books, records, and other relevant data or material in ascertaining the accuracy of any return, determining any person's tax liability, or collecting any liability; (2) to issue an administrative summons to the taxpayer or any person having possession or custody of relevant data; and (3) to take the summoned person's testimony under oath. Sections 7601 and 7602 are concerned with administrative investigations; and they are displaced or supplemented by other fact-finding devices, like discovery, if and when the tax matter is litigated.[70]

The powers of the IRS under IRC §7602 inevitably depend on constitutional and other legal trends outside the tax field and can rarely be fully assessed without surveying a broad spectrum of nontax cases. The dangers of examining IRC §7602 in isolation should be kept in mind, therefore, when

---

[68] US v. Bisceglia, 420 US 141, 145–146 (1975).

[69] Id. at 149.

[70] For the litigation of tax cases, see infra ¶43.1.

reading the material that follows, which focuses on the specific requirements of IRC §7602 and the cases decided thereunder.

2. Administrative Summons Directed to Taxpayer. In authorizing the IRS to examine books and records, issue summonses, and take testimony under oath, IRC §7602 specifies that these powers are granted

> [f]or the purpose of ascertaining the correctness of any return, making a return where none has been made, determining the liability of any person for any internal revenue tax or the liability at law or in equity of any transferee or fiduciary of any person in respect of any internal revenue tax, or collecting any such liability.[71]

This statement of purposes was augmented in 1982 by the enactment of IRC §7602(b), explicitly authorizing the IRS to issue a summons for "the purpose of inquiring into any *offense* connected with the administration or enforcement of the internal revenue laws" (emphasis added). The reference in IRC §7602 to "liability . . . for any internal revenue tax" includes, by virtue of IRC §6659(a), additions and civil penalties, as well as the underlying tax liability itself.

Although authorized to *issue* summonses, the IRS cannot *enforce* them on its own but must instead apply to a federal district court under IRC §7604(a) to compel the witness to appear, testify, and produce the specified books and other data.[72] In determining whether to enforce the summons, the court must take account of at least three statutes: IRC §7602 itself, which specifies (in the language quoted above) the purpose for which a summons can be issued by the IRS; IRC §7604(a), which authorizes courts to enforce a summons by "appropriate process," thereby vesting the court with responsibility to protect its process against abuse; and IRC §7605(b), which provides that no taxpayer "shall be subjected to unnecessary examination or investigations" and forbids more than one inspection of the taxpayer's books of account for each taxable year, unless the taxpayer requests otherwise or the IRS notifies the taxpayer in writing that an additional inspection is necessary.[73]

In *United States v. Powell,* the Supreme Court summarized the requirements of these provisions as follows:

---

[71] See US v. Euge, 444 US 707 (1980) (taxpayer required to supply examples of handwriting). For the reference in IRC §7602 to returns made by the IRS for taxpayers who have not filed their own returns, see supra ¶39.1. For the liability of transferees and fiduciaries, see IRC §6901, discussed supra ¶39.7.

[72] The district courts are also authorized to enforce IRS summonses by IRC §7402(b), which is virtually identical with IRC §7604(a). Upon failure to obey a judicial order, a person summoned can be attached as for contempt of court under IRC §7604(b).

[73] For these restrictions, see supra ¶40.1.

> [T]he Commissioner need not meet any standard of probable cause to obtain enforcement of his summons . . . He must show that the investigation will be conducted pursuant to a legitimate purpose, that the inquiry may be relevant to the purpose, that the information sought is not already within the Commissioner's possession, and that the administrative steps required by the Code have been followed . . It is the court's process which is invoked to enforce the administrative summons and a court may not permit its process to be abused. Such an abuse would take place if the summons had been issued for an improper purpose, such as to harass the taxpayer.[74]

Persons served with a summons under IRC §7602 cannot be prosecuted and punished for a good-faith refusal to comply until the defense has been presented to the court when the IRS seeks enforcement under IRC §7604(a).[75]

The principal issues that can be raised in an enforcement proceeding under IRC §7604(a) are:

1. *Relevance and materiality.* Under IRC §7602, the IRS must show that the testimony, books, records, and other data sought "may be relevant or material" to the inquiry. The "inquiry" is defined by reference to the provision's purposes—ascertaining the correctness of a return, making a return for a taxpayer who has failed to do so, determining tax liability (including the liability of transferees and fiduciaries), collecting any unpaid taxes, and inquiring into tax offenses. The testimony and data sought may be "relevant or material" to the inquiry if inspection might "shed light upon" the correctness of the taxpayer's return or the existence of a tax liability; there must be "a reasonable expectation rather than an idle hope that something may be discovered," and an overly broad summons may be whittled down to proper size by the court.[76]

2. *Privileged communications.* The Supreme Court has recognized that "evidentiary privileges such as the attorney-client privilege" are preserved from intrusion.[77] The protection presumably also encompasses such traditional privileged relationships as husband-wife, physician-patient, and priest-penitent;[78] but the litigated cases under IRC §7602 have so far involved either the

[74] US v. Powell, 379 US 48, 57–58 (1964).

[75] US v. McCarthy, 514 F.2d 368 (3d Cir. 1975).

[76] See Foster v. US, 265 F.2d 183, 187–188 (2d Cir.) ("shed light"), cert. denied, 360 US 912 (1959); US v. Harrington, 388 F.2d 520, 524 (2d Cir. 1968) ("realistic expectation").

[77] Fisher v. US, 425 US 391, 407 (1976) (accountant's work papers held by taxpayer's attorney subject to summons).

[78] 8 Wignore on Evidence §§2285–2396 (McNaughton, Ed.; Little, Brown, rev. ed. 1961); US v. Cotton, 567 F.2d 958 (10th Cir. 1977) (grounds for claiming marital privilege not established).

attorney-client privilege, which is protected, or the accountant-client relationship, which is not.[79]

The attorney-client privilege protects confidential disclosures by clients to attorneys when made to obtain legal assistance, including confidential communications by the attorney or the client to an accountant engaged to enable the attorney to advise the client properly on legal matters,[80] but not material turned over to the attorney that was not protected while in the hands of the client (such as work papers prepared by an accountant while preparing a client's tax returns).[81]

Communications to persons outside the traditional privileged relationships (e.g., banks, agents, employees, and friends) are not protected and if the communications are reduced to writing by the recipient, the documents ordinarily become part of the recipient's records, in which the taxpayer has no protected interest.[82]

3. *Privilege against self-incrimination.* The self-incrimination clause of the Fifth Amendment forbids use of IRC §7602 to compel any individual to give testimony incriminating himself, but its impact on books and records is more complex. In general, individuals cannot be compelled to produce their own papers, whether of a personal or business character, at least if they are implicitly required to testify that the documents produced are the documents demanded,[83] but the privilege does not cover (1) books and records held in a representative capacity, even if production will incriminate the representative and he is required to identify the documents;[84] (2) material prepared by other persons, even though in the witness' possession,[85] (3) personal papers that were originally protected but were surrendered to other persons, unless the transfer is a privileged communication or the transferee's custody is only tempo-

---

[79] See Couch v. US, 409 US 322, 335 (1973) (no confidential accountant-client privilege under federal law; state-created privilege not recognized in federal cases).

[80] See US v. Brown, 349 F.Supp. 420 (N.D. Ill. 1972), aff'd, 478 F.2d 1038 (7th Cir. 1973), and cases there cited.

[81] Fisher v. US, supra note 77. See In re Shapiro, 381 F.Supp. 21 (N.D. Ill. 1974) (subpoena duces tecum to appear before grand jury; preparation of tax returns does not constitute legal advice), and cases there cited; but see Colton v. US, 306 F.2d 633 (2d Cir. 1962), cert. denied, 371 US 951 (1963) (preparation of tax return may entail legal advice); see also US v. Hodge & Zweig, 548 F.2d 1347 (9th Cir. 1977) (extensive discussion, with citations).

[82] See US v. Miller, 425 US 435 (1976) (motion to suppress records obtained by subpoena from taxpayer's banks).

[83] Bellis v. US, 417 US 85, 87–88 (1974). For the implicit authentication rationale for applying the Fifth Amendment to subpoenas calling for documents rather than testimony, see Fisher v. US, supra note 77.

[84] Bellis v. US, supra note 83, at 88.

[85] Fisher v. US, supra note 77.

rary;[86] and (4) documents seized pursuant to a search warrant.[87] By responding in part to a summons, the witness may waive the right to remain silent as to related matters.[88]

4. *Investigations of criminal conduct and nontax matters.* Section 7602(b), as amended in 1982, permits the issuance of a summons for the purpose of inquiring into any offense connected with the administration or enforcement of the internal revenue laws; but the issuance of a summons and its enforcement are prohibited if a Justice Department referral is in effect with respect to the taxpayer involved.[89]

3. Third-Party Summons. Section 7602 authorizes the IRS to issue a summons requiring any person possessing books of account with entries relating to the taxpayer's business or "any other person the [IRS] may deem proper" to produce books and records or give testimony that may be relevant or material to the inquiry. A series of pre-1976 litigated cases held that if a summons was issued to a third party under IRC §7602, the target of the inquiry could intervene in order to show that the summons was issued solely to gather evidence for a criminal prosecution or called for disclosure of privileged communications between the taxpayer and the witness,[90] but there was no formal procedure giving the target notice of the summons so that such challenges could be presented. Concluding in 1976 that "many of the problems in this area would be cured if the parties to whom the [summoned] records pertain were advised of the service of a third-party summons and were afforded a reasonable and speedy means to challenge the summons where appropriate," [91] Congress enacted IRC §7609, which was amended in 1982, establishing special procedures for third-party summonses, the principal features of which are:

1. *Coverage.* Section 7609 applies to summonses requiring any "third-party recordkeeper" to produce records of the business transactions or affairs of an identified person other than the person summoned, subject to certain exceptions. The term "third-party recordkeeper" is defined by IRC

---

[86] See Couch v. US, supra note 79.

[87] Andresen v. Maryland, 427 US 463 (1976).

[88] See Rogers v. US, 340 US 367 (1951) (petitioner testified before grand jury that she held office in the Communist Party and once had possession of its books; contempt sentence for refusing to disclose to whom she transferred the books upheld).

[89] IRC §7602(c)(1). For prior law, see US v. LaSalle Nat'l Bank, 437 US 298, 318 (1978).

[90] See Donaldson v. US, 400 US 517 (1971); Reisman v. Caplin, 375 US 440 (1964); see generally US v. Genser, 582 F.2d 292 (3d Cir. 1978) (validity of third-party summons can be challenged in criminal prosecution; extensive analysis).

[91] S. Rep. No. 94-938, reprinted in 1976-3 CB (Vol. 3) 49, 406. This report contains a detailed explanation of IRC §7609.

§7609(a)(3) as a bank or similar financial institution, consumer reporting agency, issuer of credit cards, broker, attorney, accountant, or barter exchange.[92] The status of summonses served on other persons, such as the taxpayer's suppliers, customers, or employees, is unaffected by IRC §7609 and hence depends on pre-1976 law, as it may develop hereafter.[93]

2. *Notice to target of inquiry.* When a summons subject to IRC §7609 is served, notice must be given in a prescribed manner to the person identified in the summons within three days of the day of service, but not later than the twenty-third day before the records are to be examined.

3. *Right to intervene and stay compliance.* A person entitled to notice of the third party summons under IRC §7609(a) has the right under IRC §7609(a), on giving notice to the witness and the IRS, to institute a proceeding to quash the summons. These rights, which supersede any other law or rule of law (e.g., IRC §7421, forbidding injunctions against the assessment or collection of taxes), insure that targets of an inquiry will be able to present any defenses they may have to enforcement of the summons, either at the IRC §7604(a) enforcement hearing or at the proceeding to quash under IRC §7609(b)(2). To forestall dilatory tactics, however, IRC §7609(b), enacted in 1982, requires the third-party record-keeper to proceed to assemble the records requested, despite the motion to quash the summons, and to be prepared to produce them on the date specified in the summons.

4. *John Doe summons.* In *United States v. Bisceglia* the Supreme Court held that a summons could be properly issued under IRC §7602 to obtain a bank's records even though no specifically identified taxpayer was under investigation.[94] To insure judicial supervision when IRC §7602 is used not in seeking to investigate taxpayers but in seeking taxpayers to investigate, Congress enacted IRC §7609(f), under which a summons that does not identify the person under investigation can be issued only after a judicial proceeding establishing that (1) the summons relates to the investigation of a particular person or ascertainable group or class of persons; (2) there is a reasonable basis to believe that the person, group, or class may fail or may have failed to comply with any tax law; and (3) the information sought and the identity of the persons whose liability is involved cannot be readily obtained from other sources.[95]

---

[92] See US v. Exxon Co., 450 F.Supp. 472 (D.Md. 1978) (records of issuer of credit cards were its records, not taxpayer's); US v. Income Realty & Mortgage Co., 612 F.2d 1224 (10th Cir. 1979); (records of commissions paid by company to its salesmen not covered); US v. New York Telephone Co., 45 AFTR2d 1424 (E.D.N.Y. 1980), remanded 644 F.2d 953 (2d Cir. 1981) (records of taxpayer's telephone calls charged to credit card covered by IRC §7609(a)(3)(C)). For the meaning of the term "barter exchange" see IRC §6045(c)(3).

[93] See supra note 90.

[94] US v. Bisceglia, supra note 68.

[95] See US v. South Cent. Bell Tel. Co., 43 AFTR2d 931 (M.D. Tenn. 1979) (not

5. *Records of banks and other financial institutions.* The Right to Financial Privacy Act of 1978 restricts the government's access to the records of certain financial institutions by forbidding them to disclose records of their customer's financial transactions, except pursuant to one of five procedures: (1) customer authorization, valid for not more than three months and subject to revocation at any time before disclosure; (2) administrative summons or subpoena; (3) search warrant obtained in accordance with the Federal Rules of Criminal Procedure; (4) judicial subpoena; or (5) written request, provided the agency lacks the power to issue a summons or subpoena, subject to prescribed restrictions.[96]

4. Constitutional Restrictions. In addition to constitutional issues growing out of the use of administrative summonses by the IRS, other investigative techniques can create constitutional issues that, depending on the circumstances, a taxpayer or witness may raise by refusal to respond to some action by the IRS, suit to restrain the objectionable activity, suit for damages, motion to suppress the evidence before trial, or motion to exclude the evidence at the trial itself. Because these issues are ordinarily not unique to tax cases and indeed may appear in a tax context only as a remote ripple created by a great legal wave elsewhere, the major issues can only be briefly summarized here.

1. *Right to counsel.* The Constitution guarantees the right of counsel only in criminal prosecutions, but there appears to be no effort by the IRS to prevent taxpayers from being accompanied by counsel during audits, investigative interviews, hearings pursuant to an administrative summons, or conferences. Special agents of the Criminal Investigation Division are instructed by the IRS to state at the initial meeting with a taxpayer that they have the function of investigating the possibility of criminal tax fraud, that the taxpayer cannot be compelled to incriminate himself by answering questions or producing documents, and that he has the right to consult counsel before responding. This warning is not constitutionally required in routine investigations even if fraud is suspected, but there is some authority for suppressing evidence ob-

---

officially reported) (telephone company ordered to give IRS names and addresses of persons with unlisted telephone numbers, so they can be given notice under IRC §7609 before additional information is supplied); US v. Brigham Young Univ., 679 F.2d 1345 (10th Cir. 1982) (enforcing John Doe summons to obtain names of persons contributing gifts in kind to university because, on evidence that gifts were overvalued by all donors whose returns had been audited, there was "reasonable basis" for believing that some of the remaining donors may have overvalued their gifts).

[96] See generally H. Rep. No. 95-1383, reprinted in 1978-2 CB 454. The prohibition against voluntary disclosure except with the customer's consent forces the IRS to employ its power to issue an administrative summons, unless the taxpayer consents, which triggers the procedural rules of IRC §7609.

tained by a revenue agent who breaches this self-imposed operating procedure.[97]

2. *Privilege against self-incrimination.* As a shield during the investigation of tax matters, the privilege against self-incrimination protects the taxpayer against being compelled to answer questions or produce documents that might incriminate him.[98]

3. *Required documents doctrine.* Under the Emergency Price Control Act, in force during World War II, persons engaged in business were required to make and keep prescribed records. In *Shapiro v. United States,* decided in 1948, a sharply divided Supreme Court held that the privilege against self-incrimination was not violated by a subpoena requiring a businessman to produce records of his sales during a specified period, because the privilege does not encompass "records required by law to be kept in order that there may be information of transactions which are the appropriate subjects of governmental regulation." [99] Four dissenting Justices feared that the required records doctrine would expand "to the limits of its logic";[100] but in fact it has fallen into desuetude so far as federal regulations are concerned, and its current status is unclear.

The government has not displayed any desire to exploit the required records doctrine—no doubt because its rationale is inconsistent with the customary assumptions and practices of law-enforcement agencies and defense counsel. The IRS, for example, regularly honors claims by individuals who refuse to produce their tax records on self-incrimination grounds; and the courts are also responsive to these claims, provided the threat of incrimination is not feigned and the privilege is not waived.[101] Because of this uneasy truce, it has not been necessary for the courts to determine whether, assuming that Congress *could* require individual taxpayers to produce incriminating tax records, it has manifested an intent to do so.

4. *Trickery or misrepresentation.* Nonfraud, civil fraud, and criminal fraud possibilities are inextricably interwoven in virtually all investigations and taxpayers are ordinarily aware of this fact. For this reason, the courts usually suppress evidence supplied in response to an agent's request only if the taxpayer makes a clear and convincing showing of affirmative misrepresentation,

---

[97] For the IRS formula, see Statement of Procedural Rules, 26 CFR §601.107(b)(2); see also US v. Jobin, 535 F.2d 154 (1st Cir. 1976), and cases there cited; US v. Ersbo, 394 F.Supp. 1074 (D.Minn. 1975) (substantial compliance sufficient; test is whether agents misled taxpayer into believing investigation was civil in nature).

[98] See supra, text at note 83 (re IRC §7602).

[99] Shapiro v. US, 335 US 1 (1948).

[100] Id. at 71.

[101] See, e.g., Hill v. Philpott, 445 F.2d 144 (7th Cir.), cert. denied, 404 US 991 (1971) (physician's financial records protected by privilege against self-incrimination).

such as a statement by the agent that the investigation is purely civil in character.[102]

5. *Searches and seizures.* Business records and other evidence seized pursuant to a proper search warrant are admissible, even though incriminating, because the *taxpayer* is not compelled to produce the incriminating material,[103] with the result that this investigation technique avoids the self-incrimination obstacle encountered when an individual is ordered by an administrative summons issued under IRC §7602 to produce documents.[104] To comply with the Fourth Amendment, a search warrant can be issued only on probable cause, supported by oath or affirmation, and the place to be searched and the person or things to be seized must be described with particularity. Because the IRS must persuade the Department of Justice of the need for a search warrant, they are seldom used in tax investigations.[105]

6. *Use of unconstitutionally obtained evidence in civil cases.* The Tax Court held in *Suarez v. CIR* that the exclusionary rule prohibited use of constitutionally tainted evidence in a civil tax case, whether the improper seizure was conducted by state or federal officers.[106] Only four years later, however, the Supreme Court held in *United States v. Janis* that evidence improperly seized by state or local officers could be properly introduced in a federal civil tax case, since the function of the exclusionary rule—to deter improper police practices—did not require the evidence to be barred from a case that was so far "outside the offending officer's zone of primary interest." [107] The Court pointedly declined to consider the applicability of the exclusionary rule to civil proceedings involving evidence seized improperly by *federal* officials, so that the status of *Suarez* as respects evidence improperly seized by federal officials is now uncertain.[108]

5. Rewards to Informers. The IRS is empowered by IRC §7623 to pay rewards for detecting and bringing persons guilty of violating the tax laws to

---

[102] See US v. Prudden, 424 F.2d 1021 (5th Cir. 1970); US v. Tweel, 550 F.2d 297 (5th Cir. 1977).

[103] Andresen v. Maryland, supra note 87; see also Shaffer v. Wilson, 523 F.2d 175 (10th Cir. 1975), cert. denied, 427 US 912 (1976) (dentist's records seized by IRS pursuant to search warrant).

[104] See supra, text at note 71.

[105] For the constitutional requirements, see Andresen v. Maryland, supra note 87; Gordon v. CIR, 63 TC 51 (1974) (search warrant against betting establishment), aff'd on other issues, 572 F.2d 193 (9th Cir. 1977), cert. denied, 435 US 924 (1978).

[106] Suarez v. CIR, 58 TC 792 (1972).

[107] US v. Janis, 428 US 433, rehearing denied, 429 US 874 (1976).

[108] See McDonald's Est. v. US, 43 AFTR2d 415 (N.D. Cal. 1979) (not officially reported) (IRS use of evidence illegally seized by other federal officials not constitutionally objectionable; alternative ground for decision).

trial and punishment.[109] Although the statutory language seems to refer solely to information leading to criminal convictions, the regulations stress instead the monetary value of the informer's assistance, providing that rewards shall be based on the district director's judgment of "adequate compensation in the particular case, normally not to exceed ten percent of the additional taxes, penalties, and fines" collected as a result of the information provided.[110] The IRS' determination of the amount due, if any, is conclusive, unless the claimant shows an abuse of discretion in making the determination.[111]

6. Power of Taxpayers to Obtain Information. During the audit and investigative stages of a tax matter, taxpayers seeking information to buttress claims presented to the IRS or to respond to adverse IRS determinations must rely primarily on their powers of persuasion. The IRS cannot be compelled to disclose the files or investigative reports on which revenue agents and appellate conferees rely in making recommendations and proposing deficiencies.[112] If, however, the taxpayer is seeking rulings and other documents that might influence the IRS in passing on the merits of the taxpayer's case, it may be possible to compel disclosure under IRC §6110 or the Freedom of Information Act.[113] But IRS officials are not supposed to use unpublished rulings and similar determinations as precedents,[114] and the courts seldom impose an obligation of consistency on administrative agencies,[115] so success in ferreting out documents of this type is likely to be a hollow victory.

As for information in the hands of third persons, taxpayers are not vested with any authority to compel disclosure, comparable to the power of the IRS to issue administrative summonses under IRC §7602. Once litigation ensues, however, the taxpayer has the usual powers of a litigant and can engage in

---

[109] See also United States ex rel. Roberts v. Western Pac. R.R., 190 F.2d 243 (9th Cir. 1951) (qui tam actions, allowed when government has been defrauded, not permissible in tax cases in absence of official consent under IRC §7401); IRC §7214(a) (next to last sentence) (judicial awards to informers on conviction of tax officials for fraud, etc.).

[110] Treas. Regs. §301.7623-1(c); see also US v. Cortese, 614 F.2d 914 (3d Cir. 1980) (reversing district court, which had refused to enforce IRS summons because based on data supplied by informer with improper purpose).

[111] See Saracena v. US, 508 F.2d 1333 (Ct. Cl. 1975) (payment of about 1.3 percent of amount recovered by United States not abuse of discretion).

[112] The Privacy Act of 1974 does not apply to information compiled by the government in reasonable anticipation of a civil action or for law-enforcement purposes. See S. Rep. No. 93-1183 (1974), reprinted in 1975-1 CB 448, 485–489. See also IRC §§6103(c) and 6103(e) (power to inspect taxpayer's own tax returns and return information and similar documents relating to persons with whom taxpayer has material relationship), discussed supra ¶39.2.

[113] See supra ¶38.5.

[114] Rev. Proc. 78-24, 1978-2 CB 503, §7.01(4); see also supra ¶38.5.

[115] See supra ¶38.5.

discovery proceedings, take depositions, issue interrogatories, and subpoena witnesses as permitted by the rules of the court in which the suit is pending.

¶40.3 REFUNDS

1. Introductory. Taxpayers may overpay their tax liability by excessive withholding from wages, inflated declarations of estimated tax, and arithmetic errors on returns, and they may sustain operating losses in later years that generate carrybacks. Overpayments resulting from these factors are usually conceded by the IRS and either credited or refunded automatically; but these credits and refunds are provisional in the sense that the IRS may find, on auditing the return, that there was a deficiency instead of an overpayment. Credits and refunds are also noncontroversial if they result from shifting items from one taxable year to another on audit, assuming the taxpayer agrees with the adjustment. The IRS' authority to allow these voluntary credits and refunds (with interest), provided the applicable statute of limitations has not run, derives from IRC §6402.

If, however, the taxpayer discovers an error on a previously filed return or believes that the government's determination of an overpayment is too niggardly, the stage is set for a claim for refund or credit. Refund claims have a dual function: First, the claim sets in motion the IRS' administrative procedure for an examination of the taxpayer's case; second, by virtue of IRC §7422, it is a prerequisite to a judicial proceeding by the taxpayer if the IRS refuses to credit or refund the amount claimed.[116]

2. Form and Content of Refund Claims. Under the IRS rules as amended in 1976, the form for claiming a credit or refund of an overpayment is the tax return for the pertinent taxable year if the overpayment is shown on the return itself (e.g., over-withholding or excessive payments of estimated tax) or an amended return if the return as filed did not disclose the overpayment (e.g., because of an after-discovered error).[117] Under a long line of pre-1976 cases, however, letters, marginal notations on tax returns for related later years, and other informal statements can constitute claims for refund despite their formal

---

[116] Infra, text preceding note 124.

[117] Treas. Regs. §301.6402-3.

For the person entitled to receive a refund, see IRC §6402(a) (the "person who made the overpayment"); Treas. Regs. §301.6402-2(f); McGraw-Hill, Inc. v. US, 623 F.2d 700 (Ct. Cl. 1980) ("fatal category" of volunteers who pay the taxes of other persons cannot obtain refunds; on facts, taxpayer not a volunteer); see also Rev. Rul. 74-611, 1974-2 CB 399 (overpayment on joint return cannot be credited against husband's liability on separate return filed for prior year, where tax on joint return was paid by wife).

inadequacies if they are timely and adequately advise the IRS of the taxpayer's demand.[118] The 1976 designation of returns and amended returns as the proper route to a refund or credit was presumably not intended to repudiate these decisions.

Even if the claim is submitted on the proper form, the regulations provide that it will not be considered "for any purpose as a claim for refund or credit" unless it sets forth in detail each ground on which the credit or refund is claimed, with facts sufficient to apprise the IRS of the exact basis thereof, and is verified by a written declaration that is made under the penalties of perjury.[119] Until the statute of limitations runs, these requirements are innocuous, since a claim that is unverified, imprecise, or inadequately documented can be amended or, if beyond repair, replaced by a better-prepared claim. Once the statute of limitations has run, however, the taxpayer is bound—shackled may be a more descriptive term—by the claim, as submitted, since the regulations state that no refund or credit will be allowed after the statutory period except on the grounds set forth in a claim filed before the expiration of the period.[120]

The requirement of specificity is mitigated by two intertwined principles: (1) the possibility of waiver by the IRS if it proceeds to investigate the taxpayer's claim and thereby learns more about the issues, and (2) the taxpayer's right to amend the claim to make it more specific, even after the statutory period for filing an original claim has expired.[121] Under these principles, amendments frequently salvage vague or imprecise claims and cure variances, but the "metamorphosis" must not be too complete.[122] If, however, the claim is rejected, it cannot be amended after the statutory period even if an amendment before rejection would have been permissible.[123]

The application of these long-standing principles to the use of amended tax returns as claims for refund remains to be worked out. If a dollar amount with a broad label (e.g., "gross receipts," "salaries and wages," or "cost of goods sold") is changed by the amended return, the change does not identify any particular item within the affected category, nor does it explain why the original return was wrong. It may, therefore, be advisable for taxpayers to supplement the amended return before the statutory period runs if the item in

---

[118] See, e.g., US v. Kales, 314 US 186 (1941) (letter stating that taxpayer "will claim the right to a refund" tolled statute of limitations and could be amended by filing a formal claim after lapse of normal statutory period); Kearney v. A'Hearn, 210 F.Supp. 10 (S.D.N.Y. 1961), aff'd per curiam, 309 F.2d 487 (2d Cir. 1962) (letter).

[119] Treas. Regs. §301.6402-2(b)(1).

[120] Id.

[121] US v. Andrews, 302 US 517, 524 (1938); for a review of later cases in this area, see Union Pac. R.R. v. US, 389 F.2d 437 (Ct. Cl. 1968).

[122] US v. Henry Prentiss & Co., 288 US 73, 84 (1933).

[123] See US v. Memphis Cotton Oil Co., 288 US 62 (1933).

dispute is buried in a sea of other amounts so that the ground of the claim is obscure.

In addition to its use by IRC §6511(b)(1), the term "claim" is used by IRC §7422(a), forbidding judicial proceedings for the recovery of taxes "until a claim for refund or credit has been duly filed" with the IRS in accordance with the applicable regulations. Although the IRS may have the authority to establish separate channels for claims submitted solely for administrative consideration and those that the taxpayer may wish to pursue in court if satisfaction is not obtained at the administrative level, all claims move through a single channel under current practice and this means that the specificity, waiver-amendment, and other principles determining whether a claim is adequate are the same under both IRC §6511(b) and §7422.

3. Time for Filing Claims. To be considered at the administrative level by the IRS or used as the basis of judicial proceedings, refund claims must ordinarily be filed within the period prescribed by IRC §6511(a)—three years from the time the return was filed or two years from the time the tax was paid,[124] whichever is later. The usual rule under which early returns are treated as filed on the due date applies; but in the case of late returns, the filing date controls, whether the due date was extended or not.[125] An untimely claim cannot be revived by IRS consideration of its merits[126]; under IRC §6514(a)(1), a credit allowed on the basis of a barred claim is void; and if a refund is made, it can be recovered by the government by suit pursuant to IRC §§6532(b) and 7405.[127]

A claim filed within the prescribed period, even though valid, will not necessarily entitle the taxpayer to a credit or refund for the entire overpayment, since IRC §6511(b)(2) imposes secondary limits on the dollar amount recoverable. If the claim is filed within the three-year period specified by IRC §6511(a), the credit or refund may not exceed the amount paid within that period, plus any extensions of time for filing the return. If the claim is filed within the two-year period allowed by IRC §6511(a) but not within the three-year period, the recovery is limited to the amount paid during the two-year period immediately preceding the filing of the claim.[128]

---

[124] For the time when a tax is "paid," see Ford v. US, 618 F.2d 357 (5th Cir. 1980) (analysis of when remittance constitutes "payment" of tax), and cases there cited.

[125] IRC §6513(a); Treas. Regs. §301.6513-1.

[126] Kearney v. A'Hearn, supra note 118.

[127] For suits of this type, see US v. Wurts, 303 US 414 (1938) (government's claim barred by time; refund is "made" when taxpayer receives check, not when check is cashed).

[128] See Allstate Ins. Co. v. US, 550 F.2d 629 (Ct. Cl. 1977) (method of marshaling taxes and claims when two-year and three-year periods apply to different refund claims).

The two-year and three-year periods prescribed by IRC §6511(a) for claiming refunds and credits are modified or displaced by a number of special provisions, which establish longer periods for claims based on specified events, usually because it is difficult or impossible to ascertain the pertinent facts within the normal period.[129]

4. IRS Procedure in Refund Cases. On receiving a claim for refund or credit, the IRS follows substantially the same procedure as when returns are originally examined, including the administrative appeal rights accorded to taxpayers. Since the entire return is examined, not merely the claim for credit or refund, taxpayers sometimes refrain from pressing debatable claims, lest they wind up writing a check to the IRS rather than receiving one. Moreover, even if a refund or credit is allowed, the assertion of a deficiency at a later time is not barred, provided the statutory period has not expired.[130]

Refunds and credits in excess of $200,000 must be reported to the Joint Committee on Taxation under IRC §6405 and cannot be made until thirty days after the report is submitted.

If a claim is disallowed, the IRS usually asks the taxpayer to waive a formal notice of disallowance under IRC §6532(a)(3). If executed, the waiver permits the taxpayer to bring a judicial proceeding for a refund immediately, and the two-year statute of limitations on such actions starts to run at the same time.[131]

SELECTED BIBLIOGRAPHY

Bennion, How and Where to Settle a Federal Income Tax Dispute—A Practicing Lawyer's Views, 1969 So. Calif. Tax Inst. 9, 15–20.

Caplin, Government Access to Independent Accountants' Tax Accrual Workpapers, 1 Va. Tax Rev. 57 (1981).

Donaldson, Techniques in Presenting and Settling a Case Before the Internal Revenue Service: The Agent; District Conference; Appellate Division, 27 NYU Inst. on Fed. Tax. 1343 (1969).

---

[129] The special situations include claims based on (1) taxes subject to an extension of time for assessment under IRC §§6501(c)(4), 6511(c); (2) bad debts and worthless securities, IRC §6511(d)(1); (3) net operating loss, capital loss and investment credit carrybacks, IRC §§6511(d)(2) (net operating loss and capital loss carrybacks), 6511(d)(4) (investment credit); (4) foreign tax credits, IRC §6511(d)(3); and (5) adjustments under IRC §§1311–1315.

[130] Burnet v. Porter, 283 US 230 (1931).

[131] For refund suits, see infra ¶43.7.

AUDITS, DEFICIENCIES, & REFUNDS

Homer, Comment—Auditing Partnership Tax Shelters: IRS Procedures and Taxpayer Liability, 60 Neb. L. Rev. 564 (1981).

Housemann, Executing Forms 870 and 870-AD, 14 Tul. Tax Inst. 285 (1965).

Kurtz & Panel, Discussion on "Questionable Payments," 32 Tax Lawyer 13 (1978).

Magges, Section 7122 of the Internal Revenue Code: The Offer in Compromise, 11 Gonz. L. Rev. 481 (1976).

Mahon, Privileged Communications and Self-Incrimination, 32 NYU Inst. on Fed. Tax. 1251 (1974).

Namorato, The Government's Tools in the Investigation of a Criminal Fraud Case, 34 NYU Inst. on Fed. Tax. 1019 (1976).

Nash, Effective Internal Revenue Service Appellate Division Practice, 35 NYU Inst. on Fed. Tax. 325 (1977).

Nuzum, The Third-Party Recordkeeper Provisions of Section 7609, 34 Tax Lawyer 657 (1981).

Stigamire, The Internal Revenue Service Case Settlement Procedure, 1979 So. Calif. Tax Inst. 1073.

U.S. Comptroller General, Report to the Joint Committee on Internal Revenue Taxation, Who's Not Filing Income Tax Returns? IRS Needs Better Ways to Find Them and Collect Their Taxes (GGD 79-69, 1979).

Warden, Rules for Administrative Summonses Completely Revamped Under 1976 Act, 46 J. Tax. 32 (1977).

Yurow & Parker, Claims for Refund, 31 NYU Inst. on Fed. Tax. 1553 (1973).

CHAPTER 41

Statutes of Limitations

¶41.1 INTRODUCTORY

The Internal Revenue Code contains statutes of limitations to regulate many different aspects of the tax enforcement process. Section 6501, the most important of these provisions, prescribes the period within which income taxes must be assessed.[1] Section 6511 specifies the time allowed for a claim for the credit or refund of an overpayment.[2] Both of these basic provisions are "mitigated" by IRC §§1311–1314, which extend the time for a corrective assessment of a deficiency (or refund or credit of an overpayment) in certain circumstances involving inconsistencies by the IRS, the taxpayer, or specified persons

[1] See infra ¶41.2.

[2] See infra ¶41.8.

related to the taxpayer.[3] In unusual circumstances, the normal operation of the statutes of limitations can also be suspended or altered by the judicially developed doctrines of estoppel and equitable recoupment.[4] In the absence of a statute of limitations, it is generally held that the government is not barred by the equitable doctrine of laches in enforcing its rights.[5]

In addition to the general statutes of limitations on assessments and on claims for credit or refund, there are a number of time limitations to govern more specialized areas.[6] The Code and regulations prescribe numerous other time limits for making elections and taking other action, which resemble statutes of limitations in their respective jurisdictional spheres, particularly if the IRS is not authorized to extend the specified time.[7] Finally, state statutes of limitations are applicable to some areas, such as the life of a judgment obtained in an action to collect an assessed tax.[8]

The Internal Revenue Code's statutes of limitations not only bar any remedy, but also extinguish the liability. Belated payments by repentant taxpayers to the Treasury's so-called conscience fund, however, are treated not as tax payments (which would have to be refunded if received after expiration of the allowable time for making an assessment), but as gifts to the United States; and they are used to reduce the national debt.

¶41.2 ASSESSMENT OF TAX

Section 6501(a) requires income, estate, and gift taxes to be assessed, as a general rule, within three years after the return was filed and provides that no court proceeding for the collection of an unassessed tax shall be begun after the three-year period has run. Expiration of the three-year period bars the use of any mode of collection, including distraint,[9] and converts voluntary payments into "overpayments," which are subject to refund or credit within the statutory period prescribed by IRC §6511.[10]

The "assessment" required by IRC §6501(a) is effected by "recording the liability of the taxpayer" in the appropriate IRS office pursuant to IRC

---

[3] See infra ¶41.9.

[4] See infra ¶41.10.

[5] US v. Weintraub, 613 F.2d 612 (6th Cir. 1979) (extensive analysis).

[6] For statutes of limitations pertaining to specialized areas, see, e.g., IRC §6229 (partnerships), infra ¶41.2; for other specialized statutes of limitations, see infra ¶41.2.

[7] See generally Rev. Proc. 79-63, 1979-2 CB 578 (factors bearing on whether IRS will extend time limits fixed by regulations).

[8] See supra ¶39.7.

[9] See Bowers v. New York & Albany Lighterage Co., 273 US 346, 349 (1927).

[10] See Rev. Rul. 74-580, 1974-2 CB 400 (payment of time-barred tax does not operate as waiver of statute of limitations; IRC §6402(a) requires refund).

§§6202–6204.[11] Taxpayers are entitled to receive copies of the assessment record, but the assessment is timely if recorded before the three-year period expires, even if notice is not sent to the taxpayer until thereafter.[12]

The three-year period for assessment of the tax begins to run on the day after the tax return is filed, if it is filed on or after the prescribed date;[13] but an early return is treated by IRC §6501(b)(1) as filed on the last day prescribed by law for filing, and the timely mailed, timely filed principle of IRC §7502 evidently means that a return is filed when postmarked or due, whichever is later, not when received by the IRS.[14]

The basic three-year statute of limitations is subject to numerous qualifications, of which the most important are:

1. Fraud. In the case of false or fraudulent returns or a willful attempt to evade the tax, there is no statute of limitations on assessment or collection.[15]

2. Over-25-Percent Omission. The three-year period is supplanted by a six-year period if gross income is understated by more than 25 percent, under principles discussed below.[16]

3. No Return. There is no statute of limitations if the taxpayer fails to file a return, even if a return is executed for the taxpayer by the IRS under IRC §6020(b).[17]

4. Wrong Form. The statute of limitations does not ordinarily commence to run if the taxpayer files the wrong type of return, but this rule is mitigated by IRC §6501(g), providing that if a taxpayer determines in good faith that it is a trust or partnership, a return filed on that basis starts the

---

[11] See Treas. Regs. §301.6203-1; supra ¶39.7.

[12] See Filippini v. US, 200 F.Supp. 286 (N.D. Cal. 1961), aff'd on other grounds, 318 F.2d 841 (9th Cir.), cert. denied, 375 US 922 (1963).

[13] See Burnet v. Willingham Loan & Trust Co., 282 US 437 (1931) (day of filing does not count; assessment on March 15, 1926 was within four-year limitations period applicable to return filed on March 15, 1922). If the taxpayer files an amended return, the period runs from the filing of the original return, not the amended one. See Goldring v. CIR, 20 TC 79 (1953) and cases there cited.

[14] Hotel Equities Corp. v. CIR, 546 F.2d 725 (7th Cir. 1976); for IRC §7502, see supra ¶39.1.

[15] See infra ¶41.3.

[16] See infra ¶41.4.

[17] IRC §6501(b)(3); for IRC §6020(b), see supra ¶39.1; see also Rev. Rul. 79-178, 1979-1 CB 435 (delinquent correct return starts the running of the statute of limitations even if failure to file on time was due to fraud).

running of the statute of limitations even if the taxpayer is later determined to be a corporation.[18]

5. Request for Prompt Assessment. In certain situations involving the taxes of decedents and dissolving corporations, the IRS must assess the tax within eighteen months after a written request from the taxpayer.[19]

6. Partnership Returns. By the enactment in 1982 of IRC §6231, Congress amended the statutes of limitations to insure that adjustments triggered by audits of partnership returns would not be barred by the statute of limitations applicable to the individual returns of the partners. These changes, which apply to both partnership items and so-called affected items (any item on the partner's return to the extent that it is affected by the proper treatment of a partnership item), gear the statute of limitations to the partnership return. The basic period for assessments based on partnership and affected items is three years from the date of filing the partnership return or, if later, the last date for filing the return without regard to extensions.[20] Assessments with respect to partnership and affected items may be made at any time against partners signing or actively participating in a fraudulent return, and the period for assessment is extended from three or six years for any other partners affected by such a return. The period of assessment for partnership and affected items is also six years if there is an over 25 percent omission from partnership gross income. Moreover, in certain cases in which a partner is not properly identified on the partnership return or treats partnership items in a manner not consistent with the partnership's treatment and fails to disclose this fact, the period does not expire until one year after the name, address, and taxpayer identification number of the partner are furnished to the IRS. Certain partnerships with no more than 10 partners, all of whom are natural persons, are exempt from these rules.[21]

7. Miscellaneous. The normal three-year period is supplanted by longer periods in the case of (1) deficiencies attributable to the carryback of net operating losses, capital losses, and certain credits;[22] (2) joint returns filed after

[18] Similar rules apply to returns filed in good faith under IRC §§6033 and 6011(c)(2) relating to exempt organizations and DISCs. Even though the wrong return may start the statute of limitations to run, it does not take the place of the proper return for all purposes; see, e.g., Knollwood Memorial Gardens v. CIR, 46 TC 764, 795 (1966) (negligence penalty imposed despite filing of information return).

[19] See IRC §6501(d); Treas. Regs. §301.6501(d)-1; R.B. Griffith Co. v. CIR, ¶73,050 P-H Memo TC (1973) (contents of request for prompt assessment), and cases there cited.

[20] IRC §6229(a).

[21] See IRC §6231(a)(1)(B) for this exception for small partnerships.

[22] See IRC §§6501(h) (net operating losses and capital losses), 6501(i) (foreign taxes), 6501(j) (investment, work incentive, and new employee credits).

the filing of separate returns;[23] and (3) many special items that are treated by the Code in a particular way tentatively, subject to readjustment on the subsequent breach of a condition or the occurrence of a specified event.[24]

The applicable statute of limitations can also be extended by an agreement between the IRS and the taxpayer [25] and is suspended by certain events, such as the issuance of a statutory notice of deficiency ("ninety-day letter") and proceedings in the Tax Court.[26]

¶41.3 FALSE OR FRAUDULENT RETURNS

In the case of a false or fraudulent return with intent to evade tax or a willful attempt to defeat or evade tax in any manner, the tax can be assessed at any time, or a proceeding in court to collect the tax can be begun without assessment.[27] In determining whether the taxpayer's conduct is fraudulent for statute of limitations purposes, the criteria governing imposition of the 50 percent fraud penalty are applicable,[28] and the IRS has the burden of proof and must establish fraud by clear and convincing evidence.[29] If a return is fraudulent in any respect, however, all items on the return can be audited and corrected without regard to the passage of time;[30] but if two or more taxable years are involved, fraud must be proved separately for each year.[31]

¶41.4 OMISSION OF MORE THAN 25 PERCENT FROM GROSS INCOME

Section 6501(e)(1) extends normal three-year period of limitations to six years if the taxpayer omits from gross income an amount in excess of 25 percent of the gross income stated in the return, even if the error was commit-

---

[23] See IRC §§6501(1), 6013(b)(3), 6013(b)(4).

[24] See, e.g., IRC §183(e)(4) (assessment within two years at end of five-year or seven-year period in determining whether activity is conducted for profit); IRC §§1033(a)(2)(C), 1033(a)(2)(D) (replacement of involuntarily converted property); IRC §1034(j) (sale and replacement of principal residence).

[25] See, e.g., IRC §6501(c)(4); infra ¶41.5.

[26] Phoenix Elecs., Inc. v. US, 164 F.Supp. 614, 615 (D.Mass. 1958), infra ¶41.6.

[27] IRC §§6501(c)(1), 6501(c)(2), 6229(c)(1). The later filing of a nonfraudulent amended return may start the statute of limitations running, if the IRS has used the amended return. See Dowell v. CIR, 614 F.2d 1263 (10th Cir. 1980); compare Bennett v. CIR, 30 TC 114 (1958) (failure to file).

[28] See IRC §6653(b), discussed infra ¶42.3.

[29] See IRC §7454(a) (burden of proof); Drieborg v. CIR, 225 F.2d 216 (6th Cir. 1955).

[30] Lowy v. CIR, 288 F.2d 517 (2d Cir. 1961), cert. denied, 368 US 984 (1962).

[31] See Shaw v. CIR, 27 TC 561 (1956) (Acq.), aff'd, 252 F.2d 681 (6th Cir. 1958).

ted in good faith.[32] In determining the amount omitted from gross income, IRC §6501(e)(1)(A)(ii) provides that items disclosed in the return or on an attached statement are disregarded if the disclosure is adequate to apprise the IRS of the item's nature and amount.[33]

Being concerned with "omissions" from gross income, IRC §6501(e)(1) is not brought into play by errors that understate gross income without omitting anything (e.g., an understatement of gross income resulting solely from overstating the basis of property in computing gain on its sale). A fortiori, deducting excess amounts *from* gross income in computing taxable income does not result in a tainted omission from gross income.[34] On the other hand, the use of an erroneous accounting method can bring the six-year statute into play if the result is an omission from gross income of amounts properly includable therein.[35]

¶41.5 CONSENTS TO EXTEND STATUTORY PERIOD

Section 6501(c)(4) permits the IRS and the taxpayer to extend the statute of limitations by an agreement in writing before the expiration of the time otherwise applicable, such as the normal three-year period prescribed by IRC §6501(a), the six-year period prescribed by IRC §6501(e)(1), or the time fixed by an earlier agreement under IRC §6501(c)(4). Because a consent under IRC §6501(c)(4) must be executed before the statute has run, the validity of a consent may turn on whether the three-year or six-year statute is applicable or on whether a prior consent was timely.[36] Consents under IRC §6501(c)(4) are encountered in practice whenever additional time is required to examine a return or when a disputed issue is taken to the IRS Appeals Office.

---

[32] See Hale's Est. v. CIR, 1 TC 121 (1942) ("honest mistake" does not preclude application of extended statutory period).

[33] Quick Trust v. CIR, 54 TC 1336, 1347 (1970), aff'd without discussion of this point, 444 F.2d 90 (8th Cir. 1971) (detailed revelation of each and every underlying fact is not necessary); Benderoff v. US, 398 F.2d 132 (8th Cir. 1968) (individual return referred to Subchapter S corporation return; held, both returns considered together made adequate disclosure). Disclosure on a related party's return is not adequate. See Corrigan v. CIR, 155 F.2d 164 (6th Cir. 1946) (items reported on fiduciary return; omission from individual return not excused by disclosure of omitted amount on fiduciary return).

[34] See Phoenix Elecs., Inc. v. US, supra note 26.

[35] See Bond-Gleason, Inc. v. CIR, ¶59,002 P-H Memo TC (1959) (retail store's erroneous use of cash method, resulting in omission of accounts receivable from gross income).

[36] See Romine v. CIR, 25 TC 859, 871 (1956) (Acq.) (consent signed more than three but less than five years after return was filed; IRS has burden of proving over-25-percent omission from income to validate consent); Treas. Regs. §301.6501(c)-1(d) (later agreements must be executed before expiration of period previously agreed upon).

¶41.6 SUSPENSION OF STATUTORY PERIOD BY NINETY-DAY LETTER

When the IRS mails a statutory notice of deficiency ("ninety-day letter"), the running of the period of limitations on the assessment and collection of the deficiency is suspended for the period prescribed by IRC §6213(a)—ninety days from the mailing of the notice or, if the addressee is outside the United States, 150 days—and, if a petition in respect of the deficiency is docketed with the Tax Court, until its decision becomes final and for sixty days thereafter.[37] When this period ends, the applicable statute of limitations begins to run again. The Tax Court has jurisdiction to determine the correct liability even if it exceeds the amount stated in the ninety-day letter;[38] subject to this qualification, the suspension applies only to the deficiency asserted in the notice, not to any additional deficiency asserted in a later notice of deficiency.[39]

¶41.7 COLLECTION OF TAX AFTER ASSESSMENT

Once a timely assessment is made,[40] IRC §6502 permits the tax to be collected by levy or by a proceeding in court only if the levy or proceeding is begun within six years of the assessment. The six-year period on *collection* applies even if the return was fraudulent.[41] If the collection is by levy, the notice of seizure must be given within the six-year period.[42] If collection is by judicial proceeding, the date on which the complaint is filed controls.

If a collection proceeding is commenced within the prescribed six-year

---

[37] IRC §6503(a)(1); see also Treas. Regs. §301.6503(a)-1(a), Example; supra ¶40.1.

[38] See IRC §6214(a); Teitelbaum v. CIR, 346 F.2d 266 (7th Cir. 1965) (Tax Court can decide all claims that could have been asserted in notice of deficiency).

[39] Treas. Regs. §301.6503(a)-1(a)(1) (last sentence); CIR v. Wilson, 60 F.2d 501 (10th Cir. 1932).

[40] For the statute of limitations on assessments, see supra ¶41.2.

[41] See Payne v. US, 247 F.2d 481 (8th Cir. 1957), cert. denied, 355 US 923 (1958); but see Gum Prods., Inc. v. CIR, 38 TC 700 (1962) (IRC §6502 applies only to assessed amounts; fraud penalties not barred because not previously assessed).

[42] IRC §6502(b); US v. Saslavsky, 160 F.Supp. 883 (S.D.N.Y. 1957) (turnover order to enforce lien constitutes "proceeding in court" in applying six-year time limit). A timely complaint can be amended after the six-year period and actions to foreclose liens are also ancillary to the original complaint and relate back to its date. See US v. Hardy, 7 AFTR2d 957 (E.D. Va. 1961) (not officially reported), aff'd without discussion of this issue, 299 F.2d 600 (4th Cir. 1962) (date of filing controls despite delay in serving complaint); US v. Besase, 319 F.Supp. 1064 (N.D. Ohio 1970) (amended complaint relates back to date of original complaint; additions and changes in parties also relate back in absence of prejudice, etc.).

period, the judgment can be enforced at any time during its legal life, since the enforcement of the judgment is not viewed as a tax collection proceeding within the meaning of IRC §6502.[43] On the other hand, a judgment neither extends nor curtails the time allowed by IRC §6502 for a levy.[44]

Like the three-year period applicable to the assessments of taxes, the six-year period for the collection of assessed taxes by levy or judicial proceedings can be extended by agreement within the period. The six-year period for collection also resembles the three-year period for assessments in that both are suspended by the issuance of a statutory notice of deficiency (ninety-day letter) for the ninety-day or 150-day period allowed for filing a petition in the Tax Court and, if a petition is docketed, until sixty days after the Tax Court's decision becomes final.[45] The period is also suspended by IRC §§6503(b) and 6503(c) while the taxpayer's assets are in the control or custody of a federal or state court and for six months thereafter and while the taxpayer is absent from the United States for a continuous period of six months or more.

¶41.8 CREDITS AND REFUNDS OF OVERPAYMENTS

The statute of limitations on claims for credit or refund of an overpayment of income taxes is extended for many special situations, such as claims based on bad debts, worthless securities, and net operating loss carrybacks.[46] On filing a timely claim for a credit or refund, a taxpayer seeking judicial action is subject to a supplemental statute of limitations—the suit cannot be brought until six months after the claim is filed, unless the IRS acts on it during this waiting period, and it cannot be brought more than two years after the date when the IRS mails a notice of disallowance to the taxpayer by certified or registered mail.[47]

¶41.9 MITIGATION OF STATUTE OF LIMITATIONS—INCONSISTENT POSITIONS, ETC.

1. Introductory. Once the statute of limitations has run on assessing a deficiency or filing a claim for credit or refund for a taxable year, errors by either the taxpayer or the IRS cannot ordinarily be corrected; and the same is true if the year is closed by a closing agreement or the doctrine of res

[43] See Investment & Sec. Co. v. US, 140 F.2d 894 (9th Cir. 1944) (tax liability merged in judgment).

[44] IRC §6502(a) (last sentence); Treas. Regs. §301.6502-1(a)(3).

[45] IRC §6503(a); supra ¶41.6.

[46] See supra ¶40.3.

[47] See infra ¶43.7.

judicata. Without these statutory and judicial barriers, the taxpayer's liability for ancient years could be reexamined whenever new evidence or a novel theory came to light. But these methods of insuring repose are "mitigated" by IRC §§1311–1314 in closely defined circumstances, primarily involving inconsistencies by the taxpayer, a related person, or the IRS. When these mitigating rules apply, the IRS can assess deficiencies and allow refunds and credits even though they would otherwise be barred by the statute of limitations or some other law or rule of law.[48] Section 1311(a) authorizes a corrective adjustment if the year is closed by *any* "law or rule of law," not merely the statute of limitations, including (1) a statutory closing agreement under IRC §7121; (2) the doctrine of res judicata, based on a prior judicial determination of the taxpayer's liability; and (3) IRC §§6212(c) and 6512(a), providing that the filing of a petition in the Tax Court precludes the IRS from issuing an additional statutory notice of deficiency and from allowing a credit or refund for the same taxable year.

Inconsistencies can be corrected by IRC §§1311–1314 not only if they were committed by one taxpayer, but also if they involve two or more related taxpayers—for example, the successful assertion of a deficiency against the grantor of a trust for an item of income that was received and reported by the trustee. The relationships warranting corrective adjustments, as set out in IRC §1313(c), include husband-wife, grantor-fiduciary, fiduciary-beneficiary, and members of an affiliated group of corporations. The relationship must have existed during the taxable year of the error, but not necessarily when the erroneously treated transaction occurred.[49] Although IRC §§1311–1314 are primarily concerned with inconsistencies by the taxpayer or the IRS, they also sanction corrective adjustments for a different class of errors—situations in which the taxpayer or the IRS assigns an item of gross income or a deduction to the wrong year and finds, when its claim is rejected, that the correct year is barred, although it was open when the wrong year was originally picked.

2. Inconsistent Positions. Under IRC §1312, a corrective adjustment is warranted in six circumstances, each entailing a determination (as defined) that adopts a position inconsistent with the error. If the adjustment would result in a credit or refund, the inconsistent position must be maintained by the IRS; if the adjustment would result in a deficiency assessment, the inconsistent position must be maintained by the taxpayer with respect to whom the determination is made.[50]

---

[48] IRC §§1311–1314, however, do not apply to compromise settlements under IRC §7122, summarized supra ¶40.1.

[49] See Treas. Regs. §1.1313(c)-1; for an additional requirement if the corrective adjustment is a deficiency assessment against a related taxpayer, see IRC §1311(b)(3).

[50] See Mondshein v. US, 338 F.Supp. 786 (E.D.N.Y. 1971), aff'd per curiam, 469 F.2d 1394 (2d Cir. 1973) (reference in legislative history to "active inconsistency"

1. *Double inclusion in gross income.* The first circumstance authorizing an adjustment, described by IRC §1312(1), is the inclusion in gross income of an item that was erroneously included in the taxpayer's gross income for another taxable year or in the gross income of a related taxpayer. Although the term "item" as used by IRC §1312(1) is not ordinarily controversial, it may be troublesome in some situations. For example, an error in favor of the IRS in computing an amount included in income is not regarded as the erroneous inclusion of an item.

A related aspect of this issue is that the determination must adopt a position maintained by the taxpayer or the IRS, as the case may be, that is inconsistent with an *erroneous* inclusion of an item in gross income. A determination that an "item" is includable in one year usually ipso facto establishes that inclusion of the same item in the same taxpayer's return for another year was erroneous. But the determination does not always do double duty. For example, if *A* receives a check for $5,000 from *X* and endorses it over to *B*, who includes it in gross income, a determination that the payment was includable in *A*'s gross income does not prove that it was erroneously reported by *B*, since *A* might have earned the fee by performing services for *X* and *B* might have earned the same amount by performing services for *A*. Even if *A* erroneously failed to deduct the payment to *B*, an adjustment under IRC §1311-1314 is not warranted, since the determination that the amount was includable in *A*'s gross income is not inconsistent with either *A*'s failure to deduct the payment or its inclusion in *B*'s gross income.

2. *Double allowance of deduction or credit.* Section 1312 provides for a corrective adjustment if the determination allows a deduction or credit that was erroneously allowed to the taxpayer for another year or to a related taxpayer.

3. *Double exclusion of item of gross income.* Section 1312(3)(A) authorizes a correction if the determination requires the exclusion from gross income of an item that (1) was included on a return filed by the taxpayer or with respect to which tax was paid and (2) was erroneously excluded or omitted from the taxpayer's gross income for another taxable year or from a related taxpayer's gross income. For example, assume (1) that the taxpayer received $10,000 in 1982 for services performed in 1980 and included the payment in gross income for 1982; (2) that the IRS, after the statute of limitations ran on 1980, issued a notice of deficiency for 1982 based on other items; (3) that the taxpayer filed a petition with the Tax Court asserting that the payment was

---

requires more than acceptance of contention actively asserted by opposing party; "passive inconsistency" in acceding to other party's position not sufficient); Chertkof v. CIR, 66 TC 496, 507-508 (1976), on merits, 72 TC 1113 (1979), aff'd, 649 F.2d 264 (4th Cir. 1981) ("active inconsistency" does not require knowing and deliberate action to obtain tax advantage; corrective adjustment authorized whether inconsistency is fortuitous or result of design); see also another installment in the *Chertkof* litigation, 676 F.2d 984 (4th Cir. 1982).

includable not in 1982 when received but in 1980 when earned; and (4) that the Tax Court held that the taxpayer was on the accrual basis, should have reported the item in 1980, and hence was not taxable on the item in 1982. In these circumstances, an adjustment is authorized for 1980, even though a correction for that year is otherwise barred by the statute of limitations.

Section 1312(3)(A) applies only if, in addition to excluding the item from the return for the proper year, the *taxpayer* includes the item on a return for another year (or pays tax thereon, ordinarily in response to the IRS' assertion of deficiency) and then takes the initiative by asserting that the item is not includable in that year's gross income. If the determination requires the item to be excluded and adopts the taxpayer's claim that it should have been included in a different year, the inconsistency is the result of action by the taxpayer, not by the IRS.

A taxpayer who omits the item from *both* returns, however, can avoid IRC §1312(3)(A), if, when the IRS asserts a deficiency for the wrong year, he petitions the Tax Court for a redetermination of the deficiency, since the item will not have been "included in a return filed by the taxpayer" and tax will not have been paid with respect to the item. If, however, the taxpayer responds to the deficiency notice by paying the tax and claiming a refund, the resulting inconsistency will satisfy IRC §1312(3)(A), since the item will then be one "with respect to which tax was paid." [51]

Section 1312(3)(A) can apply even if the double exclusion is not wholly attributable to the taxpayer's conduct, provided the taxpayer affirmatively participated in it. In *Chertkof v. CIR,* for example, the taxpayer reported an item in 1966; but believing that it was properly reportable in 1965, the IRS asserted a deficiency for that year, determined an overassessment for 1966, and refunded the amount of the overassessment.[52] The taxpayer accepted the refund check, paid the 1965 deficiency, sued for a refund of the amount paid on the ground that the amount was properly taxable in 1966, and won on that ground. The IRS then asserted a deficiency for 1966, for which the statute of limitations on assessments had run; and the Court of Appeals for the Fourth Circuit held that the statute was mitigated by IRC §1312(3)(A), even though the amount was erroneously excluded from gross income in 1966 by virtue of the overassessment and refund (which the taxpayer accepted), rather than solely by reason of the taxpayer's independent action.

4. *Correlative deductions and inclusions for trusts, estates, and beneficiaries.* Section 1312(5) authorizes a corrective adjustment if the determination allows or disallows certain deductions in computing the taxable income of a

---

[51] Birchenough v. US, 410 F.2d 1247 (Ct. Cl. 1969); but see the debatable contrary holding in Kappel's Est. v. CIR, 615 F.2d 91 (3d Cir. 1980) (payment of deficiency not fatal if correct year was barred when deficiency was asserted; Treas. Regs. §1.1312-3, Example (1)(ii), held invalid; divided court).

[52] See, e.g., Chertkof v. CIR, supra note 50.

trust or estate or requires or denies certain inclusions in the taxable income of the beneficiaries, heirs, or legatees, provided there was a correlative error in computing the taxable income of the related taxpayer.[53]

5. *Correlative deductions and credits of affiliated corporations.* Under IRC §1312(6), a corrective adjustment is authorized if a deduction or credit is erroneously allowed, omitted, or disallowed in respect of a member of an affiliated group of corporations and the determination allows or disallows the deduction or credit in computing the income of another member of the same group.

6. *Basis of property after erroneous treatment of prior transaction.* Section 1312(7) provides for a corrective adjustment if the determination determines the basis of property and if (1) one of the following errors occurred in a prior transaction on which the property's basis depends or that was erroneously treated as affecting its basis: (a) an erroneous inclusion in or omission from gross income; (b) an erroneous recognition or nonrecognition of gain or loss; (c) an erroneous deduction of an item properly chargeable to capital account; or (d) an erroneous capitalization of a properly deductible item; and (2) the taxpayer with respect to whom the error occurred is one of the following: (a) a taxpayer with respect to whom the determination is made; (b) a taxpayer who acquired title to the property in the erroneously treated transaction and from whom the taxpayer with respect to whom the determination is made derived title in such a manner as to obtain a basis ascertained by reference to the basis of the taxpayer who acquired title in the erroneously treated transaction; or (c) a taxpayer who had title to the property at the time of the erroneously treated transaction and from whom the taxpayer with respect to whom the determination is made derived title, but only if the latter's basis is determined under IRC §1015(a), relating to property acquired by gift.

To bring IRC §1312(7) into play, the judicial decision or other determination must *determine* the basis of property, not merely *affect* its basis.[54]

3. Wrong Year Errors. Sections 1312(3)(B) and 1312(4) are concerned with situations in which the taxpayer or the IRS picks the wrong year to include an item in gross income or to take a deduction or credit *at a time when the correct taxable year is still open,* only to find, when liability for the wrong year is determined, that the correct year is no longer open.

1. *Items omitted from income.* If the determination requires the exclusion from gross income of an item not included in the taxpayer's return and with respect to which tax was not paid, IRC §1312(3)(B) authorizes a correc-

---

[53] For examples, see Treas. Regs. §1.1312-5.

[54] See Brennen v. CIR, 20 TC 495 (1953) (Acq.) (determination that bond premium was deductible in 1944 affected, but did not determine, basis of bonds in computing gain or loss on sale in 1945).

tive adjustment if the item is includable in the taxpayer's gross income for another taxable year or in the gross income of a related taxpayer—but only if assessment of a deficiency for the proper year or against the related taxpayer was not barred by any law or rule of law when the IRS first maintained (in a statutory notice of deficiency or before the Tax Court) that the item should be included in the gross income of the taxpayer for the taxable year to which the determination related.[55]

2. *Double disallowance of deductions or credits.* If the determination disallows a deduction or credit that should have been—but was not—allowed to the taxpayer for another taxable year or to a related taxpayer, IRC §1312(4) authorizes a corrective adjustment, provided the resulting credit or refund was not barred by any law or rule of law when the taxpayer first maintained in writing before the IRS or the Tax Court that he was entitled to the deduction or credit for the taxable year to which the determination relates. This type of correction is the converse of the correction authorized by IRC §1312(3)(B) and similarly requires no inconsistency. For example, assume that (1) the taxpayer claimed an ordinary loss of $10,000 on a timely return for 1981 and (2) it is determined, after the statute of limitations has run on 1982, that the loss should have been reported in 1981 as a capital loss, deductible as such only to the extent of $4,000 in 1981, and that the balance should have been carried forward and applied against $6,000 of capital gain in 1982. Under Rev. Rul. 68-152, a correction is authorized for 1982, because that year was not barred when the taxpayer deducted the loss on the return for 1981.[56]

Adjustments under IRC §§1312(3)(B) and 1312(4) are authorized only if the correct year was open when the IRS or the taxpayer, as the case may be, picked the wrong year in the manner described by IRC §1311(b)(2). The function of this requirement becomes apparent when the consequences of eliminating it are envisioned. For example, if the taxpayer erroneously omitted an item of gross income in 1950, the IRS could arbitrarily assert a deficiency for 1982 (or any other open year) and, when the taxpayer successfully contested the unwarranted deficiency for 1982, employ IRC §1312(3)(B) to open up 1950. Conversely, a taxpayer who failed to claim a deduction in 1950 could claim it in 1982 and, when the IRS successfully contested this spurious claim, obtain a corrective adjustment for 1950 under IRC §1312(4). Both of these gambits are prevented by the "open year" requirement.[57]

---

[55] For examples, see Treas. Regs. §1.1312-3(b); Perkins v. CIR, 36 TC 313 (1961) (determination that note was not dividend to taxpayer in 1949 authorized adjustment for 1951, when note was received in liquidating distribution, since 1951 was an open year when IRS issued notice for deficiency for 1949).

[56] Rev. Rul. 68-152, 1968-1 CB 369; Rev. Rul. 70-43, 1970-1 CB 176.

[57] See Mondshein v. US, supra note 50 (requirement that correct year be open when claim is made for wrong year avoids "subverting the basic aims of the statute of limitations").

4. Requirement of "Determination." The statute of limitations and similar barriers are mitigated by IRC §§1311–1314 only if the error to be corrected is manifested by a formal "determination" of the type described by IRC §1313(a). As defined by IRC §1313(a), a "determination" means:

1. A final decision by the Tax Court or other court of competent jurisdiction.

2. A closing agreement under IRC §7121.[58]

3. A final disposition of a claim. For this purpose, a disposition is final (1) as to items allowed by the IRS, when a refund or credit is allowed or when a notice of disallowance by reason of offsetting items is mailed, and (2) as to items disallowed in whole or in part and items applied to reduce a refund or credit, when the time for instituting suit expires, unless suit is instituted before then.

4. An agreement pursuant to regulations issued under IRC §1313.

Every determination, as defined by IRC §1313(a), has a twofold function: It is a jurisdictional prerequisite to a corrective adjustment and it marks the beginning of a one-year period during which the correction can be assessed as a deficiency or claimed as a refund. In effect, therefore, a qualifying determination mitigates the existing statute of limitations (or similar barrier) by substituting a new statute of limitations.

5. Amount and Method of Adjustment. Section 1314 prescribes rules determining the amount of the corrective adjustment under IRC §1311–1314, the effect of errors other than the one being adjusted, the method of making the adjustment, and the time during which it can be made.

1. *Amount of adjustment for year of error.* Computation of the amount of the adjustment for the taxable year of the error starts with the tax previously determined for that year—the amount shown on the return plus amounts previously assessed and less rebates.[59] The liability is then recomputed by treating correctly the item that was the subject of the error, and the difference is the increase or decrease in tax attributable to the correction.

2. *Effect of other items.* In ascertaining the amount of the adjustment, the statute of limitations or similar barriers are lifted solely to permit correction of the error covered by the determination under IRC §§1311–1314; neither the taxpayer nor the IRS can ransack the return in search of additional errors. On the other hand, the recomputation must take account of any automatic consequences of the correction, such as an increased deduction for

---

[58] Treas. Regs. §1.1313(a)-2; see generally supra ¶40.1.

[59] IRC §1314(a); Treas. Regs. §1.1314(a)-1(a).

charitable contributions resulting from an increase in the taxpayer's adjusted gross income and hence in the percentage limit on such deductions.[60]

3. *Other years.* If the adjustment for the year of the error creates, increases, or reduces a net operating loss or a capital loss that can be carried to another year, a corrective adjustment for the latter year is authorized by IRC §1314(a)(2). The adjustment is computed in substantially the same manner as the adjustment for the year of the error.[61]

4. *Method of adjustment.* The adjustment described above is made by an assessment or a refund of the corrective amount, depending on whether it reflects an increase or a decrease in tax, as if it were a deficiency or overpayment for the year of the error to which the normal assessment, collection, or refund procedures apply.

¶41.10 EQUITABLE ESTOPPEL AND RECOUPMENT

In addition to IRC §§1311–1314, mitigating the statute of limitations and similar barriers by permitting past errors to be corrected in closely defined circumstances, mistakes committed in closed years are occasionally redressed, in whole or in part, by the uncertain and confusing judge-made doctrines of equitable estoppel and recoupment.

Equitable estoppel, which is almost never applied at the behest of taxpayers, is based on a duty of consistency;[62] but the elements traditionally required for an estoppel at common law are not usually present: (1) conduct (including silence when there is a duty to speak) amounting to a false representation or concealment of material facts, (2) an intent or expectation that the conduct will influence the other party's conduct, (3) actual or constructive knowledge of the facts, (4) the other party's ignorance of the truth and lack of means of ascertaining the truth, (5) good-faith reliance on the conduct, and (6) action or inaction to the detriment of the person relying on the conduct.[63] Inconsistencies by taxpayers rarely exhibit all these elements, since representations made by tax returns ordinarily concern either matters of law or a mixture of legal and factual matters, rather than naked facts, and the IRS has sweeping powers of investigation that distinguish it from private victims of misrepresentations.

---

[60] See IRC §1314(a)(2); Treas. Regs. §1.1314(a)-1(e), Example.

[61] See Treas. Regs. §1.1314(a)-2(b); Treas. Regs. §1.1314(a)-2(d), Example.

[62] See Wichita Coca-Cola Bottling Co. v. US, 152 F.2d 6 (5th Cir. 1945) (taxpayer's belated effort to shift from treating amounts received for returnable containers as sale proceeds rather than deposits); Continental Oil Co. v. Jones, 177 F.2d 508 (10th Cir. 1949) (attempt to use higher basis on selling property than on receiving it); Grayson v. US, 437 F.Supp. 58 (N.D. Ala. 1977) (distributions by pension plan taxable when received because not included in gross income when earned).

[63] 28 Am. Jur. 2d, Estoppel & Waiver §35 (1966).

In addition, whenever IRC §§1311–1314 apply, they permit the error in the otherwise closed year to be corrected directly, thus putting the IRS in the same position it would have occupied if the error had not occurred. In these circumstances, the IRS is not injured by the taxpayer's error, and there is therefore no reason to estop the taxpayer from treating the later transaction properly.[64]

Another equitable remedy for inconsistencies is recoupment—permitting a taxpayer to offset a tax collected erroneously against a proper assessment, provided the two both arise out of the same taxable event, or, if the taxpayer sues for a refund, allowing the IRS to offset an otherwise barred deficiency against the amount owing.[65] Because recoupment applies only if a single transaction is subjected to two taxes on inconsistent legal theories—a rare event—it provides no remedy for the much more common situation of inconsistency in the treatment of two related transactions.[66] Moreover, recent cases espouse the persuasive theory that recoupment, even if otherwise applicable, is not warranted if the inconsistency can be corrected directly by an adjustment under IRC §§1311–1314. Finally, the Supreme Court has held that the Tax Court lacks jurisdiction to apply recoupment.[67] In short, recoupment is honored more in the breach than in the observance.

SELECTED BIBLIOGRAPHY

Bell, Recent Developments Amid the Mysteries of Mitigation, 17 U.C.L.A. L. Rev. 542 (1970).

Coleman, Mitigation of the Statute of Limitations, 31 NYU Inst. on Fed. Tax. 1575 (1973).

King, Internal Revenue Code Section 6501: The Code's Statute of Limitations, 11 Gonz. L. Rev. 607 (1976).

---

64 See Benenson v. US, 385 F.2d 26 (2d Cir. 1967) (equitable remedies neither intended by Congress nor required when IRC §§1311–1314 apply). For equitable estoppel where IRC §1311–1314 did not authorize a corrective adjustment, see Sangers Home for Chronic Patients, Inc. v. CIR, 72 TC 105 (1979).

65 Bull v. US, 295 US 247 (1935) (taxpayer allowed offset of erroneously paid tax against proper assessment); Rev. Rul. 71-56, 1971-1 CB 404 (same); see also Stone v. White, 301 US 532 (1937) (government allowed to offset barred deficiency in beneficiary's tax against refund owing to trustees of testamentary trust).

66 Rothensies v. Electric Storage Battery Co., 329 US 296 (1946); for extended review of this area, with citations, see Wilmington Trust Co. v. US, 610 F.2d 703 (Ct. Cl. 1979).

67 CIR v. Gooch Milling & Elevator Co., 320 US 418 (1943); see infra ¶43.2.

STATUTES OF LIMITATIONS

Maguire, Surrey & Traynor, Section 820 of the Revenue Act of 1938, 48 Yale L.J. 509, 719 (1939).

Mintz & Plumb, Taxing Income in Years Not Realized Under Doctrine of Equitable Estoppel, 1954 So. Calif. Tax Inst. 481.

Note, Equitable Recoupment in Tax Law, 42 NYU Law Rev. 537 (1967).

CHAPTER 42

Interest, Civil Penalties, and Tax Crimes

¶42.1 INTEREST ON UNDERPAYMENTS OF TAX

If all or any part of a tax is not paid when due, interest on the underpayment is charged by IRC §6601(a) at a rate fixed from time to time pursuant to IRC §6621, compounded daily.[1] Interest rates are determined on January 1 and July 1 of each year for the following six-month period on the basis of the average adjusted prime rate charged by commercial banks during the six-month period ending on the prior September 30 for the January 1 date and ending on the prior March 31 for the July 1 date. The interest, which is assessed and collected in the same manner as the underlying tax and is subject to the same statute of limitations,[2] is computed from the last date prescribed for payment of the tax until the date of payment, without regard to whether the time to file the return was extended.[3] Interest on underpayments is deduct-

---

[1] Daily compounding is required by IRC §6622(a), enacted in 1982. Underpayments of estimated tax are not subject to interest, but to a penalty that is tantamount to interest although it is not compounded; see IRC §§6601(h) and 6654(a), discussed supra ¶39.6.

[2] See IRC §§6601(e)(1) (same assessment and collection procedures), 6601(g) (same period of limitations).

[3] See IRC §6601(b)(1); Rev. Rul. 54-426, 1954-2 CB 39 (interest runs during extensions of time for filing return and thereafter until tax is paid); Treas. Regs. §301.6601-1(a) (date of payment is date of receipt by Treasury); but see IRC

ible by cash-basis taxpayers under IRC §163 when paid; partial payments of a tax bill are applied by the IRS as the taxpayer directs, but, in the absence of direction, first to tax, then to penalties, and finally to interest, starting with the earliest period.[4]

Taxpayers wishing to stop the running of interest on a proposed deficiency can do so by executing Form 870 (waiver of restrictions on assessment of the deficiency) pursuant to IRC §6213(d).[5] If notice and demand for payment are not made within thirty days after the waiver is filed, IRC §6601(c) provides that interest will not be charged from the end of the thirty-day period until notice and demand are made.

The taxpayer's obligation to pay interest on deficiencies is matched by the government's obligation to pay interest on overpayments.[6] In the case of concurrent deficiencies and overpayments, the obligations are ordinarily offset, and interest is payable on the net amount due.[7] There are, however, many exceptions to this reciprocity principle. A taxpayer receiving a refund that results from over-withholding or excessive payments of estimated tax, for example, is not entitled to interest if the IRS makes payment within forty-five days after the due date (the filing date, if the return is filed after the due date) of the return;[8] but if a deficiency is later determined for the same year, interest on the underpayment must be paid from the due date of the return, including the forty-five-day period during which the government had the interest-free use of the taxpayer's money. The courts have tended to leave correction of these inequities—so-called restricted interest situations—to Congress, even when attributable to inexplicable statutory quirks.[9]

¶42.2 INTEREST ON OVERPAYMENTS OF TAX

Interest is paid by the government on overpayments, whether refunded or credited against tax liabilities for other years, at the same rate used to

---

§7502 (payment sent by mail treated as received when postmarked, with certain exceptions); Rev. Rul. 74-235, 1974-1 CB 347 (when filing date is extended because it falls on Saturday, Sunday, or legal holiday, interest accrues from original due date unless payment is made on or before extended due date).

[4] See Rev. Rul. 73-305, 1973-2 CB 43; supra ¶15.3.

[5] Supra ¶40.1.

[6] See infra ¶42.2.

[7] Rev. Proc. 60-17, 1960-2 CB 942, §2.01(1) (detailed explanation of "restricted interest" situations); IRC §6601(f).

[8] See IRC §§6611(e), 6611(b)(2), 6611(b)(3); Treas. Regs. §301.6611-1(g); Rev. Rul. 56-445, 1956-2 CB 958. A return is not filed for these purposes until it is filed in "processible" form, IRC §6611(i).

[9] For "restricted interest," see Rev. Proc. 60-17, supra note 7; but see Avon Prods., Inc. v. US, 588 F.2d 342 (2d Cir. 1978) (refusing to charge interest on deficiency during period taxpayer had overpaid tax).

compute interest payable by taxpayers on underpayments.[10] Interest is computed from the date of the overpayment, defined by the regulations as the date when the first amount is paid that, when added to previous payments, exceeds the tax liability (including any interest, additions, or additional amounts).[11] Amounts paid before the return is due, payments of estimated tax, and credits for amounts withheld from wages are treated as paid on the last day prescribed for the filing of the return; hence, they do not bear interest between the date of actual payment and the date when they are credited against the tax shown on the return.[12] An overpayment that is credited against tax liability for another period bears interest until the due date of the amount against which it was credited; but if the credit is applied to the following year's estimated tax, interest is not allowed.[13]

When refunding overpayments, the IRS is allowed an interest-free grace period of forty-five days from the due date of the return (the filing date, if the return was filed after the due date), determined without regard to extensions. If the refund is not paid within this period, however, interest runs in the taxpayer's favor from the due date or the filing date, if later, of the return until a date, determined by the IRS, not more than thirty days prior to the refund check.[14]

Taxpayers expecting the IRS to assert a deficiency sometimes seek to halt the running of interest by making remittances before the amount is assessed and without filing a tax return acknowledging liability. The cases and rulings prevent taxpayers from earning interest on their spare cash "by merely dumping money as taxes [on the IRS] by disorderly remittances . . . of amounts not computed in pursuance of the actual or reasonably apparent requirements of the Code,"[15] but advance payments earn the equivalent of interest by cutting off the running of interest on a deficiency, if paid in good faith against claims that the IRS is reasonably expected to assert.

---

[10] IRC §6611; see also IRC §6602 (interest payable on erroneous refunds recoverable by suit under IRC §7405); supra ¶42.1 (interest rate prescribed by IRC §6621).

[11] See Treas. Regs. §§301.6611(b), 301.6611(c); Republic Oil Ref. Co. v. Granger, 98 F.Supp. 921, 936 (W.D.Pa. 1951) (interest computed from date check was received by IRS, not from date of IRS deposit), aff'd on other issues, 198 F.2d 161 (3d Cir. 1952).

[12] IRC §6611(d); see Treas. Regs. §301.6611-1(d).

[13] See Treas. Regs. §§301.6611-1(h)(1) (general rule), 301.6611-1(h)(2)(vii) (credit against estimated tax).

[14] See IRC §§6611(e), 6611(b)(2), 6611(b)(3); Treas. Regs. §301.6611-1(g); Rev. Rul. 76-74, 1976-1 CB 388 (interest not payable if delay in delivering check is not due to the fault of the government or results from taxpayer's delay in providing proof of guardianship or similar evidence).

[15] S. Rep. No. 221, 78th Cong., 1st Sess., reprinted in 1943 CB 1314, 140 (recommending enactment of statutory predecessor of IRC §6401(c)); IRC §6401(c); Rev. Proc. 82-51, 1982-35 IRB 11; see also Northern Natural Gas Co. v. US, 354 F.2d 310 (Ct.Cl. 1965) (extensive discussion of earlier cases).

¶42.3 CIVIL PENALTIES

1. Introductory. The Internal Revenue Code contains numerous civil penalties, imposed for diverse but sometimes overlapping delinquencies, such as failure to file, negligence, and fraud. Virtually all civil penalties are assessed, collected, and subject to statutes of limitations in the same manner as taxes.[16] As a class, therefore, they differ from fines and jail sentences in being imposed by civil rather than criminal procedures;[17] and they differ from the civil penalties imposed by most regulatory statutes in qualifying for the summary procedures used to assess and collect taxes. Because of their remedial character, civil tax penalties survive the wrongdoer's death, and they constitute taxes that are not discharged in bankruptcy.[18]

2. Failure to File Return or Pay Tax at Prescribed Time. Section 6651(a), the basic delinquency provision, imposes additions to the tax for any failure (1) to file a return on the prescribed date (determined with regard to extensions of time for filing), (2) to pay the tax shown as due on a return by the prescribed due date (determined with regard to extensions of time for payment), and (3) to pay any amount required to be shown on the return (but not so shown) within ten days from notice and demand—unless, in each case, the failure is due to reasonable cause and not willful neglect. Although assessed and collected like taxes by virtue of IRC §6660(a), delinquency penalties are subject to a different procedure so far as judicial challenge is concerned: if the IRS asserts a deficiency, it can be redetermined by the Tax Court along with any delinquency penalties under IRC §6551; but penalties, in the absence of a deficiency, cannot be redetermined by the Tax Court. In this situation, the taxpayer can get judicial review of the penalty only by paying and suing for a refund.[19] The administrative procedure relating to assessed delinquency penalties includes a penalty appeals officer who is empowered to abate the penalty if good cause is shown.[20]

---

[16] IRC §§6660(a), 6671(a).

[17] See Helvering v. Mitchell, 303 US 391, 401 (1938) (50 percent fraud penalty upheld as civil remedy imposed "primarily as a safeguard for the protection of the revenue and to reimburse the Government for the heavy expense of investigation and the loss resulting from the taxpayer's fraud").

[18] See Kirk v. CIR, 179 F.2d 619 (1st Cir. 1950) (survival of fraud penalty); Larson v. US, 340 F.Supp. 1197 (E.D. Wis. 1972) (same as to 100 percent penalty for failure to pay over employment taxes).

[19] See IRC §6659(b).

[20] IRM MS No. 5G-69 (April 18, 1977) (Administration), reprinted in 2 CCH Int. Rev. Man. 9389.

1. *Failure to file.* The failure-to-file penalty, which is imposed by IRC §6651(a)(1) and must be paid in addition to interest, is 5 percent of the amount that should have been shown on the return if the failure is for not more than one month, plus an additional 5 percent for each additional month (or fraction thereof) of continuing delinquency, up to an aggregate of 25 percent.[21] In computing the amount "required to be shown as tax" on the delinquent return, payments of estimated tax and amounts withheld from the taxpayer's wages are credited, and the addition is based on the net amount due.[22] If the return is not filed within sixty days of the prescribed filing date, the penalty imposed under IRC §6651(a)(1) cannot be less than the lesser of $100 or 100 percent of the tax required to be shown on the return.

There is an immense body of litigation involving taxpayer claims that a failure to file was "due to reasonable cause and not due to willful neglect," which the regulations test by an objective rather than subjective standard.[23] The double-barreled statutory requirement that the taxpayer show "reasonable cause" and negate "willful neglect" is usually conflated into a single requirement—reasonable cause—since if that is shown willful neglect is automatically negated. The converse, however, is not true; forgetfulness, for example, is not willful neglect, but it does not constitute reasonable cause.[24]

As excuses for a failure to file by the prescribed due date, the *Internal Revenue Manual* recognizes serious illness or death of the taxpayer or a member of his or her immediate family, the taxpayer's "unavoidable absence," destruction of the taxpayer's business premises or records by fire or other casualty, postal delay (even if insufficient stamps were affixed to the envelope), mailing a return within the allowable time but to the wrong IRS office, and inability to get the proper form because of shortages at the district director's office.[25] Reliance on a qualified and seemingly competent professional's advice

---

[21] For computation of the number of months of delinquency, see Treas. Regs. §301.6651-1(b).

For proof that the taxpayer was required to file a return, see US v. Francisco, 614 F.2d 617 (8th Cir. 1980) (proof that taxpayer's gross receipts exceeded cost of goods sold sufficient; taxpayer has burden of proving business expenses).

For cases determining whether an unsigned, wrong-form, tentative, incomplete, or otherwise deficient document is a "return" that will avoid the no-filing or late-filing penalty, see supra ¶39.1.

[22] See IRC §6651(b); Treas. Regs. §301.6651-1(d); Treas. Regs. §301.6651-1(f), Example (1).

[23] Treas. Regs. §301.6651-1(c)(1).

[24] See West Virginia Steel Corp. v. CIR, 34 TC 851, 860 (1960).

[25] IRM 4562.2(1)(d), 4562.2(1)(e), 4562.2(1)(f) ("unavoidable absence" not explained; for absence from the country, see IRC §6081(a)), 4562.2(1)(g). In the case of a corporate return, death or serious illness as an excuse is qualified by the caveat that it must affect the sole person authorized to execute the return (or his immediate family). See Harris v. CIR, ¶69,049 P-H Memo TC (1969) (ill health, chaotic home life because of divorce, imprisonment, and continuous controversy with local authorities over rental

that no return is required is an acceptable excuse if the taxpayer has no reason to doubt the adviser's opinion, provided the advice was timely sought and based on full disclosure of the relevant facts.[26] More commonly, however, the delinquent taxpayer knows quite well that a return is required and is also aware of the due date, but relies on a busy, procrastinating, disabled, or negligent tax expert to prepare the return and watch the calendar; and it has been held in these circumstances that the taxpayer has a "personal nondelegable duty" to file on time that is not discharged by passing the buck to his lawyer, accountant, or other preparer.[27] This approach leaves a little room for reliance on advisers by less sophisticated taxpayers, especially if the delay is very short;[28] but April 15 is now as well known as Christmas.

Taxpayers who decide for themselves that a return is not required or is not yet due are likely to be told that self-reliance is not "reasonable cause" for failing to file by the due date,[29] unless a layman might reasonably have believed that a return was not required.[30] Reliance on advice from IRS personnel that a return was not required or that an extension of time to file had been granted excuses a failure to file or a delay in filing, as the case may be, but it may be difficult to convince the IRS or the Tax Court that the erroneous advice was actually received.[31]

2. *Failure to pay tax shown on return.* A penalty is imposed by IRC §6651(a)(2) for failure to pay "the amount shown as tax" on an income tax

---

property; held, sufficient to avoid penalty, at least in case where IRS had burden of proof because issue was raised by amended answer in Tax Court pleadings).

[26] See, e.g., CIR v. American Ass'n of Eng'rs Employment, 204 F.2d 19 (7th Cir. 1953) (reasonable to rely on counsel's advice that taxpayer was exempt); Coldwater Seafood Corp. v. CIR, 69 TC 966 (1978) (foreign corporation's reliance on CPA's advice that returns were not required was reasonable; advice not so clearly wrong as to permit inference that taxpayer's reliance was negligent or willfully disregarded the law).

[27] Kroll v. US, 547 F.2d 39 (7th Cir. 1977) (reviews earlier cases).

[28] See Sanderling, Inc. v. CIR, 571 F.2d 174 (3d Cir. 1978) (taxpayer's accountant and IRS both confused about due date); DiPalma's Est. v. CIR, 71 TC 324 (1978) (Acq.) (attorney advised inexperienced fiduciary that estate tax return was not required until family dispute was settled); Fisk's Est. v. CIR, 203 F.2d 358 (6th Cir. 1953) (taxpayer excused where attorney was responsible for delay of one day in filing return that was completed on time).

[29] See Brittingham v. CIR, 66 TC 373 (1976), and cases there cited.

[30] See Dillin v. CIR, 56 TC 228, 247-248 (1971) (Acq.) (expatriated citizen); but see Stevens Bros. Foundation, Inc. v. CIR, 39 TC 93, 129-134 (1962) (Acq.) (extensive discussion, rejecting theory that "any real, nonfrivolous dispute concerning liability for a particular tax constitutes reasonable cause for failure to file the appropriate return, regardless of whether the taxpayer can show that competent, fully informed tax counsel advised him not to file the return," despite earlier appellate decisions to this effect), aff'd in part, rev'd in part on other issues, 324 F.2d 633 (8th Cir. 1963), cert. denied, 376 US 969 (1964).

[31] See IRM 4562.2(1)(c); Haley v. CIR, ¶77,348 P-H Memo TC (1977) (reliance on IRS advice).

return on or before the due date prescribed for payment (taking into account any extension of time for payment), unless the failure is due to reasonable cause and not willful neglect. The penalty is based on the net amount due, defined by IRC §6651(b)(2) as the amount shown as tax on the return, less credits and payments on or before the beginning of the month for which the addition is computed.[32] The penalty is 0.5 percent of the amount shown on the return if the failure is for not more than one month (measured from the return's due date), plus an additional 0.5 percent for each additional month (or fraction thereof) of delinquency, up to an aggregate of 25 percent. Although the "addition" prescribed by IRC §6651(a)(2) resembles interest, it is payable in addition to interest on the underpayment and cannot be deducted either as interest or as a business expense.[33]

If both the failure-to-file and the failure-to-pay penalties apply to the same month, the former is reduced by the latter,[34] so that the combined penalties cannot exceed 5 percent per month; but, while the failure-to-file penalty reaches its maximum in five months, the failure-to-pay penalty, accruing at a lower rate, does not reach its 25 percent maximum for a much longer period of time.[35]

The "reasonable cause" excuse for failing to pay the amount shown on a return is explained as follows by the regulations:

> A failure to pay will be considered to be due to reasonable cause to the extent that the taxpayer has made a satisfactory showing that he exercised ordinary business care and prudence in providing for payment of his tax liability and was nevertheless either unable to pay the tax or would suffer an undue hardship . . . if he paid on the due date.[36]

3. *Failure to pay tax required to be shown on return.* Section 6651(a)(3) assesses a penalty for failure to pay any tax *required to be shown* on a return if it is not paid within ten days of notice and demand, unless the failure to pay is due to reasonable cause and not willful neglect. The penalty, which begins on the date of notice and demand, runs at the same rate as the failure-to-pay penalty imposed by IRC §6651(a)(2).[37]

---

[32] If a deficiency is determined and it is not paid within ten days after notice and demand, the penalty for failure to pay is computed under IRC §6651(a)(3) rather than §6651(a)(2). For extensions of time for payment, see IRC §6161(a)(1), supra ¶39.6.

[33] See May v. CIR, 65 TC 1114 (1976).

[34] The addition to tax under IRC §6651(a)(1) cannot be reduced below the lesser of $100 or 100 percent of the tax required to be shown on the return. See IRC §6651(c)(1)(A).

[35] See IRC §6651(c)(1)(A) (reduction of failure-to-file penalty by failure-to-pay penalty); Treas. Regs. §301.6651-1(f), Example (2) (relationship of two penalties).

[36] Treas. Regs. §301.6651-1(c)(1); for "undue hardship" as an excuse, see Treas. Regs. §1.6161-1(b).

[37] The maximum penalty under IRC §6651(a)(3) is reduced by any failure-to-file

3. Negligence or Intentional Disregard of Rules and Regulations. If any part of an underpayment of tax is due to negligence or intentional disregard of rules and regulations (but without intent to defraud), IRC §6653(a) imposes a penalty of 5 percent of the underpayment plus 50 percent of the interest attributable to the portion of the underpayment that was caused by negligence or intentional disregard of rules and regulations.[38]

As used in tort law, negligence is the failure to exercise the care that an ordinarily prudent person would use under the circumstances, and occasionally the negligence penalty is imposed on taxpayers who are merely careless in determining their tax liability.[39] Ordinarily, however, negligence penalty cases involve failures to keep proper records, substantial omissions, or exaggerated or unwarranted deductions that cannot be attributed to mistake or the taxpayer's resolution of reasonable doubts in his own favor but that do not entail destruction of records, concealment, barefaced lies, and other hallmarks of tax fraud.[40] Within this broad area, much depends on the trial court's assessment of the taxpayer's testimony; and this makes it impossible to fit the cases into a neat pattern. Since penalties can be upheld judicially only if they are proposed by the IRS, simple deficiency cases sometimes involve behavior

---

penalty (other than the "minimum" penalty) attributable to the tax stated in the notice and demand; see IRC §6651(c)(1)(B); Treas. Regs. §301.6651-1(f), Example (1)(b). See Rev. Rul. 76-562, 1976-2 CB 430 (failure-to-pay penalty not imposed where return was prepared by IRS, though this action terminated the failure-to-file penalty).

[38] IRC §6652(a)(2) provides that the penalty for the failure to file certain information returns and statements shall not be less, in most cases, than 10 percent of the aggregate amount of items required to be reported when such failure is caused by intentional disregard of the filing requirement. In this situation, the maximum penalty of $50,000 in any calendar year does not apply.

[39] See Hatch v. CIR, ¶80,110 P-H Memo TC (1980); see also Leroy Jewelry Co. v. CIR, 36 TC 443, 445-446 (1961) (omission from gross sales of about 20 percent was honest error by bookkeeper; negligence penalty imposed on taxpayer who made no effort to check bookkeeper's accuracy); see also IRM 4563.2 (common-law tort standard; must have more than "mere error or a difference of opinion on some controversial question").

[40] See, e.g., Wilhelm v. CIR, ¶78,443 P-H Memo TC (1978) (large unsubstantiated business deductions); Burke v. CIR, ¶79,195 P-H Memo TC (1979) (understatement of gross income, even though seventeen W-2 forms attached to return disclosed total amount; error not intentional, but denotes negligence). For cases on the fraud borderline, in which negligence penalties were proposed and upheld, see Porter v. CIR, ¶79,104 P-H Memo TC (1979) (understatement of income, overstatement of deductions, etc., in disregard of "clear and unequivocal statutory provisions," for which no explanation was offered or, in the court's view, possible); Wesenberg v. CIR, 69 TC 1005, 1015 (1978) (considering taxpayer's education and intellectual ability, "difficult to believe that he envisioned [a trust] as anything other than a flagrant tax avoidance scheme"). Cases rejecting penalties for negligence include Harris v. CIR, ¶77,358 P-H Memo TC (1977) (honest mistakes, misunderstanding of law, and bona fide dispute re other issues); Carter v. CIR, ¶77,322 P-H Memo TC (1977) (constructive dividend; "complex legal issue on which there can be an honest difference of opinion").

that seems as egregious as the conduct described in cases upholding negligence penalties; but, in some of these cases the taxpayer may have escaped a penalty only because the conduct, as viewed before trial, seemed less blatant than in the light of hindsight.[41]

Section 6653(a) does not contain a "reasonable cause" escape hatch as do some other penalties;[42] but since negligence is the antithesis of reasonable behavior, a showing of reasonable cause for the underpayment in effect negates the existence of negligence.[43] The cases are not very clear on the effect of a taxpayer's reliance on bookkeepers and other employees to assemble the relevant facts and make the necessary computations. There is a tendency to look for "personal" negligence (e.g., employment of an unqualified employee, inadequate supervision, or an unreasonable failure to detect the error before signing the return), rather than to impute the employee's negligence to the employer on a respondeat superior theory.[44] In the case of a large enterprise, however, a refusal to impute low-level negligence to the top management would virtually immunize the company against the negligence penalty.

The "intentional disregard of rules and regulations" component of IRC §6653(a) was enacted in 1921, evidently because of concern that taxpayers were ignoring regulations thought to be invalid without flagging this act on their returns. But the penalty is rarely applied to conduct of this type, and there is a widespread assumption that taxpayers believing in good faith and on reasonable grounds that an administrative ruling is erroneous are not required to advise the IRS that they have ignored it.[45] Intentional disregard of rules and regulations that are *not* being challenged is something else again; for example, the negligence penalty is often imposed on underpayments attributable to the failure to keep adequate records, as required by IRC §6001 and the regulations thereunder.[46]

---

[41] See, e.g., Cherubini v. CIR, ¶78,512 P-H Memo TC (1978) (dentist deducted commuting expenses and unsubstantiated business expenses and omitted value of use of corporate car for personal driving).

[42] Supra, text at notes 23 and 24.

[43] See, e.g., Morrman v. CIR, 26 TC 666, 680 (1956) (Acq.) (reliance on attorney, who did not correct taxpayer's erroneous belief); Golden Nugget, Inc. v. CIR, ¶69,149 P-H Memo TC (1969) (reliance on accountant).

[44] See Pritchett v. CIR, 63 TC 149 (1974) (failure to catch accountant's error on review); Ross v. CIR, ¶78,380 P-H Memo TC (1978) (no proof taxpayer supplied accountant with necessary information).

[45] See ABA Committee on Professional Ethics, Opinion No. 314, 51 A.B.A.J. 671 (1965) (if bona fide dispute exists over validity of a rule, the taxpayer can appropriately assert his position without flagging the item); see also Journal Co. v. CIR, 46 BTA 841 (1942), rev'd, 134 F.2d 165 (7th Cir. 1943).

[46] See, e.g., Fischer v. US, 212 F.2d 441 (10th Cir. 1954) (involving author of *Mind Your Own Business,* recommending methods of keeping records to avoid income tax difficulties!).

When applicable, the negligence penalty is 5 percent of the underpayment, as defined by IRC §§6653(c)(1) and 6211(a), even if only a portion of the deficiency is attributable to the taxpayer's negligence. The additional penalty of 50 percent of the interest applies only to the interest attributable to that portion of the underpayment caused by negligence or intentional disregard of rules and regulations.[47] If the return was filed on time, the taxpayer is credited with all previous payments (e.g., estimated taxes and amounts withheld from wages) in computing the underpayment, as well as with any amount shown as due on the return even if not paid. If the return was not filed on time, however, the "underpayment" on which the penalty is based is specially defined as the entire amount of the tax, even if the belated return accurately computed the tax liability and the amount shown was satisfied in full by payments before the return's due date.[48]

The negligence penalty is imposed in addition to interest and is often combined with the failure-to-file and failure-to-pay penalties of IRC §§6651(a)(1) and 6651(a)(2), respectively. If the fraud penalty is imposed, however, it displaces the negligence penalty.[49]

4. Civil Fraud. Section 6653(b) provides that if any part of an underpayment (as defined) is due to fraud, the taxpayer is subject to a penalty of 50 percent of the underpayment and 50 percent of the interest payable under IRC §6601 with respect to that portion of the underpayment that is attributable to fraud. In its instructions to revenue agents, the IRS describes the guidelines for imposition of the civil fraud penalty as follows:

> To successfully maintain a charge of fraud in a tax case, it is necessary to establish that a part of the deficiency is due to a false material representation of facts by the taxpayer and that he/she had knowledge of its falsity and intended that it be acted upon or accepted as the truth. Such a charge must be proved by clear and convincing evidence and not rest merely upon suspicion or presumption.[50]

Fraud cases ordinarily involve systematic or substantial omissions from gross income or fictitious deductions, accompanied by the falsification or destruction of records or false or inconsistent statements to the investigating agents, especially where records are not kept by the taxpayer.[51] The taxpayer's education and business experience are also relevant,[52] as is the extent to which

---

[47] IRC §6653(a)(2).

[48] IRC §6653(c)(1) (parenthetical clause).

[49] IRC §§6653(a), 6653(b)(3); Treas. Regs. §301.6653-1(b)(2).

[50] IRM 4563.41(1), 4563.42(1).

[51] For failure to keep adequate books and records as evidence of fraud, see Cooperberg v. CIR, ¶79,102 P-H Memo TC (1979).

[52] See, e.g., Stolzfus v. US, 398 F.2d 1002 (3d Cir. 1968), cert. denied, 393 US 1020

he assisted or obstructed the investigating agents.[53]

Deficiencies caused by items involving the exercise of judgment are seldom the basis for a fraud penalty, unless the intent to evade tax is almost inescapable.[54] Similarly, the fraud penalty is seldom asserted and even less frequently upheld in cases where the deficiency results from a transaction complying with the letter but not the spirit of the law, in the absence of concealment.[55] In recent cases, however, the penalty has been successfully imposed on tax protestors who deliberately understated their taxable income, even though their returns usually exude a spirit of defiance rather than concealment.[56] It remains to be seen whether the IRS can nip this growth industry in the bud by drastic action against its pioneers.

To sustain a fraud penalty, the IRS has the burden of proving that the taxpayer was guilty (in a civil, not criminal, sense) of fraud with intent to evade tax [57] and must establish this issue by clear and convincing evidence.[58] Taxpayers who pleaded guilty to willful tax evasion or were convicted under IRC §7201 are barred by collateral estoppel from denying that the return was fraudulent and that there was an underpayment.[59] In many cases, the IRS

(1969) (penalty imposed on taxpayer with limited formal education but extensive business experience); but see Windsberg's Est. v. CIR, ¶78,101 P-H Memo TC (1978) (fraud penalty not imposed on estate of deceased IRS tax law specialist who deducted loss on vacation cottage rented for only one season during twelve-year period of ownership; education and experience indicated he should have known better and was grossly negligent but there was insufficient evidence of fraud, despite misstatements during investigation—an effort by the Tax Court to reverse the maxim that "the evil that men do lives after them"?).

[53] See, e.g., Riddle v. CIR, ¶76,205 P-H Memo TC (1976) (cooperative taxpayer); Granat's Est. v. CIR, 298 F.2d 397 (2d Cir. 1962) (refusal to cooperate).

[54] It is sometimes difficult to account for the failure of the IRS to assert a fraud penalty; see, e.g., Fixler v. CIR, ¶78,423 P-H Memo TC (1978) (partner in accounting firm deducted entertainment expenses, including cost of son's Bar Mitzvah party, despite conceded absence of related business discussions required for deduction); Imhoff v. CIR, ¶79,057 P-H Memo TC (1979) (former military inspector general's unsubstantiated deductions, including "a dental bill for a miniature poodle who was a part of the [taxpayer's] internal security system").

[55] See Court Holding Co. v. CIR, 2 TC 51, 538 (1943), rev'd, 143 F.2d 823 (5th Cir. 1944), aff'd, 324 US 331 (1945).

[56] See, e.g., Anderson v. CIR, ¶78,444 P-H Memo TC (1978) (return with rider asserting that "Gestapo is alive and well and living under the name of the IRS"); but see Tranquilli v. CIR, ¶80,010 P-H Memo TC (1980) (fraud penalty does not apply to protester listing antiwar organizations as dependents on return).

[57] IRC §7454(a). Although IRC §6653(b) refers only to fraud, and not to "fraud with intent to evade tax," IRC §7454(a) is applicable; see George v. CIR, 338 F.2d 221 (1st Cir. 1964).

[58] See, e.g., Green v. CIR, 66 TC 538 (1976) (Acq.).

[59] See Armstrong v. US, 354 F.2d 274, 290–291 (Ct.Cl. 1965), and cases there cited; Stone v. CIR, 56 TC 213 (1971); see also Mickler v. Fahs, 243 F.2d 515 (5th Cir. 1957) (plea of nolo contendere); Goodwin v. CIR, 73 TC 215 (1979) (Acq.) (divided

relies on the conviction to establish fraud and then relies on the presumption of correctness to shift to the taxpayer the burden of proving that the understatement was less than the amount determined by the statutory notice of deficiency ("ninety-day letter").[60] An acquittal in a criminal case under IRC §7201, however, does not protect the taxpayer from the civil penalty, since the government's burden of proof in a civil fraud case ("clear and convincing evidence") is less exacting than its burden in the prior criminal case (guilt "beyond a reasonable doubt"). Imposition of a civil fraud penalty after a criminal prosecution does not constitute double jeopardy, because of the penalty's remedial character.[61]

When the IRS does not have the benefit of a prior criminal conviction or plea of guilty to establish fraud, the taxpayer's subjective intent must almost always be inferred from his or her entire course of action, the most damaging items being a pattern of substantial understatements over a period of years, absence of accurate records, destruction of evidence, concealment of bank accounts and other assets, and attempts to obstruct the investigation.[62] Chiseling on low-income returns rarely elicits action by the IRS, and it is sometimes brushed aside by the courts.[63]

When a fraud penalty is based on a joint return, each spouse must be viewed independently; if one is innocent of fraud, the penalty can be assessed and collected only from the guilty one.[64] Both spouses are liable, however, for the underpayment itself, interest, and any nonfraud penalties, unless the "innocent spouse" rule of IRC §6013(e) applies.[65]

---

court—extensive analysis of collateral estoppel where taxpayer pleaded guilty to filing false and fraudulent returns.)

If the taxpayer was convicted of a tax crime other than willful evasion under IRC §7201, collateral estoppel may or may not be applicable, depending on the elements of the crime. See Goodwin v. CIR, supra (taxpayer convicted of filing false return under IRC §7206(1)); held, estopped to deny that action was fraudulent but entitled to deny underpayment of tax); see also Connor v. CIR, ¶77,121 P-H Memo TC (1977) (conviction for willful failure to file under IRC §7203 does not establish fraud), and cases there cited.

[60] US v. Bartone, 41 AFTR2d 520 (N.D. Ohio 1977) (not officially reported).

[61] See Helvering v. Mitchell, 303 US 391 (1938).

[62] See Stone v. CIR, ¶77,147 P-H Memo TC (1977), and cases there cited.

[63] See Castells v. CIR, ¶61,275 P-H Memo TC (1961) (waiter reported tips of $865 rather than $2,593; IRS agents "in a mistakenly zealous crusade have lost sight of the forest in their preoccupation with something that is not even a small tree—more like a blade of grass"; penalty rejected—only one year was involved).

[64] IRC §6653(b)(4). One spouse's conviction in a criminal case does not collaterally estop the other spouse from denying fraud. See Rodney v. CIR, 53 TC 287, 306-310 (1969).

[65] See supra ¶39.3; since one spouse's fraud prevents the statute of limitations from running on the other spouse's liability for the deficiency and nonfraud penalties (Van-

If a fraud penalty is assessed for an underpayment of tax required to be shown on a return, IRC §§6653(b)(3) and 6653(d) respectively forbid imposition of a negligence penalty under IRC §6653(a) or a delinquency penalty under IRC §6651.

5. Failure to Withhold and Collect Third-Party Taxes. Amounts withheld from employees' wages can be "a tempting source of ready cash to a failing corporation beleaguered by creditors." [66] To forestall this tactic, the IRS can order the withholding entity to open a special bank account as trustee for the United States and to deposit all "collected taxes" within two banking days after collection;[67] but if this remedy is not administered promptly, the IRS may find itself with an uncollectible claim against an insolvent employer. If the insolvency results from fraudulent conveyances, the IRS may be able to collect the unpaid amounts from the transferees under IRC §6901.[68]

In addition, under IRC §6672, any person "required to collect, truthfully account for, and pay over any tax"—a so-called responsible person—who fails in these duties or who "willfully attempts in any manner to evade or defeat any such tax" is personally liable for a penalty equal to the amount of tax that was evaded, not collected, or not accounted for and paid over.[69] Section 6672 (which is buttressed by IRC §7202, a criminal provision using almost identical language) is concerned with defaults with respect to so-called collected and withheld taxes ("third-party taxes"), such as taxes withheld from employee wages or from interest and dividends. IRS practice is to use IRC §6672 only as a "collection device" and to content itself with collecting the basic amount only once.[70] A few cases have exonerated otherwise responsible persons because of serious neglect by the government in pursuing the employer, which is the principal obligor.[71]

Liability under IRC §6672 requires two converging circumstances:(1) a "responsible person" and (2) a willful failure to collect, account for, and pay over a tax or a willful attempt to evade or defeat the tax or payment thereof.[72]

---

naman v. CIR, 54 TC 1011 (1970), see supra ¶41.3), the latter's only escape is via IRC §6013(e)(1).

[66] Slodov v. US, 436 US 238, 243 (1978).

[67] IRC §7612; violators of such an order can be prosecuted under IRC §7215.

[68] For discussion of transferee liability, see supra ¶39.7.

[69] For procedure under IRC §6672, see Rev. Proc. 57-26, 1957-2 CB 1093; Rev. Proc. 61-27, 1961-2 CB 563; Rev. Proc. 69-26, 1969-2 CB 308.

[70] Bolding v. US, 565 F.2d 663, 669 n.3 (Ct. Cl. 1977) (IRS policies).

[71] See Tozier v. US, 16 AFTR2d 5626 (D.Wash. 1965) (not officially reported) (IRS permitted payment of prior claims by bankruptcy court, released seized assets, etc.); but see Datlof v. US, 370 F.2d 655 (3d Cir. 1966), cert. denied, 387 US 906 (1967) (no defense that IRS failed to use due diligence to collect from corporation).

[72] See generally Waghalter v. US, 45 AFTR2d 409 (S.D. Tex. 1979) (not officially reported) (extensive review of cases).

1. *Responsible persons.* Shareholders, directors, lenders, and others having responsibility for payment of the withholding entity's debts have been subjected to the 100 percent penalty.[73] Responsibility need not be exclusive: Two or more persons can be responsible simultaneously for the crucial acts,[74] and the "shield of organizational form" [75] cannot be used to protect the top managers by vesting nominal authority in junior members of the staff.

2. *Willfulness.* Section 6672 does not "impose liability without personal fault." [76] The element of fault is embodied in the statutory requirement that the responsible officer must have acted "willfully," a term that is defined as "a voluntary, conscious, and intentional failure to collect, truthfully account for, and pay over the taxes withheld from the employees." [77] Since withheld and collected taxes constitute trust funds by virtue of IRC §7501 as soon as they are collected or withheld, the "willfulness" required by IRC §6672 is established if the responsible person deliberately uses the funds to pay other creditors, even if there is a reasonable expectation that sufficient funds will be on hand when payment to the government is required.[78]

6. Valuation Overstatements. Section 6659 imposes a penalty for "valuation overstatements," defined as a claim on any return that the value or adjusted basis of property exceeds 150 percent of the amount determined to be correct. The penalty applies only (1) to individuals, closely held corporations as defined by IRC §465(a)(1)(C) (at-risk rules),[79] and personal-service corporations as defined by IRC §414(m)(3) (qualified employee benefit plans), (2) if the underpayment of tax attributable to the overstatement is $1,000 or more; and (3) if the property has been held by the taxpayer for five years or less. The IRS can waive all or any part of the addition if the taxpayer shows that there was a reasonable basis for the amount claimed on the return and the claim was made in good faith.

The penalty is 10 percent of the underpayment attributable to the overstated claim if the amount claimed is between 150 and 200 percent of the correct amount, 20 percent of the underpayment if the claim is between 200 and 250 percent of the correct amount, and 30 percent of the underpayment if the claim exceeds 250 percent of the correct amount.

---

[73] See generally Adams v. US, 504 F.2d 73 (7th Cir. 1974) (finance company), and cases there cited.

[74] See, e.g., Cella v. US, 45 AFTR2d 1071 (E.D.N.Y. 1980) (corporate treasurer who could not sign checks over $1,000 without co-signature held liable).

[75] Pacific Nat'l Ins. Co. v. US, 422 F.2d 26 (9th Cir.), cert. denied, 398 US 937 (1970).

[76] Slodov v. US, supra note 66, at 254.

[77] Newsome v. US, 431 F.2d 742, 745 (5th Cir. 1970).

[78] Id.

[79] Supra ¶12.8.

7. Promoting Abusive Tax Shelters. Section 6700 imposes a penalty on any person who organizes, assists in the organization of, or participates in the sale of any interest in a partnership, other entity, investment plan, or any other plan or arrangement and who makes or furnishes (1) a statement that the person knows or has reason to know is false or fraudulent as to any material matter with respect to the securing of a tax benefit by reason of the holding of an interest in the entity or plan, or (2) a statement of the value of property or services that exceeds 200 percent of the correct value if the value is directly related to the amount of any deduction or credit allowable to the holder of an interest. While the "reason to know" standard permits the IRS to rely on objective evidence of a person's knowledge—promoters and salesmen would ordinarily be deemed to have knowledge of the facts contained in the sales materials—it is not intended to impose a duty of inquiry concerning the transaction on one whose role in the transaction does not require knowledge of the matter at issue.[80] A matter is material if it would have a substantial impact on the decision making process of a reasonably prudent investor.[81] The IRS has the authority to waive all or part of any penalty provided for a valuation overstatement if it can be shown that there was a reasonable basis for the valuation and that it was made in good faith.[82]

The penalty imposed is the greater of $1,000 or 10 percent of the gross income derived or to be derived from the endeavor by the person subject to the penalty. In determining the amount of income yet to be derived the IRS may look only to unrealized amounts which the person may reasonably expect to realize.[83] A person against whom the penalty is assessed may obtain judicial review by paying at least 15 percent of the penalty and suing for refund.[84] The burden of proof in such a proceeding is on the IRS.

In addition to the penalty imposed by IRC §6700, IRC §7408 gives the IRS the authority to bring an action to enjoin any persons from further engaging in conduct subject to penalty under IRC §6700.

8. Substantial Understatement. Section 6661(a) imposes a penalty equal to 10 percent of the amount of any underpayment of tax attributable to an understatement, defined as the excess of the amount of tax required to be shown on a tax return for the taxable year over the amount of tax shown, if the understatement exceeds the greater of 10 percent of the tax required to be shown on the return or $5,000 ($10,000 in the case of a corporation other than a Subchapter S corporation or a personal holding company).

---

[80] Conf. Rep, H.R. Rep. No. 97-760 (1982).

[81] S. Rep. No. 97-494 (1982).

[82] IRC §6700(b)(2).

[83] S. Rep. No. 97-494, supra note 81.

[84] IRC §6703(c).

In the case of items other than "tax shelter" items, the amount of the understatement is reduced by the portion of the understatement attributable to an item if (1) the tax treatment of that item on the return is supported by substantial authority or (2) the relevant factors affecting the item's tax treatment are adequately disclosed in the return or in a statement attached to the return. In the case of "tax shelter" items, the amount of the understatement is reduced only if the tax treatment of the item is supported by substantial authority *and* the taxpayer reasonably believes that the tax treatment of such item on the return was more likely than not the proper treatment. For this purpose, a "tax shelter" is a partnership, other entity, investment plan, or other plan or arrangement the principal purpose of which is the avoidance or evasion of federal income tax. A taxpayer can establish belief that the tax treatment of an item on a return was more likely than not proper by showing good faith reliance on a professional opinion to that effect.[85]

The IRS has the authority under IRC §6661(c) to waive all or any part of the penalty on a showing that there was a reasonable cause for the understatement and the taxpayer acted in good faith.

In addition to the penalty for substantial understatement, a person who aids in the preparation or presentation of any portion of a tax return or other tax-related document knowing that it will be used in connection with any material matter arising under the tax laws and that it will result, if used, in an understatement of the tax liability of another person is subject to a penalty of $1,000 for each such return or other document ($5,000 in the case of a corporate return or other document).[86]

¶42.4 CRIMINAL FRAUD AND OTHER TAX CRIMES

1. Introductory. Chapter 75 of the Internal Revenue Code creates more than a score of crimes and "other offenses" against the federal revenue laws. Referring to those concerned with income taxes, the Supreme Court has said that "singly or in combination [they] were calculated [by Congress] to induce prompt and forthright fulfillment of every duty under the income tax law and to provide a penalty suitable to every degree of delinquency." [86.1] This portrayal of the enforcement arsenal as a hierarchy of finely calibrated penalties—like a graduated rate schedule?—is appealing, but it would be more realistic to say that the government can usually choose from a hodgepodge of overlapping sanctions, depending on how heinous the misconduct seems to the

[85] S. Rep. No. 97-494, supra note 81.

[86] IRC §6701. For coordination with other return preparer penalties, see IRC §6701(f).

[86.1] Spies v. US, 317 US 492, 497 (1943).

IRS and the Department of Justice, and that prosecutors who feel cramped by this choice can sometimes also call upon provisions of the Criminal Code having no specific relationship to the income tax, such as the general statutes punishing perjury, conspiracies, false claims, and false statements.[87]

In the audit process, the IRS unearths far more cases exuding an aroma of tax evasion than can be prosecuted. These cases must be placed on a seamless spectrum of tax delinquency, which begins at one end with taxpayers who resolve all doubts in their own favor or engage in shabby but not heinous conduct and which consists at the other end of aggravated cases of deliberate omissions, false statements, destruction of records, and payoffs to government officials. The IRS and the Department of Justice screen cases at several levels in order to weed out the weak ones; and both agencies are obviously interested in the deterrent effect of publicity as well as in retributive punishment. The principal weapons in the income tax arsenal are summarized below, and some of the procedural aspects of tax fraud cases are briefly described elsewhere in this work.[88] But it should be borne in mind that criminal tax cases are criminal cases first, and tax cases only secondarily.

The criminal fraud provisions cover much of the same ground as the 50 percent civil penalty, and although they hold the government to a higher standard of proof than required for the civil penalty, they reach a wider range of persons. Unlike the civil penalty, which usually applies only to the taxpayer himself,[89] the criminal provisions punish *anyone* engaging in the defined offense, thus permitting the government to prosecute persons aiding a corrupt taxpayer.[90] Moreover, IRC §7206(2) explicitly encompasses anyone who will-

[87] See US v. Beacon Brass Co., 344 US 43 (1952) (overlapping jurisdiction of tax and nontax criminal sanctions). For the effect of a tax conviction on the taxpayer's fitness to practice a profession, see Maryland State Bar Ass'n v. Agnew, 271 Md. 543, 315 A.2d 811 (1974); In re Spritzer, 63 N.J. 532, 309 A.2d 745 (1973) (one-year suspension from practice for lawyer convicted of failure to file returns; mitigating circumstances were desire to protect seriously ill father from detection for failure to file for thirty years); Furnish v. Board of Medical Examiners, 149 Cal. App. 2d 26, cert. denied, 355 US 827 (1957) (tax evasion conviction held grounds for suspension of physician's license); but see State ex rel. Atkins v. Missouri State Bd. of Accountancy, 351 S.W.2d 483 (Mo. App. 1961) (conviction for willful failure to file tax return not sufficient ground to revoke accountant's license under state law relating to crimes of which dishonesty or fraud is an essential element).

[88] For ancillary aspects of prosecutions for tax fraud and other offenses, see supra ¶¶40.2 (IRS investigative authority), 37.1 (indirect methods of reconstructing income).

[89] Tax preparers, as defined by IRC §7701(a)(36), are subject to civil penalties for negligence or willful attempts to understate a client's tax liability. See IRC §6694; supra ¶38.3. In addition, IRC §6701 imposes certain civil penalties on persons who aid and abet the understatement of another person's tax liability. See supra ¶42.3.

[90] See Tinkoff v. US, 86 F.2d 868, 876 (7th Cir. 1936), cert. denied, 301 US 689 (1937) (accountant who prepared fraudulent returns for client; conviction under statutory predecessor of IRC §7201 upheld); US v. Moss, 604 F.2d 579 (8th Cir. 1979)

fully "aids or assists in or procures, counsels, or advises the preparation or presentation . . . of a return, affidavit, claim, or other document, which is fraudulent or is false as to any material matter, whether or not such falsity or fraud is with the knowledge or consent of the person authorized or required to present such return, affidavit, claim, or document." In addition, IRC §7343 provides that the term "person" as used in the penalty chapter of the Code includes officers and employees of corporations and members and employees of partnerships who are obligated by virtue of their status to perform the act with respect to which a violation occurs. Finally, a prosecutor can in appropriate cases, also use the general conspiracy provision of the Criminal Code to prosecute anyone conspiring to violate any substantive prohibition covering the misconduct in question.[91]

Section 6531 prescribes a three-year period of limitations on the prosecution of tax crimes, measured from the date when the offense is committed to the date of indictment or information; but it then substitutes a six-year period for willfully attempting to evade or defeat a tax, assisting in the preparation of a false or fraudulent return or other document, willfully failing to pay, filing a false statement, conspiracy to defraud, and several other offenses.[92] The applicable time limit is tolled while the offender is a fugitive from justice or is outside the United States.

2. Willful Attempt to Evade Tax. The "capstone" [93] of the hierarchy of tax crimes is IRC §7201, providing that "any person who willfully attempts in any manner to evade or defeat any tax" is guilty of a felony, punishable by a fine of not more than $100,000 ($500,000 in the case of a corporation), imprisonment for not more than five years, or both, plus the costs of prosecution and any other penalties provided by law. The "other penalties provided by law" include not only the 50 percent civil fraud penalty but also fines and prison terms imposed by other statutory provisions if prosecution thereunder does not constitute double jeopardy.[94]

In *Sansone v. United States,* the Supreme Court summarized the elements

(conviction of anti-tax crusader as aider and abettor, based on speeches and advice, upheld; free speech claim rejected).

[91] See US v. Beacon Brass Co., supra note 87.

[92] For problems in determining when an offense is "committed," see US v. Beacon Brass Co., supra note 87 (prosecution for attempt to evade tax—offense committed when false statements were made to IRS employees).

[93] Spies v. US, supra note 86.1.

[94] For the 50 percent civil fraud penalty, see supra ¶42.3; see also US v. Beacon Brass Co., supra note 87, at 46 (reference to "other penalties provided by law" indicates congressional recognition that some methods of attempting to evade taxes violate other statutes as well).

of IRC §7201 as "willfulness; the existence of a tax deficiency; . . . and an affirmative act constituting an evasion or attempted evasion of the tax." [95]

1. *Willfulness.* The Supreme Court has indicated that the element of willfulness is satisfied by "a voluntary, intentional violation of a known legal duty." [96] Although willfulness cannot be inferred from the mere understatement of income, it need not be—in fact, almost never can be—proved directly; but it can be inferred from other facts and circumstances, such as a consistent pattern of underreporting large amounts of income and omitting income from books and records.[97] By requiring the *intentional* violation of a *known* legal duty, the Court's interpretation of willfulness excludes careless behavior, as well as the taxpayer's resolution of debatable legal issues in his own favor.[98]

Although the prompt filing of correct amended returns does not retroactively purify an earlier attempt to defraud, it may be evidence from which a lack of willfullness can be inferred, depending on the circumstances surrounding the taxpayer's change of heart; but the corrected returns can also be used by the government to the taxpayer's disadvantage as admissions against interest.[99] Under current procedures, the voluntary disclosure of fraud before the government is hot on the taxpayer's trail may also be helpful, since the IRS may decide that ostensible repentance will incline a jury to resolve doubts in the taxpayer's favor; but it does not preclude prosecution, let alone wipe the slate clean as a matter of law, and hence it is a risky tactic.[100]

---

[95] Sansone v. US, 380 US 343, 351 (1965).

[96] US v. Pomponio, 429 US 10, 12 (1976) (appellate decision holding that willfulness requires a finding of bad purpose or evil motive reversed; instruction on good faith was unnecessary); the case involved IRC §7206(1) (filing false return), but US v. Bishop, 412 US 346 (1973), held that "willfully" is used with the same meaning in both provisions.

[97] See Holland v. US, 348 US 121 (1954).

[98] See James v. US, 366 US 213 (1961) (conviction for failing to report embezzled funds reversed because violation occurred before Supreme Court overruled CIR v. Wilcox, 327 US 404 (1946), holding that embezzled funds did not constitute income); US v. Garber, 607 F.2d 92 (5th Cir. 1979) (conviction of professional blood donor for failing to report income reversed on evidence that taxability of receipts was debatable); but see Ripperger v. US, 248 F.2d 944 (4th Cir. 1957), cert. denied, 355 US 940 (1958) (attorney's claim that he did not know law required returns to be filed when he lacked funds to pay tax was so unreasonable that trial judge was justified in rejecting it); Hull v. US, 37 AFTR2d 840 (10th Cir. 1975) (not officially reported) (psychosomatic procrastination rejected as defense to prosecution of CPA for willful failure to file returns).

[99] See Hayes v. US, 227 F.2d 540 (10th Cir. 1955), cert. denied, 353 US 953 (1957), and cases there cited.

[100] US v. Choate, 619 F.2d 21 (9th Cir. 1980) (claim that IRS engaged in improper discriminatory enforcement by violating alleged voluntary disclosure policy rejected).

2. *Deficiency.* The second element of IRC §7201 according to *Sansone*— the existence of a tax deficiency—is puzzling, since the broad statutory language ("attempts in any manner to evade or defeat any tax") seems to encompass unsuccessful as well as successful attempts to evade taxes—for example, the carryback of a fictitious net operating loss, even if the fraud is detected and the claimed refund is denied. Numerous cases in the courts of appeals, however, refer to an understatement of tax liability as a requisite to prosecution under IRC §7201, and some even say that a "substantial" understatement is required;[101] but there appear to be no cases explaining why the statutory term "attempt" as used in IRC §7201 should not be given its normal meaning.[102]

3. *Affirmative act of evasion.* The third element of IRC §7201, as summarized by *Sansone,* is an affirmative act of evasion or attempted evasion. The mere failure to file returns is insufficient,[103] but almost any other evasionary tactic is encompassed by the statutory reference to a willful attempt "in any manner" to evade taxes, such as "keeping a double set of books, making false entries or alterations, or false invoices or documents, destruction of books or records, concealment of assets or covering up sources of income, handling of one's affairs to avoid making the records usual in transactions of the kind, and any conduct, the likely effect of which would be to mislead or to conceal." [104] Fraud prosecutions usually involve one or more of these elements, but taxpayers who take improper or double deductions or engage in similar tactics can also be prosecuted for tax evasion under IRC §7201, provided the requisite intent to defraud is proved beyond a reasonable doubt.[105]

3. Materially False Return or Statement Under Penalty of Perjury. Section 7206(1) provides that anyone making a return, statement, or other document "which contains or is verified by a written declaration that it is made under the penalties of perjury, and which he does not believe to be true and correct as to every material matter," is guilty of a felony, punishable by a fine of not more than $100,000 ($500,000 in the case of a corporation), imprisonment for not more than three years, or both, plus the costs of prosecution. To

---

[101] See, e.g., Willingham v. US, 289 F.2d 283 (5th Cir.), cert. denied, 368 US 828 (1961); Heasley v. US, 218 F.2d 86 (8th Cir.), cert. denied, 350 US 882 (1955) ("substantial" understatement).

[102] See US v. Petti, 448 F.2d 1257 (3d Cir. 1971) (no evidence of deficiency; government argued deficiency not explicitly required by IRC §7201; issue treated as settled by *Sansone* and conviction reversed).

[103] Spies v. US, supra note 86.1, at 497–498.

[104] Spies v. US, supra note 86.1, at 499.

[105] See, e.g., US v. Pomponio, supra note 96 (corporate advances to dominant shareholders reported as loans, though known to be taxable dividends; corporate losses wrongfully assigned to partnership).

come within this provision, a document need not be sworn to or acknowledged before a notary or other person qualified to administer oaths; the requisite perjury declaration may be simply a written statement, as on Form 1040 and other tax returns.[106] A conviction under IRC §7206(1) can be based on the willful omission of a material matter as well as on an affirmative false statement;[107] and while the defect must be "material," the government does not have to prove that the IRS relied on the statement or that there was a tax deficiency.[108]

Because conduct violating IRC §7201 can also violate IRC §7206(1) (e.g., filing a fraudulent return), separate fines and consecutive prison terms cannot be meted out for an action violating both provisions.[109]

4. Materially False Statements. Section 7202 provides that any person "who willfully delivers or discloses to the [IRS] any list, return, account, statement, or other document, known by him to be fraudulent or to be false as to any material matter," shall be fined not more than $10,000 ($50,000 in the case of corporations), imprisoned for not more than one year, or both. This misdemeanor statute overlaps both IRC §§7201 and 7206(1);[110] but unlike the latter, it does not require the false statement to be made under the penalties of perjury.[111]

5. Willful Failure to File Return or to Pay Tax. Section 7203 makes it a misdemeanor (subject to a fine of not more than $25,000 ($100,000 in the case of a corporation), a prison sentence of not more than one year, or both, plus the costs of prosecution) for any person required to file a return, keep records, supply information, or pay a tax to fail to take the prescribed action at the time required. The gravamen of the crime is not an intent to defraud the government, but an intentional failure to discharge a known legal

---

[106] For the extent to which documents submitted to the IRS must be made under the penalties of perjury, see IRC §6065; Treas. Regs. §1.6065-1; see also US v. Levy, 533 F.2d 969 (5th Cir. 1976) (IRC §7206(1) applies only to documents *required* to be filed).

[107] See US v. Tager, 479 F.2d 120, 122 (10th Cir. 1973), cert. denied, 414 US 1162 (1974) (IRC §7206(1) prohibits "knowing and willful omission of material matter"), and cases there cited.

[108] US v. Jernigan, 411 F.2d 471 (5th Cir.), cert. denied, 396 US 927 (1969) (deficiency not required); US v. Romanow, 509 F.2d 26 (1st Cir. 1975) (materiality measured by statement's potential rather than actual impact).

[109] US v. White, 417 F.2d 89, 93–94 (2d Cir. 1969), cert. denied, 397 US 912 (1970).

[110] See Sansone v. US, supra note 95 (false income tax returns covered by IRC §7207).

[111] See US v. Levy, supra note 106.

duty.[112] If the taxpayer does not admit his failure to file, the IRS relies on a computer-generated report to the effect that no return can be found for the year in question, which the taxpayer may then seek to impugn.[113]

Although it has long been established that the privilege against self-incrimination does not justify a flat refusal to file *any* return,[114] it shields the taxpayer against prosecution under IRC §7203 if claimed in good faith with respect to particular entries or questions, even if the claim turns out to be unwarranted.[115]

Section 7203 also punishes a willful failure to pay taxes or estimate taxes; but the government—concerned about the constitutional problems posed by imprisonment for debt—rarely prosecutes taxpayers for failing to pay their own taxes, as distinguished from taxes withheld from employees' wages or collected from customers, where the delinquency partakes of larceny.[116] Although a naked failure to pay is difficult to prosecute under IRC §7203, taxpayers who conceal their assets (e.g., by vesting title in dummies) may be convicted of a felony under IRC §7201 for attempting to evade and defeat their tax liabilities.[117]

6. Other Crimes. The Internal Revenue Code includes many other criminal penalties covering more narrowly defined offenses, and, at the other end of the spectrum, the Criminal Code contains several very general provisions that apply to taxes along with nontax offenses. Note should also be taken of the fact that false statements and other misconduct during the course of an audit or other investigation not only are crimes in themselves, but also extend the period for prosecution, since the statute of limitations begins to run only when the false statement is submitted.[118]

---

[112] See US v. Douglass, 476 F.2d 260 (5th Cir. 1973) ("self-styled American patriot," who filed Form 1040 with only name, address, and signature, convicted under IRC §7203 despite belief that payment of U.S. taxes constitutes treason because of communist influences on government and foreign aid to enemies of United States); US v. Pohlman, 522 F.2d 974 (8th Cir. 1975), cert. denied, 423 US 1049 (1976), and cases there cited.

[113] See US v. Liebert, 519 F.2d 542 (3d Cir.), cert. denied, 423 US 985 (1975).

[114] US v. Johnson, 577 F.2d 1304 (5th Cir. 1978), and cases there cited.

[115] See Garner v. US, 424 US 648, 663 n.18 (1976).

[116] See also supra ¶42.3 (re 100 percent penalty on responsible persons who fail to collect and pay over withholding taxes); IRC §7202 (criminal prosecution for same conduct).

[117] See Cohen v. US, 297 F.2d 760 (9th Cir.), cert. denied, 369 US 865 (1962).

[118] See US v. Beacon Brass Co., supra note 87 (false statement statute applicable in income tax cases).

SELECTED BIBLIOGRAPHY

Asimow, Civil Penalties for Inaccurate and Delinquent Tax Returns, 23 U.C.L.A. L. Rev. 637 (1976).

Comment, The Civil Penalty Triad: Delinquency, Negligence, and Civil Fraud—Prevention and Avoidance, 11 Gonz. L. Rev. 628 (1976).

Gallagher, Psychiatric Defenses in Tax Fraud Cases, 3 Pepperdine L. Rev. 252 (1976).

Graves, Civil Tax Penalties: Changes and Recommendations, 5 Pepperdine L. Rev. 465, 479–486 (1978).

Lachman, Liability Under Section 6672 of the Internal Revenue Code: Recent Developments, 57 Taxes 593 (1979).

Lyon, The Crime of Income Tax Fraud: Its Present Status and Function, 53 Colum. L. Rev. 476 (1953).

McDowell, Interest Problems in Underpayments and Overpayments of Tax, 19 NYU Inst. on Fed. Tax. 1403 (1961).

Sachs, Defense of Public Corporations in Criminal Tax Cases, 32 Tax Lawyer 69 (1978).

Sisson, The Sandman Cometh: Conspiracy Prosecutions and Tax Practitioners, 31 Tax Lawyer 805 (1978).

U.S. Comptroller General, Report to Joint Committee on Internal Revenue Taxation, IRS Can Improve Its Programs to Collect Taxes Withheld by Employers (GGD 78-14, 1978).

Vasek, The Hidden Tax Trap of I.R.C. Section 6672, 67 Ky. L.J. 27 (1978).

CHAPTER 43

Tax Litigation

¶43.1 INTRODUCTORY

The most prolific sources of tax litigation are IRS determinations of deficiencies, claims by taxpayers for refunds, and suits to enjoin the IRS from assessing or collecting taxes. The litigation spectrum, however, is not confined to these actions, but encompasses a diversity of other actions, such as suits to compel or restrain disclosure of tax information and to recover property seized by the IRS.

1. Deficiency Cases. When the IRS determines a deficiency, the taxpayer can litigate the matter in any one of three courts: the Tax Court, a federal district court, or the United States Claims Court. If the first route is chosen, the taxpayer can litigate without paying in advance; by contrast, to litigate in the district court or the Claims Court, the taxpayer must pay the tax, file a claim for refund, and then commence the lawsuit.[1] The sue-now, pay-later

[1] See Flora v. US, 362 US 145 (1960).

option often leads taxpayers to choose the Tax Court. Other factors to be taken into account in selecting the forum include the following:

1. One of the courts may have adopted a construction of the Code which is more favorable to the taxpayer.

2. Trial by jury, which may or may not be an advantage, is available only in the district courts.[2]

3. A petition to the Tax Court permits a determination of a larger deficiency than was originally asserted for the year in question, even though the year is otherwise time-barred.[3] In the district court, however, a time-barred deficiency may be used by the government only by way of setoff, not as an affirmative counterclaim.[4]

4. District court judges are generalists; Tax Court judges are specialists; and judges of the Claims Court occupy the middle ground.

5. Discovery procedures vary among the three courts.[5]

6. In the Tax Court, the taxpayer can assert any issues that would diminish or eliminate the deficiency claimed by the IRS, whether previously presented to the IRS or not; in refund suits, by contrast, the taxpayer is in general confined by IRC §7422 to the issues raised by the claim for refund.

7. The Tax Court has an optional special procedure for cases involving not more than $5,000, which permits these small cases to be tried in an informal setting under relaxed rules of evidence, without a right to appeal by either party.[6]

8. Tax Court cases are litigated and settled by IRS attorneys;[7] litigation in the district courts and the Claims Court is conducted by the Tax Division of the Department of Justice, subject to an advisory role for IRS counsel.

2. Refund Cases. Claims for the refund of an overpayment can be litigated in either the federal district court or the Claims Court, but not in the Tax Court. In choosing between the federal district court and the Claims Court, taxpayers take into account some of the facts listed above.

3. Injunctions and Declaratory Judgments. Injunctions to restrain assessment or collection of federal taxes and declaratory judgments determining tax liabilities are prohibited, with minor exceptions examined later in this chapter.[8]

---

[2] See Damsky v. Zavatt, 289 F.2d 46 (2d Cir. 1961) (exhaustive historical review of jury trial in tax cases).

[3] See IRC §6214(a), discussed infra ¶43.2.

[4] See infra ¶43.7.

[5] For Tax Court discovery rules, see infra ¶43.3.

[6] Infra ¶43.5.

[7] See IRC §7452; Rev. Proc. 78-9, 1978-1 CB 563 (procedure for docketed Tax Court cases).

[8] Infra ¶43.9.

4. Damage Actions Against the IRS or IRS Employees. Taxpayers sometimes sue the IRS or its employees for damages on various theories sounding primarily in tort; and they attempt to sidestep the defense of sovereign immunity by citing the Federal Tort Claims Act. This jurisdictional foundation is ordinarily of no help, however, because the Act explicitly excludes (1) claims based on the performance or failure to perform discretionary functions or duties, whether or not the agency's or employee's discretion is abused; (2) claims arising in respect of the assessment or collection of any tax; and (3) claims arising out of assault, battery, false imprisonment, false arrest, malicious prosecution, abuse of process, libel, slander, misrepresentation, deceit, or interference with contract rights, unless they involve the conduct of investigative or law-enforcement officers who are authorized to execute searches, seize evidence, or make arrests for violations of federal law.[9]

These statutory limitations on the scope of the Federal Tort Claims Act can be avoided if the alleged misconduct violates the taxpayer's constitutional rights, since a cause of action can then be inferred directly from the Constitution.[10] Actions of this nature are usually unsuccessful, however, because it is extremely difficult to establish that the alleged misconduct violates a clearly identifiable provision of the Constitution and that the defendant is not entitled to some form of immunity.[11]

5. Taxpayer Attorney's Fees. Section 7430 authorizes the awarding of up to $25,000 in legal fees and costs to a taxpayer who prevails in civil tax litigation in the Federal courts, including the Tax Court, if the taxpayer establishes that the government's position in the litigation was unreasonable. Within the $25,000 overall limit, the recovery can include expenses incurred by a third party acting on behalf of the taxpayer—for example, a charitable organization that paid the legal fees of a taxpayer claiming a deduction for a contribution to the organization. This provision currently applies only to cases begun between March 1, 1983, and December 31, 1985.[12]

---

[9] See 28 USC §§1346(a) (jurisdiction), 2680(a) (discretionary functions), 2680(c) (assessment or collection of taxes), 2680(h) (law-enforcement officers); see also American Ass'n of Commodity Traders v. Department of the Treasury, 598 F.2d 1233, 1235 (1st Cir. 1979); Anderson v. US, 548 F.2d 249 (8th Cir. 1977) (suit for damages under Federal Tort Claims Act, alleging malicious prosecution, abuse of process, etc., in implementing IRS program to locate dishonest tax preparers; dismissed pursuant to discretionary acts exception to Act). For refund actions, see generally infra ¶43.7.

[10] See Bivens v. Six Unknown Named Agents of Federal Bureau of Narcotics, 403 US 388 (1971) (damages for unconstitutional search and arrest).

[11] See, e.g., Jetson Mfg. Co. v. Murphy, 462 F.Supp. 807 (M.D. Pa. 1978) (suit based on IRS forcible entry into taxpayer's plant and searches and seizures without warrant; acts covered by qualified immunity, since IRS employees acted in good faith and constitutional violations were not clearly established).

[12] IRC §7430(f).

¶43.2 TAX COURT—ORGANIZATION AND JURISDICTION

1. Introductory. The Tax Court began life in 1924 as the Board of Tax Appeals, which constituted "an independent agency in the executive branch of the Government." [13] It became the Tax Court of the United States in 1942, but this change in its title (and the simultaneous conversion of its "members" into "judges") was not accompanied by a change in its statutory description.[14] In 1969, however, the Tax Court was established as a court under Article I of the Constitution; and its name was changed to the United States Tax Court.[15] The principal new power stemming from this change of status is the authority to compel the attendance of witnesses, punish for contempt, and enforce its orders. The major reasons for organizing the court as a "legislative" court under Article I of the Constitution rather than as a "constitutional" court under Article III (which confers lifetime tenure and salary protection on the judges) were evidently that (1) the Department of Justice by tradition controls all litigation in Article III courts, whereas the IRS had jurisdiction over Tax Court litigation, and (2) some legislators were reluctant to increase the number of judges with life tenure.[16]

The Tax Court is composed of nineteen judges, appointed for fifteen-year terms by the President, subject to Senate confirmation "solely on the ground of fitness to perform the duties of the office." [17] The Chief Judge, who is designated by the court itself, is authorized by IRC §7444 to divide it into "divisions" of one or more judges each. By tradition, each division consists of a single judge. Their services are augmented by the work of commissioners ("Special Trial Judges"), appointed by the Chief Judge. They conduct trials and make findings of fact in reports that are filed, with briefs by the parties, with a division of the court, which may adopt, modify, or reject the report in whole or in part; remand it with instructions; or receive additional evidence.[18] Although used to a limited extent in regular cases, commissioners are primarily assigned to small tax cases, which are subject to simplified procedures and a jurisdictional limit of $5,000.[19]

The court's principal office is in the District of Columbia, but the judges

---

[13] Revenue Act of 1924, §900(k), 43 Stat. 253, 336.

[14] Revenue Act of 1942, §504(a), 56 Stat. 798, 957.

[15] IRC §7441.

[16] See generally S. Rep. No. 91-552, reprinted in 1969-3 CB 423, 615. The Tax Court Rules of Practice and Procedure were substantially revised in 1979 (71 TC at 1177); but the prior version, promulgated in 1973, contains explanatory notes (60 TC at 1057) that are still useful.

[17] IRC §7743.

[18] Tax Ct. R. 180–182.

[19] Tax Ct. R. 183; for the special procedures applicable to small tax cases, see IRC §7463, infra ¶43.5.

are circuit riders, who conduct trial sessions in about sixty cities throughout the country.

In addition to its primary function as a forum in which IRS deficiency determinations can be challenged without paying first, the Tax Court can issue declaratory judgments in a few special situations, such as petitions involving the validity of IRS rulings relating to the tax-exempt status of charitable organizations.[20] It also has jurisdiction over actions to compel or restrain disclosure of IRS rulings and other determinations.[21]

The government is represented in Tax Court cases by the Chief Counsel for the Internal Revenue Service.[22] Taxpayers can appear either pro se or through a representative. The opportunity to act as their own lawyers appeals to many taxpayers, some of whom obviously have fools for clients; the opinions in pro se cases suggest that the judges view these self-reliant petitioners with feelings ranging from compassion tinged with exasperation to exasperation tinged with compassion. Attorneys who are members in good standing of the bar of the US Supreme Court or of the highest court of any state, territory, or the District of Columbia may be admitted to practice on application.[23] Non-lawyers must establish their qualifications by written examination.

Following the trial of a case, the judge ("division") who heard the case prepares findings and an opinion, pursuant to IRC §§7459 and 7460, which becomes the "report" of the court unless within thirty days the Chief Judge directs that it be reviewed by the entire court.[24] If the conference does not approve the division's report, it is either revised by the author or reassigned by the Chief Judge to another judge; these procedures do not entail participation by the parties either by brief or by oral argument. The opinions in court-reviewed cases are routinely published in the official *Tax Court Reports;* opinions in other cases are classified by the Chief Judge as either regular or memorandum opinions, and only the former are published in the official reports. Memorandum decisions, which involve the application of settled legal principles to the facts, are published unofficially by private publishers, but they are not ordinarily cited by the Tax Court, except when summarizing an argument that relies on a memorandum decision or when quoting an appellate decision affirming or rejecting a memorandum decision.

The Tax Court is authorized by IRC §6673 to award damages up to

---

[20] Infra text at notes 61–65.

[21] Infra text at notes 66–67.

[22] IRC §7452; see also IRC §7801(b) (Chief Counsel appointed by President, subject to Senate confirmation).

[23] Tax Ct. R. 200(a)(2); see also Tax Ct. R. 200(a)(1) (good moral character and repute), 201 (standards of practice), 202 (disqualification, disbarment, etc.).

[24] IRC §7460(b).

$5,000 for delay or if the taxpayer's position is frivolous or groundless.[25] Other sanctions for the abuse of process and for improprieties include striking scandalous or indecent matter, disciplinary actions for filing frivolous pleadings or for misconduct at the trial, and dismissal of a petition for failure to prosecute it expeditiously,[26] as well as the court's power to punish for contempt.[27]

2. Deficiency Cases. The Tax Court's primary function—the redetermination of deficiencies determined by the IRS—can be exercised only if three events concur: (1) The IRS must determine a deficiency, (2) the taxpayer must be notified of the determination, and (3) the taxpayer must file a petition with the Tax Court for redetermination of the deficiency within a prescribed period of time. These jurisdictional requirements cannot be waived by the parties or by the court, and they may be raised by the court of its own motion.[28]

1. *Deficiency determination by IRS.* The Tax Court's jurisdiction under IRC §6214(a) to "redetermine the correct amount of the deficiency" presupposes that a *deficiency* has been *determined* by the IRS.[29] The term "deficiency" is defined by IRC §6211(a) as the excess of the taxpayer's liability over the amount shown on the return, plus any amounts previously assessed or collected without assessment as a deficiency, less any rebates (credits, refunds, etc.).

The Tax Court can "redetermine" a deficiency only if it has first been "determined" by the IRS.[30] The requirement of an IRS *determination* coalesces with the requirement of a *notice* of deficiency, since the usual evidence that a deficiency has been "determined" is the notice. Payment of taxes after a notice of deficiency has been sent to the taxpayer does not eliminate the

---

[25] See Hatfield v. CIR, 68 TC 895 (1977) (warning); Wilkinson v. CIR, 71 TC 633 (1979) (damage award); but see Ritchie v. CIR, 72 TC 126 (1979) (negligence penalty awarded, but not damages).

[26] Tax Ct. R. 33 (striking improper matter; disciplinary action for willful violations or willfully filing frivolous pleadings, etc.); Freedson v. CIR, 67 TC 931 (1977) (dismissal of petition for dilatory tactics).

[27] IRC §7456(d).

[28] See, e.g., Coca-Cola Bottling Co. v. CIR, 22 BTA 686 (1931) (dismissal for lack of jurisdiction; issue raised on court's own motion); Mohawk Glove Corp. v. CIR, 2 BTA 1247 (1925) (admission of jurisdiction by IRS does not bind court); see also Musso v. CIR, 531 F.2d 772 (5th Cir. 1976) (in absence of deficiency notice, Tax Court lacks jurisdiction, even if IRS was at fault in not discharging statutory duty to issue notice).

[29] See also IRC §§6212(a) (determination of deficiency by IRS), 6213(a) (taxpayer's right to petition the Tax Court "for a redetermination of the deficiency").

[30] See Terminal Wine Co. v. CIR, 1 BTA 697 (1925) (extensive analysis); see also Heinemann Chem. Co. v. Heiner, 92 F.2d 344, 347 (3d Cir. 1937) (because notice given by IRS was not "the final notice closing the case," it did not give taxpayer an opportunity to petition Tax Court for redetermination of deficiency; hence, assessment unlawful).

deficiency so as to deprive the Tax Court of jurisdiction;[31] and taxpayers litigating deficiencies in the Tax Court sometimes pay part or all of the amount claimed after filing the petition in order to cut off liability for interest in the event of an adverse decision.

2. *Notice of deficiency.* The jurisdictional notice of deficiency is ordinarily the standard IRS "ninety-day letter," [32] so called because it gives the taxpayer ninety days to file a Tax Court petition or, if addressed to a person outside the United States, 150 days.[33] The statutory notice need not conform to any prescribed pattern; but it must give the taxpayer notice that the IRS "means to assess a deficiency tax against him and . . . give him an opportunity to have such ruling reviewed by the Tax Court before it becomes effective." [34] If the notice does not satisfy this test, the taxpayer can either (a) sit tight and sue to enjoin the IRS if it attempts to assess and collect the alleged deficiency without issuing a proper notice of deficiency [35] or (b) petition the Tax Court, in which event the petition will be dismissed because the notice is inadequate, and the IRS will again be unable to assess or collect the deficiency until it sends the taxpayer a notice qualifying as "a ticket to the Tax Court."

Letters or unusual forms sent to the taxpayer may or may not qualify as notices of deficiency.[36] A letter to the taxpayer apprising him of omitted income items or serving as a final determination of deficiency for a certain year is sufficient, but a letter that also contains a blank agreement for settlement is merely an invitation to compromise.[37]

Although a statutory notice of deficiency is entitled to a presumption of correctness,[38] the Tax Court reviews the *deficiency,* not the IRS' *reasons* for determining the deficiency. Notices, therefore, are not vitiated by vagueness,

---

[31] IRC §6213(b).

[32] Supra ¶40.1.

[33] IRC §§6212(a), 6213(a). See also IRM 4464 (contents of ninety-day letter).

[34] CIR v. Stewart, 186 F.2d 239, 241 (6th Cir. 1951).

[35] IRC §6213(a). For exceptions, see IRC §§6213(b) (mathematical or clerical errors), 6851(a)(1) (assessments terminating taxable year), and 6861 (jeopardy assessments), discussed supra ¶39.7.

[36] See Lerer v. CIR, 52 TC 358 (1969) (form letter notifying taxpayer of proposed assessment is not a notice of deficiency); Scarangella v. CIR, 60 TC 184 (1973) (notice of tax due not a deficiency notice if based on amount of tax reported on the return as filed).

[37] See Biggs v. CIR, 440 F.2d 1 (6th Cir. 1971) (letter detailing omitted income items); CIR v. Forest Glen Creamery Co., 98 F.2d 968 (7th Cir. 1938), cert. denied, 306 US 639 (1939) (letter serving as final determination); Ventura Consol. Oil Fields v. Rogan, 86 F.2d 149 (9th Cir. 1936), cert. denied, 300 US 672 (1937) (letter plus blank agreement); see also Terminal Wine Co. v. CIR, supra note 30 (discussion of what constitutes a final determination).

[38] See, e.g., Albino v. CIR, 273 F.2d 450 (2d Cir. 1960), and cases there cited. For exceptions to the presumption of correctness, see O'Connor v. CIR, 412 TC 394 (1979) (arbitrary determination), and cases there cited.

inconsistencies, or the absence of explanations for the adjustments;[39] and they do not restrict the grounds or arguments that can be adduced by the IRS in supporting the deficiency when the case is tried.[40]

3. *Timely petition.* The third jurisdictional requirement is the timely filing of a petition for redetermination of the deficiency by the Tax Court. The time prescribed by IRC §6213(a) is ninety days after the statutory notice of deficiency is mailed or, if the notice is addressed to a person outside the United States, 150 days.[41] If the last day of the period is Saturday, Sunday, or a legal holiday in the District of Columbia, the time is extended to the next following business day.

The major issues involved in determining whether a petition is timely concern (1) the date on which the period begins to run, (2) the date the petition was filed, and (3) the status of informal documents purporting to be petitions.[42]

a. *Commencement of ninety-day or 150-day period.* Section 6212(a) authorizes the IRS to send the statutory notice of deficiency to the taxpayer by certified or registered mail;[43] and IRC §6212(b) provides that in the absence of notice to the IRS of a fiduciary relationship, the notice is sufficient if mailed to the taxpayer's "last known address," a phrase construed to mean the address to which the IRS reasonably believes the taxpayer wants mail to be sent.[44] If this address is used, the notice starts the ninety-day or 150-day period running, even if it is not actually received.[45] If the deficiency concerns a joint

---

[39] See Bair v. CIR, 16 TC 90, 98 (1951), aff'd, 199 F.2d 589 (2d Cir. 1952) (Tax Court redetermines deficiencies, not IRS reasons), and cases there cited.

[40] Standard Oil Co. v. CIR, 43 BTA 973 (1941), aff'd, 129 F.2d 363 (7th Cir.), cert. denied, 317 US 688 (1942). For procedures to cure vague notices, see Tax Ct. R. 51(a), 70, 90; Allensworth's Est. v. CIR, 66 TC 33 (1976) (extensive analysis).

[41] Treas. Regs. §301.6213-1; see also Krueger's Est. v. CIR, 33 TC 667 (1960) (temporary absence from United States sufficient to invoke 150-day period); Cowan v. CIR, 54 TC 647 (1970) (trip to Mexico for afternoon does not invoke 150-day period).

[42] See also Rosenberg's Est. v. CIR, 73 TC 1014 (1980) (time not extended by former attorney's misrepresentation that a petition was properly filed; court lacks authority to extend time).

[43] For the effect of a notice sent by ordinary mail, compare Boren v. Riddell, 241 F.2d 670 (9th Cir. 1957) (effective if received), with Williams v. CIR, 13 TC 257 (1949) (contra).

[44] IRC §6212(b); Treas. Regs. §301.6212-1(b); see Delman v. CIR, 384 F.2d 929 (3d Cir. 1967), cert. denied, 390 US 952 (1968) (extensive discussion). For other cases in this area, see supra ¶40.1, notes 57-61.

[45] Cataldo v. CIR, 60 TC 522 (1973), aff'd per curiam, 499 F.2d 550 (2d Cir. 1974); but see Kennedy v. US, 403 F.Supp. 619 (W.D. Mich. 1975), aff'd by order, 556 F.2d 581 (6th Cir. 1977) (notice became effective only when received; IRS must use reasonable care and diligence in ascertaining correct address). If the notice is improperly addressed, the 90-day period begins to run only if the notice is received by the taxpayer without prejudicial delay. See Robinson v. CIR, 57 TC 735 (1972) (timely petition demonstrated taxpayer was not prejudiced by incorrect address); Kennedy v. US, 403

return, a single joint notice is permitted by IRC §6212(b)(2) unless the IRS is notified by one or both of the spouses that they have established separate residences, in which event a duplicate original of the joint notice is to be sent by certified or registered mail to each spouse at his or her last known address.[46]

b. *Filing date.* A properly addressed petition sent by mail with postage prepaid is "filed" with the Tax Court within the meaning of IRC §6213(a) if it is *postmarked* within the prescribed period *and* is actually *received,* albeit after the time expires.[47] Disputes in applying this timely-mailed, timely-filed principle—which does not apply to dates stamped by private postal meters—can be avoided by the use of registered or certified mail, since the date of registration or of the certified mail receipt is deemed to be the postmark date, and registration or certification is prima facie evidence of delivery to the addressee.[48]

If both the proper filing of the petition and proper commencement of the ninety or 150-day period are at issue, the latter issue should be considered first.[49] Under this priority principle, a decision that the notice of deficiency was invalid will ordinarily prevent the IRS from assessing and collecting the alleged deficiency without sending the taxpayer a proper notice of deficiency, thus enabling the taxpayer to litigate the substantive issue in the Tax Court.

c. *Petition.* The Tax Court Rules prescribe the form and content of petitions and contain model forms;[50] but in its discretion the court—in its own words—has "leaned over backward" to take jurisdiction by virtue of documents intended as petitions, despite departures from the prescribed form and content, "whenever the taxpayer has made a conscientious effort to comply with the Rules and intends the document he files to be a petition . . . if it is reasonable to accept the document as a petition."[51]

F.Supp. 619 (W.D. Mich. 1975), aff'd by order, 556 F.2d 581 (6th Cir. 1977) (improperly addressed notice deemed mailed on date received); Lifter v. CIR, 59 TC 818 (1973) (extensive discussion of wrong-address cases).

[46] See Camous v. CIR, 67 TC 721 (1977) (wife's vague reference to separation in phone conversation with IRS agent not assigned to case is not sufficient notice).

[47] IRC §§7502(a), 7502(b); Sylvan v. CIR, 65 TC 548 (1975) (Nonacq.) (timely-mailing, timely-filing principle embraces envelopes without postmarks if evidence establishes timely mailing; extensive analysis; five judges dissenting).

[48] See IRC §7502(c); see also Treas. Regs. §§301.7502-1(c)(2), 301.7502-1(d); Smetanka v. CIR, 74 TC 715 (1980) (use of wrong ZIP code). For private meters, see Treas. Regs. §301.7502-1(c)(1)(iii)(*b*).

[49] Shelton v. CIR, 63 TC 193 (1974) (notice of deficiency improperly addressed).

[50] For regular cases, see Tax Ct. R. 30-34 and Form 1; for small tax cases, see Tax Ct. R. 170-179 and Form 2.

[51] Castaldo v. CIR, 63 TC 285, 287 (1974) (laymen testified he removed and mailed a form included with statutory notice of deficiency—possibly Form 870?—and,

3. Redetermination of Deficiencies. In deficiency cases, the Tax Court has jurisdiction "to redetermine the correct amount of the deficiency even if the amount so redetermined is greater than the amount of the deficiency" as determined by the IRS.[52] In a 1966 case, for example, a proposed deficiency of less than $1,200 increased to more than $300,000 when the IRS attorneys in preparing for trial "found themselves swept along on a voyage of discovery which in its own way came to rival Carter's exploration of the tomb of Tutankhamen" as "tax treasures" were "unearthed from beneath an unobtrusive surface."[53]

Under Tax Court Rule 142, however, the IRS has the burden of proof with respect to new issues and increased deficiencies. Moreover, if these matters are not pleaded in the IRS' answer to the taxpayer's petition, the right to raise them at a later time is discretionary with the court, whose rules provide (1) that new issues can be tried by express or implied consent of the parties and (2) that in the absence of consent, the pertinent evidence may be received, in which event the pleadings can be amended to conform to the proof "when justice so requires and the objecting party fails to satisfy the Court that the admission of such evidence would prejudice him in maintaining his position on the merits." [54]

The Tax Court has so-called ancillary jurisdiction to determine that there was an overpayment rather than a deficiency, but only for taxes and years as to which the IRS determined a deficiency.[55]

In redetermining a deficiency, the Tax Court is required by IRC §6214(b) to "consider such facts with relation to the taxes for other years . . . as may be necessary correctly to redetermine the amount of such deficiency." This may require a determination of the way a transaction was or should have been reported on the taxpayer's return for a nondeficiency year, even if corrections for that year are barred by the statute of limitations, because of its impact on the proper treatment of the item in the deficiency year. If there was an error on the return or a deficiency or overpayment for a nondeficiency year, however, the Tax Court has no jurisdiction to determine that the tax for the nondeficiency year was overpaid or underpaid.[56] If the statute of limita-

---

on getting it back from Tax Court with blank petition form, filled out latter; held, original document intended as petition; subsequently filed proper form was amended petition relating back to filing date of original document).

[52] IRC §6214(a); but see IRC §7463 ($5,000 limit in small tax cases).

[53] Ferguson v. CIR, 47 TC 11, 25 (1966).

[54] Tax Ct. R. 41(b).

[55] See IRC §6512(b)(1); see also IRC §6512(a) (exclusive jurisdiction in Tax Court). For the amount eligible for credit or refund pursuant to a Tax Court finding of an overpayment, see IRC §6512(b)(2); see generally Wheeler's Est. v. CIR, ¶79,321 P-H Memo TC (1979) (analysis of IRC §6512(b)(2)).

[56] IRC §6214(b); Heyl v. CIR, 34 BTA 223 (1936).

tions has not run on the nondeficiency year, the error can be corrected; but a separate proceeding, based on a determination of a deficiency or a refund claim, is necessary. If, however, the normal statutory period has expired but the Tax Court's determination for the deficiency year is inconsistent with a position taken by the taxpayer or the IRS in the nondeficiency year, the inconsistency may mitigate the statute of limitations under the technical rules of IRC §§1311–1314, permitting a deficiency or refund claim to be asserted for the otherwise barred nondeficiency year.[57]

4. Jeopardy and Termination Assessments. As a general rule, the Commissioner is prohibited from assessing and collecting the tax during the ninety-day or 150-day period allowed for petitioning the Tax Court; and if a petition is filed, the ban on assessment and collection is extended until the court renders its decision.[58] This general rule is subject to exceptions for jeopardy and termination assessments, which are permitted if delay might result in an uncollectible claim.[59] The IRS, however, is required by IRC §§6851(b) and 6861(b) to issue a deficiency notice promptly, so that taxpayers can seek a redetermination of the deficiency in the Tax Court.

Jeopardy and termination assessments can be challenged by suit in a federal district court to determine whether the IRS had adequate grounds for utilizing the speedy assessment and collection procedure.[60]

5. Power to Issue Declaratory Judgments. The Tax Court is authorized to issue declaratory judgments relating to (1) the tax classification of certain exempt organizations,[61] (2) the qualification of certain retirement plans,[62] (3) the existence of a tax-avoidance purpose in the case of certain transfers involving foreign corporations and subject to IRC §367,[63] and (4) the exempt status of certain state and local obligations.[64] In each case, the statute requires an "actual controversy," an IRS determination or failure to act, and exhaustion of the petitioner's administrative remedies; the action must be brought by an appropriate private party, not by the IRS; and the court may make a declaration but is not explicitly required to do so. These declaratory judgment actions are ordinarily decided on the basis of the "administrative record" (i.e., the

---

[57] For IRC §§1311–1314, see supra ¶41.9.

[58] IRC §6213(a), discussed supra ¶40.1.

[59] See supra ¶39.7.

[60] IRC §7429, discussed supra ¶39.7.

[61] IRC §7428.

[62] IRC §7476.

[63] IRC §7477; see also Dittler Bros. v. CIR, 72 TC 896 (1979) (standard of review is existence of "substantial evidence" for IRS ruling—a test "falling somewhere between the arbitrary and capricious test and a simple redetermination"; divided court).

[64] IRC §7478.

documents and related papers submitted to the IRS), subject to certain exceptions for cases involving revocations of prior actions or state and local obligations, where the administrative record can be augmented by additional evidence.[65]

6. Actions to Compel or Restrain Disclosure of IRS Rulings and Other Determinations. Under IRC §6110 the Tax Court is empowered to restrain public disclosure of an IRS written determination or background file document on the petition of a person to whom the material pertains or who has a direct interest in maintaining its confidentiality.[66] The Tax Court also has, concurrently with the District Court for the District of Columbia, jurisdiction over actions to disclose (1) material that the IRS has refused to open to public inspection and (2) the identity of persons engaging in so-called third-party contacts with the IRS, if there is evidence in the record reasonably warranting an inference of impropriety or undue influence.[67]

7. Equity Jurisdiction. It is often said that the Tax Court does not have the power to decide "equitable questions" because its jurisdiction "exists only to the extent specifically enumerated by statute."[68] When the Tax Court determines that it cannot rewrite the Internal Revenue Code to reach a more equitable result,[69] however, its restraint is attributable not to a lack of equity jurisdiction but to its obligation to act like a court; the Supreme Court itself is not empowered to set aside a legislative command in order to achieve more equitable results. It is obvious, however, that the Tax Court, like any other court, weighs the consequences of competing interpretations of ambiguous provisions in deciding which alternative was probably intended by Congress. Moreover, the Tax Court yields to no other court in applying the principle that equity looks through form to substance, and it regularly uses such equitable notions as waiver and estoppel.[70]

---

[65] Tax Ct. R. 217.

[66] IRC §6110(f)(3), discussed supra ¶38.5.

[67] IRC §§6110(f)(4) (additional disclosures), 6110(d)(3) (third-party contacts); supra ¶38.5.

[68] See Feistman v. CIR, 587 F.2d 941, 943 (9th Cir. 1978) (Tax Court cannot extend time for appeal), and cases there cited; but see Trunk's Est. v. CIR, 550 F.2d 81, 85 (2d Cir. 1977) (in construing wills, Tax Court should admit testator's declarations of intent "in carrying out its equitable obligation to search out the truth"; proceedings in Tax Court "are equitable in nature").

[69] See, e.g., Tallon v. CIR, ¶79,423 P-H Memo TC (1979) (taxpayer's mistake does not justify relief from penalty imposed by Congress on both inadvertent and deliberate excessive contributions to individual retirement accounts; Tax Court "has no authority to order such equitable relief as that requested by the petitioners").

[70] For equitable estoppel in the Tax Court, see, e.g., Graff v. CIR, 74 TC 743 (1980) (extensive discussion of criteria; held, not satisfied by facts).

Turning to points of *genuine* divergence between the Tax Court and the federal district courts, the only substantive distinction in the exercise of so-called equitable jurisdiction appears to involve the doctrine of equitable recoupment. The Tax Court—unlike the federal district courts—does not allow a taxpayer to set off an overpayment made in a year not before the court against an underpayment in a year that is before the court.[71]

¶43.3 TAX COURT PLEADINGS AND PRETRIAL PROCEDURES

1. Introductory. Pleadings in the Tax Court consist of the taxpayer's petition, the IRS' answer, and, when required by the rules, a reply.[72] As is true of all litigation, the purpose of the pleadings is to give the parties and the court "fair notice of the matters in controversy and the basis for their respective positions." [73] The parties are informed by the court's rules that every averment "shall be simple, concise, and direct"; that "technical forms" are not required; and that pleadings are to be construed "to do substantial justice." [74] Claims and defenses may be stated alternatively or hypothetically, regardless of consistency.[75] The original of every pleading must be signed by the party or his counsel; although vertification is not required, the signature is a certification that the person signing has read the petition, that to the best of his knowledge, information, or belief there is good ground to support it, and that it is not frivolous or interposed for delay.[76]

2. Petition. The rules provide that the petition shall set out jurisdictional allegations, the amounts and years involved, assignments of every error that the petitioner claims the IRS committed in determining the deficiency (including issues as to which the IRS has the burden of proof), the facts on which the taxpayer relies (except for issues on which the IRS has the burden of proof), and a prayer for relief.[77]

---

[71] Supra ¶41.10. See CIR v. Gooch Milling & Elevator Co., 320 US 418 (1943) (Board of Tax Appeals could not apply the doctrine of equitable recoupment); Taylor v. CIR, 258 F.2d 89 (2d Cir. 1958) (when reviewing Tax Court decisions, court of appeals cannot apply recoupment where Tax Court could not do so).

[72] Tax Ct. R. 30, 37(b).

[73] Tax Ct. R. 31(a).

[74] Tax Ct. R. 31(b), 31(d).

[75] Tax Ct. R. 31(c).

[76] Tax Ct. R. 23(a)(3), 33.

[77] Tax Ct. R. 34(b). If error is not assigned as to an issue, it is deemed conceded, even if the IRS has the burden of proof. See Tax Ct. R. 34(b)(4).

3. Answer. The IRS' answer, due sixty days from the service of the petition, is required to "advise the petitioner and the Court fully of the nature of the defense" and to contain specific admissions or denials of each material allegation in the petition.[78] If the IRS lacks knowledge or information sufficient to form a belief as to the truth of an allegation, a statement to this effect constitutes a denial.[79] In addition, the IRS must state every ground, and the facts supporting it, on which it has the burden of proof, including (1) affirmative defenses, such as inapplicability of the statute of limitations, res judicata, estoppel, and waiver; (2) increases in the deficiency; (3) new matters; and (4) issues that must be proved by the IRS pursuant to statute, such as fraud and transferee liability.[80]

4. Reply. The taxpayer is required to reply (within forty-five days from the service of the answer) only if the answer contains "material allegations . . . on which the Commissioner has the burden of proof." [81] If filed, a reply is deemed to admit every allegation not specifically denied. If a reply is not filed when required, however, the affirmative allegations in the answer are deemed denied unless the IRS moves for an order that specified allegations be deemed admitted; the order may be granted unless the required reply is filed on or before the date of the hearing on the motion.[82]

5. Motions. The Tax Court Rules provide for a wide array of motions whose functions and due dates are prescribed separately for each category.[83] The court can dispose of motions summarily, or it can direct the opposing party to file a written response or order a hearing. Hearings on motions are normally held in Washington, D.C., but may be held at another location at the convenience of the parties and the court.[84]

6. Stipulations. Rule 91(a) requires the parties "to stipulate, to the fullest extent to which complete or qualified agreement can or fairly should be

---

[78] Tax Ct. R. 36(a), 36(b).

[79] Tax Ct. R. 36(b).

[80] See Tax Ct. R. 36(b), 39 (affirmative defenses), 142 (IRS burden of proof). For the scope of "new matter," see La Fargue v. CIR, 73 TC 40, 52 n.9 (1979), and cases there cited; Brown v. CIR, ¶79,443 P-H Memo TC (1979) ("amorphous" distinction between new reasons and new issues subordinated to determination of surprise or substantial detriment).

[81] Tax Ct. R. 37(a), 37(b).

[82] Tax Ct. R. 37(e).

[83] Tax Ct. R. 50-55; for circumstances warranting summary judgment in whole or in part, see Waxler v. CIR, ¶79,425 P-H Memo TC (1979).

[84] See Tax Ct. R. 50(b).

reached, all matters not privileged which are relevant to the pending case, regardless of whether such matters involve fact or opinion or the application of law to fact." Objections based on materiality or relevance should be noted, but they do not justify a refusal to stipulate.[85] Rule 91(e) provides that stipulations constitute "conclusive" admissions by the parties that cannot be qualified, changed, or contradicted, except "where justice requires." [86] The stipulation process is the "mainstay" and "bedrock" of Tax Court practice, and it must be taken seriously.[87] The Tax Court's procedures for admissions, discovery and pretrial conferences are viewed as backstops rather than substitutes for the stipulation process.[88]

7. Discovery. The Tax Court Rules provide for pretrial interrogatories and for the production of documents and things.[89] These devices encompass any matter that is not privileged, regardless of the burden of proof and even if the information is inadmissible, if the information requested appears reasonably calculated to lead to the discovery of admissible evidence.[90]

Depositions are allowed by Rule 74 for discovery purposes by consent of all parties to the case; otherwise, pretrial depositions are authorized only to perpetuate evidence where there is a substantial risk that the testimony or matter sought will not be available at the trial.[91] The Tax Court's discovery rules do not provide for the discovery of information in the possession of prospective witnesses and other third persons, except for transferees.

¶43.4 TAX COURT TRIAL PRACTICE

Pursuant to IRC §7453, Tax Court proceedings are conducted in accordance with the rules of evidence applicable to trials without jury in the District

---

[85] For procedure in case of noncompliance by one party, which can result in an order providing that particular matters are deemed to be stipulated, see Tax Ct. R. 91(f); see also Allen v. CIR, ¶79,068 P-H Memo TC (1979) (failure to comply with orders regarding stipulations resulted in dismissal for failure to prosecute case properly).

[86] See Jasionowski v. CIR, 66 TC 312, 318 (1976) (stipulations not "lightly disregarded," but court is not bound by stipulated facts that are "clearly contrary to facts disclosed by the record"), and cases there cited.

[87] Tax Ct. R. 91, explanatory note, 60 TC 1117 (1973) ("mainstay"); Branerton Corp. v. CIR, 61 TC 691, 692 (1974) ("bedrock").

[88] See Tax Ct. R. 90(a) (admissions), 110(d) (pretrial conferences).

[89] See Tax Ct. R. 71 (interrogatories), 72 (production of documents and things).

[90] Tax Ct. R. 70(b).

[91] Tax Ct. R. 81(a); see also Gauthier v. CIR, 62 TC 245 (1974) (pretrial discovery depositions "incompatible" with court's practice).

Court for the District of Columbia.[92] The court adheres to a policy of liberal admission of evidence.[93]

The petitioner has the burden of going forward with the evidence and of persuading the court that it rises to the requisite level. In addition, the determination of a deficiency is accorded a presumption of correctness.[94] The weight of authority views the presumption as a procedural device requiring the taxpayer to offer enough evidence to support a finding contrary to the IRS' determination—at which point the taxpayer must still carry the ultimate burden of persuasion, but the IRS can no longer derive any benefit from the presumption.[95] In practice, however, the burden and the presumption tend to coalesce, and it is not clear that the latter adds anything to the former.[96] In any event, the taxpayer is not required to establish the correct amount due, but only the facts on the basis of which the Tax Court can redetermine the deficiency.[97]

The Code and the Tax Court Rules shift the burden of proof to the IRS in certain cases (e.g., transferee liability and fraud under the Code), new matters, increases in deficiencies, and affirmative defenses pleaded in the answer under the Tax Court Rules.[98]

Following the trial or the submission of a case on stipulated facts, briefs are filed by the parties; oral argument can be ordered by the court but is not customary.[99] If the deficiency is rejected or upheld in its entirety, decision is entered for the taxpayer or the IRS, as the case may be; but if the findings and opinion result in an increased or decreased deficiency or an overpayment, the decision is withheld pending a computation under Rule 155. If the parties agree on the amount, it is in effect ratified by the decision. If not, either party may submit a computation, to which the other party responds and the court then determines the correct amount.

¶43.5 SMALL CASES IN TAX COURT

Section 7463 provides a statutory foundation for a simplified method of trying small tax cases in the Tax Court, which applies only if (1) neither the

---

[92] See generally Tax Ct. R. 140–151.

[93] See Tax Ct. R. 143 (evidence); Karme v. CIR, 73 TC 1163 (1980) (application of Federal Rules of Evidence).

[94] See, e.g., Welch v. Helvering, 290 US 111 (1933).

[95] See Rockwell v. CIR, 512 F.2d 882 (9th Cir.), cert. denied, 423 US 1015 (1975); Llorente v. CIR, 74 TC 260 (1980) (Acq.) (extensive discussion).

[96] Starr v. CIR, ¶76,289 P-H Memo TC (1976).

[97] Helvering v. Taylor, 293 US 507 (1935).

[98] IRC §§6902(a) (status as transferee), 7454(a) (fraud); Tax Ct. R. 142(a).

[99] Tax Ct. R. 151.

amount of the deficiency placed in dispute nor any claimed overpayment exceeds $5,000 for any one taxable year, (2) the taxpayer requests that the simplified procedure be followed, and (3) the court concurs in the request. Proceedings under IRC §7463 are to be "conducted as informally as possible consistent with orderly procedure." [100] The decision is not reviewable by any other court and is not to be treated as a precedent in any other case.[101] The decision is limited to amounts placed in dispute within the $5,000 limit, plus amounts conceded by the parties.[102]

At any time before the decision in a small tax case becomes final, either party may request that further proceedings be discontinued; and the case is then converted into a regular case if the court finds that there are reasonable grounds to believe that the disputed amounts are sufficiently in excess of the $5,000 jurisdictional limit to justify granting the request.[103]

¶43.6 APPELLATE REVIEW OF TAX COURT DECISIONS

Except for small tax cases subject to IRC §7463(b), Tax Court decisions are reviewed by the court of appeals in the same manner and to the same extent as decisions of the federal district courts in civil actions tried without a jury.[104] For taxpayers other than corporations, appellate venue is in the circuit in which the taxpayer's legal residence was located when the petition was filed.[105] For corporations, venue is in the circuit in which the corporation's principal place of business or principal office or agency was located when the petition was filed or, if none was located within any circuit, the circuit in which the IRS office with which the return was filed is located.[106] By agreement between the IRS and the taxpayer, however, decisions may be appealed to any court of appeals.[107]

The Tax Court "will follow a Court of Appeals decision which is squarely in point where appeal from the case under consideration lies to that Court of Appeals and to that court alone," even if the court would apply a different rule to cases subject to review in other circuits.[108] This principle of automatic

---

[100] Tax Ct. R. 177(b). Simplified pleadings, without briefs (unless permitted by the court) and oral arguments, are employed. See generally Tax Ct. R. 170–179.

[101] IRC §7463(b); see Kahle v. CIR, 566 F.2d 581 (6th Cir. 1977) (no jurisdiction to review "small tax case").

[102] IRC §7463(c).

[103] IRC §7463(d).

[104] IRC §7482(a).

[105] IRC §7482(b)(1)(A).

[106] IRC §7482(b)(1)(B).

[107] IRC §7482(b)(2).

[108] Golsen v. CIR, 54 TC 742, 757 (1970), aff'd without discussion of this issue, 445 F.2d 985 (10th Cir.), cert. denied, 404 US 940 (1971).

deference does not apply, however, if the Tax Court believes that the appellate decision in question has been outmoded by intervening judicial developments or is not "squarely in point." [109]

¶43.7 REFUND SUITS IN FEDERAL DISTRICT COURTS AND CLAIMS COURT

Taxpayers seeking refunds of overpayments must ordinarily sue in either the federal district court or the Claims Court.[110] (Bankruptcy courts can determine the debtor's tax liability, but lack authority to order the IRS to make a refund.) [111] The principal features of tax litigation conducted in the federal district courts and the Claims Court are:

1. Full Payment of Tax. The federal district courts and the Claims Court have concurrent jurisdiction of civil actions against the United States for "the recovery of any internal-revenue tax alleged to have been erroneously or illegally assessed or collected." [112] Full payment of the tax is required before a refund action can be brought.[113] As a result, at times it is necessary to decide whether a taxpayer's remittance of funds to the IRS constituted a payment of taxes or only a deposit against an anticipated assessment.[114] If an assessment includes interest as well as the underlying tax, the only part that must be paid before suing for a refund is the tax itself;[115] but the government can then counterclaim for the interest or proceed to collect it in an independent proceeding.

2. Refund Claim. Section 7422(a) provides that a judicial proceeding for the recovery of income taxes cannot be maintained unless a claim for refund or credit has been duly filed with the IRS. This statutory requirement coalesces

---

[109] See Kent v. CIR, 61 TC 133 (1973).

[110] For the Tax Court's "ancillary" refund jurisdiction, see supra ¶43.2.

[111] See In re Lewis, 40 AFTR2d 5135 (D.Colo. 1977) (not officially reported).

[112] 28 USC §1346(a)(1). For venue in district court suits, see 28 USC §§1402(a), 1404.

[113] Flora v. US, 362 US 145 (1960) (decision on reargument); for the Court's original opinion, see Flora v. US, 357 US 63 (1958). In the case of certain penalties, the taxpayer is required only to pay 15 percent of the assessment in order to file a claim for refund, institute suit in district court, and stay collection of the remainder of the penalty. See IRC §6703 (penalties under IRC §§6700, abusive tax shelters, 6701, aiding and abetting an understatement, and 6702, frivolous tax return).

[114] For this distinction, which also arises in determining when the statute of limitations on filing refund claims commences to run, see Rosenman v. US, 323 US 658 (1945); supra ¶40.3, text at note 124.

[115] Kell-Strom Tool Co. v. US, 205 F.Supp. 190 (D.Conn. 1962).

with the IRS' administrative rules requiring a claim as a prerequisite to allowance of a refund or credit;[116] thus, the same claim serves double duty. The claim must ordinarily be filed within the period prescribed by IRC §6511(a) unless the normal period is extended by agreement between the taxpayer and the IRS;[117] and IRC §7422(a) limits the taxpayer to the grounds set out in the refund claim, unless it is amended before the statutory period for filing claims expires or the government waives the defect.[118]

3. Timely Filing of Refund Action. A refund action cannot be brought until six months after the claim is filed with the IRS unless the IRS acts on it within this waiting period, in which event the suit can be brought immediately after the IRS' decision is rendered.[119] (A premature suit is not fatal, however, since it will be dismissed without prejudice to a timely second action.) Section 6532(a) forbids the commencement of a judicial proceeding more than two years after the date when a notice of disallowance of the claim is mailed by certified or registered mail to the taxpayer. Each of these elements—"notice of disallowance," the use of certified or registered mail, and notice "to the taxpayer"—can raise crucial interpretative problems, since the commencement of a suit within the prescribed period is a jurisdictional matter.[120]

4. Amount of Recovery. Section 6511(b) limits refunds and credits to the taxes paid within prescribed periods of time before the claim was filed.[121] These limits also apply to suits; thus, a taxpayer cannot recover a larger amount by suit than could have been allowed administratively by the IRS.

Once jurisdiction over a case is vested in a federal district court or the Claims Court, the IRS can set up any errors in the taxpayer's favor as counter-

---

[116] Statement of Procedural Rules §601.105(e). For the Statement of Procedural Rules, see 26 CFR Pt. 601.

[117] See supra ¶40.3; see also Vishnevsky v. US, 581 F.2d 1249 (7th Cir. 1978) (IRS cannot waive failure to file refund claim; but mandamus relief granted where IRS informed taxpayer within statutory period that it would issue certificate of overassessment, since remaining action was ministerial rather than discretionary).

[118] See Treas. Regs. §301.6402-2(b)(1); Tucker v. Alexander, 275 US 228 (1927) (waiver).

[119] IRC §6532(a)(1). For waiver of this defense if it is not raised by the government, see Fed. R. Civ. P. 12(h); see also IRC §6532(a)(3); Treas. Regs. §301.6532-1(c) (waiver of notice of disallowance).

[120] See, e.g., Rev. Rul. 56-381, 1956-2 CB 953 (notice by regular mail not adequate); Daniel v. US, 454 F.2d 1166 (6th Cir.), cert. denied, 409 US 843 (1972) (method of establishing mailing of notice). The parties can agree to an extension of time for filing a suit, if the agreement is executed before time expires; see IRC §6532(a)(2); Treas. Regs. §301.6532-1(b); Rev. Rul. 71-57, 1971-1 CB 405 (no authority for execution of extension agreement after two-year statutory period expires).

[121] IRC §§6511(b) and 6511(c), discussed supra ¶40.3.

claims, even if the issue was not raised previously, including liabilities growing out of nontax transactions between the taxpayer and the government.[122] If, however, the time for assessing a deficiency has run when the complaint is filed, a tax counterclaim can be used only as an offset against the taxpayer's claim, and not as the basis for a money judgment against the taxpayer.[123]

5. Overlapping Jurisdiction. Once a timely Tax Court petition has been filed, the taxpayer cannot shift the litigation to a federal district court or the Claims Court by paying the deficiency and suing for a refund. Moreover, the Tax Court has primary jurisdiction over deficiency cases, even if the taxpayer sues for a refund and the IRS determines a deficiency for the same taxable period while the refund case is pending, since IRC §7422(e) stays the proceedings in the refund suit for the period normally allowed for the filing of petitions in the Tax Court and for sixty days thereafter.[124]

6. Appeals. Decisions of the federal district courts can be appealed to the courts of appeals. Before 1982, however, the Court of Claims was subject only to the discretionary certiorari jurisdiction of the Supreme Court. For this reason, a favorable precedent in the Court of Claims enabled all subsequent taxpayers, by routing their cases to that court, to prevent a conflict among the circuits—ordinarily the prerequisite to Supreme Court review—from arising.[125] By contrast, a pro-taxpayer decision in one court of appeals protected only the taxpayers in its circuit.

7. Refund Suits Against Collectors of Internal Revenue. Before 1966, a suit for refund could be brought against the Collector of Internal Revenue

---

[122] See 31 USC §227; Panhandle E. Pipe Line Co. v. US, 408 F.2d 690 (Ct. Cl. 1969) (setoff must be pleaded as affirmative defense or counterclaim). For the extent to which the doctrines of recoupment and equitable estoppel allow the government to set off a deficiency barred by the statute of limitations as a defense in a refund action, see supra ¶41.10.

[123] See Lewis v. Reynolds, 284 US 281 (1932).

[124] See Russell v. US, 592 F.2d 1069 (9th Cir.), cert. denied, 444 US 946 (1979) (district court lost jurisdiction when taxpayer petitioned Tax Court, notwithstanding latter court's failure to resolve an issue within its jurisdiction); Peters v. US, 618 F.2d 125 (Ct. Cl. 1979) (Claims Court lost jurisdiction of refund claim to Tax Court, although latter held that statute of limitations barred assessment of deficiency, since it could have determined an overpayment).

[125] For an ingenious but unsuccessful attempt by the government to break out of this straitjacket, see US v. Russell Mfg. Co., 349 F.2d 13 (2d Cir. 1965) (suit under IRC §7405(b) to recover "erroneous" refund, which was allowed by IRS to avoid unfavorable Claims Court precedent). For 1982 changes in the structure of the Claims Court and appellate review of its decisions, see Federal Court Improvement Act of 1982, P.L. 97–164, 96 Stat. 25.

(predecessor of the district director) who collected the tax in controversy. In 1966 Congress abolished suits against the collector. If such a suit is brought—old customs die hard—the United States is substituted as the party defendant, and the case is transferred to the district where it should have been brought against the United States.[126]

¶43.8 RES JUDICATA AND COLLATERAL ESTOPPEL

When a taxpayer's income tax liability is litigated, a final judgment on the merits settles the amount of the liability for the entire taxable year, not merely the validity of the particular claims put in issue.[127] But this principle, which applies the pervasive doctrine of res judicata to income tax litigation,[128] does not prevent a litigated year from being reopened to take account of net operating loss carrybacks and similar items arising after the judgment, since they could not have been litigated in the original lawsuit.[129] Moreover, IRC §§1311–1314 explicitly authorize corrective adjustments for years otherwise closed by "any law or rule of law"—a phrase encompassing the barrier of res judicata—in specified circumstances, usually involving a reversal of position by one of the parties.[130] If a statutory provision is amended retroactively, application of the change to taxable years otherwise closed by the statute of limitations or the principles of res judicata depends on the intent manifested by Congress when enacting the new rules.[131]

A judgment concerning the taxpayer's liability for one taxable year does not, of course, settle his or her liability for another taxable year; but it is conclusive as to all matters *actually* litigated and decided. As stated by the Supreme Court in *CIR v. Sunnen,* the leading case in this area, "the prior judgment acts as a collateral estoppel only as to those matters in the second proceeding which were actually presented and determined in the first suit." [132] In order for the doctrine to be applied, it must be shown that the issue was actually presented and decided on the merits; the entry of a judgment to formalize a stipulation or compromise by the parties is insufficient.[133]

---

[126] See IRC §7422(f).

[127] CIR v. Sunnen, 333 US 591 (1948).

[128] Blackmon & Assocs. v. US, 409 F.Supp. 1264 (N.D. Tex. 1976); see also Moyer v. Mathas, 458 F.2d 431 (5th Cir. 1972) (res judicata applies to default judgment); US v. Zimmerman, 478 F.2d 59 (7th Cir. 1973) (same as to judgment entered by consent).

[129] Blackmon & Assocs. v. US, supra note 128 (carryback of foreign tax credit); see also IRC §6212(c) (after-discovered fraud).

[130] See supra ¶41.9.

[131] See US v. Zimmerman, supra note 128, and cases there cited.

[132] CIR v. Sunnen, supra note 127, at 598.

[133] US v. International Bldg. Co., 345 US 502 (1953) (collateral estoppel not

Collateral estoppel is frequently applied to prevent litigation of the same issue year after year,[134] and it is also used to prevent a second duel over the same issue for the same taxable year; for example, a taxpayer who is convicted of tax evasion for a particular year cannot relitigate the issue of fraud when contesting a civil fraud penalty for the same year.[135]

Collateral estoppel does not apply, however, if there is an intervening significant change in the facts on which the earlier decision rests.[136] On the other hand, the discovery of "additional or different evidence of historically past events and actions, which took place prior to the first decision and which are static in nature, will not prevent the operation of collateral estoppel." [137]

In *CIR v. Sunnen* the Supreme Court held that a change in the "legal atmosphere" by virtue of intervening decisions in different but comparable cases could render collateral estoppel inapplicable.[138] In *Sunnen,* the change was attributable to an important series of Supreme Court decisions; but the doctrine of collateral estoppel can also be superseded by intervening decisions of the lower federal courts, statutory changes, and modified rules and regulations, provided they depart significantly from the premises on which the earlier decision was based.[139] The issue, however, is not whether the prior decision was correct in the light of the legal climate prevailing *when it was decided,* but whether the relevant legal principles, statutes, or regulations were "vitally altered" *thereafter.* [140]

When res judicata or collateral estoppel applies to the taxpayer, persons in privity with the taxpayer, such as the taxpayer's executor and transferees, are also barred from relitigating the issue.[141] The concept of "privity," how-

---

applicable to judgment representing pro forma judicial acceptance of compromise between parties).

[134] See, e.g., Phipps v. CIR, 515 F.2d 1099 (Ct. Cl. 1975) (interpretation of partnership agreement); Driscoll v. CIR, ¶72,105 P-H Memo TC (1972) (validity of family partnership); Lea, Inc. v. CIR, 69 TC 762 (1978) (allocation of payments between covenant not to compete and goodwill); Bank of America v. US, 552 F.2d 876 (9th Cir. 1977) (classification of so-called trust as association taxable as corporation).

[135] See supra ¶42.3; see also Clough v. CIR, ¶76,155 P-H Memo TC (1976) (taxpayer convicted of attempting to evade taxes cannot raise issue of unconstitutional search and seizure in civil tax case, since issue was decided in criminal proceeding).

[136] Beirne v. CIR, 61 TC 268 (1973) (collateral estoppel not applicable); Maguire's Est. v. CIR, 50 TC 130 (1968) (whether corporation is engaged in process of liquidating depends on facts that change from year to year; collateral estoppel not applicable).

[137] Lea, Inc. v. CIR, supra note 134, at 769 (no change in facts).

[138] CIR v. Sunnen, supra note 127, at 599–600.

[139] See, e.g., Mandel v. CIR, 229 F.2d 382 (7th Cir. 1956) (intervening decision of federal court of appeals); Stanback v. CIR, 271 F.2d 514 (4th Cir. 1959) (IRS regulations); National Bank of Commerce of Seattle v. CIR, 12 TC 717 (1949) (enactment of new Code provision).

[140] Lea, Inc. v. CIR, supra note 134, at 766–767 (no change in legal atmosphere); see generally Lynch v. CIR, 216 F.2d 574 (7th Cir. 1954) (extensive discussion).

[141] See, e.g., Krueger v. CIR, 48 TC 824 (1967) (taxpayer's transferee); Hill's Est.

ever, is derived from the general law of judgments rather than from the tax law, and it is much more restrictive than the "related taxpayer" concept that is employed for various purposes by the Internal Revenue Code.[142]

¶43.9 INJUNCTIONS, DECLARATORY JUDGMENTS, AND STANDING TO SUE

1. Introductory. To prevent taxpayers from sidestepping the administrative procedures, statutes of limitations, and other elaborately fashioned rules that govern the standard judicial proceedings for challenging income tax liabilities, IRC §7421(a) prohibits the maintenance of any suit in any court by any person for the purpose of restraining the assessment or collection of any tax. In addition, the Declaratory Judgment Act excludes controversies "with respect to Federal taxes" from its coverage. These barriers are augmented by the general principles determining standing to sue in federal courts, which ordinarily prevent the validity of tax assessments, refund claims, and rulings from being litigated by anyone other than the taxpayer to whom they pertain. Finally, injunctive proceedings are also subject to an entire panoply of legal principles, developed in nonaligned litigation, such as sovereign immunity, failure to satisfy jurisdictional requirements, and presence of an adequate remedy at law, that in particular cases may require the suit to be dismissed.[143]

2. The Anti-Injunction Act. Section 7421(a), the so-called Anti-Injunction Act, provides that, subject to severely limited exceptions, "no suit for the purpose of restraining the assessment or collection of any tax shall be maintained in any court by any person, whether or not such person is the person

---

v. CIR, 59 TC 846 (1973) (taxpayer's executor); see generally Restatement of the Law of Judgments, §83.

[142] See, e.g., C.B.C. Super Markets, Inc. v. CIR, 54 TC 882, 893–894 (1970) (spouse of a taxpayer convicted of filing fraudulent return not estopped from denying fraudulent nature of return in civil penalty case; conviction of corporate officer and 70 percent shareholder for filing fraudulent corporate returns does not prevent corporation from relitigating the issue). For the troublesome problem of mutuality in collateral estoppel, see Divine v. CIR, 500 F.2d 1041 (2d Cir. 1974) (in determining whether taxpayer received a taxable dividend, IRS not collaterally estopped to relitigate amount of corporation's earnings and profits, despite decision in another circuit involving another shareholder of the same corporation).

[143] See Vorachek v. US, 337 F.2d 797 (8th Cir. 1964) (sovereign immunity; want of jurisdiction), and cases there cited; Lambert v. Kurtz, 41 AFTR2d 1050 (D.Colo. 1978) (not officially reported) (suit to recover damages and compel IRS to audit plaintiff's returns barred, in succession, by sovereign immunity, lack of statutory jurisdiction, and IRC §7421); Koin v. Coyle, 402 F.2d 468 (7th Cir. 1968) (adequate remedy at law).

against whom the tax was assessed"; and IRC §7421(b) imposes a similar prohibition on suits to restrain the assessment or collection of the liabilities of transferees and fiduciaries. Despite the use of the past tense in IRC §7421(a) ("against whom the tax *was* assessed"—emphasis added), it is well established that the statutory barrier applies not only to IRS conduct with respect to taxes already assessed, but also to activities that "are intended to or may culminate in the assessment of or collection of taxes." [144] Section 7421(a) has been construed to bar suits seeking to enjoin the IRS at virtually any stage of the taxation process, including investigations and the issuance and revocation of rulings.[145]

Section 7421(a), however, is not a stone wall but a filter, which permits injunctions to be issued in the special circumstances summarized below.

1. *Nontax matters.* Since IRC §7421(a) is concerned with the assessment and collection of taxes, it should not be construed to prohibit injunctions—if otherwise warranted—in cases involving the Freedom of Information Act, the Federal Tort Claims Act, or other nontax matters.[146]

2. *Extraordinary circumstances.* Injunctive relief is permissible despite IRC §7421(a) if the taxpayer can show *both* that collection of the tax as threatened by the IRS "would cause an irreparable injury, such as the ruination of the taxpayer's enterprise," *and* that "it is clear that under no circumstances could the Government ultimately prevail." [147] The twin conditions apply even if the suit concerns the taxes of persons other than the plaintiff; moreover, "the constitutional nature of a taxpayer's claim, as distinct from its probability of success, is of no consequence under the Anti-Injunction Act." [148] These principles leave a tiny chink in IRC §7421(a), particularly if

---

[144] US v. Dema, 544 F.2d 1373 (7th Cir. 1976) (no authority to enjoin IRS from inspecting books and records of Subchapter S corporation, its president, or his wife); see also Campbell v. Guetersloh, 287 F.2d 878 (5th Cir. 1961) (cannot enjoin the IRS' use of the bank deposit method of computing the taxpayer's tax liability).

[145] See US v. Dema, supra note 144; Bob Jones Univ. v. Simon, 416 US 725 (1974) (suit to enjoin revocation of tax-exempt ruling). For other applications of IRC §7421(a), see Cattle Feeders Tax Comm. v. Shulz, 504 F.2d 462 (10th Cir. 1974) (suit to restrain issuance and enforcement of revenue ruling); Scaife & Sons Co. v. Driscoll, 94 F.2d 664 (3d Cir. 1937), cert. denied, 305 US 603 (1938) (suit to compel IRS to accept amended return).

For subsequently enacted legislation permitting the revocation of tax exemption rulings to be challenged in declaratory judgment proceedings, see supra ¶43.2.

[146] See, e.g., Sangemino v. Zuckerberg, 454 F.Supp. 206 (E.D.N.Y. 1978) (suit against IRS employee for alleged negligent driving of motor vehicle on official business); Swanner v. US, 309 F. Supp. 1183 (M.D. Ala. 1970) (suit against government for injuries resulting from failure to provide protection to IRS informant).

[147] Enochs v. Williams Packing & Navigation Co., 370 US 1 (1962).

[148] Alexander v. "Americans United," Inc., 416 US 752, 759 (1974).

the plaintiff's grievance cannot be litigated in any other forum; but taxpayers are rarely successful in this area.[149]

3. *Statutory exceptions.* Section 7421(a) explicitly excepts three categories of matters: (1) violations by the IRS of the statutory procedures enabling taxpayers to petition the Tax Court for a redetermination of deficiencies or of the procedures relating to the imposition of penalties on withholding agents and preparers of tax returns;[150] (2) IRS levies on property of persons other than the taxpayer against whom the assessment runs, including creditors with rights superior to the government's;[151] and (3) jeopardy assessments subject to review under IRC §7429(b).[152]

3. Declaratory Judgments. The Declaratory Judgment Act excludes controversies "with respect to Federal taxes." [153] Although this language seems to be even more restrictive than the Anti-Injunction Act, the two provisions have been described as "coterminous." [154] In 1976 Congress lifted the ban on declaratory judgments for cases involving the exempt status of nonprofit organizations, employee benefit plans, and state and local obligations and the validity of IRS rulings on the transfer of property to foreign entities.[155]

4. Standing to Sue. Drawn from the general rules of federal jurisdiction rather than from the Internal Revenue Code, the rules governing a would-be plaintiff's standing to sue were summarized by the Supreme Court in 1970 as follows:

> (1) For the purposes of the "case or controversy" requirement of Article III of the Constitution it must appear "that the challenged action

---

[149] See Center on Corporate Responsibility, Inc. v. Shultz, 368 F.Supp. 863 (D.D.C. 1973) (IRS ordered to grant tax exemption to plaintiff on showing of political interference with IRS consideration of its application, based on ideological objections); National Restaurant Ass'n v. Simon, 411 F.Supp. 993 (D.D.C. 1976) (IRC §7421(a) does not bar suit for injunction against IRS enforcement of requirement that restaurants record and report tips to IRS, since only other method of testing validity of requirement was violation of law entailing subjection to fine; but case dismissed on merits); but see Investment Annuity, Inc. v. Blumenthal, 609 F.2d 1 (D.C. Cir. 1979) (absence of alternative forum does not violate due process if IRS action does not invade any property right protected by due process clause).

[150] See IRC §§6212(c), 6213(a), 6672(b), 6694(c); supra ¶¶40.1 (deficiency procedures), 39.6 (withholding agents), 38.3 (tax return preparers).

[151] IRC §§7426(a), 7426(b)(1); supra ¶39.7 (levy).

[152] IRC §7429(b); supra ¶39.7.

[153] 28 USC §2201.

[154] Investment Annuity, Inc. v. Blumenthal, supra note 149, and cases there cited.

[155] See supra ¶43.2.

has caused injury in fact, economic or otherwise"; and (2) as a matter of judicial self-restraint, the court must determine "whether the interest sought to be protected by the complainant is arguably within the zone of interests to be protected or regulated by the statute or constitutional guarantee in question." [156]

This two-pronged test is not a barrier to suits brought by plaintiffs concerned with their own tax liability, unless their real complaint is that tax revenues are being used for purposes to which they object;[157] but it is less easily satisfied if the suit concerns someone else's taxes. In several cases brought to enjoin the IRS from allowing tax benefits to organizations practicing racial discrimination, the courts held that members of the excluded group had standing to challenge the validity of the ruling.[158] The Supreme Court, however, later severely restricted this type of public interest litigation by holding that indigent citizens and the organizations representing them did not have standing to challenge an IRS ruling granting tax exemption to a nonprofit hospital that provided only emergency room services to indigents, in the absence of evidence that (1) the hospitals would offer a wider range of free services if they could not otherwise qualify for tax exemption and (2) the plaintiffs would receive these services if an injunction was issued as requested.[159]

In the handful of cases holding that litigants have standing to challenge favorable tax rulings issued to other persons, IRC §7421(a) has been treated as inapplicable because the purpose of the suit is to compel the IRS to assess and collect taxes, rather than to restrain assessments and collections. It should be noted, however, that an injunction forbidding the IRS to grant favorable

---

[156] Association of Data Processing Serv. Orgs. v. Camp, 397 US 150, 152–153 (1970).

[157] See, e.g., Anthony v. CIR, 66 TC 367 (1976) (taxpayer lacks standing to assert that payment of taxes would render him an accomplice in alleged U.S. war crimes in Vietnam); Dennison v. US, 31 AFTR2d 1348 (S.D.N.Y. 1973) (not officially reported) (same as to claim that Presidential Election Campaign Fund Act entails unconstitutional expenditure of public funds).

[158] Green v. Kennedy, 309 F.Supp. 1127 (D.D.C. 1970) (class action to enjoin grant of tax-exempt status to racially segregated private schools); McGlotten v. Connally, 338 F.Supp. 448 (D.D.C. 1972) (same as to racially segregated fraternal orders).

For a successful suit by a taxpayer injured by a favorable tax ruling issued to a competitor, see IBM Corp. v. US, 343 F.2d 914 (Ct. Cl. 1965), cert. denied, 382 US 1028 (1966), discussed supra ¶38.1.

[159] Simon v. Eastern Ky. Welfare Rights Org., 426 US 26 (1976); see also American Soc'y of Travel Agents, Inc. v. Blumenthal, 566 F.2d 145 (D.C. Cir. 1977), cert. denied, 435 US 947 (1978) (no "injury in fact" shown in challenge to tax-exempt status of organization offering tour package); Abortion Rights Mobilization v. Regan, 50 AFTR2d 5366 (S.D.N.Y. 1982) (complaint seeking to compel revocation of church's tax-exempt status; held, some but not all plaintiffs had standing to sue; extensive discussion).

tax treatment to a particular taxpayer in a particular instance may result in restraining the collection of taxes from other persons or from the same taxpayer in other years. As a result, a decision upholding the plaintiff's standing to sue may be coupled with a dismissal of the suit under IRC §7421(a) on the ground that it will restrain the assessment and collection of taxes over the long haul.

SELECTED BIBLIOGRAPHY

Adams, The Imperfect Claim for Refund, 22 Tax Lawyer 309 (1968).

Asimow, Standing to Challenge Lenient Tax Rules: A Statutory Solution, 57 Taxes 483 (1979).

Baker, Procedural and Jurisdictional Aspects of Seeking a Tax Refund, 10 Tulsa L.J. 362 (1975).

Calhoun, The New Tax Court: The Status and the Rules, 44 U. Cin. L. Rev. 207 (1975).

Crampton, Forum Shopping, 31 Tax Lawyer 321 (1978).

DePriest, Section 7502, Getting to the Tax Court on Time, 66 A.B.A.J. 654 (1980).

Ferguson, Jurisdictional Problems in Federal Tax Controversies, 48 Iowa L. Rev. 312 (1963).

Goldstein, *Res Judicata* and Collateral Estoppel, 54 A.B.A.J. 1131 (1968).

Hall, Problems Facing the United States Tax Court, 1979 So. Calif. Tax Inst. 1023.

Hamburger, Choice of Forum for Litigation: The United States Tax Court, 32 NYU Inst. on Fed. Tax. 1315 (1974).

Heckman, Collateral Estoppel as the Answer to Multiple Litigation Problems in Federal Tax Law: Another View of *Sunnen* and *The Evergreens,* 19 Case W. Res. L. Rev. 230 (1968).

Holub & Ziffren, The Concept of Reimbursement of Attorney Fees in Tax Cases—Its Past, Present and Future, 56 Taxes 507 (1978).

Lau, Discovery in the Tax Court: A Preliminary Analysis, 21 U.C.L.A. L. Rev. 1339 (1974).

Miller, A Court of Tax Appeals Revisited, 85 Yale L.J. 228 (1975).

Note, The Tax Injunction Act and Suits for Monetary Relief, 46 U. Chi. L. Rev. 736 (1979).

Pierce, Tax Refund Litigation in District Courts: Choice of Forum, Trial Procedures, and Settlement Techniques, 32 NYU Inst. on Fed. Tax. 1289 (1974).

Tannenwald, After Trial—How a Case Is Decided, 27 NYU Inst. on Fed. Tax. 1505 (1969).

Tannenwald, Tax Court Trials: A View From the Bench, 59 A.B.A.J. 295 (1973).

Winslow & Ash, Forum Shopping Has Distinct Advantages in Seeking Declaratory Judgments, 57 J. Tax. 112 (1979).

Table of Cases

[*References are to paragraphs (¶).*]

[*References are to paragraphs (¶).*]

B

[*References are to paragraphs (¶).*]

[*References are to paragraphs (¶).*]

[*References are to paragraphs (¶).*]

[*References are to paragraphs (¶).*]

[*References are to paragraphs (¶).*]

D

[*References are to paragraphs (¶).*]

E

[References are to paragraphs (¶).]

[*References are to paragraphs (¶).*]

G

[*References are to paragraphs (¶).*]

H

[*References are to paragraphs (¶).*]

[*References are to paragraphs (¶).*]

I

[*References are to paragraphs (¶).*]

[*References are to paragraphs (¶).*]

L

[*References are to paragraphs (¶).*]

[*References are to paragraphs (¶).*]

[*References are to paragraphs (¶).*]

[*References are to paragraphs (¶).*]

N

O

[*References are to paragraphs (¶).*]

[*References are to paragraphs (¶).*]

Q

R

[*References are to paragraphs (¶).*]

S

[*References are to paragraphs (¶).*]

[*References are to paragraphs (¶).*]

[*References are to paragraphs (¶).*]

T

[*References are to paragraphs (¶).*]

[*References are to paragraphs (¶).*]

[*References are to paragraphs (¶).*]

Y

Z

Table of I.R.C. Sections

[*References are to paragraphs (¶).*]

[*References are to paragraphs (¶).*]

TABLE OF I.R.C. SECTIONS

[References are to paragraphs (¶).]

[*References are to paragraphs (¶).*]

[*References are to paragraphs (¶).*]

[*References are to paragraphs (¶).*]

[*References are to paragraphs (¶).*]

[*References are to paragraphs (¶).*]

[*References are to paragraphs (¶).*]

[*References are to paragraphs (¶).*]

[*References are to paragraphs (¶).*]

[*References are to paragraphs (¶).*]

[*References are to paragraphs (¶).*]

[*References are to paragraphs (¶).*]

[*References are to paragraphs (¶).*]

[*References are to paragraphs (¶).*]

[*References are to paragraphs (¶).*]

[*References are to paragraphs (¶).*]

[*References are to paragraphs (¶).*]

Table of Treasury Regulations

[References are to paragraphs (¶).]

[*References are to paragraphs (¶).*]

[*References are to paragraphs (¶).*]

[*References are to paragraphs (¶).*]

TABLE OF TREASURY REGULATIONS

[*References are to paragraphs (¶).*]

[*References are to paragraphs (¶).*]

TABLE OF TREASURY REGULATIONS

[*References are to paragraphs (¶).*]

[*References are to paragraphs (¶).*]

[*References are to paragraphs (¶).*]

INTERNAL REVENUE REGULATIONS

PROPOSED REGULATIONS

[*References are to paragraphs (¶).*]

TEMPORARY REGULATIONS

Table of Revenue Rulings, Revenue Procedures, and Other IRS Releases

[References are to paragraphs (¶).]

REVENUE RULINGS

[*References are to paragraphs (¶).*]

[*References are to paragraphs (¶).*]

[*References are to paragraphs (¶).*]

[*References are to paragraphs (¶).*]

[*References are to paragraphs (¶).*]

REVENUE PROCEDURES

TABLE OF IRS RELEASES

[*References are to paragraphs (¶).*]

GENERAL COUNSEL'S MEMORANDUM

INCOME TAX UNIT REGULATIONS

INTERNAL REVENUE NEWS RELEASE

MIMEOGRAPHS

OFFICE DECISIONS

SOLICITOR'S OPINION

TREASURY DECISIONS

Index

[References are to paragraphs (¶).]

[*References are to paragraphs (¶).*]

[*References are to paragraphs (¶).*]

[*References are to paragraphs (¶).*]

[*References are to paragraphs (¶).*]

[*References are to paragraphs (¶).*]

[*References are to paragraphs (¶).*]

[*References are to paragraphs (¶).*]

[*References are to paragraphs (¶).*]

[*References are to paragraphs (¶).*]

[*References are to paragraphs (¶).*]

[*References are to paragraphs (¶).*]

[*References are to paragraphs (¶).*]

[*References are to paragraphs (¶).*]

[*References are to paragraphs (¶).*]

[*References are to paragraphs (¶).*]

[*References are to paragraphs (¶).*]

E

[*References are to paragraphs (¶).*]

F

[*References are to paragraphs (¶).*]

[*References are to paragraphs (¶).*]

H

[*References are to paragraphs (¶).*]

[*References are to paragraphs (¶).*]

[*References are to paragraphs (¶).*]

[*References are to paragraphs (¶).*]

J

K

L

INDEX

[References are to paragraphs (¶).]

M

[*References are to paragraphs (¶).*]

N

[*References are to paragraphs* (¶).]

[*References are to paragraphs (¶).*]

[References are to paragraphs (¶).]

[*References are to paragraphs (¶).*]

[*References are to paragraphs (¶).*]

[References are to paragraphs (¶).]

[*References are to paragraphs (¶).*]

[*References are to paragraphs (¶).*]

[*References are to paragraphs (¶).*]

[*References are to paragraphs (¶).*]

[*References are to paragraphs (¶).*]

U

[*References are to paragraphs (¶).*]

Cross-Reference Table

From FUNDAMENTALS OF FEDERAL INCOME TAXATION
(student edition)

To FEDERAL TAXATION OF INCOME, ESTATES AND GIFTS
(professional edition)

Readers of the student edition will find more extensive discussions and more detailed citations in the corresponding paragraphs (¶) of the professional edition, as indicated by the cross-references set out below.

Student Edition	*Professional Edition*
CHAPTER 1	
1.1	1.2
1.2	4.1
1.3	4.3
1.4	5.1
1.5	5.2
1.6	5.3
1.7	5.4
1.8	5.5
1.9	5.6
1.10	5.7
1.11	5.8
CHAPTER 2	
2.1	6.1
2.2	6.2
2.3	6.3
2.4	6.4
2.5	6.5
CHAPTER 3	
3.1	10.1
3.2	10.2
3.3	10.3
3.4	10.4
3.5	11.1
3.6	11.2
CHAPTER 4	
4.1	12.1
4.2	12.2
4.3	12.3
4.4	12.4
4.5	12.5
4.6	12.6
CHAPTER 5	
5.1	13.1
5.2	13.2
CHAPTER 6	
6.1	15.1
6.2	15.2
6.3	15.3
6.4	15.4

Student Edition	Professional Edition
CHAPTER 7	
7.1	14.1
7.2	14.2
7.3	14.3
7.4	14.4
7.5	14.5
7.6	14.6
7.7	14.7
7.8	14.8
7.9	14.9
7.10	16.1
7.11	16.2
7.12	16.3
7.13	16.4
CHAPTER 8	
8.1	20.1
8.2	20.2
8.3	20.3
8.4	20.4
8.5	20.5
CHAPTER 9	
9.1	21.1
9.2	21.1
9.3	21.2
9.4	21.3
9.5	21.4
9.6	22.1
9.7	22.2
9.8	22.3
9.9	22.4
9.10	22.5
9.11	22.6
9.12	22.7
CHAPTER 10	
10.1	23.1
10.2	23.1
10.3	23.1
10.4	23.1
10.5	23.1
10.6	23.2
10.7	23.3
10.8	23.5
10.9	23.6
10.10	23.7
10.11	23.8
CHAPTER 11	
11.1	24.1
11.2	24.2
11.3	24.3
11.4	24.4
CHAPTER 12	
12.1	25.1, 25.2
12.2	25.3
12.3	25.4
12.4	25.5
12.5	25.6
12.6	25.7
12.7	25.8
12.8	25.10
12.9	25.11
12.10	26.1
12.11	26.2
12.12	26.3
12.13	26.4
CHAPTER 13	
13.1	27.1, 27.2, 27.3, 27.4
13.2	27.5
13.3	27.6
13.4	27.7
CHAPTER 14	
14.1	30.1, 30.2
14.2	30.3
14.3	30.4
14.4	30.5
CHAPTER 15	
15.1	31.1
15.2	31.2
15.3	31.3

CROSS-REFERENCE TABLE

Student Edition	*Professional Edition*
Chapter 16	
16.1	32.1
16.2	32.2
Chapter 17	
17.1	33.1
17.2	33.2
17.3	33.3
17.4	33.4
17.5	33.5
17.6	33.6
17.7	33.7
17.8	33.8
17.9	33.8
Chapter 18	
18.1	34.1
18.2	34.2
18.3	34.3
18.4	34.4
18.5	34.5
Chapter 19	
19.1	35.1
19.2	35.2
19.3	35.3
19.4	35.4
Chapter 20	
20.1	36.1
20.2	36.2
Chapter 21	
21.1	37.1
21.2	37.2
21.3	37.3
21.4	37.4
21.5	37.5
21.6	37.6

Student Edition	*Professional Edition*
Chapter 22	
22.1	40.1
22.2	40.2
22.3	40.3
22.4	40.4
22.5	40.5
22.6	40.6
22.7	40.7
Chapter 23	
23.1	41.1
23.2	41.2
23.3	41.3
23.4	41.4
23.5	41.6
23.6	41.7
23.7	41.8
23.8	42.1, 42.2, 42.3, 42.4
23.9	42.5
23.10	42.6
23.11	42.7
23.12	43.1
23.13	43.2
23.14	43.3
23.15	43.4
23.16	43.5
23.17	43.6
Chapter 24	
24.1	44.1
24.2	44.2
24.3	44.3
24.4	44.5
24.5	44.6
24.6	44.7
Chapter 25	
25.1	50.1
25.2	50.2
25.3	50.3
25.4	51.1
25.5	51.2

Student Edition	Professional Edition
25.6	51.3
25.7	51.4
25.8	51.5
25.9	51.7
25.10	51.8
25.11	51.9
25.12	51.10
25.13	51.10.6
Chapter 26	
26.1	52.1
26.2	52.2
26.3	52.3
26.4	52.4
26.5	52.5
26.6	52.6
26.7	53.1
26.8	53.2
26.9	53.3
26.10	53.4
Chapter 27	
27.1	54.1
27.2	54.2
27.3	54.3
27.4	54.4
27.5	54.5
27.6	54.6
27.7	54.7
27.8	54.8
27.9	54.9
27.10	54.10
27.11	54.11
Chapter 28	
28.1	55.1
28.2	55.2
28.3	55.2.3
28.4	55.2.4
28.5	55.3
Chapter 29	
29.1	60.1
29.2	60.2

Student Edition	Professional Edition
29.3	60.4
29.4	60.5
Chapter 30	
30.1	75.1
30.2	75.2
30.3	75.3
30.4	75.4
Chapter 31	
31.1	76.1
31.2	76.2
Chapter 32	
32.1	77.1
32.2	77.2
32.3	77.3
32.4	77.4
Chapter 33	
33.1	78.1
33.2	78.2
33.3	78.3
33.4	79.1
33.5	79.2
33.6	79.4
33.7	79.5
Chapter 34	
34.1	80.1
34.2	80.2
34.3	80.3
34.4	80.4
34.5	80.5
34.6	80.6
34.7	80.7
34.8	80.8
Chapter 35	
35.1	105.1
35.2	105.2
35.3	105.3

CROSS-REFERENCE TABLE

Student Edition	Professional Edition
35.4	105.4
35.5	105.5
35.6	105.6
Chapter 36	
36.1	106.1
36.2	106.2
36.3	106.2.6
36.4	106.3
36.5	106.4
Chapter 37	
37.1	107.1
37.2	107.2
37.3	107.3
37.4	107.4
37.5	107.5
Chapter 38	
38.1	110.1
38.2	110.2
38.3	110.3
38.4	110.4
38.5	110.5
Chapter 39	
39.1	111.1
39.2	111.2
39.3	111.3
39.4	111.3.12
39.5	111.3.13
39.6	111.4
39.7	111.4.6

Student Edition	Professional Edition
Chapter 40	
40.1	112.1
40.2	112.2
40.3	112.3
Chapter 41	
41.1	113.1
41.2	113.2
41.3	113.3
41.4	113.4
41.5	113.5
41.6	113.6
41.7	113.7
41.8	113.8
41.9	113.9
41.10	113.10
Chapter 42	
42.1	114.1
42.2	114.2
42.3	114.3
42.4	114.4
Chapter 43	
43.1	115.1
43.2	115.2
43.3	115.3
43.4	115.4
43.5	115.5
43.6	115.6
43.7	115.7
43.8	115.8
43.9	115.9